THE LAW OF CONTRACTS

Other books in the *Essentials of Canadian Law Series*

Statutory Interpretation

Intellectual Property Law

Income Tax Law

Immigration Law

International Trade Law

Family Law

Legal Ethics & Professional Responsibility

Copyright Law

Remedies: The Law of Damages

Individual Employment Law

The Law of Equitable Remedies

Administrative Law

Ethics and Canadian Criminal Law

Public International Law

Environmental Law 2/e

Securities Law

Constitutional Law 2/e

Youth Criminal Justice Law

Computer Law 2/e

The Law of Partnerships and Corporations 2/e

The Law of Torts 2/e

Media Law 2/e

Maritime Law

Criminal Law 3/e

Insurance Law

International Human Rights Law

Legal Research and Writing 2/e

The Law of Evidence 4/e

The Law of Trusts 2/e

Franchise Law

The Charter of Rights and Freedoms 3/e

Personal Property Security Law

THE LAW OF CONTRACTS

JOHN D. McCAMUS

Professor of Law
Osgoode Hall Law School, York University

The Law of Contracts
© Irwin Law Inc., 2005

Published in 2005 by

Irwin Law Inc.
347 Bay Street
Suite 501
Toronto, ON
M5H 2R7

www.irwinlaw.com

ISBN: 1-55221-018-9

Library and Archives Canada Cataloguing in Publication

McCamus, John D.
    The law of contracts / John D. McCamus.

(Essentials of Canadian law)
Includes bibliographical references and index.
ISBN 1-55221-018-9

1. Contracts—Canada—Textbooks. I. Title. II. Series.

KE850.M44 2005   346.7102   C2005-906853-1
KF801.M33 2005

The publisher acknowledges the financial support of the Government of Canada through the Book Publishing Industry Development Program (BPIDP) for its publishing activities.

We acknowledge the assistance of the OMDC Book Fund, an initiative of Ontario Media Development Corporation.

Printed and bound in Canada.

1 2 3 4 5   09 08 07 06 05

SUMMARY
TABLE OF CONTENTS

PREFACE   *xxi*

CHAPTER   1:   Introduction   *1*

PART ONE: FORMATION   *29*

CHAPTER   2:   Offer and Acceptance   *31*

CHAPTER   3:   Certainty of Terms   *91*

CHAPTER   4:   Intention to Create Legal Relations   *111*

CHAPTER   5:   Bargaining in Good Faith   *137*

CHAPTER   6:   Agreements in Writing   *160*

PART TWO: ENFORCEABILITY   *209*

CHAPTER   7:   Consideration and Form   *211*

CHAPTER   8:   Waiver and Promissory Estoppel   *275*

CHAPTER   9:   Privity of Contract   *294*

PART THREE: VITIATING FACTORS   *323*

CHAPTER 10:   Misrepresentation   *325*

CHAPTER 11:   Duress, Undue Influence and Unconscionability   *364*

CHAPTER 12:   Illegality   *428*

CHAPTER 13:   Mistake   *494*

CHAPTER 14:   Frustration   *566*

PART FOUR: PERFORMANCE AND BREACH   *613*

CHAPTER 15:   Conditions, Warranties and Repudiatory Breach   *615*

CHAPTER 16:   Anticipatory Repudiation   *651*

CHAPTER 17:   Conditional Agreements   *672*

CHAPTER 18:   Representation and Warranty   *689*

PART FIVE: INTERPRETATION OF AGREEMENTS   *703*

CHAPTER 19:   General Principles of Interpretation   *705*

CHAPTER 20:   Exculpatory Clauses   *749*

CHAPTER 21:   The Implied Duty to Perform in Good Faith   *780*

PART SIX: REMEDIES   *811*

CHAPTER 22:   Damages   *813*

CHAPTER 23:   Specific Performance and Injunctions   *906*

CHAPTER 24:   Restitution and Disgorgement   *961*

TABLE OF CASES   *993*

INDEX   *1071*

ABOUT THE AUTHOR   *1095*

DETAILED
TABLE OF CONTENTS

PREFACE *xxi*

CHAPTER 1:
INTRODUCTION *1*

A. Overview *1*

    1) The Plan of This Work *2*
    2) A Study of the General Principles of Contract Law *6*
    3) The Three Meanings of "Common Law" *7*

B. Common Law and Equity *9*

C. Contract, Tort and Restitution *13*

D. Continuity and Change *18*

E. Contracts as a Work in Progress: Modern Trends *23*

Further Readings *28*

PART ONE: FORMATION *29*

CHAPTER 2:
OFFER AND ACCEPTANCE *31*

A. Introduction *31*

B. The Offer *33*

    1) Preliminary Negotiations and Offers *34*

a)   Retail Sales   37
b)   Offers to the General Public: Rewards and Other Unilateral
     Contracts   40
c)   Tenders   43
d)   Auctions   47
2)   Communication of Offer   48

C. The Acceptance   52

1)   Counteroffers, Rejections and Failed Acceptances   52
2)   The Battle of the Forms   59

D. Communication of Acceptance   67

1)   Silence as Acceptance   68
2)   The Postal Acceptance Rule   73
3)   Instantaneous Communications   76

E. Revocation of the Offer   82

1)   Communication of Revocation   83
2)   The "Flagpole Problem" and Its Solutions   85

Further Readings   89

CHAPTER 3:
CERTAINTY OF TERMS   91

A. Introduction   91

B. Incompleteness   93

C. Agreements to Agree   101

D. Vagueness   104

Further Readings   110

CHAPTER 4:
INTENTION TO CREATE LEGAL RELATIONS   111

A. Introduction   111

B. Commercial Arrangements   113

1)   Explicit Agreements Not to Be Bound   113
2)   Tendering Processes   115
3)   Letters of Comfort   118
4)   Preliminary Agreements, Letters of Intent and Agreements
     "Subject to Contract"   125

C. Domestic and Social Arrangements   129

Further Readings *135*

CHAPTER 5:
BARGAINING IN GOOD FAITH *137*

A. **Introduction** *137*

B. **Certainty of Terms** *141*

C. **Options to Renew** *144*

D. **The Conduct of Tendering Processes** *147*

E. **A Duty to Bargain in Good Faith in the Absence of a Contract?** *151*

F. **Conclusion** *156*

Further Readings *158*

CHAPTER 6:
AGREEMENTS IN WRITING *160*

A. **Introduction** *160*

B. **Agreements Required to Be in Writing: The *Statute of Frauds*** *161*

  1) Introduction *161*
  2) Undertakings Subject to Section 4 of the Statute *165*
    a) Promises to Answer for the Debt, Default or Miscarriages of Another Person *165*
    b) Promises Made upon Consideration of Marriage *167*
    c) Promise by an Executor or Administrator to Answer Damages out of His or Her Own Estate *167*
    d) Agreements Not to Be Performed within One Year *168*
    e) Contracts for the Sale of Any Interest in Land *169*
  3) The Section 4 Formalities and the Effect of Non-compliance *170*
  4) Relief from the Effects of Non-compliance *174*
    a) The Doctrine of Part Performance *174*
    b) Hiding behind the *Statute of Frauds* in Order to Perpetrate a Fraud *178*
    c) Restitution *179*
  5) Other Statutory Writing Requirements *180*

C. **Incorporation of Written Terms** *181*

  1) Introduction *181*
  2) Unsigned Documents *183*
  3) Signed Documents *190*

D. **The Parol Evidence Rule** *193*

  1) Introduction *193*

2) The Scope and Operation of the Rule 197
3) Exceptions to the Rule 199
4) Canadian Reception of the Modern Approach 203
5) Merger and Entire Agreement Clauses 206
6) Conclusion 207

Further Readings 207

PART TWO: ENFORCEABILITY 209

CHAPTER 7:
CONSIDERATION AND FORM 211

A. Introduction 211

B. Consideration 214

1) The Bargain Theory 214
    a) The Definition of Consideration 214
    b) Certainty 218
    c) Firm Offers 219
    d) Illusory Consideration 220
    e) Implied Consideration 221
    f) The "Peppercorn Theory" 222
    g) Nominal Consideration 223
    h) Forbearance 226
    i) Charitable Subscriptions 228
    j) Manufacturers' Warranties 231
2) Past Consideration 232
3) The Pre-existing Duty Rule 239
    a) Public Duty 239
    b) Duty Owed to a Third Party 242
    c) Duty Owed to the Promisor 244
4) Partial Payment of a Debt 250

C. Formality: Promises under Seal 256

D. Reform 269

Further Readings 274

CHAPTER 8:
WAIVER AND PROMISSORY ESTOPPEL 275

A. Introduction 275

B. Waiver, Estoppel by Representation and *Foakes v. Beer* 277

C. The Doctrine of Promissory Estoppel 279

1) Sword vs. Shield? *280*
2) Intended to Be Acted Upon *281*
3) The Nature of the Undertaking *283*
4) Reassertion of Rights upon Notice *285*

D. Proprietary Estoppel *287*

E. *Waltons Stores (Interstate) Pty. v. Maher*: Inching Toward Section 90 *289*

Further Readings *293*

CHAPTER 9:
PRIVITY OF CONTRACT *294*

A. Introduction *294*

B. Development and Rationale of the Rule *296*

C. Limitations on and Exceptions to the Rule *301*
1) Agency *301*
2) Trusts *303*
3) Collateral Contracts *304*
4) Tort Law *305*
5) Assignment *306*
6) Statutory Exceptions *307*
7) Additional Exceptions at Common Law *308*
   a) Provisions Limiting the Liability of Employees *308*
   b) Insurance *309*
      i) Waiver of Rights against Third Parties *310*
      ii) Coverage of Third Parties *312*
   c) The Open-Textured "Principled Exception" *313*
   d) Subsequent Variation or Annulment of the Promise *317*

D. Conclusion *319*

Further Readings *320*

PART THREE: VITIATING FACTORS *323*

CHAPTER 10:
MISREPRESENTATION *325*

A. Introduction *325*

B. The Elements of Misrepresentation *326*
1) Sales Talk *327*
2) Opinion *327*

3) Intention 328
4) Law 329
5) Materiality 330
6) Inducement 331

C. Non-disclosure as Misrepresentation 331

D. Non-disclosure and Good Faith 334

E. Rescission and Restitution 337
1) Restoration of the *Status Quo Ante* 339
2) Affirmation 342
3) Intervention of Third-Party Rights 343
4) Execution of the Agreement 343
5) Laches 345
6) Merger in a Subsequent Warranty 346
7) Restitution without Rescission 347

F. Liability in Tort 348

G. Entire Agreement and Exemption Clauses 354

H. Overview 360

I. Statutory Reform 361

Further Readings 362

CHAPTER 11:

DURESS, UNDUE INFLUENCE AND UNCONSCIONABILITY 364

A. Introduction 364

B. Duress 367
1) Introduction 367
2) The Traditional Categories of Duress 369
   a) Duress to the Person 369
   b) Duress of Goods 370
3) Economic Duress 371

C. Undue Influence 382
1) Introduction 382
2) Type 1: Actual Undue Influence 384
3) Types 2A and B: Presumptive Undue Influence 385
   a) Establishing the Presumption 385
   b) Must There Exist a Dominating Influence? 388
   c) Manifest Disadvantage 391
4) Type 3: Non-presumptive Relational Undue Influence 395

   5)   Establishing the Independence of the Plaintiff   397
   6)   Effects on Third Parties   398
   7)   Remedies   402

D. **Unconscionability**   404

   1)   Introduction   404
   2)   Elements of Unconscionability   407
   3)   Effects on Third Parties   415
   4)   Justification for the Doctrine   417
   5)   Remedies   419
   6)   Statutory Unconscionability   422

E. **Conclusion**   424

Further Readings   426

CHAPTER 12:
ILLEGALITY   428

A. **Introduction**   428

B. **Agreements Contrary to Public Policy at Common Law**   430

   1)   Agreements to Commit an Unlawful Act: Crime, Tort and the
        Defrauding of Third Parties   430
   2)   Agreements Facilitating Immoral Conduct or Undermining the
        Institution of Marriage   432
   3)   Agreements Undermining the Administration of Justice and Other
        State Interests   438
        a)   Undermining the Administration of Justice   438
        b)   Other State Interests   444
   4)   Covenants in Restraint of Trade   447

C. **Statutory Illegality**   459

D. **The Consequences of Illegality**   467

   1)   Introduction   467
   2)   Restitution   470
   3)   Collateral Claims   477
   4)   The Passage of Property   481

E. **Severance**   483

Further Readings   492

CHAPTER 13:
MISTAKE   494

A. **Introduction**   494

B. **Misunderstandings** *496*

1) Introduction *496*
2) Ambiguity *498*
3) Unilateral Mistakes as to Terms *501*
4) Misunderstanding in the Context of Mistaken Bids *504*
5) Mistake as to the Identity of the Other Contracting Party *509*
6) *Non Est Factum*: Mistakenly Signed Documents *518*

C. **Mistaken Assumptions** *526*

1) Introduction *526*
2) At Common Law *527*
3) In Equity *535*
4) Rejection of the Equitable Doctrine by the English Court of Appeal *545*
5) Unilateral Mistake in Assumptions *553*

D. **Mistakes in Integration** *555*

1) Introduction *555*
2) Proving the Antecedent Agreement *556*
3) Unilateral Mistake and Rectification *559*
4) Defences and Bars to Relief *563*

Further Readings *564*

CHAPTER 14:
FRUSTRATION *566*

A. **Introduction** *566*

B. **Development of the Doctrine** *568*

C. **The Standard Categories of Frustration** *573*

1) Impossibility *573*
2) Frustration of Purpose *575*
3) Temporary Impossibility *578*

D. **A Modern Restatement: Risk-Allocation Analysis** *579*

E. **Commercial Impracticability** *588*

F. **Agreements to Transfer Interests in Land** *591*

G. **Self-Induced Frustration** *597*

H. ***Force Majeure* Clauses** *599*

I. **Consequences of Frustration** *603*

Further Readings *610*

PART FOUR: PERFORMANCE AND BREACH *613*

CHAPTER 15:

CONDITIONS, WARRANTIES AND REPUDIATORY BREACH *615*

A. Introduction *615*

B. Promises and Conditions *617*

C. The Condition-Warranty Dichotomy: Criticisms and Cure *624*

D. Refinement of the *Hong Kong Fir* Analysis *629*

E. Applying the *Hong Kong Fir* Test *633*

F. When Is a Contractual "Condition" Not a True Condition? *636*

G. A Definition of Repudiatory Breach *639*

H. Remedies for Repudiatory Breach *641*
   1) The Right to Disaffirm *641*
   2) Damages *644*
   3) Restitution *644*

I. Is There a Doctrine of "Material" Breach? *646*

Further Readings *649*

CHAPTER 16:

ANTICIPATORY REPUDIATION *651*

A. Introduction *651*

B. The Elements of Anticipatory Repudiation *655*

C. Exercising the Right to Disaffirm *658*

D. Exercising the Right to Affirm *665*

Further Readings *671*

CHAPTER 17:

CONDITIONAL AGREEMENTS *672*

A. Introduction *672*

B. Conditions Precedent to the Existence of an Agreement *675*

C. Implied Subsidiary Obligations *679*

D. Waiver and "True" Conditions Precedent *682*

Further Readings *688*

CHAPTER 18:
REPRESENTATION AND WARRANTY *689*

A. **Introduction** *689*

B. **Pre-contractual Representation as Warranty** *690*

C. **The Measure of Relief** *695*

D. **Contractual Representations** *696*

E. **Concurrent Liability in Contract and Tort** *700*

Further Readings *701*

PART FIVE: INTERPRETATION OF AGREEMENTS *703*

CHAPTER 19:
GENERAL PRINCIPLES OF INTERPRETATION *705*

A. **Introduction** *705*

B. **Sources** *707*

    1) Introduction *707*
    2) Commercial Setting or Background *708*
    3) Prior Negotiations, Drafts and Antecedent Agreements *711*
    4) Subsequent Conduct of the Parties *713*
    5) Related Agreements *715*
    6) The Meaning of Words *716*

C. **Canons of Construction** *716*

    1) Introduction *716*
    2) Construction of the Agreement as a Whole *717*
    3) Giving Effect to All Parts of the Agreement *719*
    4) Avoiding Commercially Unreasonable or Absurd Outcomes *719*
    5) Construction *Contra Proferentum* *722*
    6) List of Particulars Followed by General Language: *ejusdem generis* *724*
    7) The Restrictive Effect of Explicit References: *expressio unius* *726*
    8) The Preference Accorded Amendments to Printed Terms *726*
    9) The Preference Accorded the Earlier of Two Inconsistent Terms *727*
    10) The Preference for a Construction That Preserves the Validity or Legality of the Agreement *728*

D. **Implied Terms** *729*

1) Introduction   729
2) Terms Implied from Custom or Usage   732
3) Terms Implied in Fact   735
4) Terms Implied in Law   743
5) Implied Statutory Terms   746

Further Readings   747

CHAPTER 20:
EXCULPATORY CLAUSES   749

A. **Introduction**   749

B. **Related Doctrines**   750

C. **The Rise and Fall of Fundamental Breach in English Law**   754

D. **Canadian Reception of the Doctrine**   765

E. **Conclusion**   776

Further Readings   778

CHAPTER 21:
THE IMPLIED DUTY TO PERFORM IN GOOD FAITH   780

A. **Introduction**   780

B. **Analysis of the Leading Cases**   784

1) Good Faith, Best Efforts and the Duty to Cooperate   785
2) Good Faith and the Control of Discretionary Powers   788
3) Good Faith and the Duty to Not Evade Contractual Obligations   792

C. **The Supreme Court of Canada and Good Faith:** *Wallace v. United Grain Growers Ltd.*   798

D. **The Definition of Good Faith**   803

E. **The Test for Implying Good Faith Duties**   805

F. **Conclusion**   806

Further Readings   808

PART SIX: REMEDIES   811

CHAPTER 22:
DAMAGES   813

A. **Introduction**   813

B. The Expectancy Principle   815

   1) The Basic Principle   815
   2) Exceptions   819

C. Justifying Expectancy   826

D. Reliance as an Alternative Measure   832

E. Applying the Expectancy Principle   837

   1) Two Formulae for Calculating Expectancy Damages   838
   2) Capital vs. Income   839
   3) Conflicting Methods of Application   840
   4) Loss of a Chance to Profit   847

F. Limitations on Expectancy Damages   850

   1) Causation   850
   2) Remoteness   854
   3) Mitigation   865

G. Time of Measurement   871

H. Intangible Injuries   875

I. Punitive Damages   879

J. Penalties and Liquidated Damages   897

Further Readings   904

CHAPTER 23:
SPECIFIC PERFORMANCE AND INJUNCTIONS   906

A. Introduction   906

B. Specific Performance   908

   1) Introduction   908
   2) Inadequacy of Damages Test   912
      a) Sale of Land   913
      b) Sale of Goods   918
      c) Sale of Shares   923
   3) Other Limitations   924
      a) Mutuality   924
      b) Difficulty in Supervision   929
      c) Unfairness   934
      d) Public Policy   937
      e) Delay   938
   4) Monetary Awards   939

C. Injunctions   947

D. Contractual Stipulation of Specific Relief *956*

Further Readings *959*

CHAPTER 24:

RESTITUTION AND DISGORGEMENT *961*

A. Introduction *961*

B. Remedies upon Breach: The Innocent Party *965*

    1) Restitution of Benefits Conferred *965*
    2) Disgorgement of Profits Secured *972*

C. Remedies upon Breach: The Guilty Party *979*

    1) Introduction *979*
    2) Money Paid *980*
    3) Goods and Services Supplied *983*

D. Restitution under Ineffective Transactions *986*

    1) Introduction *986*
    2) At Common Law *987*
    3) In Equity *988*

Further Readings *991*

TABLE OF CASES *993*

INDEX *1071*

ABOUT THE AUTHOR *1095*

PREFACE

The main objective of the present work is to provide an accurate account of the principles and doctrines of the law of contracts as it is currently understood and practised in the common law provinces of Canada. Perhaps unavoidably, this study manifests the usual "colonial parochial" style of such works that, in jurisdictions of the British Commonwealth, are written on the assumption that the doctrine of the jurisdiction in question is constituted by an amalgam of leading English authorities as modified, to a greater or lesser extent, by local authority, an amalgam in which the former source is the dominant presence. For some decades, however, the Supreme Court of Canada, in particular, has charted an independent course in matters of private law, and it is possible to identify several aspects of the Canadian common law of contracts that distinguish it from the contract law of other common law jurisdictions. The Canadian embrace of punitive damages for pure breach of contract is only the most recent illustration of this phenomenon. For obvious reasons, I have attempted to portray here all developments of this kind. The reader will also find, however, references to decisions and other sources from other Commonwealth jurisdictions and from the United States. In addition to exposition, however, I have taken seriously the boast of the common law that one of the pillars of its strength is its adaptability to changing social and economic circumstances and its ability to reformulate doctrine in the light of evolving professional attitudes and insights as to how the law can be improved. Thus, I have not hesitated to offer criticism of current doctrine where it seems warranted and to offer suggestions for future growth and development of the Canadian common law of contracts. In an early conversation with Ian Macneil, when I explained my naively ambitious plan to write a treatise on the law of restitution as my first major writing project — it was to take Peter Maddaugh and me another fifteen years to complete the work — Macneil offered the view that the writers of such works must decide whether they aspire to be soothsayers or manipulators, the implication being that the former was the only honourable career choice. I have tried to follow that advice both in my work on restitution and in the present volume. I trust that the reader will find that this volume provides an account of the law that is faithful to the raw material and that I have not commingled the objectives of exposition and constructive criticism.

In all of this, of course, I have drawn heavily on the work and insights of others and it is a pleasure to record some of my intellectual debts. My early interest in contract law was thrust upon me by the teaching assignments of my then Osgoode Dean, the Honourable Gerald E. LeDain, who assured me that I would enjoy teaching both contract and commercial law in place of my hoped-for assignments in corporate and constitutional law. Subsequent events have proven the wisdom of his choice as I have found the study and teaching of private law an immensely enjoyable preoccupation. Like so many other Canadian legal scholars, I have profited greatly from Jacob Ziegel's early mentorship and continuing encouragement of my work over the years. Shortly after beginning at Osgoode, Jacob invited me to join the research team of the Ontario Law Reform Commission project on the law of sale of goods and, in turn, a second project team, which he co-directed with Stephen Waddams, that prepared a report on the amendment of the general law of contracts. It is difficult to imagine a more fortuitous training ground for a neophyte teacher of contract law. It was in the context of those commission projects that I first attempted to unravel the mysteries of the doctrines of mistake and frustration, the latest attempts at which are to be found as chapters in this volume.

Osgoode Hall Law School has provided a very congenial home for work of this kind. My current contracts colleagues, Stephanie Ben-Ishai, Tom Johnson, Iain Ramsay, Robert Wai and Toni Williams, are the latest members of a long list of colleagues with whom I have had many fruitful conversations about matters of contract law over the years. I have also learned much from fellow contributors to the two casebooks on the law of contracts with which I have been associated, the first edited by Christine Boyle and David Percy and the second by Stephen Waddams, Michael Trebilcock, Jason Neyers, Mary Anne Waldron and myself. My intellectual indebtedness to the generations of scholars who have created the literature of the common law of contract law is, of course, profound. The identities of many of my creditors are revealed in the footnote references herein and the lists of "Further Readings" appended to the chapters of this book. Winnowing the much longer lists with which I began down to a more reasonable length was not an enjoyable task. I would be most grateful to any who would draw sins of omission to my attention. If the reader detects a particular admiration for and indebtedness to the work of Melvin Eisenberg and Allan Farnsworth, the impression will be an accurate one. Accordingly, it has been a great pleasure in recent years to be associated with Professors Eisenberg and Farnsworth in the work of the American Law Institute's Advisory Committee on the *Restatement of Restitution and Unjust Enrichment 3d*. It is sad to record that Professor Farnsworth died earlier this year. As I worked my way through the chapters of this volume, his great three-volume treatise and the *Restatement of Contracts 2d*, for which he was a co-reporter, were constant companions. His relentless attempt to get to the bottom of things, so evident in his writings, and the pleasure of his company will be sorely missed at the meetings of the advisory committee.

The idea of writing a book on contract law was first broached with me by William Kaplan, a prolific and admired author in his own right, who conceived and established the series of volumes in which this work is to appear. Although both Kaplan and Jeff Miller at Irwin Law anticipated, indeed contracted for, a much shorter volume than I have been able to produce, their patience and indulgence of my desire to write a longer book have been deeply appreciated and perhaps unfairly abused by me. I very much hope that they will feel that their seemingly inexhaustible supply of patience has been rewarded. I am also grateful to Alisa Posesorski and Pamela Erlichman, at Irwin, whose excellent editorial work was both swift and meticulous. Successive Deans of Osgoode Hall Law School, Marilyn Pilkington, Peter Hogg and Patrick Monahan, have provided much appreciated moral and financial support over the years. Through their good offices and the financial support of the Ontario Law Foundation, I have been able to retain the services of a series of remarkably talented student research assistants over the years. I am grateful to, in chronological order, Sarah Pearce, Jacklin Tabar, Sarah Valair, Ian Duke, Medard Fischer, Elissa Banach, Jesse Brodlieb and Jeffery Hershenfield for their valuable research work.

Since the fall of 2000, my understanding of "contracts-in-action" has been much enhanced through various forms of consulting work with the firm of Davies Ward Phillips and Vineberg LLP. Indeed, much of the manuscript for this book was written during evening hours at Davies and I am deeply indebted to my evening assistant at Davies, Sharon Dwight, who has been able to find time, often late at night, to devote to the typing of the bulk of the manuscript for this volume. Major contributions to this effort were also made by Katherine Casey and Linda Veres who, during otherwise very busy professional days, were miraculously able to find time to meet urgent needs on the manuscript front. Many other staff members at Davies, too numerous to mention, have pitched in from time to time. Without this support, this work simply could not have been completed within the near future. I am also grateful to Jeffrey Lem for his comments on a draft of Chapter 23. My work with the firm has kindled an interest in matters of contractual interpretation that would otherwise have been more muted. It is reflected in the contents of this volume.

An urgent need to complete drafts of some of the chapters of this volume was provoked by the kind invitation of the Honourable Georgina Jackson, of the Saskatchewan Court of Appeal, to assist in the organization of a series of conferences on contract law for federally appointed judges under the auspices of the National Judicial Institute. That work, and the resulting conferences, both of which were most pleasurable professional experiences for me, usefully created an incentive to write a number of papers that ultimately formed the basis for various chapters and parts of chapters of this volume, thereby giving the project some much needed momentum. I am also grateful to the editors of the *Canadian Business Law Journal*, the *San Diego Law Review* and the *Advocates' Quarterly* for permission to reprint here materials that, in somewhat different form, first appeared as articles in those journals.

Notwithstanding the rich array of intellectual and other resources upon which I have been able to draw, the usual disclaimer is appropriate. None of the above are responsible for any deficiencies that may be detected in the design or execution of the present work. Final versions of the chapters were submitted to the publisher *in seriatim* beginning in the spring of 2005. I was able to add some references to recent developments, however, into the summer months that followed.

On a personal level, those who have trodden similar paths well know the exactions imposed by work of this kind on one's family. It is in the nature of such work — I like to think — that it expands to fill such evening and weekend hours as can be made available and, as a result, substantially encroaches on one's private life. The abiding encouragement, support and patience of my wife, Wendy, has been simply indispensable to the completion of this project. It is to her and to our two wonderful sons, Matthew and Simon, that this volume is dedicated.

September 2005
Toronto, ON   J.D.M.

CHAPTER 1

INTRODUCTION

A. OVERVIEW

The term "contract" is often used in common parlance to refer to a written document that records an enforceable agreement between two parties. Although lawyers do often use the term in this fashion, the term is used in a more general way in legal discourse as a reference to any enforceable promise. This broader usage is necessitated by the fact—surprising to some who are new to the subject—that oral promises may be enforceable in certain circumstances, notwithstanding the fact that they are not recorded in written form.[1] As a general matter, promises, whether oral or written, are enforceable if they are included within a "bargain" between two parties. The term "bargain" does not capture the entire subject matter of contract law, however, because it is also possible for unilateral or one-sided promises to be enforceable if they are recorded in writing in a particular formalized fashion.[2] The term "promise" signals that the subject of our attention consists of enforceable commitments with respect to the future. A purely contemporaneous exchange or barter of goods in which neither party gives an undertaking of any kind with respect to the subject matter of the exchange does not include a potentially enforceable promise and is

---

1   As we shall see, a limited number of types of agreements must be recorded in writing if they are to be legally enforceable. See Chapter 6, section B.
2   See Chapter 7, section C.

therefore not a contract in the requisite sense. Further, statements of present fact do not constitute promises though, as we shall see,[3] the distinction between representations or statements of fact, on the one hand, and promises, on the other, is both difficult to draw and highly manipulable. This is not to say that a false statement of current fact is of no legal interest.[4] It is merely to say that a statement of current fact is not a promise in the requisite sense. As a legal term of art, "contracts" refers to the universe of legally enforceable promises. The law of contracts, then, is the law relating to the enforcement of promises.

1) The Plan of This Work

A brief survey of the content of the law of contracts may be accomplished by outlining the plan of this work. This volume is subdivided into six parts dealing, in turn, with (1) the formation of agreements, (2) the rules for recognizing their enforceability at law, (3) grounds for setting aside or vitiating agreements that would otherwise be enforceable, (4) performance and breach of contracts, (5) principles of interpretation of agreements and (6) the remedies available for breach of contract.

A threshold question for the law of contracts is to determine whether the parties have reached agreement on the particulars of the promises that are sought to be enforced. A variety of issues relating to the formation of contracts are examined in Part One of this volume. The basic rules for determining whether the parties have reached an agreement on certain terms — the rules of "offer and acceptance" — are examined in Chapter 2. Even though the parties may have reached a genuine agreement or *consensus ad idem* on certain matters, the terms of their agreement, if it is to be enforceable, must deal with sufficient matters to constitute a valid agreement. Otherwise, the agreement will fail for incompleteness or uncertainty. This issue is considered in Chapter 3. Further, even though the parties reach consensus on sufficient matters to constitute a valid agreement, it may not have been their intention to create an enforceable agreement. The relevancy of such an intent is explored in Chapter 4. In recent years, some courts have suggested the possibility that parties negotiating toward an agreement may be subject to a duty to bargain in good faith. The possible content of such a duty and the current status of any such doctrine are examined in Chapter

---

3   See Chapter 18, section B.
4   Thus, the inducement of contracts by the making of false statements may give rise to certain remedies. See further, Chapter 10.

5. Part One concludes in Chapter 6 with an examination of various issues concerning the formation of agreements in writing. First, the nature and effect of various statutory requirements that certain types of agreements be recorded in signed writing are examined. Second, the problem of determining whether written terms included in a document — an airline ticket, for example — that one party intends will form the basis of the agreement between the parties should be considered to be binding upon the other party. Third, consideration is given to the problem that arises where a particular written document may appear to constitute the agreement between the parties but one of the parties wishes to rely on an undertaking given either orally or in another document by the other party. The so-called parol evidence rule holds that, as a general proposition, evidence of undertakings not recorded in a document intended to be the full expression of the agreement between the parties is inadmissible.

In Part Two, we consider the question of whether the promises given by one or both parties are the kinds of promises that the law should consider to be enforceable. This is evidently an issue of central importance for the law of contracts. As we shall see, there are essentially two "rules of recognition" for identifying enforceable promises and distinguishing them from promises that do not attract the enforcement mechanisms of the law. The first rule is the venerable doctrine of consideration, which holds that a promise as contained in a bargain or exchange between the parties is enforceable. The second holds that "deeds" or "contracts under seal" are enforceable simply on the basis that they have been executed by the promisor in accordance with the formal requirements for executing instruments or documents under seal. These doctrines are examined in Chapter 7. Apart from contracts under seal, then, the common law recognizes as enforceable only those promises given in return for a bargained-for consideration or exchange of value. Thus, promises unsupported by a consideration are unenforceable even if they have foreseeably induced detrimental reliance on the part of the promisee. The limited effect that may be given to non-bargain promises inducing detrimental reliance through the doctrines of waiver and promissory estoppel is examined in Chapter 8. Finally, in Chapter 9, we examine the doctrine of privity of contract, which holds that third parties who are intended to be benefited by contracts but who have given no consideration or value in return to the promisor — so-called third-party beneficiaries — have no standing to enforce the agreement. Although this controversial doctrine has been justified as a corollary of the doctrine of consideration, this explanation for the rule will be subjected to critical scrutiny in that chapter.

In Part Three, a variety of grounds for vitiating or rendering unenforceable what might otherwise be considered to be valid and enforceable agreements are subjected to analysis. The first four of these
grounds for vitiation are concerned with remedying defects in the bargaining process. Chapter 10 considers the effect on the enforceability of an agreement when a party has been induced to enter it by a
misrepresentation of a material fact by the other party, whether that
representation has been fraudulently or innocently made. Various doctrines concerning the voluntariness of agreements—duress, undue
influence and unconscionability—are then considered in Chapter
11. In Chapter 12, the limitations imposed on the ability of parties to
enter into enforceable agreements by considerations of public policy,
whether the public policy is articulated by the courts or the legislatures, will be examined. In Chapter 13 consideration is given to the
effect on enforceability of various types of mistakes that might have
affected a party's decision to enter into an agreement, be it a mistaken
assumption concerning either one or both of the parties' reasons for
entering the agreement, a mistake as to the meaning of the terms of the
agreement or a mistake with respect to the writing up of the agreement.
Finally, in Chapter 14, an analysis is provided of the doctrine of frustration that may provide an excuse for non-performance by a party where
unanticipated intervening circumstances—in the classic case, where a
work in progress is destroyed by fire—have compromised that party's
ability to perform the agreement.

In Part Four, various issues relating to the performance or non-performance of an enforceable agreement are considered. First, in Chapter
15, the definition and significance of a repudiatory breach is examined.
The central issue is to determine whether a particular breach of contract enables the party not in breach to terminate the contractual relationship and, if loss has resulted from the breach, pursue appropriate
remedies for breach of contract. As will be seen, in determining whether a particular breach has this effect, the law also determines the order
in which the performance of the parties is to occur. Both of these sets of
issues are examined in Chapter 15. In Chapter 16, we turn to consider
the effect that an announcement made by a party, prior to the time for
performance, that performance will not be forthcoming has on the ability of the other party to treat the agreement as repudiated by breach.
This, the so-called doctrine of anticipatory repudiation, is the subject
of Chapter 16. In Chapter 17, we continue our examination of contractual arrangements that order performance and, in particular, consider
the effect of provisions that stipulate that performance of either one or
both of the parties will not be required until an event occurs—such

as the granting of necessary approval of the arrangement by a governmental authority—that is beyond capacity of the parties to achieve or, as is often said, is "entirely dependent upon the will of third parties." Finally, in Chapter 18, the effect of so-called warranties is examined. In this particular context, the term "warranty" is employed to refer to an undertaking or guarantee that a particular statement of fact is true or will continue to be true or will become true on a particular future occasion. More particularly, consideration will be given to the question of whether pre-contractual representations may be considered to have contractual force as "warranties." Further, we will examine the remedial consequences that arise if the warranted facts prove to be false, thus constituting a basis for an assertion that the contractual warranty of their truth has been breached.

In Part Five, the principles employed by courts in the course of interpreting or construing agreements are examined. The most common context in which these principles are employed is in the course of giving meaning to the provisions of an existing agreement that lacks clarity. Knowledge of the principles of interpretation of agreements is also very relevant, of course, to the task of drafting agreements with a view to ensuring that the drafter's intended meaning is the meaning that the agreement would ultimately be given by a construing court. In Chapter 19, we examine the general principles of interpretation. These principles concern the materials that can be examined by the construing court, the principles or canons of construction that will be relied upon and, finally, the various grounds upon which terms will be implied in order to fill gaps in agreements. In Chapters 20 and 21, we take up two particular interpretive issues that have generated substantial bodies of case law. In Chapter 20, the law concerning the interpretation of so-called exculpatory or limitation of liability clauses is examined. In Chapter 21, the now substantial body of case law implying terms into agreements that will require a party to perform the agreement in "good faith" is subjected to analysis. As Canadian common law courts appear to be on the brink of recognizing the existence of such an implied duty as a general principle of interpretation, an attempt is made in Chapter 21 to give some content, drawn from the cases employing the concept, to the notion of good faith.

In Part Six, an account is offered of the various remedies available to a victim of a breach of contract. The principles underlying the most commonly awarded form of relief—the claim for damages for breach of contract—are analyzed in Chapter 22. The grounds on which the much less commonly awarded forms of specific redress—specific performance and injunctions—which order the party in breach either, in the former case, to do that which was promised to be done or, in the latter, not to do that which was promised not to be done under the agreement are examined in Chapter 23. Finally, in Chapter 24, consideration is given to the various forms of relief that may achieve recovery of benefits acquired by the defendant in breach of contract. The fundamental differences between the benefit-based or restitutionary liability considered in Chapter 24 and the compensatory relief awarded in the context of claims for damages for breach of contract will be further considered in an introductory fashion in "Contract, Tort and Restitution" later in this chapter.[5]

2) A Study of the General Principles of Contract Law

As with other works of the same or a similar title to the present, this volume attempts an analysis of the general principles of the law of contracts as opposed to the specific principles that may apply to particular types of transactions. As illustrations of the latter category, it may be noted that some more particularized rules have developed in the context of particular transaction types such as contracts for the purchase and sale of goods, insurance contracts, contracts of employment, leases of both real property and chattels, bills of lading and other contracts of carriage, charter parties, construction contracts, contracts of suretyship or guarantee, contracts of agency, contracts for the purchase and sale of land, and so on. Separate texts are often published with respect to transactions of these various kinds and courses specifically devoted to the study of many of them are found in the curricula of the law schools. In a study of the general law of contracts, however, the objective is to identify and analyze principles that apply across many of the subfields or specialized areas of contract law. By way of illustration, an attempt is made in the present volume to examine general principles of contract interpretation including the principles on the basis of which terms are implied in agreements. No attempt is made, however, to catalogue or discuss the various implied terms made in the various transaction types listed above. Similarly, the general principles of the law of damages are examined herein. No attempt is made to examine the more particular applications of those principles that may have developed in the context of particular transaction types. It should be noted, however, that some tension is likely to exist between the general principles and the more particularized principles that have developed in the context of individual transaction types. The particularized rules may be vulnerable

---

5   See below this Chapter, section C.

to challenge on the basis that the particular deviation from general principle is not one that can be justified on a rational basis. Thus, for example, in the latter part of the twentieth century, the Supreme Court of Canada re-examined the rules relating to the damages that can be claimed for breach for the lessee's obligation to pay rent under leases of chattels or real property. As we shall see,[6] the Supreme Court of Canada simply overruled prior doctrine and applied the general principles for calculating damages for breach of contract to claims for losses resulting from the non-performance of this type of provision.

3) The Three Meanings of "Common Law"

This volume attempts an analysis of the law of contracts as it has developed in the Canadian common law provinces. The term "common law" has three distinct meanings, each of which is relevant to the exercise of describing the subject matter of the present work. First, the phrase is used to refer to the common law as opposed to the civilian tradition. The present volume does not include an account of the civilian contract law of the province of Quebec. The contract law of the common law provinces derives from and is much influenced by the English common law tradition. Indeed, until the abolition of appeals from Canadian courts to the Privy Council in England in 1949[7] the English common law of contracts, subject to variation by any local Canadian statutes, was binding on Canadian courts. Since 1949, however, the influence of English judicial decisions on Canadian jurisprudence has waned and it is quite clear that the contemporary Supreme Court of Canada does not feel in any sense obliged to follow English authority. The Court has assumed, as properly it should, that its mandate is to develop the law of contracts and other aspects of the law in the manner that it deems best suited to the needs arising from Canadian circumstances.[8] Nonetheless, Canadian courts continue to draw much assistance from English decisions on matters of common law and typically, in the absence of some basis for concluding that English law is different from Canadian law, English authorities are frequently relied

---

6   See Chapter 22, section B(2).
7   See generally B. Laskin, "The Supreme Court of Canada: A Final Court of and for Canadians" (1951) 29 Can. Bar Rev. 1038.
8   See, for example, *Whiten v. Pilot Insurance Co.*, [2002] 1 S.C.R. 595; *Wallace v. United Grain Growers Ltd.*, [1997] 3 S.C.R. 701.

upon as a reliable though not binding source of Canadian common law doctrine.

The term "common law" is also used to refer to judge-made law as opposed to laws generated by legislative enactment. For the most part, the general principles of contract law are common law in this sense. The general principles and the detailed rules are derived from the reasons for decision given by judges in the adjudication of contract disputes. As in other Western democracies, the law produced by judicial decision-making on matters such as the law of contracts is subject to the trump of legislative enactment. In Canada, provincial legislators are possessed of a constitutional authority to enact legislation setting forth or amending the general principles of the law of contract. With very few exceptions, however, they have refrained from doing so. Reference has already been made to legislative rules requiring certain transactions to be recorded in a signed writing.[9] As a general matter, however, the other statutory treatments of various general principles of contract law are very few in number and tend to be quite narrowly focused on rather particular issues.[10] Far more common is the legislative practice, both provincially and federally, of enacting statutes regulating the content of particular transaction types such as legislation dealing with aspects of contracts of employment, contracts for the purchase and sale of goods, insurance contracts, real estate transactions, and so on. Such legislation may either stipulate the terms deemed to be included in a particular transaction type or, more commonly, may establish default rules setting out provisions that will be deemed by statute to be included in such agreements in the absence of contrary or inconsistent stipulations in the agreements themselves. For the most part, such legislation is not discussed in the present volume, given its objective of providing an account of general principles, but will be referred to from time to time as relevant to an examination of more general issues. In particular, it will be important, from time to time, to draw attention to various aspects of consumer protection legislation enacted in some provinces that are of broad application across a range of transaction types entered into by consumers with commercial suppliers of goods and services. The common law nature of the vast majority of the law

---

9   See further, Chapter 6, section B.

10   See, for example, the discussion of the statutory overruling of the rule in *Foakes v. Beer* in a number of Canadian provinces and territories, Chapter 7, section B(4). See also, for reference to the statutory overruling of *Turney v. Zhilka* in British Columbia, Chapter 17, section D, and for reference to the statutory overruling of the doctrine of privity of contract in New Brunswick, Chapter 9, section B.

concerning general principles of the law of contracts, however, has important implications for the manner in which the conflicting demands for stability of doctrine and, on the other hand, reform or modification of the doctrine are managed by the common law system. This is, of course, a more general set of issues for common law subjects including the law of contracts, torts, restitution, property and trusts. We will return to a brief consideration of these systemic issues of continuity and reform in a later part of this chapter.

Finally, the term "common law" is used to refer to doctrines of common law as opposed to those of equity. The division of English common law into doctrines of common law in this narrower sense and equity is an idiosyncratic feature of the English common law tradition that has implications for the content of the common law of contracts. To this subject, we now turn.

B. COMMON LAW AND EQUITY

For outsiders to the common law system, it is no doubt a startling fact that until the latter part of the nineteenth century, the central institutional framework of the English legal system consisted of not one court system but two. The Royal Courts of common law—King's Bench, Common Pleas and Exchequer—developed a body of jurisprudence that has come down to us as common law in the narrow sense. For much of the history of the common law, however, there was a parallel court system, the Court of Chancery, which developed the jurisprudence referred to, at least for the past few centuries, as "equity."

The origins of equity jurisprudence are to be found in the medieval office of the Chancery, that is, the royal secretariat, and in the residual authority claimed by the King, in the early era, to administer justice personally outside the system of the common law courts.[11] Those who were dissatisfied with their treatment at common law could petition the King for relief. By the fourteenth century, the volume of such petitions or bills was such that the practice of referring them to the Chancellor had begun. The Chancellor possessed a discretion to intervene in such situations by decree and by the end of the next century issued such decrees in his own name. For present purposes, it is not necessary to record the detail of the evolution of Chancery jurisdiction from the ad

---

11   See generally J.H. Baker, *An Introduction to English Legal History*, 4th ed. (London: Butterworths LexisNexis, 2002) c. 6. See also S. Worthington, *Equity* (Oxford: Oxford University Press, 2003).

hoc and discretionary interventions of the Chancellor to the establishment of a court system and, in turn, to the establishment of that body
of jurisprudence that came to be called equity. The historical origins
of equity jurisprudence, however, assist in explaining the fact that its
role was largely seen as being a corrective to the harshness of the common law. In 1615, the presiding Chancellor explained: "the office of the
Chancellor is to correct men's consciences for frauds, breaches of trust,
wrongs and oppressions of what nature soever they be, and to soften
and mollify the extremity of the law."[12]

For petitioners, the attractions of Chancery were not only that they
might achieve different results from that attainable at common law. In
the early period at least, Chancery procedures were less cumbersome
than those of the common law. The Chancellor could grant decrees
ordering parties to do whatever conscience required rather than as,
at common law, merely ordering the payment of damages. Indeed, it
should be noted that Chancery did not, as a general matter, award damages or compensation in the manner of the common law courts. "Damages" was a remedy of the common law. Over time, the role of discretion
and conscience diminished as equity jurisprudence matured into a system of rules and precedent. Chancery cases began to be reported in the
late-seventeenth century. The first text on equity appeared in 1727[13]
and by the opening of the nineteenth century the doctrines of equity,
like the doctrines of common law before them, had hardened into legal
principles and rules. Nonetheless, the oddity remained that England
had two systems of jurisprudence, not one, and that a central mandate
of one was to correct defects in the other.

Ironically, the growth of equity jurisprudence was coupled with a
deterioration in the procedural side of equity.[14] By the nineteenth century, the expense and delay of proceedings in equity had long been a
subject of notoriety and led to substantial reforms. These reform measures culminated ultimately in the enactment of the *Judicature Acts* of
1873 and 1875, which had the effect of merging the two systems into
one court, albeit a court that retained separate divisions for common
law and equity, as it does, indeed, to the present day. Nonetheless, all
the judges of England can apply both common law and equity and the
two systems, from a procedural point of view at least, have been fused
together. Equitable principles are applied when the matter is one for
equity and are not applied when the matter is by tradition one resolved

---

12   *Earl of Oxford's Case* (1615), 1 Rep. Ch. 1 at 6.
13   R. Francis, *Maxims of Equity* (London: J. Stephens, 1727).
14   Baker, above note 11 at 111–15.

exclusively by common law doctrine. Equity remains a legal subject in the sense that there are modern textbooks on equity in England[15] and Australia[16] that are kept current in revised editions. Moreover, from time to time, one sees evidence in the jurisprudence of a resort to equity or equitable principles to fashion solutions to problems presented by the perceived inadequacies of common law doctrines.

Similar procedural reforms were achieved, often at a much later stage, in the common law jurisdictions of North America. Separate courts of equity have disappeared from all of the Canadian common law provinces and almost all of the United States. The eclipse of equity, as an academic subject or separate discipline, however, is peculiar to North American jurisdictions. Equity, as a discrete subject or discipline, has simply disappeared from the curricula of the law schools. There are no currently maintained Canadian or American texts on equity jurisprudence as such.[17] Although the disappearance of equity as a discipline or legal subject is a source of disappointment for traditionalists, the reasons for its disappearance are not obscure. The fact that a body of doctrine developed in a particular court system is, of course, of great historical interest. In North America, however, this no longer seems to be accepted as a suitable analytical framework for a coherent subject or division of the law. Nonetheless, the doctrines of equity persist and they are studied and written about in the context of subjects where they continue to play an important role. The law of contracts derives from both common law and equitable sources and is constituted, therefore, by an intermingling of common law and equity doctrines. An examination of the law of contracts thus requires an understanding of the relationship between common law and equity jurisprudence. Moreover, as the fusion of common law and equity has been procedural rather than substantive, the contemporary lawyer must maintain a familiarity with the historical origins of various aspects of the law of contracts and the basic differences between common law and equity jurisprudence.

A fundamental point concerning the relationship between the two bodies of doctrine derives from the curative role of equity. In the event

---

15   J. Martin, ed., *Hanbury and Martin, Modern Equity*, 17th ed. (London: Sweet & Maxwell, 2005); J. McGhee, ed., *Snell's Equity*, 30th ed. (London: Sweet & Maxwell, 2000).

16   R. Meagher, W. Gummow and J. Lehane, *Equity: Doctrines and Remedies*, 3d ed. (Sydney: Butterworths, 1992).

17   There are Canadian texts on particular aspects of equity. See, for example, J. Berryman, *The Law of Equitable Remedies* (Toronto: Irwin Law, 2000); R.J. Sharpe, *Injunctions and Specific Performance*, 3d ed. (Aurora, ON: Canada Law Book, 2000).

of conflict between a common law doctrine and an equity doctrine, the equity doctrine prevails.[18] Thus, for example, if an agreement is of such a nature that it would be considered to be enforceable as a matter of common law, but unenforceable as a matter of equity, the equity doctrine prevails. Further, it is essential to understand the differences between equitable and common law doctrines on questions such as the enforceability of agreements. If the agreement is unenforceable in equity, the equitable nature of the rule rendering the agreement an unenforceable one is a matter of significance. If an agreement is unenforceable on the ground that it has been induced, for example, by an innocent misrepresentation[19] or by undue influence exercised by the other party,[20] the agreement is subject to an equitable order or decree of "rescission," which has the effect of setting aside the agreement. There is no precise parallel to this type of remedy at common law and, moreover, the equitable remedy is available only on the basis of principles established in the equity jurisprudence. Thus, equitable principles or defences to rescission claims that are peculiar to equitable doctrines may apply and preclude this form of relief. In such a case, the agreement would remain enforceable as a matter of common law and, in the event of a breach of the agreement, a claim for common law damages for breach of contract could be pursued. Where agreements are unenforceable as a matter of common law doctrine, the equitable remedy and the applicable equitable principles and defences are inapplicable as a matter of common law. Whether a contract that is unenforceable at common law might also be subject to a decree of rescission in equity is not a question that admits of an easy or uniform response. In short, the tests for unenforceability and the consequences of unenforceability are different, depending on whether the doctrine rendering the agreement unenforceable is a matter of common law or equity.

Similarly, courts of equity developed what are sometimes referred to as the *in personam* or personal remedies of specific performance and injunctions as an alternative remedy to the damages claim that is typically available as a matter of common law.[21] An equitable decree of specific performance, for example, orders a promisor specifically to perform or carry out a promise set out in an enforceable agreement. Again,

---

18   This basic proposition was enshrined in the English Judicature Acts and is typically set forth in courts' administration legislation in the common law provinces. See, for example, *Courts of Justice Act*, R.S.O. 1990, c. 43, s. 96(2).

19   See Chapter 10.

20   See Chapter 11, section C.

21   See generally Chapter 23.

this form of relief, being equitable in nature, is subject to equitable principles and equitable defences of various kinds that have no parallel in the context of a claim for damages at common law. In short, the remedial mechanisms of common law and equity available for breach of contract differ in important respects.

As experience outside the common law jurisdictions amply demonstrates, this doctrinal dualism is a product of historical accident and is obviously not a necessary feature of a set of laws established to facilitate the enforcement of agreements. Nonetheless, it is an enduring feature of the jurisprudence of the common law jurisdictions and a continuing source of complexity in the law of contracts of the Canadian common law provinces. The differences between common law and equity jurisprudence will be examined as they become relevant to the various topics addressed in this volume.

C. CONTRACT, TORT AND RESTITUTION

The subdivision of the law into various branches or divisions or subjects is a matter of increasing interest to common lawyers.[22] It is also a matter of some contention. Indeed, it is not entirely clear how one would define the concept of a "branch" of the law[23] nor is it clear how one would formulate the criteria for determining whether or not a particular experiment in designing or defining a branch of the law has enjoyed success.[24] Nonetheless, the need to make such subdivisions is an inescapable part of any attempt to examine and understand legal doctrine. Moreover, notwithstanding attendant controversies, a professional consensus has emerged in the common law world in the nineteenth and twentieth centuries, to the effect that the private law of obligations can be usefully subdivided for such purposes into the law of contracts, the law of torts and the law of restitution or, as the last is sometimes called, the law of unjust enrichment.[25] A useful first step

---

22   See generally P. Birks, ed., *The Classification of Obligations* (Oxford: Clarendon Press, 1997); S.M. Waddams, *Dimensions of Private Law* (New York: Cambridge University Press, 2003).

23   For an interesting and illuminating attempt, see R.A. Samek, "Unjust Enrichment, Quasi-Contract and Restitution: A Study in Organising Legal Rules" (1969) 47 Can. Bar Rev. 1.

24   For an interesting failure, however, see J.P. Bishop, *Commentaries on the Non-Contract Law* (Chicago: T.H. Flood & Co., 1889).

25   See A. Burrows, "Contract, Tort and Restitution—A Satisfactory Division or Not?" (1983) 99 Law Q. Rev. 217.

in the examination of the law of contracts, then, is to locate contract within the private law of obligations and to compare its basic conception to those of tort and restitution.

The nature of the distinction to be drawn between "public" and "private" law is also a matter of contention. Public law is generally understood to refer to laws that define the relationship between individual citizens and the state whereas private law defines the relations between private individuals, one to another. Although the division between public law and private law is elusive, constitutional and administrative law, for example, are considered clear candidates for the category of public law, whereas contract and tort, on the other hand, are plainly within the category of private law. The private law of obligations, then, sets out the duties that private individuals owe to one another. In the common law system, those duties are typically, though not exclusively, the product of judge-made law.

At the risk of some oversimplification, the subject matter, basic animating principle and remedial objectives of these three branches of the law may be briefly described. The subject matter of the law of contracts is the enforcement of promises. The basic animating principle of the law of contracts is *pacta sunt servanda*, that is, as a matter of general principle, promises ought to be performed. The principal remedial objective of the law of contracts is to place the victim of a breach of contract in as good a position as he or she would have been in if the contract had been performed. As we shall see,[26] this principle, often referred to as the expectancy principle, provides the normal basis for the calculation of damage awards in claims for breach of contract. Damages for breach of contract are thus "forward-looking" in the sense that they attempt to achieve for the victim of the breach, to the extent that an award of money can do so, the benefits of the promised performance. Thus, a seller who breaches a contract to deliver goods will be subject to a liability to pay damages in an amount that will enable the disappointed buyer to acquire equivalent substitute goods from another source.

The subject matter of the law of torts is compensation for injuries resulting from unprivileged or wrongful conduct. In its detail, the law of torts defines the nature of the unprivileged conduct that will attract tort liability and the kinds of losses that are compensable. The animating principle of the law of torts is that the wrongdoer must compensate the victim for losses resulting from the tortfeasor's wrongful conduct. The remedial objective is compensation for the victim's loss. Damages in a tort claim are thus "backward-looking" in the sense that they are

---

26   See Chapter 22, section B.

calculated with the objective of restoring the victim to the position he or she was in before the tort occurred. In this respect, they are significantly different from the "forward-looking" measure of damages in contract. Apart from this important distinction between the remedial objectives of contract and tort, a fundamental distinction between the two bodies of doctrine is that the obligations arising under the law of contracts are, in theory at least, voluntarily assumed by the contracting parties, whereas the duties arising from the law of torts are imposed as a matter of law, regardless of the intentions or desires of the parties.

The law of contracts and, later, the law of torts were recognized in the nineteenth century as useful categories for explicating legal doctrine or, one might say, for organizing professional knowledge concerning these aspects of the law. The first treatises on contract law appeared in the early part of the century.[27] Books on tort law appeared only in the later part of the century.[28] Recognition of the utility of the third branch of the law of obligations, the law of restitution or unjust enrichment, however, occurred only more recently. The law of restitution did not emerge until the first half of the twentieth century in the United States and gained acceptance in Canadian law more recently and more recently still in England and Australia.[29] The law of restitution was essentially the invention of the American Law Institute, which published the *Restatement of Restitution*[30] as one of a series of restatements on private law, including restatements of the law of contracts[31] and the law of torts,[32] both of which are now in their second editions. The restatements constituted an attempt to provide an authoritative but informal source of doctrine in each subject area in the hope of contributing to greater consistency of doctrinal development and application in the various American state courts. The restatements adopted the format

---

27 See, for example, J. Chitty, *A Practical Treatise on the Law of Contracts* (1826).

28 See, for example, F. Pollock, *The Law of Torts* (Philadelphia: Blackstone, 1887). And see generally A.W.B. Simpson, "The Rise and Fall of the Treatise" (1981) 48 U. Chicago L. Rev. 632.

29 See generally, P.D. Maddaugh and J.D. McCamus, *The Law of Restitution*, 2d ed. (Aurora, ON: Canada Law Book, 2004) c. 1 and 2.

30 American Law Institute, *Restatement of Restitution, Quasi-Contracts and Constructive Trusts* (St. Paul: American Law Institute, 1937). For the earlier history of the underlying concept, see A. Kull, "James Barr Ames and the Early Modern History of Unjust Enrichment" (2005) 25 Oxford J. Legal Stud. 297.

31 See American Law Institute, *Restatement of Contracts 2d* (St. Paul: American Law Institute, 1981).

32 See American Law Institute, *Restatement of Torts 2d* (St. Paul: American Law Institute, 1965).

of restating the law in propositional form, followed by analytical discussions and illustrative examples of the application of each principle. They are of considerable influence in shaping American private law.[33]

The foundational idea upon which the *Restatement of Restitution* was constructed was the insight that large volumes of common law doctrine, traditionally referred to as the law of quasi-contract, and a similarly expansive body of equitable doctrine, much of which is centred on the use of the so-called constructive trust, had a great deal in common and could usefully and coherently be restated in the form of a new legal subject. In the opening section, the authors attempted to identify the fundamental principle underlying the entire subject, the principle against unjust enrichment, in the following terms: "A person who has been unjustly enriched at the expense of another is required to make restitution to the other."[34]

In the manner of the other restatements, the *Restatement of Restitution* then proceeds to restate the rules established in the existing jurisprudence concerning the recovery of benefits conferred by mistake, under duress or other forms of coercion, under ineffective transactions and in various other circumstances where retention of the benefit transferred to the defendant may be said to be unjust. In common with the duties imposed by the law of tort, the duties imposed by the law of restitution are essentially involuntary in nature. Duties to restore benefits conferred are imposed in order to prevent unjust enrichment. Unlike contract and tort, the remedial objective principle of the law of restitution is to effect a recovery of benefits unjustly acquired by the defendant. It may be described as "benefit-based" liability. This measure of relief is inherently different from the compensation measure of tort law and the expectation measure of contract law, both of which measure, albeit in different ways, losses suffered by the plaintiff. The measure of restitutionary relief is the value of the benefit received or obtained by the defendant.

An additional layer of complexity is added, however, when it is revealed that the benefit-based relief awarded in restitution cases is of two different kinds. In a typical case—say, the recovery of money paid to the defendant by mistake—the benefit has been transferred directly from the plaintiff to the defendant. The defendant's gain is the plaintiff's loss and justice requires that the money be restored to the

---

33   See generally the papers collected in a symposium on the Institute in (1998) 26 Hofstra L. Rev. 567–834 and especially J.P. Frank, "The American Law Institute 1923–1998" at 615 of that volume.

34   Above note 30, s. 1.

plaintiff. We may call this a "subtraction" case. Traditionally, however, benefit-based liability has also been imposed to achieve the objective of stripping profits made by the wrongful conduct of the defendant, whether or not those profits have been secured at the direct expense of the plaintiff. An illustration may be helpful. The law of restitution is generally assumed to include the law relating to breaches of so-called fiduciary duties. In essence, such duties preclude the fiduciary, on whom the duties are imposed, from profiting through a conflict of interest with the person to whom the duty is owed. The fiduciary might unlawfully profit from a breach of duty by extracting a benefit directly from the plaintiff, the person to whom the duty is owed. In such a case, the benefit could be said to have been acquired at the direct expense of that person and its recovery could be considered to come within the "subtraction" remedial objective of the law of restitution. The fiduciary might profit, however, by engaging in profit-making activity in which revenues or profits are acquired from third parties. Where, for example, the fiduciary establishes a business that, in breach of fiduciary duty, competes with the business of the person to whom the duty is owed, the profits from the unlawful business would be derived from revenues generated by the customers of that business rather than directly from the person to whom the duty is owed. It has long been well established, as a matter of fiduciary law, that such profits are recoverable by the person to whom the duty is owed even if they cannot be said to be at the expense of that party.[35] The fiduciary is required to disgorge the profits and, in recent years, this measure of relief has been referred to as relief in the disgorgement measure.[36]

Although the conceptual frameworks provided by contract, tort and restitution identify different bodies of doctrine, it is important to appreciate that the frameworks are overlapping in the sense that an analysis of contractual doctrine cannot take place in complete isolation from tort and restitutionary analysis. Thus, many breaches of contract may also constitute tortious wrongdoing and it must be considered whether, in addition to an action for damages for breach of contract, the victim of the breach should also be entitled to bring a claim in tort.

---

35   See generally Maddaugh and McCamus, above note 29, and Chapter 3.

36   Although the foregoing paragraph sets out what I believe to be the mainstream North American consensus on the organization or scope of restitution as a legal subject, it should be noted that the taxonomy of the law of restitution is a subject that has provided much debate in recent years, especially in English legal scholarship. See, for example, P. Birks, *Unjust Enrichment*, 2d ed. (Oxford: Oxford University Press, 2005).

This is typically referred to as the problem of concurrent liability.[37] Further, where contracts have been induced by fraudulent or negligent misrepresentations, thus leading to unenforceability of the agreement either at common law or in equity, the making of the misrepresentation may constitute a tort. Again, it must be considered whether a tort remedy should be available in such circumstances.[38] As far as restitution and contract are concerned, the victim of a breach of contract may be entitled to pursue, as an alternative to the claim in damages, benefit-based restitutionary relief either in the subtraction measure[39] or, indeed, in the disgorgement measure.[40] Moreover, where contracts are held to be unenforceable either on common law or on equitable grounds, either party may wish to seek recovery of the value of benefits conferred on the other in performance of the unenforceable agreement. Such claims are normally considered to be restitutionary in nature.[41]

D. CONTINUITY AND CHANGE

The fact that the general principles of the law of contracts are generated, for the most part, by judicial decisions on a case-by-case basis under the common law method has implications for the extent to which and the manner in which the law of contracts changes over time. A number of considerations weigh in favour of the continuity or stability of the doctrines of contract law. Elementary considerations of fairness and predictability, often associated with the notion of the "rule of law," weigh in this direction. The desirability of deciding like cases in like fashion and in enabling parties to plan their affairs and predict the outcome of litigation on the basis of reasonably stable knowledge concerning the nature of the governing legal regime creates a need for stability and certainty in the law. The common law method itself creates further pressure in this direction. The doctrine of *stare decisis* or precedent, which holds that courts are bound to follow prior judicial decisions of courts higher in the judicial hierarchy than the deciding court, draws its strength from the need for stability and certainty in doctrine.[42] Further, the fact that

---

37 For discussion of which see Chapter 18, section E.
38 See further Chapter 10, section F.
39 See Chapter 24, section B(1).
40 See Chapter 24, section B(2).
41 See Chapter 24, section D.
42 See R. Cross and J.W. Harris, *Precedent in English Law*, 4th ed. (Oxford: Clarendon Press, 1991).

judicial responsibilities are being discharged by unelected judges in adjudicative processes that are not well suited to public policy formulation is likely to lead courts to be somewhat circumspect in exercising their undoubted capacity to reformulate and modify prior doctrine.[43] It is not surprising, then, that continuities in contract doctrine can be traced over long periods of time. Thus, the history of contemporary doctrines such as the law of consideration and the law of contractual performance can be traced to their origins in medieval doctrines.[44]

At the same time, it is beyond serious question that courts in the common law system are the custodians of common law subjects like contracts, torts and restitution and that it has been judicial decision-making rather than legislative reform that has dramatically transformed the common law on these subjects over time. Although judicial decision-making in the context of statutory interpretation and constitutional law, for example, is an important but perhaps secondary source of doctrine concerning such matters, in the context of other areas of the law, such as the private law of obligations, the judicial role in the production of doctrine is of central importance. Although the importance of that role is rarely trumpeted by the courts, judicial acknowledgments of the responsibility of the courts for undertaking even major reforms of private law are occasionally to be found in reported decisions. Thus, in *Kleinwort Benson Limited v. Lincoln City Council*,[45] a decision of the House of Lords in which an important change to the law relating to the recovery of monies paid under mistake was achieved, Lord Goff observed as follows:

> We all know that in reality, in the common law as in equity, the law is the subject of development by the judges—normally, of course, by appellate judges. We describe as leading cases the decisions which mark the principal stages in this development and we have no difficulty in identifying the judges who are primarily responsible. It is universally recognized that the judicial development of the common law is inevitable. If it had never taken place, the common law would be the same now as it was in the reign of King Henry II; it is because of it that the common law is a living system of law, reacting to new events and new ideas, and so capable of providing the citizens of this country with a system of practical justice relevant to

---

43   See, for example, *Watkins v. Olafson*, [1989] 2 S.C.R. 750 at 760–61, McLachlin J.
44   See A.W.B. Simpson, *The History of the Common Law of Contract* (Oxford: Clarendon Press, 1975); S.J. Stoljar, *A History of Contract at Common Law* (Canberra: Australian National University, 1975).
45   [1998] 4 All E.R. 513 (H.L.).

the times in which they live.... When a judge decides a case which
comes before him, he does so on the basis of what he understands
the law to be. This he discovers from the applicable statutes, if any,
and from precedents drawn from reports of previous judicial decisions. Nowadays, he derives much assistance from academic writings
in interpreting statutes and, more especially, the effect of reported
cases; and he has regard, where appropriate, to decisions of judges in
other jurisdictions. In the course of deciding the case before him he
may, on occasion, develop the common law in the perceived interests
of justice, though as a general rule he does this "only interstitially."
... Occasionally, a judicial development of the law will be of a more
radical nature constituting a departure, even a major departure, from
what has previously been considered to be established principle, and
leading to a realignment of subsidiary principles within that branch
of the law.[46]

Further, the doctrine of *stare decisis* is not quite the dead weight on
reform as it is sometimes assumed to be. The doctrine did not crystal-
lize into its modern and rigid form until the late-nineteenth century.[47]
In more recent decades, the highest courts in the judicial hierarchy
both in England and in common law Canada have departed from the
previously held view that *stare decisis* precluded even those courts from
overruling prior doctrine.[48]

In subsequent chapters of this volume, attention will be drawn to
important decisions of the Supreme Court of Canada and other Canadian and commonwealth courts that have made significant contributions
to the development of the law of contracts. As Lord Goff intimated,
although such contributions are typically only "interstitial in nature,"
occasionally more dramatic change is achieved. The decision of the
Supreme Court of Canada in *A.V.G. Management Science Ltd. v. Barwell*[49]
provides a useful illustration. In this case, the Supreme Court effectively overruled the traditional English authority in *Bain v. Fothergill*,
which had imposed limits on the damages recoverable in the context

46   *Ibid.* at 534–35. See also *Trident General Insurance Company Limited v. McNiece
      Bros. Pty. Ltd.* (1988), 165 C.L.R. 107 (Aust. H.C.) at 123, Mason C.J. ("... it is
      the responsibility of this Court to reconsider in appropriate cases, common law
      rules which operate unsatisfactorily and unjustly").
47   See generally Cross and Harris, above note 42.
48   See, for example, *Practice Statement (Judicial Precedent)*, [1966] 1 W.L.R. 1234;
      Reference re Farm Products Marketing Act, [1956] S.C.R. 198 at 212; *R. v. Bell*,
      [1979] 2 S.C.R. 212 at 219–20.
49   [1979] 2 S.C.R. 43. For discussion, see generally Chapter 22, section B(2).

of an innocent failure by a vendor of land to make title. The rule in *Bain v. Fothergill* had stood, as an exception to the general expectancy rule concerning the calculation of damages for breach of contract, for approximately two centuries. Laskin C.J.C., for the Supreme Court, reasoned that the social and economic circumstances that gave rise to the rule no longer prevailed, that, accordingly, this exception to the general rule was no longer defensible and that it ought therefore to be considered overruled. In reaching this conclusion, Laskin C.J.C. made reference to the broad range of sources alluded to by Lord Goff, including experience in other jurisdictions and a report of the British Columbia Law Reform Commission[50] recommending statutory abrogation of the rule. Dramatic change of this kind, however, is a rare event and is typically anticipated by the development of a series of exceptions to an unattractive doctrine and the growth of a body of published criticism of the doctrine in judicial decisions, law reform studies and academic commentary. The more likely avenues for growth of the common law of contract are through the traditional methods of extension and confinement of existing doctrines in the light of their underlying policies and rationales.

In the latter half of the twentieth century, a number of common law jurisdictions, including some Canadian provinces, established either freestanding or *ad hoc* law reform advisory committees to study the possibility of reform of various areas of the law and recommend statutory reform. It is an interesting question, then, whether the establishment of what might be referred to as a law reform commission and legislation model of law reform within many common law jurisdictions has had the effect of decreasing the importance of the role of the judiciary in producing and reformulating the basic principles of the private law of obligations. Although a careful assessment of this rather large question is beyond the scope of the present work, it may be tentatively suggested that the evidence of the last several decades suggests that there has, in effect, been no significant diminution of the role of the courts in this respect. Although law reform commissions have enjoyed considerable success in preparing reports that have enjoyed the implementation in a great range of legal policy contexts, the private law of obligations and the law of contracts in particular appears resistant to change in this

---

50 Law Reform Commission of British Columbia, *Report on the Rule in Bain v. Fothergill* (Vancouver: Law Reform Commission of British Columbia, 1976). Legislation implementing the Commission's recommendations had been enacted at the time of the appeal but not yet proclaimed in force. See now *Property Law Act,* R.S.B.C. 1996, c. 377, s. 37.

form. Thus, shortly after its establishment in 1965, the English Law Commission announced, as its first project, the codification of the law of contract. Although work proceeded to the point of the production of an internal draft of the code, the project was abandoned before completion.[51] The very idea of codification of contract law met with predictable resistance and it seems unlikely, in retrospect, that if the Commission had recommended enactment of a contract code, that Parliament would have responded with alacrity.[52] Similarly, a more modest project undertaken by the Ontario Law Reform Commission has failed to excite the legislators' imagination. The Ontario Commission published its *Report on Amendment on the Law of Contract*,[53] recommending statutory reform of a fairly lengthy list of aspects of the general law of contracts. The recommendations have not been implemented in provincial legislation nor does there appear to be any imminent prospect of such a development. There appear to be two reasons underlying the resilience of the common law method in matters of private law. First, this may reflect a governmental perspective of an appropriate division of labour between the legislative and judicial branches of government. Governments of the day may reasonably take the view that they have more pressing issues on their agenda than reform of various aspects of the private law of obligations. Second, the common lawyer's belief in the superiority of a precedent-based, as opposed to statute-based, private law in its ability to assimilate change and apply flexibly to unanticipated fact situations, is widely held. Both points are captured in Eisenberg's[54] masterly study of the common law method in the following terms:

> The second paramount function of the courts [apart from dispute resolution] is the enrichment of the supply of legal rules. Our society has an enormous demand for legal rules that private actors can live, plan, and settle by. The legislature cannot adequately satisfy this demand. The capacity of a legislature to generate legal rules is limited, and much of that capacity must be allocated to the production of rules concerning governmental matters, such as spending, taxes, and

---

51 Although never released by the Commission, the draft has been published elsewhere. See H. McGregor, *Contract Code Drawn on Behalf of the English Law Commission* (Milan: Dott A. Giuffrè Editore, 1993).

52 For a discussion of the commission's project see, for example, H.R. Hahlo, "Here Lies the Common Law: Rest in Peace" (1967) 3 Mod. L. Rev. 241; L.C.B. Gower, "A Comment" (1967) 30 Mod. L. Rev. 241; H.R. Hahlo, "Codifying the Common Law: Protracted Gestation (1975), 38 Mod. L. Rev. 23.

53 (Toronto: Ontario Law Reform Commission, 1987).

54 M. Eisenberg, *The Nature of the Common Law* (Cambridge: Harvard University Press, 1988).

administration; rules that are regarded as beyond the courts' compe-
tence, such as the definition of crimes; and rules that are best administered by a bureaucratic machinery, such as the principles for setting
the rates charged by regulated industries. Furthermore, our legislatures are normally not staffed in a manner that would enable them to
perform comprehensively the function of establishing law to govern
action in the private sector. Finally, in many areas the flexible form
of a judicial rule is preferable to the canonical form of a legislative
rule. Accordingly, it is socially desirable that the courts should act
to enrich the supply of legal rules that govern social conduct—not
by taking on lawmaking as a free-standing function, but by attach-
ing much greater emphasis to the establishment of legal rules than
would be necessary if the courts' sole function was the resolution of
disputes.[55]

A further concern with the law reform commission and legislation
model for reforming private law doctrine arises in the context of a
federal system. As recent experience in Canada illustrates, the occasional successes of this model are likely to be limited to one or a very
few provinces with resulting decline in the uniformity of contract law
across the common law provinces. In short, the law reform commission
and legislation model appears to be incapable of delivering effective
modernization of the law of contracts across the Canadian common
law jurisdictions.

E. CONTRACTS AS A WORK IN PROGRESS: MODERN TRENDS

In the following chapters, an attempt is made to trace modern developments in various aspects of the law of contracts. By way of introduction
to which follows, however, it may be helpful to portray what appear to
be the main features of this evolving work in progress. The following
and necessarily impressionistic account is best viewed by the reader as
an hypothesis that may be tested in the context of the more specific analysis of particular doctrines and problems in the chapters that follow.

Although, as intimated above, the continuities of contract law are
such that important themes and doctrines in modern contract law can

---

55 *Ibid.* at 4–5. See also Lord Goff, "The Search for Principle" in W. Swadling and
G. Jones, eds., *The Search for Principle* (New York: Oxford University Press,
1999) 313 at 317 ("To me, the best code is one which is not binding in law").

be traced to their medieval origins,[56] the main fault lines of modern Anglo-Canadian contract law were established in the jurisprudence of the English courts in the nineteenth century. This modernization of contract law took place under a greater degree of civilian influence than is often appreciated[57] and established a framework of analysis that is recognizable in its essentials to the modern student of contract law. Often now referred to as the classical model or classical period of contract law, the modern doctrine appears to have been established around the paradigm case of a bargain or exchange entered into by autonomous and self-interested parties who were, through the medium of exchange, building the new economic order. The appropriate rule for the courts and the law of contracts, it seemed, was to refrain from interfering with the dynamic forces of economic growth and to permit the parties to give effect to their freely negotiated bargains.[58] The dominance of the freely negotiated bargain or exchange as the paradigm case around which the doctrine of contract law was ordered is manifested in the doctrine of consideration, recognizing that the promises will be enforceable only where included in a bargain. The rules on offer and acceptance were designed with a view to identifying the mutual expression of wills or *consensus ad idem* as the indispensable threshold for formation of the binding agreement. The common law, no doubt ameliorated to some extent by equitable doctrines, did not appear excessively concerned with the unfairness that might result from the inability of vulnerable people to protect themselves in a bargaining context. Thus, for example, the common law doctrine of duress was narrowly conceived. A bargain was enforceable whether or not the consideration received in return was in some sense adequate or fair.[59] The rules of contract law were often

---

56   See the works cited, above note 44.

57   With respect to the influence of civilian jurists on the development of English contract law in the 19th century, see J. Gordley, *The Philosophical Foundations of Modern Contract Doctrine* (Oxford: Clarendon Press, 1991); A.W.B. Simpson, "Innovations in 19th Century Contract Law" (1975) 91 Law Q. Rev. 247.

58   A classic and oft-quoted statement of this position is that of Jessel M.R. in *Printing & Numerical Registering Company v. Sampson* (1875), L.R. 19 Eq. 462 at 465 ("... if there is one thing which more than another public policy requires it is that men of full age and competent understanding shall have the utmost liberty of contracting and that their contracts when entered into freely and voluntarily shall be held sacred and shall be enforced by Courts of Justice").

59   For an examination of the growth of the freedom of contract ideology and its reflection in nineteenth-century contract law, see P.S. Atiyah, *The Rise and Fall of Freedom of Contract* (Oxford: Clarendon Press, 1979).

applied in a rigid and formalistic fashion even if they achieved results that, to the modern eye at least, appear indefensible.[60]

If nineteenth-century contract law can be viewed as a somewhat spartan and spare reflection of the *laissez-faire* attitudes accompanying the growth of modern capitalism and the accompanying industrialization in England, a number of ameliorating trends are apparent in twentieth-century developments. Perhaps the most dominant trend is the growth of greater exposure to liability for breach of contract. Indeed, the growth of private law doctrine generally through the twentieth century appears to move in the direction of imposing a greater range of liability on parties who have caused loss or benefited at another party's expense. With respect to the awarding of damages for breach of contract, twentieth-century contract law may be characterized by a reduction in the plaintiff's favour of the threshold test for liability for compensatory damages,[61] by the granting of compensation for injuries in the form of mental anxiety or distress[62] and, in Canada at least, by the availability of punitive damages for breach of contract.[63] The possible recognition of liability in the form of an accounting of profits secured by breach is only the most recent development of this kind.[64] Expansion of potential liability has also been achieved through the growth of exceptions to the doctrine of privity of contract,[65] and the imposition of a greater range of liability for misconduct through the implication of contract terms.[66] The recognition in the late-twentieth century of tort liability for negligent misstatements inducing agreements[67] has also substantially expanded the scope of potential liability. Movement in the direction of a more expansive approach to liability in the twentieth century has thus been quite pronounced.[68] Other important trends can, how-

---

60 For an illustration, see *Foakes v. Beer* (1884), 9 App. Cas. 605 (H.L.), for discussion of which, see Chapter 7, section B(4).

61 See Chapter 22, section F(2).

62 See Chapter 22, section H.

63 See Chapter 22, section I.

64 See Chapter 24, section B(2).

65 See Chapter 9.

66 See generally Chapter 19, section D.

67 See Chapter 10, section F.

68 Grant Gilmore, writing of the equivalent to the classical theory of contract in American law, famously wrote that "the theory seems to have been dedicated to the proposition that, ideally, no one should be liable to anyone for anything. Since the idea was not attainable, the compromise solution was to restrict liability within the narrowest possible limits. Within those limits, however, liability was to be absolute...." See G. Gilmore, *The Death of Contract* (Columbus: Ohio State University Press, 1974) at 14.

ever, be detected. Thus, the harshness of the bargain theory has been ameliorated by the greater recognition of the importance of values relating to the fairness of transactions. Recent developments in the form of broadening the grounds for duress and undue influence and setting aside bargains resulting from unfair pressure and, in North American jurisdictions, in particular, the growth of unconscionability doctrine are evident manifestations of this trend.[69] If the more expansive role for these doctrines may be said to have introduced greater attention to questions of moral conduct, the incipient recognition of an implied duty to perform in good faith would be consistent with, even if a rather substantial extension of, this trend.[70]

At a more general and abstract level, the evolution of contract doctrine often appears to have been largely in the direction of a search for underlying principle[71] and the replacement of a rigid and black-letter formulation of a rule with a restatement of the rule in terms of its underlying principle or rationale. Clear illustrations of this phenomenon are to be found in the breakdown of the traditional dichotomy between conditions and warranties in the law of performance[72] and the replacement of the rigid pre-existing duty rule by a rule based on the principle of avoiding the enforcement of bargains resulting from unfair pressure.[73] Movement in a similar direction can be observed in the modern cases considering the effect of illegality[74] on agreements and the rules excusing parties from agreements on the basis of mistaken assumptions[75] and frustration.[76] Such doctrines are more open-textured and supple in their application to the great variety of fact situations to which they must apply. These developments are commonly justified on the basis that although the modernized doctrines appear unattractively flexible and therefore uncertain in their application, their virtue is that by raising to the level of conscious articulation the underlying principles for the imposition or withholding of liability, their application becomes more predictable or reckonable.[77]

The forgoing account is not intended to suggest, however, that the common law of contracts is approaching a state of near perfection. On

---

69   See Chapter 11.
70   See Chapter 21.
71   See Lord Goff, above note 55, especially at 316–17.
72   See Chapter 15, section C.
73   See Chapter 7, section B(3).
74   See Chapter 12.
75   See Chapter 13, section C.
76   See Chapter 14, section B.
77   See, for example, the discussion of unconscionability in Chapter 11, section D(4).

the contrary, much work remains to be done. The bargain theory of enforcement in Anglo-Canadian law, at least, remains more or less resplendent with the result that injuries resulting from detrimental reliance induced by the making of gratuitous promises remains an unsolved problem.[78] Similarly, the problems created by the doctrine of privity of contract, though hobbled by a recently recognized new exception to the doctrine, retain a capacity to produce unsatisfactory results.[79] In these and many other areas of contract doctrine, there remain imperfections and deficiencies that provide opportunities for further growth and development of the law. Moreover, the progress in the development of contract law is not necessarily made on a straight line basis. Not every innovation will be considered fruitful. The Canadian invention of the doctrine of "true condition precedent" offers a case in point.[80] Further, the opportunities for fruitful adjustment of doctrine presented by some authorities may not be exploited in subsequent cases. In short, there is no sign that the opportunities for further development of this work in progress are likely to abate in the near future. Such developments are contingent on the collective ability of the profession to identify fundamental purposes to be served by legal doctrine and the kinds of adjustments of doctrine that will more successfully align the doctrine with those fundamental objectives. The emergence of a substantial body of theoretical literature in recent decades, written from a variety of perspectives, can only be of assistance as these fundamental inquiries continue into the future.[81]

---

78 See Chapter 8.
79 See Chapter 9.
80 See Chapter 17, section D.
81 For a useful survey see J.M. Feinman, "The Significance of Contract Theory" (1990) 58 U. Cin. L. Rev. 1283. And see, for example, I.R. MacNeil, *The New Social Contract* (New Haven: Yale University Press, 1980); C. Fried, *Contract as Promise* (Cambridge: Harvard University Press, 1981); S. Macaulay, "An Empirical View of Contract" (1985) Wis. L. Rev. 465; M.J. Frug, "Re-reading Contracts: A Feminist Analysis of a Contracts Casebook" (1985) 34 Am. U. L. Rev. 1065; J. Wightman, *Contract: A Critical Commentary* (London: Pluto Press, 1996); R.A. Posner, *Economic Analysis of Law*, 6th ed. (New York: Aspen, 2003) c. 4; M.J. Trebilcock, *The Limits of Freedom of Contract* (Cambridge: Harvard University Press, 1993); S.A. Smith, *Contract Theory* (Oxford: Oxford University Press, 2004). Useful collections include P. Benson, ed., *The Theory of Contract Law* (New York: Cambridge University Press, 2001); R. Craswell and A. Schwartz, eds., *Foundations of Contract Law* (New York: Oxford University Press, 1994); R. Barnett, ed., *Perspectives on Contract Law* (Frederick, MD: Aspen Law & Business, 1995); A.T. Kronman and R.A. Posner, eds., *The Economics of Contract Law* (Boston: Little, Brown, 1979).

FURTHER READINGS

P.S. ATIYAH, *The Rise and Fall of Freedom of Contract* (Oxford: Clarendon Press, 1979).

J.H. BAKER, *An Introduction to English Legal History*, 4th ed. (London: Butterworths, 2002).

P. BENSON, ed., *The Theory of Contract Law* (Cambridge: Cambridge University Press, 2001).

P.B.H. BIRKS, ed., *The Classification of Obligations* (Oxford: Clarendon Press, 1997).

D. CAMPBELL, H. COLLINS & J. WIGHTMAN, eds., *Implicit Dimensions of Contract* (Oxford: Hart, 2003).

M.R. COHEN, "The Basis of Contract" (1933) 4 Harv. L. Rev. 553.

M.A. EISENBERG, *The Nature of the Common Law* (Cambridge: Harvard University Press, 1988).

M.A. EISENBERG, "The Responsive Model of Contract Law" (1984) 36 Stan. L. Rev. 1107.

C. FRIED, *Contract as Promise* (Cambridge: Harvard University Press, 1981).

J. GORDLEY, *The Philosophical Origins of Modern Contract Doctrine* (Oxford: Clarendon Press, 1991).

R.A. HILLMAN, *The Richness of Contract Law* (Dordrecht: Kluwer, 1997).

J.M. PERILLO, "Robert J. Pothier's Influence on the Common Law of Contract" (2005) 11 Tex. Wesleyan L. Rev. 267.

R.A. SAMEK, "Unjust Enrichment, Quasi-Contract and Restitution: A Study in Organising Legal Rules" (1969) 47 Can. Bar Rev. 1.

A.W.B. SIMPSON, *A History of the Common Law of Contract* (Oxford: Clarendon Press, 1975).

S.A. SMITH, *Contract Theory* (Oxford: Oxford University Press, 2004).

M.J. TREBILCOCK, *The Limits of Freedom of Contract* (Cambridge: Harvard University Press, 1993).

S.M. WADDAMS, *Dimensions of Private Law* (Cambridge: Cambridge University Press, 2003).

W. WIEGERS, "Economic Analysis of Laws and 'Private Ordering': A Feminist Critique" (1992) 42 U.T.L.J. 170.

PART ONE

FORMATION

CHAPTER 2

OFFER AND ACCEPTANCE

A. INTRODUCTION

The analytical framework for determining whether or not the parties have in fact reached a mutual understanding on the terms of their agreement is referred to as the law of offer and acceptance. The basic idea running through the law of offer and acceptance is that the parties will be held to have reached an agreement when they have formed a mutual intention to enter into a bargain with each other and, further, are in agreement as to the terms of that bargain. It is only then that the parties have reached a true *"consensus ad idem"* or "meeting of the minds," which, in theory at least, is an indispensable requirement for the formation of an agreement. In the calculus of offer and acceptance, the communications of the parties must have created an "offer" that sets out the offeror's willingness to enter into an agreement on certain terms; this is then matched with a corresponding agreement or "acceptance" forthcoming from the other party, the offeree, which also communicates a willingness to enter into an agreement on the proffered terms. The acceptance must precisely match the terms of the offer, a proposition often referred to as "the mirror image rule." A purported acceptance that indicates different terms cannot create the required consensus. Under the orthodox analysis, the offeree must intend to accept the offer.[1] Thus, the fact that two parties send out identical offers, one to another, would not create the requisite consensus.[2] The rules of offer and acceptance, then, establish the analytical mechanism whereby the common law attempts to identify fact situations in which the parties have reached agreement and distinguish them from situations in which parties have merely negotiated unsuccessfully toward that end.

Application of the offer and acceptance analysis requires an examination of the communications between the negotiating parties with a view to isolating communications that constitute an offer in the requisite sense and a corresponding acceptance. The detailed rules articulate the basic tests for isolating offers from other forms of communication and for identifying genuine acceptances. Further, they prescribe such requirements as exist for the communication of the initial offer and the acceptance. They also determine whether and when offers may be revoked. Each of these topics will be considered below. Although there are many factual circumstances in which the application of these rules is quite straightforward, there are also many situations, including fairly common transactional patterns, in which their application is subtle and contentious. Moreover, as we shall see, application of the concepts of offer and acceptance in particular fact situations is often easily manipulated to produce the particular analyst's desired outcome. In a complex fact situation, various plausible candidates for the category of offer or acceptance may emerge. In applying the analytical framework, then, it will often be important to assess the practical implications for the parties of determining whether a particular point in time in a course of negotiations is the moment when a consensus should be considered to have been reached.

In the course of this analysis it will be useful to distinguish, from time to time, between bilateral contracts and unilateral contracts. A bilateral contract is an agreement constituted by an exchange of promises. A simple illustration of a bilateral contract would be a contract for the purchase and sale of goods under which the seller promises to deliver the described goods on a stipulated date and the purchaser promises to pay the agreed price for the goods at that time. Such an agreement would typically be formed by the utterance of an offer to sell by the seller or to buy by the buyer followed by the other party's communication of an acceptance of that offer. A unilateral contract, on the other hand, is constituted by a promise given in exchange for an act. A unilateral contract is typically formed by the communication

---

1   See, however, the discussion of rewards, below, this Chapter, section B(1).
2   *Tinn v. Hoffman* (1873), 29 L.T. 271.

of an offer that indicates that the offeror is prepared to be bound by certain promises if the offeree performs a stipulated act. In such a case, performance of the stipulated act will constitute the acceptance of the offer. Offers of rewards are a commonplace illustration of the phenomenon. An offer in the form, "I will pay you five hundred dollars if you climb to the top of the flagpole," is an offer of an agreement pursuant to which the offeror will be bound to pay a certain amount of money only if the offeree performs a particular act. A more realistic illustration is the offer of a reward for a provision of information concerning the commission of a particular crime, a promise to pay money in return for the act of providing the information in question. In the context of a unilateral contract, then, the acceptance of the offer would be the performance of a particular act—climbing to the top of a flagpole or providing the information requested in the offer of reward. As we shall see, the operation of the rules of offer and acceptance encounter different kinds of difficulties in the context of unilateral as opposed to bilateral agreements.[3]

B. THE OFFER

An offer is a communication by the offeror to the offeree indicating a willingness to enter into an agreement with the offeree on certain terms. If properly characterized as an offer, the communication will signal to a reasonable offeree that the offeree may create an agreement by simply accepting those terms. An offer thus creates a power of acceptance in an offeree. A threshold issue in determining whether a particular communication is an offer is to distinguish mere preliminary negotiations from an actual offer. A distinction is drawn between mere invitations to commence bargaining or so-called invitations to treat and actual offers. As we shall see, the application of this traditional distinction to relatively commonplace factual situations may become a matter of some difficulty. Second, it must be determined whether it is necessary to communicate a particular offer to the offeree and, assuming this to be the case, how that communication must occur. These two sets of issues will be explored below.

---

3   For the suggestion that unilateral contracts are not formed by offer and acceptance. See P.M. Tiersma, "Reassessing Unilateral Contracts: The Role of Offer, Acceptance and Promise" (1992) 26 U.C. Davis L. Rev. 1.

1) Preliminary Negotiations and Offers

An "invitation to treat" is an invitation to commence bargaining. It is typically understood as an invitation to the other party to make an offer of some kind. The critical distinction between an invitation to treat and an actual offer is drawn on the basis that an offer communicates a willingness to be bound by the next communication of the offeree. Application of the distinction obviously depends on the circumstances of the particular case and may be difficult to apply in many circumstances. Two similar cases dealing with the purchase and sale of land illustrate the difficulty of the line-drawing exercise.

In *Harvey v. Facey*,[4] an intending purchaser, Harvey, sent a telegram inquiry to the owner of Bumper Hall Pen in the following form: "Will you sell us Bumper Hall Pen? Telegraph lowest cash price—answer paid." On the same day, the owner, Facey, telegraphed back the following reply: "Lowest price for Bumper Hall Pen £900." Harvey replied immediately: "We agree to buy Bumper Hall Pen for the sum of nine hundred pounds asked by you. Please send us your title deed in order that we might get early possession." Facey denied the existence of an agreement, however, on the basis that he had merely answered the second question as to price and had not replied to the first question relating to willingness. The House of Lords agreed and held that "the mere statement of the lowest price at which the vendor would sell contains no implied contract to sell at that price to the persons making the inquiry."[5]

One might be tempted to explain the result in *Harvey v. Facey* by noting that although the parties had indicated they agreed with respect to the subject matter of the sale and the price, many of the terms of the actual sale had not been the subject of agreement.[6] In a Canadian case, however, *Canadian Dyers Association Ltd. v. Burton*,[7] an agreement was found in circumstances where, similarly, the parties had essentially agreed only to the price of the property to be sold. In *Burton*, the intending purchaser made an initial inquiry to the owner of the property indicating an interest in purchasing the property and asking for the owner's "lowest price." The defendant owner responded: "The lowest price I would care to sell at for cash would be $1,650, as anything else would not bring me in as good a return on my money as my present rental…." No deal was struck at that time but a year and a half later the plaintiff

---

4   [1893] A.C. 552.

5   *Ibid.* at 556, Lord Morris.

6   For discussion of the problem of insufficient terms preventing formation, see below, Chapter 3.

7   (1920), 47 O.L.R. 259 (H.C.J.).

made a further inquiry: "We would be pleased to have your very lowest price for 25 Hanna Avenue. Perhaps we could get closer together than the last figure given us." The defendant wrote in reply: "I beg to acknowledge receipt of your favour of the 16th instant, and in reply would say that the last price I gave you is the lowest that I am prepared to accept. In fact I feel that under present conditions that this is exceptionally low and if it were to any other party I would ask more." The plaintiff, purporting to accept this offer, forwarded a cheque for $500 and invited the defendant to prepare a deed. The defendant instructed his solicitor to prepare a draft deed. A few weeks later, however, the defendant returned the cheque and advised the plaintiff that there was no agreement between them. Middleton J. distinguished *Harvey v. Facey*, placing particular emphasis on the defendant's statement that "the price … is the lowest I am prepared to accept … if it were to any other party I would ask more." "Surely," Middleton J. observed, "unless language is used to conceal thought, this is an offer."[8] Perhaps the communications in *Burton* do more clearly indicate a willingness to sell than those in *Harvey v. Facey*. It is not surprising, however, that where the defendant's conduct immediately after receiving the purported acceptance from the plaintiff plainly indicated that he understood that a contract had been formed then the communications were construed as an offer.

Consistently with *Harvey v. Facey*, courts have held that mere quotations of prices[9] do not constitute offers. There is, however, no magic in the word "quotation." A quotation followed by an indication that the supplier would be pleased to have an order from the potential customer has been held to constitute an offer.[10] In each case, as Middleton J. observed in the *Burton* case, "it is a question to be determined upon the language used, in the light of the circumstances in which it is used, whether what is said by the vendor is a mere quotation of price or in truth an offer to sell."[11]

---

8   *Ibid.* at 262.
9   See, for example, *Johnston Bros. v. Rogers Bros.* (1899), 30 O.R. 150 (Div. Ct.) (a circular letter containing the phrase "We quote you …"); *Victoria Electrical Co. v. Monarch Electrical Co. Ltd.* (1917), 13 O.W.N. 141 (Ex.).
10   *Harty v. Gooderham* (1871), 31 U.C.R. 18.
11   Above note 7 at 260. See, for example, *Bigg v. Boyd Gibbons Ltd.*, [1971] 1 W.L.R. 913 (C.A.) ("for a quick sale, I would accept £26,000" — held to be an offer); *Calgary Hardwood & Veneer Ltd. v. Canadian National Railway Co.* (1977), 74 D.L.R. (3d) 284 (Alta. S.C.T.D.), aff'd (1979), 100 D.L.R. (3d) 302 (Alta. S.C.A.D.) ("will agree to sell" if offeree obtains necessary governmental approval—held to be an offer); *Imperial Glass Ltd. v. Consolidated Supplies Ltd.* (1960), 22 D.L.R. (2d) 759 (B.C.C.A.) ("quotation" of subcontractor held to be an offer); *Bundy v. Johnson* (1856), 6 U.C.C.P. 221 ("will sell at" held to be an offer). Compare with *Clifton v.*

Similarly, courts have held that price lists[12] and advertisements of items for sale[13] are mere invitations to treat. Underlying these decisions is the courts' awareness of the practical difficulties that would ensue if such suppliers, who have a limited stock of items for sale, could be held to have entered into a binding contract with anyone who might respond to communications of this kind.[14] Where the advertisement indicates the limited nature of the supply available, however, and offers the goods to those who first perform a particular condition, it may be that the advertisement will be held to constitute an offer. In the well-known American case of *Lefkowitz v. Great Minneapolis Surplus Store*[15] a retailer published an advertisement indicating that a Black Lapin stole, worth $139.50 would be sold for $1.00 on "a first come, first served basis" the next Saturday morning at 9 a.m. This was held to constitute an offer of a unilateral contract that was accepted when the plaintiff met the condition. The retailer had turned down the plaintiff's attempt to purchase the stole on the basis of a "house rule" that such offers were intended for women only. The court rejected this argument on the basis that it constituted an attempt to modify the offer after it had been accepted. The problem of limited supply could perhaps be addressed in a more general way by implying, in appropriate cases, an obligation on the part of the offeror to supply only a reasonable quantity or to be bound only to the extent that limited supplies remain available. Courts have applied this analysis in a limited number of cases dealing with quotations[16] and train schedules[17] and it could be applied, for example, to cases involving mail-order catalogues.[18]

As *Burton* illustrates, the fact that the parties expect to execute a further written instrument—in this case, a deed of conveyance—does not preclude a finding that a binding agreement has been created prior to its execution. Nor is an agreement precluded by the anticipation of further steps in the formalization or recording of the agreement. In

---

    Palumbo, [1944] 2 All E.R. 497 (C.A.) ("I … am prepared to offer you …" a mere invitation to treat).

12   See, for example, *Grainger & Son v. Gough*, [1896] A.C. 325 (H.L.); *Boyers and Co. v. D. & R. Duke*, [1905] 2 I.R. 617 (K.B.D.).

13   See, for example, *Partridge v. Crittenden*, [1968] 1 W.L.R 1204 (Q.B.D.). See also *Rooke v. Dawson*, [1895] 1 Ch. 480 (advertisement of scholarship examination not an offer).

14   *Grainger & Son v. Gough*, above note 12 at 334, Lord Herschell.

15   86 N.W.2d 689 (Minn. S.C. 1957).

16   See *Harty v. Gooderham*, above note 10.

17   *Denton v. Great Northern Rwy. Co.* (1856), 5 El. & Bl. 860, 119 E.R. 701.

18   Compare with *Quebec Pharmaceutical Ass'n. v. T. Eaton Co.* (1931), 56 C.C.C. 172 (Que. C.A.); *Québec (Sous-ministre du Revenu) v. Simpsons-Sears Ltd.*, [1986] R.L. 37 (Que. C.A.).

Storer v. Manchester City Council,[19] for example, the defendant municipality had embarked on a scheme of selling units of public housing to
existing tenants who wished to purchase them. The plaintiff indicated
his wish to do so and received a letter from the defendant enclosing a
draft agreement that he was asked to sign and return. The letter further
indicated that if he did so, the defendant would execute the agreement
and return a copy to him. The plaintiff executed and returned the draft
agreement. With a change in government, the scheme was abandoned.
The defendant, not having returned an executed copy to the plaintiff,
adopted the position that no agreement had been entered as this final
step in the formalization of the agreement had not taken place. The
Court of Appeal held that the defendant's letter constituted an offer
that the plaintiff had accepted by execution and return of the draft
agreement.

a) Retail Sales

Application of the principles of offer and acceptance to the sale of goods
in retail establishments open to the public gives rise to similar points
of difficulty. For example, it may be considered whether the display
of goods in the shop window, perhaps with price and terms of payment attached, constitutes an offer that may be accepted by entering
the store and indicating to the salesclerk, "I will have one of those."
The traditional view is that the display does not constitute an offer.[20]
Some, but not all,[21] such cases may be explained on the basis of the
problem of limited supply. The more general explanation offered by
one commentator[22] is that the retailer should be presumed to retain a
discretion to deal with only such customers as he or she finds suitable.
Another view is possible, however, and it may be that, in appropriate
cases, courts will find that an implied "while quantities last" term in
the offer together with an absence of any understanding that such a
discretion is preserved provides a basis for a holding that the display
constitutes an offer.

---

19 [1974] 3 All E.R. 824 (C.A.). Compare with *Gibson v. Manchester City Council*,
    [1979] 1 W.L.R. 294, [1979] 1 All E.R. 972 (H.L.), rev'g [1978] 2 All E.R. 583
    (C.A.) ("may be prepared to sell" not an offer). For discussion of agreements
    "subject to contract," see Chapter 4, section B(4).

20 See, for example, *R. v. Bermuda Holdings Ltd.* (1970), 9 D.L.R. (3d) 595
    (B.C.S.C.); *Fisher v. Bell*, [1961] 1 Q.B. 394.

21 *R. v. Bermuda Holdings Ltd.*, *ibid.*

22 P. Winfield, "Some Aspects of Offer and Acceptance" (1939) 55 Law Q. Rev. 499
    at 518.

The proper characterization of the display of goods on the shelves of a self-service retail facility was considered in the leading English case, *Pharmaceutical Society of Great Britain v. Boots Cash Chemists (Southern) Ltd.*,[23] a case involving the sale of certain regulated pharmaceuticals in a self-service pharmacy operated by the defendant, Boots. The Pharmaceutical Society challenged the legality of the arrangements under which Boots supplied such commodities in its self-service outlets. Under the governing legislation, Boots was required to supply such commodities only under the supervision of a registered pharmacist. The products in question were displayed in a section of the store near the location of the manager, a registered pharmacist, who was located in reasonable proximity to the cash desks operated by cashiers. Although the manager was authorized to prevent any sale of these substances at the cash desk, the customers were not notified of this authorization and, apparently, in the normal course of events, the manager was not directly involved in processing each sale. The question, then, was whether the sale occurred at the cash desk, in which case the transaction might have been said to be, in some sense, under the supervision of the pharmacist. The plaintiff society urged that the sale occurred prior to the customer's arrival at the cash desk, and accordingly, that the offence of unsupervised sale had been committed. In support of its position, the plaintiff argued that the display of the goods on the shelf with ticketed prices amounted to an offer of sale, an offer which is accepted when the customer places the item in question in his or her shopping basket. On this basis, an offer and acceptance would have occurred prior to the customer's attendance at the cash desk and the pharmacist would no longer be in a position to refuse to authorize the sale. The Court of Appeal rejected this view, however, on the basis that the presentation of the articles for purchase to the cashier by the customer amounted to the offer, which was then accepted by the cashier. It was a persuasive consideration, in the court's view, that if one took the position that placing the article in the shopping basket amounted to an acceptance, the customer would be in no position to substitute an article of a similar kind for the first article placed in the basket.

Although, strictly speaking, it was not necessary for the court in *Boots* to decide at exactly what point the acceptance occurred, the court appeared to be of the view that the acceptance of the price by the cashier amounted to the acceptance of the customer's offer. Other views are, however, possible. In a Canadian shoplifting case, *R. v. Dawood*,[24] the

---

23   [1953] 1 Q.B. 401 (C.A.).
24   [1976] 1 W.W.R. 262 (Alta. C.A.).

question was whether the accused, who had been charged with theft, had committed that offence or had merely acquired goods by fraud, in which case she had been charged with the wrong offence. The accused had purchased a matched set of clothing items, having removed the price ticket from one of them, thus creating the impression that the entire set could be purchased for the price of the other. If, as under *Boots*, the accused had simply made an offer, albeit a misleading one, to purchase the set at the reduced price at the cash desk, a contract had been entered into at the reduced price. On this basis, though guilty of fraud, the accused was innocent of theft. The majority of the Alberta Court of Appeal was of the view that *Boots* was applicable and, accordingly, confirmed the acquittal at trial. In dissent, however, Clement J.A. would have convicted on the basis that the display of the ticketed goods was an offer open to acceptance by the accused by tendering payment of the ticketed price. Since the accused had not done so, no contract was entered into and, for Clement J.A., the accused was guilty of theft.

Two points of interest emerge from this line of cases. First, it may be noted that the concepts of offer and acceptance, even in this rather ordinary factual situation, are quite manipulable. Although Clement J.A.'s analysis is inconsistent with *Boots*, there is nothing obviously incorrect with his suggestion that goods displayed in such circumstances constitute an offer that can be accepted by presenting the goods to the cashier, perhaps coupled with a tendering of the price. Second, these cases illustrate the application of the contractual offer and acceptance and analysis in contexts where non-contractual policy considerations are present. When criminal and quasi-criminal offences are defined, as in *Dawood* and *Boots*, in terms of contractual concepts such as "sale," it is unsurprising that courts apply the contractual analysis of offer and acceptance to determine whether or not, for example, a contract of sale has been entered. And yet, the interaction of private law and public law is less than ideal in these circumstances. A number of policy considerations may be present in the context of regulatory legislation—such as narrow construction of offences against the Crown or giving effect to the intended scope of the prohibition, that, strictly speaking, are not relevant to the contractual issue of whether an offer for sale in the contractual sense had truly occurred. Conversely, cases dealing with public law offences may or may not produce doctrine that is consistent with the objectives of contract law.

Further, when these issues are considered from a purely contractual perspective, it may well be that policy considerations will move the court in one direction rather than another in applying these highly manipulable concepts. Thus, although *Boots* maximizes the discretion retained by the retailer to refuse the transaction at the cash desk, the ruling appears to leave it open to retailers to exercise that discretion in a way that might be quite surprising to the offeree and, indeed, contrary to public policy. Thus, for example, in the infamous decision in *Christie v. York Corporation*,[25] a bartender at the tavern at the Montreal Forum refused to fill the order of the plaintiff and two friends for a glass of beer on the basis that he had been "instructed not to serve coloured persons."[26] The plaintiff's claim for breach of contract and tort as a result of the humiliation suffered did not enjoy success. The decision, while consistent with *Boots* and in accord with nineteenth-century values of freedom of contract is evidently offensive to modern sensibilities.[27] One would not be surprised to find a contemporary judge holding that a tavern's displayed price list constituted an offer accepted by the plaintiff by entering the tavern, taking a seat and placing an order.

b)   Offers to the General Public: Rewards and Other Unilateral Contracts

Offers can be made to the public at large. Typically such offers are made in the form of unilateral contracts inviting members of the public to perform a particular condition in order to become entitled to a reward of some kind. The phenomenon is illustrated in the leading case of *Carlill v. Carbolic Smoke Ball Co.*[28] The defendants were the manufacturers of a patent medicine product called the "Carbolic Smoke Ball" designed as a preventative for influenza, colds or other similar diseases. The defendants published an advertisement in a London newspaper that included the following inducement to use their product:

> £100 reward will be paid by the Carbolic Smoke Ball Company to any person who contracts the increasing epidemic of influenza, colds, or any disease caused by taking cold, after having used the ball three times daily for two weeks according to the printed directions supplied with each ball. £1000 is deposited with the Alliance Bank, Regent Street, shewing our sincerity in the matter.[29]

---

25   [1940] S.C.R. 139.

26   *Ibid.* at 141.

27   For criticism on this basis, see B. Laskin, "Tavern Refusing to Serve Negro—Discrimination" (1940) 18 Can. Bar Rev. 314.

28   [1893] 1 Q.B. 256 (C.A.) [*Carlill*]. For discussion of this case in its historical context, see A.W.B. Simpson, "Quackery and Contract Law: The Case of the Carbolic Smoke Ball" (1985) 14 J. Legal Stud. 345.

29   *Carlill, ibid.* at 257.

One week later, the plaintiff purchased a smoke ball and followed the instructions by "smoking herself" thrice daily until, approximately ten weeks later, she caught influenza.

The plaintiff's attempt to collect the reward from the defendant was rebuffed by the company on a variety of grounds, including a suggestion that the reward would only be payable if Mrs. Carlill had smoked herself at the premises of the defendant under their supervision. In response to the plaintiff's claim to enforce the promise to pay the reward, the defendant raised this point and other grounds in defence. The advertisement was said to be too vague to be enforceable. With respect to offer and acceptance, the defendant argued that the offer had purportedly been made to all the world and one simply cannot contract with the entire world. Bowen L.J. responded to this point in the following terms:

> It is not a contract made with all the world. There is the fallacy of the argument. It is an offer made to all the world; and why should not an offer be made to all the world which is to ripen into a contract with anybody who comes forward and performs the condition? It is an offer to become liable to anyone who, before it is retracted, performs the condition, and although the offer is made to the world, the contract is made with that limited portion of the public that come forward and perform the condition on the faith of the advertisement.[30]

Bowen L.J. distinguished offers to sell where the seller had a limited supply of, for example, books or houses to let, in which case the advertisement is merely an invitation to negotiate rather than an offer in the strict sense. The court made short shrift of the other defences raised. The offer was not fatally vague or uncertain. The plain meaning of the advertisement was that anyone who used the smoke ball in the prescribed way and contracted influenza or a cold while using the smoke ball would be entitled to the reward. If it was unwise of the smoke ball company to fail to explicitly require that the use of the smoke ball be supervised by the company, there was no reason why the company should not be bound by the extravagance of its promises.[31]

---

30 *Ibid.* at 268.

31 The court also rejected the defendant's argument that Mrs. Carlill had not communicated her acceptance of the offer and that silence could not constitute acceptance. See further below, this Chapter, section D(1). The court did not consider the question of whether the offer could be revoked at any time prior to the time at which Mrs. Carlill contracted influenza. See below this Chapter, section E(2).

The problem of limited supply disappears in these cases because of the nature of the condition imposed on acceptance. Thus, in *Carlill*, the only members of the public who could accept the offer were those who acquired and used the smoke ball. Accordingly, the offeror company knew the size of that potential class of persons and, indeed, controlled its size through the manufacture and distribution of smoke balls. In other typical reward cases where money is offered for the return of one's lost cat or for the provision of information leading to the arrest and conviction of a perpetrator of a particular crime, there is only one person who will find the cat and likely only a very few people who could provide the requisite information concerning the criminal.

An offer of a unilateral contract can be expressed in the form, "if you do x, I promise y." In many reward cases, the advertisement will literally take this form and in the *Carbolic Smoke Ball* case, it very nearly did so. It is not necessary that the advertisement take this form, however, provided that the reader would reasonably understand that the advertisement is making an offer of this kind. Thus, in *Goldthorpe v. Logan*,[32] a purveyor of a hair removal treatment called "electrolysis," proudly boasted in an advertisement: "Hairs ... removed safely and permanently by Electrolysis ... No marks, No scars, Results Guaranteed."[33] The plaintiff subjected herself to the defendant's electrolysis treatments without success and then brought an action for damages for breach of the guarantee in the advertisement. The claim was allowed by the Ontario Court of Appeal. Laidlaw J.A. characterized the advertisement, as it would be understood, in his view, by the public, to communicate an offer of a unilateral contract in the form: "If you will submit yourself to my treatment and pay me (certain charges) I undertake to remove hair safely and permanently by electrolysis and I promise to obtain a satisfactory result."[34] The court's concern to protect credulous potential customers from extravagant promises by suppliers of such services was abundantly apparent. Laidlaw J.A. observed: "[t]he strong cannot disregard any undertaking binding in law, however lightly given, and the weak unfortunate person, however gullible, can be sure that the Courts of this country will not permit anyone to escape the responsibility arising from an enforceable promise."[35]

---

32   [1943] 2 D.L.R. 519 (Ont. C.A.).
33   *Ibid.* at 522.
34   *Ibid.*
35   *Ibid.* at 523.

c) Tenders

Application of the law of offer and acceptance to tendering processes in Canadian law has been dramatically transformed in recent years. A typical tendering arrangement will arise in the context of a large construction or other project of some kind, often at the behest of a government agency. The process normally commences with the issuance of a "tender call" or "invitation to tenders" issued by the party who wishes to retain someone to undertake the project. The tender call will set out the nature of the project and the rules relating to the submission of bids or tenders by interested parties. The tender call will often include a draft of the building or construction contract, which it is expected or required that the successful bidder will enter upon completion of the tendering process. The next stage in the process will involve the submission of bids by interested parties. Often bids will be required to be submitted into a bid depository in order to ensure the confidentiality of the bids until the time stipulated for opening and evaluating the bids. Once that time has arrived, the next stage involves the opening and assessment of the bids and the selection of the winning bid. The final step in the process, then, would be the execution of the construction contract by the successful bidder and the issuer of the invitation. Typical features of the tender call would be a requirement that each bidder, upon submitting a bid, will also submit a deposit or performance bond that will be forfeited if the bidder in question is ultimately selected by the issuer but then refuses to enter into the building contract. The tender call may also set out very elaborate rules to be followed with respect to the evaluation of bids. The issuers often also insert so-called preference clauses that purport to protect the issuer by stipulating that the issuer is not obliged to accept the lowest or any of the bids submitted. Depending on the particulars of the preference clause, the issuer will usually be in a position to accept a higher bid, if the issuer has concerns about the quality of the lower priced bids or bidders, or may, indeed, be entitled simply to cancel the project.

Under traditional doctrine, it had been assumed that the rules of offer and acceptance apply to this process in the following manner. First, the invitation to tender was considered to be simply an invitation to treat or bargain. The submission of bids, then, constituted the submission of offers by the various bidders. When the issuer selected the winning bid, this amounted to an acceptance of that particular offer and obliged the bidder to proceed with the project and, in the typical case, execute the building contract appended to the invitation to tender. The consequence of this analysis, from the bidders' perspective, was that there was no contract of any kind relating to the tendering process. Thus, if the issuer failed, in some respect, to follow the rules of the tendering process set out in the invitation, this would not constitute a breach of contract entitling disappointed tenderers to claim that the default had caused them a loss of some kind. The advantage of the tendering process for bidders, of course, is the opportunity to compete in a more or less transparent and fair process for the project in question. Under the traditional view, however, there was no contractual guarantee that the competition would be conducted in accord with the rules set out in the invitation.

This traditional view was transformed by the decision of the Supreme Court of Canada in *Ontario v. Ron Engineering & Construction (Eastern) Ltd.*,[36] a case involving an attempted withdrawal of a bid by a successful bidder who realized, upon the opening of the bids, that it had made a major miscalculation of its bid price. The plaintiff bidder had submitted a bid on a public sector project of $2,748,000 together with a bid deposit of $150,000. Upon the opening of the bids, the plaintiff's representative discovered that the plaintiff's bid was $632,000 lower than the next lowest tender. This provoked an anxious reconsideration of the calculation of the bid and a discovery by the plaintiff that it had not included $750,058 of its own labour costs in the calculation of the tender. The plaintiff thereupon immediately contacted the issuer of the tender call and asked to be permitted to withdraw the mistaken bid. The government issuer declined the request, insisted on the plaintiff's performance of the contract and, upon the plaintiff's refusal to do so, pursuant to the terms of the tender call, forfeited the plaintiff's bid deposit.

Prior to *Ron Engineering*, a substantial line of authority had developed with respect to the legal effect of mistaken bids in circumstances such as these and the plaintiff was no doubt encouraged by that line of authority to pursue a claim for a return of the bid deposit on the theory that once the mistake infecting the offer became known to the issuer, the bid could no longer be accepted.[37] In this case, however, Estey J., for the Court, trumped this line of authority. He held that the tender call, coupled with the submission of a bid, created a binding contract—referred to as "Contract A," which was to be distinguished from "Contract B," the construction contract. Therefore, the provisions of the tender call establishing the irrevocability of bids and the forfeiture of deposits of bidders who, when selected, refuse to proceed, were contractually binding on bidders, including the plaintiff. Under

---

36   [1981] 1 S.C.R. 111.
37   For an analysis of this line of authority see Chapter 13, section B(4).

the new analysis, the tender call constituted an offer of a contract relating to the tendering process and the submission of each individual bid constituted an acceptance of that offer creating a binding contract between each individual bidder and the issuer of the tender call. Under Contract A, then, the consequence of the plaintiff's refusal to go forward was forfeiture of the deposit. Accordingly, the plaintiff's claim was dismissed. In the court's view, it was not necessary to consider the impact of the plaintiff's error, if any, upon the formation of Contract B. Any miscalculation made by the plaintiff in preparing its tender was simply irrelevant to the enforceability of Contract A. The plaintiff had intended to submit the tender in the very form it was submitted at the time of the formation of Contract A.[38]

Estey J. suggested in *Ron Engineering* that Contract A was unilateral in nature inasmuch as it was created by the act of submitting a bid and thus appeared to involve the exchange of an act for a promise. This suggestion is belied, however, by the suggested content for Contract A. For Estey J., Contract A included promissory obligations on the part of both parties. On the bidder's part, the irrevocability of the bid established an obligation to go forward, if selected, and enter Contract B. On the issuer's part, the obligations included a promise to return the deposit within sixty days of the opening of the bids to bidders who were not selected and a qualified obligation to accept the lowest tender. As Contract A thus consists of promises made by both parties to the arrangement, it is plainly bilateral in nature. The mode of acceptance of the bilateral arrangement, however, is, as stipulated in the invitation, the act of submitting a bid.[39]

In subsequent cases, the Supreme Court of Canada has confirmed the validity of the offer and acceptance analysis applied, for the first time, in *Ron Engineering* to tendering processes and the court has, in so doing, rounded out the nature of the offer implicit in the tender call by recognizing the existence of a number of implied terms.[40] Thus in *M.J.B. Enterprises Ltd. v. Defence Construction (1951) Ltd.*,[41] the Supreme Court held that Contract A included an implied term obliging the issu-

---

38   For further exploration of the role of mistake in the context of tendering processes, see Chapter 13, sections B(4) and C(5).

39   In *M.J.B. Enterprises Ltd. v. Defence Construction (1951) Ltd.*, [1999] 1 S.C.R. 619 at 631, Iacobucci J. acknowledged the criticism made by others of the characterization of Contract A as unilateral in *Ron Engineering*, but saw no need to revisit this analysis in this case.

40   For discussion of implied terms generally, see Chapter 19, section D, and of the implied terms in Contract A in particular, see section D(3).

41   Above note 39.

er to refrain from accepting non-compliant bids. In the Court's view, bidders would be unwilling to submit bids unless it was understood by all that only compliant bids could be accepted. In this case, the Crown, having accepted a non-compliant bid from a third party, was exposed to a claim by the plaintiff unsuccessful bidder for the profits the plaintiff would have made if the obligation to accept only compliant bids had been followed by the Crown. As the second lowest bidder, the plaintiff could recover the full profits it would have made had it been awarded Contract B. In *Martel Building Ltd. v. Canada*,[42] the Supreme Court held that Contract A also included an implied duty on the part of the issuer to treat all bidders fairly and equally. Allegations of breach of this term are now commonplace and facilitate close scrutiny of the conduct of issuers. Indeed, the obligations imposed on issuers by Contract A are potentially so onerous that issuers now often stipulate in invitations to tender that no contractual relationship is formed by the submission of a bid.[43]

The burdensome nature of Contract A for issuers may explain why some courts have resisted application of the *Ron Engineering* offer and acceptance analysis to other similar processes. Although the Supreme Court of Canada has held that the Contract A analysis applies to the relations between a general contractor and subcontractors who have submitted bids,[44] some courts have refused to apply the analysis to tendering processes that do not lead more or less inexorably to the execution of a Contract B in a form appended to the invitation. In some tendering contexts, issuers construct a preliminary round of competition—sometimes called a Request For Proposal (RFP) or Request for Expressions of Interest (REI)—for the purpose of identifying a select group of competitors who will compete in a final round that may be more akin to traditional tendering processes. In other contexts, where the bidder is to compete not only as to cost but also with respect to the very design of the project, the invitation may stipulate only that the issuer will attempt in good faith to negotiate Contract B with the selected bidder, reserving the right to negotiate with other bidders should those negotiations fail to produce an agreement. Some courts have held that the Contract A analysis does not apply to the initial round in these

---

42   [2000] 2 S.C.R. 860.

43   For a discussion of the intention to create legal relations issue in this context, see Chapter 4, section B(2). For discussion of the content of the implied term, see Chapter 19, section D(3).

44   *Naylor Group Inc. v. Ellis-Don Construction Ltd.*, [2001] 2 S.C.R. 943. See also *Gloge Heating & Plumbing Ltd. v. Northern Construction Co.* (1986), 27 D.L.R. (4th) 264 (Alta. C.A.).

kinds of competitions, typically on the unconvincing ground that the first round does not result in the creation of a Contract B.[45] It is difficult to discern a principled reason, however, for excluding the application of the *Ron Engineering* offer and acceptance analysis to these types of competitions. As in more traditional tendering contexts, an RFP or REI involves an invitation to participate in a competition, the rules of which are often carefully prescribed in the invitation to participate. The cost of participation will often be extremely expensive. The mere fact that success in the competition leads to a further round of bidding or an attempt to negotiate rather than an immediate Contract B does not appear to supply a convincing basis for exclusion of the Contract A analysis. Detrimental reliance by bidders on the issuer's undertaking to run a fair and proper process is present in similar measure in all of these cases.

d) Auctions

An ordinary sale by auction involves three parties: the owner of the asset to be sold, the auctioneer who will auction off the particular asset as agent of the owner and the highest bidder for the item at the auction. It is well established that the auctioneer's request for bids is merely an invitation to bid rather than an offer for sale and that the individual bids are offers made in response to that invitation that may or may not be accepted by the auctioneer on the owner's behalf.[46] The acceptance of the offer is typically communicated by the fall of the auctioneer's hammer. Prior to that point in time, as each bid is merely an offer, the offer may be revoked by the bidder. This traditional analysis is set out in the sale of goods legislation of the common law provinces in the following form: "In case of a sale by auction, ... a sale is complete when the auctioneer announces its completion by the fall of a hammer or in any other customary manner, and until such announcement is made any bidder may retract his, her or its bid."[47]

This provision is silent with respect to the ability of the auctioneer, on the owner's behalf, to withdraw the item for sale before the hammer falls. Nonetheless, it follows from the proposition that bids are

---

45 See, for example, *Buttcon Ltd. v. Toronto Electric Commissioners* (2003), 65 O.R. (3d) 601 (S.C.J.); *Mellco Developments Ltd. v. Portage La Prairie (City)* (2002), 222 D.L.R. (4th) 67 (Man. C.A.). See also *Powder Mountain Resorts Ltd. v. British Columbia*, [2001] 11 W.W.R. 488 (B.C.C.A.). Compare with *WindPower Inc. v. Saskatchewan Power Corp.* (2002), 217 Sask. R. 193 (C.A.).

46 *Payne v. Cave* (1789), 3 Term Rep. 148, 100 E.R. 502. See generally M.A. Hickling, "Auctions Without Reserve" (1970) 5 U.B.C. L. Rev. 187.

47 See, for example, *Sale of Goods Act*, R.S.O. 1990, c. S.1, s. 56(b).

merely offers, that the seller is not bound, prior to the fall of the hammer and can terminate the auction and withdraw the item for sale. The practical justification for this approach, presumably, is that the bidding may be so low that it would be unfair to commit the owner to sale of the asset to the highest bidder, however low that bid might be. Were the rule otherwise, binding the owner to the highest bidder, placing one's assets up for auction would be a perilous exercise. The legislation is also silent with respect to the effect of higher bids on lower bids. It appears to be accepted that bids that are exceeded by higher bids taken by the auctioneer lapse.[48] Accordingly, the withdrawal of a higher offer does not revive the next highest bid. Further, it has been held that the publication of an advertisement indicating that an auction of particular goods will be held does not amount to an offer to potential bidders of an undertaking to conduct the auction that can be accepted by their attendance at the appointed place and time.[49]

Where the auction is advertised as being "without reserve," however, a different approach is taken. The phrase "without reserve" is interpreted as a commitment by the auctioneer to sell the item to the highest bidder, regardless of how low the highest bid may be. In this circumstance, the advertisement has been held to constitute an offer of a unilateral contract to potential bidders accepted by them when they attend at the auction that binds the auctioneer to conduct the auction on this basis.[50] The owner of the asset to be auctioned off, however, having made no offer, is not exposed to liability when the asset is withdrawn from the auction.

2) Communication of Offer

To be effective, an offer must be communicated to the offeree. This much, at least, seems to follow from the basic requirement that there must be a *consensus ad idem* between the parties. If the offeree is unaware of the offer, how could it be accepted? It might also appear to flow logically from the *consensus ad idem* principle that where the acceptance invited by the offer involves conduct by the offeree, the offeree

---

48   Hickling, above note 46 at 189, offers the explanation that the auctioneer's receipt of a higher bid constitutes an implied rejection of the previous highest bid.

49   *Harris v. Nickerson* (1873), L.R. 8 Q.B. 286.

50   See *Barry v. Davies*, [2000] 1 W.L.R. 1962 (C.A.), confirming *dicta* to the same effect in the much earlier authority, *Warlow v. Harrison* (1858), 1 El. & El. 309, 120 E.R. 925 (Ex.). See also *Harris v. Nickerson, ibid.; Johnstone v. Boyes*, [1899] 2 Ch. 73. For discussion, see F. Meisel, "What Price Auctions Without Reserve?" (2001) 64 Mod. L. Rev. 468.

must undertake the conduct in question with the intention of accepting the offer. Although both of these propositions are well established as a matter of general principle, both have been subjected to some strain in the context of offers for rewards.

The strength of the general principle that the offer must be communicated to the offeree may be illustrated by the decision of the British Columbia Court of Appeal in *Blair v. Western Mutual Benefit Association*.[51] The plaintiff in this case was a long-term and highly valued employee of the defendant association. An indication of her reputation within the association may be drawn from the fact that at a meeting of the board of directors of the association, a resolution was carried unanimously to the effect that, in view of her association with the defendant for almost thirty years, she should be given two years' salary, as retirement pay, in the event that she should retire from her position with the association. The plaintiff came to be aware of the existence of the resolution only because of her discharge of her responsibilities as a secretary. The president of the association had dictated the minutes of the meeting, including the resolution in question, to the plaintiff who then transcribed them. When she returned the transcribed copy to the president, the minutes were signed by him. Subsequently, she resigned her position with the association and, in due course, took the position that she was entitled to a severance package of two years' salary on the basis of the board resolution. The Court of Appeal, noting that there was no evidence that the plaintiff had resigned in reliance on the existence of the resolution or on the basis of any perceived obligation that the association had to her under the resolution, held that the board resolution, in itself, could not constitute an offer of a retirement package. In order to constitute an offer, the proposition must have been communicated to the plaintiff in such fashion as to indicate that the intention expressed in the resolution was being carried out and implemented with resulting alteration in the terms of her employment. The fact that one has decided to make an offer does not constitute an offer, even where the offeree has become aware of the existence of the decision. Thus, in a similar case, relied upon by the Court of Appeal,[52] where a decision had been taken by a corporation to make a general offer to all employees, the unauthorized publication of the decision in the press was held not to constitute effective communication of the offer to the offerees.[53]

---

51   [1972] 4 W.W.R. 284 (B.C.C.A.).

52   *Ibid.* at 289.

53   *Wilson v. Belfast Corp.* (1921), 55 I.L.T. 205.

In the context of rewards, however, there is some indication of a willingness on the part of courts to presume, in the absence of plain evidence to the contrary, that a person who performs the act requested by the notice of reward, was aware of the existence of the offer of reward. Thus, in *Williams v. Carwardine*,[54] the plaintiff had witnessed a murder and was apparently an acquaintance of the murderer. When required to testify at the resulting inquest, the plaintiff did not disclose that which she knew about the crime. Sometime later, a notice of reward was published by the brother of the deceased, promising to pay a sum of money to whomever would give information leading to the conviction of the person who had murdered his brother. Subsequently, having suffered a beating at the hands of the murderer, the plaintiff, believing that she was near death, and in order to ease her conscience, provided information to the police that ultimately led to the conviction of the murderer. However, the plaintiff survived and, in due course, unsuccessfully sought the reward. Her subsequent action to enforce the offer of reward enjoyed success. Denman C.J. directed a verdict for the plaintiff on the basis that she had met the condition stated in the reward but asked the jury to determine whether the plaintiff had been induced by the offer of reward to provide the information. On this point, the jury found that she had been induced by motives other than the reward in providing the information. In an exchange with counsel, Denman C.J. had asked whether there was any doubt about whether the plaintiff was aware of the existence of the offer. Counsel replied that "she must have known of it, as it was placarded all over Hereford, the place at which she lived."[55]

On the rather similar facts of *R. v. Clarke*,[56] however, the Australian High Court reached the conclusion that an offer of reward had not been accepted. Clarke had sufficient connection with murders committed by Treffene and Coulter that he was committed for trial as an accessory. Although he initially resisted providing information to the police, he, in his own words, "began to break down under the strain"[57] and provided information concerning the murders in order to clear himself of any charge of murder. Although he had been aware of the existence of a published offer of reward at the time he provided information and ultimately testified at the trial of Treffene and Coulter, he conceded that,

---

54   (1833), 4 B. & Ad. 621, 110 E.R. 590 (K.B.). The case is also reported at 172 E.R. 1101.
55   *Ibid.* at 1104 (172 E.R.).
56   (1927), 40 C.L.R. 227 (Aust. H.C.).
57   *Ibid.* at 238.

in doing so, he "gave no consideration and formed no intention with regard to the reward."[58] *Williams v. Carwardine* was distinguished as a case in which the plaintiff knew of the reward at the time of providing the information even if the reason for doing so or motive was other than an acceptance of the offer. On the facts of *Clarke*, however, the court was forced to conclude, on the basis of the statements of Clarke himself, that the offer was not present to his mind and that he had forgotten about it when providing the information. Indeed, it was only after an unsuccessful appeal of their conviction that a police officer reminded Clarke of the existence of the reward and encouraged him to pursue it. Higgins J. did, however, suggest that a presumption might have worked in Clarke's favour but for his own statement on the question of motive.[59] Further, Higgins J. was of the view that an earlier English case[60] that had permitted a police officer to recover a reward the existence of which he became aware of only after providing the information in question was incorrectly decided and placed reliance on American authority, which insists upon an awareness of the existence of a reward on the part of the offeree.[61]

If it is correct that there exists a presumption in favour of knowledge of the offer by offerees in the case of rewards, it is perhaps not obvious why this should be so. As the *Blair* case illustrates, in the normal case in which a plaintiff offeree attempts to establish the existence of a contract with the offeror, the burden would be on the offeree to establish an awareness of the offer and an intention to accept it. The explanation for the special treatment of offers of reward, however, may well be a concern that the value of rewards as an aid to the administration of justice may be undermined by an overly technical approach to the legal analysis of their enforceability. Thus, in *R. v. Clarke* itself, it is apparent that the High Court disapproved the government's refusal to pay the reward to Mr. Clarke who had, after all, provided evidence of the greatest value to the Crown in the prosecution of Coulter and Treffene. As the court observed: "the refusal of the Crown to pay the reward in this case is likely to weaken the efficacy of such a bait when the Crown seeks information from accessories to crime hereafter."

---

58   *Ibid.* at 239.
59   *Ibid.* at 241 ("But for this candid confession of Clarke's it might fairly be presumed that Clarke, having once seen the offer, acted on the faith of it, in reliance on it; but he has himself rebutted that presumption").
60   *Gibbons v. Proctor* (1891), 64 L.T. 594.
61   *Fitch v. Snedaker*, 38 N.Y. 248 (1868).

On a strict *consensus ad idem* theory, one might also assume in cases of unilateral contracts, including rewards, where the offer invites conduct on the part of the offeree as the acceptance of the offer, the conduct must be undertaken not only with knowledge of the offer but with an intention to accept the offer. As both *Williams* and *Clarke* illustrate, however, it appears to be well accepted that the motive of the offeree in providing the conduct requested by the offeror is immaterial.[62] This, again, seems a doubtful proposition and is perhaps best explained on the basis that it is supported by a policy favouring the enforceability of rewards.

C. THE ACCEPTANCE

1) Counteroffers, Rejections and Failed Acceptances

As we have seen, an offer in the requisite sense confers upon the offeree the power of acceptance. To exercise that power effectively the offeree must communicate an unqualified commitment to the terms of the agreement that has been offered. There is no meeting of the minds or *consensus ad idem* unless the acceptance is a mirror image of the offer. In the simple case, then, where the offeree simply replies, "I accept your offer," in the absence of further negotiations by the parties, the offeree will have exercised the power of acceptance and created a contractual relationship with the offeror. If the purported acceptance, however, varies in any respect the terms of the offer, it will be treated as a proposal of new terms and classified as a counteroffer rather than an acceptance.[63] The counteroffer obviously confers the power of accept-

---

62   See also *Smirnis v. Toronto Sun Publishing Co.* (1997), 37 O.R. (3d) 440 at 444 (Gen. Div.). There is some American authority to the same effect. See *Simmons v. U.S.*, 308 F.2d 160 (4th Cir. 1962) (Simmons was aware of a brewery's contest in which a prize would be awarded to the person who caught a tagged fish, Diamond Jim III, in Chesapeake Bay—Simmons caught the fish in the course of pleasure fishing without any intention of participating in the contest—held, awareness of the offer of reward was essential but the absence of motive was irrelevant—accordingly, court agreed with the ever-vigilant plaintiff revenue authorities that as Simmons could require the brewery to make the payment, it constituted taxable income in his hands.) More generally, however, American authority appears to require that at least some portion of the conduct provided by the offeree be induced by the existence of the reward. See, American Law Institute, *Restatement of Contracts 2d* (St. Paul: American Law Institute, 1981) s. 51. And see generally E.A. Farnsworth, *Farnsworth on Contracts*, 2d ed., vol. 1 (New York: Aspen Law & Business, 1998) at 104–5.

63   See, for example, *OTM Ltd. v. Hydranautics*, [1981] 2 Lloyd's Rep. 211 (Q.B.D.).

ance on the initial offeror. If the counteroffer is not accepted, however, no agreement has been entered into by the parties. Importantly, it must be noted that the effect of the counteroffer is to remove the initial offer from the bargaining table. As is sometimes said, "the counteroffer kills the original offer."[64] Thus, an offeree who responds with a counteroffer that is rejected by the initial offeror cannot respond by accepting the initial offer. A simple illustration is provided by *Hyde v. Wrench*,[65] in which the defendant offers to sell certain property to the plaintiff for £1,000. The plaintiff replied that he would be willing to pay a price of £950. This was held to be a rejection of the initial offer with a result that the plaintiff was no longer in a position to accept the initial offer at £1,000. It is presumed, in effect, that if the initial offeree replies by way of a counteroffer, the initial offer has been rejected and can only be revived with the consent of the initial offeror.

Where, however, notwithstanding the rejection of the counteroffer, the initial offeror signals an interest in continuing the negotiations with the offeree, it may be held that the offeror's conduct has the effect of reviving the initial offer. In *Livingston v. Evans*,[66] for example, the defendant, an owner of land, offered to sell the land to the plaintiff for eighteen hundred dollars. The plaintiff replied: "Send lowest cash price. Will give $1,600 cash. Wire." The owner's agent replied: "Cannot reduce price." The plaintiff immediately responded and purported to accept the initial offer at eighteen hundred dollars. The court easily concluded that the plaintiff's initial response, suggesting a lower price, amounted to a counteroffer, which would bring to an end the initial offer for sale at eighteen hundred dollars. The difficult question, in the court's view, however, was whether the reply "Cannot reduce price" had the effect of reviving the initial offer. With some hesitation, the court concluded that this communication intimated a willingness to stand by the initial offer and accordingly that it was still open for acceptance.[67] In cases where the original offer cannot be said to survive, however, the

---

64 *Trollope & Colls Ltd. v. Atomic Power Constructions Ltd.*, [1962] 3 All E.R. 1035 at 1038, Megaw J.; *Cowan v. Boyd* (1921), 61 D.L.R. 497 (Ont. S.C.A.D.); *Scanlon v. Standish* (2002), 57 O.R. (3d) 767 (C.A.).
65 (1840), 3 Beav. 334, 49 E.R. 132.
66 [1925] 4 D.L.R. 769 (Alta. S.C.).
67 Relying on the earlier decision in *Re Cowan and Boyd,* above note 64, concerning the renewal of a lease. The landlord inquired to the tenant's inquiry concerning the renewal rate for the lease by indicating that there would be an increase. The tenant replied indicating that he could not afford an increase and would therefore appreciate an early reply. The landlord replied by indicating that he would respond by the end of the month. That response was held to keep the initial

sharp distinction between acceptance and counteroffer may produce surprising results for the offeree who, intending to accept the offer, nonetheless makes inquiries about possible changes to the terms of the offer. In circumstances where it can fairly be said, however, that the offeree is accepting the offer but merely making a further inquiry[68] or a proposal for modification of the agreement that has been concluded by acceptance,[69] the acceptance remains effective. Similarly, a request for a meaningless[70] or trivial[71] addition to the terms of the agreement will not undermine the effectiveness of a purported acceptance. The line to be drawn between counteroffers and acceptances is, however, one that can only be drawn with some difficulty.

Similar analytical difficulties arise in circumstances where the offeree purports to accept the offer in a straightforward manner but the parties nonetheless persist in negotiating the terms of their arrangement. Where the parties continue to negotiate with respect to important aspects of the arrangement, it is possible to infer that they did not understand themselves to have concluded an agreement. On the other hand, it is entirely conceivable that parties could enter into an agreement through a process of offer and acceptance and subsequently negotiate possible changes to that agreement. The inherent difficulty of the distinction is well illustrated by the facts of *Bristol, Cardiff and Swansea Aërated Bread Co. v. Maggs*.[72] Maggs had written to the plaintiff offering to sell his business premises and the goodwill of the business for £450. The plaintiff replied in plain language: "I accept your offer for shop and lease, & C ...."[73] On the next day, the purchaser's solicitors forwarded a draft memorandum of agreement that included a non-com-

---

offer open. Accordingly, the tenant's purported acceptance of the increased rate, prior to hearing back from the landlord, was held to be effective.

68   *Stevenson, Jacques & Co. v. McLean* (1880), 5 Q.B.D. 346; *Bruce v. Tolton* (1879), 4 O.A.R. 144; *Powers & Son v. Hatfield & Scott* (1916), 10 O.W.N. 198, aff'd (1916), 27 O.W.R. 666 (S.C.A.D.); *Korogonas v. Andrew*, [1994] 2 W.W.R. 173 (Alta. C.A.).

69   *Bellamy v. Debenham* (1890), 45 Ch. D. 481, aff'd on other grounds, [1891] 1 Ch. 412 (C.A.); *Andrews v. Calori* (1907), 38 S.C.R. 588.

70   *Nicolene Ltd. v. Simmonds*, [1953] 1 Q.B. 543 (C.A.) (acceptance subject to the "usual terms of acceptance" — there were, in fact, no such terms — held, condition is meaningless, acceptance is effective); *Canadian Market Place Ltd. v. Fallowfield* (1976), 71 D.L.R. (3d) 341 (Ont. H.C.J.) (term varied was, in any event, nugatory from the start).

71   *Clive v. Beaumont* (1848), 1 De G. & Sm. 397, 63 E.R. 1121; *Simpson v. Hughes* (1897), 66 L.J. Ch. 334 (C.A.); *Re Imperial Land Co. v. Marseilles* (1872), L.R. 7 Ch. App. 587.

72   (1890), 44 Ch. D. 616.

73   *Ibid.* at 617.

petition clause preventing Maggs from carrying on a similar business within a certain area for a period of five years. No such arrangement had been previously discussed by the parties. Upon receipt of the draft, Maggs' solicitor proposed an amendment to the clause. A few days later, however, without hearing back from the plaintiff with respect to the proposed modification, Maggs indicated that he no longer wished to go through with the sale and asked that it be cancelled. Although the form of the request suggests that Maggs believed that the parties had an agreement, the court held that the plaintiff's attempt to stipulate a new and very important term the day following the purported acceptance indicated that the parties were still negotiating an agreement that was not yet complete.

Similarly, in *Harvey v. Perry*,[74] the Supreme Court of Canada held that negotiations for the sale of eight oil leases were not completed when the intending seller replied to a proposed arrangement by writing "I will accept your proposition"[75] or further, when, after the exchange of a written draft of the agreement, the purchaser's solicitor stated that "the terms are acceptable."[76] The fact that the purchaser forwarded a second draft including some variations on the proposed terms indicated that "[t]here was no *consensus ad idem* because the [purchaser] was still negotiating for better terms."[77] Again, the line between continuing negotiations and circumstances in which the parties have reached a binding agreement but subsequently commenced negotiations on variations of the agreement[78] will be drawn only with difficulty in cases such as these.

To be effective, an acceptance must comply with any instructions issued by the offeror for the manner in which acceptance is to be exercised. Although the offer confers a power of acceptance on the offeree, the offeror, it is often said, is the "master of the offer" and can stipulate the manner in which the power is to be exercised.[79] Thus, for example, if an offer to sell shares stipulates that it can be accepted only by the provision by the offeree of a certified cheque for the purchase price, a purported acceptance without the required cheque will be ineffective.[80] The offeror may require that the offeree communicate the acceptance

---

74   [1953] 2 D.L.R. 465 (S.C.C.).

75   *Ibid.* at 467.

76   *Ibid.* at 471.

77   *Ibid.* at 473.

78   See, for example, *Bellamy v. Debenham*, above note 69.

79   *Manchester Diocesan Council for Education v. Commercial & General Investments Ltd.*, [1969] All 3 E.R. 1593 (Ch. D.) [*Manchester Diocesan Council*].

80   *Baughman v. Rampart Resources Ltd.* (1995), 124 D.L.R. (4th) 252 (B.C.C.A.).

by a particular mode of communication.[81] Courts are reluctant to assume, however, that the stipulation of a means of communication is intended to mean that only that means of communication can be employed. Thus, in a leading case,[82] it was said that a requirement that the acceptance be "by return of post" was to be interpreted as a requirement not that only a posted acceptance would be effective but, rather, as an indication that the acceptance, whether by letter, telegram or verbal message must be communicated within the time a letter by return post would have arrived.[83] Similarly, the offeror may stipulate the place at which acceptance is to be received. Again, however, courts may not interpret such requirements as exclusive in the absence of clear stipulation to that effect by the offeror.[84]

An offer of a unilateral contract will stipulate some form of conduct as the means of acceptance. Although there may, in a particular case, be some latitude for interpretation of the stipulation in the offeree's favour—a requirement of payment, for example, may be interpreted as a requirement to tender payment[85]—strict compliance with the stipulation is normally required. Thus, in *R. v. Clarke*,[86] for example, the plaintiff failed to accept an offer of reward when the act performed was similar to but not precisely that required by the offer. The notice of reward had offered a payment in return for "such information as shall lead to the arrest and conviction of the person or persons" who committed certain murders. The plaintiff, an apparent accomplice, provided information that led to the arrest of only one of the two murderers and led to the conviction of the two for only one of the murders committed. On both grounds, the information failed to meet the requirements set out in the notice. Accordingly, the plaintiff was not entitled to collect the reward. In an unusual Canadian decision,[87] a court asserted a discre-

---

81   See, for example, *Financings Ltd. v. Stimson*, [1962] 1 W.L.R. 1184 (C.A.) (signed acceptance required, oral acceptance ineffective). Compare with *Carmichael v. Bank of Montreal* (1972), 25 D.L.R. (3d) 570 (Man. Q.B.).

82   *Tinn v. Hoffman & Co.*, above note 2. See also *Manchester Diocesan Council*, above note 79.

83   See also *Eliason v. Henshaw*, 4 Wheaton 225 (U.S.S.C. 1819) (a stipulation of acceptance "by return wagon" interpreted as a requirement that the acceptance be communicated within the period of time the return trip would normally require.)

84   *Manchester Diocesan Council*, above note 79; *Nieckar v. Sliwa* (1976), 67 D.L.R. (3d) 378 (Sask. Q.B.).

85   *Daulia Ltd. v. Four Millbank Nominees Ltd.*, [1978] Ch. 231, [1978] 2 All E.R. 557 (C.A.). Compare with *Petterson v. Pattberg*, 161 N.E. 428 (N.Y.C.A. 1928); *Beer v. Lea* (1912), 7 D.L.R. 434 (Ont. H.C.), aff'd (1913), 14 D.L.R. 236 (Ont. S.C.A.D.).

86   Above note 56.

87   *Smirnis v. Toronto Sun Publishing Corp.* above note 62.

tion to apportion the reward in a case in which the condition had not been strictly met. The plaintiff had accurately identified one Bernardo to the police as the likely perpetrator of a series of rapes and slayings and on this basis sought payment of a reward posted by the defendant newspaper for information leading to the "arrest and conviction" of the perpetrator of one of the murders. Although the police did not follow up vigorously on the tip, later discovery of DNA evidence led to an application for a search warrant for the Bernardo residence with respect to which the plaintiff's assistance was sought and obtained. The information that effectively led to the arrest and conviction of Bernardo, however, was the confession of his spouse and accomplice in the murders. The information provided by the plaintiff was said by the court to constitute "a very minor link in the chain of cause and effect that progressed through the investigation, arrest and conviction of Bernardo."[88] Although the plaintiff's information therefore could not be said to be the proximate cause of the arrest and conviction of Bernardo, the court nonetheless concluded that it was entitled to place a value on the information provided and permit the plaintiff to recover a portion of the reward. Although inconsistent with principle, the decision obviously reflects a judicial concern to avoid a complete denial of relief that might "eliminate the encouragement of individuals to come forward."[89]

An offer must be accepted in a timely fashion. If the offer stipulates that it may only be accepted by a specified time on a specified date, a late acceptance will be ineffective.[90] Where the offeror is not available at his or her business premises shortly before the deadline, however, late delivery at the offeror's residence may provide an acceptable substitute to strict compliance.[91] Further, it is open to the offeror to waive the requirement of timeliness, in which case the late acceptance will be effective.[92] If the offer does not stipulate a deadline for acceptance, the offeree must accept the offer within a reasonable period of time. It is occasionally suggested that an offer sent by mail should be accepted by return of post or, at least, on the same day,[93] but the length of the

---

88 *Ibid.* at 446.

89 *Ibid.* The court relied on American authority to similar effect in cases where more than one informant was involved. See *Genesee County v. Pailthorpe,* 224 N.W. 418 (Mich. S.C. 1929); *Tobin v. McComb,* 156 S.W. 237 (Tex. C.A. 1913).

90 See, for example, *Carmichael v. Bank of Montreal,* above note 81.

91 *Ibid.*

92 *Manchester Diocesan Council,* above note 79 at 1598. For discussion of waiver, see Chapter 8.

93 *Shatford v. B.C. Wine Growers Ltd.,* [1927] 2 D.L.R. 759 (B.C.S.C.) (sale of perishables).

reasonable time, as Estey J. noted in *Barrick Estate v. Clark*,[94] "depends upon the nature and character and the normal or usual course of business in negotiations leading to a sale, as well as the circumstances of the offer including the conduct of the parties in the course of negotiations."[95] Further, as Estey J. also observed, the nature of the subject matter of the transaction is pertinent. Thus, a reasonable time will be shorter with respect to the sale of perishables or publicly traded shares than would be the case for a sale of farm land, which in the Court's view at that time at least was not subject to frequent or sudden fluctuations in price. In this case, Barrick made an offer to sell farm land to Clark on November 15th at a stipulated price. In his absence, Clark's wife replied in writing to the effect that her husband was out of town for a few days but would be back in about ten days and, further, requesting that the offer be kept open until his return. No reply to this overture was forthcoming from the seller. By the time Clark returned and signified his acceptance of the offer on December 10th, Barrick had already sold the property to a third party on December 6th. In the Supreme Court's view, Clark's acceptance was not timely. In the communications between the parties there were a number of signals that a more prompt reply was required. The Barrick offer of November 15th indicated that if the price was satisfactory to Clark "the deal could be closed immediately." The offer concluded with a request for a reply "as soon as possible." Further, the offer indicated that the deal would close on January 1st. An acceptance on December 10th would barely provide sufficient time for the necessary documentation to be prepared. Moreover, in his initial approach to Barrick, Clark had asked for a decision "as fast as possible." Clark's acceptance fell outside the reasonable time required for acceptance.

In *Manchester Diocesan Council for Education v. Commercial & General Investments Ltd.*,[96] Buckley J., in applying the principle, suggested that there were two possible explanations for the requirement of acceptance within a reasonable period of time. The first was that the offer might be considered to contain an implied term to this effect. The second possibility was that the defendant's failure to respond in a timely fashion may be treated by the offeror as evidence that the offeree has manifested an intention to decline the offer. The implication of the first view, for Buckley J., was that the content of the implied term would be considered settled at the time the contract was entered into. Accord-

---

94   [1951] S.C.R. 177.
95   *Ibid.* at 184–85.
96   Above note 79.

ingly, what would appear reasonable to the parties at that time would be based on their respective assessment of the then current circumstances and the circumstances that were likely, in their view, to arise in the course of the continuance of the offer. On the second explanation, however, the court would be required to determine whether on the circumstances as they ultimately emerged, the offeree's failure to respond reasonably signalled to the offeror that the offer had been rejected. On this view, the conduct of the parties after the issuance of the offer and other emerging circumstances would be relevant to the termination. Buckley J. persuasively indicated a strong preference for the latter view and applied it to circumstances where delays in the approval of the acceptance by the offeree substantially extended the period during which the offer was under consideration. In the particular circumstances, however, including an earlier intimation of an intention to accept by the offeree, the acceptance was held to come within a reasonable period of time. If the matter were considered, however, from the point of view of the first explanation of the doctrine—the implied term requiring reasonable notice—it was Buckley J.'s view that so lengthy a period would have appeared to be unreasonable.

2) The Battle of the Forms

It is very common practice that parties entering agreements purport to do so on the basis of standard forms, perhaps prepared for them by their lawyers, in which they each propose to set out the terms and conditions of their contractual relations. In a typical case, an order for goods may be placed on the buyer's standard order form. That form will state, perhaps on the back of the form and in fine print, the terms and conditions upon which the buyer proposes to deal with the seller. The order may be accepted by the seller on the basis of a standard acknowledgment form stating the seller's terms. The seller's terms may be repeated in a delivery notice or an invoice. The buyer's terms may be repeated in a form acknowledging delivery of the goods. In the drafting of any particular form, either or both of the parties may try to establish that their particular form is in some sense final and unalterable by the other party's forms. The parties' respective forms are very likely to conflict in various important respects. The seller's view of credit terms or liability in the event that the goods are defective is likely to be quite different from the buyer's. It will often be the case that neither party has explicitly agreed to the forms being utilized by the other party. In the result, it may be quite unclear which party's terms are to prevail. This commonplace scenario is often referred to as the "battle of the forms."

Under the traditional analysis, the reply of each party by a form asserting different terms and conditions from those contained in the prior form of the other party constitutes, on the basis of the "mirror image" principle, the making of a counteroffer. Applying the traditional doctrine then, each successive form constitutes a counteroffer. On the basis of the forms exchanged, no consensus is reached and the parties have failed to create an agreement. If, however, the last form utilized is followed by conduct that may be considered to constitute acceptance of the offer contained in that form, an agreement will be created. In the typical case of a sale of goods based on conflicting forms, performance of the contract either by delivery of the goods or by the acceptance of delivery of goods may be considered to constitute the conduct amounting to acceptance. Thus, for example, where the seller's last form accompanies the delivery of the goods, the conduct of the buyer in accepting delivery may be held to constitute an acceptance of the seller's last counteroffer.[97] This doctrine has been referred to as the "performance doctrine" or as the "last shot" rule on the basis that the party who "fires" the last document before performance prevails.[98] The application of the performance doctrine is illustrated by the decision in *British Road Services Ltd. v. Arthur B. Crutchley and Co. Ltd.*[99] In this case, a carrier delivered goods to a warehouseman for storage, together with a delivery note stating the carrier's terms and conditions. The warehouseman then stamped the delivery notes with a rubber stamp incorporating its own terms and conditions, whereupon the carrier deposited its goods in the warehouse. In a decision affirmed on this point by the Court of Appeal, the trial judge held that the stamping of the delivery notes constituted a counteroffer and that by then handing over the goods, the carrier had accepted the warehouseman's counteroffer.

On the orthodox analysis, then, a contract is created by a series of conflicting forms only when the last form utilized is followed by conduct amounting to acceptance of the counteroffer stated in the last form. In exceptional circumstances, however, an earlier form may prevail. In *Butler Machine Tool Co. Ltd. v. Ex-Cell-O Corp. (England) Ltd.,*[100] for example, the buyer's purchase order, the terms of which were inconsistent with earlier communications of the seller, contained a tear-off slip

---

97 *Howard Marine & Dredging Co. Ltd. v. A. Ogden & Sons (Excavations) Ltd.*, [1978] Q.B. 574 (C.A.).

98 *Butler Machine Tool Co. Ltd. v. Ex-Cell-O Corp. (England) Ltd.*, [1979] 1 All E.R. 965 at 968 (C.A.), Lord Denning M.R.

99 [1967] 2 All E.R. 785, aff'd [1968] 1 All E.R. 811 (C.A.).

100 Above note 98. See also *OTM Ltd. v. Hydranautics*, above note 63.

accepting the terms of the purchase order that the seller was requested to sign and return to the buyer. The seller signed and returned the tear-off slip under cover of a letter, however, indicating that the order was accepted "in accordance with" the seller's earlier offer of sale. The court held in favour of the buyer's form, reasoning that the buyer's purchase order was a counteroffer that killed off the seller's earlier offer of sale and that the seller's return of the tear-off slip constituted acceptance of the buyer's counteroffer. The seller's reference in its covering letter to the earlier offer was held by the court to be merely a reference to the price and identity of the subject matter of the sale. Further, as we have seen,[101] the fact that the apparent "acceptance" contains some additional terms is not necessarily fatal to its categorization as an acceptance. Thus, if the additional terms can be characterized as meaningless[102] or trivial[103] or as subsequent proposals for modification of the agreement that has been reached,[104] the "acceptance" may be considered effective. In some cases, then, as Lord Denning observed in *Butler,* "the battle is won by the man who gets the blow in first."[105]

The orthodox or traditional mode of analysis has been criticized from time to time. There are essentially two perceived problems with the current law. First, in circumstances where the parties have simply exchanged forms, the mirror image rule leads typically to the conclusion that no agreement has been entered into by the parties. Nonetheless, it may be that the parties consider themselves to have an agreement and, for example, where the seller refuses to deliver the goods ordered by the buyer, the buyer may be quite surprised to discover that there exists no agreement between the parties. The surprise for the seller may be similar but more pleasant. Second, as we have seen, where the exchange of forms is followed by performance, the likely outcome is that the terms of the agreement will be those of the party who fired the "last shot." Critics of the performance rule suggest that this is an arbitrary result. Thus, it may be typical in the case of a sale of goods transaction that the last shot is the seller's form accompanying the goods, which will be implicitly accepted when the buyer accepts delivery. It may be asked, however, whether it is either fair or consistent with the expectations of the parties that the seller's view should normally prevail. For reasons such as these, proposals for reform have emerged in

101 See above this Chapter, section C(1).
102 See authorities cited above note 70.
103 See authorities cited above note 71.
104 See authorities cited above notes 68 and 69.
105 Above note 98 at 968.

various jurisdictions. In the United States, the rules of offer and acceptance, as they apply to sale of goods transactions, have been modified in all but one state on the basis of model provisions set out in Uniform Commercial Code that are intended to provide a solution to the battle of the forms.[106]

In the *Butler* case, Lord Denning suggested that the traditional analysis is "out of date" and went to propose the following alternative analytical method: "The terms and conditions of both parties are to be construed together. If they can be reconciled so as to give a harmonious result, all well and good. If differences are irreconcilable, so that they are mutually contradictory, then the conflicting terms may have to be scrapped and replaced by a reasonable implication."[107]

On this view, the parties' agreement would be constituted by the terms that are common to their respective forms, together with implied reasonable terms. As we will see, this approach is similar to the statutory reforms enacted in the United States. Lord Denning's suggestion was not taken up, however, by the other two members of the panel, Lawton and Bridge LL.J. Further, a similar suggestion made by Lord Denning M.R. in the almost contemporaneous decision of the Court of Appeal in *Gibson v. Manchester City Council*,[108] was rejected on appeal by the House of Lords.[109] Although Lord Denning's approach has been referred to in a few Canadian cases, it has not yet been explicitly adopted and applied by a Canadian court.[110] A somewhat similar approach was followed, however, by an Ontario court in *Tywood Industries Ltd. v. St. Anne-Nackawic Pulp & Paper Co. Ltd.*[111] In this case, the dispute concerned the enforceability of an arbitration clause contained in two purchase orders issued by the defendant buyer. The defendant had initially issued a tender call that set forth various terms and conditions not including an arbitration clause. The next step was the plaintiff's bid in letter form that contained, on the reverse side, a detailed list of the seller's terms and conditions that did not include an arbitration clause. In the purchase order next issued by the defendant, however, the terms set out in the reverse side of the order form did include such a clause. On the face of the document, the order was said to be accepted by the seller subject to the terms and conditions on the reverse

---

106 Section 2-207.

107 Above note 100 at 968–69.

108 Above note 19 at 586 (C.A.).

109 Above note 19 at 974 (H.L. cited to All E.R.), Lord Diplock.

110 See, for example, *General Refractories Co. of Canada v. Venturedyne, Ltd.*, [2002] O.J. No. 54 at para. 83.

111 (1979), 100 D.L.R. (3d) 374 (Ont. H.C.J.).

side and the seller was instructed to forward an "acceptance copy" of the order promptly to the buyer. In fact, the seller neither executed nor returned a copy of the purchase order to the buyer. Performance of the contract followed. Under traditional analysis, there would be a strong argument that the purchase order constituted the "last shot," and that the seller's performance of the contract constituted an acceptance of those terms. Grange J. was of the view, however, that although the parties had tried to impose their respective terms on each other, they had not enjoyed success in doing so. The buyer had not drawn attention to the arbitration clause to the seller. Indeed, it was his view that "neither party considered any terms other than those found on the face of the documents (that is, the specifications and the price) important." Accordingly, neither party, and certainly the buyer at least, could not rely on the detailed terms on the reverse side of their respective forms. Although it was not necessary for Grange J. to address the issue, one assumes that in the event of a dispute, the parties would be able to rely upon and enforce implied reasonable terms filling in the gaps in the agreement.

The approach adopted in these cases bears some resemblance to the reforms to the legislation applicable to agreements for the purchase and sale of goods enacted in the United States.[112] The model section upon which the reforms are based, U.C.C. section 2-207, provides as follows:

Section 2-207. Additional Terms in Acceptance or Confirmation

(1) A definite and reasonable expression of acceptance or a written confirmation which is sent within a reasonable time operates as an acceptance even though it states terms additional to or different from those offered or agreed upon, unless acceptance is expressly made conditional on assent to the additional or different terms.

(2) The additional terms are to be construed as proposals for addition to the contract. Between merchants such terms become part of the contract unless:

(a)   the offer expressly limits acceptance to the terms of the offer;

(b)   they materially alter it; or

(c)   notification of objection to them has already been given or is given within a reasonable time after notice of them is received.

---

112   The provisions of Article 2 of the American Law Institute's Uniform Commercial Code [U.C.C.], have been enacted as state law in all but one state, Louisiana, of the United States.

(3) Conduct by both parties which recognises the existence of a contract is sufficient to establish a contract for sale although the writings of the parties do not otherwise establish a contract. In such case the terms of the particular contract consist of those terms on which the writings of the parties agree, together with any supplementary terms incorporated under any other provisions of this Act.

The first two subsections are evidently designed to abolish the "mirror image" rule. A "definite ... expression of acceptance" is effective as such even though it contains terms "additional to or different from" those set out in the offer. This provision essentially reverses the common law rule. Thus, if the common law position will typically favour the seller, whose form will often be last, the U.C.C. rule will typically favour the buyer, whose purchase order will often be the first form utilized. The qualification set out in subsection 1 is, however, quite important. The new rule is inapplicable if the "acceptance is expressed and remains conditional on assent to the additional or different terms." The provision thus offers an invitation to the drafter to so stipulate and such a stipulation appears to reinstate the mirror image rule. Leaving that important qualification aside, subsection 2 then provides that the "additional terms" (but not the "different terms"), are proposals for addition to the contract that could be accepted by the offeror. The provision further stipulates, however, that such proposed terms will be effective between merchants unless (1) the offer, in its own terms, precludes this outcome or (2) the offeror otherwise objects to their inclusion or (3) the additional terms constitute a "material" alteration to the offer.

Subsection 3 applies to circumstances where the documents exchanged by the parties, when subjected to the analysis under subsections 1 and 2, do not establish an agreement between the parties and it is therefore necessary to rely on the conduct of the parties to establish the existence of an agreement. Unlike the common law performance rule, however, which has the effect of establishing an agreement on the terms set forth in the last document "fired" prior to performance, subsection 3 stipulates that the agreement shall consist of the terms that are common to the respective forms of the parties together with any supplementary terms incorporated under other provisions of the Code. Those provisions, in turn, set out default rules that prescribe terms that were considered to be reasonable terms by the drafters of the Code, including, for example, an implied obligation on the seller's part to provide goods of "merchantable" or reasonable quality.[113]

---

113 U.C.C. s. 2-314.

At first impression, the American provisions appear to offer a solution to the battle of the forms that is both elegant and ingenious. An examination of American experience with these rules, however, indicates that the provisions have spawned a host of interpretive and other difficulties.[114] By way of illustration, the overruling of the mirror image doctrine in subsections (1) and (2) is vulnerable to criticism on a variety of grounds. The basic premise of subsection (1) that "a definite … expression of acceptance" may contain "additional" or "different" terms from those of the offer risks incoherence. At the very least, the distinction between "acceptances" that contain so many additional or conflicting terms that they should be characterized as rejections and those that come within subsection (1) may be difficult to apply. Moreover, the nature of the basic scheme of subsection (1) has been subject to debate. Some have argued that conflicting provisions in the offer and "acceptance" knock each other out under the scheme so that it is only those terms in the initial offer that do not conflict with the offeree's terms that constitute the agreement established by subsection (1).[115] The majority view,[116] perhaps, is that the provision is properly interpreted to include all of the offeror's terms in the subsection (1) agreement, whether or not they conflict with the offeree's terms. On this view, the provision substantially strengthens the hand of the offeror.

Further, the qualification in subsection (1) that the provision is excluded where acceptances are made conditional on assent to the additional or different terms creates the likelihood that many, perhaps most, acceptances drafted by lawyers will oust the operation of the provision by including such language. Where the subsection applies, courts have had considerable difficulty in determining whether the additional terms constitute "material" alterations to the agreement.[117] Further, the

---

114 See generally J.J. White and R.S. Summers, *Uniform Commercial Code*, vol. 1 (St. Paul: West, 1995) c. 1, ss. 1–3. See also D.G. Baird and R. Weisberg, "Rules, Standards and the Battle of the Forms: A Reassessment of s. 2-207" (1982) 68 Va. L. Rev. 1217; J. Murray, "The Chaos of the 'Battle of the Forms' Solutions" (1986) 39 Vand. L. Rev. 1307.

115 See, for example, White and Summers, *ibid.* (authors divided on the point); M.G. Shanker, "Contract by Disagreement!? Reflections on UCC 2-207" (1976) 81 Com. L.J. 453.

116 R. Duesenberg, "Contract Creation: The Continuing Struggle with Additional and Different Terms under the Uniform Commercial Code Section 2-207" (1979) 34 Bus. Law. 1477.

117 An extensive jurisprudence has developed on the question of whether the term in question results in such "hardship" and "surprise" to the other party that it should be considered "material". See, for example, *American Ins. Co. v. El Paso Pipe & Supply Co.*, 978 F.2d 1185 (10th Cir. 1992).

invitation issued in subparagraph (2)(c) to include a blanket refusal in the original offer to agree to additional terms provides a drafting device, no doubt commonly used, that simply precludes inclusion of the offeree's additional terms pursuant to subsection (2). Under subsection (2), it is only "additional" and not "conflicting" terms that can be saved as proposals for amendment. The conflicting provisions, which may, of course, matter a great deal to the offerees, simply drop off the table. These latter provisions, then, together with the basic overruling of the mirror image doctrine, further secures the dominance of the offeror in the process. It is not self-evident, as a matter of policy, why the interest of the offeror ought to so consistently prevail.

Turning to subsection (3), the basic approach of constructing an agreement upon the foundation of the common ground between the parties has, again, some intuitive appeal. Nonetheless, the exercise of finding that common ground may be a difficult one, even in the context of relatively simple contracts for the purchase and sale of goods. Further, the remainder of the agreement, apart from the common ground on issues such as subject matter and price, may constitute very important terms of the transaction. To the extent that these terms are to be based on the implied statutory terms in the Code they are likely to favour, as do the equivalent provisions of provincial sale of goods legislation,[118] the interests of the buyer. Again, it is not obvious that, in context of commercial transactions, the buyers' interests should normally prevail. The basic problem in these cases, of course, is that the parties have not reached an agreement with respect to the terms of their bargain. Accordingly, the results of common law are, unsurprisingly, both unpredictable and, in some cases at least, arbitrary. Although the Code provisions appear to shift the advantage generally in the direction of the "first blow," the initial offer, it is not at all clear that the Code provisions produce results that are either more predictable or less arbitrary. Nor is it evident that revisions to the drafting of these provisions will increase their success in dealing with what appear to be intractable difficulties. On balance, it is not clear that a statutory solution is plainly preferable to the flexible, albeit unpredictable, resolution of these problems on basic common law principles of offer and acceptance.[119] In

---

118 See generally G.H.L. Fridman, *Sale of Goods in Canada*, 5th ed. (Toronto: Carswell, 2004) c. 8.

119 For a defence of the existing common law approach, see D. Vaver, "'Battle of the Forms'; A Comment on Professor Shanker's Views" (1979–80) 4 Can. Bus. L.J. 277.

sum, then, it is difficult to make a compelling case for the enactment of reforms based on the U.S. model.[120]

D. COMMUNICATION OF ACCEPTANCE

The *consensus ad idem* theory implies that an acceptance, to be effective, must be communicated by the offeree to the offeror. The minds of the parties must meet. Indeed, this is the general principle established by the cases. In *Larkin v. Gardiner,*[121] for example, Larkin had placed property in the hands of her agent for sale. The agent received an offer in the form of a draft agreement to purchase executed by Gardiner for transmittal by the agent to Larkin. By the next day, the agent presented the draft agreement to Larkin that she thereupon signed and returned to him. Later that same day, and before receiving any communication from the agent, Gardiner notified the agent that he was withdrawing the offer. It was held that Larkin had not accepted Gardiner's offer by that time. The mere execution of the agreement, which simply remained in the possession of Larkin's agent, did not fulfil the requirement that notice of the acceptance be communicated to the offeror.

In this part, we consider whether silence or inactivity on the part of the offeree can ever constitute acceptance of an offer. We then turn to consider a variety of issues relating to the point in time at which various means of acceptance are effective. Where, for example, a notice of acceptance and a revocation of the original offer have crossed in the mails, it will be necessary to determine the point in time at which the notice of acceptance is effective. Under the traditional "postal acceptance rule," in a case where mailing an acceptance is an appropriate manner of communicating the acceptance, the acceptance will be effective upon mailing. In this hypothetical situation, then, the acceptance would occur prior to the receipt of notification of the acceptance. After considering the operation of this rule, we will turn to assess the significance, with respect to this issue, of using various other forms

---

120 The Ontario Law Reform Commission considered the possibility of recommending inclusion of similar provisions in a proposed revision to the Ontario Sale of Goods legislation. The Commission rejected the idea of including provisions based on subsections (1) and (2), because of their alleged interpretive difficulties, but favoured the inclusion of a provision based on subsection (3). See Ontario Law Reform Commission, *Report on Sale of Goods*, vol. 1 (Toronto: Ministry of the Attorney General, 1979) at 81–86.

121 (1895), 27 O.R. 125 (Div. Ct.). See also *Schiller v. Fisher*, [1981] 1 S.C.R. 593.

of communication. As well, we will consider the relevance to the application of offer and acceptance analysis of the e-commerce legislation enacted by the Canadian provinces.

1) Silence as Acceptance

Against the background of a general requirement that an acceptance, in order to effective, must be communicated to the offeror, it may be considered whether there are ever circumstances in which silence or inaction may constitute acceptance of an offer. There are essentially two different kinds of fact situations in which silence may have this effect. First, situations may arise in which the silence of the offeree is reasonably understood by the offeror to indicate an acceptance of the offer by the offeree. In such circumstances, it might be said that the conduct of the offeree has the effect of signalling the offeree's assent to the offeror. The second group of cases are situations in which the offeror has waived the normal requirement of communication of acceptance. As we shall see, such waiver is more likely to be found to occur in the context of unilateral rather than bilateral agreements.

A leading illustration of the first category of cases—silence of the offeree communicating assent—is the decision of the Supreme Court of Canada in *Saint John Tug Boat Co. v. Irving Refinery Ltd.*[122] The defendant in this case operated an oil refinery in the harbour at Saint John. The refinery was supplied with crude oil brought by large tankers, which in turn were guided through the harbour by tugboats. The defendant did not have a sufficient supply of tugboats to meet completely the need for these services and rented tugs from the plaintiff for this purpose.

Pursuant to the agreement at issue in this case, the defendant had rented one of the plaintiff's tugs to provide stand-by services at a particular rental rate. The contract was renewed twice, but after the expiry of the second renewal the plaintiff continued to provide stand-by services and invoiced the defendant at the contract rate for those services. Several months later, the defendant adopted the position that the contract had expired on the renewal expiry date and that the defendant was therefore not liable to pay for the stand-by services that had been accepted by the defendant in the subsequent months. For the Supreme Court, the issue in this case was whether an acceptance by the defendant of the plaintiff's continuing offer to supply services at the contract rate could be inferred from the defendant's conduct in simply acquiescing in the receipt of services. The test of whether conduct,

---

122 [1964] S.C.R. 614.

unaccompanied by any explicit undertaking may constitute an acceptance, in the Court's view, was an objective one. The question is whether the offeror, acting reasonably, would understand that the offeree was assenting to the terms proposed. On the present facts, this test was met and the defendant was obliged to pay for the services rendered subsequent to the expiry of the renewal period at the contract rate.[123] The general principle is well established and perhaps more obviously applies in circumstances where some positive action on the part of the offeree—such as a seller sending goods in response to an order[124] or a buyer accepting delivery of goods[125]—where the conduct in question plainly signals agreement to the terms of the offeror. As we have seen, acceptance by conduct of this kind often applies in the context of cases involving the "battle of the forms."[126] The evident purpose served by the principle is protection of the reasonable expectations of the offeror in circumstances of this kind.

In the second category of cases—waiver of the requirement of notice by the offeror—the evident purpose of the doctrine is to protect the interest of the offeree who may reasonably have assumed that notice of acceptance is not necessary. A waiver of notice by the offeror may often arise in the context of an offer of a unilateral agreement. The leading illustration of the phenomenon is *Carlill v. Carbolic Smoke Ball Co.*[127] In this case, it will be recalled, the smoke ball company published a notice of a reward to be paid to any person who suffered influenza after acquiring the smoke ball product and using it in accord with the instructions. Among the various arguments made by the defendant smoke ball manufacturer to defend against the plaintiff Carlill's claim to enforce the reward was an assertion that Mrs. Carlill had not accepted the offer of reward simply by acquiring the smoke ball, using it in the prescribed manner and then catching influenza. An agreement can only be formed between the parties, it was urged, if Mrs. Carlill had notified her acceptance of the offer to the defendant. In the absence of notification, the defendant argued "the two minds may be apart, and there is not that consensus which is necessary according to the English

---

123 *Ibid.* at 623, Ritchie J. See also *Hamilton Gear & Machine Co. Ltd. v. Lewis Brothers Ltd.*, [1924] 3 D.L.R. 367; *Welton Tool Rental Ltd. v. Douglas Aircraft Co.* (1978), 28 N.S.R. (2d) 636; *Lanka Contracting Ltd. v. Brant County Board of Education* (1986), 26 D.L.R. (4th) 708 (Ont. C.A.).

124 *Hamilton Gear & Machine Co.*, *ibid.*

125 *Howard Marine & Dredging Co. Ltd. v. A. Ogden & Sons (Excavations) Ltd.*, above note 97.

126 See above this Chapter, section C(2).

127 Above note 28. For an account of this case see above this Chapter, section C(2).

law." The defence was rejected. As Bowen L.J. explained: "... as notification of acceptance is required for the benefit of the person who makes the offer, the person who makes the offer may dispense with notice to himself if he thinks it desirable to do so ... and if the person making the offer, expressly or impliedly intimates in his offer that it will be sufficient to act on the proposal without communicating acceptance of it to himself, performance of the condition is a sufficient acceptance without notification ...."[128]

On these facts, then, it was not necessary for Mrs. Carlill to do anything other than fulfil the stipulated condition in order to accept the defendant's offer. This proposition appears to be applicable generally to notices of reward. As Bowen L.J. further explained, if a notice of reward for the finding of a lost dog is posted, it is not necessary for everyone who enters upon a search for the dog to send a note to the offeror indicating an acceptance of the offer. As soon as someone finds the dog, he or she has accepted the offer.

Although the most obvious application of the waiver principle is in the context of notices of reward and other offers of unilateral agreements, there is no reason in principle why the doctrine could not apply to an offer of a bilateral contract.[129] As "master of the offer," the offeror is entitled to stipulate whatever manner of acceptance is deemed appropriate, including conduct by the offeree that does not involve notification of the offeror. The decision in *Dominion Building Corp. Ltd. v. The King*,[130] provides an illustration. In this case an offer to purchase land from the Crown stipulated that the offer would constitute a binding contract of purchase and sale once an Order in Council authorizing the transaction was passed by the offeree and a certified copy sent to the offeror. The Privy Council held that the certified copy was unnecessary. The offer would be accepted, pursuant to its terms, when the appropriate Order in Council had been made.

It is quite another matter, however, whether an offeror can impose silence as acceptance on an offeree with the result that an offeree who makes no reply may be surprised to discover that a binding contract has been created. The leading and controversial authority is *Felthouse v. Bindley*[131] in which a nephew had been negotiating the sale of a horse to his uncle. The uncle had offered to pay a price of £30 in response to which the nephew suggested the slightly higher price of 30 guin-

128 *Ibid.* at 269.
129 *Manchester Diocesan Council,* above note 79 at 1597, Buckley J.
130 [1933] 3 D.L.R. 577 (P.C.).
131 (1862), 11 C.B. (N.S.) 869, 142 E.R. 1037 (Ex. Ch.).

eas. In reply, the uncle wrote a letter suggesting a compromise price of £30, 15 shillings, indicating that he would consider the deal done if he did not hear back from the nephew. The nephew did not reply until sometime later after an auctioneer, with whom the nephew was dealing, accidentally sold the horse that had been reserved for his uncle. The nephew had instructed the auctioneer that the particular horse had been previously sold. On this basis, the uncle brought a claim for damages for conversion relying on the auctioneer's improper dealings with the horse intended for the uncle. The court held, however, that no agreement had been entered by the uncle and the nephew and, accordingly, that no claim in conversion would lie in the uncle's favour. For Willes J. "the uncle had no right to impose upon the nephew a sale of his horse for £30, 15 shillings unless [the nephew] chose to comply with the condition of writing to repudiate the offer."[132] The point obviously has some persuasive force. The waiver doctrine protects offerees who reasonably believe that their silence has the effect of creating a contract and, as a result, remain silent as a matter of choice on the assumption that formation of the contract has occurred. In cases like *Felthouse*, on the other hand, the offeree is being forced to take positive steps in order to prevent the formation of an agreement. However appealing the point is as a matter of general principle, the result on the facts of *Felthouse* is surprising. The parties, both of whom believed that they had entered into an agreement on particular terms and who had, therefore, a genuine *consensus ad idem*, were held not to have entered into an agreement at all.

The concern identified by Willes J. appears to be particularly compelling in the context of unsolicited goods supplied to consumers. Thus, where unrequested goods arrive in the mail coupled with the supplier's offer that the goods can be purchased and that it will be assumed by the offeror that the offeree has agreed to do so unless the offeree communicates a rejection to the offeror, the offeror's conduct appears to be an intrusive imposition on the peace of mind and freedom of will of the consumer. Indeed, a number of Canadian provinces have enacted legislation relieving consumers of any potential contractual obligations in these circumstances.[133] A related problem provoked a similar legislative response. In the late 1990s, cable TV companies adopted a

---

132 *Ibid.* at 1040 (E.R.).

133 See, for example, *Consumer Protection Act, 2002*, S.O. 2002, c. 30, Sched. A, s. 13; *Consumer Protection Act*, R.S.B.C. 1996, c. 69, s. 47; *Consumer Protection Act*, R.S.N.S. 1989, c. 92, s. 23; *Unsolicited Goods and Credit Cards Act*, R.S.N. 1990, c. U-6, s. 35; *Consumer Protection Act*, S.S. 1996, c. C-30.1, ss. 72–75.

practice—often referred to as "negative option billing"—pursuant to which they provided their existing customers with a new range of services, often on a free-trial basis for a period of time, indicating that unless they were notified by their customers to the contrary, it would be assumed that they wished to order and pay for the new services. Some provinces have enacted legislation prohibiting the practice.[134]

The fact situation in *Felthouse*, however, is quite different from this pattern. Goods were not foisted by one party upon the other with, in effect, a demand for action if a contract was to be avoided. The uncle and nephew had been engaged in a voluntary negotiation in which the suggestion that the silence should constitute acceptance does not appear to be an unreasonable one. Moreover, it is evident that the nephew believed that his silence resulted in the formation of a contract. The American *Restatement of Contracts 2d*[135] would achieve a different result in *Felthouse*. The *Restatement* suggests that silence may constitute acceptance in a case "where the offeror has stated or given the offeree reason to understand that assent may be manifested by silence or inaction, and the offeree in remaining silent and inactive intends to accept the offer."[136] Under this approach, then, the critical factor is that the offeree willingly chooses to affirm the agreement by remaining silent. The American rule thus produces agreement on the *Felthouse* facts.

It is also possible, however, to conceive of circumstances where silence as acceptance can be reasonably imposed whether or not the offeree, by remaining silent, actually intends to accept the offer. In the American case of *Wheeler v. Klaholt*,[137] for example, 174 pairs of shoes had been delivered on the assumption that an agreement of sale had been entered into by the parties. When it became apparent that the parties had not, in fact, reached agreement, the seller insisted that the goods be returned at once or paid for at the stipulated price. The buyer did neither and the seller sued to enforce the contract created by the offer coupled with the buyer's silent retention of the goods. Holmes C.J., noting that the parties were not strangers, that the goods had not been foisted upon the defendant and that the defendant was subject to an obligation to return the goods when it became apparent that the parties' purported agreement had failed, held that the circumstances

---

134   See, for example, the *Consumer Protection Act*, R.S.B.C. 1996, c. 69, Part 4, s. 55; *Consumer Protection Act*, R.S.N.S. 1989, c. 92 as am. by S.N.S. 1994, c. 16, s. 2.

135   American Law Institute, *Restatement of Contracts 2d* (Philadelphia: American Law Institute, 1981).

136   *Ibid.*, s. 69(1)(b).

137   59 N.E. 756 (Mass. S.C.J. 1901).

were such that a failure to return the goods constituted acceptance of the seller's terms.[138]

2) The Postal Acceptance Rule

An exception to the general principle that an acceptance must be communicated to the offeror has developed in the context of acceptances communicated through the mails. Under the "postal acceptance rule" or "mailbox" rule, an acceptance posted by mail is effective upon posting.[139] For the rule to apply, it must be appropriate for the offeree to communicate the acceptance by mail. This would obviously be the case if the offeror transmitted the offer by mail or invited an acceptance by mail. It may be reasonable for the offeree to communicate by mail, even in a case where the offer has been presented by hand. In *Henthorn v. Fraser*,[140] for example, where the offer was intended to be open for a few days and the offeror knew that the offeree resided in a distant location and, accordingly, could reasonably be expected to take the offer home with him for a few days, acceptance by post was reasonable. In *Henthorn*, Lord Herschell stated the general proposition in the following terms: "where the circumstances are such that it must have been within the contemplation of the parties, according to the ordinary usages of mankind, the post might be used as a means of communicating the acceptance of an offer, the acceptance is complete as soon as it is posted."[141]

It is generally accepted that the rule is also applicable to the communication of an acceptance by telegram.[142] The question of when an acceptance by mail is effective may become material in a variety of circumstances. First, if the acceptance is lost in the mails, it will none-

---

138 See also American Law Institute, above note 135, s. 69(1)(c) (silence and inaction may operate as an acceptance "(c) Where because of previous dealings or otherwise it is reasonable that the offeree should notify the offeror if he does not intend to accept").

139 *Household Fire & Carriage Accident Insurance Co. v. Grant* (1879), 4 Ex. D. 216 (C.A.).

140 [1892] 2 Ch. 27.

141 *Ibid.* at 33.

142 *Stevenson Jacques & Co. v. McLean*, above note 68; *Carow Towing Co. v. The "Ed McWilliams"* (1919), 46 D.L.R. 506 (Ex. Ct.); *Melady v. Jenkins Steamship Co.* (1909), 18 O.L.R. 251 (Div. Ct.). Compare with *Smith & Osberg Ltd. v. Hollenback* (1938), 53 B.C.R. 296 (S.C.). The rule has also been applied to acceptances sent by courier. See *R. v. Commercial Credit Corp.* (1983), 4 D.L.R. (4th) 314 (N.S.S.C.A.D.).

theless be effective as against the offeror.[143] Second, if the offeror decides to revoke the offer and the notice of revocation and the letter of acceptance cross in the mails, it will be critical to determine the point at which communication becomes effective. As we shall see,[144] the offeror's notice of revocation will be effective only upon arrival. The acceptance, however, will be effective on posting and will therefore preclude revocation of the offer when the notice of revocation eventually arrives. Finally, for purposes of determining the law applicable to a particular transaction or for other procedural reasons, it may be material to identify the jurisdiction in which the contract was formed. It is well established that where the acceptance is communicated by post, the place of mailing the acceptance is considered to be the place in which the contract was created.[145]

It is occasionally suggested that the postal acceptance rule is arbitrary in the sense that there is no convincing justification for the rule.[146] On this view, an arbitrary choice was required to be made, for the various purposes indicated above, as to whether the posting or the receipt of the acceptance constituted the communication of acceptance. It would be a bit surprising, however, if the courts would depart from the general rule that the offeror must receive notice of the acceptance in the absence of any rational foundation for doing so. A number of justifications for the mailbox rule have been offered, some more convincing than others. The least convincing explanation is the suggestion, often made in the early cases, that by authorizing the use of the mails for purposes of communicating the acceptance, the postal authorities have been constituted as the agent of the offeror for the purpose of receiving such communications. Accordingly, once the acceptance is placed within the control of the authorities, the acceptance has been received on the offeror's behalf. The agency argument is an obvious fiction, however, and it fails to justify the rule. The rule is obviously favourable to

---

143 *Household Fire & Carriage Accident Insurance Co. v. Grant*, above note 139; *Moscovitch Estate v. South End Development Co. Ltd.* (1968), 4 N.S.R. (1965–69) 182 (S.C.A.D.), aff'd [1968] S.C.R. vi; *Pearce v. Transportation Fire & Casualty Co.* (1977), 83 D.L.R. (3d) 259 (Ont. Dist. Ct.); *Sibtac Corp. Ltd. v. Soo; Lienster Investments Ltd., Third Party* (1978), 83 D.L.R. (3d) 116 (Ont. H.C.J.).

144 See below this Chapter, section E.

145 *Imperial Life Assurance Co. of Canada v. Colmenares*, [1967] S.C.R. 443 at 447, Ritchie J.

146 See, for example, *Household Fire & Carriage Accident Insurance Co. v. Grant*, above note 139 at 234–36, Bramwell L.J. dissenting, who disagreed with the majority's acceptance of the postal acceptance rule. See further S.A. Smith, *Contract Theory* (Oxford: Oxford University Press, 2004) at 188–92.

the interests of the offeree in circumstances where the acceptance is lost in the mails and the question arises, therefore, whether some justification for imposing this risk on the offeror can be found. One possibility is that since the offeror, as master of the offer, could have precluded the use of the mails, it is reasonable to impose the risk of loss associated with the use of the mail on the offeror. More convincing, perhaps, is the suggestion that since it is the offeror, and not the offeree, who will be aware that no acceptance has arrived, it is appropriate to place a burden of inquiry on the offeror. Further, it has been suggested that application of the general principle that acceptance is effective upon receipt would create great inconvenience in the present context as the offeree could not confidently assume that a contract had been entered into until arrival of the acceptance had been confirmed. Under the mailbox rule, the offeree can immediately assume the contract is binding and begin to rely upon it in making further commercial arrangements.[147] Finally, it has been suggested that holding a letter of acceptance is effective only on receipt opens the door to fraud perpetrated by the offeror. With respect to this last point, it is not clear that the opportunities for fraud by the offeror would be substantially greater than those created by the mailbox rule for fraud by the offeree.

Even if one finds these justifications for the mailbox rule convincing, it is nonetheless the case that the rule can visit considerable hardship on an offeror. Thus, courts may withhold application of the rule in cases where the terms of the offer appear to suggest the offeror expects to receive notice of an acceptance. In *Holwell Securities v. Hughes*,[148] for example, an option for the purchase of real estate provided that the option "shall be exercisable by notice in writing" to the intending seller within a particular time period. The Court of Appeal held that the term "notice" indicates that the acceptance is to be drawn to the attention of the offeror. Accordingly, the mailbox rule was inapplicable. Even in the absence of such language, however, the court was prepared to hold that the mailbox rule should not apply to an arrangement of this kind. Lawton L.J. indicated that the rule would not apply, even in a case where the parties might expect a communication through the post, in circumstances where the application of the rule would produce "manifest inconvenience and absurdity." The illustrations provided for this proposition were, however, hypotheticals advanced by Bramwell

---

147 *Household Fire & Carriage Accident Insurance Co. v. Grant*, above note 139 at 224, Thesiger L.J.
148 [1974] 1 W.L.R. 155 (C.A.).

B., no friend of the mailbox rule,[149] in an earlier case.[150] The rule would be inapplicable, Bramwell B. suggested, to a letter accepting a proposal of marriage which was lost in the mails or a letter of instructions to a stockbroker to sell shares in a falling market that did not reach its destination. It is not clear, however, why the court felt that, on these grounds, the mailbox rule should be inapplicable to an option for the purchase of land and, indeed, no such general principle appears to have emerged in subsequent cases. Moreover, there was certainly no evidence of prejudice to the offeror in the *Hughes* case itself. On the facts of the case, a copy of the letter of acceptance was received by the vendor's solicitors in a timely fashion and this fact was drawn to the vendor's attention by them shortly before his departure on vacation. In response to the intending purchaser's argument that these circumstances amounted to "notice in writing," the court held that the vendor himself had not received the requisite notice. The limitation on the mailbox rule suggested in *Hughes* does not appear, however, to have created a substantial impediment to its application and, accordingly, a prudent offeror who wishes to avoid application of the rule will carefully stipulate that the offeree's acceptance will be effective only upon receipt.[151]

3) Instantaneous Communications

Acceptances may be communicated in a variety of contexts and by various means of communication other than the mailing of letters. Parties may deal with each other in "face-to-face" meetings or "*inter praesentes*" either orally or in writing. Alternatively, where they are separated by distance, they may communicate with each other by a variety of methods of communication such as telephone, telex, fax, e-mail or other electronic forms of communication. With agreements negotiated *inter praesentes*, of course, no issue will arise with respect to either when

---

149 As is indicated by his dissenting opinion in *Household Fire & Carriage Accident Insurance Co. v. Grant,* above note 139.

150 *British & American Telegraph Co. v. Colson* (1871), L.R. 6 Ex. Ch. 108.

151 In an unusual Canadian case where the offer stipulated for delivery the copy of the acceptance to the offeror, the court nonetheless applied the mailbox rule. The offer was delayed in the mails and arrived only the day before the deadline stipulated for acceptance. It would have been unreasonable for the offeror located in Newfoundland, to insist that the offeree, located in Alberta, actually deliver acceptance to the offeror's place of business in a timely fashion and, accordingly, held that the posting of the acceptance constitute valid delivery. See *Island Properties Ltd. v. Entertainment Enterprises Ltd.* (1983), 146 D.L.R. (3d) 505 (Nfld. S.C.T.D.), var'd (1986), 26 D.L.R. (4th) 347 (Nfld. C.A.).

particular communications occurred or, indeed, where they occurred. When we turn to consider parties at a distance communicating through these various means of communication, however, there exists the possibility of disputes concerning the time at which communications were made. Was the faxed acceptance made at the time of sending, or arrival or at the time of reading by the offeror? Further, disputes may arise with respect to the location of contract formation, a point that may, as we have seen, be relevant for the resolution of various procedural and other legal issues. Thus, for example, where a party in New York telephones, faxes or e-mails an offeror in Vancouver to communicate an acceptance of the offer, the question may arise as to whether the contract was formed in the state of New York or in British Columbia. If the traditional principle that an acceptance is effective when communicated to the offeror applies, the place of contract formation in these cases would be Vancouver. It may be considered, however, whether the postal acceptance rule might apply to any of these forms of communication with the result that the acceptance is effective when sent from New York.

Against application of the mailbox rule it may be argued that all of these means of communication are, potentially at least, instantaneous in nature. In this respect, they are like communications *inter praesentes*, not subject to the problem of delayed communication or at least not necessarily subject to such delay. On the other hand, in the context of some of these forms of communication, an argument can be made that the particular means of communication bears some similarity to communication by mail. The communications may be prone to getting lost or scrambled and it may be that the offeree who has sent an acceptance will be unaware of the difficulties in transmission. Further, successful communication through e-mail or fax, for example, depends on the presence and attentiveness of the offeree or a representative of the offeree at the appropriate "listening post." In some cases, it may not be clear when a message has been delivered. An e-mail message might arrive in the offeror's e-mail system but may not be accessible by virtue of some internal difficulty. Until accessed, the electronic message may or may not be in some physical sense located in Vancouver. Thus far, courts have accepted that the general principle, rather than the postal acceptance rule, normally applies to instantaneous forms of communication. At the same time, however, courts appreciate that difficulties may arise in the context of these various forms of communication that do not yield easily to a straightforward application of the traditional principle that an acceptance is communicated when it is received by the offeror.

The House of Lords examined these issues in the context of an acceptance communicated by telex in *Brinkibon Ltd. v. Stahag Stahl Und Stahlwarenhandelsgesellschaft mbH.*[152] In this case, a buyer, located in London, sent a telex to sellers located in Vienna of an offer for the purchase of goods. In order to determine certain procedural issues in a subsequent lawsuit, it was material to determine whether the contract was formed in England or in Austria. The House of Lords held that the contract had been entered in Vienna when the acceptance was there received by the offeror. Lord Wilberforce drew a distinction between "instantaneous" communications such as communications *inter praesentes* or by parties in separate locations by telephone or radio communication to which the traditional principle applies and "non-instantaneous" communication between parties at a distance from each other, to which the postal acceptance rule may apply. Telex communications, in his view, should be assimilated to other forms of instantaneous communications. Accordingly, the traditional rule would normally apply with the result that the place of contracting was the place where the acceptance was received. Lord Fraser added additional reasons for agreeing with this approach. First, it was his view that it is reasonable to treat the message as having been received once it arrives on the offeror's telex machine as it is the offeror's "responsibility to arrange for prompt handling of messages within his own office."[153] Further, the party sending the message "can generally tell if his message has not been received on the other party's (the offeror's) machine, whereas the offeror, of course, will not know if an unsuccessful attempt has been made to send an acceptance to him."[154] In his view, therefore, the burden can be placed more conveniently on the offeree to ensure that the message is received by the offeror. For these additional reasons, it was inappropriate to apply the postal acceptance rule to telex communications. Both Lords Wilberforce and Fraser agreed, however, that this analysis should apply only to the "ordinary simple case."[155] Lord Wilberforce explained as follows:

> Since 1955 the use of telex communication has been greatly expanded, and there are many variants on it. The senders and recipients may not be the principals to the contemplated contract. They may be servants or agents with limited authority. The message may not reach or be intended to reach, the designated recipient immediately: messages

---

152 [1983] 2 A.C. 34 (H.L.).
153 *Ibid.* at 43.
154 *Ibid.*
155 *Ibid.*

may be sent out of office hours, or at night, with the intention, or on the assumption, that they will be read at a later time. There may be some error or default at the recipient's end which prevents receipt at the time contemplated and believed in by the sender. The message may have been sent and/or received through machines operated by third persons. And many other variations may occur. No universal rule can cover all such cases; they must be resolved by reference to the intentions of the parties, by sound business practice and in some cases, by a judgment where the risks should lie ....[156]

Arguably, then, the general principle emerging from the reasoning in *Brinkibon* is that, in the case of instantaneous communications, the traditional rule will normally apply unless the failure of the offeror to receive the communication of acceptance sent by the offeree results from the fault of the offeror or from a defect in the communication with respect to which the offeror should be deemed to have assumed the risk. With respect to the latter point, Lord Fraser's emphasis on the importance of the fact that the sender of a telex is normally in a position to know if the message has been received by the other party weighs against the application of the mailbox rule, suggests that where this is not the case in the context of a particular form of instantaneous communication, there may be room for application of the postal acceptance rule.

In *Brinkibon*, the House of Lords confirmed the earlier decision of the Court of Appeal in *Entores Ltd. v. Miles Far East Corp.*[157] applying the traditional rule to an acceptance by telex. In *Entores*, Lord Denning also emphasized the significance of the fact that the sender of the message would normally know that the message has gone through and coupled this analysis with an exclusion of the general principle where the failure of the message to arrive results from the fault of the offeror recipient. Thus, if the offeror has allowed his teleprinter to run out of ink, the offeror will be bound, in Lord Denning's view, "because he will be estopped from saying that he did not receive the message of acceptance."[158] A similar analysis was applicable, in his view, to telephone communications. Thus, if the offeree is aware that the telephone line has gone dead during the course of the conversation with the offeror, the offeree will appreciate that there is a risk that the acceptance was not heard and accordingly, must re-contact the offeror with a view to clearly communicating the acceptance. On the other hand, if the offer-

---

156 *Ibid.* at 42.
157 [1955] 2 All E.R. 493 (C.A.).
158 *Ibid.* at 495.

or realizes that he has not clearly heard the offeree but does not trouble to seek a clarification, the offeror will be bound on the basis that he is estopped from denying receipt of the message. More generally, however, Lord Denning was of the view that instantaneous communications were quite different from communications through the post and that accordingly, as a general matter, the postal acceptance rule was inapplicable to them.

A similar approach has recently been taken with respect to faxed acceptances. In _Eastern Power Ltd. v. Azienda Comunale Energia & Ambiente_,[159] the Ontario Court of Appeal applied the reasoning in _Brinkibon_ to an acceptance that had been faxed by an offeree located in Ontario to an offeror located in Italy. The traditional rule, rather than the postal acceptance rule, was held to be applicable and the contract was held to have been formed in Italy where the facsimile transmission had been received. For the court, MacPherson J.A. also agreed with the reasoning of Lord Wilberforce in _Brinkibon_ to the effect that the traditional rule was not necessarily a universal rule and would not necessarily apply to all the possible variants on the simple case of a straightforward successful transmission of a fax from the offeree to the offeror. As he noted, there was nothing on the facts of the case to suggest that the communication between the parties was not instantaneous.[160]

In recent decades, anxiety has been expressed in various quarters concerning the ability of common law and civilian contract law to cope successfully with contract formation problems in the context of e-commerce transactions entered into through Internet connections or e-mail communications. Indeed, Canadian provinces have enacted legislation designed to facilitate the legal analysis of agreements formed through electronic communications.[161] The legislation provides that a contract is not invalid by reason only of being in an electronic form. It further provides that offers, acceptances and other relevant communications can be expressed electronically or by an act such as touching or clicking an icon on a computer screen that is intended to result in electronic com-

---

159 (1999), 178 D.L.R. (4th) 409 (Ont. C.A.).

160 _Ibid._ at para. 29.

161 See, for example, _Electronic Commerce Act, 2000_, S.O. 2000, c. 17. The provincial legislation is quite similar across the country and is based on the _Uniform Electronic Commerce Act_, drafted by the Uniform Law Conference of Canada, which, in turn, was based on a model statute prepared by the United Nations Commission on International Trade Law. For analysis, see J.D. Gregory, "Canadian Electronic Legislation" (2002) 17 B.F.L.R. 277; B.J. Freedman, "Electronic Contracts under Canadian Law—A Practical Guide" (2000) 28 Man. L.J. 1.

munication unless the parties agree otherwise.[162] Further, the statute provides default definitions, which can be supplanted by the agreement of the parties, for such concepts as sending an electronic document or receiving one. Essentially, a document is sent when it enters an information system outside the sender's control.[163] An electronic document is presumed to be received when it enters the addressee's information system and is capable of being retrieved by the addressee.[164] Electronic communications are deemed to be sent from the sender's place of business and received at the addressee's place of business,[165] and so on. The statute does not attempt to deal, however, with such issues as the time and place of formation of electronic contracts. Thus, although the statute will be of assistance in determining whether a particular communication has arrived, it does not indicate, for example, whether an electronic acceptance is effective upon being sent or, rather, upon being received. In resolving such matters, it is realistic to expect that courts will apply the reasoning that may be derived from the *Brinkibon* line of authority and, where the sender of an electronic message is able to determine that the message has been received, the traditional principle that acceptance occurs upon receipt is likely to apply, subject to the caveats expressed in the *Brinkibon* decision itself.

It is perhaps not obvious that the problems addressed in the legislation could not have been solved at common law. In *Rudder v. Microsoft Corp.*,[166] for example, an Ontario court recently appeared to have little difficulty in finding that a contract was formed on the basis of clicking an "I agree" icon on a computer screen. Further, the acceptance was held to apply to all of the terms set out in the agreement displayed on the offeror's website, including those not read by the offeree. In other words, the court was able, without apparent difficulty, to simply apply the normal rules of contract formation applicable to agreements in writing to an agreement created in an electronic format.[167] Nonetheless, the new legislation may usefully contribute to the uniform treatment of some technical issues relating to contract formation in electronic form.

---

162 *Electronic Commerce Act, 2000, ibid.*, s. 19(1).

163 *Ibid.*, s. 22(1).

164 *Ibid.*, s. 22(3).

165 *Ibid.*, s. 22(4).

166 (1999), 2 C.P.R. (4th) 474, 40 C.P.C. (4th) 394 (Ont. S.C.J.).

167 See also *Kanitz v. Rogers Cable Inc.* (2002), 58 O.R. (3d) 299 (S.C.J.) (contractual provision in website agreement entered into by subscribers with Internet services provider to the effect that the terms of the agreement could be varied from time to time by the services provider by posting notices of such changes on its website or by communicating them to subscribers by e-mail or post, held binding).

The only point of substantive contract law addressed by the statute relates to mistaken communications. The statute provides[168] that an
electronic transaction will be unenforceable if an individual, presumably the offeree, makes an error in providing information electronically
and the "electronic agent," that is, the offeror, does not provide the individual an opportunity to prevent or correct such errors and the offeree
provides prompt notification of the error to the offeror. Relief will be denied, however, if the offeree has already materially benefited by receiving the benefits provided by the offeror under the agreement. In effect,
the legislative provision provides a substantial incentive for e-commerce
suppliers to provide their customers with opportunities to review and
correct material being electronically submitted by them. The statutory
rule is quite unlike the traditional common law doctrine concerning the
effect of a mistake occurring in the process of contract formation.[169]

E. REVOCATION OF THE OFFER

Until an offer has been accepted, it is open to the offeror to withdraw
or revoke the offer, thereby precluding subsequent acceptance of the
offer by the offeree. As we shall see,[170] this remains true in the case
where the offeror has promised to keep the offer open for acceptance
for a specified period of time. At common law, so-called firm offers do
not bind the offeror unless they meet the more general requirements of
the common law relating to the enforceability of undertakings.[171] As
we have seen,[172] the acceptance must be made within a time deadline
stipulated in the offer or, in the absence of a deadline, within a reasonable time. Otherwise, the offer will lapse before acceptance. Here
we consider, however, the circumstances under which an offer can be
terminated by the offeror's decision to withdraw or revoke the offer. In
particular, two issues will be considered. First, the requirements for
communication of a revocation of an offer will be addressed. Second,
the possible solutions to the problem posed by the possibility that the

---

168 Above note 161, s. 21.
169 See generally Chapter 13.
170 See the discussion of "firm offers" Chapter 7, section B(1). And see *Byrne v. Van
     Tienhoven* (1880), 5 C.P.D. 344 [*Byrne*]; and *Dickinson v. Dodds* (1876), 2 Ch. D.
     463 (C.A.).
171 In essence, a firm offer will be binding only if it is part of an enforceable bargain
     or given in accordance with certain formalities. See Chapter 7.
172 See above this Chapter, section C(1).

offeree might engage in acts of detrimental reliance prior to revocation of the offer will be considered.

1) Communication of Revocation

Revocation of an offer by the offeror will only be effective if the intention to revocate is communicated by the offeror to the offeree. The point appears to have been considered for the first time in *Byrne v. Van Tienhoven*,[173] a case in which a mailed acceptance and a mailed revocation crossed in the mails. An offer to sell mailed on October 1st was received on October 11th by the buyers who immediately accepted the offer by telegram on the 11th. On the 8th of October, the sellers mailed a revocation of the offer that was received on October 20th. The buyers then sought to enforce the agreement and the sellers defended on the basis that the offer had been revoked on October 8th and accordingly, after that date, there was no longer any possibility of a *consensus ad idem*. It was necessary to determine, therefore, whether an uncommunicated revocation could be effective. Although Lindley J. indicated that it was his understanding that civilian doctrine supported such a view, he concluded that "an uncommunicated revocation is for all practical purpose and in point of law no revocation at all."[174] This approach might be defended on the ground that if an uncommunicated revocation were considered effective, the offeree might unwittingly continue to suffer loss in the form of detrimental reliance on the offer after the offer has been silently revoked. Although a requirement that the revocation be communicated is far from being a complete solution to the problem posed by the possibility of detrimental reliance on offers, there is persuasive force in the argument that the offeror should be required to communicate the revocation in order to prevent further loss on the part of the offeree from this point forward.

In the *Byrne* case, the mailing of the revocation on October 8 preceded the mailing of the acceptance on October 11. Accordingly, it was also necessary in *Byrne* to consider whether the notice of revocation is effective when mailed or only upon receipt by the offeree. As we have seen,[175] the postal acceptance rule holds that where communication of an acceptance by mail is appropriate, the acceptance is effective upon posting. As the postal acceptance rule was well established by the time of the *Byrne* case, the court considered whether a similar

---

173 *Byrne*, above note 170.
174 *Ibid.* at 347.
175 See above this Chapter, section D(2).

principle should apply to the posting of a revocation of an offer. The court concluded that it should not apply and that revocation should be effective only upon receipt on the unconvincing ground that the agency rationale, which was said to underlie the postal acceptance rule, was inapplicable to revocation. As noted in the above discussion of the postal acceptance rule,[176] one of the early justifications for that rule was that by expressly or implicitly assenting to the sending of an acceptance by mail, the offeror had, in effect, designated the postal authorities as an agent for the purpose of receiving the acceptance on the offeror's behalf. In *Byrne*, Lindley J. held that this principle was inapplicable to the withdrawal of an offer inasmuch as he could not find any "evidence of any authority in fact given by the plaintiffs to the defendants to notify a withdrawal of their offer by merely posting a letter."[177] If, as has been suggested above, however, the agency rationale offers an unconvincing explanation for the postal acceptance rule, its distinction in *Byrne* from the facts of revocation does not offer a convincing basis for the rule requiring communication of a revocation. Again, a more convincing justification may be found in the desirability of preventing unwitting detrimental reliance on the existence of the offer by an offeree who has not been made aware of the offeror's decision to revoke the offer.[178]

Although it is accepted that an uncommunicated revocation is of no effect, it is also accepted that the revocation may be effective if the offeree learns indirectly that the offeror is no longer willing to stand by the offer. In *Dickinson v. Dodds*,[179] the defendant, Dodds, had given a firm offer to sell Dickinson a residential property at a particular price, the offer to be held open until the following Friday, June 12th, at 9 a.m. As we have noted, a mere promise to hold the offer open for a period of time was not binding on Dodds and, accordingly, Dodds was free to withdraw the offer. On Thursday the 11th, Dickinson's agent advised him first, that he understood that Dodds was negotiating to sell the property to a third party and then, that the property had in fact been sold. Nonetheless, prior to 9 a.m. on Friday morning, Dickinson's agent

---

176   *Ibid.*

177   *Byrne,* above note 170 at 348.

178   In *Byrne,* Lindley J. suggested that making the revocation effective upon posting would result in "extreme injustice and inconvenience" as it would require the offeree who has accepted to remain insecure until enough time had passed to be quite sure that a revocation had not been posted prior to acceptance. See *ibid.* at 348.

179   *Ibid.* See also *Paterson v. Houghton* (1909), 19 Man. R. 168 at 178 (C.A.), Cameron J.A.; *Pilgrim v. Milner* (1997), 155 Nfld. & P.E.I.R. 221 at 224 (Nfld. C.A.), Cameron J.A.

presented Dodds with a copy of Dickinson's acceptance of the offer of sale. Dodds replied that the acceptance was too late and that the property had already been sold. Dickinson's action to enforce the contract of sale failed, however, on the ground that, as he had become aware that Dodds had sold the property to a third party, he was no longer in a position to accept the offer. Once the intending buyer is aware that the seller has sold the property to someone else, he is aware that the seller "has not remained in the same mind to sell it to him"[180] and a *consensus ad idem* becomes impossible.

2) The "Flagpole Problem" and Its Solutions

The fact that an offer can be withdrawn by the offeror on notice to the offeree, even in the context of so-called firm offers,[181] creates the possibility that an offeree, assuming that the offer may be accepted, will detrimentally rely on the existence of the offer. The offeree might turn down an attractive alternative offer from a third party or invest resources in investigating the opportunity presented by the offer or in preparing for performance. The possibilities for detrimental reliance of this kind are perhaps particularly intense in the context of offers of unilateral agreements. Until the offeree has completed performance of the act requested by the offeror in return for the offeror's promise, the offer can be withdrawn. Thus, an offer in the form "I will pay you $500 if you climb to the top of the flagpole" can, in theory at least, be withdrawn at any point during the offeree's attempt to climb the pole. Call this the "flagpole problem."

An extreme version of the flagpole problem is illustrated by the facts of *Errington v. Errington and Woods*.[182] In this case, a father had purchased a residential property, placing title in his own name and borrowing most of the purchase money from a building society on a loan secured by a mortgage in the society's favour on the property. The father invited his son and daughter-in-law to take possession of the house and promised that if they made all of the scheduled payments on the mortgage, he would transfer ownership of the property to them. In theory, at least, it would be open to the father to withdraw the offer at any point prior to the completion of the payment schedule. Similar, if less dramatic, problems may arise in the context of offers of rewards.

180 *Dickinson v. Dodds,* above note 170 at 474.
181 See Chapter 7, section B(1)(c).
182 [1952] 1 K.B. 290 (C.A.).

Thus, in *Carlill v. Carbolic Smoke Ball Co.*[183] a reward was offered by the smoke ball company to any person who acquired the patent medicine in question, used it in accord with the instructions and nonetheless contracted influenza. In theory, at least, the offer could be withdrawn by the smoke ball company at any point in time prior to the individual user's catching of influenza, an outcome that would surprise those who purchased the smoke ball on the faith of the advertised reward. Unsurprisingly, courts are disinclined to permit offerors to revoke in such circumstances and a number of techniques have been developed for achieving that end.

First, where the language of an offer may be considered to be ambiguous on this point, courts may lean against the construction of the offer that renders it an offer of unilateral rather than a bilateral contract. In *Dawson v. Helicopter Exploration Co.*,[184] for example, the parties had engaged in extensive negotiations concerning a proposed visit to a remote area to investigate the possibility of staking mineral claims. The plaintiff had earlier staked claims in the area, which subsequently lapsed. The defendant expressed an interest in the property and offered an arrangement to the plaintiff under which he would accompany the defendant's representatives to the area to guide them to the properties in question in return for a 10 percent interest in whatever claims the defendant might stake in the area. The defendant's offer indicated that the trip would be made only if a suitable pilot could be retained and suggested a timeframe for the visit. The plaintiff replied indicating that the proposed time was satisfactory and inviting the defendant to inform him when a pilot had been retained so that he could make appropriate arrangements for release time from his current employment in order to make the trip. In due course, the defendant investigated the properties without the plaintiff's assistance, staked the properties and prepared to undertake developmental work. In response to the plaintiff's claim for damages for breach of contract, the defendant argued that the offered agreement was unilateral in nature and could only be accepted upon the plaintiff's act of accompanying the defendant's representatives on a trip to the area in question. No such trip had occurred and, accordingly, the offer had never been accepted. The Supreme Court of Canada held, however, that the offer, properly construed, was an offer of a bilateral contract that imposed obligations on the defendant to participate in carrying out the arrangements for the planned trip. Rand J. explained the court's preference for this construction of the offer in the following terms:

---

183 Above note 28.
184 [1955] S.C.R. 868.

this interpretation of the correspondence follows the tendency of courts to treat offers as calling for bilateral rather than unilateral action when the language can be fairly so construed, in order that the transaction shall have such "business efficacy as both parties must have intended that at all events it should have." ... In theory ... an offer in the unilateral sense can be revoked up to the last moment before complete performance. At such a consequence many courts have balked; and it is in part that fact that has led to a promissory construction where that can be reasonably given. What is effectuated is the real intention of both parties to close a business bargain on the strength of which they may, thereafter, plan their courses.[185]

Properly construed, the correspondence contemplated performance by both parties subject to the condition that a pilot could be retained. In the result, then, the offer could not be revoked once the offer of a bilateral agreement had been accepted. Accordingly, the plaintiff's claim for damages for breach of contract enjoyed success.

A second solution to the flagpole problem involves careful construction of the definition in the offer of the act required by the offeror as an acceptance of the offer. Thus, in the *Carlill* case, it may well be that the proper interpretation of the offer is that the act requested by the offer of reward is the acquisition of a smoke ball or, perhaps, the acquisition of the smoke ball and commencement of its use in accordance with the instructions or, as a third alternative, completion of the course of treatment. Each of these interpretations of the offer appear plausible and would provide greater protection to the interests of the offeree than a construction to the effect that acceptance is not complete until influenza is contracted. In effect, the exercise is one of narrow construction of the offer in favour of the offeree. This technique may be illustrated by the decision in *Daulia Ltd. v. Four Millbank Nominees Ltd.*[186] In this case, the plaintiffs had been negotiating for the purchase of a portfolio of properties from the defendants. The defendants' representative, one Osgoodby, offered a unilateral agreement of sale under which the defendants would sell the properties to the plaintiffs if the plaintiffs attended at the defendants' offices by 10 a.m. the next day and provided the defendants with a certified cheque for the deposit and an executed copy of the agreement of purchase and sale, the terms of which had already been agreed to by the parties. In reliance on that offer, the plaintiffs attended at the defendants' offices in timely fashion

---

185 *Ibid.* at 874–75. For discussion of the "business efficacy" test for the implication of terms, see Chapter 19, section D(3).

186 Above note 85.

with the deposit and the signed agreement, as the pleadings stated, "ready for tender" to the defendants. They were thereupon advised by the defendants who had, in fact, received an offer of a better price from a third party, that the defendants were no longer prepared to enter into an agreement with the plaintiffs. In response to the plaintiffs' claim for breach of contract, the defendants argued that the act requested by the unilateral offer, the actual tendering of the deposit and the executed agreement, had not occurred and, accordingly, the offer had been revoked prior to acceptance. Goff L.J. held that the conduct of the plaintiffs amounted to tender and, therefore, constituted an acceptance of the offer. Buckley L.J. was of the view if the actual tendering of the documents was stultified by the defendants' announcement that they would no longer proceed with the transaction, this was not a fact on which the defendants could rely in urging that actual tender had not occurred. In short, the offer was construed in such fashion as to enable the plaintiffs to argue successfully that the offer had been accepted by attending at the premises in a state of preparedness for tender.[187]

A third technique is to find that a collateral arrangement relating to the firmness of the offer is implicit in the relationship of the parties. Thus, in *Errington v. Errington and Woods*,[188] Denning L.J. solved the flagpole problem by holding that in addition to the father's undertaking that he would transfer title to the children if they completed the mortgage payments, there was a collateral understanding under which the father implicitly promised that as long as the children made the payments to the mortgagee they would be allowed to remain in possession of the premises. It was clearly the case that the children had not committed themselves to making the payments. Thus, the collateral agreement would not appear to be bilateral. The collateral understanding could be framed, presumably, as an offer from the father of a unilateral contract in the form "if you take possession of the premises, I will per-

---

187   Compare with the differing views expressed in *Petterson v. Pattberg*, above note 85, in which a mortgagee offered to grant a discharge to the mortgagor if the balance was paid off prior to a certain date. The mortgagor arrived at the mortgagee's premises in order to tender payment but, when asked to identify himself, the mortgagee advised him that it was too late to make the payment as the mortgage had been sold to a third party. A majority held that the act requested by the mortgagee — payment of the balance — had not been completed and, accordingly, the offer could be revoked. The minority view was that the mortgagor's arrival at the mortgagee's premises in a state of preparedness for tender met the requirements of the offer and created a binding agreement. See also *Beer v. Lea*, above note 85.

188   Above note 182.

mit you to remain there as long as you continue making the mortgage payments." A similar solution was proposed as an alternative ground for the relief in the *Daulia* decision. Both Goff L.J. and Buckley L.J. agreed that if the correct view was that the offer had not been properly accepted, the defendants were nonetheless in breach of a collateral and implicit undertaking that the offeror would not prevent performance of the act that amounts to the acceptance and that this obligation arises as soon as the offeree begins to perform. Again, the arrangement could be framed as the offer of a unilateral contract in the form, "If you begin to perform the act that amounts to acceptance, I will not revoke the offer until you have had an opportunity to complete the performance of that act." The implication of such arrangements would be precluded by any explicit understanding of the parties to the contrary. It seems very likely, however, that the parties in the *Errington* case, if asked to consider the matter, could have articulated an understanding of this kind and this may be true in many cases of offers of agreements where acceptance requires a substantial investment of time, energy or resources by the offeree.

FURTHER READINGS

D.G. BAIRD & R. WEISBERG, "Rules, Standards and the Battle of the Forms: A Reassessment of S. 2-207" (1982) 68 Va. L. Rev. 1217.

M.A. EISENBERG, "Expression Rules in Contract Law and Problems of Offer and Acceptance" (1994) 82 Cal. L. Rev. 1127.

P. FASCIANO, "Internet Electronic Mail: A Last Bastion for the Mailbox Rule" (1997) 25 Hofstra L. Rev. 971.

S. GARDNER, "Trashing with Trollope: A Deconstruction of the Postal Rules in Contract" (1992) 12 Oxford J. Leg. Stud. 170.

J.D. GREGORY, "Canadian Electronic Commerce Legislation" (2002) 17 B.F.L.R. 277.

M.A. HICKLING, "Auctions Without Reserve" (1970) 5 U.B.C. L. Rev. 187.

J.M. PERILLO, "The Origins of the Objective Theory of Contract Formation and Interpretation" (2000) 69 Fordham L. Rev. 427.

M. PETTIT, "Modern Unilateral Contracts" (1983) 63 B.U.L. Rev. 551.

R.A. SAMEK, "Performative Utterances and the Concept of a Contract" (1965) 43 Australasian J. Phil. 196.

A.W.B. SIMPSON, "Quackery and Contract Law: The Case of the Carbolic Smoke Ball" (1985) 14 J. Leg. Stud. 345.

P.M. TIERSMA, "Reassessing Unilateral Contracts: The Role of Offer, Acceptance and Promise" (1992) 26 U.C. Davis L. Rev. 1.

P.M. TIERSMA, "The Language of Offer and Acceptance: Speech Acts and the Question of Intent" (1986) 74 Cal. L. Rev. 189.

A.T. VON MEHREN, "The Battle of the Forms: A Comparative View" (1990) 38 Am. J. Comp. L. 265.

V. WATNICK, "The Electronic Formation of Contracts and the Common Law 'Mailbox Rule'" (2004) 56 Baylor L. Rev. 175.

P. WINFIELD, "Some Aspects of Offer and Acceptance" (1939) 55 Law Q. Rev. 498.

CHAPTER 3

CERTAINTY OF TERMS

A. INTRODUCTION

In order for an agreement to be enforceable, the parties must have reached agreement on all the essential terms of their agreement. As is often said, the parties must make the agreement, the courts will not make it for them. Further, the parties "must so express themselves that their meaning can be determined with a reasonable degree of certainty."[1] Where the parties either fail to reach agreement on all the essential terms of the agreement or express themselves in such fashion that their intentions cannot be divined by the court, the agreement will fail for lack of certainty of terms. In such circumstances, the parties have not reached a sufficient *consensus ad idem* to enable the courts to enforce their agreement. At the same time, the requirement of certainty of terms and its underlying rationale must be balanced against the practicalities of transactional negotiations. Parties may be unable to anticipate and articulate agreements with respect to future events and may intentionally leave gaps in their agreements to provide for future and mutually satisfactory accommodations. Parties, especially those not advised by lawyers, may be unaware of the nature of all the essential terms to be stipulated in the particular context. Parties may assume that reasonable or "the usual" arrangements will apply to an undetermined matter. In

---

1   *Scammell and Nephew Ltd. v. Ouston*, [1941] A.C. 251.

all such cases, the parties may intend to enter into binding contractual arrangements and believe that they have successfully done so. Rigid application of the doctrine of certainty, therefore, could produce much mischief, especially in cases where the parties detrimentally rely on the assumption that a valid and enforceable agreement has been created. Accordingly, courts will attempt to fill gaps and find meaning in agreements in circumstances where it appears that a binding agreement was intended by the parties.

The law of certainty of terms, then, reflects this tension between a requirement that the parties reach a complete and intelligible agreement and a reluctance to defeat the expectations of the parties that an enforceable agreement has been created. As Lambert J.A. observed in *Griffin v. Martens*:[2] "As long as an agreement is not being constructed by the court, to the surprise of the parties, or at least one of them, the courts should try to retain and give effect to the agreement that the parties have created for themselves."[3] As we shall see, the leading and modern authorities tend to place particular emphasis on the need to give effect, where possible, to the expectations of the parties that they have entered into a valid and enforceable agreement.[4]

Three different aspects of the doctrine must be considered. First, an agreement may suffer from incompleteness in the sense that an essential term is simply not present. The determination of whether a particular term is essential is a matter of some subtlety. Second, where parties are aware that they cannot agree with respect to a particular matter at the time of contracting, they may stipulate in their agreement that they will reach agreement on the particular matter in the future. It must be considered whether such "agreements to agree" constitute an enforceable means of filling gaps in the agreement. Third, an important term of an agreement may suffer from vagueness or, as is sometimes said, incurable uncertainty. In such circumstances, it must be determined whether, as a result of the vagueness of a particular term, the entire agreement fails for uncertainty.

---

2   (1988), 27 B.C.L.R. (2d) 152 (C.A.).
3   *Ibid.* at 153.
4   See, for example, *Banque Brussels Lambert SA v. Australian National Industries Ltd.* (1989), 21 N.S.W.L.R. 502 at 523 (S.C.), Rogers J. ("... uncertainty, a concept so much loved by lawyers, has fallen into disfavour as a tool for striking down commercial bargains.")

B. INCOMPLETENESS

The determination of whether the parties have agreed to all the essential terms of a particular agreement rests on an assessment of whether, in a case where there are missing terms, the omitted terms are so important that they warrant the conclusion that the parties have not yet reached an agreement. In applying this test, much will turn on the commercial context of the agreement. In some commercial settings, it will not be possible or may not be customary to reach an agreement with respect to particular matters at the time of formation of the agreement. In other contexts, however, it may be entirely routine to reach agreement on rather similar matters, failure to do so thus signalling that the parties have not yet reached a sufficiently complete agreement. Further, it may be material that the parties have entered similar agreements in the past and have found them to be quite workable. Even in the context of an initial agreement between the parties, it may be material that the agreement has been partially performed with the result that the effect of holding the agreement to be unenforceable will be the unjust enrichment of one of the parties at the expense of the other. These themes can be illustrated by examination of a line of leading English authorities that are often considered to be inconsistent or, indeed, irreconcilable.

In the first of these cases, *May and Butcher Ltd. v. The King*[5] the plaintiff had entered into an agreement with the defendant Disposals Board for the purchase of army surplus "tentage" as it became available, from time to time, from the Board. The agreement required the purchaser to post a single deposit as security for carrying out its obligations and, in return, the Board agreed to sell the total stock of tentage, as it became available, to the plaintiff. The agreement further provided that such matters as the prices to be paid, the dates on which payment was to be made, the quantities available for disposal and the dates for delivery were to be agreed to by the parties in due course. Ultimately, the Board refused to perform its obligations and responded to the purchaser's claim to enforce by arguing that the agreement failed because of the missing terms. The House of Lords held that the parties had simply failed to reach an agreement and placed particular emphasis on the fact that the matter of price had been left at large. The agreement could not be saved by the fact that it contained an arbitration clause. In the absence of a binding agreement, the arbitration clause did not have the effect of creating a binding agreement. The plaintiff's suggestion that

---

5   [1934] 2 K.B. 17 (H.L.). Although not reported until 1934, the decision of the House of Lords in this case was rendered in 1929.

the price could be considered to be a "reasonable" price was similarly to no avail.[6] The parties had simply failed to reach an agreement on an essential matter.

The result in *May and Butcher* is often contrasted with the decision of the House of Lords a few years later in *Hillas and Co. Ltd. v. Arcos Ltd.*[7] This case concerned the enforceability of an arrangement between a British lumber concern and a Russian Government lumber supplier. The parties had entered into an agreement with respect to the supply of a large quantity of lumber over a two-year period. During the first year, the plaintiff had purchased over 40,000 standards of lumber. The agreement conferred an option on the purchaser for a further 100,000 standards for the 1931 season. Upon its exercise by the purchaser, the seller refused to perform, taking the position that the agreement lacked sufficient certainty of terms. The agreement, which was judicially described as "inartistic, and ... repellent to the trained sense of an equity draftsman"[8] left a number of details such as dates and quantities of particular shipments at large. The prices for 1931 were to be determined by the supplier's forthcoming 1931 price list. The description of the goods as being of "fair specification" appeared vague. The parties had, however, worked successfully with the agreement in the 1930 season, finding themselves able to agree to appropriate details as the need to do so arose. As was explained in evidence, the process of negotiation that accompanies performance of such an agreement involves the making of proposals and counterproposals by the buyer and the seller until agreement is reached on the quantity and quality of goods to be forwarded in a particular instalment.

In the Court of Appeal, in *Hillas,* Scrutton L.J. had taken the view that the outcome was preordained by the decision of the House of Lords in *May and Butcher* and concluded that the agreement was, indeed, unenforceable for lack of certainty of terms. Scrutton L.J. went on to protest

---

6   Nor was the plaintiff's position strengthened by reliance on s. 8 of the *Sale of Goods Act, 1893*, which provides that if the parties have not settled on the price, the price shall be a "reasonable price". In their Lordships' view, the Act provided for a case in which the contract was silent on the matter of price whereas the agreement at issue had indicated that there would be an agreement between the parties on this matter. Also, as the Act further provides that where the price is to be settled by the valuation of a third party and the third party refuses to make that valuation, the contract is void. Lord Buckmaster expressed the view that similarly where the parties themselves refuse to fix a price, a similar result is directed by the force of this analogy. See *ibid.* at 20.

7   (1932), 147 L.T. 503 (H.L.).

8   *Ibid.* at 514.

mildly, however, that he regretted "that in many commercial matters the English law and the practice of commercial men are getting wider apart."[9] On appeal to the House of Lords, however, the agreement was held to be an enforceable one. Lord Wright made the following observation:

> Businessmen often record the most important agreements in crude and summary fashion; modes of expression sufficient and clear to them in the course of their business may appear to those unfamiliar with the business far from complete or precise. It is, accordingly, the duty of the courts to construe such documents fairly and broadly without being too astute or subtle in finding defects.... [This,] however, does not mean that the court is to make a contract for the parties or go outside the words they have used, except in so far as there are appropriate implications of law as, for instance, the implication of what is just and reasonable to be ascertained by the court as matter of machinery where the contractual intention is clear but the contract is silent on some detail.[10]

Applying this approach to the facts at hand, Lord Wright suggested that it is commonplace in some commercial settings for many matters of detail to be adjusted in the course of performing an agreement. In the present context, it was impossible or undesirable to fix precise dates for shipments and, if in the event, the parties were unable to agree, "the standard of what is reasonable can, in the last resort, be applied by the law."[11] Lord Wright did not take exception to the fixing of prices on the basis of the seller's price list for the coming year. As far as the description that the goods were to be "of fair specification" was concerned, Lord Wright noted that the parties did not experience any difficulty in applying these terms during the 1930 season. Lord Wright concluded that the parties had intended to and did in fact enter into a complete and binding agreement.

Those who are inclined to find inconsistency between the outcomes of *May and Butcher* and *Hillas* emphasize, understandably, that the details left to be arranged by the parties—quantities, dates of delivery, price and quality—appear rather similar in each case. The difference between the two cases, arguably, rests on their commercial setting. In *Hillas*, an apparently commonly used commercial arrangement contained inherent uncertainties that could not be resolved at the time of formation of the agreement. To hold such an agreement void for un-

---

9 (1932), 40 Lloyd's Rep. 307 at 311 (C.A.).
10 Above note 7 at 514.
11 Above note 7 at 515 .

certainty simply precludes the use of what appears to be a satisfactory commercial arrangement within the industry in question. One cannot make the same kinds of claims in favour of the agreement at issue in *May and Butcher*, which amounted in effect to the conferral of a private monopoly on the acquisition of government-owned war-surplus material. In the context of contemporary public administration, such an agreement would likely be considered impermissible on the ground that the sale of such assets should occur in a competitive bidding process.

In a third case, *Foley v. Classique Coaches Ltd.*,[12] the English Court of Appeal was required to apply the doctrine laid down in *May and Butcher* and *Hillas* to a contract for the purchase of land under which the purchaser, the operator of a fleet of motor coaches, agreed to enter a supplementary agreement with the vendor, who operated a service station on adjacent land, to purchase all the fuel required for the purchaser's business from the vendor at prices to be agreed "in writing and from time to time."[13] The transaction closed and the purchaser entered the requirements agreement with the vendor and abided by it for a period of some years until deciding to acquire petrol from another supplier. Scrutton L.J. who had been overruled by the House of Lords in both *May and Butcher* and *Hillas* suggested that these cases "are not easy to fit in with each other"[14] and went on to hold that this particular agreement did not fail for incompleteness simply because of the failure to agree to a firm price for the petrol. Scrutton L.J. emphasized that the purchaser did not appear to be interested in returning the land and thus wished to have the agreement considered void with respect to only part of the *quid pro quo* promised in return for the land. Although the phase "unjust enrichment" was not mentioned by Scrutton L.J. or any other member of the Court of Appeal in this case, it is not surprising that the purchaser's attempt to escape his contractual obligations and, at the same time, enjoy the benefits of the agreement, did not enjoy success. Partial execution of the agreement, then, is likely to weigh in favour of enforceability.

Similar themes emerge from the Canadian jurisprudence. In circumstances where the parties intend to create a binding relationship, the presence of some inherent uncertainty with respect to future events that will require contractual details to be worked out in due course will not defeat the agreement. The facts of *Canada Square Corp. Ltd. v. Versa-*

---

12   [1934] 2 K.B. 1 (C.A.).
13   *Ibid.* at 3.
14   *Ibid.* at 9.

food Services Ltd.[15] provided an interesting context in which to test this thesis. The agreement in question was a letter agreement entered into by a developer, as lessor of a high-rise building then under construction, and a restaurateur, as lessee, which set out in written form the parties' "verbal understanding" relating to a lease to be entered into by the parties with respect to the operation of a restaurant on the top floor of the building. In order to accommodate a restaurant at the top of the building, it was necessary for the developer to reach an agreement at an early stage of the design and construction of the building. The letter agreement set out fourteen points of agreement, including agreement on a minimum annual rental charge, and concluded with a statement made on the part of the restaurateur that "this constitutes the general principles of our agreement with you." The letter agreement was then signed by the developer under a statement that "this agreement is hereby accepted by [the developer]." Nonetheless, it was plainly envisaged that there were a number of matters that would ultimately require more precise determination and, further, that a more sophisticated and detailed document would probably be entered into at a later stage. The Ontario Court of Appeal, placing reliance on the passage from Lord Wright's opinion in the *Hillas* case, quoted above,[16] concluded that although the letter agreement was "crudely expressed and contains some very loose language,"[17] it was sufficiently complete to constitute an enforceable agreement. The court placed some emphasis on the fact that the parties appeared to conduct themselves on the basis of an assumption that the agreement was, in fact, enforceable for a period of some nineteen months or so.[18]

As the *Foley* and *Hillas* cases both illustrate, the absence of a price term is not necessarily fatal to the enforceability of an agreement. Indeed, in the context of contracts for the sale of goods, it is assumed, in the absence of a price term, that the parties intend a reasonable price.[19] On the other hand, the presence of a price term may be considered vital to the enforceability of an agreement in a variety of contexts. In *Courtney and Fairbairn Ltd. v. Tolaini Brothers (Hotels) Ltd.*,[20] the English Court of Appeal held unenforceable on grounds of incompleteness an agreement between a developer and a builder to build a substantial

---

15 (1981), 130 D.L.R. (3d) 205 (Ont. C.A.).

16 See above note 10.

17 Above note 15 at 218.

18 See also *Boult Enterprises Ltd. v. Brissett* (1985), 21 D.L.R. (4th) 730 at 737, Esson J.A.

19 See, for example, *Sale of Goods Act*, R.S.O. 1990, c. S.1, s. 9(2).

20 [1975] 1 All E.R. 716 (C.A.).

development project at a price described as "fair and reasonable contract sums in respect of each of the three projects as they arise"[21] to be negotiated with the developer's quantity surveyor. The commitment given to the builder was given in return for the builder's introduction of the developer to parties who eventually agreed to provide financing. If the agreement were to be held void for uncertainty, the developer would thus be placed in a position of having enjoyed the benefits of this arrangement without being required to engage the builder on the project. Nonetheless, Lord Denning explained that "the price in a building contract is of fundamental importance. It is so essential a term that there is no contract unless the price is agreed or there is an agreed method of ascertaining it, not dependent on the negotiations of the two parties themselves."[22] Indeed, in his view "[n]o builder and no employer would even dream of entering into a building contract for over £200,000 without there being an estimate of the cost and an agreed means of ascertaining the price."[23]

Similarly, the absence of a price term appeared to be the critical issue in a Canadian decision, *L.C.D.H. Audio Visual Ltd. v. I.S.T.S. Verbatim Ltd.*[24] This case involved a competitive bidding exercise in which two of the bidders withdrew in return for another bidder's promise that it would, if successful, retain one of the withdrawing bidders on a subcontract to provide certain services. The contract concerned the supply of translation and audiovisual services to the Congress Centre in Ottawa. As none of the bidders provided the full range of the required services, it was suggested by the City that bidders collaborate on bids. In response, the plaintiff and the other withdrawing bidder agreed with the defendant that if they withdrew, the defendant would if successful "negotiate towards entering into a subcontract for video/visual services" with one of the two withdrawing bidders. The other of the two eventually decided to withdraw from the subcontracting arrangement, thus leaving the defendant with an obligation to negotiate with the plaintiff. Accordingly, once the contract had been awarded to the defendant, the plaintiff and the defendant entered into the negotiation of an agreement under which the plaintiff would provide the video-visual portion of the services to be supplied to the City. Although agreement on most terms was ultimately

---

21   *Ibid.* at 718.

22   *Ibid.* at 719.

23   *Ibid.* For the suggestion that Lord Denning's dictum should not be read as a rigid requirement of a price term in every conceivable building contract, see *British Steel Corp. v. Cleveland Bridge and Engineering Co.*, [1984] 1 All E.R. 504 at 511 (Q.B.), Goff J.

24   (1988), 40 B.L.R. 128 (Ont. H.C.), aff'd (Sept. 11, 1991, Doc. No. C.A. 425/88).

reached, the defendant ultimately withdrew from the negotiations and assigned the work to a newly created subsidiary. Although the defendant had thus enjoyed some benefit from the plaintiff's cooperation in withdrawing from the bidding, the trial judge, affirmed on this point by the Ontario Court of Appeal, was persuaded that the agreement entered into to negotiate a subcontract was unenforceable because it lacked an essential provision identifying the percentage of gross revenues to be paid by the plaintiff to the defendant under any such agreement.

An agreement that establishes a workable mechanism for the determination of a price at a later point in time will not fail for incompleteness. The more difficult question is whether such an agreement will fail if the established mechanism proves to be unworkable. In sale of goods legislation, it is typically provided that where a contract for the sale of goods provides that the price is to be fixed by the valuation of a third party and the third party either does not or cannot make the valuation, the agreement is avoided.[25] Similarly, under traditional doctrine, an agreement to sell land at a price to be fixed by third-party valuation, where the valuation mechanism fails to work, has been held to be unenforceable. In *Sudbrook Trading Estate Ltd. v. Eggleton*,[26] however, the House of Lords overruled this line of authority, holding that an option to purchase land granted in a lease at a price to be determined by valuers was, in fact, enforceable even in circumstances where the valuation mechanism failed to work. In this case, the option provided that each party was to appoint a valuer. The two valuers were then to reach agreement on a valuation, failing which, an umpire was to be appointed by the valuers to settle the matter. The functioning of this mechanism was derailed when the grantor refused to appoint a valuer. The majority of the House of Lords held that the evident object of the agreement was to reach terms on which the sale would occur "at a fair valuation" or "at a reasonable price." Under prior law, it was well established that if the parties had in fact agreed to a sale at a "fair price" or "fair value," a court would enforce such an agreement and determine the matter of price on the basis of relevant evidence.[27] Under traditional doctrine, however, if the parties had established a mechanism for establishing the price that proved unworkable, the courts would not order an enforcement of the agreement by, for example, appointing a valuer or ordering the vendor

25 See *Sale of Goods Act*, above note 19, s. 10(1).

26 [1983] 1 A.C. 444 (H.L.). And see *Mitsui & Co. (Canada) Ltd. v. Royal Bank of Canada*, [1995] 2 S.C.R. 187.

27 See, for example, *Re Nishi Industries* (1978), 28 C.B.R. (N.S.) 261 (B.C.C.A.). And see *Mitsui & Co. (Canada) Ltd. v. Royal Bank of Canada*, *ibid.* at 203, Major J.

to appoint a valuer. In the view of the *Sudbrook* majority, however, the real object of the agreement in issue was to establish a fair evaluation rather than to reach a price only by the means specified in the agreement.[28] Accordingly, where the mechanism failed to work, the contract should be treated as an agreement for sale at a fair or reasonable price. The sentiment underlying the majority view, similar to that manifest in Lord Wright's opinion in *Hillas*, is that the courts should not be too astute to find ways of defeating agreements by which the parties intended to be bound.

In a number of cases, it has been held that where the mechanism established by the agreement for settling a particular term is to leave it to the discretion of one of the parties, the agreement may be enforceable. In such cases, however, the courts will easily imply a term requiring that the party upon whom the discretion has been conferred must exercise the discretion reasonably. Thus, in *First City Investments Ltd. v. Fraser Arms Hotel Ltd.*,[29] for example, it was held that a mortgage loan letter of commitment that left several details at large was saved by a provision by which the borrower agreed "to give to the Lender such other documents, assurances, information, covenants as the solicitors for lender may reasonably require."[30] The court held that, pursuant to that provision, the solicitors for the lender were entitled to fill the gaps in the lending agreement by inserting in the mortgage document "such provisions as they may reasonably require."[31] Similarly, in *Mitsui & Co. (Canada) v. Royal Bank of Canada Ltd.*,[32] the Supreme Court of Canada held that an option to purchase set out in a lease of two helicopters that stipulated for a price at "reasonable fair market value ... as established by Lessor" was enforceable and that the lessor was subject to an implied "duty to act in good faith to take all reasonable steps to complete the valuation in order to allow the option to be exercised if the lessee chose [to do so]."[33]

---

28   Above note 26 at 478–79, Lord Diplock.
29   (1979), 104 D.L.R. (3d) 617 (B.C.C.A.).
30   *Ibid.* at 625.
31   *Ibid.*
32   See above note 27.
33   *Ibid.* at 205, Major J.

C. AGREEMENTS TO AGREE

In agreements suffering from some degree of incompleteness, it is not uncommon for parties to stipulate in the agreement that such matters are to be agreed upon by the parties in the future. Accordingly, the question has often arisen as to whether an "agreement to agree" gives rise to an enforceable obligation. The traditional position at common law is that no such obligation does, in fact, arise. In a well-known passage from the decision in *Hillas*, however, Lord Wright suggested that such an agreement might indeed be enforceable. He first noted that an agreement to agree in the future to a particular set of terms is simply an agreement to those terms.[34] It is one contract, not two. Even if the "second contract" is one that is not to take effect until a certain date, such an agreement is just a single agreement, the operation of which has been postponed to a future date. Lord Wright went on to observe, however, as follows:

> If, however, what is meant is that the parties agree to negotiate in the hope of effecting a valid contract, the position is different. There is then no bargain except to negotiate and negotiations may be fruitless and end without any contract ensuing; yet even then, in strict theory, there is a contract (if there is good consideration) to negotiate, though in the event of repudiation by one party the damages may be nominal, unless a jury think that the opportunity to negotiate was of some appreciable value to the injured party.[35]

Lord Wright's tentative suggestion has not, however, been embraced in either the Canadian or English jurisprudence. In the *Courtney and Fairbairn Ltd.*[36] case, Lord Denning indicated that he did not consider Lord Wright's view that a contract to negotiate could be enforceable was "well founded" and went on to explain as follows: "The reason is because it is too uncertain to have any binding force. No court would estimate the damages because no one can tell whether the negotiations

---

34   See, for example, *Morton v. Morton*, [1942] 1 All E.R. 273 (P.D.) (agreement to enter a separation agreement on certain terms); *Calgary Hardwood & Veneer Ltd. v. Canadian National Railway Co.* (1977), 74 D.L.R. (3d) 284 (Alta. S.C.), aff'd 100 D.L.R. (3d) 302 (Alta. C.A.) (real estate — vendor offers that in certain circumstances, it "will agree to sell" — held, binding contract of sale upon acceptance, not an agreement to agree in the future). See also *Bawitko Investments Ltd. v. Kernels Popcorn Ltd.* (1991), 79 D.L.R. (4th) 97 at 103–4 (Ont. C.A.), Robins J.A.

35   Above note 7 at 515.

36   See above note 20.

would be successful or would fall through; or if successful, what the result would be. It seems to me that a contract to negotiate, like a contract to enter into a contract is not a contract known to the law."[37]

Thus, where there remains a fundamental matter that is explicitly said to be subject to negotiation or agreement, the agreement fails for uncertainty. This proposition has been applied in a variety of contexts. Thus, it is well established that where there is an option to purchase land at a price to be agreed[38] or an option to lease land at a rent to be agreed,[39] the agreement is unenforceable. Indeed, an agreement for the sale of land at a fixed price with a down payment and the "balance to be arranged" has been held void on the basis, presumably, that the terms of the mortgage or some similar arrangement are essential terms of a real estate transaction.[40] In other contexts, however, "balance to be arranged" terms have been upheld on the ground that such terms pertain only to mode of payment, with respect to which reasonable terms may be implied.[41]

Agreements to agree in various forms are likely features of agreements pertaining to the extraction of natural resources. Agreements relating to the development of mines or oil and gas fields may need to be entered into at a stage where the ultimate success of the particular project is unknown.[42] Nonetheless, the enforceability, for example, of agreements to sell the minerals yet to be produced may be critical to the financing of the venture. One possible strategy for attempting to manage these uncertainties is to establish a framework of principles that are to govern future relations and then stipulate that if the parties are

---

37   *Ibid.* at 720.

38   *Murphy v. McSorley*, [1929] S.C.R. 542.

39   *Re Calford Properties Ltd. and Kelly's Billiards Ltd.* (1973), 37 D.L.R. (3d) 300. See also *Godson v. P. Burns & Co.* (1919), 58 S.C.R. 404.

40   *Ibid.* See also *Kelly v. Watson* (1921), 61 S.C.R. 482; *Jackson v. Macauley Nicholls Maitland & Co. Ltd.*, [1942] 2 D.L.R. 609 (B.C.C.A.); *Arnold Nemetz Engineering Ltd. v. Tobien*, [1971] 4 W.W.R. 373 (B.C.C.A.); *Diamond Developments Ltd. v. Crown Assets Disposal Corp.* (1972), 28 D.L.R. (3d) 207 (B.C.S.C.). There are, however, Ontario decisions inconsistent with this approach. See *McDonald v. Murray* (1883), 2 O.R. 573 (C.P.); *Thomson Groceries Ltd. v. Scott*, [1943] 3 D.L.R. 25 (Ont. C.A.) (agreement stipulates the interest rate on a first mortgage, court fills in missing terms from the statutory short form, the mortgage loan is repayable on demand).

41   See, for example, *DeLaval v. Bloomfield*, [1938] 3 D.L.R. 405 (Ont. C.A.) (sale of goods).

42   For judicial criticism of the imprecision of "letter agreements" in the oil and gas industry, see *Hudson Bay Oil & Gas Co. v. Dynamic Petroleums Ltd.* (1958), 26 W.W.R. 504 at 504 (Alta. S.C.), Egbert J.

unable to agree to the application of those principles to future facts, the particular terms of the agreement will be settled by an arbitrator. This approach draws support from the decision of the Supreme Court of Canada in *Calvan Consolidated Oil & Gas v. Manning*.[43] In this case, the parties' agreement to agree was very sparse. The agreement provided for the exchange of part interests in oil and gas permits. The agreement also envisaged that one of the parties, Calvan, would be able to sell Manning's interest in a particular permit but, in the alternative, Calvan might decide to develop the property itself. With respect to the latter eventuality, the agreement further provided that the parties would agree to the terms of an operating agreement for this purpose, and if they failed to reach agreement on its terms, the terms would be settled by an arbitrator. The Supreme Court of Canada held that such an arrangement was enforceable. Otherwise, as Judson J. observed, "contracting parties in the position of Calvan and Manning, who do not know what their ultimate intentions may be if they retain the property, must provide in detail for a contingency that may never arise unless they wish to run the risk of having the rest of their contractual efforts invalidated and declared unenforceable."[44] Judson J. agreed with the Court of Appeal below that "such a situation may be dealt with by an agreement to arbitrate and I can see no legal or practical difficulty in the way."[45]

Even in the absence of an arbitration provision, however, the fact that the parties to an agreement have agreed to agree with respect to a particular matter in the future is not necessarily fatal to the agreement. In the *Canada Square*[46] case, as we have seen,[47] the Ontario Court of Appeal held that an agreement to lease the top floor of a building in progress for use as a restaurant was enforceable notwithstanding some lack of precision in the arrangements. The agreement also provided that the lessee was to operate a food stand in the lobby of the building in an unspecified location of "up to a gross amount of 600 square feet." The precise location was obviously subject to future agreement and the court had to consider, therefore, whether the uncertainty of that term rendered the entire agreement unenforceable. The Court of Appeal adopted Williston's[48] formulation of the applicable principle in the following terms: "It is evident that the question must be one of degree:

---

43   (1959), 17 D.L.R. (2d) 1 (S.C.C.).

44   *Ibid.* at 5.

45   *Ibid.* Compare with *May and Butcher v. The King*, above note 5.

46   Above note 15.

47   See above the text at notes 15–18.

48   S. Williston, *A Treatise on the Law of Contracts*, 3d ed., vol. 1 (Mount Kisco, NY: Baker, Voorhis, 1957) at 156–57.

Is the indefinite promise so essential to the bargain that inability to enforce that promise strictly according to its terms would make it unfair to enforce the remainder of the agreement? If the contract cannot be performed without settlement of the undetermined point, each party will be bound to agree to a reasonable determination of the unsettled point in order that the main promise may be enforced."[49] This proposition was held applicable to the provision concerning the lobby food stand. Accordingly, the agreement was enforceable, notwithstanding the uncertain nature of this term and, in due course, the parties would be contractually bound to agree to reasonable arrangements.

D. VAGUENESS

If a particular term of a contract is so vague or imprecise that a court cannot give a meaning to the term that the court can comfortably enforce, the agreement will fail on grounds of uncertainty. In *Scammell (G.) and Nephew, Limited v. Ouston*,[50] for example, the phrase "hire-purchase terms" was held to be so vague as to render the contract unenforceable. The defendant dealer had agreed to sell a van to the plaintiff customer for a particular price coupled with a trade-in of the customer's current vehicle. The oral agreement of the parties was recorded by the customer in a letter that acknowledged the dealer's acceptance of the order "given on the understanding that the balance of purchase price can be had on hire-purchase terms over a period of two years." Although the dealer later arranged for hire-purchase financing for the transaction, the dealer withdrew from the transaction, alleging deficiencies in the trade-in vehicle and defended the customer's ultimate action to enforce on the basis that the agreement was so vague as to be unenforceable. The House of Lords held the agreement to be unenforceable on this basis. Lord Wright explained the approach to be taken in the following terms:

> The object of the court is to do justice between the parties, and the court will do its best, if satisfied that there was an ascertainable and determinate intention to contract, to give effect to that intention, looking at the substance and not mere form. It will not be deterred by mere difficulties of interpretation. Difficulty is not synonymous

49   Above note 15 at 223, Morden J.A. The court also quoted approvingly from *City of Los Angeles v. Superior Court*, 333 P.2d 745 (1951) and *Wong v. DiGrazia*, 386 P.2d 817 (1963).

50   Above note 1.

with ambiguity so long as any definite meaning can be extracted. But the test of intention is to be found in the words used. If these words, considered however broadly and untechnically and with due regard to all the just implications, fail to evince any definite meaning on which the court can safely act, the court has no choice but to say there is no contract.[51]

Lord Wright went on to note that there were several different ways in which a hire-purchase agreement could be arranged and concluded that it would not be right to impose any particular form of agreement on the dealer. He went on to suggest, however, that if the parties had agreed to a hire-purchase agreement on the "usual terms" and further, if the court were supplied with evidence to define what the terms of a usual hire-purchase agreement might be, sufficient meaning might be given to the term to render the agreement enforceable.

As other cases demonstrate, however, a mere reference to the "usual terms" will not address the problem of uncertainty if there are, in fact, no usual terms being referred to by that phrase. Thus, in *Nicolene Ltd. v. Simmonds*,[52] a seller who coupled acceptance of an order with a statement that he assumed that "we are in agreement that the usual conditions of acceptance apply"[53] had not successfully incorporated such conditions. In the view of Denning L.J. there were simply no usual conditions of acceptance to which this phase referred. Accordingly, the "words are meaningless. There is nothing to which they can apply."[54] The clause was "so vague and uncertain to be incapable of any precise meaning."[55] It was also the view of the Court of Appeal that quite apart from this clause, the parties had agreed to only the essential terms of the agreement and accordingly, though the "usual conditions" term must be ignored, the contract was nevertheless an enforceable one. In a Canadian case, *Buyers v. Begg*,[56] a contract for the purchase and sale of land that provided that the parties would enter "an agreement for the sale containing the usual covenants" failed for uncertainty on the ground that there was no evidence before the court indicating that there was, in fact, a usual form of such an agreement in current use within the province.[57]

---

51 *Ibid.* at 268.
52 [1953] 1 Q.B. 543 (C.A.).
53 *Ibid.* at 544.
54 *Ibid.* at 550.
55 *Ibid.* at 552.
56 [1952] 1 D.L.R. 313 (B.C.C.A.).
57 Where, however, there is a statutory form of the agreement in question, it may be that a term of this kind can be given sufficient content. Thus, in *Thomson*

Agreements that require parties to make "best efforts" or "best endeavours" to fulfil certain undertakings may appear to be unattractively vague and difficult to enforce. As a general rule, however, courts have found it possible to give sufficient content to such provisions as to render them enforceable. In *Atmospheric Diving Systems Inc. v. International Hard Suits Inc.*[58] a British Columbia trial judge surveyed the extensive prior jurisprudence on this point and concluded that "best efforts" clauses impose a higher obligation than a mere "reasonable effort" and that best efforts can be defined as requiring the promisor to take "in good faith all reasonable steps to achieve the objective carrying the process to its logical conclusion and leaving no stone unturned."[59] Further, the concept "includes doing everything known to be usual, necessary and proper for ensuring the success of the endeavour."[60] The obligation to undertake such measures is not however boundless and must be considered in the context of the particular agreement. In the judge's view, it is not necessary to establish that the promisor has acted in bad faith. On the actual facts of this case, the trial judge held that the seller of highly expensive diving suits, which amounted, in effect, to one-man submarines, who had promised the customer that it would, within one year of purchase use its "best efforts" to sell the suits on a second-hand basis to other customers, had failed to do so. Indeed, the terms offered to the potential purchaser appeared designed to discourage the sale. In *R. v. CAE Industries Ltd.*,[61] a best efforts commitment given on behalf of the Government of Canada by three cabinet ministers was held enforceable. The agreement in question related to the purchase of the Winnipeg Maintenance Base of Air Canada by a private sector purchaser. In return, recognizing that viable operation of the facility would require something in the order of 700,000 man-hours of direct labour per annum, the three ministers indicated that the Government could guarantee no more than 40,000 to 50,000 direct man-hours per year but would commit itself to "employ its best efforts to secure the additional work required from other government departments and crown corporations"[62] in order to meet the larger target. When the

---

Groceries Ltd. v. Scott, [1943] 3 D.L.R. 25 (Ont. C.A.) a real estate transaction that stipulated the amount of the mortgage loan and interest rate was held to be enforceable on the basis that the statutory short form of mortgage could supply appropriate terms. The mortgage would be payable on demand.

58   (1994), 89 B.C.L.R. (2d) 356 (S.C.).

59   *Ibid.* at 373.

60   *Ibid.*

61   [1986] 1 F.C. 129, 20 D.L.R. (4th) 347 (C.A.), leave to appeal to S.C.C. refused (1985), 20 D.L.R. (4th) 347n.

62   *Ibid.* at 140 (F.C.), 353 (D.L.R.).

additional man-hours did not materialize, the purchaser sued for enforcement of the best efforts clause. In reply, the Government argued that the term was so lacking in precision as to render it incapable of conferring legal rights and that, in any event, the term could not have the effect of requiring the Government to ignore existing contracts or, more generally, to neglect the public interest. Although the court agreed with the latter points, it held that the Government had undertaken a binding contractual obligation to make best efforts to secure additional work for the facility and that it was in breach of this obligation.

Obligations to employ best efforts are often implied in contractual provisions in order to give content to provisions that otherwise might be too vague to be enforceable. In *Wiebe v. Bobsien*,[63] for example, a real estate transaction subject to the purchaser's sale of his existing residence was held enforceable by a majority of the British Columbia Court of Appeal on the basis that the purchaser was implicitly required to use best efforts to sell his own residence. If he was able to do so, he was then bound to complete the purchase of the defendant's property. In a vigorous dissent, however, Lambert J.A. was of the view that the clause was in the category of "incurable uncertainty."[64] In Lambert J.A.'s view, the parties probably intended that the purchaser had only committed himself to selling the property at a price that he has in mind rather than a reasonable price or the best offer he might receive. Accordingly, in his view, the implied term could not be given sufficient content to render it an enforceable one. The conclusion of the majority, however, has the attractive consequence that a reasonably common provision in transactions for the sale of residential premises did not have the effect of rendering the agreement an unenforceable one.

Another common provision in real estate transactions, stipulating that the purchaser's obligation to close is subject to the obtaining of "satisfactory financing" for the transaction, raises similar concerns. Canadian courts have not taken a uniform approach to their resolution. On the one hand, some courts have refused to enforce such provisions on the basis that it is not possible to identify appropriate standards by which financing could be determined to be "satisfactory." Other courts have enforced such provisions on the basis that some objective standard or measure of compliance can be introduced. In *Pietrobon v. McIntyre*[65] a transaction

---

63   (1985), 14 D.L.R. (4th) 754 (B.C.S.C.), aff'd (1986), 20 D.L.R. (4th) 475 (B.C.C.A.).
64   *Ibid.* at 478.
65   (1987), 15 B.C.L.R. (2d) 350 (S.C.). See also *Lee-Parker v. Izzet (No. 2)*, [1972] 1 W.L.R. 775 (Ch.). And see *Graham v. Pitkin*, [1992] 1 W.L.R. 403 at 405–6 (P.C.), Lord Templeman.

"subject to the Purchaser's obtaining satisfactory personal financing" was held to be so imprecise as to be unenforceable, thus rendering the entire agreement void for uncertainty. In *Gennis v. Madore*,[66] however, a requirement that the vendor was to arrange "suitable financing" was held to be enforceable. The trial judge observed that such provisions are commonly used and that courts should make every possible effort to enforce them. The provision was interpreted to impose an implied requirement that the purchaser "use reasonable efforts to obtain financing."[67]

A similar provision was held enforceable by the British Columbia Court of Appeal in *Griffin v. Martens*.[68] The agreement in question was subject to a condition that "satisfactory financing" be obtained. Lambert J.A. examined four possible meanings that could be given to this phrase. The first possibility, that the phrase means "satisfactory to a reasonable person," was rejected on the basis that this interpretation gave no effect to the adjective "satisfactory." Such an interpretation would create a test that was purely objective in nature. On the other hand, an interpretation that was purely subjective in nature, such as "satisfactory to the particular purchaser with all his quirks and prejudices, but acting honestly" would turn the agreement into a mere option. In effect, the purchaser would be agreeing merely to close the transaction if he chooses to do so. This interpretation, in Lambert J.A.'s view, would not, therefore, reflect the intentions of the parties. What was needed, then, was an interpretation that combined both subjective and objective elements. Lambert J.A. identified two possibilities. The first interpreted the phrase as meaning "satisfactory to a reasonable person in the objective circumstances of the purchaser" and the second interpreted it as "satisfactory to a reasonable person with all the subjective but reasonable standards of the particular purchaser." Lambert J.A. favoured the second of these two possibilities on the basis that this approach gives "the most accurate interpretation to the words they chose to express their intention."[69] This alternative, in his view, gives "satisfactory" a full and subjective significance and at the same time "retains the commitment of the purchaser to use his best efforts, on a similar combined standard, to obtain the financing."[70] Further, in addition to using best efforts to obtain satisfactory financing, the purchaser was implicitly required not to "withhold his satisfaction un-

---

66   (1988), 72 Nfld. & P.E.I.R. 104 (P.E.I.T.D.).

67   *Ibid.* at 109.

68   (1988), 27 B.C.L.R. (2d) 152 (C.A.).

69   *Ibid.* at 154.

70   *Ibid.*

reasonably."[71] Again, the adoption of this approach has the attractive consequence of rendering enforceable agreements of a rather common kind that the parties in question would no doubt have assumed and intended to be enforceable.

Although it has been suggested that an agreement entered into with a party identified as a named person "or his nominee" might fail for want of certainty as to the parties,[72] this view seems unlikely to prevail. It is commonplace for agreements to contain provisions permitting one or both of the parties to assign the agreement to a third party. Such provisions plainly do not render agreements void for uncertainty. It is difficult to see, then, why an agreement that enables one party to nominate another as a substitute party should fail for uncertainty. It is true that in *Causeway Shopping Centre Ltd. v. Muise,*[73] the Supreme Court of Canada appears to have assumed that a shopping centre lease entered into with "Muise or his nominee" failed for uncertainty. However the judgment below of the Nova Scotia Court of Appeal, which was tersely affirmed by the Supreme Court, indicates that the reason underlying this conclusion is that the parties had not reached agreement on whether Muise was to be personally liable on the lease in the period prior to nomination. It was this uncertainty, not presumably the mere reference to "Muise or his nominee," that rendered the agreement void. The parties had entered the agreement on the assumption that Muise would nominate a corporation yet to be incorporated. Muise, in fact, did so and the lessor subsequently sought to hold him personally liable on the lease. Both courts held that Muise was not a party to the lease and was not vulnerable to the lessor's remedies against the lessee. Neither court held, however, that the mere use of the phrase "or nominee" rendered the agreement void, nor was it held that the lease was not binding as against the nominee. Further, other decisions have held that agreements with parties identified as "x or his nominee"[74] or "x or assigns"[75] do not fail for uncertainty.

A holding that a particular term of an agreement is incurably uncertain does not, of course, lead inescapably to the conclusion that the entire agreement is void for uncertainty. Thus, in *Nicolene v. Sim-*

71   *Ibid.*
72   *Westward Farms Ltd. v. Cadieux* (1982), 138 D.L.R. (3d) 137 (Man. C.A.).
73   [1969] S.C.R. 274. The Nova Scotia Court of Appeal had held below that there existed uncertainty as to whether Muise was to be personally liable as lessee prior to nomination and that this uncertainty was fatal to the lease.
74   *Santellii v. Bifano Enterprises Ltd.* (1981), 33 B.C.L.R. 266 (S.C.).
75   *Finlay Investments Ltd. v. Abraham* (1982), 26 R.P.R. 188 (B.C.S.C.).

monds,[76] the contract for the sale of goods said to be "subject to usual conditions of acceptance" did not fail because of the vague and un-enforceable nature of that term. In the view of the court, the parties had, in other respects, agreed to all the essential terms of an agreement for the sale of goods. Accordingly, the vague term was "severable"[77] and the remainder of the agreement was valid.

FURTHER READINGS

D.W. MCLAUCHLAN, "Intention, Incompleteness and Uncertainty in the New Zealand Court of Appeal" (2002) 18 J.C.L. 153.

R. SAMEK, "The Requirement of Certainty of Terms in the Formation of Contract" (1970) 48 Can. Bar Rev. 203.

G.L. WILLIAMS, "Contract to Make a Contract – Separation Agreement" (1942) 6 Mod. L. Rev. 81.

---

76   Above note 52.
77   *Ibid.* at 552, Lord Denning.

CHAPTER 4

INTENTION TO CREATE LEGAL RELATIONS

A. INTRODUCTION

An agreement entered into by two parties will only be enforceable if the parties have entered into the agreement with the intention of creating legal relations. Social arrangements, for example, are often made without any intention that a legally enforceable agreement has been created. In a leading case,[1] this proposition was illustrated with reference to an agreement by two parties to take a walk together, or a situation in which hospitality is offered and accepted. No one would suggest that, in ordinary circumstances at least, such arrangements would be expected by the parties to result in contracts enforceable at law. Similarly, the many agreements entered into by family members with respect to the details of daily life are not normally expected to be enforceable. In commercial contexts, it is less likely that agreements would be entered into without an expectation of enforceability. Nonetheless, there are a variety of commercial situations in which parties might wish to have an understanding that does not engage the full majesty of legal enforceability. As we shall see, courts have generally assumed an absence of intention to create legal relations in family and social settings and a presence of an intention to create legal relations in commercial settings. The test for the presence of the intention is objective. Thus, a

---

1   *Balfour v. Balfour*, [1919] 2 K.B. 571 (C.A.).

promisor's private intention that no enforceable agreement be created will not prevail if the conduct of the promisor is such that the promisee reasonably believes that a binding agreement is intended.

The requirement that parties must intend legal relations is obviously one of a cluster of doctrines designed to isolate from the universe of promising behaviour, those promises and agreements that are appropriately subject to legal enforcement. Thus, the doctrine is evidently related to the rules of offer and acceptance[2] and the doctrine of consideration.[3] Indeed, it is sometimes suggested that the doctrine of intention is indistinguishable from one or both of these doctrines.[4] Typically, however, the doctrine is treated separately and it can be distinguished, if narrowly, from those related doctrines. The doctrine of consideration holds that a promise will be enforceable where it is made in return for something of value given by the promisee. In effect, consideration doctrine limits enforceability to promises made as part of a bargain. There may be many bargains, however, especially in non-commercial settings, which fail to meet the enforceability threshold, not because of the absence of consideration but, rather, because the parties had no intention of creating legal relations. Nonetheless, at the margins of the doctrine of consideration, as we shall see,[5] it appears that courts are more likely to find the existence of consideration in circumstances where the court believes that the parties intended to create a legally binding relationship. The rules of offer and acceptance, on the other hand, are designed to determine whether the communications between negotiating parties are such that a true *consensus ad idem* has been achieved on the terms of the agreement. This is not the objective of the requirement of intention to create legal relations. On the other hand, in determining whether or not a particular communication amounts to an offer, we have seen that it is relevant to consider whether the offeror intended that the offeree could, by acceptance of the offer, create a binding agreement.[6] In this context, at least, the doctrines appear to overlap. Nonetheless, whether or not the offeror intends a legal bargain, the circumstances may be such as to establish, on the basis of an objective test, the absence of an intention to create legal relations. Thus,

---

2   See Chapter 2.
3   See Chapter 7.
4   See, for example, R. Tuck, "Intent to Contract and Mutuality of Assent" (1943) 21 Can. Bar Rev. 123; B. Hepple, "Intention to Create Legal Relations" (1970) 28 Cambridge L.J. 122.
5   See Chapter 7, section B(1).
6   See Chapter 2, section B(1).

there may be cases in which a contractual offer is intended but its acceptance does not give rise to a binding contractual relationship.

In examining the intention requirement, we turn first to a series of commercial situations in which parties might desire to avoid entanglement in a legally enforceable relationship. We then turn to consider the application of the doctrine in family and other social settings.

B. COMMERCIAL ARRANGEMENTS

Although it is generally presumed that the intention to create commercial relations is present in the making of commercial arrangements,[7] two different kinds of situations arise where the requisite intention may not be present. First, there are situations in which the parties wish to be bound in honour only. If the parties so express themselves, the absence of intent may be established. The more interesting cases, such as those arising recently in the tendering context, are those in which the parties have not explicitly so provided. Second, parties negotiating an agreement may achieve and record in writing a preliminary version of their agreement. In such cases, the question arises as to whether the preliminary arrangements are themselves intended to constitute a binding and enforceable agreement.

1) Explicit Agreements Not to Be Bound

Where commercial parties have entered into arrangements that they explicitly agree should not constitute legally enforceable agreements, there would appear to be little reason not to give effect to those intentions. The leading case relates to an informal agency agreement entered into between an English supplier of paper products and its American distributor. In *Rose and Frank Company v. J.R. Crompton and Brothers Ltd.*[8] the parties had entered into a series of binding arrangements concerning their agency relationship. In 1913, however, they entered into a new agreement that involved a third party in their arrangements and provided as follows:

---

7   See, for example, *Edwards v. Skyways Ltd.,* [1964] 1 All E.R. 494 (Q.B.) (employer orally agrees to make "*ex gratia*" payments to pilots who accept redundancy—presumption applies—onus on employer to displace it is "heavy").

8   [1923] 2 K.B. 261, aff'd [1925] A.C. 445.

This arrangement is not entered into, nor is this memorandum written, as a formal or legal agreement, and shall not be subject to legal jurisdiction in the Law Courts either of the United States or England, but it is only a definite expression and record of the purpose and intention of the three parties concerned to which they each partly pledge themselves with the fullest confidence, based upon past business with each other, that it will be carried through by each of the three parties with mutual loyalty and friendly co-operation.[9]

At trial, Bailhache J. held that the agreement was enforceable, notwithstanding the presence of the honourable pledge clause, on two grounds. First, in his view, the other provisions of the memorandum of agreement set out what appeared to be a binding agreement and the honourable pledge clause, which followed these provisions, was repugnant to them and should therefore be rejected.[10] Second, it was his view that the clause was unenforceable on the basis that it was contrary to public policy as an improper attempt to oust the jurisdiction of the courts.

In the Court of Appeal, however, the decision at trial was reversed. In a much-quoted passage, Scrutton L.J. observed as follows:

Now it is quite possible for parties to come to an agreement by accepting a proposal with the result that the agreement concluded does not give rise to legal relations. The reason of this is that the parties do not intend their agreement shall give rise to legal relations. This intention may be implied from the subject matter of the agreement but it may also be expressed by the parties. In social and family relations such an intention is readily implied, however in business matters the opposite result would ordinarily follow. But I can see no reason why, even in business matters, the parties should not intend to rely on each other's good faith and honour, and to exclude all idea of settling disputes by any outside intervention, with the accompanying necessity of expressing themselves so precisely that outsiders may have no difficulty in understanding what they mean. If they clearly express such an intention, I can see no reason in public policy why effect should not be given to their intention.

When the document was regarded in its entirety, in Scrutton L.J.'s view, it was plain that such an intention had been expressed. That clear intent could not be suppressed by the prior portions of the document. A number of orders for paper products had already been placed by the

---

9   *Ibid.* at 267.
10   For discussion of this principle of interpretation, see Chapter 19, section C(9).

plaintiff pursuant to the agreement. The Court of Appeal also held that the individual orders were unenforceable as well. The decision of the Court of Appeal was affirmed on the main point but reversed on the latter, with the result that the individual orders were held to be binding.

In retrospect, the decision at trial may appear surprising to the modern reader. It must be remembered, however, that the courts have traditionally jealously guarded their jurisdiction.[11] This approach, insofar as it also discouraged the use of arbitration clauses, has been eclipsed by modern attitudes concerning the value of arbitration[12] and alternative dispute resolution more generally.[13] Nonetheless, there remains some basis for careful judicial scrutiny of honourable pledge clauses of this kind, especially in cases where there exists an imbalance in bargaining power between the parties. Where such a clause has been inserted by the more powerful party in order to take advantage of the weaker party in the event of a dispute, courts may be and, arguably, should be, willing to continue to exercise a discretion to strike such clauses down on grounds of public policy. In the absence of such concerns, however, there appears little reason to prevent commercial parties from adopting non-enforceable arrangements of the kind at issue in this case and that is, indeed, the applicable doctrine.

2) Tendering Processes

Under traditional doctrine, a tender call followed by the submission of a bid did not create a contractual relationship. Under applicable principles of offer and acceptance, the submission of the bid was treated as an offer that would be accepted when selected by the person issuing the tender call as the winning bid. As we have seen,[14] the Supreme Court of Canada, in its decision in *Ron Engineering and Construction Eastern Ltd. v. Ontario*,[15] dramatically reformed the law of tendering and held that the tender call itself constitutes an offer that is accepted by the submission of a bid, thereby creating a contract, referred to by the Court as Contract A, relating to the bidding process itself. Under Contract A, the bidder would typically be required to enter into the building contract, referred to as Contract B, if selected by the party issuing the tender call

---

11   See below Chapter 12, section B(3)(a).
12   See generally M. Mustill and S. Boyd, *The Law and Practice of Commercial Arbitration in England* (London: Butterworths, 1982) c. 1.
13   See generally J. Macfarlane, ed., *Dispute Resolution: Readings and Case Studies*, 2d ed. (Toronto: Emond Montgomery, 2003).
14   See Chapter 2, section B(1)(c).
15   [1981] 1 S.C.R. 111.

and, upon its refusal to do so, would be required to forfeit a deposit of some kind. In later cases,[16] it has been held that Contract A requires both the issuer of the call and the bidder to follow the procedures set out in the call and, moreover, contains an implied term imposing an obligation on the issuer to treat all bidders "fairly and equally."[17] Thus, a bidder who considers that it has been unfairly treated or prejudiced through the processing of the bids or the evaluation of its tender may be able to bring an action for damages for breach of the duty of fair and equal treatment. This doctrine has been a source of frequent claims concerning tendering processes and, accordingly, it is not uncommon for parties issuing tender calls to expressly stipulate that the issuing of the tender call and the submission of a bid in response do not consti-tute a contractual relationship between the parties. In principle, such a stipulation should be effective on the basis of the reasoning in *Rose and Frank Company v. J.R. Crompton and Brothers Ltd.*[18]

The more difficult question is whether, in the absence of such a stipulation, it may be concluded, under current law, that the parties lacked an intention to create legal relations with respect to the con-duct of a particular tendering process. In *M.J.B Enterprises Ltd. v. De-fence Construction (1951) Ltd.*,[19] Iacobucci J. observed: "whether or not Contract A arose depends on whether the parties intended to initiate contractual relations by the submission of a bid in response to the in-vitation to tender."[20] In holding that such intention was present in the circumstances of that case, Iacobucci J. placed emphasis on the fact that the submission of a bid was of value to the issuer, that bids were prepared at significant cost to the bidder and were accompanied by a substantial and forfeitable deposit. Such circumstances would nor-mally be present in any tender call for a large project and, accordingly, it appears that Contract A would normally arise in such a setting.

In a recent case, however, the Manitoba Court of Appeal, in *Mellco Developments Ltd. v. Portage La Prairie (City)*[21] refrained from apply-ing the *Ron Engineering* analysis to a tendering process involving a so-called request for proposal or RFP. The tendering process in this case involved the development of a parcel of 31.2 acres of city-owned land.

---

16   See, for example, *M.J.B. Enterprises Ltd. v. Defence Construction (1951) Ltd.*, [1999] 1 S.C.R. 619.

17   See, for example, *Martel v. Canada* (2000), 193 D.L.R. (4th) 1 (S.C.C.).

18   Above note 8.

19   Above note 16.

20   *Ibid.* at 633. See also *Naylor Group Inc. v. Ellis-Don Construction Ltd.*, [2001] 2 S.C.R. 943 at para. 35, Binnie J.

21   (2002), 222 D.L.R. (4th) 67 (Man. C.A.).

Unlike a more traditional call for tenders, the RFP required bidders to develop a conceptual subdivision design for the subject property, the merits of which would have a major influence on whether the particular proposal was accepted by the city. The RFP further provided that the city would merely "negotiate" with the bidder "submitting the most attractive proposal" for a sale of the land and, in the event of the failure of negotiations, would then negotiate with the proponent of the next most attractive proposal. The RFP further provided: "[t]his is an invitation for proposals and not a tender call."[22] Like a traditional tendering situation, however, the RFP required the preparation of a rather expensive proposal and the payment of a security deposit. Nonetheless, the Court of Appeal held that the RFP was distinguishable from a call for tenders and, accordingly, was not subject to the *Ron Engineering* analysis. In the court's view, the Contract A of *Ron Engineering* appears to apply only where the final terms of Contract B are set out in the bid or, presumably, the tender call, and accordingly, there is no need for further negotiation once the winning bid has been selected. Although other courts have come to the same conclusion,[23] the *Mellco* analysis nonetheless appears to impose an artificial restriction on the *Ron Engineering* analysis. To the extent that *Ron Engineering* appears designed to impose order, albeit contractual order, on the conduct of tendering processes that involve substantial investments of resources by bidders without any effective guarantee of fair treatment on the part of the issuer of the tender call, there does not appear to be any reason not to extend such protection into the context of RFPs. The fact that the RFP process may involve subsequent negotiation with the winning bidder would not appear to reduce whatever contractual expectations the bidder might have had of procedural integrity and fair treatment in the bidding process. In other words, the fact that Contract B may only constitute an "agreement to agree"[24] does not preclude, in principle, the possibility that the parties could intend that Contract A binds the parties to participate in the bidding according to the rules set out in the

---

22   *Ibid.* at 72.

23   See, for example, *Buttcon Ltd. v. Toronto Electric Commissioners* (2003), 65 O.R. (3d) 601 (S.C.J.). See also *Powder Mountain Resorts Ltd. v. British Columbia,* [1999] 11 W.W.R. 168 (B.C.S.C.), aff'd [2001] 11 W.W.R. 488 (B.C.C.A.). See also *Toronto Transit Commission v. Gottardo Construction Ltd.* (2003), 68 O.R. (3d) 356 (S.C.J.) (*Ron Engineering* narrowly distinguished on the basis that the tender call required the submission of supplementary materials subsequent to submission of the tender — Contract A not formed until the subsequent materials were filed).

24   On agreements to agree, see Chapter 3, section C.

tender call. Interestingly, both in *Mellco*[25] and in a recent Ontario decision,[26] the courts held that notwithstanding the absence of Contract A, the issuer of the RFP was nonetheless obligated to treat tenderers fairly and equally. No clear explanation was offered as to the source of this duty. In the absence of contract, however, such a duty must be grounded in some as yet otherwise unrecognized tort duty to treat bidders fairly and equally.[27]

3) Letters of Comfort

Comfort letters are typically provided in the context of large commercial loan transactions.[28] In the usual case, the borrower is the subsidiary of a parent company. The banker or lender, for obvious reasons, would generally prefer that the parent corporation guarantee the obligations of the borrowing subsidiary to repay the loan. Where the parent is unwilling to give such a guarantee, however, the lender and the parent may agree to the terms of a so-called letter of comfort in which the parent provides assurances of various kinds concerning its relationship with the subsidiary and statements of current policy concerning the administration of the affairs of the subsidiary corporation. Letters of comfort are often the subject of intense negotiation and may provide a critical incentive for the lender to enter into the transaction with the subsidiary and may result in a reduction of the cost of borrowing. If, in the event, the subsidiary is unable to repay the loan, a dispute may arise between the lender and the parent corporation. The lender will take the position that the letter of comfort is a contractual document from which a claim for damages relating to the non-payment of the loan may arise. The parent, on the other hand, will take the position that the letter of comfort is not intended to be contractually binding, that it is a mere "matter of honour" imposing, at most, moral obligations on the parent.

The factual context of letters of comfort is conveniently illustrated by the facts of the leading English case, *Kleinwort Benson Ltd. v. Malaysia Mining Corp. Bhd.*[29] The plaintiff investment bank had agreed

---

25   Above note 21.

26   *Buttcan Ltd. v. Toronto Electric Commissioners*, above note 23.

27   See Chapter 5, section E .

28   See generally P. Perell, "Lessons About Comfort Letters" (2001) 34 Can. Bus. L.J. 421; R. Sacasas and D. Weisner, "Comfort Letters: The Legal and Business Implications" (1987) 104 Banking L.J. 313.

29   [1989] 1 All E.R. 785 (C.A.), rev'g [1988] 1 All E.R. 714 (Q.B.), leave to appeal refused, [1989] 1 All E.R. 785 at 798 (C.A.). For discussion, see D.H. Clark,

to make available a £10-million credit facility to a subsidiary of the defendant Malaysia Mining Corp. The monies were to be used by the subsidiary, MMC Metals Limited, to trade in tin on the London Metal Exchange. The bank had originally sought a guarantee of the facility from the defendant. The request for a guarantee was denied but the defendant did provide a letter of comfort that included the following terms:

[1] We hereby confirm that we know and approve of these facilities and are aware of the fact that they have been granted to MMC Metals Limited because we control directly or indirectly MMC Metals Limited.

[2] We confirm that we will not reduce our current financial interest in MMC Metals Limited until the above facilities have been repaid or until you have confirmed that you are prepared to continue the facilities with new shareholders.

[3] It is our policy to ensure that the business of MMC Metals Limited is at all times in a position to meet its liabilities to you under the above arrangements.[30]

When, in 1985, the tin market collapsed, the subsidiary ceased trading and became insolvent. The plaintiff sought repayment of the loan from the defendant. Upon the defendant's refusal to do so, the plaintiff brought an action against the defendant alleging that it had breached a contractual obligation to repay the loan contained in the above provisions of the letter of comfort.

The plaintiff urged that the comfort letter was intended to be a contractual binding document and, further, that paragraph 3 was intended as a contractual undertaking that as long as the subsidiary's liability to the banker persisted, the subsidiary would be in a position to meet its liabilities. The defendant parent conceded that the document was of contractual force and effect but argued that paragraph 3 merely constituted a statement of current policy and not an undertaking with respect to future events. At trial, Hirst J. found for the plaintiff on both points.

"Contracts—Interpretation—Creation of Legally Binding Relationship—"Cold Comfort Letter": *Kleinwort Benson Ltd. v. Malaysia Mining Corp. Bhd.*" (1990) 69 Can. Bar Rev. 753; G.A. Witthun, "*Kleinwort Benson Limited v. Malaysia Mining Corporation Berhad*—A Comparative Note on Comfort Letters" (1990) 35 McGill L.J. 490; D.D. Prentice, "Letters of Comfort" (1989) 105 Law Q. Rev. 346; R.D. Gibbens, "Letters of Comfort—*Kleinwort Benson v. Malaysian Mining Corp. Berhad*" (1989) 3 B.F.L.R. 222.

30   [1988] 1 All E.R. 714 at 718 (Q.B.).

The commercial setting of the comfort letter was such that the presumption in favour of enforceability[31] applied and the document was therefore intended to be a binding contract. Hirst J. also agreed that paragraph 3 was intended to be an undertaking, given with respect to future events, that was binding on the parent company. On Hirst J.'s reading, paragraph 3 was an undertaking that "now and at all times in the future, so long as [the subsidiary] is under any liability to [the plaintiffs], it is and will be [the defendant's] policy to ensure that [the subsidiary] is in a position to meet those liabilities."[32] Further, Hirst J. emphasized that paragraph 3 did not constitute a guarantee. Nonetheless, the liability of the parent in damages for breach of paragraph 3 was equivalent to the liability that would be incurred under a proper guarantee.

The decision of Hirst J. was overturned on appeal. The Court of Appeal held that the principal error made by the trial judge was to apply the presumption of intention to create legal relations in commercial settings not only to the document as a whole, but also to paragraph 3 in particular. In its terms, paragraph 3 was simply a statement of fact. Accordingly, the true issue to be considered was whether that representation of fact was intended as a warranty.[33] On this issue, the general presumption is of no assistance. Rather, one must consider whether the affirmation of fact contained in paragraph 3 was, in fact, intended as a warranty or promise that the statement was true and would continue to be true in the future. A number of considerations led the Court of Appeal to the conclusion that no such intention was present. First, the court was of the view that the commercial context in which the comfort letter was given was both admissible[34] and revealing. The court noted that the defendant had refused to give a guarantee and had given a comfort letter as an alternative. The plaintiff, in turn, had insisted on a higher commission rate as a result. Both the context and the wording of the provision are consistent with an understanding that the comfort letter contains "no more than the assumption of moral responsibility by the defendant in respect of the debts of [the subsidiary]."[35] Moreover, the first two paragraphs of the letter, initially drafted by the plaintiff bank were, in the view of Ralph Gibson L.J., consistent with the inter-

---

31 Hirst J. relied, *inter alia*, on *Rose and Frank Company v. J.R. Crompton and Brothers Ltd.*, above note 8 and *Edwards v. Skyways Ltd.*, above note 7.

32 Above note 30 at 724.

33 For general discussion of this issue, see Chapter 18, section B.

34 For discussion, see Chapter 19, section B.

35 [1989] 1 All E.R. 785 at 795 (C.A.), Ralph Gibson L.J.

pretation that the third paragraph imposed merely a moral obligation. The defendant's awareness and approval of the transaction and its interest in the subsidiary indicated the basis for the moral obligation established by paragraph 3. If, on the other hand, paragraph 3 constituted a promise that the defendant would ensure that the subsidiary was able to pay its debts in the future, paragraphs 1 and 2 would simply become superfluous. Hirst J.'s reading of paragraph 3 that it is an undertaking that the policy of ensuring that the subsidiary is "and will be" in the future able to meet its liabilities was borne neither by the plain meaning of the provision nor the commercial context. For the Court of Appeal, paragraph 3 was simply a statement of current policy and this construction of the term was consistent with the commercial context of the transaction. Accordingly, the plaintiff's claim was dismissed.

The reasoning in the *Kleinwort Benson* case was applied by the Ontario courts in *Toronto-Dominion Bank v. Leigh Instruments Ltd. (Trustee of)*.[36] The fundamentals of the fact situation in this case were similar to those of *Kleinwort Benson*. The plaintiff bank had advanced funds in a series of lending transactions to the now insolvent Leigh Instruments Ltd. At the time of the loans, the bank unsuccessfully sought a guarantee from Leigh's parent company and, in the event, accepted a letter of comfort from the parent that was similarly worded to the letter of comfort given in *Kleinwort Benson*. In particular, paragraph 3 read as follows: "It is our policy that our wholly-owned subsidiaries, including Leigh Instruments Limited, be managed in such a way as to be always in a position to meet their financial obligations including repayment of all amounts due under the above facility."[37]

Further increases in the borrowing were agreed to by the bank and, in each case, a comfort letter in the same terms was issued by the parent. In the final and fifth letter, however, the following provision was added: "This letter replaces our letters of 31st August 1989, 31st March 1989 and 30th June 1989 and does not constitute a legally binding commitment."[38] Upon the insolvency of Leigh Instruments, the plaintiff bank sought repayment from the defendant corporation, which, by virtue of a takeover bid, had succeeded to the position of the original parent under the series of comfort letters. The new parent refused to

---

36 (1988), 40 B.L.R. (2d) 1 (Ont. Ct. Gen. Div.), aff'd 178 D.L.R. (4th) 634 (Ont. C.A.), leave to appeal to S.C.C. refused (1999), 188 D.L.R. (4th) vi. For discussion of the decision at trial, see J. Goodman, "No Comfort by Letter of Comfort: *Toronto-Dominion Bank v. Leigh*" (1999) 14 B.F.L.R. 389.

37 *Ibid.* at 8 (B.L.R.).

38 *Ibid.* at 74.

repay the loans and an action was commenced alleging breach of the contracts constituted by the comfort letters and, alternatively, claiming damages in tort for misrepresentation.

At trial, Winkler J. found the reasoning in *Kleinwort Benson* instructive. In his view, paragraph 3 was not promissory in nature. It was a mere statement of fact describing the parent company's then current policy. As in *Kleinwort Benson*, Winkler J. found the commercial context of the comfort letters of assistance. The request for a guarantee had been rejected. The parties were sophisticated in financial matters and, in particular, the bank had a sophisticated understanding of the nature of and difficulties with comfort letters. Winkler J. was also of the view that reading paragraph 3 as a promissory undertaking with respect to the future would, as Ralph Gibson L.J. reasoned in *Kleinwort Benson*, render the other provisions of the letter of comfort redundant. Accordingly, for Winkler J., the final paragraph of the fifth comfort letter quoted above, was redundant in the sense that it merely reaffirmed the nature of the comfort letter at issue and, accordingly, the same analysis applied to all five of the comfort letters. Winkler J.'s interpretation of paragraph 3 and his dismissal of the claims for breach of contract were affirmed by the Ontario Court of Appeal.[39]

There is, however, a leading Australian decision, the decision of the New South Wales Supreme Court in *Banque Brussels Lambert SA v. Australian National Industries Ltd.*[40] in which the reasoning in *Kleinwort Benson* was distinguished and a comfort letter was held to impose a binding contractual obligation to ensure repayment of a loan. The bank had advanced a line of credit to a merchant bank, Spedley Securities Limited, of which the principal shareholder was the defendant Australian National Industries Ltd. (ANI). Following the normal pattern, the first paragraph of the comfort letter acknowledged an awareness of the loan, the second paragraph indicated that it was not the intention of ANI to reduce its shareholding in Spedley. The second paragraph went on to stipulate, however, as follows: "We would, however, provide your bank with ninety (90) days notice of any subsequent decisions taken by us to dispose of this share holding, and furthermore we acknowledge that, should any such notice be served on your Bank, you reserve the right to call for the repayment of all outstanding loans within thirty (30) days."

The practical effect of this aspect of the arrangement was to put the bank in a position where, in the event of a proposed sale of the shares,

---

39   *Ibid.*
40   (1989), 21 N.S.W.L.R. 502 (S.C.). Compare with *Commonwealth Bank of Australia v. TLI Management Pty. Ltd.*, [1990] V.R. 510 (S.C.).

it would be effectively able to ensure repayment of the loan before the transaction closed. In the event, the protection afforded to the bank by this arrangement did not succeed. In due course, ANI sold its shareholding to a third party without giving ninety days' notice to the bank and, subsequently, Spedley became insolvent before repaying the loan. The third paragraph, although quite similar to the policy statements given in the *Kleinwort Benson* and *Leigh Instruments* comfort letters contained what might be considered to be an assurance that the subsidiary would be in a position to meet its financial obligations in the future. The paragraph read as follows: "We take this opportunity to confirm that it is our practice to ensure that our affiliate Spedley Securities Limited, will at all times be in a position to meet its financial obligation as they fall due. These financial obligations include repair of all loans made by your Bank under the arrangements mentioned in this letter."[41]

In the ensuing litigation brought by the bank against ANI, then, the critical question was whether this paragraph imposed an obligation on ANI to make good Spedley's default under the lending agreement. The commercial context of the comfort letter in this case was also different in some material respects. The bank had indicated that it expected a "strong"[42] comfort letter and had made it clear that the bank's view was that the loan would not be made unless the comfort letter created "a binding obligation of ANI to [the bank]."[43]

Against this background, and in light of the insertion of the word "will" explicitly in paragraph 3, the court might have been able to accept the reasoning in *Kleinwort Benson* but distinguish it as inapplicable to the different language and different commercial setting of this particular comfort letter. In holding that the comfort letter did impose a binding contractual obligation to repay the loan upon ANI, however, Rogers C.J. went on to criticize the reasoning of the Court of Appeal in *Kleinwort Benson* and to indicate his preference for the reasons offered by Hirst J. for finding that the third paragraph of the comfort letter in that case created a binding contractual obligation. In particular, Rogers C.J. indicated that, in his view, the "minute textual analysis"[44] applied by the Court of Appeal in this case should not dominate the interpretation of commercial documents. In his view, the interpretation offered by the Court of Appeal rendered the document a mere "scrap of paper."[45]

---

41   *Banque Brussels Lambert SA v. Australian National Industries Ltd.*, *ibid.* at 504.
42   *Ibid.* at 509.
43   *Ibid.* at 513.
44   *Ibid.* at 523.
45   *Ibid.*

Nonetheless, even if one accepts the reasoning of the Court of Appeal in *Kleinwort Benson*, the *Banque Brussels* case appears to be correctly decided. The plainly binding notice provisions in paragraph 2, the differences in the wording in paragraph 3 that give it a clearer future-oriented prospect and the commercial setting of the particular comfort letter at issue in this case all point in the direction of an interpretation rendering paragraph 3 an enforceable contractual commitment and provide a basis for distinguishing this case from *Kleinwort Benson*.

In cases such as *Kleinwort Benson* and *Leigh Instruments*, where the affirmation of current policy with respect to the subsidiary meeting its obligations is held to be a mere affirmation of fact rather than a warranty or undertaking, the falsity of the affirmation, though not a breach of contract, may constitute a misrepresentation. If so, the lender may be entitled to the remedies of either rescission or, if the statement is fraudulently or carelessly false, of damages in tort.[46] The availability of those remedies will turn on a precise interpretation of the nature of the statement of fact being made and the existence of detrimental reliance on this statement by the representee. In order to provide a basis for a decree of rescission, the affirmation would have to be false at the time of entering the contract.[47] In both *Kleinwort Benson* and *Leigh Instruments*, it was common ground that the affirmation of current policy was a continuing representation and thus, if the policy of the parent corporation changed without notice to the lender, the representation would cease to be true. Accordingly, if further advances were made by the lender after the representation became false, the possibility of a tort claim would arise. In *Kleinwort Benson*, the tort analysis was not pursued. In *Leigh Instruments*, however, claims for tortious misstatement were advanced and it was necessary for the court to determine the nature of the affirmation being made and its truth or falsity on the facts of the case. The plaintiff bank urged that the proper interpretation of the paragraph 3 affirmation was that it was the parent's policy that the parent would itself manage Leigh Instruments' affairs in such a way as to ensure that Leigh Instruments would be in a position to meet its obligations to the bank. The defendant parent corporation, placing emphasis on the phrase "be managed" in the paragraph 3 statement that its subsidiaries would "be managed" in such a way as to be able to meet their financial obligations, argued that the proper interpretation was that it was current policy that subsidiaries should manage themselves in such a way as to be able to meet their financial obligations. Both the trial judge and the Court of

46   See Chapter 10, section F.
47   See Chapter 10, sections B and E.

Appeal agreed with the latter interpretation. Further, the trial judge, affirmed on this point by the Court of Appeal, held that at all material times this was, in fact, the policy of the parent corporation. Moreover, even though Leigh Instruments did eventually encounter financial difficulty, there was nothing inconsistent between a policy that subsidiaries should manage themselves to avoid such an eventuality and the eventuality actually occurring. On this basis, then, the claims for damages in tort in the *Leigh Instruments* case were dismissed.

4) Preliminary Agreements, Letters of Intent and Agreements "Subject to Contract"

In the course of negotiating an agreement, the parties may reach a stage where they consider it useful to record their agreement or, perhaps, the elements of the agreement reached thus far, in a written document, on the understanding that this preliminary agreement will be eventually recorded in a perhaps larger and more complete written memorandum. These preliminary agreements may be referred to as letters of intent, commitment letters, term sheets, MOUs (memoranda of understanding) or, indeed, may not be described by any particular epithet. Similarly, parties may enter into preliminary agreements of this kind that are explicitly said to be "subject to contract" in the sense that the parties anticipate the eventual preparation and execution of a formal agreement setting out the terms of their contractual relationship. In situations of these kinds, if one of the parties withdraws from the agreement prior to the execution of the anticipated final agreement, the question may arise as to whether the preliminary agreement was in fact itself intended as a binding agreement. If the preliminary agreement fails to deal with important aspects of the anticipated agreement, the preliminary agreement may, in any event, fail for lack of certainty of terms.[48] Further, in such circumstances the preliminary agreement may be considered to be merely an "agreement to agree" and, under traditional doctrine, will be unenforceable as such.[49] For present purposes, however, we assume that the preliminary agreement is sufficiently complete as to constitute a binding agreement if, in fact, the agreement was intended to create legal relations. In the real world, of course, a particular fact situation may require consideration of the applicability of each of these doctrines.

---

48   See Chapter 3, section B.
49   See Chapter 3, section C.

The determination of whether the parties to a preliminary agreement intended the agreement to constitute a binding contract will rest upon a careful analysis of the language employed in the preliminary agreement and the factual setting in which the preliminary agreement was articulated. It is, of course, a simple matter for parties to indicate plainly whether enforceable contractual relations are intended and, where such agreements are drafted by lawyers, the point is typically placed beyond doubt. Thus, it is a common feature of professionally drafted "letters of intent" that they will stipulate that the provisions of the letter do not create binding obligations or agreements between the parties. Indeed, some letters of intent distinguish between aspects of the letter that are intended to be binding and those that are not. In the typical case, the non-binding arrangements would relate to the terms of the projected ultimate contract whereas the binding arrangements would relate to the expectations of the parties with respect to the negotiation process. Thus, the binding provisions might stipulate obligations to maintain confidentiality, might identify a date by which negotiations are to be concluded, might indicate which of the parties is to carry the burden of drafting the agreement and, in the context of a so-called lock out provision, require one or both of the parties not to negotiate with any other party concerning the subject matter of the agreement during a particular period of time.[50]

In cases where the preliminary agreement does not explicitly stipulate its binding or non-binding nature, the fact that the preliminary agreement clearly anticipates future formalization of its terms will require a determination as to whether that future formalization is a mere formality in the sense that it implements or carries into effect the preliminary and binding agreement or, rather, constitutes the moment of formation of the only binding agreement between the parties. As Parker J. explained in *Von Hatzfeldt-Wildenburg v. Alexander*:[51]

> [I]f the documents or letters relied on as constituting a contract contemplate the execution of a further contract between the parties, it is a question of construction whether the execution of the further contract is a condition or term of the bargain or whether it is a mere expression of the desire of the parties as to the manner in which the transaction already agreed to will in fact go through. In the former case there is no enforceable contract either because the condition is unfulfilled or because the law does not recognize a contract to enter into a contract. In

---

50   See, for example, *Pitt v. PHH Asset Management Ltd.*, [1993] 4 All E.R. 961 (C.A.).
51   [1912] 1 Ch. 284.

the latter case there is a binding contract and the reference to the more formal document may be ignored. The fact that the reference to the more formal document is in words which according to their natural construction import a condition is generally, if not invariably conclusive against the reference being treated as a mere desire.[52]

This suggestion by Parker J. to the effect that the use of conditional language will be an important signal that the creation of an enforceable agreement is dependent upon or contingent upon the eventual formalization of the agreement has been widely accepted. Thus, it has generally been held that where the preliminary agreement is expressly stipulated to be "subject to contract,"[53] a device commonly used in the context of real estate transactions, this provision is normally interpreted to mean that the formation of the agreement is postponed until such time as the formal contract is agreed to by the parties. Accordingly, at any time prior to execution of the formal agreement, either party is entitled to withdraw from the proposed transaction. The question is, however, one of construction and in circumstances where the preliminary arrangements are very extensive and detailed, the presence of conditional language of this kind may not preclude the preliminary agreement from constituting an enforceable agreement.[54] Further, if the party insisting on a formal agreement waives the requirement, the intent requisite to establish the preliminary agreement as a binding contract may be found to be present.[55]

If the preliminary agreement anticipating an eventual formal agreement is described in its own terms or by the parties as a "letter of intent," the preliminary agreement is likely to be found to be subject to the formal agreement and not binding at the preliminary stage.[56] Where,

---

52   *Ibid.* at 288–89.

53   Although the precise phrase "subject to contract" is found in some of the reported cases, the doctrine applies to similarly worded provisions. See, for example, *Winn v. Bull* (1877), 7 Ch. D. 29; *Chillingworth v. Esche*, [1924] 1 Ch. 97; *Lockett v. Norman-Wright*, [1925] Ch. 56; *Eccles v. Bryant and Pollock*, [1948] Ch. 93; *Frank H. Davis of Georgia Inc. v. Rayonier Canada (B.C.) Ltd.* (1968), 65 W.W.R. 251 (B.C.S.C.); *Knowlton Realty Ltd. v. Wyder* (1971), 23 D.L.R. (3d) 69 (B.C.S.C.).

54   See, for example, *Alpenstow Ltd. v. Regalian Properties Plc.*, [1985] 1 W.L.R. 721 (Ch.); *Sylvio Construction Co. v. 678192 Ontario Ltd.* (1993), 11 B.L.R. (2d) 148 (Ont. Ct. Gen. Div.). See also *Sturgeons Ltd. v. Municipality of Metropolitan Toronto* (1968), 70 D.L.R. (2d) 20 (Ont. S.C.).

55   See, for example, *Meyer v. Davies* (1989), 45 B.L.R. 92 (B.C.S.C.).

56   *Marathon Realty Co. v. Toulon Construction Corp.* (1987), 80 N.S.R. (2d) 390; *Golden Properties Ltd. v. Imbrook Properties Ltd.* (1991), 17 R.P.R. (2d) 245 (B.C.C.A.).

however, the preliminary agreement does not explicitly make the agreement conditional upon the execution of a further agreement and where it is not described as a "letter of intent," the prospects for a finding that the preliminary agreement is enforceable are significantly enhanced. In such cases, the courts typically apply the test set out by Parker J. in the *Von Hatzfeldt-Wildenburg*[57] case to the circumstances of the particular preliminary agreement. In *Calvan Consolidated Oil & Gas v. Manning*,[58] the Supreme Court of Canada held to be binding a rather sparely expressed letter agreement concerning the exchange of partial interests in oil and gas permits. The preliminary agreement envisaged that a formal agreement would be entered into by the parties, subject to their mutual agreement, and in the event of a failure to agree, the terms of the agreement would be settled by an arbitrator. The Court held that the parties had agreed to all the essential terms of their agreement and concluded: "the parties were bound immediately on the execution of the informal agreement, that the acceptance was unconditional and that all that was necessary to be done by the parties or possibly by the arbitrator was to embody the precise terms, and no more, of the informal agreement in a formal agreement."[59] Similarly in *Canada Square Corp. Ltd. v. Versafood Services Ltd.*,[60] a preliminary agreement to enter into a lease for the top floor of a building then under construction was held to be enforceable even though it was plainly envisaged that a more detailed lease would be entered into in due course. The preliminary letter of agreement set out the "general principles of our agreement."[61] The fact that it was understood to be important, in the course of erecting the building, to know whether the top floor of the building was to be used by the lessee for this purpose may have assisted the court in coming to this conclusion.

Commitment letters are another type of preliminary agreement in common use. Commitment letters are issued by lenders in circumstances where a potential borrower wishes to know that it will be able to make certain future borrowings of a particular size and on particular terms in order to ensure that the project to be undertaken by the borrower is financially viable. In such circumstances, a lender may issue a commitment letter indicating a commitment to enter into a loan with the borrower on certain terms and conditions, it being understood that a formal

---

57   Above note 51.
58   [1959] S.C.R. 253.
59   *Ibid.* at 260.
60   (1981), 130 D.L.R. (3d) 205 (Ont. C.A.); for a brief description of this case see Chapter 3, section B.
61   *Ibid.* at 210.

lending agreement will be entered into at a later stage. In the typical case, it will be apparent from the terms of the commitment letter that a binding "commitment" is intended. Thus, it is a common feature of such arrangements that the borrower will be required to accept the commitment letter formally and to pay an initial commission or fee in return for the commitment. Provided that the parties have agreed to sufficient terms of the projected loan as to avoid the problem of lack of certainty of terms,[62] commitment letters of this kind are held to be binding agreements.[63]

C. DOMESTIC AND SOCIAL ARRANGEMENTS

The general presumption against the finding of an intention to create legal relations in family and social settings draws its strongest support from the leading case of *Balfour v. Balfour*[64] in which the plaintiff wife brought a claim against her husband to enforce a promise to pay her an allowance. The couple had been living together in Ceylon, where the husband held a government posting. On a temporary visit home in England, it became clear that, for reasons of health, the wife would not be able to return to Ceylon with her husband for at least several months. On the eve of his departure, the husband undertook to provide his wife with a monthly allowance of a certain sum. Some months later when the couple had decided to live separate and apart, the wife brought an action to enforce that undertaking. Although the wife enjoyed success at trial, the Court of Appeal reversed this decision on the basis that arrangements of this kind between husband and wife "are not contracts because the parties did not intend that they should be attended by legal consequences."[65] In a well-known passage, Atkin L.J. provided the following explanation:

> They are not sued upon, not because the parties are reluctant to enforce their legal rights when the agreement is broken, but because the parties, in the inception of the arrangement, never intended that they should be sued upon. Agreements such as these are outside the

---

62   See Chapter 3.

63   See, for example, *First City Investments Ltd. v. Fraser Arms Hotel Ltd.*, [1979] 6 W.W.R. 125 (B.C.C.A.); *Abba Ventures Inc. v. Royal Trust Corp. of Canada* (1996) 25 B.L.R. (2d) 211 (N.B.Q.B.). And see T.W. Bell, "Commitment Letters and Loan Agreements" (1988) 2 B.F.L.R. 1.

64   Above note 1. And see S. Hedley, "Keeping Contract in Its Place—*Balfour v. Balfour* and the Enforcement of Informal Agreements" (1985) 5 Oxford J. Legal Stud. 391.

65   *Balfour v. Balfour*, ibid. at. 579.

realm of contracts altogether. The common law does not regulate the form of agreements between spouses. Their promises are not sealed with seals and sealing wax. The consideration that really obtains for them is that natural love and affection which counts for so little in these cold Courts. The terms may be repudiated, varied or renewed as performance proceeds or as disagreements develop, and the principles of the common law as to exoneration and discharge and accord and satisfaction are such as find no place in the domestic code. The parties themselves are advocates, judges, Courts, sheriff's officer and reporter. In respect of these promises each house is a domain into which the King's writ does not seek to run, and to which his officers do not seek to be admitted.[66]

A similar explanation was offered by Salmon L.J. in a more recent authority[67] in the following terms:

as a rule when arrangements are made between close relations, for example, between husband and wife, parent and child, or uncle and nephew in relation to an allowance, there is a presumption against an intention of creating any legal relationship. This is not a presumption of law but of fact. It derives from experience of life and human nature which shows that in such circumstances men and women usually do not intend to create legal rights and obligations, but intend to rely solely on family ties of mutual trust and affection.[68]

In determining that the particular agreement at issue in *Balfour v. Balfour* fell into the category of informal and unenforceable family arrangements, it was of critical importance that the couple had not agreed to separate at the time of the agreement and the agreement was therefore one made, in effect, by a couple living together in amity. Where parties have agreed to live separately, however, it is clearly established that similar arrangements to provide an allowance or support are normally enforceable. As Lord Denning explained in *Merritt v. Merritt*:[69] "It is altogether different when the parties are not living in amity but are separated, or about to separate. They then bargain keenly. They do not rely on ongoing understandings. They want everything cut and dried.

---

66   *Ibid.*
67   *Jones v. Padavatton*, [1969] 2 All E.R. 616 (C.A.).
68   *Ibid.* at 621.
69   [1970] 2 All E.R. 760 (C.A.). Compare with *McKinney v. McKinney* (1980), 17 R.F.L. (2d) 308 (B.C.S.C.) (mere statements of intention not intended to create legal relations).

It may safely be presumed that they intend to create legal relations."[70] The negotiation and enforcement of so-called separation agreements is both a commonplace phenomenon and a matter that is subject to regulation by provincial family law legislation.[71]

The general presumption of unenforceability has often been applied to arrangements entered into by spouses,[72] but the presumption may apply to arrangements entered into by other family members. Thus, in a Canadian case[73] an agreement among siblings that all of the income from their late father's estate should be applied to the support of their mother was held to be an informal arrangement that was not intended to be legally enforceable. On the other hand, it is quite conceivable, of course, that family members could enter into agreements with the intention that they be enforceable. Commercial arrangements between family members may obviously be intended to create enforceable agreements. Even in non-commercial settings, however, it is quite possible for the requisite intention to be present. Thus, an individual in need of care might enter into an agreement to compensate another member of the family in return for the provision of services of this kind. Such arrangements may be intended to be enforceable.[74] In *Dugas v. Dugas' Estate*[75] an arrangement under which an adult son returned home after an unsuccessful marriage and agreed to pay for his room and board was held enforceable. So too, was an obligation to repay monies lent to him by his father.[76] In a leading English case,[77] an arrangement under which a father promised to transfer ownership of a home to his son and daughter-in-law, provided that the couple first paid all of the instalments of the purchase price, was held to be binding. As in this case, it is a common feature of the cases in which an intention to create legal relations is found to be present that the party seeking to enforce the agreement has detrimentally relied on the assumed enforceability of the agreement.

---

70 *Merritt v. Merritt, ibid.* at 762.
71 See generally S. Fodden, *Family Law* (Toronto: Irwin Law, 1999) c. 13.
72 See, for example, *Barnett and Wise v. Wise*, [1961] O.R. 97 (C.A.); *Steinberg v. Steinberg* (1963), 45 D.L.R. (2d) 162 (Sask. Q.B.); *Brody v. Brody* (1976), 1 A.R. 470 (S.C.).
73 *Rogalsky Estate v. Rogalsky* (1984), 32 Man. R. (2d) 223 (Q.B.).
74 See, for example, *Ostopowich v. Crown Trust Co.* (1959), 20 D.L.R. (2d) 514 (Man. C.A.); *Haggar v. de Placido*, [1972] 1 W.L.R. 716 (Crown Ct.). Compare with *Berryere v. Berryere* (1972), 26 D.L.R. (3d) 764 (B.C.S.C.); *Re Gonin*, [1979] Ch. 16.
75 (1978), 23 N.B.R. (2d) 199 (App. Div.).
76 See also *Jackson v. Jackson* (1960), 26 D.L.R. (2d) 686 (B.C.S.C.).
77 *Errington v. Errington*, [1952] 1 K.B. 290 (C.A.). Compare with *Hardwick v. Johnson*, [1978] 2 All E.R. 935 (C.A.).

In *Jones v. Padavatton*,[78] on the other hand, the presence of substantial detrimental reliance did not lead to a finding that the requisite intention was present. In this case, a mother had encouraged her daughter to move from Washington to London to pursue legal studies and become a qualified barrister. The mother, who lived in Trinidad, hoped that upon qualifying for the Bar, the daughter would return home to Trinidad and engage in the practice of law. The daughter was loath to leave Washington for this purpose. She had a very satisfactory position with the Indian Embassy in Washington and, as a single mother, was raising her infant son. Her mother's scheme seemed impractical. Eventually, however, the daughter was induced by her mother's promise of a specified monthly allowance for as long as she continued her studies to quit her employment in Washington and move, with her son, to London to study for the Bar. A further arrangement was made when it became clear that the daughter's living arrangements in London were unsatisfactory. The mother purchased a house in order to provide accommodation for the daughter on the basis that she would rent out some of the rooms and use the proceeds, in lieu of the monthly allowance, to defray her living expenses and the carrying costs of the house. These arrangements appeared to work satisfactorily for approximately five years. The daughter's pace as a student was measured. During the five years, she had completed studies that would normally take approximately three years. For reasons not explained in the judgment, however, the mother arrived in London in the fifth year and sought possession of the house and, in effect, termination of the arrangements. The Court of Appeal divided on the question of whether an intention to create legal relations between mother and daughter was present. For the majority, the arrangement appeared to be "one of those family arrangements which depend on the good faith of the promises which are made and are not intended to be rigid, binding agreements."[79] In a judgment concurring as to result, however, Salmon L.J. concluded that in the very particular circumstances of this case, "neither the mother nor the daughter could have intended that the daughter should have no legal right to receive, and the mother no legal obligation to pay, the [monthly allowance]."[80] In response to the suggestion that the arrangements were not enforceable because it would be unthinkable if the daughter were to consider suing the mother if the mother had fallen on hard times, Salmon L.J. responded that this consideration was not relevant in determining

---

78   Above note 67.
79   *Ibid.* at 620, Danckwerts L.J., Fenton Atkinson L.J., concurring on this point.
80   *Ibid.* at 622.

whether or not there had been an intention to create legal relations at the commencement of the arrangement. The fact that it may be likely that a party would forebear from suit in particular circumstances is not inconsistent with a finding that such an intention is present. Salmon L.J. was also of the view, however, that the mother's claim should enjoy success. The agreement was, in his view, subject to an implied term that it would endure only for a reasonable period of time. In Salmon L.J.'s view, a reasonable time could not exceed five years and, accordingly, the agreement had come to an end. If the issue had arisen at an earlier point in time, however, Salmon L.J. would have enforced the arrangement. In light of the very substantial detrimental reliance engaged in by the daughter, this does indeed appear to be the preferable view.

Under traditional doctrine, it was assumed that co-habitation agreements under which parties who agree to co-habit set forth the terms and conditions under which they will conduct their domestic affairs are unenforceable on the basis of the doctrine of *Balfour v. Balfour*.[81] In the statutory modernization of provincial family law occurring in the late-twentieth century, however, a number of provinces enacted legislation providing that such "marriage contracts" or "co-habitation agreements" could be constituted as enforceable contracts. Thus, for example, the *Ontario Family Law Act*[82] provides in section 52, as follows:

> 52(1) A man and woman who are married to each other or intend to marry may enter into an agreement in which they agree on their respective rights and obligations under the marriage or on separation, on the annulment or dissolution of the marriage or of death, including,
>
> (a) ownership in or division of property;
>
> (b) support of obligations;
>
> (c) the right to direct the education and moral training of their children, but not the right to custody of, or access to their children; and
>
> (d) any other matter in the settlement of their affairs.

---

81 Marriage settlements, on the other hand, under which property is settled upon a prospective spouse in return for the promise to marry where binding, at law, provided that such arrangements were recorded in writing as required by the *The Statute of Frauds*. On this point, see further, Chapter 6, section B(2)(b).

82 R.S.O. 1990, c. F.3, s. 52(1). See also *Matrimonial Property Act*, R.S.A. 2000, c. M-8, s. 37; *Family Relations Act*, R.S.B.C. 1996, c. 128, s. 61; *Marital Property Act*, C.C.S.M., c. M.45, s. 5; *Marital Property Act*, S.N.B. 1980, c. M-1.1; *Family Law Act*, R.S.N. 1990, c. F-2, Part IV; *Matrimonial Property Act*, R.S.N.S. 1989, c. 275, s. 23; *Family Law Act*, S.P.E.I. 1995, c. 12, Part IV; *Matrimonial Property Act*, S.S. 1997, c. M-6.11, Part VII.

The legislation further provides that such agreements are not enforceable unless they are recorded in writing, signed by the parties and witnessed.[83]

Co-habitation agreements entered into by unmarried couples faced the additional hurdle at common law that they were traditionally considered to be contrary to public policy on the basis that the underlying consideration was thought to be immoral and, accordingly, that such relationships should not be recognized at law.[84] Such objections have receded, however, with evolving social attitudes on matters of this kind. Thus, in *Chrispen v. Topham*[85] a co-habitation agreement entered into by an unmarried heterosexual couple dealing with such matters as rental payments to be paid by one to the other, utilities expenses, jointly owned property, use of a car and the conditions under which a cat could be acquired by one of the parties, was held to be enforceable at common law. Further, in a number of provinces, this point had been put beyond dispute by the legislative extension to unmarried heterosexual couples of the provisions applicable to married couples such as the Ontario provisions set out above.[86] More recently still, in light of the decision of the Supreme Court of Canada in *M v. H.*[87] to the effect that the restriction of the definition of "spouse" to partners in heterosexual relationships in family law legislation constitutes constitutionally impermissible discrimination against same-sex partners, the statutory right to enter into enforceable co-habitation agreements has been extended to same-sex couples.[88]

The presumption against the intention to create legal relations applies not only within domestic settings but in social settings more generally. Though legal disputes concerning social arrangements are perhaps unlikely to arise, disputes over such matters as entitlement to season's tickets to professional sports events and the sharing of lottery winnings have surfaced in the reported cases. In an Ontario case,[89]

---

83   R.S.O. 1990, c. F.3, s. 55(1).

84   See, for example, *Farrar v. MacPhee* (1971), 19 D.L.R. (3d) 720 at 724 (P.E.I.S.C.), Tweedy J. See also *Lazarenko v. Barowsky Estate*, [1966] S.C.R. 556.

85   (1986), 28 D.L.R. (4th) 754 (Sask. Q.B.).

86   See, for example, R.S.O. 1990, c. F.3, s. 53(1). Under these provisions, an agreement that failed to comply with formalities required by the legislation would be unenforceable. *Ibid.*, s. 55(1).

87   [1999] 2 S.C.R. 3.

88   See, for example, R.S.O. 1990, c. F.3, s. 53(1).

89   *Pobasco Ltd. v. Cogan* (1990), 72 O.R. (2d) 254 (H.C.). See also *Eng v. Evans* (1991), 83 Alta. L.R. (2d) 107 (Q.B.) (arrangements concerning season's tickets for hockey games — not enforceable).

an arrangement among business associates that the holder of season's tickets to Toronto Blue Jay games would share the tickets with his associates was held to be unenforceable for lack of intent to create legal relations. A different outcome is likely to prevail in the context of the now common practice of people creating pools to purchase provincial lottery tickets. It has now been held a number of times that where parties contribute to the purchase of lottery tickets on the understanding that the winnings, if any, will be shared, the holder of the winning ticket holds the proceeds in trust in order to give effect to those enforceable arrangements.[90] Indeed, in an English case[91] a rather informal arrangement under which a grandmother, granddaughter and boarder collaborated on a weekly submission to a Sunday newspaper competition and agreed to "go shares" if they enjoyed success was held to be enforceable.

FURTHER READINGS

S.N. BALL, "Work Carried Out in Pursuance of Letters of Intent — Contract or Restitution" (1983) 99 Law Q. Rev. 572.

T.W. BELL, "Commitment Letters and Loan Agreements" (1988) 2 B.F.L.R. 1.

A.G. CHLOROS, "Comparative Aspects of the Intention to Create Legal Relations in Contract" (1959) 33 Tul. L. Rev. 607.

D.H. CLARK, "Contracts — Interpretation — Creation of Legally Binding Relationship — 'Cold Comfort Letter': *Kleinwort Benson Ltd.* v. *Malaysia Mining Corp. Bhd.*" (1990) 69 Can. Bar Rev. 753.

M. FURMSTON, T. NORISADA & J. POOLE, *Contract Formation and Letters of Intent* (Chichester: Wiley & Sons, 1998).

R.D. GIBBENS, "Letters of Comfort — *Kleinwort Benson* v. *Malaysian Mining Corp. Berhad*" (1989) 3 B.F.L.R. 222.

J. GOODMAN, "No Comfort by Letter of Comfort: *Toronto-Dominion Bank v. Leigh*" (1999) 14 B.F.L.R. 389.

---

90   See, for example, *Taylor v. Smith* (1995), 26 O.R. (3d) 50 (Gen. Div.). And see *Ross v. Hern*, [2003] O.J. No. 1659 (S.C.J.). See also *Osorio v. Cardona* (1984), 15 D.L.R. (4th) 619 (B.C.S.C.) (pooling arrangement to share racetrack winnings).

91   *Simpkins v. Pays*, [1955] 3 All E.R. 10 (H.C.).

S. HEDLEY, "Keeping Contract in its Place—*Balfour v. Balfour* and the Enforcement of Informal Agreements" (1985) 5 Oxford J. Legal Stud. 391.

B. HEPPLE, "Intention to Create Legal Relations" (1970) 28 Cambridge L.J. 122.

P. PERELL, "Lessons About Comfort Letters" (2001) 34 Can. Bus. L.J. 421.

D.D. PRENTICE, "Letters of Comfort" (1989) 105 Law Q. Rev. 346.

R. SACASAS & D. WEISNER, "'Comfort Letters': The Legal and Business Implications" (1987) 104 Banking L.J. 313.

R. TUCK, "Intent to Contract and Mutuality of Assent" (1943) 21 Can. Bar Rev. 123.

G.A. WITTHUN, "*Kleinwort Benson Limited* v. *Malaysia Mining Corporation Berhad*—A Comparative Note on Comfort Letters" (1990) 35 McGill L.J. 490.

CHAPTER 5

BARGAINING IN GOOD FAITH

A. INTRODUCTION

In a leading Canadian decision[1] on the subject of fiduciary obligation, La Forest J. observed: "The institution of bargaining in good faith is one that is worthy of legal protection in those circumstances where that protection accords with the expectations of the parties."[2] This chapter examines the extent to which the common law of contract provides legal protection to the institution of bargaining in good faith. One possible means of affording such protection would be to recognize and enforce an obligation to bargain in good faith in certain circumstances. As we shall see, the common law thus far has been reluctant to adopt this means for encouraging good-faith negotiation. The possibility of recognizing such a duty has, however, been considered in a variety of doctrinal contexts. Before turning to consider existing Canadian common law on this topic, it may be useful to speculate as to the types of conduct that might be thought to constitute bargaining in bad faith.[3]

---

1 *Lac Minerals Ltd.* v. *International Corona Resources Ltd.* (1989), 61 D.L.R. (4th) 14 (S.C.C.).
2 *Ibid.* at 14.
3 See generally M. Furmston *et al.*, *Contract Formation and Letters of Intent* (Chichester: Wiley & Sons, 1998) c. 10; E.A. Farnsworth, "Precontractual Liability and Preliminary Agreements: Fair Dealing and Failed Negotiations" (1987) 87 Colum. L. Rev. 217; J. Cassels, "Good Faith in Contract Bargaining: General Principles and Recent Developments" (1993) 15 Advocates' Q. 56.

One possible candidate might be the withholding of information that would disabuse the other negotiating party of a mistake concerning an important fact. Although the common law, as we shall see, imposes no general duty of disclosure on negotiating parties,[4] it might be argued that a duty to bargain in good faith would impose such an obligation, at least in certain circumstances. Other types of breaches of such a duty might include bargaining with no intention of reaching agreement or otherwise misleading the other party with respect to one's intentions, reneging on a promise given in the course of negotiations, refusal to make reasonable efforts to reach agreement, breaking off negotiations in order to accept a more attractive proposal from a third party, and so on. Whether any of these or other tactics might be considered to constitute bad faith might well depend, in the particular circumstances, on whether the parties had agreed to negotiate or, indeed, had agreed to negotiate in good faith.

Although it is perhaps not obvious that any or all of these negotiating moves ought to constitute breaches of duties owed to the other party, there can be no doubt that conduct of this kind can visit injuries on the other party. In the first place, the victim of such negotiating strategies may be deprived of the possibility of entering an attractive and profitable contractual arrangement. Alternatively, a victim of bad faith bargaining may sustain substantial out-of-pocket expenses in the course of fruitless negotiations. Consider, for example, the facts of the American case of *Hoffman v. Red Owl Stores*,[5] a case of reneging on a promise. The parties were negotiating a supermarket franchise. The prospective franchisor told the prospective franchisee that an eighteen-thousand-dollar cash contribution would be sufficient. Extended negotiations followed. Thus encouraged, the franchisee sold his business, moved to another town and bought a small grocery store. Negotiations then collapsed when the franchisor insisted on a substantially higher contribution. At common law, the promise to accept the lesser contribution would be unenforceable because it was not given for good consideration.[6] The franchisor's bargaining strategy nonetheless inflicted serious losses upon the prospective franchisee.

The possible existence of a duty to negotiate or bargain in good faith imposed either by agreement of the parties or as a matter of com-

---

4   See Chapter 10.

5   133 N.W.2d 267 (Wis. 1965).

6   A different result is available in American law on this point. The plaintiff succeeded in *Hoffman v. Red Owl Stores* on the basis of promissory estoppel doctrine. For discussion of promissory estoppel, see Chapter 8.

mon law has been considered in a variety of contexts. First, the issue surfaced for analysis in the context of agreements that fail or allegedly fail for lack of certainty of terms or incompleteness.[7] In such cases, the parties have not agreed to all the essential terms of their agreement but they may have explicitly or implicitly agreed to agree in the future with respect to the content of the missing essential terms. In such cases, a plaintiff attempting to enforce the agreement against a defendant who chooses not to negotiate or agree with respect to the missing terms may argue that there is at least a breach by the defendant of a duty to negotiate or to negotiate in good faith.

Second, the possible enforceability of a duty to negotiate in good faith has arisen in the context of provisions that permit one party to extend or renew an existing agreement at a price to be agreed upon in the future. An option to renew a lease for a further term at a rent "as agreed" provides a simple illustration. In such circumstances, a plaintiff tenant seeking to enforce the option against an unwilling landlord may argue that the landlord has, at the least, an obligation to negotiate or negotiate in good faith the new rent. A related type of case in which such arguments have been made arises from agreements that provide for the review of a particular term of an agreement during the term of the agreement. A lease for a five-year term might provide, for example, that the rent will be at the rate of $1,000 per month for the first twelve months and thereafter at a rate to be agreed upon by the parties. Again, it might be argued by the party seeking to enforce the agreement that the other is under an obligation to negotiate the rental rate for the remaining four years in good faith.

In each of these categories of cases, it should be noted, the plaintiff will typically argue in the alternative that on a proper interpretation of the agreement, the missing terms can be construed to be implied "reasonable" terms. Thus, where the price term in an agreement is missing, the party who wishes to enforce will argue that the price is implied to be a "reasonable" price and that the agreement is therefore enforceable. If a court is willing to hold that the reluctant party is subject to a reasonable term or terms, the plaintiff obviously has no need to rely upon an argument that there exists at least an obligation to negotiate the terms in good faith. A finding that the agreement contains a reasonable price term may, of course, force the parties to engage in negotiations, as a practical matter. Such a holding is not, however, a recognition of the existence of a contractual obligation to negotiate or to bargain in good faith.

---

7   See generally Chapter 3.

A further context in which good-faith arguments have been attempted are disputes about the treatment of bidders in tendering processes. At least one provincial Court of Appeal has adopted the view that those who conduct tendering processes must act in good faith.[8] In the recent decision of the Supreme Court in *M.J.B. Enterprises Ltd. v. Defence Construction (1951) Ltd.*,[9] however, the Court resolved a similar dispute in the plaintiff's favour without relying on a good-faith doctrine. As we have seen,[10] Canadian law has adopted the view that one who conducts a tendering process will normally have entered into a binding contract with each tenderer relating to the tendering process. It is now well established that the contractual relationship includes an implied obligation on the part of those who invite tenders to treat all tenderers "fairly and equally." Such an obligation may be thought to be somewhat akin to a duty to negotiate in good faith.

In each of the categories of cases described above, the alleged duty to negotiate in good faith is grounded in an express or implied contractual undertaking to bargain in good faith. In a further category, there is plainly no contractual foundation for the duty. In a few cases, at least, it has been argued that parties negotiating with a view to reaching an agreement may have a duty to conduct the negotiations in good faith. Presumably, the foundation for such a duty must rest in tort law. As we shall see, the evidence in support of the proposition that such a duty has been recognized is very slender indeed.

We turn, then, to a consideration of the jurisprudence arising in each of the case types set out above. We do not consider here, however, the question as to whether non-disclosure of material information might be considered to be a failure to bargain in good faith. In American law, this issue has been framed by considering whether non-disclosure might constitute a "misrepresentation" for purposes of the law relating to rescission of agreements for misrepresentation. A similar link between non-disclosure and good faith has recently been suggested by a Canadian court.[11] We will return to a discussion of this aspect of bargaining in good faith in our more general treatment of non-disclosure as misrepresentation.[12]

---

8   *Healthcare Developers Inc. v. Newfoundland* (1996), 141 Nfld. & P.E.I.R. 34.

9   (1999), 170 D.L.R. (4th) 577 (S.C.C.).

10 See Chapter 2, section B(1)(c).

11 *978011 Ontario Ltd. v. Cornell Engineering Co.* (2001), 198 D.L.R. (4th) 615 (Ont. C.A.), for discussion of which see below, Chapter 10, section D.

12 See Chapter 10, section C.

B. CERTAINTY OF TERMS

The leading decisions of the English courts on the possible existence of
a duty to negotiate in good faith have arisen in the context of attempted
agreements that may fail because of incompleteness or uncertainty of
terms.[13] Thus, the possible existence of an enforceable duty to negotiate was first suggested in a well-known dictum of Lord Wright in the
leading case of *Hillas and Co. Ltd. v. Arcos.*[14] The plaintiffs sought to enforce an agreement for an option to purchase by instalments a quantity
of timber over the 1930 lumber season from a Russian supplier. The
agreement left a number of details at large such as the arrangements to
be made for particular instalments. The prices were to be settled by the
supplier's price list when available. The description of the goods was
arguably vague. The parties had, however, worked successfully with a
similar agreement in the previous season, finding themselves able to
agree to appropriate details as the need to do so arose. In these circumstances, Lord Wright was obliged to consider whether an "agreement
to agree" might be binding. In his view, if the agreement was to agree
to the prescribed terms of what amounted to a binding contract, the
agreement to agree would simply be that binding contract. He went on
to consider, however, what the significance might be of an agreement to
attempt to reach a binding agreement in the following fashion:

> If, however, what is meant is that the parties agree to negotiate in the
> hope of effecting a valid contract, the position is different. There is
> then no bargain except to negotiate, and negotiations may be fruit-
> less and end without any contract ensuing; yet even then, in strict
> theory, there is a contract (if there is good consideration) to negoti-
> ate, though in the event of repudiation by one party the damages may
> be nominal, unless a jury think that the opportunity to negotiate was
> of some appreciable value to the injured party.[15]

It was unnecessary for Lord Wright to consider this point further, however, as it was his view that the agreement was enforceable as the parties had implicitly agreed to "reasonable" arrangements with respect to
each of these matters. If the parties were unable to agree as to a reasonable arrangement with respect to a particular point, "the machinery (of
the law) is always available to give the necessary certainty."[16]

---

13 See generally Chapter 3.
14 [1932] All E.R. Rep. 494 (H.L.).
15 *Ibid.* at 505.
16 *Ibid.* at 506.

The suggestion made by Lord Wright that an agreement to negotiate could be enforceable has not attracted support from the English judiciary. In *Courtney and Fairbairn Ltd. v. Tolaini Brothers (Hotels) Ltd.*,[17]
the idea was rejected by Lord Denning M.R. in the following terms:

> That tentative opinion by Lord Wright does not seem to me to be well
> founded. If the law does not recognise a contract to enter into a con-
> tract (when there is a fundamental term yet to be agreed) it seems to
> me it cannot recognise a contract to negotiate. The reason is because
> it is too uncertain to have any binding force. No court could estimate
> the damages because no one can tell whether the negotiations would
> be successful or would fall through; or if successful, what the result
> would be. It seems to me that a contract to negotiate, like a contract
> to enter into a contract, is not a contract known to the law.[18]

At issue in this case was the enforceability of a building contract for a
large development project with respect to which the parties had not yet
reached an agreement on the total contract price. The Court of Appeal
concluded that price is a term of fundamental importance in a building contract. Accordingly, the agreement failed for uncertainty and the
defect could not be cured by the imposition of a duty to negotiate a
price.

The House of Lords returned to this question more recently in *Walford v. Miles.*[19] The parties had agreed in principle to the purchase and
sale of a business and related premises. This agreement was "subject to
contract" and plainly unenforceable. The parties also agreed, however,
that if the purchaser would provide a comfort letter from its bankers,
the vendor would not negotiate with anyone else with respect to the
sale of these assets for an unspecified period of time. The plaintiff purchaser sought to enforce this collateral "lockout" agreement and argued
that it contained a term "necessarily to be implied to give business
efficacy thereto" that the seller "would continue to negotiate in good
faith"[20] with the purchaser so long as the purchaser continued to desire
to sell the property. Lord Ackner rejected this argument on the basis
that an agreement to negotiate lacked sufficient certainty. He elabor-
ated on this point, as follows:

---

17   [1975] 1 All E.R. 716 (C.A.).
18   *Ibid.* at 720. Lord Denning's reasoning in the second sentence in this passage is
      dismissed by Farnsworth as a *non sequitur.* See Farnsworth, above note 3 at 264.
19   [1992] 1 All E.R. 453.
20   *Ibid.* at 458.

How can a court be expected to decide whether, *subjectively*, a proper reason existed for the termination of negotiations? The answer suggested depends upon whether the negotiations have been determined "in good faith." However, the concept of a duty to carry on negotiations in good faith is inherently repugnant to the adversarial position of the parties when involved in negotiations. Each party to the negotiations is entitled to pursue his (or her) own interest, so long as he avoids making misrepresentations. To advance that interest he must be entitled, if he thinks it appropriate, to threaten to withdraw from further negotiations or to withdraw in fact in the hope that the opposite party may seek to reopen the negotiations by offering him improved terms. Mr. Naughton, of course, accepts that the agreement upon which he relies does not contain a duty to complete the negotiations. But that still leaves the vital question: how is a vendor ever to know that he is entitled to withdraw from further negotiations? How is the court to police such an "agreement"? A duty to negotiate in good faith is as unworkable in practice as it is inherently inconsistent with the position of a negotiating party. It is here that the uncertainty lies. In my judgment, while negotiations are in existence either party is entitled to withdraw from these negotiations, at any time and for any reason. There can be thus no obligation to continue to negotiate until there is a "proper reason" to withdraw. Accordingly, a bare agreement to negotiate has no legal content.[21]

In other words, a certain amount of posturing is to be expected in the context of contract negotiations. Accordingly, for the House of Lords at least, the line between good-faith and bad-faith negotiation is too difficult to discern. On the facts of the *Walford* case, their Lordships were of the view that the lack of a specified term for the lockout meant that the agreement could only come to an end when good-faith negotiations had come to an end. Accordingly, the enforceability of the agreement rested on the enforceability of a duty to negotiate in good faith. As a result, the agreement failed for lack of certainty.

As we shall see, this English judicial scepticism with respect to the viability of an enforceable duty to negotiate in good faith has been influential in Canadian decisions.

---

21   *Ibid.* at 460–61 (emphasis in the original).

C. OPTIONS TO RENEW

Some support for the enforceability of a duty to negotiate can be found in Canadian cases considering the enforceability of options to renew leases where the new rental rate is "to be agreed" by the parties. In *Empress Towers Ltd. v. Bank of Nova Scotia*,[22] the British Columbia Court of Appeal ruled on the enforceability of an option to renew a lease for an additional five-year period at a rental "which shall be the market rental prevailing at the commencement of that renewal as mutually agreed between the Landlord and the Tenant."[23] In addressing this issue, Lambert J.A. began by emphasizing, as Lord Wright had in *Hillas*, that courts should be disposed to enforce agreements created by the parties: "It is not the function of the courts to set interim agreements aside for uncertainty because they contain a clause that is not precisely expressed. If such a clause has an ascertainable meaning, then the courts should strive to find it.… As long as an agreement is not being constructed by the court, to the surprise of the parties, or at least one of them, the courts should try to retain and give effect to the agreement that the parties have created for themselves."[24]

Although Lambert J.A. does not make this point, we may wonder whether the general disposition to enforce agreements should carry additional weight in a context, such as the present, where the parties have been able to satisfactorily perform the agreement in question for a substantial period of time. Against this predisposition, however, Lambert J.A. noted: "it is well established that if all the parties say is that they will enter into a lease at a rental to be agreed, no enforceable lease obligation is created." He went on to suggest, "there may, however, be an obligation to negotiate."[25]

As Lambert J.A. noted, if the parties had simply provided for renewal at "the market rental prevailing," the agreement could have been enforced in these terms. A difficulty arose from the additional requirement that the rate be "as mutually agreed" by the parties. The effect of that provision, for Lambert J.A., was that the landlord could not be compelled to enter into a renewal tenancy at a rate that it did not find acceptable. He went on to observe, however, as follows:

---

22   (1990), 73 D.L.R. (4th) 400 (B.C.C.A.).
23   *Ibid.* at 402.
24   *Ibid.* at 403, quoting from the earlier decision of the British Columbia Court of Appeal in *Griffin v. Martens* (1988), 27 B.C.L.R. (2d) 152 at 153 (B.C.C.A.).
25   *Ibid.* at 403.

> But, in my opinion, that is not the only effect of the requirement of mutual agreement. It also carries with it, first, an implied term that the landlord will negotiate in good faith with the tenant with the objective of reaching an agreement on the market rental rate and, secondly, that agreement on a market rental will not be unreasonably withheld.... Those terms are to be implied under the officious bystander and business efficacy principles in order to permit the renewal clause, which was clearly intended to have legal effect, from being struck down as uncertain. The key to implying the terms that I have set out is that the parties agreed that there should be a right of renewal at the prevailing market rental.[26]

The Court of Appeal upheld the trial judge's finding that the lessor had not, in fact, negotiated in good faith. On this basis, the lessor's writ of possession was dismissed. Given the nature of the proceeding, it was unnecessary for the court to consider what the measure of damages would be in an action for breach of the duty to negotiate in good faith or of the obligation not to withhold agreement unreasonably. Arguably, at least, the measure might be the difference between any reasonable proposal put forward by the lessee and rejected by the lessor and the market rate, a difference that is not likely to be substantial. The principal significance of the good-faith duty, as in *Empress Towers* itself, thus seems to be to provide a basis for continuing possession by the lessee. More than this, however, the implication of a duty to bargain in good faith and not unreasonably withhold consent appears to impose, in effect, a duty to accept an offer at a reasonable price. Refusal to accept such an offer grounds the lessee's continuing possession. If this is true, however, it is unclear what is left of Lambert J.A.'s suggestion that "the landlord cannot be compelled to enter into a renewal tenancy at a rent which it has not accepted."[27] It may thus appear that the imposition of good-faith duties in this context has the effect of imposing a reasonable price on an unwilling party and significantly undermining the contractual requirement of mutual assent.

In *Empress Towers*, the renewal provision combined an objective element — the market rate — with the need for agreement between the parties. In that case, Lambert J.A. explicitly indicated that it was not necessary to deal with the question of whether a "bare right of renewal at a rental to be agreed carries with it an obligation to negotiate in good faith or not withhold agreement unreasonably."[28] It was not to be very long before the

---

26   *Ibid.* at 404.
27   *Ibid.*
28   *Ibid.* at 405.

British Columbia Court of Appeal would be provided an opportunity to address this question in *Mannpar Enterprises Ltd. v. Canada*.[29]

The contractual term at issue in *Mannpar* provided for the renewal of a five-year contract under which the plaintiff was permitted to remove and sell sand and gravel located on an Indian reserve. The option to renew was for a second five-year period. The provision was stipulated to be "subject to satisfactory performance and renegotiation of the royalty rate and annual surface rental."[30] The provision went on to state that "under no circumstances shall the royalty rate or surface rental be less than the rates received in the preceding term." Although the plaintiff gave written notice of its intention to renew, neither the Crown nor the Indian band was willing to renew. The plaintiff argued that the refusal to negotiate a new rate constituted a breach of the Crown's obligation to negotiate in good faith. Unlike *Empress Towers*, then, the renewal provision in *Mannpar* made no reference to an objective standard such as the market rate. *Mannpar* thus raised squarely the issue left at large in *Empress Towers*.

In *Mannpar*, the British Columbia Court of Appeal reaffirmed the traditional position that an agreement to agree or an agreement to negotiate is too uncertain to be enforceable. The distinguishing feature of *Empress Towers*, then, was the presence of an objective standard or "benchmark"[31] such as "market rate" in the provision at issue in that case.[32] In reaching this conclusion, it was necessary for the court to distinguish a line of authority that treated agreements to agree upon a rental as agreements to a "fair," "reasonable" or "market" rental. In the court's view it was an important and distinguishing feature of these cases that they involved leases that provided for *review* of rental rates *during* the agreed term of the lease. The English case of *Beer v. Bowden*[33] provides an illustration. In that case, a ten-year lease provided that after five years there would be a review of the rent and the rent would become "such rent as shall thereupon be agreed between the landlords and the tenant ... and in any case not less than the yearly rental payable hereunder."[34] The English Court of Appeal held that a term should be implied to the effect that a "fair rent" would be payable for the second half of the ten-year term.

29   (1999), 173 D.L.R. (4th) 243 (B.C.C.A.).

30   *Ibid.* at 247.

31   *Ibid.* at 264.

32   See also *Edper Brascan Corp. v. 117373 Canada Ltd.* (2000), 50 O.R. (3d) 425 (S.C.J.).

33   [1981] 1 W.L.R. 522 (C.A.). See also *B.I.H. Investments v. Kim*, [1996] B.C.J. No. 49 (S.C.).

34   *Beer v. Bowden, ibid.* at 523.

If the parties could not agree on a "fair rent," it could be determined by the court. For the British Columbia Court of Appeal, then, a distinction is to be drawn between cases where a rent review process is "provided for in the course of a continuing leasehold arrangement,"[35] that is to say, *during* the term of a lease, and cases where a renewal or extension of a lease *beyond* its term is exercisable only at a rental to be agreed upon by the parties. In the former case, the court will imply an objective standard such as "reasonable" or "fair." In the latter case, the provision will be held unenforceable as lacking sufficient certainty.[36]

This distinction between reviews during the term and renewals or extensions beyond is obviously a narrow one. Its rationale might be that courts should be more reluctant to strike down a provision designed to operate during the currency of a lease than they are to strike down a renewal clause. It seems unlikely, however, that the particular expectations or detrimental reliance of the parties is likely to be contingent on whether the lease has a longer term subject to rental review or a shorter term subject to renewal. The distinction is arguably, therefore, not a tenable one and it might be preferable to imply that the parties intend a reasonable rate in both contexts. If that view were to prevail, of course, the need to rely on a duty of good-faith negotiation, in the manner of the reasoning in *Empress Towers*, would no longer be necessary.

D. THE CONDUCT OF TENDERING PROCESSES

Under traditional doctrine, an invitation to tender followed by the submission of tenders constituted initial steps in a negotiation that would conclude only when the offer constituted by a particular bid or tender was selected by the inviter of tenders, thus accepting the offer and creating a binding contract. As we have seen in Chapter 2, in *Ron Engineering & Construction Eastern Ltd. v. Ontario*,[37] the Supreme Court of Canada developed a new approach to the analysis of contract formation in this context and held that an initial contract, relating essentially to the tendering process was formed by the submission of a bid, which

---

35   Above note 29 at 259.

36   The court in *Mannpar* made no reference to an earlier Saskatchewan trial court decision enforcing an explicit agreement to negotiate in such circumstances. See *Hargreaves v. Fleming* (1995), 129 Sask. R. 136 (Q.B.), Laing J. (option to renew lease on same terms "excepting as to rental rate which shall be negotiated").

37   [1981] 1 S.C.R. 111.

constituted the acceptance of an offer constituted by the invitation to tender. Thus, this initial Contract A, as it was called, contained and rendered enforceable the terms of the tendering process set out in the invitation. In *Ron Engineering* itself the issue raised was whether the bid deposit, as indicated by the terms of the invitation, was irrevocable in the sense that if a bidder was selected and then refused to enter into the ultimate agreement to do the work, called Contract B, the deposit would be forfeited and irrecoverable. In *Ron Engineering*, the plaintiff had submitted the lowest bid. However, when selected by the defendant, the plaintiff, because of a substantial calculation error in its bid, refused to enter Contract B. The Supreme Court held that, pursuant to the terms of Contract A, the plaintiff's claim to recover its deposit must fail. In subsequent cases, it has become clearly established that Contract A also contains implied terms that have the effect of regulating the conduct of the person conducting the tendering process and requiring, in effect, that the process be conducted in a fair manner. In *Healthcare Developers Inc. v. Newfoundland,*[38] the Newfoundland Court of Appeal held that the person issuing the tender call must, under an implied term in Contract A, act in good faith, a standard that required "at a minimum ... that a party not act in bad faith."[39] Cameron J.A. further explained that "it would be acting in bad faith to award something other than Contract B, to fail to reject tenders not in compliance with the call or to award Contract B on the basis of an undisclosed preference." Other courts have formulated the implied term as a duty to treat bidders "fairly" and in good faith.[40] Still other courts, however, have imposed similar obligations by means of an implied term in Contract A to treat all bidders "fairly and equally," an implied term that contains no reference to the concept of "good faith."[41] In *Martel Building Ltd. v. Canada*[42] the Supreme Court of Canada gave its *imprimatur* to an implied contractual duty of "fair and equal treatment."[43]

38   Above note 8. See also *Martselos Services Ltd. v. Arctic College* (1994), 111 D.L.R. (4th) 65 (N.W.T.C.A.), leave to appeal to S.C.C. refused [1994] 3 S.C.R. viii.
39   *Healthcare Developers Inc. v. Newfoundland, ibid.* at 627 (D.L.R.).
40   See, for example, *Tarmac Canada Inc. v. Hamilton-Wentworth (Regional Municipality)* (1999), 48 C.L.R. (2d) 236 (Ont. C.A.); *Naylor Group Inc. v. Ellis-Don Construction Ltd.* (1999), 43 O.R. (3d) 325 (C.A.).
41   See, for example, *Vachon Construction Ltd. v. Cariboo (Regional District)* (1996), 136 D.L.R. (4th) 307 (B.C.C.A.); *Northeast Marine Services Ltd. v. Atlantic Pilotage Authority,* [1995] 2 F.C. 132 (C.A.).
42   (2000), 193 D.L.R. (4th) 1 (S.C.C.).
43   *Ibid.* at para. 85.

The concept of "fair and equal treatment" does indeed appear to capture the content of the implied term. Thus, in a number of cases, the conduct amounting to the breach of the implied term was the failure to disclose a preference for certain types of contractors, such as local contractors, that might result in unequal treatment of the competing bidders.[44] The requirement of fair and equal treatment also precludes the correction of an invalid bid by a bidder after the close of tenders even, perversely it may be thought, where it is evident that, even without the correction, the bid in question is the lowest bid.[45] It is also a breach of the implied term to evaluate bids on the basis of arbitrary criteria. In *Elite Bailiff Services Ltd. v. British Columbia*,[46] the evaluation scheme used by the defendant province to evaluate bids on a contract to provide court bailiff services applied what was considered to be an arbitrary discount in the points awarded to bidders who had no previous experience in providing court bailiff services. Although the lack of experience was considered to be a relevant criterion, it could not be the subject of an arbitrary discount that precluded a fair evaluation of those bidders who, though they lacked court bailiff experience, had other relevant experience. Unequal application of criteria in the evaluation process would also constitute a breach of the implied term. In *Martel Building Ltd. v. Canada*,[47] for example, the Government defendant unfairly attributed an additional cost related to improvement of the security system in the plaintiff's building solely to the plaintiff and not to other bidders.[48]

Other kinds of terms may be implied in Contract A in order to advance the objective of fair and equal treatment. Thus in *M.J.B. Enterprises Ltd. v. Defence Construction (1951) Ltd.*,[49] the Supreme Court of Canada held that Contract A includes an implied term imposing

---

44 *Tarmac Canada Inc. v. Hamilton-Wentworth (Regional Municipality)*, above note 40; *Chinook Aggregates Ltd. v. Abbotsford (Municipal District)* (1989), 35 C.L.R. 241 (B.C.C.A.); *Kencor Holdings Ltd. v. Saskatchewan*, [1991] 6 W.W.R. 717 (Sask. Q.B.).

45 *Vachon Construction Ltd. v. Cariboo (Regional District)*, above note 41 (discrepancy between the price stated in words and that stated in figures — even though both amounts were lower than the next highest bid, allowing the bidder to correct the bid was a breach of the implied term).

46 (2003), 223 D.L.R. (4th) 39 (B.C.C.A.).

47 Above note 42.

48 Although this attribution of additional costs was held to be a breach of the implied term requiring fair and equal treatment, the breach had not caused the rejection of the plaintiff's bid and, therefore, did not give rise to a damages claim.

49 Above note 9.

an obligation on the inviter not to accept "non-compliant" bids.[50] The defendant Crown corporation had tendered out the construction of a water-pumping distribution system for an Armed Forces base. Under the terms of the invitation, tenderers were exposed to some uncertainty as to which of several types of fill would ultimately be required. Nonetheless, tenderers were obliged to bid a firm price for the project. The lowest tender contained a handwritten note stating that the bid price of the fill could change, depending on which type of fill was ultimately required by the supervising engineer. The defendant accepted this bid, in good faith, on the assumption that the handwritten note contained merely a "clarification" that would be permissible under the tender rules rather than a "qualification" on the price that would render the bid non-compliant. The Supreme Court held that the note constituted a "qualification" and, accordingly, it followed that the lowest bid was non-compliant. Accepting that bid therefore constituted a breach of the implied term requiring rejection of non-compliant bids. On behalf of the Court, Iacobucci J. explained that the implied term rests on the basis that "it is difficult to accept that the appellant, or any of the other contractors, would have submitted a tender unless it was understood by all involved that only a compliant tender would be accepted."[51] Acceptance of the non-compliant bid thus amounted to a breach of contract. The plaintiff, being the second lowest bidder, enjoyed success in its claim for lost profits on the basis that, but for the defendant's breach, it would have been awarded the contract.

In these cases, then, Canadian courts, under the leadership of the Supreme Court of Canada, have engaged in fairly detailed scrutiny of the conduct of tendering processes. In the typical case, the invitation to tenders has been issued by a public authority of one kind or another. Although these interventions by means of terms implied in Contract A have often been justified or explained, in part at least, as involving a requirement that tendering be conducted in good faith, it appears that the better description of the content of the duty imposed is that it requires "fair and equal treatment" of bidders. This is the formulation adopted in the leading case, *Martel Building Limited v. Canada*.[52] Moreover, in cases such as *Elite Bailiff Services Limited* and *M.J.B. En-*

50　An explicit term in the invitation to tender authorizing the issuer to accept non-compliant tenders would preclude the implication of such a term. See *Kinetic Construction Ltd. v. Comox-Strathcona (Regional District)* (2004), 245 D.L.R. (4th) 262 (B.C.C.A.).

51　Above note 9 at para 30.

52　Above note 42.

terprises Ltd., there appears to be no element of bad faith present in the impugned conduct of the defendant parties. In each case, the defendant acted in good faith but failed to understand and apply the nature of the governing obligation to subject bidders to fair and equal treatment. Accordingly, the better explanation of the obligation imposed appears to be that of requiring fair and equal treatment rather than an obligation to conduct tendering processes in good faith.

E. A DUTY TO BARGAIN IN GOOD FAITH IN THE ABSENCE OF A CONTRACT?

Finally, it may be asked whether a duty to bargain in good faith could arise in circumstances where the parties were plainly at the negotiation stage of their relationship. If a duty were to be imposed in such circumstances, of course, it would appear to be tortious rather than contractual in nature. There being no contractual relationship between the parties, the enforcement of a duty to negotiate in good faith would need to find a footing in either some existing tort or in a newly recognized tort of bad-faith bargaining. Unsurprisingly, given the reluctance of common law courts to enforce contractual undertakings to bargain in good faith, the traditional view is that there exists no duty to bargain in good faith as a separate and discrete tort. A more difficult question, however, is the extent to which such a duty might be discovered to be inherent in existing categories of tortious obligation.

The possibility that a duty to bargain in good faith might be grounded in tort law or in a tort-like duty has been the subject of discussion in two recent cases. In the first, *Westcom TV Group Ltd. v. CanWest Global Broadcasting Inc.*,[53] the parties were television networks who were negotiating over the sale of programming, one to the other. The defendant network, which had no right to broadcast in the area in which the plaintiff operated, had negotiated a number of short-term agreements to sell its programs to the plaintiff in the past. The parties successfully negotiated an agreement for a new ten-year agreement but it was plainly understood that the agreement would be subject to the approval of the Chair of the Board of the defendant corporation. Such approval was not forthcoming. The plaintiff alleged that the defendant had never intended to enter into such an agreement but, on the contrary, had determined to apply for its own licence to broadcast within the plaintiff's

---

53   [1997] 1 W.W.R. 761 (B.C.S.C.).

licensed area. It was further alleged that the reason why the defendant was conducting these intentionally fruitless negotiations with the plaintiff was that the defendant had an ulterior motive of wanting to demonstrate to the regulator that it could not negotiate a successful arrangement for selling its programming to a broadcaster in the plaintiff's area of operation. The plaintiff argued that this conduct constituted a breach of duty to negotiate in good faith. The plaintiff conceded that its damages were, at best, nominal but claimed, as well, for exemplary damages in order to prevent what was alleged to be the unjust enrichment of the defendant.

The defendant's application for summary dismissal of the action enjoyed success. Lowry J. quoted from Lord Ackner's comments in *Walford v. Miles*,[54] reproduced above,[55] and suggested that negotiating parties must be permitted some latitude in misrepresenting their intentions. Lowry J. commented as follows:

> Parties involved in arm's length negotiations commonly conceal their true intentions. It is part of the negotiating process that positions are advanced that do not represent what a party truly expects or is prepared to agree to in the end. A party may well say it will pay no more than a stated amount, or agree on no more than a limited term, when in fact it would pay more or agree on a longer term in order to conclude a deal. Intentions are, in that sense, commonly "misrepresented" in the interests of achieving a better bargain in the end.[56]

Noting that Lord Ackner had indicated in *Walford* that a negotiating party must nonetheless avoid making "misrepresentations," Lowry J. went on to observe that "Lord Ackner's reference to misrepresentations could only have meant misrepresentations about the subject of the contract, not about the party's true intentions."[57] This proposition is surely a doubtful one, however, as it is well established in other contexts that a false statement of current intention may constitute misrepresentation.[58] In any event, the judge noted that the relationship of the parties in the present case was punctuated by a history of litigation and of documented lack of trust with respect to the negotiating positions taken by both parties. There were accordingly no reasonable expectations of good-faith bargaining on either side.

---

54   Above note 19.
55   In the text, above note 21.
56   Above note 53 at 766–67.
57   *Ibid.* at 767.
58   See, for example, *Edgington v. Fitzmaurice* (1885), 29 Ch. Div. 459 (C.A.).

The possibility that bargaining in bad faith might constitute the tort of negligence causing economic loss was recently considered by the Supreme Court of Canada in *Martel Building Ltd. v. Canada.*[59] The defendant government agency in this case was the prime tenant of a building owned by the plaintiff. As the end of a ten-year lease approached, the plaintiff began negotiating for a renewal of the lease. The lease itself did not commit the agency to a renewal. Nonetheless, the plaintiff was encouraged by agency officials to believe that if it agreed to a particular rent, renewal would be forthcoming. In due course, the defendant agency put out a call for tenders for leased space and entered into a lease with the lowest bidder. The plaintiff was the second lowest bidder. It was the plaintiff's view, however, that it had been badly treated throughout this process. The trial judge's findings, upheld on appeal, were that the defendant did not pursue negotiations with the plaintiff in a timely fashion, did not make the plaintiff aware of who had authority to commit the agency to a renewal, did not make its negotiating position clear to the plaintiff, did not give the plaintiff enough opportunity to consider the retrofit details required by the agency, did not set a realistic schedule and make the plaintiff aware of it, and did not make timely and pertinent information available concerning the internal agency decision-making process that led to a decision made against the plaintiff's interest. Moreover, the agency's analysis of the plaintiff's bid appeared arbitrary. The plaintiff argued that this conduct caused it to lose the benefits of a ten-year renewal of the lease.

In framing its claim at trial, the plaintiff submitted that the misconduct of the defendant constituted a breach of a tort of failure to negotiate in good faith. It was the trial judge's view, affirmed by the Court of Appeal, that although such a tort had not yet emerged in the case law, the conduct of the defendant did amount to negligence of a kind that could give rise to liability for injuries in the form of economic loss. Although the trial judge was of the view that the plaintiff was unable to establish a causal connection between the defendant's negligence and the injury that occurred, the Court of Appeal overruled her on this point and held that the negligent conduct of the defendant was the main, if not the only, cause of the plaintiff's loss of an opportunity to negotiate the lease renewal.

On further appeal to the Supreme Court of Canada, then, the question before the Court was whether the tort of negligence could extend to economic loss arising out of the conduct of pre-contractual nego-

---

59   Above note 42.

tiations. The Court applied the two-stage *Anns*[60] test, which the Court
has adopted for analyzing questions of this kind. The first stage is to
consider whether there is a sufficiently close relationship between the
parties to establish the requisite degree of "proximity." The Court concluded that the relationship between negotiating parties was such that
it was foreseeable that carelessness on the part of one negotiating party
could cause the other party economic loss and, accordingly, the requisite degree of proximity was present.

The second stage of the *Anns* analysis is to consider whether there
exist any policy considerations that should serve to negate or limit the
scope of the duty of care that might otherwise arise from the relationship of proximity. On this point, the Court concluded that there were
several considerations that compelled the conclusion that negotiating
parties should not be subject to a duty to be "mindful of another commercial party's legitimate interests in an arm's-length negotiation."[61]
Iacobucci and Major JJ., for a unanimous Court, identified a number of
such considerations. First, the very object of negotiation for each party
is to gain at the other party's expense. Negotiation is a zero-sum game,
with the result that, although wealth may be transferred between the
parties, society is not less well off as a result of the transfer. Second,
the extension of a tort duty of care to commercial contractual negotiations could "deter socially and economically useful conduct."[62] It would
"hobble the marketplace to extend a duty of care to the conduct of
negotiations, and to label a party's failure to disclose its bottom line,
its motives or its final position as negligent."[63] Such a duty would unattractively reduce the incentives to engage in due diligence and to ex-
pend resources on research or other information-gathering activities.
Third, the imposition of a tort duty would create "after-the-fact insurance against failures to act with due diligence"[64] and reduce the incentives for self-vigilance. Fourth, the recognition of such a duty would
assign to the courts a "significant regulatory function, scrutinizing the
minutiae of pre-contractual conduct."[65] Other doctrines, such as those
of undue influence, economic duress, unconscionability, negligent mis-

---

60   *Anns v. Merton London Borough Council*, [1978] A.C. 728 (H.L.); *Hercules Man-
     agements Ltd. v. Ernst & Young*, [1997] 2 S.C.R. 165; *B.D.C. Ltd. v. Hofstrand
     Farms Ltd.*, [1986] 1 S.C.R. 228. And see B. Feldthusen, *Economic Negligence:
     The Recovery of Pure Economic Loss*, 4th ed. (Toronto: Carswell, 2000).
61   Above note 42 at para. 55.
62   *Ibid.* at para. 64.
63   *Ibid.* at para. 67.
64   *Ibid.* at para. 68.
65   *Ibid.* at para. 70.

representation and deceit already apply to the negotiation context and it is unnecessary to add further scrutiny to the process by creating an additional cause of action. Finally, the Court offered the view that the recognition of a new tort duty would create needless litigation and encourage a multiplicity of lawsuits. In summary, then, "any *prima facie* duty is significantly outweighed by the deleterious effects that would be occasioned through an extension of a duty of care in the conduct of negotiations."[66]

While the Supreme Court's analysis is focused on the particular question of whether or not careless negotiation ought to be recognized as a new form of tort liability, the analysis of the policy arguments against such recognition might also seem to weigh heavily against the recognition of any other kind of duty to bargain in good faith. The Court further observed, however: "As a final note, we recognize that Martel's claim resembles the assertion of a duty to bargain in good faith. The breach of such a duty was alleged in the Federal Court, but not before this Court. As noted by the courts below, a duty to bargain in good faith has not been recognized to date in Canadian law. These reasons are restricted to whether or not the tort of negligence should be extended to include negotiations. Whether or not negotiations are to be governed by a duty of good faith is a question for another time."[67]

Thus, it remains an interesting and open question whether there are forms of bad-faith bargaining that might be captured by an as yet unrecognized duty to bargain in good faith. Presumably, in order to warrant recognition of a new duty, such conduct would not be covered by the existing causes of action in, for example, undue influence, duress, unconscionability, negligent misstatement and deceit. On the other hand, in order to be consistent with the holding in *Martel*, such conduct could not amount to mere negligence in the course of negotiation. There do appear to be bargaining tactics meeting these criteria that might be referred to as bargaining in bad faith. Conduct such as reneging on a promise given in the course of negotiations,[68] refusal to make reasonable efforts to reach agreement or the breaking off of negotiations in order to accept a more attractive proposal from a third party would appear to be neither covered by the existing causes of action nor mere negligence in the course of negotiations. The existing causes of

---

66   *Ibid.* at para. 72.
67   *Ibid.* at para. 73.
68   Arguably, this problem could be more directly and effectively addressed by a more expansive use of promissory estoppel doctrine rather than by the recognition of a duty to bargain in good faith. See generally Chapter 8.

action deal essentially with matters of fraud, coercion and misinformation. There remains, then, at least the theoretical possibility that a duty to refrain from such other types of bad-faith bargaining may yet be recognized.

In the tendering context,[69] it should be noted, there are some recent and exceptional cases[70] suggesting that even in circumstances where the intention to enter Contract A does not exist, the issuer of the tender call may nonetheless be subject to a duty to treat bidders fairly and equally. Any such obligation would appear to rest on an otherwise as yet unrecognized tort duty to treat bidders fairly and equally. Although these decisions do not provide a clear explanation of the source of this obligation, whether tortious or otherwise, they may be the harbingers of an as yet unrecognized non-contractual duty to bargain in good faith.

F. CONCLUSION

A number of points may be drawn from the foregoing analysis. First, in the context of cases where the parties have not reached agreement on all the essential terms of their agreement, an explicit or implied "agreement to agree" will not serve to fill in the gaps in the agreement. Further, there appears to be little, if any, support in the case law for the notion that such understandings might ground an enforceable duty to bargain in good faith in an attempt to fill the gaps and reach agreement.

In the context of otherwise enforceable agreements, however, where the "agreement to agree" appears, for example, in an option to renew, somewhat more support can be found for the notion that a provision of this kind creates a basis for implying obligations to bargain in good faith. Two caveats, however, should be added to this observation. First, the *Mannpar*[71] decision suggests that a good-faith obligation will be implied only where the option to renew sets forth an objective standard, such as "market rental," toward which the parties are to negotiate. Second, to the extent that the imposition of good-faith obligations has the

---

69   See above this Chapter, section D.

70   *Mellco Developments Ltd. v. Portage La Prairie (City)* (2002), 222 D.L.R. (4th) 67 (Man. C.A.); *Buttcon Ltd. v. Toronto Electric Commissioners* (2003), 65 O.R. (3d) 601 (S.C.J.). These cases narrowly restrict the *Ron Engineering* analysis by distinguishing the "requests for proposals" or "RFPs" at issue in these cases from "tender calls," which are said to be subject to *Ron Engineering* and, at the same time, retain the duty to treat bidders fairly and equally without providing any clear foundation for it either in contract or tort. See Chapter 4, section B(2).

71   Above note 29. Compare with *Hargreaves v. Fleming*, above note 36.

effect of imposing a duty to agree to a reasonable term, it may be asked whether the implication of good-faith obligations is consistent with the apparent requirement of such provisions that the parties genuinely agree to the new term. In any event, it is perhaps not surprising that where there is an existing and otherwise enforceable contractual relationship, the jurisprudence appears to lean more in the direction of enforceability than it does in the context of cases where the parties have failed to reach an original agreement. Where there is an ongoing enforceable agreement, a decision that has the effect of depriving one of the parties of the benefit of an option to renew, for example, may deprive that party of something for which it has in some sense paid and on which it may well have detrimentally relied.

In the tendering cases, Canadian courts have engaged in a fairly detailed scrutiny of the conduct of tendering processes with a view to ensuring fair and equal treatment of bidders. The doctrinal basis for such scrutiny, as we have seen, is the implication of implied terms in a contract entered into by the person who extends an invitation to tender—this constituting an offer—and the submission of the bids that constitutes acceptance of that offer. Although the implied term has often been justified or linked to a notion of good faith by Canadian judges, a more precise description of the nature of the duty imposed is that the implied term requires those conducting tendering processes to treat all bidders "fairly and equally." It is this articulation of the implied term that has received the approval of the Supreme Court of Canada in the leading case of *Martel Building Limited v. Canada*.[72]

Finally, the prospects for the recognition of a duty to bargain in good faith in the absence of a pre-existing contractual relationship do not appear to be promising. As we have seen, the Supreme Court of Canada, in *Martel Building Limited v. Canada*,[73] has firmly rejected the possibility of extending the tort of negligence into the sphere of economic loss arising from the conduct of pre-contractual negotiations. In the course of justifying that decision, the reasons advanced by the Court strongly suggest that the recognition of a duty of good-faith bargaining that would involve the courts in careful examination of the conduct of contractual negotiations is unlikely. Nonetheless, the possibility remains that conduct that falls short of the existing causes of action in duress, undue influence, unconscionability, deceit and negligent misstatement, but does not amount to negligence giving rise to economic loss, could be the subject of an as yet unrecognized duty

---

72   Above note 42.
73   *Ibid.*

to bargain in good faith. The more likely development, to be further explored in the context of a more general discussion of misrepresentation,[74] is that Canadian courts might rely on the concept of bargaining in good faith as the basis for expanding duties of disclosure in the bargaining context by recognizing non-disclosure, in an expanded range of circumstances, to constitute misrepresentation. As we shall see, this is the path that has been adopted by the American courts and that has recently been suggested to be appropriate by a Canadian provincial appellate court.[75]

FURTHER READINGS

R. BROWNSWORD, N.J. HIRD & G. HOWELLS, eds., *Good Faith in Contract: Concept and Context* (Brookfield: Ashgate, 1999).

J.W. CARTER & M. FURMSTON, "Good Faith and Fairness in the Negotiation of Contracts" (1994–95) 8 J.C.L. 1.

J. CASSELS, "Good Faith in Contract Bargaining: General Principles and Recent Developments" (1993) 15 Advocates' Q. 56.

N. COHEN, "Pre-Contractual Duties: Two Freedoms and the Contract to Negotiate" in J. Beatson & D. Friedmann, *Good Faith and Fault in Contract Law* (Oxford: Clarendon Press, 1995) c. 2.

E.A. FARNSWORTH, "Precontractual Liability and Preliminary Agreements: Fair Dealing and Failed Negotiations" (1987) 87 Colum. L. Rev. 217.

P. FINN, "Commerce, the Common Law and Morality" (1989) 17 Melbourne U.L. Rev. 87.

M. FURMSTON, T. NORISADA & J. POOLE, *Contract Formation and Letters of Intent* (Chichester: Wiley & Sons, 1998) c. 10.

E.H. HONDIUS, ed., *Pre-Contractual Liability* (Deventer: Kluwer, 1991).

F. KESSLER & E. FINE, "'Culpa in Contrahendo': Bargaining in Good Faith and Freedom of Contract: A Comparative Study" (1964) 77 Harv. L. Rev. 401.

---

74   See Chapter 10, section D.
75   See *Shelanu v. Print Three Franchising Corp.* (2003), 226 D.L.R. (4th) 577 (Ont. C.A.); compare with *Peel Condominium Corp. No. 505 v. Cam-Valley Homes Ltd.* (2001), 53 O.R. (3d) 1 (C.A.) (rejecting existence of duty to bargain in good faith).

C.L. KNAPP, "Enforcing the Contract to Bargain" (1969) 44 N.Y.U.L. Rev. 673.

J.P. KOSTRITSKY, "Bargaining with Uncertainty: A Default Rule for Pre-contractual Negotiations" (1993) 44 Hastings L.J. 621.

D.W. MCLAUGHLAN, "The Justiciability of an Agreement to Negotiate in Good Faith" (2003) 20 N.Z.U.L. Rev. 265.

J. PATERSON, "The Contract to Negotiate in Good Faith: Recognition and Enforcement" (1996) 10 J.C.L. 120.

S.M. WADDAMS, "Pre-Contractual Duties of Disclosure" in P. Cane and J. Stapleton, eds., *Essays for Patrick Atiyah* (Oxford: Clarendon Press, 1991) c. 10.

R. ZIMMERMAN & S. WHITTAKER, eds., *Good Faith in European Contract Law* (Cambridge: Cambridge University Press, 2000).

AGREEMENTS IN WRITING

A. INTRODUCTION

In a much earlier era, the common law enforced only undertakings recorded in writing and executed under seal. Such undertakings could be
enforced in medieval law in an action in *covenant*.[1] With the recognition of other kinds of claims, in particular, the action in *assumpsit*,[2] the
common law developed the capacity to enforce a much broader range
of types of undertakings, including those that were merely oral or informal. In the modern era, then, the common law enforces agreements
in writing, whether or not under seal,[3] oral agreements and agreements
that are partly oral and partly in writing. In this chapter, we consider
various doctrines relating to the formation of written agreements. First,
we examine the doctrine requiring certain agreements to be recorded
in writing and, typically, signed by the party against whom the agreement is to be enforced. Although the common law no longer requires
that agreements must be recorded in writing in order to be enforceable, there are a number of statutory schemes that require that certain
types of agreements be written in form. The most important source of

---

1   See A.W.B. Simpson, *A History of the Common Law of Contract* (Oxford: Claren-
    don Press, 1975) Part I, c. I.
2   *Ibid*.
3   As we shall see, the seal retains an important role in determining the enforce-
    ability of undertakings in some circumstances. See Chapter 7.

these rules is the English *Statute of Frauds* of 1677[4] and, from a Canadian perspective, its progeny in the common law provinces. Additionally, however, there are a number of other statutes, typically of a consumer protection nature, that require that certain types of agreements must be created in the form of a written document in order to be enforceable.

Quite apart from a legislative requirement that certain types of agreements be recorded in writing, it will, of course, often meet the convenience of one or both parties to record the terms of an agreement in writing. Where the parties have a common intention to do so, their contractual relationship will normally be constituted by the written agreement. In many circumstances, however, a written document will be furnished by one party to the other in the course of negotiating or concluding an agreement and the question may then arise as to whether terms set out in the written document are incorporated within the agreement between the parties. The jurisprudence relating to the incorporation of written terms in the agreement between the parties is the second aspect of the law relating to agreements in writing considered in this chapter.

Finally, once it is determined that a writing has been incorporated into a particular agreement, it may then be asked whether the written document should form the exclusive source of the terms of the contractual relationship between the parties. This question becomes a particularly interesting one where the parties have entered into an agreement that appears, on its face, to set out a complete set of terms with respect to the subject matter of the agreement but one of the parties has been induced to enter the agreement by a prior oral undertaking given by the other party. The common law's solution to problems of this kind, the parol evidence rule, remains a controversial one. It is the third topic examined in this chapter.

B. AGREEMENTS REQUIRED TO BE IN WRITING: THE *STATUTE OF FRAUDS*

1) Introduction

Originally titled *An Act for the Prevention of Frauds and Perjuries*, the basic purpose of the *Statute of Frauds* was to reduce the prospects for success of perjured testimony under the procedural rules in place at the time of its enactment. The basic strategy of the statute was to require

---

4   1677, 29 Car. II, c. 3.

that certain types of agreements be recorded in writing and signed by the person against whom they would be enforced in order to provide a strong evidentiary basis for a finding that such an undertaking was actually given. Section 4 of the 1677 legislation provided as follows:

> [N]o Action shall be brought whereby to charge any Executor or Administrator upon any special Promise, to answer Damages out of his own Estate or whereby to charge the Defendant upon any special Promise to answer for the Debt, Default or Miscarriages of another Person or to charge any Person upon any Agreement made upon Consideration of Marriage or upon any Contract or Sale of Lands, Tenements or Hereditaments, or any Interest in or concerning them or upon any Agreement that is not to be performed within the Space of one Year from the making thereof unless the Agreement upon which such Action shall be brought, or some Memorandum or Note thereof, shall be in writing, and signed by the Party to be charged therewith, or some other Person thereunto by him lawfully authorized.[5]

In section 17 of the statute, similar requirements were imposed on contracts for the sale of goods, wares and merchandise for the price of £10 and more.[6] Other provisions of the statute apply to certain kinds of arrangements concerning trusts. Two further categories were added to the statute by Lord Tenterden's Act[7] in the early-nineteenth century. The first category concerned undertakings by adults to ratify otherwise unenforceable contracts entered into during infancy.[8] The second category consisted of misrepresentations as to credit worthiness for which the representor was to be held liable.[9] The latter provision was added in order to avoid circumvention of the writing requirement concerning guarantees. It precluded actions against oral guarantors based on the

---

5   *Ibid.*, s. 4.
6   *Ibid.*, s. 17. The treatment of informal contracts for the sale of goods under section 17 is slightly different from the section 4 scheme. Section 17 permits enforcement if the buyer has accepted part of the goods or provides partial payment or a deposit. Otherwise a note or memorandum of the agreement signed by the party to be charged is required. The provision migrated to the sale of goods legislation in many jurisdictions, including England and the Canadian common law provinces, the threshold amount typically being set at $40.00. The provision is not in accord with the expectations of many parties and has been repealed in several provinces. See *Statute Law Amendment Act*, S.B.C. 1958, c. 52, s. 17; *An Act to Repeal the Statute of Frauds*, S.M. 1982–83–84, c. 34, s. 27; *Statute Law Amendment Act (Governmental Management and Services)*, S.O. 1994, c. 27, s. 54.
7   *Statute of Frauds Amendment Act*, 1828, 9 Geo. 4, c. 14 (U.K.) ss. 5–6.
8   See now, for example, *Statute of Frauds*, R.S.O. 1990, c. S.19, s. 7.
9   *Ibid.*, s. 8.

theory that the oral guarantee could alternatively be considered to be a representation concerning the creditworthiness of the debtor.[10] In due course, the English statute came into force in other Commonwealth jurisdictions, including the common law provinces of Canada.[11]

Over the centuries since its initial enactment, the statute has been subject to criticism on various grounds. The statute itself is very much the product of its legal and social environment in early Reformation England.[12] The statute was a reaction to the perception that with the evolution of the action in *assumpsit* in the late-sixteenth and early-seventeenth centuries, which provided a device for the enforcement of informal contracts, the procedural pendulum had swung too far in the direction of permitting spurious allegations of the existence of informal agreements to enjoy success.[13] Opportunities for this form of fraud were exacerbated by the procedural rules of the time. Thus, the parties to a particular claim and their spouses were not competent witnesses in a proceeding. Accordingly, the alleged promisor would not have an opportunity to deny personally an allegation that an oral undertaking had been given. Further, although the action in *assumpsit* brought with it the significant procedural improvement of trial by jury rather than by more archaic means, trial by jury in that era had not evolved into a modern system of fact-finding. Jurors were members of the local community, who might have knowledge of the events in question, rather than dispassionate adjudicators of the facts. Legal historians report that perjury and subornation of witnesses were commonplace at the time and that there was a perception that the citizenry was particularly litigious.[14] In

---

10   It is now clearly established that the provision applies only to fraudulent misrepresentations and would not preclude an action for negligent misrepresentations of this kind. See *Banbury v. Bank of Montreal*, [1918] A.C. 626 (H.L.); *Hedley Byrne & Co. Ltd. v. Heller & Partners Ltd.*, [1964] A.C. 465 (H.L.).

11   The statute came into force in the Canadian common law provinces by reception of English law. See J.E. Côté, "The Introduction of English Law Into Alberta" (1964) 3 Alta. L. Rev. 262. Some provinces enacted similar legislation. See, for example, *Statute of Frauds*, R.S.B.C. 1979, c. 393 (repealed 1985, c. 10, section 8); R.S.N.B. 1973, c. S-14; R.S.N.S. 1989, c. 442; R.S.O. 1990, c. S.19; R.S.P.E.I. 1988, c. S-6.

12   See generally C.D. Hening, "The Original Drafts of the Statute of Frauds (29 Car. II c. 3) and Their Authors" (1913) 61 U. Pa. L. Rev. 283; E. Rabel, "The Statute of Frauds and Comparative Legal History" (1947), 63 Law Q. Rev. 174; A.W.B. Simpson, *A History of the Common Law of Contract* (Oxford: Clarendon Press, 1975) Part II, c. XIII.

13   See Simpson, *ibid*. See also S.J. Stoljar, *A History of Contract at Common Law* (Canberra: Australian National University Press, 1975).

14   See Simpson, *ibid*.

such an environment, then, there were significant opportunities for the making of fraudulent claims. It is understandable that legislators of that time held the view that the enactment of legislation, requiring certain important types of transactions to be recorded in writing and signed by the potential defendant, would improve the administration of justice. As circumstances and procedural rules changed over time, however, the underlying rationale of the statute lost much of its force. Moreover, the scheme of the statute itself facilitated yet another kind of fraud. If a person induced another to transfer value such as money in return for an oral undertaking to transfer, for example, an interest in land, the money would have been transferred in return for an unenforceable undertaking. In such circumstances, the party giving the oral undertaking might be considered to be unjustly enriched as a result of fraudulent conduct.

The growth of dissatisfaction with the effect of the statute over time led to two different types of developments that can receive only brief treatment within the confines of the present volume. First, the statute became encrusted with an elaborate and intricate body of doctrine confining the scope of the provisions of the statute and, further, providing alternative avenues for relief where the statute had the unavoidable effect of rendering a particular undertaking unenforceable. Second, in the modern era, the *Statute of Frauds* attracted the scrutiny of various law reform agencies[15] throughout the British Commonwealth and, in turn, legislative reform or repeal.[16] On the other hand, of course, requirements of formality in the context of certain transactions may have a contemporary justification. Thus, a requirement of formality may have the beneficial effect of signalling to the party giving the undertaking that it is legally enforceable and therefore requires due deliberation.[17]

---

15   See, for example, Law Revision Committee, *Sixth Interim Report (Statute of Frauds and the Doctrine of Consideration)* Cmnd 5449 (London: HMSO, 1937); Law Reform Commission of British Columbia, *Report on the Statute of Frauds* (Vancouver: The Commission, 1977); Manitoba Law Reform Commission, *Report on the Statute of Frauds* (Winnipeg: The Commission, 1980); Institute of Law Research and Reform, *The Statute of Frauds and Related Legislation* (Edmonton: The Institute, 1985); Ontario Law Reform Commission, *Report on Amendment on the Law of Contract* (Toronto: The Commission, 1987).

16   See, for example, *Law Reform (Enforcement of Contracts) Act, 1954* (U.K.) 1954, c. 34 (modification of the statute); *Statute of Frauds, 1958*, S.B.C. 1958, c. 18 (modification); *Law Reform Amendment Act*, S.B.C. 1985, c. 10, s. 8 (repeal); *An Act to Repeal the Statute of Frauds*, S.M. 1982-83-84, c. 34 (repeal).

17   Fuller has described this as the "cautionary" effect of formality. See L. Fuller, "Consideration and Form" (1941) 41 Colum. L. Rev. 799. For discussion of the role of formality as a basis for the recognition of the enforceability of undertakings, and of Fuller's views in particular, see Chapter 7.

Further, there are particular situations in which an argument can be made for the need for a written record either because of concerns about the possibility of perjured testimony or the desirability of creating and preserving a written record of the transaction in order to facilitate the operation of registration systems as, for example, in the case of transactions concerning land. Thus, in jurisdictions that have substantially reformed the statute, formality requirements have typically been preserved with respect to guarantees and transactions in land.[18]

2) Undertakings Subject to Section 4 of the Statute

a) Promises to Answer for the Debt, Default or Miscarriages of Another Person

This provision applies to undertakings given to a third party to guarantee the performance of an existing obligation of another person to that third party. The obligation may take the form of a *debt*, that is, an existing obligation to pay money, a *default*, that is, a future obligation to pay money or liability for a *miscarriage*, that is, tortious wrongdoing. In identifying the existence of a guarantee, the critical point is that the guarantee must be a secondary form of liability in the sense that it secures the obligation of another person who has a primary liability to the third party. The guarantor's liability is contingent upon the principal debtor's failure to discharge the obligation to repay the money to the third-party creditor. A guarantee can thus be distinguished from a contract of indemnity under which a primary obligation is undertaken. Thus, if A promises a landlord, B, that A will insure that all rental payments due to B under a lease to C will be paid by A, the liability of A to B is "direct" or "original" and may be enforceable even if, for some reason, C's obligation to pay the rent may no longer be enforceable against C.[19] In particular types of fact situations, however, the distinc-

---

18   See, for example, *Law and Equity Act*, R.S.B.C. 1966, c. 253, s. 59; *Law of Property (Miscellaneous Provisions) Act 1989*, (U.K.) 1989, c. 34.

19   Thus, until the recent decision of the Supreme Court of Canada in *Crystalline Investments v. Domgroup Ltd.*, 2004 SCC 3, the line of authority beginning with *Cummer-Yonge Investments Ltd. v. Fagot*, [1965] 2 O.R. 157n (C.A.), aff'g [1965] 2 O.R. 152 (H.C.J.), which applied in circumstances where a tenant had become insolvent, with resulting discharge of its liability under the lease, the question of whether A remained liable for the lease payments turned on whether the undertaking given by A amounted to a guarantee only in which the liability, being only secondary liability, fell away with the tenant's liability or, on the other hand, an indemnity, in which case A remained liable on its direct undertaking to the landlord B. A substantial body of jurisprudence plumbed the

tion between guarantees and indemnities may be very subtle.[20] Accordingly, in 1958,[21] the British Columbia statute was reformed to include indemnities within the writing requirements. In the absence of such reforms, however, if the undertaking is properly characterized as an indemnity, it falls outside the statute and may be enforceable even though not in writing.

Guarantees may be excluded from the statute in two further situations in which guarantees may be characterized as mere incidents of a larger contractual relationship. First, a *del credere* agent is one who for an additional commission agrees to guarantee the performance and solvency of the purchaser. It has been held in this context that the guarantee is part of a larger relationship of principal and agent and therefore not subject to the statutory requirements.[22] The second is where a guarantee is given in the context of a larger transaction in order to protect the proprietary interests of the guarantor in an asset. In such a case, the guarantee may be held to be merely incidental to that larger transaction and therefore outside the statute. Thus, in *Fitzgerald v. Dressler*[23] where A sold goods to B who, in turn, resold them to C, A had retained possession of the goods and a lien over them to insure payment of the price by B. C guaranteed B's payment of the price in order to encourage release of the goods by A to C. C's guarantee was held to fall outside the statute.

Notwithstanding the obstacles to clear identification of those guarantees that are subject to the statute, it appears unlikely that the formality requirements for guarantees will disappear. Guarantees are often given in family and commercial settings where the guarantor may be under some moral or commercial pressure to give the guarantee.

---

distinction between guarantees and indemnities in this context. In *Crystalline Investments*, however, the Supreme Court overruled *Cummer-Yonge* and held that even a guarantee would remain binding upon A in the event of of C's discharge through the application of insolvency principles.

20 Contrast *Beattie v. Dinnick* (1896), 27 O.R. 285 (Q.B.) (oral assurance by president that company would discharge its obligations under a promissory note — unenforceable guarantee) with *Active Customs Brokers Limited Ltd. v. Sack* (1987), 25 O.A.C. 305 (Div. Ct.) (oral guarantee of company debt by president and owner of company — held, in essence, a promise to pay owner's debt — not covered by the *statute*). See also *Sarbit v. Hanson & Booth Fisheries (Canada) Co.,* [1950] 2 W.W.R. 545 (Man. K.B.) (guarantor has interest in debtor — direct not dependent obligation — not covered by statute), rev'd on other grounds (1950), 1 W.W.R. (N.S.) 115 (Man. C.A.).

21 *Statute of Frauds, 1958*, S.B.C. 1958, c. 18, s. 5.

22 See, for example, *Couturier v. Hastie* (1852), 8 Exch. 40, 155 E.R. 1250, rev'd on other grounds [1843–60] All E.R. Rep. 280.

23 (1859), 7 C.B. (N.S.) 374, 141 E.R. 861.

Guarantees may, of course, impose ruinous liability. Accordingly, the cautionary effect of executing guarantees in writing is rather likely to be preserved. Indeed, in Alberta, the requirements have been strengthened by requiring that guarantees be executed in the presence of a notary public who must certify that the guarantor understands the content of the guarantee.[24]

b) Promises Made upon Consideration of Marriage

Initially, it was assumed that this provision included agreements to marry.[25] In due course, however, it was settled that this was not the case and that the provision extended, essentially, only to marriage settlements, that is, promises to settle property on an intended spouse in return for the promise to marry. Law reform bodies typically view this provision as anachronistic in the sense that the making of marriage settlements does not appear to be a feature of contemporary Canadian social life. The provision has been repealed in Ontario,[26] where, however, the provision has, in effect, been replaced by legislation requiring that, in order to be enforceable, domestic agreements, including marriage contracts, co-habitation agreements and separation agreements must be recorded in writing and signed, in the presence of a witness, by the party against whom the agreement is to be enforced.[27]

c) Promise by an Executor or Administrator to Answer Damages out of His or Her Own Estate

This provision also has an archaic flavour and no longer appears warranted in the context of contemporary law concerning the administration of estates. At the time of the statute, the executor or administrator was entitled to the residuum of the estate in the absence of residuary gift in the will. This feature of then contemporary law, together with the proposition that the estate was typically not liable for the wrongful acts of the deceased, placed a certain amount of moral pressure on the executor or the administrator to give personal undertakings to grant compensation to parties suffering injury at the hands of the deceased. Under contemporary law, the executor or administrator has no entitlement to the residuum of the estate and, accordingly, such undertakings

---

24 See *Guarantees Acknowledgment Act*, R.S.A. 2000, c. G-11. For discussion, see Institute of Law Research and Reform, above note 15 at 33–45.

25 See *Philpott v. Wallet* (1682), 3 Lev. 65, 83 E.R. 579.

26 *Family Law Reform Act, 1978*, S.O. 1978 c. 2, s. 88.

27 *Family Law Act*, R.S.O. 1990, c. F.3, s. 51, as amended. For discussion of domestic agreements, see Chapter 4, section C.

are, presumably, quite rare. Law reform agencies tend to dismiss this provision as anachronistic and recommend its repeal. The provision has been repealed in some provinces.[28]

d) Agreements Not to Be Performed within One Year

The requirement that agreements not to be performed within the space of one year must be in writing appears to be based on the assumption that it would be unwise to "trust to the memory of witnesses for a longer time than one year."[29] Plainly, however, the provision is not well aligned with this rationale. The provision does not preclude reliance upon testimony concerning oral contracts at a greater distance than one year from their making. Rather, it subjects contracts of a certain class — those to be performed in more than one year — to a writing requirement. Testimony concerning an oral agreement to be performed within a shorter period of time would be admissible several years later, provided that the action to enforce was brought within the applicable limitations period.[30] Moreover, the provision appears to create rather arbitrary distinctions between agreements that are subject to the writing requirement and those that are not. Thus, an agreement of indefinite duration that could be performed within a year is not covered by the statute, even if the performance is likely to take a longer time.[31] On the other hand, an agreement that stipulates a specified period of performance of more than one year is caught by the provision even though the contract also stipulates that the contract may be terminated within that period of time.[32] Similarly, the distinction between a contract to be performed for a year, commencing the day after formation of the contract, and an agreement to be performed for a year commencing two days after formation appears artificial. The former is not within the provision as account is not taken of parts of a day with the result that the contract is to be performed within a year.[33] The latter agreement,

28 See, for example, *Statute of Frauds, 1958,* S.B.C. 1958, c. 18, s. 7; *An Act to Repeal the Statute of Frauds,* S.M. 1982–83–84, c. 34.

29 *Smith v. Westhall* (1697), 1 Ld. Raym. 316.

30 For criticism of the provision on this ground, see the English Law Revision Committee, above note 15 at 9–10.

31 See *McGregor v. McGregor* (1888), 21 Q.B.D. 424; *Adams v. Union Cinemas Ltd.,* [1939] 3 All E.R. 136 (C.A.); *Quance v. Brown* (1926), 58 O.L.R. 578, [1926] 2 D.L.R. 824 (App. Div.).

32 *Hanau v. Ehrlich,* [1912] A.C. 39 (H.L.). See also *Sherman v. Monarch Chrome Furniture Co. Ltd.* (1958), 15 D.L.R. (2d) 6 (Ont. C.A.).

33 *Smith v. Gold Coast and Ashanti Explorers Ltd.,* [1903] 1 K.B. 285, aff'd [1903] 1 K.B. 538 (C.A.).

however, is caught by the statute as it cannot be performed within a year, even if the second day is a Sunday.[34] As a result of these kinds of difficulties, law reform agencies typically recommend repeal of the provision and a few Canadian provinces have done so.[35]

e)   Contracts for the Sale of Any Interest in Land

This requirement has also spawned a series of difficult points of interpretation. A cluster of issues relates to the definition of land and more particularly, to the distinction between land and goods. Difficult distinctions are required to be drawn concerning such items as agricultural crops, the natural produce of land such as timber, rights to remove oil and gas and minerals and manufactured products attached to the land that may or may not constitute "fixtures." These difficulties are not explored here because they require an *excursus* into aspects of the law of real property and sale of goods that are beyond the scope of the present work.[36] The wording of the original English statute — any contract or sale of lands, tenements or hereditaments, or any interest in or concerning them — is in force in some provinces[37] and has been a source of further complexity. The use of the disjunctive "or" between "contract" and "sale" may be thought to suggest that the provision applies to both conveyances and agreements for the sale of interests in land. Conveyances, however, appear to be dealt with in other provisions of the statute[38] and, accordingly, it is generally assumed that "or" should be interpreted as "for." The specific mention of "tenements or hereditaments" appears to be superfluous as these would plainly constitute interests in land and, again, it is generally so assumed. Some agreements that might be thought to have the effect of transferring an interest in land have been held to fall outside the statute on the ground that the agreement in question is collateral. Thus, where a contract provided for the sale of property to the purchaser and further provided that the vendor would re-sell the property on the purchaser's behalf, it was held that the latter obligation was collateral and independent of

---

34   *Britain v. Rossiter* (1879), 11 Q.B.D. 123 (C.A.).

35   See, for example, *Law Reform Amendment Act*, S.B.C. 1985, c. 10, s. 8; *Statute Law Amendment Act (Government Management and Services), 1994*, S.O. 1994, c. 27, s. 55.

36   See, for example, M. Bridge, "The Statute of Frauds and Sale of Land Contracts" (1986) 64 Can. Bar Rev. 58. These matters are treated at varying degrees of length in the law reform commission reports referred to above note 15 and in the standard treatises on property law and sale of goods.

37   See, for example, *Statute of Frauds*, R.S.O. 1990, c. S.19, s. 4.

38   In Ontario, see *ibid.*, s. 1.

the contract to sell the land and, accordingly, fell outside the statute.[39] Considered in its own terms, the agreement to sell on the defendant's behalf was not an agreement for sale and therefore not subject to the legislation. It has also been held that agreements to divide the proceeds of a sale of land,[40] royalty agreements concerning oil extracted from the land[41] and sales of partnership assets, even though the assets include land, do not come within the statutory writing requirement.[42]

3) The Section 4 Formalities and the Effect of Non-compliance

Section 4 provides that "no action shall be brought … unless the agreement upon which such action shall be brought, or some memorandum or note thereof, is in writing and signed by the party to be charged therewith or some person thereunto by him lawfully authorized."[43] An extensive body of jurisprudence has built up over the centuries interpreting virtually every aspect of this requirement. The general effect of the doctrine is to interpret the requirement in a liberal fashion that favours compliance. Thus, the "memorandum or note thereof," which is an alternative to the provision of a written agreement, is not required to be in any particular form. For example, the "memorandum" may be constituted by correspondence,[44] a will[45] or a receipt.[46] The document need not be prepared with the intention of either creating the agreement or complying with the statute. A memorandum made for internal purposes by a firm will suffice.[47] Further, Canadian courts have held that a document repudiating the existence of the transaction may constitute a sufficient memorandum of the agreement.[48] If the document itself indicates that both parties understand that they have not reached

---

39   *Canadian General Securities Co. v. George* (1918), 43 D.L.R. 20, rev'd on other grounds (1919), 59 S.C.R. 641.

40   *Stuart v. Mott* (1894), 23 S.C.R. 384; *Harris v. Lindeborg*, [1931] S.C.R. 235. Compare with *Cooper v. Critchley*, [1955] 1 All E.R. 520 at 524, Jenkins L.J.

41   *Emerald Resources Ltd. v. Sterling Oil Properties Management Ltd.* (1969), 3 D.L.R. (3d) 630 (Alta. S.C.A.D.), aff'd (1971), 15 D.L.R. (3d) 256 (S.C.C.).

42   *Archibald v. McNerhanie* (1899), 29 S.C.R. 564.

43   Above note 5.

44   *Thirkell v. Cambi*, [1919] 2 K.B. 590.

45   *Re Hoyle*, [1893] 1 Ch. 84.

46   *Knight v. Cushing* (1912), 1 D.L.R. 331 (Alta. S.C.).

47   See, for example, *Moojelsky v. Rexnord Canada* (1989), 96 A.R. 91 (Q.B.).

48   See, for example, *Martin v. Haubner* (1896), 26 S.C.R. 142; *Adam v. General Paper Co. Ltd.* (1978), 85 D.L.R. (3d) 736 (Ont. H.C.J.).

an agreement, as where the agreement is stipulated to be "subject to contract,"[49] it appears unlikely that the memorandum would be sufficient. Certainly, English courts have held that memoranda indicating an interim agreement that is "subject to contract" will not be sufficient for purposes of this statute.[50] To the extent that the reasoning in such cases insists that the memorandum must include an "admission of the existence of the agreement,"[51] however, the reasoning would appear to be inconsistent with Canadian doctrine. As the repudiation cases indicate, there is no such requirement in Canadian law as a matter of general principle.

The statute has not been interpreted as requiring that the memorandum be created contemporaneously with the formation of the agreement. Relying on the phrase "no action shall be brought," some courts have held that the writing must come into existence, however, prior to the commencement of the action.[52] On the other hand, at least one authority[53] has held that where the written record of the agreement appears in the defendant's pleadings for the first time, the plaintiff might successfully commence a new action on the basis of that written record of the agreement. Further, courts have indicated a willingness to permit a joinder of two documents where neither document contains the whole of the agreement between the parties. Although it was initially assumed that a joinder could occur only where one document expressly referred to the other,[54] it came to be accepted that parol evidence could be given to establish the connection between two documents where the connection between them, though not express, is a matter of fair inference, but not to connect two unrelated documents.[55]

The requirement that the doctrine bear the signature of the party to be charged has also been liberally construed. Thus, initials will suffice[56] as will a hand-printed name as opposed to a written signature.[57] Indeed, the printed name of a firm at the top of a standard form document such

---

49 For discussion of agreements "subject to contract," see Chapter 4, section B(4).
50 *Tiverton Estates Ltd. v. Wearwell Ltd.*, [1975] Ch. 146 (C.A.).
51 See *ibid.* at 157, Lord Denning M.R.
52 *Lucas v. Dixon* (1889), 22 Q.B.D. 357 (C.A.); *McIntyre v. Spiernburg* (1979), 41 N.S.R. (2d) 584 (S.C.T.D.).
53 *Hardy v. Elphick*, [1974] Ch. 65 (C.A.).
54 *Boydell v. Drummond* (1809), 11 East. 142.
55 See, for example, *Doran v. McKinnon* (1916), 53 S.C.R. 609; *Harvie v. Gibbons* (1980), 109 D.L.R. (3d) 559 (Alta. C.A.). Compare with *Canadian Imperial Bank of Commerce v. Titus* (1980), 110 D.L.R. (3d) 219 (Ont. H.C.J.).
56 *Chichester v. Cobb* (1866), 14 L.T. 433.
57 See above note 47.

as an invoice has been held to meet the requirement of a signature.[58] The
signature need not appear at the foot of the document,[59] provided, however, that the signature authenticates the entire document.[60] As section 4
indicates, the signature may be affixed by a "lawfully authorized" agent.
The section does not require that the appointment of the agent be accomplished in a document that complies with section 4.[61] The agent may sign
in the name of the principal or of the agent.[62]

As far as the contents of the memorandum are concerned, although
it has occasionally been suggested that all the terms of the agreement
must be recorded in the memorandum,[63] it is well established that it is
sufficient if all the material or essential terms are recorded in the document.[64] In a contract for the purchase and sale of land, for example, it
has been held that the essential terms are "the parties, the property and
the price."[65] In the context of a leasehold agreement, the date of commencement of the term has been held to be an essential matter.[66] In a
contract of employment of definite duration, a document that failed to
mention the duration of the contract would not meet the requirements
of section 4.[67]

Where a particular term recorded in the memorandum is incomplete or obscure in its meaning, parol evidence may be admitted to
clarify the meaning of the term. Such evidence may be admitted to
identify one of the parties to the agreement. Thus, in the case where
one party was identified only by the phrase, "in consideration of you
having this day paid me the sum of £50," evidence of the identity of

---

58   *Schneider v. Norris* (1814), 2 M. & S. 287.
59   *Durrell v. Evans* (1862), 1 H. & C. 174, 158 E.R. 848; *Evans v. Hoare*, [1892] 1
     Q.B. 593; *Swim v. Amos* (1895), 33 N.B.R. 49 (C.A.).
60   *Caton v. Caton* (1867), L.R. 2 H.L. 127 (H.L.).
61   *Coles v. Trecothick* (1804), 9 Ves. 234 (Ch.); *Standard Realty Co. v. Nicholson*
     (1911), 24 O.L.R. 46 (H.C.).
62   *Graham v. Mosson* (1839), 5 Bing (N.C.) 603.
63   See, for example, *Rogers v. Hewer* (1912), 3 W.W.R. 477 (Alta. C.A.); *Saperstein v.
     Drury*, [1943] 3 W.W.R. 193 (B.C.C.A.), aff'd [1944] S.C.R. 148.
64   *McKenzie v. Walsh* (1921), 61 S.C.R. 312. And see, for example, *Smith v. Spencer*
     (1918), 42 D.L.R. 269 (Sask. C.A.).
65   *McKenzie v. Walsh*, ibid. at 313 (in the particular circumstances, the date of
     completion of the transaction was a matter of convenience only and not an es-
     sential term). And see *Chapman v. Kopitoski*, [1972] 6 W.W.R. 525 (Sask. Q.B.)
     (agreement to pay arrears of taxes is part of the price and must therefore be
     recorded).
66   *Mitchell v. Mortgage Company of Canada*, [1919] 3 W.W.R. 324 (S.C.C.).
67   *Ackerman v. Thomson & McKinnon, Auchincloss, Kohlmeyer, Inc.* (1974), 4 O.R.
     (2d) 240 (C.A.).

the person who paid the money was admitted.[68] In another case, parol evidence was admitted to identify the "proprietor" mentioned in the memorandum.[69] In the context of agreements for the purchase and sale of land, parol evidence has been admitted to identify the subject matter of the agreement referred to in the memorandum by such phrases as "the property in Cable Street,"[70] "the mill property, including the cottages in Esher Village"[71] and "24 acres of land, freehold, ... at Totmonslow."[72] In *Dynamic Transport Ltd. v. O.K. Detailing Ltd.*,[73] the Supreme Court of Canada admitted parol evidence in order to identify a parcel of land described as "four acres, more or less" within an existing parcel of 5.42 acres. Where the parol evidence is itself ambiguous, however, the memorandum will not meet the requirements of the statute.[74]

Failure to comply with the statutory writing requirements has the effect that the agreement is unenforceable. It does not have the further effect, however, of determining that the agreement is void or non-existent. Accordingly, the agreement may be relevant for various legal purposes. Under the statute itself, the view that the agreement is merely unenforceable is consistent with the proposition that a subsequent memorandum complying with the statute has the effect of rendering the agreement enforceable as of the date of its formation. If the agreement were truly void, it would be conceptually inconsistent, at least, to take the view that it could subsequently become enforceable. Further, the existence of the unenforceable agreement might provide a defence in certain circumstances. For example, in *Re Whissel Enterprises Ltd. and Eastcal Developments Ltd.*,[75] a tenant of commercial premises had an oral understanding with the landlord that the lease included the adjacent yard. When the premises were acquired by a new owner, the oral understanding constituted a defence to the latter's claim to evict the tenant from the yard. Further, the unenforceable agreement may constitute sufficient consideration to provide the basis for the enforceability of a negotiable instrument.[76] Finally, it is sometimes suggested

---

68 *Carr v. Lynch*, [1900] 1 Ch. 613.
69 *Rossiter v. Miller* (1878), 3 App. Cas. 1124. Compare with *Potter v. Duffield* (1874), L.R. 18 Eq. 4 (parol evidence inadmissible to identify a "vendor").
70 *Bleakley v. Smith* (1840), 59 E.R. 831.
71 *McMurray v. Spicer* (1868), L.R. 5 Eq. 527.
72 *Plant v. Bourne*, [1879] 2 Ch. 281.
73 [1978] 2 S.C.R. 1072.
74 *Turney v. Zhilka*, [1959] S.C.R. 578.
75 (1980), 116 D.L.R. (3d) 174 (Alta. C.A.).
76 *Jones v. Jones* (1840), 6 M. & W. 84 (Exch.); *Kinzie v. Harper* (1908), 15 O.L.R. 582 (Div. Ct.); *Low v. Fry* (1935), 152 L.T.R. 585.

that the existence of the unenforceable agreement provides a defence to a claim by an unwilling purchaser, in default under an oral agreement to purchase land, to recover a deposit.[77] A preferable explanation for the denial of relief in such circumstances, however, is that, at least in cases where the vendor is willing to perform, the retention of the deposit does not constitute an unjust enrichment of the vendor. In other circumstances, however, the enrichment may well be unjust and recovery should therefore be allowed.[78]

4) Relief from the Effects of Non-compliance

There are three doctrinal devices that offer some form of relief from the effects of non-compliance with the statute. The first two, the doctrines of part performance and the doctrine that the *Statute of Frauds* cannot be employed to commit a fraud, are doctrines of equity that provide a basis for, in effect, enforcing the oral undertaking. The third is the remedy of restitution that enables a party who has transferred value to the other party under an oral agreement to recover that value in order to prevent the unjust enrichment of the other party.

a) The Doctrine of Part Performance

Within a few years of the enactment of the statute, courts of equity began to develop a doctrine that would essentially waive compliance with the statute in circumstances where it would be unjust to refuse enforcement of the agreement.[79] The principal doctrine of this kind is the doctrine of part performance. This doctrine holds that where one party to an oral agreement partially performs his or her undertaking, the oral agreement may be enforced in order to avoid injustice to the party conferring value. The doctrine is typically applied in the context of oral transactions concerning the transfer of land in return for the provision of services. Having provided the services in question, the service provider seeks the equitable remedy of specific performance[80]

---

77   *Thomas v. Brown* (1876), 1 Q.B.D. 714; *Switzer's Investments Ltd. v. Burn* (1964), 49 W.W.R. 627 (Alta. S.C.); *Monnickendam v. Leanse* (1923), 39 T.L.R. 445 (K.B.). Compare with *Casson v. Roberts* (1862), 31 Beav. 613; *Sigvaldason v. Hitsman* (1922), 65 D.L.R. 317 (Sask. C.A.).

78   See generally P.D. Maddaugh and J.D. McCamus, *The Law of Restitution*, 2d ed. (Aurora: Canada Law Book Inc., 2004) c. 13, ss. 13:200 and 13:400.

79   *Butcher v. Stapely* (1685), 1 Vern. 363.

80   For discussion of the remedy of specific performance, see Chapter 23. Although it is sometimes suggested that the doctrine is limited to cases in which specific performance is sought of a promise to transfer land, there would appear to be no

of the agreement to transfer the land. If the doctrine is applicable, the oral agreement becomes enforceable. Articulation of the test for application of the doctrine rests on a determination of the nature of the part performance that must be demonstrated and its relationship to the unenforceable oral agreement.

In England, the doctrine of part performance has evolved from an earlier and more rigid test to a test that can be more easily met by the part performer. The classic articulation of the earlier version of the test is set out in *Maddison v. Alderson*.[81] In that case, it was held that "the acts relied upon as part performance must be unequivocally, and in their own nature, referable to some such agreement as that alleged."[82] The strictness of the test is evident from the result in this case. The plaintiff spent twenty years as an unpaid housekeeper for the deceased on the faith of an oral undertaking to leave to her, by will, the house in which they lived. For the House of Lords, the provision of unpaid services over such a period of time was not itself evidence of a contract and, more particularly, not evidence of a contract relating to the land in question. By 1962, however, it appeared that the English courts were moving to a less restrictive test. In *Kingswood Estate Co. v. Anderson*,[83] Upjohn L.J. rejected the earlier test and suggested that it would be sufficient if the acts of part performance "prove the existence of some contract, and are consistent with the contract alleged."[84] This approach received the approval of the House of Lords in the leading modern English authority, *Steadman v. Steadman*.[85] Lord Reid explained the nature of the applicable test in the following terms: "you take the whole circumstances, leaving aside evidence about the oral contract, to see whether it is proved that the acts relied on were done in reliance on a contract; that will be proved if it is shown to be more probable than not."[86]

---

reason to preclude application of the doctrine in any case where specific performance could plausibly be claimed. The more difficult question is whether, if specific performance is no longer available for some reason by the time of trial (e.g., because the land has been sold to a third party), the plaintiff might succeed in an alternative claim for damages in lieu of specific performance. On the awarding of damages in lieu of specific performance, see Chapter 23, section B(4).

81 (1883), 8 App. Cas. 467 (H.L.).
82 *Ibid.* at 479, Earl Selborne L.C.
83 (1962), [1963] 2 Q.B. 169, [1962] 3 All E.R. 593 (C.A.). See also *Wakeham v. MacKenzie*, [1968] 2 All E.R. 783.
84 *Kingswood Estate Co. v. Anderson, ibid.* at 189 (Q.B.).
85 [1976] A.C. 536.
86 *Ibid.* at 541–42.

Lord Reid rejected the earlier test requiring a part performance that was necessarily or unequivocally related to the existence of a contract relating to the land on the basis that it appeared to assume that the doctrine was essentially a rule of evidence rather than the application of an equitable principle. If the doctrine of part performance were considered to be a rule of evidence it would be understandable, in his view, that courts would insist on evidence of part performance that indicates the nature of the oral agreement concerning the land. When properly viewed, however, as a doctrine that responds to the equities constituted by detrimental reliance on the oral undertaking and the consequent enrichment of the other party, so rigid a test is not required. The facts of *Steadman* itself indicate the distance that has been travelled in English doctrine from the *Maddison v. Alderson* approach. In *Steadman*, the plaintiff and defendant, whose marriage had dissolved, compromised a claim brought by the former wife concerning arrears of maintenance and the ownership of the matrimonial home. In return for the former husband's promise to make payment of one hundred pounds on the arrears and fifteen hundred pounds for the release of her interest in the matrimonial home, the former wife agreed to execute a release of her interest in the home. The agreement was not recorded in writing. The presiding justices were advised of the agreement and the proceeding was adjourned. The former husband paid the one hundred pounds into court and advanced fifteen hundred pounds to his solicitor who, in turn, forwarded a draft release to the former wife. Upon her refusal to execute the document, the former husband sought to enforce their informal agreement. The House of Lords held, on the basis of the new version of the test, that the doctrine of part performance applied and rendered the oral agreement an enforceable one.

In a series of three cases decided prior to *Steadman*, however, the Supreme Court of Canada reaffirmed its adherence to the traditional *Maddison v. Alderson* test. Each case involved the provision of services in return for a promise to transfer land upon death. In *Deglman v. Guaranty Trust Co.*,[87] a nephew had provided what were described as odd jobs, errands and minor services for his aunt in return for a promise that she would leave him one of two properties owned by her upon her death. Although the nephew lived with the aunt for six months during the period of service provision, at no time did he live in the premises subject to the aunt's promise. Applying the *Maddison v. Alderson* test, the Supreme Court concluded that the facts of part performance were

---

87   [1954] S.C.R. 725.

"wholly neutral"[88] and had no more relation to an agreement concerning the subject premises than to the possibility that the services were provided gratuitously by the nephew to his aunt. The facts of the second and third cases might be considered to raise stronger claims on the equities than the facts of *Deglman*. In *Brownscombe v. Public Trustee of Alberta*,[89] the plaintiff, from the age of sixteen, had worked for several years on the farm of the deceased, a bachelor who suffered from health problems that severely restricted his ability to work the farm himself. In addition to the services provided, the plaintiff, essentially at his own expense and on the suggestion of the deceased, had built a house on the lands in question. On a number of occasions when the plaintiff had indicated a desire to leave the defendant's employ, the deceased had promised the plaintiff that the farm would be left to him by will. Although the Supreme Court held that not all the acts of the plaintiff could be said to be unequivocally referable to some dealing in the land, the building of the house met this test and provided a basis for enforcement of the oral agreement. Similarly, in *Thompson v. Guaranty Trust Co.*,[90] the plaintiff had provided services over a long period of time, twenty-two years, on the deceased's farm. For much of this period, the deceased was incapacitated. The plaintiff was paid for the services rendered only for the first two years of this relationship. Again, the deceased had reassured the plaintiff on several occasions that he would leave the farm to him upon his death. Although, as in *Brownscombe,* the plaintiff also made some improvements to the premises, repairing the farm house and building new granaries, the Supreme Court held on these facts that "practically every act of part performance ... [was] unequivocally referable to a contract in reference to the very lands in question."[91]

Although the Supreme Court of Canada has not had an opportunity to return to a consideration of these issues subsequently to the decision in *Steadman*, it may be argued that the fact situations in both *Brownscombe* and *Thompson* suggest the possibility of some relaxation in the traditional test. Although it might be suggested that the fact situations in *Brownscombe* and *Thompson* are more compelling than the facts of *Maddison v. Alderson*, the three cases similarly involve the provision of extensive domestic services in return for an undertaking to transfer by will of the premises in which both the service provider and the recipi-

---

88   *Ibid.* at 728, Rand J.
89   [1969] S.C.R. 658.
90   [1974] S.C.R. 1023.
91   *Ibid.* at 1034, Spence J.

ent resided. Nonetheless, in the absence of a more direct consideration of the point by the Supreme Court of Canada, it would be premature to suggest that Canadian common law has adopted a significant relaxation of the traditional test.[92]

b)   Hiding behind the *Statute of Frauds* in Order to Perpetrate a Fraud

Related to the doctrine of part performance is a more general principle of equity that one ought not be allowed to hide behind the *Statute of Frauds* in order to acquire property that it would be inequitable for the acquirer to retain. The principle is often applied in the context of informal trust arrangements. Thus, where a person acquires property on the basis of an informal understanding that it will be acquired in trust for another party, the acquirer cannot rely on the *Statute of Frauds* for the proposition that the informal trust agreement is unenforceable in order to retain the property. In such a case, the acquirer will hold the property on a constructive trust.[93] The enforcement of informal trusts, however, is not an aspect of the law of contracts. Of greater relevance, in the present context, is the possibility that the doctrine might apply to an informal undertaking to transfer an interest in land where the detrimental reliance of the proposed transferee on the undertaking does not constitute partial performance of an informal agreement. A Canadian illustration of such a fact situation is found in *Dagley v. Dagley*.[94] In this case, the father had purportedly made a gift of certain real property to his son. The arrangement was not recorded in writing. The son took possession of the land, built a home on the land at his own expense and lived in the home, with his wife, until his death some years later. Upon the death of the son, the father sought to reclaim the property from the daughter-in-law. The Nova Scotia court held that the father should not be able to set up the *Statute of Frauds*. As the court observed, although

---

92   In *Currie v. Thomas* (1985), 19 D.L.R. (4th) 594 (B.C.C.A.) the court adopted the restatement of the part performance doctrine set forth in *Steadman*. As a matter of common law, however, the point has become moot in British Columbia with the enactment in 1985 of legislation essentially adopting the modern English view. See *Law and Equity Act*, R.S.B.C. 1996, c. 253, s. 59(3). And see *Hill v. Nova Scotia (Attorney General)* (1997), 142 D.L.R. (4th) 230 (S.C.C.) (*Steadman* considered, but no definitive view expressed as to the nature of the test).

93   The leading case is *Rochefoucauld v. Boustead*, [1897] 1 Ch. 196 (C.A.). And see generally, T.G. Youdan, "Formalities for Trusts of Land and the Doctrine in *Rochefoucauld v. Boustead*" (1984) 43 Cambridge L.J. 306. See also Maddaugh and McCamus, above note 78, c. 30, s. 30:200.

94   (1905), 38 N.S.R. 313 (S.C.).

it may be that title does not pass in such circumstances, "the grantor is not allowed to claim the land after having, by his promise, induced the grantee to lay out money in improvements."[95]

c) Restitution

A restitution claim lies where the plaintiff has conferred value upon the defendant in circumstances making it unjust for the defendant to retain that value.[96] As a matter of general principle, then, such claims should lie in the context of benefits transferred under contracts that are unenforceable by virtue of non-compliance with the *Statute of Frauds*. The point may be illustrated by a leading restitution case, the decision of the Supreme Court of Canada in *Deglman v. Guaranty Trust Co.*[97] As we have seen, the Supreme Court declined in this case to apply the doctrine of part performance to the provision of services by the nephew in return for the aunt's oral undertaking to leave him a house by will. The claim for specific performance of the aunt's undertaking therefore failed. An alternative claim framed by the plaintiff for unjust enrichment, however, did enjoy success. Where such claims are made for the value of services rendered, they are typically referred to by their archaic name, as claims in *quantum meruit*, and, if successful, they result in an award measured in the reasonable value of the services provided. In *Deglman*, the claim to recover the reasonable value of services rendered was explicitly grounded on the basis that, otherwise, the aunt's estate would be "unjustly enriched." In principle, claims for other kinds of value transferred should also be recoverable in a restitutionary claim. Thus, monies paid as a partial payment of the purchase price would be recoverable.[98] As we have seen,[99] however, where the money is paid as a deposit and the vendor is willing to go forward with the transaction, it has sometimes been held that the deposit is not recoverable. In such circumstances, it may be appropriate to conclude that the enrichment is not unjust.

A second and equitable stream of restitutionary doctrine concerns the equitable remedy of constructive trust.[100] As a remedy, the constructive trust has the signal advantage of potentially conferring proprietary rights on the plaintiff. It is therefore a particularly advantageous

---

95 *Ibid.* at 317.
96 See Chapter 24. And see generally Maddaugh and McCamus, above note 78, c. 1–3.
97 Above note 87.
98 See Chapter 24.
99 See above the text at notes 76–78.
100 See generally Maddaugh and McCamus, above note 78, c. 1, 5 and 13.

remedy in the context of the defendant's insolvency. The possibility that this remedy might be available in the context of benefits conferred under a contract that is unenforceable because of non-compliance with the *Statute of Frauds* was considered by the Supreme Court of Canada in *Palachik v. Kiss*.[101] A husband had made certain payments to his wife on the basis of an informal understanding that, in due course, he would receive a half-interest in the matrimonial home that was held in her name. The husband also made substantial improvements to the property. The Supreme Court appeared to accept that, in such circumstances, constructive trust relief could be available.[102]

5) Other Statutory Writing Requirements

Although, as we have seen, a number of the provisions of the original *Statute of Frauds* appear archaic and, as a result, have been repealed or modified in various Canadian jurisdictions, the use of formality requirements in the making of agreements as an instrument of public policy continues to the present day. The continued adherence, even in those jurisdictions that have reformed the *Statute of Frauds*, to the provisions relating to guarantees and contracts for the purchase and sale of land[103] manifests a continuing belief that there is social value in such requirements. In the modern era, additional statutory schemes requiring contract formality have been enacted, typically for the purpose of attempting to redress the imbalance of power in consumer transactions by insuring the provision of certain information, in written form, to the consumer. The Ontario *Consumer Protection Act*,[104] for example, requires that all executory contracts for the sale of goods or services to consumers shall be in writing and shall contain certain information.[105] An executory contract is "not binding on the buyer"[106] unless the agreement is signed by both parties and a copy of the original agreement is in possession of each of the parties. Where the agreement includes a credit arrangement, the statute further provides that the certain information shall be provided to the purchaser that will facilitate dis-

101 [1983] 1 S.C.R. 623.
102 The analysis in the case was complicated by the application of matrimonial property and succession legislation and, in the event, a proprietary constructive trust was not awarded.
103 Above note 18.
104 R.S.O. 1990, c. C.31 (repealed and replaced by the *Consumer Protection Act, 2002*, S.O. 2002, c. 30, Sch. E, s. 3 (to come into force on proclamation)).
105 *Ibid*, s. 19.
106 *Ibid.*, s. 19(2).

closure of the true cost of borrowing.[107] The latter arrangements also apply to consumer loans. Similarly, provincial legislation regulating the conduct of real estate brokers and sales agents typically requires that an agreement retaining the services of a real estate agent will not be binding unless it is evidenced in writing.[108] As well, some consumer protection legislation confers the power on the provincial government in question to stipulate the form and content of consumer agreements to be used in the provision of particular goods and services.[109] A consumer agreement not made in accordance with the regulations would typically not be binding on the consumer.[110] The cumulative effect of statutory schemes of these kinds, of course, is to create a very substantial set of exceptions to the general principle of the common law that holds that informal agreements are enforceable.

C. INCORPORATION OF WRITTEN TERMS

1) Introduction

In many contracting contexts, parties will not explicitly negotiate all the terms of their agreement. Many of the terms may be included in a written document that, so far as the intentions of one of the parties at least is concerned, may be intended to constitute a partial or complete statement of the terms of the proposed agreement. On many such occasions, it will not be expected by the person proffering the document that the other party will sign the document. Indeed, the terms of the proposed arrangement may be merely set out in a notice of some kind displayed in the location where the agreement is made. In other circumstances, a document may be handed over to the other party without any expectation that it will be read prior to the formation of the agreement. The reading of the fine print on the back of an airplane ticket by a prospective passenger would be a surprising event for the airline representative and for those patiently waiting their turn at the counter. In other circumstances, the party proffering the document may require the other party to sign and retain a copy of the document. Indeed, we

---

107 *Ibid.*, s. 24.

108 See, for example, *Real Estate Act*, R.S.A. 2000, c. R-5; *Real Estate Act*, R.S.B.C. 1996, c. 397; *Real Estate Brokers Act*, R.S.M. 1987, c. R20; *Real Estate Agents Act*, R.S.N.B. 1973, c. R-1; *Real Estate Trading Act*, R.S.N.L. 1990, c. R-2.

109 See, for example, *Consumer Protection Act, 2002*, S.O. 2002, c. 30, s. 123(1)(b); *Trade Practice Act*, R.S.B.C. 1996, c. 457, s. 33(1)(h).

110 *Ibid.*, s. 93.

have seen that in the context of consumer transactions, some provincial legislation so requires.[111] Again, however, it will often be the expectation of either or both of the parties that the agreement will not be read prior to the signing of the document. In all these types of cases, it will be necessary to consider whether the written terms have been successfully incorporated into the agreement entered by the parties. As we shall see, in determining this issue, much will turn on whether the document has been signed by the party to whom it has been proffered.

In these kinds of situations, the document put forward will typically constitute a standard printed form that the party proffering the document invariably uses when entering transactions of this kind. The form will often be offered on a "take it or leave it" basis. In the typical case, the other party, then, will have no choice but either to agree to the terms of the standard form or to decline to enter the transaction altogether. Standard form agreements are a pervasive and indispensable feature of modern commercial life. It is simply not feasible to negotiate, in any meaningful sense, the terms of many of the transactions entered into in the course of daily life. The use of standard forms does, however, give rise to a number of potential concerns. In many contexts, standard forms are unlikely to be read, or, if read, understood by the parties signing them. The classic model of *consensus ad idem* is lacking. The terms are simply drafted by one party, without any effective involvement of the other party. The very voluntariness of the agreement is undermined in circumstances where the contract relates to the supply of a service or product that could be characterized as a necessity. Further, if, for example, a particular standard form is employed by a monopoly supplier or is in common use by all the suppliers of a particular commodity or service, people who wish to acquire the commodity or service will have no effective choice as to the terms of the agreement upon which supply will occur. If the contract is drafted in an even-handed fashion, this will perhaps occasion little concern. There is, however, the risk that such standard form contracts or "contracts of adhesion" may contain terms that are harsh or unfairly oppressive to the person who wishes to obtain the particular commodity or service.[112] Thus, in the context of regulated industries, it is not uncommon

---

111 See the text at above notes 104–7.
112 There is substantial literature on the phenomenon of standard form agreements. See, for example, F. Kessler, "Contracts of Adhesion — Some Thoughts About Freedom of Contract" (1943) 43 Colum. L. Rev. 629; A.A. Leff, "Contract as Thing" (1970), 19 Am. U.L. Rev. 131; T.D. Rakoff, "Contracts of Adhesion: An Essay in Reconstruction" (1983) 96 Harv. L. Rev. 1174; I.R. Macneil, "Bureaucracy and Contracts of Adhesion" (1984) 22 Osgoode Hall L.J. 5.

for the regulatory authority to prescribe the terms upon which goods or services will be supplied to the public by industry participants.[113] Further, in some jurisdictions, legislation has been enacted empowering the courts to strike down provisions in agreements considered to be unduly harsh.[114] Here we consider, however, the extent to which the common law responds to the phenomenon of unfair terms in standard forms by refusing to incorporate them in the agreement of the parties. As we shall see, courts are reluctant to incorporate written terms that may operate unfairly and to the surprise of one of the parties. As a result, the law of incorporation of written terms has developed certain obstacles to the incorporation of such terms.

2) Unsigned Documents

The basic principle concerning the incorporation of unsigned documents into agreements was established in the nineteenth-century "ticket" cases. In these cases, the question that arose is whether tickets issued, for example, by cloakroom or parking-lot attendants that contain a set of terms, perhaps on the reverse side of the ticket, would bind the person to whom the ticket was given. In such cases, the dispute is likely to turn on the applicability of a term that purports to exclude or restrict the liability of the issuer of the ticket in the event that a breach of contract has caused loss or injury. The customer, who has suffered the loss, will claim ignorance of the existence of the term. In a leading case, *Parker v. South Eastern Railway Co.*,[115] the dispute concerned the loss of a bag deposited by the plaintiff in the defendant railway's cloakroom, the loss having been occasioned by the negligence of the defendant's employees. At the time of depositing the bag, the plaintiff had been issued with a paper ticket that, on its back, included a

---

113 If, in such a case, the terms are not made available to the consumer at the point of sale, it may be an interesting question whether the agreement is nonetheless entered into on the basis of the regulated terms. See, for example, *B.G. Linton Construction Ltd. v. C.N.R. Co.* (1974), [1975] 2 S.C.R. 678 (terms set forth by regulation pursuant to railway legislation for the sending of telegrams held binding). Some provincial consumer protection legislation confers the power, through regulation, to stipulate the form of certain agreements for the supply of goods and services to consumers. See, for example, *Consumer Protection Act, 2002*, S.O. 2002, c. 30, s. 123(1)(b); *Trade Practice Act*, R.S.B.C. 1996, c. 457, s. 33(1)(h).

114 In England, for example, see the *Unfair Contract Terms Act, 1977*, (U.K.) 1977, c. 50. The scope of the legislation is limited to exculpatory or limitation of liability clauses. See generally Chapter 20.

115 (1877), 2 C.P.D. 416 (C.A.).

term stipulating that the defendant would not be liable in the event of the loss of deposited articles. The plaintiff claimed to be unaware of the stipulation. Mellish L.J. explained that, in the absence of a signed agreement, the question is whether the party receiving the paper containing the writing has assented to the terms set out in the document. In any case where the person receiving the paper actually knows that the paper contains a set of conditions that the party issuing the ticket intends to be the terms of their agreement, assent is easily established, whether or not the recipient actually reads the document and becomes familiar with the terms.[116] In the more difficult case, where the recipient does not have actual knowledge of the nature of the document, the question is whether the person issuing the document can reasonably assume that the other party is aware that the document contains conditions either because of the nature of the transaction or because reasonable steps have been taken to give the other party notice of this fact. Mellish L.J. illustrated the former point by suggesting that a person who ships goods by sea must be assumed to realize that the bill of lading contains the terms of the contract of carriage. Accordingly, the customer is bound by the terms on the bill of lading. The shipping company is under no obligation to explain the nature of the bill of lading to each customer.[117] In cases where it is not obvious that the document is contractual in nature, however, the test to be met is whether the party relying on the document has given sufficient notice to the other party that the document or ticket contains conditions. Thus, if the railway company "did what was reasonably sufficient to give the plaintiff notice of the condition,"[118] the plaintiff would be bound by the condition, whether or not the plaintiff had troubled to read the ticket.

The determination of whether reasonable notice of terms has been provided rests on the circumstances of the particular case. Where the person receiving the document might reasonably assume that the document has some purpose other than communicating contractual terms, courts incline to the view that reasonable notice has not been given. Thus, a ticket issued at a parking lot has been held to be reasonably understood as a receipt or voucher to be surrendered when picking

---

116 *Harris v. Great Western Railway Co.* (1876), 1 Q.B.D. 515.

117 In a Canadian case, however, it was held that in a case where the language of the bill of lading is somewhat obscure and unlikely to be understood by a person with little or no experience in shipping goods, the document might provide insufficient notice. On the other hand, a commercial party, which regularly ships goods in such circumstances, could be bound. See *Promech Sorting Systems B.V. v. Bronco Rentals and Leasing Ltd.* (1995), 123 D.L.R. (4th) 111 (Man. C.A.).

118 Above note 115 at 424.

up the car.[119] Similarly, a railway company was held unable to rely on a limitation of liability provision set out in a baggage check given to a passenger. The passenger had already purchased a rail ticket that was silent on the matter and reasonably understood the claim check to be a simple receipt.[120] Further, a ticket setting out terms in very small print that, as one judge said, "instead of being designed to inform [the customer] of the defendant's attempted limitation of his responsibility, was designed to conceal it"[121] is not likely to provide sufficient notice. The presence of signage may assist in providing reasonable notice.[122] To be effective, such signs or notices must be plainly in view at the time and place of contracting. Thus, signage at a parking lot visible only as the driver leaves the lot will be ineffective.[123] A notice tacked to the back of the door of one's hotel room will not suffice as it will be seen by the hotel guest only after the contract to rent the room has been entered into at the front desk.[124]

Tickets issued at the time of contracting, such as the baggage receipt in the *Parker*[125] case, are assumed to have been issued in a timely fashion on the theory, presumably, that a customer who read the ticket and objected to its terms could, at this stage, withdraw from the transaction. Where the ticket is issued by an automatic machine, however, such as those issuing tickets at the entrance of a parking lot, it has been held that the ticket arrives too late to provide sufficient notice. In *Thornton v. Shoe Lane Parking Ltd.*,[126] the English Court of Appeal held that the ticket cases are inapplicable to a machine-issued ticket because the ticket arrives at a time when the customer is no longer in a position

---

119 *Appleton v. Ritchie Taxi*, [1942] 3 D.L.R. 546 (Ont. C.A.). See also *Chapelton v. Barry Urban District Council*, [1940] 1 K.B. 532 (C.A.) (ticket for rental of deck chairs — understood to be mere voucher or receipt); *Lamont v. Canadian Transfer Co. Ltd.* (1909), 19 O.L.R. 291 (C.A.) (cartage contract — customer later requests receipt — terms on receipt not binding).

120 *Spencer v. C.P.R.* (1913), 13 D.L.R. 836 at 843 (Ont. S.C.A.D.), Riddell J. ("We were told that everyone should be held to have read his railway check — that people generally read their checks. Speaking for myself, I never read a check in my life till this one and never saw one read — nay, further, I have never heard of one being read until the argument in this case.")

121 *Spooner v. Starkman*, [1937] 2 D.L.R. 582 at 584 (Ont. C.A.), Henderson J.A.

122 *Samuel Smith & Sons v. Silverman* (1960), 29 D.L.R. (2d) 98 (Ont. C.A.). See also *Olley v. Marlborough Court Ltd.*, [1949] 1 All E.R. 127 at 134 (C.A.), Denning L.J.

123 *Mendelssohn v. Normand Ltd.*, [1970] 1 Q.B. 177, [1969] 3 W.L.R. 139 (C.A.). See also *Thornton v. Shoe Lane Parking Ltd.*, [1971] 2 Q.B. 163 (C.A.).

124 *Olley v. Marlborough Court Ltd.*, above note 122.

125 Above note 115.

126 Above note 123.

to refuse the transaction.[127] In offer and acceptance terms, the situation was characterized as one in which the offer is made by the proprietor of the machine who has signified the willingness of the machine to accept money. The acceptance is the customer's deposit of the requisite money in the receptacle.

Where the parties have a history of dealing on the basis of a particular set of written terms, the document may be incorporated on the basis of that course of conduct in a particular transaction even though the document arrives late or, indeed, is not provided at all. In *J. Spurling Ltd. v. Bradshaw*,[128] for example, the defendant, as he had done on numerous previous occasions, deposited goods in the plaintiff's warehouse. A few days later, the plaintiff forwarded to the defendant an invoice and "landing account" that made it clear that the warehouseman's liability was limited in certain respects. Some months later, when he came to pick up the goods and discovered they were damaged, he refused to pay the plaintiff's account, taking the position that the documents had arrived too late to be incorporated into their agreement. The Court of Appeal, noting that the defendant had received such landing accounts on many previous occasions and, indeed, had taken no objection to their late arrival in the present case, held that the written terms were incorporated into the agreement on the basis of the prior course of dealing. Incorporation on this basis requires, however, some level of frequency and consistency in the prior dealings. Thus, a car owner who has had his car repaired three or four times in the past on the basis of a standard set of terms will not be bound by them if they are not furnished on a subsequent occasion.[129]

Failure to follow a consistent practice provided one of the grounds for refusing incorporation in *McCutcheon v. David MacBrayne Ltd.*[130] McCutcheon, a farmer on the Isle of Islay, asked his brother-in-law, McSporran, to arrange for the defendant carrier to ship his car to him on the mainland. The defendant was the exclusive supplier of this service on the island. The practice of the defendant, when accepting goods for shipment, was to require the customer to sign a "risk note" containing provisions limiting the liability of the carrier in the event of loss. On this occasion, however, the defendant's clerk neglected either to

---

127 Lord Denning M.R. observed: "[The customer] may protest to the machine, even swear at it; but it will remain unmoved. He is committed beyond recall." See *ibid.* at 169.
128 [1956] 2 All E.R. 121 (C.A.).
129 *Hollier v. Rambler Motors (A.M.C.) Ltd.*, [1972] 2 Q.B. 71 (C.A.).
130 [1964] 1 All E.R. 430 (H.L.).

furnish the risk note or require a signature from McSporran. Nonetheless, when the defendant's vessel, with McCutcheon's vehicle on board, struck a rock and sank, the defendant sought to protect itself on the basis that the contract contained the usual printed terms because of a course of prior dealing with McCutcheon and McSporran. McSporran's evidence was that sometimes he was asked to sign the risk note, other times not. McCutcheon had shipped goods on four previous occasions, three of them on behalf of his employer and a fourth involving the shipment of his car. He was asked to sign a risk note on each occasion. The House of Lords held that a prior course of dealing from which the risk note would be incorporated into the oral contract entered into by McSporran on McCutcheon's behalf had not been established for a variety of reasons. The past practice was not consistent. There would be no reason for McCutcheon to assume, when an oral contract was entered into, that the terms of prior written agreements would be incorporated therein. Most of McCutcheon's experience involved a different type of transaction.

An additional point was emphasized, however, by Lord Devlin, who placed particular significance on the fact that McCutcheon, in any event, had never made himself aware of the content of the written terms. The importance of subjective knowledge of the terms was emphasized by Lord Devlin as follows: "The fact that a man has made a contract in the same form ninety-nine times (let alone three or four times which are here alleged) will not of itself affect the hundredth contract, in which the form is not used. Previous dealings are relevant only if they prove knowledge of the terms, actual and not constructive, and assent to them."[131]

Although it is readily apparent that actual knowledge of the content of the written terms acquired in a course of prior dealings might assist the argument for incorporation, Lord Devlin's suggestion that it should be a precondition of incorporation did not gain favour with his colleagues on this occasion nor has it been adopted by courts in subsequent cases. A preferable explanation for incorporation in cases where the document is not furnished in a timely fashion is that the circumstances of the prior dealing are such that the party relying on the document reasonably understands the other party to have agreed to deal on the basis of the "usual terms." Thus, in the earlier case of *J. Spurling Ltd. v. Bradshaw*,[132] there was no suggestion that the defendant had ever read and understood the terms set out in the "landing accounts." Again, in

---

131 *Ibid.* at 437.
132 Above note 128.

the later decision in *Hardwick Game Farm v. Sussex Agricultural Poultry Producers Association*,[133] the House of Lords incorporated, on the basis of prior dealings involving three to four transactions per month for the previous thirty-six months, a "sale note" limiting the supplier's liability, notwithstanding the fact that the customer had never read the document in question.

Quite apart from a prior course of dealing on written terms, there may be other circumstances in which a party relying on a document that has not been furnished in a timely fashion may reasonably understand the other party to be dealing on those terms. Thus, in *British Crane Hire Corp. v. Ipswich Plant Hire Ltd.*,[134] written terms were incorporated notwithstanding the apparent absence of any prior course of dealings between the parties. The defendant had rented a large piece of earth-moving equipment from the plaintiff. Both the plaintiff and the defendant were in the equipment rental business. On this occasion, however, the defendants were actually doing the work themselves. They contacted the plaintiffs, requesting that the equipment be supplied on an urgent basis and arrangements were reached by the parties on the telephone. The plaintiffs delivered the equipment within a few days and subsequently issued their standard written terms of hire to the defendants, requesting their signature. Before the document was signed, however, the machine sank in a marsh and the defendants refused to sign the form. The plaintiff sued to recover the cost of recovering the machine, relying on a provision to this effect in their standard terms of hire. Although nothing had been said in the telephone conversation about the conditions of hire, the defendants candidly conceded that, being in the same business, they were quite familiar with terms of this kind and, indeed, insisted on them themselves when they rented out equipment. Further, it was agreed that firms in the equipment rental trade all used terms of this kind that were typically variations on a standard form used within the industry. The defendants also admitted that when they themselves supplied equipment on an urgent basis, written terms would normally follow. Against this background, the Court of Appeal, noting that the defendants had requested the machinery urgently and that it had been supplied by the plaintiffs quickly, held that the parties had, in effect, agreed to deal on the plaintiffs' usual terms. Those terms were therefore incorporated into the transaction.

Although courts are prepared to incorporate written terms on the basis of a prior course of dealing and other circumstances giving rise to

133 [1969] 2 A.C. 31 (H.L.).
134 [1975] Q.B. 303 (C.A.).

an expectation of incorporation, courts at the same time remain concerned that incorporation not become a means for imposing harsh and oppressive terms on the other party. Thus, it is well established that the requirements for notice will escalate with the increasing harshness of the terms. Denning L.J. made the point in the *Spurling* case in the following terms: "I agree that the more unreasonable a clause is, the greater the notice which must be given of it. Some clauses which I have seen would need to be printed in red ink on the face of the document with a red hand pointing to it before notice could be held to be sufficient."

This approach may appear to manipulate the rules on incorporation in order to prevent unjust results. It is possible, however, to reconcile this approach with the general principle. In cases where incorporation is based on circumstances that do not likely include actual knowledge of the content of the terms by the other party, the party proffering a document containing surprisingly harsh terms has less reason to assume that the other party is assenting to the incorporation of such terms.

Although this requirement of special notice for harsh terms will often be relevant to the incorporation of written terms in transactions with consumers on the basis of a business supplier's standard terms, the operation of this principle is not limited to the context of consumer transactions. In *Interfoto Picture Library Ltd. v. Stiletto Visual Programmes Ltd.*,[135] for example, this principle was applied in the context of a commercial transaction involving the rental of photographic transparencies. The defendant advertising agency had approached the plaintiff, which operated a library of such transparencies, with a view to renting transparencies for a client presentation. The plaintiff delivered a bag of forty-seven transparencies in the hope that some might be found suitable. The bag included a delivery note stipulating that the transparencies were to be returned within fourteen days, after which a substantial daily holding fee would be charged. The defendant examined the transparencies and reported to the plaintiff that one or two of them could be of interest. The defendant did not read the delivery note and neglected to return the transparencies for approximately one month. The plaintiff then surprised the defendant with a rather impressive invoice. The defendants refused to pay the invoice on the ground that they were unaware of the written terms set out in the delivery note. The Court of Appeal held that the plaintiffs had not done "what was necessary to draw this unreasonable and extortionate clause fairly to [the defendants'] attention."[136] To the extent that the terms and conditions set out

---

135 [1989] Q.B. 433 (C.A.).
136 *Ibid.* at 445.

in the note were common or usual terms, regularly encountered in the transparency rental business, the enclosure of the delivery note in the package of transparencies on offer to the defendants would constitute sufficient notice. A "particularly onerous or unusual"[137] term, however, must be more directly brought to the attention of the other party.

3) Signed Documents

If an agreement is entered into on the basis of a document proffered by one party and signed by the other, it is clearly established that the agreement between the parties contains the terms expressed in the document, whether or not the signing party has read the documents. As Mellish L.J. explained in *Parker v. South Eastern Railway Company*,[138] in the absence of fraud, the agreement is proved in such circumstances by proving the fact of the signature. This rule is often referred to as the rule in *L'Estrange v. F. Graucob Ltd.*,[139] a case in which Scrutton L.J. stated the rule in the following terms:

> In cases in which the contract is contained in a railway ticket or other unsigned document, it is necessary to prove that an alleged party was aware, or ought to have been aware, of its terms and conditions. These cases have no application when the document has been signed. When a document containing contractual terms is signed, then, in the absence of fraud, or, I will add, misrepresentation, the party signing it is bound, and it is wholly immaterial whether he has read the document or not.[140]

In this case, a purchaser was bound by a provision in the contract of sale excluding the implied warranties as to quality. Having signed the agreement, it was immaterial that the customer had not read the terms.

Although this general rule is well established, it is evident that the problem of inadequate notice of unfair terms, which arises in the ticket cases, may also arise in the context of signed agreements. In many contractual settings, it will not be expected that a signing party will take the time to read the agreement. Even if the document is read, it may well be, especially in the context of consumer transactions, that the purport of particular provisions of the agreement will not be understood by the

---

137 *Ibid.* at 439.

138 Above note 115.

139 [1934] 2 K.B. 394 (C.A.). And see J.R. Spencer, "Signature, Consent and the Rule in *L'Estrange v. Graucob*" [1973] Cambridge L.J. 104.

140 *L'Estrange v. F. Graucob Ltd., ibid.* at 403.

signing party. Under traditional doctrine, then, although the fact of a signature appears to dispense with the notice issue, the opportunities for imposing harsh and oppressive terms on an unsuspecting party are, as a practical matter, as present in the context of signed documents as they are in the context of unsigned documents. Accordingly, it is perhaps not surprising that the recent jurisprudence indicates that notice requirements are migrating into the context of signed agreements.

In the important decision in *Tilden Rent-A-Car Company v. Clendenning*,[141] a car rental company was held unable to rely on a limitation of liability clause in a car rental contract signed by a customer as a result of a failure to give adequate notice of the onerous nature of the clause. The rented vehicle had been damaged while being driven by the customer, Clendenning. At the time of the accident, it was conceded that Clendenning had consumed alcohol, but it was also accepted at trial that he had been nonetheless capable of the proper control of the vehicle. The car rental company, however, took the position that the collision-damage provisions of the car rental agreement were inapplicable, as a result of exclusionary clauses, and that Clendenning was personally liable for the loss. The particular provisions stipulated that the coverage would be waived in any case where the customer operated the vehicle having "consumed any intoxicating liquor." The provisions also waived coverage if the customer operated the vehicle "in violation of any law." In the view of the Court of Appeal, this was an extremely onerous clause. It would deprive the hirer of coverage if he exceeded the speed limit by even one mile, parked in a no-parking area or consumed merely a single glass of wine. In all sorts of surprising circumstances, then, the contract purported to render the hirer completely responsible for any injury to the vehicle. Writing for a majority of the court, Dubin J.A. reasoned that, although a signature constitutes "one way of manifesting consent to contractual terms,"[142] it will not manifest consent to terms that the other party "had no reason to believe were being assented to"[143] by the party signing the document. Dubin J.A. noted that the transaction was carried out in a hurried and informal manner and that the provisions of the agreement were set out in small type, which was so faint as to be barely legible on the customer's copy. Moreover, the provisions being relied on were surprising in the sense that they appeared inconsistent with the "over-all purpose for which

---

141 (1978), 83 D.L.R. (3d) 400 (Ont. C.A.). See also *Household Movers & Shippers Ltd. v. Fitzhugh* (1989), 79 Nfld. & P.E.I.R. 171 (Nfld. S.C.T.D.).
142 *Tilden Rent-A-Car Company v. Clendenning, ibid.* at 404.
143 *Ibid.* at 405.

the contact is entered into by the hirer."[144] In such circumstances, for
Dubin J.A., a signature does not truly communicate acquiescence to
"unusual and onerous terms which are inconsistent with the true object of the contract."[145] Drawing support from earlier Canadian cases[146]
to the same effect, he reasoned as follows:

> In modern commercial practice, many standard form printed docu-
> ments are signed without being read or understood. In many cases,
> the parties seeking to rely on the terms of the contract know or ought
> to know that the signature of the party to the contract does not rep-
> resent the true intention of the signor and that the party signing is
> unaware of the stringent and onerous provisions which the standard
> form contains. Under such circumstances, I am of the opinion that the
> parties seeking to rely on such terms should not be able to do so in the
> absence of first having taken reasonable measures to draw such terms
> to the attention of the other party, and, in the absence of such reason-
> able measures, it is not necessary for the party denying knowledge of
> such terms to prove fraud, misrepresentation or *non est factum*.[147]

The practical consequence of the doctrine then is to expunge the unusually onerous provisions from the written agreement. The enforceable agreement is constituted by the remaining terms.

The evident effect of the doctrine applied in *Clendenning*, then, is to
severely restrict the operation of the rule in *L'Estrange v. Graucob* and to
require that the attention of a party invited to sign a standard form be
drawn to unusually onerous terms included in the document.[148] The standard of "unusual and onerous" terms may, of course, prove to be difficult
to apply in a particular fact situation. Thus, in *Delaney v. Cascade River*

---

144 *Ibid.*

145 *Ibid.* at 407.

146 *Colonial Investment Company of Winnipeg, Manitoba v. Borland* (1911), 1 W.W.R.
171 at 189 (Alta. S.C.), Beck J., aff'd (1911), 2 W.W.R. 960 (Alta. S.C.A.D.);
Canadian Bank of Commerce v. Foreman, [1927] 2 D.L.R. 530 at 537 (Alta. C.A.);
Jacques v. Lloyd D. George & Partners Ltd., [1968] 1 W.L.R. 625 at 630 (C.A.),
Lord Denning M.R.

147 See *Tilden Rent-A-Car Company v. Clendenning*, above note 141 at 408–9. For discussion of fraud and misrepresentation, see Chapter 10. For discussion of *non
est factum*, see Chapter 13, section B(6).

148 The *Clendenning* doctrine was held inapplicable in circumstances where a prospective employer invited an employee to draft a contract of employment and
then, on its presentation, declined to read it before affixing his signature. The
rule in *L'Estrange v. Graucob* was applicable and the rather generous severance
arrangements included in the agreement by the employee were enforceable. See
978011 Ontario Ltd. v. Cornell Engineering Co. (2001), 53 O.R. (3d) 783 (C.A.).

Holidays Ltd.,[149] for example, the British Columbia Court of Appeal divided on whether a "Standard Liability Release" signed before undertaking a "white water adventure" trip down the Fraser River contained such unusual clauses that special notice needed to be drawn to them. The action had been brought by the estate of a passenger on the trip in question who had signed the release without reading it. In a tragic accident during the subsequent trip, the passenger died. His death resulted from the supply, by the defendant operator, of inadequate lifejackets to the passengers. In dissent, Nemetz C.J.B.C. held that the limitation of liability provisions set out in the Standard Liability Release were misleading in a variety of respects. The all-embracing exclusion of liability was, in his view, so onerous and unusual that it was the duty of the tour operator to draw it more plainly to the attention of the passengers before inviting their signature. The majority, on the other hand, held that, given the nature of the adventure involved, the intent of the release was reasonably obvious and the rule in *L'Estrange v. Graucob* should, therefore, apply in the normal fashion.[150]

It is another matter, of course, if the party proffering the form misleads the signing party with respect to the significance of a particular provision. Even if there was no intention to mislead, it is well established that the party proffering the form cannot rely on the printed version of the provision.[151] If the misleading conduct was intentional it may prevent the very formation of the agreement.[152]

D. THE PAROL EVIDENCE RULE

1) Introduction

The rules of incorporation, examined earlier in this chapter[153] determine whether terms set out in writing are to be included within the

---

149 (1983), 44 B.C.L.R. 24 (C.A.).

150 See also *F. Crocker v. Sundance Northwest Resorts Ltd.*, [1988] 1 S.C.R. 1186 (dangerous contest at a ski hill — signed release not binding because (a) not sufficiently drawn to the participant's attention, and (b) participant thought he was signing only an "entry form").

151 See *Canadian Indemnity Co. v. Okanagan Mainline Real Estate Board* (1970), 16 D.L.R. (3d) 715 (S.C.C.); *Curtis v. Chemical Cleaning & Dyeing Co.*, [1951] 1 K.B. 805 (C.A.); *Trigg v. M.I. Movers International Transport Services Ltd.*, (1991), 4 O.R. (3d) 562 (C.A.), leave to appeal to S.C.C. refused (1992), 7 O.R. (3d) xii n (S.C.C.). See further this Chapter, section D(3).

152 See *Glasner v. Royal LePage Real Estate Services Ltd.* (1992), 28 R.P.R. (2d) 72 (B.C.S.C.), for discussion of which see Chapter 13, section B(3).

153 See above section C of this Chapter.

agreement entered by the parties. We now turn to consider whether the written document should be considered to be the exclusive source of the terms of the agreement. If the parties have a shared intention on this matter, of course, the issue is not a difficult one. A clear mutual agreement by the parties that a written document is to constitute the sole and exclusive expression of their contractual relationship will be effective. On the other hand, if the parties plainly agree that their agreement is to be constituted both by the terms set forth in a written document and by terms either agreed to orally or set forth in an additional document, effect will be given to that understanding. The difficult case, of course, arises where the parties have different understandings on this point. In the typical case, one party will assert that the written document constitutes the full expression of the agreement. The other party will insist that some prior and, typically, oral undertaking given by the other party also constitutes part of the agreement between the parties. The party wishing to rely on the prior oral undertaking must, however, be able to surmount the obstacle to such reliance presented by the parol evidence rule. That rule holds that, in certain circumstances, the party wishing to rely on the oral undertaking may be prevented from introducing evidence of an oral understanding that supplements or is inconsistent with the written agreement.

Although commonly referred to as the "parol evidence rule," this label is somewhat misleading. In the first place, the rule applies to all forms of prior communication, not just oral communication. The rule, if applicable, would also preclude reliance upon prior written undertakings of parties who enter a subsequent written agreement. Second, although the rule is often treated as an evidentiary rule in the sense that it provides a basis for excluding evidence at trial, the rule is more appropriately considered to be a substantive rule of contract law in that it is a rule that determines that undertakings given in certain circumstances are unenforceable. Further, even if it is true that the rule might have been inspired, in part at least, by a concern that testimony concerning oral undertakings might be generally less reliable than evidence consisting of written agreements, the rule cannot now be explained on this basis. There is, of course, no general proscription against the enforcement of oral undertakings. On the contrary, they are commonly enforced. Moreover, the various exceptions to the parol evidence rule render evidence concerning prior oral undertakings admissible. Further, evidence concerning oral undertakings given after the adoption of a written agreement is generally admissible. It would be very difficult, therefore, to defend the rule on the basis that evidence concerning oral undertakings is inherently unreliable and excluded as an evidentiary matter on that basis.

As we shall see, application of the rule may, on occasion, lead to results that are perceived to be unjust. Accordingly, the rule has been subjected to criticism by various law reform bodies.[154] Some have recommended its abolition. At least one such body, however, has concluded that reform is unnecessary.[155] These differing views rest, to some extent, on different understandings of the scope and rationale of the rule. There are essentially two different versions of the rule found in the jurisprudence.[156] The first might be referred to as the "traditional" version of the rule. This version holds that where a written agreement appears on its face to be a complete agreement, parol evidence cannot be admitted that contradicts, varies, adds to or subtracts from the terms of the written agreement. Under this version of the rule, one must determine that the written agreement appears to be, in some sense, incomplete before one can turn to consider evidence of prior communications of the parties. The second or "modern" version of the rule places emphasis on the need to demonstrate that the parties actually intended to reduce their agreement into writing as a precondition to the application of the rule. In determining whether the parties actually did intend to reduce their agreement into written form, all evidence of their prior communications relevant to this issue, oral, written or otherwise, is admissible. Under this version of the rule, then, a party could lead evidence demonstrating that a written agreement that appears complete on its face is actually merely a component of an agreement that is intended by the parties to be partly oral and partly in writing. The modern version of the rule has achieved dominance in both English[157] and American[158] jurisprudence, but its status is less clear in common law Canada. This results, in part, from a general tendency on the part of courts to refrain from identifying which of the two versions of the rule is being applied in a particular case or is considered by the court to be the correct one.

---

154 See, for example, Law Reform Commission of British Columbia, *Report on Parole Evidence Rule* (Victoria: Queen's Printer, 1980); Alberta Institute of Legal Research and Reform, *The Uniform Sale of Goods Act* (Edmonton: The Institute, 1982); Ontario Law Reform Commission, *Report on Amendment of the Law of Contracts* (Toronto: Ministry of the Attorney General, 1987).

155 English Law Commission, *Report on Parol Evidence Rule*, No. 154, Cmnd 9700 (London: HMSO, 1988).

156 See generally S.M. Waddams, "Two Contrasting Approaches to the Parol Evidence Rule" (1986–7) 12 Can. Bus. L.J. 207; S.M. Waddams, "Do We Need a Parol Evidence Rule?" (1991) 19 Can. Bus. L.J. 387.

157 See, for example, English Law Commission, above note 155.

158 See American Law Institute, *Restatement of the Law of Contracts 2d* (St. Paul: American Law Institute, 1981) s. 210, Comm. b; E.A. Farnsworth, *Farnsworth on Contracts,* 2d ed., vol. 2 (New York: Aspen, 1998) at 219–23.

There is, however, some evidence of movement in the direction of the modern rule in recent Canadian jurisprudence.

The modern version of the rule can be defended on a number of grounds. First, the modern version substantially reduces the capacity of the rule to generate unjust results. Second, the modern version is more directly linked to the most defensible justification for the rule. As we have seen, the rule cannot be justified as a rule of evidence designed to exclude unreliable testimony concerning oral undertakings. The true explanation for the rule is that, properly applied, it gives effect to the intentions of the parties. If the parties indeed intended to reduce their agreement into written form, there does not appear to be a persuasive reason for refusing to give effect to that agreement, absent fraud or some other vitiating factor.[159] The modern version of the rule, then, which renders admissible all evidence concerning this issue, is thus more directly linked to the underlying rationale of the rule.

It is the traditional version of the rule that more commonly comes under attack by law reform bodies. The traditional form of the rule excludes, in a more arbitrary way, evidence concerning the prior communications of the parties and is thus more likely to produce unjust results. Accordingly, the rule has developed a number of exceptions that, cumulatively, create at least the impression of instability and uncertainty in the rule. Further, the traditional rule is often invoked for the convenient purpose of controlling the findings of fact at the first level of litigation. In the American experience, judges minded to withdraw from the jury the question of whether a particular oral undertaking was, in fact, made, could accomplish this objective through application of the rule.[160] A similar phenomenon may occur at the appellate level. An appellate court unimpressed by fact findings concerning oral undertakings at trial would normally be precluded from disturbing the fact findings as such. The trial judgment could be overruled, however, on the basis that the parol evidence rule should have been applied at trial to preclude the admission of evidence concerning the oral undertaking. Deployment of the rule in this fashion is obviously unrelated to the purpose underlying the rule. Indeed, this approach applies the rule to accomplish an ulterior or extraneous objective. As we shall see, there is some evidence suggestive of the occurrence of this phenomenon in Canadian appellate decisions concerning the rule.

---

159 See generally S. Corbin, "The Parol Evidence Rule" (1944) 53 Yale L.J. 603.
160 See the discussion of this phenomenon in *Zell v. American Seating Co.*, 138 F.2d 641 (2d Cir. 1943).

2) The Scope and Operation of the Rule

Although Canadian courts have not normally either articulated or distinguished between the traditional and modern approaches to the parol evidence rule, there are two decisions of the Supreme Court of Canada that appear to adopt the traditional approach. At the same time, these cases illustrate some of the difficulties inherent in the traditional view of the doctrine. In the first, *Hawrish v. Bank of Montreal*,[161] the defendant solicitor had signed a guarantee on the bank's standard form guaranteeing the present and future indebtedness of a newly formed company in which he had an interest. It was the solicitor's evidence that he had been given an oral assurance by the assistant manager of the bank branch that he would be released from this guarantee once the new directors of the company executed a joint guarantee of the debt. No such understanding was recorded in the bank's standard form of guarantee executed by the defendant. In its own terms, the guarantee provided that it was "a continuing guarantee and secures the ultimate balance owing by the customer."[162] In due course, when the new company became insolvent, the bank resiled from the oral understanding and brought an action to enforce the guarantee. The trial judge admitted the evidence of the bank's oral undertaking and, finding it credible, dismissed the claim. In the Supreme Court, however, Judson J., for a unanimous Court, held that the oral undertaking was inconsistent with the provision in the guarantee stipulating that it was a "continuing" one and allowed the claim to enforce the guarantee. Judson J. offered the further reason for this result that the oral evidence was also in plain contradiction of the terms of a further stipulation in which the guarantor acknowledged that "no representations have been made to him on behalf of the bank," a point to which we will return later.

The second case, *Bauer v. Bank of Montreal*,[163] also concerned the enforcement of a bank guarantee. The defendant guarantor was a major shareholder and principal officer of the company to which a loan had been made by the plaintiff bank. As part of the lending arrangements, an assignment of book debts of the company to the bank was executed. The defendant alleged that there was an oral understanding relating to the assignment that it would be preserved by the bank for the benefit of the guarantor and reassigned to him once the company's debt was discharged. In due course, however, the bank failed to register the

---

161 [1969] S.C.R. 515.
162 *Ibid.* at 517.
163 [1980] 2 S.C.R. 102.

assignment properly with the result that, upon the insolvency of the company, the book debts became available to the general creditors of the company and were of little assistance in reducing the company's indebtedness to the bank. The bank therefore sought to enforce the guarantee, relying on a provision in the guarantee form, which stipulated that the guarantee would remain enforceable whether or not the bank abstained from perfecting any securities given by the borrower. The trial judge found that the oral undertakings had indeed been given by the bank and dismissed the claim. Again, in the Supreme Court, McIntyre J., for a unanimous Court, held that the reliance on the oral undertaking was precluded by the parol evidence rule, this being a matter that, in his view, had been settled by the decision in *Hawrish*.

Both decisions may be thought to provide evidence of the capacity of the traditional approach to produce harsh results. If one accepts that each bank did in fact give the oral undertaking in question, the bank in each case acquired additional protection from the guarantor for which it had not bargained. Each guarantor was exposed to unanticipated liability in a manner that many would consider unfair. Further, both cases also illustrate the use of the parol evidence rule as a device for interfering with what appeared at the appellate level to be unsatisfactory fact findings at trial. Thus, in *Hawrish*, Judson J. indicated that he was "not convinced"[164] that the evidence established that there was a clear intention on the part of the bank to give a binding undertaking of the kind alleged. In *Bauer*, McIntyre J. appeared sceptical of the evidentiary basis for the trial judge's finding that the oral undertaking had been given. Although he then conceded that there was "some evidence"[165] on which the trial judge could make such a finding and that the sufficiency of that finding was not "for this court to judge,"[166] McIntyre J. went on to hold, however, that the evidence was rendered inadmissible by the parol evidence rule and, on this basis, effectively reversed the fact-finding at trial.

Deployment of the doctrine in this fashion is not limited to these two cases. Indeed, in a third decision of the Supreme Court of Canada applying the rule, *Carman Construction Ltd. v. Canadian Pacific Railway*,[167] the Court suggested that there was "no evidence"[168] to support the finding at trial of an intention to give a collateral warranty. A similar

---

164   Above note 161 at 520.
165   Above note 163 at 112.
166   *Ibid.*
167   [1982] 1 S.C.R. 958.
168   *Ibid.* at 967.

concern is manifest in the decision of the Ontario Court of Appeal in *Chant v. Infinitum Growth Fund Inc.*[169] The defendant Chant had executed a standard guarantee and a mortgage to secure a corporate loan. Mr. Chant was the president and, presumably, a principal shareholder of the borrowing company. The trial judge accepted Chant's evidence that it was understood between himself and the lender that the guarantee would never be enforced against him if he "did his best and did nothing detrimental to the [borrower]."[170] Accordingly, the trial judge rectified the guarantee to reflect the parol understanding and dismissed the lender's claim to enforce the guarantee. The Court of Appeal, however, was doubtful of that fact finding and indicated that there was "considerable force" in the argument made on behalf of the lender that the finding was "patently erroneous."[171] Although the court indicated that it could not interfere with that finding, the court went on to hold that the case was not an appropriate one for rectification[172] and that the parol evidence rule precluded the trial judge's reliance on the evidence concerning the alleged oral undertaking. On this basis, the lender was permitted to enforce the guarantee. In cases such as these, it appears that the rule is being employed for reasons other than its intended purpose.

3) Exceptions to the Rule

The harshness of the traditional approach has been ameliorated over time by the growth of a reasonably lengthy series of exceptions, the scope of which, at least in some cases, remains somewhat obscure. First, the rule does not apply so as to preclude the admission of evidence that an oral undertaking has established what is, in effect, a precondition to the very enforceability of the written agreement. In the classic illustration of the point, *Pym v. Campbell*,[173] for example, the parties had orally agreed that a written agreement of sale, absolute on its face, would not be implemented unless the approval of a third party was forthcoming. Erle J. held that although the written agreement afforded a strong presumption of enforceability, evidence to show that there was no agreement without the fulfilment of the condition was admissible. The doctrine has been applied in various contractual set-

---

169   (1968), 28 D.L.R. (4th) 577 (Ont. C.A.).
170   *Ibid.* at 579.
171   *Ibid.*
172   For discussion of rectification, see Chapter 13, section D.
173   (1856), 6 E. & B. 370, 119 E.R. 903.

tings.[174] Similarly, it has been held that evidence to the effect that the enforceability of an agreement was conditioned upon a future uncertain event is admissible.[175]

Given the similarity between the function of conditions precedent and conditions subsequent,[176] one might have thought that the rule in *Pym v. Campbell* might extend to conditions subsequent. An argument to this effect was attempted in the *Hawrish*[177] case, where the guarantee was allegedly subject to an oral condition that it would terminate once a new joint guarantee had been executed by the new board of directors. The argument was rejected by the Supreme Court of Canada, however, on the basis that the rule in *Pym v. Campbell* applied only to conditions precedent to the enforceability of an agreement.

Further exceptions relate to evidence concerning the enforceability of an agreement on the ground of the passing of consideration. Thus, where a deed recites that consideration for the undertaking given has been received, parol evidence of the fact that consideration did not pass is admissible.[178] However, in the case where the deed does not show a consideration, oral evidence of its passing will be admitted.[179]

Oral evidence of collateral contracts[180] constitutes a further exception to the rule, albeit an exception of somewhat uncertain ambit. A collateral contract would arguably be constituted where an oral undertaking is given in return for the other party's act of entering into the written agreement. In an early English case, for example, a tenant agreed to enter into a lease of land that was overrun with rabbits on the faith of a promise, not recorded in the leasehold agreement, that the landlord would destroy the rabbits.[181] The verbal agreement was held to be "entirely collateral to the lease and ... founded on a good consideration."[182] Evidence of its existence was therefore admissible and the

---

174 See, for example, *California Standard Co. v. Chiswell*, [1955] 5 D.L.R. 119 (Alta. S.C.T.D.) (lease conditional upon completion of foreclosure proceedings); *Wilson v. Clarke Simpkins Ltd.* (1961), 30 D.L.R. (2d) 745 (B.C.C.A.) (car purchase subject to bank approval); *Hamelin v. Seven Mile High Group Inc.*, [1994] 6 W.W.R. 251 (B.C.C.A.) (employment agreement subject to approval of stock exchange).
175 *Western Log Exchange Ltd. v. Soucie Construction Ltd.* (1979), 14 B.C.L.R. 293 aff'd on other grounds (1980), 21 B.C.L.R. 57 (C.A.).
176 For further discussion, see Chapter 17.
177 Above note 161.
178 *Re Lang Estate*, [1919] 1 W.W.R. 651.
179 *Cleveland v. Boak* (1906), 39 N.S.R. 39 (C.A.).
180 For discussion of which, see Chapter 2.
181 *Morgan v. Griffith* (1871), L.R. 6 Ex. 70.
182 *Ibid.* at 73.

verbal agreement was enforced. As in this illustration, some collateral contracts might be said merely to "supplement" the main agreement. In other cases, however, the collateral agreement will be in conflict with the written terms. In *Long v. Smith*,[183] for example, Chancellor Boyd held that reliance on evidence of an oral agreement that a written contract of purchase could be nullified if the purchaser determined that the price represented a substantial overcharge was not precluded by a provision in the agreement stipulating that the written contract contained the entire agreement between the parties. In *Francis v. Trans Canada Trailer Sales Ltd.*,[184] an oral warranty concerning the prior use of a trailer sold to the plaintiff was held enforceable, notwithstanding a provision in the agreement excluding all representations and warranties. Similarly, in an English case,[185] a tenant of retail premises who was residing in the back of the shop, entered into a renewal of the lease in terms that precluded such occupancy, on the faith of the landlord's undertaking that the tenant would be allowed to continue to reside in the premises. The court held that evidence concerning the landlord's undertaking, which had been given in return for execution of the lease, was admissible. There are several decisions to the same effect.[186] On the other hand, there are cases in which the courts have indicated that evidence of the collateral oral agreement is admissible only if the agreement is not in any way inconsistent with or contradictory of the written agreement.[187] Thus, in *Hawrish*[188] itself, the guarantor's argument that there existed an oral, collateral agreement that the guarantee would no longer be enforceable after the joint guarantee of the new board of directors was executed was rejected, in part at least, on the basis that any such agreement was inconsistent with the provision in the guarantee, which stipulated that the guarantee was a continuing one.[189] As the *Hawrish* decision appears to indicate, it may well be that courts inclined to apply the more traditional approach to the parol evidence rule are more likely to take the view that the collateral agreement must not be inconsistent with any of the terms of the writing. Nonetheless,

---

183 (1911), 23 O.L.R. 121. See also *Ferland v. Keith* (1958), 15 D.L.R. (2d) 472 (Ont. C.A.).

184 (1969), 6 D.L.R. (3d) 705 (Sask. C.A.).

185 *City and Westminster Properties (1934) Ltd. v. Mudd*, [1959] Ch. 129.

186 See, for example, *Couchman v. Hill*, [1947] K.B. 554; *Webster v. Higgin*, [1948] 2 All E.R. 127; *Harling v. Eddy*, [1951] 2 K.B. 739; *J. Evans & Son (Portsmouth) Ltd. v. Merzario (Andrea) Ltd.*, [1976] 1 W.L.R. 1078 (C.A.).

187 See *Byers v. McMillan* (1887), 15 S.C.R. 194.

188 Above note 161.

189 See also *Carman Construction Ltd. v. Canadian Pacific Railway*, above note 167.

the cases considered above demonstrate that the practice of allowing inconsistent oral undertakings to prevail over written terms is a long-standing one.

A further cluster of exceptions to the rule applies in circumstances where various doctrines of the law of contract may affect the enforceability of some or all the terms of the written agreement. Thus, oral testimony concerning the presence of fraud, undue influence or mistake affecting the formation of the agreement is always admissible. Similarly, evidence that the oral agreement of the parties has been incorrectly recorded in the written agreement, leading to the remedy of rectification[190] is admissible. Evidence of subsequent oral agreements to vary or terminate the written agreement is admissible as is evidence tending to establish the existence of waiver or promissory estoppel.[191] Subject to the rules relating to the interpretation of agreements,[192] evidence of oral or written pre-contractual communications may be admissible for the purpose of aiding in the proper interpretation or construction of ambiguous provisions of the agreement.

Finally, evidence that a party has misrepresented, however innocently, the meaning or effect of a term in a written agreement is admissible. In such a case, the misrepresenting party cannot rely on the written version of the term. Thus, in *Canadian Indemnity Co. v. Okanagan Mainline Real Estate Board*,[193] an insurer was held unable to rely on a provision in the application for a bond that provided that the insured would indemnify the insurer with respect to all losses paid by the insurer. The defendant Board had instructed its broker to renew its existing bond on the same terms. In the course of doing so, the broker, who represented the insurer, invited the insured to execute an application form as a matter of mere formality. It was this application form that contained the indemnity clause, which made the bond virtually worthless, as far as the Board was concerned. Having misrepresented the effect of the form, the insurer could not rely on the indemnity clause.[194] In *Bank of Nova*

---

190 For discussion of which, see Chapter 11.
191 See Chapter 8.
192 See Chapter 19. And see P. Perell, "The Ambiguity Exception to the Parol Evidence Rule" (2001) 36 Can. Bus. L.J. 21.
193 Above note 151.
194 See also *Mendelssohn v. Normand Ltd.*, above note 123; *Curtis v. Chemical Cleaning & Dyeing Co.*, above note 151; *Jacques v. Lloyd D. George & Partners Ltd.*, see above note 146 at 630, Lord Denning M.R.; *Trigg v. M.I. Movers International Transport Services Ltd.* (1991), 4 O.R. (3d) 562 (C.A.), leave to appeal to S.C.C. refused (1992), 7 O.R. (3d) xii n (S.C.C.). In one case, a similar result was

Scotia v. Zackheim,[195] the Ontario Court of Appeal held that this doctrine applied in the context of a guarantee that, in its terms, applied to "all debts and liabilities present or future."[196] The lender had, however, represented to the guarantor that the guarantee would apply only to any future indebtedness of the debtor. The lender's attempt to enforce the guarantee with respect to present indebtedness failed. A similar argument was advanced without success in the *Bauer*[197] case and, indeed, it is difficult to see why the argument would not apply in any case where the effect of the guarantee has been misrepresented. In *Bauer*, however, the Supreme Court held that no such misrepresentation concerning the effect of the guarantee had in fact been made by the plaintiff bank.

4) Canadian Reception of the Modern Approach

When one couples an examination of the traditional approach with an account of the lengthy and somewhat inconsistent list of exceptions to the doctrine, the call for reform, not to say abolition, of the rule sounded by various law reform bodies[198] becomes understandable. The call for reform, however, is muted if not non-existent in jurisdictions such as the United States[199] and England[200] in which the modern version of the rule has become dominant. Under the modern approach, one applies the parol evidence rule only if it has been determined that the parties have in fact intended to reduce their agreement into written form and that the writing therefore forms the exclusive source of their agreement. If, on the other hand, the evidence concerning the communications of the parties indicates that they intended that their agreement would be both oral and recorded in writing, effect is given to the oral terms. In determining whether the parties had such intentions, all relevant evidence of prior oral and written communication is admissible. Under this approach, the presence of a written document that appears complete on its face gives rise to a strong presumption that the writing is intended to contain all the terms of the bargain. As it is only a presumption, however, it is therefore open to the parties to lead evidence of antecedent undertakings that were intended to continue

---

achieved by applying the doctrine of promissory estoppel to the pre-contractual statement. See *Bank of Montreal v. Murphy*, [1986] 6 W.W.R. 610 (B.C.C.A.).

195 (1983), 3 D.L.R. (4th) 760 (Ont. C.A.).

196 *Ibid.* at 760.

197 Above note 163.

198 See the works cited, above note 154.

199 See the works cited, above note 158.

200 See above note 157.

in force, notwithstanding the written agreement.[201] Although referred to here as an aspect of the "modern" approach to the rule, it should be noted that the idea that the parol evidence rule merely creates a presumption in favour of the written document is far from being a new idea. In *Pym v. Campbell*[202] itself, for example, Erle J. referred to the rule as creating a "strong presumption" in favour of the writing.[203] Thus, where an oral undertaking is given prior to the execution of the written agreement and it appears evident that the prior undertaking was intended to be binding, it is often held that the agreement is intended to be partly oral and partly in writing.[204]

The extent to which the modern approach represents good Canadian law at the present time remains unclear. Although the *Hawrish* and *Bauer* decisions appear to be traditional in their approach, it is nonetheless the case that in neither of these authorities did the Supreme Court of Canada either explicitly articulate the doctrine or indicate that a choice was being made among the various strands of existing authority applying the parol evidence rule and its various exceptions. Indeed, it appears possible to read these decisions as being consistent with a more modern view of the scope of the rule. Such a reading has been given in the influential decision of the British Columbia Court of Appeal in *Gallen v. Butterley*.[205] The facts of this case concerned the purchase of buckwheat seed under a written agreement that excluded any warranties pertaining to the qualities of the seed. The plaintiff had entered into the contract on the faith of oral assurances that buckwheat as a crop would blanket and smother various weeds. In the event, this proved not to be the case and the plaintiff successfully sued for breach of the oral warranty. The supplier appealed the decision on the basis that the parol evidence rule precluded the admissibility of evidence concerning the oral warranty. Lambert J.A. in his reasons made a number of points concerning the Supreme Court jurisprudence on the rule and on the operation of the rule more generally. First, Lambert J.A., emphasized that the rule cannot properly be considered to be an absolute bar to the admission of evidence of prior undertakings. Otherwise, the doctrine would become "a tool for the unscrupulous to dupe the unwary." Further, he indicated that the

---

201 See K.W. Wedderburn, "Collateral Contracts" [1959] Cambridge L.J. 58 at 60; D. McLauchlan, *The Parol Evidence Rule* (Wellington: Professional Publications, 1976).

202 Above note 173.

203 *Ibid.* at 370 (E.&B.), 905 (E.R.). See also *Gillespie Bros. v. Cheney, Eggar & Co.*, [1896] 2 Q.B. 59 at 62, Lord Russell of Killowen C.J.

204 See, for example, *J. Evans & Son (Portsmouth) Ltd. v. Merzario (Andrea) Ltd.*, above note 186.

205 (1984), 9 D.L.R. (4th) 496 (B.C.C.A.).

decisions of the Supreme Court of Canada in *Hawrish*, *Bauer* and *Carman Construction* were consistent with this view. In each of these cases, as he noted, the Court considered carefully the question of whether the evidence actually supported the existence of the oral undertaking in question. If the rule was an absolute one, no such inquiry would be necessary. Further, he noted the persistence of the important exception to the rule relating to oral misrepresentation of the content or effect of the written terms thus providing an illustration of the proposition that an inconsistent oral misrepresentation may prevail over the written agreement.

As to the general nature of the rule, Lambert J.A. stated that the effect of the Canadian jurisprudence is simply to create a presumption in favour of the written agreement. The presumption is a strong one and would be at its strongest when the alleged oral representation is contrary to the written terms and somewhat less strong when the oral representation merely adds to them. Further, it was his view that the presumption would be more rigorous in a case where the parties had themselves negotiated and prepared the written agreement than in a case where a printed form was used. Finally, it was his view that the presumption would be less strong in a case where the contest was between a specific oral representation and a general exemption or exclusion clause, in which case it may be possible to read the specific representation as intended to be an exception to the more general stipulation. On the particular facts of this case, Lambert J.A. was of the view that an oral warranty was intended and that it could be read consistently with and as an exception to the more general exclusionary clause. In the result, then, the claim enjoyed success.

The approach adopted in *Gallen* offers a reading of Canadian doctrine that is more consistent with the approach taken in contemporary law in other common law jurisdictions. Further, the *Gallen* analysis provides a sound basis for avoiding the unjust results that can be produced by a too rigid application of the traditional approach. Moreover, it is more directly linked to the underlying rationale of the rule, a policy of giving effect to genuine agreements between the parties to treat their written agreement as the exclusive expression of the terms of their agreement. Under *Gallen*, evidence relevant to the determination of whether such an agreement occurred is, of course, admissible and, if a prior oral undertaking is intended to be binding, it may prevail over the written agreement. The decision in *Gallen*, and the cases that have followed it,[206] thus

---

206 See, for example, *Corey Developments Inc. v. Eastbridge Developments (Waterloo) Ltd.* (1997), 34 O.R. (3d) 73 (Gen. Div.), aff'd on other grounds (1999), 44 O.R. (3d) 95 (C.A.); *Douglas Lake Capital Co. v. Smith* (1991), 78 D.L.R. (4th) 319

offer some evidence of movement in the direction of adoption of a modern approach to the parol evidence rule in Canadian law.

5) Merger and Entire Agreement Clauses

Parties who wish to ensure that their written agreement is the exclusive source of their contractual arrangements may, of course, plainly stipulate to this effect in the written agreement. Effect will normally be give to such "merger" or "entire agreement" clauses where they represent a genuine *consensus* of the parties on this point. More difficult is the case where the clause appears in a printed form or written agreement proffered by one party in circumstances where the other party may not be aware of the existence of the term. Such terms may, of course, create a trap for the unwary party who has relied on an oral undertaking of some kind as a basis for entering into the written agreement. Accordingly, courts have often permitted the oral understandings to prevail over terms of this kind. As we have seen, the exception to the parol evidence rule pertaining to the enforceability of collateral agreements has provided a means for giving effect to prior oral undertakings.[207] Further, as the decision of the English Court of Appeal in *J. Evans & Son (Portsmouth) Ltd. v. Merzario (Andrea) Ltd.*[208] illustrates, courts have occasionally relied on the principle of construction that an earlier undertaking may prevail over a subsequent and repugnant undertaking.[209] This case concerned the transport of equipment by sea at the request of the plaintiff importer, a frequent customer of the defendant forwarding agent. On this occasion, the defendant proposed, for the first time, to ship the equipment in open containers. Concerned that the equipment would rust if carried in open containers on the deck, the plaintiff extracted an oral undertaking from the defendant that the containers in which the equipment was placed would be stored below deck. In the event, the equipment was carried on deck and the defendant sought to defend itself from the plaintiff's claim to enforce the oral assurance on the basis that the written agreement reserved to the defendant a complete freedom in the manner of handling the equipment. The Court of Appeal held that the oral undertaking prevailed over the written agree-

---

(B.C.C.A.). See also *Ahone v. Holloway* (1988), 30 B.C.L.R. (2d) 368 at 372-73 (C.A.), McLachlin J.A.

207　For discussion, see above the text at notes 180–89.

208　*J. Evans & Son (Portsmouth) Ltd. v. Merzario (Andrea) Ltd.*, above note 186.

209　For discussion of this principle of interpretation, see Chapter 19, section C(9).

ment. Otherwise, the oral undertaking would be "wholly illusory."[210] More generally, Canadian courts have given a narrow construction to entire agreement clauses and resist their application in circumstances where adequate notice of the existence of the provision has not been given to the other party.[211]

6) Conclusion

As we have seen, the decisions of the Supreme Court of Canada in *Hawrish* and *Bauer* appear to adopt a traditional approach to the application of the parol evidence rule, which is importantly different from the modern approach taken to the application of the rule in other common law jurisdictions. More recent cases, however, have attributed a more modern approach to the interpretation of these decisions and to the application of the rule. English experience suggests that the recent Canadian movement in the direction of a modern approach to application of the parol evidence rule is likely to reduce the need for statutory reform of the rule. This development is arguably preferable to statutory abolition of the rule as it leaves undisturbed the standard and acceptable commercial practice of including entire agreement clauses in genuinely negotiated agreements. In the consumer context, however, the risk of misleading sales practices being combined with printed forms, including entire agreement clauses, has provided and will likely continue to provide incentives for statutory reform. Thus, in a number of provinces, legislation has been enacted that abolishes the application of the rule in consumer transactions.[212]

FURTHER READINGS

M. BRIDGE, "The Statute of Frauds and Sale of Land Contracts" (1986) 64 Can. Bar Rev. 58.

S. CHRISTENSEN & R. LOW, "Moving the Statute of Frauds to the Digital Age" (2003) 77 Aust. L.J. 416.

A.L. CORBIN, "The Parol Evidence Rule" (1944) 53 Yale L.J. 603.

---

210 *J. Evans & Son (Portsmouth) Ltd. v. Merzario (Andrea) Ltd.*, above note 186 at 1084, Roskill L.J.
211 For discussion of these authorities see Chapter 10, section G.
212 See, for example, *Trade Practice Act*, R.S.B.C. 1996, c. 457; *Consumer Protection Act, 2002*, S.O. 2002, c. 30, s. 18(10)).

G.H.L. FRIDMAN, "The Necessity for Writing in Contracts within the Statute of Frauds" (1985) 35 U.T.L.J. 43.

J.S. JOHNSTON, "The Statute of Frauds and Business Norms: A Testable Game-Theoretic Model" (1996) 144 U. Pa. L. Rev. 1859.

F. KESSLER, "Contracts of Adhesion — Some Thoughts About Freedom of Contract" (1943) 43 Colum. L. Rev. 629.

LAW COMMISSION, *The Parol Evidence Rule* (Law Com. 154) Cmnd 9700 (London: HMSO, 1986).

LAW REFORM COMMISSION OF BRITISH COLUMBIA, *Report on Parol Evidence Rule* (Victoria, BC: Queen's Printer, 1980).

LAW REFORM COMMISSION OF BRITISH COLUMBIA, *Report on the Statute of Frauds* (Vancouver: The Commission, 1977).

LAW REVISION COMMITTEE, *Sixth Interim Report (Statute of Frauds and the Doctrine of Consideration)* Cmnd 5449 (London: HMSO, 1937).

P. LINZER, "The Comfort of Certainty: Plain Meaning and the Parol Evidence Rule" (2002) 71 Fordham L. Rev. 799.

I.R. MACNEIL, "Bureaucracy and Contracts of Adhesion" (1984) 22 Osgoode Hall L.J. 5.

MANITOBA LAW REFORM COMMISSION, *Report on the Statute of Frauds* (Winnipeg: The Commission, 1980).

D.W. MCLAUCHLAN, "The Inconsistent Collateral Contract" (1976) 3 Dal. L.J. 136.

D.W. MCLAUCHLAN, *The Parol Evidence Rule* (Wellington: Professional Publications, 1976).

ONTARIO LAW REFORM COMMISSION, *Report on Amendment on the Law of Contract* (Toronto: Ministry of the Attorney General, 1987) c. 5 and 8.

T.D. RAKOFF, "Contracts of Adhesion: An Essay in Reconstruction" (1983) 96 Harv. L. Rev. 1174.

R.S. STEVENS, "Ethics and the Statute of Frauds" (1952) 37 Cornell L.Q. 355.

S.M. WADDAMS, "Do We Need a Parol Evidence Rule?" (1991) 19 Can. Bus. L.J. 387.

PART TWO

ENFORCEABILITY

CONSIDERATION AND FORM

A. INTRODUCTION

The giving and, indeed, exchanging of promises or undertakings is a pervasive feature of our commercial and social lives. A question of central importance for the law of contracts is to articulate a basis for distinguishing between those promises that should properly attract the attention of the legal system as enforceable promises and those that should not. Although an argument could be fashioned on the basis of moral precepts that all promises should be considered binding as a matter of honour, few observers would suggest that all promises should be legally enforceable regardless of how rash and improvident they might have been and regardless of the setting, be it commercial or non-commercial, in which the promise was made. In the English common law tradition, two criteria of enforceability or rules for the recognition of enforceable promises have developed.

The basic principle is that promises will be enforced only if they form part of a bargain. The doctrine of consideration holds that to be enforceable, a promise must be purchased in the sense of being given in return for something of value provided by the promisee or, as is said, for "good consideration." The enforcement of bargains obviously plays an important role in the functioning of a modern credit economy. It is easily seen, therefore, that a strong rationale exists for the enforcement of bargains. What is less clear, however, is whether the doctrine of consideration or, as it is sometimes called, the bargain theory, successfully identifies the proper line of demarcation between those promises that should be considered enforceable by the legal system and those that should not. Indeed, the doctrine of consideration has attracted much criticism over the years. In the present chapter, after providing an account of various aspects of the application of the doctrine, we will return to consider the prospects for its reform.

The second rule of recognition for enforceable promises rests on the formal trappings within which the undertaking is given. Thus, centuries prior to the development of the doctrine of consideration, the English legal system recognized as enforceable those promises that were made in the form of sealed instruments. Although the manner or method of sealing instruments has evolved over time, the basic principle that a promise given under seal is enforceable simply because of the formal manner in which the undertaking has been given has persisted. For much of the early history of the doctrine, the execution of an instrument under seal involved the melting of some wax or other adhesive substance on the instrument upon which an impression of a seal or signet ring or other identifier of the party executing the instrument could be made. The general enforceability of instruments executed in this fashion appears to stretch back as far, at least, as the fourteenth century.[1] In an essentially pre-literate society, it is easily seen that the affixing of the seals constituted, in effect, a form of signature. Under contemporary practice, of course, it is commonplace for people to execute agreements by placing their handwritten signature on the document. There is thus no practical necessity for the use of seals as an equivalent of signature. Nonetheless, the practice of sealing instruments and of enforcing them simply by reason of their formal nature continues in many common law jurisdictions to the present day. The contemporary version of the sealed instrument typically involves the affixing of a small round piece of red-coloured adhesive paper or "wafer" next to the signature of the promisor. Although the solemnity of the act of sealing has thus obviously declined over the centuries, the execution of instruments under seal nonetheless remains a useful alternative to consideration as it provides a device by which non-bargain promises can be rendered enforceable. At the same time, the decline in the solemnity of the form and the fact that, outside the legal profession, there is unlikely to be widespread understanding of the legal significance of the typical contemporary seal, the doctrine has attracted

---

1   See A.W.B. Simpson, *A History of the Common Law of Contract* (Oxford: Clarendon Press, 1975) at 9–52.

much criticism in the modern era. After examining the contemporary doctrine relating to sealed instruments, then, we will return to consider contemporary justifications for doctrines justifying enforceability on the basis of requirements of formality and possible measures for the reform of current formality doctrine.

The history of the development of the doctrine of consideration and its ultimate emergence in its modern form in the late-eighteenth and nineteenth centuries is both complicated and the subject of much academic investigation and controversy.[2] This complex story cannot be told here. We may note, however, that along the way various alternative formulations of the basic rule of recognition were rejected. Thus, for a time, English courts and, in particular, Lord Mansfield, toyed with the idea that contracts recorded in writing could be enforceable even in the absence of consideration. In the well-known case of *Pillans and Rose v. Van Mierop & Hopkins*,[3] Lord Mansfield offered the controversial view that the rationale of the consideration doctrine was merely evidentiary in nature and that other evidence of contractual intent, such as the recording of the agreement in writing, should suffice, even in the absence of consideration. More generally, it was his view that the absence of consideration should not defeat agreements between merchants, both formal and informal. A few years later, however, the House of Lords, in its 1778 decision in *Rann v. Hughes*,[4] rejected as erroneous Mansfield's suggestion that the fact of a writing eliminated the need for consideration. Nonetheless, the fact that the doctrine of consideration renders unenforceable some seriously intended promises, especially those given by merchants, because of the absence of consideration, continues to inspire contemporary criticism of the doctrine and may, indeed, lead to its reform.

Further, English law has rejected the idea that the fact that a promise has been followed by substantial detrimental reliance thereon by the promisee should render the promise enforceable, at least in cases where the reliance was foreseeable or, indeed, intended by the promisor.[5] Again, however, the fact that foreseeable detrimental reliance on a promise will not have the effect of rendering the promise enforceable persists as a point

---

2   See, for example, Simpson, above note 1; S.J. Stoljar, *A History of Contract at Common Law* (Canberra: Australian National University Press, 1975).

3   (1765), 3 Burr. 1663, 97 E.R. 1035 (K.B.). See K. Teeven, "Mansfield's Reform of Consideration in Light of the Origins of the Doctrine" (1991) 21 Memphis State U.L. Rev. 669. See also Simpson, *ibid.* at 617–19.

4   (1778), 4 Brown P.C. 27, 2 E.R. 18 (H.L.).

5   For discussion of early intimations of a reliance doctrine, see Teeven, above note 3 at 670–72.

of criticism of the modern doctrine of consideration. By way of contrast, the American doctrine of promissory estoppel accepts that foreseeable detrimental reliance on a promise may render the promise binding "if injustice can be avoided only by enforcement of the promise."[6] Thus far, however, although both English and Canadian courts recognize a similar doctrine of promissory estoppel, the traditional and prevailing view remains that promissory estoppel should not provide a basis for recognizing the enforceability of promises in the sense that such promises could form the basis for an action to be brought by the promisee to seek their enforcement. The possibility that recognition of a rule rendering promises enforceable on the basis of detrimental reliance could ameliorate some of the perceived difficulties with the doctrine of consideration will be further considered below[7] and in a subsequent chapter examining the doctrine of promissory estoppel.[8]

B. CONSIDERATION

1) The Bargain Theory

a) The Definition of Consideration

The doctrine of consideration identifies as enforceable those promises that have been given or made as part of a bargain or exchange. An enforceable promise is one that has been, in effect, purchased by the promisee. This central or basic concept was expressed in Sir Frederick Pollock's classic definition of the doctrine in the following terms: "An act or forbearance of the one party, or the promise thereof, is the price for which the promise of the other is bought, and the promise thus given for value is enforceable."[9]

The "consideration," then, is the act or forbearance or promise thereof given in return for the promise that one wishes to enforce. A promise for which no consideration is given in return may be said to be gratuitous. Such promises are often referred to as "bare" or "naked."

---

6   American Law Institute, *Restatement of Contracts 2d* (St. Paul: American Law Institute, 1981) s. 90.
7   See this Chapter, section D.
8   See Chapter 8.
9   P.H. Winfield, ed., *Pollock's Principles of Contract*, 13th ed. (London: Stevens & Sons, 1950) at 133. See also American Law Institute, *Restatement of Contracts 2d*, above note 6, s. 71. This definition was quoted, with approval, for example, in *Dunlop Pneumatic Tyre Co. v. Selfridge & Co.*, [1915] A.C. 847 at 855 (H.L.), Lord Dunedin.

The arrangement between the parties is sometimes referred to as a "*nudum pactum*" or may be said to fail for "want of mutuality." If something given in return for the promise constitutes consideration in the requisite sense, it may be referred to as "good," "valid" or "sufficient" consideration.

At a relatively early stage, the common law recognized that a promise to act or forbear in return for another's promise could constitute consideration rendering the latter promise enforceable.[10] Agreements in which a promise is exchanged for a promise are commonly referred to as "bilateral" contracts. Typical commercial agreements are very likely to be bilateral in form. Thus, a supplier of goods or services may promise to provide them in return for the purchaser's promise to pay the contract price. With recognition of the possibility of enforcing bilateral agreements, it became possible to enforce a wholly executory exchange in which, although the parties have exchanged promises, no performance of either promise has yet been provided. Although it is plainly established that wholly executory agreements are enforceable, the question of whether they should be enforced has been the subject of some recent controversy. This is a matter to be further pursued in the context of a discussion of the remedies available for the enforcement of wholly executory exchanges.[11]

Bilateral agreements in which a promise is exchanged for a promise may be contrasted with unilateral agreements in which the promise one wishes to enforce is exchanged for an act or forbearance. An offer of a reward provides a simple illustration of a unilateral contract. A reward posted for the provision of information that will lead to the arrest and conviction of the perpetrator of a particular act in return for a promise of a money payment invites the performance of an act as the price, one might say, of the reward. Similarly, a guarantor of a bank loan may promise to guarantee the loan in return for the bank's act of advancing funds to the borrower. In the case of an existing bank loan, the giving of a guarantee might illustrate the exchange of forbearance for an enforceable promise. Assuming that the bank does not promise to forbear from enforcement of the loan, the guarantee may take the form of an undertaking by the guarantor to guarantee repayment of the loan if the bank forbears from calling in the loan or taking other steps

---

10   See, for example, *Thorp v. Thorp* (1702), 12 Mod. 455, 88 E.R. 1448 at 1450, Holt C.J. For an examination of the history of consideration doctrine, see Simpson, *A History of the Common Law of Contract*, above note 1, c. 4–6; S.J. Stoljar, *A History of Contract at Common Law,* above note 2 at 37–85.

11   See further Chapter 22, section C.

against the borrower for a particular or, indeed, a reasonable period of time.[12] As we have seen in the context of our discussion of the rules of offer and acceptance,[13] whatever expressions the parties might have used to communicate their arrangements, an offer of a truly unilateral contract can be restated in the formula "if you do (or not do) x, I promise y." The doing of the requested act or complying with the request to forbear has the effect both of accepting the offer and of providing the consideration that renders the offeror's promise enforceable.

Consideration may be constituted by any act or forbearance or promise thereof considered to be of value by the promisor. Thus, the nature of consideration has been described in another classic statement of the doctrine, in *Currie v. Misa*,[14] in the following terms: "A valuable consideration, in the sense of the law, may consist either in some right, interest, profit, or benefit accruing to the one party, or some forbearance, detriment, loss or responsibility, given, suffered, or undertaken by the other."[15]

The fact that the benefit to the promisor and detriment to the promisee are stated as alternatives may be taken to suggest that a benefit to be conferred by the promisee on a third party may constitute consideration. That this is plainly so may be illustrated by the simple guarantee of a bank loan mentioned earlier in the chapter. The guarantor's promise to guarantee the loan is given in return for the bank's conferral of a benefit on the borrower. In such circumstances, it might be said that the guarantor does not receive a benefit in return for the promise to guarantee, but the promisee bank does suffer the detriment of conferring or promising to confer value on the borrower. Similarly, the not uncommon arrangement under which a borrower might stipulate that the moneys are to be paid to a third party is binding. Again, while it might be suggested that the borrower does not benefit from such a payment term, the lender has suffered a detriment by undertaking to make such a payment. In all such cases, of course, it may be argued that the promisor would not have requested that a benefit be conferred on a third party unless it was of some advantage to the promisor to do so. In such cases, however, it is unnecessary to find that the promisor has indirectly benefited in some fashion. Consideration is constituted

---

12   See, for example, *Royal Bank v. Kiska* (1967), 63 D.L.R. (2d) 582 (Ont. C.A.).

13   See Chapter 2, sections A and B(1)(b).

14   (1875), L.R. 10 Ex. 153, aff'd 1 App. Cas. 554. See also *Sprucegrove (Town) v. Yellowhead Regional Library Board* (1982), 143 D.L.R. (3d) 188 (Alta. C.A.); *Fleming v. Bank of New Zealand*, [1990] A.C. 577 (P.C.).

15   *Currie v. Misa, ibid.* at 162.

by the detriment suffered by the promisee. As is sometimes said, the benefit need not necessarily "move" from the promisee to the promisor. It may move from the promisee to a third party.

It is, however, a well-established feature of the traditional doctrine of consideration that consideration must "move" from the promisee or, in other words, that a detriment of some kind must be suffered by the promisee. This proposition is one of the traditional justifications for the doctrine of privity of contract, which holds that a third party upon whom benefits are to be conferred by the promisor but who has given no consideration in return has no standing to enforce the promisor's undertaking. Although, as we shall see,[16] the doctrine of privity of contract is not followed in American law and has been abrogated by statute in a number of commonwealth jurisdictions, including one Canadian province,[17] the traditional doctrine of privity remains generally applicable in other common law jurisdictions. Regardless of the status of the doctrine of privity in a particular common law jurisdiction, however, the critical point for purposes of the doctrine of consideration is to note that a valid consideration must move from the promisee and thus, as a general proposition, it is necessary to establish in every case that the promisee has suffered a detriment of some kind. For the doctrine to apply, then, it must be established that the promisee has either acted or forborne from acting in the manner requested by the promisor or has given a return promise that will, in some fashion, restrict the promisee's freedom of action in the future.

The utility of considering, when applying the consideration doctrine, whether the promisee has made a commitment that restrains freedom of action in the future rather than the more pliable concepts of benefit and detriment may be illustrated by the well-known decision in *Hamer v. Sidway*.[18] This famous case involved a promise made by a nephew to refrain from using alcohol or tobacco, swearing or playing cards until the age of twenty-one, as requested by his uncle in return for the uncle's promise to pay him $5,000. Having complied with his undertaking, the nephew, upon turning twenty-one sought to enforce the promise. The uncle acknowledged the debt and indicated that money had been set aside for the purpose of paying the young man; but the uncle was reluctant to do so while the nephew was still so young.

---

16   For discussion of the doctrine of privity of contract, see Chapter 9.

17   New Brunswick. See *Law Reform Act*, S.N.B. 1993, c. L-1.2, s. 4.

18   27 N.E. 256 (N.Y.C.A. 1891); although a New York decision, the court applied English authorities, including *Currie v. Misa,* above note 14, and is generally assumed to be consistent with English law.

After the uncle's death, the nephew sought enforcement against his estate. It was argued in defence that far from suffering a detriment as a result of complying with his uncle's wishes, the nephew had actually benefited and, accordingly, the uncle's promise was not supported by consideration. In rejecting this defence, the court reasoned that the correct approach is to consider whether the promisee has limited his legal freedom of action in return for the undertaking of the promisor. Applying this rule to the present facts, the court indicated that it was "sufficient that [the nephew] restricted his lawful freedom of action within certain prescribed limits upon the faith of his uncle's agreement, and now, having fully performed the conditions imposed, it is of no moment whether such performance actually proved a benefit to the promisor."[19] In any event, in the court's view, there was nothing in the record precluding a determination that the uncle had benefited "in a legal sense."[20] This decision is often contrasted with the earlier English case, *White v. Bluett*.[21] In this case, a son had given a promissory note to his father in acknowledgment of monies advanced to the son in the form of a loan. In response to the son's complaint that the father had been more generous to his siblings, the father indicated that if the son would stop making such complaints, he would forgive the debt. Although this arrangement took the form of an exchange of promises, Pollock C.B. opined that the suggestion that the son's promise constituted good consideration pressed a consideration analysis "to an absurdity, as a bubble is blown until it bursts."[22] In his view, "[t]he son had no right to complain for the father might make what distribution of his property he liked; and the son's abstaining from doing what he had no right to do can be no consideration."[23] It may be, however, that a more convincing explanation for the result is simply that, in such circumstances, it appears unlikely that the parties intended to create a legally binding agreement.[24]

b) Certainty

The commitment given by the promisee may be too vague or imprecise to constitute good consideration. Thus, a promise to give a "good price"

---

19   *Ibid.* at 257.
20   *Ibid.*
21   (1853), 23 L.J. Ex. 36.
22   *Ibid.* at 37.
23   *Ibid.*
24   For discussion of the requirement that the parties must have such an intention, see Chapter 4.

on a future contract would not constitute good consideration.[25] Similarly, it promised to build such residential premises as the promisor may consider appropriate would not constitute good consideration.[26] Indeed, the requirement of some degree of certainty may provide an alternative explanation for the result in *White v. Bluett*.[27] Parke B. intimated such a view when he interjected that an argument "is an agreement by a father in consideration that his son will not bore him a binding contract?"[28] On the other hand, where there has been reliance on what appears to be a rather vague promise or, perhaps, where the arrangement is a socially valuable one, the courts may incline in the direction of giving content to the undertaking. Thus, in an Australian case, *Dunton v. Dunton*,[29] an estranged husband's undertaking to provide maintenance was held to be supported by the wife's undertaking to behave in a "respectable, orderly and virtuous manner."[30]

c) Firm Offers

The requirement that the promisee give in exchange a commitment that restricts future freedom of action may preclude the enforcement of fairly common transactional patterns. Thus, a so-called firm offer under which, for example, a potential purchaser of an asset makes an offer to the owner of the asset to purchase it at a stated price and promises to keep the offer open for a particular period of time, the promise to keep the offer open would not be enforceable in the absence of any commitment on the part of the owner.[31] Notwithstanding the fact that the owner might have relied on the firm offer by, for example, turning down other attractive offers, the offeror is entitled to revoke the offer. The "firm offer" arrangement fails for want of mutuality. Occasionally,

---

25 *Gilbert Steel Ltd. v. University Construction Ltd.* (1976), 67 D.L.R. (3d) 606 (Ont. C.A.); *Canada West Tree Fruits Ltd. v. T.G. Bright & Company* (1990), 48 B.C.L.R. (2d) 91 (C.A.), leave to appeal to S.C.C. refused (1991), 52 B.C.L.R. (2d) xxxviii n. Compare with *Copycats v. Rosney* (1989), 62 Man. R. (2d) 308 (Q.B.).

26 *Rosher v. Williams* (1875), L.R. 20 Eq. 210, 44 L.J. Ch. 419.

27 Above note 21.

28 *Ibid* at 37.

29 (1892), 18 V.L.R. 114 (Vict. S.C.). See also *Main v. Main*, [1955] 2 D.L.R. 588 (B.C.S.C.), aff'd (1956), 2 D.L.R. (2d) 341 (B.C.C.A.); *Ward v. Byham*, [1956] 1 W.L.R. 496 (C.A.).

30 *Dunton v. Dunton, ibid.* at 118.

31 *Dickinson v. Dodds* (1876), 2 Ch. D. 463; *Stevenson v. McLean* (1880), 5 Q.B.D. 346; *Bristol, Cardiff & Swansea Aërated Bread Co. v. Maggs* (1890), 44 Ch. D. 616; *Davis v. Shaw* (1910), 21 O.L.R. 474 (Div. Ct.); *Fraser v. Morrison* (1958), 12 D.L.R. (2d) 612 (Man. C.A.); *Rei-Mar Investment Ltd. v. Christie* (1974), 48 D.L.R. (3d) 315 (B.C.S.C.); *Gibson v. McVeigh*, [1922] 1 W.W.R. 151 (Alta. S.C.).

it has been suggested that the law should be reformed to render firm offers binding, at least when given in a commercial context.[32] Similarly, where a supplier of goods undertakes to provide goods to a customer at certain stipulated prices, the arrangement will be unenforceable if the customer has given no commitment in return to purchase any goods whatsoever.[33] Any individual order placed by the customer, prior to withdrawal of the offer by the supplier, will, of course, create a binding agreement.[34] If, however, the customer has committed itself to the seller as the exclusive supplier of the goods in question, consideration may be found. The customer is committed, at least, to purchase the goods from no other supplier and has thus limited its freedom of action.[35] A similar analysis should apply to "output" agreements under which a customer undertakes to purchase all the supplier's production or output of a particular commodity.[36] Although the supplier may not be committed to produce any particular quantity under such an agreement, the supplier is at least committed to supply such goods to no one else.

d) Illusory Consideration

An agreement that reserves the right of one party to proceed with a transaction only if he or she wishes to do so would fail for want of mutuality. Thus, an agreement to purchase real estate subject to the purchaser's approval of the premises and various other matters failed for lack of consideration.[37] Similarly, an agreement with a corporation that was stipulated to be subject to the approval of the company's president

---

32   See, for example, Law Commission ,*Working Paper No. 60: Firm Offers* (London: HMSO, 1975); Ontario Law Reform Commission, *Report on Sale of Goods* (Toronto: Ministry of the Attorney General, 1979) at 91–96; Ontario Law Reform Commission, *Report on Amendment of the Law of Contract* (Toronto: Ministry of the Attorney General, 1987) at 25. See also Uniform Commercial Code, s. 2-205 (signed firm offer by merchant enforceable).

33   *Greenberg v. Lake Simcoe Ice Supply Co.* (1917), 39 O.L.R. 32 (H.C.J.). The point was left unanswered in *Great Northern Rwy. Co. v. Witham* (1873), L.R. 9 C.P. 16.

34   See *Greenberg v. Lake Simcoe Ice Supply Co.*, *ibid.*; *Great Northern Rwy. Co. v. Witham*, *ibid.*

35   See *The Queen v. McLean* (1884), 8 S.C.R. 210; *In Re Gloucester Municipal Election Petition*, [1901] 1 K.B. 683; *Brandon Gas & Power v. Brandon Creamery Co.* (1912), 8 D.L.R. 191 (Man. C.A.).

36   However, an agreement that confers a right but not an obligation to buy the supplier's output will fail for lack of consideration. See *Tobias v. Dick and T. Eaton Co.*, [1937] 4 D.L.R. 546 (Man. K.B.). See generally E.A. Farnsworth, *Contracts*, vol. 1, 2d ed. (New York, Aspen, 1998) at 135–40. And see *Empire Gas Corp. v. American Bakeries Co.*, 840 F.2d 1333 (U.S.C.A. 7th Cir. 1988).

37   *Black, Gavin & Co. v. Cheung* (1980), 20 B.C.L.R. 21 (S.C.).

was held to be unsupported by consideration.[38] Such arrangements have the appearance of an agreement and the parties may indeed believe that an enforceable agreement has been created by them. On more careful examination, however, it is clear that one party has made no commitment whatsoever and thus, neither party can enforce the agreement. The consideration in such cases is often said to be "illusory."

e) Implied Consideration

Occasionally, courts may address the problem presented by cases of illusory consideration by finding an implicit undertaking in the arrangement on the part of the promisee. A well-known American case is *Wood v. Lucy, Lady Duff-Gordon*.[39] The defendant was a fashion designer who entered into an agreement with the plaintiff under which he would have the exclusive right to market her designs and, subject to her approval, to place her endorsement on the designs of others. The defendant was to have no right to place her endorsements on other people's designs other than through the plaintiff's agency for a period of one year. Although the agreement placed no explicit obligation on the plaintiff to promote the defendant's designs and endorsements, the agreement did recite the existence of a business organization maintained by the plaintiff that was suited to these purposes. The parties were to share profits accruing from the plaintiff's efforts. Although the plaintiff did conduct the business in the manner expected, the defendant breached her obligations under the arrangement and placed her endorsement on the fabrics and other fashion products of others, refusing to share the profits earned thereby with the plaintiff. The defence sought to defend the plaintiff's action for breach of contract on the basis that the agreement lacked mutuality. Cardozo J., however, held that the agreement was "'instinct with an obligation,' imperfectly expressed"[40] to the effect that the plaintiff would "use reasonable efforts" to bring profits and revenues into existence."[41] Applying the traditional test for implying terms, Cardozo J. held that such a term was necessary to give "business efficacy" to the agreement.[42] A similar approach has been

---

38 *Murray McDermid Holdings Ltd. v. Thater* (1983), 42 B.C.L.R. 119 (S.C.).

39 118 N.E. 214 (N.Y.C.A. 1917). And see *Dawson v. Helicopter Exploration Co.*, [1955] 5 D.L.R. 404 (S.C.C.).

40 *Wood v. Lucy, Lady Duff-Gordon*, ibid. at 214.

41 *Ibid.* at 215.

42 For discussion of the law concerning the implication of terms, see Chapter 19, section D.

taken in numerous English and Canadian authorities.[43] Thus, for example, in *Royal Bank of Canada v. Kiska*[44] a guarantee of a bank loan by the brother of the borrower was held to be binding on the basis that it was implicit in the circumstances that the brother had implicitly requested the bank to forbear from proceeding against his brother for a reasonable period of time. Courts are unlikely to imply terms in circumstances, however, where the party now wishing to imply a term intentionally avoided assuming any responsibility under the agreement. Thus, in *Tobias v. Dick and T. Eaton Co.*[45] the plaintiff distributor had induced the defendant manufacturer "by trickery"[46] to sign an exclusive distribution agreement, which, in fact, imposed no obligations on the distributor. The manufacturer, after despairing of its ability to sell more machines to the distributor, ignored the agreement and began to sell his machines to other distributors. The manufacturer successfully defended the distributor's claim for damages for breach of contract on the basis that the agreement lacked mutuality.

f) The "Peppercorn Theory"

Application of the doctrine of consideration does not require that the consideration is in some sense adequate or equivalent in value to the promise to be enforced. It is an "elementary principle that the law will not enter into an inquiry as to the adequacy of consideration."[47] Or, as is sometimes said, consideration must be sufficient but it need not be adequate. Severe inadequacy of consideration may be relevant to determination of the existence of fraud[48] or the applicability of doctrines such as undue influence[49] or unconscionability,[50] but it does not preclude a finding of sufficient consideration. This aspect of the doc-

---

43 See, for example, *Churchward v. The Queen* (1865), L.R. 1 Q.B. 173 at 195, Cockburn C.J.; *Berliner Gramophone Co. Ltd. v. Scythes* (1916), 31 D.L.R. 789 (Sask. S.C.); *Canada Cycle and Motor Co. Ltd. v. Mehr* (1919), 48 D.L.R. 579 (Ont. S.C.A.D.); *Warren & Co. v. Agdeshman* (1922), 38 T.L.R. 588 (K.B.); *Canadian Hockey Club Inc. v. Arena Amusements Ltd.*, [1930] 1 D.L.R. 127 (S.C.C.); *Burgoyne v. Murphy*, [1951] 2 D.L.R. 556 (N.B.S.C.); *Great Eastern Oil & Import Co. Ltd. v. Chafe*, [1956] 4 D.L.R. (2d) 310 (Nfld. S.C.).

44 Above note 12.

45 Above note 36.

46 *Ibid.* at 546.

47 *Westlake v. Adams* (1858), 5 C.B. (N.S.) 248, 141 E.R. 99 at 106, Byles J. See also *Bolton v. Madden* (1873), L.R. 9 Q.B. 55 at 57, Blackburn J.; *Fleming v. Mair*, [1921] 2 W.W.R. 421 (Sask. C.A.); *Calmusky v. Karaloff*, [1947] S.C.R. 110.

48 See Chapter 10, section B.

49 See Chapter 11, section C.

50 See Chapter 11, section D.

trine of consideration is often referred to as the "peppercorn theory." In theory at least, in a bargain in which something of value is exchanged for something of even trivial value, such as a peppercorn, the exchange is enforceable.[51] In a well-known English illustration[52] of the proposition, the owner of two boilers allowed the defendant to weigh them. That consent constituted consideration for the defendant's undertaking to return them to the plaintiff in good order. It was not necessary to consider, in the court's view, the nature of the benefit the defendant expected to enjoy as a result of weighing the boilers. In another case, a newspaper's offer to provide financial advice to readers who requested such advice was said to be supported by the consideration constituted by the reader's request for the advice.[53] In an Ontario case, where a brother, on learning that his sister was about to buy a funeral plot, assured her that she could share his plot, the sister's act of refraining from purchasing her own plot constituted good consideration for his promise to share.[54] In *Bank of Nova Scotia v. MacLellan*,[55] a bank released a woman from a debt that she owed jointly with her ex-husband in return for an implicit promise that she would assist the bank in locating her husband. The Nova Scotia court held that although this consideration was "slight and of little real value"[56] it was sufficient to constitute good consideration for the bank's promise to discharge the debt.

g) Nominal Consideration

A related question is whether nominal consideration constitutes good consideration. The concept of nominal consideration generally is taken to refer to consideration of insignificant value, such as a dollar that is

51   Farnsworth has traced the peppercorn illustration through Blackstone back to Lord Coke. See Farnsworth, above note 36 at 118, n. 2.
52   *Bainbridge v. Firmstone* (1838), 8 Ad. & El. 743, 112 E.R. 1019.
53   *De la Bere v. Pearson*, [1908] 1 K.B. 280 (C.A.).
54   *Hubbs v. Black* (1918), 44 O.L.R. 545 (App. Div.).
55   (1977), 78 D.L.R. (3d) 1 (N.S.S.C.). The wife also promised to make a partial payment of the debt. This, in itself, however could not constitute good consideration for reasons further explored below, this Chapter, section B(3)(c). See also *Scivoletto v. De Dona* (1961), 35 W.W.R. 44 (Alta. D.C.) (plaintiff paid woman costs of emigration from Italy to enable marriage to plaintiff's son—woman marries defendant—plaintiff's forbearance from bringing suit against woman, even though claim worthless, held good consideration for defendant's promise to reimburse plaintiff); *Botjar v. Parker* (1979), 99 D.L.R. (3d) 147 (Ont. H.C.) ("gift" of property subject to mortgage—assumption of mortgage good consideration for the transfer), aff'd on other grounds (1979), 103 D.L.R. (3d) 577 (Ont. C.A.).
56   *Bank of Nova Scotia v. MacLellan, ibid.* at 2.

transferred in order to create the form of a transaction, thus rendering
the promise of the other party enforceable. It is a conceivable view that
such a transaction is a sham and ought not be enforced.[57] The traditional position of English common law, however, consistent with the
peppercorn theory, is that an exchange involving nominal consideration on one side is nonetheless binding. The mid-nineteenth-century
decision in *Thomas v. Thomas*[58] is a leading illustration of the point.
The executors of the deceased Thomas, believing that the deceased had
wished to provide a home for his wife in which she could reside after
his death, even though his will did not so provide, entered into an
agreement with his widow in order to accomplish this objective. The
agreement provided that she should be entitled to occupy the premises
during her life or until her remarriage, in return for the making of an
annual contribution of £1 to the ground rent for the premises, such
contribution to be paid annually to the executors. The court held that
the widow's undertaking constituted good consideration. In response
to the suggestion that she was merely accepting a gift with a burden attached, the court noted that she was not simply obliged to pay ground
rent to the superior landlord to whom it was owed but, rather, was to
pay a fresh apportionment of the rent to the executors. Accordingly, the
widow's obligation was not simply a burden that was incident to the
assignment of the property to her but was, rather, a different obligation
that could constitute valid consideration. Similarly, in a Canadian case,
a conveyance of property expressed to be for the consideration of $1 did
not fail for want of mutuality.[59]

Occasionally, however, Canadian courts have refused to give effect to transactions involving nominal consideration. In such cases,
however, it appears that the courts are concerned about an aspect of
the transaction in addition to the mere inadequacy of consideration. In
Harding v. Harding,[60] for example, an agreement under which a husband
purchased his wife's interest in the matrimonial home for $1 was held

57 There is some support for this approach in modern American law. See American
    Law Institute, *Restatement of Contracts 2d* (St. Paul: American Law Institute,
    1981) s. 71, Comment b, s. 79, Comment d. See also Farnsworth, above note 36
    at 118–22. Compare with *Restatement of Contracts 2d*, s. 84, Illus. 1.
58 (1842), 2 Q.B. 851, 114 E.R. 330. See also *Re Hogg Estate* (1987), 83 A.R. 165
    (Q.B.) (gift of house in return for donee's promise to pay capital gains tax levied
    on donor as a result of the transfer—binding).
59 *MacLauchlan v. Soper* (1965), 50 M.P.R. 339 (P.E.I.S.C.). See also *Davidson v.
    Norstrant* (1921), 61 S.C.R. 493; *Canadian Williston Minerals Ltd. v. Forseth and
    Imperial Oil Ltd.* (1962), 33 D.L.R. (2d) 72 (Sask. C.A.).
60 (1972), 28 D.L.R (3d) 358 (B.C.S.C.).

to fail for lack of mutuality. The arrangement was, however, plainly an oppressive one. The wife, having left her husband for what proved to be an unsuccessful relationship with another man wished to return to the matrimonial home and reunite with her husband. The husband took advantage of her desperate desire to do so by extracting the release of her interest in the matrimonial home. It is not surprising that a court would be reluctant to enforce such an agreement. In *Gilchrist Vending Ltd. v. Sedley Hotel Ltd.*,[61] a court refused to enforce an agreement between a hotelier and a supplier of a vending machine under which the hotelier granted the supplier an exclusive licence to install a vending machine in the hotel, but which further provided that the supplier could terminate the arrangement on payment of $1. It may be that the court was of the view that so onerous a provision ought to have been drawn to the attention of the hotelier.[62] Be that as it may, *Gilchrist Vending* was explained by the English Court of Appeal in *Mountford v. Scott*[63] as a decision that held only that possible future obligations that could be avoided by payment of $1 were illusory. On this basis, the court concluded that the decision was not inconsistent with the well-established principle "to the effect that anything of value, however small the value, is sufficient consideration to support a contract at law."[64] In this case, the Court of Appeal gave effect to an option or firm offer to purchase property given in return for £1. Where, however, a promise to pay $1 is exchanged for a promise to pay a larger sum of money, say $1,000, it is arguable that the arrangement is not a bargain, but a bare gift of $999.[65] On the assumption that this view is correct, the peppercorn theory would be restricted to cases where something of uncertain value is exchanged for money. Another view, however, is possible. The correct explanation for *Thomas v. Thomas*[66] may be that since the parties adopted the form, if not the substance, of a bargain in order to ensure enforceability, there is little reason to deny it to them.[67] If this is cor-

---

61   (1967), 66 D.L.R. (2d) 24 (Sask. Q.B.).

62   For discussion of this issue, see Chapter 6, section C.

63   [1975] 1 All E.R. 198 (C.A.).

64   *Ibid.* at 202.

65   There is American authority to this effect. See *Schnell v. Nell*, 17 Ind. 29 (1861); *Shepard & Co. v. Rhodes*, 7 R.I. 470 (1863); *In re Greene*, 45 F.2d 428 (S.D.N.Y. 1930).

66   Above note 58.

67   The rationale for enforceability would thus be similar to that rendering promises given under seal enforceable on grounds of formality. See further below, this Chapter, section C.

rect, it is not obvious that exchanges of money adopted for the same purpose should be considered unenforceable.[68]

h) Forbearance

A promise to forbear or, indeed, actual forbearance may constitute a valid consideration. The enforceability of a promise given in return for actual conduct of forbearance may arise, for example, in a context of the giving of a guarantee or further security to ensure repayment of a loan. In *Royal Bank of Canada v. Kiska*,[69] as we have seen, the request for actual forbearance as the consideration for the promise to guarantee may be implicit in the circumstances. The actual forbearance or the promise to forbear need not be for a specific or definite time. In the absence of specific agreement on this point, it would be held that the forbearance is to be for a reasonable period of time.[70] Perhaps the most common fact situation to arise is that in which a promise to forbear is given as consideration in the context of compromises of disputes. In the typical case, a promise to forbear from suit will be given in return for a promise to pay a sum of money. Such agreements are enforceable and, indeed, it may be argued that their enforceability is essential to the proper and efficient administration of justice. Where the claim lacks merit, however, it may appear that the promise to forbear lacks any significant value and accordingly, perhaps, ought not be considered to constitute consideration. Indeed, if the person making the threat is aware that the claim is invalid, the extraction of an undertaking to pay has the appearance, and perhaps the reality, of an exercise in extortion. Even a promise to forbear from bringing a doubtful claim, however, will constitute good consideration, provided that the party making the threat is acting in good faith either in the sense that the party believes the claim to be a valid one or, even if it is understood to be doubtful, the claim is believed to be a reasonable one that has a fair chance of success.[71] In

---

68 See L. Fuller, "Consideration and Form" (1941) 41 Colum. L. Rev. 799 at 820.

69 Above note 12.

70 *Fullerton v. Provincial Bank of Ireland*, [1903] A.C. 309 at 313–14, Lord McNaghten. See also *Alliance Bank v. Broom* (1864), 2 Drew. & Sm. 289; *Oldershaw v. King* (1857), 2 H. & N. 517; *Miles v. New Zealand Alford Estate Co.* (1886), 32 Ch. D. 266; *Royal Bank of Canada v. Kiska*, above note 12.

71 See *B. (D.C.) v. Zellers*, [1996] 8 W.W.R. 100 (Man. Q.B.), aff'd [1996] 10 W.W.R. 689 (Man. C.A.), leave to appeal to S.C.C. refused, [1996] 10 W.W.R. 689. See also *Callisher v. Bischoffsheim* (1870), L.R. 5 Q.B. 449; *Miles v. New Zealand Alford Estate Co.*, *ibid.* at 291–92, Bowen L.J.; *Attorney General of British Columbia v. Deeks Sand & Gravel Co. Ltd.*, [1956] S.C.R. 336 at 343–46, Kellock J.; *Ronald Elwyn Lister v. Dunlop Canada Ltd.* (1982), 135 D.L.R. (3d) 1 at 13–14, Estey

Stott v. Merit Investment Corp.,[72] for example, the defendant investment firm asserted a claim against its employee, Stott, who was a registered securities representative. Stott had decided not to extend further credit to a client of the firm. His decision, however, was overridden by his supervisor and further credit was extended with consequent loss to the firm. It was the firm's view that Stott, as the representative handling this account, was personally responsible to reimburse the firm for these losses. Stott initially entered into and began performing an agreement under which he promised to reimburse the firm. Subsequently, however, he contested the agreement on the ground, *inter alia*, that the firm's claim was not a valid one, and, accordingly, that the employer's promise not to pursue the claim did not constitute good consideration for his promise to reimburse. In the court's view, this point was not to be determined on the basis of whether the firm's claim, if pursued, would actually have succeeded but, rather, on whether the claim was a *bona fide* claim at the time it was asserted. On this basis, the promise to forebear constituted good consideration.

Even in a case where the claim is clearly invalid, as opposed to merely doubtful, a promise to forebear from suit may constitute good consideration provided that the party threatening suit is acting in good faith in the sense that there is a serious intent to pursue the claim[73] and provided that the claimant is not aware of facts that, were they known to the other party, would demonstrate the invalidity of the claim.[74] The threatened claim in *B. (D.C.) v. Zellers*[75] did not withstand scrutiny under this test. The threat arose in the context of a self-styled "loss recovery program" conducted by Zellers, a large retailing firm. Under the program, Zellers threatened civil law suits against shoppers who were caught shoplifting in Zellers' stores by their security officers. In such cases, of course, the stolen articles would be restored to Zellers. The innovative theory underlying the alleged civil claim was that Zellers was entitled to recover a contribution from each shoplifter toward what they called their "incremental" cost of shoplifting. Such costs included the employment of security personnel and other security ex-

---

J. And see *Drewry v. Percival* (1909), 19 O.L.R. 463 (Div. Ct.); *Famous Foods v. Liddle*, [1941] 3 W.W.R. 708 (B.C.C.A.); *Walters v. Walters*, [1946] 3 W.W.R. 497 (Sask. C.A.).

72   (1988), 48 D.L.R. (4th) 288 (Ont. C.A.).

73   *B. (D.C.) v. Zellers*, above note 71. See also *Cook v. Wright* (1861), 1 B. & S. 559 at 569, 121 E.R. 822 at 826, Blackburn J.; *Syros Shipping Co. SA v. Elaghill Trading Co. (The Proodos C)*, [1980] 2 Lloyd's Rep. 390 at 392, Lloyd J.

74   *Miles v. New Zealand Alford Estate Co.*, above note 71 at 284, Cotton L.J.

75   *Ibid.*

penditures. Having calculated the total of such costs and dividing them by the estimated total number of shoplifting incidents, thus arriving at an "incremental cost" per incident, Zellers claimed to be entitled to a "Civil Restitution" claim for a roughly similar amount. If the shoplifter refused to pay the prescribed settlement fee, Zellers threatened to proceed with the alleged restitution claim. If, as in *B. (D.C.) v. Zellers* itself, the shoplifters in question were children, similar threats were made against their parents. However dubious the merits of the general "Civil Restitution" claim might be, the claim asserted against parents was plainly invalid. Parents are not directly liable for torts committed by their children. As the court pointed out in *Zellers*, parents would be liable in such circumstances only if they had themselves committed a tort such as negligent supervision of the activities of their children. Nonetheless, the practice followed by Zellers was to instruct lawyers to send letters to the parents of such children threatening to pursue the purported civil claim unless the parents were willing to settle the matter out of court by paying the settlement fee. The plaintiff parent in *Zellers* initially capitulated to this remarkable demand but subsequently brought a claim to recover the money paid. The claim enjoyed success on the basis that the purported claim was plainly invalid. The court was of the opinion that Zellers neither seriously thought that the claim could succeed or seriously intended to pursue the matter if the fee was not paid. Accordingly, the promise by Zellers to forbear from suit could not constitute valid consideration.[76]

i)   Charitable Subscriptions

A simple promise to make a gift would obviously be unenforceable for want of consideration. Promises to make gifts to charities, however, may raise more subtle consideration issues. Thus, earlier Canadian and American authorities occasionally adopted the view that such promises could be held binding on various grounds. For example, some courts were prepared to hold that the individual subscription or promise to give was made in consideration for the similar promises of other subscribers.[77] Other cases suggested that the subscription might be revoc-

---

76   Shortly after the decision in this case, the Manitoba legislature enacted legislation placing the burden on parents, in such circumstances, to prove that they had exercised reasonable supervision over the child. See *Parental Responsibility Act*, C.C.S.M., c. P8.

77   See, for example, *Thomas v. Grace* (1865), 15 U.C.C.P. 462 (several signatories to one subscription document); *Sargent v. Nicholson* (1915), 25 D.L.R. 638 at 644 (Man. C.A.), Haggart J.A. See also *In re: Estate of Wheeler*, 1 N.E.2d 425 (Ill. C.A. 1936).

able up until the point at which the charity relies on the subscription and incurs obligations.[78] Still others reasoned that, in a case where the subscription identified the purpose or purposes for which the gift was to be applied, the statement of purpose constituted an undertaking, perhaps implied, to spend the moneys for the stated purpose. That undertaking could constitute good consideration for the subscriber's promise to pay.[79]

A marked departure from the results and reasoning of the earlier cases was effected, however, by the decision of the Supreme Court of Canada in *The Governors of Dalhousie College at Halifax v. The Estate of Arthur Boutilier*.[80] Boutilier had made a pledge in the course of a fundraising campaign conducted by Dalhousie College on a form that stipulated that the funds were promised by the subscriber "[f]or the purpose of enabling Dalhousie College to maintain and improve the efficiency of its teaching, to construct new buildings and otherwise to keep pace with the growing need of its constituency and in consideration of subscription of others."[81] The Court rejected the claim on the basis that the college had furnished no consideration for Boutilier's subscription. Crocket J. rejected the suggestion that the subscriptions of others could constitute the requisite consideration. Noting that the American courts had themselves departed from this theory,[82] Crocket J. suggested that the principal difficulty with the theory was simply that it bore no correspondence to the facts. In the absence of direct bargaining between subscribers, no contractual relationship was established.[83] The defendant's argument that the statement of purpose contained in the pledge constituted an implicit undertaking on the part of the college to spend the subscription moneys on the stated purpose was also rejected. There was no explicit request by Boutilier to carry out the stated objectives.

---

78 *Berkeley Street Church v. Stevens* (1875), 37 U.C.Q.B. 9; *Sargent v. Nicholson, ibid.*; *Y.M.C.A. v. Rankin* (1916), 27 D.L.R. 417 (B.C.C.A.); *Y.M.C.A. v. Wood* (1916), 27 D.L.R. 420 (B.C.C.A.). See also *Martin v. Meles*, 60 N.E. 397 (Mass. S.J.C. 1901); *Trustees of Baker University v. Clelland*, 86 F.2d 14 (C.A. 8th Cir. 1936).

79 *Hammond v. Small* (1859), 16 U.C.Q.B. 371; *Re Loblaw*, [1933] 4 D.L.R. 264 (Ont. S.C.).

80 [1934] S.C.R. 642.

81 *Ibid.* at 644.

82 *Ibid.* at 645–46. See, for example, *Presbyterian Church of Albany v. Cooper*, 112 N.Y. Rep. 517 (1889).

83 Even in a case where direct dealings have occurred, the beneficiary of the promises, the charity, would face the further difficulty posed by the doctrine of privity of contract. Under that doctrine, the charity, not having itself provided consideration, would be unable to enforce the subscribers' promises. For discussion of privity of contract, see Chapter 9.

Moreover, the broad statement of purpose essentially left Dalhousie "free to pursue what had always been its aim in whatever manner its Governors should choose."[84] Crocket J. did not doubt that "an express agreement by the promisee to do certain acts in return for a subscription is a sufficient consideration for the promise of the subscriber."[85] Such an undertaking might be implied where "the subscriber has himself either expressly requested the promisee to undertake some definite project or personally taken such a part in connection with the projected enterprise that such a request might be inferred therefrom."[86] The theory that the subscription might be a revocable offer made binding by the reliance of the charity on the subscription by incurring obligations was also rejected. Drawing support from American[87] and English cases,[88] Crocket J. held that something more than the mere incurring of liability or expenditure of money on the faith of the subscription is required. Crocket J. explained: "To hold otherwise would be to hold that a naked, voluntary promise may be converted into a binding legal contract by the subsequent action of the promisee alone without the consent, express or implied, of the promisor."[89] Although this rejection of reliance-based liability may require reconsideration in light of modern developments in the law of promissory estoppel,[90] the *Dalhousie* decision strongly reaffirms the orthodoxy that subsequent reliance on a promise does not constitute good consideration.

In the absence of an express or implied promise by the charity to do certain acts in return for the subscription, then, the *Dalhousie* decision leaves little room for the enforcement of charitable subscriptions. It is not entirely clear whether a commitment to name something, such as a building or fund, in the name of the subscriber will constitute good consideration. Such an undertaking by the charity might be considered to be a promise to do something it would not otherwise have done that

---

84   Above note 80 at 647.
85   *Ibid.* at 648.
86   *Ibid.*
87   *Hull v. Pearson*, 56 N.Y. Supp. 518 (C.A. 1899).
88   *In re Hudson* (1885), 33 W.R. 819 at 821 (Ch. D.), Pearson J. ("I am bound to say that this is an attempt to turn a charity into something very different from a charity"); *In re Cory* (1912), 29 T.L.R. 18 (Ch. D.) (plaintiff Y.M.C.A. alleged that the decision to go ahead with the building project was made after receiving the defendant's pledge — subscription not binding).
89   Above note 80 at 652. Compare with *Provincial Sanatorium v. McArthur*, [1935] 4 D.L.R. 255 (P.E.I.S.C.), leave to appeal to S.C.C. refused, [1935] 4 D.L.R. 458 (P.E.I.S.C.), a decision which appears inconsistent, however, with the views expressed by Crocket J. in the *Dalhousie* case.
90   See Chapter 8.

is of direct interest to the subscriber.[91] On the other hand, where the naming appears to be little more than an expression of gratitude on the part of the charity, the promise to name may not have the effect of converting a charitable gift into a bargain. Thus, in a recent Ontario case[92] in which a hospital undertook to name a cardiac unit after the donor, the naming promise was not held to constitute good consideration. The naming had been suggested by the hospital and appeared to be of little or no interest to the donor.

j)   Manufacturers' Warranties

It is a common practice for manufacturers of goods such as consumer durables to provide written product guarantees or warranties that may, in some fashion, accompany the product as it passes through the hands of a dealer, distributor or retailer into the hands of the ultimate buyer of the product. In the typical case, where the intermediate party is not acting as the agent of the manufacturer in dealings with the buyer, the particular manufacturer's warranty would normally not be enforceable. The ultimate buyer has provided no consideration to the manufacturer in return for the manufacturer's warranty. In cases where the ultimate buyer and the manufacturer have engaged in direct discussions that include warranties concerning the product from the manufacturer, a court may be willing to construct an agreement in the form of an offer by the manufacturer to the effect that if the buyer purchases the product from a dealer, the manufacturer will be bound by the warranty.[93] In a case where no such direct communication has occurred, however, the existence of a collateral agreement of this kind with the manufacturer could not be established. Thus, manufacturers' warranties are typically not enforceable. So startling is this proposition that legislative reform imposing statutory warranties on manufacturers in the context of consumer transactions has been recommended.[94] In a few Canadian

91   *Allegheny College v. National Chautauqua County Bank of Jamestown*, 159 N.E. 173 (N.Y.C.A. 1927) (fund established in the name of donor—held to be good consideration).

92   *Brantford General Hospital Foundation v. Marquis Estate* (2003), 67 O.R. (3d) 432 (S.C.J.).

93   *Shanklin Pier v. Detel Products*, [1951] 2 K.B. 854; *Murray v. Sperry Rand Corp.* (1979), 23 O.R. (2d) 456 (H.C.J.). See generally S.M. Waddams, *Products Liability*, 4th ed. (Toronto: Carswell, 2002) at 147–60.

94   Ontario Law Reform Commission, *Report on Consumer Warranties and Guarantees in the Sale of Goods* (Toronto: Ministry of the Attorney General, 1972).

provinces,[95] legislation imposing on manufacturers some form of direct liability to consumers for losses resulting from defective products has been enacted. It may also be the case that consideration could be found in the relatively common practice of requiring consumer buyers to record certain information concerning the purchase and the buyer on a postcard provided with the product and to forward the card to the manufacturer in order to "register" the warranty. The sending of the postcard containing the information might be said to constitute good consideration for the warranty. Although it appears artificial to suggest that the manufacturer bargained for the information in return for the product warranty, a court minded to give effect to the reasonable expectations of the ultimate buyers that manufacturers' warranties are binding might hold that sending the information constitutes the requisite "peppercorn."[96]

2) Past Consideration

It follows from the bargain theory that a promise given in recognition of or in return for benefits received by the promisor in the past is unenforceable. Such a promise is not given as the price of or as part of a bargain for the previously received benefit. Past consideration, it is often said, is no consideration. In a leading nineteenth-century authority, *Eastwood v. Kenyon*,[97] for example, the defendant husband promised to discharge a debt owed by his wife's guardian to a third party. His wife's father had died during her infancy and the guardian had borrowed the money in order to provide for her education and other needs. The husband's promise was held unenforceable on the basis that "the consideration for it was past and executed long before."[98] The past consideration may no doubt provide the promisor with a motive for the fresh promise, but it does not provide a consideration for which the

---

95   *Consumer Product Warranty and Liability Act*, S.N.B. 1978, c. C-18.1; *Consumer Protection Act*, S.S. 1996, c. C-30.1, s. 64.

96   *Trueman Maritime Auto & Trailer Sales Ltd.* (1977), 19 N.B.R. (2d) 8 (C.A.) (warranty card not sent in, warranty not binding). Occasionally, courts have apparently assumed that the warranty might be binding without addressing the consideration issue. See, for example, *Maughan v. International Harvester Co. of Canada Ltd.* (1980), 112 D.L.R. (3d) 243 (N.S.S.C.A.D.); *Kelly v. Mack Canada Inc.* (1988), 53 D.L.R. (4th) 476 (Ont. C.A.).

97   (1840), 11 Ad. & El. 438, 113 E.R. 482 (Q.B.).

98   *Ibid.* at 487 (E.R.). See also *Grant v. Von Alvensleben* (1913), 4 W.W.R. 1303 (B.C.C.A.); *Johnson v. Forbes*, [1932] 1 D.L.R. 219 (Alta. S.C.A.D.); *Re Grosch*, [1945] 3 D.L.R. 63 (Alta. S.C.A.D.).

promisor has bargained.[99] Similarly, the promise of an employer who, upon the retirement of a valued employee, promises benefits in recognition of past service that are beyond the employee's contractual entitlements would be unenforceable.[100] If, on the other hand, an employer gave such a promise prior to retirement in return for the employee's undertaking to stay on the job until retirement, the requisite element of mutuality or bargain would be present.[101]

At an early stage, however, an exception to the past consideration principle was recognized, though the explanation proffered for the exception was obscure. The past consideration principle does not apply if the initial benefit had been requested by the promisor. Thus, in the 1615 decision in *Lampleigh v. Braithwait*,[102] the defendant, having feloniously slain a third party, had requested the plaintiff to do what he could to obtain a pardon, on his behalf, from the King. The plaintiff enjoyed success in this mission, and in recognition of these valuable services, the defendant promised to pay the plaintiff £100. Even though the defendant's promise was given for a past consideration, it was held binding on the basis that "though it follows, yet it is not naked, but couples itself with the suit before."[103] This exception was obviously not applicable in *Eastwood v. Kenyon* as neither the services nor the borrowing had been requested either by the defendant or by his wife at the time of their provision.

The explanation offered in *Lampleigh* that the request has the effect of coupling the benefit with the subsequent promise is not illuminating. A preferable and, indeed, the modern explanation for the result in such a case is that, where a service is provided in circumstances where there is a reasonable expectation of compensation, a binding obligation to provide compensation, enforceable in a claim for restitution, arises. A subsequent promise to provide such compensation is enforceable on

---

99 See *Johnson v. Forbes, ibid.* at 224, McGillivray J.A. ("such a promise is based upon motive and not upon consideration"). And see the discussion of moral consideration below, the text at notes 115–25.

100 See, for example, *Blair v. Western Mutual Benefit Association*, [1972] 4 W.W.R. 284 (B.C.C.A.).

101 See, for example, *Mabley & Carew Co. v. Borden*, 195 N.E. 697 (Ohio 1935). Similarly, if an employee took early retirement in reliance on a promise of a substantial payment, the promise would be enforceable. See *Edwards v. Skyways Ltd.*, [1964] 1 All E.R. 494 (Q.B.). See also *Maier v. E&B Exploration Ltd.*, [1986] 4 W.W.R. 275 (Alta. C.A.) (altered terms of employee compensation induced continued employment on the part of the employees).

102 (1615), Hobart 105, 80 E.R. 255 (K.B.).

103 *Ibid.* at 255 (E.R.).

the basis that it gives expression or precision to an existing and enforceable legal obligation. An explanation of this kind for the exception was provided by the Privy Council in *Pao On v. Lau Yiu Long*.[104] Lord Scarman affirmed: "the mere existence or recital of a prior request is not sufficient in itself to convert what is prima facie past consideration into sufficient consideration in law to support a promise."[105] The elements of the test for applying the exception were set out by him in the following terms: "An act done before the giving of a promise to make a payment or to confer some other benefit can sometimes be consideration for the promise. The act must have been done at the promisor's request: the parties must have understood that the act was to be remunerated either by a payment or the conferment of some other benefit: and payment, or the conferment of a benefit, must have been legally enforceable had it been promised in advance."[106]

It is implicit in this statement that if the benefit was conferred as a gift, the subsequent promise would not bind. It is also the case that no restitution claim would lie for benefits conferred with a gift intention.[107] Lord Scarman did not go on to observe that, where services are rendered in the reasonable expectation of compensation, a restitutionary claim for their value would normally arise. He did appear to accept, however, that the subsequent promise either offers the best evidence of the compensation originally intended to be conferred or, alternatively, constitutes a separate "positive bargain" that would be enforceable.[108] Indeed, he indicated that it mattered not which explanation for the imposition of liability is adopted though where, as in *Pao On* itself, the subsequent promise is in the form of a written agreement, "the better analysis is that of 'positive bargain.'"[109]

The somewhat complicated facts of *Pao On* provided an unusual setting in which to apply the exception. The promise arose in the context of an asset purchase accomplished through an exchange of shares. The plaintiffs owned all the issued shares in Shing On, the company that owned the asset that the defendants wished to acquire. The defendants had caused a company they owned, Fu Chip, as the purchaser of the asset, to issue shares in favour of the plaintiffs in return for their shares

---

104 [1980] A.C. 614 (P.C.). See also *Re Casey's Patents*, [1892] 1 Ch. 104.
105 *Pao On v. Lau Yiu Long, ibid.* at 630.
106 *Ibid.* at 629.
107 See generally P.D. Maddaugh and J.D. McCamus, *The Law of Restitution*, 2d ed. (Aurora, ON: Canada Law Book, 2004) c. 3.
108 *Pao On v. Lau Yiu Long*, above note 104 at 631. See also *Re Casey's Patents*, above note 104 at 115-16, Bowen L.J.
109 *Pao On v. Lau Yiu Long, ibid.*

in Shing On. By this means, Fu Chip acquired the asset. The plaintiffs were concerned that the Fu Chip shares they were acquiring might not hold their value. Accordingly, in the initial set of transactions, they extracted a side arrangement with the defendants personally under which, or so they thought, the defendants would guarantee that the Fu Chip shares would have a particular value, failing which the plaintiffs could elect to require the defendants to repurchase the Fu Chip shares at that price. In the event, the side arrangement that was actually recorded and signed proved to be one in which the defendants had, in addition to the obligation to guarantee the value of the shares, a right to take the shares back if they reached the same value. The agreement thus deprived the plaintiffs of any benefit that would result from the Fu Chip values rising in value above their guaranteed value. When the plaintiffs ultimately understood the true nature and significance of this arrangement, they threatened to refuse to close the transaction unless a new side agreement was given by the defendants under which the defendants gave a simple guarantee of the value of the Fu Chip shares. One way of construing this second arrangement with the defendants, the court held, was that the defendants had given the second undertaking in return for the plaintiff's previous act of having entered into a contract with their company for the share transfer. On this construction, the defendant's second undertaking was given for a past consideration.

In Lord Scarman's view, the three-pronged test for application of the *Lampleigh* exception applied to these unusual circumstances. The initial act of entering into an agreement with the defendants' company was done at the request of the defendants. It was understood that the plaintiff should be rewarded, in part at least, by the giving of a personal guaranty by the defendants. Finally, if the second and subsequent undertaking had been given at the time of the original formation of the agreement, it would have been legally enforceable. Two features of this fact situation are unusual. First, unlike *Eastwood* or *Lampleigh*, where the initial act is the provision of a beneficial service, the initial act in *Pao On* is the entering into of a contract with a third party, the defendants' company. Second, the subsequent promise given in recognition of or in return for that act is, in fact, a second side agreement given personally by the defendants either as a variation of or, more probably, in substitution for an original side agreement given by them. Putting those complexities to one side, however, the court's conclusion that the threefold test is applicable appears sound.

It is unfortunate, however, that Lord Scarman, in articulating the first branch of the test, placed emphasis on the requirement of a request. Although this view is certainly consistent with earlier authority, there may well be cases where services are rendered in circumstances giving rise to liability for an unjust enrichment, even though they were not provided at the request of the subsequent promisor. Thus, for example, where beneficial services are provided to the promisor in an emergency without the promisor's request, as where the promisor is unconscious,[110] a claim in restitution would lie against the recipient of the services for the value of services rendered in order to prevent the unjust enrichment of the promisor.[111] Accordingly, if the recipient of the services subsequently gave an undertaking to compensate the service provider, it would be appropriate to apply the exception to the past consideration principle. The subsequent promise simply gives expression or precision to a prior legal obligation. Accordingly, the formulation of the exception proposed by the Ontario Law Reform Commission,[112] which places no emphasis on request, appears preferable. The commission proposed: "A promise made in recognition of a benefit previously received by the promisor or by any third party from the promisee, should be enforceable to the extent necessary to prevent unjust enrichment."[113] The commission added two further points of clarification. Obviously, where the promisee initially conferred the benefit as a gift, no unjust enrichment would arise. Further, it was the commission's view that the subsequent promise should be enforceable only if it was not disproportionate to the value of the benefit initially conferred.[114]

In the past-consideration cases, it is often apparent that the subsequent promise has been inspired by the promisor's sense of moral obligation. Thus, in *Eastwood v. Kenyon*, it would not be surprising if the defendant felt a moral obligation to repay the lender who had provided funds needed for the care of his wife when she was a child. No less a figure than Lord Mansfield was of the view that a promise given out of a sense of moral obligation ought to be binding.[115] The idea that a moral obligation constitutes good consideration was rejected, however,

---

110 See, for example, *Matheson v. Smiley*, [1932] 2 D.L.R. 787 (Man. C.A.).

111 See generally J.D. McCamus, "Necessitous Intervention: The Altruistic Intermeddler and the Law of Restitution" (1979) 11 Ottawa L.R. 297; P.D. Maddaugh and J.D. McCamus, *The Law of Restitution*, 2d ed. (Aurora, ON: Canada Law Book, 2004) c. 31.

112 Ontario Law Reform Commission, *Report on Amendment of the Law of Contract* (Toronto: Ministry of the Attorney General, 1987).

113 *Ibid.* at 33.

114 *Ibid.*

115 *Hawkes v. Saunders* (1782), 1 Cowp. 289 at 290 (K.B.) ("the ties of conscience upon an upright mind are a sufficient consideration").

in *Eastwood v. Kenyon*[116] and this has become the received wisdom of the English common law. As was said in *Thomas v. Thomas*,[117] "motive is not the same thing with consideration."[118] Nonetheless, there is some persuasive force in Lord Mansfield's position[119] and a number of American cases have applied such a theory. An appealing illustration of the phenomenon is *Webb v. McGowin*.[120] By an act of great courage, Webb had saved McGowin's life, on a construction site, by placing his own body in harm's way, with the result that he was so badly injured as to be crippled for life. In gratitude, McGowin promised to pay Webb fifteen dollars every two weeks for the rest of Webb's life. In fact, McGowin did so, but when he died his estate resisted further payment. The Alabama Court enforced the promise on the basis that McGowin had a moral obligation to compensate Webb for the valuable service he had rendered, all the more so if Webb had relied on McGowin's promise to his detriment.[121] Such a result could not be achieved on the basis of the *Pao On* test.[122] McGowin did not request Webb's intervention. Nor is it clear that the result could be achieved on the basis of the proposals of the Ontario Law Reform Commission.[123] Webb's spontaneous act of heroism was not undertaken with the view to reward. Accordingly, it is not at all clear that a restitution or unjust enrichment claim would lie for the value of the services rendered.[124] Accordingly, it may be that the granting of recovery in a case like *Webb v. McGowin* requires acceptance of the view that moral obligation can render a promise enforceable.[125]

---

116 Above note 97.
117 (1842), 2 Q.B. 851, 114 E.R. 330.
118 *Ibid.* at 333 (E.R.). See also *Johnson v. Forbes,* above note 98.
119 See, for example, S. Thel and E. Yoreo, "The Promissory Basis of Past Consideration" (1992) 78 Va. L. Rev. 1045; J. Grosse, "Moral Obligation as Consideration in Contracts" (1971) 17 Vill. L. Rev. 1.
120 168 So. 196 (Ala. App. 1935).
121 As we have seen, subsequent detrimental reliance does not render a promise enforceable. For consideration of the application of promissory estoppel to situations where detrimental reliance follows a promise, see further Chapter 8.
122 Above note 106.
123 Above note 113.
124 See generally F.D. Rose, "Restitution for the Rescuer" (1989) 9 Oxford J. Legal Stud. 167. See also W. Landes and R. Posner, "Salvers, Finders, Good Samaritans and other Rescuers: An Economic Study of Law and Altruism" (1978) 7 J. Legal Stud. 83; H. Dagan, "In Defense of Good Samaritans" (1999) 97 Mich. L. Rev. 1152.
125 Compare with *Irving v. Irving* (1988), 17 R.F.L. (3d) 318 (B.C.S.C.) (moral obligation as good consideration rejected).

As noted by Lord Denman in *Eastwood v. Kenyon*,[126] there is a further exception to the past-consideration doctrine. A subsequent promise can have the effect of reviving a prior obligation that has now been suspended by some rule of law, be it common law or statute-based.[127] Thus, for example, a promise to pay a pre-existing debt, the enforcement of which is now statute-barred by a limitations statute, would revive the obligation from the date of the subsequent promise to pay. Limitations legislation now commonly provides, however, that such promises must be recorded in writing and signed by the promisor.[128] Another illustration is provided by contracts entered by children under the age of majority that are unenforceable at common law on grounds of their lack of contractual capacity. In some circumstances, subsequent promises made by the child after reaching the age of majority to perform the earlier promise may be enforceable.[129] Similarly, it has been held that where necessaries were supplied to a child under the age of majority who, upon attaining full age, promises to pay for them, the promise would be enforceable.[130] The supplier of necessaries would also have an action, probably restitutionary in nature, during the infancy of the recipient.[131] In the case of necessaries supplied, then, the enforcement of the subsequent promise would be captured by the version of the past-consideration doctrine proposed by the Ontario Law Reform Commission[132] as the initial supply of necessaries would give rise to an unjust enrichment claim. Finally, it was established for a time at common law that a bankrupt party who, after discharge, gave a subsequent promise to pay a debt otherwise discharged by the bankruptcy could give an enforceable subsequent promise to pay the pre-existing debt.[133]

---

126 Above note 97.

127 *Ball v. Hesketh* (1697), Comb. 381, 90 E.R. 541; *Spencer v. Hemmerde*, [1922] 2 A.C. 507 (H.L.); *Surrendra Overseas Ltd. v. Government of Sri Lanka*, [1977] 1 W.L.R. 565 (Q.B.).

128 See, for example, *Limitations Act*, R.S.A. 2000, c. L-12, s. 9; *Limitation Act*, R.S.B.C. 1996, c. 266, s. 5(5); *Limitation of Actions Act*, C.C.S.M., c. L150, s. 9; *Limitation of Actions Act*, R.S.N.S. 1989, c. 258, s. 6(1); *Limitations Act, 2002*, S.O. 2002, c. 24, s. 13(10); *Statute of Limitations*, R.S.P.E.I. 1988, c. S-7, s. 6; *Limitation of Actions Act*, R.S.S. 1978, c. L-15, s. 7.

129 See, for example, *Thrupp v. Fielder* (1798), 2 Esp. 628, 170 E.R. 477. See generally D.R. Percy, "The Present Law of Infants' Contracts" (1975) 53 Can. Bar Rev. 1.

130 *Cooper v. Martin* (1803), 102 E.R. 759.

131 See, for example, *Nash v. Inman*, [1908] 2 K.B. 1 (C.A.). See generally J.D. McCamus, "Restitution of Benefits Conferred Under Minors' Contracts" (1979) 28 U.N.B.L.J. 89.

132 Above note 113.

133 *Trueman v. Fenton* (1777), 2 Cowp. 544; *Austin v. Gordon* (1872), 32 U.C.R. 621. But see *Jakeman v. Cook* (1878), 4 Ex D. 26; *Wild v. Tucker*, [1914] 3 K.B. 36.

3) The Pre-existing Duty Rule

A promise to perform an act that one is already obliged to perform is obviously vulnerable to the argument that the promisor has given no new commitment to act and therefore has not given good consideration. If consideration requires the confining of one's freedom of action in the future in some fashion, such a promisor, arguably, has adopted no new constraint. Thus, an agreement in which a promisor undertakes to pay a fee in return for the promisee's undertaking simply to perform a pre-existing duty, the promise to pay the fee may be unenforceable for want of consideration. Such arguments have enjoyed success to some extent over time but, as we shall see, there has been some refinement or confinement of the doctrine in recent years. The concern underlying the pre-existing duty rule is that the person subject to the duty may be tempted to exploit another party's urgent need to have the pre-existing duty performed by exacting an additional fee or other unfair advantage from that party. The principal criticism of the rule, as we shall see, is that by striking down all agreements to perform pre-existing duties, the rule is over-inclusive in the sense that it captures many cases where there is no factual basis for such concerns. Three different kinds of cases may be conceived. The promisee may be subject to a public duty to perform the act in question. The promisee may be subject to a pre-existing contractual duty owed to a third party to perform the act in question. We may call this a "three-party" case. Finally, in a "two-party" case, the promisee may be subject to a pre-existing duty to perform the act in a pre-existing contract with the very promisor. This latter fact situation might be characterized as a unilateral or "one-sided" variation of a contract. The promisor agrees to provide further consideration. The promisee agrees merely to perform the pre-existing contractual duties.

a) Public Duty

It is self-evident why promises given by public officials and public servants of various kinds to carry out their public responsibility are considered unenforceable.[134] If arrangements of this kind were enforceable, corrupt practices of various kinds might be encouraged. The traditional explanation for that unenforceability is that an agreement to perform a pre-existing public duty simply lacks good consideration. If it is obvious that police officers, for example, should not be able to enter into enforceable arrangements to take a fee for responding to an emergency,

---

134 See, for example, *Bridge v. Cage* (1605), Cro. Jac. 103; *Darlye's Case* (1631), Het. 175; *Herring v. Dorell* (1840), 8 Dowl. 604.

there may nonetheless be cases where police officers can be employed for a fee to provide services at a level beyond that normally provided. Such an arrangement was held to be enforceable in *Glasbrook Bros. v. Glamorgan County Council*.[135] A mine manager and the local police force were at odds with respect to the level of police protection required during a strike. The manager wished to have more officers available than the police force considered necessary and entered into an arrangement whereby the mine owners paid a fee in return for a higher level of protection. When sued for the fee, the defendant owners raised lack of consideration as a defence. The House of Lords held, however, that if the police had reasonably and in good faith determined that the additional protection was not necessary, an agreement to provide it for a fee would be an enforceable one. So too, it has been held that enforceable agreements may be entered into to provide police services at special events such as football matches[136] where the owner of the business has organized the event in such a fashion as to create a need for police services. Presumably, agreements to hire extra officers to direct traffic at shopping plazas could be enforced on similar grounds. Although the police might agree that the services are required in such situations, it is not considered offensive to public policy to require the owners of such businesses to pay for the services in question. A more difficult question is whether a police officer ought to be able to claim a reward posted for the apprehension of a criminal. Although an early English authority suggests that a constable might be able to accept and enforce an offer of reward of this kind,[137] it is arguable that the collection of rewards by police officers may be contrary to public policy. If enforceable by officers, rewards might distort the proper deployment of police officers, distract them from full performance of their obligations or create disincentives for information-sharing among officers. For reasons such as these, a court may be inclined to find that the constable's performance of a pre-existing duty does not constitute good consideration.

Ordinary citizens are also subject to public duties of various kinds and if they enter into agreements to perform such duties for a fee, they

---

135 [1925] A.C. 270 (H.L.). And see *Reif v. Page* (1882), 55 Wisc. 496 (husband's offer of reward to anyone who would rescue his wife from burning building—rescue by firefighter—held binding as firefighter not obligated to risk own life in discharge of his duties).

136 *Harris v. Sheffield United Football Club Ltd.*, [1988] Q.B. 77.

137 *England v. Davidson* (1840), 11 Ad. & El. 856, 113 E.R. 640 (permitting constable to collect reward for providing information leading to the conviction of a felon on the apparent assumption that the services were not such as the constable was bound to render).

are also vulnerable to a no-consideration argument. Thus, in an English case,[138] the plaintiff had testified under subpoena in a lawsuit on the defendant's behalf pursuant to an alleged agreement under which the defendant would pay a fee for his attendance. The agreement was held unenforceable on the ground that the subpoena subjected the plaintiff to a pre-existing duty to attend and testify. An agreement under which a parent agreed to look after his or her child in return for a fee would likely fail on the ground that parents are subject to a pre-existing duty to look after their children.[139] In *Ward v. Byham*,[140] however, an unmarried couple, who had given birth to a child and then separated, entered into an agreement whereby the mother, in return for maintenance paid by the father, undertook to look after the child, to demonstrate to the father that the child was well looked after and happy and, further, to let the child determine whether or not she wished to live with her mother. The mother was subject to a statutory duty to look after the child. Nonetheless, a majority of the Court of Appeal held that she had given good consideration for the father's promise to provide maintenance. Her undertakings to provide the father with proof of the daughter's contentedness and to allow the child to determine whether she would live with the mother were beyond her statutory obligations. Denning L.J., however, was of the view that the mother had undertaken only to do what she was legally obliged to do. Nonetheless, he further observed: "Even so, I think that there was sufficient consideration to support the promise. I have always thought that a promise to perform an existing duty, or the performance of it, should be regarded as good consideration because it is a benefit to the person to whom it is given."[141]

Although Lord Denning's views on this point have not yet achieved wide acceptance, it might indeed conduce to clarity in the law to hold, as he suggested, that the performance of a pre-existing public duty can constitute good consideration but that agreements to perform such duties will not be enforceable where they are contrary to public policy. Agreements to pay public officials a fee in order to discharge their public duties are plainly contrary to public policy. Maintenance agreements of the kind at issue in *Ward v. Byham* are clearly consistent with public policy. A public policy test, therefore, might be a better device

---

138 *Collins v. Godefroy* (1831), 1 B. & Ad. 950, 109 E.R. 1040.
139 Separation agreements, however, under which couples agree to live separate and apart and which may assign responsibility for care of the children to one spouse and require payment of support by the other are binding. See, for example, *McGregor v. McGregor* (1888), 21 Q.B.D. 424 (C.A.).
140 [1956] 2 All E.R. 318 (C.A.).
141 *Ibid.* at 319. See also *Williams v. Williams*, [1957] 1 All E.R. 305 (C.A.).

for distinguishing enforceable agreements from those that are not, rather than a pre-existing duty rule subject to the kind of manipulation favoured by the majority in *Ward v. Byham* itself.

b) Duty Owed to a Third Party

Cases in which the promisor has undertaken to the promisee to perform a contract entered into previously with a third party might be thought to engage the pre-existing duty doctrine.[142] Generally, however, courts have enforced such arrangements. In *Scotson v. Pegg*,[143] for example, a carrier had contracted to deliver a load of coal to a third party or to the order of that third party. The third party, in turn, sold the coal to the defendant and ordered the plaintiff to deliver the coal to the defendant. When a dispute arose between the plaintiff and third party, the plaintiff and defendant agreed that the plaintiff would deliver the coal to the defendant for a fresh consideration. The plaintiff did, in fact, deliver the coal to the defendant but the defendant resisted payment on the ground that the plaintiff had merely undertaken to perform a pre-existing duty to the third party. A majority of the court held that the plaintiff had provided consideration as the delivery of the coal was beneficial to the defendant. Similarly, in *Shadwell v. Shadwell*,[144] an uncle was held to be bound by a promise to his nephew that he would pay the nephew a certain allowance once the nephew married his fiancée. The uncle's estate resisted a claim to enforce the promise on the basis that the nephew was already bound by a pre-existing duty to perform his promise to marry.[145] A majority of the court held that the uncle's promise was binding on the basis that there was detriment to the nephew, who may well have relied on the promise in taking his marital vows, and benefit to the uncle, who seemed pleased at the prospect of his nephew's marriage.

An unsuccessful attempt to invoke the pre-existing duty rule was also made in the important decision of the Privy Council in *Pao On v.*

---

142 See, for example, *Jones v. Wate* (1839), 5 Bing. N.C. 341 (promise to advance money in return for undertaking to discharge pre-existing debts owed to third parties—held, not good consideration).

143 (1861), 6 H. & N. 295, 158 E.R. 121. See also *New Zealand Shipping Co. Ltd. v. A.M. Satterthwaite & Co. Ltd.*, [1975] A.C. 154 (P.C.) (carrier of consignor's goods hires stevedores to unload the vessel—held, consignor's subsequent agreement with stevedores to the same end also enforceable).

144 (1860), 9 Cl. & F. 99.

145 The action to enforce a breach of a promise to marry has been abolished in many jurisdictions. See, for example, *Marriage Act*, R.S.O. 1990, c. M.3, s. 32.

Lau Yiu Long.[146] As we have seen,[147] this case concerned a side agreement entered into between the plaintiffs and the defendants in the context of an agreement to exchange shares in their respective companies. The plaintiffs had agreed to transfer their shares to the defendants' company. In return, the defendants' company would issue shares to the plaintiffs. The plaintiffs were concerned, however, that the shares in the defendants' company might not hold their value and accordingly had originally exacted a side agreement under which the defendants themselves would guarantee the value of the shares at a certain price. The first version of this arrangement, however, contained an unexpected feature that substantially reduced the value of the agreement to the plaintiffs. Accordingly, they threatened to refuse to perform the agreement requiring the exchange of shares. In response, the defendants agreed to substitute a new personal guarantee in the form expected by the plaintiffs. As noted above, one possible construction of this fact situation was that the second guarantee was given in return for the past consideration constituted by the plaintiffs having entered into the share exchange agreement. As the court held, however, the second possible construction of these facts is that the second guarantee was given in return for the plaintiffs' undertaking to perform the pre-existing share exchange agreement. On this basis, the defendants sought to defend against the plaintiffs' claim to enforce the second side agreement on the ground that the promise to perform a pre-existing duty did not constitute good consideration. In the further alternative, the defendants argued that the second guarantee was unenforceable on the ground that it had been induced by economic duress.[148]

With respect to the pre-existing duty point, the defendants urged that arrangements to provide additional consideration to induce a party to perform a pre-existing contract with a third party are likely to be entered into on the basis of unfair pressure. Accordingly, such agreements ought to be considered illegal as being against public policy on the basis that a threat to repudiate a pre-existing contractual duty owed to a third party can be and, on the present facts was, an abuse of a dominant bargaining position. The Privy Council rejected this argument. Lord Scarman observed: "where businessman are negotiating at arms' length it is unnecessary for the achievement of justice, and unhelpful in the development of the law, to invoke such a rule of public policy."[149]

---

146 Above note 104.
147 See this Chapter, section B(2).
148 For discussion of this aspect of the decision, see Chapter 11, section B(3).
149 Above note 104 at 634.

The Privy Council went on to hold that such an agreement could be voidable on grounds of economic duress but held that no such duress was present on the facts.

The decision in *Pao On* is an important one, both with respect to the doctrine of pre-existing duty and with respect to the law of economic duress. On the latter point, the decision is an early and leading authority on the proposition that a threat to breach a contract can constitute economic duress.[150] On the pre-existing duty point, the decision suggests that a rule striking down agreements to perform a pre-existing contractual duty owed to a third party is neither necessary nor desirable. Some agreements of this kind might be the product of coercion. Cases where the agreement results from oppressive threats to breach the pre-existing duty could be met by the newly recognized doctrine of economic duress rendering such agreements unenforceable. In the absence of economic duress, however, such agreements could be enforced on the basis that "a promise to perform, or the performance of, a pre-existing contractual obligation to a third party can be valid consideration."[151] The decision in *Pao On* thus aligns the rule in these cases more closely to the underlying rationale of refusing to give effect to agreements induced by coercion. As we shall see, a rather different approach has been taken in the context of promises to perform pre-existing contractual duties owed to the promisor.

c) Duty Owed to the Promisor

In what might be referred to as a one-sided variation of an agreement, a promisor might agree to provide additional consideration under an agreement in return for the promisee's undertaking merely to perform pre-existing contractual duties. Thus, for example, a buyer might agree to pay an increased price in return for the seller's undertaking simply to perform the existing agreement. It is well established in this context that the promise to perform the pre-existing contractual duty is not good consideration. This proposition was established in a pair of late-eighteenth-century and early-nineteenth-century cases concerning agreements to pay increased wages to sailors. In *Harris v. Watson*,[152] the captain of a ship that was then in some danger promised the plaintiff increased pay in return for the extra effort required in these circumstances. Lord Kenyon dismissed the claim, basing the decision "on a principle of policy, for if sailors were in all events to have their wages,

---

150 See further Chapter 11, section B(3).
151 Above note 104 at 632, Lord Scarman.
152 (1791), Peake 101, 170 E.R. 94.

and in times of danger entitled to insist on an extra charge on such a promise as this, they would in many cases suffer a ship to sink, unless the captain would pay an extravagant demand they might proper to make."[153] The principle of public policy, evidently, was that agreements struck in circumstances where the crew might take advantage of the vulnerability of the captain ought not to be enforced. This decision was approved and applied in the later decision in *Stilk v. Myrick*.[154] In this case, two members of the crew had deserted and the captain, having failed to recruit replacements for them, promised increased wages to the crew. Rather than rest the decision on the ground of public policy invoked by Lord Kenyon, however, Lord Ellenborough placed the decision on the basis of want of consideration. The crew had "undertaken to do all they could under all the emergencies of the voyage"[155] and were "bound by the terms of their original contract to exert themselves to the utmost to bring the ship in safety to her destined port."[156] Their pre-existing duty required them to respond to any emergency resulting from the desertion or, indeed, death of two members of the crew. The agreement to pay extra wages was "void for want of consideration."[157]

The shift effected in *Stilk v. Myrick* from a rule based on policy concerns relating to coercion to a rule based on absence of consideration has achieved the status of orthodoxy. Under this approach, all agreements involving one-sided variations of existing contracts fail on the basis of the pre-existing duty rule. The doctrine produces reasonable outcomes in cases where the promise to provide additional consideration is extracted by a promisee who is exploiting the promisor's vulnerability. *Smith v. Dawson*,[158] for example, appears to be a case of this kind. The plaintiffs had agreed to build a house for a fixed price. As the project neared completion, the building was partly destroyed by fire. The plaintiffs remained liable under the contract to complete construction of the building, but when they learned that the owner had taken out insurance on the house, they refused to do so unless the insurance was paid over to them. The defendant was initially reluctant to do so because she had suffered the loss of her furniture, but finally acqui-

---

153 *Ibid.* at 94.
154 (1809), 2 Camp. 317, 170 E.R. 1168.
155 *Ibid.* at 1169.
156 *Ibid.* The result would be otherwise if, before departure, it was apparent that the voyage would be dangerous and the sailors were not, therefore, required by their contract of employment to go to sea in such circumstances. See *Hartley v. Ponsonby* (1857), 7 E. & B. 872, 119 E.R. 1471.
157 *Ibid.*
158 (1923), 53 O.L.R. 615 (S.C.A.D.).

esced to the plaintiffs' demand. The promise to turn over the insurance proceeds to the plaintiffs was held not binding for want of consideration.

The doctrine is also applicable, however, to what appear to be voluntary arrangements entered into by commercial parties with relatively equal bargaining power. The doctrine is thus overinclusive in the sense that it captures and renders unenforceable many agreements that do not result from an unfair exploitation of vulnerability. A leading Canadian illustration of the phenomenon is the decision of the Ontario Court of Appeal in *Gilbert Steel Ltd. v. University Construction Ltd.*[159] The plaintiff was a supplier of fabricated steel bars for incorporation in apartment buildings being constructed by the defendant at three separate sites. Although the supply of steel for the first two projects was completed at the contract price, by the time construction was to commence on the third site, the owners of the steel mill had notified the plaintiff of a substantial increase in the price of unfabricated steel and of the prospect of a further price increase yet to come. When the plaintiff reported this news to the defendant, the parties agreed to a new written contract with respect to the third site in which a portion of the price increase was passed on to the defendant. When the mill owners announced a further increase, further discussions took place between the parties. The plaintiff alleged that the defendant orally agreed at this time to a further increase in the contract price for steel to be supplied to the third site. The defendant denied that such an undertaking had been given. Moreover, a written agreement drafted by the plaintiff that reflected the increased price but included, as well, two clauses that, according to the trial judge, had not been discussed by the parties, was never executed by them. Nonetheless, it was held at trial that the alleged oral undertaking had been given by the defendant. The promise was held unenforceable, however, for lack of consideration.

The Court of Appeal affirmed the decision at trial. Wilson J.A. rejected the suggestion that the plaintiff's promise to give the defendant a "good price on steel for the next building" constituted good consideration. The promise was too vague and imprecise to have this effect.[160] Further, she rejected as ingenious but unpersuasive, the plaintiff's sub-

---

159 Above note 25. See B. Reiter, "Courts, Consideration and Common Sense" (1977) 27 U.T.L.J. 439. See also *Modular Windows of Canada v. Command Construction* (1984), 11 C.L.R. 131 (Ont. H.C.J.); *Francis v. Canadian Imperial Bank of Commerce* (1994), 120 D.L.R. (4th) 393 (Ont. C.A.); *Hobbs v. TDI Canada Ltd.* (2004), 246 D.L.R. (4th) 43 (Ont. C.A.).
160 See also *Canada West Tree Fruits Ltd. v. T.G. Bright & Co.*, above note 25.

mission that consideration could be found in the increased credit afforded by the plaintiff to the defendant as a result of the increase in
price. As the contract provided that payment was to be made by the
defendant within sixty days of delivery of the steel, the plaintiff argued
that, as the price had increased, a greater amount of credit was now
made available to the defendant by the plaintiff for the sixty-day period. The argument was properly rejected, presumably, on the basis that
if successful, it would preclude the application of *Stilk v. Myrick* to any
transaction that included a credit term. Nonetheless, the result in *Gilbert Steel* is unsatisfying as it appears that the arrangement between
the parties was voluntary and, from the plaintiff's perspective at least,
reasonably understood to be binding.[161]

In *Gilbert Steel*, the plaintiffs also attempted to rely upon a traditional exception to the rule in *Stilk v. Myrick,* which holds that where
the parties have agreed to a mutual rescission of the prior agreement
and the substitution of a new agreement, the new agreement is binding
even though it may place increased burdens on one party alone. Consideration for the new agreement is provided by the mutual abandon-
ment of rights under the initial contract. As *Raggow v. Scougall & Co.*[162]
suggests, the mutual promises to abandon the first agreement may be
implied. In this case, the defendant employer, suffering a loss of business during World War I, contemplated closing the business. Instead,
however, the defendant called together the employees who agreed to a
reduction in wages on the understanding that when the war concluded,
they would revert to their former terms of employment. The plaintiff
employee, however, after accepting the new salary for some months,
sued to recover the full contract rate. It was held that even though there
was no express recital setting out the existence and rescission of the
old agreement, it was nonetheless the case that the parties had "in fact
torn up the old agreement and made a new one by mutual consent."[163]
To the extent that the courts are willing to imply the existence of a
mutual rescission, of course, the doctrine of mutual rescission offers
a powerful exception to the pre-existing duty rule. At the very least,

---

161 Further, the decision creates opportunities for and appears to reward unattractively strategic behaviour. The defendant in this case accepted invoices at the
increased rate but remitted cheques in rounded amounts in such fashion that
by the completion of the agreement the increased amount of the price had been
withheld.
162 (1915), 31 T.L.R. 564 (Div. Ct.). And see *Deluxe French Fries v. McArdle* (1976),
10 Nfld. & P.E.I.R. 414 (P.E.I.S.C.).
163 *Raggow v. Scougall & Co., ibid.* at 565. See also *Morris v. Baron & Co.,* [1918] A.C.
1 (H.L.).

however, the facts must not be inconsistent with the existence of an intention to rescind mutually. Thus, the doctrine was inapplicable to the factual circumstances of the *Gilbert Steel* case. The Court of Appeal held that the inference of a mutual rescission was precluded by the fact that one of the parties had, in fact, drafted a new written agreement to which the other party had not agreed. Nor was there other evidence from which a new agreement replacing *in toto* the original contract could be inferred.

A new exception to the pre-existing duty rule appears to have emerged from the recent decision of the English Court of Appeal in *Williams v. Roffey Bros. & Nicholls (Contractors) Ltd.*[164] This case, on its facts, demonstrates the unsatisfactory nature of the traditional rule. The defendant general contractor had retained the plaintiff carpenter as a subcontractor on a project that involved the renovation of twenty-seven flats. The plaintiff was having difficulty performing the agreement as a result of financial difficulties and inadequate supervision of the work-force. The contract price of £20,000 was too low. The defendant general contractor became apprehensive about the situation because there was a penalty clause in the main construction agreement that would subject the contractor to substantial liability if the work was not completed in a timely fashion. Accordingly, the defendant approached the plaintiff carpenter and suggested an increase in the price of a further £10,300 to be paid in instalments when each flat was completed, this being a variation on the prior payment arrangements. Although the work proceeded for a time on this basis, the contractor eventually ceased making payments and, in due course, the plaintiff brought an action to recover damages on the basis of the increased contract price.

Although the Court of Appeal accepted that the plaintiff had not undertaken to provide any additional consideration, the court nonetheless declined to apply the doctrine of *Stilk v. Myrick*. Glidewell L.J., noting the reasoning of Lord Scarman in *Pao On*, suggested that the recognition of economic duress lessened the need for that "rigid adherence to the doctrine of consideration"[165] that was manifest in *Stilk v. Myrick*. Although Glidewell J.L. conceded that *Pao On* was a three-party case and thus possibly distinguishable from a two-party case like *Stilk v. Myrick*, it was his view that Lord Scarman's reasoning was equally applicable to a case where a promise to perform a pre-existing contract was made by one of the two parties to the original agreement.

---

164 [1990] 1 All E.R. 512 (C.A.). See J. Adams and R. Brownsword, "Contract, Consideration and the Critical Path" (1990) 53 Mod. L. Rev. 536.

165 *Williams v. Roffey Bros. & Nicholls (Contractors) Ltd.*, ibid. at 520.

Thus, if the plaintiff had extracted the contractor's promise to increase the price by applying economic duress, the promise to pay more would be unenforceable. Where, as in this case, however, it was the contractor who identified the problem and, as a result of making the promise "obtains in practice a benefit, or obviates a disbenefit,"[166] the benefit acquired by the promisor constitutes the valuable consideration that renders the promise enforceable. The practical benefit that Glidewell L.J. had in mind is the avoidance of the penalty for late performance of the main contract. This approach represented, in his view, a refinement of the principle of *Stilk v. Myrick* but left the principle unscathed as it would continue to apply in circumstances where the promisor did not obtain a practical benefit by giving the promise.

Russell L.J. provided a similar analysis and placed emphasis on other practical benefits secured by the contractors such as the replacement of the previously haphazard method of payment and the ability to complete the work without the need to re-employ another subcontractor. In his view, *Stilk v. Myrick* would continue to apply to a "gratuitous promise, pure and simple."[167] Where, however, "a party undertakes to make a payment because by so doing it will gain an advantage arising out of the continuing relationship with the promisee, the new bargain will not fail for want of consideration."[168] The third member of the panel, Purchas L.J., indicated a greater willingness than his colleagues to confine *Stilk v. Myrick* to the special facts of employment on the high seas. "There were," he observed, "strong public policy grounds at that time to protect the master and owners of a ship from being held to ransom by disaffected crews."[169] The modern cases, in his view, tended to apply the concept of economic duress rather than to find that the second agreement failed for lack of consideration. In cases such as the present, where both parties derived some benefit from the altered arrangement, it did not matter for Purchas L.J. that one of the parties, the plaintiff carpenter, did not suffer a detriment. The contractor had clearly gained a commercial advantage from the arrangement by securing his commercial position. For all three members of the court, then, it appears that the fact that the contractor would obtain a benefit, albeit one arising from the defendant's relationship with the owner of the flats, could serve as consideration rendering the promise to pay more an enforceable one.

---

166 *Ibid.* at 522.
167 *Ibid.* at 524.
168 *Ibid.*
169 *Ibid.* at 526.

Although the new exception recognized by the Court of Appeal in the *Roffey* case is to be welcomed inasmuch as it offers at least a partial solution to the problem posed by the rule in *Stilk v. Myrick*, it must be conceded that the reasoning of the case does not appear technically consistent with the traditional doctrine of consideration. The fact that the contractor was concerned about the possibility of being required to pay a penalty under the main construction contract obviously explains *why* the contractor was prepared to make the promise to increase the price. However, as we have seen,[170] a promisor's motive for making a promise does not constitute consideration for the promise under traditional doctrine. Moreover, the exception to the traditional approach crafted in *Roffey* does not appear to be a minor or trivial one. In many instances, promises to increase unilaterally the consideration being provided in an agreement will be given because there is considered to be some practical advantage to be gained by the promisor in doing so. Thus, *Roffey* can be interpreted as a rather substantial "refinement" of the rule in *Stilk v. Myrick*. Indeed, the decision opens up the attractive possibility that the principle in *Stilk v. Myrick* will be applied only in cases where the promise to provide additional consideration is induced by economic duress. On this basis, voluntary one-sided contractual variations would normally be binding, a proposition of law that would be more in accord with the likely understandings of the parties to such arrangements than the current rule. This approach would also have the attraction of placing the law concerning pre-existing duties on the same footing in both three-party and two-party cases. As Glidewell L.J. indicated in *Roffey*, there does not appear to be a convincing reason for distinguishing between the two. Further, as was the case with *Pao On*, a shift to this approach would more closely align the decision rule in these cases to the public policy rationale underlying the rule of refusing to enforce agreements induced by coercion.

4) Partial Payment of a Debt

A promise by a debtor to make partial payment of a debt in return for a creditor's promise to accept the partial payment as a basis for treating the debt as fully discharged does not give rise to an enforceable agreement. This proposition may be considered to be an application of or a corollary of the pre-existing duty rule. In such an agreement, the debtor is not even giving an undertaking to perform a pre-existing duty. The debtor is promising only partial performance of a pre-existing duty to

---

170 See this Chapter, section B(2).

pay the debt, and this, it is commonly accepted, cannot constitute good consideration for the creditor's promise to treat the debt as discharged. The origins of the doctrine are often traced back to comments made by Lord Coke in *Pinnel's Case*[171] in 1602 and, indeed, beyond.[172] Lord Coke observed in *Pinnel's Case* as follows:

> Payment of a lesser sum on the day in satisfaction of a greater, cannot be any satisfaction for the whole, because it appears to the judges that by no possibility, a lesser sum can be a satisfaction to the plaintiff for a greater sum: that the gift of a horse, hawk, or robe, etc. in satisfaction is good. For it shall be intended that a horse, hawk or rogue, etc. might be more beneficial to the plaintiff than the money, in respect of some circumstances, or otherwise the plaintiff would not have accepted of it in satisfaction.

The validity of this proposition was tested in a leading late-nineteenth-century decision of the House of Lords in *Foakes v. Beer.*[173] John Foakes was indebted to Julia Beer in the amount of £2,090 and 19s, an amount for which she had obtained judgment. The parties then entered into an agreement under which Foakes agreed to pay Beer regular instalments of £150 until the full amount of the debt was fully paid and satisfied, in return for a promise from Beer that once the payments had been made, no proceedings would be taken to enforce the judgment. Foakes made the requisite payments but, in due course, an action was brought by Beer to recover interest. Relying, in part, on Lord Coke's statement in *Pinnel's Case*, the House of Lords held that Beer's claim for the interest should be allowed as the agreement failed for lack of consideration. The Earl of Selborne L.C. observed that it might be an improvement in the law to recognize the enforceability of an arrangement of this kind but the absence of consideration provided by the debtor precluded this outcome.

In *Foakes v. Beer*, the debtor attempted to defend on the basis that the doctrine of "accord and satisfaction" might apply notwithstanding the absence of consideration. The doctrine of accord and satisfaction was described in the following terms by Scrutton L.J. in the later decision in *British Russian Gazette and Trade Outlook Ltd. v. Associated Newspapers Ltd.*:[174] "Accord and satisfaction is the purchase of a release from an obligation whether arising under contract or tort by means of

---

171 (1602), 5 Co. Rep. 117, 77 E.R. 237 (C.P.).
172 See Stoljar, above note 2 at 119–21.
173 (1884), 9 App. Cas. 605 (H.L.).
174 [1933] 2 K.B. 616 (C.A.).

252 THE LAW OF CONTRACTS

any valuable consideration, not being the actual performance of the obligation itself. The accord is the agreement by which the obligation is discharged. The satisfaction is the consideration which makes the agreement operative."[175] The creditor's argument, then, was that the agreement with Beer constituted an accord and the making of the payments constituted satisfaction, thereby achieving a binding release from the debt. This argument was flatly rejected in *Foakes v. Beer*. The House of Lords held that the doctrine of accord and satisfaction does not create an exception to the normal requirement of consideration.

Although the rule in *Foakes v. Beer* is well established and of ancient lineage, it is widely accepted that the rule is simply unsatisfactory. Agreements to accept a lesser sum in discharge of a larger debt are commonplace. They are typically understood by the parties to be mutually advantageous and binding. The application of consideration doctrine in *Foakes v. Beer* simply frustrates the reasonable expectations of parties to transactions of this kind. There can be no doubt of the practical advantages that such arrangements have for creditors. A Canadian judge, who would have favoured overruling the doctrine observed as follows:

> The consideration for the [creditor] ... was the immediate receipt of payment and the saving of time, effort and expense. In my opinion, it is not up to the court to judge the reasons for entering into such an agreement but rather to determine that the agreement was reached with full knowledge and consent. The court must therefore recognize the validity of the agreement. It would be foolish to suppose that financial institutions disdain the old adage, "A bird in the hand is worth two in the bush."[176]

The fact that the creditor will normally receive a practical benefit from an arrangement of this kind with a debtor, however, does not constitute consideration under traditional doctrine. As we have seen,[177] the decision of the English Court of Appeal in *Williams v. Roffey Bros. & Nicholls (Contractors) Ltd.*[178] suggested that in circumstances where a

---

175 *Ibid.* at 643–44.

176 *Robichaud v. Caisse Populiar de Pokemouche Ltée.* (1990), 69 D.L.R. (4th) 589 at 595–96 (N.B.C.A.), Angers J.A. Angers J.A. did not carry a majority of the court on this point. In a concurring judgment, Rice J.A. applied the doctrine of promissory estoppel. Ayles J.A. concurred only as to result. The fact situation at issue appears to involve a composition of creditors and the result of the case can also be justified on this ground. See the text below at notes 185–91. For discussion of promissory estoppel, see Chapter 8.

177 See this Chapter, section B(3).

178 Above note 164.

general contractor received a practical benefit from the performance of a subcontractor's pre-existing duty, the practical benefit could constitute good consideration for the general contractor's promise to pay an increase in price. In the more recent decision in *Re Selectmove Ltd.*,[179] the same court had an opportunity to consider whether the *Roffey* doctrine could apply to an agreement to discharge a debt in return for a part payment on the theory that the part payment confers a "practical benefit" in the requisite sense. Peter Gibson L.J. conceded the force of the argument and suggested that in the absence of authority there would be much to be said for the enforceability of such a contract. It was, however, the court's view that acceptance of the argument would amount to an effective overruling of *Foakes v. Beer* inasmuch as a practical benefit of this kind would be present in virtually all such arrangements. As a matter of precedent, the overruling of *Foakes v. Beer* was considered by the court, understandably, to be a matter for the House of Lords and not the Court of Appeal. Whether Canadian courts might feel less constrained in departing from *Foakes v. Beer* on this basis remains to be seen.

The unsatisfactory nature of the rule in *Foakes v. Beer* is made manifest by a line of authority that narrowly distinguishes the decision. It has long been held that if the debtor agrees to make the lesser payment in a different form, the agreement to discharge the debt may be binding. Thus, in *Sibree v. Tripp*,[180] the creditor had agreed to accept in full satisfaction of a claim for £500 three promissory notes for £125, £125 and £50. The arrangement was held to be binding. Alderson B. explained: "A man may give in satisfaction of a debt of £100, a horse of the value of £5, but not £5. Again, if the time or place of payment be different, the one sum may be a satisfaction of the other .... If for money you give a negotiable security, you pay it in a different way. The security may be worth more or less, it is of uncertain value."[181]

Perhaps not every reader will find convincing the suggestion that promissory notes totalling £300 may be of greater value than a sum of £500. Nonetheless, the rule is well established and has been accepted by the Supreme Court of Canada in *Foot v. Rawlings*.[182] In this case, the debtor owed a substantial sum to the creditor under a series of promissory notes. On the suggestion of the creditor, the parties entered into an agreement under which the creditor reduced the amount of interest be-

---

179 [1995] 2 All E.R. 531 (C.A.).
180 (1846), 15 M. & W. 23, 153 E.R. 745.
181 *Ibid.* at 752 (E.R.).
182 [1963] S.C.R. 197.

ing charged, provided that the debtor make instalment payments of $300 per month in the form of a series of postdated cheques. The Supreme Court held that the change in the mode of payment constituted good consideration and that the arrangement would continue to bind as long as the debtor continued to provide the postdated cheques in the requisite fashion, failing which the right of action on the notes would revive. Such decisions are obviously difficult to defend as a matter of logic. As Lord Denning M.R. observed in *D. & C. Builders Ltd. v. Rees*:[183] "No sensible distinction can be taken between payment of a lesser sum by cash and payment of it by cheque. The cheque, when given, is conditional payment. When honoured, it is actual payment. It is then just the same as cash."[184] The resilience of this line of authority, however, strongly suggests that judges appreciate that the rule in *Foakes v. Beer* is an unsatisfactory one and ought to be distinguished whenever possible.

Application of the doctrine to compositions of creditors would be very inconvenient. A composition of creditors occurs when a group of creditors of a particular debtor enter into an agreement that they will all accept less than full payment as discharge of the debts owed to them by the debtor. The creditors' reason for entering into such an arrangement is to facilitate an orderly and equable realization by the creditors of those assets of the debtor that can be made available to satisfy their respective claims. Although the enforcement of such arrangements would appear to be inconsistent with *Pinnel's Case* and *Foakes v. Beer*, it has long been established that compositions of creditors are binding. The initial justification for this outcome was that the consideration for each creditor's promise is the promises of the other creditors.[185] This explanation does not solve the problem that the debtor appears not to have given good consideration and therefore would not be in a position to enforce the promises given by each creditor.[186] A second explanation that has found more favour is the suggestion that enabling a creditor to ignore the composition would constitute a fraud on the other creditors and, accordingly, a claim brought by a creditor against the debtor for the unpaid balance of a particular debt ought to be dismissed.[187] Again, it is not obvious that the explanation is fully satisfying. There is a sense

---

183 [1966] 2 Q.B. 617.

184 *Ibid.* at 623.

185 *Boothbey v. Sowden* (1812), 3 Camp. 175, 170 E.R. 1346. *Good v. Cheesman* (1831), 2 B. & Ad. 328, 109 E.R. 1165.

186 The debtor does not enjoy privity of contract with the exchanges of promises among the creditors. For discussion of privity of contract see Chapter 9.

187 See *Wood v. Roberts* (1818), 2 Stark. 417, 171 E.R. 691; *Cook v. Lister* (1863), 13 C.B. (N.S.) 543, 143 E.R. 215 at 235 (E.R.).

in which Mrs. Beer committed a similar fraud on Mr. Foakes and yet *Pinnel's Case* is applied in this context with full force and effect. It is unquestionably sensible, however, to enforce compositions of creditors. This practical common sense does appear to be the correct explanation for the rule.[188] In other cases, reliance has been placed on the rule concerning compositions with creditors to uphold the proposition that payment of lesser sums by third parties to the debt may create a binding agreement to discharge the debt. Thus, in cases where fathers have offered partial payment of a son's debt in return for a discharge of the debt by the creditor, the arrangements have been held binding.[189] Again, in such cases, it has been suggested that permitting the creditor, in such circumstances, to pursue the claim against the son would be to permit the creditor to commit a fraud on the father.[190] Alternatively, it has been suggested that the effect of such an agreement, once performed, is to extinguish the initial debt.[191]

A number of Canadian provinces and territories have overruled *Foakes v. Beer* by statute.[192] The Alberta provision reads as follows:

Part performance of an obligation either before or after a breach thereof shall be held to extinguish the obligation

(a) when expressly accepted by a creditor in satisfaction, or

(b) when rendered pursuant to an agreement for that purpose, although without any new consideration.[193]

Although this provision appears to overrule successfully the very decision in *Foakes v. Beer*, the statute is vulnerable to interpretive difficulties in fact situations that stray from that pattern. Thus, for example, it would appear that the provision would not save an agreement under which the creditor agrees to complete forgiveness of a debt. The section would be engaged only if a part performance of some kind is rendered by the debt-

---

188 See *Couldery v. Bartrum* (1881), 19 Ch. D. 394 at 400, Jessel M.R. ("the agreement *inter se* supplied the additional consideration that was supposed to be necessary").

189 *Hirachand Punamchand v. Temple,* [1911] 2 K.B. 330. See also *Welby v. Drake* (1825), 1 Car. & P. 557, 171 E.R. 1315; *Cook v. Lister,* above note 187.

190 *Welby v. Drake, ibid.; Cook v. Lister, ibid.*

191 See *Hirachand Punamchand v. Temple,* above note 189 at 336–37, Vaughan Williams L.J. and 339, Fletcher Moulton L.J.

192 See *Judicature Act,* R.S.A. 2000, c. J-2, s. 13(1); *Law and Equity Act,* R.S.B.C. 1996, c. 253, s. 43; *Mercantile Law Amendment Act,* C.C.S.M., c. M120; *Mercantile Law Amendment Act,* R.S.O. 1990, c. M.10, s. 16; *Queen's Bench Act,* R.S.S. 1998, c. Q-1.01, s. 64; *Judicature Act,* R.S.N.W.T. 1998, c. J-1, s. 40; *Judicature Act,* R.S.Y. 2002, c. 128, s. 25.

193 R.S.A. 2000, c. J-2, s. 13(1).

or. Further, it is not entirely clear whether the provision would save as binding an agreement to accept lesser payment where the agreement has as yet only been partially performed. Although some cases have suggested that once the part performance has commenced, the creditor's undertaking is irrevocable,[194] it is not at all clear, however, that the provision is engaged by part performance of the payment of the lesser sum—that is, part performance of the "part performance"—which, pursuant to subparagraph (a), has not yet been expressly accepted by the creditor in satisfaction, and, pursuant to subparagraph (b), has not yet been fully rendered pursuant to the agreement with the creditor. Accordingly, it has been suggested that the creditor might be able to revive the existing debt while the arrangement remains executory.[195] Finally, it may be noted that the provision is silent with respect to the question of whether the creditor would be able to rely on defences such as economic duress, undue influence or unconscionability. The preferable view is that the statute merely deals with the consideration point and that such defences would be available in the usual fashion.[196]

C. FORMALITY: PROMISES UNDER SEAL

The rule that promises recorded in instruments executed under seal and delivered to the promisee are binding on the promisor is of ancient common law lineage. Thus, the action on the covenant, which was one of the principal procedural devices for enforcing sealed instruments, can be traced back to the early-thirteenth century.[197] The early use of seals as a means of authenticating documents and executing instruments under seal was initially the preserve of feudal elites.[198] Over time,

---

194 *Bank of Commerce v. Jenkins* (1888), 16 O.R. 215 (H.C.J.); *Hoolahan v. Hivon*, [1944] 4 D.L.R. 405 (Alta. S.C.A.D.).

195 *Rommerill v. Gardner* (1962), 35 D.L.R. (2d) 717 (B.C.C.A.). A specific right of revocation where payments have not commenced or where the debtor discontinues performance for an unreasonable period of time has been specifically provided in the Manitoba legislation. See *Mercantile Law Amendment Act*, C.C.S.M., c. M120, s. 6(4).

196 *Graham v. Voth Bros. Construction (1974) Ltd.*, [1982] 6 W.W.R. 365 (B.C. Co. Ct.). The Manitoba legislation, unnecessarily perhaps, has specifically provided a defence in cases where the arrangement is unconscionable. See *Mercantile Law Amendment Act*, C.C.S.M., c. M120, s. 6(2).

197 Stoljar, above note 2 at 4.

198 F. Pollock and W.F. Maitland, *The History of English Law*, vol. II (Cambridge: Cambridge University Press, 1968) at 223–24.

however, seals became more broadly available as "the law for the great became the law for all."[199] Moreover, although the sealing of an instrument initially involved the making of an impression on the document by impressing the seal on a wax blob or other similar substance affixed to the document, the formal requisites of sealing have relaxed over the centuries to the point where it became unnecessary for one who wished to execute a sealed instrument to actually be possessed of a personal seal. In contemporary practice, it is common to simply affix a small red sticker or wafer to the instrument in question which, as long as the promisor has, in some fashion, adopted as his or her seal, will successfully function as a seal in the requisite sense.

Although a variety of legal consequences attach to instruments under seal, the most important for present purposes is that promises made in a sealed instrument are enforceable notwithstanding the absence of consideration. Although it is sometimes said that the seal "imports consideration," such statements are evidently historically inaccurate. The enforcement of sealed instruments long antedates the development of the doctrine of consideration. Moreover, the suggestion is likely to lead to the kind of confusion evident in one Canadian case[200] in which it was held that where the instrument stated on its face that there was no consideration, the seal would not have the effect of importing consideration. Such decisions are aberrant, however, and clearly inconsistent with the general rule that promises made in sealed instruments are enforceable, notwithstanding the absence of consideration given in return.[201] Thus, for example, in the context of a so-called firm offer in which the offeror promises to keep the offer open for a stipulated period of time, that promise will not be enforceable if no consideration is furnished in return by the offeree.[202] A firm offer given in an instrument under seal, however, would bind.[203] For parties who wish to render promises binding without the necessity of exchanging

---

199 *Ibid.* at 24. Pollock and Maitland record that by the end of the 13th century the "free and lawful man usually had a seal." See *ibid.*

200 *Chilliback v. Pawliuk* (1956), 17 W.W.R. 534 (Alta. S.C.T.D.).

201 Authorities on the point stretch back over the centuries. The point was recently reaffirmed, however, by the Supreme Court of Canada in *Friedmann Equity Developments Inc. v. Final Note Ltd.* (2000), 188 D.L.R. (4th) 269 at para. 20 (S.C.C.), Bastarache J.

202 See this Chapter, section B(1).

203 *Nelson Coke & Gas Co. v. Pellatt* (1902), 4 O.L.R. 481 (C.A.); *Sanitary Refuse Collectors Inc. v. City of Ottawa* (1971), 23 D.L.R. (3d) 27 (Ont. H.C.); *Gaar Scott Co. v. Ottoson* (1911), 19 W.L.R. 472 (Man. C.A.).

consideration, then, the enforceability of sealed instruments may provide a useful device for achieving that object.

There are two further legal incidents of sealed instruments that may provide an incentive for their use. First, under traditional limitations law, still applicable in some jurisdictions,[204] a longer limitation period applies to claims brought to enforce sealed instruments as opposed to merely written or parol agreements. Under the traditional statutes, the period of time within which a claim could be brought to enforce a promise made in a "specialty" is often as long as twenty years,[205] whereas a claim to enforce a promise made in an informal agreement would be considerably less. Under modern limitation statutes, however, universal limitation periods are typically adopted that impose the same period of limitation on claims brought to enforce both formal and informal agreements.[206]

A third legal incident of a contract under seal is that only the identified parties to the agreement may sue or be sued for breach of the agreement. This rule, often referred to as the "sealed contract rule," constitutes an exception to a well-established doctrine of agency law that where a contract has been entered into by an agent on behalf of an "undisclosed principal," that is, a party whose identity has not been disclosed to the other contracting party, the undisclosed principal can sue or be sued on the agreement.[207] By creating an exception to this doctrine, then, the sealed contract rule provides a means whereby undisclosed principals can immunize themselves from liability under an agreement simply by ensuring that the agent executes the agreement under seal.[208] Thus, it is not an uncommon practice in the context of mortgage lending for a corporate borrower to execute the mortgage or other loan documents under seal in order to immunize the shareholders of the borrower, who might be considered to be undisclosed principals, from personal liability in the event that the corporate borrower is unable to repay the loan. Although the soundness of the sealed contract

204 *Limitation of Actions Act*, R.S.N.B. 1973, c. L-8, s. 2; *Statute of Limitations*, R.S.P.E.I. 1988, c. S-7, s. 13; *Limitation of Actions Act*, R.S.N.S. 1989, c. 258, s. 2(1)(c).
205 See, for example, *Limitations Act*, R.S.O. 1990, c. L.15, s. 45(1), now repealed and replaced by *Limitations Act, 2002*, S.O. 2002, c. 24, s. 4.
206 See, for example, *Limitations Act*, R.S.A. 2000, c. L-12, s. 3; *Limitation Act*, R.S.B.C. 1996, c. 266, s. 3(5); *Limitations Act, 2002*, S.O. 2002, c. 24, s. 4.
207 See generally J.B. Ames, "The Undisclosed Principal—His Rights and Liabilities" (1909) 18 Yale L.J. 443; E.J. Weinrib, "The Undisclosed Principle of Undisclosed Principals" (1975) 21 McGill L.J. 298.
208 See, for example, *Porter v. Pelton* (1903), 33 S.C.R. 449.

rule has been challenged in recent years, its continuing validity was recently reaffirmed by the Supreme Court of Canada in *Friedmann Equity Developments Inc. v. Final Note Ltd.*[209]

Contracts under seal are traditionally referred to as deeds, specialties or covenants. Although these terms are used interchangeably in contemporary professional discourse, their meaning has evolved over time. Thus, in an earlier era, the term covenant was not used to refer to sealed instruments that granted or promised to grant an interest in land. In contemporary practice, the sealed instrument used to convey ownership rights in land is typically referred to as a deed or deed of conveyance. The fact that the term "specialty" has often been used in limitations statutes to identify the special limitation period for sealed instruments has led to some distortion in the use of that term. Thus, Ontario courts, albeit in *obiter dicta*, apparently determined to avoid the application of the former Ontario twenty-year limitation period applicable to all specialties have suggested that not every agreement executed under seal constitutes a specialty in the requisite sense.[210] Similarly, a Newfoundland court, in order to avoid what was apparently considered to be the unattractive conclusion that an instrument executed by a corporation under seal gave the corporate party the advantages of the longer limitation period, held that a contract under seal was enforceable as a specialty only where the promise in question was a promise to pay money and thus constituted a debt.[211] Such decisions have been cogently criticized,[212] however, and appear to be inconsistent with traditional professional usage. As far as the Newfoundland authority is concerned, it appears to have been overtaken on this point by the decision of the Supreme Court of Canada in *Friedmann Equity*,[213] which plainly accepts that the use of a corporate seal may have the general effect of creating a sealed instrument in the requisite sense and, as a result, become subject to extended limitations periods.[214]

Although the basic requirements to constitute a sealed instrument have persisted—the instrument must be executed under seal and delivered—the nature of these requirements has evolved over time and,

---

209 Above note 201. For criticism of the rule, see *Re Zamikoff v. Lundy* (1970), 9 D.L.R. (3d) 637 at 648, Laskin J.A.

210 *872899 Ontario v. Iacovoni* (1998), 40 O.R. (3d) 715 (C.A.), aff'g (1997), 33 O.R. (3d) 561 (Gen. Div.), leave to appeal to the S.C.C. denied (1999), 236 N.R. 199.

211 *Newfoundland & Labrador Housing Corp. v. Suburban Construction Ltd.* (1987), 38 D.L.R. (4th) 150 (Nfld. C.A.).

212 See G.H.L. Fridman, "Some Words About Deeds" (2002) 81 Can. Bar Rev. 69.

213 Above note 201.

214 *Ibid.* at para. 37.

moreover, they lack precise definition under current Canadian law. In the early era, the use of the seal obviously functioned as a signature equivalent and, accordingly, there was no requirement at common law that the seal be accompanied by the signature of the promisor. With the decline of the use of personalized seals and the substitution of wafers, however, it has become a common expectation that sealed instruments will be both sealed and signed. Further, it is common to have phrases such as "given under seal at ..." preceding the signature—a so-called testimonium clause—or to have the signature witnessed by a person whose signature is preceded by a so-called attestation clause, such as the phrase "signed, sealed and delivered in the presence of ... ." Although, as Laskin J.A. pointed out in *Royal Bank v. Kiska*,[215] such attestation and testimonium clauses were not necessary to make a sealed instrument enforceable at common law, they may have a useful role to play in contemporary practice where the seal itself does not serve as a unique identifier or authorized mark of the particular promisor. What must be established, however, is that the seal has been adopted by the promisor as a seal with the intention, therefore, of executing the instrument under seal. The signature may be the most convenient way of providing an evidentiary basis for that conclusion. Thus, it is well established that if an instrument bearing a wafer or other indication of a seal is signed with the intention of executing a document as a sealed instrument, this will constitute sufficient adoption or recognition of the seal to constitute the document as a sealed instrument.[216] Even if not technically required as a matter of common law,[217] then, insistence upon a signature is prudent. Indeed, given the common expectation that sealed instruments will be signed, it may well be that courts will refuse to characterize as sealed written agreements that bear a wafer but no signature of the promisor.[218] As a practical matter, however, the kinds of documents that are likely to be sealed are also very likely to be signed and, accordingly, the issue is not likely to arise.

More difficult questions arise with respect to the requirements for the seal itself. Standard form agreements that are designed for execu-

---

215 See above note 12.
216 *Stromdale & Ball Ltd. v. Burden*, [1952] Ch. 223 at 230, Danckwerts J. In such circumstances, it was held, the traditional practice of requiring promisors to place their finger on the seal or wafer was simply unnecessary. See *ibid.*
217 Since 1925, English law has required a signature. See *Law of Property Act, 1925*, 15 & 16 Geo. V. (U.K.), c. 20, s. 73.
218 Thus, in *Friedmann Equity*, above note 201 at para. 36, the Supreme Court of Canada appears to have assumed, without discussion, that a sealed instrument must be "signed, sealed and delivered."

tion by seal may include testimonium and attestation clauses. They may also include the word "seal" or the phrase "add seal" in brackets or circled at the end of a signature line as a reminder that a wafer should be attached to the document. The letters "*l.s.*," suggesting *locus signilli* or place of the seal, may similarly be placed in brackets or in a circle for the same purpose. Alternatively, the document may bear a preprinted representation of a seal either in black and white or in colour, which may be thought to signal ambiguously either that this is the place at which the seal should be attached or that this pictorial representation ought to be considered a substitute for the wafer. The conduct and state of mind of the person executing the document is also variable. In the easy case, the person executing the document may attach a red wafer in the appropriate location and, by doing so, intend to seal the instrument. More difficult cases arise, however, when the seal is added after the execution of the instrument by a third party either with or without the explicit authorization of the promisor. More difficult still may be cases where no wafer is ever attached to the document and the question arises as to whether any of the aforesaid clauses or markings on the instrument coupled with the promisor's signature will be held to constitute sufficient evidence of an intention to seal the instrument.

Although the many decisions dealing with these various types of fact situations appear to establish a broad consensus in support of the proposition that the critical question is whether or not the document was intended by the person executing it to be a sealed instrument, no more precise consensus has emerged with respect to the significance of particular aspects of either the document itself or the conduct and state of mind of the promisor.[219] Broadly speaking, two approaches have emerged. The first places emphasis on the importance of some formal act on the part of the promisor that may be thought to constitute an adoption of the seal. Until the recent decision of the Supreme Court of Canada in the *Friedmann Equity* case, this appeared to be the minority position. In *Royal Bank v. Kiska*,[220] for example, the Ontario Court of Appeal accepted that the plaintiff bank could not treat a guarantee form signed by the brother of a borrower as sealed simply because the word "seal" was printed next to the signature line when no wafer was attached to the document. The guarantee in question did, however, contain attestation and testimonium clauses. Both the majority and Laskin J.A. in dissent agreed that the guarantee was not sealed in such

---

219 See generally A. Herschorn, "Documents under Seal: Consequences and Complications" (1989) 10 Advocates' Q. 129.
220 Above note 12.

circumstances. The majority held, however, that the guarantee was, in any event, supported by consideration in the form of the plaintiff's forebearance from taking action against the debtor. In dissent, Laskin J.A. went on to observe that although there had been a relaxation of the formalities required for sealing an instrument, neither the attestation and testimonium clauses nor the presence of the word "seal" next to the signature line constituted the instrument as a sealed instrument.

He explained as follows: "The respective words are merely anticipatory of a formality which must be observed and are not a substitute for it. I am not tempted by any suggestion that it would be a modern and liberal view to hold that a person who signs a document that states it is under seal should be bound accordingly although there is no seal on it."[221] Laskin J.A. conceded that in addition to the affixing of a gummed wafer to the document, it would be sufficient if "any representation of a seal"[222] was made by the promisor. A more difficult case, in his view, would be that in which there was an imprint of a wafer seal reproduced on the document and, on this point, he offered no opinion.

In *Kiska*, Laskin J.A. placed some emphasis on the fact that the party executing the guarantee may have lacked sophistication. Laskin J.A. noted that this was the case "where a bank thrust a printed form under the nose of a young man for his signature."[223] In such circumstances, in his view "[f]ormality serves a purpose here and some semblance of it should be preserved ...."[224] Interestingly, in the two cases applying the reasoning in *Kiska* in the years following the decision, the instruments in issue were also guarantee forms containing attestation and testimonium clauses to which no wafer had been attached.[225] More recently, the Ontario Court of Appeal, relying on *Kiska*, concluded that the mere presence of a testimonium clause, in the absence of any other evidence of sealing, did not render the document a sealed instrument.[226]

---

221 *Ibid.* at 594.
222 *Ibid.* at 593.
223 *Ibid.*
224 *Ibid.*
225 *Bank of Montreal v. Sperling Hotel Ltd.* (1973), 36 D.L.R. (3d) 130 (Man. Q.B.); *Thermo-Flow Corp. Ltd. v. Kuryluk* (1978), 84 D.L.R. (3d) 529 (N.S.S.C.T.D.). See also *Thompson v. Skill* (1909), 13 O.W.R. 887 (C.A.); *Koffman v. Fischtein* (1984), 49 O.R. (2d) 124 (H.C.), var'd (1986), 53 O.R. (2d) 671 (C.A.); *New Brunswick v. Olsen* (1984), 57 N.B.R. (2d) 321 (Q.B.).
226 *872899 Ontario Ltd. v. Iacovoni*, above note 210. See also *TCB Ltd. v. Gray*, [1986] Ch. 621; *South-West Oxford Township v. Bailack* (1990), 75 O.R. (2d) 360 (Gen. Div.).

In the majority of the modern cases, however, courts appear to yield, in varying degrees, to the temptation resisted by Laskin J.A. to find that the terms of the instrument relating to seals and the markings of various kinds commonly found on printed forms constitute some evidence upon which an intention to seal, or at least a presumption thereof, can be grounded. Thus, in *Linton v. Royal Bank of Canada*,[227] for example, a wafer was attached to a bank guarantee form after its execution, without either the consent or authorization of the guarantor. Hartt J., placing emphasis on the fact that the form contained a testimonium clause in the usual form and the word "seal" in brackets next to the signature line, held that the guarantor, having failed to delete either of those printed items, manifested an intention to execute a sealed instrument. Accordingly, in his view, the addition of the actual seal did not constitute a material alteration of the document. Similar results have been achieved in other cases.[228] In *Canadian Imperial Bank of Commerce v. Kean*,[229] a Newfoundland trial judge held that a guarantee containing a testimonium clause and the word "seal" next to the signature line was sufficient evidence of execution under seal. Goodrich J. said that he had been "tempted successfully"[230] by the suggestion that a person should be bound by a signed instrument that describes itself as being under seal even though there is no seal attached it.

The two lines of authority represented by *Kiska* and *Linton*, the former placing greater emphasis on the subjective intention to seal, the latter placing greater emphasis on the objective manifestations of intent to seal on the document, are not easily reconciled. Little guidance on the matter has been forthcoming from the appellant courts. In

---

227 [1967] 1 O.R. 315 (H.C.).
228 *Spear v. Bank of Nova Scotia* (1973), 37 D.L.R. (3d) 130 (N.B.S.C.A.D.) (testimonium clause); *Procopia v. D'Abbondanzo* (1973), 35 D.L.R. (3d) 641 (Ont. H.C.), var'd (1975), 58 D.L.R. (3d) 368 (Ont. C.A.) (testimonium and attestation clauses); *Royal Bank of Canada v. Bermuda Holdings Ltd.* (1975), 67 D.L.R. (3d) 316 (B.C.S.C.) (attestation clause); *Provincial Bank of Canada v. Whiteoak Construction Ltd.* (1976), 15 N.B.R. (2d) 408 (S.C.Q.B.) ("seal" next to the signature line); *Bank of Montreal v. Crosby Group Ltd.* (1977), 26 N.S.R. (2d) 331 (S.C.T.D.) ("Affix Seal" next to the signature line); *Bank of Nova Scotia v. Forest F. Ross & Son* (1982), 40 N.B.R. (2d) 563 (Q.B.) (attestation clauses, the words "signature and seal" under the signature line and a pre-printed representation of a seal); *Canadian Imperial Bank of Commerce v. Dene Mat Construction Ltd.*, [1988] 4 W.W.R. 344 (N.W.T.S.C.) (testimonium clause and pre-printed representation of a seal). See also *First National Securities Ltd. v. Jones*, [1978] 2 All E.R. 221 (C.A.) (attestation clause and "L.S." in a circle next to the signature line).
229 (1985), 55 Nfld. & P.E.I.R. 88 (Nfld. S.C.T.D.).
230 *Ibid.* at 89.

the *Friedmann Equity*[231] case, however, the Supreme Court of Canada offered a *dictum* evidencing a preference for the more subjective approach. Bastarache J. observed as follows:

> Today, while the creation of a sealed instrument no longer requires a waxed impression, there are still formalities which must be observed. At common law, a sealed instrument, such as a deed or a specialty, must be signed, sealed and delivered. The mere inclusion of these three words is not sufficient, and some indication of a seal is required. ... To create a sealed instrument, the application of the seal must be a conscious and deliberate act. At common law, then, the relevant question is whether the party intended to create an instrument under seal.[232]

This view appears consistent with the approach taken in *Kiska* to the effect that some semblance of formality must be maintained. The line of authority taking the more objective approach appears to assume that the signing of a printed form is likely to be understood by the signor as the giving of a binding legal undertaking, whether or not a wafer seal is attached to the document at the time of signing. This may be thought to justify a somewhat more lax or objective approach to the formality requirements. The nature of the policy choice to be made between these two approaches was not, however, further explored in the *Friedmann Equity* case.

The related and important question as to whether the affixing of a corporate seal constitutes execution of an instrument by seal was authoritatively answered in the *Friedmann Equity* decision. The case involved a claim by a mortgagee for monies advanced to a corporate borrower that had affixed its corporate seal to the mortgage upon execution of the document. The claim was brought against the defendants who, it was alleged, were the beneficial owners of the property. The plaintiff mortgagee argued that the defendants were liable on the mortgage on the theory that the corporate borrower had entered into the transaction as their agent and that they were, therefore, liable personally on the mortgage as the undisclosed principals of the borrower. The alleged beneficial owners defended on the basis that since the corporate seal of the corporate borrower had been affixed to the mortgage,

---

231 Above note 201.
232 *Ibid.* at para. 36, citing as authority for the proposition that a mere testimonium clause is insufficient, *872899 Ontario Inc. v. Iacovoni*, above note 210. No reference was made, however, to the extensive line of authority favouring a more objective approach.

the mortgage was a sealed instrument and they were entitled to rely on the sealed contract rule, which holds that only the signatories to a sealed instrument can sue or be sued with respect to obligations recorded in the document. As noted above,[233] the Court confirmed the existence of the sealed contract rule on this occasion. Accordingly, the question of whether a corporate seal constituted a seal in the requisite sense became a central issue in the case. A plausible argument in support of the view that a corporate seal is a seal in the traditional sense is that the affixing of a corporate seal is rather precisely equivalent to the earlier practices concerning the sealing of instruments, indeed, much more so than the current practices typically followed by natural persons executing sealed instruments. On the other hand, some courts have been reluctant to hold that all instruments executed under corporate seal constitute specialties.[234] In *Friedmann Equity*, the Supreme Court held that the question of whether the fact that a corporate seal was affixed to a document engaged the sealed contract rule or, indeed, the other aspects of the law applicable to sealed instruments, rested on the subjective intention of the corporate party. The mere attachment of the corporate seal, however, would not in itself constitute sufficient evidence of a corporate intent to create a sealed instrument.

Bastarache J. stated the test in the following terms: "Courts must examine the instrument itself and the circumstances surrounding its creation to determine whether the corporation intended to create a sealed instrument by affixing its corporate seal."[235] For parties who wish to ensure that the affixing of a corporate seal does create a sealed instrument in the requisite sense, then, a premium has been placed on creating a paper trail that will provide not merely evidence of the affixing of the corporate seal but the presence of a corporate intent to create a sealed instrument in the requisite sense. The Court further held, however, that in a case where a statute deems a particular type of instrument to be sealed, as is the case with some land registry statutes,[236] the corporation's intention to seal becomes irrelevant.

Apart from the affixing or adoption of a seal, the other requirement for the creation of a sealed instrument is that the instrument be

---

233 See the text above at notes 207–9.

234 See, for example, *Newfoundland & Labrador Housing Corp. v. Suburban Construction Ltd.*, above note 211; *872899 Ontario v. Iacovani*, above note 210.

235 Above note 201 at para. 37.

236 See, for example, *Land Registration Reform Act*, R.S.O. 1990, c. L.4, s. 13(1). Indeed, where the statute deems the instrument to be under seal "for all purposes" as is the case with the Ontario provision, this subjects the instrument to the "sealed contracts rule" described in the text above at notes 207–9.

delivered. This requirement has also been relaxed over the centuries; no longer is the transfer of physical possession of the instrument to the other party a necessary component of delivery in the requisite sense. It is well established that an instrument may be delivered even though the instrument remains within the possession of the promisor. Delivery may be constituted by any words or acts that indicate that the promisor intended to be bound by the instrument executed under seal.[237] Thus, it is well established that the execution of the sealed instrument in the presence of an attesting witness will constitute effective delivery of the instrument even though physical possession of the instrument is retained by the promisor.[238] On the other hand, a document executed under seal, which is then handed over to the promisor's solicitors on the understanding that it is to be held by the solicitor until further instructions are issued by the promisor, has not been delivered because there appears to be no present intention to be bound.[239]

A sealed instrument that is delivered, subject to a condition or conditions that must be fulfilled before the instrument is to become enforceable, is said to be delivered as an escrow. When the conditions have been met or have been performed, the promisor is bound by the instrument absolutely.[240] Although formerly it was said to be essential that express words were used to create an escrow, it has long been well established that no particular form of words is necessary to achieve that result. Courts will examine all the facts relating to execution of the instrument and if it is apparent that the instrument was intended to take effect only if a certain condition was met, the instrument will be held to have been delivered as an escrow.[241] Thus, where a deed guaranteeing a corporate debt was signed by some directors on the understanding that the signatory directors would be liable on the instrument only if all the directors of the corporation executed the instrument, the deed was held to be conditional on that event and therefore delivered

---

237 *Xenos v. Wickham* (1866), L.R. 2 H.L. 296. See also *Re Metropolitan Theatres Ltd.* (1917), 40 O.L.R. 345 (H.C.).

238 *Zwicker v. Zwicker Estate* (1899), 29 S.C.R. 527. See also *O'Calaghan v. Coady* (1912), 8 D.L.R. 316 (P.E.I.S.C.); *Ross v. Ross* (1977), 80 D.L.R. (3d) 377 (N.S.S.C.T.D); *Yanke v. Fenske* (1959), 21 D.L.R. (2d) 419 (Sask. C.A.).

239 *Foundling Hospital (Governors and Guardians) v. Crane*, [1911] 2 K.B. 367; *Re MacNeil Estate* (2002), 212 N.S.R. (2d) 133 (S.C.).

240 *Xenos v. Wickham,* above note 237.

241 *Molsons Bank v. Cranston* (1918), 45 D.L.R. 316 (Ont. C.A.); *Trust & Loan Company v. Ruttan* (1877), 1 S.C.R. 564; *O'Connor v. Beatty* (1876), 27 U.C.C.P. 203 (Ont. H.C.); *Huron v. Armstrong* (1868), 27 U.C.Q.B. 533.

as an escrow.[242] Similarly, in a case where a lessor executed a lease and delivered it to the lessor's solicitors on the condition that an agreement be reached with the lessee as to the date of possession and an appropriate apportionment of the rent, the lease was held to be delivered as an escrow on the condition that such arrangements were reached with the lessee.[243] As is the case with absolute delivery, an instrument may be delivered as an escrow even though it remains within the possession of the promisor.[244] Delivery as an escrow can also be made, of course, to a third party on the understanding that the deed will be delivered to the promisee when the conditions have been met. Delivery as an escrow can also be made to the promisee, as the traditional rule that delivery as an escrow must be made to a third party has not survived.[245]

The tests for both sealing and delivery, then, have evolved, from earlier and more objective standards to standards that require an assessment of subjective intent, at least in marginal cases, which are rather subtle and difficult to apply. This, together with the fact that the significance of the attachment of red wafers is probably not widely understood outside the legal profession, may call into question the validity of the rules concerning sealed instruments and their underlying rationale. In a classic article examining the possible justification for rules that render agreements enforceable on the basis of formalities attending their creation, Fuller articulated three different functions performed by legal formalities.[246] The first, the *evidentiary* function, is to provide reliable evidence of the terms of the agreement in the event of controversy. The second, the *cautionary* function, is that a requirement of formality may signal to the promisor that an event of legal significance is taking place and thus deter or prevent inconsiderate or rash behaviour. The third, the *channelling* function, is to provide a device whereby the enforceability of an undertaking is easily determined. In this respect, legal formality "offers a legal framework into which the party may fit his actions, or, to change the figure, it offers channels for the legally effective expression of intention."[247]

The rule that renders written and sealed agreements enforceable arguably does perform the functions identified by Fuller. In a straightforward

---

242 *Molsons Bank v. Cranston, ibid.* Compare with *Huggard v. Ontario & Saskatchewan Land Co.* (1908), 8 W.L.R. 866 (Sask. C.A.); *Helm v. Simcoe & Erie General Insurance Co.* (1979), 108 D.L.R. (3d) 8 (Alta. C.A.).

243 *Vincent v. Premo Enterprises (Voucher Sales) Ltd.,* [1969] 2 Q.B. 609 (C.A.).

244 *Xenos v. Wickham,* above note 237.

245 *Molsons Bank v. Cranston,* above note 241.

246 L. Fuller, "Consideration and Form" (1941) Colum. L. Rev. 799.

247 *Ibid.* at 801.

case, where the seal is affixed to the document at the time of execution, each of the three functions may be serviced. The creation of a written record of the agreement performs the evidentiary function. The affixing of the seal might be thought to emphasize the legal significance of the occasion for the signatory even if the rules relating to sealed instruments are not widely understood. The fact that sealing the instrument enables the parties, and their lawyers, to be able to virtually guarantee the enforceability of a sealed instrument in a straightforward case performs the channelling function. To be sure, the relaxation of the formality requirements in the context of sealed instruments undermines, to some degree, the cautionary function. To the extent that courts move to an objective test of the act of sealing based upon presumptions arising from the wording of a standard form document, the cautionary function of the seal itself is undermined. Even under modern practice, however, the rules relating to sealed instruments, which apply, of course, only to written agreements, continue to perform an evidentiary function by ensuring that gratuitous promises, in order to be enforceable, must be recorded in writing. Further, even though the tests for determining whether a seal has been affixed or delivery has occurred have become rather subtle, the channelling function is still performed by the rules in the sense that parties and their lawyers who wish to ensure enforceability through compliance with the rules are able to do so in a straightforward manner that will avoid these subtleties.

Of the three functions, it is perhaps the channelling function that has the most contemporary significance. As we have seen, the doctrine of consideration does not appear to capture all the different kinds of undertakings that parties might reasonably expect to be enforceable. Accordingly, it is attractive to have an alternative mechanism that can be deployed to render such undertakings enforceable in circumstances where the parties in question intend them to be so. It is no doubt for this reason that judicial sentiment appears to continue to run in favour of the continuing desirability of a formality rule of some kind. Thus, in *Friedmann Equity*,[248] Bastarache J. observed: "The seal continues to serve a useful purpose in our law. It allows a promise to be enforced without evidence of consideration."[249]

If the importance of the channelling function thus offers a justification for the preservation of a formality rule of some kind, however, it is

---

248 Above note 201.

249 *Ibid.* at para. 47. Bastarache J. went on to confirm the importance of the seal in enabling parties to ensure that no one other than the named parties to an instrument will be liable thereunder. See the text above at notes 207–9.

not entirely obvious that the current common law formality rule enforcing sealed instruments is the most optimal or suitable type of formality doctrine. Accordingly, law reform bodies, over the years, have given consideration to the possibility of reform of this rule, a matter to which we next turn.

D. REFORM

Many observers consider the common law rules for recognizing the enforceability of undertakings—the doctrines of consideration and form—to be less than ideal. As far as the rules relating to sealed instruments are concerned, they are vulnerable to the criticism that they rest on an arcane practice rarely followed in contemporary society. Further, under modern practice, it is unlikely that non-lawyers will appreciate the significance of the wafer seal with the result that the cautionary effect on the parties of the ceremonial aspects of sealing has been diminished. The doctrine of consideration is vulnerable to the criticism that it fails to capture and enforce a number of different types of undertakings that parties are likely to expect to be enforceable. The consideration rules thus create a significant risk the parties will injure themselves through reliance on agreements they mistakenly assume to be enforceable. As we have seen, the doctrine of consideration renders unenforceable, for example, firm offers, manufacturers' warranties, unilateral contractual variations and agreements whereby a creditor agrees to accept partial payment of a debt as a complete discharge of the obligation.[250] Charitable subscriptions are also not enforceable for want of consideration even in cases where the charity in question has foreseeably and detrimentally relied on the making of the subscription. More generally, the doctrine of consideration may be considered to have become overly subtle in drawing distinctions between enforceable and unenforceable contracts in such contexts, for example, as the doctrine of past consideration. It is not surprising, then, that law reform bodies have considered the possibility of recommending statutory reform of both the doctrine of consideration and the rules relating to sealed instruments.[251]

---

250 See this Chapter, section B.

251 See, for example, Law Revision Committee, *Sixth Interim Report (Statute of Frauds and the Doctrine of Consideration)*, Cmnd 5449 (London: HMSO, 1937); The Law Commission, *Working Paper No. 60, Firm Offers* (London: HMSO, 1975); Ontario Law Reform Commission, *Report on Sale of Goods* (Toronto: Attorney General,

Though obviously vulnerable to criticism, the rule that sealed instruments are enforceable has proven to be very resilient in Canadian common law jurisdictions. The Ontario Law Reform Commission, however, has argued persuasively that the ceremonial aspects of signing under seal are not likely of much significance in contemporary society.[252] Accordingly, the commission recommended that the seal could usefully be replaced by a requirement that formal agreements must be signed by the promisor in the presence of an attesting witness. In support of this proposal, it may be suggested that a signed and witnessed writing requirement would be more broadly understood by laypersons as signalling the creation of a legally binding arrangement. This proposal has not been implemented, however, and it seems unlikely that Canadian common law provinces will soon attempt this or any other reform of formality doctrine. The requirement of a seal in circumstances where deeds have been executed and delivered has, however, been abrogated in England.[253] To be enforceable as a deed, the instrument must merely be signed before an attesting witness and delivered. Extensive reforms have also been enacted in the United States. Many states have enacted legislation either abolishing the distinction between sealed and unsealed instruments or reforming, in some other fashion, the rules of formality.[254]

Reform of the law of consideration has proven to be even more elusive in common law jurisdictions. Even the sharpest critics of current doctrine, however, do not counsel abolition.[255] It is widely accepted that bargains should be enforceable. Indeed, Fuller[256] has argued that the functions performed by the formality rules considered above — their value in performing evidentiary, cautionary and channelling functions — can also offer justification for the enforcement of bargains. At least in the context of a half-completed exchange[257] where consideration

---

1979) c. 5(3); Law Reform Committee of South Australia, *Sixteenth Report Relating to the Law on Sealing of Documents* (Adelaide: The Committee, 1971); Chief Justice's Law Reform Committee, *Sealing of Documents* (Victoria: The Committee, 1975).

252   *Report on Amendment of Law of Contract* (Toronto: Ministry of the Attorney General, 1987) at 43.

253   *Law of Property (Miscellaneous Provisions) Act, 1989* (U.K.), c. 34, s. 1.

254   See generally J.M. Perillo, ed., *Corbin on Contracts*, vol. 3, rev. ed. by E.M. Holmes (St. Paul: West, 1996) c. 10.

255   See, for example, P.S. Atiyah, *Essays on Contract Law* (Oxford: Clarendon Press, 1986) at 240–43.

256   See above note 246.

257   *Ibid.* at 815–16. Fuller concedes that this argument has less persuasive force in the context of wholly executory exchanges. See *ibid.* at 816–18. For further dis-

has been delivered to the promisor, the evidence of what has occurred provides some indication of the existence of an agreement, the passing of consideration signals the importance of the occasion to the parties and the fact of creating the bargain, as every legal professional well understands, provides a predictable device for ensuring enforceability. Indeed, Fuller would justify the enforcement of bargains in which the consideration on one side is merely nominal on the same ground.[258] The enforcement of bargains can also be justified on the grounds of economic policy.[259] The obvious economic purpose and value of bargains is strengthened by their enforceability. To the extent that bargains are the unfair result of inequality of bargaining power, other doctrines can be fashioned and relied upon to meet the needs of justice in such cases.[260] Thus, critics of the doctrine of consideration typically focus on particular aspects of the doctrine that produce unattractive results rather than on wholesale abolition of the very doctrine itself.

A comprehensive set of proposals for legislative reform of the doctrine of consideration has been recommended by the Ontario Law Reform Commission, tackling each of the allegedly deficient aspects of the doctrine on a case-by-case basis.[261] With respect to the unenforceability of firm offers, the commission recommended that a firm offer made by a person in the course of a business should be enforceable for the time stated or for a reasonable amount of time not to exceed three months.[262] With respect to the problem of unilateral variations of agreements, the commission recommended that agreements in good faith modifying a contract should be enforceable even in the absence of consideration

---

cussion of the rationale for enforcing wholly executory exchanges, see Chapter 22, section C.

258 *Ibid.* at 820. For discussion of nominal consideration, see this Chapter, section B(1).

259 See, for example, M. Eisenberg, "The Principles of Consideration" (1982) 67 Cornell L.R. 640 at 643:

> The state has an independent interest in the enforcement of [bargain] promises. Exchange creates surplus, because each party presumably values what he gets more highly than what he gives. A modern free-enterprise system depends heavily on private planning and on credit transactions that involve exchanges over time. The extent to which private actors will be ready to engage in exchange, and are able to make reliable plans, rests partly on the probability that bargain promises will be kept. Legal enforcement of such promises increases that probability.

See also R. Posner, *Economic Analysis of Law*, 6th ed. (New York: Aspen, 2003) c. 4.2.

260 See generally Chapter 11.

261 Ontario Law Reform Commission, above note 252, c. 2.

262 *Ibid.* at 33.

moving from the promisee.[263] The commission recommended reform of the past-consideration rule by suggesting that a promise given in return for a past consideration should be enforceable unless either the initial benefit was conferred as a gift, or, for other reasons, the enforcement of the promise would not result in the unjust enrichment of the promisee.[264] This recommendation was coupled with a proviso that such promises should be enforceable only to the extent that the value of the promise is not disproportionate to the value of the past consideration. As we have seen,[265] a number of Canadian provinces, including Ontario, have enacted legislation overruling the rule of *Foakes v. Beer*,[266] which held that an agreement to accept partial payment as a full discharge of a debt obligation was unenforceable. The Ontario commission recommended amendments to the Ontario provisions that would cure interpretative difficulties inherent in the current Ontario version of these provisions.[267] Finally, the commission recommended enactment of a statutory rule that would render promises foreseeably relied upon enforceable to the extent that justice requires,[268] a rule based on American contract law. As noted in the "Introduction," the American doctrine of promissory estoppel holds that where a promisor should reasonably expect the promisee to rely detrimentally on the promise, the promise may be enforced if justice so requires and, further, that the remedy available for breach may be limited if justice so requires.[269] Thus, the promisee's remedy may be limited, in an appropriate case, to compensation for the actual value of the injuries sustained in reliance on the promise—reliance damages—rather than the value of the performance of the promise—the so-called expectancy measure of relief normally available for breach of contract.[270]

Again, no legislative action has been taken to implement these recommendations in Ontario or elsewhere in common law Canada. Indeed, statutory reform of the doctrine of consideration across the country does not appear to be a likely prospect. Accordingly, it may be

---

263 *Ibid.*

264 *Ibid.*

265 See this Chapter, section B(4).

266 Above note 173, for discussion of which see this Chapter, section B(4).

267 Above note 252 at 32–33.

268 *Ibid.* at 34.

269 See, for example, American Law Institute, *Restatement of Contracts 2d* (St. Paul: American Law Institute, 1981) s. 90. For discussion of the Canadian doctrine of promissory estoppel, see Chapter 8.

270 For discussion of the expectancy and reliance measures of relief, see Chapter 22, sections B and D, respectively.

considered whether judicial reform of the consideration rules is a more likely avenue for their improvement. As we shall see in Chapter 8, there does exist some possibility that the doctrine of promissory estoppel may evolve, as a matter of Canadian common law, into a rule that, on the American model, will provide a cause of action to parties who have foreseeably and detrimentally relied on a promise given without consideration in return. In other words, the commission's proposal to adopt the American promissory estoppel rule may well be achieved through judicial reform of the common law. The judicial recognition of a rule enforcing promises on the basis of foreseeable detrimental reliance would, indeed, provide a solution to some of the problems identified in the commission's catalogue of concerns with respect to consideration doctrine. Thus, with respect to the firm offer problem, a rule that permitted actions to enforce such promises to the extent that the offeree has detrimentally relied on the promise to keep the offer open might provide a generally satisfactory solution to the firm offer issue. Similarly, the enforceability of unilateral contractual variations would be significantly addressed by a detrimental reliance rule.[271] Further, judicial reconsideration of the past-consideration rule and its exceptions could produce a rule more in tune with the commission's recommendations.[272] A common law solution to the problem posed by the rule in *Foakes v. Beer* also seems possible. If the payment of a partial debt or, indeed, the promise to make a partial payment could be considered either to be the conferral of a valuable benefit on the creditor,[273] which is distinguishable from the benefit of the original debt, or a detrimental reliance on the undertaking to discharge the debt,[274] the rule in *Foakes v. Beer* could be reversed on the basis of a common law analysis. Further, charitable subscriptions could be held binding where the donor intends that the donee will detrimentally rely on the promised gift and the donee actually does so rely.[275] In sum, if the courts were minded to do so, much of the difficulty currently posed by the existing doctrine of consideration could be resolved through the traditional common law methods of doctrinal refinement and adjustment.

---

271 See Chapter 8, Section E.
272 For discussion of difficulties with the past consideration doctrine and their possible resolution, see this Chapter, section B(2).
273 See this Chapter, section B(4).
274 See Chapter 8, section C.
275 *Allegheny College v. National Chautauqua County Bank of Jamestown*, 159 N.E. 173 at 175 (N.Y.C.A. 1927), Cardozo J. See also E.A. Farnsworth, *Changing Your Mind: The Law of Regretted Decisions* (New Haven: Yale University Press, 1998) at 76–78.

FURTHER READINGS

P.S. ATIYAH, *Essays in Contract* (Oxford: Clarendon Press, 1986) c. 8.

J.P. DAWSON, *Gifts and Promises* (New Haven: Yale University Press, 1980).

M.A. EISENBERG, "Donative Promises" (1979) 47 U. Chicago L. Rev. 1.

M.A. EISENBERG, "The Bargain Principle and Its Limits" (1982) 95 Harv. L. Rev. 741.

M.A. EISENBERG, "The Principles of Consideration" (1982) 67 Cornell L. Rev. 640.

M.A. EISENBERG, "The World of Contract and the World of Gift" (1997) 85 Cal. L. Rev. 821.

G.H.L. FRIDMAN, "The Basis of Contractual Obligation" (1974) 7 Loy. L.A. L. Rev. 1.

C.J. GOETZ & R.E. SCOTT, "Enforcing Promises: An Examination of the Basis of Contract" (1980) 89 Yale L.J. 1261.

C.J. HAMSON, "The Reform of Consideration" (1938) Law Q. Rev. 223.

ONTARIO LAW REFORM COMMISSION, *Report on Amendment of the Law of Contract* (Toronto: Ministry of the Attorney General, 1987) c. 2.

R.A. POSNER, "Gratuitous Promises in Economics and Law" (1977) 6 J. Legal Stud. 411.

B.J. REITER, "Courts, Consideration and Common Sense" (1977) 27 U.T.L.J. 439.

S.A. SMITH, *Contract Theory* (Oxford: Oxford University Press, 2004) c. 6.

K.C.T. SUTTON, *Consideration Reconsidered* (St. Lucia, Queensland: University of Queensland Press, 1974).

J. SWAN, "Consideration and the Reasons for Enforcing Contracts" in B.J. Reiter & J. Swan, eds., *Studies in Contract Law* (Toronto: Butterworths, 1980).

M.J. TREBILCOCK, *The Limits of Freedom of Contract* (Cambridge: Harvard University Press, 1993) c. 8.

WAIVER AND PROMISSORY ESTOPPEL

A. INTRODUCTION

The doctrine of consideration holds that, apart from promises given under seal, promises will not be enforceable unless they are given as part of a bargain or exchange. As we have seen in Chapter 7, the doctrine of consideration usefully identifies a category of promises that ought indeed to be enforced. However, the opposite side of the consideration coin, the doctrine that *gratuitous* promises are generally unenforceable, is a rule that is capable of creating considerable inconvenience. Thus, for example, promises to vary existing contractual obligations will be unenforceable unless paid for by the promisee. Parties to agreements will often give gratuitous undertakings of this kind, however, and expect them to be enforceable and to be relied upon. In *Gilbert Steel Ltd. v. University Construction Ltd.*,[1] for example, a supplier of steel was unable to enforce the purchaser's promise to adjust the contract price upwards as the supplier's performance of the pre-existing duty to supply the steel was not good consideration. Similarly, in the leading decision in *Foakes v. Beer*,[2] a creditor's promise to discharge a debt in return for partial payment of the obligation was held to be unenforceable. The debtor's

---

1   (1976), 12 O.R. (2d) 1967 (C.A.).
2   (1884), 9 App. Cas. 605 (H.L.). See the discussion of this case above, Chapter 7, section B(4).

payment of a sum less than that required by the pre-existing contractual duty was held not to be good consideration. Decisions of this kind frustrate the reasonable expectations of the parties. Accordingly, a number of Canadian provinces reacted to the holding in *Foakes v. Beer* by enacting legislation that specifically and narrowly overruled it.[3]

Gratuitous promises to enter into contracts in the future may also give rise to hardship. In the context of building contracts, for example, a general contractor will normally rely on the quoted prices of subcontractors in calculating its bid. If the bid is successful and a subcontractor then refuses to enter into a subcontract at the quoted price, the contractor may suffer a loss. If the general contractor cannot obtain an equivalent price from another supplier, it will have relied to its detriment on the subcontractor's gratuitous promise. The failure of the doctrine of consideration to address adequately problems of this kind is a frequent source of criticism of the doctrine.

In this chapter we examine the doctrines of waiver and promissory estoppel and attempt to determine whether they provide a solution to these difficulties. Our conclusion will be that these doctrines provide, at best, only a partial solution to them. In this respect, they will be compared unfavourably to the American version of promissory estoppel doctrine that has been set out in the American *Restatement of Contracts* in the following terms:

> 90(1) A promise which the promisor should reasonably expect to induce action or forbearance on the part of the promisee or a third person and which does induce such action or forbearance is binding if injustice can be avoided only by enforcement of the promise. The remedy granted for breach may be limited as justice requires.[4]

Section 90 thus sets out a rule for the recognition of the enforceability of promises that is an alternative to the doctrine of consideration. Under American law, then, a promise would be enforceable if it is either given for good consideration or given under the circumstances described in Section 90. In examining the development of the Anglo-Canadian doctrine of promissory estoppel, it will be helpful to compare its development with the model provided by the American rule.

---

3   See Chapter 7, section B(4).

4   American Law Institute, *Restatement of Contracts 2d* (St. Paul: American Law Institute, 1979). For discussion, see P.N. Pham, "The Waning of Promissory Estoppel" (1994) 79 Cornell L. Rev. 1263; and R.A. Hillman, "Questioning The 'New Consensus' on Promissory Estoppel: An Empirical and Theoretical Study" (1998) 98 Colum. L. Rev. 580.

The Anglo-Canadian version of promissory estoppel doctrine first appeared in its modern form in 1947 with the decision of Denning J. in *Central London Property Trust Ltd. v. High Trees House Ltd.*[5] As a prelude to examining the *High Trees* decision and more recent developments, it will be useful to set out its historical antecedents—the doctrines of waiver and estoppel by representation—and, further, to consider why those early doctrines were unable to provide a solution to the problems faced by the defendant debtor in *Foakes v. Beer.*

B. WAIVER, ESTOPPEL BY REPRESENTATION AND *FOAKES V. BEER*

The doctrine of waiver is commonly illustrated by reference to the decision of the House of Lords in *Hughes v. Metropolitan Rwy. Co.*[6] In this case, a landlord had given a notice to the tenant pursuant to the terms of the lease, requiring that certain repairs be made by the tenant within six months. The tenant replied that he was willing to do the repairs but that he would like to enter into negotiations for the sale of the leasehold interest to the landlord and further indicated that he would not undertake the repairs during negotiations to that end. The negotiations broke off a few months later and when six months from the initial notice to repair had expired, the landlord purported to treat the lease as forfeited and brought an action to eject the tenant from the premises. The House of Lords dismissed the claim on the basis that the "course of negotiation ... of the parties ..."[7] had led the tenant to believe that the time limit for repairs would not be strictly enforced by the landlord and, accordingly, that the landlord would not be permitted to enforce it. The landlord had waived his right to insist on strict performance of the agreement and could not now insist on doing so.

This doctrine of waiver, as it has come to be known, is applicable in a variety of factual settings. For example, a purchaser of goods cannot waive a right to timely delivery and then refuse to accept the goods upon late delivery.[8] Often, as in *Hughes*, the doctrine will be relied on by the defendant. In other cases, however, the doctrine may be relied on by a plaintiff.[9] What is common to these situations, however, is that

---

5   [1947] 1 K.B. 130.
6   (1877), 2 App. Cas. 439 (H.L.).
7   *Ibid.* at 448.
8   *Charles Rickards Ltd. v. Oppenheim*, [1950] 1 K.B. 616 (C.A.).
9   *Ibid.*

the party relying on waiver is using the doctrine to rebut the other party's allegation that the relying party has engaged in a breach of the original contract.

For present purposes, it is useful to consider whether waiver doctrine would apply to the facts in *Foakes v. Beer*, where a debtor made a partial payment in return for the creditor's promise to forgive the entire debt. Could the debtor argue that the creditor has waived the right to full payment and cannot now be allowed to claim it? At the time of *Foakes v. Beer*, and indeed more recently, it has been commonly understood that waiver does not apply to these facts. Presumably, this is because the degree of reliance or detrimental change of position suffered in the typical waiver case is thought to be greater than that sustained by the debtor in *Foakes v. Beer*. In the typical waiver case, a party relies on the waiver by committing a breach of contract on the faith of an undertaking that it would not be considered such. In *Foakes v. Beer*, on the other hand, the debtor's reliance is simply that of making a partial payment of a larger sum owed. The debtor's change of position in making a partial payment rather than making no payment at all is, under traditional doctrine, neither good consideration nor the type of detrimental reliance that engages the doctrine of waiver.

An attempt to ground relief for the debtor in a similar case on the basis of the common law doctrine of estoppel by representation was attempted in 1854 in *Jorden v. Money*.[10] That doctrine holds that one who has induced another party to act to his detriment on the faith of a statement of fact will not be allowed in subsequent litigation to deny the truth of the fact in question. For example, where one represents that another is authorized to sell one's assets,[11] or that someone is the owner of an asset,[12] or that a particular debt is life-insured,[13] the representee who then relies detrimentally on such a statement will be able to prevent the representer from denying the truth of the statement in a subsequent lawsuit.

In *Jorden v. Money*, a debtor sought to rely on this doctrine in a case where the creditor has assured the debtor that she would not enforce the debt. The debtor's father had been kind to the creditor and she had decided to require no payment from the son. In reliance on this undertaking, the debtor concluded that he could afford to marry his betrothed and did so. Subsequently, however, the creditor sued to enforce

10   (1854), 5 H.L. Cas. 185.
11   *Spiro v. Lintern*, [1973] 1 W.L.R. 1002 (C.A.).
12   *Harnam Singh v. Jamal Pirbhai*, [1951] A.C. 688 (P.C.).
13   *O'Flaherty v. British Acceptance Corp.* (1964), 48 D.L.R. (2d) 562 (B.C.S.C.).

the debt. In that action, it was urged on the debtor's behalf that the creditor should be estopped by her representation that she had given up her right to sue on the debt. The House of Lords held, however, that the creditor's representation was not a representation of fact but rather a statement of something that the individual intends or intends not to do, in other words, an undertaking. In order for an undertaking to be enforceable, of course, it must be given in return for consideration. Accordingly, the creditor's claim was allowed. The result in *Jorden v. Money* is thus consistent with the later decision in *Foakes v. Beer*.

C. THE DOCTRINE OF PROMISSORY ESTOPPEL

A more expansive version of waiver doctrine, commonly referred to as equitable or promissory estoppel, was articulated by Denning J. in the leading case of *High Trees*.[14] The defendant, High Trees, had taken a thirty-nine-year lease of a new block of flats in London in 1937. The flats had not been fully let before the outbreak of the war. In the wartime conditions, it appeared likely that the income from the flats would not be sufficient to pay the rent reserved under the lease. Accordingly, the plaintiff landlord agreed to a reduction in the rent. The defendant then paid rent at the lesser rate through the wartime period. This continued even when the flats had been fully let at the beginning of 1945. In late 1945, the recently appointed receiver of the plaintiff company, having discovered the nature of this arrangement, wrote a letter to the defendant demanding both payment of rent at the full rate in the future and a full accounting of the arrears. In order to test its legal position, the receiver then brought a claim for rent at the full rate for the last two quarters of 1945. Understandably, the plaintiff placed reliance on *Foakes v. Beer* and *Jorden v. Money* in arguing that its undertaking to accept a reduced rent did not preclude it from reasserting its entitlement to the full rent payable under the lease. Waiver would not apply to a promise to accept a partial payment as a full discharge of an obligation. The landlord's undertaking was a promise, not a representation, and therefore could not be the subject of an estoppel.

These arguments did not enjoy success. It was Denning J.'s view that the doctrine of *Hughes* would come to the aid of the tenant at least with respect to the payments made prior to the early part of 1945. Denning J. reasoned that where one has given, albeit gratuitously, a prom-

---

14 Above note 5.

ise that was intended to be binding and intended to be acted upon and which was in fact acted upon, the promise should be considered to be binding. The *Hughes* case was relied upon by Denning J. as authority for the proposition that equity would not allow one to "go back on such a promise." "In my opinion," he said, "the time has now come for the validity of such a promise to be recognized."[15] Strictly speaking, of course, it was not necessary for Denning J. to decide whether the landlord could recover the earlier arrears. The actual claim was for the last two quarters of 1945 at a time when, according to its own terms, the landlord's undertaking might be considered to have expired. Nonetheless, it was plainly Denning J.'s view that the effect of the landlord's undertaking was to extinguish the obligation to pay full rent during the earlier period. On this basis, the doctrine of promissory estoppel, rather like waiver, would serve as an effective defence to a claim by the promisor attempting to enforce the original contractual arrangement.

1) Sword vs. Shield?

In *High Trees*, Denning J. had referred to promises such as that given by the landlord as "binding" or as having "validity."[16] A few short years later, Denning L.J. had an opportunity to reconsider the meaning of these terms in *Combe v. Combe*.[17] The parties to this lawsuit were a divorced couple. The husband had promised to pay his former wife maintenance of £100 a year. It was found at trial that the wife had given no consideration for this promise. The plaintiff wife sought to enforce this promise, however, on the basis that it was rendered binding by the doctrine of promissory estoppel. Denning L.J. was thus obliged to consider whether the doctrine could be used merely defensively as it was in *High Trees*, or could be extended to provide an affirmative basis for enforcing a gratuitous promise. If it was to play the latter role, it would of course supplement or provide an alternative to the doctrine of consideration as a means of identifying enforceable promises. In *Combe*, however, Denning L.J. dismissed the claim and held that promissory estoppel could not found a cause of action to enforce the promise itself. "The doctrine of consideration is too firmly fixed," he said, "to be overthrown by a side-wind."[18] The role of promissory estoppel doctrine was restricted to preventing parties from insisting upon their strict legal rights in situa-

15 *Ibid.* at 135.
16 *Ibid.*
17 [1951] 2 K.B. 215 (C.A.).
18 *Ibid.* at 220.

tions where it would be unjust to allow actions to enforce them. As has often been said since, Denning L.J. clearly conceded in *Combe* that the doctrine of promissory estoppel can be used only as a shield and not as a sword. Although it is commonly accepted that Denning L.J.'s view on this point is correct, this is a point to which we must return.

Assuming, however, that it is true that the doctrine of promissory estoppel is restricted to this defensive role, it is likely that it will perform this role most commonly in the context of gratuitous contractual variations. It will serve, as in *High Trees*, as a defence to a claim brought by the promisor to enforce the original agreement in its own terms. As with waiver, though the defence may be more commonly deployed by defendants, it may also be used by plaintiffs who wish to rebut an allegation of contractual breach made by a defendant.[19] It is essential, however, that the contractual variation in each case constitute a concession rather than an affirmative undertaking to provide additional benefits under the agreement. In the latter case, an attempt to enforce the promise to provide more would flounder on the sword and shield distinction. This was the problem in *Gilbert Steel*,[20] where a purchaser of steel had agreed to pay the supplier more than the original contract price. The supplier's claim for the additional compensation failed on the ground that such a claim involved using the doctrine as a sword in attempting to enforce the gratuitous undertaking to pay more. On the other hand, if a purchaser gratuitously varied the agreement by agreeing to accept late delivery, such an undertaking would be effective in the sense that the supplier's late delivery would be no answer to the supplier's claim for the original contract price. The buyer would be estopped from treating late delivery as a breach. In short, concessions can create effective defences to claims. Affirmative promises to do more are ineffective because they require enforcement.

2) Intended to Be Acted Upon

One of the issues unresolved by *High Trees* relates to the degree of reliance or acting upon the promise by the promisee that must occur for the doctrine to apply. Must the type of reliance be, in some sense, detrimental or prejudicial? Would the type of reliance that occurs in *Foakes v. Beer*[21] — partial payment of a debt — constitute reliance in the

---

19   See, for example, *Charles Rickards Ltd. v. Oppenheim*, above note 8.
20   Above note 1.
21   Above note 2.

requisite sense? Lord Denning offered his own answers to these questions in subsequent decisions.

In *D. & C. Builders Ltd. v. Rees*,[22] Lord Denning indicated his view that the doctrine of promissory estoppel would apply to the *Foakes v. Beer* fact situation. In *D. & C. Builders*, the defendant had refused to pay contractors who had supplied services to him. The defendant offered to pay something less than two-thirds of the price for the work "in settlement." The plaintiff was in dire need of money, as the defendant well knew, and accepted the payment on these terms. Ultimately, the plaintiff brought a claim for the balance and the defendant set up the plaintiff's undertaking to settle the debt as a defensive promissory estoppel. Although it was Lord Denning's view that the defence should not be available to the defendant for other reasons, he clearly indicated his opinion that promissory estoppel would apply, as a matter of principle, in these circumstances. Partial payment of a debt constituted sufficient reliance or acting upon the promise to discharge the debt to engage the doctrine. Thus, though this remains a contentious point, it was clearly Lord Denning's view that the modern doctrine of promissory estoppel had effectively overruled the decision of the House of Lords in *Foakes v. Beer*.[23]

More generally, Lord Denning expressed the view that it is not necessary that the "acting upon" the promise be in any sense detrimental. It is sufficient, in Lord Denning's view, if the promisee has been "led to act differently from what he otherwise would have done."[24] It is thus not necessary to demonstrate that the debtor who makes a partial payment has prejudiced himself thereby or to show that the tenant in *High Trees* was prejudiced by the landlord's willingness to accept less than the full rent. It is sufficient that the subsequent conduct of the promisee in each case was affected by the promise. Other judges, however, have suggested that some degree of prejudice or inconvenience must be demonstrated.

In *Post Chaser*,[25] for example, Goff J. refused to apply the doctrine in a case where there was no evidence of significant detrimental reliance by the promisee. A buyer had apparently waived a defect in the documentation of a transaction, or at least, this could reasonably be inferred by the seller from the buyer's instructions that the documents

---

22 [1966] 2 Q.B. 617 (C.A.).

23 In *High Trees*, above note 5 at 135, Denning J. suggested, rather unconvincingly, that this aspect of the matter, i.e., the doctrine of promissory estoppel, had simply not been considered by the House of Lords in *Foakes v. Beer*.

24 *W.J. Alan & Co. Ltd. v. El Nasr Export & Import Co.*, [1972] 2 Q.B. 189 at 213 (C.A.). See also *High Trees*, ibid. at 134–36.

25 *Société Italo-Belge pour le Commerce et L'Industrie S.A. V. Palm and Vegetable Oils (Malaysia) Sdn. Bhd. (sub nom. The "Post Chaser")*, [1982] 1 All E.R. 19 (Q.B.).

be presented to a sub-buyer. The seller duly presented the documents to the sub-buyer but within two days the sub-buyer rejected the documents as did the buyer in turn. The seller sold the goods to others and sued for damages. The buyer defended on the basis of the defect but the seller maintained that it had acted upon the buyer's tacit promise to waive the defect by presenting the documents to the sub-buyer and that the doctrine of promissory estoppel should apply notwithstanding the absence of any real prejudice flowing from that act. Goff J. held, however, that there must be something in the fact situation that renders it "inequitable" for the promisor to resile from the promise.[26] Here, where the sellers had received notice of the rejection very quickly, there was no evidence of prejudice of a kind that would render it inequitable to allow the buyer to resile from its undertaking. Accordingly, the doctrine of promissory estoppel did not apply.

Goff J.'s view, that some detriment or prejudice is necessary, appears more consistent with the underlying objective of the doctrine of promissory estoppel. It may, however, have the unattractive feature that it leaves at large the question of whether the reliance of the defendant in cases like *Foakes v. Beer* is sufficiently detrimental to engage the doctrine. It is, as yet, unclear whether courts will be persuaded by the argument that once the partial payment has been made, it would be inequitable to allow the creditor to recover the outstanding balance.

3) The Nature of the Undertaking

The undertaking or promise giving rise to the promissory estoppel must be voluntary in nature. In *D. & C. Builders*,[27] Lord Denning withheld application of the doctrine because the plaintiff had, in his view, taken advantage of the vulnerability of the creditor. The defendant knew of the plaintiff's need for money and took advantage of the situation to insist on a discharge of the debt in return for a partial payment. The settlement was procured by intimidation. The defendant was therefore unable to rely on the equitable doctrine. It is less than perfectly clear, however, what standard or standards should be adopted to determine voluntariness in this context. Lord Denning appears to envisage a rule resting either on the presence of facts constituting the tort of intimidation or on the notion that one who wishes to invoke an equitable doctrine must not have misbehaved in a manner attracting the censure of equity. A number of more precise doctrines of common law and equity

---

26 *Ibid.* at 26.
27 Above note 22.

have been developed to analyze the question of determining the voluntariness of undertakings in the context of contractual undertakings. Contracts entered into under duress,[28] undue influence[29] or in circumstances of unconscionability are unenforceable.[30] There appears to be no compelling basis for fashioning a different threshold test for determining the voluntariness of undertakings in the present context.

The promise or undertaking need not be explicit. It can be reasonably inferred from the words, conduct or, indeed, silence of the promisor. In the factual context of *Hughes*,[31] the undertaking was inferred from the lessor's failure to indicate to the lessee that the notice period for repairs would not be suspended during their negotiations. In *W.J. Alan & Co. v. El Nasr Export & Import Co.*,[32] Lord Denning would have inferred an undertaking to vary the currency of payment in a contract from the fact that a buyer had accepted a payment under a non-conforming letter of credit that had been established in a different currency from that prescribed by the agreement. Similarly, an optionor may, by words or conduct, lead the optionee to believe that the optionor was not insisting on timely exercise of the option.[33]

A decision of the Supreme Court of Canada in *John Burrows Ltd. v. Subsurface Surveys Ltd.*[34] may be thought to have introduced some potential for confusion on the question of inferring undertakings from conduct. In *Burrows*, the plaintiff had sold a business to the defendant, part of the purchase price having been secured by a promissory note in the amount of $42,000 given by the defendant to the plaintiff. The note provided for monthly payments and permitted the seller to claim the entire amount due under the note if any monthly payment was more than ten days in default. During a period of eighteen months or so, the defendant was consistently late in his payments but they were, on each occasion, accepted. Following a disagreement between the parties on other matters, however, the plaintiff reacted to a similarly late payment by suing the defendant for the entire amount outstanding under the note. The defendant attempted to rely upon the doctrine of promissory estoppel, inviting the Court to find that the seller's acceptance of

---

28   See Chapter 11, section B.
29   See Chapter 11, section C.
30   See Chapter 11, section D.
31   Above note 6. See also *Owen Sound Public Library Board v. Mial Developments Ltd.* (1979), 102 D.L.R. (3d) 685 (Ont. C.A.).
32   Above note 24.
33   See *Bruner v. Moore*, [1904] 1 Ch. 305; *Petridis v. Shabinsky* (1982), 35 O.R. (2d) 215 (H.C.J.).
34   [1968] S.C.R. 607.

a series of late payments without protest constituted an undertaking to accept late payments in the future.

The Supreme Court rejected this submission on essentially two grounds. First, the Court interpreted *Hughes* as a case that requires that the undertaking giving rise to waiver or estoppel must be the product of a "course of negotiation[s]" and that no such negotiations had occurred on these facts.[35] This aspect of the Court's reasoning appears to suggest that the existence of a course of negotiations is an indispensable prerequisite to the finding that an undertaking has occurred. On the contrary, however, the existence of negotiations in *Hughes* was merely part of the factual context from which the promisee could reasonably infer that such an undertaking was tacitly given. In other cases, other types of conduct or communication may give rise to such inferences.

The second aspect of the Court's reasoning, however, appears more consistent with the basic principle. The Court further suggested that in the context of this case, the seller's "friendly indulgences" with respect to the individual late payments were more consistent with an understanding that the plaintiff had not surrendered the right to timely performance.[36] On this view, the possibility of coming to a different conclusion on different facts remains open. Whether, on particular facts, the granting of indulgences should reasonably give rise to an inference that the letter of the agreement can be insisted upon only on reasonable notice is no doubt a matter of degree.[37]

4) Reassertion of Rights upon Notice

One of the questions left open by the reasoning in the *High Trees* case relates to the ability that the promisor may have to reassert rights under the original agreement upon reasonable notice to the promisee of an intention to do so. On the very facts of *High Trees*, it may be asked whether the landlord could have reasserted his entitlement to full rental in the middle of the war period, say in 1943. It was not necessary to decide this point in *High Trees* itself, of course, because no such notice was ever given. The landlord continued to accept the lesser rent beyond the point at which the flats were fully let. Accordingly, it was unnecessary for Denning J. to decide whether "the estoppel would cease when the conditions to which the representation applied came to an end, or

---

35 *Ibid.* at 615. See also above note 7 and accompanying text.
36 *Ibid.* at 617.
37 Compare with *Morrison Lamothe Inc. v. Bedok* (1986), 55 O.R. (2d) 129 (H.C.J.).

[whether] ... it would only come to an end on notice."[38] Plainly, if the promisor indicates that the promise will expire upon reasonable notice, that should govern the matter.

Where, as perhaps was the case in *High Trees*, the undertaking is expected to endure for a particular period of time, it may be asked whether notwithstanding this arrangement, the promisor can reassert strict rights under the original agreement upon reasonable notice. In order to give effect to the proposition that the promisor could not do so and that in 1943 the promise would have prospective effect into the future, it is necessary to court, if not embrace, the use of the promissory estoppel doctrine as a sword rather than a shield. That is to say, it is possible to imagine situations where giving effect to this view would require recognition of a claim by the lessee to enforce the promise.[39] As long as it is accepted, therefore, that the doctrine cannot be used as a sword, this consideration weighs against the notion that promissory estoppel has effect into the future. Similarly, if the underlying purpose served by the promissory estoppel doctrine is the protection of the promisee's reliance interest, this would suggest that the doctrine should not be considered to have a prospective effect. Arguably, the promisee's reliance interest can be protected to the extent necessary by the determination of an appropriate period of reasonable notice. On the other hand, those who favour a more expansive role for the doctrine of promissory estoppel may favour the view that the landlord's undertaking in *High Trees* would be binding throughout the war notwithstanding this incursion on the principle that the doctrine is not to be used as a sword. This approach has not yet gained clear judicial support.

In cases in which the promisor can reassert rights under the original contract upon reasonable notice, it may be asked what effect, if any, should be given to an unreasonable notice. In an English case, for example, the first notice the promisee had of such an intention was the issuance by the promisor of a claim seeking damages for breach of the original contract.[40] In a Canadian case, an insurer forwarded a lapse of policy notice to the insured that specified no future date on which the lapse notice would be effective, the insurer assuming that it was effect-

---

38 Above note 5 at 136.
39 In any case where the promisor is able to terminate performance unilaterally, for example, by refusing to accept further payments and by denying access to the rented premises, it would be necessary for the promisee to initiate a claim.
40 *Tool Metal Manufacturing Co. Ltd. v. Tungsten Electric Co. Ltd.*, [1955] 1 W.L.R. 761 (H.L.).

ive as of its own date.[41] In each case, the defendant promisee argued that the notice was unreasonable and therefore should be given no force or effect. The defendants urged that until a notice is given that is reasonable on its own terms, the promissory estoppel continues to bind the promisor. Courts have taken the view, however, that an unreasonable notice will have effect after the passage of a reasonable period of time. This is supportable on the ground that once the promisee has been made aware of the intention to resile, the promisee's reliance interest would normally be adequately protected by the expiry of a reasonable period of time before reassertion of the strict rights under the original agreement. Moreover, it would be inconvenient to adopt a rule to the effect that unreasonable notices were of no effect as it may encourage the serving of a series of notices in an attempt to ensure that at least one of them might be considered by a court to be reasonable.

D. PROPRIETARY ESTOPPEL

Although the orthodox view of the Anglo-Canadian jurisprudence is that the doctrine of promissory estoppel cannot ground a cause of action, there is a line of authority suggesting that gratuitous promises concerning the creation of interests in land appear to be enforceable in the full sense. In the typical case, an owner of land promises to another that the latter shall have an interest in the land in the expectation that the promisee will rely on that promise. Typically, the reliance involved is that the promisee will then erect a building or make other improvements upon the promisor's land in the expectation that they will be available for the benefit or the use of the promisee. In such a case, if the promisor refuses to go forward with the promised transfer of an interest, the unjust enrichment of the promisor is quite intense. For a rather long time, then, courts of equity were prepared to require owners in such circumstances to transfer the interest in question.[42] *Inwards v. Baker*[43] provides a modern illustration. A son wished to buy property,

---

41   *Saskatchewan River Bungalows Ltd. v. Maritime Life Assurance Co.* (1992), 127 A.R. 43 (C.A.), rev'd [1994] 2 S.C.R. 490. Though the Supreme Court reversed the Appeal Court decision for other reasons, it affirmed the rule set out in the text in *obiter*; see the Court of Appeal decision at 49–50 (A.R.), and the Supreme Court decision at 503 (S.C.R.).

42   See, for example, *Dillwyn v. Llewelyn* (1862), 4 De G.F. & J. 517 (C.A.) and *Plimmer v. Wellington Corp.* (1884), 9 App. Cas. 699 (P.C.).

43   [1965] 2 Q.B. 29 (C.A.).

which he could ill afford, on which to build a residence. His father encouraged him to build a residence on the father's land. The son did so and lived there for many years until the father's death. Some years thereafter, the trustees of the estate sought possession of the land. The Court of Appeal held that the son's expectation that he could continue to live on the land had been encouraged by his father and could not be defeated by the trustees. Accordingly, he was entitled to continue to occupy the residence as against the trustees.

In the subsequent case of *Crabb v. Arun District Council,*[44] the reliance of the promisee did not involve the making of improvements to the promisor's land. Crabb's predecessor in title had transferred an adjacent parcel of land to the defendant council in return, *inter alia,* for an undertaking from the council that it would build a roadway adjacent to the parcel retained by the predecessor and eventually sold to Crabb. Further, the council agreed that it would erect a fence along the boundary between the two properties and allow access from Crabb's parcel to the roadway through a gap at point A. Crabb later developed a scheme to subdivide his parcel and sell off the portion that had access to the roadway at point A, provided that the council would be willing to grant him a further access from the parcel he would retain at point B. Crabb spoke to the council about this matter and believed that he had been assured that access would be granted at point B. The council did not request payment from Crabb for this additional right of access. In due course, the defendant council erected a fence and constructed gates at point A and point B. Crabb then sold the parcel including the gap at point A and retained the back portion of the parcel that had access to the roadway through point B. Subsequently, apparently irritated by the fact that Crabb had locked the gate, the defendant council removed the gate and erected a fence across the gap at point B, thus eliminating access to the roadway from Crabb's remaining parcel.

Unlike previous cases, then, Crabb had conferred no benefit through improvement of the defendant's property. His claim to enforce what he considered to be the council's undertaking rested simply on his detrimental reliance on the promise and thus appears more precisely analogous to the issues raised by the promissory estoppel cases. The Court of Appeal held that an undertaking to grant Crabb access to the roadway was manifest at least in the act of erecting the fence and gates at points A and B. Moreover, the council was aware that Crabb intended to sell the two portions separately. Council was therefore aware that he intended to rely in this fashion on the undertaking. These circum-

---

44   [1976] Ch. 179 (C.A.).

stances were said to raise an equity in favour of Crabb that he could enforce as a plaintiff and that entitled him to a declaration that he was entitled to a right of way on the defendant council's roadway. Lord Denning described this doctrine as a species of estoppel, which he referred to as "proprietary estoppel," that uncharacteristically can provide a foundation for a cause of action to enforce the promise in question. The view that proprietary estoppel constitutes an exception to the general rule that estoppel can function only as a shield now appears to be generally accepted.

E. *WALTONS STORES (INTERSTATE) PTY. V. MAHER*: INCHING TOWARD SECTION 90

Apart from the exceptional case of proprietary estoppel, then, the current Anglo-Canadian position is that promissory estoppel may be deployed only defensively.[45] In the typical case it will enable a person who might otherwise be considered to have breached a contract to rely on the other party's undertaking that such action or inaction would not constitute a breach. In this respect, then, the Anglo-Canadian estoppel doctrine is radically different from its American counterpart. Section 90 of the *Restatement*[46] does provide a foundation for a cause of action to enforce promises and to seek damages or other appropriate remedies for their breach. This limitation on the role of Anglo-Canadian promissory estoppel is a source of criticism. Thus restricted, the doctrine appears to have little if any role outside the context of gratuitous contractual variations. And, indeed, in that context, the doctrine creates an artificial distinction between concessions granted and affirmative promises to provide greater value. As has been explained, only the former can be rendered effectively by the doctrine.[47] Moreover, within the context of concessions, it is not even clearly established that the doc-

---

45 If this is so, promissory estoppel appears to be, at most, merely a slightly expanded version of waiver doctrine. If it is expanded, the expansion would rest on whether one accepts that the requirement of reliance present in waiver has been made less stringent for promissory estoppel. See above, the text at notes 24–25. In any event, it would appear that all cases of traditional waiver would be embraced or subsumed by the doctrine of promissory estoppel. There is, however, one doubtful authority that suggests that there may be a fact situation—promise to hold open an option—that is covered by waiver doctrine but not by promissory estoppel. See *Petridis v. Shabinsky*, above note 33.

46 Above note 4.

47 See the text above at notes 19–20.

trine will provide a defence in the fact situation illustrated by *Foakes v. Beer*.[48] By comparison, then, the American doctrine appears to be a much more effective and elegant instrument for providing relief to individuals who have suffered from detrimental reliance on a broken promise that was intended to induce such reliance.

Considerations such as the foregoing may provide a foundation for the development of further exceptions or, indeed, of a more general modification of the sword versus shield doctrine. There is some evidence in the case law to this effect.[49] The important decision of the Australian High Court in *Waltons Stores (Interstate) Pty. Ltd. v. Maher*[50] expanded upon the foundations of the proprietary estoppel doctrine to develop a more comprehensive basis for permitting promissory estoppel to serve as a sword and to provide a basis for a cause of action to enforce promises. The fact situation in *Waltons* provided an appealing context within which to consider such a development. The case involved very substantial detrimental reliance on a promise to enter a lease. Waltons had been negotiating with a view to leasing a property from Maher. Waltons had indicated that its requirements could be met only if the existing building on the premises were demolished and replaced by a new facility. Waltons was aware that if its projected date of occupancy was to be met, Maher would have to commence the demolition work virtually immediately. The parties' respective solicitors reviewed a draft lease and reached an agreement on a set of amendments. Waltons' solicitor prepared a fresh lease incorporating the amendments and indicated that although Waltons had not given specific agreement to each amendment, he believed that Waltons' agreement would be forthcoming and that he would let Maher's solicitor know of any amendments not agreed to the next day. Maher's solicitor executed and returned the draft, understanding that no binding contract would be entered into until the lease was executed by Waltons. Hearing nothing further from Waltons, Maher believed that the execution of the lease was a mere formality and proceeded with the demolition work. That work was completed and 40 percent of the new facility was constructed by the time, a few months later, that Waltons advised Maher that it

---

48   See the text above at notes 21–25.

49   See *Crabb*, above note 44. See also *Commonwealth of Australia v. Verwayen* (1990), 170 C.L.R. 394; Hon. L.J. Priestly, "Estoppel: Liability and Remedy?" in D.W.M. Waters, ed., *Equity, Fiduciaries and Trusts* (Toronto: Carswell, 1993) 173 at 273; A. Robertson, "Towards a Unifying Purpose for Estoppel" (1996) 22 Monash U.L. Rev. 1; and A. Robertson, "Satisfying the Minimum Equity: Equitable Remedies After *Verwayan*" (1996) 20 Melbourne U.L. Rev. 805.

50   *Waltons Stores (Interstate) Pty. Ltd. v. Maher* (1988), 164 C.L.R. 387 (H.C.).

would not proceed with the transaction. The High Court held that Waltons' failure to communicate constituted an undertaking to enter into the lease and, further, that Waltons was aware of the reliance placed on the undertaking by Maher. The obstacle confronting Maher's claim for breach of the undertaking, of course, was that the undertaking to enter the lease was given without consideration and its enforcement would require deploying the doctrine of promissory estoppel as a sword.

The High Court allowed recovery and, in so doing, articulated a principled basis upon which an action to enforce a gratuitous promise may be allowed. The High Court did not, however, simply adopt the American detrimental reliance theory implicit in section 90. Rather, it attempted to fashion a new principle generalizing from the rule allowing relief in *Crabb*[51] and its antecedents.[52] In the High Court's view, the common thread running through such cases is that the conduct of the promisor in such cases is "unconscionable."[53] The unconscionability is said to arise from the fact that the defendant has played a part in generating "a basic assumption" upon which the other party has acted to his detriment. It would be unconscionable conduct on the part of the person who has participated in giving rise to that assumption to ignore it.[54] In *Crabb*, the assumption was that Mr. Crabb would be able to use the defendant council's roadway. The council had played a role in giving rise to that assumption and Crabb had detrimentally relied upon it. Accordingly, it would be unconscionable for the council to be allowed to resile from it. In the *Waltons* case, Waltons participated in creating Maher's assumption that a lease would be entered. In light of Maher's reliance, it would now be unconscionable for Waltons to resile. Hence, Waltons' promise to enter a lease is enforceable.

Not every reader will be attracted by the subtlety of the High Court's reasoning. Whereas section 90 straightforwardly provides a remedy for foreseeable detrimental reliance on a promise, the rule in the *Waltons* case rests on the unconscionability that results from ignoring an as-

---

51 Above note 44.

52 The court also placed some emphasis on the doctrine of "acquiescence," which holds that an owner of land who stands by and fails to intervene in the making of improvements on one's land by another who is, to the owner's knowledge, acting under a mistaken belief that it is the improver's land, is liable to the improver for the value of the improvements. See, for example, *Ramsden v. Dyson* (1866), L.R. 1 H.L. 129. Acquiescence cases, then, are not instances of reliance on a promise to transfer an interest; they are cases of acquiescing in a mistaken improvement to one's land.

53 *Waltons*, above note 50 at para. 23.

54 *Ibid.* at para. 30.

292 THE LAW OF CONTRACTS

sumption held by another party that one has played a role in creating and upon which the other has relied. One may ask whether, in substance, there is much separating the two different formulations. Would every foreseeable detrimental reliance on a promise caught by section 90 also create a situation of unconscionability because of detrimental reliance on an assumption engendered? It is conceivable that the rule articulated in the *Waltons* case is broader than section 90 because the concept of playing a role in creating an assumption might be thought to be broader than the concept of giving a promise or undertaking.[55] On the other hand, the High Court explicitly resisted adoption of section 90. It may well be that the court envisaged that some element of unfairness beyond mere detrimental reliance on a gratuitous undertaking is captured by the notion of "unconscionability." One may suggest, however, that the distinction sought is indeed an unduly subtle one and that whatever advantage of breadth may be achieved by the High Court's formulation is outweighed by the obscurity it appears to engender. Nonetheless, it is evidently the case that the High Court has broadened the basis on which a promissory estoppel can found a cause of action and has moved the law of Australia closer to the American doctrine. It may well be that the *Waltons* case will have a similar effect in other commonwealth jurisdictions. Canadian decisions, at least, manifest some inclination in this direction.[56]

---

55 The High Court's formulation—participation in the creation of an assumption—appears designed to include cases of acquiescence in another's mistake that would not be cases of broken promises. See above note 52 for a description of the acquiescence doctrine.

56 The *Waltons* decision was recently distinguished but not rejected as inconsistent with Canadian law by the British Columbia Court of Appeal. See *M. (N.). v. A. (A.T.)* (2003), 13 B.C.L.R. (4th) 73 (C.A.). The Ontario Court of Appeal has indicated, in *obiter*, views supportive of adoption of the American promissory estoppel doctrine, at least in cases of contracted variation. See *Francis v. C.I.B.C.* (1994), 120 D.L.R. (4th) 393 at 401–2 (Ont. C.A.), Weiler J.A.; *Techform Products Ltd. v. Wolda* (2001), 206 D.L.R. (4th) 171 at 185 (Ont. C.A.), Rosenberg J.A. See also *Sail Labrador Ltd. v. The Challenge One*, [1999] 1 S.C.R. 265 at para. 85, Bastarache J. (subsequent concessions held to effect an "alteration" of the agreement between the parties). In a concurring opinion, Binnie J. justified the result in the case with a more traditional estoppel analysis.

FURTHER READINGS

D.A. FARBER & J.H. MATHESON, "Beyond Promissory Estoppel: Contract Law and the 'Invisible Handshake'" (1985) 52 U. Chicago L. Rev. 903.

J.M. FEINMAN, "Promissory Estoppel and Judicial Method" (1984) 97 Harv. L. Rev. 78.

J.M. FEINMAN, "The Last Promissory Estoppel Article" (1992) 61 Fordham L. Rev. 303.

J.M. FEINMAN, "The Meaning of Reliance: A Historical Perspective" (1984) Wis. L. Rev. 1373.

R.A. HILLMAN, "Questioning The 'New Consensus' on Promissory Estoppel: An Empirical and Theoretical Study" (1998) 98 Colum. L. Rev. 580.

C.L. KNAPP, "Reliance in the Revised Restatement: The Proliferation of Promissory Estoppel" (1981) 81 Colum. L. Rev. 52.

C.L. KNAPP, "Rescuing Reliance: The Perils of Promissory Estoppel" (1998) 49 Hastings L.J. 1191.

J.A. MANWARING, "Promissory Estoppel in the Supreme Court of Canada" (1987) 10 Dal. L.J. 43.

ONTARIO LAW REFORM COMMISSION, *Report on Amendment of the Law of Contract* (Toronto: Ministry of the Attorney General, 1987) c. 2.

P.N. PHAM, "The Waning of Promissory Estoppel" (1994) 79 Cornell L. Rev. 1263.

A. ROBERTSON, "Satisfying the Minimum Equity: Equitable Remedies After *Verwayan*" (1996) 20 Melbourne U.L. Rev. 805.

A. ROBERTSON, "Towards a Unifying Purpose for Estoppel" (1996) 22 Monash U.L. Rev. 1.

M. SPENCE, *Protecting Reliance: The Emergent Doctrine of Equitable Estoppel* (Oxford: Hart, 1999).

K.M. TEEVEN, "Origins of Promissory Estoppel: Justifiable Reliance and Commercial Uncertainty before Williston's Restatement" (2004) 34 U. Mem. L. Rev. 499.

E. YORIO & S. THEL, "The Promissory Basis of Section 90" (1991) 101 Yale L.J. 111.

CHAPTER 9

PRIVITY OF CONTRACT

A. INTRODUCTION

The doctrine of privity of contract applies to situations in which one of the parties to an agreement has undertaken to confer a benefit on a third party. For example, A and B may enter into a contract where, in return for services provided to A by B, A promises to pay money to C. For convenience we shall refer to A as the promisor, to B, the party who gives consideration to the promisor, as the promisee, and to C as the third-party beneficiary. According to the doctrine of privity, C has no standing to enforce A's undertaking. C is a mere third-party beneficiary of A's undertaking and therefore not truly a party to the agreement. As has been explained, "only a person who is a party to a contract can sue on it."[1]

It is true, of course, that if A breaches his or her undertaking to pay C, B could bring an action for damages for breach of contract. This prospect may provide only cold comfort for C, however, for two reasons. First, in many third-party beneficiary cases, B will have sustained no real loss as a result of A's non-performance. Although the point is not free from difficulty,[2] it appears that where this is so, B's claim would

---

1 *Dunlop Pneumatic Tyre Co. Ltd. v. Selfridge & Co. Ltd.*, [1915] A.C. 847 at 853 (H.L.) [*Dunlop*].
2 Contrast *West v. Houghton* (1879), 4 C.P.D. 197 (P.C.) with *Lloyd's v. Harper* (1880), 16 Ch. D. 290 at 321 (C.A.), Lush L.J. In *Beswick v. Beswick*, [1968] A.C. 58 (H.L.), aff'g [1966] Ch. 538 (C.A.) [*Beswick*], for example, specific perform-

likely result in the recovery of only nominal damages. Second, quite apart from remedies issues, it may well be that B is unlikely to bring an action of this kind. B may be disinterested or may have disappeared. B may have no financial incentive for bearing the cost of a lawsuit that might result only in a benefit to C. In many cases, then, the third-party beneficiary rule will leave the third party without any effective redress against the person who promised, for good consideration, to confer a benefit on the third party.

The third-party beneficiary rule is potentially applicable in a number of commonplace transactional patterns. The phenomenon of agreements in which the promisor undertakes to pay money to the third-party beneficiary has been referred to above. In some instances of this kind, the intention of the promisee may be to confer a gift on the third-party beneficiary. In others, the promisee's intent may be to ensure a discharge of a pre-existing debt owed by a promisee to the third-party beneficiary. Many insurance contracts may give rise to third-party beneficiary issues. Insurance contracts often impose obligations on the insurer to pay money to a third-party beneficiary in certain defined circumstances. The distribution of manufactured goods through the common distribution pattern of a manufacturer selling goods to a dealer who sells, in turn, to a consumer may give rise to similar problems. If the manufacturer includes, in its contract of sale with the dealer, a manufacturer's guarantee that is intended to benefit the ultimate consumer, the consumer will be a third-party beneficiary of that guarantee.

Similar problems may arise in the context of building contracts. In the typical pattern, the owner of land hires a general contractor to construct a building. In turn, the general contractor will hire subcontractors to supply goods and services of various kinds. The owner would be a mere third-party beneficiary of the promises given by the subcontractors in their agreements with the general contractor. Another possibility arising in this context results from the common practice of owners requiring contractors to ensure that they will pay their subcontractors by purchasing a performance bond under which a surety guarantees that the subcontractors will be paid. The subcontractors are third-party beneficiaries of arrangements of this kind.

---

ance was awarded to the plaintiff in order to avoid, it would appear, resolving the question of whether C's damage might be merely nominal because A's breach caused no loss to B. See *ibid.* at 72–73, Lord Reid; and 88–89, Lord Pearce. See also *Coulls v. Bagot's Executor & Trustee Co. Ltd.* (1967), 119 C.L.R. 460 at 500–2 (Aust. H.C.), Windeyer J.

Provisions of agreements that are designed to limit the liability of one of the parties to the agreement may also be drafted with a view to restricting the liability of third parties. Thus a shipper of goods might agree with the carrier that the carrier's liability for damage to the goods may be restricted to some degree and, further, that the restriction will be applicable also to the potential liability of the carrier's employees and any independent contractors, such as stevedores, whom the carrier might hire to handle the goods. The carrier's employees and the stevedores would be third-party beneficiaries of such a provision.

Although, as we shall see, the courts and legislatures have developed techniques for providing relief to third-party beneficiaries in some of these situations, the general principle to the effect that the third-party beneficiary has no right to enforce the undertaking of the promisor is clearly established. The doctrine is capable of producing much mischief, however, and accordingly, it has been the subject of much criticism.

B. DEVELOPMENT AND RATIONALE OF THE RULE

Although there is some evidence in seventeenth- and eighteenth-century authorities of a judicial willingness to admit claims by third-party beneficiaries,[3] a rule to the contrary was clearly adopted in 1861 in *Tweddle v. Atkinson*[4] and, more importantly, reaffirmed by the House of Lords in 1915 in *Dunlop*,[5] in 1962 in *Scruttons Ltd. v. Midland Silicones Ltd.*,[6] and by numerous Canadian decisions.[7] In *Tweddle*, the father of a bride exchanged promises with the father of the groom that they each would pay monies to the groom before a certain date. After the wedding, they recorded these promises in writing that was assented to and ratified by the married couple. The agreement further stipulated that the husband was to have full power to sue either of the parties with respect to the enforcement of these promises. In the claim eventually

---

3   See generally R. Flannigan, "Privity—the End of an Era (Error)" (1987) 103 Law Q. Rev. 564.

4   (1861), 1 B. & S. 393, 121 E.R. 762 (Q.B.) [*Tweddle*].

5   Above note 1.

6   [1962] A.C. 446 (H.L.).

7   See, for example, *Canadian General Electric Co. Ltd. v. Pickford & Black Ltd.*, [1971] S.C.R. 41; and *Greenwood Shopping Plaza Ltd. v. Beattie*, [1980] 2 S.C.R. 228 [*Greenwood*].

brought against his father-in-law, however, the husband was unsuccessful on the ground that he was a "stranger to the consideration" and was not a "party" to the contract.[8]

The facts of the *Dunlop* case involved what would now be called a resale price maintenance scheme.[9] It was designed to operate in the following fashion. The plaintiff tire manufacturer, Dunlop, wished to ensure that retailers who sold its tires would not do so at prices below the manufacturer's list price. As is often the case, however, the manufacturer did not deal directly with retailers, but rather distributed its tires by selling them to its wholesale merchant who, in turn, sold the tires to retailers. In its contract with its wholesaler, Dew & Co., Dunlop provided an incentive for Dew to obtain, in its contracts with retailers, an undertaking that the retailers would observe the manufacturer's list price when dealing with their own customers. Breach of the undertaking would render the retailer liable to pay five pounds per sale directly to Dunlop. If Dew extracted such an undertaking from a retailer, Dew was entitled to sell the tires to that retailer at 10 percent below the list price. Dew had, in fact, obtained such an undertaking in its contract with the defendant Selfridge & Co., but the latter failed to live up to the agreement and sold two tires to its customers at less than the list price. Dunlop then brought an action to enforce Selfridge's undertaking and recover ten pounds. The claim was defeated by the third-party beneficiary rule. The undertaking had been given by Selfridge in its contract with Dew. Dunlop was a mere third-party beneficiary of that promise.

In explaining the decision, Viscount Haldane repeated what are often thought to be two separate justifications for the privity doctrine alluded to in the *Tweddle* case and he described them as "fundamental" principles of English law. First, "only a person who is a party to a contract can sue on it."[10] Second, if a person is to be able to enforce a contract, "consideration must have been given by him to the promisor."[11] Dunlop had entered into a contract of purchase and sale with Dew and did not itself either enter into a contract with Selfridge or provide consideration to it for Selfridge's undertaking to observe the list price.

---

8   Above note 4 at 764 (E.R.). The court rejected the suggestion that an exception obtained where the promisee was a parent of the third-party beneficiary, thereby dismissing the potential applicability of *Dutton and Wife v. Poole* (1678), 2 Lev. 210.

9   Now rendered illegal in Canada by the *Combines Investigation Act*, R.S.C. 1985, c. C-34, s. 38. See generally M. Trebilcock, D. McQueen and B. Dunlop, *Canadian Competition Policy* (Toronto: Canada Law Book, 1987).

10   Above note 1 at 853.

11   *Ibid.*

Although Lord Dunedin confessed, "this case is to my mind apt to nip any budding affection which one might have had for the doctrine of consideration,"[12] he was nonetheless confidently of the view that the privity doctrine was a well-established feature of English law.

The justifications offered for the privity doctrine in these cases are quite unconvincing.[13] The first explanation is that the third-party beneficiary is not a "party" to the agreement. It is not entirely clear what is meant by this notion and how this concept can be distinguished, if at all, from the requirement that only a party who has given consideration to the promisor can enforce a promise. In *Tweddle*,[14] for example, the son-in-law was not only named in the agreement expressly as the person to whom the payments were to be made, he also explicitly assented to and ratified the arrangement. Nonetheless, he is said not to be a "party" to the agreement. It is not entirely clear, then, what content can be given to the concept of being a party other than the requirement that in order to be a party in the requisite sense, one must have given consideration to a promisor. If there is any independent content to the notion of "party" in this context, it would appear to be a mere circularity of reasoning. One is not a party because a third-party beneficiary is not a party.

The suggestion that the privity doctrine simply flows from or is somehow deducible from the doctrine of consideration is also seriously flawed. As we have seen,[15] the doctrine of consideration is designed for the purpose of determining whether a particular promise should be considered to be legally binding. It is a test for the enforceability of promises. The doctrine, in its own terms at least, says nothing with respect to the question of who should be able to enforce a binding promise. Indeed, it might be suggested that the privity doctrine is inconsistent with consideration theory inasmuch as it will lead, in many situations, to the perverse result that a promise given for good consideration will be essentially unenforceable for all practical purposes.

The unsatisfactory nature of the Anglo-Canadian rule can be contrasted with the approach taken in other jurisdictions. Third-party beneficiaries have been accorded the right to enforce promises for their benefit in American law.[16] Further, as Viscount Haldane noted in the

---

12 *Ibid.* at 855.
13 See generally M.A. Eisenberg, "Third-party Beneficiaries" (1992) 92 Colum. L. Rev. 1358.
14 Above note 4.
15 See Chapter 7.
16 See Eisenberg, above note 13.

Dunlop case, the rule knows no parallel in a number of civilian jurisdictions.[17] The doctrine has been subjected to trenchant criticism by
judges in England,[18] Canada,[19] and Australia.[20] Frequent calls for reform are made in reports of various law reform agencies.[21] A number of
Commonwealth jurisdictions[22]—including England[23] and one Canadian province, New Brunswick[24]—have abrogated the rule by statute.
Elsewhere in common law Canada, however, the general rule has survived though, as we shall see, its force has been significantly undermined by a growing list of exceptions to the rule.

Lord Denning championed judicial reform of the rule on a number
of occasions,[25] but his attempts to overrule the doctrine in a general
manner did not enjoy success. In *Beswick v. Beswick*,[26] for example, he
mounted a persuasive attack on the rule in a case where a deceased
person had, while living, sold his business to a nephew who promised in return that after the uncle's death, the nephew would pay his
widow an annuity of £5 per week. The uncle died and the nephew
refused to pay the annuity. Lord Denning would have allowed the widow's direct claim to enforce the nephew's promise on the ground that
the third-party beneficiary rule is not commanded by earlier authority
and would lead to an unattractive result. The other two members of

---

17   Above note 1 at 853.
18   See, for example, *Woodar Investment Development Ltd. v. Wimpey Construction U.K. Ltd.*, [1980] 1 W.L.R. 277 at 291 (H.L.), Lord Salmon; and at 300, Lord Scarman; *Darlington Borough Council v. Wiltshier Northern Ltd.*, [1995] 1 W.L.R. 68 at 76 (H.L.), Steyn L.J.; and *White v. Jones*, [1995] 2 A.C. 207 at 262–63 (H.L.), Lord Goff.
19   *London Drugs Ltd. v. Kuehne & Nagel International Ltd.*, [1992] 3 S.C.R. 299 at 418–26, Iacobucci J. [*London Drugs*].
20   *Trident General Insurance Co. Ltd. v. McNiece Bros. Pty. Ltd.* (1988), 165 C.L.R. 107 at 116–24, Mason C.J.; and 169–72, Toohey J.
21   See, for example, Ontario Law Reform Commission, *Report on Amendment of the Law of Contract* (Toronto: Ministry of the Attorney General, 1987); Manitoba Law Reform Commission, *Privity of Contract* (Winnipeg: Law Reform Commis-sion, 1993); and U.K. Law Commission, "Privity of Contract: Contracts for the Benefit of Third Parties," Cm 3329 in *Law Commission No. 242* (London: HMSO, 1996).
22   New Zealand, Queensland, and Western Australia. See U.K. Law Commission, *ibid.* at 55–62.
23   *Contracts (Rights of Third Parties) Act* (U.K.) 1999, c. 31.
24   *Law Reform Act*, S.N.B. 1993, c. L-1.2, s. 4.
25   See, for example, *Smith & Snipes Hall Farm v. River Douglas Catchment Board*, [1949] 2 K.B. 500 (C.A.); and *White v. John Warwick & Co. Ltd.*, [1953] 1 W.L.R. 1285 (C.A.).
26   *Beswick*, above note 2.

the Court of Appeal,[27] however, justified a decision in the widow's favour on the basis that she had also sued the nephew in her capacity as administratrix of her husband's estate. In their view, she was entitled to succeed in that capacity and indeed should be granted a decree of specific performance ordering the nephew to make the payments to her. On appeal to the House of Lords, the latter view prevailed.[28] Their Lordships were unanimous in rejecting Lord Denning's approach and reaffirming the commonly accepted view that the third-party beneficiary rule is good law. Though there was some hesitancy on the question of whether the estate was entitled only to nominal damages,[29] the court was also unanimously of the view that the estate was entitled to a decree of specific performance.

In cases like *Beswick*, judicial reaffirmation of the traditional rule is often accompanied by an acknowledgment of its unsatisfactory nature. In *Beswick*, for example, Lord Reid observed that a strong Law Revision Committee had recommended statutory overruling of the doctrine thirty years before, in 1937.[30] He then suggested that "if one had to contemplate a further long period of Parliamentary procrastination, this House might find it necessary to deal with this matter."[31] Similarly, in the recent decision of the Supreme Court of Canada in *London Drugs*,[32] Iacobucci J., writing for a majority of the Court, rehearsed many of the standard criticisms of the doctrine in pithy fashion and acknowledged "strong reservations about the rigid retention of a doctrine that has undergone systematic and substantial attack."[33] It was nonetheless his view that major reform to such an established principle of the law of contracts must come from the legislature.[34]

After the passage of more than thirty years since the decision in *Beswick*, reforming legislation has been enacted in the United Kingdom.[35] In Canada, however, it may be legitimately questioned whether it is realistic to expect that the legislatures of the common law provinces will act

---

27   Danckwerts and Salmon L.JJ.

28   See *Beswick*, above note 2.

29   See *ibid.* at 73, Lord Reid; 78, Lord Hodson; 88–89, Lord Pearce; and 101, Lord Upjohn.

30   See *ibid.* at 72, referring to U.K. Law Revision Committee, Cmd 5449 in *Sixth Interim Report, Statute of Frauds and the Doctrine of Consideration* (London: H.M.S.O., 1937).

31   Above note 2 at 72.

32   Above note 19.

33   *Ibid.* at 437.

34   *Ibid.* at 439.

35   Above note 23.

in unison so as to overrule this anomalous doctrine. No reform or, at best, a patchwork of reform appears to be the more likely consequence of leaving this issue to the legislatures. The path of judicial reform to date, however, has plainly adopted the strategy of carving out exceptions to the doctrine on a piecemeal basis. We turn, then, to a consideration of the various means by which application of the rule can be avoided in particular fact situations through adoption of other analytical devices or through the application of exceptions to the rule itself.

C. LIMITATIONS ON AND EXCEPTIONS TO THE RULE

Application of the third-party beneficiary rule can be avoided if other doctrines, such as agency, trust, collateral contract or tort provide a foundation for a claim by the beneficiary against the promisor. As well, there are recognized exceptions to the doctrine, both statutory and at common law, that ameliorate the harsh consequences of the rule in particular circumstances.

1) Agency

Under the principles of the law of agency, where a principal authorizes an agent to enter into contracts on the principal's behalf with third parties, the result of the agent's doing so is that the principal has a direct contractual relationship with the third party.[36] In what appears to be a third-party beneficiary case, then, it might be successfully argued that the promisee, B, was acting as an agent on behalf of C, the third-party beneficiary, in extracting a promise from A to confer a benefit on C. C, then, would have a direct contractual relationship with A and the third-party beneficiary rule would be avoided. From time to time, this agency analysis has been applied to what might otherwise appear to be a third-party beneficiary case. In *McCannell v. Mabee McLaren Motors Ltd.*,[37] for example, a dispute arose in the context of a series of agreements entered into by the manufacturer of Studebaker cars and each of its Canadian dealers. In each agreement with a dealer, the manufacturer required the dealer to, in effect, respect the territories assigned to other dealers and

---

36 See generally G.H.L. Fridman, *The Law of Agency*, 7th ed. (Toronto: Butterworths, 1996); and R. Powell, *The Law of Agency*, 2d ed. (London: Pitman & Sons, 1961).

37 (1926), 36 B.C.R. 369 (C.A.).

provided for remedies for breach of this undertaking. The provision also stipulated: "[i]t is understood and agreed that this paragraph shall be construed as an agreement between dealer and all other Studebaker Dealers who have signed a similar agreement."[38] When one dealer sued another for breach of this agreement, the court held that with respect to this provision, the manufacturer acted as the agent of the several dealers to bring about privity of contract among them. Through the agency of the manufacturer, then, each dealer had entered into a contract with every other dealer concerning this matter.[39]

A similar approach was taken by the Privy Council in *New Zealand Shipping Co. Ltd. v. A.M. Satterthwaite & Co. Ltd.*,[40] a case concerning a sale of equipment to be carried by sea to the purchaser. The seller, as the consignor or sender of the goods, entered into a contract, the bill of lading, with the operator of the vessel. The bill of lading provided: "no servant or agent of the carrier (including every independent contractor from time to time employed by the carrier) shall in any circumstances whatsoever be under any liability … for any loss or damage."[41] When the purchaser or consignee of the goods received them, it became apparent that they had been damaged by the stevedores who had been hired by the carrier to unload the vessel. Although the consignee conceded that he was bound by the terms of the bill of lading with respect to any claim against the carrier, the consignee sued the stevedores in negligence and claimed that the stevedores could not rely, as third-party beneficiaries, on the provision of the bill of lading that appeared to be designed to protect them. The bill of lading further stipulated, however, that with respect to this provision, the carrier was acting as an agent on behalf of its servants or agents or any independent contractors whom it might hire. The court held that the effect of this provision was to constitute the carrier as an agent for the purpose of communicating an offer of a unilateral contract to the stevedores. In effect, the consignor and consignee offer an agreement under which they promise that any independent contractors shall be entitled to the protections set out in the bill of lading, which offer can be accepted by an independent contractor, as in this case, by performing the act of unloading the vessel. A similar approach has been adopted in this same context by the Supreme Court of Canada.[42]

---

38   *Ibid.* at 371.

39   See also *Clarke v. The Earl of Dunraven*, [1897] A.C. 59 (H.L.), aff'g [1895] P. 248 (C.A.) (*sub nom. The Satanita*).

40   [1975] A.C. 154 (P.C.) [*sub nom. The Eurymedon*] [*New Zealand Shipping*].

41   *Ibid.* at 165.

42   *ITO — International Terminal Operators Ltd. v. Miida Electronics Inc.*, [1986] 1 S.C.R. 752. See also *Dyck v. Manitoba Snowmobile Association Inc.*, [1985] 1

Although agency analysis may appear to offer a useful device for avoiding application of the third-party beneficiary rule, there are severe limitations on its utility. The application of agency principles, in the normal case, rests on the finding of a genuine intention to create a relationship of agency. Thus, strained applications of the agency concept such as that found in the *New Zealand Shipping* case are vulnerable to the charge that the parties, in fact, had no such intention. In *New Zealand Shipping*, for example, Viscount Dilhorne dissented on the ground that the provision in the bill of lading did not either expressly or impliedly contain any such offer as that found by the majority.[43] Similarly, in the *Dunlop* case,[44] the plaintiff tire manufacturer sought to ground relief on the basis that the wholesaler had entered into contracts with the retailer as an agent of the manufacturer. This argument was rejected, however, on the basis that the wholesaler had clearly bought the tires from the manufacturer as a principal and there did not appear to be any separate contractual undertaking negotiated by the wholesaler as an agent of the manufacturer. Cases such as these indicate that reliance on artificial extension of the agency analysis is a precarious device for avoiding application of the third-party beneficiary rule.

2) Trusts

In contrast to the entrenchment of the third-party beneficiary rule in the common law of contract, the courts of equity developed the law of trusts under which the rights of third-party beneficiaries were recognized.[45] Trust arises in circumstances where property is being held by a person, the trustee, subject to an obligation to deal with the property for the benefit of third persons, the beneficiaries of the trust. A parent, for example, may transfer assets into the hands of a trustee to be administered for the benefit of the children. The law of trusts recognizes that the right to enforce a contractual obligation, a so-called *chose in action*, is included among the kinds of assets that can be made the subject matter of a trust. Accordingly, if a third-party beneficiary of a contract can successfully claim that the promisee held the right to enforce the

---

S.C.R. 589 (release of Association effective to preclude tort claim in negligence against official for physical injuries). See D. Vaver, *Developments in Contract Law: The 1984–85 Term* (1986) 8 Sup. Ct. L. Rev. 109 at 137–47.

43   See above note 40 at 170.

44   Above note 1.

45   See generally E. Gillese and M. Milczynski, *The Law of Trusts*, 2d ed. (Toronto: Irwin Law, 2005); and D.W.M. Waters, *Law of Trusts in Canada*, 2d ed. (Toronto: Carswell, 1984).

promise as a trustee for the beneficiary, the beneficiary could enforce the promise on the basis of the principles of the law of trusts. Although English and Canadian courts have applied the trust analysis to third-party beneficiary cases, at least in the context of promises to pay money or to transfer land,[46] the modern authorities indicate that trust analysis will apply only in circumstances where it is clear that the parties actually intended to create a trust relationship.[47] In *Vandepitte v. Preferred Accident Insurance Co.*,[48] for example, it was argued that a provision in a father's car insurance policy that extended indemnity protection to persons driving the car with permission was held by the father in trust for the benefit of his daughter. The argument was rejected on the basis that there was no evidence that the father "had any intention to create a beneficial interest" for his daughter specifically or as a member of a described class.[49]

As with agency law, then, extended application of the law of trusts to third-party beneficiary contract cases is vulnerable to the charge that no genuine intention to create such a relationship is evident on the facts of the case. The role of trust law as a device for circumventing the third-party beneficiary rule in contracts cases is thus severely limited.

3) Collateral Contracts

As has been indicated, the distribution of manufacturer's goods through dealers who purchase the goods from the manufacturer and then sell the goods, in turn, to the consumer may give rise to third-party beneficiary problems. The consumer may be a third-party beneficiary of a manufacturer's guarantee contained in the contract of sale to the dealer. In some instances, the device of collateral contract may enable the consumer to enforce the manufacturer's undertaking directly. Such relief is likely limited, however, to cases where the manufacturer has communicated with the consumer. In *Shanklin Pier Ltd. v. Detel Products Ltd.*,[50] for example, the defendant paint manufacturer had represented to the plaintiff that its paint had certain qualities that rendered it appropriate

---

46 See, for example, *Lloyd's v. Harper*, above note 2; *Kendrick v. Barkey* (1907), 9 O.W.R. 356 (H.C.J.); and *Les Affréteurs Réunis Société Anonyme v. Leopold Walford (London) Ltd.*, [1919] A.C. 801 (H.L.).

47 See *Schebsman, In re*, [1944] Ch. 83 (C.A.); and *Fournier Van & Storage Ltd. v. Fournier*, [1973] 3 O.R. 741 (H.C.J.).

48 [1933] A.C. 70 (P.C.) [*Vandepitte*].

49 *Ibid.* at 80.

50 [1951] 2 K.B. 854. See also *Wells (Merstham) Ltd. v. Buckland Sand and Silica Ltd.*, [1965] 2 Q.B. 170; and *Murray v. Sperry Rand Corp.* (1979), 23 O.R. (2d) 456 (H.C.J.).

for use in repainting the plaintiff's pier. The plaintiff then required its painting contractor to use the defendant's paint. The contractor then purchased the paint from the defendant and applied it to the pier. When the paint proved to be unsatisfactory, the plaintiff successfully claimed damages from the manufacturer. Even though the contract for the supply of the paint was between the manufacturer and the contractor, the court held that there was a collateral unilateral contract offered by the manufacturer to the plaintiff. In effect, the manufacturer was held to have offered to the plaintiff that it would be bound by its representations concerning the quality of the paint if the plaintiff instructed its contractor to use its paint on the project. When the plaintiff did so, it accepted the manufacturer's offer and gave the consideration that rendered the manufacturer's warranty binding.

Similar unilateral contracts may be found where the advertising material of manufacturers is read by consumers prior to the purchase of goods from an independent supplier.[51] As the connection between the manufacturer and the consumer becomes more tenuous, however, the inference of contractual intentions of this kind appears more artificial and, hence, unpredictable in application.

4) Tort Law

In some cases, the breach of A's contractual duty to B may also constitute a tort imposing compensable injuries upon C. C's tort claim against A may thus appear as another device for avoiding the third-party beneficiary rule. Thus, if A supplies a defective product to B who, in turn, sells the item to C, A may be in breach of the contract with B, but this will not avail C. If, however, the defect results from negligence and causes physical injury or property damage to C, a claim may be brought by C against A on the basis of *Donoghue v. Stevenson*.[52] The development of tort principles enabling recovery of economic loss expands the possible scope of this solution to the third-party beneficiary problem.[53] Recently, for example, the Supreme Court of Canada has held that the builder of a defective building may be liable in tort to a subsequent owner of the building for the economic loss involved in repairing the defect, at

---

51   See *Murray v. Sperry Rand Corp.*, *ibid.* (purchaser relies on manufacturer's sales brochure); and *Leitz v. Saskatoon Drug & Stationery Co. Ltd.*; *T.C. Distributers (1970) Ltd., Third Party* (1980), 4 Sask. R. 35 (Q.B.) (purchaser relies on advertising tag attached to product).

52   [1932] A.C. 562 (H.L.).

53   See generally B. Feldthusen, *Economic Negligence: The Recovery of Pure Economic Loss*, 4th ed. (Toronto: Carswell, 2000).

least where the defect poses a foreseeable and substantial danger to the health and safety to the occupants of the building.[54]

Although these tort duties relating to the supply of defective goods and structures typically arise independently of the contractual duties imposed by the initial contract of supply, there are other cases in which the tort duty owed to the third party appears to arise directly from the breach of contract. In recent English cases, for example, solicitors have been held liable to prospective beneficiaries for their failure to draw up a will[55] or execute[56] it properly. Such failures would constitute breach of contractual duties owed to their clients that could not be enforced in a contract claim by the prospective beneficiaries because of the third-party beneficiary rule. Their claim in tort, which avoids the third-party beneficiary rule, appears to flow directly from the initial breach of contract.[57]

5) Assignment

The law concerning the assignment of contractual rights is a complex subject that is beyond the scope of this work.[58] For present purposes, however, contractual rights are considered to be a species of property, so-called *choses in action*, that, like other species of property, can be transferred from one person to another. The assignment of a contractual right by an assignor to an assignee will be enforceable by the assignee against the original promisor if the assignment complies with the rules[59] of common law, equity or statute relating to the effectiveness of assignments. In the context of a contract in which the promisor

---

54   *Winnipeg Condominium Corp. No. 36 v. Bird Construction Co.*, [1995] 1 S.C.R. 85.

55   *White v. Jones*, above note 18.

56   *Ross v. Caunters*, [1980] Ch. 297.

57   See also *Junior Books Ltd. v. Veitchi Co. Ltd.*, [1983] 1 A.C. 520 (H.L.) (factory owner recovers cost of repairing or replacing defective flooring from flooring subcontractor). For criticism, see D. Cohen, "Bleeding Hearts and Peeling Floors: Compensation for Economic Loss at the House of Lords" (1984) 18 U.B.C. L. Rev. 289; J. Blom, "Economic Loss: Curbs on the Way Ahead?" (1986–87) 12 Can. Bus. L.J. 275; and J.G. Fleming, *The Law of Torts*, 9th ed. (Sydney: Law Book Co., 1998) at 184–86.

58   See generally S.M. Waddams, *The Law of Contracts*, 4th ed. (Toronto: Canada Law Book, 1999) c. 8; and G.H.L. Fridman, *The Law of Contracts in Canada*, 4th ed. (Toronto: Carswell, 1999) c. 17.

59   Although common law doctrine was inhospitable to assignment, equity permitted it. Late-nineteenth-century legislation enacted in England and the Canadian provinces removed some of the obstacles to its recognition. See, for example, *Judicature Act*, R.S.A. 1980, c. J-1, s. 21(1); and *Conveyancing and Law of Property Act*, R.S.O. 1990, c. C.34, s. 53(1).

promises to confer benefits to a third-party beneficiary, then, if the promisee were to assign the benefits of the contract to the third-party beneficiary in an effective manner, the third-party beneficiary would be entitled to enforce the contract as an assignee.[60]

The possibility of assignment does not provide a general solution to the third-party beneficiary problem. Not all agreements are capable of being assigned. Contracts involving a personal or service element, for example, cannot be assigned.[61] In other cases, assignment may be inconvenient or impractical. In a narrow range of cases, however, an assignment of the promisee's rights to the third-party beneficiary could provide a solution to the third-party beneficiary problem.

6) Statutory Exceptions

Many statutory exceptions to the third-party beneficiary rule have been enacted in order to avoid unsatisfactory results. A number have been found necessary in the insurance context, and thus the beneficiary under a life insurance policy has a statutory right to enforce the policy.[62] In the context of motor vehicle insurance, an accident victim has a statutory right to claim directly against the insurer of the person who caused the accident.[63] Similarly, the problem revealed by the decision in *Vandepitte* was remedied by statute.[64] Examples from other contexts would include the statutory right of a purchaser of goods be-

---

60 As Professor Waddams has argued, the acceptance by the courts and the legislatures of the principle of assignment appears quite inconsistent with the third-party beneficiary rule. If parties can subsequently assign the right to enforce A's promise to B, what objection can there be in principle to allowing C to enforce an initial agreement by the parties to confer a benefit directly upon C? See Waddams, above note 58 at 182.

61 See *Griffith v. Tower Publishing Co. Ltd. and Moncrieff*, [1897] 1 Ch. 21; and *Sullivan v. Gray*, [1942] O.W.N. 329 (H.C.J.).

62 See, for example, *Insurance Act*, R.S.A. 1980, c. I-5, s. 264; *Insurance Act*, R.S.B.C. 1996, c. 226, s. 53; *Insurance Act*, R.S.M. 1987, c. 140, s. 172; *Insurance Act*, R.S.N.B. 1973, c. I-12, s. 156; *Insurance Act*, R.S.N.S. 1989, c. 231, s. 197; *Insurance Act*, R.S.O. 1990, c. I.8, s. 195; and *Saskatchewan Insurance Act*, R.S.S. 1978, c. S-26, s. 157.

63 See, for example, *Insurance Act*, R.S.A. 1980, c. I-5, s. 320(1); *Insurance Act*, R.S.B.C. 1996, c. 226, s. 159(1); *Insurance Act*, R.S.M. 1987, c. 140, s. 258(1); *Insurance Act*, R.S.N.B. 1973, c. I-12, s. 250(1); *Insurance Act*, R.S.N.S. 1989, c. 231, s. 133(1); *Insurance Act*, R.S.O. 1990, c. I.8, s. 258(1); and *Saskatchewan Insurance Act*, R.S.S. 1978, c. S-26, s. 210(1).

64 See, for example, *Insurance Act*, R.S.A. 1980, c. I-5, s. 305; *Insurance Act*, R.S.B.C. 1996, c. 226, s. 172; *Insurance Act*, R.S.M. 1987, c. 140, s. 267(1); *Insurance Act*, R.S.N.B. 1973, c. I-12, s. 236; *Insurance Act*, R.S.N.S. 1989, c. 231, s. 142; *Insur-*

ing carried by sea to enforce the contract of carriage (evidenced by a bill of lading) entered into by the seller and the carrier,[65] and the right of a mortgagee to sue the assignee of the mortgagor who has promised the mortgagor that it will make mortgage payments to the mortgagee.[66] Some provinces have enacted consumer protection statutes that enable consumers to enforce directly manufacturers' or sellers' product warranties, whether or not the consumers are mere third-party beneficiaries of the warranty in issue.[67]

7) Additional Exceptions at Common Law

a) Provisions Limiting the Liability of Employees

The privity rule has given rise to particularly harsh results in the context of limitation of liability clauses negotiated by employers with their customers. Where harm to the customer results from the careless conduct of employees, the employer may be immune from liability but this immunity would not extend to employees because they are merely third-party beneficiaries of the contract between their employer and the customer. An analysis of this kind was applied by the Supreme Court of Canada in *Greenwood*[68] in the context of a lease taken out by a retailer. The lessor had agreed to obtain fire insurance and not to seek compensation from the lessee in the event of a fire occurring on the premises. Nonetheless, a claim by the lessor directly against the lessee's employees who had caused a fire enjoyed success.

This point was reconsidered by the Court, however, in *London Drugs*[69] and a new exception to the privity doctrine was crafted to deal with this type of situation. In this case, the customer stored a large transformer in a warehouse and agreed that the warehouseman's liability in the event of damage to the transformer would be limited to forty dollars. The plaintiff declined to exercise an option under the storage contract to pay additional charges to effect an insurance cover for damage to the transformer. When the transformer was damaged as a

---

　　ance Act, R.S.O. 1990, c. I.8, s. 244; and *Saskatchewan Insurance Act*, R.S.S. 1978, c. S-26, s. 219.

65　*Mercantile Law Amendment Act*, R.S.O. 1990, c. M.10, s. 7(1); *Bills of Lading Act*, R.S.C. 1985, c. B-6, s. 2; and *Bills of Lading Act*, R.S.N.S. 1989, c. 38, s. 2.

66　*Mortgages Act*, R.S.O. 1990, c. M.40, s. 20.

67　*Consumer Products Warrantees Act*, R.S.S. 1978, c. C-30, s. 14(1). Compare *Consumer Product Warranty and Liability Act*, S.N.B. 1978, c. C-18.1, ss. 23, 27(1).

68　Above note 7.

69　Above note 19.

result of the negligence of the warehouseman's employees, the plaintiff brought an action directly against them in tort.

Noting that "it would be absurd in the circumstances of this case to let the appellant go around the limitation of liability clause by suing the respondent employees in tort," the Court concluded that the concept of "warehouseman" in the agreement must be taken implicitly to cover the employees of the warehouseman.[70] The Court observed that in this context the parties understand that a warehouseman performs its contractual obligation through the actions of its employees. Where the customer has agreed to a limitation of liability, the employees would not reasonably expect to be liable and holding them so would lead to "serious injustice."[71] Thus, where a limitation of liability clause negotiated by an employer either expressly or impliedly extends to cover the employees and where the employees were performing the very services contracted for by the customer in the ordinary course of their employment, the doctrine of privity, in the Court's view, should not apply. In these narrowly defined circumstances, then, employees can rely on an exception to the privity doctrine.

As noted above, however, the Court declined to affect a broader reform of the doctrine of privity on this occasion.[72] Indeed, the Court merely distinguished, rather than overruled, *Greenwood* on the grounds that a lease is rather different from a contract to provide services because it is not performed by the employees and that, in any event, the contractual provisions in *Greenwood* were not intended to confer protection on the employees.[73] It may be considered unclear, then, what result would obtain if a lease explicitly either identified as its purpose the running of a retail shop or imposed an obligation on the lessee to do so. As we shall see, however, the Court returned to consider and, perhaps, expand the exception created in *London Drugs* in a manner that might capture these kinds of arrangements.[74]

b) Insurance

Strict application of privity doctrine in the context of insurance could work a hardship in many cases. Accordingly, insurance contracts have been a fertile source of exceptions to the general rule, both at common

---

70   *Ibid.* at 444.
71   *Ibid.* at 446.
72   *Ibid.*
73   *Ibid.* at 431.
74   See the discussion of *Fraser River Pile & Dredge Ltd. v. Can-Dive Services Ltd.*, beginning in the text below at note 79.

law, and, as we have seen, in the statute books. Two different fact patterns are typically found in the cases. The first arises in the context of provisions that, in some fashion or other, waive rights that an insurer would otherwise have to pursue claims against third parties. When the insurer, in breach of such provisions, then pursues such relief, the third-party beneficiary will seek to rely on the waiver contained in the insurance contract. The second type concerns insurance agreements that extend coverage to third parties who are not, in the formal sense, parties to the agreement. The question arising in this context is whether the third parties can enforce the positive obligation of the insurer to provide coverage.

i)   Waiver of Rights against Third Parties

Where a contract of insurance provides that the insurer shall have no "recourse" against third parties or where the insurer waives a right to subrogate itself to the position of the insured for purposes of bringing a claim against a third party, it is now clearly established that such provisions are binding on the insurer. Thus, if the insurer pursues an action against a third party protected by such a provision, the third party may rely on the provision to defeat the claim, notwithstanding the third party's lack of privity. In one line of authority reaching back into the nineteenth century, insurers who issued indemnity coverage to insureds "without recourse" were held unable to bring an action against a party causing the loss who was covered by the "without recourse" stipulation.[75] The Supreme Court of Canada reached a similar conclusion in the context of a "builders' risk policy" in *Commonwealth Construction Co. v. Imperial Oil Ltd.*[76] In that case, a builders' risk policy was taken out by the owner of the project under construction. The policy covered not only the owner but the contractors and subcontractors working on the project. During the course of construction, the property was damaged by a fire resulting from the negligence of a subcontractor. Having indemnified the owner for its loss, the insurer then claimed against the subcontractor. The Supreme Court rejected the claim on two grounds. First, to permit the insurer to subrogate itself to the owner in a claim against a subcontractor would be inconsistent with the very purpose of the provision extending coverage to the contractors and subcontractors. The point of the arrangement was to spare the participants in the project "the necessity of fighting between themselves should an accident

---

75   See *Thomas & Co. v. Brown* (1899), 4 Com. Cas. 186; and *J. Clark & Son Ltd. v. Finnamore* (1972), 5 N.B.R. (2d) 467 (S.C.A.D.).

76   [1978] 1 S.C.R. 317, 69 D.L.R. (3d) 558.

occur involving the possible responsibility of one of them." Second, the Court relied upon a provision of the policy that explicitly permitted the insurer to bring subrogated claims against non-insured parties. In the Court's view, this provision plainly precluded subrogation against insured parties such as subcontractors. The third party could rely on this provision, therefore, as a basis for dismissing the claim. A recent Ontario decision has extended protection to the employees of a subcontractor on the basis that they are implicitly protected by arrangements of this kind.[77]

Although it has been suggested that the latter line of authority rests on the particular nature of builder's risk insurance,[78] the Supreme Court has now clearly established that the principle that an insurer's waiver of subrogation or recourse is binding as against third-party beneficiaries is a principle of general application. In *Fraser River Pile & Dredge Ltd. v. Can-Dive Services Ltd.*,[79] a marine insurance policy contained a waiver of subrogation by the insurer against "any charterer." The boat covered by the policy was sunk as a result of the negligence of a charterer. Subsequently, the owner of the boat and the insurer agreed to suspend the waiver of subrogation clause and the insurer brought a subrogated claim against the charterer. The charterer successfully defended the claim on the basis that the exception to the doctrine of privity established in *London Drugs* could extend to this fact situation. Understandably, the plaintiff urged that the *London Drugs* exception would apply only where the initial contract was for the supply of services and where the parties would understand that the services could only be supplied by employees or agents of the contractor. The Supreme Court rejected so narrow a reading of *London Drugs*, however, and held that the exception applies in any case in which the facts meet a twofold test. First, it must be established that the third-party beneficiary was intended by the parties to the initial contract to be benefited by the contractual provision in question. Second, the "activities performed by the third party seeking to rely on the contractual provision [are] the very activities contemplated as coming within the scope of the contract in general, or

---

77 *Madison Developments Ltd. v. Plan Electric Co.* (1997), 36 O.R. (3d) 80, 152 D.L.R. (4th) 653 (C.A.), leave to appeal to S.C.C. refused, 157 D.L.R. (4th) vii, applying the reasoning in *London Drugs*, above note 19, in support of a finding that the parties to the subcontract implicitly intended to extend protection to the employees.

78 *Ibid.* at 661 (D.L.R.); *Sylan Industries Ltd. v. Fairview Sheet Metal Works Ltd.* (1994), 89 B.C.L.R. (2d) 18 (C.A.).

79 (1999), 176 D.L.R. (4th) 257 (S.C.C.).

the provision in particular."[80] In the Court's view, the *Fraser River* facts passed these tests. The first branch was met by the explicit reference to "charterers" as a class in the initial agreement. The second branch of the test was met on the basis that the agreement envisaged that the boat would be let out to a charterer and that this is, in fact, what occurred. On the basis of this decision, then, it is clear that the exception to the doctrine of privity applicable to waivers of subrogation and similar provisions applies generally within the context of insurance agreements and is not limited to a particular class or type of policy.

ii) Coverage of Third Parties

It is commonplace for insurance policies to extend coverage not only to the party who takes out the insurance but also to other parties who may be either named or, at least, identified by reference to a category of covered persons. The question then arises as to whether such third parties can enforce the insurance policy against the insurer. A refusal to enforce such arrangements, of course, would have the effect that insurance coverage that had been paid for could not be effectively enforced by the third-party insureds. This was the problem in *Vandepitte*,[81] which held that the doctrine of privity prevented third-party insureds from enforcing such provisions. Although, as noted above, the decision in *Vandepitte* was abrogated by legislation in the context of automobile insurance, the reasoning in *Vandepitte* created a potential hazard in other insurance contexts. Nonetheless, Canadian courts appear to have adopted the practice of ignoring *Vandepitte*. In a Nova Scotia case, for example, the Appeal Division held that a mortgage-loss insurance policy taken out by a chattel mortgagor, which was payable to the mortgagee, could be enforced at the suit of the mortgagee.[82] Further, in *Scott v. Wawanesa Mutual Insurance Co.*,[83] the Supreme Court of Canada appeared to conclude that third-party insureds were effectively covered by an insurance policy even though the reasoning in *Vandepitte* would suggest that this was not so. In the recent decision in *Fraser River*, the Supreme Court confirmed: "it is time to put to rest the unreasonable

---

80   *Ibid.* at para. 32.

81   Above note 48.

82   *Trans Canada Credit Corporation Ltd. v. Royal Insurance Co. of Canada* (1983), 58 N.S.R. (2d) 280 (S.C.A.D.). Similarly, insurers who have issued indemnity coverage to insureds "without recourse" have been held unable to bring action against a party causing the loss who is covered, albeit only as a third-party beneficiary, of the "without recourse" stipulation. See *Thomas & Co. v. Brown* and *J. Clark & Son Ltd. v. Finnamore*, above note 75.

83   [1989] 1 S.C.R. 1445.

application of the doctrine of privity to contracts of insurance established by the Privy Council in *Vandepitte* ..., a decision characterized since its inception by both legislatures and the judiciary as out of touch with commercial reality."[84] With the effective overruling of *Vandepitte*, then, a further exception to the privity doctrine appears to permit the enforcement of insurance contracts by third-party insureds.

A similar development has occurred in Australia. In *Trident General Insurance Co. Ltd. v. McNiece Bros. Pty. Ltd.*,[85] the Australian High Court refused to apply the doctrine of privity in the context of a third-party claim arising from a construction project at a limestone crushing plant. The operator of the plant had taken out liability insurance that included indemnification for itself, its subsidiaries and related companies and all contractors and subcontractors at the plant. The principal contractor was held liable on a claim by an injured worker. Though merely a third-party beneficiary to the contract of insurance, it then successfully sought indemnification from the insurer. Two of the opinions[86] forming part of the majority of the court offered criticism of the third-party beneficiary rule and called for its reform. Nonetheless, the holding of the court is grounded on the recognition of a specific exception to the rule applicable to insurance contracts.

c) The Open-Textured "Principled Exception"

In *Fraser River*, the Supreme Court confirmed the existence of a "principled exception" to the doctrine of privity that is not restricted to a particular class or type of agreement. Although the principled exception was first articulated in the decision in *London Drugs*, the reasoning in that case was vulnerable to the interpretation that the exception only applied to a fact situation in which the initial contract concerned the provision of services and the parties to that agreement would have appreciated that the services could only be performed by servants or agents of the supplying party. In such circumstances, the suppliers' employees were implicitly protected by a limitation of liability provision in the initial supply contract. This narrow reading of *London Drugs* appeared to be reinforced by the Court's fine distinction of the previ-

---

84 Above note 79 at 273–74.

85 Above note 20.

86 Mason C.J. and Wilson J. in their joint opinion, and Toohey J. favoured judicial reform of the rule. Gaudron J., concurring in the result, preferred an unjust enrichment approach. Deane J. favoured the trust approach but would have allowed further evidence and submissions on the point. Brennan and Dawson JJ. dissented.

ous holding in *Greenwood*[87] in which a limitation of liability in a lease for retail premises was held to offer no protection to the employees of the lessee who negligently caused a fire. The *Greenwood* case was distinguishable, it seemed, because the initial agreement was a lease not a service agreement, and the lessees' employees could therefore not be said to be providing the very service envisaged in the initial agreement. In this respect, the charter party in *Fraser River* appears to be rather similar to the lease in *Greenwood*.

As we have seen, however, the Court in *Fraser River* held that the *London Drugs* exception to the doctrine of privity was not limited to provisions limiting liability under contracts for the supply of services. The principled exception to the doctrine, then, is of general application and is available whenever the two branches of the test set out in *Fraser River* are met. The first branch requires that the parties to the initial agreement intended to extend the benefit in question to the third party.[88] That intention may be explicit, as it was in *Fraser River Pile,* or implicit as it was in *London Drugs*. The second and somewhat opaque branch of the test is that the "very activities" of the third party come within the scope of the initial contract or provision. In *Fraser River,* the initial contract referred to "any charterer." The defendant who, in fact, chartered the boat in question was therefore engaged in the "very activity" envisaged by the agreement. The general or open-textured nature of the principled exception was emphasized by the Court in *Fraser River*. The purpose of the exception is to confer upon courts, in cases where the traditional exceptions of agency and trust do not apply, a discretion to "undertake the appropriate analysis, bounded by both common sense and commercial reality, in order to determine whether the doctrine of privity with respect to third-party beneficiaries should be relaxed in the given circumstances." The principled exception is thus not limited to a particular class or category of contracts.

In attempting to determine the reach of the "principled exception," three issues arise. First, the content of the second branch of the test requires examination. Second, it may be asked whether the application of the exception is restricted to cases where third-party beneficiaries rely upon a provision such as limitation of liability clauses and waiv-

---

87 Above note 7.
88 As formulated in *London Drugs* and *Fraser River*, the test does not require that the parties intend to confer a direct right to enforce on the third party; it is sufficient to establish an intention to benefit. For discussion of this distinction supporting the intention to benefit approach on the ground that the parties are unlikely to think of the question of direct enforcement, see *Trident General,* above note 20 at 122–23, Mason C.J. and Wilson J.

ers of subrogation in order to protect themselves against claims being brought by the original promisor. Third, the extent to which courts may be expected to apply the *Greenwood* decision in future cases may be assessed.

The scope or content of the second branch of the test is not easily discerned. Having found that the parties to the original agreement intended to benefit the third party with the provision, the second branch then requires that the third party be engaged in the "very activity" envisaged by the agreement. It is not entirely clear, however, what is contained in the second branch of the test that is not contained in the initial requirement that the third party be an intended beneficiary of the promise. In *Fraser River*, the provision was intended to protect charterers. The defendant was a charterer. Little is added to this analysis by the observation that chartering was the very activity envisaged by the agreement. Further light on the second branch may be shed by examining the role it plays in the *London Drugs* decision. Certainly, it could be said that the employees in *London Drugs* were engaged in the very activity envisaged by the agreement, that is, providing storage services. As the reasoning in *London Drugs* itself demonstrates, however, the materiality of that fact appears to be that it supports the inference that the parties must have implicitly intended to extend protection to the employees, even though the agreement does not explicitly so provide.[89] In *Fraser River*, on the other hand, where the agreement explicitly purports to confer a benefit on "charterers," it is not surprising that the second branch of the test appears to have no work to do. If this is correct, a better view of the content of the second branch of the test is that it applies only in cases where the third-party beneficiary is not explicitly referred to in the agreement and it applies in support of an inference that the agreement implicitly so provides.

The second issue is whether the principled exception could apply to a case such as *Beswick v. Beswick*,[90] where the third-party beneficiary as plaintiff brings a claim to enforce the promise, or whether its application is restricted to cases like *London Drugs* and *Fraser River*, where the third-party beneficiary as defendant, relies on a provision as protection against a claim brought by the promisor. It is true that in both *London Drugs* and *Fraser River*, the Court placed some emphasis on the nature of the reliance being placed by the third-party beneficiary on the provision in question and implicitly, one might argue, distinguished thereby cases in which a third-party beneficiary, as plaintiff, seeks to enforce a

---

89   Above note 19 at 452, Iacobucci J.
90   Above note 2.

provision. Nonetheless, there are two considerations that weigh in favour of the view that the principled exception could apply in both types of cases. First, as a matter of precedent, the overruling of *Vandepitte* in *Fraser River* offers support for the view that the exception can so apply. *Vandepitte* was a case in which the third-party beneficiary, as plaintiff, sought to enforce a promise of insurance coverage given by the promisor insurer. *Fraser River* plainly intimates that such a claim would now lie in common law Canada. Further, such a claim has been recently allowed by the Australian High Court in the *Trident General* case.[91] Second, if, as the Court states in *Fraser River,* the purpose of the exception is to withhold application of the privity doctrine in cases where considerations of "common sense and commercial reality" suggest that the doctrine should be ignored, there appears to be no convincing basis for assuming that such considerations could apply only in the context of third-party reliance on limitations of liability or waiver of subrogation provisions. We should note in passing that the second branch of the test, as formulated in *Fraser River,* does not appear to apply neatly to all cases in which third-party beneficiaries seek to enforce, as plaintiffs, promises that are intended to benefit them. Although the "insured" plaintiffs in *Vandepitte*[92] and *Trident General*[93] may appear to be engaged in the "very activity" envisaged by the agreement, that is, they suffered the defined loss or injury, the agreement in *Beswick*[94] does not envisage that the widow will engage in any particular activity, other than the receipt of money. This does not appear to be, however, a satisfactory basis for proposing different results in these cases. If, as suggested above, the true role of the second branch of the exception is to determine whether or not the third party was an intended beneficiary of the promise, this potential difficulty is made to disappear.

Finally, the breadth of the principled exception suggests that the vitality of the Court's earlier decision in *Greenwood* has been severely curtailed. Although the Court declined to overrule *Greenwood* in *London Drugs* and neglected to mention the *Greenwood* decision in *Fraser River,* it may be that *Greenwood* should now be considered to be restricted essentially to its own facts. Such an approach was adopted in a recent decision of the Ontario Court of Appeal in *Tony and Jim's Holdings Limited*

---

91 Above note 20. See also *Vandewal v. Vandewal,* [2003] O.J. No. 3269 (C.A.), and compare with *Kitimat (District) v. Alcan, Inc.* (2005), 250 D.L.R. (4th) 144 (B.C.S.C.).

92 Above note 48.

93 Above note 20.

94 Above note 2. The facts are set out in the text, above note 26.

v. *Silva*,[95] a case in which the court applied the principled exception in a fact situation similar in its essentials to that of *Greenwood*. Like *Greenwood,* the promise at issue in *Tony and Jim's* was contained in a lease in a shopping mall. The lease provided that the landlord would procure fire insurance, the premiums for which would be paid by the tenant. The policy stipulated that "all rights of subrogation are hereby waived against any corporation, firm, individual or other interest with respect to which insurance is provided by this policy." A fire occurred and the insurer brought a subrogated claim against an officer of the insured corporation, alleging that the officer's negligence had caused the fire. The Court of Appeal refused to apply *Greenwood* in the insurer's favour on the basis that *Greenwood* was a case in which the court held that the defendant employees were "strangers" to the contract. The question to be asked, after *London Drugs*, in the court's view, was whether there existed sufficient "identity of interest" between the officer and the corporation so as to warrant application of the principled exception. Such an identity of interest was established because the "parties must be taken to have understood that the corporate tenant could only be guilty of negligence through its directors or employees."[96] It is very difficult, however, to distinguish *Greenwood* on this basis. The lease in *Greenwood* imposed an obligation on the landlord to procure fire insurance and not to grant subrogation rights with respect to any loss caused by the tenant. Again, in *Greenwood* it must have been obvious to the parties that the corporate tenant could be careless only through the acts of employees. However, the result in the Ontario case is more attractive than that in *Greenwood* and it may be likely, therefore, that *Greenwood* will continue to be distinguished in the future as a case where the intention to extend protection to third parties was not clearly established[97] and that it will eventually be eclipsed by application of the principled exception to fact situations of this kind.

d) Subsequent Variation or Annulment of the Promise

To the extent that third-party beneficiaries are able to enforce promises against the promisor, consideration must be given to the question of whether such enforceable promises can be subsequently varied or

---

95   (1999), 170 D.L.R. (4th) 193 (Ont. C.A.).

96   *Ibid.* at 202.

97   A basis for distinguishing *Greenwood* on this ground is set out in *London Drugs* itself, above note 19 at 431, Iacobucci J. ("... there was little, if any, evidence to support a finding that the parties to the contract intended to confer a benefit on the employees ...").

annulled either unilaterally by the promisor or with the agreement of the promisee. Indeed, the possibility that recognition of third-party beneficiary rights would complicate or create obstacles to the exercise of variation or rescission of the initial agreement is offered by some observers as a justification for the traditional doctrine of privity.[98] On the other hand, a unilateral right to vary or rescind is capable of working injustice on third parties who have relied on the provision to their detriment. The United Kingdom legislation,[99] which abrogates the privity doctrine, resolves this difficulty by restricting the ability of the parties to the agreement to rescind or vary the agreement to the disadvantage of the third party to situations where the third party had communicated his or her assent to the arrangement to the promisor and where the promisor is either aware that the third party has relied on the term or should reasonably have foreseen that reliance. Thus, in any case where the third party either has not agreed to the term or has not relied upon it, the parties to the original agreement are free to vary or rescind its terms.

A different approach to this issue was taken by the Supreme Court of Canada in the *Fraser River* case. There the insurer and insured purported to rescind the waiver of subrogation clause after the loss had occurred so as to enable the insurer to bring a subrogated claim against the third-party beneficiary of the provision, the defendant charterer. In the view of the Supreme Court, however, once the loss had occurred, the charterer's inchoate contractual right had "crystallized" and the insurer and insured were no longer in a position to "revoke unilaterally" the charterer's rights under the waiver of subrogation clause. This approach differs from the U.K. legislative scheme in two respects. First, crystallization of the third-party's rights does not appear to be contingent upon assent to or, indeed, awareness of the original contractual term. This would appear to be the preferable approach, at least in cases where the provision in question is the normal or usual one and, perhaps, in cases where the third party is unlikely to make inquiries. Second, the position of the charterer prior to crystallization may be less secure than it would be under the U.K. scheme. The Supreme Court appears to take the view that a unilateral revocation could occur prior to crystallization even in a case where the charterer had assented to the term and, perhaps, relied upon it by refraining from taking out its own insurance. Should this matter arise, the preferable view would be that

---

98   See, for example, G.H. Treitel, *The Law of Contract*, 11th ed. (London: Sweet & Maxwell, 2003) at 588.

99   Above note 23, s. 2.

a third party who was aware of and who detrimentally relied on the existence of the provision would be protected by it until, at the least, reasonable notice of a proposed variation or rescission is given. Indeed, in a case where the arrangements in place conferring benefits on third parties are the standard arrangements and where the third parties have simply assumed that the standard arrangements are in place, it may be appropriate to dispense with any requirement that the third party have actual notice of the provision.

D. CONCLUSION

A number of considerations suggest that the doctrine of privity is vulnerable to further reform. The rule lacks a convincing policy foundation. It is capable of producing unjust and surprising results in commonplace fact situations. Its unsatisfactory nature has produced a long and growing list of exceptions, thus rendering application of the doctrine unpredictable. Though it is easy to conclude that privity doctrine is ripe for further modification, it is perhaps more difficult to identify the optimal model of reform. One possibility would be for legislatures or the courts to overrule the doctrine by adopting the principle that the absence of privity, *per se*, will not preclude an action by a third-party beneficiary to enforce a promise. The law would thus be allowed to develop on a case-by-case basis.[100] To fashion a rule that would indicate more precisely in what circumstances a third-party beneficiary should be allowed to enforce would be more difficult. As *London Drugs* strongly suggests, a rule allowing relief only to third-party beneficiaries expressly identified in the contract would be too narrow. In some circumstances it is evidently implicit in the contractual arrangements that a third party is an intended beneficiary.[101] However, a rule granting standing to enforce to every possible beneficiary of contractual performance would obviously be too broad. A contract

---

100 An approach favoured, for example, by the Ontario Law Reform Commission, above note 21.

101 The U.K. Law Commission, however, favoured limiting statutory abrogation to cases where a right is expressly conferred upon a third party identified by name, class or description. See above note 21 at 74–92. The new U.K. legislation adopts this approach. See above note 23, s. 1. See also J. Fleming, "Employer's Tort in a Contractual Matrix: New Approaches in Canada (1993) 13 Oxford J. Legal Stud. 430; and N. Siebrasse, "Third-party Beneficiaries in the Supreme Court: Categorization and Interpretation of Ambiguous Contracts" (1995) 45 U.T.L.J. 47.

to build a factory may benefit a large number of individuals and groups within a community but it would not be seriously suggested that all of them should have a right of action against a defaulting contractor. Perhaps it would be difficult to improve on the rule set out in the *Restatement on Contracts*, which distils the American experience with granting such relief and provides that the third-party beneficiary will be able to enforce the promise "if recognition of a right to performance in the beneficiary is appropriate to effectuate the intention of the parties."[102] Clearly, recognition would be inappropriate if, on a proper construction of the agreement, the promisor and promisee have agreed otherwise. The U.K. legislation[103] and American experience[104] suggests that careful thought must also be given to the question of the revocability of the promise and the extent to which supervening considerations such as frustration, illegality or non-performance by the promisee should constitute defences to the third-party beneficiary's claim. Neither the U.K. legislation nor the American experience suggests, however, that these issues cannot be satisfactorily resolved.

FURTHER READINGS

J.N. ADAMS, D. BEYLEVELD & R. BROWNSWORD, "Privity of Contract—the Benefits and Burdens of Law Reform" (1997) 60 Mod. L. Rev. 238.

J.N. ADAMS & R. BROWNSWORD, "Privity of Contract and the Idea of a Network Contract" (1990) 10 L.S. 12.

J. BEATSON, "Reforming the Law of Contracts for the Benefit of Third Parties" (1992) Curr. Legal Probs. 1.

A.L. CORBIN, "Contracts for the Benefit of Third Persons" (1930) 46 Law Q. Rev. 12.

M.A. EISENBERG, "Third-party Beneficiaries" (1992) 92 Colum. L. Rev. 1358.

---

102 American Law Institute, *Restatement of the Law of Contracts 2d* (St. Paul: American Law Institute., 1981) § 302(1). For trenchant criticism of the *Restatement's* formulation, however, see Eisenberg, above note 13 at 1381–84.

103 Above note 23, s. 3.

104 See generally *Restatement of the Law of Contracts 2d*, above note 102, § 309; U.K. Law Commission, above note 20 at 101–27; and Eisenberg, above note 13 at 1412–29.

R. FLANNIGAN, "Privity—the End of an Era (Error)" (1987) 103 Law Q. Rev. 564.

LAW COMMISSION, *Privity of Contract: Contracts for the Benefit of Third Parties*, Cmnd. 3329 (London: HMSO, 1996).

LAW REFORM COMMISSION OF NOVA SCOTIA, *Final Report: Privity of Contract (Third Party Rights)* (Halifax: Law Reform Commission of Nova Scotia, 2004).

MANITOBA LAW REFORM COMMISSION, *Privity of Contract* (Winnipeg: Law Reform Commission, 1993).

J.D. MCCAMUS, "Loosening the Privity Fetters: Should Common Law Canada Recognize Contracts for the Benefit of Third Parties?" (2001) 35 Can. Bus. L.J. 173.

R. MERKIN, *Privity of Contract: The Impact of the Contracts (Rights of Third Parties) Act 1999* (London: Lloyd's of London Press, 2000).

M. OGILVIE, "Privity of Contract and the Third Party Purchaser" (1987–88) 13 Can. Bus. L.J. 402.

ONTARIO LAW REFORM COMMISSION, *Report on Amendment of the Law of Contract* (Toronto: Ministry of the Attorney General, 1987) c. 4.

N. SIEBRASSE, "Third-Party Beneficiaries in the Supreme Court: Categorization and Interpretation of Ambiguous Contracts" (1996) 45 U.T.L.J. 47.

S.A. SMITH, "Contracts for the Benefit of Third Parties: In Defence of the Third Party Rule" (1997) 17 Oxford J. Legal Stud. 643.

A. TETTENBORN, "Covenants, Privity of Contract and the Purchaser of Personal Property" (1982) 41 Cambridge L.J. 58.

PART THREE

VITIATING FACTORS

CHAPTER 10

MISREPRESENTATION

A. INTRODUCTION

When one party has induced another party to enter into an agreement by making a material statement of fact that is false, a variety of remedies may be available to the misrepresentee, both at common law and in equity. The principal remedy is that of rescission, which, if available, has the effect of unwinding or setting aside the agreement. The remedy of rescission is available only if the parties to the agreement can be restored to their initial position in the sense that there must be possible a giving back and a taking back of benefits received by both parties. In this sense, the remedy is restitutionary in nature. The setting aside of the agreement will be accompanied by restitutionary relief for both parties. If the misrepresentation was made fraudulently, in the sense that either the misrepresentor knew that the statement was false or made the statement "recklessly and without care, whether it was true or false, and not with the belief that it was true,"[1] the resulting agreement could be rescinded at common law. In equity, however, a decree of rescission could be granted even in a case where the misrepresentation was innocently false in the sense that the misrepresentor did not make the statement with fraudulent intent. The availability of rescission, however, is curtailed by the existence of a number of traditional limita-

---

1   *Redgrave v. Hurd* (1881), 20 Ch. D. 1 at 13 (C.A.), Jessel M.R.

tions or defences and, where such limitations apply, the misrepresentee
may wish to pursue other forms of relief.

As well as or as an alternative to rescissionary relief, the misrepresentee may in certain circumstances pursue claims for compensation in
tort. Where an agreement has been induced by a fraudulent misstatement, the tort of deceit has been committed and the misrepresentee will
be entitled to recover compensatory damages. Although tortious liability
for fraudulent inducement of agreements has a lengthy history,[2] it was
not until the latter part of the twentieth century that the tort of negligence was extended to cover economic loss sustained as a result of negligent misstatements.[3] This form of liability was, in due course, extended
to embrace claims for injuries sustained as a result of entering into unattractive agreements induced by negligent misstatement.[4] The measure
of relief in tort extends to compensation for all losses occasioned by the
tortious misconduct and is thus more comprehensive than the restitutionary relief that accompanies rescission of the agreement.[5]

Before considering the various remedial alternatives available in the
context of misrepresentation, we turn to an account of the elements of
operative misrepresentation and a consideration of the extent to which
non-disclosure of a fact may constitute misrepresentation in the requisite sense. We will also consider the suggestion made by some that a
duty to disclose facts might be imposed where a standard of good-faith
conduct so requires.

B. THE ELEMENTS OF MISREPRESENTATION

In order to provide a basis for rescissionary relief, the misrepresentation must be a statement of present or past fact that is false. For these
purposes, statements of fact are distinguished from mere "sales talk,"
from statements of opinion or belief, from statements of intention or
promises and, under traditional doctrine at least, from statements of
law. Further, the fact that is misstated must be material to the decision of the misrepresentee to enter the agreement and the misstatement
must serve as an inducement to the making of that decision.

---

2   See, for example, *Derry v. Peek* (1889), 14 A.C. 337 (H.L.).
3   *Hedley Byrne & Co. v. Heller & Partners Ltd.*, [1964] A.C. 465, [1963] 2 All E.R. 575 (H.L.).
4   *Esso Petroleum Co. v. Mardon*, [1976] Q.B. 801 (C.A.); *Sodd Corp. v. Tessis* (1977), 17 O.R. (2d) 158, 79 D.L.R. (3d) 632 (C.A.).
5   For discussion of the difference between the restitutionary and tort measures of relief, see Chapter 1, section C.

1) Sales Talk

Vague and imprecise expressions or statements puffing or aggrandizing the virtues of, for example, a seller's product are not relied upon by a reasonable purchaser. Such statements are mere sales talk, "puffery" or "dealer's talk" and not statements of fact that, if false, provide a foundation for legal remedies. Thus, statements by a seller of land that the land is "improved"[6] or is an "uncommonly rich" water meadow[7] or "fertile and improvable at moderate cost"[8] or an exaggerated estimate of the value of a crop produced by the land to be sold[9] have all been held to be mere sales talk that affords no ground for relief. In some cases, however, vague commendatory language from a seller who has privileged information concerning the subject matter of the sale may be taken to include an implicit statement of fact. Thus, the statement by a seller of a used car that it was a "good little bus" was characterized as an implicit statement of fact that the vehicle met a minimum standard of roadworthiness.[10] Similarly, the seller of a house who had acted as his own contractor in building the home and who was aware of serious defects in the construction was held to have made a misrepresentation when describing the house as "well built."[11]

2) Opinion

The distinction between statements of fact and statements of opinion is similarly intended to exclude, as a basis for relief, statements upon which the misrepresentee would not reasonably rely. Thus, where an opinion is offered by someone who has no particular expertise in the matter in question, the statement would be considered to be one of opinion rather than one of fact. A reasonable person would not rely on such an opinion. Thus, an estimate by a vendor of land who estimated the sheep-bearing capacity of the land was held to have been a mere opinion on the matter.[12] Similarly, estimates of the value of assets by

---

6   *Andronyk v. Williams* (1985), 21 D.L.R. (4th) 557 (Man. C.A.), leave to appeal to
     S.C.C. refused (1986), 42 Man. R. (2d) 242n.
7   *Scott v. Hanson* (1829), 1 Russ. & M. 128, 39 E.R. 49.
8   *Dimmock v. Hallett* (1866), L.R. 2 Ch. App. 21.
9   *Rasch v. Horne*, [1930] 3 D.L.R. 647 (Man. C.A.).
10   *Andrews v. Hopkinson*, [1957] 1 Q.B. 229.
11   *Mariani v. Lemstra*, [2003] O.J. No. 750.
12   *Bisset v. Wilkinson*, [1927] A.C. 177 (P.C.). And see, for example, *Trethewey v.
     Girard* (1983), 149 D.L.R. (3d) 359 (B.C.S.C.) (private seller of boat represented
     to be sound).

non-experts are classified as matters of opinion.[13] If an opinion concerns matters over which the representor obviously has no control, it is unlikely that the statement would be characterized as one of fact.[14] However, one who possesses superior knowledge or expertise with respect to the opinion offered may be held to have made an implicit statement concerning the nature of the information upon which the opinion is based. Thus, where the seller of a hotel indicated that the current lessee was "a most desirable tenant," it was held that this amounted to a tacit assertion "that the facts peculiarly within his knowledge are such as to render that opinion reasonable."[15] Similarly, an oil company that induced a tenant to enter a lease of a service station on the basis of an inaccurate estimate of the likely volume of business at a particular intersection was held to have tacitly asserted that the study had been carefully executed.[16]

3) Intention

A representation that something will occur in the future is simply not a statement of fact. Promises are thus distinguishable from statements of fact and, if they are to bind the promisor, must meet the requirements for the enforceability of undertakings.[17] Accordingly, one who seeks to rely on a promise with respect to the future must seek a contractual undertaking in order to do so. On the other hand, a promise with respect to the future may be characterized as an implicit statement of fact concerning one's present intention. If a false statement of present intention is made, the statement is fraudulently false, and therefore gives rise to the normal remedies for fraudulent misstatement.[18]

---

13   See, for example, *Knox v. Bunch* (1913), 11 D.L.R. 377 (Alta. S.C.T.D.); *Burns v. Brouse* (1923), 24 O.W.N. 585 (S.C.A.D.); *Canada West Loan Co. Ltd. v. Virtue*, [1921] 1 W.W.R. 730 (B.C.S.C.).

14   *Rasch v. Horne*, above note 9 at 651, Robson J.A.

15   *Smith v. Land and House Property Corp.* (1884), 28 Ch. Div. 7 at 15 (C.A.), Bowen L.J.; *Northern & Central Gas Co. Ltd. v. Hillcrest Collieries Ltd.*, [1976] 1 W.W.R. 481 at 529–32, Lieberman J.

16   *Esso Petroleum Co. Ltd. v. Mardon*, above note 4. See also *Rainbow Industrial Caterers Ltd. v. Canadian National Railway Co.* (1988), 54 D.L.R. (4th) 43 (B.C.C.A.).

17   See generally Chapter 7.

18   See *Edgington v. Fitzmaurice* (1885), 29 Ch. Div. 459 at 483 (C.A.), Bowen L.J. ("the state of a man's mind is as much a fact as the state of his digestion"); *Prather v. King Resources Co.* (1972), 33 D.L.R. (3d) 112 at 118 (Alta. S.C.A.D.), Allen J.A.

4) Law

Under traditional doctrine, statements of fact are distinguished from statements of law. This may, in part, be an application to the legal context of the distinction between statements of fact and statements of opinion. If so, one would expect that a statement of opinion as to law by one who has no expertise in the subject may, in appropriate circumstances, constitute an opinion on which one ought not to reasonably rely. Thus, a vendor of a land warrant who misrepresented the legal effect of the document because he was unaware of recent legislative change was held to have made a statement of law rather than fact.[19] The distinction between statements of fact and law, however, is not typically explained as an application of the fact/opinion distinction. Perhaps this is because statements by a non-lawyer with respect to, for example, the lawfulness of certain conduct or the legal effect of a particular document would not normally be considered a legal opinion. Rather, such statements would be understood as statements of fact about the law, presumably gleaned from some reliable source. From this perspective, there appears to be little reason to distinguish between statements of fact and statements of law, and it is not surprising, therefore, that the distinction between fact and law has been notoriously difficult to apply in this and in other legal contexts. Thus, for example, statements with respect to "private rights" have been treated as statements of fact.[20] Similarly, an inaccurate representation that nothing in a deed of conveyance precluded the purchaser from carrying on his business was held to be a statement of fact.[21] In the context of restitutionary recovery of money paid under a mistake, the traditional distinction between the rule permitting recovery of money paid under mistake of fact and that denying relief where the money was paid under mistake of law, has more recently been abolished.[22] The underlying rationale for the denial of relief for representations of law has often been said to be the proposition that everyone should be taken to be cognisant of the law.[23] This is not a convincing

---

19 See *McKenzie v. Dwight* (1885), 11 O.A.R. 381 (C.A.). See also *Rule v. Pals*, [1928] 3 D.L.R. 295 (Sask. C.A.). A different result would be possible, presumably, if the representor possessed expertise with respect to the matter in question, on the basis that the legal opinion contained an implicit statement that it rested on a sound foundation.
20 *MacKenzie v. Royal Bank of Canada*, [1934] A.C. 468 (P.C.).
21 *Wauton v. Coppard*, [1889] 1 Ch. 92.
22 See *Canadian Pacific Airlines Ltd. v. British Columbia*, [1989] 1 S.C.R. 1133. And see generally P.D. Maddaugh and J.D. McCamus, *The Law of Restitution*, 2d ed. (Toronto: Canada Law Book, 2004) c. 11.
23 See, for example, *Rule v. Pals*, above note 19.

justification for the doctrine. While the assumed legal knowledge principle is evidently pertinent to the determination of guilt in a criminal proceeding or of liability in a tort claim, it appears to be singularly inapt in the present context. It is one thing to hold that an accused person cannot defend himself on the basis that he was unaware of the offence in question, quite another to suggest that since everyone is assumed to know the law, individuals who have entered into agreements on the faith of another party's false statement concerning a material aspect of the law, cannot be heard to have relied on the statement. Indeed, the latter proposition is the opposite of common sense. The victim of the misstatement of law is as surely harmed as the victim of a misstatement of fact.[24] It thus seems likely that, in due course, the distinction will be considered to be abolished in the present context as well.[25]

5) Materiality

The requirement that the misstatement of fact be material means that the misrepresentation must relate to a matter that would be considered by a reasonable person to be relevant to the decision to enter the agreement in question. Thus, statements made by the solicitor in *Redgrave v. Hurd*[26] to a prospective purchaser of his practice that the income yielded annually was a certain amount was obviously material to the decision of the purchaser to acquire the practice. On the other hand, where the misrepresentation relates to a factual matter that is not of great consequence, the materiality threshold will not be met. In a case where the vendors of property misrepresented the income yield of the property by a factor of less than 1 percent, the misrepresentation was not considered to be material.[27]

---

24   See Ontario Law Reform Commission, *Report on Amendment of the Law of Contract* (Toronto: Ministry of the Attorney General, 1987) at 242 (recommending abolition of the distinction in this context for this reason).

25   Where the misrepresentation of law is made in the context of negotiating a settlement of a dispute, however, different considerations prevail and the misrepresentee may reasonably be taken to have assumed the risk of failing to make appropriate inquiries. With respect to the role of mistake in the context of agreements of compromise, see generally Chapter 13, section C.

26   See above note 1. And see, for example, *Sanitary Refuse Collectors v. Ottawa (City)*, [1972] 1 O.R. 296 (H.C.) (misleading information re tender); *F. & B. Transport Ltd. v. White Truck Motor Sales Manitoba Ltd.* (1965), 51 W.W.R. 124 (Man. C.A.) (incorrect model year of truck); *Southwood Mall Ltd. v. Scardina*, [1981] 6 W.W.R. 569 (Man. Co. Ct.) (shopping mall—misleading estimate of "tenant's work" inducing lease).

27   *Hinchey v. Gonda*, [1955] O.W.N. 125 (H.C.J.).

6) Inducement

In addition to being shown to be material, the misrepresentation must have constituted an inducement to enter the agreement upon which the misrepresentee relied. Thus, a representee who undertakes his or her own separate investigation of the facts would not be held to have relied on the misrepresentation.[28] On the other hand, it is clearly established that the representee has no obligation to engage in "due diligence" and make such an independent investigation, even where the means of doing so are made available by the misrepresentor.[29] Further, it is clearly established that the misrepresentation need not be the exclusive or even a predominant inducement for entering the agreement.[30] It must be established, simply, that it was an inducement. Moreover, once it is established that a misrepresentation is of such a nature that it is liable to induce the misrepresentee to enter the contract, it would be presumed against the misrepresentor that such inducement did occur.[31] Although, in *Redgrave v. Hurd*,[32] Jessel M.R. suggested that an inference of law that inducement occurred arises in such circumstances, this view has not been accepted,[33] and it appears to be that the inference is one of fact rather than law.[34]

C. NON-DISCLOSURE AS MISREPRESENTATION

The traditional doctrine concerning contract formation holds that a party negotiating an agreement is not subject to a duty to disclose material facts to the other party.[35] Nonetheless, there are exceptional circumstances in which silence or non-disclosure is treated, in effect, as misrepresentation and provides a basis for rescission of the ultimate

---

28 *Attwood v. Small* (1838), 6 Cl. & F. 232, 7 E.R. 684.
29 See *Redgrave v. Hurd*, above note 1 at 13.
30 See *McCallum v. Proctor* (1914), 26 O.W.R. 481 (S.C.A.D.); *Fleming v. Boultbee* (1929), 37 O.W.N. 293 (H.C.).
31 *Mathias v. Yetts* (1882), 46 L.T. (N.S.) 497 (C.A.); *Baker v. Guaranty Savings & Loan Association*, [1931] S.C.R. 199 at 208.
32 Above note 1 at 21.
33 See, for example, *Smith v. Chadwick* (1884), 9 App. Cas. 187 at 196, Lord Blackburn (rejecting this view).
34 See, for example, *L.K. Oil & Gas Ltd. v. Canalands Energy Corp.* (1989), 60 D.L.R. (4th) 490, leave to appeal to S.C.C. refused, [1990] 1 W.W.R. lxxi n (S.C.C.).
35 *Smith v. Hughes* (1871), L.R. 6 Q.B. 597 (Div'l Ct.). And see Chapter 13, section B.

agreement.[36] First, misrepresentation has been found in the context of half-truths, that is, partial disclosure of true facts that creates a misleading impression. In a leading case,[37] the plaintiffs were purchasers of a property that they intended to use for a brickyard. The vendor himself had indicated to the purchaser that he thought there were restrictive covenants that might prevent the property's use for that purpose. The plaintiffs asked the vendor's solicitors if there were any restrictions on the use of the property. The solicitor replied that he was not aware of any. This was literally true. Unfortunately, however, the solicitor did not go on to explain that he had not checked to determine whether this was so. In fact, the land could not be used lawfully for these purposes. This half-truth made on the vendor's behalf provided a basis for rescission.

A second exception to the traditional rule relates to conduct typically referred to as "active concealment" of the truth. In a Manitoba case,[38] for example, the owner of a small apartment block who intended to put it up for sale noticed a crack in one wall that appeared to be rather serious. He sought advice from a structural engineer who recommended substantial and expensive repairs. Rather than repair the building, the owner concealed the crack by covering it over with matching bricks. The property was then placed on the market. The eventual sale was rescinded for misrepresentation. Similarly, it has been held that refusal to grant a purchaser of real estate access to the premises for fear that a visit would reveal a significant defect in the property constituted fraudulent concealment.[39]

A third exception imposes a duty to disclose where changing circumstances affect the truth of an earlier statement. In a leading case,[40] O'Flanagan, a medical doctor, accurately advised a prospective purchaser of his practice that it was bringing in £2,000 a year. Before the contract was entered into, however, O'Flanagan became ill and his prac-

---

36   See generally S.M. Waddams, "Pre-contractual Duties of Disclosure" in P. Cane and J. Stapleton, eds., *Essays for Patrick Atiyah* (Oxford: Clarendon Press, 1991) at 237–56; S. O'Byrne, "Culpable Silence: Liability for Non-Disclosure in the Contractual Arena" (1998) 30 Can. Bus. L.J. 239. And see E.A. Farnsworth, "Comment on Waddams" (1991) 19 Can. Bus. L.J. 351.

37   *Nottingham Patent Brick and Tile Co. v. Butler* (1886), 16 Q.B.D. 778 (C.A.). See also *Doon v. Wilks* (1996), 5 R.P.R. (3d) 282 (B.C.S.C.); *MacLeod v. Ruck* (1985), 3 B.C.L.R. (2d) 35 (C.A.). A similar explanation may be offered for *Souder v. Wereschuk* (2004), 245 D.L.R. (4th) 385 (Alta. C.A.) (separation agreement—non-disclosure of lottery winnings in husband's statement of assets).

38   *Gronau v. Schlamp Investments Ltd.* (1974), 52 D.L.R. (3d) 631 (Man. Q.B.).

39   See *Abel v. McDonald* (1964), 45 D.L.R. (2d) 198 (Ont. C.A.).

40   *With v. O'Flanagan*, [1936] Ch. 575 (C.A.). See also *Hogar Estates in Trust v. Shebron Holdings Ltd.* (1979), 101 D.L.R. (3d) 509 (Ont. H.C.J.).

tice became worthless. Failure to disclose this fact provided a ground for rescission.

Apart from these exceptional cases involving misleading conduct, there are a few categories of contractual relationships that are considered to be *uberrima fides* (that is, requiring the utmost good faith), with respect to which active duties to disclose are imposed. Insurance contracts are considered to be *uberrima fides* and both parties are required to disclose material facts to the other, failing which the contract is unenforceable.[41] Similarly, certain types of family arrangements involving, for example, agreements to settle disputes concerning entitlements to family assets,[42] are placed in this category. Contracts between parties who have a fiduciary relationship[43] are also classified as requiring the utmost good faith.

Beyond these traditional exemptions and contracts *uberrima fides*, however, there are cases that cannot be easily explained within the traditional doctrine. Consider, for example, *Bank of British Columbia v. Wren*.[44] In this case, the bank sued to enforce certain written guarantees given by the defendant to the bank as security for a loan made to a corporate party. Before signing the last guarantee, the defendant asked the credit manager of the bank about the current status of the collateral pledged by the borrower to secure the loan. The credit manager honestly answered that he did not know but would make inquiries. Thereupon, the defendant signed the guarantee, not realizing that the collateral had previously been released by the bank. The court held, in these circumstances, that the plaintiff "in failing to disclose material facts"[45] had made a misrepresentation to the defendant and the guarantee was rescinded.

The *Wren* case cannot easily be explained within the established categories of cases requiring disclosure. Neither can the decision of the Ontario Court of Appeal in *McGrath v. MacLean*[46] in which it was held that

41 *London Assurance v. Mansel* (1879), 11 Ch. D. 303; *Joel v. Law Union and Insurance Co.*, [1908] 2 K.B. 863 (C.A.). And see R.A. Hasson, "The Doctrine of *Uberrima Fides* in Insurance Law—A Critical Evaluation" (1969) 32 Mod. L. Rev. 615.

42 *Greenwood v. Greenwood* (1863), 2 De G. J. & S. 28, 46 E.R. 285; *Gordon v. Gordon* (1819), 3 Swans. 400; 36 E.R. 910. But not a separation agreement entered into by spouses. See also, however, *Souder v. Wereschuk*, above note 37 (rescission of separation agreement on the basis of non-disclosure of lottery winnings).

43 See *S. (F.) v. H. (C.)* (1994), 120 D.L.R. (4th) 432 (Ont. Gen. Div.), aff'd on other grounds (1996), 133 D.L.R. (4th) 767 (Ont. C.A.).

44 (1973), 38 D.L.R. (3d) 759 (B.C.S.C.). See also *Souder v. Wereschuk*, above note 37.

45 *Bank of British Columbia v. Wren*, ibid. at 762.

46 (1979), 95 D.L.R. (3d) 144 (Ont. C.A.), leave to appeal to S.C.C. refused April 7, 1979.

a vendor of land may be under a duty to disclose the existence of latent defects that render the premises "unsafe for human habitation." In an attempt to explain *Wren*, it might be argued that guarantees are a type of transaction that could or should be classified as *uberrima fides*. At the present time, however, it appears that contracts of guarantee are not so characterized.[47] It seems unlikely, moreover, that courts will consider that the negotiation of a guarantee imposes a duty on the principal creditor to disclose all material facts. Further, no such solution appears available with respect to real estate transactions. It may be then, that the *Wren* and *McGrath* decisions may be considered to be harbingers of the adoption of a more generalized exception to the traditional rule permitting non-disclosure of material facts in the context of contractual negotiations.

D. NON-DISCLOSURE AND GOOD FAITH

Under American law, an exception to the traditional rule that parties negotiating agreements have no duty to disclose material facts to one another is more "open-textured" than the more limited exceptions thus recognized to date in Canadian common law. In the American jurisprudence, the duty to disclose is often linked with a duty to act in good faith. Thus, the *Restatement of Contracts*[48] provides in section 161(b) that a representor's non-disclosure of a known fact will be treated as equivalent to a misrepresentation in the following circumstances:

> where he knows that disclosure of the fact would correct a mistake of the other party as to a basic assumption on which that party is making a contract and if non-disclosure of the fact amounts to a failure to act in good faith and in accordance with reasonable standards of fair dealing.[49]

The American cases[50] reflected in the *Restatement* rule include cases rather similar to the decisions in *Wren* and *McGrath*, discussed above.

---

47   See *Hamilton v. Watson* (1845), 12 Cl. & F. 109; *Royal Bank of Canada v. Hislop* (1990), 62 D.L.R. (4th) 228 (B.C.C.A.); *Royal Bank of Scotland plc v. Etridge (No. 2)*, [2001] 3 W.L.R. 1021 at 1059 and 1082; J. Cartwright, *Misrepresentation* (London: Sweet & Maxwell, 2002) at 348–49.

48   American Law Institute, *Restatement of Contracts 2d* (St. Paul: American Law Institute, 1981).

49   *Ibid.* at 431.

50   See, for example, *Obde v. Schlemeyer*, 353 P.2d 672 (Wash. 1960) (sale of property infested by termites); *Federal Deposit Insurance Corporation v. W.R. Grace & Co.*, 877 F.2d 614 (7th Cir. 1989) (borrower obliged to disclose circumstances rendering the proposed collateral worthless).

More generally, the American cases appear to deal with situations where the information relates to a fundamental matter that, if disclosed, would cause the other party to refrain from entering the agreement and where the non-disclosure could not be justified on the ground that the informed party should be able to take advantage of his or her superior knowledge in the particular bargaining context. Thus, where a prospective employee indicated concerns about job security, the employer's failure to disclose the insecurity surrounding the position offered constituted misrepresentation by non-disclosure.[51] Similarly, an apostate priest was held required to disclose his status when applying for appointment to the faculty of a Catholic university.[52]

Although no equivalent doctrine has yet been plainly recognized in Canadian common law, the Court of Appeal for Ontario, in a recent decision, has expressed support for the recognition of a similar duty to disclose where non-disclosure would constitute a failure to act in good faith. The disclosure issue in *978011 Ontario Ltd. v. Cornell Engineering Co.*[53] arose in the unusual context of a services agreement that had been drafted by the prospective employee. Stevens, the president and principal owner of the employer, Cornell Engineering, had been a mentor and advisor of the prospective employee, Macdonald. When recruiting Macdonald, Stevens invited him to draft a services contract. Macdonald included in the draft a rather generous termination provision. When Macdonald presented the agreement to Stevens for signature, Stevens declined to read the agreement and simply asked whether Macdonald was satisfied with the terms of the agreement. Upon the eventual termination of the employment, Macdonald sought to enforce the termination arrangement. Cornell Engineering argued that it should have been made aware by Macdonald of the unusual nature of the termination provision of the agreement. Thus, the issue raised for the court's consideration was whether a duty to disclose the nature of the term existed, notwithstanding the election of Stevens to forego a reading of the terms of the agreement. Although the Court of Appeal held that, in the circumstances, an individual who declined to examine the agreement was simply bound by its terms, the court nonetheless

51 *Pearson v. Simmonds Precision Products*, 624 A.2d 1134 (Vt. 1993).
52 *Fuller v. DePaul University*, 12 N.E.2d 213 (Ill. App. 1938). Compare with *Courtwright v. C.P. Ltd.* (1983), 5 D.L.R. (4th) 488 (Ont. H.C.), aff'd (1985), 18 D.L.R. (4th) 639 (Ont. C.A.) (similar result on basis of strained application of fiduciary duty doctrine).
53 (2001), 198 D.L.R. (4th) 615 (Ont. C.A.). Compare with *Peel Condominium Corp. No. 505 v. Cam-Valley Homes Ltd.* (2001), 53 O.R. (3d) 1 (C.A.).

went on to consider whether, in other circumstances, a duty to disclose the nature of the term might arise.

Although the court conceded that in the absence of a special relationship "the common law in Canada has yet to recognize that in the negotiation of a contract, there is a duty to have regard to the other person's interests, namely, to act in good faith,"[54] the court went on to observe that there are, in fact, "circumstances where the law requires more than self-interested dealing on the part of a party."[55] Such circumstances arise where, firstly, one party "relies on the other for information necessary to make an informed choice and, secondly, the party in possession of the information has an opportunity, by withholding (or concealing) information, to bring about the choice made by the other party."[56] In refining this analysis, the court placed reliance on an article by Finn[57] in which the author advocated recognition of a duty to disclose where required by a good-faith standard. More particularly, the court adopted the suggestion by Finn that the following five factors would indicate situations where the duty to disclose should be imposed:

(1) A past course of dealing between the parties in which reliance for advice, etc., has been an accepted feature;

(2) The explicit assumption by one party of advisory responsibilities;

(3) The relevant positions of the parties particularly in their access to information and in their understanding of possible demands of the dealing;

(4) The manner in which the parties were brought together, and the expectations that could create in the relying parties; and

(5) [W]hether "trust and confidence knowingly [has] been reposed by one party or the other."[58]

The court then applied these factors to the circumstances of this case and found that in each instance, the factors weighed against, rather than in favour, of the imposition of a duty to disclose. In essence, the relative seniority of Stevens, the mentoring relationship he had over the years with Macdonald, and his decision not to read a rather straightforward document, weighed against imposing a duty of disclosure on Macdonald. If Macdonald had been aware that Stevens was mistaken

---

54 *978011 Ontario Ltd. v. Cornell Engineering Co.*, *ibid.* at 625, Weiler J.A.

55 *Ibid.* at 626.

56 *Ibid.*

57 See P. Finn, "The Fiduciary Principle" in T. Youdan, ed., *Equity, Fiduciaries and Trusts* (Toronto: Carswell, 1989) 1 at 10–24.

58 Above note 53 at 626–27 quoting Finn, *ibid.* at 20.

as to the terms of the agreement, an error of this kind would, on traditional principles, prevent formation of the agreement.[59] This point was not pursued by the court, however, and the discussion thus appears to suggest that even in the absence of an awareness of the other party's error, the party with superior knowledge of material facts, including the terms of the agreement to be signed, could be subject to a duty to disclose on the basis of the five-factor test articulated by Finn. If such a duty is to be recognized, of course, it will require the drawing of a somewhat delicate line between situations where a party negotiating an agreement ought to be able to profit from superior knowledge and situations where such behaviour is considered inappropriate. American experience suggests that a possible guideline in making this distinction would be to consider whether the information in question was acquired intentionally by the bargainor with superior knowledge and, perhaps, where it can be argued that the financial incentive of being able to profit from the acquisition of such knowledge provides a useful stimulus to commercial activity of the kind in issue.[60] Although this criterion would itself, no doubt, be difficult to apply, it does usefully signal the importance of avoiding the imposition of disclosure obligations that will both surprise commercial actors and reduce unattractively the incentives for investing in the acquisition of superior knowledge.

E. RESCISSION AND RESTITUTION

A party who is able to establish that an agreement was induced by an operative misrepresentation may seek the remedy of rescission. In essence, the remedy of rescission involves an unwinding or setting aside of the contractual relationship between the parties. Upon rescission, the as yet unperformed obligations of the party become unenforceable. With respect to obligations that have been performed, an agreement that is subject to the remedy of rescission is voidable rather than void *ab initio*, with the consequence that the agreement is considered to be an enforceable one until a rescission of the agreement is achieved. Upon rescission, however, the parties are to be restored to their initial pre-contractual position by requiring restoration of benefits transferred

---

59 See *Smith v. Hughes* (1871) L.R. 6 Q.B. 597, for discussion of which see Chapter 13, section B.

60 See A.T. Kronman, "Mistake, Disclosure, Information and the Law of Contracts" (1978) 7 J. Legal Stud. 1; E.A. Farnsworth, *Farnsworth on Contracts*, 2d ed. (New York: Aspen, 1998) at 453–56.

under the agreement. In this sense, then, the rescission of the contract in question has a retrospective or *ab initio* effect. Thus, in the case of a rescission of a simple contract for the purchase and sale of goods, rescission will be coupled with return of the goods to the seller and a return of the purchase price to the buyer. During the period prior to rescission of the agreement, however, the fact that the agreement is voidable rather than void has the effect that property in the goods in question would pass to the buyer in the manner intended by the parties until such time as rescission has the effect of revesting the property in the goods in the seller.

There are a number of limitations or "bars" to rescissionary relief. The most important of these is that relief will not be available if it is not possible to effect a mutual restoration of the benefits conferred by the parties, one upon another, or, as is sometimes said, a restoration of the *status quo ante* or a *restitutio in integrum*. Upon an equitable decree of rescission, then, any orders required to effect a mutual restoration of benefits conferred would be issued. Indeed, courts of equity possessed a greater ability than courts of common law to tailor orders with this objective in mind. Hence, even in the case of fraudulent misrepresentation, the misrepresentee might choose to seek a decree of rescission in equity. Although the remedy of rescission for misrepresentation developed initially in equity, it ultimately came to be recognized that in cases of fraudulent misrepresentation, the courts of common law would also treat agreements induced by fraud as voidable.[61] In equity, however, the remedy was not limited to cases of fraud. Equitable rescission is available for agreements induced by merely non-fraudulent or innocent misrepresentations.

Equitable rescission of an agreement would normally be accomplished by the obtaining of a judicial decree to this effect. Nonetheless, the action of a misrepresentee in giving notice of an election to rescind the agreement to the misrepresentor may have the practical effect of achieving rescission because the ultimate decree of rescission would normally treat the rescission as effective on the date of giving notice of the election to rescind. In this limited sense, then, rescission may be considered to be a "self-help" remedy.[62] Indeed, if a mutual restoration

---

61   *Erlanger v. New Sombrero Phosphate Co.* (1878), 3 App. Cas. 1218 (H.L.). Thus, courts of common law would not allow relief to a misrepresentee who had received but not restored an asset, thus forcing the misrepresentee to seek rescission in equity, which could only be achieved by restoring the asset to the transferee.

62   See generally J. O'Sullivan, "Rescission as a Self-help Remedy: A Critical Analysis" (2000) 59 Cambridge L.J. 509; Cartwright, above note 47 at 63–66.

of the parties can be achieved without judicial intervention, the election to rescind coupled with restoration could render a judicial proceeding unnecessary. If, however, either the misrepresentor brought an action to enforce the agreement against the misrepresentee or the misrepresentee required judicial intervention in order to effect a restoration of the *status quo ante*, the misrepresentee would be required to seek a rescissionary decree in order to achieve an effective rescission of the agreement.

Although notice of an election to rescind would normally be effective upon communication of the election to the misrepresentor,[63] communication of the election to rescind may not be required in all circumstances. Thus, in *Car and Universal Finance Co. Ltd. v. Caldwell*,[64] the seller of a car was held to have effectively rescinded the agreement of sale even though no communication with the misrepresentor had taken place. In this case, a buyer, acting fraudulently, purchased the car from the seller in return for a cheque that was subsequently dishonoured. When the seller discovered the fraud, he was unable to find the purchaser but he immediately contacted the police and the automobile association. Subsequently, the buyer sold the car to a good-faith purchaser. It was held by the Court of Appeal that the seller had effectively rescinded the agreement by contacting the police and the automobile association, this being all that the seller could reasonably do in the circumstances. Accordingly, title to the car did not pass to the third-party purchaser. This exception to the general requirement that notice of the election to rescind be communicated to the misrepresentor is not likely to be extended, however, beyond the circumstances of this case.[65] Thus, in the absence of fraud or, perhaps, of a situation in which the misrepresentor has made the giving of notice impossible, the requirement of actual notice of the election to rescind is very likely to obtain.

1) Restoration of the *Status Quo Ante*

Under traditional doctrine, the decree of rescission will not be made available in a case where a restoration of the *status quo ante* is not pos-

---

63 *Abram Steamship Co. v. Westville Shipping Co.*, [1923] A.C. 773 at 781, Lord Atkinson. See also *Guarantee Co. of North America v. Gordon Capital* (1999), 178 D.L.R. (4th) 1 at para. 39, Bastarache J.

64 [1965] 1 Q.B. 525.

65 For criticism and suggested reform of the doctrine so as to require notice, see Ontario Law Reform Commission, *Report on Sale of Goods*, vol. 2 (Toronto: Attorney General, 1979) at 276.

sible.[66] Such a restoration is obviously possible where the benefits that have passed between the parties can be restored *in specie*. The more difficult question, however, is whether rescission can be granted in circumstances where this is not literally true—for example, where goods that have been transferred have perished. Similarly, in the case of the sale of a business, the possible deterioration in the value of the business and the profits made by the purchaser while in possession of the business may complicate the exercise effecting a *restitutio in integrum*. Courts of equity were able to achieve practical justice in such cases by coupling a decree of rescission with orders for an accounting of profits or an indemnity. As Lord Blackburn observed in *Erlanger v. New Sombrero Phosphate Co.*:[67] "But a court of equity could not give damages, and, unless it can rescind the contract, can give no relief. And on the other hand, it can take accounts of profits, and make allowance for deterioration. And I think the practice has always been for a court of equity to give this relief whenever, by the exercise of its powers, it can do what is practically just, though it cannot restore the parties precisely to the state they were in before the contract."[68]

The objective of such awards is restitutionary in nature, however, rather than providing a more comprehensive award of damages for injuries sustained as a result of entering into the agreement.[69] In *Whittington v. Seale-Hayne*,[70] for example, the plaintiff had entered into an agreement to lease a farm on the faith of a false representation that the property was in a sanitary condition. The plaintiff lessee took possession of the property and incurred various expenses in the course of conducting a poultry business. The plaintiff purchased poultry stock, made certain improvements to the premises in the form of repairs required by the local municipality and paid taxes on the property. The plaintiff sought, in addition to rescission of the agreement, compensation for the poultry stock that died as a result of the unsanitary conditions, for the improvements made to the premises and for the municipal taxes paid on the property. As well, the plaintiff claimed for the profits that could have been made on the poultry business were it not for the

---

66   See, for example, *Morin v. Anger* (1930), 66 O.L.R. 327 (S.C.A.D.); *Lowe v. Suburban Developers Ltd.*, [1962] O.R. 1029 (C.A.); *Blanchette v. Shabatowski* (1981), 29 A.R. 158 (Q.B.); *King v. Walmar Ventures Ltd.* (1986), 10 B.C.L.R. (2d) 15 (C.A.).

67   Above note 61.

68   *Ibid.* at 1278. See also *Wandinger v. Lake* (1977), 78 D.L.R. (3d) 305 at 315 (Ont. H.C.J.), Lerner J.

69   *Newbigging v. Adam* (1886), 34 Ch. D. 582 (C.A.).

70   (1900), 82 L.T. 49.

unsanitary condition of the premises. In the result, the plaintiff recovered only the cost of the improvements and the municipal rates, both of which expenditures had conferred value on the misrepresentor. The other items of loss required compensation of a kind that was not available in equity.

The courts are more prepared to exercise their discretionary powers to unwind a transaction in a case of fraud than in a case of innocent misrepresentation. This proposition was relied upon by the British Columbia Court of Appeal in rescinding an agreement for the purchase of a motel company in *Kupchak v. Dayson Holdings Co. Ltd.*[71] The Kupchaks had purchased the shares of a motel company from Dayson Holdings in return for two properties conveyed to the holding company and mortgages taken back by the holding company on the assets of the motel company securing payment of the remainder of the purchase price. The Kupchaks took possession of the business and operated it for only a few months before discovering that Dayson Holdings' representations with respect to the profitability of the business were fraudulent falsehoods. This discovery led to an exchange between the lawyers representing each party and a threat by the Kupchaks to withhold mortgage payments until the dispute was resolved. Subsequently, Dayson Holdings sold an undivided half-interest in one of the properties that it had acquired from the Kupchaks and erected an apartment building on the premises. More than one year later, the holding company unsuccessfully sought foreclosure of the mortgage and the Kupchaks, who remained in possession of the premises and continued operating the business, sought rescission of the agreement. In defending the rescission claim, the holding company relied on its inability to restore to the Kupchaks the now-jointly owned premises upon which the apartment building was located. The Court of Appeal held that Dayson Holdings could not resist rescission on the basis of its own dealing with property it had acquired by fraud and granted rescission of the transaction. In lieu of requiring restoration of the effected property, however, the court substituted an order requiring Dayson Holdings to compensate the Kupchaks for the value of that property at the time of the initial transfer to the holding company. Although it had been submitted by Dayson Holdings that such compensation is "more like damages" than an account or indemnity, the court held that it had the jurisdiction to order a compensation that was designed to "effect substantial restitution"[72] under a decree for rescission. We will return later in this chapter to a

---

71   (1965), 53 D.L.R. (2d) 482 (B.C.C.A.).
72   *Ibid.* at 486.

consideration of whether such monetary restitutionary awards might be made even in the absence of a decree of rescission.

2) Affirmation

Just as a party may elect to rescind an agreement on the basis of misrepresentation, so too a party may elect to affirm the transaction. Such an affirmation will be irrevocable. The affirmation can arise, however, only after the misrepresentee becomes aware of the nature of the misrepresentation. Further, to be effective, the affirmation must constitute an informed choice in the sense that it requires knowledge that the falsehood gives rise to a right to terminate the transaction. Thus, an English case[73] holds that, in circumstances where the misrepresentee obtained legal advice but was not made aware of the right to rescind for misrepresentation until he retained the services of a second solicitor, the misrepresentee retained the right to rescind until he became aware of its existence. The affirmation may be communicated by words or inferred from conduct. Thus, affirmation may be inferred from the fact that after learning of the misrepresentation, the misrepresentee continued with[74] or demanded performance of the contract.[75] Similarly, where a manufacturer was induced to lease machines on the faith of a misrepresentation, continued use of the machines after learning of the misrepresentation has been held to preclude rescission for misrepresentation.[76] The possibility of affirmation by conduct was at issue in *Kupchak v. Dayson Holdings Ltd.*[77] After learning of the misrepresentation, the Kupchaks remained in possession of and operated the hotel business for more than a year. The British Columbia court held that the conduct of the Kupchaks did not amount to affirmation. Shortly after learning of the misrepresentation, their solicitors had communicated the Kupchaks' concerns to Dayson Holdings in such a manner as to signal an intention to repudiate. Moreover, as it was not feasible for the Kupchaks to force a restoration of the hotel business upon Dayson Holdings, their conduct in continuing to manage the business was

---

73 *Peyman v. Lanjani,* [1984] 3 All E.R. 703. And see *Coastal States Pty. Ltd. v. Melevende,* [1965] V.R. 433. See also *Barron Estate v. Kelly,* [1918] 2 W.W.R. 131 (S.C.C.).

74 *Grant Campbell & Co. v. Devon Lumber Co. Ltd.* (1914), 7 O.W.N. 209 (S.C.A.D.).

75 *Panzer v. Zeifman* (1978), 88 D.L.R. (3d) 131 (Ont. C.A.).

76 *United Shoe Machinery of Canada v. Brunet,* [1909] A.C. 330 (P.C.). See also *Long v. Lloyd,* [1958] 1 W.L.R. 753 (C.A.) (continued use of lorry).

77 Above note 71. See also *Kellogg Brown & Root Inc. v. Aerotech Herman Nelson Inc.* (2004), 238 D.L.R. (4th) 594 (Man. C.A.).

reasonable in all the circumstances. Conduct that leads the misrepresentator to reasonably believe that affirmation has occurred, however, will communicate affirmation and, alternatively, may give rise to the application of estoppel doctrine.[78]

3) Intervention of Third-Party Rights

It follows from the proposition that transactions induced by misrepresentation are voidable rather than void that the title to any property acquired under the agreement by the misrepresentor is a voidable one. Until such time as the title is avoided, however, the misrepresentor holds legal title and can pass title in the asset to a *bona fide* purchaser for value without notice of the underlying equity or difficulty with the title. The policy underlying this equitable principle is evidently that if a choice must be made between favouring the interests of one who has been induced into a contract by misrepresentation and has either not discovered the problem or, if the problem has been discovered, has not taken action to effect a rescission of the contract and another party who has purchased the property in good faith from the misrepresentor, the interests of the latter should be preferred. Once the election to rescind has been taken, however, equity avoids the title of the transferor and in the contest between the misrepresentee and a subsequent purchaser of the asset, the rights of the misrepresentee are preferred. Under this approach, then, one who, albeit innocently, gives up possession of assets on the faith of a misrepresentation is at risk of the intervention of third-party rights until such time as the misrepresentation is discovered and reasonable steps have been taken to unwind the transaction. Generally, the misrepresentee who has elected to rescind must notify the misrepresentor of that election. As we have seen, however, in exceptional circumstances, where such communication is not possible, other reasonable steps may be held to constitute an effective election to rescind.[79]

4) Execution of the Agreement

Execution or performance of the agreement has been held to constitute a barrier to rescission in a variety of contexts. In the context of real estate transactions induced by innocent misrepresentation, for example, the

---

78   See, for example, *Peyman v. Lanjani*, above note 73. A subjective intent to affirm would not be necessary to ground an estoppel. See Cartwright, above note 47 at 79. And see generally Chapter 8.

79   See *Car and Universal Finance Co. Ltd. v. Caldwell*, above note 64.

execution doctrine has been applied rather rigidly to the effect that once that transaction closes by transfer of the purchase price in exchange for a conveyance of the property in question, the transaction can no longer be rescinded for misrepresentation. The rigidity of the doctrine is well illustrated by the decision of the Supreme Court of Canada in *Redican v. Nesbitt*.[80] This case involved the purchase of a leasehold property. The transaction closed with the exchange of an assignment of the lease and a cheque for the purchase money. A few days later, upon learning that the premises had been misdescribed in material respects—this being alleged by the purchaser to be the first opportunity to discover these problems—the purchaser stopped payment on the cheque and sought rescission of the agreement. In response to the argument that the execution of the contract precluded rescission, the purchaser argued that the payment by cheque was merely conditional and, as payment had not been achieved, execution had not yet occurred. The Supreme Court held that although the failure of the cheque to clear would give rise to a right of action on the part of the vendor, the parties had intended the transaction to close and the contract was therefore executed. Rescission was therefore no longer available. The Court emphasized, however, that execution of the contract would not constitute a bar to rescission in a case of fraudulent misrepresentation.[81] Presumably, the somewhat rigid approach taken to the execution bar in the real estate context may rest on a perception that it is a customary practice for purchasers to investigate title and examine the subject premises prior to the closing of the transaction. As *Redican v. Nesbitt* illustrates, however, the rule is capable of having a harsh effect in circumstances where an inspection on the premises cannot, as a practical matter, precede closing. Accordingly, the better view appears to be that execution should be considered to be a material but not dispositive factor in determining whether rescission should remain available and there exists some judicial support for this approach.[82]

Traditionally, the execution bar has also been applied in the contexts of sale of securities[83] and sale of goods so as to preclude rescission. In the latter context, however, this limitation has been applied

---

80   [1924] S.C.R. 135.
81   In this context, the Court indicated, rescission would be barred only by an inability to make *restitutio in integrum*. Where that inability results from the conduct of the wrongdoer, however, it will not constitute a bar to rescissionary relief. See *ibid.* at 152; *Kupchak v. Dayson Holdings Ltd.*, above note 71.
82   *S-244 Holdings Ltd. v. Seamore Building Systems Ltd.*, [1994] 8 W.W.R. 185 at 190 (B.C.C.A.), Cumming J.A.
83   *Seddon v. North Eastern Salt Co. Ltd.*, [1905] 1 Ch. 326.

more flexibly in the modern cases. In *Leaf v. International Galleries*,[84] Denning L.J. suggested that innocent misrepresentation might provide a ground for rescission even after execution. Denning L.J. reasoned, however, that the right to rescind for misrepresentation could not survive beyond the point in time when the right to terminate the contract for breach of contract would expire,[85] on the ground that "an innocent misrepresentation is much less potent than a breach of contract."[86] In the circumstances of this case, the time was well past for either form of relief and it was therefore not necessary for Denning L.J. to offer guidance on the nature of the limitation to be applied to rescission. It appears rather likely, however, that the courts will permit rescission until there has occurred, as the Manitoba Court of Appeal has observed, "the passage of a reasonable period of time for the purchaser to determine whether representations are true."[87]

5) Laches

Unreasonable delay in bringing a claim for rescission also constitutes an equitable defence to the claim. In an influential articulation of the defence in *Lindsay Petroleum Oil Co. v. Hurd*,[88] Sir Barnes Peacock stressed that mere delay alone would not constitute the defence. The delay must be such as to indicate that the misrepresentee has essentially waived the remedy or it must have created a situation in which the granting of relief would be unfairly prejudicial to the misrepresentor. He further explained: "But in every case, if an argument against relief, which otherwise would be just, is founded upon mere delay, the delay of course not amounting to a bar by any statute of limitations, the validity of that defence must be tried upon principles substantially equitable. Two circumstances, always important in such cases, are the length of the delay and the nature of the acts done during the interval, which might affect either party and cause a balance of justice or injustice in taking the one course or the other, so far as relates to the

---

84   [1950] 2 K.B. 86 (C.A.).

85   Under the applicable provisions of sale of goods legislation, that right would expire when, after the lapse of a reasonable period of time he retains the goods without intimating to the seller that he has rejected them. See, for example, *Sale of Goods Act*, R.S.O. 1990, c. S.1, s. 34(c).

86   *Leaf v. International Galleries*, above note 84 at 90–91. Compare, however, the opinion of Lord Evershed M.R., favouring retention of the traditional execution bar. See *ibid.* at 94–95.

87   *Ennis v. Klassen* (1990), 70 D.L.R. (4th) 321 at 331 (Man. C.A.), Huband J.A.

88   (1874), L.R. 5 P.C. 221.

346 THE LAW OF CONTRACTS

remedy."[89] The view that the availability of this defence rests on the weighing of the appropriateness of the relief from the misrepresentee's perspective against the length of the delay and any resulting prejudice to the misrepresentor is well accepted in Canadian cases.[90]

6) Merger in a Subsequent Warranty

In the drafting of commercial agreements, it is not uncommon for the parties to repeat in the agreement itself representations that have been made during the course of the negotiation of the agreement. Often such provisions will take the form that the promissor "represents and warrants" that certain statements are true.[91] When the former representation now becomes a term of the agreement, the falsity of the representation becomes a breach of contract, entitling the misrepresentee to the normal remedies for breach of contract.[92] In the present context, however, we may consider whether the rescissionary remedy for the pre-contractual misrepresentation remains available. Although the point is not free from difficulty, the traditional position at common law appears to be that once the misrepresentation becomes repeated as a term of the contract, the rescissionary remedy is no longer available. In *Pennsylvania Shipping Company Co. v. Compagnie Nationale de Navigation*,[93] a case concerning a time charter of a tanker, the charterer had asked, during the course of negotiating the agreement, for quite detailed information concerning the specifications of the vessel. The information was provided and then made the subject of explicit guarantees in the charterparty agreement. The statements were not correct with the result that the vessel was unsuitable for the charterer's purpose. The court held that rescission for pre-contractual misrepresentation was unavailable to the charterer as the pre-contractual representations had merged with the warranties or guarantees in the agreement. Thus, the charterer's rights to terminate the contract rested on the proper analysis of his remedies under the agreement itself. This approach was justified by the English Court of Appeal in *Leaf v. Inter-*

---

89 *Ibid.* at 240.
90 See, for example, *Consolidated Investments Ltd. v. Acres* (1917), 32 D.L.R. 579 (Alta. S.C.) and *Kupchak v. Dayson Holdings Co. Ltd.*, above note 71.
91 See further, Chapter 18, section D.
92 See Chapters 22–24.
93 [1936] 2 All E.R. 1167 (K.B.). See also *Woods v. Borstel* (1962), 34 D.L.R. (2d) 68 (Alta. S.C.A.D.) (sale of goods). Compare with *Compagnie Française de Chemins de Fer Paris-Orleans v. Leeston Shipping Co. Ltd.* (1919), 1 Ll. L.R. 235 at 237–38.

national Galleries[94] on the basis that once the representation becomes a contractual term, sufficient remedies are available at common law for breach of contract and thus, the intervention of equity, with a rescission decree, is either unnecessary or inappropriate. In England, this merger doctrine has been abolished by statute.[95] In Canadian common law, however, it is likely that the traditional common law persists. As a practical matter, however, the point is not likely to arise with great frequency as the kinds of commercial agreements that contain explicit contractual representations are also likely to include contractual provisions precluding remedies for pre-contractual misrepresentations.[96]

7) Restitution without Rescission

As we have seen,[97] where a partial restoration of the properties transferred to the other party remains possible, monetary compensation for that portion that cannot be restored may be substituted. A more difficult question is whether monetary restitutionary awards might be made in a case where restoration of the property transferred is completely impossible. In principle, there does not appear to be a convincing reason against allowing such relief. Under traditional equitable doctrine, however, if restitution could not be granted, no relief whatsoever could be allowed. Granting pure monetary compensation appeared to impermissibly trench on the compensatory jurisdiction of common law. The unattractive effect of this proposition, however, is that in such circumstances, the misrepresentor is simply allowed to retain the ill-gotten gain. A more satisfactory solution would be to allow, in appropriate circumstances, a monetary restitutionary claim for the benefit acquired through misrepresentation. In recent years, Canadian and English courts have, indeed, begun to recognize the availability of a monetary restitutionary claim in such circumstances in the context of transactions affected by unconscionability[98] and undue influence[99] and, indeed, of those induced by misrepresentation. Thus, the British Columbia Court of Appeal observed in *Bank of Montreal v. Murphy*[100] that courts are not "confined to the remedy of rescission where a contract is induced by a misrepresentation and the awarding of a remedy of rescission does not

---

94 Above this Chapter, section E(1).
95 See *Mispresentation Act*, 1967 (U.K.), c. 7, s. 1(a).
96 See further this Chapter, section G.
97 *Kupchak v. Dayson Holdings Ltd.*, above note 71.
98 See Chapter 11, section D.
99 See Chapter 11, section C.
100 [1986] 6 W.W.R. 610 (B.C.C.A.).

do justice between the parties. In some cases a money award may be given instead of rescission. In other cases, a money award may be given as well as rescission."[101] An innovative approach of this kind would do much to mitigate the harsh results that may otherwise flow from strict application of the various bars to rescission.

F. LIABILITY IN TORT

One who is induced to enter into an agreement on the basis of a false statement of fact made by the other contracting party may be able to pursue a claim in tort. If the statement was fraudulently false, a claim may lie in the tort of deceit. If the statement was made negligently or carelessly, a claim may lie in the tort of negligence. The claim in deceit has a longer history.[102] In the leading case of *Derry v. Peek*,[103] Lord Herschell set out the requisite intention for establishing the tort of deceit in the following terms:

> First, in order to sustain an action of deceit, there must be proof of fraud and nothing short of that will suffice. Secondly, fraud is proved when it is shown that a false representation has been made (1) knowingly, (2) without belief in its truth, or (3) recklessly, careless whether it be true or false. Although I have treated the second and third as distinct cases, I think the third is but an incident of the second, for one who makes a statement under such circumstances can have no real belief in the truth of what he states. To prevent a false statement from being fraudulent, there must, I think, always be an honest belief in its truth.[104]

The claim in *Derry v. Peek* was brought on the basis of an allegation that the directors of a corporation had made fraudulently false statements in a prospectus that had induced the plaintiff to subscribe for shares in the company. A successful defence of honest belief was raised. The claim was thus one brought against a defendant whose fraud had allegedly induced the plaintiff to enter into an agreement with a third party, the company. It is well established, however, and, indeed, it is the paradigm case, that recovery is possible where the injury suffered from

---

101 *Ibid.* at 615–16. See also *S-244 Holdings Ltd. v. Seymour Building Systems Ltd.,* above note 82.
102 See *Pasley v. Freeman* (1789), 3 T.R. 51.
103 Above note 2.
104 *Ibid.* at 374.

the defendant's fraud is to have been induced by the fraud to enter into an agreement with the defendant.[105]

Recognition of liability in negligence for carelessly made pre-contractual misstatements is, however, a more recent phenomenon. Indeed, liability for economic loss resulting from negligently false statements as a more general matter was established only in the latter half of the twentieth century. In 1963, in the leading case of *Hedley Byrne & Co. v. Heller & Partners*,[106] the House of Lords recognized for the first time that liability in negligence for economic loss could be attracted by a carelessly false statement. The defendant bank had been approached by the plaintiff for gratuitous advice concerning the creditworthiness of one of the bank's customers, with whom the plaintiff proposed to deal. The defendant gave a positive reference although, at the same time, it clearly disclaimed any liability for the accuracy of its advice. Relying on this advice, the plaintiff entered into dealings with the customer and suffered economic loss. Although the disclaimer led to the dismissal of the claim, the House of Lords nonetheless indicated that, in its absence, a claim could lie for negligent misrepresentation forseeably relied upon with resulting economic loss. Canadian courts quickly followed the House of Lords in recognizing this new liability in tort.[107] In the immediate wake of the decision in *Hedley Byrne*, however, it was not immediately apparent that this form of tort liability would be applicable in the context of pre-contractual misstatements inducing contracts with the misrepresentor. Initial resistance to the idea that it might so apply rested on an assumption that once the parties have entered into a contract, the contract itself ought to be the exclusive source of their mutual rights and responsibilities. Thus, in *Hedley Byrne* itself, Lord Reid observed: "[w]here there is a contract there is no difficulty as regards the contracting parties: the question is whether there is a warranty."[108]

---

105 See, for example, *Archer v. Brown*, [1985] Q.B. 401; *Saunders v. Edwards*, [1987] 1 W.L.R. 1116 (C.A.). A further alternative claim may be to "waive the tort" of deceit and sue for restitution of the benefits acquired by the tortfeasor through fraud. See, for example, *Amertek Inc. v. Canadian Commercial Corp.* (2003), 229 D.L.R. (4th) 419 (Ont. S.C.J.), rev'd on other grounds [2005] O.J. No. 2789 (C.A.). And see Maddaugh and McCamus, above note 22, c. 24.

106 See above note 3.

107 See, for example, *The Pas v. Porky Packers Ltd.* (1976), 65 D.L.R. (3d) 1 (S.C.C.).

108 Above note 3 at 581 (All E.R.). See also *J. Nunes Diamonds Ltd. v. Dominion Electric Protection Co.*, [1972] S.C.R. 769 at 777–78, Pigeon J. See generally S. Schwartz, "*Hedley Byrne* and the Pre-Contractual Misrepresentations; Tort Law to the Aid of Contract?" (1978) 10 Ottawa L.R. 581; C.R. Symmons, "The Problem of Affability of Tort Liability to Negligent Mis-statements in Contractual Situations: A Critique on the *Nunes Diamonds* and *Sealand* cases" (1975) 21

It seemed likely, however, that the *Hedley Byrne* form of liability would be extended into the pre-contractual sphere. *Hedley Byrne* itself, after all, was a case in which it was accepted that a negligently false statement made by A, which induced B to enter into a contract with C, could expose A to tort liability in a suit brought by B. It would not be a dramatic extension of the doctrine then to impose liability in a case where the careless inducement is uttered by C rather than A. This step was first taken by the English Court of Appeal in *Esso Petroleum Co. v. Mardon.*[109] In that case, a prospective tenant of an Esso service station was given a forecast by Esso of the estimated annual consumption of petrol at the particular location, which induced Mardon to enter into the service station lease. In the event, however, the volume of sales was much lower than had been predicted and Mardon, therefore, lost large sums of money. In a claim brought by Esso to enforce the lease, Mardon successfully counterclaimed for damages on the alternative grounds of negligent misrepresentation and collateral contract.[110] With respect to the former claim, Lord Denning M.R., observed as follows:

> [I]f a man, who has or professes to have special knowledge or skill makes a representation by virtue thereof to another—be it advice, information or opinion—with the intention of inducing him to enter into a contract with him, he is under a duty to use reasonable care to see that the representation is correct, and the advice, information or opinion is reliable. If he negligently gives unsound advice or misleading information or expresses an erroneous opinion, and thereby induces the other side into a contract with him, he is liable for damages.[111]

Two years later, the new doctrine was applied by the Ontario Court of Appeal in *Sodd Corporation Inc. v. Tessis.*[112] In that case, the plaintiff was the purchaser of the stock of a bankrupt furniture business. In preparing its tender, the plaintiff had relied on statements made by the defendant trustee in bankruptcy as to the proper method of calculating the retail value of the goods in question. The defendant's method resulted in an overestimate of approximately twice the real value of the goods. The defendant's advice on this point was held to be a negligent misstatement, giving rise to liability for the plaintiff's loss. In the years

---

McGill L.J. 79 and G.H.L. Fridman, "The Interaction of Tort in Contract" (1977) 93 Law Q. Rev. 422; N. Rafferty, "Liability for Pre-Contractual Misstatements" (1984) 14 Man. L.J. 63.

109   See above note 4.

110   With respect to this latter claim, see the discussion below, Chapter 18, section B.

111   *Esso Petroleum Co. v. Mardon*, above note 4 at 820.

112   Above note 4.

following the decision in *Sodd v. Tessis*, the doctrine has been applied or its existence has been recognized in numerous decisions of Canadian courts,[113] including the Supreme Court of Canada.[114]

In order to establish liability in negligence for pre-contractual statements, it is often said that there must be a "special relationship" between the parties. Indeed, in the immediate period following the decision of *Hedley Byrne*, it was widely assumed that in order to be held liable, the defendant must be engaged in the business of providing the advice in question. The defendant in *Hedley Byrne* was a banker. In another of the leading English cases,[115] and in *Sodd v. Tessis*, the defendants were accountants. Though it is true that the defendants in many cases were engaged in the business of providing the advice in question, this is far from true of all the *Hedley Byrne* cases.[116] As Iacobucci J. observed in *Queen v. Cognos Inc.*:[117] "The question of whether a duty of care with respect to representations exists depends on a number of considerations including, but not limited to, the representor's profession. While this factor may provide a good indication as to whether a 'special relationship' exists between the parties, it should not be treated in all cases as a threshold requirement."[118]

As a general proposition, it appears to be sufficient to establish a "special relationship" if the reliance of the representee on the representor's statement was both foreseeable by the representor and reasonable on the part of the representee.[119] Where the misrepresentor does not possess any particular expertise or access to superior skill and knowledge, reliance may well be unreasonable and the special relationship will be held not to exist.[120]

Although the definition of "misrepresentation" or the elements of misrepresentation for purposes of tort liability are fundamentally simi-

---

113 See, for example, *Sealand of the Pacific Ltd. v. Ocean Cement Ltd.* (1973), 33 D.L.R. (3d) 625 (B.C.S.C.), var'd (1974), 51 D.L.R. (3d) 703 (B.C.C.A.); *Peters v. Parkway Mercury Sales Ltd.* (1975), 58 D.L.R. (3d) 128 (N.B.C.A.) and *Nelson Lumber Co. Ltd. v. Koch* (1980), 111 D.L.R. (3d) 140 (Sask. C.A.).

114 See *Central & Eastern Trust Co. v. Rafuse*, [1986] 2 S.C.R. 147; *Rainbow Industrial Caterers Ltd. v. C.N.R.*, [1991] 3 S.C.R. 3; *Queen v. Cognos Inc.* (1993), 99 D.L.R. (4th) 626 (S.C.C.).

115 *Mutual Life Assurance v. Evatt*, [1971] 1 All E.R. 150 (P.C.).

116 See, for example, *R.H. Peden Construction Ltd. v. Resolute Construction (1977) Ltd.* (1980), 31 A.R. 453 (Q.B.); *Nelson Lumber Co. v. Koch*, above note 113.

117 See *Queen v. Cognos Inc.*, above note 114.

118 *Ibid.* at 648–49.

119 Above note 114 at 648, Iacobucci J.; *Hercules Managements Ltd. v. Ernst & Young* (1997), 146 D.L.R. (4th) 577 at para 24.

120 See *Kingu v. Walmar Ventures Ltd.* (1986), 10 B.C.L.R. (2d) 15 (C.A.).

lar to the elements of misrepresentation for purposes of a decree of rescission, there are differences between them.[121] Thus, for example, it has been said that to engage the tort of deceit, the representation must be an "active" one, thus suggesting a reduced role for non-disclosure as misrepresentation.[122] At the same time, it is accepted that "half-truths" can amount to deceit.[123] Further, it is accepted in the tort context that a misleading opinion will count as a misrepresentation for purposes of the torts of deceit and negligence, whereas opinions are distinguished from statements of fact in the rescission context. The requirement of material inducement in the rescission context has no precise parallel in the tort jurisprudence, though the requirement that the tortious misstatement caused the loss and that the misrepresentee reasonably relies on the misrepresentation may achieve a similar, if not precisely identical, analysis.

The potential role of negligence on the part of the misrepresentee may also be different in the two contexts. As we have seen, the misrepresentee who seeks rescission is under no obligation to engage in "due diligence." The plaintiff in *Redgrave v. Hurd*[124] would not be denied rescission simply because the purchasing solicitor had failed to take advantage of a means of knowledge readily available to him. Similarly, in the tort context, it is unlikely that negligence on the part of the misrepresentee would preclude or reduce the representor's liability for fraudulent misstatement. Although the defence of contributory negligence may be broadly available under modern apportionment legislation, it is unlikely that it would be applied in such fashion as to reduce liability for fraud.[125] In a tort claim for negligent misstatement, however, the negligence of the misrepresentee may well give rise to apportionment on the basis of contributory negligence. In *Avco Financial Services Realty Ltd. v. Norman*,[126] for example, the Ontario Court of Appeal applied the doctrine in a negligent misstatement claim. A husband and wife had given a mortgage and, at the same time, purchased creditors'

---

121 See generally Cartwright, above note 47, c. 1, 2 and 4.
122 *Peek v. Gurney* (1873), L.R. 6 H.L. 377 at 391 and 403.
123 *Ibid*. See also *Smith Newcourt Securities Ltd. v. Scrimgeour Vickers (Asset Management) Ltd.*, [1997] A.C. 254 at 274, Lord Steyn; *Alevizos v. Nirula* (2003), 234 D.L.R. (4th) 352 (Man. C.A.).
124 Above note 1.
125 For discussion of modern apportionment legislation and its potential application to intentional torts, see L. Klar, *Tort Law,* 3d ed. (Toronto: Carswell, 2003) at 458–62.
126 (2003), 226 D.L.R. (4th) 175 (Ont. C.A.). See also *Grand Restaurants of Canada Ltd. v. Toronto (City)* (1981), 32 O.R. (2d) 757 (H.C.J.).

insurance policies to cover the debt in the event of death, accident or sickness. Although the mortgage was renewed for successive terms, it proved to be impossible for the mortgagors to renew the insurance policies. In the interim, the wife had become ill. Upon reapplication for the insurance, the application for renewal of the insurance was rejected on grounds of her illness. The couple had not been advised by the insurance company that the life insurance policy would not be automatically renewed whenever the mortgage was renewed. Accordingly, when the mortgagee brought an action to enforce the mortgage covenant against the husband, he counterclaimed against the insurance company for damages suffered as a result of a negligent failure to inform him that the policy was not automatically renewable. This claim against the insurer succeeded, but the claim was reduced on the basis that the husband's failure to make appropriate inquiries amounted to contributory negligence. At first impression, as the Court of Appeal observed, it may appear inconsistent to hold that, in such circumstances, the husband has reasonably relied on the insurer with respect to the negligent misrepresentation but that his reliance was sufficiently careless as to engage the doctrine of contributory negligence.[127] In the court's view, however, the issue as to whether or not the reliance on the statement was reasonable from the point of view of establishing liability in negligence was not the same as whether the misrepresentee's carelessness should be taken into account in determining the extent of recovery. The first issue involves a determination as to whether a "special relationship" exists and the test of reasonable reliance, arguably, does not equate to a negligence test. When one turns to consider contributory negligence, the issue becomes one of negligence and a broader range of factors become relevant. Thus, it may be reasonable to rely on someone with whom one has a "special relationship," but one could still do so without taking reasonable precautions to protect oneself. To be sure, in the court's view, it would be unlikely to find that a misrepresentee who behaved negligently could also be held to have reasonably relied on the misrepresentation. Nonetheless, such findings could, at law, co-exist even though, on the facts of *Avco*, the court took the view that the negligent conduct of the husband was such that it precluded a finding in his favour on the issue of reasonable reliance.

---

127 See Klar, above note 125 at 227–29, for the suggestion that the doctrine of contributory negligence should be inapplicable in this context on the theory that if the reliance was careless, it could not have been reasonable and, accordingly, the claim should be dismissed.

The measure of damages in a tort claim is obviously different from the restitutionary relief awarded in the context of rescission. The plaintiff in tort is allowed to recover out-of-pocket losses or compensatory damages, with the objective of placing the plaintiff in the position the plaintiff was in prior to the occurrence of the tort. In the typical case where the value of the consideration being supplied is misrepresented, the normal measure would be the difference between the price being paid and the market value of the consideration supplied. More generally, however, the plaintiff is entitled to recover consequential losses. Thus, in *Esso Petroleum Co. v. Mardon*,[128] Mardon was entitled to recover his entire lost investment in the service station business.[129]

G. ENTIRE AGREEMENT AND EXEMPTION CLAUSES

As we have seen, misrepresentations of fact that induce agreements may give rise to a variety of remedies, including equitable rescission for misrepresentation and damages in tort where the misrepresentation is fraudulent or negligent. As we shall see,[130] if the representation can be characterized as a binding collateral warranty, the various remedies for breach of contract become available. Understandably, drafters of agreements exhibit an inclination to include provisions that seek to limit or exclude these types of liabilities. The success of such provisions in achieving these objectives will require a careful construction of the actual language of the provision. Further, however, in the interpretation of such clauses, courts appear to be influenced by a consideration

---

128 Above note 4.
129 In *Rainbow Industrial Caterers Ltd. v. C.N.R.*, above note 114, it was assumed, in unusual circumstances, that the measure of relief in tort may exceed the measure of relief in a contract claim. The plaintiff claimed that it had been induced into a food catering contract on the basis of a negligent misstatement estimating the number of meals to be supplied. The Court held that as the plaintiff would not have entered into the agreement if it had been correctly advised, it was entitled to recover its lost investment, including losses that could not be attributable to the misrepresentation. If the plaintiff had sued in contract, however, it would be awarded damages that would place it in as good a position as it would have been in if the representation had been true and therefore it would not have recovered losses that could not be related to the misrepresentation itself. See also *Wiebe v. Gunderson* (2004), 243 D.L.R. (4th) 1 (B.C.C.A.) (sale of business induced by seller's misrepresentations—role of lost profits in calculating tort damages).
130 See Chapter 18.

as to whether the particular clause has been drawn to the attention of the representee. Thus, in *Hedley Byrne*[131] itself, the defendant was excused from liability by virtue of the fact that the defendant bank had, when rendering the advice in question, explicitly stated that the advice was "for your private use and without responsibility on the part of the bank or its officials."[132] The arguments for excusing the defendants in such circumstances are obviously compelling. It is reasonable for the representor to assume that he will not be held responsible for the veracity of the statement and unreasonable for the representee to attempt to impose liability. The significance of the disclaimer becomes much more difficult, however, if it is to be found only in the subsequent agreement entered into between the parties. Indeed, one commentator has suggested that a disclaimer found in the ultimate contract arrives too late to be of any assistance to the defendant inasmuch as the representation has already had the desired effect of inducing the buyer to enter into the agreement.[133] The trap has already been set and triggered. If the contract contains a disclaimer clause, it is simply a better trap. It seems rather more likely, however, that the courts will simply construe the contractual disclaimer with a view to determining whether it truly operates as a release of the representor's liability for the prior tort and there is some evidence for this in the recent case law.

Where the disclaimer is found in the subsequent agreement, the courts evince a concern to determine whether the representee has had adequate actual notice of the significance of the representor's disclaimer. In *Roberts v. Montex Development Corporation*,[134] for example, the condominium purchase agreement included a clause to the effect that "it is understood and agreed that there are no representations, warranties, guarantees, promises or agreements other than those contained in this agreement." This provision was held to be ineffective to exclude tort liability because the plaintiff "had no independent legal advice before signing the interim agreement" and the judge was satisfied "that the escape clause meant nothing to her — if she read it, which I doubt."[135] Similarly, in *Beer v. Townsgate I Ltd.*,[136] the Ontario Court

---

131 *Hedley Byrne & Co. v. Heller & Partners Ltd.*, above note 3 at 468.
132 *Ibid.*
133 D.W. Greig, "Misrepresentation and Sales of Goods" (1971) 87 Law Q. Rev. 179 at 201–2.
134 (1979), 100 D.L.R. (3d) 660 (B.C.S.C.). See also *Zippy Print Enterprises Ltd. v. Pawliuk*, [1995] 3 W.W.R. 324, Lambert J.A. And see generally P. Perell, "A Riddle Inside an Enigma: The Entire Agreement Clause (1998) 20 Advocates' Q. 287.
135 *Roberts v. Montex Development Corporation*, *ibid.* at 664.
136 (1997), 152 D.L.R. (4th) 671 (Ont. C.A.).

of Appeal declined to give effect to an entire agreement clause where agreements for the sale of condominium units were entered into in a "frenzied" atmosphere in which there was no effective opportunity to read the clause and, accordingly, no reasonable expectation on the part of the seller that the purchasers had assented to the clause. In another Ontario case,[137] however, the court was prepared to give effect to a similar contractual disclaimer, but appeared to place great weight on the fact that the plaintiffs had, prior to signing the document, received advice from their lawyer to the effect that they were "taking an awful chance"[138] in signing a document that so severely restricted the defendant's liabilities.

In *Sodd Corporation Inc. v. Tessis*,[139] and in the decision of the Supreme Court of Canada in *Carman Construction Ltd. v. Canadian Pacific Railway Co.*,[140] disclaimers that were made available to the plaintiff at the time of the initial statement were the subject of analysis. In *Sodd v. Tessis*, the disclaimer was afforded little significance. A disclaimer appeared in the advertisement for sale by tender published by the trustee in bankruptcy and stated the following: "Tenders will be accepted on the basis that the purchaser has inspected the assets and title thereto, and no warranty or condition is expressed or can be implied as to designation, classification, quality or condition or in any manner whatsoever."[141] The trial judge expressed the view, and the Court of Appeal appeared to agree, that this clause would not reach a negligent misrepresentation and the trial judge went on to say that she found the disclaimer in the context of the advertisement somewhat misleading.

In *Carman Construction*, on the other hand, the disclaimer was seized upon as a basis for depriving the plaintiff of relief. In *Carman Construction*, the plaintiff construction company had successfully tendered for a project for the excavation of rock. Tenders were called on September 6, 1977, the printed materials requiring that the tender be

---

137 *Ronald Elwyn Lister Ltd. v. Dunlop Canada Ltd.* (1978), 85 D.L.R. (3d) 321 (Ont. H.C.), rev'd on other grounds (1979), 105 D.L.R. (3d) 684 (Ont. C.A.), but restored on further appeal (1982), 135 D.L.R. (3d) 1 (S.C.C.).

138 *Ibid.* at 332 (Ont. H.C.).

139 Above note 4.

140 (1982), 136 D.L.R. (3d) 193. For discussion, see E.J. Hayek, "Collateral Contracts and the Supreme Court of Canada: *Carman Construction Ltd. v. Canadian Pacific Railway Co.*" (1983) 7 Can. Bus. L.J. 328. For a discussion of the decisions below, see J. Swan and B.J. Reiter, "The Effectiveness of Contractual Allocations of Risk: *Carman Construction v. Canadian Pacific Railway; Ronald Elwyn Lister Ltd. v. Dunlop Canada Ltd.*" (1982) 6 Can. Bus. L.J. 219.

141 Above note 4 at 633 (D.L.R.).

submitted by 10 a.m. on September 9. The tender documents included a draft contract that contained the following provision:

> It is hereby declared and agreed by the Contractor that this Agreement has been entered into by him on his own knowledge respecting the nature and conformation of the ground upon which the work is to be done, the location, character, quality and quantities of the material to be removed, the character of the equipment and facilities needed, the general and local conditions and all other matters which can in any way affect the work under this Agreement, and the Contractor does not rely upon any information given or statement made to him in relation to the work by the Company.[142]

Mr. Fielding, the vice-president and general manager of the plaintiff, conceded that he had read this provision. During the period from September 6 to September 9, Mr. Fielding approached the defendant and indicated that a tender would be impossible by virtue of the fact that they had no knowledge with respect to the quantity of rock to be removed and no time within which to conduct a survey, the tender period being an unusually short one. In response to Fielding's inquiry, a CPR employee informed him that the volume was estimated to be 7,000 to 7,500 cubic yards of rock. This estimate was found to be carelessly erroneous, and it seriously underestimated the amount of rock to be removed. The plaintiff, having completed the extra work required by the project, brought an action for the value of the work done, pleading, *inter alia*, a negligent misstatement. The claim foundered, however, on the existence of the disclaimer contained in the tender documents. It was significant, for Martland J., writing for a unanimous Court, that Mr. Fielding had read and understood the disclaimer clause when he received the tender documents and, accordingly, the plaintiff was aware that he could not rely on any information or statement made to it by the defendant with respect to the work. The plaintiff was aware, it was held, that it would be relying on such information only at its own risk.[143] This circumstance is compelling inasmuch as it brings the facts squarely within the holding in *Hedley Byrne* itself. It may be wondered, however, whether the Court came too quickly to the conclusion that the significance of the provision in the tender documents was indeed so clearly understood by the plaintiff. On the rather special facts of this case, it might well be that Fielding would assume that a clause designed to deal with the ordinary situation, in which an examination

---

142 *Carman Construction Ltd. v. Canadian Pacific Railway Co.*, above note 140 at 195.
143 *Ibid.* at 204.

by the plaintiff was at least possible, would not apply to the discussion that took place in the present case.

In each of the cases in which the courts have been prepared to give effect to the exclusionary clause, then, they have been very careful to ensure that the existence of the disclaimer was clearly brought to the attention of the representee. This is certainly consistent with the fact situation in *Hedley Byrne*, where the disclaimer was part of the very communication that contained the misrepresentation. Where, as in *Roberts v. Montex Development Corporation* and *Beer v. Townsgate I Ltd.*, the disclaimer and the original misrepresentation are separated by time and space, there is presumably much to be said for the view that actual notice is desirable, and this indeed does seem to be a preoccupation of the courts in these cases.

Finally, are clauses that purport to preclude liability for pre-contractual misstatements subject to the usual principle concerning the interpretation of exculpatory or limitation of liability clauses? That principle holds that such provisions should be given the effect of precluding liability only where the language of the particular provision clearly so indicates. The general principle of narrow construction of limitation of liability clauses should apply in this context. The narrow approach would hold, for example, that disclaimer clauses should not be construed to exclude negligence in the absence of clear language on this point.[144] There is some support for this approach in recent cases. Thus, in *Beer v. Townsgate I. Ltd.*,[145] the Ontario Court of Appeal suggested that an entire agreement clause that stipulated "there is no representation, warranty, collateral agreement or condition affecting this agreement"[146] did not preclude liability in tort. Some courts have indicated a reluctance to apply narrow construction techniques of this kind. In *Hayward v. Mellick*,[147] Houlden J.A., in dissent, applied

---

144 Thus, if the clause does not specifically refer to negligent acts and if the defendant could be liable on grounds other than negligence, the traditional approach is to hold that liability for negligent acts is not excluded. See, for example, *Alderslade v. Hendon Laundry, Ltd.*, [1945] K.B. 189 (C.A.); *Salmon River Logging Co. Ltd. v. Burt*, [1953] 2 S.C.R.117; *Canada Steamship Lines Ltd. v. The King*, [1952] 2 D.L.R. 786 (P.C.); *Robert Simpson Regina Ltd. v. Dominion Electric Protection Co.* (1971), 19 D.L.R. (3d) 218 (Sask. Q.B.). The rule is not absolute, however. See *ITO — International Terminal Operators Ltd. v. Miida Electronics Inc.*, [1986] 1 S.C.R. 752. It will be applied less strictly to limitations of as opposed to exclusions of liability. See *Ailsa Craig Fishing Co. Ltd. v. Malvern Fishing Co. Ltd.*, [1983] 1 W.L.R. 964 (H.L.).

145 Above note 136 at 682, Brooke J.A.

146 *Ibid.* at 681.

147 (1984), 5 D.L.R. (4th) 740 (Ont. C.A.).

the traditional narrow construction of approach in this context. Thus, in his view, where a contract had been induced by a negligent misstatement, a provision to the effect that "there is no representation, warranty or collateral agreement affecting this agreement … other than as expressed herein in writing"[148] was insufficient to preclude liability for negligence. The majority opinion of Weatherston J.A., however, offered the view that so strict a construction appeared "too strained"[149] and accordingly, the provision did preclude such liability, even though liability for negligence had not been explicitly mentioned. The majority did accept, however, that a strict construction approach is generally applicable to such clauses. Moreover, the majority suggested that where the pre-contractual statement relates to "some overriding or collateral matter"[150] rather than relating merely to the quality or fitness of the subject matter of the contract, the statement falls outside the terms of the agreement and, accordingly, liability may not be precluded by such a provision.

In *Carman Construction*, the Supreme Court of Canada exhibited greater reluctance to apply the strict construction approach in circumstances where the provision in question stipulates that the representee "does not rely upon any information given or statement made" by the representor.[151] Martland J. indicated that considerable argument was submitted with respect to the capacity of the contractual provisions to exempt a tortfeasor from liability for negligence. Martland J. held, however, that this particular type of provision was not properly characterized as a clause exempting the defendant from liability but rather could be described as "a non-reliance provision, the effect of which was to prevent liability arising on the part of the [the defendant] in respect of statements made or information given by its employees."[152] One may object that it is not obvious, however, that the particular drafting format of the disclaimer clause should preclude argument about whether a strict construction technique should be followed. Be that as it may, the *Carman Construction* decision offers a clear signal to the drafter that the "non-reliance" drafting format has certain obvious advantages.

---

148 *Ibid.* at 750.
149 *Ibid.* at 749.
150 *Ibid.* at 748.
151 Above note 140 at 195.
152 *Ibid.* at 204.

H. OVERVIEW

As we have seen, the remedies available to an individual who has been induced to enter into a contract on the basis of a false statement of fact include rescission for misrepresentation and claims for damages in tort where the representation has been made fraudulently or carelessly. The remedial options available at common law and equity are summarized in Table 10.1.

Table 10.1 *Remedies for Misrepresentation*

Nature of Misrepresentation	Remedies at Common Law	Remedies in Equity
Fraudulent	contract voidable— rescission (with restitution) compensatory damages for the tort of deceit	contract voidable— rescission (with restitution)
Innocent (a) careless	compensatory damages for the tort of negligence	contract voidable— rescission (with restitution)
(b) non-careless	—	contract voidable— rescission (with restitution)

As Table 10.1 illustrates, the least attractive remedial position for a misrepresentee is to be the victim of a non-careless, innocent misrepresentation. Such a person is not able to claim common law compensatory damages in tort. Further, although a claim for rescission in equity may be possible, rescissionary relief, as we have seen, may disappear rather quickly. Thus, for example, where a consumer buyer has been led to purchase a defective item on the basis of misleading but non-careless misrepresentations by the seller, the consumer victim may be without effective redress. Such circumstances have led to a variety of ameliorating techniques such as lowering the bars to rescission and recognition of a doctrine of *error in substantialibus*,[153] the effect of the latter being one of permitting rescission at a later stage than it would be available for mere misrepresentation. Perhaps the most important ameliorating device, however, is that of transforming the representation of fact into a contractual promise through the device of "collateral contract." The analytical means by which a representation may properly be character-

---

153 See, for example, *Alessio v. Jovicka* (1973), 42 D.L.R. (3d) 242 (Alta. S.C.A.D.). For discussion of this doctrine, see G.H.L. Friedman, *"Error in Substantialibus*: A Canadian Comedy of Errors" (1978) 56 Can. Bar Rev. 603.

ized as an enforceable collateral warranty will be considered in a later chapter.[154]

I. STATUTORY REFORM

Consumer protection legislation in a number of provinces has significantly modified the law of misrepresentation as it applies to consumer transactions.[155] These statutory schemes attempt, to varying degrees, to regulate consumer sales practices within the province and to provide civil redress to consumers who have been injured by such practices. In these statutory schemes, consumer transactions are typically defined as transactions between a commercial seller and a consumer acquiring goods and certain kinds of services for personal rather than business use. With respect to the representation, these statutes typically set forth an extended definition of the notion of misrepresentation, capturing utterances made by commercial sellers that would not be caught by the common law definition of misrepresentation.[156] Typically, misleading representations by sellers are included within a larger concept of misleading conduct that, in turn, is made the subject of a provincial offence. In the Alberta statute,[157] for example, misleading representations are defined to constitute an "unfair practice."[158] The commission of an unfair practice is prohibited under the statute.[159] A consumer who has suffered loss due to an unfair practice is entitled to bring a civil action for relief. The statute confers a broad discretion upon courts, in such claims, to award damages, including punitive damages, and to make orders for specific performance, restitution of property or money or rescission of the consumer transaction.[160] In granting relief, the court is not constrained by the traditional equitable limitations on the granting of rescissionary decrees.

---

154 See Chapter 18.
155 *Fair Trading Act*, R.S.A. 2000, c. F-2; *Trade Practice Act,* R.S.B.C. 1996, c. 457; *Trade Practices Act*, R.S.N.L. 1990, c. T-7; *Consumer Protection Act, 2002*, S.O. 2002, c. 30, Sch. A; *Business Practices Act*, R.S.P.E.I. 1988, c. B-7.
156 See, for example, s. 6(4) (Alta.); s. 3(1) (B.C.); s. 5(1) (Nfld. & Lab.); s. 14 (Ont.); s. 2(1) (P.E.I.).
157 *Fair Trading Act*, R.S.A. 2000, c. F-2.
158 *Ibid.,* s. 6.
159 *Ibid., s.* 7.
160 *Ibid.,* s. 13(2).

The law of misrepresentation has been reformed in a more general way in England. The *Misrepresentation Act*[161] applies to any transaction entered into on the basis of a misrepresentation. There are four main features to this statute. First, the Act abolishes the doctrine of merger,[162] which holds that the repetition of a pre-contractual misrepresentation as a contractual term deprives the misrepresentee of the rescissionary remedy for misrepresentation. The statute provides[163] that a contractual warranty will not preclude such relief. Second, the Act broadens slightly the action for compensatory damages for misrepresentation by shifting the burden to the representor to establish that "he had reasonable ground to believe and did believe up to the time the contract was made that the facts represented were true."[164] Third, the Act somewhat reduces the right to rescission by conferring on courts a statutory discretion to award damages in lieu of rescission.[165] Finally, the Act provides that contractual terms that exclude or restrict liability for precontractual misrepresentation are enforceable only if they meet a standard of reasonableness.[166]

FURTHER READINGS

R. BIGWOOD, "Pre-Contractual Misrepresentation and the Limits of the Principle in *With v. O'Flanagan*" (2005) 64 Cambridge L.J. 94.

J. BIRDS & N.J. HIRD, "Misrepresentation and Non-Disclosure in Insurance Law—Identical Twins or Separate Issues?" (1996) 59 Mod. L. Rev. 285.

J. CARTWRIGHT, *Misrepresentation* (London: Sweet & Maxwell, 2002).

J.L. COLEMAN, D.D. HECKATHORN & S.M. MASER, "A Bargaining Theory Approach to Default Previsions and Disclosure Rules in Contract Law" (1989) 12 Harv. J.L. & Pub. Pol'y 639.

P. FINN, "The Fiduciary Principle" in T. Youdan, ed., *Equity, Fiduciaries and Trusts* (Toronto: Carswell, 1989).

---

161 1967, c. 7; see P.S. Atiyah and G.H. Treitel, "*Misrepresentation Act*" (1967) 30 Mod. L. Rev. 369; Cartwright, above note 47.

162 See this Chapter, section E.

163 Above note 161, s. 1.

164 *Ibid.*, s. 2(1).

165 *Ibid.*, s. 2(2).

166 *Ibid.*, s. 3, incorporating by reference s. 11(1) of the *Unfair Contract Terms Act*, 1977 (U.K.), c. 50.

L.C.H. HOYANO, "Lies, Recklessness and Deception: Disentangling Dishonesty in Civil Fraud" (1996) 75 Can. Bar Rev. 474.

A.T. KRONMAN, "Mistake, Disclosure, Information and the Law of Contracts" (1978) 7 J. Legal Stud. 1.

S. O'BYRNE, "Culpable Silence: Liability for Non-Disclosure in the Contractual Arena" (1998) 30 Can. Bus. L.J. 239.

P. PERELL, "A Riddle Inside an Enigma: The Entire Agreement Clause" (1998) 20 Advocates' Q. 287.

P. PERELL, "The Fraud Elements of Deceit and Fraudulent Misrepresentation" (1996) 18 Advocates' Q. 23.

N. RAFFERTY, "Liability for Pre-Contractual Misstatements" (1984) 14 Man. L.J. 63.

K.L. SCHEPPELE, *Legal Secrets: Equality and Efficiency in the Common Law* (Chicago: University of Chicago Press, 1988).

E. SHERWIN, "Nonmaterial Misrepresentation: Damages, Rescission, and the Possibility of Efficient Fraud" (2003) 36 Loy. L.A. L. Rev. 1017.

S.M. WADDAMS, "Pre-contractual Duties of Disclosure" in P. Cane and J. Stapleton, eds., *Essays for Patrick Atiyah* (Oxford: Clarendon Press, 1991).

DURESS, UNDUE INFLUENCE AND UNCONSCIONABILITY

A. INTRODUCTION

This chapter examines a cluster of doctrines applicable to circumstances where a stronger party has taken advantage of a weaker party
in the course of inducing the weaker party's consent to an agreement.
More particularly, the common law doctrine of duress and the equity
doctrines of undue influence and unconscionability will be considered.
Where applicable, each doctrine renders the agreement in question unenforceable at the option of the weaker party. These doctrines constitute, then, exceptions to or limitations on the general approach of the
common law to the effect that where two parties having contractual
capacity reach a *consensus ad idem* on an exchange of value, the resulting bargain is enforceable. These doctrines are interrelated and, in a
particular fact situation, it may be appropriate to consider the application of two or even all three of the doctrines.

The organization and interrelation of the doctrines bears the burden of the historical division of private law doctrine into doctrines of
common law and those of equity. The relationship between common
law duress and equitable undue influence illustrates the point. Both of
these doctrines consider the effect of threats of various kinds made to
induce the threatened party to enter into an agreement. Thus, the common law doctrine of duress provided relief essentially in cases of agreements induced by dire threats, such as threatened physical violence.

Equity in its traditional role of ameliorating the harsh edges of the common law, was prepared to render unenforceable agreements induced by less dire threats. This aspect of the equitable doctrine has come down to us as the doctrine of "actual" undue influence.[1]

There is a second branch to the law of undue influence, however, dealing with the inducement of agreements in circumstances where the transaction results from abuse of a relationship of trust and confidence. Where such a relationship is found to exist, the existence of undue influence is presumed and this second branch of the doctrine of undue influence is therefore often referred to as "presumptive" undue influence. Under this branch the existence of a threat of some kind is not required. Under the traditional principles of duress at common law and actual undue influence in equity, a threatened breach of contract in a commercial setting would not be considered to be a threat in the requisite sense. In the late-twentieth century, however, it became recognized that such threats might provide a ground for unenforceability of the resulting agreement. As this doctrine has been termed "economic duress," however, it appears as an expansion of the categories of common law duress rather than an expansion of the equitable category of actual undue influence. A more rational organization of this material might distinguish between agreements induced by threats (including traditional duress, actual undue influence and economic duress) as opposed to agreements induced through abuse of a relationship of trust and confidence. Nonetheless, the convention of treating these subjects according to the historical divisions of common law and equity is widely accepted and will be followed here.

Although the distinction between undue influence and unconscionability is less problematic, it is nonetheless the case that the boundary line between relationships of trust and confidence that are of such a nature as to give rise to presumptive undue influence and relationships merely subject to a doctrine of unconscionability cannot be traced with complete precision. This point is illustrated by the well-known decision of the English Court of Appeal in *Lloyds Bank v. Bundy*.[2] Bundy was an elderly farmer who mortgaged his only asset, Yew Tree Farm, to the bank in order to provide funds to his son whose business was in some difficulty. On two further occasions, the father was invited to provide additional security and guarantees in order to assist his son and he did so. By this time, the total charge against the property had come to exceed its

---

1   The doctrine of actual undue influence is not restricted, however, to situations in which threats have been uttered. See below this Chapter, section C(2).

2   [1975] Q.B. 326 (C.A.).

value. On the signing up of the third charge, the bank manager, who had recently taken over this position, appreciated that Bundy had no asset other than Yew Tree Farm and was of the view that the problems with the son's company might be deep-seated. Nonetheless, he neither insisted nor suggested that Bundy should take some time to think about the transaction or, indeed, seek some advice on the matter. When the son's difficulties were not alleviated, the bank foreclosed on the mortgage and brought an action for possession of the farm. In response, Bundy sought to set aside the transaction on equitable grounds. For the majority of the court, this series of transactions between the father and the bank had established the requisite relationship of trust and confidence and thus, on the basis of the traditional equitable doctrine of undue influence, the third and devastating transaction could be set aside. As we shall see, these facts would likely ground a finding of unconscionability, at least by a Canadian court. For a Canadian judge, then, *Bundy* might be a case of undue influence or unconscionability or, indeed, both.

The *Bundy* case has attracted a good deal of attention, but not because of its location at the borderline of undue influence and unconscionability. Rather, it was on this occasion that Lord Denning M.R. proposed, in effect, a merger of the various doctrines considered in this chapter. Lord Denning seized upon the occasion to articulate a new general principle that, in his view, could serve the useful function of reconciling the complex of common law and equitable doctrines permitting relief in situations of this kind. He began by noting: "[I]n the vast majority of cases, a customer who signs a bank guarantee or charge cannot get out of it."[3] He then listed "exceptions to this general rule" constituted by the doctrines of duress, undue influence and unconscionability.[4] Lord Denning then proposed the following rationalizing principle:

> Gathering all together, I would suggest that through all these instances there runs a single thread. They rest on "inequality of bargaining power." By virtue of it, the English law gives relief to one who, without independent advice, enters into a contract upon terms which are very unfair or transfers property for a consideration which is grossly inadequate, when his bargaining power is grievously impaired by

---

3   *Ibid.* at 336.
4   Lord Denning M.R. did not refer to the concept of unconscionability as such but identified two categories of cases where "undue pressure" provided a basis of relief, categories that appear equivalent to the doctrine referred to here as that of "unconscionability." In addition, Lord Denning listed a fifth category relating to salvage agreements as being similar in nature. See *ibid.* at 337–39.

reason of his own needs or desires, or by his own ignorance or in-firmity, coupled with undue influences or pressures brought to bear on him by or for the benefit of the other.[5]

Lord Denning then proceeded to apply this new principle to the fact situation of this case. Placing particular emphasis on the fact that the father relied implicitly on the bank to advise him with respect to the transaction and was much influenced by his affection for his son, he concluded that the case came within the new general principle. It was on this basis that he held the transaction should be set aside. Lord Denning's suggestion that these existing doctrines can be rationalized and restated in the form of a single principle of "inequality of bargaining power" is a bold and interesting one. After examining the three separate doctrines of duress, undue influence and unconscionability, we will return to consider this suggestion in the concluding section of this chapter.

B. DURESS

1) Introduction

At common law, contracts entered into on the basis of certain types of coercion categorized as duress are unenforceable. Under traditional doctrine, the categories of duress were few in number and narrowly defined. Thus, the earliest form of duress recognized at common law was actual or threatened violence to the person. It is not surprising that the common law took the view that agreements induced by actual or threatened violence could not be enforced by the person who committed or threatened violence in order to secure the other party's consent to the agreement. For much of the history of the doctrine of duress, it was not clear that the common law doctrine of duress would hold unenforceable agreements induced by any other form of duress. In the late-twentieth century, however, a new and more open-textured form of duress—economic duress—was recognized as an additional potential ground of unenforceability. It is in this latter context that the task of drawing the line between unacceptable coercion and legitimate commercial pressure has become most difficult. As we shall see, these difficulties have not been completely resolved in English or Canadian law.

In addition to rendering agreements induced by duress unenforceable, the doctrine also provides a basis for restitutionary recovery of

---

5   *Ibid.* at 339.

benefits conferred in the absence of the formation of an agreement. Thus, monies handed over in response to actual or threatened violence to the person would ground recovery of those monies in a restitutionary claim, notwithstanding the absence of any contractual arrangement to make the payment in question.[6] Our concern here, however, is the extent to which agreements that have been induced by duress are considered enforceable at common law. As the common law did not assume that any form of duress that could ground restitutionary recovery would also necessarily provide a basis for holding that an agreement entered into under such duress would be unenforceable, it is important, for present purposes, to preserve the analytical distinction between these two different forms of relief.

Occasionally, it is suggested that the effect of a finding of duress is that the contract is void *ab initio*.[7] Certainly, in cases of actual or threatened violence, it is difficult to see why the perpetrator of the violence or the threat should be entitled to rely on any of the equitable defences[8] that might be engaged by a holding that such agreements are merely voidable, rather than void.[9] On the other hand, the principal advantage to the coerced party of holding that an agreement is merely voidable rather than void is that the unenforceability of the agreement is at the option of that party. Accordingly, if the coerced party so wishes to, the agreement may be treated as enforceable. Principally for this reason, it appears to be generally accepted that the effect of a finding of duress is that the agreement in question is rendered voidable.[10] The other

---

6   For discussion of the restitutionary aspects of common law duress, see P.D. Maddaugh and J.D. McCamus, *The Law of Restitution*, 2d ed. (Aurora: Canada Law Book, 2004) c. 26 [Maddaugh and McCamus, *Restitution*].

7   See, for example, *Barton v. Armstrong*, [1976] A.C. 104 at 120 (P.C.), Lord Cross; *Saxon v. Saxon*, [1976] 4 W.W.R. 300 at 307 (B.C.S.C.), Spencer Co. Ct. J., aff'd [1978] 4 W.W.R. 327 (C.A.); *Canada Life Assurance Co. v. Stewart* (1994), 118 D.L.R. (4th) 67 at 80, Pugsley J.A. See also D.J. Lanham, "Duress and Void Contracts" (1966) 29 Mod. L. Rev. 615.

8   As, for example, where the victim is held to have acted upon or adopted the contract. See, for example, *Findlay v. Findlay*, [1951] 1 D.L.R. 185 at 188–89 (Ont. C.A.), aff'd [1952] 1 S.C.R. 96. See also *Pao On v. Lau Yiu Long*, [1980] A.C. 614 at 635 (P.C.). In the context of threatened violence, however, it may be that these defences will be interpreted generously in favour of the coerced party. See, for example, *Byle v. Byle*, (1990), 65 D.L.R. (4th) 641 (B.C.C.A.).

9   See, for example, *Saxon v. Saxon*, above note 7. And see American Law Institute, *Restatement of Contracts 2d* (St. Paul: American Law Institute, 1981) s. 176.

10 See, for example, *North Ocean Shipping Co. Ltd. v. Hyundai Construction Co. Ltd.* (*sub nom. The Atlantic Baron*), [1979] Q.B. 705 at 720; *D.P.P. for Northern Ireland v. Lynch*, [1975] A.C. 653 at 695; *Stott v. Merit Investment Corp.* (1988), 48 D.L.R. (4th) 288 at 305 (Ont. C.A.); *Byle v. Byle*, above note 8.

important effect of a determination that agreements entered into under duress are voidable rather than void is that third parties who have, in good faith, relied on the validity of the transaction would be protected on the basis of the equitable principle that in such circumstances it is too late to rescind the agreement. A number of cases have held that, in such circumstances, agreements entered into under duress will not be avoided to the prejudice of third parties.[11] Against this background, we turn to the traditional categories of duress and the recently recognized category of economic duress.

2) The Traditional Categories of Duress

a) Duress to the Person

A contract induced by actual or threatened violence to a person is unenforceable at common law. The doctrine of duress of the person extends beyond violence and threats made to the other party to the agreement to include threats made to the safety of other members of that party's family. Thus, agreements entered into on the basis of a husband's threat to kill the wife's children[12] or by one sibling to harm another in order to induce the parents to enter into an agreement[13] are voidable on the basis of duress. The doctrine extends, as well, to actual or threatened unlawful confinement or imprisonment of a person.[14] Where the duress is constituted by a threat, the threat must be believable[15] and believed.[16] Although the threat would, of course, normally be communicated directly to the party induced to enter the agreement, it is sufficient if the coerced party learns of the existence of the threat from a third party.[17]

The Privy Council stated, in *Barton v. Armstrong*,[18] that an agreement induced by duress to the person is generally accepted to be void-

---

11 See, for example, *Kesarmal S/O Letchman Das v. N.K.V. Valliappa Chettiar S/O Nagappa Chettiar*, [1954] 1 W.L.R. 380 (P.C.); *Canadian Imperial Bank of Commerce v. Boudreau* (1982), 41 N.B.R. (2d) 365 (Q.B.); *Wilgross Investments Ltd. v. Goldshlager* (1974), 51 D.L.R. (3d) 343 (Ont. Div. Ct.).

12 *Saxon v. Saxon*, above note 7.

13 *Byle v. Byle*, above note 8.

14 *Earl of Northumberland's Case* (1583), 4 Leon. 91, 74 E.R. 750; *Blanchard v. Jacobi* (1918), 43 O.L.R. 442 (H.C.).

15 *Armstrong v. Gage* (1877), 25 Gr. 1 (Ont. Ch.).

16 *Byle v. Byle*, above note 8.

17 See *ibid.* (parents enter contract with one child having learned of that child's threat to harm a sibling from a third sibling).

18 Above note 7.

able rather than void and is therefore unenforceable at the option of the victim of the violence or threat. It is sufficient if the violence or threat constituted a reason for entering the agreement and thus, as in *Barton v. Armstrong* itself, the fact that the party may have entered into the agreement even in the absence of threatened violence, the duress remains operative. In this case, in the course of a battle for control by two major shareholders of a corporation, one made a death threat to the other in order to cause the latter to enter into an agreement to buy out his shareholding. Although the evidence indicated that the threatened party believed that, in any event, some transaction of this kind was necessary for the future of the company, the death threat was held to be sufficient to engage the doctrine of duress. Further, the Privy Council held that the burden is placed upon the party issuing the threat to establish that the threat did not contribute to the decision to enter into the agreement.

b)   Duress of Goods

As a matter of restitutionary law, the common law concept of duress was extended beyond actual or threatened violence to the person to include interference with property rights. Thus, in a leading case,[19] where a pawnbroker demanded an excess payment from the pawner in order to release the pawned goods, the payment was recoverable in a restitution claim. The doctrine would also apply to payments extracted by a landlord through improper distraint of a tenant's goods.[20] The doctrine applies, more generally, to payments extracted through the improper seizure or retention of the plaintiff's personal property.[21] It is applicable both to an actual seizure of goods and to a threatened seizure.[22] Curiously, however, it has been held until recently that the doctrine of duress of goods does not apply so as to vitiate a contract induced by improper seizure or retention of an individual's goods. The leading case, *Skeate v. Beale*,[23] concerned a wrongful distraint of a tenant's goods by a landlord. Although monies paid in direct response to an improper distraint would be recoverable, the court held, in *Skeate v. Beale*, that an agreement entered into in the same circumstances would be enforceable. The tenant

---

19   *Astley v. Reynolds* (1731), 2 Str. 915, 93 E.R. 939. See also *Pople v. Dauphin* (1921), 60 D.L.R. 30 (Man. C.A.).

20   See, for example, *Fell v. Whittaker* (1871), L.R. 7 Q.B. 120.

21   It has also been suggested that the doctrine is applicable to the wrongful withholding of an interest in real property. See *Peter Kiewit Sons' Co. of Canada Ltd. v. Eakins Construction Ltd.*, [1906] S.C.R. 361 at 380, Cartwright J.

22   See, for example, *Maskell v. Horner*, [1915] 3 K.B. 106 at 120, Lord Reading C.J.

23   (1841), 11 Ad. & El. 983, 113 E.R. 688.

had given a promise to pay and the court held that the mere fear that one's goods may be lost "does not deprive anyone of his free agency who possesses that ordinary degree of firmness which the law requires all to exert."[24] This distinction between sums paid and sums promised to be paid does not appear to be defensible and would appear to be inconsistent with the decisions extending the common law of duress to duress of goods. Indeed, in *Knutson v. Bourkes Syndicate*,[25] the Supreme Court of Canada expressed doubt concerning the holding in *Skeate v. Beale* and, more recently, English courts have clearly indicated that the decision should no longer be considered to constitute good law.[26]

3) Economic Duress

Much earlier than other common law jurisdictions, the United States extended the concept of duress beyond the traditional forms of duress to other kinds of economic pressure.[27] In English law, however, recognition of economic duress as a form of coercion that could undermine the enforceability of an agreement induced thereby did not come until the late 1970s. In the leading case of *Pao On v. Lau Yiu Long*,[28] the Privy Council confirmed the earlier suggestions of English trial judges[29] to the effect that economic duress could serve to vitiate or negate consent to a contractual arrangement. In common with many of the modern duress cases, *Pao On* involved a threatened breach of contract. It will be recalled[30] that this case concerned a guarantee given in the context of a transaction involving the sale of a company owned by the plaintiffs to Fu Chip, a company owned by the defendant Lau, in return for shares in Fu Chip. In order to ensure the value of that consideration, the plaintiff had exacted a guarantee from Lau that the shares would have a certain value on a particular date, failing which the plaintiff could require Lau to purchase them at the stipulated value.

---

24   *Ibid.* at 990 (Ad. & El.).

25   [1941] S.C.R. 419.

26   See, for example, *Pao On v. Lau Yiu Long*, above note 8 at 635–36, Lord Scarman; *Dimskal Shipping Company S.A. v. International Transport Workers Federation (sub nom. The Evia Luck)*, [1992] 2 A.C. 152 at 165 (H.L.), Lord Goff of Chieveley.

27   See generally J. Dalzell, "Duress by Economic Pressure" (1942) 20 N.C.L. Rev. 237 at 341.

28   Above note 8 at 617.

29   See *Occidental Worldwide Investment Corp. v. Skibs A/S Avanti (sub nom. The Siboen and The Sibotre)*, [1976] 1 Lloyd's Rep. 293 (Q.B.); *North Ocean Shipping Co. Ltd. v. Hyundai Construction Co. Ltd. (sub nom. The Atlantic Baron)*, above note 10.

30   See Chapter 7, section B(2).

Although the intention of the guarantee was thus to protect the value of the purchase price paid for the plaintiff's company, the wording of the guarantee was such that if the value of the Fu Chip shares was in excess of the stipulated value, Lau could purchase the shares at the stipulated price and enjoy the increased value of the shares. When the plaintiff belatedly appreciated that the guarantee had taken this form, he indicated that he would refuse to close the transaction unless a new guarantee was issued by Lau enabling the plaintiff to retain the shares should their value exceed the stipulated price. Lau, confronted by the unattractive possibility of negative publicity for Fu Chip should the deal fail to close, took legal advice and decided to issue a second guarantee in the requested form. The trial judge observed that Lau did not anticipate the dramatic fall in the stock market, affecting the value of Fu Chip shares, and accordingly, probably believed that he was taking little risk in giving such a guarantee. With the subsequent fall of the market, however, the second guarantee exposed Lau to very substantial liability. Lau defended the plaintiff's action to enforce the guarantee on a variety of grounds,[31] including economic duress. Lord Scarman defined duress as "a coercion of the will so as to vitiate consent"[32] and went on to indicate that "in a contractual situation commercial pressure is not enough."[33] Again, the "compulsion had to be such that the party was deprived of 'his freedom of exercising his will.'"[34] In applying this test, Lord Scarman indicated that the following evidentiary matters could be relevant: "American judges pay great attention to such evidential matters as the effectiveness of the alternate remedy available, the fact or absence of protest, the availability of independent advice, the benefit received, and the speed with which the victim has sought to avoid the contract."[35]

In order to meet the test, then, it must be shown that the conduct coerced did not amount to a "voluntary act."[36] Applying these criteria to the facts of the *Pao On* case, Lord Scarman held that Lau had submitted to commercial pressure, but not to coercion in the requisite sense. The Privy Council accepted the trial judge's finding that "Lau considered the matter thoroughly, chose to avoid litigation, and formed the opinion that the risk in giving the guarantee was more apparent than real."[37]

---

31   Including absence of consideration. For discussion of this point, see Chapter 7, section B(3)(b).
32   Above note 8 at 635.
33   *Ibid.*
34   *Ibid.*
35   *Ibid.* at 636.
36   *Ibid.*
37   *Ibid.* at 635.

The "overborne will" threshold set by Lord Scarman in *Pao On* establishes a test that is obviously very difficult to meet. There cannot be many cases in which a party subject to economic duress could be said to have acted as a mere automaton. An individual subject to extreme commercial pressure might nonetheless understand that the decision to accept the lesser of two evils—handing over the demanded benefit rather than enduring the threatened conduct—is a conscious and intentional choice. Indeed, the overborne will approach has been criticized on the basis that, if seriously applied, the defence of economic duress would rarely, if ever, be available and on the further ground that it requires a difficult, perhaps impossible, inquiry into the psychological state of mind of the coerced party.[38] Within a few years, however, the House of Lords had an opportunity to consider the emerging economic duress doctrine in *Universe Tankships of Monrovia v. International Transport Workers' Federation*.[39] On this occasion, Lord Scarman articulated the test in somewhat different terms. The dispute concerned demands made by the defendant federation of unions of the plaintiff, an operator of a ship flying a "flag of convenience." The defendant had a policy of "blacking" such ships unless they complied with the defendant's demands. Blacking would have the effect of denying the plaintiff access to tugboat facilities and would thus prevent continuation of the ship's voyage. Essentially, the defendant's demands required the plaintiff to agree to abide by certain conditions of employment and to make various payments, including such items as back pay and membership fees for the crew and a contribution to the defendant's "Welfare Fund." The plaintiff capitulated to these demands, entered the required agreements and performed its payment obligations. After leaving port, however, the plaintiff sought recovery of the amounts paid on the basis that the agreements entered into with the defendant were voidable because of economic duress. Lord Scarman set out a twofold test for applying the concept of economic duress: "(1) pressure amounting to compulsion of the will of the victim; and (2) the illegitimacy of the pressure exerted."[40]

With respect to the first branch of the test, Lord Scarman observed that the requirement is variously stated in the authorities as "coercion

---

38 See generally H. Stewart, "Economic Duress in Canadian Law: Towards a Principled Approach" (2003) 82 Can. Bar Rev. 359; M.H. Ogilvie, "Economic Duress, Inequality of Bargaining Power and Threatened Breach of Contract" (1981) 26 McGill L.J. 289; P.S. Atiyah, "Economic Duress and the Overborne Will" (1982) 98 Law Q. Rev. 197.

39 [1983] 1 A.C. 366 (H.L.).

40 *Ibid.* at 400.

or vitiation of consent."[41] In his view, however, "[t]he classic case of duress is ... not the lack of will to submit but the victim's intentional submission arising from the realization that there is no other practical choice open to him."[42] Lord Scarman then proceeded to consider the evidentiary matters referred to in *Pao On* as relevant but not dispositive. Thus, even though the plaintiff had not protested at the time of entering into the agreements with the defendant, it was nonetheless clear that the plaintiff had no practical alternative but to submit to the arrangement.

Having satisfied the first branch of the test, then, it was necessary to determine whether or not the pressure exerted was "legitimate." On this branch of the test, inasmuch as the defendant's threat to interfere with the contractual relations of the plaintiff with service providers was clearly tortious at common law, the question became whether the applicable statutory labour relations scheme precluded the characterization of industrial action of this kind as tortious. If it did so, it was accepted that the pressure exerted by the defendant would not be illegitimate in the requisite sense. On this point their Lordships divided, the majority holding that the defendant's demand with respect to the Welfare Fund contribution was not legitimated by the applicable legislation. That payment was therefore recoverable. Under this second version of the test, then, emphasis shifts from the psychological state of mind of the coerced party to a determination as to whether, as a practical matter, the coerced party had any option but to yield to the pressure and, secondly, whether the pressure was itself illegitimate. In subsequent English cases, though some reference to the coercion of the will theory continues, emphasis is increasingly placed on the legitimacy of the threat and the lack of any practical alternative course of action.[43]

Reception of the American doctrine of economic duress into English law was anticipated in Canadian law by the development of a doctrine of "practical compulsion." In its 1941 decision in *Knutson v. Bourkes Syndicate*,[44] the Supreme Court of Canada held that monies paid in re-

---

41   *Ibid.*

42   *Ibid.*

43   See, for example, *Vantage Navigation Corporation v. Suhail and Saud Bahwan Building Materials LLC (sub nom. The Alev)*, [1989] 1 Lloyd's Rep. 138 (Q.B.); *Atlas Express Ltd. v. Kafco (Importers and Distributors) Ltd.*, [1989] Q.B. 833; *Dimskal Shipping Co. S.A. v. International Transport Workers Federation (The Evia Luck)*, above note 26; *CTN Cash and Carry Ltd. v. Gallaher Ltd.*, [1994] 4 All E.R. 714 (C.A.). For discussion of subsequent English decisions, see Stewart, above note 38 at 365–67; M.H. Ogilvie, "Economic Duress in Contract: Departure, Detour or Dead-end?" (2001) 34 Can. Bus. L.J. 194 at 207–20.

44   [1941] S.C.R. 419.

sponse to a threatened breach of contract were recoverable. This case involved a real estate transaction in which the plaintiff syndicate had agreed to purchase a parcel of land from the defendant Knutson, free and clear of a 15 percent interest in the property owned by a third party. To the knowledge of Knutson, the syndicate had, in turn, agreed to sell the land on to a subpurchaser. Sometime prior to the closing of the initial transaction, Knutson acquired the 15 percent interest from the third party and signalled his intention to insist on an additional payment of 15 percent of the purchase price to himself as a condition of closing. The syndicate protested this demand but, in due course, made the payment to Knutson. After the transaction had closed, the syndicate brought a claim against Knutson for the monies paid. The Supreme Court, drawing support from the duress-of-goods line of authority held that the payments were not voluntary in the sense required by the existing cases. Kerwin J., for the Court, concluded as follows: "In order to protect its position under the option agreement and to secure title to the lands which was under obligation to transfer to [the subpurchaser], the Syndicate was under a practical compulsion to make the payments in question and is entitled to their repayment."[45] The decision in this case has spawned its own line of authority explicating the concept of "practical compulsion."[46] The doctrine will not apply where the coercion can be characterized as ordinary commercial pressure.[47] It is of particular interest in the present context that the practical compulsion cases do not adopt an overborne will test but focus, rather, on the extent to which there were any practical alternatives available to the party subject to coercion.

In response to the recognition of the new economic duress doctrine by the English courts in *Pao On* and *Universe Tankships*, Canadian courts accepted the new doctrine as a feature of Canadian law and, in the context of cases of threatened breach of contract at least, the doctrine of practical compulsion appears to have been displaced by the doctrine of economic duress. Although *Knutson v. Bourkes Syndicate* is occasionally referred to in such cases,[48] the continuing role of practical

---

45 *Ibid.* at 425.
46 See generally Maddaugh and McCamus, above note 6, c. 26:300.10.
47 See, for example, *Peter Kiewit Sons' Co. of Canada Limited v. Eakins Construction Ltd.*, above note 21; *Morton Construction Co. Ltd. v. City of Hamilton* (1961), 31 D.L.R. (2d) 323 (Ont. C.A.). For criticism of the application of the concept in these cases, see Maddaugh and McCamus, above note 6, c. 29:200.
48 See, for example, *Adanac Realty Ltd. v. Homes Development Ltd.* (1986), 43 R.P.R. 88 (Ont. H.C.J.), a case that purports to distinguish between practical compulsion and economic duress in a threatened breach of contract context.

compulsion in Canadian law is principally that of enabling restitution-ary relief, particularly in the context of taxes, licence fees and other payments improperly exacted by public authorities.[49] With the shift to economic duress in the context of threatened breach of contract, then, it becomes critical, in an assessment of current Canadian law, to deter-mine whether Canadian courts have adopted the overborne will theory of *Pao On* or the no practical alternative coupled with illegitimate pres-sure test set forth in *Universe Tankships* or, indeed, some other theory in fashioning a Canadian version of the doctrine.

In the earliest stages of Canadian reception of the doctrine, Canad-ian courts tended to apply the overborne will theory and to cite and rely upon the evidentiary factors articulated by Lord Scarman in *Pao On* as if they constituted the elements of a rigid test.[50] In *DeWolfe v. Mansour*,[51] for example, an agreement in which one of two parties to a development agreement agreed to buy out the other was held not to have been induced by economic duress. The Nova Scotia trial judge quoted passages from *Pao On* setting out the overborne will test and applied Lord Scarman's evidentiary factors, which he referred to as the "determining factors,"[52] as a test for the applicability of the doc-trine. Given the absence of protest by the allegedly coerced party, the availability of alternative courses of action explained by his lawyer, the reasonableness of the terms of the arrangement and the absence of subsequent steps to avoid the agreement, the attempt to invoke the doctrine did not succeed.[53]

In the more recent cases, however, a test for the application of the doctrine influenced by the *Universe Tankships* model appears to have emerged. In *Stott v. Merit Investment Corp.*,[54] for example, the Ontario Court of Appeal articulated a version of the test that places emphasis on the illegitimacy of the threat and the lack of practical alternatives. In this case, a salesman, Stott, was pressured by his superiors in the de-fendant investment firm to absorb losses sustained on a customer's ac-

---

49 See, for example, *Eadie v. Township of Brantford*, [1967] S.C.R. 573. And see gen-erally Maddaugh and McCamus, above note 6, c. 22:300.30.

50 In an early case, *Ronald Elwyn Lister Ltd. v. Dunlop Canada Ltd.* (1979), 105 D.L.R. (3d) 684 at 694–95 (Ont. C.A.), Weatherston J.A., rev'd on other grounds, [1982] 1 S.C.R. 726, the Ontario Court of Appeal quoted at length from Lord Scarman's opinion in *Pao On*.

51 (1986), 73 N.S.R. (2d) 110, 33 B.L.R. 135 (S.C.).

52 *Ibid.* at 146 (B.L.R.).

53 See also *Newfoundland and Labrador Drilling Ltd. v. Miller* (1992), 97 Nfld. & P.E.I.R. 140 (Nfld. S.C.T.D.); *Roenish v. Bangs* (1993), 8 Alta. L.R. (3d) 148 (Q.B.).

54 Above note 10.

count that the customer could not repay. The particular losses had been incurred as a result of the intervention of a supervisor, Douglas, who reversed a decision of Stott and instructed him to permit the client to engage in the investment in question and provide a postdated cheque. It was this intervention by Douglas that caused the loss in question. Although there was a general policy at the firm that sales representatives guaranteed the creditworthiness of their customers, it was Stott's view that he should not be liable for losses that did not result from his own actions. Nonetheless, when pressured by a senior executive officer to do so, Stott signed an agreement accepting responsibility for the losses. The circumstances in which he assented to the arrangement involved high-pressure tactics. Stott was called into the executive officer's office unexpectedly; he was advised that if he did not sign the document forthwith it would not go well for him at the firm and he would have difficulty getting employment elsewhere. Stott asked for, but was not given, time to reflect on the matter and to consult a lawyer. Although the Court of Appeal agreed that responsibility for the losses incurred should fall upon Douglas, the critical issue in the case was whether Stott's agreement to cover the losses was unenforceable, *inter alia*, on the basis of economic duress. Finlayson J.A. quoted at length from *Universe Tankships* and articulated the test for economic duress in the following terms: "It must be a pressure which the law does not regard as legitimate and it must be applied to such a degree as to amount to 'a coercion of the will,' to use an expression found in English authorities, or it must place the party to whom the pressure is directed in a position where he has no 'realistic alternative' but to submit to it."[55] In applying the test, the court concluded that economic duress was present. No reference to overborne will was made in reaching that conclusion and it thus appears that the court was simply applying the *Universe Tankships* test. The majority of the court further concluded, however, that Stott's subsequent conduct essentially affirmed the agreement and the defence of economic duress was therefore no longer available.[56]

In another recent case, the Ontario Court of Appeal applied the reasoning in *Pao On* but did so in a fashion that is consistent with the movement in the direction of the *Universe Tankships* test. In *Gordon v. Roebuck*,[57] the trial judge had applied the evidentiary factors identi-

---

55   *Ibid.* at 305.

56   See also *North Ocean Shipping Co. Ltd. v. Hyundai Shipping Co. Ltd. (sub nom. The Atlantic Baron)* above note 10, in which affirmation was held to have occurred.

57   (1992), 92 D.L.R. (4th) 670 (Ont. C.A.). See also *Van Kruistum v. Dool* (1997), 35 O.R. (3d) 430 (Gen. Div.).

fied by Lord Scarman in *Pao On* and concluded that there did not exist a sufficient coercion of the will. The dispute, between two solicitors acting as trustees for different investors in a real estate joint venture, concerned a payment exacted by one before agreeing to provide a discharge of a mortgage needed to close a transaction concerning one of the properties owned by the joint venture. The solicitor demanding the payment, Roebuck, insisted that the party whom he represented, Satok, had lent money to the joint venture and accordingly, as a condition of providing the discharge, should be repaid his loan. The other solicitor, Gordon, took the position that Satok was an investor rather than a lender and should merely share, with the other investors, the fruits of their investment. Nonetheless, in order to close the transaction, Gordon agreed to pay a substantial sum to Roebuck, as trustee for Satok, out of the proceeds of the sale. The Court of Appeal reviewed the trial judge's findings on the evidentiary factors. Reversing the trial judge on these points, the Court of Appeal held that there had been sufficient protest and that Gordon took steps to avoid the transaction with reasonable promptness. The trial judge's suggestion that Gordon should have sought a court order requiring execution of the documents was rejected on the basis that the possibility of getting a matter of such complexity before a court and resolved in time to close the transaction was unrealistic. With respect to the trial judge's finding that there had been independent legal advice, McKinlay J.A. held that this point was quite irrelevant. Given the fact that there was "no other practical course available but to capitulate to the demands,"[58] the independent advice could only have been to recommend capitulation. On this basis, the court was prepared to find that economic duress had occurred, unless it could be found that the pressure exerted by Roebuck was "legitimate."[59] In the court's view, the onus was on Gordon to establish that Roebuck was not entitled to the funds demanded by him. Gordon had failed to meet that onus and, accordingly, the pressure exerted by Roebuck was assumed to be legitimate. Although, again, the court made reference to the overborne will test, the court's emphasis on the lack of practical alternatives available to Gordon and on the legitimacy of the pressure is consistent with the *Universe Tankships* version of the test.

---

58 *Gordon v. Roebuck, ibid.* at 674.
59 *Ibid.* In an unorthodox terminological turn, the court would have held that economic duress had occurred and that the second step was to determine whether or not it constituted "*unjustifiable* economic duress." The more orthodox analysis would be to hold that unless the pressure is illegitimate, economic duress is not established. See *ibid.* at 675.

A more straightforward embrace of the *Universe Tankships* analytic-al model is set out in the decision of the same court in *Techform Prod-ucts Ltd. v. Wolda.*[60] In this case, the plaintiff auto parts manufacturer sought to assert ownership over a valuable type of truck hinge invented by the defendant who, at the time of the invention, was retained as a consultant to the plaintiff for the purpose of inventing products of this kind. This particular invention was the product of after-hours work by the defendant. Nonetheless, it was covered by the terms of an Employee Technology Agreement (ETA) that the defendant had signed during the course of his retainer. Having developed concerns about the defend-ant's apparent intention to seek to charge the plaintiff for ownership rights to an earlier invention, the plaintiff insisted that the defendant sign the ETA, which it had drafted to deal with problems of this kind. The ETA conferred ownership rights to inventions upon the employer in circumstances of the kind at issue. Although the defendant had in-itially objected to signing the ETA, he reluctantly capitulated in doing so for fear of losing his job. His personal circumstances were such that he could ill afford to be without employment. When, in due course, the defendant invented the truck hinge in question and proposed that he be paid separately for transfer of the ownership rights to the invention, the plaintiff dismissed the defendant and sought to enforce its rights under the ETA. The trial judge, applying the evidentiary factors from *Pao On* as well as the *Universe Tankships* test, held that the ETA was not enforceable on the grounds of economic duress. The Court of Ap-peal affirmed the trial judge's view that a finding of economic duress required a determination that the coerced party had no practical al-ternative to capitulation and that the threat was illegitimate. The court reversed the trial judge, however, on the basis that she had not suffi-ciently considered the question as to whether the pressure applied by the plaintiff had been legitimate. In the court's view, the plaintiff held a *bona fide* belief at the time it insisted on the signing of the ETA that it was the owner of inventions developed by employees and consultants such as the defendant. Further, the plaintiff had allowed the defendant a period of time to consider and obtain advice with respect to the ETA. On these grounds, the pressure applied was not illegitimate and the defence of economic duress failed.

The apparent shift to the *Universe Tankships* test is a welcome de-velopment. The criteria to be applied by the test—lack of a practical alternative and illegitimacy of the threat—appear to be both more ana-

---

60   (2001), 206 D.L.R. (4th) 171 (Ont. C.A.). See also *Permaform Plastics Ltd. v. Lon-don & Midland General Insurance Co.*, [1996] 7 W.W.R. 457 (Man. C.A.).

lytically sound and more manageable to apply than those suggested by the overborne will theory. As a factual matter, it should normally be a straightforward exercise to determine whether or not the coerced party had an available alternative and practical course of action. The test of illegitimacy speaks more directly to the problem of distinguishing legitimate commercial pressure from illegitimate coercion. Where the threatened conduct constitutes a crime or as in *Universe Tankships* a tort, the illegitimacy test is easily applied. The more difficult case, of course, is that of threatened breach of contract, conduct that is, in the normal case at least, considered to be lawful.[61]

Some guidance is available, however, from the cases applying the illegitimacy test in this context. As the courts have observed, "in determining the legitimacy of the pressure, one must consider the nature of the pressure and the nature of the demand the pressure is applied to support."[62] Accordingly, even though a threat to breach a contract is normally a lawful act, it may be that the nature of the demand being made may cross the line separating legitimate from illegitimate pressure. Thus, threats that have the flavour of blackmail to them are likely to be considered illegitimate. For example, where an employer threatens to dismiss an employee and, as well, to tarnish the employee's reputation within the industry in order to coerce the employee's consent to an adjustment to his or her existing employment contract, the threat is likely to be held illegitimate.[63] On the other hand, *Gordon*[64] and *Techform*[65] suggest that if the party making the threat is seeking to enforce a right to which it believes, in good faith, it is entitled, the threat is a legitimate one.[66] *Knut-*

---

61   In *Universe Tankships,* above note 39 at 401, Lord Scarman emphasized that, as in the case of blackmail, where the threatened act is often lawful—for example, the threatened disclosure of truthful information—the threatened conduct need not be unlawful to constitute economic duress. For consideration of the relevance of the blackmail analogy, see Stewart, above note 38 at 382–83.

62   *Techform Products Ltd. v. Wolda* (2000), 5 C.P.R. (4th) 25 at 46 (Ont. S.C.J.), Sachs J., quoted with approval by the Ontario Court of Appeal, above note 60 at 185, Rosenberg J.A.

63   Such a threat was made in *Stott,* above note 10. Although the Court of Appeal did not place emphasis on this aspect of the fact situation, it may have contributed to the finding of economic duress. See also *Perkins Oil Co. v. Fitzgerald,* 121 S.W.2d 877 (Ark. 1938).

64   Above note 57.

65   Above note 60.

66   See also *CTN Cash and Carry Ltd. v. Gallaher Ltd.,* above note 43. *Pao On,* above note 8, might be considered to be a similar case on the basis that the plaintiffs were apparently insisting on a modification of the original agreement that would reflect their understanding of its originally intended effect.

son,[67] however, appears to suggest that there may be an objective limit on this aspect of legitimacy. The coercing party in that case may well have believed that he was entitled to make the claim he asserted. In the court's view, however, the transaction documents plainly did not support his claim and the charge of "practical compulsion" succeeded. Further, where a demand is made maliciously or vindictively in the sense that it is designed to harm the coerced party without any significant benefit to the person making the threat, the threat would presumably be considered illegitimate.[68] Finally, in those cases in which the threat has been found to be illegitimate, the demand typically has the character of seeking to exploit the other party's vulnerability in order to enjoy an immoderate or unfair gain. Thus, for example, the attempt to impose liability on the salesman in *Stott*[69] for losses caused by his supervisor was plainly both immoderate and unfair and, but for Stott's subsequent affirmation of the agreement, would have constituted economic duress.

The doctrine of economic duress is likely to be of increasing importance in contract law, particularly in the context of the renegotiation of existing agreements. Although many of the recent cases dealing with economic duress arise in circumstances where a threatened breach of contract has led to a renegotiation of a contract, resort is normally made to the doctrine of duress only if the agreement to amend the existing agreement is considered to be binding. Economic duress is also likely to perform a critical role, however, in the context of gratuitous undertakings to vary existing agreements. Such undertakings are, on the basis of consideration doctrine, unenforceable. Under traditional doctrine, the policing of coerced renegotiation of contracts has been achieved, not very effectively, through application of the consideration doctrine relating to the unenforceability of promises to perform a pre-existing contractual duty. Where the threatening party exacts an undertaking to provide further consideration from the other party but promises in return only to perform the pre-existing agreement, the amending agreement is unenforceable. As noted elsewhere,[70] the difficulty with this doctrine is that it is both overinclusive and underinclusive. It is overinclusive in the sense that within the class of agreements rendered unenforceable on consideration grounds, it captures both renegotia-

---

67   Above note 44.
68   See *Restatement of Contracts 2d*, above note 9, s. 176(2)(a). And see E.A. Farnsworth, *Farnsworth on Contracts*, 2d ed., vol. 1 (New York: Aspen, 1998) at 485.
69   Above note 10.
70   See Chapter 7.

tions induced by coercion and those that have been the subject of voluntary agreement. It is underinclusive in the sense that, within the class of agreements rendered enforceable on the basis of consideration doctrine, there may be many cases in which the agreement has been induced by illegitimate coercion. Accordingly, recent reforms of the pre-existing duty doctrine have taken the view that a promise to perform a pre-existing duty, in such circumstances, should constitute good consideration unless the amending agreement has been secured by duress. Further, a second possible solution to the pre-existing duty problem also appears to be qualified by a "no duress" requirement. It may be that the doctrine of promissory estoppel will be employed in the future to protect parties who have relied on gratuitous agreements to vary existing contracts. If so, however, it is likely that the doctrine will not apply where the obligation to be enforced is one that has been secured by duress.[71] Thus, even in circumstances where, under traditional doctrine, no enforceable agreement to vary an existing contract would be found, the doctrine of economic duress is likely to perform an important role in distinguishing enforceable undertakings to vary existing agreements that are the product of normal commercial pressure from those that are unenforceable on grounds of economic duress.

C. UNDUE INFLUENCE

1) Introduction

The equitable doctrine of undue influence provides a basis for setting aside a gift or a transaction where the transfer of value has been induced by an "unconscientious use by one person of power possessed by him over another."[72] If applicable, the doctrine enables the influenced party to obtain an equitable rescission of the gift or transaction. The types of circumstances giving rise to claims of undue influence have been traditionally divided into two categories. The first, so-called actual undue influence, arises when the plaintiff is able to establish the use of such power by the defendant on a particular occasion. The second category,

---

71   See Chapter 8, section C(3).

72   *Earl of Aylesford v. Morris* (1873), 8 Ch. App. 484 at 491. The term "unconscientious" may mislead for it appears, at least in cases of presumptive undue influence, that it is unnecessary to establish a lack of moral probity on the part of the influencing party. The critical question is whether the influenced party was disabled from acting independently. See further below.

undue influence arising by presumption, is engaged when the plaintiff is able to establish that the nature of the relationship between the parties is such that the use of such power on a particular occasion should be presumed. The second category can be further subdivided. First, there are situations in which the relationship is of a recognized type of relationship, such as solicitor and client, with respect to which the presumption invariably arises. Second, in the context of a relationship not so recognized, a court may hold that the particular nature of the relationship between the parties is such that a presumption should arise. In recent English case law,[73] these three types of undue influence have been referred to as Types 1 (actual undue influence), 2A (the recognized list of relationships) and 2B (presumption arising from the particular circumstances). In a recent decision,[74] the House of Lords has suggested that presumptive due influence is merely a subspecies of a broader category of "relationship" undue influence[75] in which one party has a measure of influence over the other that may be abused. Such a relationship may be established on the basis of an evidential presumption but need not be. In their Lordships' view, even if the presumption is not, for some reason, available to the influenced party, it may nonetheless be possible to establish that such a relationship did exist and was abused. We shall classify this non-presumptive relational undue influence as Type 3 and return to a consideration of this category after examining Types 1, 2A and 2B.

The plaintiff's claim for a rescission on the basis of undue influence can be defeated by the defendant on a showing that the gift or transaction was an exercise of independent will by the plaintiff. In the 2A and 2B cases, of course, the presumption has the effect of shifting the evidential[76] burden to the defendant to do so. Normally, but not invariably, the defendant will attempt to establish the fact of independence by demonstrating that the plaintiff has received independent legal advice with respect to the gift or transaction in question. Although the main features of the law of undue influence are reasonably well settled, a number of controversies have emerged in recent years, raising interesting questions relating to the test for the existence of undue influence, the role of independent legal advice and the nature of the remedies available once undue influence is found.

---

73   *Bank of Credit and Commerce International SA v. Aboody*, [1992] 4 All E.R. 955 at 964 (C.A.).

74   *Royal Bank of Scotland v. Etridge (No. 2)*, [2001] 4 All E.R. 449 (H.L.) [*Etridge*].

75   *Ibid.* at 457–58, Lord Nicholls.

76   *CIBC Mortgage Corporation v. Rowatt* (2002), 61 O.R. (3d) 737 (C.A.).

2) Type 1: Actual Undue Influence

The doctrine of actual undue influence is essentially equity's version of the common law doctrine of duress. Duress at common law, as we have seen, enables recovery of a payment made or the setting aside of a transaction where either has been induced by the making of a dire threat of some kind, such as a threat of physical violence to the person or to a near relative.[77] Actual undue influence was recognized by courts of equity to arise in the context of threats that would not engage the common law doctrine. Thus, for example, gifts and transactions have been set aside in circumstances where a caregiver on whom an elderly person has become dependent threatens to abandon that person[78] and in circumstances where a threat has been made to prosecute an individual or a close relative of the individual for a criminal offence.[79] In such cases, provided that it can be shown that the gift or transaction resulted from the threat, a decree of rescission will be available.

The decision of the English Court of Appeal in *BCCI v. Aboody*[80] indicates, however, that an explicit threat is not necessary to support a finding of actual undue influence. In that case, the defendants were husband and wife and were also the shareholders and directors of a family company that was essentially operated by the husband. The wife's practice was to sign, without inquiry, corporate documents placed before her by her husband on the assumption that the husband would operate the company for their mutual benefit. In the course of executing a series of personal guarantees and a charge on property she owned to secure the company's indebtedness, the lending bank arranged for the wife to receive independent legal advice from a solicitor. In the course of her meeting with the solicitor, the husband barged into the room and, after an angry exchange with the solicitor, his wife signed the document. Although the case was treated by the trial judge as one of actual undue influence, perhaps on the basis of the direct evidence of the husband's bullying manner, the case demonstrates that a rather fine line may exist between circumstances of actual undue influence and cases in which the past history of the relationship is such as to give rise to a presumption of a lack of independence.

In *Aboody*, the Court of Appeal went on to hold that in a case of actual undue influence, it was necessary to find not only the presence

---

77 See above this Chapter, section B.

78 *Re Craig* (1970), [1971] Ch. 95, [1970] 2 All E.R. 390.

79 *Williams v. Bayley* (1866), L.R. 1 H.L. 200 (threat against son); *Stolze v. Fuller*, [1939] S.C.R. 235 (threat against plaintiff).

80 Above note 73.

of influence but, as well, the existence of a manifestly disadvantageous transaction. On the facts, the court held that no such disadvantage inhered in the arrangements entered into by the wife and, accordingly, that the doctrine of actual undue influence did not apply. The court reached the conclusion that manifest disadvantage must be shown in reliance on the decision of the House of Lords in *National Westminster Bank plc v. Morgan*,[81] a case that held that manifest disadvantage must be shown in order to establish a presumption of undue influence. In the later decision of the House of Lords in *CIBC Mortgages plc v. Pitt*,[82] however, the Court of Appeal was overruled on this point on the basis that actual undue influence is a species of fraud and accordingly "[l]ike any other victim of fraud, a person who has been induced by undue influence to carry out a transaction which he did not freely and knowingly enter into is entitled to have that transaction set aside as of right."[83] It is of some importance, as will be seen, to note that the decision of the House of Lords in *Pitt* indicates that the effect of actual undue influence is to vitiate consent. Once consent is vitiated, the transaction falls, whether or not the transaction itself can be said to be disadvantageous in some sense. Thus, if, as a result of actual undue influence, an elderly person sells his or her home to a party exercising actual undue influence, the transaction may be set aside, whether or not the contract price is a fair one.

3) Types 2A and B: Presumptive Undue Influence

a) Establishing the Presumption

If the plaintiff can establish a presumption of undue influence, relief will be available unless the presumption can be rebutted by the defendant. In a 2A case, the presumption arises by virtue of the fact that the relationship between the parties is of a kind prescribed in a defined list of relationships that give rise to the presumption. The list includes the relationships of solicitor and client,[84] doctor and patient,[85] trustee and beneficiary,[86] parent

---

81 [1985] 1 All E.R. 821 (H.L.).

82 [1993] 4 All E.R. 433 (H.L.).

83 *Ibid.* at 439.

84 *Wright v. Carter*, [1903] 1 Ch. 27 (C.A.); *Rochdale Credit Union Ltd. v. Barney* (1984), 14 D.L.R. (4th) 116, 48 O.R. (2d) 676 (C.A.).

85 *Mitchell v. Homfray* (1881), 8 Q.B.D. 587 (C.A.); *Ralston v. Tanner* (1918), 43 O.L.R. 77 (S.C.).

86 *Ellis v. Barker* (1871), L.R. 7 Ch. App. 104; *Jenyns v. Public Curator* (1953), 90 C.L.R. 113.

and child,[87] and religious advisor and follower.[88] The prescribed list does not include husband and wife,[89] employer and employee or banker and customer, though, as will be seen, in the particular circumstances of relationships such as these, a 2B presumption may apply.

A 2B presumption arises where the history of a particular relationship between two parties can be characterized as establishing a relationship of "trust and confidence." The test for the kinds of circumstances giving rise to the presumption and the difficulty inherent in applying the test are illustrated in *Geffen v. Goodman Estate*.[90] In *Geffen*, the dispute arose in the context of conflict among four siblings, the three Geffen brothers and their sister, Goodman, concerning the disposition of their mother's estate. Goodman had a history of mental illness and, in order to provide her with needed support, the mother had initially made a will leaving her entire estate to her daughter for life, with the remainder to be divided equally among all her grandchildren. When the mother died, it was discovered that she had made a second will in which she transferred her home outright to the daughter, made small bequests to her brothers and left the rest of the estate to the daughter for life, with the remainder to her children only. The brothers were disappointed with this change, which had the effect of excluding their children from any interest in the estate. They were also concerned that the sister might make an unwise disposition of the house, given her psychological history, and effectively divest herself of a necessary means of support.

In these circumstances, the four siblings retained counsel to give advice as to whether or not the second will was valid. Having been satisfied that it was, a suggestion was made to the effect that Goodman might transfer title to the house immediately to the grandchildren, leaving herself a life interest in it. Goodman rejected this suggestion and thereafter there was only "casual contact"[91] between Goodman and her brothers. She continued to seek the advice of the lawyer, however, and in due course she conveyed the property to trustees under a trust of the property for her life, provided that the trustees would consider a sale of the property if they considered the sale to be in her interest, with any

---

87 *Lancashire Loans Ltd. v. Black*, [1934] 1 K.B. 380; *Cox v. Adams* (1904), 35 S.C.R. 393; and others in a parental role, such as guardian and ward, *Hylton v. Hylton* (1754), 2 Ves. Sr. 547, 28 E.R. 349.

88 *McKinnon v. McPherson* (1910), 44 N.S.R. 402 (C.A.); *Allcard v. Skinner* (1887), 36 Ch. D. 145.

89 *Yerkey v. Jones* (1939), 63 C.L.R. 649 (Aust. H.C.).

90 [1991] 2 S.C.R. 353, 81 D.L.R. (4th) 211.

91 *Ibid.* at 215 (D.L.R.).

remaining value of the house to be divided among all the grandchildren upon her death. After Goodman's death, her executor brought this claim to set aside that transaction on the ground that it was procured by the undue influence of her brothers. On these facts, the Supreme Court of Canada divided as to whether, in the aftermath of the death of her mother, there existed a situation in which Goodman had placed her trust and confidence in her brothers to help her straighten out her legal and financial situation and that a presumption of undue influence would arise in these circumstances. Two members of the Court, who placed emphasis on the psychological vulnerability of Goodman, would have applied the presumption. Two other members of the Court, placing emphasis on the trial judge's finding of an absence of a close relationship among the siblings, would not have. The fifth member of the panel stated that it was unnecessary to decide the point because the Court also held unanimously that, at the time of the transfer, no undue influence could be established. At that time, there was very little contact between the brothers and their sister. Moreover, the sister did receive some independent legal advice from the lawyer she consulted and, as well, the trust instrument was in accord with her wishes.

Family settings, such as that in *Geffen*, provide an obvious context within which relationships of trust and confidence may develop.[92] In other cases, the presumption of undue influence has been applied in favour of parents influenced by their children[93] and spouses influenced by their partners.[94] Beyond the family context, however, such trust and confidence has been presumed to exist, for example, in the relationships of an elderly gentleman who often relied on a neighbour for advice,[95] of a customer who placed confidence in the advice of a bank manager[96] and of a junior employee who was subject to the influence of the employer.[97]

As confirmed by the Supreme Court in the *Geffen* case[98] itself, the requisite relationship of trust and confidence is typically one in which the influenced party places trust and confidence in the stronger party on the basis of a belief by the former that the latter is acting in his or

---

92   See, for example, *Inche Noriah v. Shaik Allie Bin Omar*, [1929] A.C. 127 (P.C.) (nephew and elderly aunt).

93   *Bank of Montreal v. Stuart*, [1911] A.C. 120. Compare with *Bank of Montreal v. Duguid* (2000), 185 D.L.R. (4th) 458 (Ont. C.A.).

94   *Albert v. Albert* (1981), 33 N.B.R. (2d) 689 (Q.B.).

95   *Goldsworthy v. Brickell*, [1987] 1 All E.R. 853 (C.A.).

96   *Lloyd's Bank v. Bundy*, [1975] Q.B. 326 (C.A.).

97   *Credit Lyonnais Bank Nederland NV v. Burch*, [1997] 1 All E.R. 144 (C.A.).

98   Above note 90.

her best interests. In principle, however, the 2B presumption is not restricted to such cases. It would be available, for example, where a pattern of the weaker party doing the stronger party's bidding arises from a pattern of intimidation rather than of misplaced confidence.[99] The important element is the existence of a degree of influence that undermines the influenced party's capacity for independent action. The willingness of the courts to find that the circumstances of a particular relationship support the presumption will be influenced by the degree of vulnerability of the influenced party[100] and by the level of intimacy of the relationship between the parties.[101] Thus, though husband and wife is not a relationship on the prescribed list, the potential for dependency is increased by the emotional intimacy of the relationship. Further, where the impugned transaction is "extravagantly improvident,"[102] the finding that the relationship gives rise to the presumption will more readily be drawn.

b)   Must There Exist a Dominating Influence?

In recent years, a controversy has arisen as to whether a 2B presumption of undue influence rests on a finding that the stronger party exercised a "dominating influence" on the weaker party. The existence of such a requirement was suggested by Lord Scarman in *National Westminster Bank plc v. Morgan*.[103] In this case, a husband in financial difficulty with his business sought to refinance loans secured by a mortgage on the matrimonial home that he owned jointly with his wife, by securing a further legal charge on that home. As the matter was urgent, the bank manager visited the wife at her home and invited her to execute the charge. The wife expressed concern that the charge should not secure her husband's business debts. The bank manager incorrectly advised her that it did not do so. In due course, when the bank attempted to realize its security, the wife sought to rescind the charge on the ground of undue influence. Lord Scarman, with the full concurrence of his colleagues, rejected the claim of undue influence on the ground that the relationship between

---

99   See, for example, *Re Craig,* above note 78.
100   See, for example, *Geffen v. Goodman Estate,* above note 90. Evidence of infirmity of various kinds is a frequent factual element of 2B cases.
101   *Barclays Bank plc v. O'Brien,* [1993] 4 All E.R. 417; *Bank of Montreal v. Stuart,* above note 93. This principle would apply to "all other cases where there is an emotional relationship between cohabitees." See *O'Brien* at 431.
102   *Credit Lyonnais Bank Nederland NV v. Burch,* above note 97 at 155, Millett L.J. ("The transaction gives rise to grave suspicion. It cries aloud for an explanation." *Ibid.* at 152).
103   Above note 81.

the wife and the bank manager had not "crossed the line"[104] from the normal relationship of banker and customer to a relationship in which the bank had developed "a dominating influence"[105] over the wife. As we shall see, it may be that under more recent authority, the bank may be under an obligation, in such circumstances, to advise the wife to seek independent advice. The question remains, however, whether "dominating influence" is an element of the 2B presumption test.

In the later case of *Goldsworthy v. Brickell*,[106] the Court of Appeal considered at some length and rejected the notion that "dominating influence" must be established. Nourse L.J. suggested that it would be sufficient to engage the 2B presumption if one established the degree of trust and confidence between two parties that is typical of those relationships identified by the 2A list. The principle underlying the 2A and 2B presumptions, in his view, is the same: "It is that the degree of trust and confidence is such that the party in whom it is reposed, either because he is or has become an adviser of the other or because he has been entrusted with the management of his affairs or everyday needs or for some other reason, is in a position to influence him into effecting the transaction of which complaint is later made."[107] Just as it would be unnecessary to establish that the client is dominated by the solicitor or that the patient is dominated by the doctor in order to engage the 2A presumption,[108] so too it should be unnecessary to establish domination in order to engage the 2B presumption. Moreover, Nourse L.J. reviewed the leading English cases and observed that support could not there be found for a requirement of domination.[109] On its particular facts, *Goldsworthy* was a case in which an elderly farmer had become quite dependent upon the advice of his neighbour. The Court of Appeal held that although the relationship fell short of being one of domination, the farmer had nonetheless reposed such trust and confidence in the neighbour that a presumption of undue influence was established.

In the *Geffen*[110] case, the Supreme Court turned its attention to this controversy. As has been indicated, a panel of five members of the Court held unanimously that undue influence was not established on the facts of this case. Both Wilson J., with whom Cory J. concurred,

---

104 *Ibid.* at 831.
105 *Ibid.*
106 Above note 95.
107 *Ibid.* at 865.
108 *Ibid.* at 868. ("Even in jest such cases must be rare ... it is not the function of a presumption to presume the generally improbable.")
109 *Ibid.* at 866–68.
110 Above note 90.

and La Forest J., with whom McLachlin J. concurred, favoured the view that the presumption should arise only in a case where "one person is in a position to dominate the will of another."[111] In a brief concurring opinion, Sopinka J. indicated that having found there was no undue influence, any discussion of the nature of the presumption was "unnecessary and *obiter*."[112] The members of the Court did not note that the language of dominating influence had earlier found its way into the Supreme Court jurisprudence. In 1941, in *McKay v. Clow*,[113] Crocket J. opined that the "established rule" is that where an immoderate gain is achieved by a person occupying "such a position in relation to his or her supposed benefactor as to give the recipient a dominating influence over the latter"[114] a presumption of undue influence arises. Nor did the Court offer, in *Geffen*, a detailed rebuttal of the various points made by Nourse L.J. in his critique of the requirement of dominating influence.

While the discussion of dominating influence in the *Geffen* case may be unsatisfying to some observers, it seems rather likely that lower courts will adopt the view that dominating influence is an element of the 2B presumption test in Canadian law. There is some evidence of this in the post-*Geffen* case law.[115] It must be asked, however, whether much of significance turns on the recognition or adoption of this requirement. The notion of "dominating influence" or "domination" is rather vague.[116] In her opinion in *Geffen*, Wilson J. also restated the test as requiring "that the relationship between [the siblings] was such that a potential existed for the brothers to exercise a *persuasive influence* over their sister."[117] There would appear to be little, perhaps nothing, separating this test from that favoured by the court in *Goldsworthy v. Brickell*. Moreover, it would seem entirely possible for a court to apply the test as formulated by the Court in the *Geffen* case and agree with Lord Scarman that the limited contact between the bank manager and the wife in *Morgan*[118]

---

111 *Ibid.* at 227, Wilson J, and at 239, La Forest J. (D.L.R.).
112 *Ibid.* at 241.
113 [1941] 4 D.L.R. 273 (S.C.C.).
114 *Ibid.* at 290.
115 *Williams v. Downey-Waterbury*, [1995] 2 W.W.R. 609 at 614 (Man. C.A.); *Rutkowski Estate v. Brandhorst* (1997), 19 E.T.R. (2d) 209 at 211 (Alta. C.A.); *Dmyterko Estate v. Kulikowsky* (1992), 47 E.T.R. 66 at 92 (Ont. Ct. Gen. Div.); and *Dell'Aquila Estate v. Mellof*, [1996] 6 W.W.R. 445 at 459 (Sask. Q.B.).
116 See P. Birks and C.N. Yin, "On the Nature of Undue Influence" in J. Beatson and D. Friedmann, eds., *Good Faith and Contract Law* (Oxford: Clarendon Press, 1995) 57 at 69.
117 Above note 90 at 228 (D.L.R.) (emphasis added).
118 Above note 103.

was insufficient to raise a presumption and, at the same time, agree with the Court of Appeal that the history of dependency exhibited in *Goldsworthy* provided a factual foundation for a 2B presumption. In short, it is unlikely, that the "dominating influence" test articulated in *Geffen* is likely to reduce or otherwise affect the traditional scope of undue influence doctrine.

c)   Manifest Disadvantage

A second ground identified by the House of Lords in *Morgan* for depriving the wife of relief was that the impugned transaction did not exhibit a "manifest disadvantage" to the wife. The lending transaction was a short-term loan at a commercial rate of interest that was necessary to ward off foreclosure on the prior mortgage and preserve the wife's interest in the matrimonial home. It was Lord Scarman's view that the presumption of undue influence would not arise unless "the transaction itself was wrongful in that it constituted an advantage taken of the person subjected to the influence which, failing proof to the contrary, was explicable only on the basis that undue influence had been exercised to procure it."[119] Moreover, it was his view that the reported cases invoking the presumption appeared invariably to involve transactions exhibiting manifest disadvantage and this provided support, in his view, for the proposition that such disadvantage is a requirement.

In *Geffen*, the trial judge found that the trust agreement entered into by Goodman was not "manifestly disadvantageous" and, accordingly, the Supreme Court was required to consider whether the manifest disadvantage principle, from *Morgan*, should be considered to be a feature of Canadian undue influence law. Wilson J. found the reasoning of Lord Scarman in *Morgan* persuasive and adopted the view that manifest disadvantage must be established in order for the presumption to arise, at least in the context of commercial transactions.[120] Wilson J. defended this approach on the basis that it was necessary to "accord some degree of deference to the principle of freedom of contract and the inviolability of bargains."[121] Accordingly, in addition to establishing that a relationship of dominance exists, the plaintiff must demonstrate

---

119 *Ibid.* at 827.

120 Above note 90 at 226–28 (D.L.R.).

121 *Ibid.* at 228. It may well be, as La Forest J. intimated in his concurring judgment, that Wilson J. has here confused the presumption with the doctrine itself. It was Lord Scarman's suggestion that the presumption should not arise, not that undue influence *per se* requires a finding of manifest disadvantage. See *ibid.* at 239, La Forest J. The doctrine itself does not require a showing of "manifest disadvantage." See below this Chapter, section C(4).

"that the contract worked unfairness either in the sense that he or she was unduly disadvantaged by it or that the defendant was unduly bene-fited by it."[122] In the context of gifts and bequests, however, it was Wilson J.'s view that it would be inappropriate to require that disadvantage be demonstrated. The issue in such cases, she said, "is that such acts of beneficence not be tainted." In other words, it appears that the presumption arises in the context of gifts and bequests simply on the basis of a concern that the donor's or testator's consent was not genuine. A refinement of this approach, with a view to excluding ordinary birthday or Christmas gifts from scrutiny for undue influence, has recently been suggested by the House of Lords.[123] Where a relationship of trust and confidence exists between donor and donee, it may be appropriate to require that the presumption arises only where "the transaction is not readily explicable by the relationship of the parties."[124]

La Forest J. declined to take a position on the manifest disadvantage issue. Although he noted that it "*may* not be unreasonable to require that there be some showing of undue disadvantage or benefit in a commercial transaction before the presumption will arise,"[125] La Forest J. indicated that the issue did not arise in the present case, which was not one involving a commercial transaction. More generally, he observed that the difference of opinion in the English jurisprudence as to whether or not manifest disadvantage should be required "stems from different views on what the doctrine on undue influence is designed to protect."[126] He articulated these views as follows:

> One view is that it should protect against abuses of trust, confidence or power. From this prospective, the focus is upon the process of the undue influence itself, rather than result. Manifest disadvantage to the person influenced is not a requirement, but merely evidence that goes to show whether or not an abuse of confidence took place. The opposing view is that the law should not interfere with reasonable bargains, and that the doctrine of undue influence should only address abuses of trust or confidence resulting in a significant and demonstrable disadvantage to the person influenced.[127]

---

122 *Ibid.*
123 *Royal Bank of Scotland v. Etridge (No. 2)*, above note 74 at 460–61, Lord Nicholls. Lord Nicholls asserted that this factor must be established in any case of presumptive undue influence.
124 *Ibid.*
125 Above note 90 at 239 (D.L.R.) (emphasis added).
126 *Ibid.* at 240.
127 *Ibid.*

Having thus framed the controversy concerning manifest disadvantage, La Forest J. declined to align himself with either of the opposing views. Sopinka J., it will be recalled, expressed his view that discussion by the court of the test for undue influence was "unnecessary and *obiter*."[128] In the result, therefore, two members of the panel in *Geffen,* Wilson and Cory JJ., favoured recognition of the manifest disadvantage requirement and three declined comment. This issue remains unresolved.

In England, the manifest disadvantage test has been abandoned. In *Royal Bank of Scotland v. Etridge (No. 2),*[129] Lord Nicholls indicated that the label "manifest disadvantage" has been "causing difficulty."[130] In place of this requirement, it was held that, in addition to the relationship of trust and confidence, one must establish that "the transaction is not readily explicable by the relationship"[131] in order to engage the presumption. Thus, for example, while relations between solicitor and client and doctor and patient are those of trust and confidence, the presumption does not apply to "an agreement whereby a client or patient agrees to be responsible for the reasonable fees of his legal or medical advisor."[132] Such transactions do not suggest that "something may be amiss."[133] Where, however, "a solicitor has bought property from his client and it is properly put in issue that the purchase was at an undervalue *or* that the client's consent may have been improperly obtained,"[134] the presumption is established. In short, unless "the transaction cannot be readily accounted for by the ordinary motives of ordinary persons in that relationship,"[135] the evidential burden shifts to the party who allegedly exercised undue influence. Under current English law, then, it is not necessary to establish that the impugned transaction is itself a manifestly disadvantageous one.

The status of the manifest disadvantage test in Canadian law is much less clear. Although Wilson J.'s comments on manifest disadvantage are obviously *obiter dicta*, which did not attract the support of the majority of the Court, it is nonetheless possible that lower courts will apply a manifest disadvantage test in presumptive undue influence cases. Indeed, there is some evidence to suggest that trial judges, at

128 *Ibid.* at 241.
129 Above note 74.
130 *Ibid.* at 461.
131 *Ibid.* at 460.
132 *Ibid.* at 461.
133 *Ibid.*
134 *Ibid.* at 482, Lord Hobhouse (emphasis added).
135 *Ibid.* at 459, Lord Nicholls.

least, have begun to do so.[136] Arguably, this would be an unfortunate development. Of the two opposing views framed by La Forest J., the view that undue influence is concerned with process is the more compelling.[137] If undue influence is present, the consent of the influenced party is undermined and therefore there appears to be no sound reason to give effect to the transfer or transaction whether or not it is a reasonable and fair one. The idea that the presumption is rooted in a concern about the genuineness of consent is consistent with the proposition that the presumption can be rebutted by demonstrating that the transfer or transaction was the product of independent judgment.[138] Further, we have noted that manifest disadvantage is not required, at least by the House of Lords,[139] in cases of actual undue influence. Accordingly, it is clearly the case, in English law at least, that a finding of undue influence does not require that the transaction itself exhibits manifest disadvantage. The doctrine is targeted at vitiated consent, not the fairness of the terms. The issue addressed in the recent English cases is whether a presumption should arise in the absence of disadvantage. As noted, the House of Lords held in *Etridge* that the requirement is not a helpful one in that context.

It would be unfortunate if Canadian courts adopted manifest disadvantage as a prerequisite for the presumption or, worse still, as an element of undue influence itself. As traditionally understood and as recently reaffirmed by the House of Lords,[140] the doctrine of undue influence is intended to relieve parties whose consent derives from the abuse of confidential relationships, whether or not the resulting transaction is at the market rate. If the relationship is established as being one of trust and confidence, it is difficult to see why "manifest disadvantage," an element not required by the doctrine, should be required by the presumption. Disadvantage may assist in giving rise to the presumption, but if the relationship itself bespeaks of a lack of consent, arguably, the evidential burden ought to shift. It may well be, then, that manifest disadvantage will disappear from Canadian cases and it may also be that Canadian courts will follow the lead of the House of Lords in *Etridge* in substituting, as a requirement for the presumption, a showing that the transaction is not, like a birthday gift between relatives or a lawyer's

---

136 *Fowler Estate v. Barnes* (1996), 13 E.T.R. (2d) 150 at 166–67 (Nfld. S.C.T.D.); *Roenish v. Bangs,* above note 53 at 165–66.

137 See generally P. Birks and C.N. Yin, above note 116.

138 See further below, this Chapter, section C(5).

139 Above note 82. See also *Etridge,* above note 74 at 458.

140 *Etridge,* above note 74 at 458.

fee, "readily explicable by the relationship of the parties."¹
trine of manifest disadvantage does, however, gain a foothol
ian case law, one might predict that courts, in order to avoi͟u ͟.͟.͟,
inclined to find actual undue influence rather than apply the presumption or, as it was Wilson J.'s view that the requirement would apply only
to commercial transactions, that a particular transaction does not have
a commercial character. Alternatively, in cases where the problem is
that the influenced party did not wish to enter the transaction at all,
a court could hold that a manifest disadvantage is established by that
fact alone, whether or not the terms of the bargain are unfair or oppressive.[142] A further alternative would be to recognize the existence of and
apply the Type 3 category, to which we now turn.

4) Type 3: Non-presumptive Relational Undue Influence

In *Etridge*,[143] the House of Lords clarified the role of the evidential presumption in presumptive undue influence and emphasized that it is
merely a "forensic tool"[144] to assist in establishing that there exists "a
relationship between two parties where one has acquired over another
a measure of influence, or ascendancy, of which the ascendant person
then takes unfair advantage."[145] The burden of establishing the existence of undue influence falls upon the person claiming to have been
wronged. "The evidence required to discharge the burden of proof depends on the nature of the alleged undue influence, the personality
of the parties, their relationship, the extent to which the transaction
cannot readily be accounted for by the ordinary motives of ordinary
persons in that relationship, and all the circumstances of the case."[146]
The party alleging undue influence may rely on the presumption to
shift the burden of proof to the other party where it is established that
trust and confidence have been reposed in the other and that the transaction is not readily explicable by the relationship. The *Etridge* court
emphasized, however, that it would be possible to establish that abuse

---

141 *Ibid.* at 460, Lord Nicholls.
142 Wilson J. places some emphasis on the idea that contract law does not set aside
    agreements simply because the process is tainted. This view appears to ignore
    the doctrines of mistake, misrepresentation and fiduciary obligation under
    which transactions, fair in their terms, can be set aside on process grounds. See
    Geffen v. Goodman Estate, above note 90 at 226.
143 Above note 74.
144 *Ibid.* at 459.
145 *Ibid.* at 457.
146 *Ibid.* at 458–59.

of a relationship of trust and confidence had occurred without reliance on the presumption. A plaintiff alleging undue influence could thus succeed in a case where the presumption is inapplicable as "for instance, where the impugned transaction was not one which called for an explanation."[147]

For the House of Lords, then, it appears to be sufficient to engage the doctrine if the consent of the unduly influenced party has been vitiated by an abuse of a relationship of trust and confidence, whether or not the transaction itself is such as to arouse suspicion. The requirement that the transaction calls for an explanation is a necessary element in raising the presumption but not a necessary element of undue influence itself. These views were anticipated by the suggestion made in Geffen[148] by La Forest J. to the effect that one possible view is that a showing of manifest disadvantage might be an element in the presumption but not necessarily in the doctrine itself. In the context of non-presumptive relational undue influence, then, it is clearly the case, as La Forest J. intimated, that "the focus is upon the process of undue influence itself, rather than the result."[149] The transaction may be a reasonable one, then, in the sense that it is, for example, at the market rate, but if the influenced party's consent is procured by abuse of a relationship of trust and confidence the transaction may be set aside.

Recognition of the possibility of establishing non-presumptive relational undue influence in Etridge offers a useful clarification of the nature of relationship undue influence and the role played by the evidential presumption in the cases. While it may be that some apparent unfairness in the transaction must be established in order to engage the presumption, an abuse of a relationship of trust and confidence may be established without reliance on the presumption. Where the transaction does not call for an explanation, then, the party alleging undue influence must establish not only the existence of the relationship of trust and confidence but also that, as a matter of fact, the influenced party's consent was procured by an abuse of that relationship. In such a case, the unfairness and the reason for judicial intervention resides in the lack of genuine consent rather than in some imbalance in the terms of the values exchanged. A similarly useful clarification of the Canadian law of undue influence may follow in the wake of the Etridge decision. If so, this would involve a rejection of the position advocated

---

147 Ibid. at 459.
148 Above note 90, in the passage quoted in the text above at note 127.
149 Ibid.

by Wilson J. in *Geffen*[150] to the effect that agreements will be set aside for undue influence only where "manifest disadvantage" exists. The doctrine would apply in any case where it is established that genuine consent is absent because of an abuse of a relationship of trust and confidence.

5) Establishing the Independence of the Plaintiff

The defendant in an undue influence case will seek to defend an actual undue influence claim or rebut the presumption in a case of presumed undue influence by establishing that the act of the plaintiff was "the result of the free exercise of independent will."[151] The most common, though by no means the only, means of establishing independence is to demonstrate that the plaintiff has received independent advice, normally from a lawyer, with respect to the content and consequences of the transaction being entered and the circumstances surrounding its formation. Independent legal advice, however, is neither a necessary nor a sufficient basis for establishing independence. It is not necessary because there may be other circumstances that will demonstrate that a transaction was entered as an independent act or that a gift is the result of acting "spontaneously and independently."[152] It is not sufficient to establish independence in the sense that the jurisprudence indicates that the finding of independence will often turn on the quality of the advice offered. Thus, it is said that the advice must be fully informed and such as would be given "solely in the interests of the donor,"[153] that it should normally be given in the absence of the influencing party,[154] and that the advice should fully explain "the nature and effect of the transaction."[155]

Even the most perfect independent legal advice may not avail the defendant in a case where the degree of influence is severe. The more profound the influence, the less likely it is that the individual is capable of following the advice. In *Credit Lyonnais Nederland NV v. Burch*,[156] the plaintiff employee had entered into a potentially ruinous person-

---

150 Above note 90 at 226–28.

151 *Inche Noriah v. Shaik Allie Bin Omar*, above note 92 at 135.

152 *Re Brocklehurst*, [1978] Ch. 14 at 40, Bridge L.J.

153 Above note 92 at 136.

154 *Green v. Perley* (1989), 103 N.B.R. (2d) 181 at 202 (Q.B.).

155 *Inche Noriah v. Shaik Allie Bin Omar*, above note 92 at 135. In *Etridge,* above note 74 at 469–71, Lord Nicholls set forth an extensive list of the kinds of information to be made available when providing independent legal advice to a guarantor.

156 Above note 97. See also *Powell v. Powell*, [1900] 1 Ch. 243.

al guarantee for the business debts of her employer. In commenting on the quality of independent legal advice that would be necessary to rebut the presumption obviously arising in such circumstances, Millet L.J. commented: "it is not sufficient that she should have received independent advice unless she has acted on that advice. If this were not so, the same influence that produced her desire to enter into the transaction would cause her to disregard any advice not to do so."[157] Moreover, in such circumstances, the solicitor is under a duty to "satisfy himself that the transaction is one which his client could sensibly enter into if free from improper influence; and if he is not so satisfied to advise her not to enter it, and to refuse to act further for her if she persists."[158] In *Etridge*,[159] however, the House of Lords cautioned that this approach is appropriate only in cases where "it is glaringly obvious that the [influenced party] is being grievously wronged"[160] and that, more generally, "it is not for the solicitor to veto the transaction"[161] by refusing to confirm that independent advice has been given. Nonetheless, in a limited range of cases the failure to follow the independent legal advice, properly given, is itself an evidence of the lack of an independent frame of mind.

6) Effects on Third Parties

A finding of undue influence has the potential to affect third parties in two kinds of situations. First, where A, acting under B's undue influence, enters a transaction that has the effect of passing property to B and B, in turn, sells the property to C, C's title to the asset will be affected by the undue influence exercised by B if C is aware of the influence. A will be entitled to rescind the transaction with the effect that the property is revested in A because C has notice of the defect in the initial transaction. C is not a *bona fide* purchaser for value without notice. On the other hand, if C had no notice, C would take title as it would now be too late to rescind. Third-party rights have intervened.

A second transactional setting in which third-party rights may be affected arises commonly in the context of personal guarantees. In a situation where C extends credit to B, C may require that a personal guarantee of B's indebtedness be given by A. If B secures A's guarantee

---

157 *Credit Lyonnais Nederland NV v. Burch*, above note 97 at 156.
158 *Ibid.*
159 Above note 74.
160 *Ibid.* at 469.
161 *Ibid.*

by undue influence, the question arises as to whether C might be affected by A's equity, as between A and B. Such cases often arise in the context of married couples. A husband seeking a bank loan for business purposes may be required by the lending bank to obtain a personal guarantee signed by the wife or to secure the loan with a mortgage on a jointly owned matrimonial home. Plainly, in such circumstances, if the bank has actual notice of the undue influence exercised by the husband, the wife is entitled to rescission of the guarantee or charge. Similarly, the bank will be vulnerable to rescission if it can be held that the husband was acting as the bank's agent in securing the wife's agreement. Greater difficulty arises in circumstances where the bank is not aware of the undue influence. Nonetheless, both Canadian and English courts have taken the view that in cases where a wife guarantees or executes a charge to secure her husband's business debts, the bank will be affected by any undue influence exercised by the husband unless special precautions are taken to ensure that the wife's consent to the arrangement is fully informed and independent. In *E & R Distributors*,[162] the British Columbia Court of Appeal indicated that it would be sufficient if the bank provided a "proper explanation" of the transaction to the wife before inviting her signature. In *Barclays Bank plc v. O'Brien*,[163] the House of Lords held that, on such facts, the bank had constructive notice of the undue influence and was under a duty to take reasonable steps to ensure that the wife's consent is based on an adequate understanding of the nature and effect of the transaction and that her consent is true and informed. In a normal case, this burden would be discharged and constructive notice would be avoided if the bank insists that the wife meet privately with a representative of the bank and that she be advised of "the extent of her liability as surety, warned of the risk she is running and urged to take independent legal advice."[164] In cases where knowledge of further facts suggests that undue influence is not merely possible but probable, "the creditor to be safe will have to insist that the wife is separately advised."[165] The Supreme Court of Canada[166] has

---

162 *E & R Distributors v. Atlas Drywall Ltd.* (1980), 118 D.L.R. (3d) 339 (B.C.C.A.).

163 Above note 101. See generally M.H. Ogilvie, "No Special Tenderness for Sexually Contracted Debt? Undue Influence and the Lending Banker" (1996) 27 Can. Bus. L.J. 365; B. Fehlberg, "The Husband, The Wife and Her Signature — the Sequel" (1996) 59 Mod. L. Rev. 675; J. Cartwright, "Taking Stock of *O'Brien*" [1999] R.L.R. 1.

164 *Barclays Bank plc v. O'Brien*, ibid. at 430.

165 *Ibid.*

166 *Gold v. Rosenberg* (1997), 152 D.L.R. (4th) 385 at 402 (S.C.C.), Iacobucci J., and at 408, Sopinka J.

expressed its approval of the *O'Brien* decision, thus tacitly signalling, perhaps, that the burden imposed on the banker in *E & R Distributors* is not sufficiently onerous. These principles apply not only to married couples but also to others living in circumstances of intimacy.[167] The doctrine of constructive notice can apply where a junior employee gives a manifestly improvident guarantee of the employer's indebtedness secured by a second charge given over the employee's flat.[168] Indeed, in *Etridge,* the House of Lords held that there was simply no limit on the kinds of relationships that could be subject to the *O'Brien* principle. The critical question is whether the circumstances are such that the lender is put upon inquiry.[169] That would invariably be true, in the court's view, in the context of a non-commercial guarantee.[170] Further, it has been held that where a lending transaction is voidable on grounds of constructive notice, so too will be a second transaction substituted for the first as a condition of its discharge.[171]

Constructive notice will not arise, however, where the transaction is, on its face, beneficial to the potentially influenced party. Thus, in *CIBC Mortgages plc v. Pitt,*[172] where a husband and wife signed a joint application for a substantial loan to be secured by a mortgage on a jointly owned matrimonial home, explaining to the bank that the money would be used to discharge a previous mortgage and purchase a holiday home, the money was duly advanced and deposited in their joint bank account. As the wife knew, however, the money was intended by the husband to be used for purchasing shares on the stock market. The wife had opposed these plans and entered into the transaction only because of undue influence exercised upon her by the husband. When the husband's investments lost their value and he was unable to maintain the mortgage payments, the bank sought possession of the matrimonial home. The wife's claim of undue influence failed on the ground that from the bank's perspective, this transaction appeared to be nothing other than a normal advance of borrowed monies to a husband and wife for their joint benefit. The mere existence of a husband and wife relationship did not constitute constructive notice of undue influence. *O'Brien* may apply, however, to a loan taken out by a corpora-

---

167 *Barclays Bank plc v. O'Brien,* above note 101 at 431. The presumption may arise even though the parties having an intimate relationship do not co-habit. See *Massey v. Midland Bank plc,* [1995] 1 All E.R. 929 (C.A.).

168 *Credit Lyonnais Bank Nederland NV v. Burch,* above note 97.

169 Above note 74 at 474–76.

170 *Ibid.* at 476.

171 *Yorkshire Bank plc v. Tinsley,* [2004] 3 All E.R. 463 (C.A.).

172 Above note 82.

tion in which both husband and wife own shares even when the wife holds a directorship or executive office in the company. The facts must be examined to determine who actually is responsible for the conduct of the company's business.[173]

In cases where constructive notice does arise, the bank's obligation to take reasonable steps may be satisfied by the giving of a warning, even if, in the event, the independent legal advice is unsatisfactory for some reason. Where, however, the advice is given by the solicitor to the bank or to the husband or by a member of the same law firm, it may be held, as it was in a Canadian case, that the bank "was aware, or ought to have been aware, that this woman had not had the benefit of independent legal advice with respect to a transaction which, from a business viewpoint, was manifestly disadvantageous to her."[174] Recent English decisions, on the other hand, take the view that reliance can be placed on legal advice given by the solicitor to the husband's corporation, to which the advance is made,[175] or by a member of the firm of solicitors retained by the husband.[176] Indeed, the English Court of Appeal recently held that unless the bank has reason to know of any deficiency, the bank can rely on advice given by a solicitor it has retained and instructed to provide the advice. In such circumstances, the court held, the bank is entitled to assume that the solicitor in question has discharged satisfactorily his or her responsibilities to the party being advised. In all such cases, however, solicitors must carefully consider whether there is any reason their involvement would not be in the best interests of the vulnerable party and, if there is, either decline the retainer or, if such circumstances should later become apparent, cease to act.[177] In Canada, however, the prudent course is to ensure that the advice is given by a solicitor who will be perceived to be truly independent of the interests of the lender and the borrower.

The obligation on the party subject to constructive notice is of a lesser nature than that assumed by the influencing party. The latter must demonstrate that an independent decision was made and is therefore vulnerable to any deficiencies in the quality of the independent advice. In considering the bank's position as a third party, however, the question is how the transaction appeared to the bank. Once advised by a solicitor that proper advice has been given, the bank is under no

---

173   *Etridge*, above note 74 at 466.
174   *Bertolo v. Bank of Montreal* (1986), 33 D.L.R. (4th) 610 at 620 (Ont. C.A.).
175   *Massey v. Midland Bank plc*, above note 167.
176   *Barclays Bank plc v. Thomson*, [1997] 4 All E.R. 816 (C.A.).
177   *Etridge*, above note 74 at 472.

obligation to make further inquiries with respect to the precise nature of that advice. If, however, the bank is in possession of information not available to the solicitor that suggests a lack of free will, the bank must pass this information on to the solicitor.[178] If it has not been, or if the bank knows or ought to know that the solicitor has not offered adequate advice, the solicitor's advice is of no assistance to the bank.[179]

A finding that there exists constructive notice does not, of course, settle the question of whether undue influence did exist. A burden remains on the party alleging undue influence to establish either actual undue influence occurred or that a presumption of undue influence arises that cannot be successfully rebutted. Thus, in *Bank of Montreal v. Duguid*,[180] a case in which a wife guaranteed her husband's investment loan from the bank, the existence of a close relationship and a disadvantageous transaction gave rise to constructive notice on the part of the bank, but did not, in itself, give rise to the presumption of undue influence. Indeed, a majority of the court held that the fact that the wife was a real estate agent who would have understood the nature of and the risks involved in the transaction, together with the absence of evidence of a relationship in which the wife placed her trust and confidence in the husband with respect to financial matters, precluded a finding of presumed undue influence.

7) Remedies

Once undue influence is found, the remedy traditionally available to the unduly influenced plaintiff is an equitable rescission of the impugned transaction. As in other rescissionary contexts, there are limits on the availability of this relief. The traditional bars to relief preclude rescission in circumstances where the transaction has been affirmed, where a return to the *status quo ante* cannot be effected, where third-party rights to the subject matter of the transaction have arisen or where the defence of laches arises as a result of the passage of a reasonable period of time within which to seek relief.

It is important to note, however, that the requirement of a restoration of the *status quo ante*—a giving back and a taking back on both sides—has been ameliorated by an increased willingness on the part of the courts to substitute monetary compensation for a specific restoration of the *status quo ante*. Thus, transactions may be set aside, even

---

178 *Ibid.* at 473.
179 *Ibid.* at 468 and 473.
180 Above note 93.

where precise restoration is impossible, by requiring the defendant to couple rescission with the payment, for example, of reasonable compensation for deterioration in the value of property[181] or, perhaps, by requiring the plaintiff to compensate the defendant for the value of services rendered.[182] When granting equitable rescissionary relief, courts have a discretion to devise an order that seeks to restore the parties "substantially" to the *status quo*.[183]

A more controversial question is whether the courts could grant monetary compensation in complete substitution for a rescission of the transaction. If A, unduly influenced by B, sells property to B and B then, in turn, sells the property to C, who is unaware of the undue influence, rescission is precluded by the intervention of C's good-faith acquisition of the property. In such circumstances, could A seek compensation from B for the difference between the contract price and the market value of the asset transferred? A persuasive case can be made for such relief. B has made a profit at A's expense by means of undue influence. As a matter of principle, it is difficult to articulate a convincing basis for the traditional proposition that B's initiative in transferring the property to C should have the effect of cutting off A's ability to reverse the unjust enrichment of B. A solution to this problem may be found in the renewed vitality accorded by Canadian and other Commonwealth courts to the concept of "equitable compensation,"[184] especially in the context of fiduciary relationships.[185] This revival of equitable compensation as a concept opens up the possibility that monetary awards might be available in other equitable contexts such as undue influence.

A recent English case suggests that equitable compensation could, indeed, constitute a complete substitution for rescissionary relief in an undue influence setting. The facts of *Mahoney v. Purnell*[186] were the following. The plaintiff, Mahoney, and his son-in-law, Purnell, operated a hotel business owned by a corporation in which they were ap-

---

181 *Kupchak v. Dayson Holdings Ltd.* (1965), 53 D.L.R. (2d) 482 (B.C.C.A.).

182 *O'Sullivan v. Management Agency and Music Ltd.,* [1985] 3 All E.R. 351.

183 *Alati v. Kruger* (1955), 94 C.L.R. 216 at 224 (Aust. H.C.). The authorities are gathered in *O'Sullivan, ibid.*

184 See generally, J.D. McCamus, "Equitable Compensation and Restitutionary Remedies: Recent Developments" in *L.S.U.C. 1995 Special Lectures, Law of Remedies* (Toronto: Carswell, 1995) at 295.

185 *Guerin v. Canada,* [1984] 2 S.C.R. 335 is the first of a lengthy list of Supreme Court authorities on point. See generally J.D. McCamus, "Prometheus Unbound: Fiduciary Obligation in the Supreme Court of Canada" (1997) 28 Can. Bus. L.J. 107.

186 [1996] 3 All E.R. 61 (Q.B.).

proximately equal shareholders. In circumstances that it was agreed amounted to undue influence, Purnell pressured his father-in-law to enter into a transaction under which he sold his shares to Purnell at a price that proved to be dramatically less than their true value. Mahoney was to receive approximately two hundred thousand pounds over ten years. Shortly thereafter, the hotel was sold, in a rising market, for £3.3 million. In due course, the company, now wholly owned by Purnell, lost these profits in other ventures. Under traditional doctrine, the sale of the hotel to a third party would preclude rescissionary relief. In this case, however, the trial judge held that equitable compensation could be made available. The plaintiff was awarded the difference between the value of the interest he transferred to Purnell and that which he had received in return.

The measure of relief awarded in *Mahoney v. Purnell* is restitutionary in nature. Mahoney recovered the unpaid-for value of the asset he had transferred to Purnell. It was no defence to Purnell that he had squandered that value in unprofitable ventures. Such a result, though innovative, appears to be sound in terms of general principle and it therefore appears likely that such an approach will be taken in Canadian common law. The more general recognition of the unjust enrichment principle in Canadian law,[187] coupled with the recent embrace by the Supreme Court of Canada of a revitalized concept of equitable compensation provides a doctrinal foundation for accepting *Mahoney v. Purnell* as good Canadian law. Moreover, there is some Canadian authority that assumes the existence of and exercises a discretion to substitute compensation for rescission.[188]

D. UNCONSCIONABILITY

1) Introduction

In addition to the jurisdiction to set aside agreements resulting from abuse of confidential relationships on the basis of the doctrine of undue influence, courts of equity asserted a jurisdiction to set aside agreements where, even in the context of bargaining by complete strangers, unfair agreements resulted from an inequality of bargaining power. In *Waters v. Donnelly*,[189] Chancellor Boyd described the jurisdiction in the

---

187 See generally Maddaugh and McCamus, above note 6, c. 2.
188 *Treadwell v. Martin* (1976), 67 D.L.R. (3d) 493 (N.B.C.A.).
189 (1884), 9 O.R. 391 (Ch.).

following terms: "[I]f two persons, no matter whether a confidential relationship exists between them or not, stand in such a relation to each other that one can take an undue advantage of the other, whether by reason of distress, or recklessness, or wildness, or want of care, and when the facts shew that one party has taken undue advantage of the other by reason of the circumstances I have mentioned, a transaction resting upon such unconscionable dealing will not be allowed to stand."[190]

Where such circumstances are present, "the principle is applied of requiring the one who gets the benefit to prove that the transaction was fair, just and reasonable."[191] The facts of this case are illustrative. The parties apparently had no relationship prior to the negotiation of the impugned transaction. The plaintiff, a young and unsophisticated man who was not a business person and who was described as being "weak-minded and very easily led,"[192] was persuaded by the defendant, a shrewd business person, to trade his Niagara peach orchard and seven hundred dollars in return for the defendant's livery stable. The transaction rested on a substantial exaggeration of the value of the defendant's property. Moreover, it included a mortgage obligation that the plaintiff was unlikely to have fully understood. The plaintiff was "over-matched and overreached; without information, and without advice he made a most improvident exchange."[193] The transaction was set aside. Although the term "fraud," is often used in these cases to refer to the defendant's conduct, it is clearly established, as Chancellor Boyd noted,[194] that it is not necessary to establish that fraud in the common law sense of deceit must have occurred. The elements of the doctrine articulated by Chancellor Boyd establish a form of "equitable" or "constructive" fraud.

Although this doctrine of unconscientious dealing or, as it is now more commonly described, unconscionability is applicable to dealings between complete strangers, it may also apply to dealings between parties that have a pre-existing relationship. Thus, it may occur that in a particular fact situation consideration may be given to whether either one or both of the doctrines of undue influence and unconscionability

---

190   *Ibid.* at 401, quoting from a leading formulation of the doctrine set out by Sullivan M.R. in *Slator v. Nolan* (1876), 11 I.R. Eq. 367 at 386–87. See also *Black v. Wilcox* (1976), 70 D.L.R. (3d) 192 at 196 (Ont. C.A.), Evans J.A. References to the earlier English authorities are collected in *Fry v. Lane* (1888), 40 Ch. D. 312.
191   *Waters v. Donnelly,* above note 189 at 402.
192   *Ibid.* at 392, Osler J.A.
193   *Ibid.* at 406, Boyd C.
194   *Ibid.* at 401–2.

might apply. Nonetheless, the doctrines have separate and discrete functions. In a leading case, *Morrison v. Coast Finance Ltd.*,[195] Davey J.A. outlined the difference between the two doctrines in the following terms:

> The equitable principles relating to undue influence and relief against unconscionable bargains are closely related, but the doctrines are separate and distinct. ... A plea of undue influence attacks the sufficiency of consent; a plea that a bargain is unconscionable invokes relief against an unfair advantage gained by an unconscientious use of power by a stronger party against a weaker. On such a claim the material ingredients are proof of inequality in the position of the parties arising out of the ignorance, need or distress of the weaker, which left him in the power of the stronger, and proof of substantial unfairness of the bargain obtained by the stronger. On proof of those circumstances, it creates a presumption of fraud which the stronger must repel by proving that the bargain was fair, just and reasonable ... or perhaps by showing no advantage was taken.[196]

In determining the scope of the doctrine, then, it is necessary to consider the requisite degree of the inequality of bargaining power present in a particular fact situation and the requisite degree of the advantage taken or the unfairness or inprovidency of the transaction. In attempting to discern the scope of the doctrine, it is also necessary to consider whether the doctrine is primarily or, indeed, exclusively, targeted at what has been referred to as problems of "procedural" unconscionability, or whether it may extend to cases of "substantive" unconscionability as well.[197] If the doctrine is merely procedural in nature, it may apply only to situations in which one of the bargaining parties suffers from a severe inability to engage in effective bargaining. If the doctrine is substantive in nature, however, it might be considered to apply, for example, to transactions entered into by consumers of normal bargaining capacity dealing with commercial actors, such as large corporations, that have a much greater bargaining power. If the doctrine is applicable to oppressive terms contained in ordinary consumer transactions, the doctrine might be thought to constitute an effective means of implementing broad policies of consumer protection. As we shall see, the

---

195 (1965), 55 D.L.R. (2d) 710 (B.C.C.A.).

196 *Ibid.* at 713. This passage has been quoted with approval in several Canadian cases. See, for example, *Knupp v. Bell* (1968), 67 D.L.R. (2d) 256 at 259 (Sask. C.A.), Woods J.A.; *Granville Savings and Mortgage Corp. v. Campbell* (1992), 93 D.L.R. (4th) 268 at 290 (Man. C.A.), Huband J.A.

197 See A.A. Leff, "Unconscionability and the Code — The Emperor's New Clause" (1967) 115 U. Pa. L. Rev. 485.

role of the doctrine at common law as an instrument of such a policy is, at best, a limited one. The doctrine has, however, been given statutory expression in a number of provincial legislative schemes that do implement broadly based policies of this kind.[198]

2) Elements of Unconscionability

In order to set aside a transaction on the ground of unconscionability, one must establish both inequality of bargaining power in the sense that one party is incapable of adequately protecting his or her interests and undue advantage or benefit secured as a result of that inequality by the stronger party. The combination of these two factors is well illustrated in the leading case of *Morrison v. Coast Finance Ltd.*[199] The plaintiff was an elderly widow, Mrs. Morrison, preyed upon by two young men, Lowe and Kitely. A woman of modest means, Morrison's principal income came from renting out three rooms in her home. Kitely had been a roomer for a month or two before he and Lowe successfully persuaded Morrison to mortgage her home to the defendant finance company in order to be able to lend the monies thereby secured to Lowe and Kitely. The monies were to be used by Lowe to repay a loan advanced to him by the same finance company and by the two men to each buy a car from a related automobile company that operated as a car dealer. Kitely was an alcoholic; the two men represented to Morrison that her loan to them would enable Kitely to make a start in the automobile sales business. The transaction was handled by one Crawford, the office manager for both the finance company and the automobile company. Under his supervision, the cheque for the proceeds of the mortgage was endorsed by Morrison in favour of Lowe and Kitely, who in turn returned the cheque to Crawford. Crawford deposited the amount in the account of the automobile company, from which amount the outstanding balance on Lowe's loan was restored to the finance company. The unfairness of the transaction was no doubt evident to Crawford who, later that day or the next day, required Lowe to execute a promissory note in favour of Morrison for the amount advanced and further, required the execution of conditional sale contracts for the two cars in question between the automobile company and Lowe and Kitely and assigned the vendor's interest therein to Morrison. As Davey J.A. observed, "[T]he extreme folly of this old woman mortgaging her home in order to borrow money which she could not repay out of her own resources, for the purpose

---

198 See below this Chapter, section D(6).
199 Above note 195.

of lending it to the two men, who were comparative strangers, is self-evident."[200] This was not a simple case of a mortgage being made on the usual terms to a person intending to use the money for his or her own purposes. This was a mortgage designed to put funds into the hands of the finance company and the automobile company by taking advantage of the obvious vulnerability of Morrison. It was "a gross abuse of over-whelming inequality between the parties."[201] Accordingly, Morrison's action to have the mortgage set aside on the ground that it constituted an unconscionable bargain enjoyed success.

Many of the unconscionability cases deal with situations in which the inequality of bargaining power arises from the mental infirmities that may come with advancing years.[202] In other cases, such as *Waters v. Donnelly*,[203] the inequality results from a lack of intelligence or education coupled with a lack of sophistication in business matters.[204] A more recent illustration is provided by *Harry v. Kreutziger*.[205] In this case, the plaintiff sought to set aside the sale of his fishing boat to the defendant at a price of approximately four thousand dollars. The boat, with its salmon fishing licence, was worth approximately sixteen thousand dollars. The plaintiff was a "mild, inarticulate, retiring person ... not widely experienced in business matters."[206] He was "partially deaf, easily intimidated and ill-advised."[207] Although initially reluctant to sell the boat, the defendant induced him into the sale by a "process of harassment"[208] to which he ultimately succumbed. Quite apart from the underevaluation of the boat, the plaintiff failed to appreciate the extreme difficulty he might encounter in attempting to get another fishing licence. For his part, the defendant pursued the transaction aggressively and with full knowledge of the true value of the boat. The British Columbia Court of Appeal held that the transaction was obviously improvident and that it resulted from the inequality of bargaining power

---

200 *Ibid.* at 714.

201 *Ibid.* at 716.

202 See, for example, *Knupp v. Bell*, above note 196; *Marshall v. Canada Permanent Trust Co.* (1968), 69 D.L.R. (2d) 260 (Alta. S.C.T.D.).

203 Above note 189.

204 See, for example, *Easton v. Sinclair* (1912), 3 D.L.R. 652 (Ont. H.C.J.); *Hnatuk v. Chretian* (1960), 31 W.W.R. 130 (B.C.S.C.); *Pridmore v. Calvert* (1975), 54 D.L.R. (3d) 133 (B.C.S.C.); *Buchanan v. Canadian Imperial Bank of Commerce* (1979), 100 D.L.R. (3d) 624 (B.C.S.C.), var'd (1980), 125 D.L.R. (3d) 394 (B.C.C.A.); *Stephenson v. Hilti (Canada) Ltd.* (1989), 63 D.L.R. (4th) 573 (N.S.S.C.T.D.).

205 (1978), 95 D.L.R. (3d) 231 (B.C.C.A.).

206 *Ibid.* at 231–32, McIntyre J.A.

207 *Ibid.* at 242, Lambert J.A.

208 *Ibid.*

between the parties. Other signals of inequality of bargaining power include emotional distress,[209] illiteracy,[210] inability to understand the language in which the transaction is conducted[211] and drunkenness at the time of the transaction.[212] There is no rigid limitation, however, on the kinds of factors that might establish that one party suffers from an unusual inability to protect his or her own interests in entering into a transaction with a stronger party.[213]

Similarly, there are no rigid limitations on the type of advantage taken as a result of the inequality of bargaining power. A recurring fact pattern, however, concerns the sale of land at much less than its true value, often in circumstances where the land is the only significant asset of the person in question. In *Knupp v. Bell*,[214] a transaction under which an elderly woman, suffering some of the effects of senility, had entered into a transaction to sell her property to a neighbour at a price much less than its true value, was held unenforceable. Similarly, in *Marshall v. Canada Permanent Trust Co.*,[215] Marshall, an elderly man then resident in a rest home who had suffered from some brain damage as a result of hardening of the arteries and a recent stroke, agreed to sell his farm property for considerably less than its actual value. The transaction was set aside. In *Morrison*,[216] the land was employed by Morrison as security for a loan entered into with the defendant finance company. Other typical cases include the sale of goods at an undervalue,[217] the giving of improvident guarantees,[218] disadvantageous releases of

---

209 See, for example, *Mundinger v. Mundinger* (1968), 3 D.L.R. (3d) 338 (Ont. C.A.), aff'd [1970] S.C.R. vi; *Gillett v. Gillett* (1979), 100 D.L.R. (3d) 247 (Alta. S.C.T.D.); *Natuk v. Kawula* (1979), 104 D.L.R. (3d) 288 (Man. C.A.).
210 See, for example, *Paris v. Machnik* (1972), 32 D.L.R. (3d) 723 (N.S.S.C.T.D.); *Taylor v. Armstrong* (1979), 99 D.L.R. (3d) 547 (Ont. H.C.J.); *Shoppers Trust Co. v. Dynamic Homes Ltd.* (1992), 96 D.L.R. (4th) 267 (Ont. Ct. Gen. Div.).
211 See, for example, *Gladu v. Edmonton Land Co.* (1914), 19 D.L.R. 688 (Alta. S.C.); *Bertolo v. Bank of Montreal*, above note 174; *Royal Bank of Canada v. Hussain* (1997), 37 O.R. (3d) 85 (Gen. Div.).
212 See, for example, *Black v. Wilcox*, above note 190; *Stubbs v. Erickson* (1981), 34 B.C.L.R. 45 (S.C.).
213 See, for example, *Osorio v. Cardona* (1984), 15 D.L.R. (4th) 619 (B.C.S.C.), a case of unconscionability resulting from threatened breach of contract. The case might more appropriately be analyzed as an instance of economic duress. See above this Chapter, section B(3).
214 Above note 196.
215 Above note 202.
216 Above note 195.
217 See, for example, *Harry v. Kreutziger*, above note 205.
218 See, for example, *Bertolo v. Bank of Montreal*, above note 174; *Bomek v. Bomek* (1983), 146 D.L.R. (3d) 139 (Man. C.A.).

claims executed by parties who have suffered personal injuries[219] and agreements concerned with domestic arrangements such as separation agreements.[220]

In cases of obviously unfair agreements resulting from severe inequality of bargaining power, of course, the double-barrelled test of inequality coupled with undue advantage will be easily applied. At the margin, however, no simple formula will draw the line between sufficient and insufficient inequality and sufficient or insufficient improvidence. In *Harry v. Kreutziger*,[221] however, Lambert J.A. attempted to devise a formula that might be of assistance. Lambert J.A. began his analysis by suggesting that the isolation of separate questions relating to degree of inequality and degree of improvidence was unhelpful as the two questions "are really aspects of one single question,"[222] which he formulated in the following terms:

> That single question is whether the transaction, seen as a whole, is sufficiently divergent from community standards of commercial morality that it should be rescinded. To my mind, the framing of the question in that way prevents the real issue from being obscured by an isolated consideration of a number of separate questions; as, for example, a consideration of whether the consideration was grossly inadequate, rather than merely inadequate, separate from the consideration of whether bargaining power was grievously impaired, or

---

219 See, for example, *Pridmore v. Calvert*, above note 204; *Towers v. Affleck*, [1974] 1 W.W.R. 714 (B.C.S.C.); *Woods v. Hubley* (1995), 130 D.L.R. (4th) 119 (N.S.C.A.), leave to appeal to S.C.C. refused, 136 D.L.R. (4th) vii. Compare with *Gissing v. T. Eaton Co.* (1911), 25 O.L.R. 50 (C.A.); *Gindis v. Brisbourne* (2000), 183 D.L.R. (4th) 431 (B.C.C.A.).

220 See, for example, *Mundinger v. Mundinger*, above note 209; *B. (J.F.) v. B. (M.A.)* (1999), 178 D.L.R. (4th) 340 (Ont. S.C.J.), aff'd (2001), 203 D.L.R. (4th) 738 (Ont. C.A.). Compare with *Rosen v. Rosen* (1994), 3 R.F.L. (4th) 267 (Ont. C.A.); *Clayton v. Clayton* (1998), 40 O.R. (3d) 24 (Gen. Div.); *Leopold v. Leopold* (2000), 51 O.R. (3d) 275 (S.C.J.). Provincial legislation may create a statutory jurisdiction to set aside such agreements on the same or similar grounds. See, for example, *Family Law Act*, R.S.O. 1990, c. F.3, s. 56(4). Similar problems can arise with marriage or co-habitation agreements. The question of whether a "no support" provision in such an agreement is binding on the termination of the relationship is also typically subject to provincial statutory treatment. See, for example, *Family Law Act*, R.S.O. 1990, c. F.3, s. 33(4)(a). And see *Scheel v. Henkelman* (2001), 195 D.L.R. (4th) 531 (Ont. C.A.). Compare with *Phillips-Renwick v. Renwick Estate* (2003), 229 D.L.R. (4th) 158 (Ont. S.C.J.). See generally D. Majury, "Unconscionability in an Equality Context" (1990–91) 7 Can. Fam. L.Q. 23.

221 Above note 205.

222 *Ibid.* at 241.

merely badly impaired. Such separate consideration of separate questions produced by the application of a synthetic rule tends to obscure rather than aid the process of decision.[223]

Although, in Lambert J.A.'s view, the answer to this question is to be found through an examination of the decided cases, the nature of the inquiry suggests that priority should be given to certain categories of cases: "In that examination, Canadian cases are more relevant than those from other lands, where different standards of commercial morality may apply, and recent cases are more germane than those from earlier times when standards were in some respects rougher and in other respects more fastidious."[224]

In his view, however, the inquiry was not restricted to an examination of decided cases. He further suggested, "it is also appropriate to seek guidance as the community standards of commercial morality from legislation that embodies those standards in law."[225] Thus, Lambert J. indicated that he had examined provincial consumer protection legislation with this object in view. Lambert J.A.'s emphasis on the evolving nature of the doctrine is no doubt a helpful one. Indeed, some of the modern authorities now have a somewhat dated appearance to them.[226] More generally, however, it appears likely that Lambert J.A.'s suggestion—that the question to be addressed is whether the transaction as a whole is sufficiently divergent from community standards—is intended to illuminate and supplement rather than supplant the traditional twofold test of inequality of bargaining power coupled with improvidency of the transaction.[227]

An important issue that has not received much discussion in the Canadian authorities is whether, for the doctrine to apply, the stronger party must be aware of the vulnerability of the other party. At least one Canadian authority has suggested that there is no such requirement. In *Marshall v. Canada Permanent Trust Co.*,[228] the agreement to sell the parcel of farm land at considerably less than its market value was held unconscionable even though the purchaser had no knowledge

---

223 *Ibid.*
224 *Ibid.*
225 *Ibid.*
226 See, for example, *Griesshammer v. Ungerer and Miami Studios of Dancing* (1958), 14 D.L.R. (2d) 599 (Man. C.A.); *Gaertner v. Fiesta Dance Studios Ltd.* (1973), 32 D.L.R. (3d) 639 (B.C.S.C.). For criticism, see Maddaugh and McCamus, *Restitution*, above note 6, c. 29:200.
227 See *Cougle v. Maricevic* (1983), 64 B.C.L.R. (2d) 105 at 110 (C.A.), Lambert J.A.
228 Above note 202.

of the seller's vulnerability. The purchaser was unaware of the fact that the vendor had suffered brain damage and the court held that nothing in the vendor's behaviour signalled such difficulties to the purchaser. The court held that it was "not material"[229] whether the purchaser was aware of the vendor's inability to protect his own interests. It would be surprising, however, if a stronger party who lacked knowledge of the inequality and whose behaviour was circumspect would nonetheless be subject to a finding of unconscionability. Arguably, therefore, the preferable rule may be that it is necessary to establish that the circumstances of the transaction are such that a reasonable person in the position of the stronger party would have realized the possibility that the weaker party suffered from a disadvantage of some kind. Thus, in the *Marshall* case itself, the vendor was resident in a rest home. That fact, together with the apparent inability of the vendor to appreciate the value of his land, might be considered to have put the purchaser on notice of the potential inequality of bargaining power. Other commonwealth courts have expressed the governing principle in such terms.[230] In an appropriate case, however, it may be that the extreme improvidence of the transaction itself provides a basis for finding the existence of a constructive notice of the vulnerability of the other party.[231]

Finally, it may be considered whether the doctrine may be applicable in circumstances where the weaker party is an individual who possesses the normal strengths of intellect and character of natural persons entering into contractual relationships but where the more powerful party nonetheless is able, because of its superior ability to protect itself, to extract terms that appear substantially unfair. Again, there is little explicit discussion of this question in the authorities. As we have seen, however, in the typical case, the weaker party is an individual suffering from unusual bargaining disabilities or disadvantages. Thus, it may be said, in the usual case, the unconscionability in issue has a procedural quality to it in the sense that the process by which the agreement was achieved is defective.[232] If, however, in the absence of procedural problems of this kind, an agreement can be set aside for

---

229 *Ibid.* at 263.

230 See *Commercial Bank of Australia Ltd. v. Amadio* (1983), 151 C.L.R. 447 (Aust. H.C.); *Nichols v. Jessup*, [1986] 1 N.Z.L.R. 237 (C.A.).

231 *Hart v. O'Connor*, [1985] A.C. 1000 (P.C.). Apart from such circumstances, however, the Privy Council held that, in the context of contracts entered into by parties suffering from mental incapacity, actual knowledge by the other party of the incapacity is a prerequisite to finding that the contract is unenforceable on grounds of mental incapacity.

232 See Leff, above note 197.

unconscionability simply on the basis of the unfairness of its terms, the doctrine would have a role in policing the outcome of bargaining processes or the substantive fairness of transactions in a more general way. To the extent that the doctrine may have a substantive role of this kind, it would constitute a more sweeping instrument for the striking down of unfair agreements, which consumer advocates, at least, would surely welcome. There is very little evidence in the decided cases, however, that a more powerful role of this kind is envisaged for the doctrine at common law. Nonetheless, some support for such an approach might be drawn from the decision of the House of Lords in *Schroeder Music Publishing Co. Ltd. v. Macaulay.*[233]

The *Schroeder* case concerned a long-term agreement entered into by a young and unknown songwriter with a music publisher. Under the agreement, the writer was obliged to assign full copyright for songs written during the currency of the agreement to the publisher. Royalties would be payable only if the publisher decided, in its discretion, to publish a particular song. An initial five-year term was renewable automatically if the royalty revenues exceeded a certain sum. The publisher alone could terminate the contract on one month's notice. Although the publisher thus made no commitment under the agreement to undertake initiatives with the writer's material, the payment of an advance of fifty pounds on future royalties was evidently thought to provide sufficient consideration to render the agreement enforceable. The House of Lords was unanimous in holding that the consequent restriction of the ability of the songwriter to sell his work product in the marketplace constituted an unreasonable and therefore unenforceable restraint of trade.[234] A majority of their Lordships, however, provided an additional explanation for the granting of relief on the basis that this one-sided agreement, offered to the writer on a "take it or leave it" basis, constituted an "unconscionable bargain."[235] Lord Diplock noted that the publisher was quite prepared to enter into genuine negotiations with songwriters who had an established reputation. Thus, the fact that the publisher was able to impose so unfair an arrangement on an unknown songwriter indicated that the publisher had used its bargaining power to drive an unconscionable agreement. Because there was no suggestion that the songwriter suffered from any of the usual *indicia* of inequality of bargaining power, the decision in *Schroeder* of-

---

233 [1974] 1 W.L.R. 1308 (H.L.). See also *Clifford Davis Management Ltd. v. W.E.A. Records Ltd.*, [1975] 1 W.L.R. 61 (C.A.).

234 For discussion of the law of restraint of trade, see Chapter 12, section B(4).

235 Above note 233 at 1316, Lord Diplock.

414 THE LAW OF CONTRACTS

fers a somewhat solitary illustration of the doctrine of unconscionability being applied on an essentially substantive basis.

The decision in *Schoeder* has been criticized, however, essentially on the ground that it involves an attempt to regulate the content of contract terms within the music publishing industry, a task that courts are ill equipped to undertake. More particularly, Trebilcock[236] has argued persuasively that the effect of the decision is not likely to have the intended result that music publishers will enter into more generous arrangements with unknown songwriters by, for example, agreeing that the songwriter also has a right to terminate the agreement on short notice. As he observes, "legal liability rules are unlikely to be able to affect the broad balance of advantage between buyers and sellers."[237] The much more likely outcomes are that publishers will be less willing to enter agreements with unknown songwriters or will exact other trade-offs, perhaps in the form of lower royalties, in order to compensate for the likely loss of investments made in promoting the interests of particular unknown songwriters. Moreover, even if such judicial intervention in the marketplace could be effective, some would argue that judicial regulation of the marketplace through unconscionability constitutes an unattractive incursion on the basic principles of freedom of contract that facilitate the proper functioning of the marketplace.[238] Whether or not courts find such considerations persuasive, it is nonetheless true that the *Schroeder* decision has not given birth to a body of Canadian or other commonwealth authority developing a doctrine of substantive unconscionability. Indeed, a Canadian case[239] that applies unconscionability doctrine to the renegotiation of a franchise contract in circumstances where the franchisees do not appear to suffer from any inherent disability in protecting themselves in negotiations is probably better analyzed as a case of economic duress. The franchisees had agreed in principle with the new owner of the franchisor that they would enter into a new franchise agreement. In due course, they reluctantly agreed to a new franchise agreement containing harsh terms when threatened by the franchisor with the prospect of the franchisor opening up a competing business across the street. This fact situation

---

236 See M.J. Trebilcock, "The Doctrine of Inequality of Bargaining Power: Post-Benthamite Economics in the House of Lords" (1976) 26 U.T.L.J. 359.

237 *Ibid.* at 383.

238 See, for example, R.A. Epstein, "Unconscionability: A Critical Reappraisal" (1975) 18 J.L. & Econ. 293.

239 *A & K Lick-a-Chick Franchises Ltd. v. Cordiv Enterprises Ltd.* (1981), 119 D.L.R. (3d) 440 (N.S.T.D.).

appears to engage the criteria for economic duress[240] in which case, of course, there exists no requirement to establish a particular bargaining disability of the type present in the typical unconscionability case.

3) Effects on Third Parties

In the context of our discussion of undue influence, it was material to consider whether a third party to the relationship of undue influence might be affected by the doctrine.[241] Thus, for example, where one spouse unduly influences another spouse to guarantee the first spouse's repayment of borrowings from a bank, it may be asked whether the bank is affected by the fact that the guarantee has been secured only through the undue influence of the first spouse. In recent years, the courts have developed a doctrine of constructive notice under which the bank may be held to be subject to the equity of the undue influence if the circumstances were such that the bank should have appreciated that undue influence might be present. In such a case, the guarantee is unenforceable by the bank unless it has taken reasonable steps to ensure that the guaranteeing spouse has taken independent legal advice. In such circumstances, then, the bank is subject to the doctrine, not because it has itself exercised undue influence but, rather, because it has reason to be aware of the possibility of undue influence being exercised by the first spouse. Here we consider whether a constructive notice doctrine of this kind might have some role to play in the context of unconscionable transactions.

As *Morrison v. Coast Finance Ltd.*[242] illustrates, three-party situations of a similar kind can arise in the context of unconscionable transactions. In this case, Morrison was pressured by Lowe and Kitely to borrow money from Coast Finance. In order to determine whether or not the doctrine of unconscionability applies to the transaction between Morrison and Coast Finance, one must determine whether Coast Finance is fixed with adequate knowledge of the vulnerability of Morrison. In the actual case, there were signals of this vulnerability of which Coast Finance's manager, Crawford, was aware. The British Columbia Court of Appeal was convinced that Crawford must have heard Morrison say, when she learned the amount of the mortgage, "Frank, that is more than I agreed to lend you" and further, heard her ask the solicitor

---

240 See above this Chapter, section B(3).
241 See above this Chapter, section C(6).
242 Above note 195.

present at the transaction "Should I sign this?"[243] The circumstances were such that a reasonable person would have been aware of the potential difficulty of Morrison's situation.

Similar results were achieved in cases where vulnerable parties gave what were in effect, though not in form, guarantees of the existing indebtedness of a romantic partner or family member. In *McKenzie v. Bank of Montreal*,[244] the plaintiff unwisely executed a mortgage in favour of the bank to secure the existing indebtedness of the man with whom she co-habited. The trial judge held that the bank was aware of her emotional relationship with her partner, of her partner's previous fraudulent activities and of his precarious financial situation. In such circumstances, the transaction was unconscionable and the bank was obliged to ensure that she fully appreciated and intended the consequences of her actions. In *Imperial Bank of Commerce v. Ohlson*,[245] an elderly woman entered into a loan agreement with the defendant bank; secured by a mortgage on her property, the monies had already been advanced to her adult son. The mother thus derived no advantage from the transaction. The Alberta Court of Appeal held that the relationship of elderly parent to adult child is "frequently one of dependency and therefore one which can be subject to abuse or pressure."[246] Accordingly, when an elderly parent is risking an asset solely for the benefit of a child, the bank is under an obligation to ensure that independent advice is obtained by the parent.

Although the cases have not yet developed a formal doctrine of constructive notice in the manner of the undue influence cases, then, it is nonetheless the case that a similar principle applies in the context of unconscionable transactions. In particular, if the circumstances are such that a reasonable person would appreciate the possibility that the party with whom he or she was dealing was in a weakened and vulnerable state because of the actions of another party such as a spouse or child, this will constitute sufficient awareness of the party's vulnerability to engage the first branch of the unconscionability test. As far as the second branch of the test is concerned, it will be necessary to show an advantage taken as a result of the inequality of bargaining power. In each of these three cases, it is easily seen that the finance company and the banks enjoyed an unfair advantage as a result of their ability to exploit the weakness of the other party.

---

243   *Ibid.* at 715.
244   (1975), 55 D.L.R. (3d) 641 (Ont. H.C.J.), aff'd (1976), 70 D.L.R. (3d) 113 (Ont. C.A.).
245   (1997), 154 D.L.R. (4th) 33 (Alta. C.A.).
246   *Ibid.* at 49, Conrad J.A.

4) Justification for the Doctrine

The doctrine of unconscionability, which has enjoyed something of a renaissance in the latter part of the twentieth century, at least in North American common law jurisdictions, has proven to be controversial within the academic literature. Unsurprisingly, the main charge levelled at the doctrine by its critics are that it introduces an undesirable element of instability or uncertainty into the law of contracts. Disparaged by one writer as little more than "an emotionally satisfying incantation"[247] and by another as a "poor substitute for the clear articulation of rational standards,"[248] the unstructured or open-textured nature of the doctrine arguably leads to some unpredictability in application. Others deride the effectiveness of the doctrine as an instrument of consumer protection. The modern growth of the doctrine in the latter half of the twentieth century was accompanied by and might be thought to be a reflection of an increasing social awareness of consumer protection issues. Critics observe that, as an instrument of consumer protection, the doctrine is sporadic in its application and available only to parties who can afford to litigate. The doctrine fails to correct what might appear to be systemic problems in the consumer marketplace.[249] Finally, as we have noted, to the extent that the doctrine is used in a substantive fashion to strike down unfair terms in the absence of unusual bargaining vulnerabilities, the doctrine has been criticized on the basis that it attempts essentially to regulate the fairness of contract terms and that this is not a suitable role for the courts.[250]

The doctrine of unconscionability appears, however, to be quite immune to criticisms of these kinds. The existence of the doctrine has not been questioned by a Canadian court. The explanation for this resilience is not difficult to discern. If, for example, one considers the fact situation in *Morrison v. Coast Finance Ltd.*,[251] it is difficult to disagree with the sentiment expressed by Davey J.A. in that case to the effect that "I cannot believe that the law is so deficient that it cannot reach

---

247 Leff, above note 197 at 558.

248 D. Tiplady, "The Judicial Control of Contractual Unfairness" (1983) 46 Mod. L. Rev. 601 at 614.

249 See, for example, Leff, above note 197; R.A. Hasson, "Unconscionability in Contract Law and in the New Sales Act—Confessions of a Doubting Thomas" (1979–80) 4 Can. Bus. L.J. 383.

250 See above this Chapter, section D(2). And see M.J. Trebilcock, "An Economic Approach to the Doctrine of Unconscionability" in B.J. Reiter and J. Swan, eds., *Studies in Contract Law* (Toronto: Butterworths, 1980) c. 11.

251 Above note 195.

and remedy such a gross abuse of overwhelming inequality between the parties."[252] The result in this case and in other leading cases of this kind is plainly just and the elements of the doctrine of unconscionability appear to offer a coherent explanation of why this is so. The doctrine of unconscionability also enjoys some support from academic writers and law reform bodies. Supporters of the doctrine tend to deploy a strategy of confession and avoidance with respect to the criticisms typically levelled at the doctrine. Thus, many would accept that the doctrine appears, in some sense at least, to be less crisp or certain in its definition than some other doctrines of the law of contract but maintain, nonetheless, that some degree of uncertainty is a price worth paying for producing just results in cases of this kind.[253] Similarly, although it is often conceded that the doctrine does not provide a major solution to problems of consumer protection, the doctrine is nonetheless defended on the basis that it provides a workable solution to certain kinds of cases that, when they appear before the courts, require a just resolution.[254] In response to those who would suggest that the doctrine should be strictly limited to cases of procedural unconscionability in order to avoid the risk that the courts may engage in misguided attempts to regulate the content of contractual terms in various commercial settings, a number of arguments are made. The drawing of a rigid line between procedural and substantive unconscionability required by this view has been opposed on the ground that the distinction between the two is not easily drawn. Further courts, it is said, are not likely to engage in excessive review of the fairness of contractual terms.[255] Certainly, the absence of a body of doctrine applying the decision of the House of Lords in the *Schroeder* case[256] suggests that there is some validity to the latter point.

An argument in favour of recognition of the doctrine that many have found persuasive was set forth by Karl Llewellyn, the principal architect of the unconscionability provisions of the American Uniform Commercial Code.[257] In essence, Llewellyn's position was that courts are

252 *Ibid.* at 716.
253 See, for example, M.A. Eisenberg, "The Bargain Principle and its Limits" (1982) 95 Harv. L. Rev. 741 at 769–70.
254 See, for example, B.J. Reiter, "Unconscionability: Is There a Choice? A Reply to Professor Hasson" (1979–80) 4 Can. Bus. L.J. 403.
255 See Ontario Law Reform Commission, *Report on Amendment of the Law of Contract* (Toronto: Ministry of the Attorney General, 1987) at 128.
256 Above note 233.
257 Uniform Commercial Code, § 2-302 (1962), for discussion of which see Leff, above note 197.

irresistibly drawn to refusing to enforce unconscionable transactions. In the absence of an explicit doctrine of unconscionability, then, courts manipulate other doctrines such as those relating to offer and acceptance, illegality and principles of contractual interpretation in order to achieve less directly a result that could be attained more directly by an explicit doctrine of unconscionability. Manipulation of other doctrines in order to accomplish this purpose leads to uncertainty and unpredictability in those doctrines. In Llewellyn's memorable aphorism, "Covert tools are never reliable tools."[258] On this view, recognition of an explicit unconscionability doctrine thus leads to greater predictability in the application of the doctrine.

5) Remedies

Under traditional unconscionability doctrine, the remedy available to the weaker party caught up in an unconscionable transaction was to seek rescission of the agreement in equity. It was also the case that if the stronger party brought an action specially to enforce the impugned agreement against the weaker party, equity would refuse to grant such relief.[259] In the case of equitable rescission,[260] a variety of defences may be available to the stronger party. Thus, inability to effect restitution, the intervention of third-party rights, the passage of an inordinate amount of time or the subsequent affirmation of the agreement by the weaker party may have the effect of precluding relief. As one would expect, however, these defences appear to be interpreted generously in favour of the weaker party in the context of unconscionable bargains.[261] Moreover, as in the context of undue influence,[262] there is some authority for the proposition that even where one of the defences or bars to relief precludes rescissionary relief, a claim for compensation for the true value of the benefit conferred on the stronger party may be available in lieu thereof.[263]

In fashioning rescissionary decrees, courts have demonstrated some creativity in imposing terms on the decree that will afford appropriate

258 K. Llewellyn, "Book Review" (1939) 52 Harv. L. Rev. 700 at 703. See also S. Waddams, "Unconscionability in Contract" (1976) 39 Mod. L. Rev. 369.
259 See, for example, *Knupp v. Bell*, above note 196; *Marshall v. Canada Permanent Trust Co.*, above note 202.
260 See Chapter 24, section D(3).
261 See, for example, *B. (J.F.) v. B. (M.A.)*, above note 220.
262 See above this Chapter, section C(7).
263 See *Paris v. Machnick* (1972), 32 D.L.R. (3d) 723 (N.S.T.D.); *Junkin v. Junkin* (1978), 86 D.L.R. (3d) 751 (Ont. H.C.J.).

protection to the weaker party. In *Morrison v. West Coast Finance*,[264] for example, it will be recalled that the monies borrowed from the finance company by Morrison had been advanced by her to Lowe and Kitely. In turn, they had paid the money to the automobile company to acquire two cars and to the finance company to repay Lowe's loan. In order to afford some protection to Morrison, the manager of the finance company required Lowe to execute a promissory note in favour of Morrison for the amount of the loan and had insisted that Lowe and Kitely execute conditional sale contracts identifying the automobile company vendor and then assigned the vendor's interest to Morrison. Morrison was left, then, with what was likely to be a worthless remedy against the two rogues. Davey J.A. indicated that the entire transaction ought to be set aside but that, in the absence of Lowe and Kitely who were not before the court, this would not be possible. In order to achieve substantial justice, however, the court set aside Morrison's mortgage without requiring her to repay the monies advanced, thereby allowing the payment of Lowe's debt and the sale of the automobiles to the two men to stand. Further, rescission in favour of Morrison was conditioned on a term requiring Morrison to re-transfer her interest in the conditional sale agreements to the finance company and to transfer to the finance company Lowe's promissory note. Thus, Morrison, who never benefited from the transaction, was released from any obligation and the finance company was left with its position against Lowe and Kitely, albeit a position that had worsened, in reliance on the impugned mortgage with Morrison, as a result of having sold cars to Lowe and Kitely without much prospect of recovering their prices.

More controversially, it may be asked whether the weaker party, rather than seeking rescission of the entire agreement, may seek to set aside the particularly oppressive term of the contract and enforce the remaining terms of the unconscionable bargain. The principal argument against the granting of such relief, of course, is that it has the effect of enforcing an agreement to which the stronger party never agreed. And yet, the striking out of particular terms is a standard form of relief under American unconscionability doctrine.[265] Under English and Canadian law, however, the doctrine has traditionally been employed either to enable rescission or to deny specific performance but not to delete a particular term from the unconscionable bargain. More recently, however, the Supreme Court of Canada or, more particularly, Dickson C.J.C., has suggested that the doctrine of unconscionability

264 Above note 195.
265 See generally Farnsworth, above note 68 at 554–78.

may be employed in the context of "disclaimer" or "limitation of liability" clauses to render the clause itself unenforceable with the result that the reminder of the agreement could be enforced.

As noted elsewhere,[266] the Supreme Court of Canada in *Hunter Engineering Co. Inc. v. Syncrude Canada Ltd.*,[267] reconsidered the applicability in Canadian law of the doctrine of fundamental breach. Under this doctrine, disclaimer clauses had been held unenforceable in the context of a "fundamental breach" of the contract. In *Syncrude*, the Court took the view that the doctrine of fundamental breach should be revised. Unfortunately, however, the Court reached no consensus on the nature of that revision. For Dickson C.J.C., the doctrine could be replaced by a doctrine of unconscionability. For Wilson J., however, the doctrine of unconscionability was an unsuitable substitute for fundamental breach and, accordingly, she preferred a doctrine that preserved a discretion on the part of the courts to withhold enforcement of a disclaimer clause where the circumstances of the breach were such as to render application of the clause unfair and unreasonable. On this occasion, however, neither Dickson C.J.C. nor Wilson J. attracted the support of a majority of the members of the Court. Lower courts have typically responded to this ambiguity in the doctrine of fundamental breach by holding that particular provisions are either "unfair or unreasonable or, indeed, unconscionable."[268] It is thus not clear whether the contemporary Canadian doctrine applicable to disclaimer clauses is, in fact, the traditional doctrine of unconscionability being applied to an unconscionable term. A further source of complexity is that in a number of the cases applying this ambiguous analysis, it appears that the traditional indicia of conscionability are not present.[269] Although the ultimate shape of the new Canadian doctrine on fundamental breach and its relationship to the traditional doctrine of unconscionability thus remains to be discovered, it is at least conceivable that Canadian cases applying the doctrine of unconscionability to disclaimer clauses will be the harbinger of an expanded jurisdiction of unconscionability doctrine enabling courts to strike down individual clauses and to do so on what appear to be substantive rather than purely procedural grounds.

---

266 See Chapter 20, section D.

267 [1989] 1 S.C.R. 426.

268 *Fraser Jewellers (1982) Ltd. v. Dominion Electric Protection Co.* (1997), 148 D.L.R. (4th) 496 at 503 (Ont. C.A.), Robins J.A.

269 See, for example, *Solway v. Davis Moving & Storage Inc.* (2002), 222 D.L.R. (4th) 251 (Ont. C.A.); *Atlas Supply Co. of Canada Ltd. v. Yarmouth Equipment Ltd.* (1991), 103 N.S.R. (2d) 1 (C.A.), leave to appeal to S.C.C. granted but discontinued, [1991] S.C.C.A. 256.

6) Statutory Unconscionability

Two different types of statutory schemes incorporating the concept of unconscionability have been enacted at the provincial level across Canada. The first type, typically titled, *Unconscionable Transactions Relief Act*, has been enacted by all ten provinces.[270] These statutes are quite narrowly focused on the issue of excessive interest charged in lending transactions. Typically, the statutes apply only to transactions involving "money lent" and then confer remedial powers on the courts where "the court finds that, having regard to the risk and to all the circumstances, the cost of the loan is excessive and that the transaction is harsh and unconscionable."[271] In such a case, the court may (1) re-open the transaction and take an accounting between the parties, (2) re-open any previous settlement of the obligations between the parties and relieve the debtor with respect to any sums not fairly due, and (3) set aside or revise the agreement either wholly or in part and, in particular, order the creditor to indemnify the debtor with respect to any losses resulting from the creditor having parted with collateral given by the debtor to secure the loan.[272] It is clear that the statutory unconscionability remedy is in addition to, rather than in place of, whatever relief might be available to the debtor on the basis of the equitable doctrine of unconscionability[273] and some of the statutes clearly so stipulate.[274]

A second generation of "trade practices" or "business practices" legislation incorporating the concept of unconscionability has been enacted in five Canadian provinces.[275] These statutes typically apply

---

270 *Unconscionable Transactions Act*, R.S.A. 2000, c. U-2; *Consumer Protection Act*, R.S.B.C. 1996, c. 69; *Unconscionable Transactions Relief Act*, R.S.M. 1987, c. U20; *Unconscionable Transactions Act*, R.S.N.B. 1973, c. U-1; *Unconscionable Transactions Relief Act*, R.S.N.L. 1990, c. U-1; *Unconscionable Transactions Relief Act*, R.S.N.S. 1989, c. 41; *Unconscionable Transactions Relief Act*, R.S.O. 1990, c. U.2; *Unconscionable Transactions Relief Act*, R.S.P.E.I. 1988, c. U-2; *Civil Code of Quebec*, S.Q. 1991, c. 64, Art. 1437; *Unconscionable Transactions Relief Act*, R.S.S. 1978, c. U-1. See generally R.C. Cuming, "The Credit Consumer in Trouble: Remedies of Canadian Consumer Creditors" (1969) 15 McGill L.J. 48.

271 See, for example, R.S.O. 1990, c. U.2, s. 2.

272 *Ibid.*

273 See *Canadian Imperial Bank of Commerce v. Ohlson* (1997), 154 D.L.R. (4th) 33 (Alta. C.A.).

274 R.S.O. 1990, c. U.2, s. 5 (nothing in the Act "derogates from the existing powers or jurisdiction of any court").

275 *Fair Trading Act*, R.S.A. 2000, c. F-2; *Trade Practice Act*, R.S.B.C. 1996, c. 457, (rep. S.B.C. 2004, c. 2 (to come into force on regulation)); *Trade Practices Act*, R.S.N.L. 1990, c. T-7; *Business Practices Act*, R.S.O. 1990, c. B.18 (repealed 2002, c. 30, Sch. E, s. 1 (to come into force on proclamation), and replaced with

more broadly to all consumer transactions in which commercial parties are providing goods and services to ordinary or non-business consumers. With respect to such transactions, the statutes typically provide remedies where such transactions have been induced by misrepresentation[276] or where the transaction is determined by a court to be unconscionable. To assist the court in making the latter determination, a number of the statutes set out lists of factors that may be taken into account. The lists vary to some extent from one statute to another but the Ontario list, which is illustrative, sets out the following factors:

(i)   that the consumer is not reasonably able to protect his or her interest because of physical infirmity, ignorance, illiteracy, inability to understand the language of an agreement or similar factors,

(ii)   that the price grossly exceeds the price of which similar goods or services are readily available to like consumers,

(iii) that the consumer is unable to receive a substantial benefit from the subject-matter of the consumer representation,

(iv)   that there is no reasonable probability of payment of the obligation in full by the consumer,

(v)   that the proposed transaction is excessively one-sided in favour of someone other than the consumer,

(vi)   that the terms or conditions of the transaction are so adverse to the consumer as to be inequitable,

(vii) that he or she is making a misleading statement of opinion on which the consumer is likely to rely to his or her detriment,

(viii) that he or she is subjecting the consumer to undue pressure to enter into the transaction.[277]

Where the supplier "knows or ought to know"[278] of the presence of one or more of these factors, a finding of unconscionability may be made. The statutes typically provide both civil redress in the form of rescis-

---

Consumer Protection Act, 2002, S.O. 2002, c. 30, Sch. A (to come into force on proclamation)); *Business Practices Act*, R.S.P.E.I. 1988, c. B-7. See generally E.P. Belobaba, "Unfair Trade Practices Legislation: Symbolism and Substance in Consumer Protection" (1977) 15 Osgoode Hall L.J. 327.

276   See Chapter 10, section I.

277   *Business Practices Act*, R.S.O 1990, c. B.18, s. 2(2). The Ontario Act adopts the awkward device of providing relief only where there has occurred an "unconscionable consumer representation" thus suggesting that in addition to one or more of the listed factors, there must be a representation of some kind made by the supplier. Presumably, however, any representation made in the unconscionable circumstances would suffice and this requirement should normally be easily met.

278   *Ibid.*

sion, with the possible alternative of an award of damages and criminal penalties in the form of a quasi-criminal offence. These statutes substantially expand the role of the doctrine of unconscionability in the context of consumer transactions. Thus, the listed factors plainly extend beyond procedural concerns to matters of substantive unconscionability. Indeed, it is only the first and last factors in the list that are plainly restricted to procedural matters. Whether, however, court-ordered civil redress of this kind is of much practical significance to the average consumer is another matter. Accordingly, it may well be that the more significant provisions of these statutes are those providing for extensive administrative remedies. Under each of the statutes, a public official is given extensive authority to investigate and obtain cease and desist orders with respect to unconscionable practices.[279]

E. CONCLUSION

It remains, then, to consider whether there is merit in Lord Denning's suggestion in *Lloyds Bank v. Bundy*[280] that the three doctrines of duress, undue influence and unconscionability or, as he called it, "undue pressure," should be merged or synthesized into an overarching principle of inequality of bargaining power. On its facts, the *Bundy* case sits in the area where the doctrines of undue influence and unconscionability, at least as understood in Canada, tend to overlap. The finding of a majority of the Court of Appeal that the relationship between Bundy and the bank was a relationship of trust and confidence, thus giving rise to the doctrine of undue influence, was arguably a slightly generous one though perhaps within the scope of the traditional doctrine. On the other hand, under Canadian law at least, the facts of *Bundy* appear to engage the doctrine of unconscionability.[281] The bank was aware of the relationship of the father to the son and the fact that Bundy was placing charges on his one and only valuable asset that exceeded its value in order to guarantee the debts of his son's business. As well, the bank appeared to appreciate that the son's business was in a precarious state. These circumstances could ground a finding that the bank had sufficient awareness of the improvidence of the agreement and the inequality of bargaining power between itself and Bundy to render the agreement unenforceable. It is an interesting question, then, whether

---

279 See, for example, R.S.O. 1990, c. B.18, ss. 5–15.
280 Above note 2. And see above this Chapter, section A.
281 See above this Chapter, section D(3).

the fact that these categories may not appear to have precise bound-aries constitutes a sound reason for adopting Lord Denning's approach of simply abolishing the distinctions between them and analyzing cases with a single principle operating at a higher level of generality. This question does not admit of an easy answer.

As a matter of doctrine, Lord Denning's suggestion of a new prin-ciple was not adopted by his colleagues in the *Bundy* case. Moreover, the suggestion has been plainly rejected by the House of Lords.[282] Can-adian courts[283] have been more welcoming but it would not be cor-rect to suggest that Canadian courts have abandoned the traditional categories of analysis. Indeed, it appears unlikely that they will do so. Cases involving threats, for example, are rather different from the kinds of fact situations that invite application of the doctrines relating to relationships of trust and confidence and unconscionable bargains. Similarly, the core cases of presumptive undue influence where there exists an ongoing relationship between two parties that is likely to in-fluence consent is rather different from the typical unconscionability case in which an individual suffering from unusual bargaining frailties of some kind is taken advantage of by a complete stranger. Arguably, then, the traditional categories assist rather than obscure the analysis required to assemble relevant authorities and decide like cases in like fashion. Moreover, the level of abstraction of the "inequality of bar-gaining power" principle does not appear to offer much assistance in the difficult task of determining whether relief should be accorded in a particular case. Indeed, it seems possible, as Lambert J.A. indicated in *Harry v. Kreutziger*,[284] that Lord Denning's new general principle "was clearly not intended as a touchstone, since the liberal employment of adjectives makes it too flexible for that purpose, but rather as a dem-onstration that the categories of grounds for rescission are interrelated and based on a common foundation."[285] Identifying commonalities be-tween differing categories is, of course, a useful exercise in the search for improved doctrine. On this occasion, however, it appears not to have produced a new rule.

---

282 See *National Westminster Bank Plc. v. Morgan*, [1985] A.C. 686 (H.L.).

283 *McKenzie v. Bank of Montreal*, above note 244; *Royal Bank of Canada v. Hinds* (1978), 88 D.L.R. (3d) 428 (Ont. H.C.J.); *A & K Lick-a-Chick Franchises Ltd. v. Cordiv Enterprises Ltd.*, above note 239.

284 *Harry v. Kreutziger*, above note 205.

285 *Ibid.* at 241.

FURTHER READINGS

P. BENSON, "Abstract Right and the Possibility of a Nondistributive Conception of Contract: Hegel and Contemporary Contract Theory" (1989) 10 Cardozo L. Rev. 1077.

R. BIGWOOD, "Coercion in Contract: The Theoretical Constructions of Duress" (1996) 46 U.T.L.J. 201.

P.B.H. BIRKS & C.N. YIN, "On the Nature of Undue Influence" in J. Beatson & D. Friedmann, eds., *Good Faith and Contract Law* (Oxford: Clarendon Press, 1995).

M.A. EISENBERG, "The Bargain Principle and its Limits" (1982) 95 Harv. L. Rev. 741.

R.A. EPSTEIN, "Unconscionability: A Critical Reappraisal" (1975) 18 J.L. & Econ. 293.

B. FEHLBERG, *Sexually Transmitted Debt* (Oxford: Oxford University Press, 1997).

R.A. HASSON, "Unconscionability in Contract Law and in the New Sales Act — Confessions of a Doubting Thomas" (1979–80) 4 Can. Bus. L.J. 383.

D. KENNEDY, "Distributive and Paternalist Motives in Contract Law and Tort Law, With Special Reference to Compulsory Terms and Unequal Bargaining Power" (1982) 41 Md. L. Rev. 563.

L.A. KORNHAUSER, "Unconscionability in Standard Forms" (1976) Cal. L. Rev. 1152.

A.A. LEFF, "Unconscionability and the Code — The Emperor's New Clause" (1907) 115 U. Pa. L. Rev. 485.

D. MAJURY, "Unconscionability in an Equality Context" (1990–91) Can. Fam. L.Q. 23.

M.H. OGILVIE, "Economic Duress in Contract: Departure, Detour or Dead-End?" (2000) 34 Can. Bus. L.J. 194.

M.H. OGILVIE, "No Special Tenderness for Sexually Contracted Debt? Undue Influence and the Lending Banker" (1996) 27 Can. Bus. L.J. 365.

ONTARIO LAW REFORM COMMISSION, *Report on Amendment of the Law of Contract* (Toronto: Ministry of the Attorney General, 1987) c. 6.

A. SCHWARTZ, "A Reexamination of Nonsubstantive Unconscionability" (1977) 63 Va. L. Rev. 1053.

H. STEWART, "A Formal Approach to Contractual Duress" (1997) 47 U.T.L.J. 175.

H. STEWART, "Economic Duress in Canadian Law: Towards a Principled Approach" (2003) 82 Can. Bar Rev. 359.

M.J. TREBILCOCK, "An Economic Approach to the Doctrine of Unconscionability" in B.J. Reiter & J. Swan, eds., *Studies in Contract Law* (Toronto: Butterworths, 1980) c. 11.

M.J. TREBILCOCK, "The Doctrine of Inequality of Bargaining Power: Post-Benthamite Economics in the House of Lords" (1976) 26 U.T.L.J. 359.

S. WADDAMS, "Unconscionability in Contract" (1976) 39 Mod. L. Rev. 369.

M.A. WALDRON, "Spousal Guarantees and Conceptual Complexity: Can We Find a Better Solution?" (2001) 16 B.F.L.R. 391.

ILLEGALITY

A. INTRODUCTION

The rules determining whether a particular agreement is unenforceable by reason of illegality[1] are normally divided into two categories, those determined to be contrary to public policy as a matter of common law and those determined to be unlawful by statute. For the most part, this division of the topic is a satisfactory one. Agreements contrary to public policy at common law rest on a judicial determination that the type of agreement in question is sufficiently inconsistent with public policy that it should be treated as unenforceable. In the context of statutory illegality, however, the discretion of the courts to determine public policy is, in theory at least, constrained by the fact that the policy determination with which the agreement is in conflict has been made by the legislature. For example, the determination that contracts restraining one's ability to trade[2] should be considered unenforceable rest on a determination of public policy made by the courts themselves as a matter of common law. On the other hand, in the extensive network of regulatory schemes under which the sale and distribution of goods and services of various kinds are commonly regulated, the legislature has articulated public policies of various kinds that may include an express or implied prohibition of cer-

---

1   See generally R.A. Buckley, *Illegality and Public Policy* (London: Sweet & Maxwell, 2002); N. Enonchong, *Illegal Transactions* (London: Lloyd's of London Press, 1998).

2   See below this Chapter, section B(4).

tain types of agreements. Such agreements are held to be unenforceable on the basis of so-called statutory illegality.

The distinction between common law and statutory illegality becomes more difficult to apply in the context of agreements that involve the commission of acts that constitute statutory offences. At common law, it was determined that a contract to commit a criminal offence, such as an agreement to commit an assault on a third party, is unenforceable.[3] The agreement is unenforceable as a matter of common law, even though the offence may be defined by statute, because the determination that the agreement is unenforceable is a decision made by the court that is not preordained by the legislation defining the offence of assault. The category of statutory illegality is reserved, in theory at least, for situations in which it is the statute, rather than the judiciary, that determines that the contract is illegal and unenforceable. In fact, however, it is a rare event that a statutory scheme explicitly stipulates that particular types of agreements are void or unenforceable. The application of the doctrine of statutory illegality therefore typically rests on a judicial determination as to whether a particular statute implicitly provides that a particular type of agreement is unenforceable by reason of the illegality. The question, it is often said, is whether the statute impliedly "prohibits" the contract in question. Plainly, where the statutory illegality in question is one that occurs during the performance of the contract, but is not required by the terms of the agreement, the issue is classified as a matter of statutory illegality and it is widely accepted that the correct analysis of the issue under current law requires a careful analysis of the structure and underlying purposes of the statute in question, with a view to determining whether or not the statute, in addition to stipulating the offence, is properly construed as requiring that the agreement in question is an unenforceable one.[4]

The more difficult case to classify, however, is one in which the agreement requires, in effect, the commission of a statutory offence. Some courts and writers treat this as a case of common law illegality as the contract is one that has been entered for the purpose of committing an offence. Similarly, where the regulatory offence prescribes an act that is contractual in nature, such as a prohibition of the sale of certain goods in specified circumstances, there is a possibility that the agreement in question will be classified as an agreement to commit an offence and, accordingly, embraced by the common law category. At the same time, however, in both of these situations, it appears relevant

3   *Allen v. Rescous* (1676), 2 Lev. 174, 83 E.R. 505.
4   See below this Chapter, section C.

to ask whether the legislature intended not only to create an offence of sale but also implicitly determined that the contract of sale should itself be unenforceable. In other words, such cases appear to be appropriate candidates for the category of statutory illegality. Indeed, where the statutory offence in question is embedded in a regulatory scheme of some kind, it is surely relevant to the determination as to whether it is implicit in the scheme that the related agreement should be considered unenforceable to consider the structure and purposes of the regulatory scheme and deploy the analytical methods that have been developed in the statutory illegality cases. Accordingly, the better view, and the view followed here, is that in the context of regulatory offences, agreements that involve the commission of such offences should be classified as matters of statutory illegality rather than as agreements to commit offences subject to the common law doctrine. Nonetheless, it will be useful to return to this issue in the context of the discussion of the common law category of agreements to commit an offence.

B. AGREEMENTS CONTRARY TO PUBLIC POLICY AT COMMON LAW

1) Agreements to Commit an Unlawful Act: Crime, Tort and the Defrauding of Third Parties

Agreements to commit crimes or torts are unenforceable at common law. An agreement to commit an assault on a third party is obviously unenforceable.[5] So too, for example, are agreements to commit extortion of third parties,[6] to evade currency controls,[7] to deal in prohibited retail stamps,[8] to distribute obscene material,[9] to print libellous material[10] or to obtain goods by false pretences.[11] A contract entered into for the purpose of committing the tort of inducement of breach of contract is unenforceable.[12] In a perhaps predictable Canadian illustration, an

---

5   *Allen v. Rescous*, above note 3.
6   *Byron v. Tremaine* (1898), 31 N.S.R. 425, aff'd 29 S.C.R. 445.
7   *Bigos v. Bousted*, [1951] 1 All E.R. 92.
8   *United Dominion Promotion Sales Inc. v. Shaw* (1957), 119 C.C.C. 380 (N.B. Co. Ct.).
9   *Fores v. Johnes* (1802), 4 Esp. 97, 170 E.R. 654; *Poplett v. Stockdale* (1825), Ry. & Mood. 337, 171 E.R. 1041.
10 *Apthorp v. Neville & Co.* (1907), 23 T.L.R. 575.
11 *Berg v. Sadler and Moore*, [1937] 2 K.B. 158.
12 *Harrington v. Victoria Graving Dock Co.* (1878), 3 Q.B.D. 549. See also H. Lauterpacht, "Contracts to Break a Contract" (1936) 52 Law Q. Rev. 494.

agreement intended to induce a hockey player to break an existing contract and join a new team was held unenforceable on this ground.[13]

Agreements entered into for the purpose of defrauding or otherwise injuring third parties are unenforceable under this common law doctrine. A substantial line of authorities holds unenforceable agreements that are structured so as to facilitate a fraud being perpetrated on revenue authorities. In *Alexander v. Rayson*,[14] for example, a lease stating a falsely low rental term, coupled with a side agreement charging handsomely for various services, designed to misrepresent the rateable value of the premises to the municipality and thereby reduce tax liability was unenforceable. An agreement permitting a broker to sell shares in a company structured in such fashion as to prevent securities regulators from detecting an unlawful level of remuneration for the broker was held unenforceable.[15] Similarly, a contract for the sale of a business falsely representing a low price in order to induce bank financing[16] and a transaction for the purchase of an apartment block falsely representing a high price in order to secure a higher mortgage loan than the lender would otherwise advance[17] were both held to be illegal. In an early Ontario case,[18] a transaction that amounted to a pyramid scheme designed to exploit third parties was struck down. A sale of shares undertaken with a view to enabling the seller to engage in share purchases that would "rig the market" by creating the impression that there was a substantial demand for the shares in question was struck down as an unlawful attempt to mislead the public.[19] Transactions such as these, entered into for an unlawful purpose, will be unenforceable by any party to the agreement that shared the unlawful intention.[20]

In *St. John Shipping*,[21] Devlin J. appears to have assumed that the common law rules striking down agreements entered into with the intention of committing a crime apply to all statutory offences. Rigid

---

13   *Wanderers' Hockey Club v. Johnson* (1913), 5 W.W.R. 117 (B.C.S.C.).

14   *Alexander v. Rayson*, [1936] 1 K.B. 169 (C.A.). See also *Napier v. National Business Agency Ltd.*, [1951] 2 All E.R. 264 (C.A.) (employment contract—income tax); *Stuart v. Kingman* (1978), 91 D.L.R. (3d) 142 (Ont. H.C.J.) (land transfer tax); *Tucker Estate v. Gillis* (1988), 53 D.L.R. (4th) 688 (N.B.C.A.) (sales tax—false identification of purchaser).

15   *Williams v. Fleetwood Holdings Ltd.* (1973), 41 D.L.R. (3d) 636.

16   *Menard v. Genereux* (1982), 138 D.L.R. (3d) 273 (Ont. H.C.J.).

17   *Letkeman v. Zimmermann*, [1978] 1 S.C.R. 1097.

18   *Bonisteel v. Saylor* (1890), 17 O.A.R. 505 (C.A.).

19   *Scott v. Brown, Doering, McNab & Co.*, [1892] 2 Q.B. 724.

20   *Alexander v. Rayson*, above note 14 at 182; *St. John Shipping Corp. v. Joseph Rank Ltd.*, [1957] 1 Q.B. 267 at 283 [*St. John Shipping*].

21   *St. John Shipping*, *ibid.*

application of a doctrine of this kind, however, could lead to unsatisfactory results, especially in the context of regulatory offences, and ought not be followed. This approach could justify, for example, the result in *Kingshott v. Brunskill*,[22] a well-known Ontario decision striking down an agreement between two farmers for the purchase and sale of ungraded apples. Under the applicable legislation and regulations, apples were required to be graded before sale. The sale thus constituted an offence. In fact, however, it was the expectation of the parties that the purchasing farmer would grade the apples before reselling them to the public. Nonetheless, the regulations, which admitted no exception for such circumstances, captured the transaction and rendered it unlawful. The Ontario Court of Appeal struck down the transaction even though the mischief presumably aimed at by the statute—sale of ungraded apples to the public—was not present. The seller therefore could not recover the price of the apples, notwithstanding the fact that the purchaser had subsequently graded them and resold them to the public. As we shall see,[23] this decision has been criticized by subsequent Canadian courts and is generally considered to be unsatisfactory. Cases of this kind are likely to be more satisfactorily analyzed as instances of statutory illegality, with respect to which a careful analysis of the objectives and structure of the regulatory scheme is required. Alternatively, if such cases are to be considered to be subject to the common law illegality doctrine, it will be important to recognize that the rule striking down agreements that require commission of an offence is not an absolute one. For example, it will not be applied where, as in a case such as *Kingshott*, an examination of the objectives of the statutory scheme of which the offence forms a part and of the disproportionate nature of the penalty imposed, indicates that holding the agreement unenforceable would produce an unjust result.[24]

2) Agreements Facilitating Immoral Conduct or Undermining the Institution of Marriage

Courts have traditionally asserted a jurisdiction to deny enforcement of contracts conducing to immoral conduct or undermining the institution of marriage. A number of the particular illustrations of the application of this principle now have a dated appearance to them and, in a

---

22   [1953] O.W.N. 133 (C.A.).
23   See below this Chapter, section C.
24   At the very least in such a case, a claim in restitution for the value of the apples sold ought to be available to the seller. See below this Chapter, section D(2).

number of instances, have been overtaken by evolving social attitudes and, indeed, statutory reform. In particular, abolition of the claim for breach of promise to marry,[25] increasing recognition of the enforceability of domestic agreements[26] and evolving social attitudes toward co-habitation outside marriage have rendered much of the traditional doctrine irrelevant to contemporary social life. Nonetheless, the jurisdiction to strike down agreements on the basis of their tendency to promote immoral conduct remains and it may well be that courts will face difficult decisions with respect to such matters in the years ahead.

Under traditional doctrine, agreements to marry were held void in circumstances where they were considered to be inconsistent with the current marital status of one of the parties. Thus, promises by a married man to marry another woman upon the death of his wife were held to be unenforceable.[27] Such agreements were considered to promote separation between a husband and wife or encourage immoral behaviour, such as adultery. Similarly, a promise by a married person to marry a third party upon divorce of the current marriage is also unenforceable.[28] Such a promise would be enforceable, however, if given after divorce proceedings had been initiated and a decree *nisi* of divorce had been obtained.[29] In jurisdictions in which the cause of action for breach of a promise to marry has been abolished, of course, such doctrine is no longer relevant.

Agreements by married persons to live separate and apart were also considered unenforceable under traditional doctrine as being inconsistent with the institution of marriage. Thus, an agreement, signed by a couple prior to their marriage, providing that they would live separate and apart after marrying has been held to be unenforceable.[30] Under traditional doctrine, an agreement made in anticipation of a future separation of spouses was void as against public policy.[31] Modern legislation concerning domestic agreements, however, typically enables married couples and other co-habitants subject to such legislation, to stipulate a set of arrangements that will obtain in the event of a future separation

---

25   See, for example, *Marriage Act,* R.S.O. 1990, c. M.3, s. 32.
26   See Chapter 4, Section C.
27   *Spiers v. Hunt,* [1908] 1 K.B. 720; *Wilson v. Carnley,* [1908] 1 K.B. 729.
28   *Skipp v. Kelly,* (1926), 42 T.L.R. 258 (H.L.).
29   *Fender v. St. John-Mildmay,* [1938] A.C. 1 (H.L.). See also *Skipp v. Kelly, ibid.*
30   *Brodie v. Brodie,* [1917] P. 271.
31   *Harrison v. Harrison,* [1910] 1 K.B. 35. Exceptionally, the doctrine would not apply where the married couple had lived separate and apart for a time but had reunited on the basis of an agreement as to what the arrangements would be in the event of a second separation. See *ibid.*

of the parties.[32] Separation agreements entered into by couples who are living separate and apart are enforceable at common law.[33]

The perceived importance of preserving, indeed fostering, public attitudes concerning the sanctity of marriage may also explain the traditional rule that marriage brokerage contracts are unenforceable. A contract under which a marriage broker undertakes to seek to arrange a marriage for a client with an identified individual for a fee is plainly unenforceable. In a leading case, *Hermann v. Charlesworth*,[34] the broker undertook, for an initial fee, to introduce the plaintiff client to a number of potential spouses with a larger fee to be paid in the event that a marriage took place. When the arrangement did not enjoy success, the plaintiff sought to recover the initial fee on the theory that the contract was one of marriage brokerage and therefore unenforceable at common law, thus providing a basis for restitution of the monies paid. The defendant broker argued that as no identified individual was stipulated as the target of the exercise, the agreement should not be considered to be a marriage brokerage contract in the requisite sense. The Court of Appeal rejected this argument and explained that the basis underlying the general principle "is the introduction of the consideration of a money payment into that which should be free from any such taint."[35] It may be wondered, then, whether modern dating and introduction services of various kinds are subject to a similar principle. The answer rests, in turn, on identifying the proper basis for the traditional rule. One possibility would be that marriage brokerage contracts were perceived to be exploitative and, more particularly, took advantage of the particularly vulnerable status of unmarried women in an earlier era. If this is so, it may be that evolving social attitudes and legal norms concerning gender equality may have undermined the basis of the traditional rule to some extent. Second, it may be that the better rubric for determining the enforceability of such agreements is the doctrine of unconscionability.[36] On this view, the arrangements concerning modern dating and introduction services might be considered valid unless, in the particular circumstances, they constitute the taking of undue advantage of an inequality of bargaining power.

---

32   See, for example, *Family Law Act*, R.S.O. 1990, c. F.3, ss. 52–53. And see Chapter 4, section C.

33   *Merritt v. Merritt*, [1970] 2 All E.R. 760 (C.A.). And see Chapter 4, section C.

34   [1905] 2 K.B. 123 (C.A.).

35   *Ibid.* at 130.

36   See Chapter 11, section D.

Given the common law's concern with the sanctity of marriage, it is not surprising that traditional doctrine took a dim view of unmarried co-habitation. Thus, an agreement to transfer an interest in property on the understanding that the parties would engage in future unmarried and therefore elicit co-habitation was considered void.[37] Both social attitudes and legal norms with respect to unmarried co-habitation have evolved, however, over time. Some courts were able to enforce similar agreements by holding that the true consideration for the agreement in question was not the future elicit co-habitation. Thus, in a Saskatchewan case,[38] the court held that the consideration for the transfer of property was not the understanding that the parties would co-habit but, rather, the work to be done by the transferee on the property. With increasing social acceptability of unmarried co-habitation, the rights of co-habiting couples are commonly treated to some extent in provincial family law legislation.[39] At common law, it has been accepted for some time that a lease to a co-habiting couple would not be unenforceable simply because of the nature of their relationship.[40] As far as co-habitation agreements themselves are concerned, provincial legislation dealing with the enforceability of domestic agreements typically extends enforceability to the co-habitation agreements of unmarried couples.[41] Moreover, it now appears to be accepted that as a matter of common law, such agreements are enforceable. In *Chrispen v. Topham*,[42] in response to the defendant's argument that an agreement concerning the financial arrangements of unmarried co-habitants was void on public policy grounds, the trial judge observed that "present day social acceptance of common-law living counters that argument."[43]

Agreements related to the conduct of prostitution are considered void at common law. In a leading case, *Pearce v. Brooks*,[44] the defendant had contracted with the plaintiff coach builders to acquire a fancy

---

37   For a relatively recent application of the doctrine, see *Prokop v. Kohut* (1965), 54 D.L.R. (2d) 717 (B.C.S.C.).

38   *Kutsenko v. Wasilenko* (1959), 19 D.L.R. (2d) 665 (Sask. C.A.). See also *Farrar v. MacPhee* (1971), 19 D.L.R. (3d) 720 (P.E.I.S.C.) (even though a co-habitation agreement would be void as contrary to public policy, this did not preclude a restitutionary claim for the value of housekeeping services rendered to the deceased).

39   See, for example, *Family Law Act*, above note 32, s. 30.

40   *Heglibiston Establishments v. Heyman* (1978), 36 P. & C.R. 351 (Eng. C.A.).

41   See, for example, *Family Law Act*, above note 32, s. 52.

42   (1986), 28 D.L.R. (4th) 754 (Sask. Q.B.), aff'd on other grounds (1987), 39 D.L.R. (4th) 637 (Sask. C.A.).

43   *Ibid.* at 758 (Q.B.), Kindred J.

44   (1866), L.R. 1 Ex. 213.

brougham, a horse-drawn carriage. It was known to the plaintiff that the defendant was a prostitute and that she intended to use the carriage to assist in her vocation. The agreement provided that the defendant could terminate the lease on the payment of a penalty. The plaintiff sought to enforce this arrangement without success. On appeal, Pollock C.B. observed: "any person who contributes to the performance of an illegal act by supplying a thing with the knowledge that it is going to be used for that purpose, cannot recover the price of the thing so supplied."[45] On similar grounds, it has been held that a lease of premises to the mistress of a man from whom the moneys available to pay the rent would have originated was unenforceable.[46] The trial judge had refused to apply the *Pearce v. Brooks* doctrine on the basis that its application should be strictly limited to cases of prostitution. The Court of Appeal reversed, however, on the basis that the precise nature of the immoral conduct was irrelevant to the outcome. The results in such cases are, however, open to question. It is not obvious that parties engaged in an extramarital affair should be entitled, in effect, to free rent. Moreover, the line drawn between the tools of the trade and the basic necessities of life will be difficult to draw in cases like *Pearce v. Brooks*. Agreements concerning the latter, no doubt, would be considered enforceable. Agreements concerning the conduct of a business providing the services of prostitution, however, are likely to be held unenforceable. In a Canadian case,[47] a contract of fire insurance on a house being operated as a bawdy house was held void. It is not entirely obvious, however, how this line of authority will or should be applied to agreements relating to the provision of services other than prostitution that have a dimension of sexuality to them, such as the provision of pornography in its various forms. The recent English decision in *Armhouse Lee Ltd. v. Chappel*[48] involved an agreement to publish magazine advertisements concerning the sale of telephone pre-recorded messages and live telephone conversations of a sexual nature. The service provider resisted the publisher's claim for payment for the advertisements on the basis of the immoral nature of its own business. The Court of Appeal held that whether or not the agreements entered into with subscribers to the service were void on grounds of public policy, the advertising contracts were not. Accordingly, the publisher was able to enforce the agreements and recover the price of the advertisements.

---

45   *Ibid.* at 217.
46   *Upfill v. Wright*, [1911] 1 K.B. 506.
47   *Dominion Fire Insurance Co. v. Nakata* (1915), 26 D.L.R. 722 (S.C.C.).
48   [1996] E.W.J. No. 211; *The Times*, August 7, 1996.

It is possible that new heads of public policy rendering contracts un-enforceable at common law on moral grounds might be recognized by the courts in the future. With the increasing involvement of legislatures in the regulation and prohibition of conduct that is considered to be anti-social in various ways, however, the role for the courts in determining such questions as a matter of common law appears to have diminished. Nonetheless, there may be situations in which legislatures are reluctant to intervene and the courts may be required, as a matter of common law, to determine the shape of public policy on a particular issue. The phe-nomenon of gestational or surrogacy contracts offers an illustration of this possibility. Although such arrangements may take a variety of forms, a common pattern would be an arrangement under which a fertile gesta-tional mother would, for a fee, bear a child conceived through artificial insemination of the sperm of a fertile husband of a married couple ex-periencing fertility problems. The understanding of the parties, typically, would be that, upon birth, custody of the infant would be turned over to the married couple by the gestational mother. In such circumstances, the gestational mother is also the biological mother of the child. A dispute concerning the enforceability of the surrogacy agreement is likely to arise if the gestational mother refuses to grant custody of the infant to the mar-ried couple. Litigation of this kind has arisen in the United States. Some American courts have taken the view that such arrangements may be en-forced.[49] In other states, however, courts have held such agreements void on the basis that they are contrary to public policy.[50] Such courts are con-cerned about the potentially exploitative nature of these agreements and the fact that they mandate the compulsory separation of a child from the biological mother and, in effect, require the adoption of the child in cir-cumstances where no determination has been made as to the suitability of the adoptive parents. A Canadian Royal Commission[51] expressed the view that surrogacy agreements are incompatible with Canadian social values and, accordingly, recommended that federal legislation prohibit the practice of paying for surrogacy services. Although such legislation has been enacted,[52] it does not dispose of the question of the enforceabil-ity of such agreements at common law.[53]

---

49   See, for example, *Johnson v. Calvert*, 19 Cal. Rep.2d 494 (1993).

50   See, for example, *Re Baby M*, 537 A.2d 1227 (N.J. 1988).

51   Royal Commission on New Reproductive Technologies, *Proceed with Care: Final Report of the Royal Commission on New Reproductive Technologies* (Ottawa: The Commission, 1993).

52   *Assisted Human Reproduction Act*, S.C. 2004, c. 2, ss. 6(1) and (5).

53   For discussion, see A.H. Young, "New Productive Technologies in Canada and the United States: Same Problems, Different Discourses" (1998) 12 Temp. Int'l

3) Agreements Undermining the Administration of Justice and Other State Interests

Another group of cases concerns agreements that have the potential effect of undermining the functioning or integrity of certain public institutions. The largest category of these cases deals with agreements that may interfere with the proper administration of justice. Other cases concern the proper functioning of other governmental institutions and relations with foreign governments.

a) Undermining the Administration of Justice

Agreements with witnesses that might be considered to create an incentive for perjury are unenforceable. Thus, an agreement to compensate a witness for providing evidence that the payer must have realized would not be true is unenforceable.[54] Contracts to provide a reward in return for evidence leading to the conviction of a person or persons who have committed a particular offence are, of course, unexceptionable and commonly employed.[55] On the other hand, an agreement to pay an informer to provide testimony leading to the conviction of a third party in which the fee was to be paid upon a sliding scale corresponding to the length of the sentence of the accused was held to be so direct an incentive to perjury as to be contrary to public policy and unenforceable.[56] Agreements to withhold testimony are also inconsistent with the proper adjudication of disputes. Accordingly, a provision in an agreement settling a patent infringement claim stipulating that the party in question would not testify in other proceedings concerning possible infringements of the same patent was held to be void and unenforceable.[57]

& Comp. L.J. 43; L. Shanner, "The Right to Procreate: When Rights Claims Have Gone Wrong" (1995) 40 McGill L.J. 823.

54   *Hendry v. Zimmerman*, [1947] 4 D.L.R. 550 (Man. K.B.). The court further held that if the purpose of the agreement was to compensate the witness for providing accurate evidence for a fee in excess of the statutory witness fee in circumstances where the witness was within the jurisdiction and subject to subpoena, the agreement would be unenforceable for lack of consideration. See *ibid.* at 554. See also *Collins v. Godefroy* (1831), 1 B. & Ad. 950, 109 E.R. 1040. And see generally Chapter 7, Section B(3)(a).

55   See, for example, *Williams v. Cawardine* (1833), 4 B. & Ad. 621, 110 E.R. 590 (K.B.).

56   *Symington v. Vancouver Breweries Ltd.*, [1931] 1 D.L.R. 935 (B.C.C.A.).

57   *Flexi-Coil Ltd. v. Smith-Roles Ltd.*, [1981] 1 F.C. 632 (T.D.), aff'd [1982] 1 F.C. 553 (C.A.). See also *Kearley v. Thomson* (1890), 24 Q.B.D. 742 (C.A.) (an agreement by a solicitor for a creditor of an insolvent party not to attend at the public examination of the bankrupt and oppose discharge held unenforceable).

An agreement to stifle a prosecution either by withdrawing a prosecution already instituted or by agreeing not to initiate such a prosecution in the future is void as contrary to public policy.[58] Thus, an agreement by relatives of an embezzler to repay moneys embezzled from a financial institution in return for the latter's promise not to prosecute the embezzler is unenforceable.[59] The agreement to stifle the prosecution may be inferred, as where prosecution has been threatened and the person making the threat must have realized that the subsequent agreement was entered into on the assumption that there would be no prosecution.[60] Under traditional English doctrine, a distinction was drawn between threats to stifle a felony as opposed to a mere misdemeanour, with the effect that agreements would be plainly void only if they concerned the former category of offences. With respect to misdemeanours, a distinction was drawn between prosecutions of a merely private rather than public nature. Agreements to stifle prosecutions of a merely private nature could be enforced.[61] The distinction between felonies and misdemeanours was rejected by Canadian courts in favour of a general proposition that agreements to stifle are void only where the offence is injurious to the community more generally rather than merely confined in its effect to the other party to the agreement.[62] This distinction appears to be based on the relative gravity of the offence. Thus, obtaining money by false pretences has been held to be an offence against the community more generally, notwithstanding the fact that its principal impact is upon the victim of the crime.[63] Further, agreements to stifle prosecutions for domestic violence or harassment

58 *Collins v. Blantern* (1767), 2 Wils. K.B. 341, 95 E.R. 847; *Pachal v. Schiller* (1914), 20 D.L.R. 851 (Sask. S.C.); *Boon v. Fair* (1916), 11 O.W.N. 177 (H.C.); *Johnson v. Musselman*, [1917] 2 W.W.R. 444 (Alta. C.A.); *Newell v. Royal Bank of Canada* (1997), 147 D.L.R. (4th) 268 (N.S.C.A.).

59 See *Jones v. Merionethshire Permanent Benefit Building Society*, [1892] 1 Ch. 173. See also *Peoples' Bank of Halifax v. Johnson* (1892), 20 S.C.R. 541.

60 *Boon v. Fair*, above note 58. See also *Newell v. Royal Bank of Canada*, above note 58; *Fuller v. Stoltze*, [1938] 1 D.L.R. 635 (Sask. C.A.), aff'd [1939] 1 D.L.R. 1 (S.C.C.).

61 *Keir v. Leeman* (1844), 6 Q.B. 308, 115 E.R. 118, aff'd (1845), 9 Q.B. 371, 115 E.R. 1315 (Ex. Ch.); *Fisher v. Appollinaris* (1875), 10 Ch. App. 297; *Windhill Local Board of Health v. Vint* (1890), 45 Ch. D. 351; *Kerridge v. Simmonds* (1906), 4 C.L.R. 253 (Aust. H.C.). See also A.H. Hudson, "Compromises of Criminal Liability" (1980) 43 Mod. L. Rev. 532.

62 *Dwight v. Ellsworth* (1852), 9 U.C.R. 539; *Leggatt v. Brown* (1899), 30 O.R. 225 (H.C.J.); *Morgan v. McFee* (1908), 18 O.L.R. 30 (C.A.).

63 *Morgan v. McFee, ibid.*

have been held void.[64] Where, however, the agreement to stifle is a component of an agreement that is essentially a compromise of a civil claim related to a minor offence, the agreement may be enforceable.[65] An agreement to stifle an indictable offence may constitute the crime of compounding an offence.[66] It is not necessary, however, that the parties have committed this offence in order to establish that their conduct constitutes an agreement to stifle a prosecution.[67]

Agreements to oust the jurisdiction of the courts are unenforceable at common law on the basis that there is a strong public interest in ensuring that citizens have access to the courts for the resolution of their disputes. Although it is accepted that parties may agree to assign their disputes for resolution by a domestic tribunal, both in respect to questions of fact and questions of law, a provision in the agreement that purported to preclude access to the courts for the ultimate resolution of questions of law would be unenforceable as an unlawful attempt to oust the jurisdiction of courts.[68] Thus, a provision of a lease that stipulated that the tenant was to pay an amount of money with respect to repairs would be "final and not subject to challenge in any manner whatsoever" was held to constitute an unenforceable attempt to oust court jurisdiction.[69] At common law, the same principle would apply to an agreement to submit disputes to arbitration,[70] though it was accepted that an agreement could lawfully require that a determination of a point of law by an arbitrator be made as a condition precedent to the commencement of court proceedings.[71] At the same time, it is well accepted, as a matter of public policy, that there exists a strong interest in allowing parties to insulate themselves from the inconvenience of legal proceedings by agreeing to final and binding arbitration of their contractual disputes. The precise balance between the competing interests of access to the courts and access to alternative means of dispute

---

64   *Hadfield v. Hadfield* (1996), 30 B.C.L.R. (3d) 131; *K. (E.) v. K. (D.)* (2003), 233 D.L.R. (4th) 101 (B.C.S.C.). Compare with *Keir v. Leeman*, above note 61 at 395 (Ex. Ch.), Tindal C.J. (agreement to stifle prosecution for assault not void).

65   See, for example, *Fisher v. Apollinaris*, above note 61 (trademark infringement); *Kerridge v. Simmonds*, above note 61 (libel).

66   *Criminal Code*, R.S.C. 1985, c. C-46, s. 141.

67   *Morgan v. McFee*, above note 62.

68   *Lee v. Showmen's Guild of Great Britain*, [1952] 2 Q.B. 329 at 342, Lord Denning; *Baker v. Jones*, [1954] 2 All E.R. 553; *Enderby Town Football Club v. Football Association Ltd.*, [1971] 1 Ch. 591.

69   *In re Davstone Estates Ltd.'s Leases*, [1969] 2 Ch. 378.

70   *Czarnikow v. Roth, Schmidt & Co.*, [1922] 2 K.B. 478 (C.A.).

71   *Scott v. Avery* (1856), 5 H.L. Cas. 881.

resolution is typically resolved in common law jurisdictions through the enactment of arbitration legislation,[72] analysis of which is beyond the scope of the present work.

Agreements under which one party supports or obtains a share of proceeds of another party's lawsuit are unenforceable at common law on the basis of the doctrines of maintenance and champerty. Maintenance is defined as the improper giving of encouragement or support to another person in the assertion or defence of legal proceedings in which the person providing the support or encouragement has no legitimate interest. Champerty is an aggravated form of maintenance in which the parties agree that the maintainer will obtain a share of the proceeds of the lawsuit.[73] Agreements involving maintenance or champerty are void as against public policy at common law. Maintenance and champerty have also been considered to be both common law crimes[74] and torts.[75] In Ontario, the invalidity of champertous agreements was also confirmed by a nineteenth-century statute, *An Act Respecting Champerty*.[76] The historical origins of these doctrines can be traced back to the early medieval period. They were initially designed to curtail the unattractive practices of royal officials and members of the nobility who officiously intermeddled, for personal gain, in the litigation of less powerful persons.[77] Although such practices have long since disappeared, the modern justification for these doctrines must be a perceived need to reduce the incentives for speculation in lawsuits or the stirring up of contentious proceedings. The modern trend, however, is one of narrowly confining the scope of these ancient doctrines.

In determining whether a particular arrangement amounts to maintenance or champerty, it is critical to find the presence of an improper motive. As is often said, there must be "an officious intermeddling, stir-

---

72 See, for example, *Arbitration Act, 1991*, S.O. 1991, c. 17, s. 45.
73 *Trendtex Trading Corporation v. Credit Suisse*, [1980] Q.B. 629 at 663, Oliver L.J. See generally P. Puri, "Financing of Litigation by Third-Party Investors: A Share of Justice?" (1998) 36 Osgoode Hall L.J. 515.
74 And thus were considered to be crimes in Canadian law until the abolition of common law crimes in 1953. See *Criminal Code*, R.S.C. 1985, c. C-46, s. 9.
75 See, for example, *Frind v. Sheppard*, [1940] 4 D.L.R. 455 (Ont. C.A.), rev'd [1941] 4 D.L.R. 497 (S.C.C.). These torts were abolished in England and in some Australian states. See, for example, *Criminal Law Act, 1967* (U.K.), c. 58, s. 14(2). See generally J.G. Fleming, *The Law of Torts*, 9th ed. (Sydney: Law Book Company, 1998) at 688–93.
76 R.S.O. 1897, c. 327.
77 See generally P.H. Winfield, "The History of Maintenance and Champerty" (1919) 35 Law Q. Rev. 50.

ring up of strife or other improper motive."[78] The mere fact that one is providing financial support to a lawsuit is thus not sufficient. It must be established that the party providing support does not have a legitimate interest in the outcome of the lawsuit. The concept of legitimate interest does, however, appear to be broadly construed.[79] Thus, if the maintainer intervened on the compassionate ground that the party requiring support would not otherwise be able to bring the lawsuit, the maintainer's interest would be legitimate.[80] A shared practical interest in the outcome of the litigation would suffice. Thus, a mutual protection society of anglers was held to have a legitimate interest in supporting the lawsuit of a particular anglers' group advancing a claim concerning pollution in a particular river.[81] A car dealer was held to have a legitimate interest in supporting its customers' claims for repair costs against the provider of an extended warranty that the dealer had sold to them.[82] A trade union has a legitimate interest in supporting its executives in libel actions relating to the discharge of their responsibilities.[83] The fact that the provider of support is a creditor of the plaintiff who is likely to be repaid only if the lawsuit enjoys success, constitutes a legitimate interest.[84] One who provides expertise essential to the success of the claim may have a sufficient interest.[85]

---

78   *Monteith v. Calladine* (1964), 47 D.L.R. (2d) 332 at 342 (B.C.C.A.), quoted with approval in *Buday v. Locator of Missing Heirs Inc.* (1993), 16 O.R. (3d) 257 at 267–68 (C.A.), Griffiths J.A. See also *McIntyre Estate v. Ontario (Attorney General)* (2002), 218 D.L.R. (4th) 193 at 204–6 (Ont. C.A.), O'Connor A.C.J.O., rev'g (2001), 198 D.L.R. (4th) 165 (Ont. S.C.J.).

79   *In re Trepca Mines Ltd. (No. 2)*, [1963] Ch. 199 at 219 (C.A.), Lord Denning M.R., quoted with approval in *McIntyre Estate v. Ontario (Attorney General), ibid.* at 205, O'Connor A.C.J.O.

80   *Findon v. Parker* (1843), 11 M. & W. 675, 152 E.R. 976 (Ex. Ct.); *R. v. Goodman*, [1939] S.C.R. 446 at 450, Kerwin J. Financial support from relatives is unexceptionable. See *Bradlaugh v. Newdegate* (1883), 11 Q.B.D. 1 at 11, Lord Coleridge.

81   *Martell v. Consett Iron Co. Ltd.*, [1955] Ch. 363 (C.A.). See also *Young v. Young*, [1993] 4 S.C.R. 3 (religious society supporting member's divorce proceeding).

82   *American Home Assurance Co. v. Brett Pontiac Buick GMC Ltd. (No. 2)* (1992), 116 N.S.R. (2d) 319 (C.A.).

83   *Hill v. Archbold*, [1968] 1 Q.B. 686 (C.A.).

84   *Fredrickson v. Insurance Corp. of British Columbia* (1986), 28 D.L.R. (4th) 414 (B.C.C.A.), aff'd (1988) 49 D.L.R. (4th) 160 (S.C.C.) (assignment of the claim in such circumstances does not amount to maintenance). See also *Societa Italiana Assicurazioni Transporti v. Canadian Marine Underwriters Ltd.* (1994), 26 C.C.L.I. (2d) 283 (Ont. Ct. Gen. Div.). See also *Trendtex Trading Corporation v. Credit Suisse*, above note 73 (effect on an assignment).

85   *Buday v. Locator of Missing Heirs Inc.*, above note 78; *Pielak v. Crown Forest Industries Ltd.* (1992), 64 B.C.L.R. (2d) 207 (S.C.). Compare with *Smythers v. Armstrong* (1989), 67 O.R. (2d) 753 (H.C.J.).

Champerty is a species of maintenance with the added element that the maintainer will share in the proceeds of the litigation. Accordingly, to establish that an agreement is champertous, it must be found that the maintainer has an improper motive. As is often said, without maintenance, there can be no champerty.[86] Thus, courts have enforced agreements that might have otherwise been condemned as champertous because of the presence of a legitimate motive on the part of the party supplying support to the litigation.[87] Although the doctrine of champerty would apply to any maintainer, regardless of his or her professional relationship, if any, to the party being supported,[88] application of the doctrine to agreements under which lawyers provide litigation services are of particular interest as their use in this context has been subject to much professional debate over the years. At common law, an agreement under which a lawyer agrees to provide litigation services to a client on the understanding that the lawyer will receive a share, typically a percentage share, of the proceeds of the lawsuit as a fee and, typically, will not otherwise be compensated for the services rendered is considered to be champertous.[89] The underlying concern is that a champertous arrangement might provide an incentive for the lawyer to engage in unethical conduct.[90]

Increasingly, however, it has come to be recognized in many jurisdictions that contingency fee arrangements provide a device whereby lawyers may, by taking the risk of loss of the lawsuit, provide access to court proceedings that might otherwise be denied to parties with meritorious claims. Thus, lawyers' contingency fee agreements have been rendered lawful in many jurisdictions, including all the Canadian

86 *Newswander v. Giegerich* (1907), 39 S.C.R. 354 at 359, 362–63; *Neville v. London Express Newspaper Ltd.*, [1919] A.C. 368 at 378–79, 382–83 (H.L.); *R. v. Goodman*, above note 80 at 449, 453–54; *McIntyre Estate v. Ontario (Attorney General)*, above note 78 at 204 (Ont. C.A.).

87 *Galati v. Edwards Estate* (1998), 27 C.P.C. (4th) 123 (Ont. Ct. Gen. Div.); *S. v. K.* (1986), 55 O.R. (2d) 111 (Dist. Ct.); *R. v. Goodman, ibid.*; *Stribbell v. Bhalla* (1990), 73 O.R. (2d) 748 (H.C.J.); *Buday v. Locator of Missing Heirs Inc.*, above note 78.

88 *Cole v. Booker* (1913), 29 T.L.R. 295; *Buday v. Locator of Missing Heirs Inc., ibid.*

89 *Re Solicitor* (1907), 14 O.L.R. 464 (H.C.J.); *Wallersteiner v. Moir (No. 2)*, [1975] Q.B. 373 (C.A.); *Trendtex Trading Corp. v. Credit Suisse*, above note 73; *Awwad v. Geraghty & Co.*, [2000] 1 All E.R. 608 (C.A.). Exceptionally, however, it has been held that if the litigation had been commenced before the lawyer in question was retained, the agreement may not be champertous. See *Monteith v. Calladine*, above note 78.

90 *In re Trepca Mines Ltd. (No. 2)*, above note 79 at 219–20, Lord Denning.

provinces[91] except Ontario. In Ontario, contingency agreements have been given legislative approval only in the context of class actions.[92] More generally, lawyers' contingency fee agreements remain subject to *An Act Respecting Champerty*[93] and have traditionally been considered unenforceable. In the leading decision of the Ontario Court of Appeal, in *McIntyre Estate v. Ontario (Attorney General)*,[94] however, it was held that the effect of that legislation was simply to apply the common law doctrine of champerty to such agreements and, further, the court held that the common law treatment of lawyers' contingency fee agreements should be considered to have evolved over time. Such agreements would no longer be considered to be, *per se*, champertous. In reaching this conclusion, the court drew support from the policy considerations relating to access to justice that favour the use of contingency fee arrangements and the reforms made in other jurisdictions.[95] At the same time, the Court of Appeal concluded that contingency fee agreements could overcompensate a lawyer to such a degree that the agreement would be unreasonable or unfair to the client and therefore would constitute an agreement to maintain with an improper purpose.[96] Accordingly, the enforceability of the contingency fee arrangement in a particular case must often be determined in light of the ultimate result and the extent of compensation thereby afforded to the lawyer in question.

b) Other State Interests

More generally, agreements that tend to undermine the proper functioning of public institutions are considered void as against public policy. Thus, an agreement entered into by a Member of Parliament to vote in accordance with the instructions of a third party, for reward, would appear to be an unlawful constraint on the Member's ability to vote in accordance with his or her own opinions.[97] Agreements entered into

---

91 A survey of the provisions is set out in the appendix to the reasons given at first instance in *McIntyre Estate v. Ontario (Attorney General)*, above note 78 at 190–92 (Ont. S.C.J.).

92 *Class Proceedings Act, 1992*, S.O. 1992, c. 6, s. 33(1).

93 Above note 76.

94 Above note 78.

95 *McIntyre Estate v. Ontario (Attorney General)*, *ibid*. at 211–20 (Ont. C.A.). A similar shift in professional attitudes has occurred with respect to contingency fee arrangements entered into by accountants. See *Johnson v. Lazzarino* (1998), 39 O.R. (3d) 724 (Gen. Div.), aff'd (1999), 43 O.R. (3d) 253n (C.A.).

96 *McIntyre Estate v. Ontario (Attorney General)*, *ibid*. at 220 (Ont. C.A.). See also *Thai Trading Co. v. Taylor*, [1998] Q.B. 781 at 788–90.

97 *Amalgamated Society of Railway Servants v. Osborne*, [1910] A.C. 87 at 115, Lord Shaw of Dunfermline.

with a minister of the Crown,[98] or a municipal authority,[99] with a view to committing a government to a particular course of legislative decision-making are unenforceable on the ground that they represent an unlawful constraint on the capacity of a legislative authority to legislate in the best interests of the electors. Similarly, an agreement requiring a municipal body to ignore procedural requirements in the form of a public hearing for the exercise of its legislative mandate is unenforceable.[100] The payment of a bribe to a public official constitutes a common law offence[101] and an agreement to do so would no doubt be void on public policy grounds. An assignment or mortgage of the salary of the public official is also unenforceable on the ground, presumably, that it creates the risk of diminished capacity to perform or of a relationship of dependency on the assignee or mortgagee.[102] An agreement under which one undertakes to procure an honour or, presumably, a public office, assumed to be free from such influences is also unenforceable.[103] More generally, agreements to engage in what might now be referred to as "influence peddling" have traditionally been considered unenforceable at common law on policy grounds. Thus, where a person claiming to be influential in government circles agrees to bring that influence to bear, in return for a fee, in order to influence the outcome of what is generally perceived to be an objective decision-making process, the agreement is unenforceable. Thus, in *Montefiore v. Menday Motor Components Co.*,[104] the plaintiff, who had agreed to attempt to procure for the defendant government contracts for the making of aircraft parts,

---

98 *Provincial Court Judges Association (Saskatchewan) v. Saskatchewan (Minister of Justice)*, [1995] 6 W.W.R. 626 (Sask. Q.B.), rev'd on other grounds [1996] 2 W.W.R. 129 (Sask. C.A.). Election promises have been held to be unenforceable on similar grounds. See *Canadian Taxpayers Federation v. Ontario (Minister of Finance)* (2004), 73 O.R. (3d) 621 (S.C.J.); *Hogan v. Newfoundland (Attorney General)* (2000), 183 D.L.R. (4th) 225 (Nfld. C.A.).

99 *Vancouver v. Registrar of Vancouver Land Registration District* (1955), 15 W.W.R. 351 (B.C.C.A.). In *Pacific National Investments Ltd. v. Victoria (City)*, [2000] 2 S.C.R. 919, the Supreme Court of Canada held that an implicit agreement with a developer under which a municipality undertakes not to change the zoning of a particular parcel was contrary to public policy as an unlawful fetter on the municipality's capacity to legislate in the best interests of the residents and, accordingly, *ultra vires* the municipality and unenforceable.

100 *Finney v. Township of McKellar* (1982), 133 D.L.R. (3d) 351 (Ont. C.A.).

101 *Regina v. Whitaker*, [1914] 3 K.B. 1283.

102 *Re Mirams*, [1891] 1 Q.B. 594; *Angers v. Gauthier*, [1924] S.C.R. 479.

103 *Parkinson v. College of Ambulance*, [1925] 2 K.B. 1. See also *Egerton v. Brownlow* (1853), 4 H.L. Cas. 1, 10 E.R. 359.

104 [1918] 2 K.B. 241. See also *Norman v. Cole* (1800), 3 Esp. 253, 170 E.R. 606.

was held unable to recover the agreed upon commission with respect to agreements allegedly resulting from his efforts. A Canadian case suggested that this principle might apply to a similar agreement entered into for the purpose of bringing influence to bear on a friendly foreign government.[105] The line between influence peddling at common law and the activities of the modern lobbyist may well be difficult to draw and will turn, presumably, on a distinction between advocacy services that are presumably not corrupt and simply trading on personal connections that, under traditional common law at least, could not be the subject of an enforceable agreement. The importance of a free press in a democratic society has also been identified as a matter of public policy at common law. Thus, an agreement under which a newspaper owner agreed, for a fee, to refrain from commenting on the activities of a particular group of companies was held unenforceable as an unlawful restraint on the ability of the newspaper to comment freely on matters of public interest.[106]

Agreements inconsistent with government interests concerning relations with foreign countries may be unenforceable at common law. Thus, an agreement entered into for the purpose of committing an illegal act in a foreign country will not be enforced. In a leading case,[107] a contract to supply whisky into the United States during prohibition was held unenforceable. This principle has been applied in circumstances where the arrangement, though not illegal in the foreign jurisdiction, is contrary to the public policy of that jurisdiction.[108] If a state of war exists with a foreign nation, agreements entered into with residents of the foreign nation will be unenforceable on the basis that they constitute "trading with the enemy" and may have the effect of enhancing the resources available to the enemy state.[109] The principle is territorial in nature. Thus, a Canadian or a citizen of a neutral state resident in

---

105 *Carr-Harris v. Canadian General Electric Co.* (1921), 61 D.L.R. 434 at 435 (Ont. S.C.A.D.), Meredith C.J.C.P. The other members of the majority did not find it necessary to deal with this issue. Two judges dissented on this point. See also *Lemenda Trading Co. v. African Middle East Petroleum Co.*, [1988] Q.B. 448.

106 *Neville v. Dominion of Canada News Co. Ltd.*, [1915] 3 K.B. 556.

107 *Foster v. Driscoll*, [1929] 1 K.B. 470. See also *Shiesel v. Kirsch*, [1931] O.R. 41 (Ont. C.A.); *Regazzoni v. K.C. Sethia (1944) Ltd.*, [1958] A.C. 301 (H.L.); *Royal Boskalis Westminster NV v. Mountain*, [1999] Q.B. 674.

108 *Lemenda Trading Co. v. African Middle East Petroleum Co.*, above note 105.

109 *Porter v. Freudenberg*, [1915] 1 K.B. 857 at 868, Lord Reading C.J. See also *Furtado v. Rogers* (1802), 3 Bos. & P. 191, 127 E.R. 105; *Ertel Bieber & Co. v. Rio Tinto Co.*, [1918] A.C. 260. War must be declared, not merely imminent. See *Janson v. Driefontein Consolidated Mines Ltd.*, [1902] A.C. 484 (H.L.).

or carrying on business in the foreign jurisdiction would be subject to the principle.[110] Conversely, a national of the enemy nation resident in a neutral territory will not be subject to the principle unless it is apparent that the assets to be acquired under the agreement by the enemy national are destined for the enemy territory.[111]

4) Covenants in Restraint of Trade

For centuries, the courts of common law have invalidated arrangements that have as their object the reduction of competition in the marketplace.[112] The common law's intolerance of anticompetitive practices was comprehensive. Thus, for example, in the early-seventeenth century there were common law decisions striking down a royal grant of a monopoly[113] and the by-law of a tailors' guild restricting the practice of that trade in a particular municipality to tailors associated with or approved by the guild.[114] In the modern era, of course, the control of monopolies and other anticompetitive practices is accomplished by legislative prohibition and administrative regulation.[115] What remains as a matter of common law, however, is the doctrine that consensual agreements under which one party agrees to refrain from competing with the other party—so called covenants in restraint of trade—are generally considered unenforceable at common law on the ground that they are contrary to public policy. The basic concept has been defined in the following terms: "A contract in restraint of trade is one in which a party (the covenantor) agrees with any other party (the covenantee) to restrict his liberty in the future to carry on trade with other persons not parties to the contract in such manner as he chooses."[116] Such covenants are commonly found in employment contracts and in contracts for the purchase and sale of a business. As we shall see, however, they are also commonly found in other commercial contexts.

---

110 *Porter v. Freudenberg,* above note 109.
111 *Lampel v. Berger* (1917), 38 D.L.R. 47 (Ont. S.C.).
112 The early history is reviewed in M.J. Trebilcock, *The Common Law of Restraint of Trade* (Toronto: Carswell, 1986) c. 1 and J.D. Heydon, *The Restraint of Trade Doctrine,* 2d ed. (Sydney: Butterworths, 1999) c. 1.
113 *Darcy v. Allen (The Case of Monoplies)* (1602), Moore (K.B.) 671.
114 *Ipswich Tailors' Case* (1614), 77 E.R. 1218.
115 *Competition Act,* R.S.C. 1985, c. C-34. See generally B. Dunlop, D. McQueen and M. Trebilcock, *Canadian Competition Policy* (Toronto: Canada Law Book, 1987).
116 *Petrofina (Great Britain) Ltd. v. Martin,* [1966] Ch. 146 at 180, Diplock L.J. And see *Esso Petroleum Co. Ltd. v. Harper's Garage (Stourport) Ltd.,* [1968] A.C. 269 at 317, Lord Hodson.

Although covenants in restraint of trade are generally unenforceable, it is not the case that all such covenants are void. Thus, the principal task for the law of restraint of trade is to distinguish those covenants that are void from those that are considered to be enforceable. To come within the latter category, a restraint must be ancillary to or a component of a larger transaction or relationship. As is sometimes said, a "bare" restraint is void. The leading illustration of this proposition is a decision of the Privy Council in a case arising in British Columbia, *Vancouver Malt and Sake Brewing Co. Ltd. v. Vancouver Breweries Limited.*[117] In this case, the defendant, who was in the business of brewing sake but who also possessed a non-transferrable licence to brew beer, purported to sell to the plaintiff—the only beer brewer in Vancouver—the goodwill associated with the beer-brewing business authorized by the licence. It also gave a covenant not to compete in the beer business in return for a payment by the plaintiff of fifteen thousand dollars. The obvious point of the arrangement was to eliminate the seller as a potential competitor of the plaintiff in the beer business. The Privy Council characterized the arrangement as a "bare covenant not to compete"[118] and, as such, unenforceable at common law. Where, however, the covenant is merely a component of a larger transaction, such as an agreement to purchase and sell a business, the covenant is potentially enforceable if it meets the requisite standard of reasonableness.

The classic statement of the test for measuring the reasonableness of a particular restraint was set out in *Nordenfelt v. Maxim Nordenfelt Guns & Ammunition Co.*[119] by Lord Macnaghten in the following terms:

> The public have an interest in every person's carrying on his trade freely: so has the individual. All interference with individual liberty of action in trading, and all restraints of trade themselves, if there is nothing more, are contrary to public policy, and therefore void. That is the general rule. But there are exceptions: restraints of trade and interference with individual liberty of action may be justified by the special circumstances of a particular case. It is a sufficient justification, and indeed, it is the only justification, if the restriction is reasonable—reasonable, that is, in reference to the interests of the parties concerned and reasonable in reference to the interests of the public, so framed and so guarded as to afford adequate protection to the party in whose favour it is imposed, while at the same time it is in no way injurious to the public.[120]

---

117 [1934] A.C. 181.
118 *Ibid.* at 190.
119 [1894] A.C. 535 (H.L.).
120 *Ibid.* at 565.

The basic reasonableness test, generally referred to as the "*Nordenfelt* test," thus has two dimensions or branches—reasonableness in light of the interests of the parties and reasonableness in light of the public interest in access to a competitive marketplace. Application of the reasonableness test is contingent upon the "peculiar circumstances of a particular case,"[121] including the nature of the transaction within which the restraint is located, the nature of the commercial activity restrained, the interests of the parties protected or undermined by the restraint and the general nature of the particular market within which the restraint is designed to operate.

In the context of the purchase and sale of a business, the typical covenant in restraint of trade precludes the seller of the business from competing with the purchaser of the business within a particular geographical area for a specified period of time. Applying the first branch of the *Nordenfelt* test in this context, it may be noted that both the seller and the purchaser of the business have a legitimate interest in the enforceability of the restraint for it is only if the restraint can be enforced that the seller can effectively transfer the goodwill of the business. It is in the interest of the buyer to acquire the goodwill and in the interest of the seller to receive consideration for its transfer. Nonetheless, the scope of the restraint must be reasonable in terms of its duration, geographical scope and the type of activity restrained. With respect to the last point, the activity restrained must generally be limited to the nature of the business sold.[122] Thus, in *Nordenfelt* itself, which concerned the sale of a business engaged in the manufacture of guns and ammunition, a covenant on the part of the seller to refrain from competing in any way, with any business carried on by the buyer, was considered too wide. On the other hand, the seller's covenant not to compete in the trade or manufacture of guns or ammunition was held to be enforceable. Generally speaking, the geographical scope of the restraint must be limited to the area in which the seller's business had been active.[123] A worldwide restraint was upheld in *Nordenfelt*, however, on the basis that although the seller had only a few customers, they were spread around the world. Occasionally, it has been suggested that the fact that the parties had anticipated an expansion of the business might

---

121 *J.G. Collins Insurance Agencies Ltd. v. Elsley*, [1978] 2 S.C.R. 916 at 923, Dickson J.
122 See *British Reinforced Concrete Engineering Co. v. Schelff*, [1921] 2 Ch. 563; *Goldsoll v. Goldman*, [1915] 1 Ch. 292 (C.A.).
123 See, for example, *Connors Bros. Ltd. v. Connors*, [1940] 4 All E.R. 179 (P.C.); *Giannone & Stampeder Motor Hotel Ltd.* (1963), 41 D.L.R. (2d) 242 (Alta. S.C.T.D.); *McAllister v. Cardinal* (1964), 47 D.L.R. (2d) 313 (Ont. H.C.J.); *Greening Industries Ltd. v. Penny* (1966), 53 D.L.R. (2d) 643 (N.S.S.C.).

be taken into account in assessing the reasonableness of a constraint broader in scope than the area in which the seller's business is actually being conducted.[124] As far as the temporal duration of the covenant is concerned, reasonably lengthy periods, including periods of indefinite length have been upheld.[125] At the same time, the temporal dimension of the restraint remains subject to a reasonableness test.[126]

A doctrine of severability is applied to the context of agreements to sell a business. If the offensively broad provisions can be deleted, thus leaving a reasonable residue, courts will, in effect, strike out the offending portions of the covenant and enforce the remainder. Thus, as intimated above, the *Nordenfelt* court deleted that portion of the covenant that committed the seller to "compete in any way with [any business] for the time being carried on by the [buyer]."[127] In another case involving the sale of an imitation jewellery business conducted in London, the seller undertook not to compete with the buyer with respect to the sale of either real or imitation jewellery in the United Kingdom, France, Spain, the United States and Russia. The court deleted as too broad the references to real jewellery and to each of the foreign countries.[128] It is generally accepted that severance should be permitted only where it can be accomplished by deletion of terms rather than a rewriting of the terms. This is the so-called blue-pencil test.[129] Occasionally, however, partial enforcement of an otherwise offensive provision has been achieved by interpreting the covenant in question narrowly in light of the commercial context of the agreement.[130] The pervasiveness of the blue-pencil approach, however, has inspired a drafting technique pursuant to which covenants are drafted in a series of subclauses setting out constraints of increasing scope and duration coupled with a final

---

124 See, for example, *Tank Lining Corp. v. Dunlop Industrial Ltd.* (1982), 40 O.R. (2d) 219, 140 D.L.R. (3d) 659 (Ont. C.A.); *McAllister v. Cardinal,* above note 123.

125 *Connors Bros. Ltd. v. Connors,* above note 123; *Cope v. Harasino* (1964), 48 D.L.R. (2d) 744 (B.C.C.A.).

126 See, for example, *Pelow v. Ivey* (1933), 49 T.L.R. 422; *Bodmin Bros. v. Langestone & Lavery* (1911), 31 N.Z.L.R. 200; *Brown v. Brown,* [1980] 1 N.Z.L.R. 484; *Bliss & Laughlin Industries Incorporated v. Doerner* (1978), 42 C.P.R. (2d) 74 (Ont. C.A.), aff'd [1980] 2 S.C.R. 865, 117 D.L.R. (3d) 547.

127 Above note 119 at 536.

128 *Goldsoll v. Goldman,* above note 122.

129 The validity of this approach in the broader context of illegal contracts more generally has been reconsidered in recent years by the Supreme Court of Canada. See further this Chapter, section E.

130 See, for example, *Mizon v. Pohoretzky* (1917), 40 O.L.R. 239 (S.C.A.D.); *Latimer v. Fontaine* (1905), 2 W.L.R. 191 (N.W.T.S.C.); *E.P. Chester Ltd. v. Mastorkis* (1968), 70 D.L.R. (2d) 133 (N.S.S.C.A.D.).

clause indicating that any provisions determined to be offensive on restraint of trade grounds shall be severed from the remainder of the covenant.[131]

Application of the first branch of the *Nordenfelt* test in the context of an employment contract gives rise to different considerations. In the typical case, the employee will covenant, as part of the employment agreement, that, upon termination of the employment relationship, the employee will not compete with the employer in a particular area for a particular period of time. For a number of reasons, restraint of trade doctrine is applied more vigorously in the context of postemployment restraints. In contrast to the sale of business context, the employer and employee do not have a similar commonality in their interest in the enforceability of the restraint as do the buyer and seller of a business. Further, as Dickson J. observed in *J.G. Collins Insurance Agencies Ltd. v. Elsley*,[132] in the employment context, "an imbalance of bargaining power may lead to oppression and a denial of the right of the employee to exploit, following termination of employment, in the public interest and in his own interest, knowledge and skills obtaining during employment."[133] Such concerns are not present to the same degree or may not be present at all in the context of restraints that operate during the period of employment. Accordingly, covenants given by an employee not to compete with the employer during the course of the employment contract are generally considered to be enforceable.[134] Postemployment restraints, on the other hand, that are intended simply to restrict competition with the employer by the former employee are invalid. A postemployment restraint designed to serve legitimate interests of the employer may, however, survive scrutiny under the *Nordenfelt* test.

---

131 The *reductio ad absurdum* of this drafting technique is to be found in an Australian case in which the trial judge estimated that 82,152 different combinations of the various subclauses could be devised and held the agreement unenforceable on the grounds of uncertainty. See *Austera Tanks Pty. Ltd. v. Running*, [1982] 2 N.S.W.L.R. 840.

132 Above note 121.

133 *Ibid.* at 924.

134 *Warner Bros. Pictures Inc. v. Nelson*, [1937] 1 K.B. 209. This point cannot be generalized beyond the employment context, however, as it is clearly established that in other kinds of relationships such as music publication contracts and solus agreements, covenants restraining competition during the term of the agreement may be subject to the doctrine. See, for example, *A. Schroeder Music Publishing Co. Ltd. v. MacAulay*, [1974] 3 All E.R. 616 (H.L.); *Stephens v. Gulf Oil* (1975), 65 D.L.R. (3d) 193 (Ont. C.A.), leave to appeal to S.C.C. refused (1976), 11 O.R. (2d) 129n.

452 THE LAW OF CONTRACTS

A postemployment restraint will be valid only if it is designed to protect legitimate "proprietary" interests of the employer and does so in a manner that is not excessive. The covenant must provide merely "reasonable protection to trade secrets, confidential information and trade connections of the employer."[135] Where the purpose of the clause, however, is properly characterized as an attempt to incapacitate the former employee as a potential competitor, the restraint is void. The employer in *Mason v. Provident Clothing & Supply Co.*,[136] was in the business of signing up householders to participate in a scheme enabling them to benefit from discounts achieved through bulk purchases of clothing and other goods and it employed canvassers for this purpose. The employer extracted from a canvasser who worked one small district of London a postemployment covenant that prevented him from engaging in such work within 25 miles of London. The covenant was held void on the basis that it was an attempt to preclude the former employee from deploying his talents as a canvasser in a competitive fashion rather than to protect the employer's trade secrets or other confidential information from unfair exploitation by the former employee. In a particular employment context, the line between the employee's skill-set and the employer's trade secrets and confidential information may be difficult to draw. In *Herbert Morris Ltd. v. Saxelby*,[137] for example, the defendant had worked as a draftsman and then engineer for several years for the plaintiff, a leading manufacturer of lifting devices. During his time as an engineer, he was privy to a good deal of confidential scientific information concerning the plaintiff's manufacturing processes. The defendant's postemployment covenant not to compete within the United Kingdom for seven years was held unenforceable, however, on the ground that it was essentially designed to prevent the defendant from employing his skill-set in the service of competitors, a skill-set that included the general knowledge he had acquired of the plaintiff's "scheme of organization and methods of business."[138] On the other hand, in *Littlewoods Organisation Ltd. v. Harris*,[139] a covenant was enforced against the defendant who was the former executive director of the plaintiff's mail-order business. The defendant had acquired strategic marketing information, such as sales trends, sources of manufac-

---

135 Above note 121 at 924.

135 Above note 121 at 924.
136 [1913] A.C. 724 (H.L.).
137 [1916] 1 A.C. 688 (H.L.).
138 *Ibid.* at 704. See also *Drake International Ltd. v. Miller* (1976), 61 D.L.R. (3d) 420 (Ont. H.C.J.) (employment agency).
139 [1978] 1 All E.R. 1026 (C.A.).

tured goods, market research and the company's plans for the future. This was considered by the Court of Appeal to be confidential know-how that could be protected by a postemployment restraint.[140]

The protection of the employer's proprietary interest in trade connections typically involves an attempt by the employer to protect relations with customers who may, because of the nature of the employment, have formed a connection with or attachment to the employee in question. Again, in this context, a difficult line must be drawn between the former employee's skill-set or reputation and a capacity to unfairly exploit relationships with the employer's customers developed through the course of the employment relationship. In some cases, at least, it has been held that where the customers are likely to be attracted by the former employee's personal skills, a postemployment restraint will not be enforced.[141] However, if the particular employee's role in the employer's business is one in which a relationship of loyalty between the customer and the employee is likely to arise, a postemployment restraint will be valid. The leading decision of the Supreme Court of Canada, *J.G. Collins Insurance Agencies Ltd. v. Elsley*,[142] involved the sale of a general insurance agency to another general insurance agency pursuant to which the seller became the general manager of the combined businesses and eventually signed an employment agreement containing a postemployment restraint. The seller, *Elsley*, managed the combined businesses for seventeen years. Dickson J. described his relationship with the customers of the combined businesses as follows: "During the seventeen-year period Elsley dealt with the customers of the agency to the almost total exclusion of Collins. To them Elsley was the business, Collins little more than a name. Elsley met the customers, telephoned them frequently, placed their insurance policies and answered their queries. ... People became accustomed to doing business with him on a personal basis and he looked after their insurance needs."[143]

Dickson J. further noted that when the postemployment restraint was drafted "it was known that Elsley had, or would acquire, a special and intimate knowledge of the customers of his prospective employer and the means of influence over them." The Supreme Court held that the postemployment restraint was valid in these circumstances.

---

140 See also *Commercial Plastics Ltd. v. Vincent*, [1965] 1 Q.B. 623 (C.A.) (information concerning evolving methods of manufacturing adhesive tape constitutes confidential know-how).

141 *Attwood v. Lamont*, [1920] 3 K.B. 571 (C.A.) (skilled tailor); *Northern Messenger & Transfer Ltd. v. Fabbro* (1964), 49 W.W.R. 115 (Man. Q.B.) (talented canvasser).

142 Above note 121.

143 *Ibid.* at 920.

Similar decisions have been made with respect to postemployment restraints in the context of employed lawyers[144] and medical practitioners.[145] Where, on the other hand, the nature of the service provided by the employee on the employer's behalf to customers is such that the customer would be indifferent to the identity of the employee, a postemployment restraint would be unenforceable.[146]

Assuming that a legitimate proprietary interest of the employer has been identified, issues similar to those arising in the context of a sale of the business concerning the reasonableness of the scope and duration of the restraint arise in the employment context.[147] In addition, however, courts have identified as an issue in the employment context whether the nature of the employer's interest in its customer relationships is such as to render an outright ban on competition in the postemployment restraint or, on the other hand, is such that it could be reasonably protected by a mere ban on solicitation of customers by the former employee. If a ban on solicitation is considered sufficient, an outright ban on competition would be unenforceable. As the Supreme Court noted in *Elsley*, an outright ban on competition can be justified only in exceptional circumstances.[148] The exceptional nature of the circumstances in *Elsley* were indicated, in Dickson J.'s view, by the fact that, notwithstanding Elsley's claim that he had not solicited former clients, something in the order of two hundred clients switched their custom to his new place of business. Although solicitation bans have been approved as reasonable in the context of professional services,[149] such approval is not automatic. In a recent Ontario case, for example, *Lyons v. Multari*,[150] the defendant was a young oral surgeon who went into practice with an experienced oral surgeon in Windsor, Ontario, and agreed to a postemployment non-competition restraint that was to preclude the opening up of a practice within 5 miles of the plaintiff's

---

144 *Fitch v. Dewes*, [1921] 2 A.C. 158 at 165 (H.L.), Lord Birkenhead L.C. (the employee "should not be in a position to use the intimacies and knowledge which he had acquired in the course of his employment in order to create a practice of his own in that same place and by doing so undermine the business and connection of the [employer]").

145 *Routh v. Jones*, [1947] 1 All E.R. 758 (C.A.); *Mills v. Gill*, [1952] 3 D.L.R. 27 (Ont. H.C.J.).

146 See, for example, *S.W. Strange Ltd. v. Mann*, [1965] 1 All E.R. 1069 (Ch.); *Winnipeg Livestock Sales Ltd. v. Plewman* (2000), 192 D.L.R. (4th) 525 (Man. C.A.).

147 See generally Trebilcock, above note 112 at 99–106.

148 Above note 121 at 926.

149 See, for example, *Fitch v. Dewes*, above note 144; *Mills v. Gill*, above note 145.

150 (2000), 50 O.R. (3d) 526 (C.A.).

office for a period of three years. Shortly after terminating the relationship, the defendant opened an oral surgery practice in contravention of the covenant. The Court of Appeal held that the plaintiff had a proprietary interest in the identity of the dentists who regularly referred patients to him and in the identity of his patients but that this proprietary interest could be adequately protected by a non-solicitation clause. Accordingly, the non-competition covenant was unenforceable.

Courts are much less willing to apply the doctrine of severance in order to cure unreasonable restraint in the employment context. The traditional view is that the vulnerability of the employee in a typical case weighs against heroic efforts to save the clause. Lord Moulton explained the basis for the traditional approach in *Mason v. Provident Clothing & Supply Co.*[151] in the following terms:

> It would in my opinion be *pessimi exempli* if, when an employer had exacted a covenant deliberately framed in unreasonably wide terms, the courts were to come to his assistance and, by applying their ingenuity and knowledge of the law, carve out of this void covenant the maximum of what he might validly have required. It must be remembered that the real sanction at the back of these covenants is the terror and expense of litigation, in which the servant is usually at a great disadvantage, in view of the longer purse of the master. ... [T]he hardship imposed by the exaction of unreasonable covenants by employers would be greatly increased if they could continue the practice with the expectation that, having exposed a servant to the anxiety and expense of litigation, the court would in the end enable them to obtain everything which they could have obtained by acting reasonably.[152]

On this basis, severance would not be permitted. However, there are cases where courts have read down overly broad constraints on the basis of interpretative principles.[153] Further, there are a number of cases in which covenants containing both non-solicitation clauses and non-competition clauses have been severed with the result that the non-solicitation clauses remain enforceable.[154] Although the Supreme Court

---

151 Above note 136.

152 *Ibid.* at 745. See also *Attwood v. Lamont*, above note 141 at 596, Younger L.J.

153 See, for example, *Haynes v. Doman*, [1899] 2 Ch. 13 (C.A.); *Home Counties Dairies Ltd. v. Skilton*, [1970] 1 All E.R. 1227 (C.A.); *Marion White Ltd. v. Frances*, [1972] 3 All E.R. 857 (C.A.); *Littlewoods Organisation Ltd. v. Harris*, above note 139.

154 See, for example, *Stenhouse Australia Ltd. v. Phillips*, [1974] A.C. 391 (P.C.); *Creditel of Canada Ltd. v. Faultless* (1977), 18 O.R. (2d) 95 (H.C.J.); *W.R. Grace & Co. of Canada Ltd. v. Sare* (1980), 28 O.R. (2d) 612 (H.C.J.). See also *Computer Centre*

of Canada indicated a preference for the traditional view in an *obiter dictum* in *Elsley*,[155] there is some prospect that, at least in cases where the particular covenant is not patently unreasonable nor an obvious exercise in exploiting the vulnerability of employees, courts may be willing to apply the techniques of interpretation and severance to cure an otherwise unenforceable restraint.

The second branch of the *Nordenfelt* test measures the reasonableness of the covenant in light of the public interest in access to competitive markets. Application of the second branch of the test also varies to some extent between the sale of business cases and those involving postemployment restraints. In the sale of business context, the principal concern evident in the analysis of the public interest branch of the test is to ensure that compliance with the covenant does not have the effect of creating a "pernicious monopoly."[156] It has been suggested, however, that the second branch of the test may have a broader application in this setting and may involve consideration of, for example, whether enforcement of the covenant might have an unduly negative impact on an important industry in a particular region.[157]

When one turns to the employment context, the second branch of the test may have less of a role to play inasmuch as the employee's interest in being able to compete in the marketplace and earn a living is quite consistent with the public interest in access to a competitive marketplace. In measuring the reasonableness of postemployment restraints, however, courts will consider the question of whether the unavailability of the services of the particular former employee will have a negative impact on consumers. Thus, in *Elsley*, Dickson J. considered it noteworthy that the removal of *Elsley* himself from the marketplace of general insurance would leave the consumers in the region with nothing less than twenty-two alternative suppliers of the service.

Such concerns are most likely to arise in the context of medical services. Thus, in *Sherk v. Horwitz*,[158] the defendant obstetrician had agreed to a postemployment restraint upon termination of his employment with a medical clinic in St. Catharines, Ontario. In a decision upheld

---

Personnel Ltd. v. Lagopoulous (1975), 58 D.L.R. (3d) 352 (Ont. H.C.J.) (non-competition clause survives).

155 Above note 121 at 925–26.

156 *Attorney General of Australia v. Adelaide Steamship Co.*, [1913] A.C. 781 at 796 (P.C.), Lord Parker. See also *Connors Bros. Ltd. v. Connors*, above note 123; *Doerner v. Bliss & Laughlin Industries Incorporated*, above note 126 (S.C.C.).

157 *Tank Lining Corporation v. Dunlop Industrial Ltd.*, above note 124.

158 [1972] 2 O.R. 451 (H.C.J.), aff'd on other grounds [1973] 1 O.R. 360 (C.A.), leave to appeal to S.C.C. refused (1972), 9 C.P.R. (2d) 119n (S.C.C.).

by the Ontario Court of Appeal on other grounds, the trial judge found
that there was a shortage of obstetricians in St. Catharines and held the
restraint unenforceable on the basis of the second branch of the *Nordenfelt* test.[159] In *Sherk*, it was also suggested that the nature of the doctor-
patient relationship is such that patients ought not be deprived of access
to the physician in whom they have placed their confidence.[160] Similarly,
Lord Denning has taken the view that the relationship between solicitor
and client is of such a nature that it would be contrary to public policy
to deprive a client of the choice of a solicitor through enforcement of
a postemployment restraint.[161] A later decision of the Privy Council,
however, has rejected this approach, placing emphasis on the fact that
firms would be reluctant to hire younger associates if postemployment
restraints were unenforceable, thus creating the risk of loss of firm clients.[162] The preferable view may be, however, that the nature of the relationship may vary in its intensity from one area of specialization to
another, both in medicine and in law. It does appear contrary to public
policy to deprive a patient of access to a chosen psychiatrist or an accused person to a chosen defence counsel on the basis of a postemployment restraint. At the present time, however, there is slender support
in the authorities for the proposition that such considerations may be
taken into account in striking down such provisions.

Although the great bulk of the restraint of trade cases deal with
restraints operative in the context of contracts to sell businesses and
employment contracts, the doctrine has also been applied in a broad
range of other commercial settings. Thus, for example, the doctrine has
been applied to "requirements" or "solus" agreements entered into by oil
companies with retailers, typically garages or service stations, supplying oil and gasoline products for use in automobiles. Such agreements
will typically require the garage operator to purchase all requirements
for oil and gasoline from the particular supplier and, further, not to sell
the products of other suppliers. In *Esso Petroleum Co. Ltd. v. Harper's
Garage (Stourport) Ltd.*,[163] the House of Lords applied restraint of trade
doctrine to such an arrangement. The first of two solus agreements entered into by the defendant restrained the sale of competitive products
for a period of four and a half years. This restraint survived scrutiny, but

---

159 See also *Baker v. Lintott* (1981), 54 C.P.R. (2d) 200 (Alta. Q.B.). Compare with
     Routh v. Jones, above note 145.
160 Above note 158 at 454 (H.C.J.) ("choosing a physician or surgeon is not akin to
     commercial transactions").
161 *Oswald Hickson Collier & Co. v. Carter-Ruck*, [1984] 2 All E.R. 15 (C.A.).
162 *Deacons (A Firm) v. Bridge*, [1984] A.C. 705 (P.C.).
163 Above note 116.

a second, which was contained in a mortgage, and was to last for twenty-one years, was held unenforceable. In *Stephens v. Gulf Oil*,[164] the Ontario Court of Appeal held that the doctrine did not apply to an individual who acquires a service station subject to an existing constraint. On this view, the doctrine is applicable only to an operator who is already in possession of a service station before entering a solus agreement. Further, the doctrine has been applied to contracts between songwriters and music publishers. In *A. Schroeder Music Publishing Co. v. Macaulay*,[165] the House of Lords applied the doctrine to an agreement under which a young songwriter committed all of his work product to the plaintiff publisher for a period of ten years in return for a small consideration and virtually no commitment on the part of the publisher to publish the materials. The commitment to refrain from supplying compositions to other publishers was held to be an unreasonable restraint of trade. A further illustration is found in the "retain-or-transfer" rules of professional sports leagues, under which teams can effectively preclude their players from contracting to provide future services to another team. In *Eastham v. Newcastle United Football Club Ltd.*,[166] such an arrangement was held to constitute a postemployment restraint that was unreasonable and unenforceable. In *Tank Lining Corp. v. Dunlop Industrial Ltd.*,[167] the doctrine was applied to a provision in a licensing agreement under which a Canadian company employed, under licence, the technology developed by an American company for "lining" railway cars. The provision stipulated that in the event of termination of the agreement by either party, neither party would engage in the railcar-lining business in Canada for two years following the termination. Notwithstanding the unusual commercial setting of the arrangement, the Ontario Court of Appeal held that the arrangement was subject to the doctrine of restraint of trade. In the court's view, however, in the circumstances of the particular case, the restraint was not an unreasonable one and could be enforced.

In sum then, the doctrine of restraint of trade is flexible in its application and may apply in a variety of transactional settings. The illus-

---

164 (1975), 65 D.L.R. (3d) 193 (Ont. C.A.), leave to appeal to S.C.C. refused (1976), 65 D.L.R. (3d) 193n (S.C.C.). See also *Cleveland Petroleum Co. v. Dartstone Ltd.*, [1969] 1 All E.R. 201 (C.A.).

165 Above note 134. See also *Clifford Davis Management Ltd. v. WEA Records Ltd.*, [1975] 1 All E.R. 237 (C.A.).

166 [1964] Ch. 413. See also *Blackler v. New Zealand Rugby Football League*, [1968] N.Z.L.R. 547; *Buckley v. Tutty* (1971), 125 C.L.R. 353 (Aust. H.C.). Compare with *Detroit Football Co. v. Dublinski*, [1956] O.R. 744 (H.C.J.), rev'd on other grounds [1957] O.R. 58 (C.A.).

167 Above note 124.

trations set out above, however, do not exhaust the kinds of situations in which the doctrine has been applied and, indeed, may be applied in the future. The potential scope of the doctrine is as broad as the imaginations of those who would devise new forms of anticompetitive contractual arrangements.

C. STATUTORY ILLEGALITY

Agreements that are in conflict with a statutory scheme of some kind may be considered to be illegal and unenforceable at common law. Where a statute specifically provides that a particular type of agreement is unenforceable,[168] of course, the agreement in question is plainly unenforceable. In such a case, a court has no discretion to exercise on the question of enforceability. The issue is authoritatively resolved by the statute. Such provisions do not appear to be common, however, and in the more typical case, the issue of statutory illegality arises in the context of a statute that does not plainly determine the question of enforceability but, rather, creates a prohibition or a set of regulatory requirements that appear to render either the formation or the performance of a particular agreement inconsistent, in some fashion, with the statutory scheme. Where the statute is silent on the point, then, courts are evidently required to exercise judgment as to whether the contract in question should be determined to be illegal and unenforceable. The analytical method applied by the courts in resolving such questions has evolved over time. Under the earlier or traditional doctrine, courts were inclined to assume that a contract that was in conflict with a statutory scheme in some fashion was necessarily illegal and void. A more modern approach has emerged in recent decades in which the courts take a more flexible approach and consider whether enforcement of the contract would be consistent with, or on the other hand, subvert the policies underlying the statutory enactment. If enforcement of the agreement would undermine the policy objectives of the statutory scheme, courts refuse to enforce the agreement in question. On the other hand, where enforcement would not subvert those objectives, courts exercise a discretion to enforce the agreement. Enforcement is often justified on the basis that the courts ought to exercise restraint in interfering with the rights conferred by the ordinary law of contracts, on the basis that non-enforcement imposes a penalty on the contract-

---

168 See, for example, *Consumer Protection Act*, S.O. 2002, c. 30, Sch. A, s. 23.

ing party that is out of proportion with the gravity of the statutory conflict, or on the basis that enforcement is necessary in order to prevent the unjust enrichment of one party at the expense of the other.[169]

The rigidity of the traditional approach may simply reflect a judicial desire for certainty of contractual doctrine typical of an earlier era. Alternatively, it may be that the traditional approach crystallized in an era preceding the modern growth of the regulatory apparatus of the state that now touches on many aspects of both commercial and private life. However the emergence of the modern approach may be explained, it appears to be increasingly accepted that the traditional approach is capable of producing unjust results and needs to be supplanted by a more modern and flexible approach. As one judge observed, "[M]odern judicial thinking has developed in a way that has considerably refined the knee-jerk reflexive reaction to a plea of illegality."[170] The modern view, as characterized by another judge, has two characteristics. First, the modern approach "rejects the understanding that simply because a contract is prohibited by statute it is illegal and, therefore, void *ad initio*."[171] The second distinguishing feature "is that enforceability of a contract is dependent upon an assessment of the legislative purpose or objectives underlying the statutory provision."[172]

A central feature of the traditional approach to the analysis of statutory illegality is an overly broad conception of an interpretive principle concerning the implicit statutory prohibition of agreements. Courts were inclined to assume that if the making or performance of a contract involved a failure to comply with a statutory prohibition or regulation, the contract itself was implicitly prohibited by the statute. This aspect may be illustrated by the decision of the Supreme Court of Canada in a nineteenth-century authority, *Bank of Toronto v. Perkins*.[173] The Court in that case was required to consider the effect of a provision of the *Banking Act*[174] that prohibited banks from lending money

---

169 An alternative method of achieving this latter objective, however, would be to enforce the contract but to allow a restitutionary claim for the value of benefits conferred. Under the traditional approach, however, the difficulty with this solution was that if the plaintiff was the party in breach of the statutory prohibition or scheme, restitution would normally be denied. This approach also appears to have yielded into a more modern approach. See below this Chapter, section D(2).

170 *Royal Bank of Canada v. Grobman et al.* (1977), 18 O.R. (2d) 636 at 651–52 (H.C.), Krever J.

171 *Still v. Minister of National Revenue*, [1998] 1 F.C. 549 at 573 (C.A.), Robertson J.A.

172 *Ibid.*

173 (1882), 8 S.C.R. 603.

174 1987 (U.K.), 34th Vic., c. 5, s. 40.

on the security of an interest in land. The plaintiff bank sought to enforce such an arrangement. The claim was dismissed by the Supreme Court, however, on the basis that the transaction must be taken to be implicitly avoided by the statutory provisions. Strong J. reasoned as follows: "Whenever the doing of any act is expressly forbidden by statute, whether on grounds of public policy or otherwise the English courts hold the act, if done, to be void, though no express words of avoidance are contained in and of itself."[175]

On this approach, then, it was unnecessary for the court to reflect on the policy reasons underlying the statutory prohibition and determine whether avoidance of the transaction is an appropriate means of carrying out those policies. The bank had argued that the prohibition was not based on considerations of public policy but, rather, related to the internal management of the bank, relying on American authority suggesting that the transaction should be considered enforceable. Strong J., however, rejected the attempt to rely on American authority that in his view "admits considerations of the policy of an enactment as influencing its interpretation to an extent to which the decisions of the English courts are distinctly opposed."[176] The principal English authority relied upon by Strong J. for this proposition, *Cope v. Rowlands*,[177] is another well-known nineteenth-century illustration of the traditional approach. This case involved a claim by an unlicensed stockbroker to enforce a contract for the supply of services in buying and selling stock. The statute requiring the licence created an offence of unlicensed dealing but was silent as to the effect of the statute on service contracts entered into by unlicensed brokers. The claim was dismissed, however, on the basis that it is "clear that a contract is void if prohibited by a statute, though the statute inflicts a penalty only, because such a penalty implies a prohibition."[178] Under the traditional view, then, the fact that one of the parties is engaged in the commission of a prohibited act leads more or less directly to the conclusion that the contract itself is, by implication, rendered unenforceable by the statute.

The traditional approach has been applied in numerous Canadian authorities.[179] Nonetheless, it also is recognized that the doctrine, if zealously applied, can lead to unjust results. The leading illustration of

175 Above note 173 at 613.
176 *Ibid.*
177 (1836), 2 M. & W. 149, 150 E.R. 707.
178 *Ibid.* at 710 (E.R.).
179 See, for example, *Brown v. Moore* (1902), 32 S.C.R. 93; *Advance Rumely Thresher Co. v. Yorga*, [1926] S.C.R. 397; *Wirth v. Kutarma*, [1955] 5 D.L.R. 785 (Sask. C.A.); *Kocotis v. D'Angelo*, [1958] O.R. 104 (C.A.).

the phenomenon is *Kingshott v. Brunskill*,[180] a decision of the Ontario Court of Appeal involving the sale of ungraded apples from one farmer to another. The sale of ungraded apples was prohibited by provincial regulation, an obvious instrument of consumer protection that was designed to prevent the sale of ungraded apples to the public. In this case, however, it was established that the parties expected that the purchasing farmer would grade the apples before resale to the public and this is, indeed, what occurred. Nonetheless, the Court of Appeal held that the selling farmer's claim for the purchase price was precluded by the fact that the contract involved the commission of an illegal act. The result of the case appears to effect a substantial unjust enrichment of the purchasing farmer. Given the fact that the transaction did not offend the underlying purpose of the regulation, there would appear to be no harm and some justice in permitting the selling farmer to enforce the agreement.

The rigid application of the traditional approach to agreements entered into in non-compliance with the *Lord's Day Act*,[181] which prohibited the making of contracts on a Sunday, offers another illustration. Although the legislation was ultimately found to be unconstitutional,[182] it was accepted, during the period when the statute was in force, that agreements entered into on a Sunday were illegal and unenforceable.[183] Again, however, rigid application of this view was capable of producing harsh results. In *Rogers v. Leonard*,[184] an American purchaser entered into a contract with a Canadian vendor to buy a cottage on a Sunday. Although the American purchaser was unaware of the *Lord's Day Act* prohibition, the Canadian purchaser admitted her awareness of the prohibition and later sought to defend against the purchaser's action for specific performance on the basis of illegality doctrine. The purchaser, who had acted in "good faith and with a genuine intent to comply with all laws"[185] had, with the vendor's consent, taken possession of the cottage. Notwithstanding the fact that the trial judge was of the view that the defendant seller had acted in "gross bad faith,"[186] Haines J. allowed what he evidently considered to be a technical and unmeritorious de-

---

180 Above note 22.
181 R.S.C. 1970, c. L-13, s. 4. Violation of the prohibition against contracting on Sunday exposed the offender to a fine of "not less than $1 and not exceeding $40." See *ibid.*, s. 12.
182 *R. v. Big M Drug Mart Ltd.*, [1985] 1 S.C.R. 295.
183 *Neider v. Carda of Peace River District Ltd.*, [1972] S.C.R. 678 at 685, Hall J.
184 (1973), 39 D.L.R. (3d) 349 (Ont. H.C.J.).
185 *Ibid.* at 362.
186 *Ibid.*

fence to the claim. The purchaser's alternative claim for expenses incurred in reliance on the agreement was also dismissed.

A countertrend favouring a greater reluctance to hold agreements void on grounds of public policy, however, has been evident in judicial decisions for quite some time. Thus, in *Vita Food Products Inc. v. Unus Shipping Co.*,[187] Lord Wright observed: "Nor must it be forgotten that the rule by which contracts not expressly forbidden by statute are declared to be void are in proper cases nullified for disobedience to a statute is a rule of public policy only, and public policy understood in the wider sense may at times be better served by refusing to nullify a bargain save on serious and sufficient grounds."[188] A similar observation was made by Devlin J. in the leading decision of *St. John Shipping Corp. v. Joseph Rank Ltd.*[189] in the following terms: "Caution in this respect is, I think, especially necessary in these times when so much of commercial life is governed by regulations of one sort or another, which may easily be broken without wicked intent."[190]

The decision of Devlin J. in *St. John Shipping* is an exemplar of the modern approach to statutory illegality. The claim was brought by a shipowner to recover a claim for freight charges. The defendant, whose goods had been transported across the Atlantic, defended the claim on the basis that the boat had been overloaded, in breach of the applicable merchant shipping legislation, to such an extent that the load line was still submerged when it arrived at the port of Birkenhead. Although the master of the ship had been prosecuted for this offence and fined the maximum fine in the circumstances of twelve hundred pounds, the amount of freight earned by commission of the offence was almost double that amount. The defendants, by resisting payment of the freight, sought to take the profit out of the defendant's misconduct. Although the case was, in this sense, a sympathetic one, Devlin J. approached the matter as one requiring a careful analysis of the purpose and structure of the statutory scheme with a view to determining whether the unenforceability of the individual carriage contracts was a suitable civil sanction for the courts to add to the penal sanctions set out in the statutory scheme. Devlin J. noted that as a sanction, unenforceability of the agreement had a potentially draconian effect: "A shipowner who accidentally overloads by a fraction of an inch will not be able to recover from any of the shippers or consignees a penny of the

---

187 [1939] A.C. 277.
188 *Ibid.* at 293.
189 Above note 20.
190 *Ibid.* at 288.

freight."[191] Moreover, holding such agreements unenforceable would result in "inconveniences and injury to maritime business."[192] Accordingly, and noting "how important it is that the courts should be slow to imply the statutory prohibition of contracts,"[193] Devlin J. held that the contract of carriage was enforceable, notwithstanding the unlawful manner of its performance. Although, to be sure, the sanctions imposed by the statute appeared to be inadequate from a financial point of view, the solution to this problem lay with Parliament and not with the judicial imposition of a civil sanction that appeared ill suited to the task of punishing the offence.

The reasoning in *St. John Shipping* may thus be characterized as requiring, against the background of the general policy of the common law to enforce agreements, an analysis of the objectives and structure of the statutory scheme in question in order to determine whether unenforceability of the particular transaction is either a necessary or a desirable common law complement to the statutory scheme. It has been applied many times in English[194] and Canadian[195] cases. In *Sidmay Ltd. v. Wehttam Investments Ltd.*,[196] for example, a borrower sought a declaration that a mortgage given to secure a loan was illegal and unenforceable as the lender was not registered under the Ontario *Loan and Trust Corporations Act*.[197] The lender had therefore committed the statutory offence of carrying on the business of a loan corporation while not registered with the result, it was urged, that the mortgage transaction was unenforceable. The Ontario Court of Appeal applied the analytical model deployed by Devlin J. in *St. John Shipping* and analyzed the intent and objects of the statute and of its historical antecedents. The court concluded that the purpose of the statute was to provide a form of control over corporations engaged in the business of lending funds obtained

---

191 *Ibid.* at 281.
192 *Ibid.* at 289.
193 *Ibid.*
194 See, for example, *Shaw v. Groom*, [1970] 2 Q.B. 504 (C.A.); *Phoenix General Ins. Co. of Greece S.A. v. Halvanon Ins. Co. Ltd.*, [1988] Q.B. 216 (C.A.); *Howard v. Shirlstar Container Transport Ltd.*, [1990] 3 All E.R. 366 (C.A.).
195 See, for example, *Maschinenfabrik Seydelmann K-G. v. Presswood Bros. Ltd.* (1965), 53 D.L.R. (2d) 224 (Ont. C.A.), rev'g on other grounds (1964), 47 D.L.R. (2d) 214 (Ont. H.C.J.); *Albert E. Daniels Ltd. v. Sangster* (1976), 12 O.R. (2d) 512 (Co. Ct.); *Lasenby v. Lamp Holdings & Developments Ltd.* (1980), 117 D.L.R. (3d) 181 (Ont. Div. Ct.); *C. Battison & Sons Inc. v. Mauti* (1986), 34 D.L.R. (4th) 700 (Ont. Div. Ct.); *Alberta Turkey Producers v. Leth Farms Inc.*, [1999] 7 W.W.R. 12 (Alta. Q.B.).
196 (1967), 61 D.L.R. (2d) 358 (Ont. C.A.), aff'd [1968] S.C.R. 828.
197 R.S.O. 1960, c. 222, s. 133(3). See now R.S.O. 1990, c. L.25, s. 214(1).

from a variety of sources including depositors, debenture holders and other creditors of the corporation. The lender in this case was a private corporation and therefore did not require such regulatory supervision. In the court's view, although the defendant lender was subject to the prohibition on a literal reading of its terms, the statute should not be construed to apply to a corporation such as the defendant. The court went on to hold that even if an offence had been committed, the mortgage transaction nonetheless remained enforceable. As Kelly J.A. observed, "[T]he underlying purpose of the Act to afford greater security to the depositors, creditors and security holders of the corporation would be defeated if its assets became depleted by the inability to recover from the borrower the money lent on the security of real estate."[198]

In *Love's Realty & Financial Services Ltd. v. Coronet Trust*,[199] the Alberta Court of Appeal applied an avowedly modern approach to the analysis of a claim brought for a real estate commission by an unlicensed real estate agent. Although the plaintiff had contravened the statute in entering into the listing agreement, the court held that the statute did not render the transaction itself unenforceable. As Kerans J.A. observed, "[O]ne can refuse to apply the traditional rule [rendering the transaction unenforceable] in a case when to apply it would have a harsh effect *and* is not required to affirm the legislative policy."[200] The plaintiff's claim was no doubt assisted by the fact that by the time the service of finding a purchaser for the property was rendered, a licence had been obtained.[201] Similarly, in *Johnson v. Lazzarino*,[202] an Ontario court enforced a claim by a chartered accountant to enforce an agreement that provided for a contingency fee, notwithstanding the fact that contingency fees were prohibited by the rules of the governing regulatory body. Sharpe J. noted that although the plaintiff might be subject to disciplinary sanctions, nothing about the agreement rendered it inherently wrong or contrary to public policy, as evidenced by the fact

---

198 Above note 196 at 375.

199 (1989), 57 D.L.R. (4th) 606 (Alta. C.A.). See also *Canada (Attorney General) v. Becker*, [1999] 4 W.W.R. 347 (Alta. C.A.).

200 *Love's Realty & Financial Services Ltd. v. Coronet Trust, ibid.* at 616 (emphasis in original).

201 See also *Beer v. Townsgate I Ltd.* (1997), 152 D.L.R. (4th) 671 (Ont. C.A.) (sale of condominium by vendor not registered under home warranties legislation — registration achieved by the time of closing — agreement not rendered unenforceable by reason of its non-compliance with the statute); *Morrell v. Cserzy* (2002), 14 C.L.R. (3d) 94 (Ont. S.C.J.) (absence of renovation licence not a bar to contractor's claim on contract to perform renovations).

202 Above note 95.

that the governing rules had ultimately been changed to permit such arrangements.

In *Still v. Minister of National Revenue*,[203] the Federal Court of Appeal provided a sustained analysis of the differences between the traditional or "classical" model of illegality doctrine and the modern approach. The classical model—exemplified, in part, by the reasoning in *Kingshott v. Brunskill*[204]—was rejected by the court for two reasons. First, Robertson J.A. observed that "the classical model has long since lost its persuasive force and is no longer being applied consistently."[205] Second, in his view, the classical model "fails to account for the reality that today a finding of illegality is dependent, not only on the purpose underlying the statutory prohibition, but also on the remedy being sought and the consequences which flow from the finding that the contract is unenforceable."[206] On its facts, *Still* was a case in which an immigrant who had achieved permanent resident status improperly took employment without obtaining the required work permit. When ultimately laid off by the employer, the plaintiff sought unemployment benefits. The benefits were initially denied, however, on the basis that the contract of employment was an illegal one. In determining, then, whether the plaintiff was entitled to unemployment insurance benefits, Robertson J.A. indicated that the modern view is to exercise a discretion to grant or withhold relief on the basis of the following proposition that was, he indicated, a "principle" rather than a "rule": "where a contract is expressly or impliedly prohibited by statute, a court may refuse to grant relief to a party when, in all of the circumstances of the case, including regard to the objects and purposes of the statutory prohibition, it would be contrary to public policy, reflected in the relief claimed, to do so."[207] Noting that the plaintiff had acted in good faith and on the basis of a misunderstanding of the applicable rules, Robertson J.A. was of the view that the denial of employment benefits would be a sanction that was quite disproportionate to the gravity of the statutory breach. Accordingly, the contract was not void for the purpose of determining whether it constituted insurable employment. The court ordered that the application for unemployment benefits should enjoy success.

---

203 [1998] 1 F.C. 549.
204 Above note 22.
205 Above note 203 at 575.
206 *Ibid.*
207 *Ibid.* at 578.

As has been noted above,[208] an agreement entered into with the deliberate intention of committing an unlawful act is considered unenforceable as a matter of common law. As the unlawful act in question could constitute the breach of a statutory prohibition, the dividing line between common law illegality of this kind and statutory illegality is not easily drawn. As Devlin J. observed in *St. John Shipping*, however, in the absence of a deliberate intent to commit an unlawful act, the proper analysis of the question of enforceability of a contract is that of statutory illegality and therefore rests on a determination as to whether the statute in question is properly construed either to expressly or impliedly prohibit the agreement. In determining this question, however, no distinction is drawn between contracts that involve the commission of a prohibited act at the time of formation as opposed to contracts that do not require but may involve an illegal mode of performance. The latter was the case in *St. John Shipping*. In all cases of statutory illegality, as Devlin J. observed, the question is whether or not the contract "as made or as performed [is] a contract that is prohibited by the statute."[209] Thus, in cases like *Sidmay, Love's Realty* and *Johnson*, the illegality affected the making or formation of the agreement rather than its performance. Nonetheless, the question in each case was whether the particular contract should be considered to be prohibited by the statute in light of the objectives of the statute and the general policy of the common law favouring the enforcement of agreements.

D. THE CONSEQUENCES OF ILLEGALITY

1) Introduction

The determination that an agreement is either void at common law on grounds of public policy or void by reason of statutory illegality carries with it the conclusion that an action for damages for breach of the agreement cannot succeed. The parties to such agreements, however, may have conferred value on each other or may have suffered losses in reliance on the assumed enforceability of the agreement. In some instances at least, complete denial of relief for losses suffered or of the ability to recover the value of benefits transferred may be considered to work an injustice. Accordingly, we consider here whether claims, other

208 See above this Chapter, section B(1).
209 Above note 20 at 284.

than the claim for damages for breach of contract, might be available to vindicate the interests of parties in such circumstances.

The starting point for the analysis of this set of issues must be the famous statement of general principle offered by Lord Mansfield in *Holman v. Johnson*[210] in the following terms:

> The principle of public policy is this: *Ex dolo malo non oritur actio.* No Court will lend its aid to a man who founds his cause of action upon an immoral or illegal act. If, from the plaintiff's own stating or otherwise, the cause of action appears to arise *ex turpi causa*, or the transgression of a positive law in this country, there the court says he has no right to be assisted. It is upon that ground the court goes; not for the sake of the defendant, but because they will not lend their aid to such a plaintiff. So if the plaintiff and defendant were to change sides, and the defendant was to bring his action against the plaintiff, the latter would then have the advantage of it; for where both are *equally* at fault, *potior est conditio defendentis.*[211]

In considering the types of remedies, other than enforcement of the agreement, that might be available to parties to illegal agreements, then, it must be determined whether there are other types of claims that are not properly said to be "founded" upon the illegal or immoral act. If the claim is so founded, and the parties are equally at fault, "*potior est conditio defendentis*," that is to say, in such circumstances, it is better to be in the position of the defendant. For a party who has transferred value to the other party under the illegal agreement, the most obvious type of claim to be considered would be a claim for restitution of the value of the benefit conferred. Alternatively, where the value transferred takes the form of a transfer of ownership of an asset, it may be considered whether the transferor's interest in the asset has, indeed, been successfully transferred to the other party. If not, the transferor may retain ownership of the asset and be entitled to pursue proprietary relief in some form. To the extent that a party has suffered loss in reliance on the illegal contract, the possibility of pursuing claims in tort or with respect to a collateral agreement of some kind would hold out the only possible prospects for success. Each of these types of claims will be considered here.

As a preliminary point, however, it is useful to note that there exists a relationship or, indeed, a tension between the threshold issue of enforceability and these consequential issues. If, in cases of a transfer of

---

210 (1775) 1 Cowp. 341, 98 E.R. 1120.
211 *Ibid.* at 343 (Cowp.).

value or reliance losses, it appears just to award some form of relief and, further, if these other types of claims are not available because of the illegality involved, the court may be tempted to hold that the agreement itself is not illegal in order to avoid an unjust result. This point may be illustrated by reference to the facts of *Kingshott v. Brunskill*,[212] the case involving the sale of ungraded apples by one farmer to another. It will be recalled that the Ontario Court of Appeal held that the contract was unenforceable because it contravened regulations designed to prevent the sale of ungraded apples to the public. The fact that the purchasing farmer who then graded the apples and sold them to the public has achieved a windfall benefit by virtue of a technical breach of the regulatory scheme appears to constitute an unjust enrichment at the expense of the farmer who initially owned the apples. If the initial selling farmer is unable to bring a successful restitutionary claim for the value of the apples transferred to the second farmer, it may appear that the only device available to the court to prevent such an unjust enrichment is to hold that the agreement itself is not illegal, thus enabling the first farmer to bring an action for the contractual price. Conversely, if the initial farmer is entitled to recover in a restitutionary claim the value of the apples transferred, the pressure to find that the agreement is an enforceable one is relieved. In such cases, it may be that the better solution to the problem rests on a greater willingness to award restitutionary relief in such circumstances.

A similar point may be made with respect to the question of proprietary relief. To the extent that parties who have transferred assets under an illegal agreement are unable to recover their value in a restitutionary claim, a court may be tempted to find that property in the asset has not passed thereby enabling the transferor to pursue a proprietary claim in order to avoid the unjust enrichment of the transferee. Holding that the property does not pass, however, will typically create a division between ownership and possession of assets with consequent risk of harm to third parties who may purchase the assets in question from a possessor who is unable to pass good title. Again, the better solution to the problem may be an increased recognition of the availability of restitutionary relief coupled with a determination that property in the asset passes to the transferee. As we shall see, there does appear to be some movement, in recent decades, in the direction of greater recognition of the availability of restitutionary relief for benefits conferred under illegal transactions.

---

212 Above note 22.

2) Restitution

The traditional view is that, generally speaking, the *Holman v. Johnson* principle applies to restitutionary claims with the result that restitutionary claims for the value of benefits conferred under illegal contracts are normally denied. To the extent that such relief is allowed, then, it comes by way of recognized exceptions to the general principle. Traditionally, there are four well-recognized categories of cases in which relief is allowed. In each category, the relationship of the plaintiff to the illegality in question is such that it may be said that the plaintiff and defendant are not equally at fault or, not *in pari delicto*, thus avoiding Lord Mansfield's proscription that "where both are equally in fault, *potior est conditio defendentis*."[213] First, a party who is genuinely unaware of the factual circumstances leading to the illegality of the transaction may be permitted to recover value transferred to the other party in a restitutionary claim. One of the few illustrations of the point concerns an agreement that involved trading with the enemy.[214] The plaintiff had paid premiums on an insurance contract relating to goods en route from Russia. The agreement was unenforceable as a state of war existed between England and Russia at the time. The plaintiff was allowed to recover the premiums on the basis that he was not aware, at the time of contracting, of the outbreak of hostilities.

A second exception is applicable in situations where the statutory scheme that renders the transaction unenforceable is designed to protect persons in the position of the plaintiff. Where the plaintiff is a member of a class of persons intended to be protected from the actions of persons in the position of the defendant, it would be consistent with the objectives of the statutory scheme to allow restitutionary recovery of any benefits transferred by the plaintiff to the defendant. In the leading case, *Kiriri Cotton Co. Ltd. v. Dewani*,[215] a tenant had paid "key money" to a landlord in violation of rent control legislation designed, in part, to protect tenants from extra charges of this kind. The Privy Council awarded recovery of the "key money" on the basis that the plaintiff was a member of a protected class. Denial of relief in such circumstances would defeat the very purpose of the legislation. Similar results have been achieved in Canadian cases.[216] A third exception ap-

---

213   Above note 210 at 343 (Cowp.).
214   *Oom v. Bruce* (1810), 12 East 225, 104 E.R. 87.
215   [1960] A.C. 192 (P.C.).
216   *Burgess v. Zimmerli* (1914), 17 D.L.R. 708 (B.C.C.A.); *Haug & Nellermoe v. Murdoch* (1916), 26 D.L.R. 200 (Sask. S.C. en banc); *North Saskatchewan Seeds Ltd. v. Couch* (1960), 32 W.W.R. 253 (Sask. Dist. Ct.); *D'Amore v. McDonald* (1973), 32

plies in circumstances where the defendant has engaged in wrongful conduct such as fraud, oppression or undue influence.[217] In such cases, it appears not to be required that the technical prerequisites of a finding of fraud have been met. It is sufficient if the defendant's conduct is wrongful and the plaintiff is not equally at fault.[218] Nor is it necessary in such a case to show that the plaintiff is entirely free of blame, provided that the plaintiff is less complicit than the defendant in the wrongful activity.[219]

The fourth exception extends restitutionary relief to a party who, though initially *in pari delicto* with the other party, has made a timely decision to resile from the transaction. Such a party is said to have a *locus poenitentiae* or a place or position from which repentance is possible, thus clearing the way for a successful restitutionary claim. The precise boundaries of the doctrine of *locus poenitentiae* are obscured by two points of difficulty. First, although, as a matter of general principle, it is established that repentance must occur before the objects of the agreement have been substantially achieved, application of this principle to particular fact situations is a matter of some subtlety. Second, there exists some uncertainty on the question of whether the repentance must be genuine in the sense that a moral choice to resile from the contract must be made at a time when the achievement of its objectives remain possible. If genuine repentance in this sense is a requisite element of the doctrine, a claimant who resiled from the transaction because the illicit scheme was either frustrated or no longer necessary from the claimant's perspective, would not succeed in a restitutionary claim.

Where the performance of the illegal contract is complete and the illicit objective has been accomplished, the doctrine of *locus poeniten-*

D.L.R. (3d) 543 (Ont. H.C.J.), aff'd 40 D.L.R. (3d) 354 (Ont. C.A.); *Kasprzycki v. Abel* (1986), 55 O.R. (2d) 536 (Dist. Ct.); *Outson v. Zurowski* (1985), 63 B.C.L.R. 89 (C.A.).

217 See, for example, *Smith v. Cuff* (1817), 6 M. & S. 160, 105 E.R. 1203; *Williams v. Bayley* (1866), L.R. 1 H.L. 200; *Fairweather v. McCullough* (1918), 43 D.L.R. 525 (Ont. S.C.A.D.); *Erwin v. Snelgrove*, [1927] 4 D.L.R. 1028 (Ont. S.C.A.D.); *Stoltze v. Fuller*, [1939] S.C.R. 235; *Mule v. Royal Bank of Canada* (1997), 147 D.L.R. (4th) 268 (N.S.C.A.).

218 See, for example, *Mohamed v. Alaga & Co.*, [1999] 3 All E.R. 699 (C.A.) (plaintiff Somali speaker agrees to provide translation services as part of an arrangement under which the plaintiff refers Somali-speaking clients to the firm in return for a share of the firm's fees—fee-splitting arrangements of this kind rendered unlawful by professional regulation—plaintiff entitled to recover in restitution for translation services).

219 *Goodfriend v. Goodfriend*, [1972] S.C.R. 640; *Gateway Hotel (1985) Ltd. v. Schur* (1990), 66 Man. R. (2d) 305 (Q.B.); *Koe v. Earl* (1993), 82 Man. R. (2d) 297 (Q.B.).

472 THE LAW OF CONTRACTS

tiae is clearly inapplicable. Short of this, it is less clear when the objective of the agreement will be considered to have been "substantially performed,"[220] with the result that restitutionary relief is no longer available. An examination of leading English cases suggests that restitution will remain available as long as such relief is not inconsistent with the policy underlying the particular rule that has rendered the transaction unenforceable. Thus, in *Taylor v. Bowers*,[221] for example, the plaintiff had transferred his stock and trade to a friendly party in order to defeat his creditors. Subsequently, the transferee further transferred the assets to one of the plaintiff's creditors. Prior to the eventual sale by auction of the plaintiff's assets, the plaintiff sought to repudiate the initial transaction and recover the assets. Such recovery was permitted and is evidently consistent with the creditor protection rationale underlying the rule rendering the initial transfer illegal. Conversely, in *Kearley v. Thomson*[222] the plaintiff was a friend of a bankrupt who made a payment to solicitors for one of the creditors in return for their undertaking not to attend the public examination of the bankrupt and not to oppose his discharge. Prior to the discharge of the bankrupt, the friend sought recovery of the bribe. Although it may be that the correct outcome in this case is not self-evident, it is not surprising that the court dismissed the claim to recover what was, in effect, a bribe. In *Hermann v. Charlesworth*,[223] a case of marriage brokerage, the defendant broker had agreed, for an initial fee, to provide introductions to suitable young men with a further fee to be paid in the event of a successful match. After a few introductions were made, the plaintiff client sought recovery of the initial payment. Because the rule rendering such agreements unenforceable is designed to protect people in the position of the plaintiff, it is unsurprising that recovery was allowed. In each of these cases, one might take the view that substantial performance had occurred or, conversely, that the ultimate objective of the agreement had not been achieved. The seeming inconsistency in the results, however, can be explained on the basis that restitutionary relief did not undermine the rule rendering the transaction unenforceable in either *Taylor* or *Hermann*, but that it might be considered to do so in *Kearley*. The traditional justification for the differing results, however, would be that the performance was substantial in *Kearley* but not sufficiently so as to deny relief in *Taylor* and *Hermann*.

---

220 *Letkeman v. Zimmermann*, above note 17 at 1105, Martland J.
221 (1876), 1 Q.B.D. 291 (C.A.).
222 (1890), 24 Q.B.D. 742 (C.A.).
223 [1905] 2 K.B. 123 (C.A.).

The second limitation on the doctrine of *locus poenitentiae*—the requirement of genuine repentance—is controversial and has been reconsidered and possibly rejected in recent years. A leading illustration of the requirement is to be found in the controversial decision in *Bigos v. Bousted*.[224] This case involved an illegal agreement designed to evade English currency controls. The Italian defendant had agreed to supply Italian currency to the English plaintiff's wife and child during a visit to Italy in return for which the plaintiff would supply English currency to the defendant on a visit to England. The plaintiff had posted security with the defendant to secure repayment. When the defendant failed to live up to his side of the bargain, the plaintiff sought recovery of the security. The claim failed on the basis that the plaintiff's repentance was not genuine. The plaintiff had resiled from the scheme only because the scheme had been frustrated by the defendant's failure to carry out his part of the scheme.

The imposition of a requirement that the plaintiff's repentance be genuine, in this sense, has been criticized on the basis that it artificially restricts the availability of restitutionary relief. Even in cases where the illicit plan has been frustrated or has been rendered unnecessary by changing circumstances, justice may be better served by the awarding of restitution.[225] Both English and Canadian courts appear to have taken the view that repentance in this moral sense does not constitute a prerequisite to restitutionary relief. In *McDonald v. Fellows*,[226] the Alberta Court of Appeal held that genuine repentance is not a condition of restitutionary relief. The plaintiff was allowed to recover a deposit paid in a real estate transaction entered into on a Sunday in contravention of the *Lord's Day Act*,[227] notwithstanding the plaintiff's apparent lack of remorse. The English Court of Appeal has similarly concluded that "restitution should not be confined to the penitent."[228] In *Tribe v. Tribe*,[229] a father had transferred ownership of the shares of a family company into his son's hands in order to shield the asset from a landlord of premises leased to the father with respect to which the father had anticipated certain claims. When, in due course, the dispute with the landlord was settled, the son resisted the father's claim for a return

---

224 [1951] 1 All E.R. 92 (K.B.).
225 See, for example, R. Merkin, "Restitution by Withdrawal from Executory Illegal Contracts" (1981) 97 Law Q. Rev. 420 at 444. See also J.K. Grodecki, "*In Pari Delicto Potior est Conditio Defendentis*" (1955) 71 Law Q. Rev. 254.
226 (1979), 105 D.L.R. (3d) 434 (Alta. C.A.).
227 Above note 181.
228 *Tribe v. Tribe*, [1995] 4 All E.R. 236 at 260 (C.A.).
229 *Ibid.*

of the shares on the basis of the illicit nature of the arrangement. Recovery for the father was allowed, notwithstanding the fact that the reason for the claim was that the need for deception had passed rather than a timely change of heart on the father's part. It appears likely, then, that the *locus poenitentiae* exception will be potentially available in the future in any case where the illicit objective has not been achieved.

Apart from the possibility of some modest expansion in the availability of the *locus poenitentiae* exception, the traditional exceptions permit restitution only in circumstances where the plaintiff seeking restitution is, in some sense, less at fault or not *in pari delicto*, with the defendant. For the party at fault, however, restitution is traditionally unavailable. Nonetheless, there are cases where such relief is doubtlessly appropriate and application of the traditional doctrine leads to unjust results. Perhaps the most startling illustration of this phenomenon arises under the English moneylenders legislation.[230] Under this legislation, moneylending agreements are required to be recorded in writing and the writing must include certain details of the transaction. Accidental omission of a detail, as in a case where the parties failed to record the date of advancing the borrowed monies because they were uncertain as to when the transaction would, in fact, close,[231] renders the transaction unenforceable. None of the traditional exceptions are available to the moneylender, who has failed to comply with the statute and is, therefore, the party at fault. The remarkable consequence is that the borrower is entitled to retain the monies advanced with no enforceable obligation to repay them or to pay interest.[232] As we have seen, Canadian courts avoided an unsatisfactory result of this kind in *Sidmay Ltd. v. Wehttam Investments Ltd.*,[233] by holding that the mortgage loan advanced in that case was not rendered unenforceable by the *Loan and Trust Corporations Act.*[234] Indeed, it may well be that the court's tentative conclusion that if the mortgage loan was unenforceable, restitution of the monies advanced

---

230 *Moneylenders Act, 1927* (U.K.), 1927, c. 21, ss. 1 and 6.

231 See, for example, *Barclay v. Prospect Mortgages Ltd.*, [1974] 1 W.L.R. 837 (Ch.).

232 Exceptionally, where the borrower seeks equitable relief to recover assets pledged to secure repayment of the loan, the granting of such relief may be conditioned on repayment of the loan. See *Lodge v. National Union Investment Co. Ltd.*, [1907] 1 Ch. 300. The history of *Lodge's* case, however, is one of being narrowly distinguished and it is unlikely, under English law, that even this form of "passive" protection will be available to the lender. See generally P.D. Maddaugh and J.D. McCamus, *The Law of Restitution*, 2d ed. (Aurora: Canada Law Book, 2004) c. 15:500.

233 Above note 196.

234 R.S.O. 1960, c. 222, s. 133(3). See now R.S.O. 1990, c. L.25, s. 214(1).

would not normally be available may have created an environment in which the enforceability of the agreement seemed an attractive solution.[235] As intimated above,[236] the unavailability of restitutionary relief may create some pressure to find a just result by holding the agreement itself to be enforceable. A preferable solution in such cases may be to expand the role of restitutionary relief and this, indeed, is the direction that has been pursued by Canadian courts in recent years.

In particular, Canadian courts have recognized that a restitution claim in favour of the party who has committed the unlawful act may well provide an appropriate result where a denial of restitution would confer an inappropriate windfall on the other party. In *Berne Developments Ltd. v. Haviland*,[237] for example, restitution of moneys advanced by a second mortgagee on the sale of a residential property was allowed even though the mortgage itself was unenforceable because of the second mortgagee's involvement in non-disclosure of the existence of the second mortgage to the first mortgagee in order to secure the latter's consent to the transaction. The trial judge, Saunders J., observed as follows: "In recent years there has been a recognition of the desirability [of] balancing the need to preserve public policy by not enforcing illegal agreements and the need to avoid unjust enrichment."[238] Saunders J. further observed that "the striking of the balance may depend in each case on the extent of the illegality and the unjust enrichment."[239] Although the conduct of the second mortgagee was sufficiently reprehensible to preclude enforcement of the second mortgage and its interest term, it was nonetheless appropriate to require the mortgagor to repay the principal sum of the moneys advanced. A similar result has been achieved in a case involving work performed by an unlicensed tradesman.[240]

Support for this approach can be drawn from a variety of sources. First, the analysis offered in cases like *Berne Developments* is essentially

---

235 A similar phenomenon may have occurred in *St. John Shipping Corp. v. Joseph Rank Ltd.,* above note 20. Devlin J. appeared to accept, in that case, that if the carriage agreement was unenforceable, no relief would be available in restitution for the value of services rendered. See *ibid.* at 283–84.
236 See above this Chapter, section D(1).
237 (1983), 40 O.R. (2d) 238 (H.C.J.).
238 *Ibid.* at 250; Saunders J. placed reliance upon a *dictum* of Masten J.A. in *Steinberg v. Cohen,* [1930] 2 D.L.R. 916 at 928 (Ont. C.A.) where Masten J.A. observed: "It is possible that each case should depend upon its own facts, and upon a balancing by the court of the public interest on the one hand and the private injustice on the other."
239 *Berne Developments Ltd. v. Haviland, ibid.*
240 *Monticchio v. Torcema Construction Ltd.* (1979), 102 D.L.R. (3d) 462 (Ont. H.C.J.).

an application to the question of restitutionary liability of the modern contextual analysis of illegality issues applied in *St. John Shipping* to the threshold question of the enforceability of the agreement. If, as in *St. John Shipping*, the guilty party may, in appropriate circumstances, be able to enforce the agreement itself, it must follow that there may be cases where the guilty party should be afforded the lesser remedy of holding the agreement unenforceable but permitting that party to obtain restitutionary relief. Indeed, the idea that the modern contextual approach to the enforceability issue ought to be applied to the restitutionary issue was explicitly drawn out in the reasoning of Robertson J.A. of the Federal Court of Appeal in *Still v. Minister of National Revenue*.[241] As we have seen,[242] the decision in *Still* offered a critique of the traditional approach to the enforceability question and advocated the adoption of the more modern approach illustrated by Devlin J. in the *St. John Shipping* case. Robertson J.A. also explicitly indicated, however, that this analysis should be applied to the various forms of relief that might be available in the context of an illegal transaction.[243] Under this approach, then, even though the agreement itself may properly be considered to be unenforceable on illegality grounds, it is a separate question whether restitutionary relief might be made available, even to a party that is implicated in the illegal conduct. The adoption of the modern approach to the analysis of the restitutionary rights of the party *in delicto* also draws support from the reports of law reform bodies,[244] scholarly writing[245] and from important recent decisions from the Australian High Court.[246] In general

---

241 Above note 203.

242 See above this Chapter, section C.

243 Above note 203 at 578. Further, Robertson J.A.'s account of the traditional authority included both cases dealing with the enforceability question and cases dealing with the availability of restitutionary relief.

244 See, for example, Law Reform Commission of British Columbia, *Report on Illegal Transactions* (Vancouver: The Commission, 1983); Ontario Law Reform Commission, *Report on Amendment of the Law of Contract* (Toronto: Ministry of the Attorney General, 1987) c. 11. See generally R. A. Buckley, "Illegal Transactions: Chaos or Discretion" (2000) 20 L. S. 155.

245 See, for example, J.D. McCamus, "Restitutionary Recovery of Benefits Conferred under Contracts in Conflict with Statutory Policy—The New Golden Rule" (1987) 25 Osgoode Hall L.J. 787; P.B.H. Birks, "Recovering Value Transferred under an Illegal Contract" (2000) 1 Theor. Inq. L. 155. And see J.W. Wade, "Benefits Obtained under Illegal Transactions—Reasons for and against Allowing Restitution" (1946) 25 Tex. L. Rev. 31; and J.W. Wade, "Restitution of Benefits Acquired Through Illegal Transactions" (1947) 95 U. Pa. L. Rev. 261.

246 *Pavey and Matthews Pty Ltd. v. Paul* (1987), 69 A.L.R. 577 (Aust. H.C.) (builder performing work under oral contract rendered unenforceable by statute—restitutionary relief for value of services rendered allowed). See J. Beatson, "Unjust

terms, then, such relief will be available where permitting restitution will not undermine the objectives of the rule rendering the transaction unenforceable or where denial of restitutionary relief would constitute a disproportionate penalty to impose on the party performing the unlawful act. At a more abstract level, it might be said that restitution will be made available to the party in default where failure to do so will result in the unjust enrichment of the other party.[247]

3) Collateral Claims

Although the principle of *Holman v. Johnson*[248] may preclude enforcement of an agreement or even, unless one of the exceptions to the principle applies, a successful restitutionary claim for the value of benefits conferred on the other party, the principle does not preclude the assertion of collateral or independent claims that are not "founded" on the immoral or illegal act.[249] Three types of collateral claims have been enforced—independent tort claims, claims on collateral agreements and the enforcement of proprietary rights. The leading illustration of enforcement of an independent tort claim is the decision of the English Court of Appeal in *Saunders v. Edwards*.[250] This case concerned an agreement to purchase a leasehold interest in a flat tainted by the fact that the parties had inflated the value of the chattels included in the transaction with a view to reducing the liability for stamp tax. Notwithstanding the illegal nature of the agreement, the purchaser was permitted to pursue a claim in tort for the loss resulting from a fraudulent misrepresentation made by the seller concerning the extent of the premises included within the lease. Agreements that are collateral to the illegal agreement may be enforced in appropriate circumstances. Thus, a contractor who performed renovations on the defendant's premises without the

---

Enrichment in the High Court of Australia" (1988) 104 Law Q. Rev. 13. The second case, *Nelson v. Nelson* (1995), 184 C.L.R. 53 (Aust. H.C.) applies the modern analysis to an equitable proprietary claim. For discussion of this case, see below this Chapter, section D(3).

247 The modern analysis has also been adopted in the U.S. jurisprudence. For a recent statement of the American rule, see American Law Institute, *Restatement of Restitution and Unjust Enrichment*, T.D. No. 3 (Philadelphia: American Law Institute, 2004) s. 32.

248 Above note 210.

249 *Ibid.* at 343 (Cowp.).

250 [1987] 1 W.L.R. 1116 (C.A.). See also *Shelley v. Paddock*, [1980] 1 Q.B. 348 (C.A.). Compare with *Thackwell v. Barclays Bank Plc*, [1986] 1 All E.R. 676 (Q.B.).

requisite ministry approvals was nonetheless entitled to enforce the defendant's collateral undertaking to acquire such approvals.[251]

The possibility of asserting a collateral proprietary claim is likely to arise only in circumstances where the transferor of an asset has retained a limited proprietary interest in the asset in question. As we shall see,[252] the general principle applicable to the passage of property under an agreement tainted by illegality is that the intention to pass proprietary interests under an illegal agreement will normally be effective, notwithstanding the illegality. In the normal case, then, an illegal contract for the purchase and sale of a chattel will result in the transfer of ownership of the chattel to the purchaser. Thus, the seller, who is unable to enforce the illicit agreement, will not be able to assert proprietary rights to the chattel. If the transferor retains a limited interest in the chattel, however, that interest may be asserted, notwithstanding the illegality of the overall agreement. The leading illustration of this proposition is the decision in *Bowmakers Ltd. v. Barnet Instruments Ltd.*[253] In this case, the plaintiff had purchased three sets of machine tools and then let them out on hire-purchase agreements to the defendant. The initial purchase and the hire-purchase agreements were all unenforceable on grounds of illegality. The defendant breached the agreements by improperly selling two sets of tools to third parties, and by refusing payment on the third agreement. The defendant resisted the owner's claim for the value of the tools on the basis that the transaction was tainted by illegality. Although the plaintiff was unable to enforce the hire-purchase agreements, claims to assert proprietary claims as the true owner of the machine tools enjoyed success. In theory, the owner is entitled to assert ownership rights without relying on the illicit agreement whereas the defendant, whose defence rests on the illegality of the transaction, cannot rely on the illegality to defeat the owner's claim. Although this decision results in an unattractive distinction between outright sales, where no claim would arise, and transfers of limited interests, where the true owner retains the capacity to assert proprietary rights, the decision in *Bowmakers Ltd. v. Barnet Instruments Ltd.* has been accepted, it appears, on the basis that it provides at least

---

251 *Strongman (1945) Ltd. v. Sincock*, [1955] 2 Q.B. 525 (C.A.). See also *Archbolds (Freightage) Ltd. v. S. Spanglett Ltd.*, [1961] 1 Q.B. 374 (C.A.); *Munro v. French* (1979), 103 D.L.R. (3d) 91 (Sask. Q.B.).

252 See below this Chapter, section D(4).

253 [1945] 1 K.B. 65 (C.A.).

some relief from the general reluctance of the common law to award restitution in favour of a party who has committed an illegal act.[254]

The *Bowmakers* principle has also been held to apply to equitable proprietary interests. Under the equitable doctrine of resulting trust, where a gratuitous transfer of legal title in an asset is made to a transferee, it is presumed in the absence of evidence to the contrary that it is intended that the asset be held by the transferee beneficially on behalf of the transferor. The transferor thus has an equitable proprietary interest in the asset. Application of this doctrine in the context of an illegal transaction might arise, for example, where a transferor makes a gratuitous transfer in order to shield the asset in question from creditors or the revenue authorities on the understanding that, when danger has passed, the transferee will restore the asset to the transferor. When the transferee subsequently refuses to abide by that understanding, the transferor will attempt to assert an equitable proprietary claim. The transferee would resist such a claim on the basis that the transaction is tainted by its immoral purpose. In *Tinsley v. Milligan*,[255] the House of Lords held that the *Bowmakers* principle applied to circumstances of this kind with the result that the transferor is entitled to assert an equitable proprietary claim. In this case, unmarried co-habitants jointly purchased a house, placing title in the name of one partner in order to facilitate fraudulent social security claims by the other. Upon severance of the relationship, the partner with title refused to share the home with the other partner. The latter partner was held able to assert an equitable proprietary interest, notwithstanding the illegal purpose of the transaction, with the result that the partner with legal title was determined to hold the property beneficially on their joint behalf in equal shares. An earlier Ontario case had come to the same conclusion.[256] The explanation given for such results is that the equitable proprietary claim is independent of the transaction and that it is, therefore, the spouse with legal title that must ground a defence to the claim on the illegality of the transaction.

The decision in *Tinsley* has been criticized on various grounds,[257] not least on the ground that the doctrine appears to apply, no matter

---

254 See generally B. Coote, "Another Look at *Bowmakers v. Barnet Instruments*" (1972) 35 Mod. L. Rev. 38; C.J. Hamson, "Illegal Contracts and Limited Interests" (1949) 10 Cambridge L.J. 249.

255 [1993] 3 All E.R. 65 (H.L.).

256 *Gorog v. Kiss* (1977), 78 D.L.R. (3d) 690 (Ont. C.A.), leave to appeal to S.C.C. refused (1977), 18 N.R. 484 (S.C.C.). See also *Scheuerman v. Scheuerman*, [1916] 52 S.C.R. 625.

257 See, for example, N. Enonchong, "Illegality: The Fading Flame of Public Policy" (1994) 14 Oxford J. Legal Stud. 295; H. Stowe, "The 'Unruly Horse' Has Bolted"

how heinous the misconduct of the transferor may have been. Moreover, the decision leads to artificial distinctions between cases where
the resulting trust *simpliciter* applies as against cases where it is rebutted by the equitable presumption of advancement. The latter principle
holds that if a parent[258] pays for or contributes to the price of property
placed in a child's name or a husband transfers property gratuitously
to his wife, equity assumes, in the absence of contrary evidence, that
an outright transfer or "advancement" of the property to the transferee
is intended. Thus, if a married couple engaged in the conduct exemplified by the *Tinsley* case, with the husband placing property in his wife's
name in order to perpetrate a fraud, the husband's equitable proprietary claim would fail. The presumption of resulting trust would be
countered by the presumption of advancement and the husband would
be left with the need to produce evidence of the unlawful transaction
in order to demonstrate a lack of intent to transfer the equitable interest
and thus justify the proprietary claim. Inconsistent results of this kind
are difficult to justify and courts are likely to strain to avoid them.[259]

A more satisfactory approach was adopted by the Australian High
Court in *Nelson v. Nelson*.[260] In this case, a mother had transferred property to her children to facilitate the commission by her of a fraud on
the veterans' affairs authorities by claiming a subvention for the purchasing of a house. This benefit was available only to widows of army
veterans who did not already own a home. The scheme was carried out
but, upon sale of the first property, the children refused to share the
proceeds with the mother. Under the *Tinsley* reasoning, the mother's

---

(1994) 57 Mod. L. Rev. 441; G. Virgo and J. O'Sullivan, "Resulting Trusts and Illegality" in P.H.B. Birks and F. Rose, eds., *Restitution and Equity*, vol. 1 (London:
Mansfield Press, 2000) c. 6.

258 Under English law, the presumption applies only to fathers and children. It has
been recognized, however, in Canada that the principle also applies to transfers
between mother and child. See, for example, *Rupar v. Rupar* (1964), 46 D.L.R.
(2d) 553 (B.C.S.C.); *Dagle v. Dagle Estate* (1990), 70 D.L.R. (4th) 201 (P.E.I.C.A.),
leave to appeal to S.C.C. refused 74 D.L.R. (4th) viii; *Dreger (Litigation Guardian of) v. Dreger* (1994), 91 Man. R. (2d) 171 (Q.B.), aff'd [1994] 10 W.W.R. 293
(Man. C.A.).

259 See, for example, *Tribe v. Tribe,* above note 228, which involved a transfer of an
asset from father to son in order to shield the asset from a landlord. As we have
seen, when the danger of a claim by the landlord had passed, the son refused
to return the transferred asset. The father was allowed to enforce his equitable
proprietary interest, however, on the basis of a somewhat innovative application
of the *locus poenitentiae* doctrine. See above this Chapter, section D(2).

260 Above note 246. For discussion, see P. Creighton, "The Recovery of Property
Transferred for Illegal Purposes" (1997) 60 Mod. L. Rev. 102.

equitable proprietary claim based on the presumption of resulting trust would be met by the presumption of advancement applicable to a transfer from parent to child and the claim would be defeated. In *Nelson*, however, the Australian High Court adopted the innovative approach of examining the underlying purposes and structure of the legislation with a view to determining whether the granting of recovery would either undermine or be consistent with the statutory scheme. The court examined, *inter alia*, the sanctions imposed for misconduct of this kind by the statutory scheme itself and concluded that denying the mother equitable proprietary relief would impose an additional and inappropriate common law sanction on the mother that was disproportionate to the wrong committed by her. *Nelson v. Nelson*, it may be observed, applies the approach taken in *St. John Shipping* to the enforceability question[261] to an evaluation of the merits of the independent equitable proprietary claim. In so doing, the Australian High Court avoids both the inconsistent results flowing from the *Tinsley* decision and the difficulty that the approach in *Tinsley* appears to apply regardless of how grave the wrongful conduct of the transferor has been. Under the *Nelson* reasoning, equitable proprietary relief could be denied in a case where, in light of the gravity of the wrongdoing, it appeared appropriate to deprive the wrongdoer of equitable proprietary relief. The *Nelson* reasoning is consistent with the analysis offered by the Federal Court of Appeal in *Still v. Minister of National Revenue*[262] and may well represent the future course of Canadian doctrine on this issue.

4) The Passage of Property

Where an illegal agreement purports to pass the property or ownership rights to an asset from a transferor to a transferee, an issue arises as to whether the effect of the illegality is to prevent the passage of property under the agreement. Although this is evidently an important question, it is not one that admits of a clear answer. The traditional position appears to be that a contract that is illegal and void is of no force and effect and, accordingly, that property in assets transferred does not pass pursuant to the terms of the agreement.[263] At the same time, it is some-

---

261 For discussion, see above this Chapter, Section C.
262 Above note 203. The court in *Still* suggested that the modern analytical approach should be applied to any form of relief sought by the party complicit in an illegal transaction. See above this Chapter, section D(2).
263 *Maschinenfabrik Seydelmann K-G v. Presswood Bros. Ltd.*, above note 195. See also *Brown v. Moore* (1902), 32 S.C.R. 93.

times said that the transferor has no right to recover property transferred or moneys paid under an illegal agreement.[264] The unattractive
combined effect of these two propositions may be that the transferee
will be unjustly enriched if, for example, the price has not been paid,
though occasionally it has been suggested that the transferor is entitled
to assert a proprietary claim.[265] A second unfortunate consequence of
a "no passage of property" rule is that it may lead to the separation of
ownership and possession with consequent risk that a *bona fide* third
party purchasing the asset in question from the transferee will suffer
an injury as the transferee in such circumstances would be unable to
pass good title to the purchaser. On the other hand, it has also been
suggested that property may pass through delivery of the goods.[266] Indeed, the English Court of Appeal has held that where a dealer in goods
delivers the goods directly to the customer buying the goods on credit
but transfers title thereto to a finance company under an illegal agreement, transfer of title to the finance company occurs through the mere
"execution" of the agreement, notwithstanding the absence of delivery
of the goods to the finance company.[267]

A more direct assault on the traditional view was taken by the Privy
Council in *Singh v. Ali*.[268] This case involved the sale of a lorry pursuant to the terms of which the parties intended to deceive the transport
authorities by retaining the registration of the vehicle in the name of the
seller. The seller had repossessed the vehicle and the purchaser brought
a successful claim in trespass. The Privy Council held that the transfer
of property under an illegal agreement is effective. Although this appears to be the preferable view, it must be coupled with a recognition
that in certain cases, where the policy underlying the rule rendering
the transaction unenforceable would be undermined by a holding the
property passes, a court should not hold that property passes, notwithstanding the illegality. In *Singh v. Kulubya*,[269] for example, the transfer
of protected "Mailo" lands in breach of a statutory scheme requiring
official approval of such transactions was held ineffective to pass property in the subject lands. Allowing the property to pass would defeat
the very purpose of the statutory scheme. A similar explanation may be

264 *Lapointe v. Messier* (1913), 49 S.C.R. 271; *Boulevard Heights v. Veilleux* (1915), 52 S.C.R. 185; *Steinberg v. Cohen*, [1930] 2 D.L.R. 916 (Ont. S.C.A.D.).
265 See, for example, *Maschinenfabrik Seydelmann K-G v. Presswood Bros. Ltd.*, above note 195 at 221 (Ont. H.C.J.).
266 See, for example, *Pimvicska v. Pimvicska* (1974), 50 D.L.R. (3d) 569 (Alta. S.C.).
267 *Belvoir Finance Co. Ltd. v. Stapleton*, [1971] 1 Q.B. 210 (C.A.).
268 [1960] A.C. 167 (P.C.).
269 [1964] A.C. 142 (P.C.).

offered for a Canadian case refusing to hold that property passes under an agreement that was not in compliance with the statutory protection of "dower" rights.[270] In sum, then, the preferable view, which appears to draw substantial support from modern authorities, is that property in assets transferred under illegal agreements will normally pass unless such a holding is inconsistent with or would serve to undermine the objectives of the rule rendering the transaction illegal and unenforceable.

E. SEVERANCE

In cases where a provision of an agreement has been found to be illegal, the doctrine of severance may enable a court to excise the offending provision from the agreement and permit each party to enforce the remainder of its terms that are untouched by the illegality. As with other aspects of illegality doctrine, a determination as to whether or not a particular contractual provision is severable in this sense may rest on a subtle analysis of the policy factors underlying the rule offended by the provision and the particular contractual setting. In essence, the test for determining whether a particular provision is severable is twofold. First, it must be considered whether, as a practical matter, the remainder of the agreement, after excision of the offending term, constitutes an agreement that can sensibly be enforced. Second, it must be determined whether the nature of the illegality is such that enforcement of the remainder of the agreement would be inconsistent with the policy considerations underlying the rule that renders the provision illegal and unenforceable. Under traditional doctrine, there is, however, a further requirement. It must be possible to effect the excision of a term only by deletion of words from the agreement. This, the so-called blue-pencil test, had the consequence that although courts could delete a provision or parts of a provision from the agreement, they could not revise or add to the terms of an agreement and, so it was said, "make the agreement for the parties." Under this approach, then, courts could delete provisions only in the metaphorical sense of drawing a line through them. As we shall see, however, the Supreme Court of Canada[271] has, in recent years, departed from this traditional view and has adopted a concept

---

270 *Shopsky and Shopsky v. Danyliuk* (1959), 23 D.L.R. (2d) 501 (Alta. S.C.).
271 *Transport North American Express Inc. v. New Solutions Financial Corp.* (2004), 235 D.L.R. (4th) 385 (S.C.C.), rev'g (2002), 214 D.L.R. (4th) 44 (Ont. C.A.), rev'g (2001), 200 D.L.R. (4th) 560 (Ont. S.C.J.). And see *Thomas Brown & Sons Ltd. v. Fazal Deen* (1962), 108 C.L.R. 391 (Aust. H.C.).

of "notional severance" under which a provision might, in effect, be rewritten so as to avoid conflict with the rule that rendered the original version of the provision unenforceable.

In determining whether, as a practical matter, the offending provision can be severed from the remainder of the agreement, it must be considered whether the offending provisions "are in substance so connected with the others as to form an indivisible whole which cannot be taken to pieces without altering its nature."[272] Thus, for example, in a case involving a service station lease containing an unenforceable provision requiring the lessee to purchase gasoline exclusively from the lessor oil company, the Privy Council held that this requirement was an indispensable part of the arrangement and that the "tie" could not be severed from the lease so as to enable the lessee to remain in possession of the premises and conduct the business by purchasing its gasoline supplies from other sources.[273] Further, where the offending provisions essentially amount to the whole consideration provided by one party, it would not be sensible to sever the offending provisions and enforce what thus becomes an essentially one-sided arrangement.[274] Assuming that the offending provisions can be deleted from the agreement without impermissibly affecting the nature of the agreement, the second branch of the test requires a determination as to whether the nature of the illegality is such that the entire agreement is tainted. In a colourful illustration of the point offered by an Australian judge, one would not expect a court to sever and enforce the remaining provisions contained in an agreement that provided for the carrying out of an assassination.[275] Less dramatically, a line of cases holds, for example, that agreements entered into for the purpose of defrauding the revenue authorities will not be subject to severance.[276]

---

272 *McFarlane v. Daniell* (1938), 38 S.R. (N.S.W.) 337 at 345, a statement approved by the Privy Council in *Carney v. Herbert*, [1985] 1 All E.R. 438. See also *Transport North American Express Inc.*, above note 271 at para. 55 (S.C.C.), Bastarache J.
273 *Amoco Australia Pty. v. Rocca Bros. Motor Engineering Co.*, [1975] A.C. 561 (P.C.).
274 See, for example, *Bennett v. Bennett*, [1952] 1 K.B. 249 (separation agreement in which the consideration flowing from the wife was an unenforceable undertaking not to invoke the jurisdiction of the court—provision not severable—agreement unenforceable). See also *Alec Lobb v. Total Oil GB*, [1985] 1 All E.R. 303.
275 *McFarlane v. Daniell*, above note 272 at 346.
276 See, for example, *Miller v. Karlinski* (1945), 62 T.L.R. 85; *Napier v. National Business Agency Ltd.*, above note 14. See also *Taylor v. Bhail*, [1996] C.L.C. 377 (repair contract including obligation to provide an inflated estimate of the value of the work to enable the employer to defraud an insurer—offending provision not severable—agreement unenforceable).

Canadian courts have considered and refined the doctrine of severance in a series of cases arising from the criminal rate of interest provisions of the Canadian *Criminal Code*.[277] Section 347 of the *Code* prohibits the entering into of agreements to receive interest at a rate that exceeds 60 percent *per annum*. The provision further defines the concept of "interest" expansively to include "all charges and expenses, whether in the form of a fee, fine, penalty, commission or other similar charge or expense or in any other form"[278] paid or payable with respect to the advancing of credit. This provision was included in the *Criminal Code* as a feature of the legislation repealing the federal *Small Loans Act*.[279] The latter legislation had been originally inspired by the apparent need to regulate small consumer loans at a time when banks and other financial institutions had not substantially entered the consumer loan market. The legislation was thought to be unnecessary, however, once banks and other responsible lenders had entered the consumer market at competitive lending rates. At the same time, however, it was thought desirable to provide the law enforcement community with a means to deal with non-market loan-sharking activities and for this purpose, section 347 was introduced into the *Criminal Code*.[280] The provision was drafted, however, without any evident awareness of commercial practices in the context of high-risk, especially short-term, commercial loans. Accordingly, although the provision appears to have been rarely invoked against actual loan sharks, the expansiveness of the provisions[281] has captured numerous commercial lending transactions entered into by sophisticated commercial parties, often acting on the basis of professional advice.[282]

The facts of a leading case, *William E. Thomson Associates Inc. v. Carpenter*,[283] neatly illustrate the problem. The plaintiff investment

---

277 *Criminal Code*, R.S.C. 1985, c. C-46, s. 347 [*Code*].
278 *Ibid.*, s. 347(2).
279 R.S.C. 1970, c. S-11.
280 Parliament, Standing Senate Committee on Banking, Trade and Commerce, October 29, 1980, 29:9-21:10.
281 The provisions have also been interpreted expansively. See *Garland v. Consumers Gas Co.*, [1998] 3 S.C.R. 112.
282 The potential for this sort of difficulty did not go unnoticed at the time of enactment. See J.S. Ziegel, "Bill C-44; Repeal of the Small Loans Act and Enactment of a New Usury Law" (1981) 59 Can. Bar Rev. 188; J.S. Ziegel, "The Usury Provisions in the Criminal Code: The Chickens Come Home to Roost" (1986) 11 Can. Bus. L.J. 233. See also M.A. Waldron, *Proposed Amendments to Section 347 of the Criminal Code* (Ottawa: Uniform Law Conference of Canada, 2003).
283 (1989), 61 D.L.R. (4th) 1 (Ont. C.A.), leave to appeal to S.C.C. refused (1990), 65 D.L.R. (4th) viii.

banker had entered into an arrangement to provide interim financing to a corporation experiencing financial difficulties in order to provide a period of time during which the borrower's affairs could be put in order with a view to attracting conventional financing. In due course, the borrower proved to be unable to arrange a refinancing and defaulted on the loan. Accordingly, the lender sought to enforce guarantees executed by two directors of the borrower. The guarantors defended the claim on the basis that the interest charges contravened section 347. The various charges associated with the interim financing, including interest charges, a facility fee and reimbursement of the plaintiff's legal fees and other costs, were all considered to be interest within the meaning of section 347 and cumulatively amounted to an annual rate in excess of 60 percent. Accordingly, both the loan and the associated guarantees constituted illegal transactions and were unenforceable. The problem in such cases is not that the lender might be prosecuted under the *Code* for commission of the section 347 offence. This eventuality is most unlikely.[284] Rather, the problem is that borrowers in such circumstances will take the position that as the entire transaction is unlawful, neither the interest nor the principal must be paid to the lender with resulting enrichment of the borrower at the lender's expense. The net and, presumably, unintended effect of section 347 in this context, then, is to increase the risk of this kind of financing and, we may assume, reduce its availability. For obvious reasons, however, considerable attention has been focused in these cases on the question of the severability of the unlawful interest provisions.

Initially, Canadian courts sought to distinguish between transactions in which the interest provisions could be considered to be collateral to the primary purpose of the transaction, in which case the interest provisions were severable,[285] and those in which the interest yield was said to be the central purpose of the transaction, in which case the provisions could not be severed.[286] More recently, however, Canadian courts have accepted that the interest provisions in these cases are severable even in a straightforward lending context where the very point of the transaction from the lender's perspective is to earn

---

284 Section 347(7) stipulates that no proceedings may be brought under this provision without the consent of the provincial Attorney General. Accordingly, prosecution on the facts of cases like *Thomson* are exceedingly unlikely and, as yet at least, appear not to have occurred.

285 *Mira Design Co. Ltd. v. Seascape Holdings Ltd.*, [1982] 4 W.W.R. 97 (B.C.S.C.) (commercial mortgage — primary purpose to secure repayment of the purchase price — held not fundamentally illegal).

286 *Croll v. Kelly* (1983), 48 B.C.L.R. 306 (S.C.).

interest. In such cases, the lender is at least entitled to a return of the principal.[287] As well, in cases where the criminal rate of interest stipulated in the agreement contains a number of components, courts have adopted the view that provisions relating to particular components can be deleted to the point at which the amount of interest payable under the remaining provisions is less than the criminal rate. The lender can then enforce the remainder of the agreement, including the undeleted interest provisions, and recover not only the principal but an amount of interest that is calculated at less than the criminal rate.[288]

In the *Thomson* case itself, the guarantees were enforced and the court offered a restatement of the severance doctrine that has proven to be influential in this line of cases. The court noted that the two considerations to be addressed in applying severance doctrine are first, "whether severance is possible … without affecting the substance of the obligation to repay the principal of the loan and without making a new agreement for the parties,"[289] and second, "whether public policy prevents the severance of the agreement because it is tainted by illegality."[290] Blair J.A. then proceeded to identify four principles, drawn from the decided cases, to be taken into account in applying these tests: "The first consideration is whether the purpose and policy of s. 347 would be subverted by severance. … The second consideration is whether the parties entered into the agreement for an illegal purpose or with an evil intention. … The third consideration is the relative bargaining position of the parties and their conduct in reaching the agreement. … The fourth consideration … is whether the appellants can be considered to have been unjustly enriched at the expense of the company."[291]

On the *Thomson* facts, it was Blair J.A.'s view that each of these considerations weighed in favour of severance. Because the purpose of the transaction was to "curb the reprehensible practice of loan sharking"[292] that purpose would not be undermined by enforcing the balance

---

287 See *William E. Thomson Associates Inc. v. Carpenter*, above note 283; *Olympia Enterprises v. Dover Financial Corp.* (1995), 147 N.S.R. (2d) 121 (S.C.).

288 *Milani v. Banks* (1997), 145 D.L.R. (4th) 55 (Ont. C.A.); *Boyd v. International Utility Structures Inc.* (2002), 216 D.L.R. (4th) 139 (B.C.C.A.). Compare with *TerraCan Corp. v. Pine Projects Ltd.* (1993), 100 D.L.R. (4th) 431 (B.C.C.A.). See also *Vandekerkhove v. Litchfield* (1995), 121 D.L.R. (4th) 571 (B.C.C.A.), leave to appeal to S.C.C. refused, 126 D.L.R. (4th) vii (restitution of interest paid under lawful provisions denied).

289 Above note 283 at 8.

290 *Ibid.*

291 *Ibid.* at 11–12.

292 *Ibid.* at 11.

of the terms of the present transaction. Second, this was not a case in which the parties had entered into the agreement with the intention of committing an illegal act or of accomplishing an illegal purpose. Third, the parties were sophisticated commercial parties acting on the basis of professional advice. This was not a case of a desperate borrower dealing with a usurious lender. Fourth, receipt of the principal without a corresponding obligation to repay constituted an inappropriate enrichment of the borrower. For Blair J.A., then, the lending agreement, even though tainted by illegality, should not be considered to be completely unenforceable. More particularly, the guarantors were held liable for the principal amounts subject to the guarantees.

Under traditional doctrine, there exists the further requirement that severance will only be available if it can be achieved through deletion rather than revision of provisions in the agreement.[293] This requirement that the court must be able to sever rather than revise an offending provision, referred to as the blue-pencil test, was considered until recently at least, to be generally applicable to illegality cases in Canadian common law. Exceptionally, there may be one situation in which severance is not permitted and application of the blue-pencil test may be withheld. As we have noted, English and Canadian courts have applied severance doctrine in the context of covenants in restraint of trade. Rather than simply excise the offending provision, courts may sever portions of the covenant, thus enabling enforcement of the remaining portions of the restraint. In the context of employment contracts, however, it has been suggested that where a restrictive covenant contains a series of restraints, at least one of which failed because of its breadth, the entire covenant should be struck down as unenforceable.[294] Courts should not enable employers to rely on such clauses *in terrorem*, and then, when the matter is litigated, allow the employer to enforce a reasonable version of the clause by applying the blue-pencil test. Applying the blue-pencil test in this context, then, virtually invites employers to draft unreasonably broad restraints confident in the knowledge that they will at least be able to enforce a judicially designed reasonable version of them in the event of a dispute. In other cases, however, both English and Canadian courts have held in employment cases that if the lawful constraint can be said to be a separate covenant

---

293 See above this Chapter, section B(4).

294 *Mason v. Provident Clothing & Supply Co.,* above note 136 at 745, Lord Moulton; *Attwood v. Lamont,* [1920] 3 K.B. 571 at 593, Younger L.J.; *J.G. Collins Insurance Agencies Ltd. v. Elsley,* [1978] 2 S.C.R. 916 at 925–26, Dickson J. And see *Gordon v. Ferguson* (1961), 30 D.L.R. (2d) 420 (N.S.S.C.).

from the unlawful restraint, the latter can be severed with the result that the lawful restraint is enforceable.[295] On this view, there would appear to be no special rule precluding the application of severance doctrine in the employment context.

A more fundamental breach in the universality of the blue-pencil test has recently been established, however, by the decision of the Supreme Court of Canada in *Transport North American Express Inc. v. New Solutions Financial Corp.*[296] The facts of *New Solutions* were similar to those of the *Thomson* case. The plaintiff lender had extended a substantial and high-risk loan to the defendant borrower on an urgent basis. The lender had initially suggested that, in light of the risks involved, it should take an equity position in the borrower. The borrower resisted this overture, however, and the parties agreed to a substantial payment in lieu of this device. This commitment together with other fees and charges were held to constitute interest in the requisite sense and cumulatively amounted to an effective annual interest rate of 30.8 percent. The arrangement also included interest in the traditional sense, however, at a rate of 4 percent per month calculated daily and this, to the apparent surprise of the parties, amounted to an effective annual interest rate of 60.1 percent, thus itself exceeding the criminal rate of interest. The total "interest" yield was thus 90.9 percent. Under the *Thomson* ruling, as it has been more recently applied[297] a possible outcome of the lender's claim to enforce the contract would be to sever the barely but plainly offensive 60.1-percent interest-rate covenant and enforce the covenants creating an effective annual 30.8-percent interest-rate burden. At trial, however, in a ruling overturned by the Ontario Court of Appeal[298] but restored on further appeal,[299] Cullity J. offered the innovative view that it was open to the court to reduce the overall effective rate to 60 percent on the basis of the proposition that "severance might be effected notionally by reading down provisions so that the criminal rate of interest would not be exceeded and not merely by striking out words."[300] Cullity J. suggested that the blue-pencil test was

---

295 *Putsman v. Taylor*, [1927] 1 K.B. 637, aff'd [1927] 1 K.B. 741 (C.A.). See also *Hall v. More*, [1928] 1 D.L.R. 1028 (B.C.C.A.); *Garbutt Business College Ltd. v. Henderson*, [1939] 3 W.W.R. 257 (Alta. C.A.); *E.P. Chester Ltd. v. Mastorkis* (1968), 56 C.P.R. 139 (N.S.S.C.A.D.).
296 Above note 271.
297 See authorities referred to above note 288.
298 Above note 271.
299 *Ibid.* (S.C.C.).
300 *Ibid.* at 572 (Ont. S.C.J.).

a "relic of a bygone era"[301] characterized by a more rigid approach to the interpretation of contracts. The traditional defence of the blue-pencil test to the effect that the courts should not remake the agreement for the parties was rejected by Cullity J. on the basis that in any case where severance doctrine is applied, the courts have, in effect, imposed a new agreement on the parties.

On appeal, a divided Supreme Court of Canada favoured the approach taken by Cullity J. For the majority, Arbour J. also found the traditional justification of the blue-pencil test unconvincing. She observed that the changes to an agreement effected by the traditional blue-pencil technique "will often fundamentally alter the consideration associated with the bargain and do violence to the intention of the parties."[302] In her view, the doctrine of severance gives rise to a spectrum of available remedies. At one end of the spectrum, in the context of traditional loan-sharking arrangements, the court could denounce such practices by simply refusing to apply the doctrine of severance. In the middle of the spectrum would be cases where it might be appropriate to withhold enforcement of the interest provisions but uphold the borrower's obligation to repay the capital. At the other end of the spectrum, "in the case of a good faith commercial transaction,"[303] where the equities favour the lender and severance does not undermine the policy of the legislation, she indicated that a court may sever only those provisions of the loan agreement that put the effective rate of interest over 60 percent, leaving intact the borrower's obligations to repay the principal and to pay some interest. In exercising the discretion to sever, however, courts should not be restricted by the blue-pencil test that was, for Arbour J., capable of producing artificial results depending on the structure of the agreement. On the present facts, it would produce a 30.8-percent interest rate. If the parties had agreed to a single provision providing for 90.9-percent interest, however, no interest would be recoverable. If the lender had the good fortune to have stipulated for 60 percent interest in one provision together with 30.9-percent interest in others, 60 percent would be recoverable. Erratic results of this kind can be avoided, in her view, by the application of a doctrine of notional severance, reducing the rate to 60 percent even though no actual provision of the agreement so stipulated.

In determining whether notional severance should be applied to the *New Solutions* facts, Arbour J. applied the four factors articulated

---

301 *Ibid.* at 573 (Ont. S.C.J.).
302 *Ibid.* at para. 28 (S.C.C.).
303 *Ibid.* at para. 31 (S.C.C.).

in the *Thomson* case as a test for determining whether notional severance should be available. Accordingly, she considered whether the policy underlying section 347 of the *Code* would be subverted by notional severance, whether the parties had entered the agreement for an illegal purpose or with an evil intention, the relative bargaining position of the parties and the potential for the borrower to enjoy an unjustified windfall in the absence of notional severance.[304] Noting that the purpose of section 347 related to the prohibition of loan sharking rather than the broad range of commercial and consumer transactions actually captured by the provision, she concluded that there was no reason to prefer the 30.8-percent result achieved by the blue-pencil test to the 60-percent rate achieved by notional severance in terms of the purposes underlying section 347. Further, as there was no evil intent present and no inequality of bargaining power between the parties, the equities of the situation favoured the lender and the imposition of a 60-percent rate.

Recognition of the doctrine of notional severance may be thought to offer an attractive device for ameliorating the harsh and unexpected impact of section 347 of the *Code* in the context of transactions that fall outside the intended target of loan sharking activity. It may be asked, however, whether the Supreme Court intended to provide a new remedial device available across the broad range of illegal transactions. Although the discussion of notional severance offered by Arbour J. in *New Solutions* appears quite focused on the problems posed by section 347, there is no reason, in principle, why notional severance would not be more broadly available.[305] Indeed, Bastarache J., in dissent, criticized the idea of notional severance on the ground that there was no principled basis for restricting notional severance to the section 347 context. In his view, therefore, recognition of the device created a source of greater uncertainty in the law across the whole field of illegal transactions. However, application of the concept to covenants in restraint of trade in the context of employment contracts, for example, would surely exacerbate the problem, noted above[306] that the application of severance doctrine might encourage employers to take the calculated risk of drafting very broad restraints secure in the assumption that the court will impose a reasonable and, perhaps, notionally severed, provision.[307]

---

304 *Ibid.* at para. 42 (S.C.C.).

305 See *ibid.* at para. 59 (S.C.C.).

306 See the discussion of *Mason v. Provident Clothing & Supply Co.*, above note 136, in this Chapter, section B(4).

307 Bastarache J. indicated particular reservations about applying notional severance in the restraint of trade context. See above note 271 at para. 61 (S.C.C.).

Indeed, this may be a more general difficulty with the idea of notional severance. It may be useful, therefore, for courts to identify this concern as a further basis, in addition to the four-factor test from *Thomson*, for withholding application of the notional severance concept.[308]

FURTHER READINGS

J. BEATSON, "Repudiation of Illegal Purpose as a Ground for Restitution" (1975) 91 Law Q. Rev. 313.

P.B.H. BIRKS, "Recovering Value Transferred under an Illegal Contract" (2000) 1 Theor. Inq. L. 155.

R.A. BUCKLEY, *Illegality and Public Policy* (London: Sweet & Maxwell, 2002).

R.A. BUCKLEY, "Illegal Transactions: Chaos or Discretion?" (2000) 20 Leg. Stud. 155.

B. COOTE, "Another Look at *Bowmakers v. Barnet Instruments*" (1972) 35 Mod. L. Rev. 38.

N. ENONCHONG, *Illegal Transactions* (London: Lloyd's of London Press, 1998).

J. FLEMING, "Insurance for the Criminal" (1971) 34 Mod. L. Rev. 176.

M. FURMSTON, "The Analysis of Illegal Contracts" (1967) 16 U.T.L.J. 267.

W. GELLHORN, "Contracts and Public Policy" (1935) 35 Colum. L. Rev. 679.

J.K. GRODECKI, "*In Pari Delicto Potior est Conditio Defendentis*" (1955) 71 Law Q. Rev. 254.

M.J. HIGGINS, "The Transfer of Property under Illegal Transactions" (1962) 25 Mod. L. Rev. 598.

---

308 In *New Solutions*, *ibid.*, Fish J., in dissent, was indeed of the view that this consideration should prevent application of the concept of notional severance, assuming that it is available, to the very facts of the *New Solutions* case. See *ibid.* at para. 120 (S.C.C.). It may be, however, that such concerns are adequately addressed by the first and third elements of the *Thomson* test, i.e., the potential for undermining the rule rendering the transaction unenforceable and inequality of bargaining power.

LAW REFORM COMMISSION OF BRITISH COLUMBIA, *Report on Illegal Transactions* (Vancouver: The Commission, 1983).

J.D. MCCAMUS, "Restitutionary Recovery of Benefits Conferred under Contracts in Conflict with Statutory Policy—The New Golden Rule" (1988) 25 Osgoode Hall L.J. 787.

ONTARIO LAW REFORM COMMISSION, *Report on Amendment of the Law of Contract* (Toronto: Ministry of the Attorney General, 1987) c. 11.

M.J. TREBILCOCK, *The Common Law of Restraint of Trade* (Toronto: Carswell, 1986).

MISTAKE

A. INTRODUCTION

A party who has entered into an agreement labouring under a mistake of some kind may wish to seek redress in either one of two different forms. First, the party may wish to rely upon the mistake as an excuse for non-performance of his or her obligations under the agreement. Alternatively, such a party may wish to seek a revision of the agreement that will bring the agreement into alignment with his or her own mistaken perception of the nature of the obligations imposed by the agreement. In this chapter, we examine the possibilities for relief of these two different kinds.

Different kinds of mistakes may affect a party's decision to enter into an agreement. One might be mistaken about the meaning of the terms of the agreement. One might enter into an agreement motivated by a reason that rests on false information or assumptions. One might sign a written agreement that does not reflect one's understanding of the agreement reached through the negotiation process. The nature of the relief available for mistake varies from one type of mistake to another and, accordingly, a threshold question to be addressed in any examination of the law of contractual mistake is to fashion appropriate categories of the kinds of mistakes that may affect a transaction. Although various terms are used by different writers to refer to the various categories of mistake, there is a broad consensus that there exists a basic division between mistakes that prevent formation of the agreement, here referred to as "misunderstandings," and mistakes concerning some matter relevant to the decision to enter the agreement, here referred to as "mistaken assumptions."[1] In some contexts, the two categories are referred to, respectively, as mistakes as to "terms" and mistakes as to "motive."[2] In cases of misunderstanding, the parties have failed to reach an adequate *consensus ad idem*.[3] The parties may, for example, have different ideas about what the terms of the contract mean. There is, one might say, no genuine or true agreement between the parties. In a mistaken assumptions case, on the other hand, the parties have reached an adequate *consensus ad idem*.[4] They share an understanding of what the contract means but either one or both of the parties may have entered into the agreement on the basis of a factual assumption that proves to be false. A mistaken assumption relates to the reasons for entering into the agreement rather than one's awareness of the actual terms of the agreement. Whether the mistake is a misunderstanding with respect to the terms of the agreement or a mistaken assumption relating to the motives or reasons for entering the agreement, the effect of the mistake may be to make the transaction surprisingly unattractive for one of the parties, once the truth is revealed. The party who has been disadvantaged by the mistake will wish to be excused from the agreement. As we shall see, a variety of doctrines developed, both at common law and in equity, that may achieve this result in an appropriate case. We will also see that there is some as yet unresolved tension in the interaction between doctrines of common law and equity in some aspects of the law of mistake.

A third type of mistake, here referred to as a "mistake in integration," occurs when the agreement as negotiated by the parties is incorrectly recorded in what is intended by the parties to be an accurate written record of the agreement. Thus, in a contract for the purchase and sale of land, the description of the land in the written agreement

---

1   For an illuminating discussion of classification questions, see G. Palmer, *Mistake and Unjust Enrichment* (Columbus: Ohio State University Press, 1962) c. 1.
2   See, for example, *Calgary v. Northern Construction Co.*, [1986] 2 W.W.R. 426 (Alta. C.A.).
3   See generally Chapter 2.
4   Thus, yet another set of categories that expresses the distinction between misunderstandings and mistaken assumptions divides mistakes into those that "negative" consent in the sense of demonstrating that genuine consent did not occur (here referred to as misunderstandings) and those that operate so as to "nullify" consent in the sense of providing a basis for relief even though consent was initially secured (here referred to as mistaken assumption). See *Bell v. Lever Brothers Ltd.*, [1932] A.C. 161 at 217 (H.L.), Lord Atkin, rev'g [1931] 1 K.B. 557 (C.A.).

may describe a parcel that is larger or smaller than the parcel the parties intended to transfer. The party who has been disadvantaged by the mistake is likely to wish either to withdraw from the agreement or have the written document revised so as to accord with the initial understanding of the parties. Courts of equity developed the remedy of rectification to provide the latter form of relief. In a clear case where the parties reached a prior agreement that is not accurately recorded in the written version of the agreement, such relief will normally be available. The more difficult question is whether such relief should be available in other circumstances.

In this chapter, then, we consider the various doctrines developed by the courts of common law and the courts of equity to provide relief of various kinds from agreements affected by misunderstandings, mistaken assumptions and mistakes in integration.[5] In what follows, the term "*unilateral* mistake" is used to refer to situations in which only one of the parties to the agreement labours under a mistake. Thus, a unilateral mistake with respect to the meaning of a term would occur where one party suffers from such a mistake but the other party to the agreement is aware of the correct meaning of the term. The term "*common* mistake" will be used to refer to situations where both parties to the agreement share the same mistake. Thus, a common mistaken assumption occurs where both parties suffer from the same incorrect assumption concerning some factual circumstance that is material to the decision of one or both of the parties to enter into the agreement.

B. MISUNDERSTANDINGS

1) Introduction

A misunderstanding occurs where one party is not clear about the correct meaning of a term or terms of the agreement or where both parties understand the meaning of a term or terms differently, neither under-

---

5   Mistakes may also arise in the context of the performance of an agreement. Thus, for example, one might pay a debt for a second time, having forgotten that the debt had already been paid. In the normal case, such a second payment should be and is recoverable in a restitutionary claim for the recovery of the money paid under a mistake. See generally P.D. Maddaugh and J.D. McCamus, *The Law of Restitution*, 2d ed. (Aurora: Canada Law Book, 2004) c. 10. The problem of mistaken overperformance and the restitutionary relief therefor does not raise issues concerning the enforceability of contractual obligations and will not be further considered here.

standing being, in the requisite sense, the correct meaning of the agreement. In a case of misunderstanding, the critical question is whether the parties have reached a true *consensus ad idem*. The mere fact that one party suffers from a misunderstanding of one or more of the terms of an agreement does not necessarily lead to the conclusion that no *consensus* has been achieved. Where the other party correctly understands the meaning of the agreement, a *consensus* may be achieved on the basis of the objective theory of contract formation. Notwithstanding the misunderstanding, the other party to the agreement may be entitled to rely on the mistaken party's objective manifestation of assent as a basis for the creation of a valid and binding *consensus*. As Blackburn J. observed in *Smith v. Hughes*:[6] "If whatever a man's real intention may be, he so conducts himself that a reasonable man would believe that he was assenting to the terms proposed by the other party and that the other party upon that belief enters into the contract with him, the man thus conducting himself would be equally bound as if he had intended to agree to the other party's terms."[7] Thus, even where a *consensus* may be said to fail at a subjective level, the *consensus* may be achieved on an objective basis and the contract so created is an enforceable one. A *consensus* may fail, however, where each party has a different understanding of a term that is so ambiguous or vague or imprecise that neither party can insist on his or her own meaning as being the true or correct meaning of the term of which the other party has objectively assented. In such a circumstance, the common law of contract formation holds that no enforceable contract has been created. Similarly, a *consensus* will fail where one party is aware of the other party's mistaken understanding of a particular term. Again, the lack of *consensus* leads to the conclusion that no contract has been created at common law. We consider both of these types of cases below.

Under traditional common law doctrine, there are two further instances in which particular types of mistakes may lead to the conclusion that a *consensus ad idem* has not been achieved. First, where a party enters into an agreement with one person, believing that person to be someone else—a so-called mistake of identity—it was held at common law that no enforceable agreement had been created, at least in circumstances where the other party was actively involved in inducing the mistake. A second type of error induced by the other party that may give rise to a finding of no *consensus* is a mistake as to the very nature of the agreement entered—typically by executing a written

---

6   (1871), L.R. 6 Q.B. 597 (Div. Ct.).
7   *Ibid.* at 607.

agreement—by the mistaken party. These are cases of so-called *non est factum*. If the doctrine is applicable, the mistaken party is allowed to assert that he or she did not assent to the signed agreement and it should therefore be considered to be a nullity at common law. Both of these doctrines are, however, controversial because of the potential impact they may have on third parties. In the context of an unenforceable contract for the purchase and sale of goods, for example, where the purchaser has induced the error rendering the contract unenforceable, a third party may have innocently repurchased the subject matter of the sale from the purchaser. Since, if either doctrine applies, the agreement is a nullity at common law, no property interest in the subject matter of the sale will have passed to the purchaser who induced the error, typically referred to as the "rogue," and the rogue, in turn, will not have passed an interest in the goods to the third-party purchaser. The innocent third party is thus exposed to a claim by the seller for the innocent purchaser's unwitting conversion of the goods. In such cases, the common law, when faced by the dilemma of preferring the interests of one innocent party, the original seller, over those of another innocent party, the third-party purchaser, chose to favour the former. As we shall see, critics of these common law doctrines suggest that their role ought to be reduced, if not eliminated, with the result that the original seller's claim in conversion in such a case would fail and the seller would be left to those remedies available against the rogue on the basis of the rogue's fraudulent misrepresentation. The equitable remedy of rescission for misrepresentation would not prevent the initial formation of the contract and would, as a consequence, afford protection to the innocent third party until the point in time at which rescission occurs.

2) Ambiguity

An agreement that contains a term that is either ambiguous or so vague and imprecise that each party can reasonably have a different understanding of the meaning of the term may be held to fail for lack of *consensus ad idem*. The leading illustration of the phenomenon is the fact situation in *Raffles v. Wichelhaus*.[8] The plaintiff had agreed to sell certain bales of cotton to the defendant to arrive "ex *Peerless*" from

---

8   (1864), 2 H. & C. 906, 159 E.R. 375. See generally R. Birmingham, "Holmes on 'Peerless'; *Raffles v. Wichelhaus* and the Objective Theory of Contract" (1985) 47 U. Pitt. L.R. 183; A.W.B Simpson, "Contracts for Cotton to Arrive: The Case of the Two Ships Peerless" (1999) 11 Cardozo L. Rev. 287.

Bombay. As it happened, there were two vessels named *Peerless* due to sail from Bombay, one in October and the other in December. Although, in the actual case, the matter was discussed only in the context of an interim proceeding, the court appears to have assumed that if the parties had different ships *Peerless* in mind, the contract would be unenforceable, Subsequent generations have assumed that the case stands as authority for the proposition that the contract would be unenforceable in such circumstances for failure of *consensus ad idem*.

The conventional understanding of *Raffles v. Wichelhaus* is that it would not have been possible in that case for one party to establish that his understanding of which ship *Peerless* was intended by the agreement was the more reasonable one. If, on the other hand, the buyer, for example, was able to establish that his meaning was the reasonable one in the circumstances, the contract would be formed on that basis. The party whose understanding of the term can be established to be the reasonable or conventional understanding is able to rely upon the objective theory of contract formation. Thus, in *Lindsey v. Heron & Co.*[9] Middleton J. embraced the following proposition:

> The apparent mutual assent of the parties essential to the formation of a contract must be gathered from the language employed by them, and the law imputes to a person an intention corresponding to the reasonable meaning of his words and acts. It judges of his intention by his outward expressions and excludes all questions in regard to his unexpressed intention. If his words or acts, judged by a reasonable standard manifesting attention to agree in regard to the matter in question, that agreement is established, and it is immaterial what may be the real or unexpressed state of his mind on the subject.[10]

On this basis, then, a private and unreasonable interpretation of a term of the agreement would not prevent its formation. In *Hobbs v. Esquimalt & Nanaimo Railway Company*,[11] for example, the defendant railway company was unable to defeat an agreement under which it purported to sell land to the plaintiff on the basis of its private understanding of the meaning of the term "land." According to the defendant's evidence, it had adopted the practice of selling only the surface rights to land and not the mineral rights relating to a particular parcel. Accordingly, when it entered into an agreement to sell land to Mr. Hobbs, it intended to convey only the surface rights. Mr. Hobbs claimed that he had relied,

---

9   (1921), 50 O.L.R. 1, 64 D.L.R. 92 (C.A.). See also *Smith v. Hughes*, above note 6.
10   See *ibid.* at 98–99 (D.L.R.).
11   (1899), 29 S.C.R. 450.

in entering the agreement, on the ordinary meaning of the term "land," as normally including both surface rights and mineral rights. The Supreme Court held that the railway company's private understanding of the meaning of the term was unreasonable. Accordingly, Hobbs was entitled to enforce the agreement on the basis that it required transfer of the full ownership rights to the land.

In *Lindsey v. Heron & Co.*[12] itself, the parties to a contract for the purchase and sale of shares had in mind different companies with similar-sounding names. The seller had approached the defendant and asked, "What will you give me for seventy-five shares of Eastern Cafeterias of Canada?" The defendant replied that he would look into the question and later responded, "I will give you ten dollars and fifty cents a share for your Eastern Cafeterias." The plaintiff replied, "I accept your offer." In fact, the defendant had in mind purchasing shares in Eastern Cafeterias Ltd., an apparently more valuable stock. Applying the objective approach to this exchange of communications, however, the majority of the Court of Appeal took the view that the defendant led the plaintiff seller to understand that he was prepared to pay ten dollars and fifty cents per share, for shares in Eastern Cafeterias of Canada. Had the plaintiff offered to sell shares in "Eastern Cafeterias," however, the term would have been ambiguous and there would have been no contract. In dissent, Lennox J. would have held that the offer to buy "your Eastern Cafeterias," which was accepted by the plaintiff, suffered from an ambiguity in the sense that the parties each had different ideas of the shares being referred to. Accordingly, he would have held that, as the parties were not referring to the same subject matter, there was no *consensus ad idem*.

Application of the objective theory of contract formation arose in quite unusual circumstances in *Staiman Steel Ltd. v. Commercial & Home Builders Ltd.*[13] In the typical case in which reliance is placed on the objective theory of contract formation, it is the non-mistaken party who relies on the theory in order to enforce the agreement on the terms as understood by the non-mistaken party. In *Staiman Steel*, on the other hand, it was the mistaken party who sought to enforce the objective version of the agreement against the non-mistaken party. The plaintiff purchased a bulk lot of steel from the defendant at an auction. The plaintiff mistakenly believed that the lot included both building steel and used steel whereas, in the court's view, the defendant seller correctly understood that the lot included used steel only. Evidently, the

---

12   Above note 9.
13   (1976), 13 O.R. (2d) 315, 71 D.L.R. (3d) 17 (H.C.).

plaintiff had been able to make the agreement at an attractive price, as he wished to go ahead with the transaction even if the lot contained only used steel. The seller, however, refused to go forward with the transaction unless the purchaser would sign a waiver releasing any claim he might have against the seller for a lot that included building steel. The purchaser refused to do so and, in due course, the purchaser brought an action against the seller for damages for non-delivery. In these circumstances, then, the purchaser, who did not understand the terms of the agreement and therefore did not subjectively assent to them, wished to enforce the agreement on an unwilling party who actually understood the agreement. Although the circumstances of this case are therefore somewhat unusual, it is difficult to see why the seller should not be required to abide by its own reasonable understanding of what the agreement meant. The court applied the objective theory against the non-mistaken party and held the seller liable for damages for breach of contract. The seller had no right to insist on a waiver of any claim the purchaser might have to building steel as a condition of delivery. This was simply an attempt to unilaterally introduce a new term to the agreement and did not provide an excuse for non-delivery.

3) Unilateral Mistakes as to Terms

Where, prior to formation of a contract, one party is mistaken with respect to the meaning of a term of the contract and the other party is aware of that mistake, the contract will fail for lack of a *consensus ad idem*. A party who attempts to enforce an agreement, the significance of which, he or she realized at the time of formation, was misunderstood by the other party, will not be rewarded by enforcement of the agreement. This proposition is set forth in the decision in *Smith v. Hughes*,[14] a case involving the sale by sample of a quantity of oats. The buyer, a trainer of race horses, mistakenly concluded that the oats in question were *old* oats rather than *new* oats, the former being more suitable for his purposes. It appeared that the seller may have been aware of the fact that the buyer was mistaken on this point, but insisted that he had not contracted to supply old oats. The decision involved a review of the instructions put to the jury at trial. The court concluded that the jury had not been properly instructed as to the difference between a situation in which the seller was aware of the buyer's mistake as to the quality of the oats as opposed to a situation in which the seller was aware that the buyer understood that the contract stipulated that the oats in question

---

14   Above note 6.

were old oats. With respect to the former situation, the doctrine of *caveat emptor* applied and the seller was under no obligation to disabuse the purchaser of his mistaken assessment of the quality of the oats.[15] However, if the seller was aware that the purchaser believed that the seller had warranted that the oats were old, the contract would fail for lack of *consensus ad idem*. Where the mistaken term is included in an offer, the problem is often referred to as "snapping up an offer." An offeree who is aware that the offeror does not intend the offer in the terms in which it is expressed cannot snap up the offer and create an enforceable contract. That result is precluded by the rule in *Smith v. Hughes*.

Formation of a contract may also be prevented where the non-mistaken party does not have actual knowledge of the other party's mistake as to terms. Thus, where the non-mistaken party has conducted the negotiations with the intention of causing such an error, the agreement will fail. In *Glasner v. Royal Lepage Real Estate Services Limited*,[16] for example, the non-mistaken party had made a minor adjustment to the draft agreement provided by the ultimately mistaken party in the hope that the mistaken party would not notice the change. The mistaken party had extended a written offer to purchase a residential property that contained a warranty that the building had never been insulated with a particular substance. The vendor, who had, on a previous occasion, removed the substance from the premises, adjusted the draft agreement to state that there was currently no such insulation on the premises and, further, instructed his agent not to advise the potential purchaser of the change in the draft. The purchaser signed the agreement, not noticing the change. Having ultimately been advised by the agent of the alteration to the draft, the purchaser refused to close the transaction. The vendor's action to enforce the agreement failed for lack of *consensus*.

Similarly, there are cases where the circumstances are such that it can reasonably be concluded that the non-mistaken party either "must have known" or "ought to have known" of the error. In *Hartog v. Colin & Shields*,[17] an offer to sell Argentine hare skins at so much "per pound" was accepted by an offeree even though the negotiations had proceeded on a "per piece" pricing basis, as was the custom of the

---

15   To the extent that courts may require, in particular circumstances, that parties make disclosures concerning the subject matter of the contract, the doctrine of *caveat emptor* is obviously undermined. With respect to the treatment of certain kinds of non-disclosure as misrepresentation, see further Chapter 10, section C.

16   (1992), 28 R.P.R. (2d) 72 (B.C.S.C.).

17   [1939] 3 All E.R. 566 (K.B.). See also *McMaster University v. Wilchar Construction Ltd.* (1971), 22 D.L.R. (3d) 9 (Ont. H.C.J.), aff'd (1973), 12 O.R. (2d) 512n, 69 D.L.R. (3d) 400n (C.A.).

trade. It was held that the buyer must be taken to have known of the error and, accordingly, that the contract had not been validly created. Negligent inducement of error may also preclude enforcement of the agreement. In *Scriven Brothers & Co. v. Hindley & Co.*,[18] an auctioneer was precluded from enforcement of a contract to sell tow to the defendant buyer because the misleading nature of his catalogue had led the buyer to assume that the goods up for auction were hemp rather than tow. Although the auctioneer realized that the defendant had put in a high bid for tow, he reasonably believed that the defendant's mistake was one as to the value of the tow. Nonetheless, as the auctioneer's negligence had induced the buyer's error, the fact that the parties were not *ad idem* as to the subject matter of the sale precluded enforcement of the agreement.

Under traditional doctrine, the inability to enforce agreements entered into on the basis of a unilateral mistake as to terms is explained on the basis of a lack of *consensus ad idem*. On this basis, such agreements are simply void at common law. Occasionally, however, the results have been explained on the basis of estoppel doctrine. Thus, in *Scriven Brothers & Co. v. Hindley & Co.* itself, the court held that the auctioneer's negligence prevented it "from being able to insist upon a contract by estoppel."[19] Although the possible distinction between failure of *consensus ad idem* and estoppel is not explored in this case, it is possible that the distinction is of some significance. Thus, if the true explanation for the results in these cases is that the non-mistaken party is precluded from relying on an "estoppel" that might otherwise be effective, it would appear that the mistaken party should not be precluded from relying on the objective theory of contract formation.[20]

The failure of *consensus* approach in the unilateral mistake as to terms context leads to the conclusion that where the vitiating doctrine is applicable, it renders the contract void at common law. In *Taylor v. Johnson*,[21] the Australian High Court has made the interesting suggestion that agreements affected by such mistakes should be considered valid at common law but subject to rescission in equity. In this case, the parties had entered into an option agreement for the purchase and

18 [1913] 3 K.B. 564.
19 *Ibid.* at 569. See also *Colonial Investment of Winnipeg v. Borland* (1911), 1 W.W.R. 171 (Alta. S.C.), aff'd (1912), 2 W.W.R. 960 (Alta. C.A.). And see J.R. Spencer, "Signature, Consent and the Rule in *L'Estrange v. Glaucob*" (1973) 32 Cambridge L.J. 104.
20 Compare with *Staiman Steel Ltd. v. Commercial & Home Builders Ltd.*, above note 13.
21 (1983), 151 C.L.R. 422 (Aust. H.C.).

sale of two parcels of land, each of about five acres, for a total price of fifteen thousand dollars. The vendors believed, however, that the price was fifteen thousand dollars per acre. The purchaser suspected error and made a point of not referring to the price in subsequent conversations with the vendors and, in other ways, deliberately sought to ensure that the vendors were not disabused of their mistake. As we have seen, such an agreement would likely fail in Canadian law for lack of a *consensus ad idem*. A majority of the High Court, however, held that the contract was valid at common law but subject to rescission in equity. In reaching this conclusion, the High Court drew support from similar developments in other aspects of the law of contractual mistake. As we will see later in this chapter,[22] in such areas as mistake of identity, *non est factum* and mistaken assumptions, English and Canadian courts have restricted the effect of common law mistake doctrines that render agreements void and permitted such agreements to be rescinded only in equity. The objective in doing so is the protection of third parties who might be negatively affected by agreements that are void rather than voidable for mistake. The High Court applied this approach in the present context and held that where, as in *Taylor v. Johnson*, the parties "have to all outward appearances agreed with sufficient certainty on the same terms on the same subject matter,"[23] the agreement should be considered to be enforceable at common law. The agreement would be subject to equitable rescission, however, on the basis that the purchaser was aware of circumstances indicating that the vendors were labouring under a serious error and, further, deliberately attempted to prevent them from its discovery. Arguably, the restriction of common law doctrines rendering contracts void for mistake appears to be a useful development of the law of mistake.[24] Accordingly, the decision of the Australian High Court in *Taylor v. Johnson* may prove to be a useful model for courts in other common law jurisdictions.

4) Misunderstanding in the Context of Mistaken Bids

Until the dramatic reshaping of the law of tendering by the Supreme Court of Canada in *Ron Engineering & Construction Eastern Ltd. v. Ontario*,[25] there was some judicial support for the proposition that the law

---

22　See below this Chapter, sections B(5), B(6) and C(3).

23　Above note 21 at 429, quoting from *Solle v. Butcher*, [1950] 1 K.B. 671 at 691, Denning L.J., for discussion of which see below this Chapter, section C(3).

24　See below this Chapter, sections B(5) & (6) and C(3) & (4).

25　[1981] 1 S.C.R. 111, 119 D.L.R. (3d) 267.

concerning unilateral mistake as to terms might have some application in the context of mistaken bids. In the typical case, the problem is that a bidder who submits a bid in response to an invitation to tenders has made an important mistake, typically mathematical in nature, in calculating the bid price. When the bids are opened, the mistaken bidder discovers that its bid is very substantially below the second lowest bid, thus leading to an investigation that reveals the error. Under traditional doctrine, the bid was considered, under the law of offer and acceptance,[26] to be an offer extended by the bidder. The selection of a particular bid constituted acceptance of that offer with the result that a contract was entered into on the basis of the terms as set out in the bid. Thus, if the mistaken bidder discovers the error and draws it to the attention of the issuer of the invitation to tender prior to acceptance, it is at least arguable that the issuer of the invitation is unable to "snap up" the mistaken bid that is now known to be affected by error. The bidder's unilateral error, with respect to the bid price, is known to the issuer of the invitation and therefore prevents formation of the agreement.

In order to successfully apply this analysis to a mistaken bid, it is necessary to be able to properly characterize the bid that is based on a mistaken calculation as containing a mistake as to "terms." Prior to the decision in *Ron Engineering*, although Canadian courts differed to some extent on the point, it appeared to have been established that the unilateral mistake doctrine would preclude acceptance of the bid by the issuer once the existence and nature of the mistake was communicated by the bidder to the issuer. In *Imperial Glass Ltd. v. Consolidated Supplies Ltd.*,[27] however, the British Columbia Court of Appeal held that a bid based on a mistaken calculation did not contain a mistake as to a "term." The mistaken bid in question was prepared by a subcontractor who was to supply window glass to a general contractor bidding on a construction project. The general contractor relied on the bid when calculating its own eventually successful bid. After the general contractor's bid was accepted, it sought and received confirmation of the bid price from the subcontractor and placed the order for the glass. By this point in time, the general contractor was in fact aware that the subcontractor's bid was mistaken but considered that it was not subject to a duty to disclose the problem to the subcontractor. The British Columbia Court of Appeal confirmed that no such duty existed and held that the subcon-

---

26 See Chapter 2.
27 (1960), 22 D.L.R. (2d) 759 (B.C.C.A.). For criticism, see M. Carr, "Contract—Mistake—Unilateral Mistake of Offeror and Basis of Offer" (1961) 39 Can. Bar Rev. 625.

tractor's mistake did not constitute a mistake as to a term. Accordingly, the general contractor was able to accept the subcontractor's offer, notwithstanding its awareness of the latter's mistake. The court reasoned as follows: "The mistake was not in the offer. All that is claimed is that the offer would not have been made had the mistake been detected. The mistake was therefore in the motive or reason for making the offer, not in the offer. There was consequently a consensus and a valid contract."[28] In the court's view, therefore, under the rule in *Smith v. Hughes*,[29] the general contractor was at liberty to accept the offer.

Later cases, however, attempted to bring similar fact situations within the rule concerning unilateral mistake of terms. In *McMaster University v. Wilchar Construction Limited*,[30] for example, the unilateral mistake as to terms rule was applied to a situation in which a bidder had mistakenly omitted the entire first page of the bid. That page contained an escalator clause to cover the predictably higher costs of labour to be incurred during the duration of the contract. The court held that the issuer, who was aware of the error at the time it purported to accept the bid, could not create an enforceable contract by doing so. The agreement failed for lack of *consensus ad idem*. Indeed, the court went on to hold that even if the nature of the error had not been communicated to the issuer of the invitation, the error was sufficiently obvious that the issuer would be precluded from acceptance on this basis.[31] The failure to include the first page of the bid in *McMaster University* is evidently more easily characterized as a mistake as to "terms" than the miscalculation error in *Imperial Glass*. The failure of consensus approach was also taken, however, in the later case of *Belle River Community Arena Inc. v. W.J.C. Kaufmann Co.*,[32] a case involving a calculation error and thus more closely analogous to *Imperial Glass*. In *Belle River*, the bidder discovered that it had failed to include approximately $70,000 of costs in a bid price of approximately $615,000. The bidder discovered its error after the opening of the bids and communicated the problem to the issuer of the invitation prior to any purported attempt at acceptance. On these facts, the Ontario Court of Appeal held that "an offeree cannot accept an offer which he knows has been made by a mistake and which *affects* the fundamental term of the contract."[33] Arnup J.A. went

---

28   *Imperial Glass Ltd. v. Consolidated Supplies Ltd.*, *ibid.* at 763, Coady J.A.
29   Above note 6.
30   Above note 17.
31   *Ibid.* at 22 (D.L.R.).
32   (1978), 87 D.L.R. (3d) 761 (Ont. C.A.).
33   *Ibid.* at 766 (emphasis added).

on to observe: "In substance, the purported offer, because of the mistake, is not the offer that the offeror intended to make, and the offeree knows that."[34] In this case, then, the Court of Appeal extended *Smith v. Hughes* beyond cases of mistakes as to terms to mistakes that "affect" a fundamental term of the contract. Once aware of such a mistake, the offeree cannot "snap up" the offer.

This approach was rejected by the Supreme Court of Canada in *Ron Engineering*. As noted elsewhere,[35] the Court held that the invitation to tender itself constituted an offer that was in turn accepted by the bidder by the submission of a bid. This initial agreement, referred to as Contract A, relates to the tendering process itself. Under Contract A, the issuer of the invitation becomes bound to conduct the tendering process in accord with any commitments made in the invitation. The bidder also becomes bound by any undertakings required of bidders by the invitation. In *Ron Engineering*, the bidder had submitted a bid at a price of approximately two million seven hundred thousand dollars that mistakenly failed to include costs of approximately six hundred thousand dollars. The error was discovered by the bidder shortly after the opening of the bids and quickly communicated to the issuer of the invitation. Relying on the decision in *Belle River*, the bidder took the position that the bid was therefore incapable of being accepted and sued for recovery of its bid deposit. The Supreme Court held that the claim was precluded by the provision of Contract A, which stipulated that the bid deposit was irrevocable and could not be recovered if the bidder refused to abide by the issuer's acceptance of its bid. Estey J., for a unanimous Court, held that the mistaken calculation had no impact on the creation of Contract A. The plaintiff bidder had argued that since the bid was a product of a mistaken calculation, it was incapable of acceptance and accordingly could not form the basis for a construction contract, Contract B. In turn, therefore, or so it was argued, the bid could not be subject to the terms of Contract A. In response, Estey J. reasoned as follows: "The fallacy in this argument is twofold. Firstly, there was no mistake in the sense that the contractor did not intend to submit the tender as in form and substance it was. Secondly, there is no principle in law under which the tender was rendered incapable of acceptance by the appellant."[36] For Estey J., then, there was simply no mistake as to the terms of Contract A and no basis for holding that Contract A failed for a lack of *consensus ad idem*.

---

34   *Ibid.*
35   See Chapter 2, section B(1)(c).
36   Above note 25 at 275 (D.L.R.).

Estey J. appeared to envisage only two means of escape from the vice-grip of Contract A. First, he conceded that a different result might be appropriate, where, as in the *McMaster University* case, the mistake in the bid was apparent on the face of the document. Estey J. did not explain the technical means by which formation of Contract A would be precluded in such circumstances. Presumably, however, such a bid does not constitute a successful acceptance of the offer of Contract A contained in the invitation to tenders.[37] A second escape route, tentatively envisaged by Estey J., was that there might be a form of tender "so lacking as not to amount in law to a tender in the sense of the terms and conditions established in the call for tenders."[38] Such a tender, he suggested could not be "snapped up" by the owner and, accordingly, "would not operate to trigger the birth of contract A."[39] As *Ron Engineering* itself demonstrates, however, the mere fact that the bid price is based on a major miscalculation of price does not necessarily constitute a basis for preventing the formation of Contract A.

In *Ron Engineering*, the actual decision dealt with the irrecoverability of the bid deposit and the Court abstained from offering a view as to whether or not the mistaken calculation could have the effect of preventing the formation of Contract B. In the later decision of the Alberta Court of Appeal in *Calgary v. Northern Construction Co.*,[40] however, it was held that this question is, in a sense, immaterial. Again, the case involved a bid price based on a mistaken calculation. Upon discovery of the error after the opening of the bids, the bidder notified the issuer of the problem. Nonetheless, the issuer subsequently purported to accept the bid, which was the lowest bid. Upon the bidder's refusal to proceed with Contract B, the issuer brought an action for damages for breach of contract. The Court of Appeal held that it was unnecessary to decide whether or not the ultimate construction contract, Contract B, could be successfully created, notwithstanding the error. The bidder had made a commitment in Contract A to enter into Contract B. Accordingly, when it refused to assent to Contract B, it committed a breach of this provision of Contract A and exposed itself to a damages claim. The damages were to be calculated on the basis of the difference between the bid price and the price that the issuer was required to pay to the alternate bidder who eventually agreed to enter Contract B.

---

37   See, for example, *Ottawa (City) Non-Profit Housing Corp. v. Canvar Construction (1991) Inc.* (2000), 13 O.A.C. 116 (C.A.).

38   Above note 25 at 277 (D.L.R.).

39   *Ibid.*

40   Above note 2.

In summary, then, with the advent of the *Ron Engineering* doctrine, the doctrine of unilateral mistake as to terms appears to be irrelevant in the context of mistaken bids unless the error is either a palpable one on the face of the document or the bid is so badly botched as not to constitute a tender in the requisite sense. A bidder's mistake relating to the calculation of the bid price has no impact in relieving the bidder from Contract A or in relieving the bidder from liability under Contract A for refusal to enter into Contract B. If, however, the mistake in calculation does not constitute a mistake as to a *term* in the requisite sense, it must be a mistake with respect to an assumption underlying or motivating the bidder's decision to enter Contract A on the terms and conditions set out in the bid. On this view, the mistaken bid is properly characterized as a unilateral mistake as to an *assumption* underlying the formation of Contract A and it may be considered whether relief should be made available, in any circumstance, on the grounds that a unilateral mistake in assumption, at least a very severe one, ought to provide a basis for rescission of Contract A. This solution was proposed in the concurring judgment of Kerans J.A. in the *Northern Construction* case and, as we shall see,[41] it does reflect the treatment accorded this issue in the American law of contractual mistake. This is a point to which we will return in the context of a discussion of mistaken assumptions doctrine.

5) Mistake as to the Identity of the Other Contracting Party

A contract entered into by a party who is mistaken with respect to the identity of the other contracting party may fail for lack of a *consensus ad idem*. If so, the agreement will be void at common law. In the typical case, A is induced fraudulently by B to enter into a contract with B on the understanding that B is someone other than B. For example, A may sell goods to B under such false pretences. B's cheque for the price then proves to be worthless. Such an agreement is, of course, vulnerable to rescission on the ground of B's misrepresentation.[42] A's remedies against B, however, may prove to be ineffective. Accordingly, if, prior to rescission, B has resold the goods to C, A will wish to consider whether a remedy against C is available. If C purchased the goods from B in good faith in the sense of being unaware of the circumstances of B's fraud, it will be material to determine whether the transaction between A and B is not merely voidable for rescission but, rather, void at common law

41   See below this Chapter, section C(5).
42   For discussion of misrepresentation, see Chapter 10.

because of the failure of *consensus ad idem*. If the transaction is merely voidable for misrepresentation, legal title to the goods will have passed from A to B under the initial transaction and B will therefore be able to pass good title to C prior to rescission. Under equitable doctrine, A's right to rescind for misrepresentation is lost once the goods have been purchased in good faith by C. If the initial transaction is void for mistake, however, no property will pass to B or C and C will be liable in a conversion claim to A for the value of the goods.

Application of the common law doctrine rendering contracts void for mistakes in identity thus typically arises in the context of contests between two innocent parties, A, who unsuspectingly sold the goods to B and C, who purchased the goods in good faith from B. The question of which of the two innocent parties must suffer for the loss occasioned by B, the "rogue," will be determined by finding that the transaction between A and B is either void at law, in which case A prevails, or merely voidable in equity, in which case, prior to rescission, C prevails. As we shall see, the question as to which of these two parties should generally suffer the loss has proven controversial.

The first two of the leading cases on this point arose in the context of transactions entered into by correspondence. The other leading cases deal with situations in which A and B have dealt with each other on a face-to-face basis. In the first, *Cundy v. Lindsay*,[43] a rogue named Blenkarn ordered by letter a substantial quantity of handkerchiefs from the plaintiff Lindsay, a linen manufacturer. The order was written in such fashion as to create the impression in Lindsay that the order was being placed by one Blenkiron & Co., a highly respected firm known to Lindsay and carrying on business at an address similar to Blenkarn's. Lindsay accepted and filled the order, believing it had been placed by Blenkiron & Co. Blenkarn's fraud, achieved in part by a deceptive signature, was intentional. Having received delivery of the handkerchiefs from Lindsay, Blenkarn sold them to the defendant Cundy who was unaware of the fraud practised by Blenkarn. Blenkarn failed to make payment and Lindsay brought a successful conversion claim against Cundy for the value of goods obtained by Cundy from Blenkarn. The House of Lords held that no contract had been made by Lindsay with Blenkarn. Lindsay had intended to deal with Blenkiron & Co. and knew nothing of Blenkarn. Lord Cairns M.R. observed that in such circumstances "there was no consensus of mind which could lead to any agreement or any contract whatever."[44] Accordingly, title remained in the hands of

---

43   (1878), 3 App. Cas. 459.
44   *Ibid.* at 465.

Lindsay and Cundy was therefore liable to Lindsay for the value of the linen.

The decision in *Cundy v. Lindsay* may be contrasted with the decision of the Court of Appeal in the later case of *King's Norton Metal Co. Ltd. v. Edridge, Merrett & Co. Limited.*[45] In this case, the rogue, Wallis, did not purport to be another existing entity but, rather, created a fictional persona for himself. Wallis set himself up in business as "Hallam and Co." and created stationery for Hallam and Co. of an impressive nature, falsely identifying a number of locations at which Hallam and Co. purported to carry on business and graced with a pictorial representation of a large factory adorned with several chimneys. When Wallis sought a quote for the supply of brass rivet wire from the plaintiff metal manufacturers, the plaintiffs were no doubt suitably impressed. The plaintiff quoted a price, Wallis placed an order and, upon receipt of the goods, sold them in turn to the defendant metal merchants. The defendant was unaware of the fraud practised on the plaintiffs by Wallis. The cheque from Hallam and Co. to the plaintiffs proved worthless. The plaintiffs thereupon sued the defendant in conversion for the value of the rivet wire. For obvious reasons, the plaintiff relied on *Cundy v. Lindsay*. The Court of Appeal rejected the claim, however, on the basis that unlike *Cundy v. Lindsay*, there was here only one entity, Wallis, albeit one trading under an *alias* and, accordingly, that the contracts had been entered into with that individual. For *Cundy v. Lindsay* to apply, it was necessary to establish that the plaintiff believed itself to be dealing with an actual and existing entity, whom the rogue purported to be. In *King's Norton*, the plaintiff was clearly contracting with the writer of the letters, albeit under the false belief that the writer was a substantial business rather than a rogue. This distinction between the two cases has often been subsequently explained as resting on the distinction between mistakes as to identity and mistakes as to attributes. Lindsay thought he was dealing with an existing and known person other than Blenkarn. The plaintiff in *King's Norton* knew that it was dealing with the writer of the letters but merely thought the writer had more attractive attributes than proved to be the case. The distinction between identity and attributes may be thought to capture a genuine distinction between the facts of the two cases. It is not at all clear, however, that the distinction offers a convincing reason for their differing results.

The distinction between mistakes as to identity and mistakes as to attributes proved to be of more uncertain application in the context of face-to-face dealings between the parties. The difficulty is illustrated

45   (1897), 14 T.L.R. 98 (C.A.).

by two cases that are famously difficult to distinguish. In *Phillips v. Brooks*,[46] the rogue, North, entered the plaintiff's jewellery shop and selected pearls and a ring for purchase. He then produced a chequebook and wrote out a cheque for the purchase price stating, "You see who I am, I am Sir George Bullough," and giving an address on St. James' Square. The plaintiff was aware of the existence of such a person and, upon checking in a directory, confirmed that Sir George lived at that address. The plaintiff invited North to take the items with him but North protested and suggested that, pending clearing of the cheque, he would take only the ring. North subsequently pledged the ring to the defendant who, in good faith, advanced moneys to him in return. When North's cheque was dishonoured, the plaintiff jeweller sought his remedy in conversion against the defendant. The plaintiff relied on *Cundy v. Lindsay*. The trial judge dismissed the claim, however, on the basis that, in his view, "the seller intended to contract with the person present, and there was no error as to the person with whom he contracted, although the plaintiff would not have made the contract if there had not been a fraudulent misrepresentation."[47] Accordingly, the transaction was merely voidable in equity and the defendant, as *bona fide* purchaser, acquired title to the ring. Inasmuch as the plaintiff was aware of the existence of Sir George Bullough and thought he was dealing with him, the facts in *Phillips v. Brooks* appear to be materially similar to those of *Cundy v. Lindsay*. Thus, the rejection of its application in *Phillips* may be taken to suggest that *Cundy v. Lindsay* will rarely apply in the context of face-to-face dealings. On the very similar facts of the later decision in *Ingram v. Little*,[48] however, the doctrine of *Cundy v. Lindsay* was applied.

In *Ingram v. Little*, the plaintiffs were three joint owners of a car who had advertised it for sale. Approached by a rogue who offered to purchase the car, the plaintiffs negotiated a price. When the rogue produced his chequebook, the plaintiffs advised him that they were prepared to sell only for cash. Thereupon, he falsely represented himself to be one P.G.M. Hutchinson of Stanstead House in Caterham and indicated that he had substantial business interests. One of the plaintiffs authenticated the fact that a person of that name and address was listed in the telephone directory and the deal was concluded. Before the fraud was uncovered, the car had been sold to a car dealer who was unaware of the fraud. The cheque proved worthless and the plaintiffs sued

---

46   [1919] 2 K.B. 243.
47   *Ibid.* at 248–49.
48   [1961] 1 Q.B. 31 (C.A.).

the defendant dealer in conversion for the value of the car. Although the facts appear virtually indistinguishable from *Phillips v. Brooks*, the plaintiffs in *Ingram* succeeded.

The court held that the offer to sell the car was intended for Hutchinson, that the rogue knew this and that, accordingly, the rogue could not accept the offer. The contract was void and title did not pass either to the rogue or the defendant. The difficulty in distinguishing *Phillips v. Brooks* was conceded by Sellers L.J. who suggested that it might be distinguished on its facts as a case in which the jeweller intended to deal with North.[49] Pearce L.J. accepted the view that *Phillips* might be distinguished as a case in which the contract had been entered into once the price had been agreed and prior to the discussion concerning the cheque.[50] In dissent, Devlin L.J. would have held that *Phillips v. Brooks* was dispositive and that the decision was supportable on the basis of the opposition that where parties are addressing each other in person, rather than by correspondence, it is presumed that "a person is intending to contract with the person to whom he is actually addressing the words of contract."[51]

After *Ingram v. Little*, then, the law of mistaken identity in face-to-face dealings appeared to be in a rather unsatisfactory state. The question of whether a *bona fide* purchaser of goods in these circumstances would be protected rested on the distinction between void and voidable contracts. That distinction, in turn, appeared to rest on a subtle line to be drawn between the facts of *Phillips v. Brooks*, where the plaintiff, in theory, may not have intended to make the offer exclusively to Sir George Bullough and *Ingram v. Little* where, it was held, the offer could be accepted only by P.G.M. Hutchinson. An alternative explanation of the seemingly inconsistent results on the basis of a distinction between mistakes of identity and mistakes as to attributes appears to be similarly unilluminating. The facts of both cases might be characterized as mistakes concerning the identity of the other contracting party or, alternatively, as mistakes concerning the attribute of creditworthiness of the other contracting party. The distinction between the cases was not only difficult to discern, however, it appeared unrelated to the merits of the defendant's position in such cases. Arguably, at least, if the defendant's interests were worthy of protection in *Phillips v. Brooks*, it is difficult to see why they were not similarly worthy of protection in *Ingram v. Little*.

---

49   *Ibid.* at 51.
50   *Ibid.* at 60.
51   *Ibid.* at 66.

The English Court of Appeal returned to these issues in the later case of *Lewis v. Averay*[52] and offered a new approach to the problem. The court favoured a solution that would give a preference to the rights of the *bona fide* purchaser by restricting the range of situations in which a mistake as to identity would render the contract void at common law, thus leaving the seller to pursue such remedies as might be available against the rogue for misrepresentation. The rationale for giving preference to the interests of the good-faith purchaser was placed explicitly by Lord Denning M.R. on the basis that "it was the seller who let the rogue have the goods and thus enabled him to commit the fraud."[53] Thus, as between the seller and a purchaser who knew nothing of what passed between the seller and the rogue, the purchaser's interests should be preferred. In Lord Denning's view, therefore, when "two parties have come to a contract — or rather what appears, on the face of it, to be a contract — the fact that one party is mistaken as to the identity of the other does not mean that there is no contract, or that the contract is a nullity and void from the beginning. It only means that the contract is voidable, that is, liable to be set aside at the instance of the mistaken person, so long as he does so before third parties have in good faith acquired rights under it."[54] All members of the court were critical of the reasoning in *Ingram v. Little*. Lord Denning M.R., in particular, disparaged the purported distinction between *Phillips v. Brooks* as a case where the contract had been entered into prior to the discussion of the cheque and *Ingram v. Little* as a case where formation had not taken place before the fraudulent misrepresentation was made. The two cases were, in his view, simply indistinguishable. Moreover, the distinction between mistakes as to identity and mistakes as to attributes was "a distinction without a difference."[55] As he explained, "a man's very name is one of his attributes. It is also a key to his identity. If then, he gives a false name, is it a mistake as to his identity? or a mistake as to his attributes? These fine distinctions do no good to the law."[56] The court appears to have been unanimously of the view that when a seller is dealing with a person who is physically present, the fact that the person has misrepresented his or her identity will not prevent formation of the contract though it may render the contract voidable in equity. The facts in *Lewis v. Averay* were very similar to those of *Phillips v.*

---

52   [1972] 1 Q.B. 198 (C.A.).
53   *Ibid.* at 207.
54   *Ibid.*
55   *Ibid.* at 206.
56   *Ibid.*

Brooks and *Ingram v. Little.* In *Lewis,* the rogue presented himself to the plaintiff seller as Richard Greene, the then well-known film actor, producing a special film studio admission pass as proof of identity. The plaintiff was persuaded by this ruse, turned over possession of his car to the rogue and accepted payment by cheque. Subsequently, the rogue sold the car to the defendant, a *bona fide* purchaser. When the rogue's cheque proved worthless, the plaintiff sought recovery of the car or its value from the defendant. The court held that the plaintiff had entered into an agreement with the rogue which, though vulnerable to rescission on equitable grounds, was not void at common law. Accordingly, the claim failed.

The approach adopted by the Court of Appeal in *Lewis v. Averay* has also been advocated by various law reform bodies and has found support both in the American case law[57] and in the Uniform Commercial Code.[58] Both the Ontario Law Reform Commission[59] and the English Law Reform Committee[60] have recommended that the distinction between void and voidable title should be abolished in the present context and that in all cases the *bona fide* purchaser should obtain a good title unless the owner avoided the transaction before resale of the goods by the rogue. Such reforms would effect a broader change than that accomplished in *Lewis v. Averay.* The reasoning in *Lewis v. Averay* appears to be confined to situations where the parties are dealing on a face-to-face basis. Thus, in cases where the parties are dealing with each other through correspondence, the reasoning in *Cundy v. Lindsay* may still be applicable, thereby rendering the transaction void in a case where the seller acted in the belief that the purchaser was someone other than the person actually writing the letters upon which the seller relied. Arguably, then, extension of the *Lewis v. Averay* principle to agreements entered into by correspondence may require legislative reform. In the Canadian context, however, where legislation on such a matter across the provinces is very unlikely, a preferable solution would be judicial extension of the *Lewis v. Averay* principle to such agreements.

---

57   American Law Institute, *Restatement of Contracts 2d* (St. Paul: American Law Institute, 1981) § 153, Comm. g; *Silver Dollar City v. Kitzmiller Construction Co.,* 931 S.W.2d 909 (Mo. App. 1996); *Potucek v. Cordeleria Lourdes,* 310 F.2d 527 (10th Cir. 1962). Compare with G. Williams, "Mistake as to a Party in the Law of Contract" (1945) 23 Can. Bar Rev. 271 at 380.

58   Art. 2-403(1)(a).

59   Ontario Law Reform Commission, *Report on Sale of Goods,* vol. 1 (Toronto: Ministry of the Attorney General, 1979) at 106.

60   Law Reform Committee, *Twelfth Report (Transfer of Title to Chattels),* Cmnd 2958 (London: HMSO, 1996) at para. 15.

If legislation to deal with the point remains necessary, however, recent English experience suggests that the provisions need to be very carefully drawn. The English *Hire Purchase Act, 1964*[61] includes a provision designed to protect good-faith purchasers of motor vehicles that are subject to hire-purchase agreements entered into on the basis of mistakes in identity. In the provision, however, the rogue who has acquired the car under a hire-purchase agreement in such circumstances is referred to as the "debtor." In *Shogun Finance Ltd. v. Hudson*,[62] the English appellate courts were called upon to decide whether or not this statutory protection of good-faith purchasers extended to a situation where the finance company and the rogue had arguably not had direct dealings but had entered into the hire-purchase agreement through the exchange of written documents. The rogue had acquired the vehicle in question from a car dealer who had, in turn, arranged for hire-purchase finance with the plaintiff on the rogue's behalf. The rogue had falsely identified himself to the dealer as a Mr. Patel of a certain address. The dealer filled in this information on the application for hire-purchase financing. The finance company performed a credit check on Mr. Patel and approved the application. Subsequently, the rogue sold the car to a good-faith purchaser, Hudson, and then vanished without a trace. The finance company brought a claim against Hudson to assert its rights as owner of the car.

In the Court of Appeal,[63] a majority, applying *Cundy v. Lindsay*, held that since there were no face-to-face dealings and since the identity of the rogue was of vital importance to the finance company, the hire-purchase contract entered into between the company and the rogue was void. Accordingly, the rogue hirer did not constitute a "debtor" within the statutory provision and the protection afforded by the legislation to *bona fide* purchasers in such circumstances was therefore unavailing.[64] By this interpretation of the statute, its application appears to have been undermined in the perhaps very typical fact situation in which there are no direct face-to-face dealings between the finance company and the consumer.

---

61   (U.K.) 1964, c. 53, s. 27, as amended.
62   [2002] 4 All E.R. 572 (C.A.), aff'd [2003] UKHL 62, [2004] 1 A.C. 919, [2004] 1 All E.R. 215.
63   *Ibid.* (C.A.).
64   In dissent, Sedley L.J. adverted to the policy considerations favouring a broader application of the *Lewis v. Averay* principle but would have granted relief on the basis that since the dealer had acted on the rogue's behalf in arranging the hire-purchase agreement, the face-to-face principle could be said to apply and the purchaser was therefore protected by the provision.

On further appeal to the House of Lords,[65] the decision of the majority of the Court of Appeal was upheld on the basis of a more searching analysis of the coherence, or lack of same, of the law of mistaken identity. Noting the apparent conflict between *Ingram v. Little* and *Lewis v. Averay*, their Lordships considered whether preference should be accorded to one or the other. As well, the possibility of extending the modern approach taken in *Lewis v. Averay* to the context of agreements entered into by correspondence was considered. In the event, both the traditional approach to agreements by correspondence manifest in *Cundy v. Lindsay* and the modern approach to face-to-face dealings manifest in *Lewis v. Averay* were left undisturbed. A majority of three who favoured dismissing the appeal consisted of Lords Hobhouse, Phillips and Walker, each of whom offered slightly different reasons for doing so. Of the three, only Lord Hobhouse adopted the view that the approach taken by Lord Denning in *Lewis v. Averay* was incorrect.[66] The finance company, in his view, was only willing to deal with an identified party, Mr. Patel. Accordingly, there was no *consensus ad idem*. Lord Hobhouse appeared to accept, then, that a mistake of identity, as such, precludes formation of an agreement both in the context of agreements by correspondence and in face-to-face dealings. The other two members of the majority, however, Lords Phillips and Walker, generally favoured the approach adopted in *Lewis v. Averay* to face-to-face transactions of applying a strong presumption in favour of finding that an agreement, albeit a voidable one, was entered into with the physical person with whom one was dealing. Such an approach was not to be extended, in their view, to agreements by correspondence, however, where the form of the written agreement itself governs. The finance company had approved an agreement with Patel. That agreement was a nullity. In dissent, Lords Nicholls and Millett not only favoured the approach in *Lewis v. Averay*, they favoured its extension to agreements by correspondence. As Lord Nicholls explained, in facing the difficult choice of which of the two innocent parties to favour, the finance company or the third-party purchaser, "the loss is more appropriately borne by the person who takes the risks inherent in parting with his goods without receiving payment."[67] In his view, therefore, these cases should be resolved on the basis that a person "is presumed to intend to contract with the person with whom he is actually dealing, *whatever the mode*

---

65   Above note 62 (H.L.).

66   *Ibid.* (H.L.) at para. 47, though no detailed reasons for this conclusion are set forth.

67   *Ibid.* at para. 35.

518 THE LAW OF CONTRACTS

of communication."[68] On this view, *Cundy v. Lindsay* would be overruled and *Ingram v. Little,* presumably, would be considered to be wrongly decided.[69] Although Lords Nicholls and Millett did not attract majority support in this case, their views may well receive a more favourable reception by Canadian courts minded to bring greater coherence to the law of mistaken identity than it enjoys at the present time.

6) *Non Est Factum*: Mistakenly Signed Documents

The doctrine of *non est factum* holds that a very particular kind of fraudulent inducement that leads a party to sign a written document, including an agreement, is void at common law on the basis that the person affixing the signature has not genuinely agreed to the document. Where the signature has been induced by a fraudulent representation as to the nature of the document, the signatory may defend an action brought to enforce any undertaking given in the document on the basis that the signing was not a consensual act. The defendant can plead *non est factum*, that is, that the signature was not his act or, as is sometimes said in the cases, his mind did not go with the signature.[70] It is as if the document were a forgery. As we have seen, a fraudulent misrepresentation that induces an agreement normally gives rise to voidability of the agreement.[71] The effect of *non est factum*, however, is to render the document or agreement void at common law. Hence the doctrine of *non est factum*, like the doctrine of mistake as to the identity of the other contracting party[72] creates risks for third parties. Thus, the leading cases typically involve situations in which A, on the basis of a fraudulent inducement of this kind, signs a document that has the effect of transferring property to B and B then further transfers the property to C, an innocent third-party purchaser for value who has no notice of the underlying defect in the first transfer. Because the initial transfer is void at common law, no property passes to B or to C and C is vulnerable to a claim by A, for example, in trespass or conversion. If the initial transaction was merely voidable for fraudulent misrepresentation, A would be entitled to rescind the transaction in the typical case, but property could transfer to B and, in turn, to C at any point in time prior to the actual rescission of the agreement. In this context,

---

68   *Ibid.* at para. 36 (emphasis added).
69   *Ibid.* at para. 87, Lord Millett.
70   *Non est factum* may be translated as "It is not his deed."
71   See Chapter 10.
72   See this Chapter, section B(5).

as in others, there has been some restriction of the scope of this common law doctrine in recent years with the apparent object of affording greater protection to such third parties.

The doctrine of *non est factum* has a lengthy history. In *Thoroughgood's Case*,[73] decided in 1582, the doctrine was applied to a release of all claims executed by a landlord under seal at the urging of the tenant, one William Chicken. Chicken advised the landlord falsely that the deed would have the effect only of releasing the landlord's claim to arrears of rent. In fact, the deed had the effect of releasing to Chicken, the landlord's entire claim to the land. The landlord was illiterate but, when advised by a bystander that the deed was as described by Chicken, the landlord affixed his seal. Chicken subsequently sold the land to an innocent third party. The landlord successfully pleaded *non est factum* and neither Chicken nor the third party acquired his interest in the land. Although, as this case illustrates, the doctrine originally applied to instruments under seal and was available only to the illiterate, the doctrine was extended, over time, to protect even literate people who had been defrauded in a similar manner and to cover written documents not executed under seal, including written agreements.

Three aspects of the doctrine of *non est factum* have proven to be contentious over the years. First, the extent to which the doctrine might be available to a person who is literate remains unclear. Second, the role of negligence on the part of the signer has, until recently, been a point of some difficulty. Third, traditional English doctrine has identified as material mistakes those relating to the class or character of the document rather than to its contents. Although this distinction has been abolished for purposes of English law, its status in Canadian law remains obscure. These issues are interrelated as, in each case, these doctrines offer a means for limiting the scope of the doctrine. The connection between the first two points is particularly intimate. To the extent that one refuses to recognize the signatory's negligence as relevant, one might be tempted to restrict the doctrine to signatories suffering from severe vulnerability with a resulting need for special protection. However, if negligence on the part of the signatory precludes application of the doctrine, restriction of the defence to unusually vulnerable persons may appear less necessary or desirable. In resolving these difficulties, it is well accepted that the policy considerations underlying the doctrine are those identified by Lord Wilberforce in the leading decision in *Saunders v. Anglia Building Society*[74] in the following terms: "[the law] ... has two

---

73   (1582), 2 Co. Rep. 9a.
74   [1971] A.C. 1004 (H.L.).

520 THE LAW OF CONTRACTS

conflicting objectives: relief to a signer whose consent is genuinely lacking … protection to innocent third parties who have acted upon an apparently regular and properly executed document. Because each of these factors may involve questions of degree or shading, any rule of law must represent a compromise and must allow to the courts some flexibility in application."[75] In attempting to achieve an appropriate balance between these objectives, the significance to be attributed to carelessness on the part of the signer of the document appears critical.

In the leading nineteenth-century English case indicating the modern scope of the doctrine, *Foster v. Mackinnon*,[76] it was suggested that negligence should preclude the application of the doctrine in a contest between the signer and an innocent third party.[77] The defendant had endorsed a bill of exchange on the basis of an understanding, fraudulently induced by a third party, Callow, that he was signing a guarantee of Callow's debt. An innocent endorsee claimed to enforce the endorsement against the defendant. Byles J. observed as follows:

> It seems plain, on principle and on authority, that, if a blind man, or a man who cannot read, or who for some reason (not implying negligence) forbears to read, has a written contract falsely read over to him, the reader misreading to such a degree that the written contract is of a nature altogether different from the contract pretended to be read from the paper which the blind or illiterate man afterwards signs; then, at least if there be no negligence, the signature so obtained is of no force. And it is invalid not merely on the ground of fraud, where fraud exists, but on the ground that the mind of the signer did not accompany the signature; in other words that he never intended to sign, and therefore in contemplation of law never did sign, the contract to which his name is appended.[78]

The court concluded that the defendant had "never intended to endorse a bill of exchange at all, but to sign a contract of an entirely different nature."[79] Although it is true that Byles J. emphasized the importance of limiting the application of *non est factum* in the context of negotiable instruments because they "are not only assignable, but they form part

---

75 *Ibid.* at 1023–24, quoted with approval by Estey J. in *Marvco Color Research Ltd. v. Harris*, [1982] 2 S.C.R. 774 at 787, 141 D.L.R. (3d) 577 at 587.

76 (1869), L.R. 4 C.P. 704.

77 In a contest between the signer and the fraudulent party, negligence of the signer is surely irrelevant.

78 Above note 76.

79 *Ibid.* at 712.

of the currency of the country,"[80] the passage set out above indicates that it was the court's view that negligence on the part of the signer would, as a general matter, preclude reliance on *non est factum*. Nonetheless, in the later case of *Carlisle & Cumberland Banking Co. v. Bragg*[81] it was held that the correct interpretation of English law was that the negligence of the signer precluded the availability of *non est factum* only in the case of the signing of a negotiable instrument. This development was considered by many to be an unfortunate one in the sense that it would appear that in striking the balance between the interests of the person who signed the instrument and the third party who has suffered loss because of it, carelessness on the part of the signer should indeed be relevant. Nonetheless, English law remained in this unsatisfactory state until the decision of the House of Lords in *Saunders*[82] in 1971.

In 1956, the Supreme Court of Canada applied the then-current English doctrine in *Prudential Trust Co. Ltd. v. Cugnet*,[83] a case in which a retired farmer executed an assignment and transfer of a half-interest in the petroleum and natural gas in the lands in question to an oil company upon the fraudulent misrepresentation of the company's agent that he was signing a document granting merely an option on a ninety-nine-year lease on the petroleum and natural gas rights on those lands. The rights were subsequently resold to an innocent third-party purchaser. The farmer, Cugnet, apparently reluctant to interrupt a card game in which he was then engaged, did not read the document he signed. In a contest between Cugnet and the third party, the Supreme Court held that even if Cugnet had acted carelessly, the negligence of a signer was simply irrelevant to a pleading of *non est factum*. The irrelevance of negligence was defended by Locke J. on the basis that carelessness would be relevant only if it could be established that a duty of care in tort to sign the document carefully was owed to the public at large. In his view, no such duty could be established.[84] Cugnet therefore succeeded in a trespass claim against the third party. Cartwright J., in dissent, anticipated future developments in English law. In his view, Cugnet's conduct was clearly careless and ought to provide a basis for precluding his reliance on the *non est factum* doctrine at the expense of the third party. In order to reach such a conclusion, it was not necessary to be able to hold that Cugnet owed a duty in negligence to

---

80   *Ibid.*
81   [1911] 1 K.B. 489 (C.A.).
82   Above note 74.
83   [1956] S.C.R. 914.
84   *Ibid.* at 929.

the public at large. Rather, Cugnet's carelessness gave rise to an estoppel preventing Cugnet from denying the validity of the document as against a purchaser for value in good faith. Cugnet was a literate man with experience in buying and selling properties. In the circumstances, his failure to read the document amounted to such carelessness as to preclude reliance on the *non est factum* doctrine.

A similar view was taken by the House of Lords in the *Saunders* case.[85] Again, in this case, the contest was between the signer of the document and an innocent third party. The plaintiff was an elderly woman, Mrs. Gallie, who had been victimized by a trusted nephew, one Parkin. Gallie had previously advised Parkin that she would be leaving her house to him in her will. Parkin then asked her to transfer the property to him immediately so that he could borrow money on the security of the property. In return, it was understood that Mrs. Gallie could remain in the house for the rest of her life. In the event, Parkin presented Gallie with a deed of conveyance to a friend, one Lee, representing to Gallie that the document was a deed of gift to himself. Gallie signed the document and, as her glasses were broken at the time, did not attempt to read it. Indeed, the evidence suggested that in any event she was unlikely to understand the legal significance of the document. In due course, the property was mortgaged to an innocent third party by Lee and in the ultimate contest between Gallie and the third party, an allegation of negligence was made by the third party against Gallie. The House of Lords analyzed the history of English jurisprudence on the relevance of negligence to the *non est factum* plea and held that in a contest between the signer of the document and an innocent third party, negligence on the part of the signer should preclude reliance on the doctrine. Negligence, in this context, did not require the recognition of a tort duty owed to the public at large. The concept simply refers to carelessness on the part of the signer. Moreover, in contrast to the position taken by Cartwright J. in the *Cugnet* case, it was not correct to suggest that negligence operates in this context by way of estoppel. In the normal case, estoppel arises from misstatements rather than negligence. More importantly, to rest the doctrine on grounds of estoppel would place the burden of proof on the third party, the person who purports to have relied on the estoppel. As Lord Pearson observed, this places the burden of proof on the wrong party. The burden should be placed on the signer who is aware of the lack of knowledge and intention with which the document is signed and who should, therefore, have the burden of establishing that it was signed without negligence on his

---

85   Above note 74.

or her part.[86] In the particular circumstances, however, it was held that Mrs. Gallie's conduct did not amount to carelessness. Her plea of *non est factum* failed, however, on the ground that her mistake was not of a sufficiently fundamental nature, a matter to which we will shortly return.

The Supreme Court of Canada had an opportunity to reconsider the negligence point in 1982 in *Marvco Color Research Ltd. v. Harris*[87] and on this occasion, the Court followed the lead of the House of Lords in *Saunders* and confirmed the position taken by Cartwright J. in dissent in the *Cugnet* case. On its facts, *Marvco* was again a case in which documents transferring an interest in land were signed without being read. The signers were a married couple, the Harrises, who had previously mortgaged their home to the Bank of Montreal in order to assist the co-habitant of their daughter to acquire an interest in a business. The further document signed by them at his urging was represented to be a new version of the first mortgage correcting the date in that mortgage. Thus assured, both husband and wife signed the new document that was, in fact, a further mortgage of the home for a rather more substantial sum to another mortgagee. Both husband and wife were literate, English-speaking and familiar with mortgages, having executed mortgages on at least three prior occasions. Both the trial judge and the provincial appellate court held that their conduct in signing the second mortgage was careless, a finding that was not disturbed on further appeal to the Supreme Court of Canada. Estey J., on behalf of the Court, emphasized that negligence in this context connotes mere "carelessness" rather than negligence in the sense of tortious liability.[88]

In *Marvco*, the Supreme Court offered little guidance with respect to the kinds of circumstances that will ground a finding of carelessness beyond indicating "[t]he magnitude and extent of the carelessness, the circumstances which may have contributed to such carelessness, and all other circumstances [are to be] taken into account in each case."[89]

---

86   *Ibid.* at 1038.

87   Above note 75.

88   *Ibid.* at 785–86 (S.C.R.). Although Estey J. indicates that carelessness will give rise to an "estoppel," it is not clear that the Court had in mind estoppel *stricto sensu* with the result, as noted by Lord Pearson in the *Saunders* case, above note 74, that the burden of establishing the estoppel and the requisite state of mind of the signer would therefore be placed upon the innocent third party. The better view, surely, is that the doctrine developed in the *Marvco* case is like estoppel in the sense that it precludes denial of assent to the initial agreement but is unlike estoppel in that it places the burden of proof on the estopped party to prove that the requisite state of mind was present.

89   *Marvco Color Research Ltd. v. Harris, ibid.* at 787 (S.C.R.).

As the facts of *Marvco* illustrate, however, the most obvious basis for a finding of carelessness arises in situations in which literate parties decline to read documents they are signing.[90] Other cases,[91] including *Saunders*,[92] demonstrate that where the literate signer is unlikely, however, to be able to understand the legal significance of the document to be signed, carelessness will not be established. Other instances of carelessness could include failure to make reasonable inquiries as to the nature of the document being signed.[93] More generally, as Lord Reid observed in *Saunders*,[94] parties, whatever their level of sophistication, must take "such precautions as they reasonably can."

The wisdom of extending the protection of the *non est factum* doctrine beyond the initial cases of blind and illiterate signers, or people in equivalent circumstances such as those signing documents in a foreign language, has occasionally been questioned.[95] Nonetheless, it appears to be well established that the doctrine can apply to a signer who is both literate and reasonably sophisticated. Thus, in *Saunders*, Lord Reid observed:

> I do not say that the remedy can never be available to a man of full capacity. But that could only be in very exceptional circumstances: certainly not where his reason for not scrutinising the document before signing it was that he was too busy or too lazy. In general, I do not think that he can be heard to say that he signed it in reliance on someone he trusted. But, particularly when he was led to believe that the document which he signed was not one which affected his legal rights, there may be cases where this plea can properly be applied in favour of a man of full capacity.[96]

---

90   See *National Bank of Canada v. Taylor* (1986), 45 Alta. L.R. (2d) 301 (Q.B.).

91   See, for example, *National Bank of Canada v. Digest Reporting Service Limited*, [1985] 6 W.W.R. 481 (Man. C.A.).

92   Above note 74.

93   *Coss (Trustee of) v. Shuckett* (1990), 79 C.B.R. (N.S.) 149 (Man. C.A.); *Caisse Populaire de La Salle Credit Union Ltd. v. River Ridge Properties Ltd.* (1997), 115 Man. R. (2d) 115 (C.A.); *Canadian Imperial Bank of Commerce v. P.E.I. Mussel King Inc. and Vandenbrent* (1984), 49 Nfld. & P.E.I.R. 173 (P.E.I.S.C.); *Royal Bank of Canada v. Gill* (1986), 6 B.C.L.R. (2d) 359 (S.C.), aff'd [1988] 3 W.W.R. 441 (B.C.C.A.).

94   Above note 74 at 1016. Executing a document in blank is likely to be considered careless. See *United Dominions Trust Ltd. v. Western*, [1976] Q.B. 513 (C.A.).

95   See, for example, *Howatson v. Webb*, [1908] 1 Ch. 1 at 3–4 (C.A.), Farwell J., aff'g [1907] 1 Ch. 537. See also *Prudential Trust Co. Ltd. v. Cugnet*, above note 83 at 933–34, Cartwright J.

96   Above note 74 at 1016.

Further, in *Marvco*, the signing husband and wife were precluded from relying on the document by their carelessness rather than by the fact that they were literate and had had previous experience in the signing of mortgage documents.

Finally, the requisite nature of the signer's mistake must be considered. Prior to the decision in *Saunders*, English law had established that the mistake must relate to the character and class of the signed document rather than to its mere contents. As the cases illustrated, however, such a distinction is vulnerable to manipulation. Thus, in *Howatson v. Webb*,[97] the signer was invited to execute some deeds "transferring the Edmonton property." In fact, the signer was invited to sign and did sign a mortgage document containing a covenant on the part of the signer to repay a mortgage debt. On one view, a document that attracts a significant personal obligation of this kind might be thought to be in a different class from a mere transfer that would have exposed the signer to no liability. Nonetheless, the court held that both a deed of conveyance and a mortgage relate to a transfer of the property and, accordingly, the mistake in question related merely to the contents rather than to the class or character of the document. The correct application of this distinction was not perfectly obvious in the *Cugnet* case. The signer in that case believed that he was executing the grant of an option on a ninety-nine-year lease of oil and natural gas rights, whereas the document in fact included, as well, an outright transfer of an undivided half-interest in those rights. For the majority of the Supreme Court, this was a difference in the class or character of the document. For Cartwright J. in dissent, the differences between the documents as understood and as signed were not significant enough to engage the *non est factum* doctrine. Similarly, in *Saunders* itself, application of this distinction was problematic. Mrs. Gallie believed she was executing a deed of gift in favour of her nephew, whom she trusted to live up to an undertaking that she would be permitted to reside in her home for the rest of her natural life. In fact, she executed a deed of conveyance to his associate, Mr. Lee, who, in turn, sold the property on to a third party. On the one hand, the document both as understood and as signed was a deed of conveyance. On the other hand, from Mrs. Gallie's perspective, the transaction was quite importantly different from that which she understood herself to be signing. It was in *Saunders*, however, that the House of Lords abandoned the distinction between the class or character of documents and the mere contents. The critical question was said to be that the document as signed must be "fundamentally different" or

---

97   Above note 95.

"radically different" or "totally different" from the document as understood.[98] Unfortunately, it is not clear, however, that this adjustment to the doctrine has been accepted into Canadian law. In the *Marvco* case, the Supreme Court, having resolved the dispute on the basis of the carelessness of the signing parties, felt it unnecessary to consider this point. Nonetheless, the persuasiveness of the reasoning in the *Saunders* case, together with the scepticism concerning the distinction exhibited by Cartwright J. in dissent in *Cugnet*,[99] suggests that Canadian courts are likely to adopt this approach in due course.

C. MISTAKEN ASSUMPTIONS

1) Introduction

The law of "mistaken assumptions" enables courts to treat as unenforceable agreements that have been entered into on the basis of erroneous assumptions concerning the context of the agreement in question where enforcement of the agreement would inflict an injustice on one of the parties. In a mistaken assumptions case, the parties reach agreement on the terms of their contract but share an error with respect to some important contextual circumstance that has motivated one or both of the parties to enter the agreement. The parties might not appreciate, for example, that goods that are the subject matter of a sale had been destroyed by fire prior to the entering into of the agreement. In determining whether an agreement should be considered unenforceable by reason of the mistaken assumption that infects its creation, courts must engage in a delicate exercise of balancing the competing values of contractual stability and the provision of relief in cases of severe injustice.

Doctrines that have the effect of enabling the parties to escape from their liabilities under an agreement entered on the basis of a mistaken assumption developed at both common law and equity. As we shall see, the relationship between common law and equitable doctrines has been and, in England particularly, continues to be a source of controversy. After examining the development of common law and equitable doctrines concerning contracts entered into on the basis of a shared or "common" mistaken assumption, we will consider whether relief from a transaction might appropriately be awarded in a case of a "unilateral"

---

98   Above note 74 at 1039, Lord Pearson and 1017, Lord Reid.
99   Above note 83 at 931.

mistaken assumption where one of the parties suffers from such a mistake, but the other does not.

2) At Common Law

Much controversy surrounds the common law doctrine rendering contracts void on the basis that the agreement in question has been entered into by the parties on the basis of a common and mistaken assumption concerning a material fact. Nonetheless, it is clear that relief in this form is available in two classes of cases. The first, referred to as *res extincta*, holds agreements for the sale of goods void in circumstances where the parties are unaware that the goods had ceased to exist at the time of contracting. The most frequently cited illustration of this proposition is *Couturier v. Hastie*,[100] a case holding void a contract for the sale of a cargo of corn that, unbeknownst to the parties, had ceased to exist at the time of contracting. This common law doctrine was enshrined by Sir MacKenzie Chalmers[101] in the English sale of goods legislation.[102] Relief would not be available, however, if the seller had explicitly or implicitly warranted the existence of the goods.[103] The second category, cases of *res sua*, are those in which a purchaser later discovers that at the time of contracting he or she already owned the subject matter of the sale. Such agreements are also void at common law. Interestingly, the authority most frequently cited for this proposition is in fact a decision of a court of equity. In *Cooper v. Phibbs*,[104] a lease of a fishery was set aside on the ground that the lessee, at the time of entering the lease, was already entitled to an equitable life estate in the property. As we shall see, the precise significance to be attached to the equitable nature of this authority has been a matter of some controversy. Nonetheless, it appears to be well accepted that, in a case of *res sua*, the contract is void at common law.

Beyond these two categories, the scope of the common law doctrine has been and, indeed, remains rather unclear. Certainly, however, com-

100 (1856), 5 H.L.C. 673, 10 E.R. 1065.
101 M. Chalmers, *Sale of Goods Act, 1893*, 2d ed. (London: W. Clowes and Sons, 1894) at 17.
102 *Sale of Goods Act, 1893* (56 & 57 Vict., c. 71) s.6, a provision repeated in the sale of goods legislation in the common law provinces of Canada and in other Commonwealth jurisdictions. See, for example, *Sale of Goods Act*, R.S.O. 1990, c. 5.1, s. 7.
103 *McRae v. Commonwealth Disposals Commission* (1951), 84 C.L.R. 377 (Aust. H.C.).
104 (1867), L.R. 2 H.L. 149.

mon law courts have held agreements void in a range of circumstances beyond those of *res extincta* and *res sua*. The difficulty lies, however, in articulating the basis on which other types of circumstances will ground a holding that the agreement is void for mistake. The various versions of the requirements articulating the test for operative mistake may be characterized as being either "narrow" or "broad." Though the narrow versions of the test appear more restrictive or difficult to apply than the broader and seemingly more flexible versions of the test, it may well be that the precise nature of the test will not be dispositive of the outcomes in particular cases. The narrow conception of the common law doctrine is applicable only where, by way of extension of the doctrine of *res extincta*, it can be said that the "subject matter" of the agreement "ceases to exist" because of a mistake. In *Strickland v. Turner*,[105] for example, it was held that the purchase of an annuity where the annuitant was in fact already dead at the time of sale was void. This result can be explained on the basis that the subject matter of the agreement—an annuity on the life of a living person—had ceased to exist at the time of contracting. A similar explanation can be offered for the decision in *Scott v. Coulson*,[106] a case in which the sale of a life insurance policy on the life of one A.T. Death was held void when it was discovered that, by the time of contracting, Death had in fact died. The value of the policy was thus very different from what the parties had initially assumed. If one defines the subject matter of the agreement to be "a life insurance policy on the life of a living person," the agreement could be held void on the basis that that subject matter did not exist at the time of contract.[107] Similarly, in the much-taught American case of *Sherwood v. Walker*,[108] the sale of a cow, Rose 2d of Abalone, which, although assumed by the parties to be barren, was with calf at the time of contracting, could be held to be void on the basis that the subject matter of the agreement, a barren cow, did not exist at the time of entering the agreement. In reply, of course, it would be argued that the subject matter of the contract is a cow or, indeed, Rose 2d herself. As these decisions illustrate, the "non-existence of the subject matter" test is a highly manipulable one. One can artfully characterize the subject matter of the contract in such a way as to either deny relief or make it

---

105 (1852), 7 Ex. 208, 155 E.R. 919.

106 [1903] 2 Ch. 249 (C.A.).

107 Such an explanation of the result in *Scott v. Coulson* was offered by Greer L.J. in the Court of Appeal decision in the leading case of *Bell v. Lever Brothers Ltd.* (*sub nom. Lever Brothers Ltd. v. Bell*), above note 4 at 595 (K.B.).

108 33 N.W. 919 (Mich. S.C. 1887).

available. The test thus offers little guidance as to when the common law doctrine will apply.

Other judges tend to articulate a broader test in terms that stress the "basic" or "fundamental" nature of the mistake in question. Thus, in *Scott v. Coulson* itself, Vaughan Williams L.J. explained the result on the basis that "both parties entered into this contract on the basis of a common affirmative belief that the insured was alive; but as it turned out that this was a common mistake, the contract was one which cannot be enforced. This is so at law ..., if the basis which both parties recognize as the basis is not true."[109] Romer L.J. reasoned that the defendant "must be taken to have known that the basis on which the contract had been entered into, and the common belief on which both parties had acted, did not exist. That was a circumstance which went to the root of the matter, and rendered it improper to insist upon the completion of the contract."[110] Although Romer L.J.'s reference to the fact that the basis for the agreement did not exist shows traces of the non-existence of the subject-matter test, the emphasis placed on the mistake being required to be one with respect to a matter that forms the *basis* of the agreement appears somewhat broader than the subject-matter test.

A similar approach was taken by Blackburn J. in *Lord Kennedy v. Panama, New Zealand and Australian Royal Mail Co. (Ltd.)*,[111] a case involving a purchase of shares on the basis of a prospectus that falsely stated that the company had secured an attractive agreement with the government of New Zealand to provide mail services. Blackburn J. articulated the test for holding the agreement void for mistake in the following terms: "the difficulty in every case is to determine that the mistake or misapprehension is as to the substance of the whole consideration, going, as it were, to the root of the matter, or only to some point, even though a material point, an error as to which does not effect the substance of the whole consideration."[112] Applying this test to the circumstances of the case, Blackburn J. concluded that although the mistake had formed a material part of the motive for applying for the shares, the mistake did not prevent the shares from "being in substance those [the plaintiff] applied for."[113] These broader tests in terms of fundamental error may be supported on the basis that they are more flexible in the sense that they avoid the verbal manipulations inherent

---

109 Above note 106 at 252.
110 *Ibid.* at 253.
111 (1867), L.R. 2 Q.B. 580 (Q.B.).
112 *Ibid.* at 588.
113 *Ibid.* at 589.

in the narrower tests. On the other hand, they may be thought to suffer from an unattractive degree of generality or vagueness.

On the basis of such authorities, then, the doctrine of mistaken assumptions at common law had obviously remained in a rather unsatisfactory state. There appears to have been no clear consensus as to the nature of the test to be applied. Moreover, the reasoning in the cases does not provide a convincing explanation for either the granting or the withholding of relief. The difference between *Strickland v. Turner* and *Lord Kennedy's* case appears to be that the purchaser in the latter case assumed the risk that the description of the company's business in the prospectus might not be perfectly accurate, whereas the purchaser in the former case did not assume the risk that the annuity being purchased might be valueless. The one fact that appears to be common to the actual cases granting relief is that the mistaken assumption has led to a drastic miscalculation of the value being acquired by one of the parties to the agreement. However, considerations such as these, while no doubt present in the minds of the judges deciding these cases, had found no explicit basis in the articulated tests for determining that the contracts are void from mistake at common law. The mistake must relate to the existence "or substance" of the subject matter of the contract or, in some sense, to a matter that is the "basis" of the agreement the parties have entered. Such was the unsatisfactory state of the law prior to the decision of the House of Lords in the leading case of *Bell v. Lever Brothers Ltd.*[114]

In this well-known case, Lever Brothers had entered into agreements to terminate the employment contracts of two senior employees in order to facilitate a proposed reorganization of the employer's corporate structure. As it was the employer's view that the employees had both provided valuable services in senior management positions in a subsidiary trading in Africa, the arrangements reached were generous in nature. When, however, after receiving the moneys, one of the employees disclosed that they had both been secretly trading in cocoa on their own account, Lever Brothers sought to set aside the agreements on the basis that had it been aware of the circumstance, the employees could have been dismissed for cause. At trial, the jury held that although this misconduct had not been present in the minds of the employees at that time of negotiating the agreements, Lever Brothers, on the other hand, if it had been aware of these circumstances, would have

---

114 Above note 4 (H.L.). For a detailed examination of the factual circumstances of the case, see C. MacMillan, "How Temptation Led to Mistake: An Explanation of *Bell v. Lever Brothers Ltd.*" (2003) 119 Law Q. Rev. 625.

exercised its right to dismiss the employees summarily and without compensation. At trial, Wright J., as he then was, quoted with approval[115] the test articulated by Blackburn J. in *Lord Kennedy's* case[116] and held that the mistake went to the substance of the whole consideration and that the agreement was either void at common law or could be set aside in equity. In the Court of Appeal, however, both the narrow and the broader versions of the test attracted some support. Scrutton L.J. framed the test in terms of a mistake that relates to "the continuance of a particular state of things [that] is in the contemplation of both parties fundamental to the validity of the contract."[117] He suggested, however, that the application of the test could be expressed either as an implication of the term in the agreement or as the application of an "assumed foundation" test. He explained as follows:

> One may describe the result as either that the contract is void because of an implied term that its validity shall depend on the existence at the time of the contract, and during its term of performance, of a particular state of facts, or (which is only another way of putting the proposition) that there is a mutual mistake of the parties, who make the contract believing that a particular foundation to it exists, which is essential to its existence, a fundamental reason for making it. In either case the absence of the assumed foundation makes the contract void.[118]

This suggestion that the doctrine can be formulated in the alternative form of an implied term was to be taken up by Lord Atkin in the House of Lords. The other members of the Court of Appeal simply contradicted each other on the relevance of the non-existence of the subject-matter test.[119] All members of the Court of Appeal were, however, satisfied that the test had been met on the present facts and that the appeal should be dismissed.

On further appeal to the House of Lords, however, the appellants enjoyed success. The leading opinion of Lord Atkin appears to adopt what might be considered a variation of the narrower version of the test. Lord Atkin began with a survey of the existing doctrine concerning cases of *res extincta* and *res sua*, characterizing the former as a "mistake

---

115 *Lever Brothers Ltd. v. Bell*, above note 4 at 566 (K.B.).
116 Quoted in the text above at note 112.
117 Above note 4 at 584 (K.B.).
118 *Ibid.* at 585.
119 *Ibid.* at 595, Greer L.J. favouring a "fundamental basis" test and at 590, Lawrence L.J. applying the "non-existent" subject-matter test.

as to the existence of the subject-matter"[120] and the latter as "mistake as to title."[121] In such cases, he stated, the agreement is "void" rather than "voidable." Neither category of these cases being applicable to the facts at hand, Lord Atkin went on to consider the doctrine applicable to a case where the mistake relates to the *quality* of the subject matter of the agreement rather than its existence or ownership. He reasoned as follows: "Mistake as to quality of the thing contracted for raises more difficult questions. In such a case a mistake will not affect assent unless it is the mistake of both parties, and is as to the existence of some quality which makes the thing without the quality essentially different from the thing as it was believed to be."[122]

Although this test moves away from the literal language of the "non-existence of the subject-matter" test, the movement is not dramatic. Under Lord Atkin's test, one must establish not that the subject matter fails to exist but rather that it has become something essentially different from what it was believed to be. Like the non-existence of the subject-matter test, however, Lord Atkin's new version of the test appears to be a highly manipulable one. A pregnant cow is essentially different, one could say, from a barren cow. Indeed, as we shall see, Lord Atkin's opinion itself offers some evidence of this feature of the test.

Curiously, having apparently opted for a narrow version of the test for operative mistake, Lord Atkin then introduced a note of ambiguity in his opinion by embracing the more open-textured approach adopted in the Court of Appeal by Scrutton L.J. Like him, Lord Atkin suggested that there was an "alternative mode of expressing the result of a mutual mistake."[123] Drawing support from the now discredited implied contract theory of frustration doctrine, Lord Atkin indicated his agreement with the following proposition formulated by counsel: "Whenever it is to be inferred from the terms of a contract or its surrounding circumstances that the consensus has been reached upon the basis of a particular contractual assumption, and that assumption is not true, the contract is avoided: i.e., it is void *ab initio* if the assumption is of present fact and it ceases to bind if the assumption is of future fact."[124]

In Lord Atkin's view, few would disagree with this statement but he cautioned that care must be taken with the meaning of the terms "basis" and "contractual assumption." In determining whether a particular as-

---

120 Above note 4 at 218 (A.C.).
121 *Ibid.*
122 *Ibid.*
123 *Ibid.* at 224.
124 *Ibid.* at 225, quoting Sir John Simon.

sumption is a condition of a contract, Lord Atkin quoted from the "important judgment of Scrutton L.J. in the present case"[125] and found the expressions "[i]n the contemplation of both parties fundamental to the continued validity of the contract" and "a foundation essential to its existence" to be helpful.[126] A third phrase employed by Scrutton L.J., "a fundamental reason for making it," could in Lord Atkin's view be "misleading" because one's motive for entering into an agreement could be mistaken in some respect without giving rise to a finding that "the new state of facts makes the *contract* something *different in kind* from a contract in the original state of facts."[127] Moreover, such a term is not to be implied unless it was necessary to do so in order to give, in the language of the traditional test for implying terms, "business efficacy to the transaction."[128] Oddly, then, Lord Atkin appears at one and the same time both to adopt the broader language of the test formulated by Scrutton L.J. in the Court of Appeal and, as well, equate that test to what appears to be the narrower test of requiring the mistake to be of such nature that the contract itself is different in kind from the contract as initially contemplated.

The narrow versions of the test articulated by Lord Atkin thus appear to include the initial suggestion that the mistake is as to a "quality that makes the thing without the quality essentially different from the thing as it was believed to be,"[129] a test that appears to apply to the *subject matter* of the agreement and the later suggestion that the mistake must make the *agreement* itself "different in kind."[130] It may or may not be that these versions are intended by Lord Atkin to be overlapping or indeed co-extensive. Although the two tests appear to be applied interchangeably by Lord Atkin, no guidance on this point is forthcoming. In any event, the difficulty one encounters in applying the latter version of the test is manifest in the following passage from Lord Atkin's opinion:

> Is an agreement to terminate a broken contract different in kind from an agreement to terminate an unbroken contract, assuming that the breach has given the one party the right to declare the contract at an end? I feel the weight of the plaintiffs' contention that a contract immediately determinable is a different thing from a contract for an

125 *Ibid.* at 226.
126 *Ibid.*
127 *Ibid.* (emphasis added).
128 *Ibid.*
129 *Ibid.* at 218.
130 *Ibid.* at 226.

unexpired term, and that the difference in kind can be illustrated by the immense price of release from the longer contract as compared with the shorter. And I agree that an agreement to take an assignment of a lease for five years is not the same thing as to take an assignment of a lease for three years, still less a term for a few months. But, on the whole, I have come to the conclusion that it would be wrong to decide that an agreement to terminate a definite specified contract is void if it turns out that the agreement had already been broken and could have been terminated otherwise. The contract released is the identical contract in both cases, and the party paying for release gets exactly what he bargains for.[131]

Application of the "difference in kind" test to the facts of *Bell v. Lever Brothers* is no easy matter. Indeed, it may be that whatever test is employed to determine the scope of operative mistake, its application to the facts of *Bell v. Lever Brothers* will involve a difficult decision. Nonetheless, the real problem with the "difference in kind" test is not that it is difficult to apply but, rather, that it does not raise for consideration the criteria or factors that appear to be relevant to the choice to be made.

The real dilemma confronted by the court in *Bell v. Lever Brothers* is to determine whether or not the risk of the kind of error that occurred should be considered to have been assumed by an employer in the context of negotiating a termination agreement. One could justify the result in *Bell v. Lever Brothers* on the basis that, generally, employers negotiating such agreements should make whatever inquiries they deem fit prior to entering such an agreement and, that in the absence of fraud or other misleading conduct by the employees, employers should be considered to have taken the risk that their inquiries were inadequate. Once the agreement has been entered, the time for such inquiries has passed. As a general matter, employers are aware of the risk of such errors and one could reasonably hold that the risk of inadequate inquiry is assumed by the employer in these circumstances.

Alternatively, if so general a proposition was found unattractive by the deciding court, the result in *Bell v. Lever Brothers* could be justified on the basis that on the particular facts, the employer's generosity in recognizing the valuable contribution made by these particular employees led the employer, in effect, to waive proper inquiries and make what, in retrospect, may appear to be, in effect, a somewhat foolhardy gift. In such circumstances, again, the risk of error may be considered to have been assumed by the employer. In any event, the important

---

131 *Ibid.* at 223.

point for present purposes is that it is considerations such as these that are plainly relevant to the making of the decision in this case. Yet they are not directly required or, indeed, encouraged to be considered by the "difference in subject matter" or "difference in kind" test.

Whether one finds Lord Atkin's analysis satisfactory or not, however, it can fairly be said that his opinion is not entirely free of ambiguity. In particular, it is not clear what role Lord Atkin had in mind for a formulation of the test adverting to mistaken assumptions "fundamental to the continued validity of the contract."[132] Greater clarity cannot be easily purchased by examining the other opinions written in this case. The panel divided three to two and can be fairly described as reaching no definitive conclusion on the precise nature of the test for operative mistake.[133] Accordingly, Lord Atkin's "difference in the subject matter" or "difference in kind" test did not clearly express the opinion of the House of Lords on this occasion. Indeed, the three other members of the panel who offered a view on the point appeared to prefer a more flexible formula of the kind offered in *Lord Kennedy's* case by Blackburn J.[134]

3) In Equity

In 1950, in the decision of the Court of Appeal in *Solle v. Butcher*,[135] Denning L.J. was afforded an opportunity to consider the effect of *Bell v. Lever Brothers* and the role played by mistaken assumptions doctrine

---

132 *Ibid.* at 225.

133 Thus, Lord Thankerton, who concurred with Lord Atkin, found attractive the analysis offered in *Lord Kennedy's* case and articulated the nature of the requisite mistake as being with respect to a matter that the parties "accepted in their minds as an essential and integral element of the subject-matter [of the contract]." See *ibid.* at 235. The third member of the majority, Lord Blanesburgh was content to decide the case on the basis that "mutual mistake had not been pleaded." See *ibid.* at 189. In dissent, Lord Warrington, with whom Viscount Hailsham concurred, offered a further definition of operative mistake, indicating that the error must be "of such a fundamental character as to constitute an underlying assumption without which the parties would not have made the contract they in fact made" and concluded that the actual error in *Bell v. Lever Brothers* "was as fundamental to the bargain as any error one can imagine." See *ibid.* at 208.

134 Thus, many editions of *Anson on Contract* have explained that "where the parties contract under a false and fundamental assumption, going to the root of the contract, and which both of them may be taken to have had in mind at the time they entered into it as the basis of their agreement, the contract may be void." See, for example, J. Beatson, ed., *Anson's Law of Contract*, 28th ed. (Oxford: Oxford University Press, 2002) at 319.

135 Above note 23.

in the equitable context. In this important case, Denning L.J. offered a very restrictive interpretation of the scope of the common law mistake doctrine and suggested that a more flexible doctrine for setting aside agreements on the basis of mistaken assumptions was available in equity. Denning L.J.'s summary of the effect of *Bell v. Lever Brothers* was as follows:

> The correct interpretation of that case, to my mind, is that, once a contract has been made, that is to say, once the parties, whatever their inmost states of mind, have to all outward appearances agreed with sufficient certainty in the same terms on the same subject-matter, then the contract is good unless and until it is set aside for failure of some condition on which the existence of the contract depends, or for fraud, or on some equitable ground, neither party can rely on his own mistake to say it was a nullity from the beginning, no matter that it was a mistake which to his mind was fundamental, and no matter that the other party knew that he was under a mistake.[136]

It is evident that Denning L.J. is here giving the narrowest possible interpretation of the effect of *Bell v. Lever Brothers*. The only justification for so narrow a reading in the opinions in that case is to be found, of course, in Lord Atkin's suggestion that unless the mistake makes the contract or its subject matter different in kind from the original contract or its subject matter, the mistake is inoperative. If, notwithstanding the mistake, the subject matter of the contract remains the same or the kind of contract remains the same, Lord Atkin appears to suggest that the contract must be binding. Hence the arguable legitimacy of Lord Denning's suggestion that if the parties agree "in the same terms on the same subject-matter,"[137] the common law doctrine is inapplicable.

Applying this test to the facts of *Solle v. Butcher*, the common law doctrine was, in Denning L.J.'s view, inapplicable. Solle and Butcher had collaborated on the renovation of a building owned by Butcher containing five flats. Acting on Solle's advice that the renovations were of a sufficient extent to render the rent control legislation inapplicable, Butcher rented one of the flats to Solle at a rental considerably in excess of that which would otherwise have been permissible under the legislation. If applicable, the legislation would have obliged Butcher to comply with the necessary statutory formalities for the increase in prior rent. After a falling out between the parties, Solle took the position that the legislation did in fact apply and that he had been charged an unlawful

---

136 *Ibid.* at 691.
137 *Ibid.*

amount of rent under the agreement. In due course, it was held that the legislation did, in fact, apply. The parties had thus entered the lease under a common mistake as to their respective rights under the rent control legislation. Though the error was induced by Solle, the error was innocent on his part in the sense that he had received professional advice on the point before passing on this view to Butcher. For Denning L.J. common law mistake doctrine did not apply in such circumstances. Although the lease may have been entered into on the basis of a shared assumption concerning a fundamental matter, nonetheless, the parties had agreed in the same terms on the same subject matter and the lease was therefore enforceable at common law.

For Denning L.J., however, that was not the end of the matter. He then turned to "consider mistakes which render a contract voidable, that is, liable to be set aside on some equitable ground."[138] Controversially, Denning L.J. asserted that there existed a well-established equitable jurisdiction to set aside agreements that were enforceable at common law. Drawing support from the *res sua* case, *Cooper v. Phibbs*,[139] Denning L.J. claimed that a court of equity could relieve for common mistake "so long as it could do so without injustice to third parties . . . whenever it was of opinion that it was unconscientious for the other party to avail themselves of the legal advantage which he had obtained."[140] Denning L.J. indicated that the notion of what would be considered "unconscientious" had developed over time and summarized various grounds for setting aside agreements in equity, adding to this list a doctrine of equitable mistake in the following terms: "A contract is also liable in equity to be set aside if the parties were under a common misapprehension either as to facts or as to their relative and respective rights, provided that the misapprehension was fundamental and that the party seeking to set it aside was not himself at fault."[141]

This doctrine was available to the tenant in the present case. Indeed, in Denning L.J.'s view, the injustice of allowing the tenant to take advantage of the mistake that equity were so rigid that they could not remedy such an injustice, "it is time we had a new equity to make good the omissions of the old" but fortunately, in his view, "the established rules are amply sufficient for this case."[142]

---

138 Above note 23 at 692.
139 Above note 104.
140 *Solle v. Butcher*, above note 23 at 692.
141 *Ibid.* at 693.
142 *Ibid.* at 695.

There are two particularly controversial features of this reasoning. First, it is sometimes said that Denning L.J.'s reading of the common law doctrine is unduly restrictive.[143] Second, it is sometimes argued that historically there simply was no separate definition of operative mistake in equity and that Denning L.J.'s assertion in this regard is simply inaccurate.[144] As we shall see, these criticisms of Denning L.J.'s reasoning came to preoccupy the Court of Appeal in the recent decision in *The Great Peace*.[145] It should be noted, however, that Denning L.J. was not reticent about his reasons for wanting to constrain or, indeed, replace common law mistake doctrine with an equitable version of the rule. In Denning L.J.'s view, the common law doctrine was unsatisfactory from a policy prospective as it creates a potential for severe injustice for third parties who have innocently acquired for value the subject matter transferred by the initial void contract. This point was spelled out quite plainly in the following terms:

> In order to see whether the lease can be avoided for this mistake it is necessary to remember that mistake is of two kinds: first, mistake which renders the contract void, that is, a nullity from the beginning, which is the kind of mistake which was dealt with by the courts of common law; and, secondly, mistake which renders the contract not void, but voidable, that is, liable to be set aside on such terms as the court thinks fit, which is the kind of mistake which was dealt with by the courts of equity. Much of the difficulty which has attended this subject has arisen because, before the fusion of law and equity, the courts of common law, in order to do justice in the case in hand, extended this doctrine of mistake beyond its proper limits and held contracts to be void which were really only voidable, a process which was capable of being attended with much injustice to third persons who bought goods or otherwise committed themselves on the faith that there was a contract.[146]

As an illustration of the harmful effects of the common law doctrine, Denning L.J. referred to *Cundy v. Lindsay*,[147] the famous mistake of identity case, in which an innocent third-party purchaser of the subject mat-

---

143 See, for example, *Associated Japanese Bank (International) Ltd. v. Crédit du Nord SA*, [1989] 1 W.L.R. 255 at 267, [1988] 3 All E.R. 902, Steyn J.

144 See, for example, C. Slade, "The Myth of Mistake in Contract" (1954) 70 Law Q. Rev. 385; W.E.D. Davies, "Mistake in Equity: *Solle v. Butcher* Re-examined" (1969) 2 Man. L.J. 79.

145 *Great Peace Shipping Ltd. v. Tsavliris Salvage (International) Ltd.*, [2002] 4 All E.R. 689 (C.A.).

146 Above note 23 at 690–91.

147 Above note 43, for discussion of which see above this Chapter, section B(5).

ter of the original sale was held liable in conversion to the original seller for its value. Equity, on the other hand, would protect the *bona fide* purchaser for value in such a case by withholding the remedy of rescission from the initial purchaser. The fusion of law and equity, in Denning L.J.'s view, made it possible to reverse this historical process of extending inappropriately the doctrines of the common law. Accordingly, at common law "only those contracts are now held void in which the mistake was such as to prevent the formation of any contract at all."[148]

From a policy perspective, these views appeared to be undeniably sound. Void for mistake is an unsatisfactory doctrine and its restriction in *Solle v. Butcher* is surely a welcome development. Moreover, as we have seen, the constraint of void for mistake is an approach that has surfaced in other contexts. Limitations have been imposed on the scope of the common law doctrines of *non est factum*[149] and mistake of identity.[150] In each case, transactions that were originally treated as void at common law are now to be considered valid at common law but unenforceable in equity, thereby protecting third parties and leaving the mistaken parties to pursue equitable rescissionary relief.

The remedy fashioned by Denning L.J. in *Solle v. Butcher* is also controversial. Purporting to rely on the flexibility in fashioning rescissionary remedies said to be manifest in *Cooper v. Phibbs*, Denning L.J. conditioned rescission on a willingness of the landlord to offer a lease for the unexpired portion of the term at the rate that could have been secured by compliance with the rent control legislation and, further, on the condition that the tenant would pay a fair and economic rent for the occupation of the premises enjoyed thus far. Similar results, it may be noted, have been achieved in American law.[151] Bucknill L.J. agreed

---

148 Above note 23 at 691.
149 *Saunders v. Anglia Building Society*, above note 74, for discussion of which see above this Chapter, section B(6).
150 *Lewis v. Averay*, above note 52, for discussion of which see above this Chapter, section B(5). The validity of this approach has recently been affirmed by the House of Lords. See *Shogun Finance Ltd. v. Hudson*, above note 62.
151 Thus, Illustration 3 to § 152 *Restatement of Contracts 2d* reads:

> A contracts to sell and B to buy a tract of land. B agrees to pay A $100,000 in cash and to assume a mortgage that C holds on the tract. Both A and B believe that the amount of the mortgage is $50,000, but in fact it is only $10,000. The contract is voidable by A, unless the court supplies a term under which B is entitled to enforce the contract if he agrees to pay an appropriate additional sum, and B does so....

> If the court of equity is restricted to either granting or withholding rescission, the unattractive result in such a case is that either the contract will be enforced

with the terms of the proposed order but, apart from observing that he had read Denning L.J.'s reasons, offered no view on the nature of the relationship between common law and equitable mistake doctrine. Jenkins L.J. dissented on the ground that the mistake was one of law and that an error of this kind could not be the foundation for the right to rescind.

The equitable mistake doctrine articulated by Denning L.J. in *Solle v. Butcher* appears to have been accepted into the fabric of Canadian contract law and, at least prior to the recent decision in *Great Peace Shipping Ltd. v. Tsavliris Salvage (International) Ltd.*,[152] into the fabric of English law as well. Although it is true that in English law a number of the early decisions involved Lord Denning himself, the doctrine has now been applied on a number of occasions and most recently by decisions of the Court of Appeal in which Lord Denning played no part. In *Grist v. Bailey*,[153] an agreement for the sale of land was set aside by Goff J., as he then was, on the basis that the parties had erroneously believed that the land was subject to an existing tenancy. Free of the tenancy, the land was worth more than double the contract price. In *Magee v. Pennine Ins.*,[154] an agreement of compromise under which an insured paid a claim under an accident insurance policy was set aside on the ground that the parties shared an erroneous belief that the policy was valid and binding. In *Laurence v. Lexcourt Holdings Ltd.*,[155] a long-term lease of property for use as business premises was set aside as the parties had failed to appreciate that the zoning permitted this use of the premises only for the first two years of the term. In *Associated Japanese Bank (International) Ltd. v. Crédit du Nord SA*,[156] a guarantee of a debt secured by a sale and lease-back of non-existent goods was held void at common law on the basis that the *res extincta* analogy was a close one. Steyn J., as he then was, went on to observe, "[t]oday it is clear that mistake in equity is not circumscribed by common law definitions. A contract affected by mistake

---

as is, with resulting unjust enrichment of the purchaser B who pays 40% less than anticipated for the land or the contract is rescinded in which case B is unfairly deprived of the opportunity to purchase the property at the agreed price. The ability of the court to condition rescission upon the enabling of B to enforce the agreement by paying the additional $40,000 provides a solution of which neither A nor B can reasonably complain. See American Law Institute, *Restatement of Contracts 2d*, vol. 1, above note 57 at 387.

152 Above note 145.
153 [1967] Ch. 532, [1966] 2 All E.R. 875.
154 [1969] 2 Q.B. 507, [1969] 2 All E.R. 891 (C.A.).
155 [1978] 2 All E.R. 810, [1978] 1 W.L.R. 1128 (Ch.).
156 Above note 143.

in equity is not void but may be set aside on terms."[157] Further, Steyn J. indicated that if it was incorrect to hold the guarantee void at common law, he would have considered it to be voidable in equity. For Steyn J. "a narrow doctrine of common law mistake (as enunciated in *Bell v. Lever Brothers Ltd.*), supplemented by the more flexible doctrine of mistake in equity (as developed in *Solle v. Butcher* and later cases), seems to me to be an entirely sensible and satisfactory state of the law."[158] In *William Sindall Plc. v. Cambridgeshire County Council*,[159] the Court of Appeal refused to apply the equitable doctrine, which it assumed to be well established, to set aside a sale of land for development purposes where the parties had failed to appreciate the existence of a sewer running under the land. In the view of the Court of Appeal, the existence of an express term subjecting the transaction to easements precluded application of equitable mistake doctrine. Within the past few years, the existence of the doctrine has been assumed in two decisions of the English Court of Appeal[160] and a decision at trial.[161]

Although the list of Canadian decisions applying the equitable doctrine is not as lengthy, the correct view would be that the doctrine has been accepted as a feature of Canadian law.[162] One of the leading cases, *Toronto Dominion Bank v. Fortin (No. 2)*,[163] like *Magee v. Pennine Ins.*, applies the doctrine to an agreement of compromise. In the Canadian case, the agreement of compromise was held to be voidable on the ground that the agreement was based on a common and erroneous assumption concerning the validity of the initial claim. The court distinguished, quite correctly, a decision of the Supreme Court of Canada that enforced a compromise based on a similar mistaken assumption where, however, the parties had each sought legal advice on the very issue in question. In other cases, the doctrine was held applicable to

---

157 *Ibid.* at 266 (W.L.R.).

158 *Ibid.* at 267–68.

159 [1994] 3 All E.R. 932, [1994] 1 W.L.R. 1016 (C.A.).

160 *Nutt v. Read* (1999), 32 H.L.R. 761 (C.A.); *West Sussex Properties Ltd. v. Chichester DC*, [2000] All E.R. (D) 887 (C.A.).

161 *Clarion Ltd. v. National Provident Institution*, [2000] 2 All E.R. 265 (Ch.).

162 See, for example, *McMaster University v. Wilchar Construction Ltd.*, above note 17 at 18–19 (Ont. H.C.J.). See also *Vandekerhove v. Litchfield* (1993), 103 D.L.R. (4th) 739 (B.C.S.C.), rev'd on other grounds (1995), 121 D.L.R. (4th) 571 (B.C.C.A.), leave to appeal to S.C.C. refused (1995), 126 D.L.R. (4th) vii; *Stellar Properties Ltd. v. Botham Holdings Ltd.*, [1994] 8 W.W.R. 639 (B.C.C.A.). And see S.M. Waddams, *The Law of Contracts*, 5th ed. (Aurora: Canada Law Book, 2005) at 272–78; G.H.L. Fridman, *The Law of Contract in Canada*, 4th ed. (Toronto: Carswell, 1999) at 276–78.

163 (1978), 88 D.L.R. (3d) 232, [1978] 5 W.W.R. 302 (B.C.S.C.).

circumstances where the parties to a real estate transaction mistakenly assumed that the property was twice as large as it in fact was,[164] where it was discovered that the monthly payments agreed upon in the context of the long-term agreement for the purchase and sale of land and chattels would never retire the balance the purchase price[165] and where, in the context of a real estate transaction, the parties had mistakenly believed that a dwelling house was located on the lot in question.[166]

Prior to the decision of the English Court of Appeal in *The Great Peace*,[167] then, to which we will shortly turn, one would have concluded rather confidently that in both England and in common law Canada the equitable mistake doctrine articulated in *Solle v. Butcher* was a recognized feature of the law. In passing, it is of interest to note that in virtually all of these English and Canadian cases, literal performance of the contract remained possible. Thus, if one were to attempt to apply to these cases the version of the doctrine articulated by Lord Atkin in *Bell v. Lever Brothers*, it would be necessary to manipulate the concept of the "subject matter of the contract" in each case in order to be able to conclude that the subject matter of the contract was different from that assumed because of mistake. Such arguments could be made, of course, with varying degrees of artificiality in these various fact situations.

The strength of Denning L.J.'s opinion in *Solle v. Butcher*, then, is its effect in restricting the scope of the common law doctrine of void for mistake and supplanting it with an equitable doctrine that affords protection to the interests of innocent third parties. Indeed, it is not obvious that Denning L.J., at least, would apply common law doctrine beyond the well-established categories of *res extincta* and *res sua*, these being cases, it should be noted, in which true owner claims against a third party do not typically arise. Non-existent goods are not likely to be resold to a third party who would, in any event, not take possession of the goods. Goods already owned by the purchaser can, of course, be successfully transferred for value to third parties.

The weakness of the opinion, however, is that it appears to offer very little guidance with respect to the test for operative mistake to be applied in equity. Beyond the suggestion that there must be a "common and fundamental misapprehension" either as to facts or as to relative and respective rights, the opinion offers virtually no guidance as to the factors to be taken into account to determine whether or not such

---

164 *Hyrsky v. Smith* (1969), 5 D.L.R. (3d) 385 (Ont. H.C.J.).
165 *Ivanochko v. Sych* (1967), 60 D.L.R. (2d) 474 (Sask. C.A.).
166 *Marwood v. Charter Credit Corp.* (1971), 20 D.L.R. (3d) 563 (N.S.S.C.A.D.).
167 Above note 145.

a misapprehension is present in a particular fact situation. American experience[168] strongly suggests that the competing tensions of contractual stability and relief for egregious error are best reconciled by attempting to determine whether the parties have explicitly or implicitly allocated the risk of error in their agreement[169] and, if not, in considering whether the presence of error has given rise to a severe and surprising imbalance in the values being exchanged under the affected transaction. Thus, the basic mistaken assumptions principle set out in section 152 of the *Restatement of Contracts 2d*[170] is as follows:

§152. When Mistake of Both Parties Makes a Contract Voidable

(1) Where a mistake of both parties at the time a contract was made as to a basic assumption on which the contract was made has a material effect on the agreed exchange of performances, the contract is voidable by the adversely affected party unless he bears the risk of the mistake under the rule stated in §154.

(2) In determining whether the mistake has a material effect on the agreed exchange of performances, account is taken of any relief by way of reformation, restitution, or otherwise.[171]

The key criteria for application of the test set out in the first subparagraph, then, are first, that the mistake has had a "material"[172] effect on the agreed exchange of performances and second, that the adversely affected party does not bear the risk of the error that has occurred. As §152(1) indicates, the requirement that the adversely affected party does not bear the risk of the error in question is further explicated in §154:

§154. When a Party Bears the Risk of a Mistake

A party bears the risk of a mistake when
(a) the risk is allocated to him by agreement of the parties, or

---

168 For a brief account of which see the text below at notes 170–77.

169 This approach has also been advocated by Commonwealth scholars. See, for example, Waddams, above note 162 at 284-85; P.S. Atiyah, "Judicial Techniques and the English Law of Contract" (1968) 2 Ottawa L. Rev. 337, revised and reprinted as "Judicial Techniques and the Law of Contract" in P.S. Atiyah, *Essays on Contract* (Oxford: Clarendon Press, 1986) c. 9; L.B. McTurnan, "An Approach to Common Mistake in English Law" (1963) 41 Can. Bar Rev. 1.

170 American Law Institute, *Restatement of Contracts 2d*, above note 151, s. 152.

171 *Ibid.* at 385. See also E. Allan Farnsworth, *Farnsworth on Contracts*, 2d ed., vol. 2 (New York: Aspen, 1998) at 569–82.

172 In this context, "material" means basic or fundamental in the sense that "the resulting imbalance in the agreed exchange is so severe that [the disadvantaged party] cannot fairly be required to carry it out. See above note 151 at 388.

    (b) he is aware, at the time the contract is made, that he has only limited knowledge with respect to the facts to which the mistake relates but treats his limited knowledge as sufficient, or

    (c) the risk is allocated to him by the court on the ground that it is reasonable in the circumstances to do so.[173]

Subparagraphs (a) and (b) identify situations where the affected party may reasonably be held to an understanding that the risk has been assumed. Subparagraph (c), however, is apparently intended to deal with situations where, although an inference of this kind is unwarranted, the circumstances are nonetheless such that the affected party ought to be held to have assumed the risk of error. The illustrations of this last proposition offered in the *Restatement* would not alarm or, indeed, surprise an English or Canadian reader. Thus, Illustration 3 offers a variation of *Scott v. Coulson*[174] and suggests that the annuitant is not dead at the time of contracting but, rather, suffers from an incurable, fatal disease.[175] In such a case, the illustration concludes, a court would hold that the purchaser had assumed the risk of that kind of error. Other illustrations indicate that contractors will be taken to have assumed the risk that subsoil conditions are such as to render a construction contract more expensive to complete[176] or that increased costs resulting from a contractor's mistaken estimate of the amount of labour required increase the cost to complete a particular project.[177]

    If one revisited the facts of *Bell v. Lever Brothers* under sections 152 and 154, one would be directed to consider whether the error led to a material effect on the exchange, which is undoubtedly the case, but one would then be directed to consider what appears to be the critical issue in *Bell v. Lever Brothers*, that is, whether an employer either generally or on the particular facts of this case should be taken to have assumed the risk of error resulting from what might be considered to be the inadequate investigation concerning the performance of the particular employees. The actual decision in *Bell v. Lever Brothers* can be defended on the basis that the risk of such errors was indeed assumed by Lever Brothers. Indeed, it is perhaps not too much to suggest that a risk-assumption analysis of this kind is implicit in the English and Canadian

173 *Ibid.* at 402–3.
174 Above note 106.
175 Above note 57 at 405.
176 *Ibid.*, Illustration 4.
177 *Ibid.*, Illustration 6.

decisions on mistaken assumptions.[178] Interestingly, Steyn J. observed in *Associated Japanese Bank (International) Ltd. v. Crédit du Nord SA*[179] that before setting aside an agreement either at law or in equity, one must first consider "whether the contract itself, by express or implied condition precedent or otherwise, provides who bears the risk of the relative mistake."[180] Similarly, in *William Sindall Plc. v. Cambridgeshire County Council*,[181] Hoffman L.J. similarly emphasized the importance of risk-allocation analysis. A more explicit adoption of this approach offers the prospect of more rational and coherent foundation for the analysis of mistaken assumptions cases.

4) Rejection of the Equitable Doctrine by the English Court of Appeal

In *The Great Peace*,[182] both the trial judge and the Court of Appeal had occasion to reconsider the existence of the equitable jurisdiction to avoid agreements on the basis of mistaken assumptions articulated by Denning L.J. in *Solle v. Butcher*. The trial judge, Toulson J., reached the "bold conclusion"[183] that the views expressed by Denning L.J. in *Solle* were incorrect. In Toulson J.'s view, equity simply did not possess a jurisdiction to set aside agreements on such grounds. The Court of Appeal agreed with these views and concluded that the equitable jurisdiction invoked by Denning L.J. and by subsequent English courts was a mere "chimera."[184] The reasons offered by the Court of Appeal for this conclusion set forth a lengthy analysis of the history of mistaken assumptions doctrine, placing considerable emphasis on a detailed dissection of the reasoning in *Bell v. Lever Brothers* and *Solle v. Butcher* itself. After briefly describing the reasons provided for the Court of Appeal by Lord Phillips M.R., a critique[185] of the decision will be offered.

---

178 See Atiyah, above note 169; P.S. Atiyah and F.A.A. Bennion, "Mistake in the Construction of Contracts" (1961) 24 Mod. L. Rev. 421.
179 Above note 143.
180 *Ibid.* at 268 (W.L.R.).
181 Above note 159.
182 Above note 145.
183 *Ibid.* at 692, Lord Phillips M.R.
184 *Ibid.* at 723.
185 For more extended treatment, see J.D. McCamus, "Mistaken Assumptions in Equity: Sound Doctrine or Chimera?" (2004) 40 Can. Bus. L.J. 46. And see D. Sheehan, "Vitiation of Contracts for Mistake and Misrepresentation of Law" [2003] R.L.R. 26.

The facts of the case are uncomplicated. En route from Brazil to China, a vessel, *The Cape Providence*, suffered serious structural damage, with consequent risk to both the vessel and its crew. The defendant salvor was retained to provide assistance. The defendant sought assistance from a third party, Marint, in locating a tug. When it appeared that the tug would only be available in five or six days, Marint was asked to try to locate another vessel in the vicinity of *The Cape Providence* that might be prepared to offer assistance with the evacuation of the crew, should that become necessary. Marint advised that *The Great Peace*, owned by the plaintiffs, was the vessel closest to the current location of *The Cape Providence* and that it should be able to rendezvous with *The Cape Providence* in about twelve hours. Acting on the instructions of *The Cape Providence*, the defendant commenced negotiations with the plaintiff for suitable arrangements by which *The Great Peace* would alter its course and proceed to the location of *The Cape Providence*. Within a few hours, such arrangements were reached and *The Great Peace* altered its course. The arrangements included a term permitting the defendant to cancel the agreement on payment of a minimum five-day fee.

Within a few hours, it became apparent that *The Great Peace* was actually 410 miles, rather than the initially estimated 35 miles, away from *The Cape Providence*. At this point, the defendants advised Marint that they were expecting to cancel *The Great Peace* but would not do so yet, because they wished to determine whether a closer vessel could be identified. Shortly thereafter, having learned that *The Cape Providence* had been passed by a vessel called the *Nordfarer*, the defendants contracted with the owners of the *Nordfarer* for similar assistance and instructed Marint to cancel the arrangements with the plaintiffs. Marint then confirmed the cancellation and indicated that it would recommend, in the circumstances, the payment of a lesser cancellation fee of two days' hire. The defendants were unwilling, however, to pay any sum at all to the plaintiff, with respect to the cancellation of the agreement.

In response to the plaintiff's claim for the five-day cancellation fee payable under the agreement, the defendants argued, both at trial and in the Court of Appeal, that the agreement had been entered into on the basis of a shared fundamental assumption that *The Great Peace* was "in close proximity"[186] to *The Cape Providence*, whereas, in fact, she was not. Accordingly, the agreement was either void at common law or, at least, voidable in equity and subject to rescission. These defences were rejected both at trial and on appeal and the claim enjoyed success. On

---

186 Above note 145 at 696.

behalf of the Court of Appeal, Lord Phillips M.R. began his reasons with a careful examination of the reasoning at all levels in *Bell v. Lever Brothers*. Lord Phillips quoted at particular length from the opinion of Lord Atkin, which he considered to represent a consensus of the majority of the panel. Lord Phillips observed that the matter had been considered both at common law and in equity at trial and further, that Lord Atkin had indicated that the result in *Cooper v. Phibbs*,[187] the principal authority upon which Denning L.J. had relied upon as evidence at the existence of an equitable jurisdiction, should have been that the agreement is void at common law rather than voidable in equity. Accordingly, Lord Phillips suggested that Denning L.J.'s conclusion in *Solle v. Butcher* that the House of Lords in *Bell v. Lever Brothers* had simply not considered the possible application of an independent equitable jurisdiction to relieve the mistake was simply "not realistic."[188]

With particular reference to Lord Denning's reliance on *Cooper v. Phibbs*, Lord Phillips accepted the view advanced by Matthews[189] that it might well have been a case in which a contract valid at common law was rescinded in equity for mistake.[190] The plaintiff's perceived need to resort to equity may have rested on the ground that the plaintiff's life estate was equitable in nature and might not well have been recognized by a court of common law. Nonetheless, the type of mistake that the court appeared to recognize in *Cooper v. Phibbs* as providing a basis for rescission was an instance of *res sua* in which a party agrees to purchase a title that he already owns. The court was merely applying the common law doctrine of *res sua* to the purchase of an equitable interest. The width of the jurisdiction in equity would not therefore appear to be remarkable. Further, Lord Phillips quoted passages from the opinions in *Norwich Union Fire Insurance Society Ltd. v. Wm. H. Price Ltd.*[191] in support of the proposition that in *Bell v. Lever Brothers*, the House of Lords had equated "the test of common mistake in *Cooper v. Phibbs* with one that renders a contract void at common law."[192] Accordingly, it was simply "not correct to state that *Cooper v. Phibbs* as interpreted by Denning L.J. was 'in no way impaired by *Bell v. Lever Brothers Ltd.*' or that it had been 'fully restored' by *Norwich Union*."[193]

---

187 Above note 104.
188 Above note 145 at 722.
189 P. Matthews, "A Note on *Cooper v. Phibbs*" (1989) 105 Law Q. Rev. 599.
190 Above note 145 at 715–18.
191 [1934] A.C. 455 at 462–63 (H.L.).
192 Above note 145 at 723.
193 *Ibid.* at 722.

Lord Phillips then turned to consider the various subsequent decisions of the lower courts and of the Court of Appeal that purported to follow and apply *Solle v. Butcher.* The collective support offered by those authorities for the notion that the doctrine of *Solle v. Butcher* had become a recognized proposition of English law was undermined by Lord Phillips on three grounds. First, on a careful parsing of the decisions, it was his view that these cases do not "define satisfactorily different qualities of mistake, one operating in law and one in equity."[194] Second, Lord Phillips appeared to offer some scepticism with respect to the appropriateness of the results in at least some of the subsequent cases. There was, in his view, a common factor in *Solle v. Butcher* and in the later cases in that the "effect of the mistake has been to make a contract a particularly bad bargain for one of the parties."[195] Third, it was his view that the difficulties with *Solle v. Butcher* had not been fully canvassed in the decisions that appear to accept its legitimacy.

If the equitable doctrine is to be thus dispatched, it must be asked what version of the common law doctrine would, in the view of the Court of Appeal, remain in place. The answer is that the common law doctrine of mistaken assumption is perceived by the Court of Appeal in *The Great Peace* as being very restrictive in nature. Lord Atkin's views did not escape unscathed. Thus, Lord Phillips questioned whether there was a solid jurisprudential basis for the "quality of the subject-matter" test fashioned by Lord Atkin.[196] It was Lord Phillips' view that a surer footing could be found in analogous principles in the law of frustration. Thus, after a review of the evolution of frustration doctrine from its origins in implied contract theory to the more modern statement in the *Davis Contractors* case,[197] he concluded: "The avoidance of a contract on the ground of common mistake results from a rule of law under which, if it transpires that one or both of the parties have agreed to do something which it is impossible to perform, no obligation arises out of that agreement."[198]

Therefore, building on a rather restrictive view of the doctrine of frustration, Lord Phillips articulated the test for operative mistake at common law in the following terms:

[T]he following elements must be present if common mistake is to avoid a contract:

---

194 *Ibid.* at 728.
195 *Ibid.*
196 *Ibid.* at 705.
197 *Davis Contractors Ltd. v. Fareham Urban District Council,* [1956] A.C. 696 (H.L.).
198 Above note 145 at 708.

(i)   there must be a common assumption as to the existence of a state of affairs;

(ii) there must be no warranty by either party that that state of affairs exists;

(iii) the non-existence of the state of affairs must not be attributable to the fault of either party;

(iv) the non-existence of the state of affairs must render performance of the contract impossible;

(v)   the state of affairs may be the existence, or vital attribute, of the consideration to be provided or circumstances which must subsist if the performance of the contractual adventure is to be possible.[199]

The conclusion that mistake will be operative only where performance of the contract has become impossible appears to offer very little scope for the operation of the doctrine. On the other hand, like the "non-existence of the subject matter" test, it may be possible to manipulate the concept of the "contractual undertaking" in such a way as to be able to conclude that although literal performance of the agreement remains possible, performance of the true contractual undertaking has become "impossible." Indeed, Lord Phillips appears to envisage this sort of manipulation:

In consideration whether performance of the contract is impossible, it is necessary to identify what it is that the parties agreed would be performed. This involves looking not only at the express terms but at any implications that may arise out of the surrounding circumstances. In some cases, it will be possible to identify details of the "contractual adventure" which go beyond the terms which are expressly spelled out, in others it will not.[200]

Nonetheless, the narrowness of the conception of common law mistake doctrine envisaged by Lord Phillips is underlined by his suggestion that it may be difficult to reconcile *Bell v. Lever Brothers*[201] with *Scott v. Coulson*,[202] the case involving the sale of a life insurance policy on a person who, contrary to the parties' assumptions, was deceased at the time of contracting. In Lord Phillips' view, this decision is often erroneously treated as being on all fours with *Strickland v. Turner*,[203]

---

199 *Ibid.* at 708–9.
200 *Ibid.* at 708.
201 Above note 4.
202 Above note 106.
203 Above note 105.

the case applying mistake doctrine to the sale of an annuity on the life
of a deceased person. The annuity in *Strickland* was "self-evidently a
nullity,"[204] whereas this could not be said of the life insurance policy in
Scott v. Coulson. Although Lord Phillips did not explicitly suggest that
Scott v. Coulson should no longer be considered to be good law, he suggested that the decision could only be explained on the basis that "a life
policy before decease is fundamentally different from a life policy after
decease, so that the contractual consideration no longer existed."[205] In
such a case, presumably, it may be argued that it has become "impossible" to perform the contractual undertaking.

Finally, then, it remained for the Court of Appeal to apply this test
to the present facts. Unsurprisingly, the court concluded that the mistake as to the distance between the two vessels did not "render the
contractual adventure impossible of performance."[206] The fact that the
boats were farther apart than first assumed did not render the services
"essentially different" than those originally envisaged. Curiously, although the Court of Appeal quoted, with apparent approval, passages
from the judgment of Steyn J. in the *Associated Japanese Bank* case[207]
and Hoffman L.J. in *William Sindall plc*[208] to the effect that an appropriate first step in the analysis of a mistaken assumptions problem is to
attempt to determine whether the parties have allocated the risk of the
kind of error that has occurred to one of them, the Court of Appeal did
not apply this analysis to the facts of this case. Had the Court of Appeal done so, it may well be that the fact that the parties had included
a termination provision in their agreement that permitted termination
by the hirer only upon the payment of five days' hire might have been
considered to have assigned a risk of early termination to the hirer. In
the final paragraph of the judgment, Lord Phillips adverts to the importance of the termination clause in the following terms: "The parties
entered into a binding contract for the hire of *The Great Peace*. That contract gave the parties an express right to cancel the contract subject to
the obligation to pay the 'cancellation fee' of five-days' hire. When they
engaged the *Nordfarer* they cancelled *The Great Peace*. They became liable in consequence to pay the cancellation fee. There is no injustice in
this result."[209] It is unfortunate that the court did not consider whether,

---

204 Above note 145 at 711.
205 *Ibid.*
206 *Ibid.* at 730.
207 Above note 143 at 268 (W.L.R.), quoted by Lord Phillips, above note 145 at 709.
208 Above note 159 at 1035 (W.L.R.), quoted by Lord Phillips, above note 145 at
    709–10.
209 Above note 145 at 731.

in the light of this provision, the risk of early termination for whatever reason had been implicitly assigned to the hirer by the agreement.

Although one must concede that there is some truth in the Court of Appeal's suggestion[210] that in *Solle v. Butcher* Denning L.J. attempted to confine the doctrine of mistaken assumptions at common law as articulated by Lord Atkin in *Bell v. Lever Brothers*, the decision in *The Great Peace* appears to be an unfortunate one for a variety of reasons.[211] First, the test for operative mistake defined by the Court of Appeal in *The Great Peace* appears unduly restrictive and is likely, therefore, to lead to the manipulations characteristic of the earlier narrow versions of the test. If courts are required to assert that performance has become impossible, it seems very likely that in a case where relief appears warranted, a court will find that the nature of the contractual undertaking is such that its performance has become "impossible." Further, the suppression by the Court of Appeal of the relevance of the impact of the error on the values being exchanged appears to direct the analysis away from what must surely be a relevant criterion or factor.[212] What could one mean by "fundamental" or "basic" error other than that the error has had a severe or devastating impact on the equivalency of the exchange? It is ironic, then, as Daniel Friedmann has observed, that "the element that the parties (and possibly also the jury) usually consider to be the most important, is, under the common law, totally irrelevant."[213] Moreover, by failing to address the very problem identified by Denning L.J. in *Solle v. Butcher*—the impact of the common law void for mistake doctrine on the interests of third parties—the Court of Appeal has breathed renewed life into a doctrine that is quite unattractive from a policy perspective. Indeed, in this respect, *The Great Peace* is quite inconsistent with other developments in the modern English law of contractual mistake in which the courts have quite deliberately restricted the scope of doctrines rendering contracts void for mistake with a view to reducing the harsh impact of these doctrines on innocent third parties.[214] Finally, the attempted suppression of the equitable doctrine carries with it, at least for the purposes of English law, the suppression of the remedial flexibility afforded by that doctrine. The result is to

---

210 *Ibid.* at 722.

211 See generally McCamus, above note 185 and Sheehan, above note 185.

212 Above note 145 at 728–29.

213 D. Friedmann, "The Objective Principle and Mistake and Involuntariness in Contract and Restitution" (2003) 119 Law Q. Rev. 68 at 74.

214 See above this Chapter, section B(5) (mistakes in identity), this Chapter, section B(6) (*non est factum*). And see the discussion of *Taylor v. Johnson*, above note 21 in this Chapter, section B(3).

leave mistaken assumptions doctrine in a very unsatisfactory state as, indeed, the Court of Appeal appears to concede in this case.[215] Indeed, Lord Phillips conceded the force of Denning L.J.'s reservations concerning the common law doctrine that, ironically, the court had just reinstated, and called for legislative reform of the doctrine.[216] The call for legislative reform of the doctrine, after displacing the reforms achieved in *Solle v. Butcher*, is particularly unhelpful in the Canadian context. It is most unlikely that any and certainly not all of the Canadian common law provinces would deal with these issues by statute. At most, it might be expected that a few provinces could address the problem with a resulting patchwork of doctrine across the common law provinces. Moreover, the reform is, in any event, likely to simply restate the general approach taken in *Solle v. Butcher* of rendering agreements voidable rather than void for mistake. In short, it would be unfortunate if Canadian courts were to follow the lead of the English Court of Appeal in *The Great Peace* and abolish the equitable doctrine of mistaken assumptions. Indeed, it may well prove to be the case that *The Great Peace* will not be the last word on this topic in English jurisprudence.[217]

On the other hand, the Court of Appeal has made a valuable contribution in *The Great Peace* by reaffirming that it is critical in situations where the possibility of applying mistaken assumptions doctrine is being considered that a court attempt to make an assessment of the risk allocation effected by the agreement itself. Although the Court of Appeal has unhelpfully commingled the risk allocation analysis with the determination of whether performance has become "impossible,"[218] it is nonetheless an important step forward for the court to assert that it is necessary to "determine whether on true construction of the contract one or other party has undertaken responsibility for the subsistence of

---

215 Above note 145 at 730.

216 See *ibid.*, where Lord Phillips M.R. stated: "We can understand why the decision in *Bell v. Lever Brothers Ltd.* did not find favour with Denning L.J. An equitable jurisdiction to grant rescission on terms where a common fundamental mistake has induced a contract gives greater flexibility than a doctrine of common law which holds the contract void in such circumstances. Just as the *Law Reform (Frustrated Contracts) Act 1943* was needed to temper the effect of the common law doctrine of frustration, so there is scope for legislation to give greater flexibility to our law of mistake than the common law allows."

217 Thus, it is of interest that the modern restriction on void for mistake in identity achieved in *Lewis v. Averay*, above note 52, has recently been reaffirmed by the House of Lords in *Shogun Finance Ltd. v. Hudson*, above note 62. For discussion, see above this Chapter, section B(5).

218 Above note 145 at 708–9, quoted in the text above at notes 198 and 199.

the assumed state of affairs."[219] As noted above, however, it is unfortunate that the Court of Appeal did not apply this test to the facts of *The Great Peace*, as it appears that the existence of a cancellation fee provision provided a satisfactory basis for inferring that the risk of early termination for whatever reason was assumed by the hirer.

5) Unilateral Mistake in Assumptions

It is generally assumed to be a feature of Anglo-Canadian law concerning mistaken assumptions that the mistake will be operative only if it is common in the sense of being shared by both parties. American law, on the other hand, recognizes the possibility that unilateral mistake in assumptions might provide a basis for rescission of an agreement. In a recent Canadian case concerning a mistakenly calculated bid, an Alberta judge has suggested the adoption of an approach that appears to be very similar to the American rule. The traditional emphasis on the requirement of common mistake may be illustrated by the decision in *Bell v. Lever Brothers Ltd.*[220] In order to successfully make the argument that the contract could be vitiated by common mistake, it was necessary for Lever Brothers to argue that the employees shared their mistake. It will be recalled that the severance agreement at issue in that case, which provided for generous payments to the employees, was entered into by Lever Brothers on the false assumption that the employees could not be dismissed for cause on the basis of their prior misconduct. In order to establish that the mistake was common, Lever Brothers successfully argued that the prior misconduct and its significance was not present in the minds of the employees when they negotiated the severance agreement. Thus, the mistake was common. Ironically, then, the employees would be in a much better position if they were aware of the mistaken assumption at the time of contracting because, in this case, the mistake would be merely unilateral and the employees would be able to exploit the employer's ignorance. On such facts, the employer would be left to attempt to mount the difficult argument that the employees had an obligation to disclose their previous misconduct.[221] The apparently perverse effect of the common mistake requirement in this context suggests that it may merit further consideration.

An attractive context within which to consider the application of a unilateral mistaken assumptions doctrine arises in the context of mis-

---

219 *Ibid.* at 711.
220 Above note 4.
221 See Chapter 10, sections C & D, for a discussion of duties of disclosure.

takenly calculated bids. As we have seen in Chapter 2,[222] the decision of the Supreme Court of Canada in *Ron Engineering & Construction Eastern Ltd. v. Ontario*[223] held that one who submits a bid in response to an invitation to tender has entered into a binding contract, Contract A, as it is called, relating to the tendering process. On this basis, the Supreme Court held that even though the bid in question had been based on a severely mistaken calculation, the mistake was irrelevant to the formation of Contract A. Thus, Contract A remained binding, including a provision stipulating that a bidder who, when selected, refuses to enter the construction contract, Contract B, forfeits its bid deposit. Thus when, upon its selection as the winning bidder, the plaintiff bidder refused to enter into Contract B, it was required to forfeit its deposit. The consequence of the *Ron Engineering* doctrine, then, is that in these circumstances the mistaken calculation infecting the bid is merely a unilateral mistaken assumption underlying the bid. That assumption is that the bid price has been correctly calculated and it has, in the Supreme Court's view, no significance with respect to the enforceability of Contract A. Further, as the Alberta Court of Appeal held in *Calgary v. Northern Construction Co.*,[224] since Contract A requires the selected bidder to enter into Contract B, the mistaken bidder who refuses to enter Contract B will be liable for damages sustained by the party who issued the invitation to tenders by eventually entering into a Contract B with a higher bidder. In a severe case, then, a mere technical slip or, indeed, an undetected typographical error could expose the mistaken bidder to liabilities that appear rather draconian. A unilateral mistaken assumptions doctrine might offer an appropriate means for ameliorating such situations.

In the *Northern Construction Co.* case itself, the defendant mistaken bidder was held liable under Contract A for the expectancy damages sustained by the issuer of the invitation when it was required to enter Contract B with a higher bidder. In a concurring judgment, however, Kerans J.A. suggested that, in a severe case, where the effect of Contract A is to impose a "grossly disproportionate burden" upon the mistaken bidder, it would be "unconscionable"[225] for the issuer to hold the bidder

222 See Chapter 2, section B(1)(c).
223 Above note 25.
224 Above note 2.
225 This test has been misinterpreted by one trial judge as requiring "unconscionability" in the sense of inequality of bargaining power. See *Ottawa (City) Non-Profit Housing Corp. v. Canvar Construction (1991) Inc.* (1999), 46 C.L.R. (2d) 116 (Ont. Ct. Gen. Div.). For Kerans J.A., it appears that a grossly disproportionate burden establishes the requisite element of unconscionability. The decision at

to his mistaken bargain. In such circumstances, in his view, notwithstanding the unilateral nature of the bidder's mistaken assumption, Contract A would not be enforceable. Although Kerans J.A. did not refer to American doctrine in his reasons, it is of some interest that the American rule mirrors rather precisely the approach that he articulated in this case. The American rule is set out in section 153 of the *Restatement of Contracts 2d*[226] in the following terms:

> 153. Where a mistake of one party at the time a contract was made as to a basic assumption on which he made the contract has a material effect on the agreed exchange of performances that is adverse to him, the contract is voidable by him if he does not bear the risk of the mistake under rule stated in §154, and (a) the effect of the mistake is such that enforcement of the contract would be unconscionable, or (b) the other party had reason to know of the mistake or his fault caused the mistake.[227]

The rule set out in this section is similar to the American law on common mistake[228] with the exception that in order to obtain relief on the basis of mere unilateral error, the effect of the mistake on the exchange must be so severe that the enforcement of the agreement would be considered to be "unconscionable." Interestingly, the illustrations set out in the *Restatement*, drawn from American case law, include the granting of relief for unilateral mistake in the context of a mistakenly calculated bid.

D. MISTAKES IN INTEGRATION

1) Introduction

A mistake in integration occurs when the parties reach agreement in the course of their negotiations and an error is made in the subsequent recording of the agreement in writing. In the clear case of an antecedent oral agreement between the parties that is not accurately recorded in the written agreement, the equitable remedy of rectification is available

---

trial in *Canvar* was reversed on appeal on the basis that the gross error was apparent on the face of the tender, which therefore did not give rise to Contract A. See (2000), 13 O.A.C. 116 (C.A.). And see above this Chapter, section B(4).

226 Above note 57.

227 *Ibid.* at 394. Section 154 is set out in the text above at note 173.

228 See section 152 of the *Restatement* set out in the text above note 171.

to either party. If satisfied that an error of this kind has occurred, the court will order reformation of the instrument to bring it into accord with their antecedent agreement.[229] Unlike the previously considered categories of mistake, mistakes in integration do not normally give rise to a conflict between the interest of one party in the enforcement of reasonable expectations and the interest of the other in obtaining relief from an oppressive bargain or preventing an unjust enrichment. In the paradigm case of mistaken integration of an antecedent agreement, the reasonable expectations of both parties can be easily accommodated by reformation of the written agreement.

A number of issues may arise in the context of a claim for rectification. First, the nature and extent of the prior agreement required to apply the doctrine must be considered. Second, as the proponent of rectification has the burden of persuading the court that a written agreement, typically signed by the proponent, does not accurately reflect the prior understanding of the parties, such claims have been hedged in with certain requirements concerning the nature of the proof required to establish satisfactorily the antecedent oral agreement. Further, where the mistake is unilateral in the sense that one party believes that the written instrument accords with the antecedent understanding of the parties, whereas the other party is aware, or perhaps, should have been aware of the fact that the terms of the written agreement do not do so, it must be considered whether rectification should be made available. Finally, as the remedy is equitable in nature, it is subject to various bars or defences recognized on equitable grounds. Each of these issues will be considered in turn.

2) Proving the Antecedent Agreement

Although it is often said that the party seeking rectification must establish a prior "agreement" between the parties, it is plainly the case that it is not necessary to establish the existence of an antecedent binding agreement.[230] The more difficult question is whether the antecedent agreement must be a complete one in the sense that the parties had agreed to all the essential terms of the agreement. Any such requirement would appear to be inconsistent with the practice in rectification cases.

---

229   *H.F. Clarke v. Thermidaire Corp. Ltd.* (1973), 33 D.L.R. (3d) 13 at 20–21 (Ont. C.A.), Brooke J.A., rev'd on other grounds (1974), 54 D.L.R. (3d) 385 (S.C.C.).

230   *United States v. Motor Trucks Ltd.*, [1924] A.C. 196 (P.C.) (rejecting the argument that a prior oral agreement to transfer an interest in land could not provide a standard for rectification because of the lack of formality).

In cases involving the purchase and sale of land, for example, where the parties have, by antecedent understanding, reached agreement on the parcel of land to be transferred, a misdescription of the parcel in the subsequent writing will normally be rectified without anxious consideration of whether all the essential terms of an agreement for the purchase and sale of land had been the subject of antecedent agreement.[231] This point was specifically addressed, however, by the English Court of Appeal in *Joscelyne v. Nissen*.[232] This decision held that if the parties were in agreement on a particular point, up to the time of execution of the formal agreement, the agreement could be rectified to embody an appropriate term even though the parties had not yet reached agreement on other essential matters prior to the time of execution. In this case, a father had transferred a business to his daughter on the basis of an understanding that he would be given a right of occupation of certain premises free of all rent and outgoings of any kind. The daughter acted on this understanding for a time until ultimately advised that the written agreement did not impose such an obligation upon her. The Court of Appeal, rejecting suggestions to the contrary in some earlier authorities, ordered rectification, notwithstanding the fact that the parties had evidently not reached agreement on a number of relevant terms and conditions prior to execution. It is sufficient, then, to find a common continuing intention with respect to the matter in question. The court also indicated its view that an antecedent agreement between the parties could provide a basis for rectification even though the prior understanding had been expressed to be "subject to contract."[233]

There is a significant burden of persuasion on a party who asserts that a signed written agreement does not reflect the prior intention of the parties. Indeed, it has often been suggested that there exists an unusual burden of proof in rectification claims, departing from the normal civil standard of balance of probabilities. Thus, the Supreme Court of Canada has, on previous occasions, suggested that the parties seeking rectification must establish proof of the antecedent agreement "beyond reasonable doubt"[234] or leaving "no 'fair and reasonable

---

231 See, for example, *Devald v. Zigeuner* (1958), 16 D.L.R. (2d) 285 (Ont. H.C.J.); *Sylvan Lake Golf & Tennis Club v. Performance Industries Ltd.* (2002), 209 D.L.R. (4th) 318 (S.C.C.).

232 [1970] 1 All E.R. 1213 (C.A.). See also *Dynamex Canada Inc. v. Miller* (1998), 161 Nfld. & P.E.I.R. 97 at para. 23 (Nfld. C.A.). And see *Crane v. Hegeman-Harris Co. Inc.*, [1939] 1 All E.R. 662 (Ch.).

233 *Joscelyne v. Nissen, ibid.* at 1222–23.

234 *M.F. Whalen (The) v. Pointe Anne Quarries Ltd.* (1921), 63 S.C.R. 109 at 127, 63 D.L.R. 545, Duff J. See also *Brisbois v. Chamberland* (1990), 77 D.L.R. (4th) 583 (Ont. C.A.).

doubt.'"[235] A less burdensome standard of "convincing proof," however, now appears to be generally accepted.[236] Binnie J. in *Sylvan Lake Golf & Tennis Club v. Performance Industries Ltd.*[237] expressed the current view of the Supreme Court in the following terms: "The modern approach, I think, is captured by the expression 'convincing proof,' i.e., proof that may fall well short of the criminal standard but which goes beyond the sort of proof that only reluctantly and with hesitation scrapes over the low end of the civil 'more probable than not' standard."[238]

Noting that critics have suggested that nothing more than the ordinary civil standard proof is necessary,[239] Binnie J. concluded that preservation of a higher standard would avoid dilution of the "demanding preconditions to rectification" by marginal cases. It is not obvious, however, that anything other than applying the normal civil standard to a situation in which the proponent of rectification must typically overcome the substantial obstacle of a signed written agreement that the other party claims to represent the intentions of the parties is at work in this context. Further, no similar special standard is applied to claims based on collateral contracts that appear to raise rather similar issues.[240]

The types of evidence that may be found persuasive by a court entertaining a claim for rectification are illustrated by the decision of a Saskatchewan court in *Bercovici v. Palmer*,[241] a case involving a dispute concerning the subject matter of a contract for the purchase and sale of land. The vendors claimed to have intended to sell only two business properties to the defendant. The conveyance included a cottage property that was not contiguous to the business premises. The facts that persuaded the trial judge that the cottage was not intended to be included in the transaction concerned both the conduct of negotiations and the post-execution conduct of the parties. The purchaser had expressed interest in buying the business premises but never mentioned the cottage that was not, in any respect, related to the business premises. A memorandum of instructions to the solicitor, jointly prepared by the parties, made no mention of the cottage. The purchase price

---

235 *Hart v. Boutilier* (1916), 56 D.L.R. 620 at 630 (S.C.C.), Duff J.
236 *Joscelyne v. Nissen,* above note 232 at 1222. See also *Augdome Corp. v. Gray,* [1975] 2 S.C.R. 354 at 371, Spence J.
237 Above note 231.
238 *Ibid.* at 333.
239 Referring to S. Waddams, *The Law of Contracts,* above note 162 at para. 343. See also G.H.L. Fridman, *The Law of Contract in Canada,* above note 162 at 878.
240 See also *Coderre (Wright) v. Coderre,* [1975] 2 W.W.R. 193 at 199 (Alta. S.C.T.D.), D.C. McDonald J.
241 (1966), 59 D.L.R. (2d) 513 (Sask. Q.B.), aff'd (1966), 59 D.L.R. (2d) 516 (Sask. C.A.).

appeared to have been calculated without the cottage being present to the mind of either party. After execution of the agreement, the purchaser did not demand possession of either the cottage or its keys, nor did the purchaser appear to have ever taken a look at the cottage after the transaction closed. The purchaser never paid taxes on or sought to insure the cottage. Although the purchaser and the vendors quarrelled from time to time about apparently less important matters, they had no discussion concerning the cottage. The agreement of sale listed the contents of the business premises but not the cottage. On these grounds, the trial judge was satisfied "beyond any fair and reasonable doubt" that the cottage was not intended to be included in the transaction.[242] Where, on the other hand, the evidence in support of the antecedent agreement amounts essentially to a bare assertion that there was such an agreement, uncorroborated in any respect, the claim for rectification is likely to fail.[243]

In *Bercovici*, much of the evidence was parol evidence that had been produced in an attempt to obtain a variation of the ultimate written agreement. Such evidence is admissible in rectification claims. Accordingly, evidence relevant to a claim for rectification constitutes a well-established exception to the parol evidence rule.[244] In *Bercovici*, an appeal was taken on the admissibility of evidence concerning the post-execution behaviour of the purchaser. As the appellate court held, however, it appears to be well established that evidence of subsequent conduct consistent with the antecedent agreement is relevant and admissible.[245] It is sometimes said, as it was in *Bercovici v. Palmer*, that the evidence must include some documentary evidence consistent with the antecedent agreement.[246] As Binnie J. noted in the *Sylvan Lake Golf & Tennis Club* case, however, "modern practice has moved away from insistence on documentary corroboration."[247]

3) Unilateral Mistake and Rectification

A unilateral mistake in integration occurs where one party, the mistaken party, fails to appreciate that the antecedent agreement is not re-

242 *Ibid.* at 514.
243 See, for example, *Coderre (Wright) v. Coderre,* above note 240.
244 For discussion of which, see Chapter 6, section D.
245 *Bercovici v. Palmer,* above note 241. See also *M.F. Whalen (The) v. Pointe Anne Quarries Ltd.,* above note 234 at 568 (D.L.R.).
246 *Bercovici v. Palmer, ibid.* at 517–18. See also *M.F. Whalen (The) v. Pointe Anne Quarries Ltd., ibid.*
247 Above note 231 at 334. See also *Augdome Corp. v. Gray,* above note 236.

corded in the written agreement but the other party, the non-mistaken party, reads and understands the meaning of the written agreement. In English law, in a case of unilateral mistake, the remedy of rectification appears to be available only in circumstances where the non-mistaken party either knew of the mistake or engaged in unconscionable conduct designed to divert the attention of the eventually mistaken party from discovering the error. Thus in *A. Roberts & Co. Ltd. v. Leicestershire County Council*[248] a contractor tendered a contract to erect a school for the defendant council at a certain price, the work to be completed in eighteen months. The council, however, prepared a construction agreement that provided for completion in thirty months, a material change that made the contract more burdensome for the contractor. Before execution of the agreement, the council learned that the contractor was unaware of the change but proceeded to execute the agreement without correcting the contractor's error. On these facts, rectification to the contractor's understanding of eighteen months was allowed. Further, in *Commissioner for the New Towns v. Cooper*,[249] the defendant conducted negotiations in such a way as to obscure from the mistaken party the true significance of the language forming part of the oral antecedent agreement and the ultimate written agreement. The defendant had diverted the mistaken party's attention from documentation that would have revealed the full significance of the arrangement by making false and misleading statements. The result of the defendant's conduct was that the mistaken party made the very mistake intended. The non-mistaken party, however, merely suspected but did not know that the mistaken party was, in fact, unaware of the significance of the arrangement. In such circumstances, the unconscionable nature of the defendant's conduct was held to be a ground for rectifying the agreement so as to accord with the mistaken party's antecedent understanding. On the other hand, in *Riverlate Properties v. Paul*,[250] where the defendant neither knew of the mistaken party's error nor engaged in "sharp practice," rectification was denied.

The Canadian law on rectification appears to differ from English law in two respects. First, it is clearly established in Canadian law that rectification may be available where the defendant either "knew or ought to have known of the error and the plaintiff did not."[251] The content of the "ought to have known" branch of this test is not entirely clear but

---

248   [1961] Ch. 555.
249   [1995] 2 All E.R. 929 (C.A.).
250   [1975] Ch. 133 (C.A.).
251   *Sylvan Lake Golf & Tennis Club*, above note 231 at 330.

it would appear to be slightly broader than the "sharp practice" test envisaged by English law. Second, in a case where a Canadian court would hold that the defendant did not know but "ought to" have known of the plaintiff's error, the court retains a discretion to grant rescission to the mistaken party but to condition that rescission with an option to be exercised by the non-mistaken party to have the agreement rectified to the antecedent understanding of the parties. The advantages of this form of relief appear to be twofold. First, where the party who "ought to have known" is guilty of no sharp practice, this approach avoids imposing on the non-mistaken party, an agreement to which he or she did not genuinely assent. The non-mistaken party assented to the agreement as written. On the other hand, this approach avoids the all or nothing solution of the English doctrine that refuses any relief whatsoever to the mistaken party where the non-mistaken party ought to have known of the error but has engaged in no sharp practice.

The Canadian approach, resting on earlier English authority, is illustrated in *McMillen v. Chapman and S.S. Kresge Co. Ltd.*[252] In this case, the parties had orally agreed to a five-year lease at an agreed rent. The lessee instructed his solicitor to draft a lease and to insert a clause, not previously discussed with the lessor, conferring upon the lessee the right to terminate the lease on ninety-days' notice to protect himself in the event that his business should fail. He also indicated that if the lessor was not prepared to agree to such an arrangement, he would not insist upon it. The written version of the lease erroneously conferred such a right to terminate upon the lessor, rather than the lessee. When the lessor read the lease, he noticed this advantageous arrangement, had no objection to it and executed the lease in that form. The lessee sought to rectify the lease by deleting the termination clause that had not been part of the antecedent oral agreement. McRuer C.J.H.C. rejected the claim for rectification. In his view, where a mistake is only unilateral, relief should be available only where the non-mistaken party is guilty of fraud or conduct equivalent to fraud and, even in such a case, the court should not grant compulsory rectification but, rather, should put the non-mistaken party to an election between having the transaction annulled altogether on a rescission or submitting to rectification of the agreement in accordance with the antecedent understanding of the parties. On the facts of this case, the trial judge was of the view that since the lessor had acted "in perfect good faith,"[253] there should be no relief available whatsoever. In *Devald v. Zigeuner*,[254] a case in which the seller's barn was mistakenly included in a real estate transaction, a fact apparently known to the purchaser who thus might be thought to have engaged in a sharp practice, the same trial judge granted rescission of the agreement to the seller subject to the purchaser's right to elect for rectification of the deed to exclude the barn.

The absence of more recent Canadian authority imposing this solution, together with the rejection of this approach by the English Court of Appeal in the *Roberts*[255] case, might be thought to render the current status of this doctrine somewhat uncertain. Professor Waddams has defended this approach, however, on the basis that in a case where a court is reluctant to find fraud, even though it is strongly suspected, the remedy of rescission subject to rectification provides a solution that avoids imposing an agreement not genuinely assented to on either party.[256] If rescission is decreed, the mistaken party will be disappointed by the loss of the antecedent agreement but will not be forced to comply with the unexpected terms in the written agreement. Under this form of relief, the non-mistaken party is either released from the bargain or enabled to affirm the transaction voluntarily on the mistaken party's terms. Where the party clearly has engaged in sharp practice, however, it may be appropriate to hold the non-mistaken party to the terms as understood by the mistaken party, as is the case under current English law, by the granting of a compulsory rectification.[257] Such relief was, indeed, awarded by the Supreme Court of Canada in *Sylvan Lake Golf & Tennis Club*[258] on the basis that the non-mistaken party had engaged in fraudulent conduct concerning the execution of the written agreement.

---

254 Above note 231.

255 Above note 248.

256 S.M. Waddams, "Contracts-Mistake-Rectification with Optional Rescission" (1975) 53 Can. Bar Rev. 339.

257 *A. Roberts & Co. Ltd. Leicestershire County Council*, above note 248. In this case, however, there does not appear to have been an antecedent agreement to which the agreement could be reformed. Arguably, then, the case is one where unilateral mistake as to a term prevents formation of the agreement. See above this Chapter, section B(3). Possible explanations for the result, however, are that on an objective theory of formation, the antecedent agreement was created by the fact that the contractor's intent had been expressed on several occasions with the acquiescence and, therefore, apparent agreement of the council or, alternatively, that the council's behaviour at the time of formation created a reasonable belief on the plaintiff's part as to the content of the written agreement by which the council is now bound. See. G. Palmer, *The Law of Restitution*, vol. 3 (Boston: Little, Brown & Co., 1978) at 24–33, 48–53.

258 Above note 231.

4) Defences and Bars to Relief

Rectification is an equitable remedy and accordingly its award is in the discretion of the court.[259] Further, the usual range of defences or bars to equitable relief may have the effect of denying this particular form of relief. Thus, an order of rectification will not be granted where its effect would be to work an unfair prejudice on an innocent third party. In *Wise v. Axford*,[260] for example, rectification was denied where its effect would have been to retract a portion of a property conveyed to an innocent third-party purchaser. The vendor had sold two contiguous lots to separate purchasers. In the first transaction, the vendor and purchaser both mistakenly understood that the lot line of the lot to be sold included a portion of the second lot. After the first transaction closed, the second lot was sold to a second purchaser who was unaware of any difficulties relating to the first transaction. When the first purchaser sought rectification of the deed to include a portion of the second parcel, rectification was denied. The impact on the innocent third party must, however, be prejudicial in some sense. Thus, in a case where the effect of rectification is simply to substitute one creditor for another, where the identify of the creditor is plainly a matter of indifference to the debtor, rectification was allowed.[261] Further, as in other equitable contexts, undue delay[262] or affirmation of the agreement in its written version[263] may provide a basis for denying this form of relief.

In the *Sylvan Lake Golf & Tennis Club* case,[264] it was argued that the plaintiff should be denied the remedy of rectification on the ground that the plaintiff's want of due diligence in refraining from reading the written agreement ought to provide a basis for denying rectification. The written document in this case related to the purchase of a golf club property by the parties and provided, in part, that a certain portion of the property would be reserved to the plaintiff for development purchases. That portion was described by referring to its length and width as 480 yards and 110 feet. The original understanding of the parties had been that the width measurement was also in yards. Further, it appeared the other party substituted the word "feet" for the intend-

---

259 See *Sylvan Lake Golf & Tennis Club*, above note 231 at 340.

260 [1955] 1 D.L.R. 508 (Ont. C.A.).

261 *Augdome Corp. v. Gray*, above note 236.

262 *Hart v. Boutilier*, above note 235.

263 *A.L. Gullison & Sons Ltd. v. Corey* (1979), 24 N.B.R. (2d) 638 (Q.B.), rev'd (1980), 29 N.B.R. (2d) 86 (C.A.); *Shorb v. Public Trustee* (1953), 8 W.W.R. (N.S.) 657 at 672–673 (Alta. S.C.), aff'd (1954), 11 W.W.R. (N.S.) 132 (Alta. C.A.).

264 Above note 231.

ed yards with fraudulent intent. In such circumstances, the Supreme Court of Canada held, the alleged want of due diligence could not serve as a defence to the rectification claim. One who is guilty of fraud simply cannot raise an argument of this kind. More generally, however, the Court's view was that a plaintiff seeking rectification is not subject to a demonstration of due diligence in reviewing the written document. As Binnie J. observed, "[M]ost cases of unilateral mistake involve a degree of carelessness on the part of the plaintiff."[265] An argument based on due diligence is not persuasive in the rectification context because the plaintiff "seeks no more than enforcement of the prior oral agreement to which the defendant has already bound itself."[266] However, as the remedy is discretionary in nature, the conduct of the plaintiff is a relevant consideration and therefore, in an appropriate case, the negligence of a plaintiff seeking a rectification is a consideration to be taken into account in determining whether it would be unjust to impose this form of relief on a defendant in a particular case.

FURTHER READINGS

P.S. ATIYAH, "Judicial Techniques and the Law of Contract" in P.S. Atiyah, *Essays on Contract* (Oxford: Clarendon Press, 1986) c. 9.

R. BIRMINGHAM, "Holmes on 'Peerless': *Raffles v. Wichelhaus* and the Objective Theory of Contract" (1985) 47 U. Pitt L. Rev. 183.

E.A. FARNSWORTH, *Alleviating Mistakes* (Oxford: Oxford University Press, 2004).

G.H.L. FRIDMAN, "Error in Substantialibus: A Canadian Comedy of Errors" (1978) 56 Can. Bar Rev. 603.

G.H.L. FRIDMAN, "Tendering Problems" (1987) 66 Can. Bar Rev. 582.

D. FRIEDMANN, "The Objective Principle and Mistake and Involuntariness in Contract and Restitution" (2003) 119 Law Q. Rev. 68.

A. KULL, "Mistake, Frustration, and the Windfall Principle" (1991) 43 Hastings L.J. 1.

A. KULL, "Unilateral Mistake: The Baseball Card Case" (1992) 70 Wash. L. Rev. 57.

---

265 *Ibid.* at 338.
266 *Ibid.* at 338–39.

C. MACMILLAN, "How Temptation Led to Mistake: An Explanation of *Bell v. Lever Brothers Ltd.*" (2003) 119 Law Q. Rev. 625.

P. MATTHEWS, "A Note on *Cooper v. Phibbs*" (1989) 105 Law Q. Rev. 599.

J.D. McCAMUS, "Mistaken Assumptions in Equity: Sound Doctrine or Chimera?" (2004) 40 Can. Bus. L.J. 46.

L.B. McTURNAN, "An Approach to Common Mistake in English Law" (1963) 41 Can. Bar Rev. 1.

G. PALMER, *Mistake and Unjust Enrichment* (Columbus: Ohio State University Press, 1962).

R. SAMEK, "Some Reflections on the Logical Basis of Mistake of Identity of Party" (1960) 38 Can. Bar Rev. 479.

S. SCHWARTZ, "*Non Est Factum* in Canada after *Marvo Colour Research Ltd. v. Harris*" (1985) 35 U.N.B.L.J. 92.

D. SHEEHAN, "Vitiation of Contracts for Mistake and Misrepresentation of Law" (2003) R.L.R. 26.

A.W.B. SIMPSON, "Contracts for Cotton to Arrive: The Case of the Two Ships Peerless" (1999) 11 Cardozo L. Rev. 287.

S.M. WADDAMS, "Contracts—Mistake—Rectification with Optional Rescission" (1975) 53 Can. Bar Rev. 339.

FRUSTRATION

A. INTRODUCTION

The doctrine of frustration may provide an excuse for non-performance to a party whose ability to perform has been compromised by supervening events that occur after formation of the agreement.[1] In an agreement to rent a concert hall, for example, the owner's ability to perform would be severely compromised if the building were to be destroyed by fire.[2] A contract to sell and ship goods from India to an Italian buyer becomes more expensive to perform when the Suez Canal is unexpectedly closed.[3] A contract to rent rooms on Pall Mall with a view of the coronation procession of Edward VII becomes pointless when the procession is cancelled.[4] A contractor is hired to construct a particular facility and is then ordered by the government to discontinue the work under wartime regulations.[5] In such cases, provided that the matter

---

1   See generally G.H. Treitel, *Frustration and Force Majeure*, 2d ed. (London: Thomson Sweet & Maxwell, 2004); E. McKendrick, ed., *Force Majeure and Frustration of Contract*, 2d ed. (London: Lloyd's of London Press, 1995) [McKendrick]. And see D. Percy, "The Application of the Doctrine of Frustration in Canada" in G.H.L. Fridman, ed., *Studies in Canadian Business Law* (Toronto: Butterworths, 1971) c. 3.
2   *Taylor v. Caldwell* (1863), 3 B. & S. 826, 122 E.R. 309 (Q.B.).
3   *Tsakiroglou & Co. v. Noblee Thorl G.m.b.H.*, [1962] A.C. 93.
4   *Krell v. Henry*, [1903] 2 K.B. 740 (C.A.).
5   *Metropolitan Water Board v. Dick, Kerr & Co. Ltd.*, [1918] A.C. 119 (H.L.).

has not been specifically provided for in the agreement, the doctrine of frustration may have the effect of discharging the agreement, thereby releasing the parties from any further obligation to perform.

In cases of this kind, the parties have entered into an agreement on the assumption that such problems would not materialize. Cases of frustration are thus quite similar to cases of mistaken assumptions concerning the facts existing at the time an agreement is entered into, a matter that we consider elsewhere.[6] While mistaken assumptions cases deal with assumptions concerning facts in existence at the time of formation of the contract, frustration cases deal with assumptions concerning future events. The close relationship between mistaken assumptions and frustration cases can be neatly illustrated by reference to the coronation cases arising from the postponed coronation of Edward VII. If the contract entered into to rent rooms on Pall Mall had been entered into at a time when the originally planned coronation procession had already been cancelled, the case would be one of mistaken assumptions as to existing facts.[7] If, however, the cancellation of the procession was announced only after the contract had been entered into, the case would be one of frustration. As with mistaken assumptions doctrine, then, frustration doctrine must find an appropriate balance between the inclination to hold people to their bargains, notwithstanding the fact that the bargain has become unexpectedly less attractive to them, and, on the other hand, an inclination to relieve parties from their bargains where a refusal to do so appears unjust and may result in the unjust enrichment of the other party.

In this chapter, the development of the doctrine of frustration and the traditional categories of its application will be considered. It will be suggested that the analytical model that has developed in the law of mistaken assumptions—risk-allocation analysis—may also be fruitfully employed in the context of cases of frustration. We shall then turn to consider the application of frustration doctrine in the particular contexts of increased expense or commercial impracticability, agreements to transfer interests in land and frustration resulting from choices made by the party subject to the obligation to perform. Obviously, parties who anticipate the possibility of interference with contractual performance by supervening events may wish to stipulate for the consequences of such events. Such provisions typically relieve parties from the burden of performance when certain stipulated events of this kind occur. The interpretation of these so-called *force majeure* clauses will

---

6   See Chapter 13, section C.
7   *Griffith v. Brymer* (1903), 19 T.L.R. 434.

be briefly considered before turning to an account of the consequences of frustration at common law.

B. DEVELOPMENT OF THE DOCTRINE

The evolution of the doctrine of frustration in English law may be characterized as having three phases or stages of development. In the earliest phase, the common law appeared to be most reluctant to permit changing circumstances to provide an excuse for non-performance of an agreement. The leading case of *Paradine v. Jane*,[8] decided in 1647, was accepted by the courts[9] as establishing the rule of absolute contracts. Under this approach, unexpected changes in circumstances that substantially undermine the value of a contract for a promisor constitute no defence to a claim brought by the promisee to enforce the agreement against the promisor. On its facts, *Paradine v. Jane* involved a twenty-one-year lease of a farm. After six years of occupancy, the tenant had been dispossessed, as a result of the actions of enemies of the King, for a period of approximately two years. The tenant refused to pay rent for the period during which he could not work the land. The landlord's claim for the rent enjoyed success, however, as the tenant was obliged to perform his contractual obligations "notwithstanding any accident by inevitable necessity, because he might have provided against it by his contract."[10] In the absence of so providing, however, the obligation is absolute. Thus, "if the lessee covenant to repair a house, though it be burnt by lightning or thrown down by enemies, yet he ought to repair it."[11]

Even at this early stage of development, however, there was some authority for the existence of exceptions to this general rule of absolute contracts. The death of the promisor in a contract of personal service[12] and the enactment of subsequent legislation rendering performance illegal[13] were recognized defences to the promisee's claim. A substantial inroad on the doctrine was not made, however, until the second phase in the development of the doctrine initiated by Blackburn J.'s decision

---

8   (1647), Aleyn 26, 82 E.R. 897.

9   See, for example, *Walton v. Waterhouse* (1673), 2 Wms. Saund. 420, 85 E.R. 1233; *Hadley v. Clark* (1799), 8 T.R. 259, 101 E.R. 1377; *Atkinson v. Ritchie* (1809), 10 East 530, 103 E.R. 877.

10   Above note 8 at 27 (Aleyn).

11   *Ibid.*

12   *Hyde v. Dean of Windsor* (1597), Cro. Eliz. 552, 78 E.R. 798.

13   *Abbot of Westminster v. Clerke* (1536–37), 1 Dyer 27a, 73 E.R. 59.

in *Taylor v. Caldwell*,[14] some two hundred years later. In this case, a music hall burned down after a contract to rent the hall for four days had been entered into, but before the time for performance had arrived. The owner of the hall defended against the hirer's claim for damages for breach of contract on the basis that the fire rendered his performance impossible. In permitting the defence, Blackburn J. merely extended the operation of a principle then well recognized[15] that a bailee's duties were discharged if the goods in his care perished without fault on his part. In *Taylor* the court held that the perishing without fault of the premises to be let discharged the owner's obligations under the contract of hire. In articulating reasons for this holding, however, Blackburn J. put forward an explanation that dominated English judicial thinking on the subject until the latter part of the twentieth century. Having conceded that the contract did not expressly provide for discharge in the event of a fire, Blackburn J. went on to observe:

> a condition is implied that the impossibility of performance arising from the perishing of the person or thing shall excuse the perform-ance ... that excuse is by law implied, because from the nature of the contract it is apparent that the parties contracted on the basis of the particular person or chattel. In the present case, looking at the whole contract, we find that the parties contracted on the basis of the continued existence of the Music Hall ... that being essential to their performance.[16]

Hence, the contract was construed by Blackburn J. as subject to an im-plied condition that the owner be excused. In *Taylor v. Caldwell*, then, performance will be excused in the changed circumstances because this solution is dictated by what the agreement reveals about what must have been the actual intent of the parties.

The search, mandated by *Taylor v. Caldwell*, for subjective intent as a basis for implying a term could, however, only provide a satisfac-tory explanation for a limited range of cases. It might seem obvious to some that where the subject matter of the contract has been destroyed, it is reasonable to assume that the parties must not have intended the contract to continue in force. Yet even in these cases, it is clear that the inquiry does not concern the actual intent of the parties, but the pre-sumed intent of the parties acting as reasonable persons. As one judge was later to observe, "there is something of a logical difficulty in see-

---

14   (1863), 3 B. & S. 826, 122 E.R. 309.

15   *Williams v. Lloyd* (1629), Jones, W. 179, 82 E.R. 95.

16   *Taylor v. Caldwell*, above note 14 at 839 (B. & S.).

ing how the parties could even impliedly have provided for something which *ex hypothesi* they neither expected nor foresaw."[17] The obvious inadequacy of the implied-term theory provoked a third phase in the development of the doctrine in which the implied-term approach ultimately met its eclipse and was replaced by a rule that is formally divorced from speculation concerning the subjective intent of the parties.

An approach that found favour with a number of judges was first articulated in 1916 by Viscount Haldane in his dissenting opinion in *Tamplin Steamship Co. v. Anglo Mexican S.S. Co.*[18] The case involved a charter party interrupted by governmental requisition of the ship for use as a troop carrier. The majority held that no term could be implied in the charter party to excuse the parties in the event of interruptions of this kind. In dissent, Viscount Haldane suggested that the charter party could be considered to be dissolved on the following basis: "Although the words of the stipulation may be such that the mere letter would describe what has occurred, the occurrence, itself, may yet be of a character and extent so sweeping that the foundation of what the parties are deemed to have had in contemplation has disappeared, and the contract itself has vanished with that foundation."[19]

Although Viscount Haldane thus avoided reference to the intent of the parties, and the implied-term theory, it is nonetheless the case that an attempt to discern the true "foundation" of the agreement, must rest ultimately on construction of the agreement. Thus, Viscount Haldane indicated that enforcement of the contract should be rejected because it would "in reality impose new and different terms on the parties."[20] Viscount Haldane's approach requires one to determine whether, on a proper construction, the contract requires performance to continue in the changed circumstances.

In the course of construing an agreement, of course, it may be necessary to give a reading of the agreement that rests on an objective standard of reasonableness. Some jurists, however, appeared to favour reliance on a reasonableness standard that was divorced from the exercise of construing the agreement between the parties. On this formulation of the doctrine, frustration could be characterized simply as a "device by which the rules as to absolute contracts are reconciled with the special excep-

---

17   *Davis Contractors Ltd. v. Fareham Urban District Council*, [1956] A.C. 696 at 728 (H.L.), Lord Radcliffe.
18   [1916] 2 A.C. 397 (H.L.).
19   *Ibid.* at 406–7.
20   *Ibid.* at 407.

tion which justice demands."[21] Thus, some judges characterized the doctrine as one that permits the courts to exercise a discretion to vary or supplement the terms of the agreement in order to achieve a just and reasonable result. Both Lord Wright[22] and Lord Denning strongly supported this position, the latter in *British Movietonews Ltd. v. London and District Cinemas*[23] in the following words: "In these frustration cases, as Lord Wright said, the court really exercises a qualifying power—a power to qualify the absolute, literal or wide terms of the contract—in order to do what is just and reasonable in the new situation."[24]

Applying this approach, the Court of Appeal qualified the language of a supplemental agreement the parties had entered to deal with wartime restrictions on newsreel films and held that the agreement was frustrated. This approach is vulnerable to the criticism, however, that it offers little insight that would be of assistance in an attempt to apply the doctrine. Indeed, it amounts to little more than a statement of the obvious fact that the purpose served by the doctrine is the pursuit of justice. This view becomes controversial, however, insofar as it is taken as suggesting that the court's power to discharge the promisor is derived from something other than its jurisdiction to construe the agreement between the parties. The decision of the Court of Appeal in *British Movietonews* was, however, reversed by the House of Lords. The views of Lord Denning were expressly rejected and the court asserted that the touchstone of judicial intervention was, as Viscount Simon indicated, the "true construction" of the agreement.[25]

A few years later, however, the House of Lords adopted an explanation of frustration doctrine that, on first impression, may appear to be more consistent with the views of Lords Wright and Denning than with the construction approach. In *Davis Contractors Ltd. v. Fareham Urban District Council*,[26] Lord Radcliffe stated that application of the doctrine turned on what the parties "as fair and reasonable men, would presumably have agreed upon if, having such possibilities in view, they had made express provisions as to their several rights and liabilities

21 *Hirji Mulji v. Cheong Yue S.S. Co. Ltd.*, [1926] A.C. 497 at 510, Lord Summer.
22 See *Joseph Constantine S.S. Line Ltd. v. Imperial Smelting Corp. Ltd.*, [1942] A.C. 154 (H.L.); *Denny, Mott & Dickson v. James B. Fraser & Co. Ltd.*, [1944] A.C. 265; Lord Wright, *Legal Essays and Addresses* (Cambridge: Cambridge University Press, 1939) at 258–59.
23 [1951] 1 K.B. 190 (C.A.), rev'd on appeal, [1952] A.C. 166 (H.L.).
24 *Ibid.* at 200 (C.A.).
25 *Ibid.* at 183–86 (H.L.), Viscount Simon. See also *ibid.* at 187 (H.L.), Lord Simonds.
26 Above note 17.

in the event of its occurrence."[27] And he added: "the spokesman of the fair and reasonable man, who represents after all no more than the anthropomorphic conception of justice, is, and must be, the court itself."[28] If an analysis based on an attempt to attribute intentions to the parties is to be abandoned, what is to take its place? Lord Radcliffe provided the following answer to this question:

> perhaps it would be simpler to say at the outset that frustration occurs whenever the law recognizes that without default of either party a contractual obligation has become incapable of being performed because the circumstances in which performance is called for would render it a thing radically different from that which was undertaken by the contract. *Non haec in foedera veni.* It was not this that I promised to do.[29]

Thus, the appropriate starting point for inquiry when applying the doctrine is to ask whether the promisor's obligation has radically changed as a result of the intervening events. Lord Radcliffe went on to emphasize, however, that the application of frustration doctrine rests ultimately on a proper construction of the agreement entered into by the parties.[30] It is only by such means that one could determine "that which was undertaken by the contract." This reaffirmation of construction as the foundation of the doctrine suggests, however, that the distance travelled from the "implied-contract" theory to the *Davis Contractors* test is not vast. The principal difference achieved in the movement of the doctrine from the abandoned implied-contract theory to the modern construction theory thus appears to be a greater willingness, when construing the agreement, to employ an objective standard of reasonableness in qualifying the literal terms of the agreement when a radical change of circumstances has occurred.

In Canada, the implied-term theory has met a similar fate. Although Lord Denning's seemingly more radical views were adopted by the British Columbia Court of Appeal,[31] the more cautious statements of Lord Radcliffe in the *Davis Contractors* case were quoted with approval by the Supreme Court of Canada in 1960[32] and by other Canadian courts

---

27   *Ibid.* at 728, quoting from *Dahl v. Nelson* (1881), 6 App. Cas. 38 at 59, Lord Watson.
28   *Ibid.* at 728.
29   *Ibid.* at 728–29.
30   *Ibid.* at 729. See also *ibid.* at 719, Lord Reid. And see below this Chapter, section D.
31   *Cahan v. Fraser*, [1951] 4 D.L.R. 112 (B.C.C.A.).
32   *Peter Kiewit Sons' Co. of Canada v. Eakins Construction Ltd.*, [1960] S.C.R. 361 at 368. See also *Naylor Group Inc. v. Ellis-Don Construction Ltd.*, [2001] 2 S.C.R. 943 at paras. 52–59. And see *Swanson Construction Co. v. Government of Manitoba*

in more recent years.[33] Accordingly, the modern approach of construing the agreement in light of the "radical change in the nature of the obligation" may be considered to be the prevailing view in Canada.

C. THE STANDARD CATEGORIES OF FRUSTRATION

The doctrine of frustration has provided an excuse for non-performance on the basis of changing circumstances in three kinds of situations. First, the doctrine has been applied in cases where the frustrating event has rendered performance impossible. Second, there are a small number of cases in which, though performance remains possible, the purpose for which one or both of the parties have entered the agreement has been undermined. Third, there are cases in which temporary impossibility has grounded discharge for frustration.

1) Impossibility

As we have seen,[34] even at the time of *Paradine v. Jane*,[35] courts had recognized exceptions to the rule of absolute contracts. Thus, in a contract to provide personal services, the death of the service provider discharged the agreement.[36] Similarly, the enactment of subsequent legislation prohibiting the contractual performance in question brought the agreement to an end.[37] In such cases, performance might be said to be, in some sense, impossible. Similarly, in *Taylor v. Caldwell*,[38] the destruction of the concert hall by fire might be said to render performance impossible. Although the rule in the *Taylor* case is commonly referred to as the doctrine of "impossibility by destruction of specific subject matter," it is clear that the rule has a wider application than this designation would indicate. The term "subject matter"

(1963), 40 D.L.R. (2d) 162 (Man. C.A.); *Electric Power Equipment v. R.C.A. Victor Co.* (1964), 41 D.L.R. (2d) 727, var'd (1965), 46 D.L.R. (2d) 722 (B.C.C.A.).

33   See, for example, *Capital Quality Homes v. Colwyn Construction Ltd.* (1975), 61 D.L.R. (3d) 385 (Ont. C.A.). And see *Focal Properties Ltd. v. George Wimpey Canada Ltd.* (1975), 73 D.L.R. (3d) 387 (Ont. C.A.), aff'd on other grounds (1977), 78 D.L.R. (3d) 129 (S.C.C.).

34   See above this Chapter, section B.

35   Above note 8.

36   Above note 12.

37   Above note 13.

38   Above note 14.

for example, does not refer merely to the performance promised under the agreement but as well to a specific person or thing necessary for performance of the promisor's undertaking. In *Nickoll & Knight v. Ashton Edridge & Co.*,[39] for example, the rule was applied to discharge an agreement to sell goods "to be shipped by the steamship Orlando" on the basis that the ship in question had been stranded. Further, it is clear that the rule applies in circumstances short of physical destruction of the "particular person or chattel." It is enough that there exists an incapacity to perform.[40]

Shortly after the decision in *Taylor*, the doctrine was applied to a case where the performance of the promisor was said to be prevented by an act of the legislature. In *Baily v. De Crespigny*,[41] the defendant had covenanted that he would refrain from building a structure on certain lands. The fact that the legislature had subsequently intervened and permitted a railway company to expropriate the defendant's land and build a station on it was held to be a complete defence to the plaintiff's claim for breach of contract. Performance had been rendered impossible by statute. Similar considerations would apply, of course, when the promised performance of the promisor is itself prohibited[42] by the law of the jurisdiction in which it is to be performed,[43] or when a declaration of war has the effect of rendering further performance of the contract trading with the enemy.[44] Although some of the pre-*Taylor* case law had recognized a doctrine of impossibility of performance caused by operation of law,[45] it was in the *Baily* case that this doctrine was placed squarely on the implied-contract theory.

In sum, the doctrine of impossibility will discharge a promisor where, without his fault, (a) in a contract requiring the personal performance of the promisor, the promisor dies or is incapacitated through illness, (b) in a contract where performance requires the continued existence of a specific thing, that thing perishes or is otherwise unavailable for performance; and (c) performance is subsequently prevented or prohibited by operation of law.

---

39 [1901] 2 K.B. 126.

40 See, for example, *ibid.* (sale of cargo—ship temporarily stranded by perils at sea); *Robinson v. Davison* (1871), L.R. 6 Ex. 269 (temporary illness—personal services contract).

41 (1869), L.R. 4 Q.B. 180.

42 *Metropolitan Water Board v. Dick, Kerr & Co. Ltd.*, above note 5.

43 *Ralli Bias v. Compania Naviera Sota & Aznar*, [1920] 2 K.B. 287.

44 *Atkinson v. Ritchie*, above note 9.

45 *Brewster v. Kitchell* (1697–98), 1 Salk. 198, 91 E.R. 177.

2) Frustration of Purpose

A well-known series of cases arising from the postponement of the coronation of Edward VII presented problems that could not easily be resolved by resort to the doctrine of impossibility. In the leading case of *Krell v. Henry*,[46] for example, the defendant had agreed to hire a flat from which the coronation procession could be observed. The agreement made no reference to the coronation. In fact, however, the owner of the flat was aware of the hirer's purpose for renting the flat. Postponement of the coronation destroyed the value of the agreement for the hirer, but did not render impossible the performance of the expressly stated obligations of either party. Nonetheless, the Court of Appeal, in rejecting the owner's claim for the fee, held that the *Taylor* case applied to this set of circumstances. Vaughan Williams L.J., writing for the court, noted that the *Taylor* rule had been extended to cases "where the event which renders the contract incapable of performance is the cessation or non-existence of an express condition or state of things, going to the root of the contract, and essential to its performance."[47] In his view, the only novel point that arose here was whether the court should look to circumstances beyond the terms of the agreement in applying the rule. He answered this question affirmatively in the following manner:

> I think that you first have to ascertain, not necessarily from the terms of the contract, but if required, from necessary inferences, drawn from surrounding circumstances recognized by both contracting parties, what is the substance of the contract and then to ask the question whether that substantial contract needs for its foundation the assumption of the existence of a particular state of things. If it does, this will limit the operation of the general words, and in such case, if the contract becomes impossible of performance by reason of the non-existence of the state of things assumed by both contracting parties as the foundation of the contract, there will be no breach of the contract thus limited.[48]

Hence, on a narrow reading, the decision may be said merely to create an exception to the parol evidence rule that permits the courts to take a broad view of the obligations assumed by the parties. The *Krell* decision has, however, been generally considered to accomplish much more than simply displacing the parol evidence rule in certain cases. The

46   Above note 4.
47   *Ibid.* at 748.
48   *Ibid.* at 749.

broader view is that the case establishes a doctrine independent from considerations of impossibility to the effect that where the occurrence of some event may be said to be the basis of a contract, even though it may not be expressly mentioned in the agreement, the parties will be discharged if that event does not occur. In order to extend the rule in this fashion, however, the decision in *Krell* restates the basic principle broadly on terms of the cessation or non-existence of a state of things forming the foundation of the agreement. Lord Loreburn adopted this wider statement of the rule in *Tamplin Steamship Co. v. Anglo-Mexican Petroleum*[49] and linked it to the failure of the purpose of the agreement. The court's task, he suggested, is "to examine the contract and the circumstances in which it was made, not of course to vary, but only to explain it, in order to see whether or not from the nature of it the parties must have made their bargain on the footing that a particular thing or state of things would continue to exist."[50] In such cases, Lord Loreburn observed, a term would be implied to that effect, if "the discontinuance is such as to upset altogether the purpose of the contract."[51] By linking the doctrine to a failure of the purpose of the agreement, Lord Loreburn focuses more particularly on the impulse underlying the decision in *Krell v. Henry*. Both owner and hirer understood what the purpose of the agreement had been; supervening events had made it unattainable. It is not surprising then that the rule is often referred to as relating to "frustration of the commercial purpose."

By eliminating references to impossibility of performance and by formulating the rule in terms of a cessation or non-existence of a "state of things" going to the root of the contract, the *Krell* decision cast the rule in broad enough form to embrace all of the impossibility cases as well as situations such as *Krell* in which no question of impossibility arises. The "state of things" that ceases to exist in the impossibility cases is the ability of the party to perform. This broader version of the rule, then, had the capacity to become the only rule. Moreover, the *Krell* version of the rule was quite similar to the then-current version of the mistaken assumptions rule.[52] Adoption of the broader test, then, would have had the attractive feature of emphasizing the fundamental similarity of frustration and mistaken assumptions cases. This rationalization of the doctrine was not to occur, however, and the doctrines of impossibility and frustration were received as and continue to be re-

---

49　Above note 18.
50　*Ibid.* at 403.
51　*Ibid.*
52　See Chapter 13, section C.

garded as two separate doctrines and the parallels between frustration and mistaken assumptions cases are infrequently observed.[53]

The potential scope for the operation of the frustration of purpose rule has not been treated expansively by the courts. The very correctness of the *Krell* decision has itself been questioned,[54] and Lord Wright has said of the decision that it "is certainly not one to be extended."[55] Further, the decision has been narrowly distinguished on occasion. In *Herne Bay Steam Boat Company v. Hutton*,[56] another of the coronation cases, the Court of Appeal held that the defendant, who had hired the plaintiff's boat, as the agreement of hire stated, "for the purpose of viewing the naval review and for a day's cruise round the fleet,"[57] was not discharged from his agreement by the cancellation of the coronation-related naval review. The occurrence of the naval review did not "lay the foundation"[58] and was not the sole basis for the contract.[59] Nonetheless, it is generally accepted that the *Krell* decision was itself correctly decided and that the doctrine of frustration of the commercial purpose is an accepted feature of English[60] and Canadian[61] law. At the same time, however, the practical effect of the doctrine appears to be insubstantial. Judicial recognition of its existence is typically accompanied by a decision that it does not apply to the facts at hand.[62]

---

53 Through the evolution of the doctrine, however, various judges, whether intentionally or not, have formulated the frustration test in terms approximating the then-current test for mistaken assumptions. Thus, in the nineteenth century, whereas mistake related to the non-existence of the subject matter of the agreement, frustration related to the destruction of the subject matter. For a modern illustration, see Laskin J.A., in his dissenting opinion in *Parrish & Heimbecker Ltd. v. Gooding Lumber Ltd.* (1968), 67 D.L.R. (2d) 495 at 498 (Ont. C.A.) framing his analysis of frustration in terms of the failure of "mutual assumptions by parties that underlie their commercial relations," a test that closely parallels the modern analysis of mistaken assumptions issues. See Chapter 13, section C.

54 By Viscount Finlay in *Larrinaga v. Société Franco-Américaine des Phosphates de Medulla, Paris* (1922), 29 Com. Cas. 1 at 7, [1923] All E.R. Rep. 1 at 6 (H.L.).

55 *Maritime National Fish Ltd. v. Ocean Trawlers*, [1935] A.C. 524 at 529.

56 [1903] 2 K.B. 683.

57 *Ibid.* at 684.

58 *Ibid.* at 689, Vaughan Williams L.J.

59 *Ibid.* at 691, Romer L.J., "... it cannot be said that by reason of the failure to hold the naval review there was a total failure of consideration."

60 See, for example, *Horlock v. Beal*, [1916] 1 A.C. 486 at 513 (H.L.), Lord Shaw of Dunfermline.

61 See, for example, *Capital Quality Homes Ltd. v. Colwyn Construction Ltd.* (1975), 61 D.L.R. (3d) 385 at 390 (Ont. C.A.), Evans J.A.

62 See, for example, *British Movietonews Ltd. v. London and District Cinemas Ltd.*, above note 23.

3) Temporary Impossibility

The term "frustration" seems to have been first introduced into English law in cases where prolonged delay in performance severely reduced the value of the performance to the promisee or dramatically
increased the burdens shouldered by the promisor in discharging his
duty. Most frequently, these problems arose in maritime cases where
either the shipowner or the charterer sought a discharge from his obligations under a charterparty agreement.[63] The term "frustration of the
adventure" was initially employed by the courts to refer to the situation where the shipowner, by virtue of his own breach of a contractual
duty, had so delayed his performance that it was no longer of any real
value to the charterer. In such cases the charterer would be entitled to
a discharge from his agreement to hire the vessel. Two decisions in the
1870s applied this analysis to situations where the delay was caused
by circumstances beyond the shipowner's control. In *Geipel v. Smith*[64]
the defendant shipowner was permitted to treat the charter party as at
an end by reason of the fact that war had broken out and delayed the
promised voyage for the foreseeable future. The state of war "was likely
to continue so long and so to disturb the commerce of merchants, as
to defeat and destroy the object of a commercial adventure like this."[65]
Accordingly, the charterer was denied the right to require a delayed
performance. In *Jackson v. Union Marine Insurance Co.*,[66] however, it
was the shipowner who wished to enforce the charter party. Here the
shipowner's delay, although excusable, was held to have so diminished
the value of performance that the charterer was entitled to repudiate
the agreement.

The principles developed in these cases have been extended beyond
the maritime context and applied in a long series of decisions involving
prolonged delay in performance that had resulted from circumstances
for which the party in delay was not to be held responsible. In particular, the interruptions in performance of contractual commitments
caused by World War I generated a series of cases[67] in which these
doctrines were firmly established. In one of the wartime cases, *Tamplin
v. Anglo-Mexican S.S. Co.*,[68] the House of Lords indicated that the pro-

---

63   See generally R.G. McElroy and G.L. Williams, *Impossibility of Performance*
     (Cambridge: University Press, 1941) c. 6.
64   (1872), L.R. 7 Q.B. 404.
65   *Ibid.* at 414–15.
66   (1874), L.R. 10 C.P. 125.
67   See McElroy and Williams, above note 63, c. 7.
68   Above note 18. See also *Horlock v. Beal*, above note 60 at 512–13, Lord Shaw.

longed delay cases were all of a piece with the principles established in *Taylor v. Caldwell*[69] and *Krell v. Henry*.[70] Although there is therefore some justification for speaking of a generalized doctrine of frustration that embraces these three distinguishable lines of authority, this merger of the doctrines has not occurred. The three lines of authority are commonly treated as distinguishable.

D. A MODERN RESTATEMENT: RISK-ALLOCATION ANALYSIS

The adoption of the *Davis Contractors* test in England and Canada effected a flat rejection of the implied-contract theory of frustration doctrine and its underlying assumption that one can determine whether performance is still required, notwithstanding the changed circumstances, by a careful examination of the parties' intentions with respect to the matter. The *Davis Contractors* test places emphasis on whether the changed circumstances in which performance is called for would "render it a thing radically different from that which is undertaken by the contract."[71] Under the *Davis Contractors* test, then, emphasis shifts from an attempt, presumably futile, to determine what the parties actually intended with respect to the unforeseen event to a determination of the nature of the contractual undertaking of the affected party and whether the changed circumstances have radically changed the nature of that obligation. In determining the nature of the contractual undertaking, it will be necessary to engage in a careful construction of the terms of the contract. As Lord Reid noted in the *Davis Contractors* case: "It appears to me that frustration depends, at least in most cases, not on adding any implied term, but on the true construction of the terms which are in the contract read in the light of the nature of the contract and of the relevant surrounding circumstances when the contract was made."[72]

---

69 Above note 14.
70 Above note 4.
71 Above note 17 at 729.
72 *Ibid.* at 720–21. See also Lord Radcliffe's observation, at 729, that "[t]here is no uncertainty as to the materials upon which the court must proceed" followed by his quotation, with approval, of the following statement of Lord Wright: "The data for decision are, on the one hand, the terms and construction of the contract, read in light of the then existing circumstances, and on the other hand the events which have occurred." See *Denny, Mott & Dickson Ltd. v. James B. Fraser & Co. Ltd.*, above note 22 at 274–75, Lord Wright.

Application of the *Davis Contractors* test, then, sets in motion an exercise in construing the terms of the agreement with a view to determining whether the performance as envisaged by the contract has been radically transformed by the changing circumstances. Very little direct guidance is given in the *Davis Contractors* case itself, however, as to the manner in which this process of construction should proceed. A careful reading of the jurisprudence applying the doctrine of frustration, however, strongly suggests that the critical consideration is a determination of whether, on its proper construction, the agreement in question allocates the risk of the occurrence of the changing circumstances in question to either one of the parties. If the agreement assigns the risk to the party who wishes to be excused from performance, the agreement is enforceable against that party. If the risk has been assumed by the other party or by neither party, however, the doctrine of frustration may apply so as to excuse both parties from further performance.[73] Taking the facts of *Krell v. Henry*[74] as illustrative, we may ask whether the risk of the non-occurrence of the coronation procession was assumed by either party. If it had been assumed by the renter, the owner of the rooms would have been entitled to enforce the agreement. If the risk was assumed by the owner or by neither party, the contract would be discharged by frustration and neither party would be liable for non-performance.

Although the centrality of risk-allocation analysis in the construction of agreements in the context of frustration cases is rarely acknowledged explicitly by the courts, there are occasional judicial statements acknowledging its importance. Thus, in *National Carriers Ltd. v. Panalpina (Northern) Ltd.*,[75] for example, Lord Roskill made the following observations concerning the doctrine of frustration:

---

73   The significance of a finding that the party seeking to excuse non-performance bears the risk leads invariably to the conclusion that the excuse of frustration is not available. The significance of a finding that the other party has "assumed the risk" varies from one context to another. In some circumstances—for example, a finding that the seller of goods retains the risk of accidental loss of the goods until delivery to the buyer—it will have the consequence that the party bearing the risk remains liable to perform the agreement. In other contexts—for example, a finding that the risk of destruction by fire at an existing factory in which a supplier has been installing duct work falls upon the owner—the consequence may be to discharge both parties. See, for example, *Appleby v. Myers* (1867), L.R. 2 C.P. 651; *Parsons Bros. Ltd. v. Shea* (1965), 53 D.L.R. (2d) 86 (Nfld. S.C.). If the risk of the frustrating event has not been assumed by either party, the doctrine will apply.

74   Above note 4.

75   [1981] A.C. 675 (H.L.).

The doctrine is principally concerned with the incidence of risk — who must take the risk of the happening of a particular event especially when the parties have not made any or any sufficient provision for the happening of that event? When the doctrine is successfully invoked it is because in the event which has happened, the law imposes a solution, casting the incidence of that risk on one party or the other as the circumstances of a particular case may require, having regard to the express provisions of the contract into which the parties have entered.[76]

Reference to the incidence of risk is much more likely to occur, however, when courts refrain from applying the doctrine. In explaining the reason for refusing to permit the party wishing to be excused from a duty to perform to rely on the doctrine of frustration, courts often explain that the risk of the changing circumstances in question has been assumed by that party. Thus, in *Davis Contractors* itself, the House of Lords held that the risk of delay in construction is one borne, in the circumstances of that case, by the contractor. Lord Reid observed as follows: "In a contract of this kind, the contractor undertakes to do the work for a definite sum and he takes the risk of the cost being greater or less than he expected."[77] Similarly, Lord Radcliffe observed: "To my mind it is useless to pretend that the contractor is not at risk if delay does occur, even serious delay."[78]

Cases such as *Davis Contractors* not only signal the importance of risk-allocation analysis to the construction of agreements in the frustration context, but they also indicate the kinds of factors that courts will take into account in determining the incidence of risk. Thus, *Davis Contractors* indicates that a performer assumes the risk of circumstances making performance more onerous of a kind that are normal or even somewhat abnormal in the industry in question. If, on the other hand, the circumstances are utterly abnormal, the doctrine of frustration may apply. In *Davis Contractors*, Lord Reid observed, "[i]t may be that delay could be of a character so different from anything contemplated that the contract was at an end, but in this case, in my opinion, the most that could be said is that the delay was greater in degree than was expected."[79]

---

76 *Ibid.* at 712. Location of risk is commonly discussed in the application of frustration doctrine to agreements for the sale of goods and for the transfer of interests in land. See Treitel, above note 1 at 76–124. And see below this Chapter, section F.

77 Above note 17 at 724.

78 *Ibid.* at 731.

79 *Ibid.* at 724.

Similar points were made in the 1922 decision of the Supreme Court of Canada in *Canadian Government Merchant Marine Ltd. v. Canadian Trading Co.*[80] The defendant had contracted to transport lumber for the plaintiff to Australia in two vessels then under construction by a third party. In the event, the vessels were not ready on time and the defendant was unable to undertake the voyages in question. The defendant's attempt to defend against the plaintiff's claim for damages on the basis of frustration doctrine failed. Although dressed in the language of the implied term theory, Duff J. alluded to risk allocation in the following terms: "it is most important to remember that no such terms should be implied when it is possible to hold that reasonable men could have contemplated the taking the risk [*sic*] of the circumstances being what they in fact proved to be when the time for performance arrived."[81]

There was nothing in the evidence to indicate that the delay and the completion of the vessels arose from any extraordinary occurrence. Thus, Duff J. suggested that the destruction of the vessels by fire might well constitute a different case. As a general matter, then, performance that is rendered more onerous by changing circumstances that are foreseeable are not likely to ground a frustration defence.[82] The mere fact that a particular change in circumstance was foreseeable or foreseen may not necessarily lead to the conclusion, however, that the risk of its occurrence has been assumed.[83]

Further, some cases suggest that a change in circumstances that reduces, but does not eliminate, the value of performance for the other party will not constitute frustration. In one of the coronation cases, *Herne Bay Steamboat Company v. Hutton*,[84] the defendant had chartered a boat for the purpose of taking passengers on a cruise to see the naval fleet and a Naval Review associated with the coronation of Edward VII. With the cancellation of the Naval Review, the defendant refused to

---

80   (1922), 64 S.C.R. 106.

81   *Ibid.* at 111.

82   See, for example, *Kesmat Investments Inc. v. Industrial Canadian Indemnity Co.* (1985), 70 N.S.R. (2d) 341 (S.C.A.D.) (in return for a sewer easement across Kesmat's land, Industrial promised to obtain a re-zoning in a subdivision of Kesmat's property — expensive environmental study required — agreement not frustrated). See further, below this Chapter, section E.

83   See, for example, *Bank Line Ltd. v. Arthur Capel & Co.*, [1919] A.C. 435 (H.L.) (requisition of chartered ship foreseen and provided for, in part, by agreement — impact of prolonged requisition on owner of vessel not foreseen — frustration doctrine applied). See also *W.J. Tatem v. Gamboa*, [1939] 1 K.B. 132 at 138, Goddard J.; *Ocean Tramp Tankers Corp. v. V/O Souvfracht (The Eugenia)*, [1964] 2 Q.B. 226 at 239, Lord Denning M.R.

84   Above note 56.

go ahead with the transaction. The owner's claim for the rental charge succeeded, however, on the basis that a day's cruise around the fleet retained some value even in the absence of the Naval Review. Similarly, in *Claude Neon General Advertising Ltd. v. Singh*,[85] a contract to construct and lease a neon sign to a restaurant was not frustrated when wartime lighting restrictions prohibited the use of outdoor lighted signs between sunset and sunrise. The sign remained of value during the hours of sunlight.

The cases applying the doctrine of frustration also offer evidence of factors relevant to a risk-allocation analysis. The impossibility cases, for example, suggest that, as a general matter, courts assume that the risk that performance will become impossible as a result of supervening circumstances has not been allocated by the agreement to the party charged with performance.[86] At the same time, of course, it is conceivable that a person could give a guarantee of performance that might bind even in the event that performance was to become impossible.[87] The cases on temporary impossibility indicate that the risk of short-term delay is normally assigned to the party awaiting performance but that prolonged delay resulting from supervening circumstances is not allocated to either party, with the result that the doctrine of frustration is applicable.

Where the risk allocation under an agreement is perfectly obvious, even though not expressed, the proper construction of the agreement will likely reflect the actual intentions of the parties. Thus, in the context of a long-term contract for the purchase and sale of goods, it is very likely that the parties would commonly understand that fluctuations in the market price of the goods in question are at the risk of the seller if it rises and of the buyer if it should fall. In less obvious cases, however, the parties may have differing assumptions with respect to such matters or may have no expectation whatsoever. In these cases, as in all cases of interpretation, "an objective standard based on reasonableness will be needed to resolve the conflict."[88] At this point, as Lord Radcliffe colourfully stated in the *Davis Contractors* case, "there rises the figure of the fair and reasonable man ... the court itself."[89] In fashioning a reasonable-risk allocation in the particular circumstances, courts may

85   [1942] 1 D.L.R. 26 (N.S.S.C.). For discussion of English, Australian and American "black-out" cases, see Treitel, above note 1 at 296–301.
86   See above this Chapter, section C(1).
87   *Clifford v. Watts* (1870), L.R. 5 C.P. 577 at 585, Willes J.
88   E.A. Farnsworth, "Disputes over Omission in Contracts" (1968) 68 Colum. L. Rev. 860 at 876.
89   Above note 17 at 728.

give consideration to trade custom, to evidence concerning the assumptions on which the parties entered into the agreement and any other inferences that may be drawn from the structure of the agreement into which they have entered.[90] Thus, for example, if an agreement such as a charter party or lease has a lengthy term, it may be more reasonable to hold that the charterer or tenant has assumed the risk of changing circumstances during that term.[91] An obligation to insure or indeed, a past practice of taking insurance[92] or an abnormally high price[93] might signal the assumption of a particular risk. An agreement that is plainly speculative in nature may have been entered for the very purpose of settling the incidence of certain risks in advance.[94]

The relevance of risk-allocation analysis is also supported by the analogy of the mistaken assumptions cases. As we have seen,[95] the importance of risk-allocation analysis in this context has been recognized by the English judiciary. Mistaken-assumptions analysis applies, as we have noted, to mistaken assumptions concerning circumstances believed to be in existence at the time the contract is created. Frustration analysis, on the other hand, applies to assumptions concerning future circumstances that prove to be unfounded. The doctrines thus perform

---

90   In a well-known article, Posner and Rosenfeld have argued that the best method for locating the incidence of risk is to determine which of the two parties is the "superior risk bearer" and imposing the risk on that party. Identification of the superior risk bearer rests on whether a party is (a) in a better position to prevent the risk from materializing or (b) the cheaper insurer. In determining the latter, one would consider the relative ability of the parties to appraise the likelihood and magnitude of the loss and to absorb the transaction costs through, for example, pooling the risk or self-insuring. See R.A. Posner and A.M. Rosenfeld, "Impossibility and Related Doctrines on Contract Law" (1977) 6 J. Legal Stud. 83. Trebilcock has offered a telling critique of this proposal, however, noting that the various criteria identified by these authors will spring up often, perhaps typically, pointing in opposite directions. See M. Trebilcock, *The Limits of Freedom of Contract* (Cambridge: Harvard University Press, 1993) at 135–36. See also A. Kull, "Mistake, Frustration, and the Windfall Principle of Contract Remedies" (1991) 43 Hastings L.J. 1.

91   See *Dominion Coal Co. v. Lord Strathcona Shipping Co. Ltd.*, [1926] A.C. 108 (P.C.); *National Carriers Ltd. v. Panalpina (Northern) Ltd.*, above note 75.

92   See *Frustrated Contract Act*, R.S.B.C. 1996, c. 166, s. 6(1). See also *Tamplin S.S. Co. v. Anglo-Mexican Petroleum Co.*, above note 18.

93   *Tatem v. Gamboa*, above note 83 as explained by Professor Atiyah. See P.S. Atiyah, *An Introduction to the Law of Contract*, 5th ed. (Oxford: Clarendon Press, 1995) at 241.

94   *Larrinaga & Co. Ltd. v. Société Franco-Américaine des Phosphates de Medulla, Paris*, above note 54.

95   See Chapter 13, section C.

similar and related functions and it is appropriate, therefore, that the analytical frameworks they employ would also be similar. As with mistaken assumptions doctrine then, it would be useful to articulate more plainly that the determination of whether the doctrine of frustration applies in a particular fact situation rests on a careful construction of the agreement undertaken with a view to determining whether the risk of loss resulting from changing circumstances has been allocated to either party and, if not, whether that loss is so substantial that the doctrine of frustration should apply. Failure to discuss risk allocation and the factors relevant to its determination under a proper construction of the agreement is likely to lead to manipulative use of other concepts. Thus, if the test is considered to be simply one of determining whether performance is "impossible," it is likely that courts will employ heroic efforts to determine the precise nature of the undertaking that has become "impossible" if it appears inappropriate to saddle the performer with the risk of changing circumstances.[96] Similarly, and here the parallel with mistaken assumptions doctrine is quite striking, if it is required to establish that the "existence of a particular state of things" is the "foundation of the contract,"[97] the concept of "a particular state of things" can be made to do the necessary work to avoid an inappropriate allocation of risk.

A number of these themes may be illustrated by a comparison of two of the cases arising from the closure of the Suez Canal in 1956. In the first case, *Société Franco Tunisienne D'Armement v. Sidermar*,[98] the dispute concerned a voyage charter under which the shipowner provided the vessel for the purpose of a voyage from an Indian port to Genoa. The parties envisaged that the voyage would take a route through the Suez Canal and, indeed, required the captain of the vessel to telegraph a party in Genoa on passing the canal. With the closure of the canal, the vessel was required to go around the Cape of Good Hope, thereby doubling the length of the voyage. The shipowner successfully

---

96   Compare with *Great Peace Shipping Ltd. v. Tsavliris Salvage International Ltd.*, [2002] 4 All E.R. 689 (C.A.), in which the Court of Appeal suggests the importation of an impossibility test from frustration doctrine into the context of mistaken assumptions law, but cautions that in doing so one must carefully determine the details of the "contractual adventure" that may not be expressly spelled out in the contract. See *ibid.* at 708. For discussion see Chapter 13, section C(4).

97   This is the test articulated in *Krell v. Henry*, above note 4 at 754. The "state of things" that failed to be in existence in that case was "rooms *to view the coronation procession*" (emphasis added). See *ibid.* at 754.

98   [1961] 2 Q.B. 278.

claimed that the charter was discharged by the frustrating event of canal closure and that it was therefore entitled to recover the reasonable value of the service rendered. In the second case, *Tsakiroglou & Co. v. Noblee Thorl G.m.b.H.*,[99] however, a claim that closure of the Suez Canal frustrated the agreement at issue failed. This case concerned a sale of Sudanese groundnuts c.i.f. Hamburg,[100] thereby signalling that the seller assumed the risk of paying the necessary freight charges. Both the seller and the buyer of the groundnuts envisaged that the goods would be transported to the buyer upon a vessel that would proceed through the Suez Canal. The contract made no reference, however, to the canal. Upon closure of the canal, the seller unsuccessfully claimed that the contract of sale was discharged by frustration and was held to be subject to a continuing duty to perform in the changed circumstances. The seller's obligation to supply groundnuts had not been "fundamentally" altered or rendered "radically different"[101] by the closure of the canal.

In the first place, we may note that the concept of "impossibility" appears to be highly manipulable in this context. If one interprets the agreement as requiring travel through the Suez Canal, one may conclude that performance of the contract has been rendered "impossible." In *Sidermar*, on the one hand, the court offered this as part of its explanation for the result. In *Tsakiroglou*, on the other hand, the court held that travel through the Suez Canal was not required. Indeed, Viscount Simonds suggested that even if there was an implied term to utilize the Suez route, the closure of the canal would not necessarily frustrate the agreement.[102] The fact that one agreement referred to the Suez Canal whereas the other did not thus does not appear to offer a satisfactory explanation for the differing results in the two cases.

When examined from the perspective of a risk-allocation analysis, however, differences between the two cases can be discerned.[103] The agreement in *Tsakiroglou* was an agreement of sale whereas the agreement in *Sidermar* was a voyage charter. For the seller, then, the cost of freight was merely one of the cost components entering into the calcu-

---

99 [1961] 2 All E.R. 179 (H.L.).

100 An agreement under which the sale price includes the costs of the goods, insurance and freight charges.

101 *Ibid.* at 184, Viscount Simonds.

102 *Ibid.* at 182–83.

103 Another possible view, of course, is that the cases are simply irreconcilable and that, as *Tsakiroglou* is a decision of the House of Lords, whereas *Sidermar* is a decision at trial, the latter must be considered to be incorrectly decided. See, for example, *Ocean Tramp Tankers Corp. v. V/O Souvfracht (The Eugenia)*, above note 82 at 239, Lord Denning M.R.

lation of this sale price. For the ship owner, the length of the voyage is the defining feature of the agreement. Moreover, the contract of sale in *Tsakiroglou* was c.i.f. A seller who did not wish to undertake such a risk, as Beatson has observed[104]would have entered into a free on board (f.o.b.)[105] agreement under which freight charges are assigned to the buyer. From a risk-allocation perspective, then, there is at least a plausible basis for the different outcomes in the two cases. In *Tsakiroglou,* the increase in freight charges was not a sufficiently fundamental matter to bring the facts outside the risk allocation set out in the agreement. For the shipowner in *Sidermar,* however, the agreement did not assign to the shipowner a risk that the voyage would be approximately twice the expected length. Indeed, it is of interest that in *Sidermar,* the trial judge explicitly distinguished c.i.f. sales contracts as being quite different in nature and subject to a different analysis on the frustration point.[106]

A clearer focus on the risks assigned by the agreement in a Canadian crop failure case, *Parrish & Heimbecker Ltd. v. Gooding Lumber Ltd.,*[107] might have led to a different result. It is well established that where a farmer, for example, promises to sell a crop grown from his own land, the failure of the crop will constitute a frustration of the agreement.[108] *Parrish & Heimbecker,* however, is the more difficult case where the parties no doubt contemplated a particular source of supply but did not stipulate that source in the agreement. In this case, the defendant trucker had entered into an agreement to supply corn to a Toronto grain dealer. It was understood by the parties, though not recorded in their written agreement, that the defendant would acquire the corn from farmers who were located near the defendant's place of business in Parkhill, some distance from Toronto. In due course, weather conditions affected the crop yield in that region and the defendant was unable to meet its commitments to the plaintiff buyer. A majority of the Ontario Court of Appeal held that since the agreement did not stipulate a particular source, the defendant was contractually obliged to try to find other sources of corn to meet his obligations to the buyer. In the majority view, it was "immaterial"[109] that the plaintiff's agent knew of

---

104 See J. Beatson, "Increased Expense and Frustration" in F.D. Rose, ed., *Consensus ad Idem* (London: Sweet & Maxwell, 1996) 121 at 133.
105 An agreement under which the seller undertakes, typically, to place the goods "free on board" a particular vessel. In such an agreement, it is understood that the freight charges are to be borne by the buyer.
106 Above note 98 at 306–7.
107 Above note 53.
108 *Howell v. Coupland* (1876), 1 Q.B.D. 258.
109 Above note 53 at 497.

the defendant's intention to purchase from particular sources. In dissent, however, Laskin J.A. examined factors suggesting that the ability of the defendant to acquire the corn from identified sources was a mutual assumption underlying the relationship of the parties. As the plaintiff knew, the defendant was "a lumber company engaged also in trucking" and "not in any professional or business sense a grain broker."[110] To require the defendant to acquire corn from other sources would change the fundamental character of the agreement. For all practical purposes, the defendant "was in a factoring position as between the plaintiff and the farmers in the area."[111] For Laskin J.A., then, the defendant's occupation and the mutual assumption of the parties with respect to the source of the corn indicated that the defendant had not undertaken the risk of a crop failure in his region with the consequent need to acquire corn from alternate suppliers in other parts of the province. Similar results have been achieved in American law.[112]

E. COMMERCIAL IMPRACTICABILITY

Historically, discharge of the promissor on the basis of unexpected changes of circumstances has been rooted in a concept of impossibility. Accordingly, a seller of goods will be excused from a duty to deliver where transportation facilities are simply not available[113] but not where they have merely become considerably more expensive than originally anticipated.[114] Similarly, in the leading case of *Davis Contractors*,[115] it was stated that the mere fact that "there has been an unexpected turn of events, which renders the contract more onerous than the parties had contemplated ... [is not] by itself a ground for relieving a party of the obligation he has undertaken."[116] On the basis of such authorities, one might conclude that the mere fact that performance has become

---

110 *Ibid.* at 498.

111 *Ibid.*

112 See, for example, *Squillante v. California Lands,* 42 P.2d 81 (Cal. App. 1935); *Snipes Mountain Co. v. Benz Bros. & Co.,* 298 P.2d 714 (Wash. 1931). See generally E.A. Farnsworth, *Farnsworth on Contracts,* 2d ed. (New York: Aspen Law & Business, 1998) at 601–2. In the absence of English authority, Treitel has suggested that similar results would be achieved under English law. See Treitel, above note 1 at 184–85.

113 *Vancouver Milling & Grain Co. v. C.C. Ranch Co.,* [1924] S.C.R. 671.

114 *Tsakiroglou & Co. Ltd. v. Noblee Thorl G.m.b.H.,* above note 99.

115 Above note 17.

116 *Ibid.* at 716, Viscount Simonds.

so expensive as to be commercially impracticable, rather than literally or physically impossible, does not constitute a frustrating event under English or Canadian common law. In principle, however, it is difficult to discern a rational basis upon which extreme increases in the cost of performance could never constitute frustration of an agreement. Applying the *Davis Contractors* test itself, it would seem that, for example, a hundredfold[117] increase in the cost of performance should be considered to be a change in circumstances that renders performance "a thing radically different from that which was undertaken by the contract,"[118] notwithstanding the fact that the performance remains literally possible.

American law has plainly recognized a test of commercial impracticability rather than impossibility for the application of frustration doctrine.[119] Although the doctrine of commercial impracticability has rarely been applied to cases where the changing circumstances merely involve increased expense of performance, the doctrine has been applied in such cases to a limited degree. Thus, for example, in *Aluminium Co. of America v. Essex Group Inc.*,[120] severe increases in the cost of electricity resulting from OPEC initiatives were held to constitute a frustrating event. Similarly, in *Florida Power & Light Co. v. Westinghouse Electric Co.*,[121] extreme increases in the projected costs of disposing of spent fuel, with no commercially practicable alternative method available, constituted a frustrating event.

Little direct support can be found in Commonwealth authorities, however, for the proposition that commercial impracticability may constitute a frustrating event. There are occasional *dicta* in support of the proposition. Thus, in a Canadian case, *Kesmat Investments Inc. v.*

---

117 Compare with *Brauer & Co. (Great Britain) Ltd. v. James Clark (Brush Materials) Ltd.*, [1952] 2 All E.R. 497 (C.A.), a case holding that the mere fact that the seller's minimum export price to acquire the goods to be supplied under an agreement of sale was now more than the buyer's purchase price did not constitute *force majeure* within the contractual *force majeure* clause. The mere fact that the contract was now unprofitable did not constitute *force majeure* but the court further suggested that a hundredfold increase in cost might well excuse performance. See *ibid.* at 500, Singleton L.J. and 501, Denning L.J.

118 Above note 17 at 729.

119 See American Law Institute, *Restatement of Contracts 2d* (St. Paul: American Law Institute, 1981) s. 261 ("Where after a contract is made, a party's performance is made impracticable without his fault by the occurrence of an event the non-occurrence of which was a basic assumption on which the contract was made, his duty to render that performance is discharged, unless the language or the circumstances indicate the contrary.").

120 499 F. Supp. 53 (W.D. Pa. 1980).

121 826 F.2d 239 (4th Cir. 1987).

Industrial Machinery Co. and Canadian Indemnity Co.,[122] a case in which increased cost of performance was found not to constitute frustration, McDonald J.A. nonetheless expressed the applicable test in the following terms: "Courts have, however, interpreted impossibility of performance to encompass not only absolute impossibility but also impossibility in the sense of impracticality of performance due to extreme and unreasonable difficulty, expense, injury or loss."[123]

Moreover, there are a few authorities in which increased expense has been treated as a frustrating event. In an English case, *William Cory & Son Ltd. v. London Corporation*,[124] it appears to have been accepted that in the context of an agreement under which barge owners agreed to transport refuse, the enactment of by-laws requiring inordinately expensive refitting of the barges constituted a frustrating event. In a decision of the Australian High Court, *Codelfa Construction Pty. Ltd. v. State Rail Authority of NSW*,[125] it was held that the granting of an injunction directing that no construction work could take place between 10 a.m. and 6 p.m. so severely increased the cost of constructing railway tunnels that the contractor's obligations were discharged by a frustrating event. Accordingly, the contractor was entitled to claim for the value of the work done on a *quantum meruit* basis. Further, as Beatson has argued,[126] some support for the recognition of impracticability as a frustrating event can be drawn from maritime cases dealing with the shipowner's obligation to repair a chartered vessel. Under the prevailing rule, even though repair of the vessel may be possible, the shipowner is not obliged to make the repairs if the cost of effecting the repairs is unreasonably high.[127] In an extreme case of increased expense of performance, then, it may well be that Canadian courts will more plainly recognize that commercial impracticability rather than literal impossibility is the threshold that must be met in applying the doctrine of frustration.

---

122   Above note 82.
123   *Ibid.* at 348. And see *Lieberman v. Roseland Theatre Ltd.*, [1946] 1 D.L.R. 342 (N.S.S.C.).
124   [1951] 1 K.B. 8, aff'd [1951] 2 K.B. 476 (C.A.).
125   (1982), 149 C.L.R. 337 (Aust. H.C.).
126   See generally Beatson, above note 104 at 137–40.
127   See, for example, *Assicurazioni Generali & Schenker & Co. v. S.S. Bessie Morris & Co. Ltd.*, [1892] 2 Q.B. 652.

F. AGREEMENTS TO TRANSFER INTERESTS IN LAND

The application of the doctrine of frustration to agreements to transfer an interest in land has proven to be a contentious matter. On one view, as long as it is possible to transfer the interest in question, there is simply no room for application of the doctrine of frustration. This point is sometimes explained on the basis that such agreements are not mere contracts. Rather, they convey or create an interest in land and, accordingly, are inherently not susceptible to the application of frustration doctrine. When the interest passes, the contract is performed. On the other hand, the view has been taken, especially in the context of leases, that there is, in principle, no reason why an agreement to lease land could not be subject to the doctrine if a supervening event undermines the very purpose for which the agreement was entered. Further, though this is a matter of some controversy, similar views have been adopted, by Canadian courts in particular, with respect to the potential application of the doctrine to agreements for the purchase and sale of land.

In *Cricklewood Property and Investment Trust Ltd. v. Leighton's Trust Investment Ltd.*,[128] the House of Lords divided on the question of whether the doctrine of frustration could, in principle, apply to a lease of land. This case involved a ninety-nine-year lease of a building estate under which the lessee covenanted to erect a shopping centre within a certain period of time after having been given notice by the lessor to do so. Rental became payable one year after the giving of such notification. Although notices had been served by the lessor, the commencement of war and consequent wartime building restrictions prevented the construction of the centre. The lessee resisted making the required rental payments on the basis that the lease had been frustrated. The House of Lords divided on the question of whether, in principle, the doctrine of frustration could apply to a lease. Viscount Simon offered the view that neither authority nor principle precluded the application of the doctrine to a lease. He conceded that it was very difficult to imagine circumstances in which a simple lease of land for a period of years under which the lessee was free to use the land in any fashion desired could be subject to determination on the basis of a frustrating event. Where, however, a lease has been entered into for the express purpose of using the land for a particular purpose, such as erecting a building on the land that would ultimately benefit the lessor on termination of

---

128 [1945] A.C. 221 (H.L.).

the lease, it was easier, in his view, to imagine circumstances in which it might be appropriate to apply frustration doctrine. On the present facts, however, the lease had more than ninety years to run and the length of the interruption resulting from the wartime regulations was likely to be a small fraction of the whole term of the lease. Accordingly, the doctrine did not apply. Although Lord Wright was in agreement on the point of principle, two members of the panel[129] were of the view that the doctrine of frustration was simply inapplicable to a lease of land. Even if circumstances developed that made it difficult or impossible for one party to carry out some of its obligations under the lease, the lease would still be effective. As Lord Russell explained, "the estate and the land would still be vested in the tenant."[130] The fifth member of the panel[131] reserved on the point as the doctrine would not be applicable to the facts in issue, in any event.

The House of Lords returned to the point of principle, however, in 1980 in *National Carriers Ltd. v. Panalpina (Northern) Ltd.*[132] On this occasion, the matter was resolved in favour of the proposition that the doctrine of frustration can apply to leases. The argument to the contrary that a lease is more than a mere contract because it conveys an interest in land was rejected on the basis that there may be situations in which the mere transfer of the leasehold estate may not accomplish the purpose of the agreement. On this point, Viscount Simon's illustration of a building lease was considered persuasive.[133] Further, their Lordships were of the view that a distinction between agreements creating estates in land and other types of contracts would be artificial. Thus, as the doctrine of frustration plainly applies to leases of vessels, it was not at all clear why it could not also apply to leases of land.[134] Some support was also drawn from American experience, including a line of cases holding that leases of liquor saloons had been frustrated by prohibition.[135] In response to the further argument that it should be accepted as a general principle that on execution of a lease, risk passes to the lessee, it was suggested that while this may be generally the case, especially in the context of a long-term lease, there was no reason why the

---

129 Lords Russell of Killowen and Goddard.
130 *Ibid.* at 234.
131 Lord Porter.
132 Above note 75.
133 See, for example, *ibid.* at 694–95, Lord Wilberforce.
134 See *ibid.* at 690, Lord Hailsham; 694, Lord Wilberforce; 701, Lord Simon of Glaisdale; and 713, Lord Roskill.
135 See *ibid.* at 695, Lord Wilberforce; 702, Lord Simon; and 716, Lord Roskill.

risk of a particular supervening event might not fall upon the lessor.[136] Again, on the particular facts of this case, however, it was concluded that the doctrine was inapplicable. The defendant had leased a warehouse for a period of ten years. A road that provided the only vehicular access to the warehouse was closed by the municipality to facilitate repairs to a neighbouring building for a period estimated to be twenty months. Although the road closure amounted to a severe dislocation, it did not rise to the "gravity of a frustrating event."[137]

Canadian courts appear to have accepted that the doctrine of frustration may apply to leases.[138] The doctrine has also been held applicable to an agreement to lease, as where the agreement relates to premises not yet in existence that fail to materialize because of an expropriation of the property.[139] The more difficult question, however, is whether the doctrine of frustration may apply to a sale of land. In *Capital Quality Homes Ltd. v. Colwyn Construction Ltd.*,[140] the Ontario Court of Appeal appeared to assume that if the doctrine may apply to leases, it should also apply to sales of land. Once the agreement of sale is executed, of course, title to the land has been transferred and there would not appear to be much room for the operation of frustration doctrine.[141] The contract has been fully executed. In such circumstances, the risks attendant upon ownership appear to have been visited upon the new owner. In this respect, a sale is unlike a lease, the latter of which retains some executory obligations after the transfer of the leasehold interest. Even in the context of an agreement for the sale of land yet to be executed, however, the traditional English position has been that the risk of supervening events that may have some impact on the value of the land pass to the purchaser at the time of contracting.[142] In *Amalgamated Investment Property Co. v. John Walker and Sons Ltd.*,[143] for example,

---

136 *Ibid.* at 691, Lord Hailsham; 695, Lord Wilberforce; 705, Lord Simon; and 712, Lord Roskill.

137 *Ibid.* at 697, Lord Wilberforce.

138 *Capital Quality Homes Ltd. v. Colwyn Construction Ltd.*, above note 61; *Turner v. Clark* (1983), 30 R.P.R. 164 (N.B.C.A.). Some landlord and tenant legislation provides that the doctrine of frustration of contract will apply to residential or other tenancy. See, for example, *Tenant Protection Act, 1997*, S.O. 1997, c. 24, s. 10; *Commercial Tenancy Act*, R.S.B.C. 1996, c. 57, s. 30.

139 *Re Dennis Commercial Properties Ltd. v. Westmount Life Insurance Co.* (1969), 7 D.L.R. (3d) 214 (Ont. H.C.J.), aff'd 8 D.L.R. (3d) 688n (Ont. C.A.).

140 Above note 61 at 397, Evans J.A.

141 Above note 75 at 705, Lord Simon.

142 The leading case is *Paine v. Meller* (1801), 6 Ves. 349. See generally Treitel, above note 1 at 103–24. See also *Lysaght v. Edwards* (1876), 2 Ch. D. 499.

143 [1976] 3 All E.R. 509 (C.A.).

a contract had been entered into for the purchase of a warehouse for occupation or redevelopment at a price based on the assumption that this would prove to be possible. On the day after the transaction was entered into, however, the Department of Environment notified the vendor that the building had been listed for preservation as a building of special architectural or historic interest. Development of such a property was not necessarily precluded but it would require special permission. In explaining that no relief was available to the purchaser in such circumstances, Buckley L.J. reasoned as follows:

> It seems to me that the risk of property being listed as property of architectural or historical interest is a risk which inheres in all ownership of buildings. In many cases it may be an extremely remote risk. In many cases, it may be a marginal risk. In some cases it may be a substantial risk. But it is a risk, I think, which attaches to all buildings and it is a risk that every owner and every purchaser of property must recognize that he is subject to.[144]

Purchasers who did not wish to assume such risks, of course, could insert an appropriate condition in the agreement of purchase and sale. Otherwise, the risk of supervening events is assumed by the purchaser. Obviously, an argument can be made that risk generally or some particular type of risk ought to pass at some other point in time. For example, a plausible case could be made for transferring the risk of physical destruction of buildings located on the property by fire upon either the transfer of possession or the closing of the transaction. The traditional approach of imposing risk generally on the purchaser from the moment of contracting has been defended, however, on the basis that it promotes certainty by avoiding fine determinations as to the circumstances in which risk generally, or some particular risks, ought to pass at some other point in time. [145]

Canadian courts, on the other hand, appear to be more willing to impose the risk of some supervening events on the vendor. The opportunities for the application of frustration doctrine in this context, however, appear limited. In the *Capital Quality Homes Ltd.*[146] case, the supervening event was such that it rendered literal performance of the agreement actually impossible. The agreement provided for the separate conveyance of twenty-six building lots each of which, in turn, comprised a part of existing lots within a registered plan of subdiv-

---

144 *Ibid.* at 517.
145 See Treitel, above note 1 at 111–12.
146 Above note 61.

ision. Structuring the transaction in this fashion avoided any need for further planning permission. Before the transaction closed, however, legislation came into effect that restricted the vendor's right to effect a transfer in this fashion without obtaining additional consents. Given the short time frame, the obtaining of such consents was not a practical possibility. The Ontario Court of Appeal held that the "very foundation of the agreement"[147] had been destroyed and that "impossibility of performance"[148] had been established. The agreement was therefore discharged by the doctrine of frustration. This case represents what must be a very unusual fact situation, then, in which the very act of carrying out the execution of the agreement to convey the property has been rendered impossible.

In other cases, Canadian courts have held that the risk of rezoning may rest with the vendor and thus, discharge the agreement on the basis of frustration doctrine. In these cases, however, there appear to be special circumstances that may support the proposition that the current zoning of the property is in some sense fundamental to the agreement. In *British Columbia (Ministry of Crown Lands) v. Cressy Development Corp.*,[149] for example, the defendant had purchased ninety acres of land from the plaintiff for the purpose of subdividing and developing the lots. Under the agreement, the purchaser explicitly covenanted that it would not resell the lots in any way other than as serviced lots. When the necessary rezoning of the property was not completed in a timely fashion, the purchaser sought to resile from the transaction on the basis of frustration doctrine. The British Columbia Court held that the failure to rezone the property "destroyed the very foundation of the agreement"[150] and that the purchaser was therefore excused on the basis of frustration doctrine. In the particular circumstances of this transaction, however, it is evident that the development of the property was critical to both parties and it is not surprising, therefore, that frustration doctrine was successfully invoked. A similar conclusion was reached by the British Columbia Court of Appeal in *KBK No. 138 Ventures Ltd. v. Canada Safeway Ltd.*[151] in circumstances in which it might also be said that the preservation of the existing zoning was a fundamental assumption shared by both parties. The vendor had advertised

---

147 *Ibid.* at 394.
148 *Ibid.*
149 [1992] 4 W.W.R. 357 (B.C.S.C.).
150 *Ibid.* at 371.
151 (2000), 185 D.L.R. (4th) 650 (B.C.C.A.). See also *Focal Properties Ltd. v. George Wimpey (Canada) Ltd.* (1975), 73 D.L.R. (3d) 387 (Ont. C.A.).

a property for sale, describing its current zoning and permitted density ratio. The ultimate agreement of purchase and sale contained an escalator clause that would increase the price in the event that greater density was ultimately permitted. In due course, however, the director of planning in the particular municipality took the rather unusual step of bringing an application on his own motion to rezone the property in a manner that would substantially restrict its development potential and reduce the value of the land by approximately 30 percent. The court held that this most unusual initiative on the part of the director was a change of circumstances "so fundamental as to be regarded as striking at the root of the agreement and as entirely beyond what was contemplated by the parties when they entered into the agreement."[152] It had, as a result, "transformed the contract into something totally different from what the parties intended."[153]

In the absence of unusual circumstances of this kind, however, it appears likely that the traditional rule,[154] imposing the risk of supervening events on the purchaser, will apply. Thus, in *Victoria Wood Development Corp. v. Ondrey*,[155] the plaintiff had entered into a contract to buy ninety acres of land with the intention of subdividing and developing the property. Subsequent to entering the agreement, the legislature enacted legislation restricting development on the property. The purchaser's attempt to resile from the transaction on the basis that it had been frustrated did not enjoy success. Osler J. reasoned as follows:

> a developer in purchasing land is always conscious of the risk that zoning or similar changes may make the carrying out of his intention impossible, or may delay it. He may attempt to guard against such risk by the insertion of proper conditions in the contract and thereby persuade the vendor to assume some of the risk. In the present case he has not done so and, indeed, there is no evidence that he has attempted to do so. "The very foundation of the agreement" is not affected and there is no room for the application of the doctrine of frustration.[156]

In Osler J.'s view, the ability of the purchaser to develop the land thus did not form part of the foundation of the agreement. The ability of the parties to perform their obligations under the agreement was not affected by the supervening legislation.

---

152   *KBK No. 138 Ventures Ltd. v. Canada Safeway Ltd.*, *ibid.* at 660.
153   *Ibid.*
154   *Paine v. Meller*, above note 142.
155   (1977), 74 D.L.R. (3d) 528 (Ont. H.C.J.).
156   *Ibid.* at 532–33.

G. SELF-INDUCED FRUSTRATION

The doctrine of frustration applies to cases where supervening events that have occurred, as it is commonly said, "without default of the contract-or,"[157] have prevented the party from performing the agreement. Where the frustrating event arises by virtue of the non-performing parties' own "fault," the frustration is said to be "self-induced" and the doctrine of frustration is inapplicable. Thus, where performance of a contract is contingent on the approval of a third party, the non-performing party is not excused by the absence of approval in a case where the non-performing party did not trouble to apply for that approval.[158] Similarly, where the contract imposes an obligation to make best efforts to obtain such approval, failure to act reasonably in pursuing that objective constitutes self-induced frustration.[159] Similarly, it appears to be accepted that a frustrating event that results from the negligence of the performing party will preclude reliance on the doctrine. Thus, if a shipowner claimed frustration on the basis that the vessel required to carry out the contract had been lost, the frustrating event would be self-induced if it resulted from the negligence of the shipowner's own employees.[160]

More difficult problems arise where the performing party has a number of customers and the effect of the frustrating event is to partially rather than wholly prevent the performer's ability to perform the contractual obligations owed to the customers. In such a case, the frustrated party may choose to perform some contracts but not others. It is very likely that the decision to refuse to supply some customers will be characterized as an act of self-induced frustration. The leading case is *Maritime National Fish Ltd. v. Ocean Trawlers Ltd.*[161] The plaintiff had rented a trawler, the *St. Cuthbert*, from the defendant for twelve months. The *St. Cuthbert* was fitted out with an "otter trawl" that was essential to its operation for the intended purpose. The defendant also operated four other trawlers fitted with otter trawls. At the time of contract, the

---

157 *Taylor v. Caldwell*, above note 2 at 834 (B. & S.), 312 (E.R.).

158 *S.F. Silver Falcon Holding Co. v. Agricultural Development Co. of Saskatchewan* (1990), 81 Sask. R. 195 (Q.B.). See also *Graham v. Wagman* (1976), 73 D.L.R. (3d) 667 (Ont. H.C.J.) (contract to rent parking spaces in building to be constructed — inability to obtain financing for construction does not constitute frustration), var'd on another point (1978), 21 O.R. (2d) 1 (C.A.).

159 *Dinicola v. Huang & Danczkay Properties* (1996), 135 D.L.R. (4th) 525 (Ont. Ct. Gen. Div.), aff'd on other grounds (1998), 163 D.L.R. (4th) 286 (Ont. C.A.).

160 *J. Lauritzen A.S. v. Wijsmuller B.V. (The Super Servant Two)*, [1989] 1 Lloyd's Rep. 148 at 156 (Q.B.), aff'd [1990] 1 Lloyd's Rep. 1 (C.A.).

161 [1935] A.C. 524 (P.C.).

parties were aware that licences would be required for the operation of these vessels with otter trawls. In due course, the defendant made the appropriate application to the Ministry of Fisheries but was eventually advised that the permission of the minister was granted with respect to only three otter trawls. When requested to identify which of its vessels were to be licensed, the defendant did not select the *St. Cuthbert*. In response to the plaintiff's claim for damages for breach of the charter party, the defendant relied on the doctrine of frustration. The Privy Council held, however, that it was the defendant's election to assign the three licences to other trawlers that frustrated the agreement. Accordingly, the doctrine was inapplicable on the basis that the election constituted a self-induced frustration. This result appears unattractive, however, on the basis that if the defendant had failed to obtain any licences, the doctrine of frustration would have applied to each of the five charter parties concerned. Accordingly, the fact that only partial approvals were obtained effectively forced the defendant into a position of breaching some contracts without the protection of the doctrine of frustration. Nor, apparently, would it be of any assistance to the non-performing party in such a case if the "selection" occurred prior to the frustrating event. Thus, in *The Super Servant Two*,[162] a shipowner had agreed to transport a heavy drilling rig on either one of two identified large self-propelled barges. The contract stipulated that the particular barge to be utilized would be selected at the shipowner's option. The shipowner selected one of the two vessels and assigned the other to contracts with third parties. After the owner did so, the selected vessel sank. The shipowner's attempt to rely on the doctrine of frustration foundered on the basis that the selection of the vessel constituted self-induced frustration.

Similar problems may arise in the context of partial inability to supply fungibles such as agricultural crops and minerals. Where a farmer, for example, has entered into agreements to supply produce to a group of customers and a partial crop failure occurs, a decision by the farmer to supply some customers but not others would presumably constitute self-induced frustration under the *Maritime National Fish* doctrine.[163] Indeed, even if the farmer adopted the reasonable course of pro-rating the supply on an equitable basis among the customers, the self-in-

---

162 *J. Lauritzen A.S. v. Wijsmuller B.V.*, above note 160.

163 *Hollinger Consolidated Gold Mines Ltd. v. Northern Canadian Power*, [1923] 4 D.L.R. 1205 (Ont. S.C.A.D.) (electrical power); *Samuel v. Black Lake Asbestos and Chrome Co.* (1920), 58 D.L.R. 270 (Ont. S.C.A.D.), rev'd on other grounds (1921), 62 S.C.R. 472 (chrome ore).

duced frustration rule would still prevent reliance on the doctrine of frustration. If, however, the individual contracts of supply contained *force majeure* provisions[164] and the supervening event constituted *force majeure*, the equitable pro-rating of supply among customers would appear to be satisfactory and subject to the protection of the clause.[165]

H. *FORCE MAJEURE* CLAUSES

Parties who are sensitive to the possibility of disruption of their contractual arrangements by supervening events may decide to include in the agreement a provision that relieves one or both of the parties from further performance if certain specified events of this kind should occur. Such provisions are typically referred to as *"force majeure"* clauses.[166] The general nature of *force majeure* clauses was characterized by Dickson J. in *Atlantic Paperstock Ltd. v. St. Anne-Nackawic Pulp & Paper Co.*,[167] in the following terms: "An act of God clause or *force majeure* clause ... generally operates to discharge a contracting party when a supervening, sometimes supernatural, event, beyond control of either party, makes performance impossible. The common thread is that of the unexpected, something beyond reasonable human foresight and skill."[168]

Although *force majeure* is the term used to refer to the French civilian doctrine that most resembles the doctrine of frustration, use of the term to refer to contractual provisions of this kind is not considered to import into the common law system or, more particularly, into the interpretation of such provisions at common law, the French version of frustration doctrine.[169] Occasionally, however, parties drafting commercial agreements may use the actual phrase *"force majeure"* in referring to the supervening events that excuse the performance of one or both parties. Accordingly, common law judges are occasionally required to give some content to the phrase. Thus, in a series of English cases, it has been held that the phrase *"force majeure,"* when employed

---

164 For discussion of which see below, this Chapter, section H.
165 *J. Lauritzen A.S. v. Wijsmuller B.V.*, above note 160 at 158–59.
166 See generally W. Swadling, "The Judicial Construction of *Force Majeure* Clauses" in McKendrick, above note 1, c. 1; G. Treitel, above note 1, c. 12.
167 [1976] 1 S.C.R. 580.
168 *Ibid.* at 583.
169 See Swadling, above note 166 at 5–8. See also B. Nicholas, "*Force Majeure* in French Law" in McKendrick, above note 1, c. 2.

in a provision of this kind, does not excuse performance on the basis of the kinds of interruptions, such as bad weather, that commonly interrupt the flow of work in a particular workplace[170] or, more generally, acts resulting from the "act, or negligence, or omission, or default" of the person relying on the clause.[171] Although some of these authorities refer to civilian sources,[172] a contractual reference to the concept of *force majeure* itself does not appear to carry a meaning that is appreciably different from the concept of frustration at common law.

The far more common drafting technique for *force majeure* clauses, however, is to list a sometimes rather lengthy series of supervening events that would constitute an excuse for one or both of the parties.[173] The following is illustrative:

> Neither party shall be liable in damages to the other for any act, or omission or circumstance occasioned by or in consequence of any acts of God, strikes, lock-outs, acts of the public enemy, wars, blockades, insurrections, riots, epidemics, landslides, land subsidence, lightning, earthquakes, fires, storms, floods, washouts, arrests and restraints of rulers and people caught in civil disturbances, explosions and any other cause, whether of the kind wherein enumerated, or otherwise, not within the control of the party claiming suspension and which by the exercise of due diligence such party is unable to prevent or overcome.

The advantages of such a clause are obvious. One can clearly stipulate the kinds of events that excuse non-performance rather than leave the matter to the uncertainties of the common law. Thus, if it is not clear that a strike would constitute frustration at common law, it is clear that it would constitute an excuse under a provision such as that quoted above. Further, one can stipulate in such provisions remedial measures

---

170 *Matsoukis v. Priestman & Co.*, [1915] 1 K.B. 681 (nor did it cover such items as a coal strike interrupting supply of coal and the attendance of employees at football matches and a funeral—the phrase did apply, however, to delay caused by a breakdown in machinery).

171 *Lebeaupin v. Richard Crispin & Co.*, [1920] 2 K.B. 714 at 721, McCardie J. See also *The Concadoro*, [1960] 2 A.C. 199 (P.C.) (failure of master of ship to leave on voyage because of insufficient funds not *force majeure*); *Brauer & Co. (Great Britain) Ltd. v. James Clark (Brush Materials) Ltd.*, [1952] 2 All E.R. 497 (C.A.) (substantial increase in price, not *force majeure*).

172 See, for example, *Lebeaupin v. Richard Crispin & Co.*, ibid. at 721.

173 If the term "*force majeure*" is itself included in the list, it has been said that the phrase should be "construed in each case with a close attention to the words which precede or follow it, and with a due regard to the nature and general terms of the contract." See *Lebeaupin v. Richard Crispin & Co.*, ibid. at 720.

of a kind not contemplated by the common law. The common law either discharges the agreement or leaves it an enforceable state. A *force majeure* clause, on the other hand, may stipulate that reasonable efforts must be taken to solve the problem caused by a supervening event of a stipulated kind, failing which, the non-performance would not be excused. Thus, such a provision might stipulate as follows: "Such causes affecting performance by either party, however, shall not relieve it of liability in the event of its contributory negligence or misconduct or in the event of its failure to use due diligence to remedy the situation and remove the cause in an adequate manner and with all reasonable dispatch." Although the common law may achieve a similar result by refusing to hold that a supervening event amounts to frustration where due diligence could have remedied the problem, provisions such as the above more clearly achieve this result and provide clearer guidance to the parties as to the conduct expected of them in the event of a supervening event.

Force majeure clauses are interpreted in the light of their general purpose of excusing non-performance upon the occurrence of supervening events that make performance impossible. Thus, in the *St. Anne* case, for example, a clause that did not plainly indicate that the particular supervening event must arise from circumstances beyond the control of the party relying on the clause was interpreted in a manner consistent with such a requirement.[174] The dispute concerned an agreement under which the plaintiff, Atlantic, sold substantial quantities of waste paper to the defendant, St. Anne, to be used in the manufacture of corrugating medium, a product used in the manufacture of cardboard. This was a new business for St. Anne and accordingly, as a result of a concern that it may not have adequate markets for its corrugating medium, the list of supervening events in the *force majeure* clause in the agreement included "non-availability of markets" as an event that would excuse St. Anne from its purchase obligations. The provision committed St. Anne to purchase a certain minimum quantity of waste paper "unless as a result of an act of God, the Queen's or public enemies, war, the authority of the law, labour unrest, or strikes, the destruction of or damages to production facilities, or the non-availability of markets for pulp or corrugating medium."[175] As a result of a variety of circumstances, the market for St. Anne's corrugating medium was not buoyant. Accordingly, St. Anne advised Atlantic that it would no longer purchase waste paper from Atlantic. St. Anne defended At-

---

174 Above note 167. And see E. Veitch, "Contracts—Frustration—*Force Majeure* Clauses—Non-Availability of Market" (1976) 54 Can. Bar Rev. 161.

175 *Atlantic Paperstock Ltd. v. St. Anne-Nackawic Pulp & Paper Co., ibid.* at 582.

lantic's subsequent claim for damages on the basis of the *force majeure* clause. It was the view of the Supreme Court, however, that the basic cause of the non-availability of markets resulted from the conduct of St. Anne. The whole corrugating medium project was "misconceived"[176] in a number of respects. St. Anne had an inadequate marketing plan, inordinate operating costs and, unlike other actors in the industry, a lack of captive outlets. For these and other reasons, the principal cause of the inability of St. Anne to market its corrugating medium was "a condition which it brought upon itself."[177]

More generally, where the *force majeure* clause has been inserted in the agreement for the benefit of one party, the construction of the agreement should be subject to the normal principle of *contra proferentum*.[178] Beyond this point, however, it is less clear whether the especially narrow construction approach taken to exemption clauses[179] should apply to *force majeure* clauses. It may be argued that a *force majeure* clause merely defines the obligations imposed by an agreement rather than limits or excludes liability for the breach of obligations already imposed by the agreement. On this basis, *force majeure* clauses might be considered to constitute a distinct category from exemption clauses.[180] The distinction between the two types of clauses, however, is at best a subtle one.[181] Thus, at least in cases where the *force majeure* clause may be thought to be inconsistent with the fundamental object of the agreement, a narrow construction approach like that applied to exemption clauses is likely to apply. It has been held, for example, that in the absence of an explicit reference to negligence, non-performance resulting from negligent acts is not excused.[182] Further, it appears to be well established that, as with an exemption clause, the burden of proof that the clause is applicable to the particular fact situation is upon the party, typically the defendant, who wishes to rely on the clause.[183]

---

176 *Ibid.* at 587.

177 *Ibid.*

178 See *Lebeaupin v. Richard Crispin & Co.*, above note 171. See generally Chapter 19, section B.

179 See Chapter 20.

180 See, for example Swadling, above note 166 at 10–18.

181 Compare with the similar and unsatisfactory distinction drawn by some between exemption clauses and limitation of liability clauses, for discussion of which see Chapter 20, section C.

182 *J. Lauritzen A.S. v. Wijsmuller B.V.* (*The Super Servant Two*), above note 160 (C.A.).

183 See, for example, *Bremer Handelsgesellschaft mbH v. C. Mackprang Jr.*, [1979] 1 Lloyd's Rep. 221 (C.A.); *P.J. Van der Zijden v. Tucker & Cross*, [1975] 2 Lloyd's Rep. 240.

I. CONSEQUENCES OF FRUSTRATION

The most obvious effect of the application of frustration doctrine is to relieve the party whose performance has been prevented or interrupted by the supervening event from its obligation to performance of the agreement. The other party's obligation to performance is also discharged. Though the other party's discharge is often explained as a consequence of frustration,[184] it may also be explained by the failure of consideration resulting from non-performance. Thus, the other party who has received no performance from the party relying on frustration doctrine may treat the contract as at an end because of non-performance, whether or not the doctrine of frustration applies, so as to excuse the non-performance. If the doctrine does apply, of course, it has the effect of precluding the other party from bringing an action for damages for breach of contract against the non-performing party.

The more difficult question, however, is whether either one or both of the parties will have a claim in restitution for the value of benefits conferred on the other party prior to the discharge of the agreement through frustration.[185] In England, a rather unsatisfactory response to this question was provided by the common law that was, however, reformed by the enactment of the English *Law Reform (Frustrated Contracts) Act* of 1943.[186] In Canada, support for the English legislative reform led to the adoption of a *Uniform Frustrated Contracts Act*[187] that was virtually identical to the English statute. The model statute was adopted in one territory[188] and in all the Canadian common law provinces except British Columbia, Nova Scotia and Saskatchewan. The unsatisfactory nature of the English statute soon became apparent, however, and was the subject of critical scrutiny by various law reform bodies.[189] Acting on the advice

---

184 See, for example, *Taylor v. Caldwell*, above note 2 at 840 (B. & S.), Blackburn J.; *Hirji Mulji v. Cheong Yue S.S. Co.*, above note 21 at 507, Lord Sumner. See generally Treitel, above note 1 at 60–66.

185 See generally P.D. Maddaugh and J.D. McCamus, *The Law of Restitution,* 2d ed. (Aurora: Canada Law Book, 2004) c. 18.

186 VI and VII Geo., c. 40.

187 Conference of Commissioners on Uniformity of Legislation in Canada, *Proceedings of the 30th Annual Meeting, 1948* at 18 and appendix G.

188 R.S.N.W.T. 1988, c. F-12.

189 See D.J. Mullan, Nova Scotia Law Reform Advisory Commission, *Frustrated Contracts Law* (Halifax: Nova Scotia Law Reform Advisory Commission, 1976); Ontario Law Reform Commission, *Report on Amendment of the Law of Contract* (Toronto: Ministry of the Attorney General, 1987) c. 14; Law Reform Commission of Saskatchewan, *Tentative Proposals for a Frustrated Contracts Act* (Saskatoon: Law Reform Commission of Saskatchewan, 1987). See also G. Williams,

604 THE LAW OF CONTRACTS

of its law reform commission, British Columbia enacted a new *Frustrated Contracts Act*[190] that, in turn, was adopted as a new model *Uniform Act*.[191] The new *Uniform Act* has been adopted by the Yukon Territory[192] and, in modified form, by Saskatchewan.[193] In Canada, then, there is a statutory scheme of either one of two kinds in operation in almost all the common law provinces. In Nova Scotia, however, the issue is left to be determined as a matter of common law. In this province, then, the question that must be considered is whether the common law should be considered to be frozen in the unhappy state it had achieved in English law by 1943 or, rather, should be considered to be subject to reinterpretation in the light of more general developments in the Canadian law of restitution.

An account of Canadian law concerning the consequences of frustration may conveniently begin, then, with an account of the position at common law in England and the statutory reform thereof effected in 1943. The traditional position at English common law combined a reluctance to grant restitutionary relief with a rigid view of the effect of frustration on the enforceability of the contractual obligations of the parties. Generally speaking, restitution was denied.[194] Consistent with the idea that a frustrated contract is enforceable up to the moment of frustration but not thereafter, English law further held that obligations that had accrued prior to the frustrating event remained enforceable, whereas those accruing after the event were not. However logical, this approach was capable of producing quite perverse results. *Chandler v. Webster*,[195] one of the coronation cases, illustrates the difficulty. In *Chandler*, an agreement to rent a room with a view of the coronation procession was frustrated by the subsequent cancellation of the procession as a result of the illness of Edward VII. By the time of the cancellation, the renter had already paid part of the rental price and, indeed, the remainder of the rent had fallen due. The renter was unable to obtain restitution of the monies paid prior to the moment of frustration

---

The Law Reform (Frustrated Contracts) Act, 1943 (London: Stevens & Sons, 1944).

190 S.B.C. 1974, c. 37. See now *Frustrated Contract Act*, R.S.B.C. 1996, c. 166.

191 Conference of Commissioners on Uniformity of Legislation in Canada, *Proceedings of the Annual Meeting 1973*, at 27 and *Proceedings of the Annual Meeting 1974* at 28.

192 *Frustrated Contracts Act*, R.S.Y. 2002, c. 96.

193 *Frustrated Contracts Act*, S.S. 1994, c. F-22.2.

194 For a defence of the traditional approach of letting the losses lie where they have fallen, see A. Kull, "Mistake, Frustration, and the Windfall Principle of Contract Remedies" (1991) 43 Hastings L.J. 1.

195 [1904] 1 K.B. 493 (C.A.).

on the theory that restitution would be available only where monies had been paid on a contract that was *void ab initio.* As the remaining rent had become payable, however, the landlord was entitled to bring an action to enforce the payment obligation. As a result of the timing of the payment obligation, then, the renter became liable to pay the entire rental for the room, even though the contract had been frustrated by the cancellation of the procession.

The harshness of the common law position on the restitution point was addressed, in part at least, by the decision of the House of Lords in *Fibrosa Spolka Akcyjna v. Fairbairn Lawson Combe Barbour Ltd.*,[196] a decision rendered a short time before the enactment of the 1943 legislation. The claim in *Fibrosa* was brought by a Polish firm that had made a partial payment on the purchase price of machinery to be supplied by an English manufacturer. The occupation of a Polish port by enemy forces frustrated the agreement. The House of Lords overruled *Chandler* on the restitution point and held that the monies paid were recoverable, provided that the plaintiff had suffered a "total failure of consideration" in the sense that it had received nothing of value in return for the payment. Although this decision obviously improved the position at common law, several difficulties remained. The total failure of consideration requirement appears indefensible. It is not at all clear why the receipt of some value by the purchaser should be a basis for complete rejection of the claim. Surely, such value as had been received could simply be deducted from the purchaser's restitutionary claim. Further, the decision in *Fibrosa* left untouched the English rule relating to restitutionary recovery of benefits conferred other than money under frustrated agreements. The decision in *Appleby v. Myers*[197] held that where the obligation to supply services is "entire" and not "severable," the plaintiff can recover the value of the services supplied only if the contract is fully performed. Thus, partial performance prior to a frustrating event would not provide a basis for a restitutionary claim.[198] Further, the decision in *Fibrosa* did not touch the second branch of the *Chandler* case that held that obligations that accrued prior to the moment of frustration would remain enforceable. Finally, as Viscount Simon noted in the *Fibrosa* case,[199] the common law was incapable of providing a solution

---

196   [1943] A.C. 32 (H.L.).

197   Above note 73.

198   In the context of a partial delivery of goods, however, both at common law and
  under sale of goods legislation, if the buyer retains or accepts the goods, the
  buyer must pay for the goods at the contract rate. See, for example, *Sale of Goods
  Act*, R.S.O. 1990, c. S.1, s. 29(1).

199   Above note 196 at 49.

to the problem presented by someone who had endured expenses in preparation for the performance of a contract prior to the frustrating event but had not conferred value on the other party. In the absence of value being conferred, no restitution claim could lie. The allocation of losses of this kind, if appropriate, could only be achieved by statutory reform.

The English legislation[200] and, in turn, the first Canadian *Uniform Act*[201] effected essentially four critical reforms of the position at common law. The first two reforms overruled the two branches of the *Chandler* decision. Thus, the old *Uniform Act* provides that sums payable but not paid prior to the frustrating event "cease to be payable."[202] Under the statute, then, the landlord's claim in *Chandler* would be denied. Second, the Act provides that sums paid prior to the frustrating event are recoverable.[203] Unlike the decision in *Fibrosa*, however, the Act does not condition recovery of sums paid on a requirement that there has been a total failure of consideration. The recoverability of the sums paid is subject, however, to two further reforms achieved by the legislation. The third confers a discretion on the courts to set off monies paid or payable against the cost of any performance-related expenses incurred by the party receiving the payment prior to the frustrating event.[204] The party that incurred the expenses may retain the sums paid or recover the sums payable to the extent necessary to compensate for those expenses. The Act thus appears to assume that the point of a prepayment is to fund the expenses incurred in preparing to perform the contract by the payee. Accordingly, such expenses should be either set off against the payer's statutory claim to recover the monies paid or, if the monies are merely payable, and not paid, should be recoverable by the party who has suffered expenses. Thus, under this legislation, there could be no apportionment of losses incurred in the absence of a payment being paid or payable prior to the frustrating event. The fourth reform confers a discretion on courts to allow recovery for the value of benefits conferred "other than a payment of money" on the other party.[205] Thus, in any case where non-monetary benefits have been conferred, whether or

---

200 Above note 186. For discussion see Williams, above note 189 and Treitel, above note 1.

201 Above note 187. The *Uniform Act* has been enacted in six Canadian provinces. See *Frustrated Contracts Act*, R.S.A. 2000, c. F.27; C.C.S.M., c. F190; R.S.N.B. 1973, c. F-24; R.S.N.L. 1990, c. F-26; R.S.O. 1990, c. F.34; R.S.P.E.I. 1988, c. F-16.

202 *Ibid.*, s. 4(1).

203 *Ibid.*

204 *Ibid.*, s. 4(2).

205 *Ibid.*, s. 4(3).

not a prepayment has been made, a judicial discretion to allow restitutionary relief was created. Where monies had been paid, of course, the claim for the value of non-monetary benefits conferred would amount to a counterclaim for the value of those benefits, albeit one that would enjoy success only upon the exercise of a judicial discretion to grant relief.

Although the first *Uniform Act* represents a substantial improvement on the position at common law, several difficulties remain. Thus, it is not clear why it was considered necessary to confer only discretionary rights to achieve restitutionary recovery for the value of benefits conferred other than money. Second, the loss apportionment provisions of the first *Uniform Act* were considered, by many, to be inadequate. Loss apportionment could occur only where a contract stipulated for a prepayment prior to the moment of frustration. Further, the statute does not offer clear guidance with respect to perhaps the most troublesome fact situation, the case where the effect of the frustrating event is to destroy the value of benefits conferred on the other party. The statute simply allows recovery for the value of benefits conferred "before the parties were discharged."[206] This might suggest that if valuable benefits are conferred before the moment of discharge, restitutionary recovery could be allowed, even though the value of those benefits may be destroyed by the frustrating event. On the other hand, Canadian cases have held that where the value has been so destroyed, no restitutionary claim should lie under the statute. In a Canadian case, *Parsons Bros. Ltd. v. Shea*,[207] for example, restitutionary recovery was denied to a plaintiff heating contractor who had installed ductwork in the defendant's premises prior to the destruction of the building by fire. In such circumstances, the Newfoundland Court held, recovery should be denied because the defendant had ultimately received no value from the plaintiff. A preferable solution in such cases, arguably, would be to allow a *prima facie* right to recover but to allow a set-off for some portion of the defendant's expenses, thus effecting an allocation of the losses suffered as a result of the frustrating event.[208] On the theory that the parties in

---

206 *Ibid.*

207 (1965), 53 D.L.R. (2d) 86 (Nfld. S.C.). See also *Can-Truck Transportation Ltd. v. Fenton's Auto Paint Shop Ltd.* (1993), 101 D.L.R. (4th) 562 (Ont. C.A.). Compare with *Hubbard v. Walker* (1856), 13 U.C.R. 205; *Angus v. Scully*, 57 N.E. 674 (Mass. S.J.C. 1900).

208 See, for example, W.A. Seavey, "Problems in Restitution" (1954) 7 Okla. L. Rev. 247; B.J. Reiter, "Real Estate—Agreement of Purchase and Sale—Down Zoning Before Closing: How Frustrating?" (1978) 56 Can. Bar Rev. 98; J. Swan, "The Allocation of Risk in the Analysis of Mistake and Frustration" in B.J. Reiter &

such a case have together suffered a "contractual accident," in effect, some commentators have proposed a solution of this kind.[209] This is, indeed, also the solution adopted by the British Columbia legislation[210] and the new Canadian *Uniform Act*.[211]

There are three principal reforms of the first *Uniform Act* achieved in the second *Uniform Act*. First, the new Act creates a straightforward entitlement to recover, as of right, in a restitutionary claim, the value of benefits conferred prior to the frustrating event.[212] Second, the Act imposes a loss apportionment scheme to deal with any case where the expenditures of one party have not conferred value on the other party or, alternatively, though value has been conferred, that value has been destroyed by the frustrating event. This is achieved by defining the concept of "benefit" for purposes of restitutionary recovery to include "something done in fulfilment of contractual obligations, whether or not the person for whose benefit it was done received the benefit."[213] The statute then further provides that where a restitutionary claim is brought for a "benefit," any total or partial loss in the value of the benefit "shall be apportioned equally."[214] Thus, in a case where wasted expenditures have not produced an actual benefit or where the expenditures resulted in the conferral of an actual benefit but its value has been destroyed by the frustrating event, the losses will be apportioned equally between the parties. Third, the Act provides that recovery may be denied in a case where the circumstances of the particular case, including a prior course of dealing between the parties or trade custom, suggests that the party who has endured the expenditures should "bear the risk" of their loss.[215] Thus, for example, the fact that the prior course of dealing between parties indicates that the party enduring the expenditures

---

J. Swan, eds., *Studies in Contract Law* (Toronto: Butterworths, 1980) at 181; C. Fried, *Contract as Promise* (Cambridge: Harvard University Press, 1981) c. 5. See also P.D. Maddaugh and J.D. McCamus, above note 185, c. 18.

209 For differing views as to whether the English legislation is amenable to an interpretation of this kind, see *Gamerco S.A.* v. *ICM/Fair Warning (Agency) Ltd.*, [1995] 1 W.L.R. 1226 at 1237 (Q.B.), Garland J.; *B.P. Exploration Co. (Libya) Ltd.* v. *Hunt (No. 2)*, [1979] 1 W.L.R. 783 at 800 (Q.B.), Goff J., aff'd [1981] 1 W.L.R. 232 (C.A.), aff'd [1983] 2 A.C. 352 (H.L.).

210 Above note 190.

211 Above note 191. The new uniform legislation has been adopted in the Yukon, above note 192 and, in modified form, in Saskatchewan, above note 193.

212 Above note 191, s. 5(1).

213 *Ibid.*, s. 5(4). And see *Cassidy* v. *Canada Publishing Corp.* (1989), 41 B.L.R. 223 (B.C.S.C.).

214 *Ibid.*, s. 5(3).

215 *Ibid.*, s. 6(1).

has normally effected insurance against such losses may be evidence of a "course of dealing" suggesting that it is the understanding of the parties that a loss of this kind would be borne by the party effecting such insurance.

It remains, then, to consider whether, in a common law jurisdiction such as Nova Scotia that has not enacted either of the *Uniform* statutes, the common law must be considered to be the common law as it existed in England in 1943 before the enactment of the English legislation. As there are no leading Canadian cases modernizing the law of restitution in the context of frustrated agreements, it is possible to argue that the English common law of 1943 persists in the absence of legislative reform. The preferable view, however, is that modern developments in the more general law of restitution[216] have implications for the current state of the common law in the context of restitutionary recovery for benefits conferred under frustrated agreements. Thus, for example, Canadian courts no longer appear to insist on the requirement that there be a total failure of consideration in the context of claims for the value of money paid.[217] Second, the reluctance of English courts to allow recovery for the value of services rendered in this context appears to be explained, in part at least, by the notion that it is difficult to "imply" a contractual obligation in the face of an actual agreement, albeit one that is frustrated, to provide the services in question.[218] This implied-contract theory of restitutionary liability has been discredited in Canada.[219] Accordingly, it is possible that the kind of restitutionary remedy available for the conferral of non-monetary benefits conferred under the new *Uniform Act* may be recognized as available as a matter of common law. The problem of apportioning loss for wasted expenditures is more difficult at common law. It is possible, however, that Canadian courts may take their cue from the new *Uniform Act* and find, as a matter of common law, that restitutionary claims should lie for the value of "benefits" conferred in the form of partial performance (the concept of benefits being broadly construed to include all performance-related expenditures) and then subjecting such claims to a counterclaim for half the value of either wasted expenditures or any loss in the value of the performance resulting from the occurrence of the frustrating event.

216 See generally Maddaugh and McCamus, above note 185, c. 3.
217 See *ibid.*, c. 4, s. 200:10.
218 See *ibid.*, s. 18:200.
219 *Deglman v. Guaranty Trust*, [1954] S.C.R. 725. And see generally Maddaugh and McCamus, above note 185, c. 1.

FURTHER READINGS

J. BEATSON, "Increased Expense and Frustration" in F.D. Rose., ed., *Consensus ad Idem* (London: Sweet & Maxwell, 1996) c. 6.

E.A. FARNSWORTH, "Disputes over Omission in Contracts" (1968) 68 Colum. L. Rev. 860.

C. FRIED, *Contract as Promise* (Cambridge: Harvard University Press, 1981) c. 5.

D. IBBETSON, "Absolute Liability in Contract: The Antecedents of *Paradine v. Jayne*" in F.D. Rose, ed., *Consensus ad Idem* (London: Sweet & Maxwell, 1996) c. 1.

A. KULL, "Mistake, Frustration, and the Windfall Principle" (1991) 43 Hastings L.J. 1.

LAW REFORM COMMISSION OF BRITISH COLUMBIA, *Report on the Need for Frustrated Contracts Legislation* (Victoria: The Commission, 1971).

LAW REFORM COMMISSION OF SASKATCHEWAN, *Tentative Proposals for a Frustrated Contracts Act* (Saskatoon: Law Reform Commission, 1987).

R.G. MCELROY & G.L. WILLIAMS, *Impossibility of Performance* (Cambridge: Cambridge University Press, 1941).

E. MCKENDRICK, ed., *Force Majeure and Frustration of Contract*, 2d ed. (London: Lloyd's of London Press, 1995).

E. MCKENDRICK, "The Regulation of Long-Term Contracts in English Law" in J. Beatson & D. Friedmann, eds., *Good Faith and Fault in Contract Law* (Oxford: Oxford University Press, 1995).

NOVA SCOTIA LAW REFORM ADVISORY COMMISSION, *Frustrated Contracts Law* (Halifax: Nova Scotia Law Reform Advisory Commission, 1976).

D. PERCY, "The Application of the Doctrine of Frustration in Canada" in G.H.L. Fridman, ed., *Studies in Canadian Business Law* (Toronto: Butterworths, 1971) c. 3.

R.A. POSNER & A.M. ROSENFELD, "Impossibility and Related Doctrines in Contract Law" (1977) 6 J. Legal Stud. 83.

A. STEWART & J.W. CARTER, "Frustrated Contracts and Statutory Adjustment: The Case for a Reappraisal" (1992) 51 Cambridge L.J. 66.

L. TRAKMAN, "Loser Take Some: Loss Sharing and Commercial Impossibility" (1985) 69 Minn. L. Rev. 471.

L. TRAKMAN, "Frustrated Contracts and Legal Fictions" (1983) 46 Mod. L. Rev. 39.

M. TREBILCOCK, *The Limits of Freedom of Contract* (Cambridge: Harvard University Press, 1993) c. 6.

G.H. TREITEL, *Frustration and Force Majeure,* 2d ed. (London: Sweet & Maxwell, 2004).

G. WILLIAMS, *The Law Reform (Frustrated Contracts) Act, 1943* (London: Stevens & Sons, 1944).

PART FOUR

PERFORMANCE AND BREACH

CHAPTER 15

CONDITIONS, WARRANTIES AND REPUDIATORY BREACH

A. INTRODUCTION

Parties to enforceable agreements will often require an answer to either one or both of two interrelated questions. First, if an agreement does not plainly stipulate the order in which the performance of the respective parties is to occur, a party may wish to know whether its performance of a particular obligation must precede the other party's performance of its corresponding obligation. Thus, a party that has agreed to make a payment in return for the performance of certain services may wish to know whether the payment is required to be made before the provision of the services or only after they have been received. A second issue that may arise relates to the ability of a "victim" of a breach of contract (also referred to here as the "innocent party" or "the party not at fault" or "not in default") to bring an end to a contractual relationship on the basis of the other party's breach. An employer, for example, may wish to know whether certain breaches of the employment contract on the part of the employee entitle the employer to terminate the employment relationship. Again, this issue could be the subject of stipulation in the employment contract. In the absence of such a provision, however, the common law must be able to determine whether the innocent party is entitled to terminate the agreement on the basis of the other party's breach of contract.

These two rather different issues are interrelated for the following reasons. In determining the order of performance required by the contract, one will also, as a consequence, identify circumstances in which a failure to perform by one party will provide the other party with a basis for withholding performance or, indeed, terminating the agreement. Thus, in the context of an agreement under which a payer agrees to pay money in return for services to be provided by the other party, if it is determined that the provision of services must precede payment, it will follow that a failure by the service provider to provide the contractually required services will provide the payer with a basis for refusing to make payment and to terminate the contractual relationship. Under traditional doctrine, both of these sets of issues were determined on the basis of whether the particular provisions of the agreement in issue were properly classified as either "conditions" or as mere "warranties." In determining whether a breach of contract would entitle the other party to terminate the relationship, traditional doctrine would consider whether the provision breached was properly classified as a "condition" of the agreement. If so, the innocent party had the ability to terminate the agreement. With respect to the order of performance, traditional doctrine would determine whether the performance of a particular obligation was not merely the performance of a "condition" but the performance of a "condition precedent" to the enforceability of the obligation of the other party. The party whose obligation to perform is a condition precedent to the enforceability of the other party's obligation must obviously "go first." Further, if that party fails to perform the condition precedent, the victim of the breach will be entitled to treat the contract as discharged by that breach.

Although much of the law on this topic adopted its modern shape by the end of the nineteenth century, the rigid classification of terms as being either "conditions" or "warranties" upon which it was based created a doctrine that was considered by many to be unduly rigid and therefore subject to manipulation in order to achieve satisfactory results in particular cases. In the latter part of the twentieth century, however, the doctrine underwent a substantial transformation. One of the principal objectives of this chapter is to assess the nature and extent of that doctrinal modification.

A major difficulty inherent in addressing this topic is terminological in nature. The terms "rescission" and "repudiation" are bandied about in discussions of this topic as if they were subject to hard and fast meanings, whereas, alas, they are not. The term "rescission" is used to refer to equitable rescission for misrepresentation or on other equitable grounds; or, to the discharge or termination of an agreement for breach. The term "repudiation" is used to refer to a severe breach of contract; or, alternatively, to the election by the party not at fault to treat the contract as discharged by the breach. In *Photo Production Ltd. v. Securicor Transport Ltd.*,[1] Lord Wilberforce observed as follows:

> A vast number of expressions are used to describe situations where a breach has been committed by one party of such a character as to entitle the other party of refuse further performance: discharge, rescission, termination, the contract is at an end, or dead; or displaced; clauses cannot survive or simply go. I have come to think that some of these difficulties can be avoided; in particular the use of the term "rescission" even if distinguished from rescission *ab initio*, as an equivalent for discharge, though justifiable in some contexts … may lead to confusion in others. To plead for complete uniformity may be to cry for the moon.[2]

The safest course, in my view, is to use the term "rescission" rather strictly to refer only to rescission on equitable grounds. The type of breach of contract giving rise to the innocent party's right to "terminate" the contract or treat it as "discharged" by breach is perhaps most clearly referred to as "repudiatory breach." Without unrealistically "crying for the moon," these usages are at least followed in this book. But there are other terminological difficulties. As we shall see, the use of the term "condition" has changed over time. The term "warranty" has more than one meaning. The concept of "fundamental breach" creates its own set of hazards.

The primary task of this chapter is to articulate the rules identifying particular breaches of contract as "repudiatory," thus giving rise to the innocent party's right to terminate for breach. The chapter provides an account of the development of the condition-warranty dichotomy and the modern reform thereof and then briefly sketches the remedial options open to the victim of a repudiatory breach of contract. The chapter concludes with brief discussions of the remedies available for breaches of terms drafted in the form of representations and warranties and of the concept of material breach.

B. PROMISES AND CONDITIONS

Although the point of a contract or of contract law may be said to create or recognize the existence of enforceable promises or undertakings,

---

1   [1980] A.C. 827 (H.L.). See also *Guarantee Co. of North America v. Gordon Capital Corp.* (1999), 178 D.L.R. (4th) 1 (S.C.C.).
2   *Photo Production Ltd. v. Securicor Transport Ltd., ibid.* at 844.

contracts are not simply composed of a string of promises given by each of the parties to the agreement. Contracts also typically set forth arrangements, referred to usually as conditions, that stipulate a state of affairs that must exist before one or more of the obligations of one or more of the parties to the agreement is to be enforceable. For example, the obligations of the parties to close a transaction for the purchase and sale of land may be stipulated to be contingent upon or conditional upon the rezoning of the land by a certain date by the municipality in which the land is located. If that state of affairs does not exist by the stipulated date, the obligation to close is not enforceable against either party. Such arrangements may also have the effect of ordering the performance of the promises given by each party: "The employer is not obliged to pay the architect until the drawings are completed." Completion of the drawings is a state of affairs that must exist before the obligation of the employer to make payment becomes enforceable. The architect "goes first."

The typical contract, then, can be seen to be composed of two different kinds of terms: on the one hand, promises or contractual undertakings that set out the obligations of the parties and, on the other hand, conditions that stipulate states of affairs under which one or more contractual undertakings are enforceable by the promisee in question and that may stipulate the order in which the contractual undertakings are to be performed by the parties.

Conditions stipulating circumstances in which an obligation or obligations are enforceable can be subdivided into conditions precedent and conditions subsequent. A condition that stipulates a state of affairs that must exist before a particular undertaking becomes enforceable is a condition precedent. The condition relating to rezoning in the hypothetical real estate transaction referred to above would be a condition precedent to closing. A condition that stipulates a state of affairs under which the obligations of the parties cease to be enforceable is a condition subsequent. A provision in a lending contract that stipulates that the lender's obligations to advance monies will terminate upon the insolvency of the borrower would be a condition subsequent.

For convenience, we will defer consideration of certain controversies concerning the nature of conditions. It is possible that certain types of conditions precedent are correctly considered to stipulate states of affairs that must exist before the very contract comes into existence rather than merely conditioning the enforceability of particular undertakings within a binding contract.[3] Further, though it is generally assumed that

---

3   For a helpful discussion of this issue, see *Wiebe v. Bobsien*, [1985] 1 W.W.R. 644 (B.C.S.C.).

conditions inserted for the benefit of one party may be waived by that party with the result that the obligations of the parties rendered contingent by that condition remain enforceable, Canadian courts—alone it would appear in the common law world—have invented a doctrine of "true condition precedent" pursuant to which some such conditions cannot be waived. This is the infamous rule in *Turney v. Zhilka*,[4] the continuing validity of which was reaffirmed by the Supreme Court of Canada in the decision in *Barnett v. Harrison*.[5] These issues are further explored in a subsequent chapter.[6]

It is evident that a condition could stipulate that the performance of one party's promise is a state of affairs that must exist before the other party's obligation to perform becomes enforceable. The above example of the employment of an architect is a simple illustration of this phenomenon. The arrangement is that the employer's promise to pay the fee is not enforceable until the architect has performed his or her promise to provide the drawings. Such "promissory" conditions precedent, where the state of affairs that must occur is the performance of another party's promise, may be distinguished from "non-promissory" or "contingent" conditions precedent, where the state of affairs that must exist is the occurrence of something other than the performance of a contractual promise. The rezoning of the land said to be a condition precedent of the closing of the real estate transaction referred to above would be an obvious illustration of a non-promissory condition precedent. Neither party has promised that the rezoning will occur. Accordingly, failure of rezoning is not a state of affairs that results from non-performance of one party's promise. To be sure, it may be held to be implicit in such a non-promissory condition precedent that one or both of the parties will promise to cooperate in the making of an application for rezoning, but the condition precedent itself nonetheless remains a non-promissory condition precedent. Promissory conditions precedent, as the architect's arrangements illustrate, have the effect of determining the order in which the effected promises of the parties will be performed.[7]

---

4   [1959] S.C.R. 578.

5   [1976] 2 S.C.R. 531.

6   See Chapter 17.

7   Parenthetically, we may note that Canadian lawyers often reserve the term "condition precedent" for non-promissory conditions precedent and refer to promissory conditions precedent simply by describing the promise itself as a "condition." Usage on this point is not consistent, however, and there are frequent references in the jurisprudence to promissory conditions precedent as "conditions precedent."

Where parties expressly stipulate not only the promises or undertakings given by each party but also the conditions of their enforceability, a court will have little difficulty in giving effect to the latter. If the agreement plainly stipulates that completion of the drawings is a state of affairs that must exist before the employer's obligation to pay the architect is enforceable, such an arrangement or condition will be easily interpreted and applied by a court. Difficulties arise, however, when the parties do not so plainly stipulate. In an earlier stage of the development of the common law of contract, these problems were addressed through the doctrine of dependent and independent terms.[8] If a promise was determined to be "dependent" on some other promise, the first promise would be enforceable only if the second promise had been performed. Thus, if the buyer's promise to pay for goods was "dependent" on the seller's promise to deliver them, the promise to pay is enforceable only if the goods are delivered. We might express the same idea by stating that where the first promise is dependent on the second, enforcement of the first is "contingent" upon or "conditional" upon performance of the second promise. If the first promise was independent, however, it could be enforced whether or not any other promise had been performed. The effect of the doctrine was succinctly stated by Sergeant Williams in his notes on *Pordage v. Cole*[9] as follows:

> where there are several covenants, promises or agreements, which are independent of each other, one party may bring an action against the other for a breach of his covenants, & c. without averring a performance of the covenants, & c. on his, the plaintiff's part; and it is no excuse for the defendant to allege in his plea a breach of the covenants, & c. on the part of the plaintiff. ... But where the covenants & c. are *dependent*, it is necessary for the plaintiff to aver and prove a performance of the covenants, & c. on his part, to entitle himself to an action for the breach of covenants on the part of the defendant.[10]

In the earliest stages of the development of this doctrine, the common law took the position that mutual promises were considered to be independent or separately enforceable, unless the parties plainly stipulated to the contrary.[11] Thus, in a contract of employment in which the employer promises to pay a wage and the employee promises to provide

---

8   S.J. Stoljar, *A History of Contract at Common Law* (Canberra: Australian National University Press, 1975) c. 12.

9   (1669), 1 Wms. Saund. 319, 85 E.R. 449.

10   *Ibid.* at 320 (Wms. Saund.).

11   See Stoljar, above note 8 at 148–50.

services, the employee could sue to enforce the employer's wage obligation even if no service had been provided. Similarly, a seller of goods could sue for the price even though the goods had not been delivered.[12] Recognition of the more modern notion of "concurrent conditions" had not yet occurred.

With the wisdom of the hindsight afforded by several centuries, we can easily see that the doctrine of independency would not survive. The examples just given illustrate the potential for harsh results for the employer and the buyer whose obligations to pay remain enforceable, notwithstanding the absence of performance by the employee and seller. On the other hand, where conditional words are used in the contract, harsh results are possible in cases where substantial but not complete performance has been rendered, but the obligation of the other party, being contingent, is unenforceable. Legal historians tell us that in order to solve problems of these kinds, the courts manipulated the independent-dependent distinction in such a way as to bring about just results.[13] Further, courts demonstrated an increasing willingness to find the existence of dependency and, indeed, by the late-eighteenth century, at least, the notion of what we would now consider to be concurrent conditions—that is, mutual obligations to tender performance—received the approval of Lord Mansfield. With respect to the problem of substantial but incomplete performance, the courts indicated a willingness to find that even though conditional language was present in the agreement, an undertaking could be found to be independent, thus permitting one who had not completely performed to bring an action to enforce the other party's obligation subject to a counterclaim being brought by the other party for the deficiency. In short, the courts were prepared to manipulate the independent-dependent distinction to "achieve reasonable results."[14]

The complexity and evolution of the doctrine of dependent and independent terms need not be examined in depth here. Two developments, however, are of importance. First, the distinction between dependent and independent terms came to be seen as turning on a distinction between obligations going to the "whole of the consideration" rather than merely to "part" of the consideration provided by a party. A leading exposition of this point is to be found in the decision of Lord Mansfield in *Boone v. Eyre*[15] in 1779. The case concerned the sale of a

12   Early cases to this effect are cited by Stoljar, *ibid.*
13   Stoljar, *ibid.* at 151–55.
14   *Ibid.* at 155.
15   (1779), 1 H. Bl. 273n, 126 E.R. 160.

West Indian plantation, including a group of slaves. The seller sought to enforce the agreement even though, contrary to his undertaking, he did not possess title to the slaves. For Lord Mansfield, a distinction was to be drawn between mutual covenants that "go to the whole of the consideration on both sides"[16] so that they become conditioned upon each other as opposed to undertakings where the consideration goes "only to a part" so that the breach thereof sounds only in damages. The undertaking at issue in *Boone v. Eyre* fell into the latter category for otherwise, as Lord Mansfield explained, failure to own even one slave would bar the seller's action. The seller's action for the price was therefore allowed subject to the buyer's counterclaim for damages for the deficiency.

Boone v. Eyre concerned an executed contract and held, in effect, that a partial breach would not preclude the seller's action for the price. The distinction between obligations concerning the whole of rather than part of the consideration came to be applied, however, to executory agreements as well. In the famous case of *Bettini v. Gye*,[17] a singer, Bettini, had agreed to perform in concerts and operas for Gye during a period of four months. He agreed, as well, "without fail" to arrive in London at least six days prior to the commencement of the engagement for rehearsals. Bettini fell ill and arrived late. Gye refused to allow him to perform and Bettini brought an action for damages. Blackburn J. noted that the question of whether the defendant was justified in refusing to allow Bettini to perform "depends on whether this part of the contract is a condition precedent to the defendant's liability, or only an independent agreement a breach of which will not justify a repudiation of the contract, but will only be a cause of action for compensation and damages."[18] For Blackburn J., the test to apply required one to make the following determination: "whether the particular stipulation goes to the root of the matter, so that a failure to perform it would render the performance of the rest of the contract a thing different in substance from what the dependent has stipulated for; or whether it merely partially affects it and may be compensated for in damages."[19]

On the particular facts, it was Blackburn J.'s view that given, *inter alia*, the length of the contract, the failure to arrive in time for rehearsals did not "go to the root of the matter so as to require us to consider it a condition precedent." If Gye wanted to be able to terminate Bettini for late arrival at rehearsal, he should have stipulated that "if Mr. Bettini is

---

16   *Ibid.*
17   (1876), 1 Q.B.D. 183.
18   *Ibid.* at 187.
19   *Ibid.* at 188.

not there at the stipulated time, Mr. Gye may refuse to proceed further with the agreement." In short, then, by the end of the nineteenth century, it had come to be accepted that the distinction between dependent and independent terms rested on a distinction between stipulations going to the root of the contract and those that did not. This distinction or test has found its way into the modern law of conditions and warranties.

The second development of contemporary significance is evident in the language of Blackburn J. in *Bettini v. Gye*. At least by the late-nineteenth century, where a breach of contract went to the root of the contract, the undertaking that was breached came to be itself referred to as a "condition" of the agreement. A stipulation of lesser importance came to be referred to as a mere "warranty," breach of which sounds only in damages. We thus arrive at modern terminology, more familiar to us, in which the undertakings or promises in a contract are themselves classified as either conditions or warranties. Breach of the former gives rise to the right of the party not at fault to terminate the contract in addition to suing for damages, whereas breach of the latter gives rise only to a damages claim. Instead of asking, then, whether, in a case like *Bettini v. Gye*, a court should imply (or not) a condition in a form such as, for example, "performance of Bettini's undertaking to arrive in a timely fashion is a state of affairs that must exist before Gye's obligations under the agreement become enforceable," one is directed to ask whether Bettini's *promise* to arrive is a condition or a mere warranty. On this view, rather than determine the nature of any conditions that are implied into the agreement in order to condition the enforceability of particular promises, one classifies each of the promises set out in the agreement as being either conditions or warranties. As will be seen, this shift in the analytical model is thought by many to have brought with it undesirable consequences. Nonetheless, its adoption in the late-nineteenth century was confirmed by, if not in the main achieved by, the adoption of this analytical model in the *Sale of Goods Act*[20] of 1893. Though the terms "condition" and "warranty" are not defined in the legislation, the Act provides—in a section copied in the sale of goods legislation of common law Canada and of other Commonwealth jurisdictions—as follows: "Whether a stipulation in a contract of sale is a condition a breach of which may give rise to a right to treat the contract as repudiated or a warranty, a breach of which may give rise to a claim for damages but not to a right to reject the goods and treat the contract as repudiated depends in each case on the construction of the contract, and a stipulation may be a condition, though called a warranty in the contract."

---

20   See, for example, *Sale of Goods Act*, R.S.O. 1990, c. S.1, s. 12(2).

The Act then goes on to provide in various sections that in the absence of contractual language to the contrary, contracts for the sale of goods shall be deemed to include implied conditions as to merchantability, fitness for purpose, conformity with description and so on. The underlying analytical model on which this provision is based appears to assume that contractual undertakings can be divided into two and only two categories, the more important category being that of conditions and the lesser being that of warranties. Critics of the "condition-warranty" dichotomy have suggested that because of its defects the newer approach ought to be restricted in its application to sale of goods agreements *per se.* Undoubtedly, however, the condition-warranty analysis has spread out beyond the particular context of contracts for the sale of goods and has come to be seen as an aspect of the general law of contracts.

C. THE CONDITION-WARRANTY DICHOTOMY: CRITICISMS AND CURE

A number of criticisms are commonly made of the condition-warranty analytical model, and in recent decades a more flexible and, arguably, rational analytical method for determining the consequences of a breach of contract appears to have been adopted by the courts.[21] A basic conceptual attack on the condition-warranty dichotomy is that it rests on a confusion of the concepts of promise and condition. Conditions, as traditionally understood, are not promises. They are arrangements that stipulate circumstances under which promises may be either enforceable or unenforceable. Thus, to use the term "condition" to refer to particular promises in an agreement introduces an element of terminological confusion. This is all the more so inasmuch as contractual stipulations that are properly regarded as conditions in the traditional sense are also frequently included in agreements. Thus, the condition concerning rezoning in the hypothetical real estate transaction is plainly a condition in the traditional sense of an arrangement or term stipulating circumstances under which the undertakings to close the transaction are enforceable or not. A possible response to this criticism is that this modern use of the term "condition" to refer to and classify particular contractual undertakings may be seen as simply an elliptical way of referring to the more complicated notion that this particular

---

21   See, for example, F.M.B. Reynolds, "Warranty, Condition and Fundamental Term" (1963) 79 Law Q. Rev. 534.

undertaking is one that is subject to an understanding that its performance is a state of affairs that must exist if the other party's obligations are to be enforceable. Certainly, it is in any event a common drafting technique to use the term "condition" in this elliptical fashion and to stipulate that certain undertakings in the agreements are conditions, by which the drafter means to suggest that their breach will entitle the other party to treat the contract as discharged by breach. The call for conceptual clarity in the use of the term "condition" thus comes a little late in the day to be effective. We shall return to this drafting point.

A more telling criticism of the condition-warranty dichotomy is that it leads to an unnecessary and unhelpful rigidity in the determination of the consequences of particular breaches of contract. By focusing on the importance of the term rather than the significance of the actual breach of contract for the party not at fault, the condition-warranty dichotomy envisages a bipolar world in which a term must be classified either as one in which, the term being a condition, any conceivable breach of the undertaking will give rise to the right to disaffirm the contract or, being classified as a warranty, every conceivable breach of the undertaking must be considered to sound only in damages. Thus, the condition-warranty dichotomy appears to preclude the possibility that an undertaking could be of such a nature that some breaches should give rise to the right to disaffirm whereas others, being less severe in their impact on the party not at fault, should not have that effect. And yet, there are surely many contractual stipulations of this kind in fact. In the case of such stipulations, the condition-warranty dichotomy requires an all-or-nothing choice between condition, that is, treating all breaches, however trivial, as repudiatory or warranty, that is, treating none as repudiatory, however devastating the consequences of a particular breach might be.

A compelling illustration of this problem is to be found in the facts of *Hong Kong Fir Shipping Co. Ltd. v. Kawasaki Kisen Kaisha Ltd.*,[22] a decision of the English Court of Appeal in which a modern reformulation of the condition-warranty dichotomy was fashioned. This was a claim by the owners of a vessel for hire payable by the defendant charter-

---

22   [1962] 2 Q.B. 26 (C.A.). For Canadian acceptance of the *Hong Kong Fir* analysis, see *First City Capital Ltd. v. Petrosar Ltd.* (1987), 61 O.R. (2d) 193 (H.C.J.); *Lehndorff Canadian Pension Properties Ltd. v. Davis Management Ltd.* (1989), 59 D.L.R. (4th) 1 (B.C.C.A.); *First City Trust Co. v. Triple Five Trust Corp. Ltd.* (1989), 57 D.L.R. (4th) 554 (Alta. C.A.); *Ramrod Investments Ltd. v. Matsumoto Shipyards Ltd.* (1990), 47 B.C.L.R. (2d) 86 (C.A.); *Krawchuk v. Ulrychova* (1996), 40 Alta. L.R. (3d) 196 (Prov. Ct.); *Shelanu Inc. v. Print Three Franchising Corp.* (2003), 226 D.L.R. (4th) 577 (Ont. C.A.).

ers under a charter party of twenty-four months' duration. The charter party contained an undertaking by the owner to, in effect, maintain the vessel in a state of seaworthiness. The charter party further provided that no hire would be paid for time lost for repairs in excess of twenty-four hours and, at the charterers' option, that such periods of time could be added to the length of the charter. The defendant charterers had refused payment on the grounds that in addition to an initial period of five weeks required for repairs to the vessel's engines, the vessel was going to be off hire for a further fifteen weeks in order to undertake repairs as a result of the charterers' subsequent discovery that the engines were in a very sorry state. If one applied the condition-warranty dichotomy to this situation, one would have to determine whether the owner's undertaking as to seaworthiness was either a condition or a warranty. Obviously, it could be argued that seaworthiness "goes to the root" of a charter party and that breach of the obligation therefore gives the charterers a right to terminate the agreement. On the other hand, it would be obvious that minor repairs required from time to time, though equally breaches of the seaworthiness undertaking, would not be unexpected and should not constitute a basis for termination of the agreement. Following this line of analysis, if the seaworthiness undertaking were classified as a warranty, however, no breach of the seaworthiness provision, no matter how disastrous its impact on the charterers might be, could give rise to a right to terminate the agreement.

Confronted by this dilemma, the Court of Appeal in *Hong Kong Fir* adopted what may have appeared to be an innovative approach.[23] Diplock L.J., having noted that either the parties or Parliament might stipulate that any breach of a particular undertaking could provide a basis for termination of the contract by the party not at fault, went on to criticize the rigidity of the condition-warranty dichotomy. In Diplock L.J.'s view, the central flaw in the approach dictated by the condition-warranty dichotomy is that it focuses on the nature of the undertaking rather than the circumstances of the particular breach of that undertaking and fails to appreciate that there will be contractual undertakings, perhaps many of them, with respect to which some breaches should give rise to the ability on the part of the party not at fault to terminate the agreement and others should not have this effect. It was therefore

---

23   The analysis may be regarded, however, as a revival of an approach implicit if not indeed explicit in earlier authorities. See R. Goff, "The Search for Principle" in W. Swadling and G. Jones, eds., *The Search for Principle* (New York: Oxford University Press, 1999) 313 at 316–17.

necessary, in his view, to recognize the existence of a third category of terms, neither conditions nor warranties, which, when breached, give rise to the necessity to examine the consequences of the particular breach in issue and determine whether, in light of those circumstances, the party not at fault should be entitled to disaffirm or terminate the contract or, rather, be left to a damages claim.

The effect of the approach adopted by Diplock L.J., then, was to narrowly confine the existing categories of conditions and warranties and insert between them a new and rather large category of what are sometimes referred to as "innominate," that is, unnameable or unclassifiable, and sometimes as "intermediate" terms. He reasoned as follows:

> No doubt there are many simple contractual undertakings, sometimes express, but more often because of their very simplicity ("It goes without saying") to be implied, of which it can be predicated that every breach of such an undertaking must give rise to an event which will deprive the party not in default of substantially the whole benefit which it was intended that he should obtain from the contract. In such a stipulation, unless the parties have agreed that breach of it shall not entitle the non-defaulting party to treat the contract as repudiated, is a "condition." So, too, there may be other simple contractual undertakings of which it can be predicated that *no* breach can give rise to an event which will deprive the party not in default of substantially the whole benefit which it was intended that he should obtain from the contract; and such a stipulation, unless the parties have agreed that breach of it shall entitle the non-defaulting party to treat the contract as repudiated, is a "warranty."
>
> There are, however, many contractual undertakings of a more complex character which cannot be categorized as being "conditions" or "warranties." ... Of such undertakings, all that can be predicated is that some breaches will, and others will not, give rise to an event which would deprive the party not in default of substantially the whole benefit which it was intended that he should obtain from the contract; and the legal consequences of the breach of such an undertaking, unless provided for expressly in that contract, depend on the nature of the event to which the breach gives rise and do not follow automatically from a prior classification of the undertaking as a "condition" or a "warranty."[24]

---

24 Above note 22 at 69–70.

Turning to the facts of the present case, Diplock L.J. observed that the owner's obligation as to seaworthiness was of this complex and un-classifiable character. The stipulation is one that "can be broken by the presence of trivial defects easily and rapidly remediable as well as by defects which must inevitably result in a total loss of the vessel." Noting that a substantial number of previous cases on this point did not ap-pear to take the view that this problem could be solved by determining whether the undertaking is a condition rather than a warranty, Diplock L.J. went on to observe that the correct approach to the analysis of this stipulation was as follows:

> What the judge had to do in the present case, as in any other case where one party to a contract relies on a breach by the other party as giving him a right to elect to rescind the contract, was to look at the events which had occurred as a result of the breach at the time in which the charterers purported to rescind the charterparty, and to decide whether the occurrence of those events deprived the char-terers of substantially the whole benefit which it was the intention of the parties as expressed in the charterparty that the charterers should obtain from the further performance of their own contractual undertakings.[25]

Applying this approach, Diplock L.J. agreed with the trial judge that the present breaches were not such as to deprive the charterers of sub-stantially the whole benefit that it was the intention of the parties that the charterers should obtain from further use of the vessel. Accord-ingly, the charterers were not entitled to terminate the charter party for breach.

The innominate term analysis advanced in *Hong Kong Fir* thus pro-vides an elegant solution to the rigidity and inflexibility of the analysis based on the condition-warranty dichotomy. As Diplock L.J. intimates in *Hong Kong Fir*, however, it may be noted that the inflexibility of the condition-warranty dichotomy may, at least in part, result from the col-lapsing of the distinction between promises and conditions culminating in the provisions of the *Sale of Goods Act* referred to above. The condi-tion-warranty dichotomy requires that one simply analyze the terms of the contract itself and determine whether this particular provision in the context of this particular contract goes to the root of the contract. Such an analysis can and, indeed, should be made without regard to the actual circumstances of the particular breach that has occurred. This ap-proach does appear to flow naturally from a decision that each contractual undertaking must be classifiable as either a condition or a warranty. If, however, one reverts to the traditional analysis and asks whether a traditional condition (in the sense of a stipulation that a particular state of affairs must exist if a particular promise is to be enforceable) is to be implied with respect to the owner's undertaking as to seaworthiness, the analyst might more easily come to the conclusion that it would be appropriate to imply a condition to the effect that the charterer's obligations to pay hire under the charter party will be unenforceable only in the event of a very substantial breach of the seaworthiness obligation. In Diplock L.J.'s view, the adoption of the condition-warranty dichotomy obscured our view of the fact that it is the "event" of breach that engages the condition. That is to say, once one focuses on the importance of the circumstances of the breach, it becomes easier to see that, in many cases, the appropriate course will be to imply a condition that only some but not other breaches of a particular undertaking will constitute a state of affairs rendering the other party's obligations unenforceable.

In *Hong Kong Fir*, however, Diplock L.J. attempts to put these terminological muddles behind us by suggesting that it is possible to classify the undertakings in an agreement into one of three categories: "true" conditions, we might say, being undertakings of which every conceivable breach would deprive the party not in default of substantially the whole benefit of the contract; "true" warranties, that is terms of such lesser importance that no conceivable breach could have such an effect and thirdly, innominate terms, that is, terms that cannot be classified as either true conditions or true warranties and with respect to which the actual circumstances of the breach and their impact on the party not at fault must be examined in order to determine whether that party should be accorded a right to disaffirm the contract in addition to the right to pursue a claim in damages. Thus, Diplock L.J.'s innominate term analysis allows us to reintroduce flexibility in the sense of grounding the decision as to whether a particular breach is repudiatory by examining the effects of the breach on the party not at fault. At the same time, it does not require us to abandon the modern orthodoxy that some promises, at least, can be classified as "conditions" and some others, at least, as mere "warranties."

D. REFINEMENT OF THE *HONG KONG FIR* ANALYSIS

Two refinements of the *Hong Kong Fir* analysis have emerged in the subsequent cases. First, the extent of the adjustment, if any, to existing doctrine effected by the *Hong Kong Fir* definition of the nature of conditional terms has been examined. Second, the applicability of the *Hong Kong Fir* analysis to sale of goods cases has been considered.

The stringent test proposed by Diplock L.J. in *Hong Kong Fir* for the recognition of "true" conditions—a term of such a nature and importance that every conceivable breach would deprive the other party of substantially the whole benefit of the contract might, if literally or vigorously applied, radically restrict the types of terms that would be considered to be conditions at common law. Indeed, such an approach might be thought to require reconsideration of bodies of common law doctrine developed over the years with respect to the recognition at common law of conditions in familiar transactional types or patterns. It may be asked, then, whether so substantial an overhauling of prior doctrine was contemplated by the Court of Appeal in *Hong Kong Fir* and, if so, whether so extensive a program of reform of the common law is desirable.

These issues surfaced for consideration in *Bunge Corp., New York v. Tradax Export S.A., Panama.*[26] This case concerned a buyer's failure to comply with a contractual requirement to provide the seller with "at least 15 consecutive days' notice" of the probable readiness of a vessel on which the goods would be shipped. The sellers claimed that the late notice was a repudiatory breach, disaffirmed the agreement and sued for expectancy damages. As the agreement did not expressly stipulate that the notice requirement was a condition, the buyer invoked the innominate term analysis of *Hong Kong Fir*, arguing that minor lateness did not deprive the seller of the advantage of the contract. The appeal of the argument is obvious. A timeliness obligation can be breached gravely with a major effect on the party not at fault or trivially with no harmful consequence. Under the *Hong Kong Fir* analysis, only the former breaches should be considered repudiatory. The House of Lords rejected this argument, however, and in so doing may be taken to have indicated a note of caution with respect to the comprehensiveness of the reform achieved by *Hong Kong Fir.* Lord Wilberforce suggested that it was an error to attempt to apply Diplock L.J.'s "seminal judgment"[27] to a time clause in a mercantile agreement where the parties have an interest in being able to determine with a degree of certainty whether the terms of the agreement have been met. While he commended the "greater flexibility in the law of contracts to which *Hong Kong Fir* points the way,"[28] he nonetheless did not doubt that "in suitable cases, the

---

26   [1981] 2 All E.R. 513 (H.L.).
27   *Ibid.* at 541.
28   *Ibid.* at 542.

courts should not be reluctant, if the intentions of the parties as shown by the contract so indicate, to hold that an obligation has the force of a condition, and that indeed they should usually do so in the case of time clauses in mercantile contracts."[29]

Similarly, Lord Roskill expressed the view that the innominate term analysis should not be considered to be applicable to "stipulations as to time in mercantile contracts."[30] Such an approach would be inconsistent with earlier authority. Further, while characterizing Diplock L.J.'s judgment as a "landmark"[31] of twentieth-century contracts' jurisprudence and recognizing the value of the "modern approach and not being overready to construe terms as conditions unless the contract clearly requires the court to do so,"[32] Lord Roskill observed that "none the less, the basic principles of construction for determining whether or not a particular term is a condition remain as before."[33] Moreover, to the extent that Diplock L.J.'s judgment in *Hong Kong Fir* might be taken to suggest that in the absence of an express stipulation of "condition" in the contract, the innominate term approach applies, Lord Roskill emphasized that, on a proper construction, a contract might be interpreted to include an implied condition, "always bearing in mind on the one hand the need for certainty and, on the other hand, the desirability of not, when legitimate, allowing rescission where the breach complained of is highly technical and where damages would clearly be an adequate remedy." For Lord Roskill, the correct reading of Diplock L.J.'s tripartite analysis of what has been referred to here as "true" conditions, "true" warranties and innominate terms, is that this analysis only applies once it has been determined, on the basis of more traditional analytical methods, that a particular term is not a condition.

In *Bunge*, then, the House of Lords, though welcoming the increased flexibility of the *Hong Kong Fir* analysis, signalled that the desirability of certainty in contractual interpretation for the parties may ground a finding that an agreement is properly construed to contain a term that is implicitly a condition of the agreement even though it is not true that every conceivable breach thereof will deprive the party not at fault of the substantial benefits of the agreement. Moreover, there is a suggestion in *Bunge* that the prior common law identifying particular terms as conditions—at least to the extent that it rests on a construction of the

---

29 *Ibid.*
30 *Ibid.* at 552.
31 *Ibid.* at 550.
32 *Ibid.* at 551.
33 *Ibid.*

agreement giving effect to the intentions of the parties—is not swept aside by the *Hong Kong Fir* test for repudiatory breach. The same view has been judicially expressed on other occasions.[34]

The innominate term analysis would have no application, of course, to a contractual provision that was stipulated by legislation such as the *Sales of Goods Act* to be an implied condition of the agreement. Thus, any breach, however minor, of the implied condition as to merchant-ability or fitness for purpose in a sale of goods contract would give the buyer a right to disaffirm the contract and reject the goods. A more difficult question is whether the sale of goods legislation provision quoted above[35] was intended to create a statutory condition-warranty dichotomy with the result that the innominate term analysis would never apply to a sale of goods transaction. In *Hong Kong Fir*, Diplock L.J. appeared to concede that the innominate term analysis might, indeed, be excluded in contracts for the sale of goods. Subsequent cases, however, have clarified the point and have concluded that provisions of a sale of goods agreement that are not classified as conditions by the *Sale of Goods Act* are amenable to this analysis. In *Cehave NV v. Bremer Handelsgesellschaft mbH*,[36] the Court of Appeal considered the significance of a comparatively minor breach of a contractual stipulation providing that "shipment to be made in good condition." The buyer, arguing that the *Sale of Goods Act* created a statutory condition-warranty dichotomy, defended rejection of the goods on the basis that a contractual stipulation relating to the "good condition" of the goods must be a condition rather than a mere warranty and, accordingly, that any breach thereof entitled the buyer to reject. The Court of Appeal held, however, that the innominate term analysis did apply. Lord Denning explained that the intermediate term analysis of the *Hong Kong Fir* case simply pointed to the existence of a substantial body of prior law dealing with terms that were neither warranties nor conditions and with respect to which the right to terminate for repudiatory breach rested on an assessment of the gravity of the particular breach. As the applicability of the general principles of the common law to contracts for the sale of goods is expressly preserved by section 61(2) of the 1893 English Act—at least to the extent not inconsistent with the sale of goods provisions of the Act—the innominate term analysis of *Hong Kong Fir* is also applicable to such agreements. The particular term at issue was, in Lord Denning's

---

34 See, for example, *The Mihalis Angelos*, [1971] 1 Q.B. 164 at 200–1, Edmund Davies L.J. and 205, Megaw L.J.

35 See above this Chapter, section B; and see *Sale of Goods Act*, above note 20.

36 [1975] 3 All E.R. 739 (C.A.).

view, one that could be breached either in a serious and substantial way or in a minor way. Accordingly, it was subject to the innominate term analysis and, on the particular facts, a right to reject goods was not an appropriate response to the seller's breach. In another case, this approach was adopted by the House of Lords.[37] Canadian courts have followed the lead of the English courts and have also applied the *Hong Kong Fir* analysis to contracts for the sale of goods.[38]

E. APPLYING THE *HONG KONG FIR* TEST

Where a breach of contract constitutes a breach of a term properly classified as a "condition" of the contract, either by statute or by contractual stipulation or, as we have seen, by proper construction of the agreement at common law, the breach of contract is a repudiatory breach giving rise to an option on the part of the victim of the breach to terminate the contract. Where the term breached is not properly so classified, however, the victim must then turn to the *Hong Kong Fir* analysis in order to determine whether or not the particular breach is repudiatory in the requisite sense. In *Hong Kong Fir* itself, Diplock L.J. articulated the test as one of determining whether the breach deprived the party not at fault of "substantially the whole benefit which it was intended that [the party not at fault] should obtain from the contract."[39] In *Sail Labrador Ltd. v. Challenge One*,[40] Bastarache J. referred to the test as one

---

37   *Reardon Smith Line v. Yngvar Hansen-Tangen*, [1976] 1 W.L.R. 989 (H.L.).

38   *Krawchuk v. Ulrychova*, above note 22. Section 61(2) of the English Act has its equivalents in the Canadian legislation. See, for example, *Sale of Goods Act*, R.S.O. 1990, c. S.1, s. 57(1).

39   Above note 22 at 69. This test received the *imprimatur* of Wilson J. in *Hunter Engineering Co. Inc. v. Syncrude Canada Ltd.*, [1989] 1 S.C.R. 426 at 499, referring there to Lord Diplock's articulation of the test in these terms in *Photo Production Ltd. v. Securicor Transport Ltd.*, above note 1 at 849, though it is unclear whether Wilson J. was here confusing the Diplock test for repudiatory breach with the test for breaches that may restrict the application of an exculpatory clause.

40   [1999] 1 S.C.R. 265 at 281–82 (contract requiring 35 payments by certified cheque—payer provides non-certified postdated cheques that payee accepts, one of which is rejected by the drawee bank in error—held, no substantial non-performance—Binnie J., concurring, relied on the doctrine of waiver). In the *Cehave* case, above note 36 at 747, Lord Denning articulated the test as one of "serious and substantial" divergence from the terms. In these cases, both Bastarache J. and Lord Denning refer to the alternative formulation of a breach that goes "to the root of the contract," thereby embracing the metaphor traditionally used to identify dependent terms and ultimately "conditions."

of "substantial non-performance." It may be asked, however, whether some guidance can be gleaned from the cases as to the considerations that may or should be brought to bear in determining whether, in the circumstances of a particular breach, this test has been met.

A number of factors or guidelines for application of the *Hong Kong Fir* test can be drawn or inferred from the *Hong Kong Fir* decision itself and from other cases finding the presence or absence of a repudiatory breach. Thus, *Hong Kong Fir* may be taken to suggest that one should consider the proportional effect of the breach on the total value of the performance being rendered by the party at fault. The vessel in *Hong Kong Fir* was off hire for repairs for a total of twenty weeks. On the other hand, the charter was to last for twenty-four months. Moreover, the period of time off hire could be added to the contract at the charterer's option. Similarly, it has been held in the context of an instalment contract for the sale of goods that minor shortages with respect to particular instalments would not constitute a repudiatory breach.[41] The fact that the parties stipulated, in *Hong Kong Fir*, for the consequences of time off hire also may be taken to suggest that the parties to the charter party anticipated problems of this sort and that the difficulties that emerged in *Hong Kong Fir* were considered to be within the range of the kinds of problems one may anticipate in a contractual arrangement of this kind. The fact that a particular defect in performance is foreseeable, indeed foreseen, may weigh against termination of an agreement that does not itself provide for such relief.

A number of cases offer support for the proposition that the consequences of a particular breach may be considered in the light of the known purposes for which the contract was entered by the party not at fault. Where, in the light of those purposes, the value of the performance is destroyed or, perhaps, substantially undermined, a repudiatory breach will be found. Two contrasting Canadian cases illustrate the point. First, *Shun Cheong Holdings B.C. Ltd. v. Gold Ocean City Supermarket Ltd.*[42] concerned the lease of retail premises in which the tenant operated a grocery store. The seepage of a greasy, smelly liquid from the premises of another tenant of the landlord on an intermittent basis during a four-month period not only constituted a health and safety hazard in the trial judge's view, but created the impression on customers that the store suffered from unsanitary conditions. The British Columbia Court of Appeal agreed that these circumstances, together with

---

41   *Agrifoods International Corp. v. Beatrice Goods Inc.* (1997), 34 B.L.R. (2d) 294 (B.C.S.C.).

42   (2002), 216 D.L.R. (4th) 392 (B.C.C.A.).

the landlord's failure to solve the problem, constituted a repudiatory breach of an implied condition of quiet possession and entitled the tenant to terminate the lease. In *Krawchuk v. Ulrychova*[43] the purchase of an eight-year-old Arabian horse for use as a riding horse by the purchaser's eleven-year-old daughter could not be considered to be repudiated when the purchaser discovered that the horse suffered from a "cribbing" condition. The condition was correctable by the wearing of a "cribbing collar" and did not prevent its use as a riding horse. It was a breach of the guarantee as to soundness, therefore, that sounded only in damages.

Where the breach gives rise to a reasonable belief in the party not at fault that the other party is unreliable and therefore unlikely to perform acceptably in the future, the breach is likely to be considered repudiatory. In *Sanko Steamship Co. v. Eacon Timber Sales Co.*,[44] the plaintiff shipping company had agreed to carry lumber for the defendant. Upon the commencement of insolvency proceedings in Japan concerning the plaintiff and the withdrawal of the charter of one of the ships being used by the plaintiff to carry the defendant's lumber because of the plaintiff's failure to pay the hire, the defendant reasonably concluded that the plaintiff's reliability had been seriously impaired and, accordingly, was held entitled to terminate the contract on the basis of the plaintiff's repudiatory breach. Similarly, a purchaser of software design services was entitled to repudiate on the basis that the defects in the software already delivered and delays in its supply together with the probability of further serious delay enabled the purchaser to terminate for repudiatory breach.[45] Similarly, where the nature of the breach suggests that the defaulting party

---

43   Above note 22. See also *Majdpour v. M&B Acquisition Corp.* (2001), 206 D.L.R. (4th) 627 (Ont. C.A.) (notwithstanding various breaches by the franchisor, the franchise business carried on intact and the commercial purpose of the franchise agreement was not destroyed).

44   (1986), 32 D.L.R. (4th) 269 (B.C.S.C.). See also *Shelanu Inc. v. Print Three Franchising Corp.*, above note 22 (franchisor's breaches not sufficient to evince an intention not to be bound). And see *Maple Flock Co. Ltd. v. Universal Furniture Products (Wembley) Ltd.*, [1934] 1 K.B. 148 (C.A.) (sale of goods by instalments—defect in one instalment not likely to be repeated—breach not repudiatory). *A fortiori*, a breach of whatever gravity when coupled with an express indication by the party in breach of an intention to no longer be bound by the agreement constitutes a repudiatory breach. See *Freeth v. Burr* (1874), L.R. 9 C.P. 208; *Canadian Doughnut Co. Ltd. v. Canada Egg Products Ltd.*, [1954] 2 D.L.R. 77 (Sask. C.A.), aff'd [1955] S.C.R. 398. With respect to repudiation prior to the time for performance, see Chapter 16.

45   *Imperial Brass Ltd. v. Jacob Electric Systems Ltd.* (1989), 72 O.R. (2d) 17 (H.C.J.). Compare with *United Systems Ltd. v. Clearwater Lobsters Ltd.* (1986), 58 Nfld. & P.E.I.R. 138 (Nfld. S.C.T.D.). (similar context—breach not repudiatory).

is unreliable in the sense that it cannot be trusted or counted upon to perform with integrity, a repudiatory breach is likely to be found. In *968703 Ontario Ltd. v. Vernon*,[46] the defendant had hired an auctioneering firm to sell off some of its assets. Under the agreement, all proceeds were to be deposited by the plaintiff auctioneer into a joint bank account with a view to the ultimate distribution of the funds to the parties. The plaintiff's failure to deposit the funds in such an account undermined the defendant's confidence in the plaintiff and constituted a repudiatory breach entitling the defendant to terminate the agreement. The decision in *Computer Workshops Ltd. v. Banner Capital Market Brokers Limited*[47] concerned the supply of computer software and hardware installation services. The defendant disclosed to the plaintiff its software program, which was to be adapted to the plaintiff's needs, a program that was unique and copyrighted by the defendant. The plaintiff's disclosure of the software program to one of the competitors of the defendant was held to be a repudiatory breach of an implied term to maintain confidentiality that entitled the defendant to terminate the agreement.

In applying the *Hong Kong Fir* test, then, the consequences of the breach for the party not at fault must be considered in light of such factors as those identified above in order to determine whether the rights of the party not at fault are sufficiently vindicated by the awarding of damages for breach of contract or whether the circumstances are such that conferring upon the party not at fault the option to treat the contract as at an end is the more appropriate form of relief.

F. WHEN IS A CONTRACTUAL "CONDITION" NOT A TRUE CONDITION?

It is trite law that the parties can effectively stipulate that the breach of a particular provision will entitle the party not at fault to disaffirm the contract and refuse further performance, preserving, at the same time, a right to sue for damages flowing from the breach. Where such arrangements are spelled out plainly and in detail, courts will have little difficulty interpreting and applying them. A common drafting technique, however, for achieving this objective is simply to stipulate that the following undertakings of a party or the parties are "conditions" of this agreement. We may ask, then, whether this common, though less explicit, drafting

46 (2002), 58 O.R. (3d) 215 (C.A.).
47 (1988), 50 D.L.R. (4th) 118 (Ont. H.C.J.), aff'd 74 D.L.R. (4th) 767 (C.A.).

device will invariably achieve the desired objective. Where, on the particular facts, the effect of such a provision appears oppressive, we may expect that courts would incline against an interpretation that achieves such a result. This problem arose in the English decision in *L. Schuler A.G. v. Wickman Machine Tool Sales Ltd.*[48] The defendant Schuler, a German manufacturing firm, had granted the plaintiff Wickman exclusive distribution rights for certain of its products in a territory that included the United Kingdom. In order to ensure that vigorous marketing efforts directed at car manufacturers would be undertaken by Wickman, Schuler stipulated in the agreement as follows:

7.   Promotion [Wickman]
(a)   Subject to Clause 17 [Wickman] will use its best endeavours to promote and extend the sale of Schuler products in the Territory.
(b)   It shall be condition of this Agreement that:
   (i)   [Wickman] shall send its representatives to visit six [largest U.K. car manufacturers] at least once in every week for the purpose of soliciting orders for panel presses;
   (ii)   that the same representative shall visit each firm on each occasion unless there are unavoidable reasons preventing the visit from being made by that representative in which case the visit shall be made by an alternative representative and [Wickman] will ensure that such a visit is always made by the same alternate representative.[49]

When Wickman failed to comply strictly with its obligations under 7(b) by missing a few visits, Schuler terminated the agreement on the basis that the missed visits constituted a breach of condition and entitled Schuler to bring the agreement to an end. Wickman's claim for damages, however, enjoyed success. In the Court of Appeal, Lord Denning M.R. distinguished the technical or legal meanings of the term "condition" from the meaning of this term in common usage, which, accordingly to the *Oxford English Dictionary* is simply that of "a provision, a stipulation." Lord Denning opined that the parties probably did not intend to use the term condition in clause 7 in a technical sense but rather were simply using the term with its common meaning. Accordingly, failure to comply with 7(b) was not a repudiatory breach giving rise to the right on the part of Schuler to terminate the agreement. It was merely a breach of the contract that was not repudiatory in nature and that sounded, therefore, only in damages.[50]

---

48   [1972] 2 All E.R. 1173 (C.A.), aff'd [1973] 2 All E.R. 39 (H.L.).
49   *Ibid.* at 1176–77 (C.A.).
50   *Ibid.* at 1179–82 (C.A.).

On appeal to the House of Lords, Lord Denning's proposition that a contractual stipulation referring to a term as a condition might be using the word "condition" in its common rather than technical meaning was subject to divided opinion. Lord Wilberforce was of the view that use of the word "condition" indicated that the term was one that, when breached, entitled the aggrieved party to treat the contract as at an end.[51] Lord Reid conceded that the term is frequently used in this sense and, indeed, that it may be presumed to have that meaning in a formal legal document.[52] Lord Reid further observed, however, that the term is also used with a less stringent meaning as in the familiar phrases "conditions of sale" and "for conditions see back," printed on a ticket. In such contexts the term simply refers to "the terms of the contract."[53] Since the term "condition" was plainly not being used in clause 7(b) as a title for or reference to "the terms of the agreement," it might appear that the appropriate conclusion to draw was that the German manufacturer was entitled to terminate the agreement. Lord Wilberforce, however, was alone in this view. The other members of the panel were able to construe clause 7 in such a way as to avoid this result. Lord Reid, for example, placed emphasis on clause 11 of the agreement that provided for a power to determine the agreement in the following terms:

> Duration of Agreement
> (a) This Agreement and the rights granted hereunder to [Wickman] shall commence ... and shall continue in force ... unless and until determined by either party upon giving to the other not less than 12 months' notice in writing ... PROVIDED that Schuler or [Wickman] may by notice in writing to the other determine this Agreement forthwith if:
>   (i) the other shall have committed a material breach of its obligations hereunder and shall have failed to remedy the same within 60 days of being required in writing so to do or
>   (ii) the other shall cease to carry on business or shall enter into liquidation.[54]

For Lord Reid, then, the question became whether clause 11(a)(i) was intended to apply to all material breaches of the agreement that are capable of being remedied, including breaches of clause 7. Having concluded that this was indeed the scope of clause 11(a)(i), it then needed to be considered

---

51 *Ibid.* at 54 (H.L.).
52 *Ibid.* at 44 (H.L.).
53 *Ibid.*
54 *Ibid.* at 42–43 (H.L.).

whether a failure to make a few visits was a breach that could be "remedied" within the meaning of clause 11(a)(i). In Lord Reid's view, failure to make a particular visit was indeed a type of breach that could be cured or remedied by making a subsequent visit. Accordingly, clause 11(a)(i) was applicable and provided the only basis upon which the agreement could be terminated for a breach of clause 7. Such a construction of the agreement, in Lord Reid's view, made it possible to avoid the unreasonable conclusion that failure to make even one visit would enable the manufacturer to terminate the agreement. In short, although the phrase "it is a condition of this Agreement that" will normally have the effect of creating a true condition in a formal legal document, courts will search for another plausible meaning of the phrase in circumstances where the consequences of so interpreting the phrase are absurd or unreasonable.

G. A DEFINITION OF REPUDIATORY BREACH

From the foregoing account, a definition of the concept of repudiatory breach can be devised in the following terms:

A repudiatory breach, giving the party not at fault a right to terminate the agreement, occurs where the breach is a breach of a term that is properly classified as

a) a "condition," being a term so classified by any one of the following means:
   i) legislation imposing statutory conditions in particular contract types such a those for the sale of goods;
   ii) stipulation of a term as a "condition" within an agreement though, in the absence of plain language, the courts may lean against construing a particular provision as a "condition," even where it is identified as a "condition" in the agreement where so construing the term would lead to unreasonable results and another interpretation of the provision is plausible;
   iii) where not expressly so stipulated in an agreement, nonetheless a proper construction of the agreement indicates that it is the intention of the parties that the particular term be treated as a condition, with respect to which construction, the existing common low doctrine identifying particular contractual terms as being conditions will be considered helpful; or
   iv) on the basis of the *Hong Kong Fir* test, the term is of such a nature that every conceivable breach of the term gives rise to an event that "will deprive the party not in default of substantially

the whole benefit which it was intended that he should obtain from the contract," or

b) an innominate or intermediate term where, on the basis of the *Hong Kong Fir* test, the particular breach that has occurred is an event that deprives the party not at fault of substantially the whole benefit which it was intended that he or she should have obtained from the contract.

This brief summary requires some elaboration. First, with respect to (a)(i), we have seen that even though, as in the case of the *Sale of Goods Act*, a number of statutory conditions are imported into a type of contract by a legislative scheme, the *Hong Kong Fir* innominate term analysis may nonetheless apply to other terms in such agreements.

With respect to (a)(ii), it is not necessary of course to use the term "condition" to stipulate that breach of a particular term will give rise to the right of the other party to elect to treat the contract as discharged. Use of the term "condition" may be the most common device employed for this purpose, but plain language indicating the consequence of breach would obviously also suffice.

With respect to (a)(iii) and (a)(iv), some tension may exist between the traditional doctrine briefly restated in (a)(iii) and the *Hong Kong Fir* analysis stated in (a)(iv). While the judicial consensus that has emerged in the wake of *Hong Kong Fir* appears to be that the traditional doctrine is preserved, it nonetheless also appears to be the case that, influenced by *Hong Kong Fir*, contemporary courts are likely to exhibit a greater reluctance to classify a term as a condition than might have been the case under the traditional doctrine. The traditional doctrine will be helpful, especially in the context of well-established interpretations of standard transactional types, though perhaps not dispositive, in light of the greater flexibility introduced by the *Hong Kong Fir* analysis.

With respect to paragraph (b), it is understandable that some judges and commentators have taken to refer to this doctrine as a doctrine of "fundamental breach." This usage can mislead, however, and create confusion with the doctrine of "fundamental breach" as it applies to exculpatory clauses.[55] There is a consequent risk that the notion of repudiatory breach will be confused with whatever doctrine we may still have restricting the effect of exculpatory clauses in particular circumstances. From an analytical perspective, the question as to whether a particular breach is repudiatory is quite distinct from the question as

---

55   As noted above, see the opinion of Wilson J. in *Hunter Engineering Co. Inc. v. Syncrude Canada Ltd.*, above note 39. See also *Majdpour v. M.&B. Acquisition Corp.*, above note 43.

to whether an exculpatory clause should be held effectively to limit or exclude liability for breach. The doctrine of "fundamental breach" in the latter sense will be examined in a subsequent chapter.[56]

H. REMEDIES FOR REPUDIATORY BREACH

In the context of a repudiatory breach, the party not at fault has available a variety of remedial options both at common law and in equity. The possible availability of the equitable remedies of specific performance and injunctions will not be considered here.[57] Our focus at this point is on the ability to treat the contract as at an end and the availability of the common law remedies of damages and restitution. At common law, the party not at fault confronted by a repudiatory breach may exercise a right to terminate or disaffirm the contract and suspend further performance. Further, whether that party decides to affirm or disaffirm the contract, a claim for damages for breach of contract may be pursued in either event.[58] In certain circumstances, the party not at fault may be able to pursue, as an alternative to the claim for damages, a claim in restitution for the value of benefits conferred on the party in default.[59] Each of these options is considered briefly below.

1) The Right to Disaffirm

A repudiatory breach does not, in itself, bring an end to a contract. Rather, it confers upon the innocent party a right of election to treat the contract at an end, thereby relieving the parties of further performance though not, of course, relieving the party guilty of repudiatory breach from its liabilities for contractual breach.

As a general rule, the party not at fault must make the election and communicate it to the repudiating party. As Asquith L.J. stated in *Howard v. Pickford Tool Co. Ltd.*,[60] "An unaccepted repudiation is a thing writ in water and of no value to anybody; it affords no legal rights of any sort or kind."[61] Thus, failure to communicate a decision to terminate may, in appropriate circumstances, have the effect of affirming the contract. The

---

56   See Chapter 20.
57   See Chapter 23.
58   See Chapter 22.
59   See Chapter 24.
60   [1951] 1 K.B. 417 (C.A.).
61   *Ibid.* at 421.

employee in *Pickford Tool* was denied a declaration that the employer's repudiatory breach had discharged the agreement as he had continued on with his employment for some months. On the other hand, the election to disaffirm can be communicated by conduct and, in an appropriate case, mere silence or inactivity may be a sufficient signal of an election. In *Vitol S.A. v. Norelf Ltd.*[62] the buyer wrongfully repudiated a contract for the sale of goods. The seller failed to take any of the normal steps, such as the tendering of shipping documents, to perform the agreement. This was held to be sufficient evidence of an election to disaffirm.

The party terminating for repudiatory breach is not under an obligation to communicate the reason for termination to the party in breach.[63] The terminating party may nonetheless rely on the breach that occurred if later called upon to justify the termination. Indeed, it is accepted that even if an incorrect reason for termination is specified at the time of communicating the decision to terminate, the innocent party may later rely on an actual repudiatory breach of the party in breach, even one of which the terminating party was unaware at the time of the decision to terminate, as a later justification for termination.[64] A recent illustration is provided by *Glencore Grain Rotterdam BV v. Lebanese Organisation for International Commerce.*[65] In the context of a contract to buy a large quantity of wheat f.o.b. a vessel to be supplied by the buyer, the seller purported to terminate the contract when the buyer's vessel arrived one day late. Although the late arrival was held not to constitute a valid reason for termination, the seller was able to subsequently justify the termination on the basis of the buyer's failure to have submitted a conforming letter of credit. Although the seller had protested the terms of the letter of credit at the time of its presentation, a conforming letter of credit had not been supplied by the buyer in a timely fashion. The seller first relied on the non-conforming letter as a basis for termination, however, during the ensuing litigation. Nonetheless, the court applied the basic principle that a party who is entitled to terminate for repudiatory breach is not deprived of the right to do so by giving an incorrect reason for termination if there existed an actual

---

62   [1996] A.C. 800 (H.L.).

63   *British & Beningtons Ltd. v. North Western Cachar Tea Co. Ltd.*, [1923] A.C. 48; *Connaught Laboratories Ltd. v. Canada* (1983), 49 N.R. 332 (Fed. C.A.); *Scandinavian Trading Co. A/B v. Zodiac Petroleum S.A. and William Hudson Ltd. (The Al Hofuf)*, [1981] 1 Lloyd's Rep. 81 (Q.B.).

64   *Ibid.* The parties may, however, stipulate in their agreement that notice of the reason for termination must be provided, failing which the termination would not be effective. See *Connaught Laboratories Ltd. v. Canada, ibid..*

65   [1997] 4 All E.R. 514 (C.A.).

repudiatory breach, whether or not the terminating party was aware of the actual breach at the time of termination.[66]

This basic principle is subject, however, to two limitations. First, if the actual repudiatory breach upon which termination is later justified is of such a nature that the breach could have been cured if attention had been drawn to it at the time of termination, the principle does not apply.[67] This limitation was unavailable to the buyer in *Glencore Grain* as the date for submission of a conforming letter of credit had passed by the date of the seller's termination. The second limitation on the basic rule is that it is subject to the doctrines of waiver and estoppel. Accordingly, if the party in default detrimentally relies on a representation made by the terminating party, whether by conduct or otherwise, to the effect that strict compliance with the agreement on a particular matter will not be insisted upon, the terminating party is precluded from later justifying termination on the ground of this particular failure to comply.[68] Thus, in a real estate transaction, where the purchaser is informed by the seller of a misrepresentation made on his behalf by his agent and the purchaser indicates an intention to close the transaction notwithstanding the misrepresentation, the purchaser cannot later justify an incorrect termination of the transaction on the basis of the misrepresentation.[69]

A contract discharged by breach is not, of course, rescinded or avoided *ab initio*. The parties are both released from further performance. Nonetheless, the agreement remains a valid and binding contract in the sense that the terms are enforceable against the defaulting party in claims for damages for past and future[70] defaults and for other remedies.

---

66   *Ibid.* at 526, Evans L.J., relying on the formulation of the rule set forth by Greer J. in *Taylor v. Oakes Roncoroni & Co.* (1922), 127 L.T. 267 at 269. See also *Carr v. Fama Holdings Ltd.* (1989), 63 D.L.R. (4th) 25 (B.C.C.A.) (termination of employment contract); *RDA Film Distribution Inc. v. British Columbia Trade Development Corp.*, [2001] 2 W.W.R. 88 (B.C.C.A.) (termination of guarantee of film financing loan).

67   *Heisler v. Anglo-Dal Ltd.*, [1954] 2 All E.R. 770 at 773 (C.A.), Somervell L.J.

68   *Glencore Grain Rotterdam BV v. Lebanese Organisation for International Commerce*, above note 65 at 527–31. This appears to be accepted as the correct explanation for what appeared to be a broader limitation of refusing to apply the basic rule where it would be "unfair or unjust" to do so arguably suggested by the language of Lord Denning M.R.'s opinion in *Panchaud Frères SA v. Etablissements General Grain Company*, [1970] 1 Lloyd's Rep. 53 at 57 (C.A.). See *Glencore Grain*, above note 65. See also *Bremer Handelsgesellschaft mbH v. Vanden Avenne-Izegem PVBA*, [1978] 2 Lloyd's Rep. 109 (H.L.).

69   *Samson v. Lockwood* (1998), 40 O.R. (3d) 161 (C.A.).

70   Although the defaulting party is released from further performance if the contract is disaffirmed, the defaulting party nonetheless remains liable in damages

2) Damages

Every breach of contract, whether or not repudiatory, potentially gives rise to a claim for damages for breach of contract if loss has been caused by the breach. Thus, whether the victim of a repudiatory breach elects to affirm or disaffirm the agreement, a damages claim will lie. If the breach is not a repudiatory breach, of course, a damages claim will also lie. The law relating to the quantification of damages for breach of contract will be considered in a subsequent chapter.[71]

3) Restitution

It is perhaps less well known that the victim of a repudiatory breach who elects to disaffirm the contract may, as an alternative to the claim for damages, pursue a claim in restitution for the value of benefits conferred on the defaulting party.[72] Such a claim may be attractive for a variety of reasons. First, where the transaction is not a profitable one from the victim's perspective, the measure of relief in restitution may be of greater value than the contractual damages claim. Second, there may be problems involved in proving the nature of the damages claim that could be avoided simply by pursuing a claim for the return of monies paid to the party in breach or for the recovery of the value of other benefits conferred.

The law concerning restitution for benefits conferred under agreements discharged by breach is rather complex and will be considered in Chapter 24, which provides a more general analysis of restitutionary remedies. Under traditional doctrine, a distinction existed between the recovery of monies paid by the innocent party as opposed to other types of benefits conferred. The rules applying to the recovery of these two different types of benefits differed in one important respect. With respect to monies paid to the defaulting party, the traditional learning with respect to this claim is that it will lie only if the innocent party has received no value in return from the party in default. Restitution is available only if there has been a "total failure of consideration." This anomalous requirement is a holdover of the medieval claim in *money*

---

for injuries resulting from non-performance of those future obligations. See, for example, *Moschi v. Lep Air Services Ltd.*, [1973] A.C. 331 (H.L.); *Photo Production Ltd. v. Securicor Transport Ltd.*, above note 1 at 849, Lord Diplock; *Guarantee Co. of North America v. Gordon Capital Corp.*, above note 1 at para. 41, Bastarache J.

71   See Chapter 22.

72   See generally P.D. Maddaugh and J.D. McCamus, *The Law of Restitution*, 2d ed. (Aurora: Canada Law Book, 2004) c. 19:200.

had and received. It lacks a convincing rationale and is, as shall be argued below,[73] likely to be ignored by a contemporary Canadian court. When one turns to restitutionary recovery of non-monetary benefits conferred under a contract discharged by breach, the total failure of the consideration requirement miraculously vanishes. Recovery for the value of services rendered, for example, will normally lie in a *quantum meruit* claim. As a general matter, then, the victim of repudiatory breach who disaffirms that agreement is entitled to recover, as an alternative to the damages claim, restitution of the value of benefits conferred on the party in default.

At this point it is useful to note another linguistic point of confusion involving the term "rescission." Just as the election to terminate for repudiatory breach is sometimes referred to as rescission in a way that might lead to confusion with the equitable concept of rescission, so too the seeking of restitutionary recovery of benefits conferred under agreements discharged for breach is sometimes referred to as rescission. This usage brings with it the same potential for confusion with equitable doctrines. This confusion is heightened by the total failure of consideration requirement that looks, to the untrained eye, as being something equivalent to the equitable requirement that, upon rescission, there must be a "giving back" and "taking back" on both sides. Simply stated, the equitable doctrines relating to rescission have no application to the context of discharge for breach. The decision to terminate a contract for repudiatory breach is not complicated by any such requirement of a "giving back" and "taking back" on both sides. Although it is true historically that in this context, when one sought restitutionary recovery of monies paid to the other party, the total failure of consideration requirement was imposed, it seems most unlikely, as suggested above, that such a requirement would be imposed by a contemporary Canadian court.

By way of summary, then, it may be useful to display the traditional common law[74] remedies for breach of contract, both repudiatory and non-repudiatory, as shown in Table 15.1.

---

73   See Chapter 24.
74   For discussion of the equitable remedies for breach of contract see Chapter 23.
     It has recently been suggested that a further alternative form of relief — disgorgement of the profits secured by breach — may be available in a limited range
     of cases. In principle, such relief could be available, in an appropriate case,
     whether or not the innocent party elected to disaffirm the contract. For discussion of this possibility, see Chapter 24, section B(2).

Table 15.1 *Common Law Remedies for Breach of Contract*

Type of Term	Option to Terminate	Exercise of the Option	Damages	Restitution
Condition	Yes	a) affirm	Yes	No
		b) disaffirm	Yes	Yes
Innominate (a) with grave consequences	Yes	a) affirm	Yes	No
		b) disaffirm	Yes	Yes
Innominate (b) with less grave consequences	No	–	Yes	No
Warranty	No	–	Yes	No

I. IS THERE A DOCTRINE OF "MATERIAL" BREACH?

There are many similarities between the American law of contracts and Anglo-Canadian contract law. There are also important differences between the two systems, of course, as the rules relating to third-party beneficiaries,[75] estoppel as a sword[76] and good faith[77] illustrate. With respect to the present topic—the consequences of repudiatory breach—there are both terminological and substantive differences between American doctrine and Canadian common law. From a terminological perspective, although American usage also is somewhat variable, the term "material breach" is commonly used to refer to what an English or Canadian lawyer would describe as "repudiatory breach." From a substantive perspective, American law has recognized that the perpetrator of a material breach of contract ought normally to be given a reasonable opportunity to cure the defective performance. When a defective performance has been cured, the right of the party not at fault to terminate the contract for material breach is defeated and the contract remains in full force and effect. The recognition of the right to cure appears to have been first accomplished in the context of sale of goods transactions as an improvement upon the "perfect tender rule." The latter rule still forms a part of Anglo-Canadian sale of goods law. The right to cure has been recognized as a more general proposition, however, and is restated in the pertinent articles of the American Law Institute's *Restatement of Contracts 2d.*[78]

---

75 See Chapter 9.
76 See Chapter 8.
77 See Chapters 5 and 21.
78 (St. Paul: American Law Institute, 1981) ss. 237 and 241.

Anglo-Canadian law, on the other hand, does not recognize a right to cure in the context of repudiatory breach,[79] nor has the practice yet developed of referring to repudiatory breach as "material breach" in the American manner. Nonetheless, the terms "material" and "materiality" may arise in the context of discussions of repudiatory breach for a number of reasons. First, parties may use the concept of material breach in the language of their agreements and provide, for example, that certain remedies are available in the event of material breach. While a carefully drawn agreement would define that term, it is not invariably the case, of course, that this occurs. Second, as we have seen, the test for operative misrepresentation inducing a contract requires that the representation be "material" and, accordingly, it is not uncommon in contractual drafting to stipulate that a breach of the term of the agreement setting out "representations and warranties" occurs only where the contractual misstatement is false "in a material respect." Accordingly, it may be useful to consider whether the term "material breach" has acquired a technical or commonly understood meaning in the Anglo-Canadian law of repudiatory breach.

As a matter of ordinary usage, the adjective "material" has a number of possible interpretations. As we have seen, American usage in the present context treats "material" as being equivalent to "substantial" or to what is often referred to, albeit confusingly, as "fundamental breach" in Canadian law. On the other hand, when material is distinguished from its opposite, "non-material," "material" acquires a meaning of non-trivial, relevant or significant. In the context of misrepresentation doctrine, it appears to have a meaning of this kind. The misrepresentation inducing the contract need not be fundamental in some sense. It is sufficient if it is material in the sense of being relevant to the decision to enter the contract.

This ambiguity in the use of the term "material" appears to be present in the Anglo-Canadian cases in which the term has been utilized

---

79 Although something rather similar appears to have occurred in *Sail Labrador Ltd. v. Challenge One*, above note 40. It will be recalled that this case concerned the issue of whether one erroneously rejected cheque in a series of instalment payments would constitute a repudiatory breach. It was argued that the failed payment prevented the payer from being able to exercise an option to purchase that was conditioned on instalment payments being made promptly and in accordance with the contractual schedule. Bastarache J. was of the view that a doctrine of "spent breach" would apply that would allow the optionee to exercise an option if defects in performance had been corrected by the time of exercising the option. Since the payer had promptly corrected the problem with the payment, the option remained open for exercise.

in the present context. Thus, there are occasional judicial references to "material breach" that suggest that the judge in question treats the term as being synonymous with "repudiatory breach." In *Nowlan v. Midland Transport*,[80] for example, Bastarache J.A., as he then was, referred to "fundamental or material breach giving [a] right to resiliation of the contract."[81] On the other hand, there are cases in which contractual references to material breach are treated as including both substantial and non-substantial breaches of contract. In the case of *L. Schuler A.G. v. Wickman Machine Tool Sales Limited*,[82] the House of Lords considered whether a contractual provision allowing the party in default to remedy "the material breach of its obligations" would apply to a failure by the distributor to simply miss one visit to the English car manufacturers. The House of Lords concluded that the clause did apply to such a breach and thus, plainly, must have interpreted the phrase "material breach" as referring to virtually any breach of the distributor's obligations, whether substantial or not.

The concept of materiality may also arise in situations where contractual performance is conditioned upon the conduct of an inspection on certain terms and conditions. In *Veba Oil Supply & Trading GmbH v. Petrotrade Inc.*,[83] a contract for the sale of gas and oil was conditioned on the approval of a mutually agreed upon independent inspector applying customary methods of inspection. The inspector departed from the customary methods in a minor way and the issue arose as to whether the condition failed because of that failure to follow normal practice. The Court of Appeal held that the condition would fail only if the departure from the contractual instructions was "material" by which the court meant that it must not be "trivial or *de minimis*" in the sense that it would obviously not be a matter of significance for either party. The court held that the departure was not material in this sense and, accordingly, the contract remained enforceable.

Where the concept of materiality arises in the context of contractual "representations and warranties," it is important to maintain a distinction between the requirement of materiality that may be applicable to the misrepresentation and the separate notion of repudiatory breach. Thus, to establish breach it may be necessary to demonstrate that a particular misrepresentation (or non-disclosure where disclosure is re-

---

80   (1996), 174 N.B.R. (2d) 81 (C.A.), leave to appeal to S.C.C. refused (1996), 179 N.B.R. (2d) 319 (S.C.C.).

81   *Ibid.* at 89 (C.A.).

82   Above note 48, for discussion of which see above this Chapter, section F.

83   [2002] 1 All E.R. 703 (C.A.).

quired) is material in order to prove that the term has been breached. In this context, "material" is likely to be construed as synonymous with "relevant." It is a separate question, however, whether the breach is, in turn, a repudiatory breach giving rise to the right to treat the contract as at an end. In the typical commercial agreement, that matter will be placed beyond doubt by explicitly stipulating that such a breach is a breach of a condition of the agreement or is a breach that entitles the other party to, for example, refuse to close the transaction. If the agreement did not so provide, it would be necessary to invoke the common law test(s) for repudiatory breach rather than to rely on a test of materiality.[84]

In summary, then, the answer to the question posed in the title of this section should be in the negative. There is no standard use of the term material breach in the context of the Anglo-Canadian doctrine of repudiatory breach. Rather, the terms "material" or "materiality" must be carefully construed in light of the particular doctrinal or contractual context in which the terms are being employed.

FURTHER READINGS

E.G. ANDERSON, "A New Look at Material Beach in the Law of Contracts" (1988) 21 U.C. Davis L. Rev. 1073.

J.H. BAKER, "Contract: Construction of 'Condition'" (1973) 32 Cambridge L.J. 196.

R. BROWNSWORD, "*L. Schuler A.G. v. Wickman Machine Tool Sales Ltd.*: A Tale of Two Principles" (1974) 37 Mod. L. Rev. 104.

R. CHILDRES, "Conditions in the Law of Contracts" (1970) 45 N.Y.U.L. Rev. 33.

A.L. CORBIN, "Conditions in the Law of Contracts" (1919) 28 Yale L.J. 739.

D.W. GREIG, "Condition — or Warranty?" (1973) 89 Law Q. Rev. 93.

---

84   It is not entirely clear that this distinction between the "materiality" requirement for representations and the test for repudiatory breach is clearly preserved in the reasoning in the *Guarantee Co. of North America* case, above note 1 at para. 44.

T.J. HOLDYCH, "Warranties and Conditions in the Sale of Goods: A Market-Based Assessment of English and European Community Warranty Law" (1998) 29 Cambrian L. Rev. 73.

J. HONNOLD, "Buyer's Rights of Rejection" (1949) 97 U. Pa. L. Rev. 457.

G.L. PRIEST, "A Theory of the Consumer Product Warranty" (1981) 90 Yale L.J. 1311.

G.L. PRIEST, "Breach and Remedy for the Tender of the Non-Conforming Goods under the Uniform Commercial Code: An Economic Approach" (1978) 91 Harv. L. Rev. 960.

J.A. SEBERT, "Rejection, Revocation and Cure under Article 2 of the Uniform Commercial Code: Some Modest Proposals" (1990) 84 Nw. U.L. Rev. 375.

S.J. STOLJAR, "Conditions, Warranties and Descriptions of Quality in Sales of Goods" (1952) Mod. L. Rev. 425.

S.J. STOLJAR, "The Contractual Concept of Condition" (1953) 69 Law Q. Rev. 585.

ANTICIPATORY REPUDIATION

A. INTRODUCTION

An anticipatory repudiation of an agreement occurs when one party manifests, through words or conduct, an intention not to perform or not to be bound by provisions of the agreement that require performance in the future. We have previously considered whether failure to perform a contractual obligation at the time stipulated for performance constitutes a repudiatory breach of contract entitling the party not in breach to terminate the agreement and pursue such remedies as may be available with respect to losses caused by the breach of contract.[1] In this chapter, we consider whether an anticipatory repudiation of contractual obligations may similarly give rise to an entitlement on the part of the innocent party to bring the agreement to an end and pursue any available remedies for contractual breach. The basic approach taken by the common law to this question holds that an anticipatory repudiation of a future obligation has the same effect on the rights of an innocent party as an actual breach of the obligation in question. Thus, if an actual breach of the provision in question would entitle the innocent party to treat the contract as discharged by breach, an anticipatory repudiation of that obligation would confer a similar option on the innocent party. More than this, however, it is well established that

---

1   See Chapter 15.

where the innocent party elects to disaffirm the contract on the basis of an anticipatory repudiation, the innocent party may immediately commence an action for breach. The innocent party need not postpone the commencement of such an action until the date for performance has arrived. Although this proposition is often referred to as the doctrine of anticipatory *breach*, it has frequently been observed that it is difficult to see how one could breach an obligation prior to the date for performance. Accordingly, anticipatory *repudiation* is perhaps a more felicitous description of the factual phenomenon.

The general principle was established in the leading decision in *Hochster v. De La Tour*.[2] The plaintiff in this case had been hired on April 12, 1852, by the defendant to act as the defendant's courier on a trip abroad. The assignment was to begin on June 1st of that year. On May 11th the defendant wrote to the plaintiff and cancelled the assignment. The plaintiff immediately commenced an action for damages for breach of contract. Prior to June 1st, the plaintiff secured alternative employment with a third party to commence on June 4th. The defendant had the temerity to argue that the plaintiff, being himself in breach of contract by accepting alternative employment prior to the date for performance was himself in breach of contract and therefore not entitled to sue. The jury's verdict for the plaintiff was upheld on appeal. Lord Campbell C.J. rejected the argument that the plaintiff was entitled to relief only if he had maintained his availability for work for the defendant on June 1st, reasoning as follows:

> it is surely much more rational, and more for the benefit of both parties, that, after the renunciation of the agreement by the defendant, the plaintiff should be at liberty to consider himself absolved from any future performance of it, retaining his right to sue for any damage he has suffered from the breach of it. Thus, instead of remaining idle and laying out money in preparations which must be useless, he is at liberty to seek service under another employer, which would go in mitigation of the damages to which he would otherwise be entitled for a breach of the contract.[3]

As has often been pointed out, however, this reasoning does not necessarily lead to the conclusion that the plaintiff should be entitled to bring an action immediately after the anticipatory repudiation. It would be sufficient to meet Lord Campbell's concern that the plaintiff be in a position to mitigate to hold that the innocent party, when confronted

---

2   (1853), 2 El. & Bl. 678, 118 E.R. 922.
3   *Ibid.* at 926 (E.R.).

by an anticipatory repudiation, is immediately at liberty to mitigate loss by pursuing other contractual arrangements but is nonetheless not entitled to bring action until the date for the repudiating party's performance has arrived.

A second explanation for the recognition of an immediate right of action offered by Lord Campbell C.J., however, avoids this conceptual difficulty. He explained as follows: "Another reason may be that where there is a contract to do an act on a future day there is a relation constituted between the parties in the meantime by the contract, and that they impliedly promise that in the meantime neither will do any thing to the prejudice of the other inconsistent with that relation. As an example, a man and woman engaged to marry are affianced to one another during the period between the time of the engagement and the celebration of the marriage."[4]

On this view, the anticipatory repudiation becomes a present breach of an implied obligation to maintain a preparedness or willingness to perform the future obligation that, if sufficiently grave, confers upon the innocent party an immediate right to terminate the arrangement and pursue the usual remedies for breach of contract. The implication of such a term might be justified by the usual rules relating to implied terms.[5] In some circumstances, the implication of such a term may appear artificial. It may be, therefore, that the true explanation for the doctrine of anticipatory repudiation lies in the practical convenience of enabling the innocent party to settle his or her rights immediately upon the anticipatory repudiation, especially in cases where the repudiating party's obligation or obligations to perform are set in the distant future. Moreover, in the absence of a doctrine of anticipatory repudiation, the fact that the agreement would remain binding on the innocent party in the period prior to breach could lead to unattractive consequences for the innocent party. A further and important consideration is that where the repudiating party's obligations are to be performed in a series of instalments, the doctrine of anticipatory repudiation avoids the necessity of a series of lawsuits to enforce those obligations. Finally, the recognition of an immediate right of action may be considered to respond to the economical reality that the promissor's binding obligation of future performance is of present economic value to the promisee and, accordingly, that the anticipatory repudiation by the promisor diminishes that

---

4   *Ibid.*
5   See Chapter 19, section D.

value.[6] If the underlying rationale of the rule remains to some extent obscure, however, there can be no doubt that the recognition of an immediate right of action in response to an anticipatory repudiation is a well-established feature of English and Canadian common law.[7]

As we have seen,[8] in the context of a repudiatory breach of an agreement, the victim of the breach is entitled either to affirm or disaffirm the agreement and, in either event, pursue remedies for breach of contract. Similarly, in the context of anticipatory repudiation, the effect of the repudiation is to confer an option upon the innocent party either to disaffirm or affirm the contract.[9] Thus, although the innocent party is entitled to disaffirm the agreement immediately and sue, that party may prefer to affirm the agreement and encourage or insist upon performance by the repudiating party or, more passively, simply wait and see whether the repudiating party does in fact eventually refuse to perform his or her contractual obligations when they fall due. As we shall see, however, there are risks associated with the latter courses of action as there may occur some subsequent and supervening event that may provide an excuse for the eventual default of the repudiating party.[10]

We next turn, then, to a consideration of the elements of or definition of anticipatory repudiation with a view to determining the type of conduct on the part of the repudiating party that will amount to an anticipatory repudiation. We will then consider the manner in which the innocent party may exercise the option to treat the contract as disaffirmed by the anticipatory repudiation and the consequences of that choice. Consideration will then be given to the implications of a decision on the part of the innocent party to affirm the contract and either await or encourage performance.

---

6   For an analysis of the economic implications of the doctrine, see generally T.H. Jackson, "'Anticipatory Repudiation' and the Temporal Element of Contract Law: An Economic Inquiry into Contract Damages in Cases of Prospective Non-Performance" (1978) 31 Stan. L. Rev. 69.

7   See, for example, *Frost v. Knight* (1872), L.R. 7 Ex. 111; *Moschi v. Lep Air Services Ltd.*, [1973] A.C. 331 (H.L.); *Gold v. Stover* (1920), 60 S.C.R. 623; *Kloepfer Wholesale Hardward & Automotive Co. v. Roy*, [1952] 2 S.C.R. 465.

8   See Chapter 15.

9   See, for example, *Heyman v. Darwins Ltd.*, [1942] A.C. 356 (H.L.).

10   See below, this Chapter, section C.

B. THE ELEMENTS OF ANTICIPATORY REPUDIATION

An anticipatory repudiation consists of an "intimation of an intention to abandon and altogether to refuse performance of the contract."[11] Such an intention may be intimated either by words or by conduct. The determination as to whether such an intention has been evinced by conduct may, of course, require the making of difficult factual inferences. As Devlin J. observed in a leading English case,[12] the basic test to be applied is "whether the party renunciating has acted in such a way as to lead a reasonable person to the conclusion that he does not intent to fulfil his part of the contract."[13] Such conduct could include, for example, the sale of the subject matter of the agreement to a third party[14] or otherwise making one's performance impossible,[15] preventing the innocent party from performing[16] or purporting to exercise contractual rights that do not exist, such as a non-existent right to cancel the agreement.[17]

The problem of determining how grave the anticipated non-performance must be in order to treat the agreement as terminable on grounds of anticipatory repudiation is precisely parallel to the problem of determining whether an actual breach of contract provides a basis for the innocent party to elect to treat the contract as discharged by breach. As we have seen,[18] the conceptual framework within which this issue is analyzed in the context of actual breach has evolved to some extent over time. Under the modern analysis, the test for determining whether a repudiatory breach giving rise to the right to terminate the agreement has occurred is to consider whether the consequences of the breach in the particular circumstances of the case deprive the innocent

---

11   *Freeth v. Burr* (1874), L.R. 9 C.P. 208 at 213, Lord Coleridge C.J., a passage often quoted in Canadian cases. See, for example, *Midland Railway Co. v. Ontario Rolling Mills* (1882), 2 O.R. 1 (Q.B.D.), aff'd (1884), 10 O.A.R. 677 at 685 (C.A.); *Pugsley v. Fowler* (1909), 4 N.B. Eq. 122 at 136–37 (S.C.). See also *Heyman v. Darwins Ltd.*, above note 9 at 361.
12   *Universal Cargo Carriers Corp. v. Citati*, [1957] 2 Q.B. 401, aff'd on other grounds [1957] 2 Lloyd's Rep. 191 (C.A.).
13   *Ibid.* at 436 (Q.B.).
14   See *Sawyer v. Pringle* (1891), 18 O.A.R. 218 at 225 (C.A.), Hagarty C.J.O.
15   See, for example, *Gilbert v. Campbell* (1869), 12 N.B.R. 474 (S.C.).
16   See, for example, *Boon v. Bell and Bell*, [1932] 2 W.W.R. 304 (Sask. C.A.); *Alexander Hamilton Institute v. McNally* (1919), 53 N.S.R. 303 (App. Div.).
17   See, for example, *Adolph Lumber Co. v. Meadowcreek Lumber Co.* (1919), 58 S.C.R. 306; *Clausen v. Canada Timber and Lands Ltd.*, [1923] 4 D.L.R. 751 (P.C.).
18   See Chapter 15, sections B and C.

party of "substantially the whole benefit"[19] that it was the intention
of the parties that the innocent party would obtain from performance
of the agreement. In the context of anticipatory repudiation, then, the
parallel test would be whether the future performance that the repudiating party evinces an intention not to perform meets this threshold.
The validity of this approach was confirmed by Lord Diplock in *Afovos
Shipping Co. S.A. v. Pagnan*,[20] in the following terms:

> The doctrine of anticipatory breach is but a species of the genus re-
> pudiation and applies only to fundamental breach. If one party to
> a contract states expressly or by implication to the other party in
> advance that he will not be able to perform the particular primary
> obligation on his part under the contract when the time for perform-
> ance arrives, the question whether the other party may elect to treat
> the statement as a repudiation depends upon whether the threatened
> non-performance would have the effect of depriving that other party
> of substantially the whole benefit which it was the intention of the
> parties that he should obtain from the primary obligations of the
> parties under the contract then remaining unperformed. If it would
> not have that effect there is no repudiation, and the other party can-
> not elect to put an end to such primary obligations remaining to be
> performed. The non-performance threatened must itself satisfy the
> criteria of a fundamental breach.[21]

Consistently with the history of the doctrine of repudiatory breach itself, a variety of expressions have been used to attempt to characterize
the level of gravity of the threatened non-performance that is required
to engage the doctrine of anticipatory repudiation, including the classic formulation that the threatened breach must "go to the root" of the
contract.[22]

---

19   *Hong Kong Fir Shipping Co. Ltd. v. Kawasaki Kisen Kaisha Ltd.*, [1962] 2 Q.B. 26
     at 70 (C.A.), Diplock L.J. For discussion, see Chapter 15, section C.
20   [1983] 1 W.L.R. 195 (H.L.).
21   *Ibid.* at 203. For discussion of Lord Diplock's distinction between primary and
     secondary contractual obligations, see Chapter 20, section C. See also *Decro-
     Wall v. Practitioners in Marketing Ltd.*, [1971] 2 All E.R. 216 at 232 (C.A.), Buck-
     ley L.J. ("... the threatened breach must be such as to deprive the injured party
     of a substantial part of the benefit to which he is entitled under the contract")
     quoted with approval in *Odeco Drilling of Canada Ltd. v. Hickey Estate* (1985), 54
     Nfld. & P.E.I.R. 116 at 133 (Nfld. S.C.T.D.), aff'd (1986), 59 Nfld. & P.E.I.R. 150
     (Nfld. C.A.).
22   *Cromwell v. Morris* (1917), 34 D.L.R. 305 at 309 (Alta. C.A.), Beck J.; *Robert
     Bell Engine & Thresher Co. v. Farquharson* (1918), 39 D.L.R. 625 at 627 (Sask.
     S.C.A.D.), Lamont J. See also *Decro-Wall v. Practitioners in Marketing Ltd., ibid.*

The fact that repudiating parties may have acted in good faith in the sense that they genuinely believed that they were entitled to terminate the agreement on the basis of the other party's default appears to be irrelevant. Thus, in a Canadian case[23] concerning the sale of an interest in timber licences, a repudiating purchaser who mistakenly believed that the timber did not live up to the representations made by the seller and, indeed, sought unsuccessfully to rescind the agreement on this ground was nonetheless held to have engaged in an anticipatory repudiation of the agreement. This proposition draws indirect support from numerous cases that simply do not consider whether the repudiating party had an honest belief in its entitlement to refuse further performance.[24] If, however, the repudiating party is entitled to bring the agreement to an end as a result of the other party's misconduct, it is obvious that the repudiation does not constitute an anticipatory repudiation giving rise to the usual remedies therefor.[25] Moreover, as in the context of repudiatory breach, a repudiation explicitly based on an unsatisfactory justification can be justified by the repudiating party on the basis of facts subsequently discovered that would have justified the repudiation at that time.[26] An anticipatory repudiation, then, must be unjustified in the sense that the repudiating party lacks a legal justification for refusing to be further bound by the agreement in question.

Some support can be found for an exception to the general principle of anticipatory repudiation in cases where the repudiation occurs after the repudiating party has received all the agreed consideration from the other party. In *Melanson v. Dominion of Canada General In-*

---

at 232, Buckley L.J. Having rehearsed a number of the traditional formulations, Buckley L.J. went on to observe as follows (at 232): "I venture to put the test in my own words as follows: will the consequences of the breach be such that it would be unfair to the injured party to hold him to the remedy in damages as and when a breach or breaches may occur? If this would be so, then repudiation has taken place."

23 *Cromwell v. Morris* above note 22. See also *Clausen v. Canada Timber & Lands Ltd.*, above note 17.

24 See, for example, *Denmark Productions Ltd. v. Boscobel Productions Ltd.*, [1969] 1 Q.B. 699 (C.A.) (abandoned by road manager, "The Kinks" dismiss his employer that had contracted to provide this service to the band); *Estate-Gard Services of Canada Ltd. v. Loewen Management Corp.* (1989), 38 B.C.L.R. (2d) 362 (C.A.) (wrongful dismissal of funeral services provider for failure to attend meetings and lack of profitability).

25 See, for example, *Paragon Farms Ltd. v. H.D. Linn Dev. Services Inc.*, [1988] 6 W.W.R. 417 (Sask. Q.B.).

26 *Universal Cargo Carriers Corp. v. Citati*, above note 12. For discussion of this point in the context of repudiatory breach, see Chapter 15, section H(1).

surance Co.,[27] for example, the plaintiff had duly filed a proof of loss with the defendant insurer under an accident insurance policy. The defendant then repudiated liability under the policy. Prior to the expiry of the sixty-day period for the payment of claims stipulated in the policy, the plaintiff commenced this action. The New Brunswick appellate court held that the action was premature. The doctrine of anticipatory repudiation applied, it was held, only where some obligation of the plaintiff remained unperformed or executory. Having filed the proof of claim, the plaintiff had done all that it was required to do under the agreement. Accordingly, or so it was suggested, the doctrine of anticipatory repudiation did not apply. There does not appear to be a coherent justification for this exception, however, and accordingly, its status must be considered to be rather insecure. The implicit suggestion that where there remains only moneys to be paid, the doctrine of anticipatory repudiation is inapplicable is simply inconsistent with the general principle and its underlying rationale.[28] Thus, for example, if the obligation of the insurer were to make a series of payments over a number of years, refusal to apply the doctrine of anticipatory repudiation would produce that multiplicity of actions that the doctrine is designed to avoid. It seems possible, then, that the approach taken in *Melanson* is neither likely to be extended beyond its own fact situation nor, indeed, likely to survive further judicial scrutiny.

C. EXERCISING THE RIGHT TO DISAFFIRM

When confronted by an anticipatory repudiation, then, the innocent party has the right to elect to terminate the agreement or, as is sometimes misleadingly said, to "accept" the repudiation as discharging the agreement.[29] The effect of exercising the right to disaffirm the agree-

---

27   [1934] 2 D.L.R. 459 (N.B.S.C.A.D.).

28   A similar doctrine has emerged in the American jurisprudence. See, for example, *Phelps v. Herro*, 137 A.2d 159 (Md. 1957). Farnsworth disparages the doctrine as an irrational remnant of the scepticism that greeted the general principle's first appearance in American doctrine. See E.A. Farnsworth, *Farnsworth on Contracts*, 2d ed., vol. II (New York: Aspen Law & Business, 1998) at 531–32.

29   The term "accept" is misleading inasmuch as it may lead to confusion with a mutual agreement to terminate or cancel an agreement. See, for example, *Jones v. DeWolfe* (1883), 23 N.B.R. 356 (C.A.). Unlike a decision to disaffirm the agreement for anticipatory repudiation and pursue remedies for breach of contract, a mutual agreement to terminate or abandon the contract would be intended

ment is to relieve the innocent party of any further obligation to perform the agreement and, as we have seen, to enable the innocent party to pursue immediately remedies available for the breach of contract constituted by the anticipatory repudiation. A number of legal issues relate to the manner in which the right to disaffirm in response to an anticipatory repudiation is to be exercised. The right need not be exercised immediately after the innocent party becomes aware of the anticipatory repudiation, but the right to elect may be lost if the passage of time before election results in prejudice to the repudiating party or is of sufficient length to constitute evidence of affirmation of the agreement.[30] Further, the mere fact that the innocent party has encouraged retraction of the repudiation or has attempted to negotiate a compromise will not preclude timely exercise of the right to disaffirm.[31] If, however, during the period of time prior to the innocent party's exercise of that right, the repudiating party retracts the repudiation and resumes performance of the agreement, the innocent party's option to disaffirm will have vanished.[32]

An innocent party who wishes to disaffirm must engage in conduct that amounts to an exercise of the election to disaffirm the contract.[33] Although the most obvious manner of exercising the right would be to explicitly communicate a decision to disaffirm to the repudiating party, it is not required that such communication must take place. A decision to terminate can be communicated by conduct. Thus, for example, the issuance of a writ claiming damages for breach of contract has been held to be an exercise of the election to disaffirm.[34] The question of whether the election needs to be explicitly communicated to

to waive or compromise any rights that might otherwise have been available to pursue such remedies. See generally D.M. McRae, "Repudiation of Contracts in Canadian Law (1978) 56 Can. Bar Rev. 233 at 253–56.

30   See *Allen v. Robles*, [1969] 3 All E.R. 154 (C.A.). See also *Dresser Industries Inc. v. Raven Muds Ltd.* (1976), 1 A.R. 616 at 637 (S.C.A.D.), Morrow J.A. and see *Scarf v. Jardine* (1882), 7 App. Cas. 345 at 360, Lord Blackburn.

31   *McCowan v. McKay* (1901), 13 Man. R. 590 (C.A.); *Dot Developments Ltd. v. Fowler* (1980), 118 D.L.R. (3d) 371 (B.C.S.C.); *Yukong Line Ltd. of Korea v. Rendsburg Investments Corp. of Liberia*, [1996] 2 Lloyd's Rep. 604 (C.A.); *Stocznia Gdanska S.A. v. Latvian Shipping Co. (No. 2)*, [2002] 2 Lloyd's Rep. 436 (C.A.).

32   *Stocznia Gdanska SA v. Latvian Shipping Company (No. 2)*, ibid. This principle is subject, presumably, to potential application of the doctrine of promissory estoppel if the innocent party has detrimentally relied on the anticipatory repudiation. For discussion of promissory estoppel, see Chapter 8.

33   *Johnstone v. Milling* (1886), 16 Q.B.D. 460 at 467, Lord Esher M.R.; *McCowan v. McKay*, above note 31 at 604.

34   *Canada Egg Products Ltd. v. Canadian Doughnut Co. Ltd.*, [1955] S.C.R. 398.

the repudiating party was considered inconclusively by the Supreme Court of Canada in *American National Red Cross v. Geddes Bros.*[35] In this case, a seller indicated to the buyer, prior to the date for delivery, that he would not be able to perform the contract. The buyer marked the contract "cancelled" in its files but did not explicitly communicate its election to disaffirm the contract to the seller. Subsequently, the seller purported to exercise the contractual right to deliver. Upon the buyer's refusal to accept the goods, the seller sued for the price. The Supreme Court of Canada dismissed the claim but divided on the question of whether the election to disaffirm must be communicated to the other party. Sir Louis Davies C.J. opined that "an actual notice of acceptance is not necessary"[36] and went on to explain as follows: "a letter to the renouncing party, though a prudent and businesslike course, is not an essential necessary to complete the adoption in cases where facts proved allow of a fair inference of acceptance of renunciation being drawn."[37] Davies C.J. was of the view that in light of proven facts of this case, including the "unequivocal and absolute"[38] nature of the seller's repudiation, the seller would have reasonably inferred that the buyer had disaffirmed the agreement.

In a concurring opinion, Anglin J. was able to agree as to result on different grounds but indicated that, in his view, the plea of anticipatory repudiation failed because of a failure to communicate the election to disaffirm. In dissent, Mignault J. expressed similar views. Duff and Idington JJ. agreed with the result favoured by the Chief Justice but did not find it necessary to deal with the communication point. It may be that the preferable analysis of a fact situation of this kind would be to simply apply an estoppel analysis. If the failure to clearly communicate the decision to disaffirm induces detrimental reliance on the part of the repudiating party, the innocent party could be estopped from exercising the right to disaffirm. No such prejudice seems likely on the facts of the *Geddes Bros.* case. Although subsequent cases appear to establish the proposition that the election to terminate the agreement must be communicated,[39] the Supreme Court of Canada seems to have accepted, in a later decision,[40] the proposition advanced by Davies C.J.

35   (1920), 61 S.C.R. 143.
36   *Ibid.* at 145.
37   *Ibid.* at 147.
38   *Ibid.* at 145.
39   *Canada Egg Products v. Canadian Doughnut Co. Ltd.*, above note 34; *Ginter v. Chapman & Keen* (1967), 60 W.W.R. 385 (B.C.C.A.).
40   *Kamlee Construction Ltd. v. Town of Oakville* (1960), 26 D.L.R. (2d) 166 at 182 (S.C.C.), Ritchie J. (innocent party demands resumption of work by a certain date

to the effect that even in the absence of communication of the election, disaffirmation will be effective if it can be reasonably inferred from the conduct of the innocent party in the particular circumstances of the case that the repudiation has been accepted as a discharge of the agreement. Where such an inference cannot be reasonably drawn, the innocent party who fails to explicitly communicate an election to disaffirm evidently runs the risk that the failure to communicate will be taken as a basis for inferring that the contract has been affirmed by the innocent party. Once the election to disaffirm has been effectively made, the election is said to be irrevocable in the sense that the innocent party cannot later reaffirm the agreement and insist on performance by the repudiating party.[41]

The consequences for the parties of an election to disaffirm for an anticipatory repudiation are parallel to those of disaffirmation for repudiatory breach.[42] As in the context of repudiatory breach, use of the term "rescission" may mislead in the present context.[43] An election by the innocent party to disaffirm for anticipatory repudiation does not rescind the contract in the sense of avoiding the contract *ab initio* and requiring the parties to be restored to the *status quo ante*. Rather, the contract is discharged by the breach. Thus, although the repudiating party is not obliged to continue performing, that party nonetheless remains responsible for past and future non-performance in the sense of being exposed to the innocent party's entitlement to pursue remedies for breach of contract.[44] The innocent party is fully excused of further performance in the sense that further non-performance does not constitute a breach of contract. Thus, for example, the vendor of land who has elected to disaffirm on the basis of the purchaser's anticipatory repudiation is not obliged to tender a deed at the date of closing.[45]

— parties negotiating compromise — innocent party fails to respond to repudiating party's last offer (even though having undertaken to do so) by stipulated date — disaffirmation can be reasonably inferred from such circumstances).

41   *Johnstone v. Milling* above note 33 at 467, Lord Esher M.R.; *MacNaughton v. Stone*, [1950] 1 D.L.R. 330 (Ont. H.C.J.); *Osmack v. Stan Reynolds Auto Sales Ltd.*, [1974] 1 W.W.R. 408 (Alta. S.C.A.D.), aff'd [1976] 2 W.W.R. 576 (S.C.C.).

42   See Chapter 15.

43   See Chapter 15, section A.

44   *Heyman v. Darwins Ltd.*, above note 9 at 399, Lord Porter; *Johnson v. Agnew*, [1980] A.C. 367 (H.L.); *Abraham v. Wingate Properties Ltd.*, [1986] 1 W.W.R. 568 (Man. C.A.).

45   *McCallum v. Zivojinovic* (1977), 79 D.L.R. (3d) 133 (Ont. C.A.), leave to appeal to S.C.C. refused (1977), 19 N.R. 539. Similarly, tender by an innocent buyer disaffirming because of vendor's repudiatory breach is unnecessary. See *Hobart Investment Corp. Ltd. v. Walker* (1977), 76 D.L.R. (3d) 156 (B.C.C.A.).

Nor would a defective tender constitute a breach of contract in circumstances where the tender itself was unnecessary.[46] Similarly, where a contract for the sale of goods has been wrongfully repudiated by the buyer, the disaffirming seller is not obliged to tender delivery as a prerequisite to enforcement of the bargain.[47] A further illustration may be drawn from the insurance context. If an insurer wrongfully repudiates liability under an insurance contract when informed of a loss by the insured, the insured can enforce the policy notwithstanding any failure to comply with a contractual requirement to file a written proof of loss with the insurer within a particular period of time.[48]

If, however, the repudiating party can establish that, quite apart from the impact of the anticipatory repudiation, the innocent party would not, in any event, have been able to perform the agreement, that is a matter that may be taken into account in assessing the innocent party's damages. In *The Mihalis Angelos*,[49] for example, a vessel had been chartered for the purpose of loading mineral ore at a particular port on or about July 1, 1965. The charter party further provided that in the event that the vessel was not ready to load at that port by July 20, 1965, the charterer had an option to terminate the agreement. On July 17th the charterer purported to cancel the agreement on the grounds of *force majeure* on the basis that sufficient quantities of iron ore were not available as a result of warlike conditions. This was arguably an improper repudiation of the charter party. It subsequently became apparent, however, that the ship could not have been available for loading by July 20. The English Court of Appeal held that even if this was a wrongful anticipatory repudiation entitling the owner to terminate the charter party, the fact that the vessel would not have been available in timely fashion and, consequently, that the charterer would have

---

46   *Mastercraft Construction Corp. v. Baker* (1978), 86 D.L.R. (3d) 121 (Ont. H.C.J.), aff'd 104 D.L.R. (3d) 767n (Ont. C.A.).

47   *British & Beningtons Ltd. v. North Western Cachar Tea Co. Ltd.*, [1923] A.C. 48 (H.L.).

48   *Battle v. Fidelity & Casualty Co. of New York* (1923), 54 O.L.R. 24 (H.C.), aff'd (1924), 55 O.L.R. 330 (S.C.A.D.); *Beury v. Canada National Fire Ins. Co.* (1917), 35 D.L.R. 790 (Ont. S.C.), aff'd (1917), 37 D.L.R. 105 (Ont. S.C.A.D.); *Magrath v. Sydenham Mutual Fire Ins. Co.*, [1923] 3 D.L.R. 44 (Ont. S.C.); *West Coast Securities Ltd. v. Continental Ins. Co.* (1975), 66 D.L.R. (3d) 278 (B.C.S.C.). Compare with *Guarantee Co. of North America v. Gordon Capital Corp.* (1999), 178 D.L.R. (4th) 1 (S.C.C.) (principle held inapplicable to insured's failure to comply with contractual time limitation within which legal proceedings against the insurer could be commenced by the insured).

49   *Maredelanto Compania Naviera SA v. Bergbau-Handel G.m.b.H.* (*The Mihalis Angelos*), [1971] 1 Q.B. 164 (C.A.).

been entitled to terminate the charter party without liability, was a relevant factor to the determination of the true extent of the owner's loss. On these facts, the owner was entitled merely to nominal damages. In short, although the innocent party is not required to tender performance, the innocent party's ultimate inability to perform is a fact that may be taken into account in reducing the damages available to the innocent party.

The more difficult question is whether the repudiating party should be able to rely on the subsequent incapacity of the innocent party to perform as an excuse for the initial repudiation, thus providing, as it were, an "after the fact" justification for the repudiating party's decision to terminate the agreement. It is well established that if the repudiating party repudiated for an incorrect or unlawful reason but, nonetheless, was subsequently able to discover that there existed *at the time of repudiation* an alternative and satisfactory ground for repudiation, the repudiating party is entitled to rely on the alternative and correct ground as a sufficient justification for the repudiation.[50] In *The Mihalis Angelos*, however, the Court of Appeal assumed that *subsequent inability to perform* would have an impact on the loss suffered by the innocent party but would not legitimate the initial anticipatory repudiation.[51]

The remedies available to the innocent party who has elected to disaffirm for an anticipatory repudiation are parallel to those available to a party who disaffirms for repudiatory breach.[52] The principal remedial option is a claim for damages for breach of contract.[53] In the alternative, the innocent party may be entitled to bring a restitutionary claim for the value of benefits conferred on the repudiating party.[54] Indeed, restitutionary remedies may be available to the repudiating party, provided that the agreement does not plainly stipulate that the value of

50   *British & Beningtons Ltd. v. North Western Cachar Tea Co. Ltd.*, above note 47.
51   See also *Braithwaite v. Foreign Hardwood Co.*, [1905] 2 K.B. 543 (C.A.); *Taylor v. Oakes, Roncoroni & Co.* (1922), 127 L.T. 267 (C.A.). See also F. Dawson, "Waiver of Conditions Precedent on a Repudiation" (1980) 96 Law Q. Rev. 239 (suggesting that the rule ought to be that where the repudiating party can establish that, at the time of repudiation, the innocent party was either disposed not to complete the contract or had become disabled from performing his contract, the repudiation should be considered to be justified).
52   See Chapter 15, section H.
53   The claim for damages is subject to the usual limitations including the obligation of the innocent party to take reasonable steps to mitigate loss. See Chapter 22, section F(3).
54   See Chapter 24, section B.

benefits conferred on the innocent party by the repudiating party will be forfeited in the event of the latter's breach of contract.[55]

Traditionally, it was held that the doctrine of anticipatory repudiation and the ability of the innocent party to disaffirm the agreement and pursue a damages claim with respect to the future non-performance of the agreement was simply inapplicable to leases of land. The traditional approach taken to a lessee's breach of the leasehold covenant to pay rent was that the landlord, in such circumstances, may pursue one of three mutually exclusive avenues of redress.[56] First, the landlord might do nothing to alter the relationship of landlord and tenant but simply insist on performance of the terms of the contract and enforce the tenant's rental obligations as they become due. Second, the landlord could terminate the lease, in which case the landlord would retain only the right to sue for rent due and payable or other damages up to the date of termination of the lease. Third, the landlord could advise the tenant that the property would be re-let on behalf of the tenant with the result that the landlord could retake possession of the premises and continue to enforce the tenant's obligation to pay rent, subject to a deduction for any rent secured by the landlord from a new tenant on the original tenant's account. What was unavailable to the landlord as an avenue of redress, however, was the doctrine of anticipatory breach whereby the landlord could simply terminate the lease on the basis of the tenant's anticipatory repudiation of the future rent obligations and bring an action for damages for breach of contract relating to that future non-performance. As Laskin J. explained in the leading decision of the Supreme Court of Canada in *Highway Properties Ltd. v. Kelly, Douglas & Co. Ltd.*,[57] the traditional position was based on a theory that a lease was not a mere contract, but, rather, created an interest in land. Accordingly, or so it was thought, upon surrender of the premises to the landlord and termination of the lease, the leasehold interest expires and the covenants in the lease became unenforceable against the tenant. In *Kelly, Douglas*, Laskin J., on behalf of the Supreme Court, suggested that the traditional doctrine should be overruled and that the general doctrine of anticipatory breach should apply to leases. He justified this view on the following grounds:

> It is no longer sensible to pretend that a commercial lease, such as the one before this Court, is simply a conveyance and not also a con-

---

55 See Chapter 24, section C.

56 An account of the traditional doctrine is provided in *Highway Properties Ltd. v. Kelly, Douglas & Co. Ltd.*, [1971] S.C.R. 562 at 570, Laskin J.

57 *Ibid.*

tract. It is equally untenable to persist in denying resort to the full armoury of remedies ordinarily available to redress repudiation of covenants merely because the covenants may be associated with an estate in land. Finally, there is merit here as in other situations in avoiding multiplicity of actions that may otherwise be a concomitant of insistence that a landlord engage in instalment litigation against a repudiating tenant.[58]

On its facts, *Kelly, Douglas* concerned the termination of the lease of a major tenant in a shopping mall. The tenant had repudiated the lease. The owner of the mall resumed possession of the premises, notifying the tenant that it would be held liable for any losses resulting from its wrongful repudiation of the lease. The courts below had held that when the owner had retaken possession of the premises occupied by the tenant, there had been a surrender of the lease and, accordingly, the owner could recover only damages flowing from breaches occurring prior to the date of surrender. The Supreme Court held, however, that the doctrine of anticipatory repudiation applied to such circumstances. Accordingly, the owner of the mall was entitled to elect to disaffirm the lease and pursue an action for damages for the injuries resulting from the tenant's future non-performance of the obligation to pay rent.

D. EXERCISING THE RIGHT TO AFFIRM

When confronted by an anticipatory repudiation, the innocent party also has the option of affirming the contract and, subject to the limitations discussed below, awaiting performance of the agreement. As we have noted above,[59] the fact that the innocent party has urged the repudiating party to retract the repudiation or has attempted to settle the dispute will not constitute an affirmation that precludes subsequent disaffirmation by the innocent party. Further, a mere failure to communicate an election to disaffirm to the repudiating party will not preclude a subsequent election to disaffirm unless the passage of time has resulted in significant prejudice to the repudiating party or, in the circumstances, the silence of the innocent party is reasonably

---

58   *Ibid.* at 576. Compare with *Total Oil (Great Britain) Ltd. v. Thompson Garages (Biggin Hill) Ltd.*, [1972] 1 Q.B. 318 at 324 (C.A.), Lord Denning M.R. (doctrine of anticipatory repudiation inapplicable to leases).

59   See above this Chapter, section C. See also, for example, *Allen v. Robles*, above note 30.

interpreted as evidence of a decision to affirm the agreement.[60] If the innocent party does affirm the agreement, however, the election is sometimes said to be irrevocable.[61] Arguably, however, the better view is that unless the repudiating party has suffered prejudice as a result of the affirmation, the innocent party should be considered to retain a right to disaffirm up to the time for performance.[62] Otherwise, the innocent party, having been irrevocably committed to the contract by the affirmation, would be obliged to continue to perform the agreement, notwithstanding the unretracted and persisting anticipatory repudiation of the repudiating party.

Affirmation of the agreement must be distinguished from a waiver by the innocent party of the proposed breach by the repudiating party. Waiver of a proposed breach of contract excuses the repudiating party from the breach and may prevent the innocent party from seeking redress for losses sustained as a result.[63] Affirmation of the agreement in the face of an anticipatory repudiation, however, preserves the rights of the innocent party against the innocent party and affirms the repudiating party's obligation to perform. An election to affirm, however, carries with it certain risks for the innocent party. Thus, as the affirmed agreement remains in full force and effect, the repudiating party is entitled to take advantage of any subsequent events that may provide the repudiating party with a defence to the innocent party's claim for damages for breach of contract. As the affirming innocent party is under a continuing obligation to perform the agreement, subsequent breach by the innocent party may provide a defence for the repudiating party. Thus, a service provider confronted with an anticipatory repudiation who affirms the agreement must maintain a readiness and willingness to perform.[64] A claim to enforce a contract for the sale of goods based on the buyer's anticipatory repudiation failed on the basis that the seller, who had affirmed the contract, failed to comply with certain conditions precedent to the closing of the transaction.[65] Similarly, subsequent events may make performance of the contract by the

---

60   See, for example, *McCowan v. McKay*, above note 31.

61   *Stocznia Gdanska SA v. Latvian Shipping Co.*, [1997] 2 Lloyd's Rep. 228 (C.A.), rev'd on other grounds [1998] 1 W.L.R. 574 (H.L.).

62   See G.H. Treitel, "Affirmation after Repudiatory Breach" (1998) 114 Law Q. Rev. 22 for support of this position.

63   See Chapter 8.

64   *McLellan v. Winston* (1886), 12 O.R. 431 (C.P.).

65   *Fletton Ltd. v. Peate Marwick* (1988), 50 D.L.R. (4th) 729 (B.C.C.A.), leave to appeal to S.C.C. refused (1988), 50 D.L.R. (4th) vii (S.C.C.). See also *Cromwell v. Morris*, above note 22; *Fercometal S.A.R.L. v. Mediterranean Shipping Co. S.A.*,

repudiating party impossible or unlawful, thus providing a defence to the innocent party's claim.[66] Subsequent events may also have the effect of reducing the innocent party's loss with subsequent benefit to the repudiating party.[67] If the contract has been affirmed, the repudiating party may have a change of heart and decide to perform. In such circumstances, the innocent party is obliged to accept that performance.[68]

Although the affirming innocent party has lost the right to disaffirm on grounds of anticipatory repudiation, the innocent party retains, of course, an entitlement to bring an action for damages for breach of contract against the repudiating party for any past and future breaches of the repudiating party's obligations.[69] As an alternative, however, it may be that the innocent party can bring an action for specific performance of the future obligation. Such relief has been awarded in the context of contracts for the purchase and sale of land, though the decrees granted would not be enforceable until the date for performance of the obligation.[70] A more difficult question, however, is whether the innocent party's decision to affirm the contract is constrained by a duty to mitigate loss. Thus, in a case where continuing to affirm the contract will run up damages that might otherwise be avoided by disaffirmation and mitigation by the innocent party, it may be considered whether the innocent party is obliged to disaffirm and take reasonable steps in mitigation of loss. The policy considerations that support the general principle precluding recovery for avoidable loss[71] suggest an affirmative answer to this question. A somewhat surprising decision of the House of Lords in *White & Carter (Councils) Ltd. v. McGregor,*[72] however, appeared to suggest that the innocent party was not substan-

---

[1989] A.C. 788 (H.L.); *Norfolk v. Aikens* (1989), 64 D.L.R. (4th) 1 (B.C.C.A.); *Homestar Industrial Properties Ltd. v. Philps,* [1993] 1 W.W.R. 163 (B.C.C.A.).

66 *Avery v. Bowden* (1855), 5 El. & Bl. 714, 119 E.R. 647 (outbreak of Crimean War made continued performance of a charterparty unlawful). For discussion of the doctrine of frustration, see Chapter 14.

67 *Tai Hing Cotton Mill Ltd. v. Kamsing Knitting Factory,* [1979] A.C. 91 (P.C.) (buyer's damages reduced by decline in market price of goods to be supplied by repudiating seller).

68 *Johnstone v. Milling,* above note 33; *Pamarta Holdings Ltd. v. Routledge* (1974), 52 D.L.R. (3d) 19 (Ont. H.C.J.).

69 *Bentsen v. Taylor, Sons & Co.,* [1893] 2 Q.B. 274; *Hain S.S. Co. Ltd. v. Tate & Lyle Ltd.* (1936), 41 Com. Cas. 350.

70 *Kloepfer Wholesale Hardware & Automotive Co. v. Roy,* [1952] 2 S.C.R. 465; *Hasham v. Zenab,* [1960] A.C. 316 (P.C.).

71 See Chapter 22, section F(3).

72 [1962] A.C. 413 (H.L.).

tially constrained, in exercising the right to affirm the contract, by a duty of mitigation of this kind. In this case, the plaintiff was a provider of advertising services in the form of making space available on litter bins supplied to municipal councils. The defendant had agreed to a three-year renewal of a contract to take advertising space of this kind and shortly thereafter resiled from the agreement. The plaintiff purported to affirm the contract, began performance and then sued to recover the full price to be paid by the defendants. The claim for the full price was based on an escalator clause in the agreement that stipulated that, in the event of the defendant's failure to make payments, the entire amount to be paid during the agreement became immediately due and payable. The defendant resisted the claim on the basis that, as the contract has been repudiated before any performance had been undertaken, the plaintiff was restricted to a claim for damages that, in turn, should be subject to a duty to mitigate loss. The plaintiff had not made any effort to mitigate losses by finding a substitute advertiser. A majority of the House of Lords held that in the circumstances the innocent party was indeed entitled to affirm the agreement and enforce the escalator clause, with the result that the entire contract price was recoverable as damages for breach. Lord Reid did suggest "if it can be shown that a person has no legitimate interest, financial or otherwise, in performing a contract rather than claiming damages, he ought not be allowed to saddle the other party with an additional burden with no benefit to himself."[73] Lord Reid did not explain, however, the nature of the legitimate interest advanced by the plaintiff in the present case. In dissent, two members of the panel opined that the majority view was simply inconsistent with the general principle that victims of a breach of contract are subject to an obligation to mitigate their losses.[74]

The decision in *White & Carter (Councils)* evidently runs a serious risk of encouraging economically wasteful activity. On its own facts, the encouragement of the plaintiff's conduct in proceeding with advertisements that were unwanted by the defendant colourfully illustrates the point. More recent Canadian cases suggest that the doctrine of *White & Carter (Councils)* will be narrowly confined and that, perhaps, the views of the dissenting members of the panel in that case more closely approximate current Canadian law. In *Finelli v. Dee,*[75] Laskin J.A., for the Ontario Court of Appeal, indicated scepticism with respect to the majority reasoning in *White & Carter (Councils)* and went on to distin-

---

73   *Ibid.* at 431.
74   For discussion of the mitigation principle, see Chapter 22, section F(3).
75   (1968), 67 D.L.R. (2d) 393 (Ont. C.A.).

guish the case as inapplicable to the facts of the case before the court. The agreement at issue in *Finelli* related to the pavement of a driveway. The customer had repudiated the agreement prior to the selection of a date for the work to be done. The paving company affirmed the agreement, in effect, by paving the driveway while the defendant was away from home and then sued for the price. Laskin J.A. distinguished *White & Carter (Councils)* on the basis that in *Finelli*, affirmation and continued performance by the innocent party would require the assent and cooperation of the party in breach. The *White & Carter (Councils)* approach was simply inapplicable to circumstances of this kind.[76]

In *Asamera Oil Corp. Ltd. v. Sea Oil & General Corp.*,[77] the Supreme Court of Canada confined the *White & Carter (Councils)* approach to some extent by stressing the importance of the innocent party's "substantial and legitimate interest" in affirming the contract. The agreement at issue in this case obliged the defendant to redeliver to the plaintiff certain shares that had been lent by the plaintiff to the defendant. When the time for redelivery arose, the defendant refused to return the shares and the plaintiff commenced an action. The issue in dispute was whether the plaintiff was obliged, within a reasonable period of time, to acquire substitute shares. Thus, although the case concerned the application of the duty of mitigation in circumstances of repudiatory breach rather than anticipatory repudiation, the Court nonetheless made certain observations concerning the decision in *White & Carter (Councils)*. Estey J. for the Supreme Court observed that the reasoning of the court in *White & Carter (Councils)*, to the extent that it required, in cases of affirmation for anticipatory repudiation, a "substantial and legitimate interest in looking to performance of a contractual obligation"[78] represented an "eminently reasonable position."[79] In Estey J.'s view, however, an innocent party asserting such an interest as the plaintiff should seek the remedy of specific performance, at

---

76 See also *Council of London Bureau Council v. Twickenham Garden Developments Ltd.*, [1971] Ch. 233, in which a building contractor dismissed by the employer and owner of the land refused to discontinue the work. The employer, a municipal council, sought an injunction to remove the builder from the building site. The court dismissed the application on the ground that the licence to occupy the site granted to the builder by the council was irrevocable during the term of the contract. The court also held that the rule in *White & Carter (Councils)* was inapplicable to facts of this kind, on the basis that the builder's continued performance required the cooperation of the council.

77 [1979] 1 S.C.R. 633, (1978), 98 D.L.R. (3d) 1.

78 *Ibid.* at 668 (S.C.R.).

79 *Ibid.*

least in the context of agreements to purchase a particular piece of real estate or a block of shares. Only where a plea for specific performance failed would the losses be considered to be unavoidable and, therefore, recoverable. In other words, for Estey J., to meet the requisite threshold, the substantial and legitimate interest of the innocent party in affirming the agreement must be so pressing that a plausible argument can be made for specific relief on the basis that damages would constitute an inadequate remedy in all the circumstances of the case.

A similar approach was advocated by the English Court of Appeal in *Attica C. Carriers Corp. v. Ferrostaal Poseidon Bulk Reederei G.m.b.H.*,[80] a case in which the owner of a vessel refused to accept redelivery of the vessel unless the charterer completed extensive and expensive repairs and continued to pay charter hire during the period required for the repairs. The charterers defended on the basis that although they were liable for damages for the state of disrepair of the vessel, the owner should not be entitled to affirm the contract, require them to retain possession of the vessel and continue to pay charter hire. The owner relied on *White & Carter (Councils)* in support of its position that it was entitled to affirm the contract and hold the charterers to their obligation to repair. The Court of Appeal rejected this position on the basis that damages constituted an adequate remedy for the owner. Lord Denning suggested that the decision in *White & Carter (Councils)* would not be applicable in circumstances where the innocent party's refusal to disaffirm the contract and seek redress in the form of a damages claim was unreasonable since damages would have constituted an adequate remedy.[81] Thus, although the rather generous view of the right to affirm set forth by the House of Lords in *White & Carter (Councils)* has not been flatly rejected by either English or Canadian courts, more recent decisions strongly suggest that the innocent party's right to affirm the contract will usually be subject to a duty to mitigate loss by disaffirming and pursuing damages relief in the typical case where damages at common law would be an adequate remedy.

---

80   [1976] 1 Lloyd's Rep. 250 (C.A.). See also *Clea Shipping Corp. v. Bulk Oil International Ltd. (No. 2)*, [1984] 1 All E.R. 129 (Q.B.).

81   *Ibid.* at 255.

FURTHER READINGS

J.W. CARTER, "The Embiricos Principle and the Law of Anticipatory Breach" (1984) 47 Mod. L. Rev. 422.

F. DAWSON, "Metaphors and Anticipatory Breach of Contract" (1981) 40 Cambridge L.J. 83.

F. DAWSON, "Waiver of Conditions Precedent on a Repudiation" (1980) 96 Law Q. Rev. 239.

T.H. JACKSON, "'Anticipatory Repudiation' and the Temporal Element of Contract Law: An Economic Inquiry into Contract Damages in Cases of Prospective Non-Performance" (1978) 31 Stan. L. Rev. 69.

D.M. McRAE, "Repudiation of Contracts in Canadian Law" (1978) 56 Can. Bar Rev. 233.

F.D. ROSE, "The Effects of Repudiatory Breaches of Contract" (1981) 34 Curr. Legal Probs. 235.

S.J. STOLJAR, "Some Problems of Anticipatory Breach" (1974) 9 Melbourne U.L. Rev. 355.

S. WILLISTON, "Repudiation of Contracts" (1901) 14 Harv. L. Rev. 317.

CHAPTER 17

CONDITIONAL AGREEMENTS

A. INTRODUCTION

The terms of a contract are of two kinds. First, enforceable agreements contain promises or undertakings in which the promisor typically undertakes to do certain things in the future. Contractual promises may also take the form of a promise or guarantee that a particular statement is or will continue to be true.[1] Second, the typical agreement will contain terms, though they may often be implied rather than express terms, that stipulate or prescribe states of affairs that must exist, or not exist, if one or more of the undertakings in the agreement is to be enforceable. Under traditional usage, terms setting out these kinds of arrangements are referred to as "conditions." A simple building contract, for example, could contain a promise to build a house according to certain specifications on the part of the builder and a promise by the hirer to pay a certain contract price. Either expressly or by implication, the agreement may contain a further term that stipulates that the completion of the building by the builder is a state of affairs that must exist before the obligation of the hirer to pay the contract price becomes enforceable. Where the subject matter of the condition, as in this illustration, is the performance of one of the promises set out in the agreement, the condition is often referred to as a "promissory condition." A

---

1   See Chapter 18, section D.

condition will often prescribe something other than the performance of a promise as the state of affairs that must exist before one or more of the promises in the agreement becomes enforceable. Thus, for example, the building contract might provide that the promises to build and to pay respectively are not enforceable until such time as a building permit has been issued by the local municipality. Such a condition may be referred to as a "non-promissory condition" because neither party has promised that the municipality will issue a building permit. If the municipality refuses, for some reason, to issue a building permit, neither the builder nor the hirer is obliged to perform its contractual promises and neither is in breach of its contractual obligations.

Conditions may also be subdivided into "conditions precedent" and "conditions subsequent." A condition precedent describes a state of affairs that must exist before one or more of the promises set out in the agreement becomes enforceable. The enforcement of the obligation, it is sometimes said, is suspended. If neither party has promised to fulfil the condition—to obtain the building permit in our example—we may describe this arrangement as a non-promissory condition precedent. In such circumstances, the condition relating to the building permit is a condition precedent to the obligations to build and to pay. A condition subsequent prescribes a state of affairs that will bring an already enforceable and binding obligation to an end. A simple illustration would be a term in a contract of guarantee that stipulates that the promise of guarantee will no longer be binding on the promisor once a new board of directors is appointed to the debtor company. Although the guarantee is binding on the guarantor until that event occurs, it terminates on the occasion of the appointment of the new board. Such an arrangement may be referred to as a non-promissory condition subsequent.

In a previous chapter,[2] we examined the transformation in the use of the term "conditions" as it refers to promissory conditions precedent. In the late-nineteenth century, it became common professional usage to refer to the promise, the performance of which is a condition that must be fulfilled before one or more of the other parties' undertaking becomes enforceable, as itself a condition. Under this usage, the promise of the builder to build the home is categorized as a "condition," it being understood that so classifying the term had the consequence that failure to perform the promise would render the hirer's promise to pay unenforceable. This rather elliptical use of the term "condition" was adopted in the sale of goods legislation enacted in the late-nineteenth

---

2   See Chapter 15, section B.

century in England[3] and elsewhere in the British Commonwealth,[4] including the Canadian common law provinces, and it remains standard professional usage when referring to promissory conditions. As we have seen, the law of promissory conditions has evolved over time and is the critical analytical tool in determining whether a particular breach of contract enables the other party to terminate the agreement and, further, in determining the order in which the undertakings in the agreement are to be performed.[5] With respect to the latter point, where it appears appropriate to infer that the appropriate solution is that certain promises of both parties should be performed at the same time, the promises are referred to as "concurrent conditions." In a contract for the sale of goods, for example, it is normally implied by statute that the seller's obligation to deliver the goods and the buyer's obligation to pay for the goods should be performed contemporaneously.[6] The effect of these obligations being concurrent conditions is that each party must tender performance at the time stipulated for delivery in order to be able to enforce the other party's obligation.

In this chapter, we examine the effect of non-promissory conditions on the enforceability of agreements. Three questions will be considered. First, it may be asked whether the non-fulfilment of a non-promissory condition precedent may lead to the conclusion that no contract was ever in existence. As we shall see, although it is reasonably common for judges to refer to non-promissory conditions precedent as being conditions precedent to the very existence of an agreement or obligation, the actual circumstances in which such a condition precedent will be held to be a condition precedent to the very existence of the agreement are quite unusual. The much more common phenomenon is to find that a condition precedent is a condition of the enforceability of one or more of the undertakings in an agreement but not of the existence of the agreement itself. Second, we consider the kinds of circumstances in which courts will imply subsidiary promissory obligations on the part of one or both of the parties to assist or cooperate in achieving fulfilment of the non-promissory condition precedent. In our simple building contract example, then, we may ask whether a court is likely to imply a term in which the builder undertakes to obtain the building permit or, perhaps, to make reasonable efforts to do so. Third, we consider whether and when it is possible for a party who wishes to do

---

3   *Sale of Goods Act*, 1893 (U.K.), 56 & 57 Vict., c. 71.
4   See, for example, *Sale of Goods Act*, R.S.O. 1990, c. S.1.
5   See Chapter 15.
6   See, for example, Ontario *Sale of Goods Act*, above note 4, s. 27.

so to waive fulfilment of the non-promissory condition precedent and enforce the contract nonetheless. On this point, Canadian courts have developed a doctrine of "true condition precedent" pursuant to which a non-promissory condition precedent cannot be waived, even in circumstances where the provision has been inserted into the agreement in order to benefit or protect one of the parties and that party now wishes to proceed with the agreement in the absence of that benefit or protection.

The focus of our attention in this chapter is on non-promissory conditions precedent rather than subsequent. The issues examined are more likely to arise in the context of conditions precedent. Conditions subsequent do not place at risk the very existence of the agreement. Their fulfilment can arise only in the context of a binding and enforceable agreement. Although, in theory at least, implied subsidiary obligations and unilateral waiver could arise in the context, they are less likely, as a practical matter, to do so. The guarantor whose obligations expire on the fulfilment of a condition subsequent is not likely to wish to elect to waive that release from further exposure. There are other differences between conditions precedent and subsequent. Thus, the burden of establishing that the condition precedent has been fulfilled will be on the plaintiff, whereas the burden of establishing that a condition subsequent has been fulfilled falls on the defendant. Further, it is perhaps more likely that the party benefiting from a condition precedent rather than subsequent will be required to give notice to the other party of its fulfilment. In either case, however, the question of whether such an obligation arises rests on a proper construction of the agreement.[7]

B. CONDITIONS PRECEDENT TO THE EXISTENCE OF AN AGREEMENT

It is not uncommon to find judicial statements to the effect that the non-fulfilment of a particular condition precedent prevents the formation or existence of an agreement or the existence of a particular obligation within the agreement. Such statements are to be viewed with caution. In *Aberfoyle Plantations Ltd. v. Cheng*,[8] the parties had agreed to the purchase and sale of a rubber estate. A minor portion of the es-

---

7   Where fulfilment of the condition is within the peculiar knowledge of one party, construction in favour of a duty to give notice is more likely. Compare, however, *Sky Ranches Ltd. v. Nelson* (1980), 30 B.C.L.R. 162 (C.A.).

8   [1960] A.C. 115 (P.C.).

tate had been leased by the vendor under leases that required renewal. Accordingly, the sale agreement stipulated that the purchase was "conditional on the vendor obtaining ... a renewal of the ... leases" by a specified date and further stipulated that "if for any cause whatsoever, the vendor is unable to fulfil this condition, this agreement shall become null and void and the vendor shall refund to the purchaser the ... deposits already made." In the event, the leases had not been renewed either by the agreed date or by a revised deadline to which the parties had agreed. Nonetheless, the vendor sought to enforce the agreement on the ground that consent would likely be forthcoming in due course. The purchaser, however, purported to terminate the contract and claimed for return of the deposit. Unsurprisingly, the court held that the vendor's failure to fulfil the condition precluded enforcement and the purchaser was awarded recovery of its deposit. In the course of explaining the result, however, Lord Jenkins described the effect of the condition relating to the renewal of the leases in the following terms: "It was thus made plain beyond argument that the condition was a condition precedent on the fulfilment of which the formation of a binding contract of sale was made to depend."[9]

Lord Jenkins thus appears to suggest that there was no binding contract in existence prior to fulfilment of the condition and the vendor and the purchaser were therefore at liberty to withdraw from the arrangement without penalty prior to its fulfilment. It seems unlikely that Lord Jenkins meant to suggest that the relationship prior to fulfilment of the condition did not constitute a binding contractual relationship. No such finding was necessary in order to explain the result that rests, simply, on the vendor's failure to meet the condition precedent to the purchaser's obligation to close the transaction. Moreover, the enforceability of the arrangement prior to fulfilment is a matter to be tested, surely, by the ordinary rules of formation[10] and enforceability.[11] If Lord Jenkins did intend to suggest that no binding agreement had been entered into, this proposition appears to be incorrect. Thus, in a later English case,[12] in the context of a contract for the sale of a lease that was "subject to" the vendor obtaining the requisite consent from the landlord, the contract was held to be binding. In this case, the cor-

---

9   *Ibid.* at 128.
10   See Chapters 2–6.
11   See Chapter 7.
12   *Property & Bloodstock Ltd. v. Emerton; Bush v. Property & Bloodstock Ltd.,* [1968] Ch. 94 (C.A.).

rectness of Lord Jenkin's observations in the *Aberfoyle* decision was doubted.[13]

Where, however, the condition precedent essentially reserves a unilateral discretion to withdraw from the apparent agreement, there would appear to be no agreement in existence until such time as the condition is fulfilled. Thus, in a British Columbia case,[14] a contract for the purchase and sale of a hotel was "subject to [the purchaser's] inspection of and approval of premises and chattels, subject to [the purchaser's] approval of the financial statements and subject to [the purchaser] increasing the present 2nd mortgage by $140,000." Taylor J. held that an arrangement under which the purchaser has committed to purchasing the property only if he chooses to do so is not a binding agreement subject to a condition precedent of purchaser approval. Rather, it is simply a bare offer to sell to the purchaser from which the offeror could withdraw prior to the purchaser's communication of the necessary approvals. Similarly, in another case,[15] it was held that an apparent agreement between the parties that stated that the plaintiff's offer to purchaser was "subject to" the approval of the company president was a bare offer that, unsupported by consideration flowing from the purchaser, could be withdrawn. This analysis rests, essentially, on the acceptable proposition that in the absence of a commitment of any kind on the part of the offeree, no consideration has been provided in return for the offeror's undertaking to keep the offer open for a particular period of time. A promise by a purchaser to purchase property if, in his absolute discretion, he decides that he likes the property does not constitute good consideration. If, on the other hand, an undertaking to keep the offer open is given for consideration or, indeed, under seal,[16] an offer to sell a property to a purchaser, subject to the purchaser's approval, would function simply as an enforceable option to purchase.[17]

---

13 *Ibid.* Danckwerts L.J. observed, at 116, with respect to the *Aberfoyle* decision: "Lord Jenkins thought that the contract was so conditional that even the relationship of vendor and purchaser was never created by it. This is a proposition which, with all respect, I find it very difficult to accept."

14 *Black Gavin & Co. v. Cheung* (1980), 20 B.C.L.R. 21 (S.C.).

15 *Murray McDermid Holdings Ltd. v. Thater* (1982), 42 B.C.L.R. 119 (S.C.).

16 See Chapter 7, section C.

17 In both *Black Gavin & Co. v. Cheung,* above note 14 and *Murray McDermid Holdings Ltd. v. Thater,* above note 15, the trial judge held that the payment of a deposit in either case by the purchaser did not constitute consideration. The critical question is whether, if the purchaser should decide not to go forward with the transaction, the deposit would be forfeited. If not, the payment of the deposit would not constitute good consideration. In the trial judge's view in these cases, the deposits would not become subject to forfeiture until the pur-

A second circumstance in which non-fulfilment of a condition precedent could prevent the existence of an agreement is where the condition is expressed in such vague language that the apparent agreement fails for uncertainty.[18] For example, an agreement for the purchase and sale of land that is subject to the purchaser "obtaining financing" may lack sufficient precision to create an enforceable agreement. Thus, in one Canadian decision,[19] it was held that a condition precedent contingent upon the purchaser "obtaining satisfactory personal financing," was too imprecise to constitute a binding agreement. Such arrangements are common, however, and courts are likely to attempt to construe such clauses in such fashion as to render them enforceable. In another Canadian decision,[20] the British Columbia Court of Appeal was able to give sufficient content to a condition precedent contingent on "satisfactory financing" to render the agreement enforceable. The provision was interpreted as meaning "satisfactory to a reasonable person with all the subjective but reasonable standards of the particular purchaser."[21] In the court's view, this interpretation offered an appropriate and enforceable blend of subjective and objective elements. While the term "satisfactory" was given a subjective component, the "reasonable standards" element enabled the court to enforce an obligation on the purchaser's part to use "best efforts."

A similar approach was taken by the British Columbia Court of Appeal in *Wiebe v. Bobsien*,[22] to the interpretation of a condition precedent in a real estate transaction rendering the agreement subject to the purchaser being able to sell his existing residence on or before a particular date. Prior to the fulfilment of the condition by sale of the purchaser's existing home, the vendor withdrew from the transaction and sold the property at a better price to a third party. The purchaser persisted, however, in his attempt to fulfil the condition and did sell his existing

---

chaser in each case approved the sale. At that point only would the purchaser be subject to an enforceable obligation to close and only at that point in time, then, would non-completion by the purchaser lead to forfeiture of the deposit. If, on the other hand, the parties had agreed that if the purchaser simply does not approve the transaction, the deposit would not be returnable, the transaction would function as an enforceable option. See *Mark 7 Development Ltd. v. Peace Holdings Ltd.* (1991), 53 B.C.L.R. (2d) 217 (C.A.).

18   See Chapter 3.

19   *Pietrobon v. McIntyre* (1987), 15 B.C.L.R. (2d) 350 (S.C.).

20   *Griffin v. Martens* (1988), 27 B.C.L.R. (2d) 152 (C.A.).

21   *Ibid.* at 154. See also *Gennis v. Madore* (1988), 72 Nfld. & P.E.I.R. 104 (P.E.I.S.C.T.D.).

22   (1984), 14 D.L.R. (4th) 754 (B.C.S.C.), aff'd (1986), 20 D.L.R. (4th) 475 (B.C.C.A.).

home in timely fashion and then sought to enforce the agreement. The trial judge held that the condition precedent relating to the purchaser's sale of his existing home to a third party did not prevent the formation of a binding agreement. Accordingly, as the purchaser had fulfilled the condition, the transaction was enforceable. Although this decision was upheld by the British Columbia Court of Appeal, Lambert J.A. in dissent, would have held that the meaning of the condition precedent was so uncertain that no binding contract had been entered. Certainly, in his view, the provision did not, in effect, impose an obligation on the purchaser to sell his existing home to the highest bidder. Rather, the purchaser probably expects that the sale "can only take place at a price that he considers reasonable and is willing to accept."[23] A condition, the fulfilment of which is so subjective was, in Lambert J.A.'s view, so uncertain that the agreement failed for uncertainty; the interim agreement between the parties was simply a standing offer that could be withdrawn, and was withdrawn by the vendor prior to the fulfilment of the condition. The majority, however, was of the view that sufficient content could be given to the condition precedent by implying terms requiring that "the purchaser would act in good faith and use all reasonable efforts to sell his home."[24] Such implied terms gave the condition precedent sufficient content to avoid the uncertainty problem and, moreover, the implied commitments to act in good faith and use all reasonable efforts constituted good consideration for the vendor's undertaking to hold the offer open for the specified period of time. The device adopted in these cases of implying undertakings in the agreement that both provide consideration and render the fulfilment of the condition a sufficiently certain or objective matter that the term may be enforced is commonly used in the context of interpreting and applying conditions precedent. To this matter, we now turn in more detail.

C. IMPLIED SUBSIDIARY OBLIGATIONS

Where an agreement is subject to a non-promissory condition precedent, such as being conditional upon the approval of a third party, courts will often imply subsidiary promissory obligations on the part of one or both of the parties. One reason for doing so is to give effect to the reasonable expectations of the parties as to how the condition may be fulfilled. In the leading case of *Dynamic Transport Ltd. v. O.K. Detailing*

---

23   *Ibid.* at 478 (B.C.C.A.).
24   *Ibid.* at 477.

Ltd.,[25] for example, a transaction for the purchase and sale of land was subject to a condition precedent that the parcel to be transferred be subdivided from the parcel of which it then formed a part. When the purchaser sought specific performance of the agreement, the vendor defended on the basis that subdivision approval had not been obtained and, further, that the agreement was silent as to whether it was the vendor or purchaser who should obtain this approval. The Supreme Court of Canada held that a court will "readily imply"[26] a promise on the part of each party to do all that is necessary to facilitate or cooperate in the fulfilment of the condition in a contract of this kind. With respect to the determination of which of the parties had the burden of going forward with an application for subdivision, the Court noted that the applicable planning legislation stipulated that the person who proposed to subdivide the property had the burden of applying for permission. Accordingly, the Court concluded that it was the vendor who was under an implied duty to make the appropriate application. Similarly, in *Smallman v. Smallman*,[27] where a separation agreement was "subject to the approval in due course of the court," the parties were subject to an implied obligation to seek court approval. Sometimes, the subsidiary obligation is said to be one imposing a duty to exercise "due diligence" in seeking fulfilment of the condition precedent.[28] The implied duty to cooperate may include an obligation to provide financial statements where the request for the information is a reasonable one.[29] In these cases, parties who are subject to the implied promise to facilitate or cooperate in the fulfilment of the condition precedent will be in breach of contract should they fail to do so and subject, therefore, to the normal remedies for breach of contract.[30]

Another reason for implying undertakings that are subsidiary to the condition precedent is to impose a contractual obligation on one or both parties to refrain from engaging in conduct that will defeat fulfilment of the condition precedent. In *Multi-Malls Inc. v. Tex-Mall Properties Ltd.*,[31] where an agreement for the purchase and sale of land was subject to a condition that the site be rezoned to permit construc-

---

25   [1978] 2 S.C.R. 1072.

26   *Ibid.* at 1084.

27   [1971] 3 All E.R. 717 (C.A.).

28   See *Hargreaves Transport Ltd. v. Lynch*, [1969] 1 W.L.R. 215 (C.A.).

29   See *100 Main Street Ltd. v. W.B. Sullivan Construction Ltd.* (1978), 88 D.L.R. (3d) 1 (Ont. C.A.).

30   See Chapters 22–24.

31   (1980), 108 D.L.R. (3d) 399 (Ont. H.C.J.), aff'd (1981), 128 D.L.R. (3d) 192 (Ont. C.A.).

tion of a shopping centre by the purchaser, the seller substantially reduced the prospects of obtaining rezoning of the parcel by acquiring and developing a mall on another nearby property. This was held to be a breach of the vendor's implied duty not to do any act that would make the securing of the consent less likely, giving rise to a claim for damages.[32] Similarly, a party must not enter into contractual relationships with third parties that disable it from cooperating in the fulfilment of the condition precedent. In *Victoria Queen Investments Ltd. v. The Savarin Ltd.*,[33] for example, an agreement for the sale of land was subject to approval by the Liquor Licence Board. The purchaser entered into a loan agreement in order to finance the transaction with a lender who required that its identity not be disclosed to third parties. As a result, the purchaser was unable to comply with the requirements of the board that the identity of lenders be disclosed and the transaction could not close. This was held to be a breach of an implied term of the contract requiring the purchaser to comply with reasonable requests for information by the board, thus exposing the purchaser to a claim by the vendor for damages for breach of contract.

Finally, a subsidiary obligation may be implied in order to avoid the conclusion that non-fulfilment of a particular condition precedent has the effect that no agreement was in existence. Thus, in a case where an agreement appears to confer a unilateral discretion to fulfil or not fulfil a condition precedent, a subsidiary undertaking may be implied in order to constrain or give some structure to that discretion so as to avoid the conclusion that the promisor has not given consideration or that the condition and the agreement fail for uncertainty. *Wiebe v. Bobsien*[34] provides an illustration. The agreement of purchase and sale was subject to a condition precedent that the purchaser must sell his existing property to a third party. As we have seen, the British Columbia Court of Appeal avoided the conclusion that prior to fulfilment of the condition precedent there was simply no agreement in existence by holding that the contract implicitly imposed an obligation on the purchaser to "act in good faith and use all reasonable efforts to sell his home."[35] Again, failure to do so would constitute a breach of contract giving rise to the usual remedies.

---

32 There calculated as the value of the lost chance to obtain rezoning. See Chapter 22, section E(4).

33 (1980), 101 D.L.R. (3d) 353 (Ont. H.C.J.).

34 Above note 22.

35 *Ibid.* at 477 (B.C.C.A).

682 THE LAW OF CONTRACTS

D. WAIVER AND "TRUE" CONDITIONS PRECEDENT

The parties to an agreement subject to a non-promissory condition precedent may mutually agree to waive the fulfilment of the condition. Where this is done, the obligations subject to the condition become enforceable. Obviously, a mutual waiver cannot be achieved in cases such as *Dynamic Transport Ltd. v. O.K. Detailing Ltd.*,[36] where the transaction could not close unless the subdivision of the original parcel was effected. The more difficult question is whether there are circumstances in which a unilateral waiver of a condition precedent may be effective. In other common law jurisdictions, it is possible for a party that is the intended beneficiary of a non-promissory condition precedent to unilaterally waive fulfilment of the condition and enforce the obligations of the agreement that were subject to the condition.[37] The benefited party cannot unilaterally waive, however, if the other party has an interest in fulfilment of the condition that would be prejudiced by waiver. Thus, in *Heron Garage Properties Ltd. v. Moss*,[38] a contract for the purchase and sale of land was subject to a condition precedent that planning permission for use of the property as a service station be obtained. The purchaser was unable to waive the condition because the seller retained adjacent property on which he planned to sell cars and thus had an interest in the fulfilment of the condition. In the absence of such an interest in the other party, the party benefiting from the condition is normally entitled to waive its fulfilment. In common law Canada, however, this issue has become much complicated by a doctrine of "true" condition precedent developed by the Supreme Court of Canada in a line of cases beginning with *Turney v. Zhilka*[39] in 1959. Although the ambit of the rule established in that case remains uncertain, it is clear that it establishes a uniquely Canadian limitation on the right of unilateral waiver.

The facts of *Turney v. Zhilka* were uncomplicated. A contract for the purchase and sale of land was subject to the following condition preced-

---

36   Above note 25.
37   See, for example, *Wood Preservation, Ltd. v. Prior (Inspector of Taxes)*, [1968] 2 All E.R. 849 (Ch.), aff'd [1969] 1 All E.R. 364 (C.A.); *Graham v. Pitkin*, [1992] 2 All E.R. 235 (P.C.); *Gange v. Sullivan* (1966), 116 C.L.R. 418 (Aust. H.C.); *Donaldson v. Tracy*, [1951] N.Z.L.R. 684 (S.C.); *Funke v. Paist*, 52 A.2d 655 (Pa. 1947); *Richardson v. Snipes*, 330 S.W.2d 381 (Tenn. 1959).
38   [1974] 1 All E.R. 421 (Ch.).
39   [1959] S.C.R. 578.

ent: "Providing the property can be annexed to the Village of Streets-
ville and a plan is approved by the Village council for subdivision."[40]
After inquiries of the village council were made by the purchaser, it
became clear that the possibility of annexation was remote. Nonetheless, the purchaser wished to proceed with the purchase and purported
to waive fulfilment of the condition precedent. The trial judge held that
as the condition was one that had been introduced solely for the benefit
of the purchaser, the purchaser was entitled to waive and proceed with
the purchase. Although the Supreme Court of Canada expressed doubt
about the basis for the factual inference that the condition was for the
exclusive benefit of the purchaser, the Court held that, in any event,
the decision should be disposed of on "broader grounds."[41] Judson J.,
on behalf of a unanimous Court, briefly discussed cases in which a
party benefiting from a promissory condition precedent was held to be
entitled to waive performance of the promise. These were described
as cases in which "one party to a contract may forego a promised advantage or may dispense with part of the promised performance of the
other party which is simply and solely for the benefit of the first party
and is severable from the rest of the contract."[42] The present facts were
to be distinguished, however, on the following basis: "But here there
is no right to be waived. The obligations under the contract, on both
sides, depend upon a future uncertain event, the happening of which
depends entirely on the will of a third party—the Village council. This
is a true condition precedent—an external condition upon which the
existence of the obligation depends. Until the event occurs there is no
right to performance on either side."[43] Noting that neither party has
promised that the future uncertain event will occur, Judson J. suggested that this was "an attempt by one party, without the consent of the
other, to write a new contract."[44]

It is not entirely clear which of the factors mentioned by Judson J.
is the critical indicator of the existence of a true condition precedent.
If the doctrine applies whenever the fulfilment of a condition is a "future uncertain event," the doctrine would apply to virtually every non-
promissory condition precedent. If the critical point is that fulfilment
is dependent "entirely on the will of the third party," the application
of the doctrine is narrowed to some extent though the extent of the

---

40   *Ibid.* at 582.
41   *Ibid.* at 583.
42   *Ibid.*
43   *Ibid.* at 583–84.
44   *Ibid.* at 584.

narrowing remains unclear. If being dependent on the will of a third party means that a decision or action of some kind must be taken by a third party, such as a municipal council or a bank, the doctrine will have a very broad sweep. On the other hand, if the doctrine will not apply where one of the parties must be actively involved in obtaining or provoking the decision or action, the scope of the doctrine will be narrowed. A third possibility is that the key factor is that the "obligations under the contract, on both sides" are subject to the contingency. If this is the test for the application of the true condition precedent doctrine, the test would have the advantage of flexibility. In a case where unilateral waiver appears to be appropriate, a judge could reason, albeit with some circularity, that on the particular facts, the obligations on both sides were not subject to the contingency. To be consistent with *Turney v. Zhilka,* however, a judge could not simply conclude from the fact that a condition benefited one party alone, that the obligation of both parties was not subject to the condition. Such a view would ignore the "broader grounds," however elusive they may be.

The result in *Turney v. Zhilka,* in the view of many observers, is plainly unsatisfactory. The parties to such an agreement would likely be surprised by the result. The decision appears to offer the vendor an unbargained-for option to withdraw from the transaction in a rising market.[45] Unsurprisingly, perhaps, provincial appellate courts have attempted to confine the doctrine from time to time. In *Beauchamp v. Beauchamp,*[46] for example, the Ontario Court of Appeal declined to apply *Turney v. Zhilka* to a financing condition in a real estate transaction. The contract of purchase and sale was subject to a condition that the purchaser be able to obtain a first mortgage in the amount of ten thousand dollars at current rates and a second for twenty-five hundred dollars. In the event, the purchaser was able to arrange a first mortgage for twelve thousand dollars and, accordingly, had no need for a second and none was obtained. When the vendor refused to close on the ground that the financing condition had not been completely fulfilled, the purchaser sought to enforce the agreement. Specific performance of the agreement was granted. The Court of Appeal distinguished the *Turney v. Zhilka* line of authority on the basis that "the condition herein is not such as is dealt with in those cases."[47] It is not abundantly apparent, however, that *Turney v. Zhilka* can be so easily distinguished. The obtaining of financing was a future uncertain event dependent upon

---

45   See *Barnett v. Harrison,* [1976] 2 S.C.R. 531 at 536, Laskin C.J.C.
46   [1973] 2 O.R. 43, 32 D.L.R. (3d) 693 (C.A.).
47   *Ibid.* at 695 (D.L.R.).

the will of lenders. On the other hand, application of *Turney v. Zhilka* to these facts would lead to a most surprising result. An appeal of this decision to the Supreme Court of Canada was dismissed.[48] A more vigorous attack on *Turney v. Zhilka* mounted by the British Columbia Court of Appeal in *O'Reilly v. Marketers Diversified Inc.*[49] did not enjoy success. The contract of purchase and sale of land in this case was subject to a condition that the purchaser be able to purchase an adjacent lot. The Court of Appeal held that this was a stipulation for the exclusive benefit of the purchaser that he could therefore waive. *Turney v. Zhilka* was distinguished as a case where the condition was to be "wholly performed by a third party." On appeal, the Supreme Court of Canada briefly explained, in an opinion authored by Judson J. that neither party had an enforceable agreement without fulfilment of the condition.[50]

Although the rule in *Turney v. Zhilka* was applied by the Court in *O'Reilly* and in the almost contemporaneous decision of the Court in *F.T. Developments Ltd. v. Sherman*,[51] the matter was obviously a contentious one. In each case, the appeal was first argued before a panel of five judges and then, again, before the full Court.[52] The correctness of *Turney v. Zhilka* surfaced again for consideration before the Supreme Court in 1976 in *Barnett v. Harrison*,[53] a case in which, again, the appeal was twice argued. The condition in this case was a rather more complicated one. Although the transaction for the purchase and sale of land was subject to obtaining the necessary approvals to the site plan and proposed changes in zoning, the timing of the closing of the transaction was explicitly linked to the granting of those approvals and was to occur sixty days after the date of the final approval. This aspect of the condition gave the vendor the further argument that if the approvals were not forthcoming, the agreement failed to stipulate a closing date. Although the purchaser made certain attempts to obtain the requisite approvals, he did not enjoy success. When it became apparent that the purchaser would have to simply accept the existing zoning, he purported to waive the condition and communicated a willingness to close the transaction in sixty days.[54] For the majority of the Court, however,

---

48   [1974] S.C.R. v.
49   (1968), 1 D.L.R. (3d) 387 (B.C.C.A.), rev'd [1969] S.C.R. 741.
50   *Ibid.* (S.C.R.).
51   [1969] S.C.R. 203 (offer conditional upon purchaser obtaining rezoning of the land—*Turney v. Zhilka* applied in a brief judgment authored by Judson J.).
52   See *Barnett v. Harrison*, above note 45 at 533, Laskin C.J.C.
53   *Ibid.*
54   As the agreement further provided that the purchaser may, at his option agree to any necessary amendments to the proposal site plan, the appellant argued

this was a situation in which *Turney v. Zhilka* applied and the purchaser was unable to enforce the agreement. Dickson J. noted that the approval sought was "a future uncertain event" that was "entirely dependent upon the will of third parties."[55] Dickson J. conceded that the doctrine was not applied in other common law jurisdictions but indicated that as the rule had been in effect since 1959 and applied many times, it should be preserved in the "interests of certainty and predictability in the law."[56] Dickson J. also attempted to defend the rule, however, on a more principled basis. First, he suggested that the distinction drawn in *Turney v. Zhilka* between promissory and non-promissory conditions was a valid one. Further, it was his view that application of the rule avoids determination of two difficult questions. The first is whether the condition precedent is for the benefit of only one party or for their joint benefit. The second is whether the condition is severable from the balance of the agreement. The former point made by Dickson J. strongly suggests, then, that even if the condition can be fairly characterized as being exclusively for the benefit of one party, that party cannot unilaterally waive its fulfilment.

In a vigorous dissent, Laskin C.J.C. sought to confine the operation of *Turney v. Zhilka*. In his view, the proper explanation for the rule in that case was the holding of the Court that the "obligations under the contract, *on both sides*, depend upon a future uncertain event."[57] The rule should therefore not be applied in a case where the provision has been inserted in the agreement for the purchaser's benefit alone. Accordingly, it was incorrect of the Court to have applied *Turney v. Zhilka* to the facts of the *O'Reilly*[58] case. Similarly, for Laskin C.J.C., the condition on the facts of *Barnett* was for the sole benefit of the purchaser. The provision should be subject to a unilateral waiver and, if waived, the transaction would close sixty days after the purchaser's waiver of fulfilment of the condition.

---

that this unlimited right of amendment must include a right to simply accept the existing zoning. This argument was accepted below by Jessup J.A. in dissent in the Ontario Court of Appeal. See [1973] 2 O.R. 176 (C.A.). For the majority in the Supreme Court, however, Dickson J. held that the provision conferred merely a right to "alter or correct or improve" the plan in response to the demands of the authorities. See above note 45 at 557, Dickson J.

55　*Ibid.* at 557.
56　*Ibid.* at 559.
57　*Ibid.* at 541, quoting Judson J. from *Turney v. Zhilka,* above note 39 at 583 (emphasis added by Laskin C.J.C.).
58　Above note 49.

Barnett v. Harrison thus appears to affirm the proposition that a zoning condition inserted for the exclusive benefit of a purchaser cannot be waived by the purchaser in the absence of explicit language to this effect in the agreement. Moreover, the reasoning of the majority in *Barnett* appears to suggest that the rule in *Turney v. Zhilka* is to be broadly applied, at least in cases where the fulfilment of the condition can be said to be "entirely dependent upon the will of third parties."[59] The unsatisfactory nature of the doctrine, however, would suggest that courts will likely lean against an expansive interpretation of the doctrine and, indeed, it may well be that the doctrine will be subject to reconsideration on a future occasion. In British Columbia,[60] however, such heroics have been rendered unnecessary by the statutory overruling of *Turney v. Zhilka*.

Some evidence of judicial ambivalence concerning the doctrine may be found in the later decision of the Supreme Court of Canada in *McCauley v. McVey*.[61] In this case, there were two transactions involved. The owner of two lots of land arranged to sell them to McVey. Under that agreement, McVey undertook to arrange for and bear the cost of any surveys required in order to permit a transfer of title. Prior to the closing of that transaction, McVey had entered into a further agreement to sell one of the lots to McCauley. Under the second agreement, the obligations of the parties were subject to a condition to the following effect: "This agreement to be contingent upon the herein named vendor having title to the herein mentioned property by the date set for the closing of this sale."[62]

Under the first transaction, McVey did make arrangements with a surveyor, but the surveys, through no fault of McVey's, were not completed in timely fashion. Accordingly, the first transaction had not closed by the closing date for the sale to McCauley. For the courts below and, indeed, for McIntyre J. in dissent from the decision of the Supreme Court of Canada granting the appeal, this was a straightforward situation for application of the rule in *Turney v. Zhilka*. McIntyre J. emphasized that the vendor had not undertaken to fulfil the condition of acquiring title. Moreover, the fulfilment of the condition was completely dependent, in his view, upon the performance by the original third-party vendor of the obligation to transfer title to McVey. McVey was guilty of no intentional default. The condition was not fulfilled

59 Above note 45 at 557.
60 *Law and Equity Act*, R.S.B.C. 1990, c. 253, s. 54.
61 (1979), 98 D.L.R. (3d) 577 (S.C.C.).
62 *Ibid.* at 578.

and neither party could enforce the agreement. Laskin C.J.C., however, writing for a majority of the Supreme Court that included Dickson J., held that *Turney v. Zhilka* could be distinguished and that McCauley's action for specific performance would enjoy success. For the majority, McVey was under an implied obligation to give title. Accordingly, this was not a case in which the obligations of the parties were subject to a future uncertain event, the happening of which depends entirely on the will of a third party. While the decision in *McCauley v. McVey* thus leaves the rule in *Turney v. Zhilka* intact, it does suggest that the implication of a promissory obligation may be a device that can be employed to blur the distinction between true conditions precedent and those that can be unilaterally waived.

FURTHER READINGS

J.S. EWART, *Waiver Distributed* (Cambridge: Harvard University Press, 1917).

G. DAVIES, "Conditional Contracts for the Sale of Land" (1977) 55 Can. Bar Rev. 289.

ONTARIO LAW REFORM COMMISSION, *Report on Amendment of the Law of Contract* (Toronto: Ministry of Attorney General, 1987) c. 13.

B.J. REITER & J. SWAN, "Contracts and the Protection of Reasonable Expectations" in B.J. Reiter & J. Swan, eds., *Studies in Contract Law* (Toronto: Butterworths, 1980).

R.J. SMITH, "Conditional Contracts for the Sale of Land" (1974) 33 Cambridge L.J. 211.

S.J. STOLJAR, "The Contractual Conception of Condition" (1953) 69 Law Q. Rev. 485.

G.H. TREITEL, "'Conditions' and 'Conditions Precedent'" (1990) 106 Law Q. Rev. 185.

REPRESENTATION AND WARRANTY

A. INTRODUCTION

As we have seen in Chapter 10, a variety of remedies are available to an individual who is induced into an agreement by a misrepresentation. Whether the misrepresentation is fraudulently or innocently false, the misrepresentee may be able to rescind the agreement. If the misstatement is made fraudulently or negligently, the misrepresentor may be liable in tort to claim for compensatory damages. A further alternative form of relief may be available if a misrepresentation inducing a contract can be characterized as being subject to an implicit undertaking that the representation is true. In such circumstances, it may be possible to render that undertaking enforceable either as a collateral contract that is subsidiary to the main contract induced by the representation or, indeed, as part of that main contract itself. In either case, the falsity of the representation would constitute a breach of the implicit undertaking and would give rise to a claim for damages for breach of contract. If the undertaking is a simple warranty that the statement is true, liability will be strict and not dependent on a finding of fraud or negligence. The measure of damages in a claim for breach of contract would be in the expectancy measure, a measure of relief that is potentially more comprehensive than a compensatory award in tort as it may include an element of the profit that would have been secured if the statement had, in fact, been true.[1] A statement of fact inducing the contract may also be repeated explicitly in the induced agreement itself and thus become subject to the remedies available for breach of contract. Further, an agreement may contain representations that are made for the first time in the agreement itself and that have contractual force and effect. In all these various circumstances in which representations may be given contractual force, it must be considered whether the misrepresentee should be able to pursue claims in both tort and contract concurrently.

B. PRE-CONTRACTUAL REPRESENTATION AS WARRANTY

If a representation can be properly characterized as a contractual warranty, the falsity of the statement constitutes a breach of a contractual term. Accordingly, the misrepresentee will be entitled to bring a claim for damages calculated in the expectancy measure. Thus, even a victim of a false or negligent misstatement, who may be entitled to pursue a claim in tort, may prefer to be able to characterize the misrepresentation as a contractual warranty that brings the advantage of the contractual measure of relief.

For the victim of a wholly innocent or non-careless misrepresentation, however, the contract damages claim may be the only available remedy. There would be no claim for tort damages because of the absence of negligence. The equitable claim for rescission of the agreement would be potentially available but it may vanish rather quickly as a result of the operation of various applicable bars to rescission, especially that of execution.[2] In such circumstances, it will be especially attractive to a representee to be able to characterize the representation in question as not merely a representation but as an enforceable contractual term. Indeed, courts have adopted this view on the basis of a finding that the particular representation, though, in form, a statement of fact, is implicitly an undertaking or guarantee that the fact is true and that this undertaking forms part of a collateral enforceable contract entered into by the representor and representee.

Under this collateral contract analysis, then, the representation made prior to the formation of the contract is transformed into a term of a unilateral contract that is collateral to that "main" contract. A uni-

---

1   For discussion of the difference between contractual and tort measures of relief, see Chapter 1, section C.

2   For an account of the bars to rescission, see Chapter 10, section E.

lateral contract is a contract consisting of a promise exchanged for an act.[3] The offer of a unilateral contract can be expressed in the formula "if you do x, I promise y." In the unilateral collateral contract, the "if x" is "if you enter into the main contract with me" and the "I promise y" is "I promise or guarantee that the representation I am making is true."[4] The device is neatly illustrated by the facts of the leading traditional English authority, *Heilbut, Symons & Co. v. Buckleton*.[5] The defendants were rubber merchants who had underwritten a large number of shares in the Filisola Company, with a view to selling the shares to the public. The plaintiffs purchased a substantial number of the shares from the defendants having been assured by them that the company in question was a "rubber company." The statement was not made fraudulently. The availability of rescission for innocent misrepresentation was barred by execution of the main contract. The jury held that the Filisola Company could not be accurately described as a "rubber company." Accordingly, the issue on appeal was whether the statement that the shares on offer were shares in a rubber company was a mere misrepresentation inducing the contract (in which case, no relief would be available) or, rather, could be considered to be a collateral warranty that created a binding contractual obligation guaranteeing that the Filisola Company was properly so described. To establish such a claim, Lord Moulton explained, the claimant must show that the representation made by the defendants was actually intended as a "warranty," that is, a contract collateral to the main contract to take the shares, whereby the defendants, in consideration of the plaintiff entering into a contract to take the shares, promised that the company in question was a rubber company. Parenthetically, we may note that the term "warranty" is being used here in a generic sense as equivalent to "contractually binding undertaking," rather than in its more modern and technical sense as referring to a contractual term, breach of which sounds only in damages.[6]

In Lord Moulton's view, such a collateral contract was conceivable and would possess in full "the character and status of a contract."[7] He went on to suggest, however, that such agreements, which have the ef-

---

3   See Chapter 2, sections A and B(1)(b).

4   There could also be a collateral contract analysis in circumstances where the offeror invites the offeree to enter into a contract with a third party. For example, a manufacturer could offer to guarantee the quality of a product if the offeree purchases the product from a third-party dealer or retailer. See, for example, *Murray v. Sperry Rand Corporation* (1979), 96 D.L.R. (3d) 113 (Ont. H.C.J.).

5   [1913] A.C. 30.

6   See generally Chapter 15.

7   Above note 5 at 47.

fect of altering the terms of the main contract — an effect that might be achieved more naturally by actually amending the main contract rather than executing a collateral contract, are "viewed with suspicion by the law."[8] A rather stringent test for establishing such agreements was then set out in the following terms: "They must be proved strictly. Not only the terms of such contracts but the existence of an *animus contrahendi* on the part of all the parties to them must be clearly shown. Any laxity on these points would enable parties to escape from the full performance of the obligations of contracts unquestionably entered into by them and more especially would have the effect of lessening the authority of written contracts by making it possible to vary them by suggesting the existence of verbal collateral agreements relating to the same subject matter."[9] In formulating this test Lord Moulton relied on a remark that he attributed to Holt C.J. to the effect that "an affirmation at the time of sale is a warranty, provided it appear on evidence to be so intended."[10] The test is a stringent one in the sense that the representee who has reasonably relied on the representation in making the decision to enter the contract and who may well believe that the representation is binding in some sense may nonetheless have difficulty establishing that the representation was uttered with "contractual intent" on the speaker's part.

Later courts, however, have taken a less stringent view of the burdens to be discharged by a party seeking to claim that a representation made prior to the time of sale, for example, amounted to a collateral warranty. Such claims are likely to receive a warmer reception, perhaps, in the context of consumer transactions. Thus, in *Dick Bentley Productions Ltd. v. Harold Smith (Motors) Ltd.*,[11] the English Court of Appeal held that a representation made by the seller of the used car that the car had done only 20,000 miles since being fitted with a replacement engine was not

---

8   *Ibid.*

9   *Ibid.*

10 *Ibid.* at 49, referring indirectly to Holt C.J.'s judgments in *Crosse v. Gardner* (1689), Carth. 90 and *Medina v. Stoughton* (1700), 1 Salk. 210, summarized in these terms by Buller J. in *Pasley v. Freeman* (1789), 3 T.R. 51. As Atiyah has pointed out, Buller J.'s emphasis on intention to contract is quite defensible in *Pasley* as he was concerned to distinguish an earlier case, *Harvey v. Young* (1603), Yelv. 21 in which the plaintiff purchaser unsuccessfully claimed for losses resulting from reliance on seller's puffery as to the value of the asset purchased. See P.S. Atiyah, *Essays on Contract* (Oxford: Clarendon Press, 1986) at 277–78. Notwithstanding these fragile historical foundations, the contractual intention test has been widely accepted.

11 [1965] 1 W.L.R. 623 (C.A.).

merely an innocent misrepresentation but was a warranty in the requisite sense. Lord Denning, after quoting the pithy statement of the contractual intention test attributed to Holt C.J. upon which Lord Moulton relied in *Heilbut Symons*, went on to explain how the "intention" test is to be applied: "Looking at the cases once more, as we have done so often, it seems to me that if a representation is made in the course of dealings for a contract for the very purpose of inducing the other party to act on it, and it actually induces him to act on it by entering into that contract, that is *prima facie* ground for inferring that the representation was intended as a warranty. It is not necessary to speak of it as being collateral. Suffice it that the representation was intended to be acted upon and was in fact acted on."[12] It will be apparent that Lord Denning's version of the "*animus contrahendi*" test appears to be perilously close to and, perhaps, indistinguishable from the test for operative misrepresentation. Further, Lord Denning appears to reject the need for finding a unilateral collateral warranty and is prepared to conclude, more simply, that the apparent representation simply becomes a term of the main contract in the form of a promise that the stated fact is true.

In *Dick Bentley*, Lord Denning distinguished his own previous reasoning in *Oscar Chess Ltd. v. Williams*,[13] a case involving a misrepresentation by a non-commercial seller. The seller had purchased a car and received with it a logbook, or title document, identifying 1948 as the year of manufacture of the car. When he resold the car to the plaintiff buyer, the seller simply repeated the information contained in the logbook, representing that the car was manufactured in 1948. The seller was completely innocent of fault and was not in a position to look behind the information provided in the logbook. On such facts, in Lord Denning's view, the inference of warranty was rebutted. By contrast, the seller in the *Dick Bentley* case was a dealer who was in a position to know or at least find out the history of the vehicle. On this view, then, the test for warranty appears to be that in circumstances where the representor has expertise or privileged access to information not possessed by the representee and, presumably, where the representee reasonably relies on the truth of the statement in entering into the contract, the affirmation in question will be treated as a warranty. Although such a test appears to be a less stringent one[14] than the contractual in-

---

12   *Ibid.* at 627.
13   [1957] 1 W.L.R. 370 (C.A.).
14   In *J. Evans & Son (Portsmouth) v. Merzario (Andrea) Ltd.*, [1976] 2 All E.R. 930 at 933 (C.A.), Lord Denning M.R. observed that much of what was said in *Heilbut, Symons* is "entirely out of date."

tention test set out in *Heilbut Symons & Buckelton*, it does offer a more realistic basis for identifying circumstances in which the representee would reasonably assume that the representor is, in some sense, bound by the representation. A similar approach has been adopted in modern Canadian cases.[15]

If a contractual warranty guaranteeing the truth of a representation is found, liability for its falsity will be strict in the sense that it is not dependent on a finding of fraud or negligence. It is possible, however, that the warranty might be construed as one to provide carefully researched information. In such a case, the misrepresentor will be liable for breach of the contractual warranty only if the information is carelessly obtained or provided. In *Esso Petroleum Co. v. Mardon*,[16] as noted above, a prospective tenant was induced into a service station lease by the company's presentation of a carelessly prepared report that overestimated the projected volume of business or "through-put" at the particular intersection at which the station was to be located. It would be unrealistic, in such circumstances, to infer that the oil company was warranting or guaranteeing that there would, in fact, be such a volume of business in the future. The English Court of Appeal held, however, that the oil company had given an implicit warranty that the report had been prepared with reasonable skill and care. A finding that the report had not been so prepared grounded a claim for damages for breach of contract.[17]

Contractual liability for pre-contractual misrepresentations may be precluded by an effectively drawn "entire agreement" clause.[18] Such stipulations, commonly included in commercial agreements, typically include language such as the following: "this agreement is the entire agreement between the parties and there are no inducements, promises or agreements oral or otherwise between the parties not embodied herein." Such clauses have considerable potential for unpleasantly surprising parties induced into agreements by misrepresentations and collateral warranties. Accordingly, they are often construed narrowly against the party for whose benefit they were included. In *Sodd Corporation Inc. v. Tessis*,[19] for example, the agreement provided that "no warranty or condition is expressed or can be implied" with respect

---

15   See, for example, *Murray v. Sperry Rand Corp.*, above note 4; *Dellelce Construction and Equipment v. Portec Inc.* (1990), 73 O.R. (2d) 396 (H.C.J.).

16   [1976] Q.B. 801 (C.A.).

17   See generally J. Cartwright, *Misrepresentation* (London: Sweet & Maxwell, 2002) at 208–11.

18   For further discussion of entire agreement clauses, see Chapter 10, section G. And see generally Chapter 6, section D.

19   (1977), 79 D.L.R. (3d) 632 (Ont. C.A.).

to the matter in dispute. The Ontario Court of Appeal assumed that the clause would not preclude enforcement of a collateral warranty. Similarly, though the point is not free from difficulty, English courts have held that "entire agreement" clauses do not necessarily preclude actions to enforce collateral agreements constituted by pre-contractual misrepresentations. The collateral agreement, arguably, is a separate contractual arrangement and thus not inconsistent with the clause.[20] On the other hand, enforcement of the collateral agreement is obviously inconsistent with the underlying purpose of the entire agreement clause and some courts have precluded enforcement on that ground.[21]

C. THE MEASURE OF RELIEF

The transformation from representation to term brings the representation into the remedial context of remedies for breach of contract. Thus, breach of a promise that the stated fact is true will give rise to a claim for damages calculated in the expectancy measure of relief. In the usual case, then, the plaintiff misrepresentee would be entitled to recover an amount of money calculated so as to place the plaintiff in the position he would have been in if the promise of the truth of the statement had been fulfilled.[22] The difference between the contractual measure of damages and the damages that might be available in tort for fraudulent or negligent misstatement can be quite striking, as may be illustrated by the facts of *Leaf v. International Galleries*.[23] In this case, the plaintiff buyer bought a painting from the defendant for eighty-five pounds. It was a painting of Salisbury Cathedral, represented by the seller to be by the artist Constable. When, in due course, the painting was discovered by the buyer not to be a Constable, the buyer sought rescission of the contract, a claim that failed on grounds of lateness. The claim in tort for misrepresentation, however, if it had been available, would have yielded damages calculated by subtracting from eighty-five pounds the value of the painting actually received. The plaintiff would be placed back in his pre-contract position. However, if the representation were considered to be a collateral warranty sounding in contractual damages,

---

20 See, for example, *McGrath v. Shah* (1987), 57 P. & C.R. 452. See also *Brikom Investments Ltd. v. Carr*, [1979] Q.B. 467 at 480 (C.A.), Lord Denning M.R.

21 See, for example, *Inntrepreneur Pub. Co. v. East Crown*, [2000] 2 Lloyd's Rep. 611 at 614.

22 See generally Chapter 22.

23 [1950] 2 K.B. 86 (C.A.).

the expectancy measure of relief would yield whatever (presumably impressive) amount was needed to buy an actual Constable painting of Salisbury Cathedral, less eighty-five pounds.

On the other hand, if the undertaking is construed as being one to provide truthful or carefully researched information and the provision of truthful or carefully researched information would have persuaded the misrepresentee to refuse to enter the agreement, the tort and contractual measures may coincide. Thus, in *Esso Petroleum Co. v. Mardon*[24] itself, if the implicit undertaking that the estimate of the volume of business or through-put had been carefully done were true, it would reveal that the proposed transaction was not a profitable one and, accordingly, the prospective tenant would have refused to enter the lease. Thus, the contractual measure of relief would place the tenant in the position he would have been in if he had not entered the lease. To accomplish this objective, he would be awarded his out-of-pocket losses, a measure of relief that would be similar to that available in a tort claim on the theory of a negligent misrepresentation that the study was carefully undertaken.[25] Similarly, where the effect of the representation is to warrant that a particular task need not be undertaken as part of a larger project, the contract and tort measures may coincide. In *BG Checo International Limited v. British Columbia Hydro and Power Authority*,[26] a claim brought by a construction company hired to construct a hydro line, the employer had warranted to the contractor that the clearing of the site had been undertaken and completed by another party. The contractor was held entitled to recover the cost of doing that work but not a profit component. Awarding the latter would place the contractor in a better position than if the contract had been performed. If the site had been cleared, no profit would have been earned on the extra work of clearing the site. The same measure of relief — out-of-pocket loss — would be available in a claim for tort damages on the basis that the underlying representation was made negligently.

D. CONTRACTUAL REPRESENTATIONS

Under the foregoing analysis, a pre-contractual misrepresentation may be characterized as a warranty that is either enforceable as a term of a unilateral collateral contract that is ancillary to the main contract or,

---

24   Above note 16.
25   *Ibid.* at 820–21.
26   [1993] 1 S.C.R. 12.

indeed, as a term of the main contract itself. Representations may also appear as explicit warranties in an agreement. Indeed, it is a commonplace drafting technique to set out "representations" in commercial agreements. In a typical transaction for the sale of a business involving a sale of the assets of the business, for example, there will be a provision, perhaps titled "Representations and Warranties," providing more or less the following: "The Vendor represents and warrants to the Purchaser as follows and acknowledges that the Purchaser is relying on such representations and warranties in connection with its purchase of the Purchased Assets."

The provision will then go on to stipulate numerous representations and warranties dealing with such matters as the fact that the vendor is validly incorporated, that the annexed financial statements are accurate, that the vendor has title to the purchased assets, and so on. As these few examples suggest, many of the subparagraphs will consist of simple statements of fact rather than promises. If the agreement is carefully drawn, it will further stipulate, perhaps elsewhere in the agreement, the remedial consequences that arise, if any of the "representations and warranties" should prove to be false. Thus, it may be stipulated that the purchaser's obligation to close the transaction is conditioned upon the "representations and warranties of the vendor contained in this agreement being true and correct." The vendor's solicitor may insist that the phrase "in all material respects" be added in an attempt to confine the vendor's obligation to serious and important inaccuracies. The agreement may go on to provide explicitly that non-compliance by the vendor enables the purchaser to refuse to close the transaction and to terminate the contractual relationship of the parties.

Use of the verb "represents" in such provisions does not lead to the conclusion that the representations are mere representations and not proper terms (i.e., undertakings) of the contract. Such representations are terms of the contract in the sense that they are the subject of a promise that they are true, and accordingly, when the statements prove to be false, they give rise to the normal remedies for breach of contract. Thus, the representee will be entitled to claim for damages for breach of contract, calculated on the contractual measure and, if the breach is repudiatory in nature, may elect to disaffirm or terminate the agreement.[27] It is entirely possible, however, that the parties might

---

27   See generally Chapters 15 and 22. This point has recently been reaffirmed by the Supreme Court of Canada in *Guarantee Co. of North America v. Gordon Capital Corp.* (1999), 178 D.L.R. (4th) 1 (S.C.C.), especially para. 44. In an *obiter dictum*, however, Bastarache J. went on to suggest that when one is entitled to

stipulate for some other remedial regime. Indeed, this issue has arisen in the recent decision of the Supreme Court of Canada in *Guarantee Co. of North America v. Gordon Capital Corp.*[28]

In *Gordon Capital*, an insurer contested its liability under a fidelity bond on the basis that the insured broker had made a misrepresentation in its application for the bond. The representations made in the application were explicitly incorporated within the bond and subject to an undertaking that "[t]he Insured represents that the information furnished in the application for this bond is complete, true and correct." The bond then further stipulated as follows: "Any misrepresentation, omission, concealment or incorrect statement of a material fact, in the application or otherwise, shall be grounds for the rescission of this bond."[29]

The insurer had learned of the false statement subsequent to the filing of a claim by the insured. Accordingly, the insurer argued that use of the term "rescission" enabled the insurer to rescind the bond *ab initio*, thus escaping all liability on the bond. The insured countered that, as the representation constituted a term of the contract, the misrepresentation gave rise only to a right on the part of the insurer to treat the misrepresentation as a repudiatory breach, thus giving it a right to disaffirm the contract and treat it as being at an end merely prospectively from the time of disaffirming. Thus, the bond would be enforceable at the time of filing the claim. The question before the Court, then, was whether use of the term "rescission" to stipulate the remedy for contractual misrepresentation in this agreement established an entitlement to the remedy of rescission *ab initio* in the equitable sense. As the Court observed, a simple reference to the concept of rescission is ambiguous. It is sometimes used to refer to a situation in which a repudiatory breach of contract is followed by an election by the victim to terminate the contract. It is also used to refer to the equitable remedy of setting

---

disaffirm an agreement for breach of a contractual representation, the contract will be void *ab initio*. See para. 47. This view is not supported, however, either by earlier authority or by the authors referred to and appears to incorrectly conflate the remedies for pre-contractual misrepresentation with those available for breach of contractual representations. The traditional view is that if a pre-contractual representation reappears as a term of the agreement, the remedies available when the now contractual representation proves false are those available for contractual breach, i.e., damages and, if the breach is repudiatory, an option to disaffirm the agreement. See, for example, *Woods v. Borstel* (1962), 34 D.L.R. (2d) 68 (Alta. S.C.A.D.). And see above this Chapter, section C.

28   *Guarantee Co. of North America v. Gordon Capital Corp., ibid.*
29   *Ibid.* at 17.

aside the agreement on the basis that it has been induced by a misrepresentation. Although the Court noted that the term "rescission," in proper usage, refers to the equitable remedy for misrepresentation, the Court went on to observe as follows: "Since 'rescission' has frequently been used to describe an accepted repudiation, courts must be sensitive to the potential for misuse. To that end, courts must analyse the entire context of the contract and give effect, where possible, to the intent of the parties. If they intended 'rescission' to mean 'an accepted repudiation,' then the contract should be interpreted as such."[30]

In the context of the fidelity insurance contract in issue, however, it was the Court's view that since rescission was coupled with the concept of misrepresentation and since the agreement also provided for the return of premiums paid by the insured, the term "rescission" should be given its correct or ordinary meaning of equitable rescission *ab initio*. Moreover, in the Court's view, "[f]or sophisticated parties, it will take strong evidence to displace the meaning suggested by the parties' choice of language in the contract itself." On this basis, then, there appears to be a presumption, at least in the context of agreements drafted by sophisticated parties, that contractual provisions stipulating for the remedy of "rescission" for contractual misrepresentation will be interpreted as stipulating for a rescission *ab initio* rather than for termination of the agreement on the basis of an accepted repudiatory breach. In this case, the Court expressed no opinion on the question of whether, when a contract is "rescinded" on the basis of a contractual provision of this kind, damages would be available to the victim of the breach.[31] Obviously, however, the prudent drafting practice would be to stipulate clearly the consequences of a misrepresentation both in terms of its impact on the enforceability of various portions of the agreement and in its implications for liability for damages or other forms of contractual relief.

---

30   *Ibid.* at 16.
31   *Ibid.* at 17. On the one hand, contractual damages would not normally be available in the context of rescission for misrepresentation. See generally Chapter 10. On the other hand, however, the "misrepresentation" in such circumstances is, in fact, a breach of the contract and accordingly, as such, would normally give rise to a contractual damages remedy. Presumably, this conundrum should be resolved by, in similar fashion to the analysis of the rescission issue in this case, attempting to determine, in the particular contractual context, whether the parties intended to preclude or not preclude the victim of the breach from pursuing damages recovery in addition to the contractually-based "rescission."

E. CONCURRENT LIABILITY IN CONTRACT AND TORT

Representations of fact that have been made fraudulently or negligently may attract liability in damages in a tort claim. As we have also seen, misrepresentations that have induced agreements may be properly characterized as warranties in the form of a unilateral agreement collateral to the main agreement or as terms of the main agreement itself, thus making available to the misrepresentee the normal remedies for breach of contract. Further, we have noted that it is a common practice to draft an explicit term of an agreement giving an undertaking that a particular set of representations is true. In such circumstances, then, it may be asked whether the maker of the misrepresentation may be liable both in tort and in contract for the making of a particular false statement. The traditional doctrine, treating the question of whether an individual who has breached a contract in such fashion that the conduct also amounts to a tort that may be liable concurrently in both contract and tort, is rather subtle and complex.[32] As a general principle, the traditional doctrine held that once the parties had entered into a contractual relationship, the terms of the contract ought to provide the exclusive source of the parties' mutual rights and obligations. This principle was, in turn, subject to a number of limitations and exceptions of uncertain ambit. In recent years, however, this subject has been greatly simplified by the decision of the Supreme Court of Canada in *BG Checo International Ltd. v. British Columbia Hydro & Power Authority*.[33] In this case, the defendant tendered out a project involving the construction of a hydro line. The invitation to tender negligently misrepresented that a right of way for the line had been cleared by others. This negligent misstatement was repeated as a term of the construction contract entered into by the plaintiff, the successful bidder. In this case, the Supreme Court confirmed that the remedies available for the breach of contract constituted by the misrepresentation would be the normal contractual remedies for breach of contract. The Court went on to consider, however, whether it might be possible to claim tort damages in such a case if the breach of contract (i.e., the false representation) also constituted the tort of negligent misstatement. The *BG Checo* decision is the leading Canadian decision on concurrency of liability

---

32 See W. Poulton, "Contract or Tort" (1966) 82 Law Q. Rev. 346; G. Fridman, "The Interaction of Tort and Contract" (1977) 93 Law Q. Rev. 422.

33 Above note 26. And see M. Ogilvie, "Concurrent Liability in Contract and Tort: Cautionary Tales from the Supreme Court of Canada" (1997) J. Bus. L. 372.

in tort and contract where a breach of contract also constitutes tortious misconduct. For purposes of Canadian law, the Supreme Court swept aside the remarkable complexity of the traditional doctrine of concurrent liability and adopted a straightforward principle that parties who are guilty of tortious misconduct when breaching a contract will be liable concurrently in contract and tort, unless the agreement between the parties stipulates to the contrary. A dissenting opinion in this case evidenced some lingering attraction to the traditional approach. Iacobucci J. would have held that if the tortious misconduct also constituted a breach of an express contractual term, the liability in contract would extinguish liability in tort.[34] On this view, where the contractual liability was based on an implied term — such as an implied term to exercise reasonable skill and care — concurrent liability in tort would be preserved. In the majority view, this consequence was perverse. It would be unsatisfactory to deny concurrent liability in the context of an express term but impose it in cases where the contractual obligation was so obviously implicit in the relationship that it had not been made the subject of an express term.

In the context of a contractual misrepresentation, then, if the misrepresentation is either fraudulently or negligently false, the party in breach will be vulnerable to claims in both contract and tort. Concurrent liability in contract and tort is not limited, of course, to breaches of contract that constitute fraudulent or negligent misstatement. The fraudulent or negligent performance of any obligation could attract concurrent liability in tort. In portraying a picture of the remedies available in the context of terms of agreements that set forth representations, however, it is important to note the possible existence of the tort remedy. Tort liability for contractual misrepresentation is, however, subject to the application of any terms of the agreement limiting or precluding tortious liability.[35]

FURTHER READINGS

D.K. ALLEN, *Misrepresentation* (London: Sweet & Maxwell, 1988) c. 5.

P.S. ATIYAH, *Essays on Contract* (Oxford: Clarendon Press, 1980) c. 10.

---

34   *BG Checo International Ltd. v. British Columbia Hydro & Power Authority, ibid.* at 67–69.

35   For discussion of provisions limiting liability for pre-contractual misrepresentations see Chapter 10, section G. And see generally Chapter 20.

J. BLOM, "Tort Recovery for Economic Loss and the Intersection between Contract and Tort" (1996) 54(3) The Advocate 367.

M. BRIDGE, "The Overlap of Tort and Contract" (1982) 27 McGill L.J. 872.

J. CARTWRIGHT, *Misrepresentation* (London: Sweet & Maxwell, 2002) c. 6.

F. DAWSON, "Parol Evidence, Misrepresentation and Collateral Contracts" (1982) 27 McGill L.J. 403.

G.H.L. FRIDMAN, "The Interaction of Tort and Contract" (1977) 93 Law Q. Rev. 422.

D.W. MCLAUCHLAN, "The Inconsistent Collateral Contract" (1976) 3 Dal. L.J. 136.

B. MORGAN, "The Negligent Contract Breaker" (1980) 58 Can. Bar Rev. 299.

M.H. OGILVIE, "Concurrent Liability in Contract and Tort: Cautionary Tales from the Supreme Court of Canada" (1977) J. Bus. L. 372.

ONTARIO LAW REFORM COMMISSION, *Report on Amendment of the Law of Contract* (Toronto: Ministry of the Attorney General, 1987) c. 12.

ONTARIO LAW REFORM COMMISSION, *Report on Consumer Warranties and Guarantees in the Sale of Goods* (Toronto: Ministry of the Attorney General, 1972).

W. POULTON, "Contract or Tort" (1966) 82 Law Q. Rev. 346.

K.W. WEDDERBURN, "Collateral Contracts" (1959) Cambridge L.J. 58.

PART FIVE

INTERPRETATION OF AGREEMENTS

GENERAL PRINCIPLES OF INTERPRETATION

A. INTRODUCTION

The law of contracts provides an institutional framework within which parties who wish to do so can establish an enforceable agreement giving effect to their mutual intentions. The law of interpretation of agreements addresses the difficult task of determining, on the basis of the parties' actual agreement, what those intentions should be considered to be. The process of interpretation is an exercise of giving meaning to the terms adopted by the parties in formulating their agreement.[1] It is often said that the process of interpretation is an exercise in attempting to ascertain the "true intentions" of the parties. In *Consolidated-Bathurst Export Ltd. v. Mutual Boiler & Machinery Insurance Co.*,[2] for example, Estey J. observed as follows: "the normal rules of construction lead a court to search for an interpretation of which, from the whole of the contract, would appear to promote or advance the true intent of the parties at the time of entry into the contract."[3]

---

1   See generally K. Lewison, *The Interpretation of Contracts,* 3d ed. (London: Sweet & Maxwell, 2004). See also E.W. Patterson, "The Interpretation and Construction of Contracts" (1964) 64 Colum. L. Rev. 833; R. Sullivan, "Interpreting Contracts in Practice and Theory" (2000) 13 Sup. Ct. L. Rev. (2d) 369.

2   (1979), 112 D.L.R. (3d) 49 (S.C.C.).

3   *Ibid.* at 58.

For a variety of reasons, however, the "true intentions" of the parties may be an elusive quarry. As a matter of fact, in a particular case, the parties might have quite different intentions at the time of contracting, with respect to the meaning or significance of various aspects of their arrangements. The agreement may be entered into on the basis of a standard or printed form that at least one of the parties and perhaps both of them have neither read nor, if read, understood. The meaning of individual terms or phrases in the agreement may be obscure and may not have been clearly considered by the parties at the time of contract formation. The language employed may be ambiguous. The parties may have attached different meanings to particular terms of the agreement.

It would not be sensible for courts, in many if not all of these kinds of circumstances, simply to throw up their hands and conclude that since the "true intentions" of the parties cannot be established, the contract has no meaning and will not be enforced. Inescapably, then, the process of construction or interpretation of agreements must have an objective component, enabling the interpreter to attribute meaning to the agreement even in the absence of "true intentions." Such an approach could rest and does in fact to some extent rest on a presumption that the parties intended the terms of the agreement be given their literal meaning regardless of whether either party understood that meaning at the time of contract formation. Taken to an extreme, this objective or literal approach would simply render the actual intentions of the parties irrelevant.

The law of interpretation, however, does not exclusively embrace either the subjective or objective perspective. On the contrary, the law of contract interpretation represents a subtle blend of subjective and objective elements attempting to determine what the parties probably did intend on the one hand and, on the other hand, relying on objective methods of interpretation to settle points of difficulty that cannot be resolved on a more subjective basis. Thus, for example, it is traditionally accepted that it is appropriate to look at the parties' objectives in entering into the transaction to determine how to interpret a particular provision of the agreement. The approach is to determine what the parties actually intended the agreement to mean. However, a party that wishes to assert that the agreement means something other than the meaning conveyed by a literal interpretation of the terms used faces the full weight of the objective element in the law of contract interpretation.

In this chapter and in Chapters 20 and 21, the law of interpretation is subdivided into five separate topics. In section B of this chapter, we consider first the law concerning the sources that may be examined for the purpose of interpreting an agreement. Although the law of interpretation applies, in principle, to both written and oral agreements, the rules of interpretation have developed principally in the context of interpreting written agreements. The first question to be addressed, then, is to determine the nature of other documents or factual information — often referred to as "extrinsic aids" — that may be examined to assist in the interpretation of the written agreement. We will then turn to consider the traditional principles or maxims, canons or guidelines to interpretation that provide the interpreter with some assistance in the exercise of attributing meaning to the terms of an agreement. In section D of this chapter, we consider the basis upon which courts imply terms in agreements, typically to fill gaps in the agreement left by the parties. As we shall see, the process of implication is sometimes one of giving effect to the "true intentions" of the parties but probably more often is an exercise in attributing hypothetical intentions to parties that they would, as reasonable persons, have articulated if they had considered the matter in question. Indeed, in a certain range of cases, courts imply terms in agreements that may be considered to be imposed as a matter of judicial policy rather than inferred from the actual or hypothetical intentions of the parties. Two discrete problems that have attracted much judicial discussion will be given separate treatment in Chapters 20 and 21. In Chapter 20, an account is given of the history and current status of the doctrine of fundamental breach, a doctrine that has developed with respect to the interpretation or control of the use of exculpatory or limitations clauses. In Chapter 21, the question of whether, under Canadian common law, courts have fashioned a doctrine requiring parties to perform their obligations in good faith will be examined. As will be suggested, it appears that such a doctrine is slowly emerging in the form of an implied term to this effect.

B. SOURCES

1) Introduction

The first step in the process of interpretation is to identify the target of interpretation, the communications between the parties that constitute the terms of their agreement. In the typical case, the object of interpretation will be an agreement between the parties that has been recorded in writing. As we have seen, the parties will be bound by the terms of a written agreement that they have signed[4] or, indeed, by the

---

4   See Chapter 6, section C(3).

terms of an unsigned document that they nonetheless had reason to believe constituted the terms of the agreement being formed.[5] Agreements may also be composed, however, of more than one document or of a document or documents combined with oral communications between the parties. It is at this stage of the analysis — identification of the target of interpretation — that the parol evidence rule becomes relevant. As we have seen,[6] the parol evidence rule holds, essentially, that where a written agreement has been entered into by the parties with an intention that it constitute the exclusive expression of their agreement, evidence that would tend to add, vary, supplement or contradict the terms of the written agreement is inadmissible. In a typical dispute under the parol evidence rule, one party will wish to rely on certain oral undertakings given in addition to the written agreement by the other party. The other party will insist that evidence of those undertakings is inadmissible on the basis of the rule. In such contests, the role of the rule is to assist in determining the identity of the materials that constitute the agreement between the parties. In our discussion of the rule, we noted the existence of numerous exceptions to the principle of inadmissibility. Further, we noted that the parol evidence rule does not preclude the admissibility of evidence used as an aid in interpretation or construction of agreements. The rules concerning the admissibility of evidence that can be relied upon by courts in aid of interpretation of the agreements, which are the focus of discussion here, thus operate independently of the rule. Thus, for example, if a court is entitled under the rule considered below[7] to admit and consider evidence relating to the circumstances surrounding the formation of the transaction, including the "aim" and "genesis" of the transaction, that evidence is admissible whether or not the written agreement entered into by the parties is subject to the parol evidence rule. Against this background, then, we turn to consider the principal sources to which a court is permitted to turn to provide assistance in the interpretation or construction of an agreement.

2) Commercial Setting or Background

In attempting to determine the correct interpretation of contractual provisions, courts may have regard to the surrounding circumstances or commercial context of the agreement. Accordingly, evidence of the

---

5   See Chapter 6, section C(2).
6   See Chapter 6, section D.
7   See below this Chapter, section B(2).

commercial setting or "factual matrix" of the agreement as opposed to the subjective intentions of the parties is admissible. Lord Wilberforce stated the basic principle in *Reardon Smith Line Ltd. v. Yngvar Hansen-Tangen*[8] in the following terms:

> No contracts are made in a vacuum: there is always a setting in which they have to be placed. The nature of what is legitimate to have regard to is usually described as "the surrounding circumstances" but this phrase is imprecise: it can be illustrated but hardly defined. In a commercial contract it is certainly right that the court should know the commercial purpose of the contract and this in turn presupposes knowledge of the genesis of the transaction, the background, the context, the market in which the parties are operating.[9]

Similarly, in *Prenn v. Simmonds*,[10] Lord Wilberforce stated: "[T]he time has long since passed when agreements ... were isolated from the matrix of facts in which they were set and interpreted purely on internal linguistic considerations."[11] English law was not to be considered to have been "left behind in some island of literal interpretation."[12] In particular, regard may be had to "evidence of the 'genesis' and objectively the 'aim' of the transaction."[13] Canadian courts routinely admit evidence of surrounding circumstances on this basis.[14]

Evidence of surrounding circumstances may obviously have a critical role in the interpretation of particular terms. Words often derive

---

8   [1976] 1 W.L.R. 989 (H.L.). See also *Charrington & Co. v. Wooder*, [1914] A.C. 71 at 82–83, Lord Dunedin.

9   *Reardon Smith Line Ltd. v. Yngvar Hansen-Tangen, ibid.* at 995–96, placing reliance *inter alia* on *Utica City National Bank v. Gunn*, 118 N.E. 607 at 608 (N.Y. 1918), Cardozo J. (indicating the relevance of "the genesis and aim of the transaction"). This passage has received the approval of Canadian courts. See, for example, *Hi-Tech Group Inc. v. Sears Canada Inc.* (2001), 52 O.R. (3d) 97 (C.A.).

10 [1971] 1 W.L.R. 1381 (H.L.).

11 *Ibid.* at 1383–84, placing reliance on *River Wear Commissioners v. Adamson* (1877), 2 App. Cas. 743 at 763, Lord Blackburn.

12 *Prenn v. Simmonds, ibid.* at 1384.

13 *Ibid.* at 1385. For approval of this passage by Canadian courts, see, for example, *Canada Square Corp. v. Versafood Services Ltd.* (1981), 130 D.L.R. (3d) 205 at 215–16; *Atlific (Nfld.) Ltd. v. Hotel Buildings Ltd.* (1994), 120 Nfld. & P.E.I.R. 91 (Nfld. C.A.), leave to appeal to S.C.C. refused (1995), 185 N.R. 400n.

14 See, for example, *Canada Law Book Co. v. Boston Book Co.* (1922), 64 S.C.R. 182 at 185, Duff J. and at 200–1, Anglin J.; *Wenzoski v. Klos*, [1940] 1 W.W.R. 523 (Man. C.A.); *Qualico Developments Ltd. v. Calgary (City)*, [1987] 5 W.W.R. 361 (Alta. Q.B.); *Privest Properties Ltd. v. Foundation Co. of Canada Ltd.* (1977), 145 D.L.R. (4th) 729 (B.C.C.A.); *Toronto-Dominion Bank v. Leigh Instruments Ltd. (Trustee of)* (1999), 178 D.L.R. (4th) 634 at 639.

their precise meaning from their use in a particular context. Discernment of the particular meaning attributed to words by the parties will often depend on an appreciation of the aims and objectives of the transaction. It has recently been suggested that the concept of surrounding circumstances is not adequately captured by the phrase "factual matrix." In *Investors Compensation Scheme Ltd. v. West Bromwich Building Society*,[15] Lord Hoffmann sought to improve upon Lord Wilberforce's use of that expression in the following terms: "The background was famously referred to by Lord Wilberforce as the 'matrix of fact' but this phrase is, if anything, an understated description of what the background may include. Subject to the requirement that it should have been reasonably available to the parties … it includes absolutely anything which would have affected the way in which language of the document would have been understood by a reasonable man."[16]

As a practical matter, it is not clear that this seemingly broader definition of the concept of commercial background or surrounding circumstances would have a dramatic impact on the scope of the admissibility of evidence concerning such matters. The most important limiting factor on the admissibility of such evidence, as Lord Hoffman himself noted in the *Investors Compensation Scheme Ltd. v. West Bromwich Building Society* case,[17] is that evidence of the subjective intentions of a party is inadmissible and must be distinguished from the factual matrix.[18] One party's declaration of subjective intent is not considered material to the determination of the common intention of the parties. Moreover, such evidence is likely to be suspect on the basis that it is self-serving.[19]

Evidence of the factual matrix is not dependent upon a finding that the agreement is ambiguous in some respect. Evidence concerning the surrounding circumstances of the transaction is always admissible. Indeed, when the words of the agreement are viewed in the light cast by the surrounding circumstances, ambiguity, sometimes referred to

---

15   [1998] 1 W.L.R. 896 (H.L.).

16   *Ibid.* at 912–13. See also *B.C.C.I. v. Ali*, [2002] 1 A.C. 251 at 269, Lord Hoffmann; *Sirius International Insurance Co. (Publ) v. FAI General Insurance Ltd.*, [2005] 1 All E.R. 191 at 199–201 (H.L.), Lord Steyn. For discussion, see G.R. Hall, "A Curious Incident in the Law of Contract: The Impact of 22 Words from the House of Lords" (2004) 40 Can. Bus. L.J. 20.

17   [1998] 1 W.L.R. 896 at 912–13.

18   *Prenn v. Simmonds*, above note 10 at 1385; *Eli Lilly and Co. v. Novopharm Ltd.* (1998), 161 D.L.R. (4th) 1 at para. 54. See also *White v. Central Trust Co.* (1984), 7 D.L.R. (4th) 236 at 248 (N.B.C.A.), La Forest J.

19   See Sir C. Staughton, "How Do the Courts Interpret Commercial Contracts?" [1999] Cambridge L.J. 303 at 304–6.

as a "latent" ambiguity, may be uncovered.[20] When a latent ambiguity has been revealed, the courts may obviously examine and consider the sources permitted by the ordinary rules of interpretation. In addition, however, it has been held that in the case of a latent ambiguity that a court may examine directly the intentions of the parties.[21]

3) Prior Negotiations, Drafts and Antecedent Agreements

As a general rule, evidence of the prior negotiations of the parties is inadmissible for the purpose of construing the eventual agreement. There are two reasons underlying this general principle. First, as we have seen,[22] evidence of the subjective intentions of a party is inadmissible on the ground that it is irrelevant to the task of determining the intentions of both parties and, more particularly, to the task of determining what the other party would reasonably have understood the contract to mean. To the extent that a party may seek to introduce evidence of preliminary negotiations in order to establish the existence of subjective intentions, the evidence would be inadmissible on the same ground. The principal rationale for excluding such evidence, however, is that it is generally irrelevant to the task of determining the nature of the final consensus of the parties. In *Prenn v. Simmonds*,[23] Lord Wilberforce provided the following explanation:

> The reason for not admitting evidence of these exchanges is not a technical one or even mainly one of convenience (though the attempt to admit it did greatly prolong the case and add to its expense). It is simply that such evidence is unhelpful. By the nature of things, where negotiations are difficult, the parties' positions, with each passing letter, are changing and until the final agreement, though converging, still divergent. It is only the final document which records a consensus. If the previous documents use different expressions, how does construction of those expressions, itself a doubtful process, help on

---

20   *Alampi v. Swartz*, [1964] 1 O.R. 488 (C.A.); *Leitch Gold Mines Ltd. v. Texas Gulf Sulphur Co.* (1968), [1969] 1 O.R. 469, 3 D.L.R. (3d) 161 (H.C.J.); *Trans-Canada Pipelines Ltd. v. Northern & Central Gas Corp.* (1983), 41 O.R. (2d) 447 at 452 (C.A.), Cory J.A.; *Arthur Andersen Inc. v. Toronto-Dominion Bank* (1994), 17 O.R. (3d) 363 at 372 (C.A.), Grange and McKinlay JJ.A. For discussion of the *Texas Gulf Sulphur* case, see P. Perell, "The Ambiguity Exception to the Parol Evidence Rule" (2001) 36 Can. Bus. L.J. 21.

21   See, for example, *The Curfew*, [1891] P. 131; *Bank of New Zealand v. Simpson*, [1900] A.C. 182; *Leitch Gold Mines Ltd. v. Texas Gulf Sulphur Co.*, *ibid.* at 527–28 (O.R.).

22   See above this Chapter, section B(2).

23   Above note 10.

the construction of the contractual words? If the same expressions are used, nothing is gained by looking back; indeed, something may be lost since the relevant surrounding circumstances may be different. And at this stage there is no consensus of the parties to appeal to.[24]

Lord Wilberforce, however, did concede that previous documents could be examined in order to determine the commercial or business object of the agreement[25] but he was insistent that the prior negotiations could not be looked to for evidence of the objective of one of the parties. As Lord Wilberforce noted, in the realm of contractual negotiation, parties often have to be satisfied with less than they want and, accordingly, "it would be a matter of speculation how far the common intention was that the particular objective should be realized."[26] In his view, therefore, the Court of Appeal had erred in admitting evidence of the particular concerns of one of the negotiating parties. Canadian courts have applied this reasoning in excluding evidence of previous negotiations.[27] In *Craighampton Investments Ltd. v. Ayerswood Developments Ltd.*,[28] the Ontario Court of Appeal observed: "it verges on idle activity for a court to rehash the negotiations, activities and conduct of the parties and hear their now professed expression of what their intentions were at an earlier time."[29]

Drawing the line between evidence concerning surrounding circumstances, including the "aim" and "genesis" of the transaction, as opposed to evidence of "subjective intentions," may prove to be a subtle matter in some cases. Thus, earlier correspondence may be admissible to establish the aim of the transaction[30] but inadmissible for the purpose of establishing subjective intention.[31] Moreover, the fact that the parties were engaged in negotiations and the reasons for those negotiations may well constitute admissible evidence of the commercial objectives of the parties as part of the factual matrix of the agreement.[32]

---

24   *Ibid.* at 1384–85.

25   *Ibid.* at 1385.

26   *Ibid.*

27   See, for example, *Black Swan Mines v. Goldbelt Resources Ltd.*, [1997] 1 W.W.R. 605 (B.C.C.A.); *Kentucky Fried Chicken v. Scott's Food Service Inc.* (1998), 41 B.L.R. (2d) 42 (Ont. C.A.). See also *Toronto-Dominion Bank v. Leigh Instruments Ltd. (Trustee of)* (1998), 40 B.L.R. (2d) 1 at 105–9, Winkler J.

28   (1984), 4 O.A.C. 124 (C.A.).

29   *Ibid.* at 126, MacKinnon A.C.J.O.

30   *Re Broughton Collieries Ltd.*, [1944] 1 D.L.R. 530 (N.S.C.A.).

31   *Black Swan Mines v. Goldbelt Resources*, above note 27.

32   *Langley Lo-Cost Builders Ltd. v. 474835 B.C. Ltd.*, [2000] 7 W.W.R. 46 at 54 (B.C.C.A.), McEachern C.J.B.C.

Indeed, it may be that the rule could usefully be reformulated in terms of its rationale. Rather than suggesting that there is a blanket exclusion of evidence concerning prior negotiations, it may be preferable to hold that such evidence is generally inadmissible but may be admitted where it is relevant either to show the aim and genesis of the transaction or, stating the point more generally, where it may be of assistance in the interpretation of the terms of the agreement. Thus, a New Zealand judge has recently suggested that a prior draft of the agreement might be of assistance in determining the meaning, from an objective and reasonable point of view, of the words of the eventual agreement.[33] The American rule is framed in these terms.[34]

Preliminary drafts of the eventual agreement are, as evidence included within the concept of prior negotiations, generally inadmissible for the reasons identified above. Antecedent *agreements* are, however, another matter. If, as suggested in *Prenn v. Simmonds*,[35] the rationale for excluding prior negotiations, including draft agreements, is that they are irrelevant to the task of determining the nature of the final consensus of the parties, the same objection cannot be made to antecedent agreements. Thus, there are some authorities indicating that antecedent agreements may be admissible.[36] Where it is clear that the subsequent agreement is intended to supersede rather than merely implement the earlier agreement, however, the earlier agreement will obviously be of limited assistance.[37]

4) Subsequent Conduct of the Parties

Both Canadian and English courts have differed, over time, on their approach to the question of whether the evidence considering the subsequent conduct of the parties to an agreement is admissible for the purpose of interpreting their agreement. In English law, it now appears

---

33   *Yoshimoto v. Canterbury Golf International Ltd.*, [2001] 1 N.Z.L.R. 523. See also G. McMeel "Prior Negotiations and Subsequent Conduct" (2002) 119 Law Q. Rev. 272.

34   See American Law Institute, *Restatement of Contracts 2d* (St. Paul: American Law Institute, 1981) s. 214(c) ("Agreements and negotiations prior to or contemporaneous with the adoption of a writing are admissible in evidence to establish ... (c) the meaning of the writing....").

35   Above note 10.

36   See, for example, *Punjab National Bank v. de Boinville*, [1992] 1 W.L.R. 1138 at 1149 (C.A.), Staughton L.J.

37   *H.I.H. Casualty & General Insurance Ltd. v. New Hampshire Insurance Co.*, [2001] 2 Lloyd's Rep. 161 at 179, Rix L.J.

to be settled, as a result of the decision of the House of Lords in *James Miller & Partners Ltd. v. Whitworth Street Estates (Manchester) Ltd.*[38] that it is not legitimate to examine subsequent conduct of the parties as an aid in construction of the agreement. Canadian courts, however, have been more willing to consider subsequent conduct of the parties as being of some assistance in determining the proper construction of the agreement. Thus, in a Saskatchewan case,[39] Thomson J. observed that in the attempt to resolve an ambiguity in an agreement, "there's no better way of determining what the parties intended than to look at what they did under it."[40] Lambert J.A. of the British Columbia Court of Appeal offered the following summary of the Canadian position in *Re Canadian National Railway and Canadian Pacific Ltd.*:[41]

> In Canada the rule with respect to subsequent conduct is that if, after considering the agreement itself, including the particular words used in their immediate context and in the context of the agreement as a whole, there remain two reasonable alternative interpretations, then certain additional evidence may be both admitted and taken to have legal relevance if that additional evidence will help to determine which of the two reasonable alternative interpretations is the correct one. It certainly makes no difference to the law in this respect if the continuing existence of two reasonable alternative interpretations after an examination of the agreement as a whole is described as doubt or as ambiguity or as uncertainty or as difficulty of construction.[42]

Although there is an Alberta decision expressing scepticism with respect to the approach described by Lambert J.A.,[43] the majority view

---

38 [1970] A.C. 583.
39 *Bank of Montreal v. University of Saskatchewan* (1953), 9 W.W.R. (N.S.) 193 (Sask. Q.B.).
40 *Ibid.* at 199.
41 (1978), 95 D.L.R. (3d) 242 (B.C.C.A.).
42 *Ibid.* at 262. See also *Leitch Gold Mines Ltd. v. Texas Gulf Sulphur Co.*, above note 20 at 238 (D.L.R.), Gale C.J.O.; also *Manitoba Development Corporation v. Columbia Forest Products Ltd.*, [1974] 2 W.W.R. 237 (Man. C.A.); *Delisle v. Bulman Group Ltd.*, [1991] 4 W.W.R. 637 (B.C.S.C.); *Arrowhon Exploration Ltd. v. Northstar Energy Corp.* (1993), 108 D.L.R. (4th) 709 (Alta. Q.B.); *Palasky v. Palasky* (1993), 89 Man. R. (2d) 1 (Q.B.); *1043545 Ontario Inc. v. 2748355 Canada Inc.* (1998), 19 R.P.R. (3d) 190 (Ont. Ct. Gen. Div.); *Norton v. Margesson* (2001), 47 R.P.R. (3d) 237 (Ont. S.C.J.); *Weyerhauser Can. v. IWA Can., Local 1-207* (2003), 16 Alta. L.R. (4th) 321 (Q.B.).
43 *Paddon-Hughes Development Co. v. Chiles Estate*, [1992] 3 W.W.R. 519 (Alta Q.B.). See also *Northwestern Mechanical Installations Ltd. v. Yukon Construction Co.* (1982), 136 D.L.R. (3d) 685 (Alta C.A.).

appears to be that evidence of subsequent conduct of the parties is admissible for the purpose of resolving difficulties in the interpretation of an agreement. The Ontario Court of Appeal, for example, clearly accepted this proposition in *Montreal Trust Co. of Canada v. Birmingham Lodge Ltd.*[44] In this case, the court was required to interpret a debenture that stipulated that "as between the Guarantors and the Lender the guarantors shall be considered as primarily liable."[45] In construing this provision, the court derived assistance from the subsequent conduct of the lender in describing the guarantors simply as a guarantor and not as a primary debtor in subsequent offers to renew the mortgage on the subject property. The court quoted with approval the passages set out above from Thomson J. and Lambert J.A. and indicated that subsequent conduct may be used to interpret a written agreement because it offers evidence of the meaning the parties attributed to the agreement after its execution and, by reasonable inference, what might have been intended at the time of execution.

5) Related Agreements

Many transactions, especially large commercial transactions such as the purchase and sale of a large and complex business, may involve the execution of several agreements. In such contexts, it is an interesting question, then, whether in the interpretation of one of the agreements, regard may be had to the others. The basic principle is that such regard may be had only where the agreements essentially form components of one larger transaction. Where each agreement is entered into on the faith of the others being executed and where it is intended that each agreement form part of a larger composite whole, assistance in the interpretation of any particular agreement may be drawn from the related agreements.[46] Thus, in *Mechanical Pin Resetter Co. Ltd. v. Canadian Acme Screw & Gear Ltd.*,[47] the Supreme Court of Canada read together four interrelated agreements in order to give content to the geographical scope of a licence to manufacture conferred in one of them.

44 (1995), 24 O.R. (3d) 97 at 100 (C.A.), Laskin J.A. See also *Arthur Andersen Inc. v. Toronto-Dominion Bank,* above note 20 at 372.
45 *Montreal Trust Co. of Canada v. Birmingham Lodge Ltd., ibid.* at 105.
46 See, for example, *Smith v. Chadwick* (1882), 20 Ch. D. 27 at 62, Jessel M.R.; *Samuel v. Jarrah Timber and Wood Paving Corp. Ltd.,* [1904] A.C. 323.
47 [1971] S.C.R. 628. See also *McKnight v. Robertson* (1910), 17 O.W.R. 454 (C.A.); *Cooke v. Anderson and Anderson,* [1945] 2 D.L.R. 698 at 707 (Alta. S.C.A.D.), Ford J.A.; *Tsiribis v. Panopoulos* (1981), 21 R.P.R. 58 (Ont. H.C.J.).

6) The Meaning of Words

The words used in an agreement are normally to be construed in accord with their "natural"[48] or ordinary or, as has been said, in their "plain ordinary and popular sense."[49] Where useful in determining the nature of that meaning, courts may make reference to standard dictionary definitions.[50] References to standard dictionaries are commonplace in the reported decisions. Where agreements contain technical or scientific terms, courts may admit evidence of their meaning.[51] Agreements drafted by lawyers will often include legal terms of art. Such terms are to be interpreted in accord with their technical meaning in law.[52] Evidence may be admitted to indicate that the parties utilized particular terms in a specialized sense[53] or in accord with customary usage in a particular trade.[54] Where it is evident from the face of the agreement that the parties have used a term with their own particular meaning[55] or where the parties have stipulated definitions for terms in the agreement[56] courts will give effect to the parties' special use of the terms in question.

C. CANONS OF CONSTRUCTION

1) Introduction

In this section, we examine the traditional principles or maxims or canons of construction. Although the canons are often referred to as principles or rules, they are not rules in any meaningful sense. They are, rather, guidelines or aids to interpretation that may suggest fruitful

---

48 *North Eastern Rwy. Co. v. Hastings*, [1900] A.C. 260 at 263 (H.L.), Earl of Halsbury L.C.

49 *Robertson v. French* (1803), 4 East 130 at 135, 102 E.R. 779, Lord Ellenborough C.J.

50 See, for example, *Marquis Camden v. Inland Revenue Commissioners*, [1914] 1 K.B. 641; *Mills v. Continental Bag & Paper Co.* (1918), 45 D.L.R. 389 (Ont. S.C.A.D.); *Milliken v. Young*, [1929] 3 D.L.R. 64 at 68–69 (Sask. C.A.), Martin J.A.

51 See, for example, *Shore v. Wilson* (1839), 9 Cl. & F. 355, 8 E.R. 450; *Baldwin & Francis Ltd. v. Patents Appeal Tribunal*, [1959] A.C. 663 (H.L.).

52 See, for example, *Sydall v. Castings Ltd.*, [1967] 1 Q.B. 302 (C.A.); *London & Lancashire Fire Insurance Co. Ltd. v. Bolands Ltd.*, [1924] A.C. 836 (H.L.).

53 See *Scragg v. United Kingdom Temperance & General Provident Institution*, [1976] 2 Lloyd's Rep. 227; *Lovell & Christmas Ltd. v. Wall* (1911), 104 L.T. 85.

54 *Provincial Insurance Co. v. Connolly* (1879), 5 S.C.R. 258 at 269–71, Henry J.; *Industrial & Technical Press v. Jack Canuck Publishing Co. Ltd.* (1920), 17 O.W.N. 409.

55 See, for example, *Lloyd v. Lloyd* (1837), 2 My. & Cr. 192, 40 E.R. 613.

56 See, for example, *Re George & The Goldsmiths & General Burglary Insurance Assoc. Ltd.*, [1899] 1 Q.B. 595.

lines of analysis but they rarely point in the direction of an inescapable conclusion. Further, in any case of interest, it is very likely that several canons will be engaged or relied upon by the parties, some pointing in one direction, some in the other. In short, the construction or interpretation of agreements is an art, not a science. The canons are the toolkit with which the artisan must work. The principal canons are briefly examined below.

2) Construction of the Agreement as a Whole

Agreements are to be construed in such fashion as to effectuate the intentions of the parties as can best be determined from the entirety of the agreement. Individual terms are thus to be construed in the light of their relationship to other parts of the agreement and the overall objectives of the agreement. In *BG Checo International Ltd. v. British Columbia Hydro & Power Authority*,[57] La Forest and McLachlin JJ. stated the basic principle in the following terms: "It is a cardinal rule of the construction of contracts that the various parts of the contract are to be interpreted in the context of the intentions of the parties as evident from the contract as a whole."[58]

Each term must be interpreted, to the extent that it may bear the appropriate meaning, harmoniously with the other terms of the agreement. Accordingly, when so construed, the term in question may bear a meaning other than its most obvious meaning.[59] In *McClelland & Stewart Ltd. v. Mutual Life*,[60] for example, the Supreme Court of Canada was required to construe a life insurance policy taken out by an author in favour of the plaintiff publisher. The issue in the case was whether the insurer, upon the death of the author, was exempt from liability under the policy as a result of the operation of a self-destruction clause. The clause excluded liability arising from self-destruction of the author within two years of the "effective date" of the policy. On a plain reading of the clause, together with the application form completed for the

---

57 [1993] 1 S.C.R. 12. See also *Milliken v. Young*, above note 50; *Morgan v. Hudson Bay Mining & Smelting Co.*, [1930] 2 D.L.R. 587 (Man. K.B.); *Cook v. Cook* (1968), 66 D.L.R. (2d) 285 (N.S.S.C.); *Bowater Newfoundland Ltd. v. Newfoundland & Labrador Hydro* (1978), 15 Nfld. & P.E.I.R. 301 (Nfld. C.A.); *Consolidated-Bathurst Export Ltd. v. Mutual Boiler & Machinery Insurance Co.*, [1980] 1 S.C.R. 888 at 901, Estey J.

58 *BG Checo International Ltd. v. British Columbia Hydro & Power Authority*, ibid. at 23–24.

59 See, for example, *Elderslie Steamship Co. Ltd. v. Borthwick*, [1905] A.C. 93.

60 [1981] 2 S.C.R. 6.

policy, a strong argument could be made that the effective date of the policy for purposes of the self-destruction clause was the date on which the policy had been delivered to the insured rather than the date to which the policy had been backdated by the parties. Dickson J., after noting that the terms, when read in isolation, offered strong support for the insurer's interpretation, nonetheless held that when the documents were construed in their entirety, the earlier date was the effective date of the policy for all purposes, including the proper interpretation of the self-destruction clause.

Further, a term that appears to have a plain meaning may, when construed in the context of the entire agreement, be rendered ambiguous.[61] In order to resolve the ambiguity, resort may then be made to other principles of interpretation or extrinsic aids. The principle of construction of the agreement as a whole also suggests that where a term is employed in various contexts in an agreement, regard may be had to all uses of the particular term. The use of a particular term in one portion of an agreement may obviously be of some assistance in clarifying the meaning of the same term in another part of the agreement.[62] However, there does not appear to be a rule of construction that particular words are presumed to be used consistently throughout an agreement.[63]

Construction of individual provisions in light of the intentions of the parties as manifest in the agreement as a whole may have the effect of resolving inconsistencies between terms. A standard technique for reconciling a conflict between a more general provision and one that deals inconsistently with a more specific matter is to read the latter provision as an exception to or qualification of the more general term. In *BG Checo*, for example, an agreement relating to the construction of a hydro transmission line provided that the defendant hydro authority was to clear the land on which the line was to be erected. A more general provision of the agreement, however, provided that the contractor assumed responsibility for satisfying himself as to site conditions and assumed responsibility for any misunderstandings with respect to the condition of the site. The contractor successfully claimed for losses resulting from the hydro authority's failure to have properly cleared the site on the basis that its more specific obligation to do so was an exception to the general exclusion of liability with respect to the condition of the work site.

---

61   *Hillis Oil & Sales Ltd. v. Wynn's Canada Ltd.*, [1986] 1 S.C.R. 57 at 66, Le Dain J.
62   *Re Birks*, [1900] 1 Ch. 417.
63   *Watson v. Haggitt*, [1928] A.C. 127. See also *National Trust Co. v. Palace Theatre Ltd.*, [1928] 2 D.L.R. 739 (Alta. S.C.A.D.).

3) Giving Effect to All Parts of the Agreement

The basic principle that terms are to be interpreted in the context of the entire agreement between the parties is often coupled with the instruction that effect should be given, if possible, to all parts of the agreement. No provision of the agreement, it is sometimes said, should be considered to be "otiose" or "redundant" or mere surplusage.[64] In *Re Strand Music Hall Co. Ltd.*,[65] Lord Romilly M.R. provided the following statement of the general principle: "The proper mode of construing any written instrument is, to give effect to every part of it, if this be possible, and not to strike out or nullify one clause in a deed, unless it be impossible to reconcile it with another in a more express clause in the same deed."[66] Thus, courts will lean against an interpretation of an agreement that will render one of the terms meaningless.[67] At the same time, it is appreciated that agreements, especially agreements drafted by lawyers, will often contain language that is duplicative as Lord Hoffmann recently suggested, as a result of the "lawyer's desire to be certain that every conceivable point has been covered."[68] For this reason, he suggested "the argument from redundancy is seldom an entirely secure one."[69]

4) Avoiding Commercially Unreasonable or Absurd Outcomes

In choosing among possible constructions of an agreement, courts will avoid an interpretation that produces a commercial result that is considered unreasonable. In *Consolidated-Bathurst Export Ltd. v. Mutual Boiler & Machinery Insurance Co.*,[70] Estey J. expressed the principle in the following terms: "Where words may bear two constructions, the more reasonable one, that which produces a fair result, must certainly be taken as the interpretation which would promote the intention of the parties. Similarly, an interpretation which defeats the intentions of

---

64   See, for example, *Wardle v. Manitoba Farms Loans Association*, [1954] 4 D.L.R. 572 at 578 (Man. C.A.), Adamson J.A., rev'd on other grounds [1955] 5 D.L.R. 673 (S.C.C.).

65   (1865), 35 Beav. 153, 55 E.R. 853.

66   *Ibid.* at 856 (E.R.).

67   See, for example, *Steinberg Inc. v. Tilak Corp.* (1991), 2 O.R. (3d) 165 at 168–69 (Gen. Div.).

68   *Beaufort Developments (N.I.) Ltd. v. Gilbert-Ash N.I. Ltd.*, [1999] 1 A.C. 266 at 274 (H.L.).

69   *Ibid.*

70   Above note 2. See also *Sirius International Insurance Co. (Publ) v. FAI General Insurance Ltd.*, above note 16.

the parties and their objective in entering into the commercial trans-action in the first place should be discarded in favour of an interpreta-tion of the policy which promotes a sensible commercial result."[71] In this case, the Supreme Court avoided an interpretation of an insurance policy that, in the Court's view, "would render the endeavour on the part of the insured to obtain insurance protection nugatory."[72]

The principle is often expressed in terms of avoiding "absurdity" or "absurd consequences."[73] In this context, however, the concept of absurdity appears to be used interchangeably with the notion of com-mercial unreasonableness. It is not necessary to establish that the un-attractive interpretation of the agreement produces a result that is, in some sense, an outrageous one. Thus, in *Guarantee Co. of North America v. Gordon Capital Corp.*,[74] for example, the Supreme Court of Canada was confronted with a choice between two plausible interpretations of a fidelity insurance bond under which a brokerage was insured against losses caused by dishonest and fraudulent acts of its employees. The dispute concerned, first, the proper interpretation of a provision that enabled "rescission" of the agreement by the insurer in the event that false statements had been included in the application for the bond and, second, the effect of an improper exercise of the right to rescind by the insurer on the contractual limitation periods stipulated elsewhere in the bond as binding on the insured. The insured had notified the insurer of a substantial loss. The insurer, having discovered what it considered to be a material misrepresentation in the original application, purported to "rescind" the bond. The insured then commenced this action. The insurer defended the insured's claim, however, on the basis that the insured had not commenced its claim within the applicable two-year limitation period stipulated in the bond. For purposes of a prelimin-ary motion on the limitations point, it was accepted by the parties that the insurer had engaged in an improper rescission of the bond. The interpretation preferred by the insured was that the insurer, having im-properly purported to rescind the bond, had committed a repudiatory breach[75] and could not rely on the procedural protections—including the stipulated limitations period for claims by the insured—otherwise

---

71   *Ibid.* at 58.
72   *Ibid.* at 59.
73   See, for example, *Tillmanns & Co. v. S.S. Knutsford Ltd.*, [1908] 2 K.B. 385 at 402, Farwell L.J. ("there is a presumption that business men do not intend to do anything absurd, which is some slight guide; but in all cases it is a matter of construction").
74   (1999), 178 D.L.R. (4th) 1 (S.C.C.), rev'g (1998), 157 D.L.R. (4th) 643 (Ont. C.A.).
75   See generally Chapter 15.

available to it under the bond. The Ontario Court of Appeal agreed with the position of the insured on this point.[76] The interpretation preferred by the insurer, however, was that the procedural protections of the limitation period, at least, remained in place. The Supreme Court of Canada reversed the Court of Appeal and accepted the insured's interpretation on the basis that the consequences of the insured's interpretation would lead to a commercial absurdity because it would mean that in any case where the insurer mistakenly attempted to rescind the agreement, such protections would be lost. The insurer "would be exposed to a longer period of uncertainty concerning future claims from an insured who has purportedly engaged in misrepresentation than one who has complied with all the statutory terms."[77] Although the term "absurdity" is employed here, the interpretation offered by the insured was at least a plausible one—as the decision of the Court of Appeal would tend to suggest—but the Supreme Court was evidently of the view that the insurer's interpretation was the more commercially reasonable one.

As one would expect, the more unreasonable or absurd a particular interpretation appears, the greater will be the judicial effort expended in attempting to find a more reasonable interpretation. In *L. Schuler A.G. v. Wickman Machine Tool Sales Ltd.*,[78] for example, a German manufacturing firm had retained an English distributor under an agreement that required the distributor, as a "condition" of the agreement, to visit the six largest British car manufacturers once a week. The manufacturer purported to terminate the agreement on the basis that the distributor, having missed a few visits, had breached a "condition" of the agreement, thereby entitling the manufacturer to terminate the relationship. The manufacturer's position was a plausible one. As we have seen,[79] if the term is, indeed, properly characterized as a condition—and a stipulation to that effect would normally be dispositive—the manufacturer would be entitled to terminate for any breach of the term in question. The result, however, was plainly unattractive. Lord Reid characterized the idea that the term should be interpreted in such fashion that even one failure to make a visit could lead to termination was "so unreasonable that it must make me search for some other possible meaning of the contract."[80] He further observed: "The fact that a particular construction leads to a very unreasonable result must be a relevant consideration. The more

---

76   (1998), 157 D.L.R. (4th) 643 (Ont. C.A.).
77   Above note 74 at para. 62 (S.C.C.), Bastarache J.
78   [1973] 2 All E.R. 39 (H.L.).
79   See Chapter 15, section C.
80   Above note 78 at 45.

unreasonable the result the more unlikely it is that the parties can have intended it, and if they do intend it the more necessary it is that they shall make that intention abundantly clear."[81]

Relying on provisions of the agreement relating to the ability of the manufacturer to require the distributor to "cure" material breaches, the court was able to conclude that, notwithstanding the use of the term "condition," the parties did not intend that any breach of the visitation requirement, however minor, would permit the manufacturer to terminate the agreement. Conversely, of course, the less unreasonable the meaning of the provision, the less likely it is that such heroics will be undertaken.[82] As these cases tend to illustrate, however, the open-textured nature of concepts such as "commercial absurdity" or "commercial unreasonableness" leave them, perhaps inescapably, to some extent in the eye of the beholder.

5) Construction *Contra Proferentum*

The principle of construction *contra proferentum* holds that provisions in agreements and other written documents that suffer from ambiguity are to be construed against the interest of the person who drafted or proferred the ambiguous provision. The doctrine was described by Estey J. in *McClelland & Stewart Ltd. v. Mutual Life Assurance Co. of Canada*[83] in the following terms: "That principle of interpretation applies to contracts and other documents on the simple theory that any ambiguity in the term of the contract must be resolved against the author if the choice is between him and the other party to the contract who did not participate in its drafting."[84]

The apparent rationale for the rule is that the author of the agreement, having had an opportunity to protect his or her interest, ought to be able to take advantage of such protections as have been inserted only to the extent that they are clearly communicated in the language of the agreement to the other party. The doctrine works against unfair surprise of the non-drafting party.[85] A further underlying concern may be to preclude any incentive that might otherwise exist for the author to strategically draft provisions that are deliberately obscure, with the intention of

---

81 *Ibid.*

82 See, for example, *Yorkwood Homes (Georgetown) Inc. v. Law Development Group Georgetown (No. 2) Ltd.* (1999), 45 O.R. (3d) 257 (C.A.).

83 Above note 60.

84 *Ibid.* at 15.

85 See *Arthur Andersen Inc. v. Toronto-Dominion Bank*, above note 20 at 395, Abella J.A.

preserving the opportunity of asserting a more generous interpretation at a later date.[86] It is consistent with the underlying rationale of the principle that resort may be made to construction *contra proferentum* only if the provision in question is ambiguous and this requirement is well established.[87] Where the authorship of the provisions in question are fairly attributable to both parties, the principle is inapplicable.[88]

Although construction *contra proferentum* is applicable, in principle, to any type of transaction,[89] it is especially likely to be applied where the author of the document is in a stronger bargaining position than the other party and is able to deal on the basis of the author's own standard terms on a "take it or leave it" basis. Insurance contracts, for example, are frequently construed *contra proferentum* against the interests of the insurer.[90] Similarly, in the context of guarantees that, in the usual case, are drafted by someone other than the guarantor, provisions imposing burdens on the guarantor will be construed against the interests of the person who drafted the guarantee.[91] Perhaps the most frequent target of construction *contra proferentum* are exemption or limitation of liability clauses drafted by parties intending to restrict their own liability for breach of contract for the losses caused thereby to the other party. Such provisions, it is often said, are strictly construed against their author. Thus, if a limitation of liability clause does not expressly exclude liability for negligence and, if the provision can reasonably be interpreted as excluding some other type of liability, the clause will be interpreted as not

---

86 See *Eli Lilly and Co. v. Novopharm Ltd.*, above note 18 at 26, Iacobucci J. (the doctrine "operates to protect one party to a contract from deviously ambiguous or confusing drafting on the part of the other party by interpreting any ambiguity against the drafting party"). See also American Law Institute, *Restatement of Contracts 2d* (St. Paul: American Law Institute, 1981) s. 206 Comment.

87 See, for example, *McClelland & Stewart Ltd. v. Mutual Life Assurance Co. of Canada*, above note 60 at 15; *Eli Lilly and Co. v. Novopharm Ltd.*, ibid. at 26, Iacobucci J.; *Manulife Bank of Canada v. Conlin*, [1996] 3 S.C.R. 415 at 425, Cory J.; *TransCanada Pipelines Ltd. v. Potter Station Power Limited Partnership* (2003), 226 D.L.R. (4th) 262 at 267, Simmons J.A. And see *Chilton v. Co-operators General Insurance Co.* (1997), 143 D.L.R. (4th) 647 at 654 (Ont. C.A.), Laskin J.A. ("The court should not strain to create an ambiguity where none exists.").

88 See, for example, *Birrell v. Dryer* (1884), 9 App. Cas. 345.

89 *Hillis Oil & Sales v. Wynn's Canada Ltd.*, above note 61 at 69, Le Dain J.

90 See, for example, *Consolidated-Bathurst Export Ltd. v. Mutual Boiler & Machinery Insurance Co.*, above note 2; *McClelland & Stewart Ltd. v. Mutual Life Assurance Co. of Canada*, above note 60; *Zurich Life Insurance Co. of Canada v. Davies*, [1981] 2 S.C.R. 670.

91 See, for example, *Manulife Bank of Canada v. Conlin*, above note 87; *Bank of Montreal v. Korico Enterprises Ltd.* (2000), 50 O.R. (3d) 520 (C.A.).

protecting the author against liability for negligence.[92] The application of the *contra proferentum* to exculpatory clauses thus appears to be particularly vigorous. In a case involving a bill of lading entered into by sophisticated commercial parties, however, the Supreme Court of Canada has emphasized that the rule is not an absolute one and that, especially in the context of an agreement in which commercial parties are essentially determining which of the parties is to bear the cost of insurance at various stages of the agreement, the provision should be construed in the context of the whole agreement. In such circumstances, it may be appropriate to treat the provision as excluding liability for negligence even though an express reference to negligence has not been made.[93] Further, the House of Lords has drawn a distinction between exculpatory clauses excluding liability as opposed to those merely limiting liability and has suggested that clauses of the latter type, though subject to *contra proferentum*, would not be subject to the "specially exacting standards, applicable to such clauses."[94] It is difficult, however, to justify the drawing of a stark distinction between clauses that limit, as opposed to those that exclude, liability. A more defensible distinction might be drawn between commercial and consumer transactions, with the particularly exacting standards being reserved for the latter context. The problem of interpreting limitation and liability clauses has also inspired the development of the doctrine of so-called fundamental breach. The history and current status of this doctrine will be reviewed in a later Chapter.[95]

6) List of Particulars Followed by General Language: *ejusdem generis*

Where a provision lists a series of particular items that share a common characteristic of some kind, and the list is then completed by a more general phrase, the *ejusdem generis* principle holds that the scope of the

---

92   *Canada Steamship Lines Ltd. v. The King*, [1952] 2 D.L.R. 786 (P.C.); *Salmon River Logging Co. Ltd. v. Burt*, [1953] 2 S.C.R. 117; *Canadian Pacific Forest Products Ltd. v. Belships (Far East) Shipping (Pte.) Ltd.* (1999), 175 D.L.R. (4th) 449 (Fed. C.A.). Conversely, a reference in the clause to a limitation of liability "whether or not from negligence or gross negligence" has been held inapplicable to losses resulting from deliberate misconduct. See *Meditek Laboratory Services Ltd. v. Purolator Courier Ltd.* (1995), 125 D.L.R. (4th) 738 (Man. C.A.).

93   *I.T.O.—International Terminal Operators Ltd. v. Miida Electronics Inc.*, [1986] 1 S.C.R. 752 at 799, McIntyre J.

94   *Ailsa Craig Fishing Co. Ltd. v. Malvern Co. Ltd.*, [1983] 1 W.L.R. 964 at 970 (H.L.), Lord Fraser of Tullybelton.

95   See Chapter 20.

general phrase is limited by the common characteristics or the class or genus of the particularized items. Thus, a well-known illustration of the point concerned a lease that provided for an abatement of rent if occupancy was interrupted by "fire, flood, storm, tempest or other inevitable accidents." It was held that the phrase "inevitable accident" does not refer to accidents caused by either of the contracting parties. The particularized items indicate that the phrase refers to accidents resulting from circumstances beyond their control.[96] The principle was applied to a *force majeure* clause in *Atlantic Paper Stock Ltd. v. St. Anne-Nackawic Pulp & Paper Co.*[97] The clause was contained in a requirements contract that excused the purchaser from a minimum-purchase requirement in various circumstances beyond the control of the parties including acts of God, war, labour unrest, the destruction of production facilities "or the non-availability of markets for pulp or corrugating medium." The purchaser had suffered a decline in the market for his own product and sought to excuse its obligations under the requirements contract on the basis of the latter phrase. The Supreme Court held, however, that the *ejusdem generis* principle applied and, accordingly, the "non-availability of markets" also must result from circumstances beyond the control of the parties. On the particular facts, the Court was of the view that the purchaser's lack of satisfactory markets resulted in the main from its own poor planning, inadequate marketing efforts and soaring production costs. Accordingly, the *force majeure* clause did not excuse the purchaser from meeting its minimum commitment.

Like other canons of construction, *ejusdem generis* is a guide to interpretation rather than a rule. Its application is dependent on a careful assessment of the context of the particular clause. Indeed, the common sense underlying the canon is that the particular items in a list are suggestive of the object of the provision and it is generally appropriate, of course, to interpret a clause in the light of its object.[98] It has been said that the doctrine "is a very valuable servant, but it would be a most dangerous master."[99] The principle will not be of assistance in a case where the itemized particulars do not share a common characteristic.[100] Obviously, parties minded to avoid application of the maxim may draft provisions that signal a contrary intention by including phrases such as "from any cause whatsoever" or "whether or not similar to the foregoing."[101]

---

96 *Saner v. Bilton* (1878), 7 Ch. D. 815.
97 [1976] 1 S.C.R. 580.
98 See *Sun Fire Office v. Hart* (1889), 14 App. Cas. 98 at 104, Lord Watson.
99 *Anderson v. Anderson*, [1895] 1 Q.B. 749 at 755, Lopes L.J.
100 *S.S. Magnhild v. McIntyre Bros. & Co.*, [1920] 3 K.B. 321 at 329–31, McCardie J.
101 *Chandris v. Isbrandtsen-Moller Co. Inc.*, [1951] 1 K.B. 240 at 245, Devlin J.

7) The Restrictive Effect of Explicit References: *expressio unius*

An express reference to a particular person, thing, condition or exception may, when considered in context, amount to an exclusion of unmentioned alternatives. The principle that explicit reference to the one may constitute an exclusion of the alternatives is often expressed in the Latin maxim *expressio unius est exclusio alterius*. In an often referred to illustration of the point, a deed transferring a group of properties specifically mentioned that the fixtures in some of the properties were included in the conveyance. The court concluded that the explicit reference to fixtures in some cases was to be interpreted as excluding a transfer of fixtures with respect to the other properties.[102] If the parties had made no mention of fixtures at all, the fixtures would normally pass as part of the realty. The common sense underlying the analysis is that since the parties obviously knew how to express themselves when they wished to include fixtures, the absence of a reference to fixtures with respect to some properties is of significance.[103] The maxim is to be applied cautiously, however, as it is well understood that the missing reference may be an accidental omission rather than an intended exclusion.[104]

8) The Preference Accorded Amendments to Printed Terms

Parties dealing with each other on the basis of standard printed terms may make handwritten or typed amendments to the form that may

---

102 *Hare v. Horton* (1833), 5 B. & Ad. 715, 110 E.R. 954. See also *Blackburn v. Flavelle* (1881), 6 App. Cas. 628 (P.C.); *Pearson v. Adams* (1912), 27 O.L.R. 87 (Div. Ct.), rev'd 28 O.L.R. 154 (C.A.), rev'd 50 S.C.R. 204; *Miller v. Emcer Products Ltd.*, [1956] Ch. 304.

103 Often the point is expressed in more or less these terms. See, for example, *Scott v. Wawanesa Mutual Insurance Co.*, [1989] 1 S.C.R. 1445, in which La Forest J., in dissent, would have interpreted a fire insurance policy as providing coverage to a homeowner under a fire insurance policy excluding liability for injuries caused by an "insured." The fire in question was caused by the son of the plaintiffs who, as a member of the household, was an included "insured." In the provision of the policy excluding liability for vandalism, however, the term explicitly included loss caused by members of the household. For La Forest J., that explicit reference signalled that losses caused by members of the household were not excluded from the more general provision concerning losses caused by fire. In the majority view, however, the policy plainly excluded all losses caused by an "insured," including all members of the household. See also *Torchia v. Royal Insurance Co. of Canada* (2003), 64 O.R. (3d) 775 (S.C.J.).

104 *Colquhoun v. Brooks* (1887), 19 Q.B.D. 400, aff'd (1889), 14 App. Cas. 493. See also *Pearson v. Adams*, above note 102.

conflict with the printed terms and conditions. If that conflict cannot be resolved by the usual techniques of construction,[105] it is well established that handwritten or typed terms take priority to the inconsistent terms in the printed standard form.[106] The evident rationale for the rule is that preference should be given to terms that the parties have clearly chosen for themselves and therefore constitute the best evidence of their intentions.

9) The Preference Accorded the Earlier of Two Inconsistent Terms

As we have seen earlier in this chapter,[107] courts attempt to give a harmonious reading to two apparently inconsistent terms. Where such a reading cannot be found, however, the terms are said to be repugnant and preference is given to the provision that first appears in the agreement.[108] As we have seen earlier,[109] in *J. Evans & Son (Portsmouth) Ltd. v. Merzario (Andrea) Ltd.*,[110] Lord Denning relied on this principle as a means of avoiding application of the parol evidence rule to a prior oral undertaking that conflicted with an exemption clause in the subsequent written agreement. In Lord Denning's view, the agreement was intended to be partly oral and partly written, and the written exemption clause was to be rejected as repugnant to the earlier oral undertaking. The arbitrariness of the rule is readily apparent where the inconsistent terms appear in a single written document. It is not surprising,

---

105 See, for example, *Bayoil S.A. v. Seawind Tankers Corp.*, [2001] 1 Lloyd's Rep. 533.
106 *Robertson v. French* (1803), 4 East. 130, 102 E.R. 779; *Glynn v. Margetson & Co.*, [1893] A.C. 351; *Mann v. St. Croix Paper Co.* (1912), 5 D.L.R. 596 (N.B.C.A.); *Baldwin v. Canada Foundry* (1914), 6 O.W.N. 152, aff'd 6 O.W.N. 364 (S.C.A.D.); *British Whig Publishing Co. v. E.B. Eddy Co.* (1921), 62 S.C.R. 576; *Knight Sugar Co. v. Webster*, [1930] S.C.R. 518; *Templin v. Alles*, [1944] O.W.N. 96; *Blanco v. Nugent*, [1949] 3 D.L.R. 19 (Man. K.B.); *The Athinoula*, [1980] 2 Lloyd's Rep. 481; *Homburg Houtimport B.V. v. Agrosin Private Ltd.*, [2003] 2 W.L.R. 711 (H.L.).
107 See above this Chapter, section B(3).
108 *Forbes v. Git*, [1922] 1 A.C. 256 at 259 (P.C.), Lord Wrenbury; *Cotter v. General Petroleums Ltd.*, [1951] S.C.R. 154 at 158, Kerwin J. and 170–71, Cartwright J.; *Hassard v. Peace River Co-operative Seed Growers Association*, [1954] 2 D.L.R. 50 at 54 (S.C.C.), Kellock J.; *Independent Lumber Co. v. David* (1911), 1 W.W.R. 134 at 140 (Sask. C.A.), Lamont J.; *Continental Insurance Co. v. Law Society of Alberta* (1984), 14 D.L.R. (4th) 256 at 262 (Alta. C.A.), Lieberman J.A. A different rule applies to the construction of wills, where the later provision will prevail. See, for example, *Re Hammond*, [1938] 3 All E.R. 308.
109 See Chapter 6, section D(5).
110 [1976] 1 W.L.R. 1078 (C.A.).

therefore, that courts treat the principle as, in effect, a principle of last resort. As Scrutton L.J. observed in *Rose & Frank Co. v. J.R. Crompton and Brothers Ltd.*,[111] "before this heroic method is adopted, … it must be clearly impossible to harmonize the whole of the language the parties have used."[112]

10) The Preference for a Construction That Preserves the Validity or Legality of the Agreement

When confronted with a choice between an interpretation that will render an agreement or a term invalid or one that will render it valid, courts prefer the construction that supports validity.[113] Thus, courts will avoid, if possible, an interpretation of an agreement that renders the agreement void.[114] Similarly, for example, if a particular interpretation of an agreement will have the effect that one of the parties has no effective obligation under the agreement, thus rendering the agreement a mere sham, a construction imposing some obligation on that party, if possible, will be preferred.[115] The same principle may be applied to save a particular term of an agreement.[116] The principle is often expressed in the form of a Latin maxim: *verba ita sunt intelligenda ut res magis valeat quam pereat* or, in English, "words should be so understood that the matter in question may have effect rather than fail." The principle may also apply where the parties have entered into an agreement that may fail for lack of certainty of terms. In a leading case on that issue, *Hillas & Co. Ltd. v. Arcos Ltd.*,[117] Lord Wright, noting that commercial agreements are often recorded in crude and apparently incomplete fashion, went on to observe as follows:

> It is, accordingly, the duty of the court to construe such documents fairly and broadly, without being too astute or subtle in finding defects; but, on the contrary, the courts should seek to apply the old maxim of English law, *verba ita sunt intelligenda ut res magis valeat quam pereat*. That maxim, however, does not mean that the court is

---

111   [1923] 2 K.B. 261 (C.A.).

112   *Ibid.* at 287. See also *Cotter v. General Petroleums Ltd.*, above note 108 at 170–71, Cartwright J.

113   See, for example, *Langston v. Langston* (1834), 2 Cl. & F. 194, 5 E.R. 908 (H.L.).

114   *Detomac Mines Ltd. v. Reliance Flourspar Mining Syndicate Ltd.*, [1952] O.R. 423 at 430 (H.C.J.), Gale J., aff'd [1952] O.R. 783 (C.A.).

115   *Aita v. Silverstone Towers Ltd.* (1978), 19 O.R. (2d) 681 at 687 (C.A.), Arnup J.A.

116   *Ibid.*; *Hayne v. Cummings* (1864), 16 C.B. (N.S.) 421, 143 E.R. 1191.

117   (1932), 147 L.T. 503.

to make a contract for the parties, or go outside the words they have used, except so far as there are appropriate implications of law as, for instance, the implication of what is justice and reasonable to be ascertained by the court as a matter of machinery where the contractual intention is clear but the contract is silent on some detail.[118]

As we have seen, in that case, the House of Lords was prepared to fill in some of the gaps left by the parties by imposing standards of reasonableness.[119]

On similar grounds, where an agreement admits of two possible constructions, one of which renders the agreement lawful and the other of which renders it unlawful, courts will give preference to the former interpretation.[120]

D. IMPLIED TERMS

1) Introduction

In the course of construing or interpreting agreements, courts often conclude that the parties have not given complete expression to their agreement and that gaps in the agreement must be filled in with implied terms. Gaps or omissions may arise because the parties have contented themselves to agree only to the main or essential terms of the agreement. Alternatively, the parties may simply not have foreseen and provided for a point of difficulty or a contingency that emerges in the course of their contractual relationship. The practice of implying terms in such circumstances is well established. Implied terms constitute an important and pervasive source of contractual obligation. At the same time, courts frequently observe that they will not construct agreements for the parties and further, that the implying of contractual terms is an analytical device to be used sparingly and with caution. This traditional view was set forth by Cory J.A., as he then was, in the following terms:

> When may a term be implied in a contract? A court faced with that question must first take cognizance of some important and time-honoured cautions. For example, the courts will be cautious in their

---

118 *Ibid.* at 514.
119 See Chapter 3, section B.
120 *Fausset v. Carpenter* (1831), 2 Dow & Cl. 232, 6 E.R. 715; *Perry v. Brandon* (1914), 32 O.L.R. 94 at 98 (S.C.A.D.), Middleton J.; *Cantor Art Services Ltd. v. Kenneth Bieber Photography Ltd.*, [1969] 1 W.L.R. 1226 (C.A.).

approach to implying terms to contracts. Certainly a court will not rewrite a contract for the parties. As well, no term will be implied that is inconsistent with the contract. Implied terms are as a rule based on the presumed intention of the parties and should be founded on reason. The circumstances and background of the contract, together with its precise terms should all be carefully regarded before a term is applied. As a result, it is clear that every case must be determined in its own particular facts.[121]

It is important to note that, in this passage, Cory J.A. is referring to implied terms based on the presumed intentions of the parties. There are two different categories of implied terms resting on presumed intentions. The first consists of implied terms incorporating custom or usage. The second category consists of terms implied that appear to be made necessary by or are, in some sense, obvious from the circumstances of the particular transaction. Such terms are often referred to as being implied in fact.[122] Implied terms in either category rest on the presumed intentions of the parties and, as Cory J.A. suggests, their implication would be defeated, therefore, by the presence of an explicit and inconsistent term of the parties' agreement. There is, however, a third category of implied terms, terms implied by law,[123] to which these propositions do not apply or do not apply to the same degree. Terms implied by law were characterized by Le Dain J. in *Canadian Pacific Hotels Ltd. v. Bank of Montreal*[124] as "the third category of implication, which does not depend on presumed intention—the implication of terms as legal incidents of a particular class or kind of contract, the nature and content of which have to be largely determined by implication."[125] As we shall see, terms implied by law may be quite inconsistent with the actual and unexpressed intentions of one of the parties, but are implied in the agreement in order to ensure that the agreement between the parties is, in the court's view, a fair and reasonable one. Further, although inconsistent terms in an agreement normally trump terms that otherwise would be implied by law, courts may be reluctant

---

121 *G. Ford Homes Ltd. v. Draft Masonry (York) Co. Ltd.* (1983), 43 O.R. (2d) 401 at 403 (C.A.), Cory J.A., a passage quoted with approval by the Supreme Court of Canada in *ter Neuzen v. Korn*, [1995] 3 S.C.R. 674 at 712–13, Sopinka J. See also *Luxor (Eastbourne) Ltd. v. Cooper*, [1941] A.C. 108 at 137 (H.L.), Lord Wright.
122 *Machtinger v. HOJ Industries Ltd.*, [1992] 1 S.C.R. 986 at 1008, McLachlin J.
123 *Ibid.*
124 [1987] 1 S.C.R. 711.
125 *Ibid.* at 776.

to conclude that a particular contractual provision is, indeed, truly inconsistent with a term implied by law.

The implication of terms resting on the presumed intentions of the parties—whether based on custom or usage or on the particular circumstances of the agreement—may appear to be justifiable on the basis that the court is engaging in an exercise designed to give effect to the will of the parties. The phrase "presumed intention of the parties" is, however, an inherently ambiguous one. Glanville Williams captured this ambiguity by suggesting the following as two different types of implied terms: "(i) ... terms that the parties ... probably had in mind but did not trouble to express; (ii) ... terms that the parties, whether or not they actually had them in mind, would probably have expressed if the question had been brought to their attention."[126]

As Williams noted, the first type of implication is an attempt to determine what the parties were actually thinking. In this category, it is presumed that the implied term is what the parties actually intended but did not express. The second type is an attempt to discern a hypothetical intention that the parties would have formulated if they had anticipated the problem in question. If the first category represents what is essentially a factual inquiry, the second is obviously more speculative. As a practical matter, of course, it may be difficult to draw a clear distinction between these two types of implications. This ambiguity is present in judicial discussions of the implication of terms. Although reference is frequently made to "presumed intentions," it is often not entirely clear whether a particular judge is referring to presumed actual intentions or to the presumed hypothetical intentions of the parties to the agreement. It is important to note, however, that notwithstanding occasional references in the judicial rhetoric surrounding the implication of terms to the need to give effect to the "intentions" of the parties—thus intimating, perhaps, that the court is confined to a search for the actual intentions of the parties—it is plainly the case that terms implied in fact are commonly implied on the basis of presumed hypothetical intentions. In the typical case, there is little or no evidence and little or no judicial discussion of the question of whether the parties actually intended that which is being implied and simply neglected to "write it down." Accordingly, the implication of terms in fact sits uneasily on a rationale of simply giving effect to the will of the parties. Inescapably and, perhaps, seamlessly, the exercise becomes one of implying into the agreement, on an objective basis, reasonable terms that, it is assumed, the parties would or ought to have agreed to if the matter

---

126 G. Williams, "Language and the Law" (1945–46) 61 Law Q. Rev. 71 at 401.

had been raised at the time of contracting. Ultimately, the rationale for the implied in fact term may be that, when required to fill a gap left in the agreement between the parties, courts should attempt to fill that gap with an implied term that accords with fundamental notions of reasonableness and fair dealing.[127]

Williams distinguished the first two categories of implied terms from a third, which corresponds to the category referred to here as terms implied by law. He described this third category as follows: "(iii) ... terms that, whether or not the parties had them in mind or would have expressed them if they had foreseen the difficulty, are implied by the Court because of the Court's view of fairness or policy or in consequence of rules of law."[128] Terms implied by law could conceivably correspond to the intentions of the parties if the parties are both fair and reasonable people who share the court's view of the appropriateness of the particular implied term. In such circumstances, the term implied by law may correspond precisely to the actual or presumed hypothetical intentions of the parties. As Williams notes, however, the important point is that the presence of such intentions is irrelevant to the court's determination that such a term should be implied by law.

We turn, then, to consider the three categories of implied terms: those implied on the basis of custom or usage, those implied in fact and those implied by law. Finally, brief mention will be made of the phenomenon of implied statutory terms.

2) Terms Implied from Custom or Usage

Where there are, in particular trades or commercial contexts, established customs or usages relating to the terms on which parties deal with each other, such custom or usage may provide a basis for an implied term. In *Hutton v. Warren*,[129] Parke B. offered the following influential explanation for this proposition:

> It has long been settled, that, in commercial transactions, extrinsic evidence of custom and usage is admissible to annex incidents to

---

127 See generally E.A. Farnsworth, *Farnsworth on Contracts*, 2d ed., vol. II (New York: Aspen Law & Business, 1998) at 331–37. For discussion of the relationship of consent-based rationales for contractual obligation and implied terms, see, for example, C. Fried, *Contract as Promise* (Cambridge: Harvard University Press, 1981) c. 5; R. Barnett, "The Sound of Silence: Default Rules and Contractual Consent" (1992) 78 Va. L. Rev. 821.

128 *Ibid.*

129 (1836), 1 M. & W. 466, 150 E.R. 517.

written contracts, in matters with respect to which they are sound. The same rule has also been applied to contracts in other transactions of life, in which known usages have been established and prevailed; and this has been done upon the principle of presumption that, in such transactions, the parties did not mean to express in writing the whole of the contract by which they intended to be bound, but a contract with reference to those known usages.[130]

In this passage, Baron Parke plainly rests the implication of terms setting forth known usages on the basis that the parties are presumed to have intended to deal on that basis. This theme is pervasive in the jurisprudence concerning this topic. Thus, in *Liverpool City Council v. Irwin*,[131] for example, Lord Wilberforce observed: "[w]here there is, on the face of it, a complete bilateral contract, the courts are sometimes willing to add terms to it, as implied terms: this is very common in mercantile contracts where there is an established usage: in that case the courts are spelling out what both parties know and would, if asked, unhesitatingly agree to be part of the bargain."[132] As is often said, the custom or usage must be "notorious."[133] Similarly, in the decision of the Supreme Court of Canada in *Georgia Construction Co. v. Pacific Great Railway Co.*,[134] Duff J. made the following observation: "Usage, of course, where it is established, may annex an unexpressed incident to a written contract; but it must be reasonably certain and so notorious and so generally acquiesced in that it may be presumed to form an ingredient of the contract."[135] In this case, the plaintiff alleged the existence of a custom in the railway industry relating to the method for calculating charges for a particular kind of work. Duff J. observed that the argument failed because the custom was not "so well recognized, so well known among persons engaged in railway construction, and so widely prevailing as to justify a presumption that everybody who enters into a contract for such work does so with the intention of being bound by that usage."[136]

The custom or usage must relate to the terms on which parties deal with each other in the particular commercial context. Thus, in *Canad-*

---

130 *Ibid.* at 521 (E.R.).

131 [1977] A.C. 239.

132 *Ibid.* at 253, quoted with approval in *Canadian Pacific Hotels Ltd. v. Bank of Montreal*, above note 124 at 774, Le Dain J.

133 See, for example, *Turner v. Royal Bank of Scotland*, [1999] 2 All E.R. (Comm) 664 at para. 39 (C.A.).

134 [1929] S.C.R. 630.

135 *Ibid.* at 633.

136 *Ibid.* at 636.

ian Pacific Hotels Ltd.,[137] the plaintiff bank sought to imply a term based on an alleged custom under which a sophisticated customer would have a system of internal accounting controls that would include a monthly bank conciliation and a practice of reporting discrepancies to the bank within a reasonable period of time. Failure to comply with the custom, or so the bank argued, would constitute a breach of the implied term. Le Dain J. indicated that the mere fact that it might be true that sophisticated customers did engage in such practices would not "support an inference of an understanding between the bank and the customer that the customer would examine his bank statements with reasonable care and report any discrepancies within a reasonable time, failing which he would be precluded from setting up the discrepancies against the bank."[138] Further, the custom must not be contrary to law[139] and, as Duff J. noted in *Georgia Construction*, it must be "reasonably certain." Thus, in a case involving an alleged custom for charging for burial services within a particular religious community, which involved three different methods of calculating the fee, one of which involved considerable discretion, the trial judge held that the custom was too uncertain to form the basis of an implied term.[140] As custom or usage is admitted into the contract on the basis of presumed intentions, it is obvious that the custom can be defeated by inconsistent terms in the agreement between the parties.[141]

Canadian cases in which the plaintiff has successfully established a custom providing the basis for an implied term include *David v. Arnott-Smith Timber Co.*,[142] in which a contract for the purchase of lumber ordered various types or sizes of lumber without specifying the amount of any particular type that was to be provided. The lumber actually supplied was predominantly of the less commercially valuable variety. Although the lumber supplied technically complied with the specifications, it was held that the defendant supplier was in breach of an implied term based on a custom of the industry that under such contracts the supplier would send a fair proportion of each of the respective types of lumber. In another case, it was held that a contract to rent a trailer included an

---

137 Above note 124.

138 *Ibid.* at 775.

139 *Turner v. Royal Bank of Scotland*, above note 133 at para. 39.

140 *Schara Tzedeck v. Royal Trust Co.* (1951), 1 W.W.R. (N.S.) 760 (B.C.S.C.), aff'd (1952), 5 W.W.R. (N.S.) 279 (B.C.C.A.), aff'd on other grounds [1953] 1 S.C.R. 31.

141 *Imperial Grain & Milling Co. v. Slobinski Bros. & Sons*, [1922] 3 W.W.R. 221 (Man. K.B.).

142 (1952), 7 W.W.R. (N.S.) 306 (B.C.S.C.).

implied promise reflecting an understanding within the industry that rented equipment was to be returned in its original condition subject to reasonable wear and tear.[143] In a contract for the purchase of a cow, a term was implied on the basis of a code of ethics of a cattle association that imposed on the vendor of a cow mistakenly believed to be pregnant an obligation to compensate the purchaser for the loss of a calf.[144]

3) Terms Implied in Fact

The second category of terms implied on the basis of the presumed intentions of the parties are terms said to be necessary or obvious in light of the particular circumstances of the transaction between the parties. Two orthodox and overlapping tests for determining whether such a term can be implied were articulated in the traditional English cases and have been accepted in Canadian common law. First, the so-called officious bystander test was set out by MacKinnon L.J. in *Shirlaw v. Southern Foundries (1926) Ltd.*[145] in the following terms: "*Prima facie* that which in any contract is left to be implied and need not be expressed is something so obvious it goes without saying; so that if, while the parties were making their bargain, an officious bystander were to suggest some express provision for inclusion in their agreement, they would testily suppress him with a common 'Oh, of course!'"[146] The officious bystander test, it may be noted, is quite consistent with the presumed hypothetical intention test articulated by Glanville Williams.[147] The second classic formulation of the test is that set out by Bowen L.J. in *The Moorcock*[148] as follows: "In business transactions such as this, what the law desires to effect by the implication is to give such business efficacy to the transaction as must have been intended at all events by both parties who are businessmen."[149]

The business efficacy and officious bystander tests are often stated in the alternative on the assumption that they are essentially synonymous.[150] In *Canadian Pacific Hotels Ltd.*,[151] Le Dain J. characterized the

---

143 *Con-force Products Ltd. v. Luscar Limited* (1982), 27 Sask. R. 299 (Q.B.).
144 *Banks v. Biensch* (1977), 3 Alta. L.R. (2d) 41 (S.C.T.D.).
145 [1939] 2 K.B. 206.
146 *Ibid.* at 227.
147 Above note 126.
148 (1889), L.R. 14 P.D. 64.
149 *Ibid.* at 68.
150 See, for example, *Reigate v. Union Manufacturing Co.*, [1918] 1 K.B. 592 at 605 (C.A.), Scrutton L.J.
151 Above note 124.

test for implied terms in fact as being the implication of a term "as necessary to give business efficacy to a contract *or as otherwise meeting* the 'officious bystander' test as the term the parties would say, if questioned, that they had obviously assumed."[152] Le Dain J. thus appears to suggest the officious bystander test might be slightly broader than the business efficacy test, perhaps with a view to capturing cases of a non-commercial nature where a business efficacy standard may not fit.[153] There is, however, no body of authority distinguishing between the two tests and it appears to be broadly accepted, as a practical matter, that the tests are essentially overlapping means of achieving the same objective of identifying the presumed intentions of the parties with respect to the matter in dispute.

Although the concepts of business efficacy or obviousness are evidently to some extent open-textured or difficult to define, it is clearly the case that the test is something other than a simple test of filling gaps in an agreement, implying the terms to which reasonable parties would have agreed. In *Liverpool City Council v. Irwin*,[154] Lord Denning suggested that the necessity test was an unrealistic one and that, in practice, what the courts actually do is imply terms when it is "reasonable in all circumstances to do so."[155] On further appeal to the House of Lords, however, Lord Denning's view was rejected and the necessity test was reaffirmed.[156]

Assuming, as both English and Canadian courts accept, that the necessity standard is the appropriate standard, the relationship between that test and ideas of reasonableness is nonetheless a subtle one and a potential source of confusion. Thus, it is plainly the case that the implied terms must themselves be reasonable.[157] One would not expect a court to imply terms into an agreement that it considered to be unreasonable. Further, keeping in mind that the implied in fact term rests on the presumed intentions of the parties, courts quite understandably

---

152 *Ibid.* at 775 (emphasis added).
153 Conversely, however, it was observed in *R v. Marshall* (1999), 177 D.L.R. (4th) 513 at 540 (S.C.C.), Binnie J., that courts will imply terms "where it is necessary to assure the efficacy of the contract, for example, where it meets the 'officious bystander' test," thereby suggesting, perhaps that the "efficacy" test is the broader of the two.
154 [1976], Q.B. 319 (C.A.).
155 *Ibid.* at 330.
156 *Liverpool City Council v. Irwin,* [1977] A.C. 239 at 254 (H.L.), Lord Wilberforce and 265, Lord Edmund-Davies.
157 *B.P. Refinery (Westernport) Pty. Ltd. v. Shire of Hastings* (1977), 52 A.J.L.R. 20 (P.C.).

presume intentions that are reasonable. In other words, in attributing to the parties hypothetical intentions as to what they would have agreed to if the matter had been raised at the time of contracting, courts assume that the parties would behave reasonably and would agree to a reasonable term. Indeed, in the absence of actual but unexpressed intentions it is inescapable that courts would apply a reasonable intentions standard. In other words, although necessity appears to be the threshold that must be met before engaging in the exercise of implying the term, the formulation of the term to be implied is very much an exercise that rests on a concept of reasonableness. At the same time, however, the implied term is tailored to the needs of the actual transaction of the actual parties rather than to some hypothetical reasonable transaction; accordingly, to the extent that relevant actual intentions of the parties are manifest in the transaction, they must form a basis for the implied term.[158] Most obviously, a term will not be implied that is inconsistent with an express term.[159] The actual intentions of the parties could be relevant, however, in other ways. For example, even though the parties failed to address explicitly in their agreement the unanticipated contingency that has occurred, they may have elsewhere in the agreement dealt with similar problems in a particular fashion. In such circumstances, it might well be appropriate for a court to determine that since a term must be implied to make the transaction an efficacious one, it is appropriate in light of the actual intentions of these parties, with respect to an analogous matter, to imply a similar term dealing with the unanticipated matter. A court could and perhaps should do so, even if the court might also feel that some abstract set of reasonable parties might have come to a different solution. In the absence of relevant information concerning the actual intentions of the parties, however, the exercise of implying a term is essentially indistinguishable from asking what the parties would, as reasonable people, have agreed to if the matter had been raised at the time of contracting.

In addition to being reasonable, the implied term must be capable of clear expression.[160] The implied term must be lawful and not contrary to public policy. The latter requirement was applied by the Supreme Court of Canada recently in *Pacific National Investments Ltd. v. Victoria (City)*[161]

---

158 *M.J.B. Enterprises Ltd. v. Defence Construction (1951) Ltd.*, [1999] 1 S.C.R. 619 at 635–36, Iacobucci J.

159 *Toronto Gravel Road & Concrete Co. v. County of York* (1885), 12 S.C.R. 517; *Hydro Electric Power Commission of Ontario v. Coniagas Reduction Co. Ltd.*, [1933] 3 D.L.R. 337 (P.C.); *Cooke v. CKOY Ltd.*, [1963] 2 O.R. 257 (H.C.J.).

160 *Marinangeli v. Marinangeli* (2003), 228 D.L.R. (4th) 376 (Ont. C.A.).

161 (2000), 193 D.L.R. (4th) 385 (S.C.C.).

to a development agreement entered into by the plaintiff developer and
the defendant municipality. The agreement authorized a two-stage development, the first stage residential and the second commercial. The
lands were zoned appropriately by the municipality. Once the first phase
was completed, however, the new residents objected to the commercial
phase of the development. In response to this pressure, a newly elected
council rezoned the lands in question so as to preclude the second phase
of the development. The plaintiff sued to enforce the agreement on the
basis of an implied term that the defendant would not rezone the land in
this fashion for a reasonable period of time. Although the Supreme Court
of Canada divided on the point, a majority held that an implied term of
this kind would be unlawful and contrary to public policy as an unlawful fetter on the legislative powersof the defendant council.[162]

A great variety of terms have been implied on the grounds of business efficacy or obviousness. A contract to supply a staircase to a house
under construction was held subject to an implied term that the staircase would comply with the building code.[163] A contract to supply news
was held to contain an implied term that the news will be accurate.[164]
Some implied terms have as their object the facilitation of performance
of the agreement. A building contract imposes an implied obligation
upon the owner of the land to facilitate the work of the contractor.[165]
In a contract between a client and a brokerage, the broker is implicitly
required to give reasonable notice of a decision to refuse to transact
further business on behalf of the client.[166] In a separation agreement
providing for an adjustment in the amount of support in the event of a
material change in the husband's circumstances, a term was implied to
require the defendant husband to disclose such changes to the plaintiff
wife.[167] Where the approval of a third party is necessary in order to en-

---

162 A subsequent claim by the developer for the value of a number of amenities constructed in anticipation of the second phase of development did, however, enjoy
success. See *Pacific National Investments Ltd. v. Victoria (City)* (2004), 245 D.L.R.
(4th) 211 (S.C.C.).
163 *G. Ford Homes Ltd. v. Draft Masonry (York) Co. Ltd.*, above note 121.
164 *Allan v. Bushnell T.V. Co. Ltd.* (1968), 1 D.L.R. (3d) 534 (Ont. H.C.J.).
165 *Penvidic Contracting Co. Ltd. v. International Nickel Co. of Canada Ltd.* (1975), 53
D.L.R. (3d) 748 (S.C.C.); *Marentette Bros. Ltd. v. City of Sudbury* (1974), 45 D.L.R.
(3d) 321 (Ont. C.A.).
166 *Venture Capital USA Inc. v. Yorkton Securities Inc.* (2003), 66 O.R. (3d) 760
(S.C.J.), rev'd on appeal (2005), 75 O.R. (3d) 325 (C.A.) (an explicit term permitting the broker to refuse the customer's instructions trumped the usual implied
term in agency agreements of indefinite duration that the agent may terminate
only upon reasonable notice).
167 *Marinangeli v. Marinangeli*, above note 160.

able a contract to proceed, it may be implied that the party in a position to seek that approval must make reasonable efforts to do so.[168] In other cases, courts have implied undertakings that the promisor will not do anything to impede performance of the contract.[169] The idea underlying both lines of authority appears to be an implied duty to cooperate in the fulfilment of the objectives of the contract. In other cases, courts imply terms that are designed to control the exercise of discretionary powers conferred by agreements. Thus, in the context of a real estate agency business, a provision in the employment contracts with agents enabling the employer to divide a commission among the agents involved in a particular sale "at the sole discretion of the employer" was held subject to an implied obligation to exercise the discretion in a manner consistent with the purpose for which the term was included in the agreement, that is, effecting appropriate compensation of the employees involved.[170] In a subsequent chapter[171] it will be suggested that cases implying duties to cooperate and limiting the exercise of contractual discretions are some evidence of a judicial willingness to imply terms requiring performance of contracts in good faith.

Numerous authorities have considered whether, in a contract of indefinite duration, a term should be implied to permit one or both of the parties to terminate the arrangement upon reasonable notice to the other. Initially, the common law took the position that if the parties did not stipulate in the agreement a method of termination, the agreement should be presumed to be perpetual in nature.[172] The presumption could be set aside if the party alleging an entitlement to terminate, perhaps on reasonable notice, was able to demonstrate either from the wording of the agreement or its nature that the presumption should be set aside. Modern authorities appear to accept, however, that the matter is to be determined simply on the basis of ordinary principles of interpretation, without the aid of a presumption in favour of perpetu-

---

168 *Dynamic Transport Ltd. v. OK Detailing Ltd.*, [1978] 2 S.C.R. 1072. See also *Brauer & Co. (Great Britain) Ltd. v. James Clark (Brush Materials) Ltd.*, [1952] 2 All E.R. 497 (C.A.); *Metropolitan Trust Co. of Canada v. Pressure Concrete Services Ltd.* (1973), 37 D.L.R. (3d) 649 (Ont. H.C.J.), aff'd (1975), 9 O.R. (2d) 375 (C.A.).

169 *Multi-Malls Inc. v. Tex-Mall Properties Ltd.* (1980), 108 D.L.R. (3d) 399 (Ont. H.C.J.), aff'd 128 D.L.R. (3d) 192n (Ont. C.A.), leave to appeal to S.C.C. refused, 41 N.R. 360n.

170 *Greenberg v. Meffert* (1985), 18 D.L.R. (4th) 548 (Ont. C.A.), leave to appeal to S.C.C. refused, 30 D.L.R. (4th) 268n.

171 See Chapter 21.

172 *Llanelly Railway & Dock Co. v. London & North Western Railway Co.* (1875), L.R. 7 H.L. 550.

ity.[173] The fact that the agreement in question would require the provision of goods or services of inflating cost at a fixed price in perpetuity weighs in favour of the implication of a term permitting termination upon reasonable notice by the supplier.[174] In the context of distributorship agreements, for example, where a finding that the agreement is perpetual would leave one party, the manufacturer, at the mercy of the distributor, an implied term to terminate on reasonable notice will probably be found.[175] The presence of an express termination clause that does not explicitly permit termination on reasonable notice may suggest that a clause to this effect should not be implied,[176] but the presence of such a provision is not dispositive.[177] While the trend of the modern cases appears to lie in the direction of implying rights to terminate on reasonable notice, there is no reason, in principle, precluding parties from agreeing to indefinite or perpetual obligations and if, on the proper construction of the agreement, a perpetual obligation is intended, it will be enforced. Thus, for example, in *Shaw Cablesystems Manitoba Ltd. v. Canadian Legion Memorial Housing Foundation (Manitoba)*,[178] it was held that an agreement entered into with a non-profit seniors' residential facility to supply cable TV services at a steeply dis-

---

173   See, for example, *Crediton Gas Co. v. Crediton Urban District Council*, [1928] 1 Ch. 174; *Re Spenborough Urban District Council's Agreement*, [1968] Ch. 139; *Martin-Baker Aircraft Co. Ltd. v. Canadian Flight Equipment Ltd.*, [1955] 2 Q.B. 556; *Winter Garden Theatre (London) Ltd. v. Millennium Productions Ltd.*, [1948] A.C. 173 (H.L.); *Toronto Type Foundry Ltd. v. Miehle-Goss-Dexter* (1968), 5 D.L.R. (3d) 578 (Ont. H.C.J.); *A & K Lick-a-Chick Franchises Ltd. v. Cordiv Enterprises Ltd.* (1981), 119 D.L.R. (3d) 440 (N.S.S.C.T.D.); *Rapatax (1987) Inc. v. Cantax Corp.* (1997), 145 D.L.R. (4th) 419 (Alta. C.A.), leave to appeal to S.C.C. refused (1997), 149 D.L.R. (4th) vii; *Gutka v. Cargill Ltd.* (1994), 127 Sask R. 126 (Q.B.).

174   *Staffordshire Area Health Authority v. South Staffordshire Waterworks Co.*, [1978] 1 W.L.R. 1387. On this occasion, Lord Denning proposed, in effect, a reversal of the presumption but his view did not carry a majority of the court nor has it found favour in subsequent authority.

175   *Martin-Baker Aircraft Co. Ltd. v. Canadian Flight Equipment Ltd.*, above note 173. See also *Bernard-Norman Specialties Co. v. S.C. Time Inc.* (1989), 71 O.R. (2d) 278 (H.C.J.); *Treen Gloves & Safety Products Ltd. v. Degil Safety Products (1989) Inc.* (1990), 33 C.P.R. (3d) 74 (B.C.S.C.).

176   See, for example, *Reigate v. Union Mfg. Co. (Ramsbottom) Ltd. and Elton Cop Dyeing Co. Ltd.*, above note 150; *Cook v. CKOY Ltd.*, above note 159; *Ev's Truck & Equipment Inc. v. Mack Canada Inc.* (1993), 50 C.P.R. (3d) 94 (B.C.S.C.); *Re Berker Sportcraft Limited's Agreements* (1947), 177 L.T. 420.

177   See, for example, *Treen Gloves & Safety Products Ltd. v. Degil Safety Products (1989) Inc.*, above note 175; *Bernard-Norman Specialties Co. v. S.C. Time Inc.*, above note 175.

178   (1996), 135 D.L.R. (4th) 501 (Man. Q.B.).

counted rate was a perpetual agreement. The fact that the price was discounted from a fluctuating price and that the agreement provided for termination on notice by the facility but not by the plaintiff cable company were of assistance to the court in reaching this conclusion. In *Town of Fort Frances v. Boise Cascade Canada Ltd.*,[179] the Supreme Court of Canada held that an agreement under which an energy supplier had acquired land and water and power privileges from a municipality in return for an undertaking to supply the municipality with its electricity requirements at a fixed rate was intended to last indefinitely. The Court reasoned that the fact that the agreement, on its correct interpretation, provided a cap on the annual amount of electricity to be supplied at the fixed rate pointed in the direction of perpetual obligation.

The dual standard for implying terms—necessary for business efficacy or obvious to an officious bystander—are evidently somewhat open-textured standards that are capable of interpretation to varying degrees of strictness. It is difficult to ascertain or, indeed, generalize with respect to the level of strictness imposed by Canadian courts in applying the standard. If one might imagine a scale of "necessary for business efficacy" running from a strict standard of absolute necessity to a more liberal standard of reasonable necessity, a recent series of Canadian cases dealing with tendering issues suggests that a more liberal standard is being applied. In 1981, the Supreme Court of Canada held, for the first time, that a tender call or an invitation to bids or tenders constituted an offer that is accepted by the submission of a tender creating a so-called Contract A relating to the bidding process.[180] In the intervening years, Canadian courts and, in particular, the Supreme Court of Canada, have imposed a series of substantive obligations on the issuer of the invitation through the medium of implied terms. Thus, in the absence of a term stipulating that the issuer is not obliged to accept the lowest or any of the bids—a so-called privilege clause—it has been held that the issuer has an implicit obligation to accept the lowest bid.[181] In *M.J.B. Enterprises Ltd. v. Defence Construction (1951) Ltd.*,[182] the Supreme Court of Canada held that under either the business efficacy or officious bystander tests, it was also appropriate to interpret Contract A as including an implied obligation on the part of the issuer

179 (1983), 143 D.L.R. (3d) 193 (S.C.C.).
180 *Ron Engineering & Construction Eastern Ltd. v. Ontario*, [1981] 1 S.C.R. 111. For discussion of the contract formation issue arising in this context, see Chapter 2, section B(1).
181 *Chinook Aggregates Ltd. v. Abbotsford (Municipal District)*, [1990] 1 W.W.R. 624 (B.C.C.A.); *Kencor Holdings Ltd. v. Saskatchewan*, [1991] 6 W.W.R. 717 (Sask. Q.B.).
182 [1999] 1 S.C.R. 619.

to reject non-compliant bids, that is, bids that do not comply with the rules for bidding set out in the tender call. The plaintiff was the second lowest bidder in a tender call issued by the defendant government agency. The lowest bid had contained a schedule of prices concerning one particular item, whereas the call required tenders to submit a fixed price. The defendant, considering the schedule to be merely a "clarification" rather than a non-compliant "qualification," accepted the bid in good faith. For the Court, Iacobucci J. reasoned that he would "find it difficult to accept that the [plaintiff], or any of the other contractors, would have submitted a tender unless it was understood by all involved that only a compliant tender would be accepted."[183] Accordingly, in his view, it was "reasonable to find an implied obligation to accept only a compliant tender."[184] Accordingly, the plaintiff's claim for damages representing the profit that it would have enjoyed if it had been selected as the successful bidder was successful.

Further, in *Martel Building Ltd. v. Canada*,[185] the Supreme Court held that Contract A also included an implied term requiring the issuer to treat all bidders fairly and equally. In so doing, the Court gave its *imprimatur* to a substantial body of decisions in the lower courts that had imposed such a duty. Again, the implication of the term was defended by Iacobucci J. on the basis that it was "necessary to give business efficacy to the tendering process."[186] This doctrine has continued to provide a substantial incentive for litigation by unsuccessful bidders who have enjoyed success where, for example, agents of the issuer had engaged in post-tender negotiations with bidders in an attempt to reach a more attractive arrangement concerning price than those contained in the bids,[187] where the issuer makes the selection on the basis of criteria—such as a preference for local contractors—that was not discussed in the call for tenders,[188] where the issuer allowed a bidder to correct a patent mathematical error after the tenders had been closed[189] and where the valuation of the tenders was not conducted in a suf-

---

183 *Ibid.* at 636.

184 *Ibid.*

185 [2000] 2 S.C.R. 860.

186 *Ibid.* at 894.

187 *Stanco Projects Ltd. v. British Columbia (Ministry of Water, Land and Air Protection)* (2004), 242 D.L.R. (4th) 720 (B.C.S.C.).

188 *Chinook Aggregates Ltd. v. Abbotsford (Municipal District)*, above note 181.

189 *Vachon Construction Ltd. v. Cariboo (Regional District)* (1996), 136 D.L.R. (4th) 307 (B.C.C.A.) (contract price expressed differently in words and numerals—both numbers lower than the second lowest bid—issuer's permission to make correction held to be a breach of Contract A).

ficiently even-handed fashion.[190] In the complex tendering processes that are likely to accompany contemporary large-scale public and private projects, the potential burdens imposed by these implied terms are substantial. Indeed, issuers are well advised to contract out of such liabilities where it is practicably feasible to do so. The fact that such provisions are now not uncommon may be thought to undermine the initial suggestion that such implied terms are necessary to give business efficacy to tendering arrangements. At the very least, this line of authority suggests that Canadian courts currently apply a standard of necessity approximating a "reasonably" necessary rather than an "absolutely" necessary standard.

4) Terms Implied in Law

As Le Dain J. observed in *Canadian Pacific Hotels Ltd.*,[191] terms implied by law do not rest on the presumed intentions of the parties. Indeed, as McLachlin J. noted in *London Drugs Ltd. v. Kuehne & Nagel International Ltd.*[192] "the court, where appropriate, may as a matter of policy imply a term in a particular type of contract, even where it is clear that the parties did not intend it."[193] Thus, terms implied by law are said to constitute "legal incidents" of particular kinds of contractual relationships.[194] Although the test for implying a term as a matter of law is said to be one of "necessity," the term "necessity" is being used, in this context, in a somewhat different sense from its use in the context of terms implied by fact. A distinction is drawn between "the search for an implied term necessary to give business efficacy and the search, based on wider considerations, for a term which the law will imply as a necessary incident of a definable category of contractual relationship."[195] The distinction may be illustrated by the holding in *Liverpool City Council v. Irwin*,[196] in which a term was implied in a tenancy agreement that the landlord had an obligation to maintain the common parts of the build-

---

190 *Martel Building Ltd. v. Canada*, above note 185.
191 Above note 124 at 776.
192 [1992] 3 S.C.R. 299.
193 *Ibid.* at 457.
194 *Canadian Pacific Hotels Ltd. v. Bank of Montreal Ltd.*, above note 124 at 762, Le Dain J.; *Machtinger v. HOJ Industries Ltd.*, above note 122 at 1009, McLachlin J.
195 *Scally v. Southern Health & Social Services Board*, [1992] 1 A.C. 294 at 307, Lord Bridge. See also *Liverpool County Council v. Irwin*, above note 156 at 255, Lord Wilberforce; *Lister v. Romford Ice & Cold Storage Co. Ltd.*, [1957] A.C. 555 at 579, Viscount Simonds.
196 *Liverpool County Council v. Irwin*, *ibid.*

ing in a good state of repair. As McLachlin J. observed of this decision in *Machtinger v. HOJ Industries Ltd.*,[197] "while the tenancy agreement could have continued without this term, it was necessary in a practical sense to the fair functioning of the agreement, given the relationship between the parties."[198] The implied at law term in issue in *Machtinger* was the implied obligation of an employer, in a contract of employment of indefinite duration, to provide the employee with a reasonable notice of termination of the relationship. McLachlin J. observed that such an obligation is a "necessary condition"[199] of the relation between employer and employee and further, that the attachment of a necessary legal incident to a contract is essentially a judicial exercise in imposing a legal duty.[200]

Terms are implied by law, then, to ensure the fair functioning of agreements in the context of standard transaction types such as contracts of employment, insurance, leases and so forth. In the employment context, for example, apart from the employer's implied obligation to give reasonable notice of termination, the employee is obliged to provide services at a reasonable level of skill and care,[201] and is obliged to not disclose confidential information[202] or betray secret processes.[203] The employer is obliged to take reasonable care to ensure that the tools, equipment and system of work provided to the employee are safe.[204] The irrelevance, as a matter of principle, of the presumed intentions of the parties to the implication of terms by law is conveniently illustrated by the employer's implied obligation to provide reasonable notice of termination. The fact that the particular employer might have assumed or privately intended that he would be entitled to dismiss an employee peremptorily is simply irrelevant to the implication of the duty to provide reasonable notice at common law. More difficult questions arise, however, if the explicit terms of the agreement signal an employer intention of some kind with respect to a question of termination. In *Machtinger* itself, the employment agreement at issue explicitly provided for notice that was less than the amount of notice required by the applicable provincial employment standards legislation. The contractual provision was therefore unenforceable, but it remained to consider whether the ex-

---

197 Above note 122.
198 *Ibid.* at 1010.
199 *Ibid.* at 1012.
200 *Ibid.*
201 *Lister v. Romford Ice & Cold Storage Co. Ltd.*, above note 195.
202 *Robb v. Green*, [1895] 2 Q.B. 315.
203 *Amber Size & Chemical Co. v. Menzel*, [1913] 2 Ch. 239.
204 *Williams & Clyde Coal Co. v. English*, [1938] A.C. 57 (H.L.).

press indication of an intention on the part of the employer to provide something less than reasonable notice would preclude the implication by law of the common law duty to provide reasonable notice. In her concurring judgment, McLachlin J. concluded that the explicit term did not have that effect. The explicit term was null and void and, accordingly, could not displace the common law rule.[205]

Even where the explicit inconsistent term is a lawful one, however, courts may lean against an interpretation of the explicit term that renders it plainly inconsistent with the term that otherwise would be implied by law. In *Ceccol v. Ontario Gymnastic Federation*,[206] the employer's common law duty to provide reasonable notice of termination was again at issue. In this case, the employee was retained on a series of one-year contracts and was in the sixteenth year of the employment relationship when the employer served notice of termination, offering a severance payment equivalent to three months of her salary. The employee sued for wrongful dismissal relying on the implied term obliging the employer to provide reasonable notice of termination, which would have been considerably in excess of three months. The employer defended on two grounds. First, it was argued that the individual one-year contracts were fixed-term contracts rather than contracts of indefinite duration and, accordingly, the implied duty was not applicable. This argument was rejected on the ground that the arrangement amounted, in substance, to a continuous employment relationship of indefinite duration rather than sixteen separate fixed-term agreements. The employer further argued, however, that in each agreement it was stipulated that the employer and the employee "agreed to abide by the *Ontario Employment Standards Act* and regulations concerning notice of termination of employment."[207] Under that legislation, the employee would be entitled merely to eight weeks' notice.[208] Conceding that the employer's interpretation of the provision was "a plausible one,"[209] the Ontario Court of Appeal nonetheless concluded that the failure of the agree-

---

205 The majority opinion reached the same conclusion on the ground that the "presumption" of reasonable notice could not be rebutted by a provision that failed to comply with employment standards legislation. Having decided the matter on this "narrower" ground, the majority was able to avoid the "complex" issue of the relationship between intention and implied terms. See above note 122 at 998, Iacobucci J.

206 (2001), 204 D.L.R. (4th) 688 (Ont. C.A.).

207 *Ibid.* at para. 5.

208 *Employment Standards Act,* R.S.O. 1990, c. E-14. See now *Employment Standards Act, 2000*, S.O. 2000, c. 41, s. 57(1)(h).

209 Above note 206 at para. 37.

ment to stipulate plainly that this provision was applicable to dismissal without cause rendered the provision an ambiguous one and held that the provision should be read as being consistent with the common law requirement of reasonable notice in the event of such a termination. On this basis, the trial judge's holding that the plaintiff employee was entitled to sixteen months' notice in damages, subject to a deduction of four months' wages for failure to mitigate, was affirmed. If, on the other hand, a lawful period of notice had been plainly stipulated, it would preclude implication of the implied term of reasonable notice.[210] In sum, terms implied by law, like terms implied by fact, are "default" rules that can displaced by a contrary stipulation by the parties. In the context of terms implied in law, however, courts may place greater emphasis on a requirement that the contrary stipulation be clear and explicit.

5) Implied Statutory Terms

Legislatures have frequently adopted the device of implying terms in agreements between private parties in the context of standard transactional patterns such as the purchase and sale of goods, insurance agreements of various kinds and leases. Often such rules are default rules in the sense that they are subject to contrary stipulation by the parties. Thus, for example, sale of goods legislation typically provides that the seller is subject to an implied obligation to provide goods that are merchantable[211] and fit for any specified purpose[212] and that the obligations of the parties to tender delivery of the goods and payment of the price are implicit mutual conditions.[213] All these statutory implied terms are displaced by any explicit contractual terms to the contrary. In other contexts, however, such as residential leases[214] or contracts to supply goods and services to consumers,[215] particular implied statutory conditions may not be subject to contrary stipulation. Many, though far from all, of these terms have historical antecedents in the form of terms implied at common law. In retrospect, some might be considered to have been implied in fact; others implied in law. The historical origins

---

210 See, for example, *MacDonald v. ADGA Systems International Ltd.* (1999), 41 C.C.E.L. (2d) 5 (Ont. C.A.), leave to appeal to S.C.C. refused (1999), 127 O.A.C. 396n.

211 See, for example, *Sale of Goods Act*, R.S.O. 1990, c. S.1, s. 15(2).

212 *Ibid.*, s. 15(1).

213 *Ibid.*, s. 27.

214 See, for example, *Tenant Protection Act*, S.O. 1997, c. 24, ss. 16 and 24.

215 See, for example, *Consumer Protection Act, 2002*, S.O. 2002, c. 30, Sched. A., s. 9.

of statutory terms are, however, a matter of indifference.[216] If the statute is applicable to the transaction in question and the implied term is not displaced by a contrary stipulation of the parties, the implied statutory term becomes a term of the agreement.

FURTHER READINGS

A. BARAK, *Purposive Interpretation in Law* (Princeton: Princeton University Press, 2005).

R. BARNETT, "The Sound of Silence: Default Rules and Contractual Consent" (1991) 78 Va. L. Rev. 821.

G.R. HALL, "A Curious Incident in the Law of Contract: the Impact of 22 Words from the House of Lords" (2004) 40 Can. Bus. L.J. 20.

L. HOFFMAN, "The Intolerable Wrestle with Words and Meanings" (1997) 114 S.A.L.J. 656.

K. LEWISON, *Interpretation of Contracts*, 3d ed. (London: Sweet & Maxwell, 2004).

E. MCKENDRICK, "The Interpretation of Contracts: Lord Hoffman's Restatement" in S. Worthington, ed., *Commercial Law and Commercial Practice* (Oxford: Hart, 2004) c. 6.

D.W. MCLAUCHLAN, "A Contract Contradiction" (1999) 30 V.U.W.L.R. 175.

D.W. MCLAUCHLAN, "Common Assumptions and Contract Interpretation" (1997) 113 Law Q. Rev. 237.

G. MCMEEL, "Prior Negotiations and Subsequent Conduct" (2002) 119 Law Q. Rev. 272.

G. MCMEEL, "The Rise of Commercial Construction in Contract Law" (1998) L.M.C.L.Q. 382.

E.W. PATTERSON, "The Interpretation and Construction of Contracts" (1964) 64 Colum. L. Rev. 833.

---

216 Where the statutory term does have a common law antecedent, however, the common law doctrine explicating the nature of the term may, of course, be relevant to the exercise of interpreting the statutory term.

E.A. POSNER, "The Parol Evidence Rule, the Plain Meaning Rule, and the Principles of Contractual Interpretation" (1998) 146 U. Pa. L. Rev. 533.

S.A. SMITH, *Contract Theory* (Oxford: Oxford University Press, 2004) c. 8.

C. STAUGHTON, "How Do the Courts Interpret Commercial Contracts?" (1999) Cambridge L.J. 303.

J. STEYN, "The Intractable Problem of the Interpretation of Legal Texts" (2003) 25 Sydney L. Rev. 5.

R. SULLIVAN, "Interpreting Contracts in Practice and Theory" (2000) 13 Sup. Ct. L. Rev. (2d) 369.

G. WILLIAMS, "Language and the Law" (1945) Law Q. Rev. 71 at 179, 293 and 384.

CHAPTER 20

EXCULPATORY CLAUSES

A. INTRODUCTION

The use of exculpatory clauses in written agreements is a pervasive practice in both commercial and consumer transactions. Exculpatory clauses are used to limit the potential liability of a party for breach of contract. Such clauses may completely preclude liability for breaches of certain stipulated kinds. Others may concede liability but impose a limitation on the extent of liability, such as return of the purchase price or a numerical cap on the extent of liability assumed. Other clauses may impose strictures on the manner in which losses resulting from breach are to be claimed by imposing, for example, a short period of notice within which claims are to be advanced. Exculpatory clauses are referred to by a variety of labels, such as disclaimers, limitation of liability clauses and exclusion, exceptions or exemption clauses. When such clauses are used deliberately by the parties to consciously allocate the risk of certain kinds of losses to one party or the other, they perform a valuable function. On the other hand, where they have been inserted by one party in a written agreement that, for whatever reason, is unlikely to be read by the other party, the use of such provisions may surprise that party and lead to what may be considered to be harsh and unjust consequences. Such problems are most likely to arise, of course, in the context of transactions involving the supply of goods and services to consumers on the basis of standard forms drafted by the supplier. Understandably, then, the courts have attempted to devise various techniques for effecting some degree of judicial control over the use of exculpatory clauses.

In this chapter, we examine the development of the doctrine of so-called fundamental breach that has been the principal, but not the exclusive means, for achieving this objective. Although controversy continues as to the precise nature of the doctrine, it is widely accepted that it is, for the most part at least, an aspect of the law of contract interpretation. The basic idea underlying the doctrine of fundamental breach is that there may be breaches of contract that are so severe that exclusion clauses, however drafted, should be either narrowly interpreted or otherwise confined by the courts in such a way as to withhold the protection of the particular clause in such circumstances. The doctrine of fundamental breach emerged in the middle of the last century from a series of decisions by the English Court of Appeal in which Lord Denning played a prominent role. Over the next few decades, an extended debate between the Court of Appeal and the House of Lords concerning the nature of and proper role of the doctrine unfolded. The view advanced by Lord Denning and the Court of Appeal was that the doctrine held that in circumstances of a fundamental breach of contract, an exculpatory clause would not be permitted to protect the party in breach from liability on the basis of a "rule of law" to this effect. The view advanced by the House of Lords was that the proper approach to the judicial control of exculpatory clauses is merely one of narrow construction of the clauses against the interests of those relying upon them. Unsurprisingly, the views of the House of Lords were to prevail. The course of the debate, however, reveals a number of the difficulties involved in fashioning a doctrine of this kind. Accordingly, the leading English cases will be reviewed here before turning to an account of the Canadian reception of the doctrine. As a preliminary matter, however, it is useful to identify and distinguish certain doctrines with which the doctrine of fundamental breach may be confused.

B. RELATED DOCTRINES

The doctrine of fundamental breach is not the only device devised by the courts to effect control over the effects of exculpatory clauses. As we have seen,[1] the rules relating to the incorporation of written terms in agreements have developed in such a way as to reject incorpora-

---

1   See Chapter 6, section C.

tion of unfair exculpatory clauses in circumstances where the affected party has not had adequate notice of the inclusion of the clause in the written document. The requirement of special notice of unduly harsh exculpatory clauses has been applied in the context of both signed agreements and unsigned documents forming the basis of a contractual relationship. It is often the case that the party not in breach will want to rely both on the rules relating to incorporation and on the doctrine of fundamental breach. The effect of the two doctrines is, however, quite distinct. If the rules of incorporation apply to prevent inclusion of the term in the agreement, the provision should, in theory at least, be of no force and effect whatsoever. The doctrine of fundamental breach comes into play, however, only if the exculpatory clause is included within the agreement and thus appears to be potentially capable of shielding the party in breach from liability. If the doctrine applies, it holds that an otherwise enforceable clause does not protect the party in breach from liability for a fundamental breach of contract.

Two further devices that may have the effect of controlling reliance on exculpatory clauses arise in the context of the parol evidence rule.[2] That rule precludes reliance on prior representations or undertakings to supplement, vary or contradict the terms of a written agreement that is intended to be the full expression of the agreement between the parties. There are a number of exceptions to this rule, two of which are of particular interest in the present context. The first holds that where a party has misrepresented the effect of a clause of the agreement, the other party may rely upon and enforce the term as represented rather than in priority to the term in its written form.[3] The application of this exception may have an impact on the enforceability of an exculpatory clause. Where the party relying on the clause misrepresents its effect, the clause will be interpreted on the basis of the misrepresentation rather than the written form. In *Curtis v. Chemical Cleaning & Dyeing Co.*,[4] for example, the defendant laundry was held unable to rely on an exculpatory clause because of a misrepresentation concerning its effects. The plaintiff had entrusted a white satin wedding dress to the defendant for cleaning. Upon noticing the exculpatory clause on the receipt, the plaintiff inquired as to its effect. The defendant's clerk represented that it protected the defendant with respect to injuries to the

---

2   See Chapter 6.
3   See Chapter 6, section D(3).
4   [1951] 1 K.B. 805 (C.A.). See also *Trigg v. M.I. Movers International Transport Services Ltd.* (1991), 4 O.R. (3d) 562 (C.A.), leave to appeal to S.C.C. refused (1992), 7 O.R. (3d) xii (S.C.C.).

beads and sequins on the dress only. Accordingly, when the dress itself was stained as a result of the cleaning process, the defendant could not rely on the broader language contained in the clause to protect itself from liability.

The second exception to the rule relevant to the present context relates to prior oral undertakings as to the mode of performance of an agreement. It has been held that evidence of a prior oral undertaking as to the manner in which a contract will be performed is admissible and may take priority over an exculpatory clause in the written agreement that would, if enforced, have the effect of rendering the initial undertaking illusory. In *Mendelssohn v. Normand Ltd.*,[5] for example, the plaintiff had deposited his car in a garage operated by the defendant on the faith of an undertaking that his car would remain locked. The defendant's attendant failed to live up to that undertaking with the result that valuable possessions were stolen from the plaintiff's car. The defendant proprietor of the garage was unable to rely on a printed term excluding liability for lost articles as it would have the effect of nullifying the prior undertaking.

Perhaps the most important source of confusion relating to the doctrine of fundamental breach is its relationship with the concept of repudiatory breach. As we have seen,[6] it is the doctrine of repudiatory breach that determines whether, when confronted by a breach of contract, the innocent party is entitled to disaffirm the contract and be released, therefore, from any further obligation to perform. The effect of a repudiatory breach is to entitle the innocent party to elect either to affirm or disaffirm the agreement. Whichever choice is made, the party in breach is liable for damages for breach of contract. It is not necessary to repeat here an account of the intricacies of the doctrine of repudiatory breach. The important point for present purposes is that similar phrases are used to describe the nature of some types of repudiatory breach and the nature of fundamental breach. As a result there exists a significant potential for confusion of the two concepts. Indeed, this particular confusion is an important and continuing source of difficulty.

Briefly stated, a breach is considered repudiatory in three types of situations. First, the breach is repudiatory when it constitutes a breach

---

5   [1969] 2 All E.R. 1215 (C.A.). See also *J. Evans & Son (Portsmouth) Ltd. v. Merzario (Andrea) Ltd.*, [1976] 1 W.L.R. 1078 (C.A.). Compare with *Solway v. Davis Moving & Storage Inc.* (2002), 222 D.L.R. (4th) 251 (Ont. C.A.) (similar result achieved through application of fundamental breach doctrine). See also *Canadian Indemnity Co. v. Okanogan Mainline Real Estate Board* (1970), 16 D.L.R. (3d) 715 (S.C.C.) (indemnity clause held unenforceable on similar grounds).

6   For discussion of repudiatory breach, see Chapter 15.

of a "condition" of the agreement. The parties may themselves stipulate which provisions of the agreement are considered conditions in
the requisite sense. Contractual conditions may also be stipulated by
statute or recognized at common law as being implicit in certain transaction types. In all of these cases, the particular breach of contract
may have either major or minor consequences for the innocent party.
However, since the breach in question is a breach of a "condition," the
breach is repudiatory in nature.

The second and third categories of repudiatory breach constitute
particular sources of confusion with the doctrine of fundamental
breach. In the second, if the terms of the agreement cannot be determined to be "conditions" by any of the above means, courts may imply
that a particular term of the contract is a condition where the term is
so important that any failure to perform it may be considered to be fundamental or essential or of such a nature that it "goes to the root of the
contract" and so on. In the third, even where it cannot be determined
that the term in question is a condition on the basis of this analysis,
a breach of a term may be held to be repudiatory where the particular
breach has such grave consequences for the innocent party that the
breach itself may be characterized as being fundamental or of such a
nature that it goes to the root of the contract and so on. Use of the term
"fundamental" and related expressions in these latter two contexts of
repudiatory breach, then, may lead and has led to confusion between
the doctrines of repudiatory breach and fundamental breach. Thus, an
English formulation of the definition of fundamental breach for the
purposes of the doctrine of repudiatory breach[7] has been relied on by
some members of the Supreme Court of Canada as a definition of the
concept of fundamental breach for the purposes of the doctrine of fundamental breach that is applicable to exclusion clauses.[8]

More importantly, in English law, for a time at least, there appeared
to be a confusion or merger of the two doctrines in such a way as to
lead to quite unsatisfactory results. The two doctrines, however, have
importantly different functions. The doctrine of repudiatory breach,
including those categories in which a concept of fundamentality is involved, identifies breaches of contract that are of such a nature as to entitle the innocent party to treat the contract as at an end. The doctrine
of fundamental breach, on the other hand, is designed to determine

---

7   *Photo Production Ltd. v. Securicor Transport Ltd.*, [1980] A.C. 827 at 849 (H.L.),
    Lord Diplock.
8   *Hunter Engineering Co. Inc. v. Syncrude Canada Ltd.*, [1989] 1 S.C.R. 426 at 499,
    Wilson J.

whether, in the event of a breach, the guilty party ought to be permitted to rely on an exclusionary clause. It is entirely possible that a breach could be of such a nature as to give rise to the right to terminate but not be so severe as to preclude the guilty party from relying on the exculpatory clause in the agreement. The test for applying each doctrine therefore cannot be the same.[9] This point is all the more obvious in the context of repudiatory breaches of contractual stipulations that are determined to be "conditions" by various means. Breaches of such stipulations, though nonetheless repudiatory, might not be of major or fundamental consequence for the innocent party and, in such a case, could not conceivably give rise to the application of the doctrine of fundamental breach. Thus, even if similar language is used to define the tests for application of the doctrines of repudiatory breach and fundamental breach, the test in each case is being applied for a different purpose and is, no doubt, applied differently. In examining the doctrine of fundamental breach, then, it is important to maintain a clear view of the difference between these two doctrines and the potential for confusion between them.

C. THE RISE AND FALL OF FUNDAMENTAL BREACH IN ENGLISH LAW

The doctrine of fundamental breach, in its initial formulation, held that where a breach of contract constituted a radical or fundamental departure from the obligations set out in the contract, an exculpatory clause that would otherwise have insulated the party in breach from liability would not have that effect. An influential articulation of the doctrine by its leading proponent, Lord Denning, is found in *Karsales (Harrow) Ltd. v. Wallis*.[10] The defendant had agreed to purchase a secondhand automobile from a dealer on financing arranged through the plaintiff hire-purchase company. The plaintiff let out the car to the defendant on hire-purchase terms that included an exclusion of liability with respect to any defects in the car. When the defendant had initially inspected the car, it was in excellent condition. Upon delivery, however, it was in a deplorable state, having been substantially damaged by interven-

---

9   *Suisse Atlantique Société d'Armement Maritime S.A. v. N.V. Rotterdamsche Kolen Centrale*, [1967] 1 A.C. 361 at 431, Lord Wilberforce, a passage quoted by Dickson C.J.C. in *Hunter Engineering Co. Inc. v. Syncrude Canada Ltd., ibid.* at 463.

10   [1956] 2 All E.R. 866 (C.A.).

ing events of some kind. The defendant refused to take delivery of the car and, in due course, was sued by the plaintiff finance company for non-payment of monthly hire-purchase charges. The Court of Appeal dismissed the claim. The hire-purchase contract contained an implied term that the car would be maintained in suitable condition pending delivery, a term that had obviously been breached. The exculpatory clause was unavailing, it was said, as a result of recent developments in the law. Lord Denning observed as follows:

> The law about exempting clauses, however, has been much developed in recent years, at any rate about printed exempting clauses, which so often pass unread. Notwithstanding earlier cases which might suggest the contrary, it is now settled that exempting clauses of this kind no matter how widely they are expressed, only avail the party when he is carrying out his contract in its essential respects. ... They do not avail him when he is guilty of a breach which goes to the root of the contract.[11]

Lord Denning further observed that the principle can be expressed as being applicable where a supplier provides something "different in kind" from that contracted for or has breached a "fundamental term" or a "fundamental contractual obligation."[12] All of these expressions were comprehended in his view, "by the general principle that a breach which goes to the root of the contract disentitles the party from relying on the exempting clause."[13] Support for this approach could be found in the context of a sale of goods contract where the goods delivered are "different in kind" from those contracted for,[14] in the bailment context where the bailee hands over the goods to someone other than the bailor,[15] and in the context of carriage of goods where the carrier undertakes a substantial deviation from the agreed route.[16] In such settings, courts had held that the exculpatory clause in the agreement could

---

11   *Ibid.* at 868–69.

12   *Ibid.* at 869.

13   *Ibid.*

14   *Andrews Bros. (Bournemouth) Ltd. v. Singer & Co. Ltd.*, [1934] 1 K.B. 17 (C.A.) (contract to deliver "new Singer cars"—Singer with substantial mileage delivered—exclusion of express and implied warranties concerning quality held ineffective to exclude liability).

15   *Woolf v. Collis Removal Service*, [1948] 1 K.B. 11 (C.A.); *Alexander v. Railway Executive*, [1951] 2 K.B. 882. See also *Sze Hai Tong Bank Ltd. v. Rambler Cycle Co. Ltd.*, [1959] A.C. 576 (P.C.).

16   *James Thorley Ltd. v. Orchis Steamship Co. Ltd.*, [1907] 1 K.B. 660 (C.A.); *Hain S.S. Co. Ltd. v. Tate & Lyle Ltd.*, [1936] 2 All E.R. 597 (H.L.).

not insulate the party in breach from liability for failing to perform such essential obligations. As envisaged by Lord Denning, the doctrine did not rest on construction of the particular clause or the agreement more generally. The doctrine applied as a "rule of law." The effect of the doctrine, it should be noted, was not to render the exculpatory clause generally unenforceable. Rather, the clause was inapplicable, as a matter of law, to the fundamental breach of contract.

The doctrine of fundamental breach was applied with some enthusiasm by English courts, especially in the context of consumer transactions.[17] The House of Lords had an opportunity to consider the soundness of the doctrine, however, in *Suisse Atlantique Société d'Armement Maritime S.A. v. N.V. Rotterdamsche Kolen Centrale*,[18] a commercial case involving the application of a demurrage clause in a charter party. The plaintiff had chartered a vessel from the defendant for the purpose of carrying shipments of coal across the Atlantic for a period of two years. The plaintiff claimed that as a result of the defendant's failure to load and unload the vessel in timely fashion, it had been denied six additional voyages that should have been performed within the two-year period. The plaintiff claimed for the profits lost as a result of this breach of contract. The defendant relied on the demurrage clause, which stipulated that the defendant would only be obliged to pay one thousand dollars per day in the event of delay and that the plaintiff was therefore limited in its claim to this amount for each day of delay beyond that required for timely performance of its obligations. On the assumption that a demurrage clause can be characterized as an exculpatory clause,[19] the plaintiff invoked the doctrine of fundamental breach and urged that the claim could succeed, notwithstanding the apparent limitation on liability contained in the clause. The House of Lords rejected the rule of law approach of the *Karsales* case and held that the correct view was that the application of an exceptions clause to circumstances of fundamental breach was a matter to be determined on the basis of the true construction of the agreement. Lord Wilberforce did suggest that the rule of law approach might apply in a marginal case where the clause appears to "have so wide an ambit as in effect to deprive one party's stipulations of all contractual force."[20] To construe the clause as having this effect

---

17   See, for example, *Yeoman Credit Ltd. v. Apps*, [1962] 2 Q.B. 508; *Charterhouse Credit Co. Ltd. v. Tolley*, [1963] 2 Q.B. 683 (C.A.); *Astley Industrial Trust Ltd. v. Grimley*, [1963] 1 W.L.R. 584 (C.A.).

18   Above note 9.

19   An assumption with which a majority of their Lordships did not agree.

20   Above note 9 at 432.

would "reduce the contract to a mere declaration of intent"[21] and a court would not give the clause that effect. Apart from such cases, however, the construction approach would apply.

Viscount Dilhorne and Lord Hodson straightforwardly rejected the rule of law approach and asserted that the question of the applicability of the exceptions clause to a particular breach of contract was a straightforward matter of construction. The views expressed by Lords Reid and Upjohn were, however, more complex. Indeed, it may be said that both fell into error in confusing the doctrine of fundamental breach as it applies to exceptions clauses and the doctrine of repudiatory breach entitling the innocent party to disaffirm the contract.[22] As a result, both concluded that where the innocent party disaffirmed the contract, the contract came to an end and accordingly, in their view, the exceptions clause was no longer of any force and effect. Lord Reid reasoned as follows:

> General use of the term "fundamental breach" is of recent origin and I can find nothing to indicate that it means either more or less than the well known type of breach which entitles the innocent party to treat it as repudiatory and to rescind the contract. ... If fundamental breach is established, the next question is what effect, if any, that has on the applicability of other terms of the contract. This question has often arisen with clauses excluding liability, in whole or in part, of the party in breach. I do not think that there is generally much difficulty where the innocent party has elected to treat the breach as a repudiation, bring the contract to an end and sue for damages. Then the whole contract has ceased to exist including the exclusion clause, and I do not see how that clause can then be used to exclude an action for loss which will be suffered by the innocent party after it has ceased to exist, such as loss of the profit which would have accrued if the contract had run its full term.[23]

If, on the other hand, the innocent party affirms the contract, the contract remains in full force and effect and, in Lord Reid's view, the exceptions clause is applicable, though subject to proper and narrow construction of its terms.

Similarly, Lord Upjohn explained the consequences of disaffirmation of the agreement for breach in the following terms: "[T]he principle upon which one party to a contract cannot rely on the clauses of

---

21   *Ibid.*
22   In his opinion, Lord Wilberforce warned against such confusion. See *ibid.* at 431.
23   *Ibid.* at 397–98.

exception or limitation of liability inserted for his sole protection, is ... if there is a fundamental breach accepted by the innocent party the contract is at an end; the guilty party cannot rely on any special terms in the contract."[24]

This reasoning leads to the unsatisfactory conclusion that although the contract remains enforceable after disaffirmation, the exceptions clause is not enforceable. Accordingly, the effect of this analysis, whether intended or not, is to dramatically enhance the "rule of law" approach and apply it to every case in which a contract is disaffirmed for breach. Given that a repudiatory breach may be less severe than a "fundamental breach" in the *Karsales* sense, it follows that in the context of disaffirmation, exclusion clauses would be inoperative, as a matter of law, in a broader range of situations than those envisaged in the original *Karsales* doctrine. Indeed, a few years later, in *Harbutt's "Plasticine" Ltd. v. Wayne Tank & Pump Co. Ltd.*,[25] Lord Denning seized upon this aspect of the reasoning of Lords Reid and Upjohn as a justification for a substantial expansion of the role of the rule of law approach.

The facts of the *Harbutt's* case uniquely illustrate the essential difficulty with the rule of law approach. Where, in a commercial setting, the exceptions clause represents a consensual exercise by the parties in allocating the risk of certain types of losses to one party rather than the other, the rule of law approach would, if applicable, simply strike down that voluntary agreement. The plaintiff, an owner of a plasticine factory, had hired the defendant to design and install certain equipment to be used in the plaintiff's manufacturing processes. The design was deficient with the result that the equipment caused a fire that destroyed the factory. The plaintiff was insured for losses occasioned by fire and, within weeks, received substantial sums from the insurer and began the rebuilding of the factory. When it was ultimately discovered that the cause of the fire was negligence on the part of the defendant, the plaintiff's insurer brought a subrogated claim in the plaintiff's name against the defendant for the cost of rebuilding the factory. Lord Denning, relying on the passages from the opinions of Lords Reid and Upjohn quoted above, suggested that the effect of the *Suisse Atlantique* case was to affirm the rule of law approach as it applied to cases where a party disaffirmed the contract. The construction approach would apply, in his view, only if the innocent party affirmed the contract. By extension, the rule of law approach was applicable, in his view, to a case like *Harbutt's*, where the effect of the breach was to frustrate the con-

---

24   *Ibid.* at 425.
25   [1970] 1 Q.B. 447 (C.A.).

tract in the sense that there was simply no point in either affirming or disaffirming the contract. In a case such as this, the contract was "*automatically* at an end without the innocent party having an election."[26] For Lord Denning, then, the party in breach cannot rely on the exculpatory clause in such circumstances because the breach of contract has itself brought the contract to an end. Accordingly, the subrogated claim of the insurer enjoyed success. On the basis of this reasoning, presumably, the rule of law approach would apply in any case where there was no need to disaffirm the contract. As there is no point in disaffirming the contract once it has been fully executed, it might well have been Lord Denning's view that the rule of law approach would apply even in the case of a merely executed contract where no frustrating event such as a fire had occurred.

This dramatic expansion of the rule of law approach was, however, short-lived. In what would become the leading English decision on fundamental breach, *Photo Production Ltd. v. Securicor Transport Ltd.*,[27] Lord Denning's treatment in *Harbutt's* of the reasoning of the House of Lords in *Suisse Atlantique* attracted vigorous criticism on the basis that it simply ignored the reasoning of the majority of the opinions offered in that case. Moreover, on the merits of the proposed doctrine, the doctrine in *Harbutt's* was said to contain unsatisfactory reasoning with respect to the effect of the termination of the agreement. As Lord Wilberforce indicated, there appears to be no reason in principle for disregarding, upon termination of the agreement, what the agreement itself says about damages.[28] *Harbutt's* was explicitly overruled in the *Photo Production* case.

With respect to the doctrine of fundamental breach more generally, the House of Lords confirmed, in *Photo Production*, that the construction approach was to be applied in determining whether or not an exculpatory clause applied in the context of a particular breach of contract. Their Lordships noted, however, that the legal landscape had changed in an important respect since the decision in *Suisse Atlantique*. Acting on the advice of the English and Scottish Law Commissions,[29] Parliament had enacted the *Unfair Contracts Terms Act 1977*.[30] This legisla-

---

26 *Ibid.* at 466 (emphasis in original).
27 Above note 7.
28 *Ibid.* at 844.
29 U.K., Law Commission and Scottish Law Commission, *Exemption Clauses, Second Report* (Law Com.; no. 69, H.C. 605; Scottish Law. Com.; no. 39) (London: HMSO, 1975).
30 (U.K.) 1977, c. 50. See generally N. Palmer and D. Yates, "The Future of the *Unfair Contract Terms Act 1977*" (1981) 40 Cambridge L.J. 108; J. Adams and R.

tion applies to exemption clauses in consumer contracts and standard forms. It renders certain kinds of exemption clauses ineffective and subjects others to a test of reasonableness. With respect to the latter test, the statute instructs the courts to consider, *inter alia*, the relative bargaining strength of the parties and the extent to which the party not relying on the clause knew or ought to have known of its existence.[31] The fact that legislation addressing these issues in these contexts had been enacted enabled the House of Lords to focus the attention of the common law on negotiated commercial arrangements. Moreover, the fact that the legislation was restricted in its focus was itself considered to be an important signal of Parliament's intentions with respect to the treatment of exculpatory clauses in the commercial setting. Lord Wilberforce explained:

> It is significant that Parliament refrained from legislating over the whole field of contracts. After this Act, in commercial matters generally, when the parties are not of unequal bargaining power, and when risks are normally borne by insurance, not only is the case for judicial intervention undemonstrated, but there is everything to be said, and this seems to have been Parliament's intention, for leaving the parties free to apportion the risks as they think fit and for respecting their decisions.[32]

Lord Wilberforce, with whom Lords Keith and Scarman concurred,[33] reaffirmed the view that he had stated in *Suisse Atlanique* to the effect that whether and to what extent an exculpatory clause will apply to a fundamental breach is "a matter of construction."[34]

Properly construed, the clause at issue in the *Photo Production* case applied to the loss that had occurred and, accordingly, insulated the defendant from liability. The defendant had been engaged to provide security services in the form of nightly patrols of the plaintiff's factory for a modest fee. One of the defendant's employees had started a fire that resulted in the destruction of the factory. The exculpatory clause, however, clearly indicated that the defendant would not be responsible for such losses. Lord Wilberforce noted that although the clause should be construed *contra proferentum*, the intent of the clause was clear. More-

---

Brownsword, "The *Unfair Contract Terms Act*: A Decade of Discretion" (1988) 104 Law Q. Rev. 94.

31 *Unfair Contracts Terms Act 1977, ibid.,* Schedule 2.

32 Above note 7 at 843.

33 Separate concurring opinions were filed by Lords Diplock and Salmon.

34 Above note 7 at 843.

over, as the defendant would have had no knowledge of the value of the plaintiff's factory or of the plaintiff's fire precautions, "nobody could consider it *unreasonable*, that as between these two equal parties the risk assumed by Securicor should be a modest one, and that the [plaintiff] should carry the substantial risk of damage or destruction."[35]

In a concurring judgment, Lord Diplock rejected the rule of law approach and affirmed that the proper approach involves construction of the clause. Lord Diplock, however, engaged in a more extensive and complex analysis of the nature of the construction approach. Indeed, Lord Diplock devised a novel conceptual apparatus for the purpose of identifying more precisely the nature of the "narrow construction" involved in the interpretation of exculpatory clauses. Lord Diplock divided contractual obligations into two types, primary and secondary. The primary obligations are the undertakings that promise that "some thing will be done."[36] The primary obligations are both express and implied and the parties are, generally speaking, free to determine what their primary obligations under the agreement will be. Implied primary obligations are the product of either judicial determination or legislative enactment. Breaches of primary obligations were said by Lord Diplock to "give rise to substituted or secondary obligations on the part of the party in default."[37] These secondary obligations are, essentially, the obligation to pay damages for breach of contract, and the obligation to do so was termed by Lord Diplock the "general secondary obligation." As Lord Diplock observed, in the absence of repudiatory breach and a resulting termination of the agreement by the innocent party, the primary obligations of the party in breach remain unchanged. Upon disaffirmation for repudiatory breach, however, the parties are released from further performance, though the party in breach remains liable in damages for past and future losses resulting from the breach. Lord Diplock introduced a further complexity in this analysis by using the phrase "anticipatory secondary obligation"[38] to describe the situation in which a contract is terminated for a repudiatory breach with the result that the innocent party is excused from further performance and is nonetheless entitled to recover damages with respect to the future and unperformed obligations of the party in breach. The obligation of the party in breach to compensate for future non-performance in such circumstances is the anticipatory secondary obligation. The

---

35 *Ibid.* at 846 (emphasis added).
36 *Ibid.* at 848.
37 *Ibid.*
38 *Ibid.* at 849.

general secondary obligation and the anticipatory secondary obligation are, for Lord Diplock, implied obligations and, like implied primary obligations, subject to modification by the parties. In principle, then, there can be no objection to the inclusion of an exculpatory clause in an agreement that has the effect of modification of the general or anticipatory secondary obligations. This general principle, however, was subject, in Lord Diplock's view, to two limitations.

First, parties are not free to modify the implied secondary obligations to such an extent that the agreement no longer retains "the legal characteristics of a contract."[39] This point is reminiscent of the suggestion made by Lord Wilberforce in *Suisse Atlantique* to the effect that an exculpatory clause would not be construed so broadly as to preclude any form of liability and, therefore, "reduce the contract to a mere declaration of intent."[40] The second limitation arises from a presumption in favour of the implied primary and secondary obligations. In Lord Diplock's view, courts should lean in favour of maintaining the integrity of the implied obligations, if possible, when construing an exculpatory clause. He explained this approach in the following terms:

> Since the obligations implied by law in a commercial contract are those which, by judicial consensus over the years or by Parliament in passing a statute, have been regarded as obligations which a reasonable businessman would realise that he was accepting when he entered into a contract of a particular kind, the court's view of the *reasonableness* of any departure from the implied obligations which would be involved in construing the express words of an exclusion clause in one sense that they are capable of bearing rather than another, is a relevant consideration in deciding what meaning the words were intended by the parties to bear.[41]

Lord Diplock emphasized, however, that this approach is operative only where the exclusion clause is truly ambiguous. He went on to state: "this [approach] does not entitle the court to reject the exclusion clause, however *unreasonable* the court itself may think it is, if the words are clear and fairly susceptible of one meaning only."[42]

The rather complex analysis offered by Lord Diplock, then, appears designed to offer a justification for the application of a *contra proferentum* approach in the context of provisions that modify the implied

---

39   *Ibid.* at 850.
40   Above note 9.
41   Above note 7 at 850–51 (emphasis added).
42   *Ibid.* at 851 (emphasis added).

primary and secondary obligations in an agreement. It is not at all clear that this analysis is either necessary or illuminating. The principle of *contra proferentum* appears to apply generally to the interpretation of exculpatory clauses drafted by one of the parties to the agreement and, more particularly, applies whether or not the primary obligation in question is express or implied. Moreover, it is not at all clear that one's understanding of the rules of contract law that require a party in breach to compensate the innocent party is enhanced by considering the obligation to arise from implied terms of the agreement, the general and anticipatory secondary obligations. Perhaps because of the unattractive complexity of the analysis, it does not appear to have been adopted by subsequent courts to any significant degree.[43]

With the enactment of the *Unfair Contract Terms Act 1977*, the role of the doctrine of fundamental breach in English contract law has been very much reduced. In essence, the doctrine applies to negotiated commercial agreements, a context within which the construction approach, as the House of Lords noted in the *Photo Production* case, has much to commend it. At common law, such clauses are to be construed *contra proferentum*. Even Lord Denning appears to have accepted, however, that where the language of the provision has a clear meaning, heroic efforts and strained interpretations of the language to confine the applicability of the clause are inappropriate. In *George Mitchell Ltd. v. Finney Lock Seeds Ltd.*,[44] a farmer had purchased seeds on the basis of a standard form agreement that restricted liability in the event of loss caused by defective seeds to return of the purchase price. The supplier had supplied the wrong type of seed and caused a considerable loss of profit. Lord Denning was of the view that the language of the supplier's exemption clause was so clear that he was obliged by the reasoning in *Photo Production* to give effect to the clause and limit the supplier's liability at common

---

43   In *George Mitchell Ltd. v. Finney Lock Seeds Ltd.*, [1983] Q.B. 284 at 300–1 (C.A.), aff'd [1983] 2 A.C. 803 (H.L.), Lord Denning was dismissive of the analysis ("I do hope, however, that we shall not often have to consider the newfound analysis of contractual obligations into 'primary obligations' 'secondary obligations' 'general secondary obligations' and 'anticipatory secondary obligations'. No doubt it is logical enough but it is too esoteric altogether. It is fit only for the rarefied atmosphere of the House of Lords. Not at all for the chambers of the practitioners. Let alone for the student at the university"). Compare with *Hunter Engineering Co. Inc. v. Syncrude Canada Ltd.*, above note 8 at 499, Wilson J., where reliance on Lord Diplock's analysis appears to have induced a confusion between the doctrines of repudiatory breach and fundamental breach in the exculpatory clause sense.

44   *George Mitchell Ltd. v. Finney Lock Seeds Ltd.*, ibid.

law to return of the price. The circumstances under which the supplier's standard form had been employed, however, engaged the statutory jurisdiction to withhold enforcement if it would "not be fair or reasonable to allow reliance upon the term."[45] Lord Denning noted that the clause had not been negotiated between persons of equal bargaining power. It had simply been imposed on the farmer without negotiation. Moreover, it was the practice of the seed merchant not to rely on the clause in meritorious cases. Further, Lord Denning noted that it appeared that the supplier had been seriously negligent. In these circumstances, it would not be "fair or reasonable" to allow the merchant to rely on the clause. Lord Denning was affirmed on both points by the House of Lords.[46]

In the *George Mitchell* case, however, Lord Denning objected to the suggestion made in another decision of the House of Lords to the effect that the principles applicable to exclusion clauses ought not be applicable "in their full rigour"[47] to clauses merely limiting liability. Clauses of the latter type would be read *contra proferentum* but not judged by the "specially exacting standards"[48] applicable to exclusion clauses. As Lord Denning noted, however, this distinction is difficult to defend in principle and had been rejected by earlier authority.[49] Moreover, now that the standard for construction has become less "strained" than it was prior to the enactment of the *Unfair Contract Terms Act 1977*, there would appear to be no reason to refrain from subjecting a limitation of liability clause to the same *contra proferentum* approach that is now applicable to exclusion clauses in the pure sense.[50] The only special rule, then, that appears to apply to exclusion clauses in English law is that courts will resist interpreting an exclusion clause in order to give it so wide an ambit as to effectively deprive the agreement of any contractual force and effect. Apart from such cases, a simple *contra proferentum* approach appears to be applicable.[51]

---

45 *Supply of Goods (Implied Terms) Act 1973*, (U.K.) 1973, c. 13, s. 4. See now *Unfair Contract Terms Act 1977*, (U.K.) 1977, c. 50.

46 Above note 43.

47 *Ailsa Craig Fishing Co. Ltd. v. Malvern Co. Ltd.*, [1983] 1 W.L.R. 964 at 970 (H.L.), Lord Fraser of Tullybelton.

48 *Ibid.*

49 Above note 43 at 301 (C.A.). The authority in question was *Atlantic Shipping and Trading Co. v. Louis Dreyfus and Co.*, [1922] 2 A.C. 250 at 260, Lord Sumner. The distinction was also criticized as untenable by Wilson J. in *Hunter Engineering Co. Inc. v. Syncrude*, above note 8 at 518.

50 Indeed, in the *Ailsa Craig* case Lord Fraser had suggested that limitation of liability clauses would be subject to *contra proferentum* but not subject to the "specially exacting standards" applied to exclusion clauses. See above note 47.

51 In the *George Mitchell* case, Lord Denning suggested that the result in the *Photo Production* case is explicable on the basis that both Lord Wilberforce and Lord

D. CANADIAN RECEPTION OF THE DOCTRINE

Canadian courts accorded the doctrine of fundamental breach set out by Lord Denning in the *Karsales*[52] case a warm reception. The doctrine was applied on numerous occasions, many of them involving disputes concerning commercial agreements.[53] In these cases, the courts typically reasoned that the contract performance provided by the person relying on the clause was so defective that the other party had essentially not received the bargained-for consideration. With the advent of the decision of the House of Lords in *Suisse Atlantique*,[54] however, Canadian courts accepted the soundness of the decision in that case and began to employ, at least in appearance, the construction approach. In *B.G. Linton Construction Ltd. v. C.N.R. Co.*,[55] a majority of the Supreme Court of Canada, following the reasoning in *Suisse Atlantique*, held that the defendant, which had badly botched the sending of the plaintiff's bid on a construction project by telegraph, was able to rely on a comprehensive exculpatory clause. In dissent, however, Laskin C.J.C. would have applied the principle that an exculpatory clause cannot be given the effect of completely negating any obligation that the agreement might have appeared to contemplate. In his view, "[t]here must be a residue of obligation that is not cancelled out by concurrent exemp-

---

Diplock considered that in the particular circumstances of the case the exclusion clause was a "reasonable" one. See the italicized portion of the quotations from the opinions of Lords Wilberforce and Diplock set out in the text above at notes 34 and 40. The suggestion that a reasonableness standard applies even in the context of commercial agreements not subject to the *Unfair Contract Terms Act 1977*, however, appears inconsistent both with the statutory scheme and the general thrust of the decision in *Photo Production*. The point was not further pursued by Lord Denning himself in the *George Mitchell* case, nor has it been adopted in subsequent English decisions.

52   Above note 10.
53   See for example, *Schmidt v. International Harvester Co. of Canada Ltd.* (1962), 38 W.W.R. 180 (Man. Q.B.); *Knowles v. Anchorage Holdings Co. Ltd.* (1964), 43 D.L.R. (2d) 300 (B.C.S.C.); *Western Processing and Cold Storage Ltd. v. Hamilton Construction Co. Ltd.* (1965), 51 D.L.R. (2d) 245 (Man. C.A.); *Canadian-Dominion Leasing Corporation Ltd. v. Suburban Super Drug Ltd.* (1966), 56 D.L.R. (2d) 43 (Alta. S.C.A.D.); *Keelan v. Norray Distributing Ltd.* (1967), 62 D.L.R. (2d) 466 (Man. Q.B.); *F.&B. Transport Ltd. v. White Truck Sales Manitoba Ltd.* (1965), 49 D.L.R. (2d) 670 (Man. C.A.).
54   Above note 9.
55   [1975] 2 S.C.R. 678.

tion; otherwise, it is illusory to speak of a contract."[56] The majority did
not disagree with this proposition but held that the case was one of
negligent performance rather than fundamental breach.

Although the *Suisse Atlantique* approach was accepted and purportedly applied in a number of subsequent Canadian cases, it was not
apparent, at the level of the actual results of these cases, that much
had changed as a result of the shift to the construction technique. In
cases involving consumer purchases of vehicles, for example, a series
of defects in the vehicle in question was held to constitute a fundamental breach that the exculpatory clause, on its proper construction, did
not reach.[57] Similar results were achieved in the context of commercial
transactions on the basis of the construction approach. Thus, for example, in *R.G. McLean Ltd. v. Canadian Vickers Ltd.*,[58] the supplier of a
defective printing press was unable to rely on a broadly worded exclusion clause. The defects had resulted in a performance that was "totally
different from what the parties had in contemplation."[59] Accordingly,
on its proper construction, the clause did not preclude the action for
damages for breach of warranty.

Canadian cases in the post–*Suisse Atlantique* era, however, also
contained, on occasion, more aggressive assertions of a "rule of law"
approach reminiscent of Lord Denning's views. In a consumer transaction case, *Davidson v. Three Spruces Realty Ltd.*,[60] a British Columbia
trial judge, drawing on prior statements of Lord Denning to the same
effect,[61] asserted a jurisdiction to withhold enforcement of an exculpatory clause where, in all the circumstances, "it is unreasonable and
unconscionable"[62] to enforce the clause. The plaintiffs had placed valuables in "safety deposit" vaults operated by the defendant. The circum-

---

56   *Ibid.* at 684. A separate dissenting judgment was filed by Spence J., with whom
Dickson and Beetz JJ. concurred, applying the *Karsales* version of the doctrine.
57   See, for example *Lightburn v. Belmont Sales Limited* (1969), 6 D.L.R. (3d) 692
(B.C.S.C.); *Gibbons v. Trapp Motors* (1970), 9 D.L.R. (3d) 742 (B.C.S.C.). Compare
with *Peters v. Parkway Mercury Sales Ltd.* (1975), 58 D.L.R. (3d) 128 (N.B.C.A.);
Keefe v. Fort (1978), 89 D.L.R. (3d) 275 (N.S.C.A.).
58   (1970), 15 D.L.R. (3d) 15 (Ont. C.A.).
59   *Ibid.* at 20.
60   (1977), 79 D.L.R. (3d) 481 (B.C.S.C.), Anderson J.
61   See *Gillespie Brothers & Co. Ltd. v. Roy Bowles Transport Ltd.*, [1973] Q.B. 400
at 416 ("[the law] will not allow a party to exempt himself from his liability
at common law when it would be quite unconscionable of him to do so"). See
also *Levison v. Patent Steam Carpet Cleaning Co. Ltd.*, [1978] Q.B. 69 at 81 (C.A.)
("the doctrine of fundamental breach ... still applies in standard form contracts
where there is inequality of bargaining power").
62   Above note 60 at 493.

stances considered relevant by the trial judge included the fact that the agreement was set out on a standard form, that the customers' attention had not been drawn to the exemption clause nor, indeed, were they provided with copies of the agreement. These factors, it may be noted, are rather similar to those that English courts are required to consider under the *Unfair Contract Terms Act 1977.*[63] Further, in *Davidson*, the agreements were executed by the plaintiffs after receiving representations that proper precautions would be taken by the defendant to ensure the security of their valuables. A suggestion had also been made by the defendant that there was no need for the plaintiffs to acquire insurance against loss by theft or otherwise. The trial judge's view that exemption clauses can be ignored where it would be unreasonable and unconscionable to apply them is, of course, quite inconsistent with the reasoning in the *Suisse Atlantique* case.

Similarly, in the decision of the Ontario Court of Appeal in *Beaufort Realties (1964) Inc. v. Belcourt Construction (Ottawa) Ltd.*[64] — a decision ultimately appealed to the Supreme Court of Canada[65] — the Court refused to apply a waiver of lien clause executed by a subcontractor in the context of a construction project where the general contractor had wrongfully refused to pay the subcontractor for what it considered to be unsatisfactory work. Wilson J.A., speaking for the Court of Appeal, acknowledged that the Supreme Court of Canada had approved *Suisse Atlantique* in the *Linton Construction*[66] case and further acknowledged that Lord Reid, in *Suisse Atlantique,* had stated that "there is no indication in the recent cases that the courts are to consider whether the exemption is fair in all circumstances or is harsh and unconscionable."[67] Nonetheless, Wilson J.A. went on to suggest that it was open to the court to determine "whether it is fair and reasonable that [the exemption clause] survive the disintegration of its contractual setting."[68] For the Court of Appeal, the waiver of lien stipulation, even though it simply deprived the subcontractor of the additional remedy of a lien, was

---

63   Above note 31.

64   *Sub nom. Chomedy Aluminium Co. Ltd. v. Belcourt Construction (Ottawa) Ltd.* (1979), 97 D.L.R. (3d) 170 (Ont. C.A.).

65   [1980] 2 S.C.R. 718.

66   Above note 55.

67   Above note 64 at 177, quoting Lord Reid in *Suisse Atlantique*, above note 9 at 406.

68   In her view, the question is not whether the clause itself, considered in its contractual setting is fair and reasonable but, rather, whether in the circumstances that have occurred, it is "fair and reasonable" that the exemption clause should continue to be binding.

considered to be an exculpatory clause. Further, non-payment by the general contractor on the mistaken assumption that the subcontractor was in breach was held to constitute a fundamental breach of the agreement. Accordingly, the general contractor could not rely on the waiver and the statutory lien was held to revive. Otherwise, the result would be unfair and unreasonable. Again, it is not possible to find in *Suisse Atlantique* support for the proposition that a court can withhold enforcement of an exculpatory clause in circumstances where it considers application of the clause to be "unfair and unreasonable." Further, the result in this case might be considered to constitute a rather aggressive application of the doctrine of fundamental breach.

Against this background, the decision of the Supreme Court of Canada in the *Beaufort Realties* case occasions some surprise. Subsequent to the decision of the Ontario Court of Appeal, and prior to the argument of the appeal to the Supreme Court of Canada in this case, the decision of the House of Lords in *Photo Production* was released.[69] In a rather short judgment on behalf of the Supreme Court, Ritchie J. quoted at length from Lord Wilberforce's reasons in *Photo Production* in which Lord Wilberforce strongly criticized the views of Lord Denning and reaffirmed the construction approach favoured in *Suisse Atlantique*. Consistently with the position taken in the *Linton Construction* case, then, the Supreme Court reaffirmed its support for the construction approach. At the same time, however, the Court, somewhat surprisingly, affirmed the holding of the Ontario Court of Appeal that the waiver of lien clause ceased to bind the subcontractor as a result of the general contractor's fundamental breach of contract. If, at the level of formal doctrine, the construction approach had been reaffirmed by the court in this case, the result belied some continuing influence of Lord Denning's views.

A more open embrace of an independent Canadian doctrine of fundamental breach was to await the decision of the Supreme Court of Canada in 1989 in *Hunter Engineering Co. Inc. v. Syncrude Canada Ltd.*[70] This case involved a commercial transaction under which gearboxes were designed and supplied by Hunter for the plaintiff Syncrude's tar sands operations in Western Canada. Under a second agreement, Allis-Chalmers supplied a conveyer system that included a further set of Hunter-designed gearboxes. Under both contracts, warranties were given with respect to the gearboxes but, under a separate provision, the warranties in each case expired either twenty-four months from delivery of the

---

69   Above note 7.
70   Above note 8.

equipment or twelve months from its commencement in service, whichever should first occur. When, after expiry of the warranty period, the
gearboxes failed as a result of design defects, Syncrude launched actions
against Hunter and Allis-Chalmers, both of whom relied on the limitation of liability clauses. Syncrude sought to disarm the clauses on the
basis of the doctrine of fundamental breach. Although the Court was
unanimous in the view that the plaintiff's claims were to be dismissed, a
majority view as to the nature of the doctrine of fundamental breach did
not emerge. Extensive discussions of the doctrine were offered both by
Dickson C.J.C. and Wilson J., but neither view attracted majority support. Each attracted a concurring vote. The fifth member of the panel
declined to choose between the competing views.[71]

Both Dickson C.J.C. and Wilson J. noted that the *Photo Production* case had reaffirmed the construction approach advocated in *Suisse
Atlantique* and adopted by the Supreme Court of Canada in the *Beaufort Realties* case. They acknowledged as well, however, that although
Canadian courts appeared to have paid lip service to the construction
approach, they had persisted in applying fundamental breach doctrine
in a manner that had some similarity to the rule of law approach to
the doctrine. Further, both acknowledged that the more restrictive approach taken by the House of Lords in the *Photo Production* case was
facilitated by the enactment in England of the *Unfair Contract Terms
Act 1977*. They further noted that in Canada, however, the absence of
such legislation meant that the doctrine of fundamental breach would
have to continue to develop on a common law basis. Accordingly, both
sought to clarify the role of the doctrine. Unfortunately, however, the
nature of the clarification offered by each differs in what may appear to
be material respects.

Wilson J. adopted an approach to the doctrine reminiscent of the
views she had expressed as a member of the Ontario Court of Appeal
in the *Beaufort Realties* case. In her view, courts should be able to refuse to enforce exclusion clauses in circumstances where it would be
unfair and unreasonable to enforce them in strict accordance with their
terms. Wilson J. rejected the idea that it might be open to courts to
"require that the exclusion clause be *per se* a fair and reasonable contractual term in the contractual setting or bargain made by the parties."[72] Courts are, she suggested, unsuited to the task of determining

---

71 L'Heureux-Dubé J. concurred with Wilson J. La Forest J. concurred with Dick-
    son C.J.C. McIntyre J., in a very short judgment, declined further comment on
    the fundamental breach doctrine.
72 Above note 8 at 508.

the fairness or reasonableness of terms negotiated by the parties. In her view, however, it was "an entirely different matter for the courts to determine *after a particular breach has occurred* whether an exclusion clause should be enforced or not."[73] In that context, it should be open to a court to determine whether "it was fair and reasonable to enforce the clause in favour of the party that committed that breach even if the exclusion clause was clear and unambiguous."[74] Although Wilson J. provided very little guidance as to when the nature of a particular breach would be, such that it would be unfair and unreasonable to apply an exculpatory clause, she did suggest that a party that is "seeking to escape almost entirely the burdens of the transaction"[75] should not be able to rely upon such a clause.

Wilson J. then considered the possibility that the doctrine of unconscionability might serve as a suitable alternative to retention of her proposed version of the doctrine of fundamental breach. Unfortunately, this discussion does not clearly distinguish between the traditional doctrine of unconscionability[76] and the notion of unconscionability as it appeared to be developing in some of the decisions of Lord Denning in the exculpatory-clause context. Under the traditional doctrine, agreements that have been entered into on the basis of an unfair advantage taken of an inequality of bargaining power may be rescinded by the weaker party. In the normal exculpatory-clause case, of course, there is no question of rescission. The party not in breach wishes to enforce the contract but, at the same time, ignore the exculpatory clause. It was Lord Denning's suggestion that one might be able to ignore the clause in circumstances where applying the clause would itself be a matter of unconscionability. This novel use of the concept of unconscionability to, in effect, delete a clause rather than rescind an agreement has not, of course, been accepted by the House of Lords as forming a part of the English law of fundamental breach. It did, however, form a part of the analysis offered by the British Columbia court in *Davidson v. Three Spruces Realty Ltd.*[77] In her opinion in *Hunter*, however, Wilson J. includes references both to the traditional doctrine and to the use of the concept in the *Davidson* case, without indicating either that a difference existed between them or that one was to be preferred, in her view. More generally, however, Wilson J. was of the view that unconscionability

---

73   *Ibid.* at 509 (emphasis in original).
74   *Ibid.* at 510.
75   *Ibid.*
76   See Chapter 11, section D.
77   Above note 60.

was not a satisfactory alternative to a clarified doctrine of fundamental breach as its adoption would restrict the application of the doctrine to circumstances of inequality of bargaining power. Even in cases of relatively equal bargaining power, in her view, "there is some virtue in a residual power residing in the court to withhold its assistance on policy grounds in appropriate circumstances."[78] Accordingly, for Wilson J., the doctrine of fundamental breach would apply in a case where the nature of the breach is such that it would be unfair and unreasonable to apply the clause.

For Dickson C.J.C., however, unconscionability provided the solution to the fundamental breach puzzle. Dickson C.J.C. specifically rejected the approach suggested by Wilson J. of requiring the court to assess the reasonableness of enforcing the exculpatory clause in the circumstances of the particular breach. Rather, he was inclined to the view that the doctrine of fundamental breach should be replaced by a doctrine that generally holds the parties to the terms of their agreement but relieves the weaker party therefrom in circumstances of unconscionability. Again, there is ambiguity in Dickson C.J.C.'s judgment, as there was in that of Wilson J., as to whether or not the term "unconscionability" is being used to refer to the traditional doctrine enabling rescission of the entire agreement in the context of inequality of bargaining power or, on the other hand, to a new and innovative doctrine that would restrict the application of an exculpatory clause in circumstances of unconscionability. Certainly, Dickson C.J.C. referred to the doctrine as one in which the terms of the agreement normally apply, "provided the agreement is not unconscionable"[79] thus suggesting that the traditional doctrine is being invoked. On the other hand, at a later point in his opinion he suggests that unconscionability and inequality of bargaining power enables the courts to "focus expressly on the real grounds for refusing to give force to a contractual term,"[80] thereby suggesting that he had in mind the doctrine envisaged by Lord Denning and applied in *Davidson v. Three Spruces Realty Ltd.*[81]

Although divining the correct interpretation of the effect of the Supreme Court's decision in *Hunter* is not an easy task, there is at least some common ground between Dickson C.J.C. and Wilson J. First, both agree that in a typical commercial transaction, the construction approach is appropriate and the parties should be left to the terms to

---

78   Above note 8 at 517.
79   *Ibid.* at 456.
80   *Ibid.* at 462.
81   Above note 60.

which they have agreed. Both also agree, however, that the *Photo Production* approach, of a rigid rule of construction only of all exculpatory clauses, is not suitable for Canadian common law. In attempting to reconcile the differences between the two opinions, it may be useful to make the assumption that Dickson C.J.C. did, in fact, have in mind a doctrine of unconscionability that would not rescind the agreement for reasons of inequality of bargaining power but would have the effect of restricting application of the exculpatory clause in circumstances where doing so would lead to an unconscionable result. Indeed, it is unlikely that Dickson C.J.C. would have intended to apply the traditional doctrine of unconscionability with resulting rescission of the agreements to which it applied. Such an approach would simply make nonsense of the typical case in which the weaker party is seeking to enforce the agreement but, at the same time, attempting not to be bound by the exculpatory clause inserted into the agreement to protect the other party. If one can make this assumption, the difference between the two opinions can be made to diminish, if not disappear. Both Wilson J. and Dickson C.J.C., on this basis, might be seen to favour the retention of a judicial discretion to withhold application of an exculpatory clause where, in Wilson J.'s terms, doing so would be "unfair and unreasonable" or in Dickson C.J.C.'s terms, "unconscionable." There appears to be very little separating the meaning of these two concepts in the present context. Indeed, they have been used interchangeably in the fundamental breach cases by Lord Denning and in the Canadian decision, *Davidson v. Three Spruces Realty Ltd.*[82] The remaining point of distinction between the two opinions, then, would be that although Dickson C.J.C. appears to be of the view that fundamental breach should be restricted in its application to classic cases of inequality of bargaining power, Wilson J. was of the view that the doctrine should have a broader sweep than this. As we have seen,[83] the traditional doctrine of inequality of bargaining power is restricted in its application to very severe cases of inequality. It would not provide a basis for rescission, for example, in any case where an ordinary consumer enters into a contract with a supplier on the supplier's standard terms. Although there is an inequality of bargaining power in such circumstances, it is not of sufficient degree to engage the traditional unconscionability doctrine. It appears unlikely, therefore, that Dickson C.J.C. intended to

---

82   Above note 60 at 492–93.
83   See Chapter 11, section D.

restrict the new fundamental breach doctrine to so limited a context.[84] If that is so, the preferable reading of his opinion would be that the doctrine could potentially apply to any case where the agreement is not the product of free negotiations between parties of relatively equal bargaining strength, provided that application of the clause would lead to a result considered to be "unconscionable." On this basis, it is not only the case that the difference between the two opinions would further diminish, it would also appear to be the case that the Canadian common law doctrine has moved significantly in the direction of the approach adopted in the English *Unfair Contract Terms Act 1977*.

Some support for this reading of the decision of the Supreme Court in *Hunter* can be drawn from the subsequent cases applying the doctrine of fundamental breach set out in that case. Thus, it seems to be accepted that very little distinction is to be drawn between the approach of Dickson C.J.C. to the effect that an intervention should occur only where there exists "unconscionability" as opposed to that of Wilson J. that the courts should retain a discretion to withhold enforcement of exculpatory clauses where the result would otherwise be "unfair and unreasonable." In *Fraser Jewellers (1982) Ltd. v. Dominion Electric Protection Co.*,[85] for example, the Ontario Court of Appeal appears to have elided the two tests by considering whether, in the particular circumstances, there was anything "unfair or unreasonable or, indeed, unconscionable in giving effect to this term of the agreement."[86] Further, as one would expect, it appears unlikely that this threshold will be met in the case of an ordinary commercial transaction. In *Fraser Jewellers*, where an agreement to provide security services had been entered into between the plaintiff jeweller and the defendant security firm, the latter operating under the name "ADT," it was held that the exculpatory clause in the agreement affording protection to ADT in the event of

---

84 Support for this reading of his opinion might be drawn from his statement that "[o]nly where the contract is unconscionable, *as might arise* from situations of unequal bargaining power between the parties, should the courts interfere with agreements the parties have freely concluded" (emphasis added) thereby suggesting that unconscionability could be present in other circumstances. See above note 8 at 462. And see *Solway v. Davis Moving & Storage Inc.* (2002), 222 D.L.R. (4th) 251 at 255 (Ont. C.A.), Labrosse J.A.

85 (1997), 148 D.L.R. (4th) 496 (Ont. C.A.). See also *Newcourt Credit Group Inc. v. Hummel Pharmacy Ltd.* (1998), 38 O.R. (3d) 82 (Div. Ct.); *Carleton Condominium Corp. No. 32 v. Camdev Corp.* (1999), 47 C.L.R. (2d) 224 (Ont. C.A.); *Solway v. Davis Moving & Storage Inc.*, *ibid.*

86 *Fraser Jewellers (1982) Ltd. v. Dominion Electric Protection Co.*, *ibid.* at 503, Robins J.A.

loss was binding. Accordingly, even though losses occasioned by theft may have been exacerbated by ADT's failure to respond promptly to the alarm, the plaintiff's claim to recover those losses was subject to the cap set out in the limitation of liability provisions in the agreement. Moreover, in determining whether application of the clause is fair and reasonable, it may be relevant to consider whether the clause is intended to effect a reasonable allocation of risk between the parties. In *Fraser Jewellers*, Robins J.A. addressed this point in the following terms:

> Having regard to the potential value of property kept on a customer's premises, and the many ways in which a loss may be incurred, the rationale underlying this type of limitation clause is apparent and makes sound commercial sense. ADT is not an insurer and its monitoring fee bears no relationship to the area of risk and the extent of exposure ordinarily taken into account in the determination of insurance policy premiums. Limiting liability in this situation is manifestly reasonable. The clause, in effect, allocates risk in a certain fashion and alerts the customer to the need to make its own insurance arrangements. ADT has no control over the value of its customer's inventory and can hardly be expected, in exchange for a relatively modest annual fee, to insure a jeweller against negligent acts on the part of its employees up to the value of the entire jewellery stock whatever that value, from time to time, may be.[87]

Exceptionally, however, the doctrine will apply in a commercial setting where the conduct of the party relying on the clause is sufficiently offensive as to be characterized as "unconscionable" or "unfair, unreasonable or contrary to public policy."[88] In *Plas-Tex Canada Ltd. v. Dow Chemical of Canada Ltd.*,[89] the defendant supplied defective resin to a group of companies, including the plaintiff pipe manufacturer. The pipe manufactured by the plaintiff was employed by other members of the group in the construction of natural gas pipelines. The defect had the effect that the pipe manufactured with the defendant's resin as an ingredient was hazardous. The pipe had a tendency to crack, thus allowing natural gas to escape. At the time of contracting with the plaintiff, the defendant was aware of the defect and its effect on early failure of the pipes. Rather than disclose this information, the defendant "chose to protect itself from liability by inserting liability-limiting

---

87   *Ibid.* at 506.
88   *Plas-Tex Canada Ltd. v. Dow Chemical of Canada Ltd.* (2004), 245 D.L.R. (4th) 650 at para. 50 (Alta. C.A.), Picard J.A.
89   *Ibid.*

clauses"[90] in its agreement with the plaintiff. In the view of the Alberta Court of Appeal, such conduct was unconscionable and the exculpatory clauses could not be relied upon by the defendant.

The doctrine is likely to receive more ready application in the context of consumer transactions. Thus, suppliers of vehicles that are so defective as not to be in workable condition may not be able to hide behind an exculpatory clause.[91] A more difficult fact situation is posed by *Solway v. Davis Moving & Storage Inc.*[92] The plaintiffs had entered into a contract with the defendant moving company to remove and store their household goods before delivering them to their new home. The plaintiffs had understood that the goods would be stored in a locked trailer in the defendant's parking lot. The trailer was, however, left on the street to facilitate snow removal on the lot and the trailer and its contents were stolen from that location. The terms of the agreement were stipulated by statute and included a limitation of liability clause limiting the defendant's liability to a modest sum per pound. A majority of the Ontario Court of Appeal applied the fundamental breach doctrine on the ground that it would be unconscionable, unfair or unreasonable to allow the defendant to rely on the clause in these circumstances. The plaintiff was therefore allowed to recover the substantial losses resulting from the theft. The case is, however, a difficult one. The clause was stipulated by statute and might be thought to represent a reasonable allocation of risk between the owner of the chattels, who knows their value, and the moving company, who will not likely have such knowledge. Further, in this particular case, it appears that the plaintiffs were aware of the nature of the limitation of liability and, indeed, had taken out some additional insurance. For reasons such as these, Carthy J.A., in dissent, would not have applied fundamental breach doctrine.[93]

---

90   *Ibid.* at para. 54.
91   See, for example, *Scarborough Tire & Spring Service Ltd. v. Campbell Graphics Inc.* (1994), 17 B.L.R. (2d) 118 (Ont. Ct. Gen. Div.); *Bagnell's Cleaners & Launderers Ltd. v. Eastern Automobile Co.* (1991), 111 N.S.R. (2d) 51 (S.C.T.D.). These cases do not, however, refer to the *Hunter* analysis.
92   Above note 84.
93   For criticism of the majority opinion from a law and economics perspective, see A.J. Duggan, "Stolen Goods, A Cruise Disaster and a Right of Way Gone Wrong: Three Unconscionable Contracts Cases from a Law and Economics Perspective" (2004) 40 Can. Bus. L.J. 3. A similar exchange of views occurred in a Nova Scotia case involving two commercial parties. See *Atlas Supply Co. of Canada Ltd. v. Yarmouth Equipment Ltd.* (1991), 103 N.S.R. (2d) 1 (S.C.A.D.), leave to appeal to S.C.C. granted and discontinued, [1991] S.C.C.A. No. 256 (sale of franchise—misleading projections of future business—"merger" and "independent investigation" clauses held unconscionable). For criticism, see V.W.

Finally, it appears to be accepted that the application of the unconscionable or unfair and unreasonable test does not, if successfully met, lead to the rescission of the agreement. The cases applying *Hunter* assume that the effect of fundamental breach doctrine, if applicable, is to withhold the application of the term to the particular fact situation rather than to rescind either the agreement itself or the particular term.

E. CONCLUSION

The nature and scope of the doctrine of fundamental breach has varied over time in both England and in Canada. In England, with the enactment of the *Unfair Contract Terms Act 1977*,[94] the evolution of the doctrine appears to have been completed. With the discretion conferred by that statute on the courts to control the application of exculpatory clauses in consumer contracts and other standard form agreements, the need for a common law doctrine conferring a similar discretion has disappeared. Accordingly, under English law, the doctrine of fundamental breach appears to have settled into a simple matter of applying the usual techniques of contract interpretation, including the principle of *contra proferentum*, to exculpatory clauses in agreements not subject to the legislation. In common law Canada, in the absence of similar legislation, the courts have persisted, however, in developing a common law device for controlling the application of disclaimer clauses. Nonetheless, there remain some similarities between the English and Canadian versions of the doctrine. In both systems, in the case of an ordinary commercial transaction, a construction approach will be followed. Further, it appears that in both systems, an exculpatory clause will not be applied or interpreted in such fashion as to render nugatory or illusory the obligations of one party.[95] Further, Canadian courts continue to interpret clauses strictly on the basis of the *contra proferentum* principle.[96]

DaRe, "Atlas Unchartered: When Unconscionability 'Says It All'" (1996) 27 Can. Bus. L.J. 426. And see *F. Mendelssohn v. Normand Ltd.*, above note 5 (parked car—attendant promising to lock the car—car not locked with resulting theft of valuables left in the car—garage owner not protected by exculpatory clause).

94 Above note 30.

95 This principle was accepted by the Supreme Court of Canada in *Beaufort Realties* case, above note 64 and by Wilson J. in *Hunter,* above note 8 at 510.

96 *Canadian Pacific Forest Products Ltd. v. Belships (Far East) Shipping (Pte.) Ltd.* (1999), 175 D.L.R. (4th) 449 (Fed. C.A.) (*contra proferentum* or strict construction approach not overtaken by the decision in *Hunter Engineering*). See also *Meditek Laboratory Services Ltd. v. Purolator Courier Ltd.* (1995), 125 D.L.R.

Beyond these points of similarity, however, it is clearly established that an independent doctrine of fundamental breach has been developed in Canadian common law that differs in material respects from the current English doctrine. In *Hunter,* both Dickson C.J.C. and Wilson J. accepted the proposition that in the absence of Canadian legislation[97] equivalent to the *Unfair Contract Terms Act 1977*, there exists a continuing need for a residual judicial discretion to intervene and withhold application of exculpatory clauses that bring about results that are either "unconscionable" in Dickson C.J.C.'s terms or "unfair and unreasonable" in the terms adopted by Wilson J. Although the failure of the Supreme Court either to speak with one voice or offer a majority view in *Hunter* leaves the precise nature of the Canadian doctrine in a somewhat uncertain state, it is nonetheless possible to identify the main features of the doctrine. First, it appears to be generally accepted that the doctrine is one that has the effect of withholding the application of an exculpatory clause in what might be referred to as an "extreme case" rather than having the effect of providing a basis for rescission of the agreement. Further, it therefore seems unlikely that Dickson C.J.C. used the term "unconscionable" to refer to the traditional doctrine of unconscionability that would lead to rescission, nor does it appear likely that he intended to refer to the severe imbalances in bargaining power that are engaged by that doctrine. On this basis, there appears to be very little separating the concepts of "unconscionability" and "unfair and unreasonable"; indeed, Canadian courts seem to accept that this is the case. It may be observed that the Canadian common law doctrine, which appears to confer a residual discretion on courts to refrain from applying exculpatory clauses in cases where this would lead to unconscionable, unfair and unreasonable results, appears to have some similarity to the English statutory scheme that enables courts to withhold enforcement of such clauses "except in so far as … the contract term satisfies the requirement of reasonableness."[98] It would, however, be an exaggeration to suggest that Canadian courts have achieved at common law what has been achieved in England by Parliament. Indeed, the similarities between the approach developed in *Hunter* and the English legislation appear to have gone unnoticed in the

---

(4th) 738 (Man. C.A.). For discussion of the *contra proferentum* principle, see Chapter 19, section C.

97   As Wilson J. noted in *Hunter,* consumer protection legislation enacted in some provinces may be capable of achieving somewhat similar results in the context of consumer transactions; see *Hunter,* above note 8 at 511–12. For discussion of this legislation, see Chapters 10 and 11.

98   Above note 30, s. 3.

Canadian jurisprudence. It may well be, however, that over time the English jurisprudence on fairness and reasonableness in the context of exculpatory clauses may be of some assistance in fashioning the Canadian jurisprudence on the *Hunter* doctrine.

In whatever form the Canadian doctrine may ultimately assume, the doctrine of fundamental breach is likely to continue to attract criticism from some quarters. The open-textured nature of the doctrine, resting on such broad concepts as "unconscionability," "fairness" and "reasonableness" will appear too vague and uncertain to many observers. On the other hand, the history of the doctrine in both English and Canadian common law strongly suggests that the urge to intervene and prevent unjust results resulting from the application of harsh exculpatory clauses is simply irresistible. If this is the case, the law concerning exculpatory clauses is likely to be more rather than less predictable if the underlying concern is openly recognized, as it is in *Hunter*, rather than suppressed and achieved indirectly through the subterfuge of strained interpretation of such terms.

FURTHER READINGS

J. ADAMS & R. BROWNSWORD, "The *Unfair Contract Terms Act*: A Decade of Discretion" (1988) 104 Law Q. Rev. 94.

K.F. BERG, "Israeli Standard Contracts Law 1964: Judicial Controls of Standard Form Contracts" (1979) 28 I.C.L.Q. 560.

B. COOTE, *Exception Clauses* (London: Sweet & Maxwell, 1964).

V.W. DARE, "Atlas Unchartered: When Unconscionability 'Says it All'" (1996) 27 Can. Bus. L.J. 426.

A.J. DUGGAN, "Stolen Goods, A Cruise Disaster and a Right of Way Gone Wrong: Three Unconscionable Contracts Cases from a Law and Economics Perspective" (2004) 40 Can. Bus. L.J. 3.

R.D. FLANNIGAN, "*Hunter Engineering*: The Judicial Regulation of Exculpatory Clauses" (1990) 69 Can. Bar Rev. 514.

R.A. HASSON, "The Nine Lives of Fundamental Breach" (1985) 10 Can. Bus. L.J. 80.

LAW COMMISSION, *Exemption Clauses in Contracts, First Report: Amendments to the Sale of Goods Act, 1893* (London: HMSO, 1969).

E. MacDonald, *Exemption Clauses, Penalty Clauses and Unfair Terms* (London: Butterworths, 1999).

M.H. Ogilvie, "Fundamental Breach Excluded But Not Extinguished: *Hunter Engineering v. Syncrude Canada*" (1990) 17 Can. Bus. L.J. 75.

M.H. Ogilvie, "'Reasonable' Exemption Clauses in the Supreme Court of Canada and the House of Lords" (1991) 25 U.B.C. L. Rev. 199.

Ontario Law Reform Commission, *Report on Consumer Warranties and Guarantees in the Sale of Goods* (Toronto: Ministry of the Attorney General, 1972).

D. Yates, *Exclusion Clauses in Contracts*, 2d ed. (London: Sweet & Maxwell, 1982).

THE IMPLIED DUTY TO PERFORM IN GOOD FAITH

A. INTRODUCTION

The general principles upon which terms can be held to be implicit in contracts have been considered in a previous chapter.[1] Here we consider whether Canadian common law recognizes the existence of a general duty, perhaps in the form of an implied term, requiring contracting parties to perform their agreements in good faith. Civilian systems typically recognize the existence of a general duty of this kind. Indeed, the origins of the concept can be traced to Roman law.[2] English common law, on the other hand, has been resistant to the idea. In 1989, Bingham L.J. compared the English and civilian systems in the following terms:

> In many civil law systems, and perhaps in most legal systems outside the common law world, the law of obligations recognises and enforces an overriding principle that in making and carrying out contracts parties should act in good faith. … English law has, characteristically, committed itself to no such overriding principle but has developed piecemeal solutions in response to demonstrated problems of unfairness.[3]

---

1   See Chapter 19, section D.
2   See R. Powell, "Good Faith in Contracts" (1956) 9 Curr. Legal Probs. 16.
3   *Interfoto Picture Library Ltd. v. Stiletto Visual Programmes Ltd.*, [1989] Q.B. 433 at 439 (C.A.).

Although English interest in the civilian doctrine of good faith performance has been sharpened by the increasing influence of European law on the English law of contracts,[4] a general duty to perform contracts in good faith has not yet emerged in English law.

A very different story unfolded in the United States. The recognition of a general duty of good faith performance was given a substantial impetus in American law and, indeed, a statutory base, when such a duty was explicitly provided for in the Uniform Commercial Code,[5] a model law, in the 1950s. The Code, in turn, was enacted as state law across the country. There are several references to good faith in the Code.[6] In due course, the influence of the American Code and the vast body of case law on good faith that surrounded and, to some extent, preceded it led to the inclusion of an article on good faith in the *Restatement of Contracts 2d*,[7] published in 1981. Section 205 of the *Restatement* provides as follows: "Every contract imposes upon each party a duty of good faith and fair dealing in its performance and its enforcement." Alone among the common law jurisdictions, then, the United States appears to have adopted a generalized duty of good faith contractual performance.

The interest of Canadian common law lawyers in the duty of good faith appears to have been stimulated, in part at least, by the work of the Ontario Law Reform Commission on sale of goods law[8] and contract law.[9] In its reports on both topics, the commission recommended that legislation be enacted giving recognition to the doctrine of good faith. In the latter report, the commission reasoned that "statutory recognition of the doctrine of good faith would serve to synthesize the various strands of good faith analysis in the case law. Moreover, the literature reveals that a generalized doctrine of good faith would conform

---

4   See generally G. Teubner, "Legal Irritants: Good Faith in British Law or How Unifying Law Ends Up in New Divergences" (1998) 61 Mod. L. Rev. 11; R. Brownsword, "'Good Faith in Contracts' Revisited" (1996) 49 Curr. Legal Probs. 111.

5   Ss. 1-203, 2-103. See generally R.S. Summers "'Good Faith' in General Contract Law and in the Sales Provisions of the Uniform Commercial Code" (1968) 54 Va. L. Rev. 195.

6   Article 1-203, for example, provides as follows: "Every contract or duty within this Act imposes an obligation of good faith in its performance or enforcement." And see E.A. Farnsworth, "Good Faith in Contract Performance" in J. Beatson and D. Friedmann, eds., *Good Faith and Fault in Contract Law* (Oxford: Clarendon Press, 1995) 153 at 155.

7   (St. Paul: American Law Institute, 1981).

8   Ontario Law Reform Commission, *Report on Sale of Goods* (Ottawa: Ministry of the Attorney General, 1979).

9   Ontario Law Reform Commission, *Report on Amendment of the Law of Contract* (Toronto: Ontario Law Reform Commission, 1987).

to commercial realities."[10] To date, however, although some provinces have enacted legislation imposing good faith or fair dealing duties in the specific context of franchise agreements,[11] neither Ontario nor any other common law province has enacted general legislation of the kind recommended by the commission. In recent years, however, Canadian courts have frequently made reference to the duty of good faith performance and, in numerous cases, appear to have assumed that such a duty is an existing feature of the Canadian common law of contracts.[12] In this chapter, we examine the leading cases in which recognition of the doctrine is either assumed or advocated. As well, an attempt will be made to identify recurring themes in the factual patterns of these cases, with a view to demystifying the doctrine and giving the doctrine more concrete content. In turn, this exercise may provide a working definition of the concept of good faith. Before turning to examine the case law, however, we begin by briefly describing the Canadian debate concerning recognition of the duty and identifying the principal arguments advanced by the doctrine's advocates and its detractors.

There are two principal arguments made by advocates of recognition of a generalized duty of good faith performance, both of which appear to have had some influence of the thinking of the Ontario commission. The first argument minimizes the extent of the change involved in recognizing the doctrine and suggests that the common law has already, in effect, recognized such a doctrine, though not by name. Thus, it has been suggested that recognition of the doctrine "would simply consolidate existing doctrinal approaches and provide a more

---

10   *Ibid.* at 174. And see E.P. Belobaba, "Good Faith in Canadian Contract Law" in Law Society of Upper Canada, *Special Lectures 1985, Commercial Law: Recent Developments and Emerging Trends* (Don Mills, ON: R. de Boo, 1985) at 73, a revised version of a background paper prepared for the Commission.

11   *Franchises Act*, S.A. 2000, c. F-23, s. 7; *Arthur Wishart Act (Franchise Disclosure) 2000*, S.O. 2000, c. 3, s. 3. And see *Shelanu Inc. v. Print Three Franchising Corp.* (2003), 226 D.L.R. (4th) 577 (Ont. C.A.). And see generally S. O'Byrne, "Breach of Good Faith in Performance of the Franchise Contract: Punitive Damages and Damages for Intangibles" (2004) 83 Can. Bar Rev. 431.

12   See generally S.K. O'Byrne, "Good Faith in Contractual Performance: Recent Developments" (1995) 74 Can. Bar Rev. 70; D. Stack, "The Two Standards of Good Faith in Canadian Contract Law" (1999) 62 Sask. L. Rev. 201; J.D. McCamus, "Abuse of Discretion, Failure to Cooperate and Evasion of Duty: Unpacking the Common Law Duty of Good Faith Contractual Performance" (2004) 29 Advocates' Q. 72. For a discussion that includes recent developments in Australia and New Zealand, see A.T. Mason, "Contract, Good Faith and Equitable Standards in Fair Dealing" (2000) 116 Law Q. Rev. 66.

precise remedial vocabulary."[13] Indeed, as Bingham L.J. appears to concede, there is considerable force to the argument that many existing common law doctrines—some of which will be examined in this chapter—appear to manifest a policy of encouraging good faith or punishing bad faith. The second argument in support of recognition is that explicit adoption of a good faith duty will bring the law more into accord with the expectations of contracting parties. Commercial actors, and others, expect that the people with whom they enter into transactions will act in good faith. By explicitly recognizing the existence of such a duty, the common law of contract will simply give effect to those reasonable expectations. This thesis, it may be noted, is not entirely consistent with the first argument. This is an argument for reforming the law in order to bring it into closer alignment with the reasonable expectations of contracting parties. Current law, it is argued, does not fully achieve this laudable objective and can be improved by adopting a generalized duty of good faith. A third argument, sometimes made in favour of recognition, draws on comparative material. If, as noted above, the duty of good faith contractual performance is recognized in civilian legal systems, including the law of Quebec,[14] and in the United States, recognition of the doctrine in Canadian common law would simply bring our legal system into line with other jurisdictions.

The principal argument against recognition, of course, is the concern that recognition of the good faith duty will bring an unattractive degree of uncertainty to the law. With increased uncertainty comes increased difficulty in giving advice and the prospect of more protracted litigation.[15] For critics of the doctrine, the existing common law approach in which discrete rules have developed to deal with particular instances of bad faith is not only satisfactory, it is preferable to the adoption of a vague general standard. Further, some detractors of good faith have examined the comparative experience and find it either wanting or not easily transportable into the common law context. For one observer, the recognition of such a doctrine is of such significance that this development would require a wholesale rethinking of the nature of contractual obligation, something that should be undertaken, in

---

13   See, for example, Belobaba, above note 10 at 78–79.
14   See, for example, *Banque Canadienne Nationale v. Soucisse*, [1981] 2 S.C.R. 339; *Houle v. Banque Canadienne Nationale*, [1990] 3 S.C.R. 122. And see Civil Code of Quebec, L.Q. 1991, c. 64, arts. 6 and 7.
15   See, for example, M. Bridge, "Does Anglo-Canadian Contract Law Need a Doctrine of Good Faith?" (1984) 9 Can. Bus. L.J. 385 at 412–13. Compare with E.A. Farnsworth, "Comments on Michael Bridge's Paper" (1984) 9 Can. Bus. L.J. 426 at 430.

his view, only by the legislature.[16] Whether it is realistic to think that Canadian provincial legislatures will take an interest in such issues is, of course, another matter.

B. ANALYSIS OF THE LEADING CASES

The debate concerning the desirability of recognizing an explicit duty of good faith performance has attracted increasing judicial attention in recent years. Accordingly, it may be asked whether Canadian common law now recognizes the existence of such a duty. The answer to this question lies in a careful examination of what appear to be the leading decisions making reference to good faith. An examination of these cases will also provide some insight into the extent to which the common law already addresses, through more traditional means, problems that might be addressed by the concept of a duty of good faith performance.

Before turning to an examination of the decisions, however, a number of preliminary observations may be made. First, as we shall see, it is a striking fact that in not one of these cases is the analysis of or reference to the good faith performance obligation necessary to the decision in question. In each case, the result could have been, and indeed was, explicitly grounded in the application of traditional contract doctrine. On the basis of these authorities, then, it would be difficult to make a compelling argument that a duty of good faith performance has now been recognized at common law in Canada. Further, the Canadian cases in which the concept of good faith is invoked appear to fall into three categories: those imposing duties to cooperate in achieving fulfilment of the objectives of the agreement; those imposing limits on the exercise of contractual discretionary powers; and those precluding parties from evading contractual obligations. Whatever might be said to be the status of the doctrine of good faith performance at the present time, the recognition, in appropriate cases, of implicit contractual obligations of these three kinds appears to be an established feature of Canadian contract doctrine. Thus, these decisions offer some support for the argument that a good faith performance obligation is manifest

---

16   See P. Girard, "'Good Faith' in Contract Performance: Principle or Placebo?" (1983) 5 Sup. Ct. L. Rev. 309. See also R. Hasson, "Good Faith in Contract Law—Some Lessons from Insurance Law" (1987–88) 13 Can. Bus. L.J. 93 (suggesting that "good faith" has produced "bizarre" results in insurance law and questioning the wisdom of extending the doctrine throughout contract law).

in a number of existing common law doctrines that, in effect, require the performance of contractual obligations in good faith.[17] Interestingly, the fact situations in which Canadian courts have considered application of the duty to perform in good faith bear a remarkable similarity to those covered by the good faith performance rubric in American law. Thus, the illustrations of the American doctrine identified in the *Restatement*[18] typically involve either the control of the exercise of discretionary contractual powers or the imposition of obligations to cooperate in the accomplishment of the objectives of the agreement or, at least, to refrain from engaging in evasive strategies to defeat the objectives of the agreement. Accordingly, it appears that much, though possibly not all, of the work being accomplished by the good faith doctrine in the United States is being accomplished in Canadian common law by more traditional means.

1) Good Faith, Best Efforts and the Duty to Cooperate

Advocates of the good faith duty place considerable importance on the decision at trial in *Gateway Realty Ltd. v. Arton Holdings Ltd.*,[19] a decision upheld, in the result, by the Nova Scotia Court of Appeal.[20] This case involved a dispute between owners of neighbouring mall properties. Zellers was initially the anchor tenant in the mall owned by Gateway. Hotly pursued by developer Arton, Zellers eventually moved its business to the Arton mall and Arton took an assignment of the remaining seventeen years of Zellers' lease with Gateway. That lease had permitted Zellers to occupy the premises, leave them vacant, or assign the lease to a third party, all without Gateway's consent. The upshot, then, was that Gateway's major competitor, Arton, was now the assignee of the anchor lease without any obligation to occupy the premises or seek a suitable subtenant. This problem appeared to be solved, however, when the parties entered into an agreement to "use their best efforts" to lease the space formerly occupied by Zellers. When it became apparent to Gateway that Arton was refusing to sublet to prospective tenants that Arton considered would give Gateway a competitive advantage, Gateway brought an action claiming that Arton was in breach

---

17   See, for example, Belobaba, above note 10.
18   Above note 7. The illustrations given in the *Restatement of Contracts 2d* to section 205, the good faith section, fall (with one possible exception—Illus. 9, which might be considered to be an estoppel case) into these three categories.
19   *Gateway Realty Ltd. v. Arton Holdings Ltd. and LaHave (No. 3)* (1991), 106 N.S.R. (2d) 180 (S.C.T.D.).
20   (1992), 112 N.S.R. (2d) 180 (S.C.A.D.).

of its contractual obligation to use best efforts and, alternatively, was in breach of a duty of good faith performance.

At trial, Kelly J. came relatively easily to the conclusion that the obligation to undertake "best efforts" is an enforceable and not uncommon obligation in business agreements and that the conduct of Arton constituted a breach of this contractual provision. Kelly J. went on, however, to engage in a lengthy and erudite analysis of the alternative ground urged by the plaintiff, the existence and breach of a duty of good faith performance owed by Arton to Gateway. Placing reliance on existing references to the idea of good faith in Canadian cases and on the American experience, Kelly J. articulated a doctrine of good faith performance in the following terms:

> The law requires that parties to a contract exercise their rights under that agreement honestly, fairly and in good faith. This standard is breached when a party acts in a bad faith manner in the performance of its rights and obligations under the contract. "Good faith" conduct is the guide to the manner in which the parties should pursue their mutual contractual objectives. Such conduct is breached when a party acts in "bad faith" — a conduct that is contrary to community standards of honesty, reasonableness or fairness. The insistence on a good faith requirement in discretionary conduct in contractual formation, performance, and enforcement is only the fulfilment of the obligation of the courts to do justice in the resolution of disputes between contending parties.[21]

Applying this standard to the facts, Kelly J. concluded that Arton was under an obligation to exercise its discretion to sublease the premises in a reasonable manner and not in bad faith and that Arton was in breach of its obligation. In terms of remedy, Kelly J. concluded that the breach of contract was so serious as to justify termination of the assignment to Arton.

On appeal, the decision at trial was upheld. In a brief oral opinion, the Court of Appeal reiterated and affirmed the central factual findings of Kelly J. and concluded that the failure of Arton "to exercise their 'best efforts' to find a suitable tenant or tenants had the effect of literally destroying the viability of Gateway's plaza shopping centre, contrary to any expectation in the original lease."[22] The court offered no opinion on the existence or applicability of a duty of good faith performance. Although Kelly J.'s articulate embrace of the good faith duty no doubt

---

21   Above note 19 at 191–92.
22   Above note 20 at 183.

makes a valuable contribution to judicial discussion of good faith, it must be noted that, as a matter of authority, the analysis of good faith in his opinion is pure makeweight. The result of the case rests firmly on the express undertaking of Arton to use "best efforts." The discussion of good faith is simply unnecessary.

In the absence of an explicit undertaking to exercise best efforts, however, Canadian courts have found such duties to be implicit in contractual relations in appropriate cases.[23] Indeed, courts have implied more generalized duties to cooperate in the fulfilment of contractual obligations. Occasionally, such implied obligations have been linked to actions of good faith. Where, for example, performance of the contract is subject to a condition precedent, the fulfilment of which requires the cooperation of one of the parties, an undertaking to provide such cooperation will be readily implied. Although such cases contain references to a requirement to make "best efforts" or to act in "good faith," this doctrine has not yet been linked to the debate concerning the recognition of a good faith performance obligation. Nonetheless, such cases constitute a prime example of existing common law doctrine that appears to implement a requirement of good faith performance.

The leading Supreme Court of Canada decision, *Dynamic Transport Ltd. v. O.K. Detailing Ltd.*[24] was rendered in 1978, a few years before the debate concerning the recognition of a good faith performance doctrine emerged in common law Canada. This case involved an action for specific performance of a contract for the purchase and sale of land. The agreement was subject to a condition precedent that subdivision approval be obtained, but the agreement was silent as to whether the vendor or the purchaser would obtain that approval. Dickson J., for the Court, held that the person who proposes to carry out the subdivision prior to sale is the vendor and, accordingly, construed the agreement as containing an implied undertaking on the part of the vendor to make a proper application for a subdivision and "use his best efforts" to obtain the approval. He further explained that "the vendor is under a duty to act in good faith and to take all reasonable steps to complete the sale."[25] As Dickson J. noted, this holding was based on a substantial body of case law standing for the more general proposition that "the court will

---

23 See, for example, *Bercovici v. Palmer* (1966), 59 D.L.R. (2d) 513 (Sask. C.A.); *Atmospheric Diving Systems Inc. v. International Hard Suits Inc.* (1994), 89 B.C.L.R. (2d) 356 (S.C.).

24 (1978), 85 D.L.R. (3d) 19 (S.C.C.).

25 *Ibid.* at 28, a passage relied upon by Kelly J. in *Gateway Realty*. See above note 19 at 192.

readily imply a promise on the part of each party to do all that is necessary to secure performance of the contract."[26]

2) Good Faith and the Control of Discretionary Powers

Canadian judges have referred to a duty of good faith in a series of recent cases involving what one might refer to as abuse of a discretionary power conferred by contract. In each case, the defendant was required to exercise the power in question in a reasonable fashion. In *Mesa Operating Ltd. Partnership v. Amoco Canada Resources Ltd.*,[27] for example, the underlying transaction involved the sale by the plaintiff of oil and gas properties to the defendant. The agreement of sale reserved a royalty to the seller. The agreement further provided that the defendant could "pool" properties for royalty payments. The dispute arose from a decision by the defendant to pool one of the properties it purchased from the plaintiff with one of its own properties in a manner that had the effect of reducing by half the amount of royalties that would be received by the plaintiff. Although the trial judge did not find that his exercise of the contractual power to pool was dishonest or fraudulent, it was nonetheless a decision that ignored current industry practice.

At trial, Shannon J., placing substantial reliance on the opinion of Kelly J. in *Gateway Realty*, articulated a duty of good faith in the following terms: "the common law duty to perform in good faith is breached when a party acts in bad faith, that is, when a party acts in a manner that substantially nullifies the contractual objectives or causes significant harm to the other, contrary to the original purposes or expectations of the parties."[28] When applied to the facts of this case, it was Shannon J.'s view that the discretion to pool conferred by the contract is "not an unfettered discretion because 'the defendant is obliged to act in good faith vis-à-vis the royalty holder.' Such a term exists by implication."[29]

The decision at trial was upheld on appeal, but the Alberta Court of Appeal expressed itself much more cautiously on the issue of good faith. Indeed, Kerans J.A. expressed the view that a "general obligation expressed in terms of good faith is not an obvious part of contract law

---

26   *Dynamic Transport Ltd. v. O.K. Detailing Ltd., ibid.* at 27. Similarly, it will be implied that a party should not engage in conduct likely to obstruct performance of the agreement. See *Multi-Malls Inc. v. Tex-Mall Properties Ltd.* (1980), 108 D.L.R. (3d) 399 (Ont. H.C.), aff'd (1981), 128 D.L.R. (3d) 192 (Ont. C.A.), leave to appeal to S.C.C. dismissed (1982), 41 N.R. 360n (S.C.C.).

27   (1992), 129 A.R. 177 (Q.B.), aff'd (1994), 19 Alta. L.R. (3d) 38 (C.A.).

28   *Ibid.* at 218 (Q.B.).

29   *Ibid.* at 214.

in England and Canada."[30] Further, Kerans J.A. was concerned that use of the term "good faith" would blur the distinction between obligations imposed on parties that arise from the agreement as opposed to obligations imposed by the law despite the agreement of the parties. The doctrines of illegality and unconscionability, for example, fit within the latter category. The obligation imposed in the present case, in his view, comes within the former category, as an obligation that "turns on a rule founded in the agreement of the parties, not in the law."[31] For Kerans J.A., then, it was unnecessary to delve further into the matter of "good faith." He explained, as follows:

> The rule that governs here can, therefore, be expressed much more narrowly than to speak of good faith, although I suspect it is in reality the sort of thing some judges have in mind when they speak of good faith. As the trial judge said, a party cannot exercise a power granted in a contract in a way that "substantially nullifies the contractual objectives or causes significant harm to the other contrary to the original purposes or expectations of the parties."[32]

When framed in this fashion, according to Kerans J.A., the rule applied in this case is analogous to the rule applied in other cases where parties on whom contractual discretionary powers are conferred are required to act reasonably and responsibly.

In two earlier decisions of the Ontario Court of Appeal, the reading in of requirements to act reasonably in the exercise of contractual powers was coupled with references to a good faith obligation. In *LeMesurier v. Andrus*,[33] a purchaser of land had seized upon a minor discrepancy concerning the title as a basis for repudiating the transaction, relying on the standard provision of the agreement relating to objections to title. Relying on an earlier decision of the Supreme Court of Canada to this effect, Grange J.A. held that one who seeks to take advantage of a clause of this kind "must exercise his right reasonably and in good faith and not in a capricious or arbitrary manner."[34] The purchaser's reliance upon the clause in this case was, in the court's view, "capricious or arbitrary." Grange J.A. went on to observe:[35] "The approach may be merely an example of the development of an independent doctrine of

---

30   *Ibid.* at 43 (C.A.).
31   *Ibid.* at 44.
32   *Ibid.* at 45.
33   (1986), 25 D.L.R. (4th) 424 (Ont. C.A.).
34   *Ibid.* at 430, quoting from *Mason v. Freedman*, [1958] S.C.R. 483 at 487, Judson J.
35   *LeMesurier v. Andrus, ibid.* at 430–31.

good faith in contract law at least in the performance of contracts, one explicitly set forth in the American Uniform Commercial Code and in the American *Restatement* and exhibited, although perhaps in disguised form, in many English and Canadian cases—see the lecture of Professor Belobaba." On this view, then, a well-established principle requiring that a particular type of contractual discretionary power be exercised in a manner that is not arbitrary and capricious is a manifestation of what may be an emerging independent doctrine of good faith.

In *Greenberg v. Meffert*,[36] the Ontario Court of Appeal was required to consider what limitations, if any, should be imposed on the exercise of a discretion conferred upon an employer in a contract for the employment of a real estate agent. The contract provided that agents were entitled to commissions only if the particular sale occurred during the course of their employment. Commissions on properties listed by an agent but sold after the termination of the employment were to be "disbursed at the company's discretion."[37] On the particular facts, the plaintiff had obtained a listing for a property that was sold after the termination of his employment. The selling agent then bribed the office manager to pay him the listing agent's commission that would otherwise have been paid to the plaintiff. The plaintiff sued for that commission and the employer defended on the basis that its discretion to pay was absolute in character.

The Court of Appeal framed the issued as requiring a determination of whether the discretion conferred was subject to an objective standard or was merely subjective in nature. In the latter case, the discretion would be essentially uncontrolled. Relying on English and American authority in this effect, Robins J.A. explained: "In any given transaction, the category into which such a provision falls will depend upon the intention of the parties as disclosed by their contract. In the absence of explicit language or a clear indication from the tenor of the contract or the nature of the subject-matter, the tendency of the cases is to require the discretion ... to be reasonable."[38]

Robins J.A. further noted that the provision had been drafted by the employer and that the principle of *contra proferentum* supported his conclusion that the discretion was one that, on a proper construction of the agreement, could only be exercised reasonably. Robins J.A. then added, however, a reference to good faith in the following fashion:

---

36   (1985), 18 D.L.R. (4th) 548 (Ont. C.A.).
37   *Ibid.* at 549.
38   *Ibid.* at 554.

Apart altogether from the question of reasonableness, a discretion must be exercised honestly and in good faith. That proposition is so fundamental as to require no elaboration. The collusive conduct here clearly deprived the discretion of those qualities and contaminated the decisional process. That patently improper conduct vitiated not only the reasonableness required in the objective criteria but the good faith and honesty required whether the discretion is objective or subjective. In either case the decision to deprive the appellant of any commission was not made honestly and in good faith and cannot stand. Fair dealing is implicit in the contract. The clause in issue, in my opinion, ought not to be construed so as to shield the company's improper exercise of discretion from any review.[39]

This passage suggests, then, that a duty to exercise the discretion in good faith provides a second justification for the imposition of liability. To be sure, however, the good faith duty appears to arise by proper construction of the agreement rather than as a result of the imposition of an independent and free-standing good faith duty.

In sum, these cases establish the proposition that where discretionary powers are conferred by agreement, it is implicitly understood that the powers are to be exercised reasonably. The concept of reasonableness in this context implies a duty to exercise the discretion honestly and in light of the purposes for which it was conferred. The basic idea is a familiar one that parallels the controls imposed on the exercise of discretionary powers conferred upon administrative bodies under well-established principles of public law.[40]

---

39   *Ibid.* at 556. See also *Marshall v. Bernard Place Corp.* (2002), 58 O.R. (3d) 97 (C.A.) (vendor-purchaser agreement conditional upon approval of inspection report—purchaser's "sole and absolute discretion" to approve must be exercised in good faith); *McKinlay Motors Ltd. v. Honda Canada Inc.* (1989), 80 Nfld. & P.E.I.R. 200 (Nfld. S.C.T.D.) (manufacturer's discretion to allocate vehicles to dealers to be exercised in good faith). For a similar Australian authority, see *Renard Constructions (ME) Pty. Ltd. v. Minister for Public Works* (1992), 26 N.S.W.L.R. 234 (C.A.). And see *Valley Equipment Ltd. v. John Deere Ltd.* (2000), 4 B.L.R. (3d) 282 (N.B.Q.B.) (termination of dealership—no explicit provision in agreement permitting termination without cause—discretion to terminate must be exercised reasonably, not arbitrarily and in good faith).

40   A parallel specifically noted in an English decision concerning the exercise of a contractual discretion. See *Paragon Finance Plc. v. Staunton*, [2002] 2 All E.R. 248 (C.A.).

3) Good Faith and the Duty to Not Evade Contractual Obligations

In other cases, defendants have attempted to evade contractual duties by engaging in conduct that they considered was not strictly precluded by the letter of the terms of their agreement. In the typical case, the conduct is held, on a more expansive construction, to be a breach of the express terms of the agreement. The underlying idea is a not unfamiliar one in the law of contractual interpretation—one cannot do indirectly what one has covenanted not to do directly.[41] Occasionally, however, courts have invoked the concept of good faith performance in this context. In *MDS Health Group Ltd. v. King Street Medical Arts Centre Ltd.*,[42] for example, the plaintiff medical laboratory, MDS, sought to enforce a restrictive covenant in its lease with the defendant, King Street, which limited the right of the defendant to lease premises in the building to a competitive medical laboratory service. Together with a number of doctors and dentists, MDS was a tenant in a medical arts building owned by King Street. The tenants, including MDS, owned the shares in King Street and the relationship of the shareholders was governed by a shareholders' agreement.

After MDS refused to agree to a substantial increase in rent proposed by King Street, a group of doctor shareholders opened a "Physicians' Lab" in which laboratory specimens were taken from their patients and sent out to a third-party lab for processing. Unsurprisingly, the establishment of the physicians' lab had the effect of reducing significantly the volume of business directed to MDS. MDS sought to enjoin this activity as a breach both of the restrictive covenant in the lease and of similar arrangements contained in the shareholders' agreement. The defendants argued that the covenants precluded leasing to a competitive lab but did not preclude the defendants from establishing a lab of the kind in issue to meet the needs of their patients. Haley J. held that the establishment of the physicians' lab contravened the restrictive covenant in the lease and the injunction was issued. As well, however, Haley J. made extensive reference to the reasoning of Kelly J. in *Gateway Realty* and held that the establishment of the competing lab was also a "breach of the good faith required (by) the law of parties to

---

41   See, for example, *Re Penn Central Transportation Co. v. Canada Southern Railway Co.*, [1971] 3 O.R. 247 at 262 (H.C.J.), Fraser J.; *Cradle Pictures (Canada) Ltd. v. Penner* (1975), 10 O.R. (2d) 444 at 447 (H.C.J.), Holland J. See also *Johnston v. St. Andrews Church* (1877), 1 S.C.R. 235 at 282, Ritchie J.

42   (1994), 12 B.L.R. (2d) 209 (Ont. Ct. Gen. Div.).

a contract."[43] Again, this reliance on good faith is, of course, not necessary to the decision. The defendant breached the restrictive covenant in the lease. It is irrelevant whether the breach was committed either in bad faith or, in some sense, innocently or in good faith. In the absence of such a covenant, of course, it is most unlikely that the establishment of a competitive enterprise would be considered to be precluded by an implied duty to act in good faith.[44]

Disputes concerning the evasion of rights of first refusal have generated a subtle body of jurisprudence.[45] In the typical contractual right of first refusal, the grantor of the right undertakes that, as owner of the property subject to the right, it will not accept a *bona fide* offer from a third party to purchase the property without first giving the grantee of the right an opportunity to purchase the property on the same terms and conditions as those of the third party's offer. In the main, resolution of disputes concerning such rights appears to rest on the proper interpretation of the language of the particular right of first refusal. Thus, for example, attempts to frustrate or evade a right of first refusal may be met by the implication of a term that renders the means of evasion a breach of the right. In a leading English case, *Gardner v. Coutts & Co.*,[46] a grantor's attempt to avoid the right of first refusal when giving the property to a third party on the assumption that a gift, as opposed to an offer of purchase, would not trigger the right, failed. The grantee's claim to enforce succeeded on the basis that the agreement, properly construed, included an implied term that the right of first refusal would also be triggered by a gift of the property. In the trial judge's view: "[I]t is implicit in a grant of first refusal that the person who has to offer the property to the other party, should not be entitled to give it away without offering it and so to defeat the first refusal."[47] A recent Ontario decision, however, suggests that an alternative basis on which attempts to evade rights of first refusal might constitute contractual breach can be found in the implied duty to perform contractual obligations in good faith.

---

43   *Ibid.* at 223.
44   *947101 Ontario Ltd. v. Barrhaven Town Centre Inc.* (1995), 121 D.L.R. (4th) 748 (Ont. Ct. Gen. Div.).
45   See generally P.M. Perell, "Options, Rights of Purchase and Rights of First Refusal as Contracts and as Interests in Land" (1991) 70 Can. Bar Rev. 1; R. Flannigan, "The Legal Construction of Rights of First Refusal" (1997) 76 Can. Bar Rev. 1; C.D. Johnson and D.J. Stanford, "Rights of First Refusal in Oil and Gas Transactions: A Progressive Analysis" (1999) 37 Alta. L. Rev. 316.
46   [1968] 1 W.L.R. 173 (Ch.).
47   *Ibid.* at 179.

In *GATX Corp. v. Hawker Siddeley Canada Inc.*,[48] the defendant Hawker Siddeley, the grantor of the right, was the owner of a 55-percent shareholding of a company, CGTX. The other 45 percent of the shares were held by the grantee, GATX. Hawker Siddeley and GATX had entered into a Shareholders' Agreement that created rights of first refusal in the event that either Hawker Siddeley or GATX received an offer to purchase that it "proposed to accept" or if either proposed to "sell or otherwise dispose" of its shares in CGTX. In due course, Hawker Siddeley wanted to sell its control block. Both GATX and a third party, Procor, which was a major competitor in the same line of business as CGTX, were anxious to acquire Hawker Siddeley's shares. Following unsuccessful negotiations with GATX, Hawker Siddeley entered into a carefully structured agreement to sell the shares to Procor on the assumption that the structure of the transaction was such that it would not trigger GATX's right of first refusal. At Hawker Siddeley's insistence, the right of first refusal had been drafted in such a way as to exempt intercompany transfers of shareholdings within the Hawker Siddeley's group of corporations on the theory that purely internal rearrangements within its group of affiliated companies should not require GATX's consent. Hawker Siddeley's attempt to evade the right of first refusal in its dealings with Procor rested on this exemption. In essence, Hawker Siddeley incorporated a subsidiary for the purpose of transferring the 55-percent shareholding in CGTX to the third party. The control block was transferred from Hawker Siddeley to the subsidiary that, in turn, agreed to be bound by the terms of the right of first refusal. On Hawker Siddeley's view of the matter, this being an intercompany transfer, the right of first refusal was not triggered. Hawker Siddeley then distributed to its own shareholders its shareholdings in the subsidiary. At this point, then, Hawker Siddeley's reorganization had resulted in the creation of a public company, the sole asset of which was the control block of shares of CGTX formerly owned by Hawker Siddeley. The next step in the transaction was the purchase by Procor of the shares in the subsidiary from the new shareholders. On Hawker Siddeley's view, then, this was a purchase of the subsidiary, rather than the control block itself, and accordingly, this step in the transaction also did not trigger the right of first refusal.

GATX successfully challenged the transaction entered into by Hawker Siddeley and Procor on a number of grounds, including a claim that the transaction did in fact trigger the right of first refusal. The Shareholders' Agreement provided that neither party would "sell

---

48   (1996), 27 B.L.R. (2d) 251 (Ont. Ct. Gen. Div.).

or otherwise dispose" of shares in CGTX without the consent of the other party, that party having had an opportunity to exercise a right of first refusal. GATX successfully argued that the transaction with Procor, though perhaps technically not a "sale" of the control block, certainly was captured by the phrase, "or otherwise dispose" in the right of first refusal. On this basis, which was evidently a sufficient basis for granting the claim, the trial judge, Blair J., held that the transaction with Procor had indeed triggered the right of first refusal and therefore granted GATX a decree of specific performance against Hawker Siddeley. Following what now appears to be a well-trodden path, however, Blair J. went on to hold that there was "another basis" upon which this result could be justified. Blair J. opined: "[I]t is well established that the grantor of a right of first refusal must act reasonably and in good faith in relation to that right, and must not act in a fashion designed to eviscerate the very right which has been given. This is an illustration of the application of the good faith doctrine of contractual performance, which in my view is part of the law of Ontario."[49]

Support for this proposition was drawn from *Landymore v. Hardy and White Rose Properties Ltd.*,[50] a Nova Scotia trial decision dealing with a situation in which the grantors of a right of first refusal sought to evade the right by transferring the subject property to a corporation that they owned at a price substantially higher than they would have accepted in a market transaction. Unsurprisingly, the *Landymore* trial judge held that the transaction was a sham that did not defeat the right of first refusal. Saunders J. drew support from *Gardner v. Coutts & Company* for the proposition that "[t]he grantor of a right of first refusal is not entitled to frustrate it by conveying the property in such a way as to avoid having to give the right in the first place."[51] Rather than simply rely on the implied term analysis of the *Gardner* case, however, the trial judge went on to observe that relations between the grantor and grantee of a right of first refusal "must be characterized by good faith and reasonableness."[52] Support for this proposition was drawn from the doctrine relating to third-party offers to purchase the subject matter of the right for a price composed of both cash and an in-kind consideration, a point to which we will return later.

The decision in *GATX* does not significantly advance the case for recognition of a general implied duty of good faith contractual perform-

---

49   *Ibid.* at 276.
50   (1991), 110 N.S.R. (2d) 2 (S.C.T.D.).
51   *Ibid.* at 16.
52   *Ibid.* at 16–17.

ance. The reliance of the trial judge on good faith in GATX is simply unnecessary. Blair J.'s holding that the transaction is captured by the phrase "or otherwise dispose" is a sufficient basis for the granting of relief. Further, even if the phrase "or otherwise dispose" were deleted from the contractual right, it might nonetheless be argued, relying on the *Gardner* analysis, that it is implicit in a right of first refusal of this kind that the right of first refusal cannot be evaded by a transaction structured in this fashion for the exclusive purpose of defeating the right. In the further alternative, it might be argued that the exemption for intercompany transfers does not save a transaction of this kind. Arguably, that exemption was inserted for the purpose of intercompany transfers other than those undertaken for the sole purpose of evading the right. Thus, even in the absence of explicit language capturing the Procor transaction, the traditional techniques of contractual interpretation may have been invoked to achieve the same result. Even in that circumstance, then, there appears to be no need to invoke a doctrine of good faith contractual performance. Conversely, if, on the proper construction of a particular right of first refusal, the grantor's disposition of the asset does not trigger the right of first refusal, it may appear doubtful that a court should be encouraged to hold that the disposition nonetheless constitutes a breach of an implied duty of good faith. Indeed, given the importance to the parties—grantors, grantees and third parties alike—of being able to determine their legal position with respect to the enforceability of a right of first refusal, it is not surprising that courts have often held that rights of first refusal are to be strictly construed.[53] Be that as it may, one might nonetheless ask whether the invocation of good faith in GATX can be defended on the ground that it merely generalizes a duty of good faith concerning the performance of rights of first refusal that has emerged in the particular context of cases dealing with offers to purchase by third parties in which the price consists of both cash and an in-kind consideration. As we have seen, the decisional law on this point was invoked in the *Landymore* decision.

The problem that arises in the situation where the *bona fide* third-party offer stipulates a price consisting of both cash and an in-kind contribution is that the grantee of the right may have no practical ability to match such an offer and, accordingly, the receipt of such an offer might well render the right a meaningless one. Where, for example, a component of the purchase price to be paid by the third party is a parcel of land, the grantee will have no effective capacity to match the of-

---

53   See, for example, *Pierce v. Empey*, [1939] 4 D.L.R. 672 (S.C.C.). And see Flannigan, above note 45 at 11–12.

fer. Accordingly, if the grantor is able to accept such offers, the right of first refusal will be undermined and, indeed, opportunities for strategic evasive behaviour by the grantor may be facilitated. One solution to this problem — and this would appear to have been the existing law prior to what is arguably a recent Canadian shift to a good faith standard — is that the right of first refusal could be interpreted as requiring, in such a case, that the grantor offer to sell the subject property to the grantee at a price that does not exceed the total of the cash offered by the third party together with the equivalent cash value of the non-cash component of the purchase price. This was the approach taken by the English Court of Appeal in *Manchester Ship Canal Co. v. Manchester Racecourse Co.*[54] Under this approach, then, the grantor is not precluded from bargaining for non-cash consideration from a third party, but must offer the property to the grantee at a price including a cash equivalent for that portion of the consideration. Although this rule is admirably clear and easy to apply, it may be thought to work a hardship on grantors who may have a legitimate interest in obtaining the particular non-cash consideration, such as a parcel of land having unique value for the grantor, but who may be forced to sell to the grantee for a cash consideration. This potential hardship to the grantor apparently troubled the Ontario High Court in *Baggots Brass Beds Ltd. v. Neal Leasing Inc.*[55] In this case, the court took the view that the grantee's offer of a cash equivalent did not match the terms and conditions of the third party's offer of cash together with property and therefore did not constitute an effective exercise of the right of first refusal. Southey J. did not refer to the *Manchester Ship Canal* case but relied, instead, on a line of American authority[56] that takes the view that the grantee's offer of a cash equivalent is not a proper exercise of the right, provided, however, that the grantor can demonstrate that it is acting in good faith in the sense that the grantor can provide a "reasonable justification" for wanting to accept the non-cash consideration from the third party. Southey J. accepted the grantor's evidence to the effect that the property it would acquire from the third party had a particular strategic value for the grantor and this established to his satisfaction that the insistence on

---

54   [1901] 2 Ch. 37.

55   (1989), 4 R.P.R. (2d) 316 (Ont. H.C.J.).

56   *Matson v. Emory*, 676 P.2d 1029 (Wash. App. 1984). See also *Prince v. Elm Investment Co. Inc.*, 649 P.2d 820 (Utah 1982); *West Texas Transmission L.P. v. Enron Corporation*, 907 F.2d 1554 (5th Cir. 1990), cert. denied, 915 F.2d 695.

accepting the third party's offer rather than a cash equivalent from the grantee met the test of "reasonableness and good faith."[57]

We may note in passing that the approach taken by Southey J. in the *Baggots* case has been criticized,[58] principally on the ground that it has muddied the otherwise clear waters flowing from the *Manchester Ship Canal* case. Of more importance in the present context is whether the adoption of a good faith standard in the context of the mixed or unmatchable consideration cases should provide a springboard for the recognition of a more generalized duty on the part of grantors, and perhaps grantees, to exercise rights or perform duties under rights of first refusal in good faith. Certainly, there is no necessary or inescapable inference that once a good faith standard is recognized (assuming that it has been) in the context of the mixed consideration cases, that a generalized duty of good faith should be recognized more generally in the context of rights of first refusal. Moreover, it is not entirely clear what it would mean to say that the right must be exercised by the grantee in good faith in the sense that the grantee must, in deciding to exercise the right, take into account the interests of the grantor. Apart from constraining evasive activities, it is not clear how the addition of a good faith duty would expand the obligations of a grantor under a right of first refusal. As far as evasive strategies themselves are concerned, it appears that the courts are quite capable of dealing with these problems by either construing the contractual language or implying terms that will prevent the grantor from, in effect, doing indirectly what it cannot do directly, that is, selling the property to the third party without offering it to the grantee. Accordingly, and notwithstanding the vigour of the *obiter dicta* concerning good faith in the *GATX* decision, this case neither stands for the proposition that the duty has been recognized in this particular context nor, it seems, does it point to a set of problems for which the recognition of a generalized implied duty of good faith performance provides the obvious solution.

C. THE SUPREME COURT OF CANADA AND GOOD FAITH: *WALLACE V. UNITED GRAIN GROWERS LTD.*

The Supreme Court of Canada was provided with a recent opportunity to consider the desirability of recognizing a duty of good faith contrac-

57   Above note 55 at 322.
58   See Flannigan, above note 45 at 13–14.

tual performance at common law in *Wallace v. United Grain Growers Ltd.*[59] This case involved a claim for damages for wrongful dismissal. The plaintiff was employed under an agreement that was terminable at will. The plaintiff Wallace had been lured by the defendant from a rival company and for a period of some fourteen years he performed as one of the defendant's top salespersons. When the defendant fired Wallace, it did so without giving reasonable notice and was liable, therefore, for damages flowing from this clear breach of contract, that is, replacement of the income he would have earned during the notice period. Wallace sought other damages as well, however. The defendant maintained that it fired Wallace for cause and it maintained this position up to the moment of trial. These groundless allegations caused Wallace substantial mental distress, leading him to require psychiatric assistance. As well, Wallace was unsuccessful in obtaining secure employment with another employer. In short, the manner of Wallace's dismissal allegedly caused further injury for which he sought compensation. In support of these claims, it was argued before the Supreme Court that the defendant was subject to a duty, either in tort or in contract, to refrain from dismissing an employee "in bad faith." In other words, it was submitted that the defendant was subject to a duty to dismiss only in good faith or, that is, for cause or other legitimate business reasons, and that the defendant clearly breached this duty.

Before turning to consider the reasoning of the Supreme Court in this case, it may be useful to briefly portray the law relating to claims for injuries resulting from the *manner* of a wrongful dismissal as it was understood prior to the decision in *Wallace*. The history of claims for intangible injuries resulting from the manner of a wrongful dismissal is a lengthy one. In the well-known decision of the House of Lords in *Addis v. Gramaphone Co. Ltd.*,[60] it was held that damages could not be assessed in an action for wrongful dismissal for injured feelings resulting from the harsh and oppressive circumstances of a dismissal or, indeed, for the extent to which the manner of dismissal might make it more difficult for the employee to obtain re-employment. If libel or slander accompanied the dismissal, the employee should resort to the appropriate tort claim.

With the recognition, in the 1970s, of the possibility of claims for intangible injuries such as mental distress in contract cases,[61] renewed

---

59   (1997), 152 D.L.R. (4th) 1 (S.C.C.).
60   [1909] A.C. 488 (H.L.).
61   *Jarvis v. Swans Tours Ltd.*, [1973] Q.B. 233 (C.A.), for discussion of which see Chapter 22.

attempts were made on behalf of dismissed employees to recover damages for mental injury resulting from the manner of the wrongful dismissal. This issue surfaced for the consideration of the Supreme Court of Canada in *Vorvis v. Insurance Corporation of British Columbia*.[62] In this case, the plaintiff coupled his claim for damages for lack of reasonable notice with a claim for aggravated damages for mental distress resulting from the oppressive conduct of the manager prior to his dismissal. Briefly stated, the holding in *Vorvis* was that although a claim for damages for mental distress may conceivably lie in the context of a breach of an employment contract, it was necessary to demonstrate that the mental injury foreseeably flowed from either the wrongful dismissal itself, that is, the lack of reasonable notice, or from another actionable breach of contract or, indeed, a tort. This factor was missing in *Vorvis*. The conduct of the manager, however offensive, did not constitute a breach of contract and was apparently not tortious. The offensive conduct did not arise from the dismissal, it preceded it. Accordingly, there was no link between the actionable wrong, the failure to give reasonable notice, and the mental distress.

In *Wallace*, then, the plaintiff sought to find the breach of duty that was missing in *Vorvis* by alleging that the defendant employer was subject to an implied duty to dismiss only in good faith. Writing for the majority of the Court, Iacobucci J. rejected the plaintiff's suggestion that there existed either a contract or a tort obligation to refrain from engaging in "bad faith discharge." At the same time, however, it was his view that "where the manner of dismissal has caused mental distress but falls short of an independent actionable wrong, the employee is not without recourse. Rather the trial judge has discretion in these circumstances to extend the period of reasonable notice to which an employee is entitled."[63] In other words, even though the mental distress resulting from the offensive behaviour has not been caused by an actionable wrong, either in contract or in tort, the injury may be compensable indirectly through extension of the period of notice held to constitute reasonable notice.

Rejection of the existence of a duty to discharge in good faith was explained by Iacobucci J. on the basis that recognition of the duty would be inconsistent with the principle that an employment contract of indefinite length is terminable at will by either party. He explained this point as follows:[64]

---

62   [1989] 1 S.C.R. 1085, for discussion of which see Chapter 22.

63   Above note 59 at 27.

64   *Ibid.* at 28. This appears to be the majority view in American jurisprudence. See Farnsworth, above note 6 at 160. Compare with "Note, Protecting at Will

A requirement of "good faith" reasons for dismissal would, in effect, contravene these principles and deprive employers of the ability to determine the composition of their workforce. In the context of the accepted theories on the employment relationship, such a law would, in my opinion, be overly intrusive and inconsistent with established principles of employment law, and more appropriately, should be left to legislative enactment rather than judicial pronouncement.

Having rejected the idea of a duty to dismiss only for good faith reasons, Iacobucci J. did not appear to consider explicitly the alternative possibility that the Court might imply or impose an obligation to exercise the right to dismiss only in a good faith *manner*. Such a duty would constrain the manner in which the employer treated the employee upon the occasion of dismissal. Although Iacobucci J. did not discuss this alternative possibility, we may assume that it is also rejected by a majority of the Court. An implied duty of this kind was proposed by McLachlin J. in dissent and not taken up by the majority. Rather, the majority view was that mental distress resulting from the manner of dismissal was not separately actionable but could be taken into account in extending the period of required reasonable notice.

The desirability of providing some compensation for mental distress resulting from the manner of dismissal, albeit in this indirect fashion, was justified by Iacobucci J. in the following terms:

> The point at which the employment relationship ruptures is the time when the employee is most vulnerable and hence, most in need of protection. In recognition of this need, the law ought to encourage conduct that minimizes the damage and dislocation (both economic and personal) that result from dismissal ... the manner in which employment can be terminated is equally important to an individual's identity as the work itself. ... By way of expanding upon this statement, I note that the loss of one's job is always a traumatic event. However, when termination is accompanied by acts of bad faith in the manner of discharge, the results can be especially devastating. In my opinion, to ensure that employees receive adequate protection, employers ought to be held to an obligation of good faith and fair dealing in the manner of dismissal, the breach of which will be compensated for by adding to the length of the notice period.[65]

Employees Against Wrongful Discharge: The Duty to Terminate in Good Faith"
(1980) 93 Harv. L. Rev. 1816; S.R. Ball, "Bad Faith Discharge" (1994) 39 McGill
L.J. 568.

65 *Wallace v. United Grain Growers Ltd., ibid.* at 33.

Again, then, the "obligation of good faith" is not the type of duty that gives rise to a separate actionable wrong. Rather, it is a factor to be taken into account in determining the relevant notice period.

Iacobucci J. further noted that two types of injuries could result from a bad-faith dismissal. First, such a dismissal might exacerbate the problem of finding alternative employment. In such a case, in his view, this would be an appropriate matter to take into account in calculating the length of the reasonable notice period. Second, the bad-faith manner of dismissal could simply cause intangible injuries such as mental distress that, in his view, "merit compensation in and of themselves"[66] through extension of the period of reasonable notice.

In sum, then, the majority opinion in *Wallace* adopted the rather unusual device of imposing an obligation (to dismiss in a sensitive manner) that does not constitute a contractual or tortious duty but that may give rise to compensation when another actionable wrong (failure to give reasonable notice of termination of employment) occurs. With respect to the present topic, then, the decision of the majority in *Wallace* is curiously unhelpful. Certainly, *Wallace* does not constitute the breakthrough decision that recognizes the existence of a duty to perform contracts in good faith. The majority's discussion of good faith is limited quite narrowly to wrongful dismissal. There is no consideration of the possibility of recognizing a more generalized duty of good faith performance. Further, the rejection of this more narrowly defined good faith duty offers no encouragement for those who favour recognition of the general duty of good faith performance. On the other hand, the fact that the majority was prepared to give some recognition to a good faith obligation, albeit indirectly, may be counted by some as a halting half-step forward in the direction of recognition of the general duty.

The majority opinion in *Wallace* was vigorously criticized by McLachlin J. in her dissenting reasons. In her view, the reasoning of the majority failed to honour "the principle that damages must be grounded in a cause of action."[67] For McLachlin J., the manner of dismissal should be relevant to the calculation of the reasonable notice period only where the manner of dismissal in fact has an impact on the ability of the employee to find re-employment. Adopting this approach, in her view, would make the calculation of such damages more predictable. At the same time, she agreed with the majority that employers should be subject to an obligation to act in good faith when dismissing an employee. The appropriate vehicle for imposing such an obligation, how-

66   *Ibid.* at 36.
67   *Ibid.* at 40.

ever, was to recognize the existence of an "implied contractual term to act in good faith in dismissing an employee."[68] On this view, the good faith duty, it should be emphasized, would relate to the manner of dismissal alone. Both the employer and the employee would remain free to terminate the employment relationship without cause.

Predictably, perhaps, academic opinion has been kinder to the dissenting reasons than those of the majority in *Wallace*.[69] The idea that there exists a legal obligation that does not give rise to an enforceable duty but that may provide a basis for additional compensation when another enforceable duty is breached does not appear to have struck a responsive chord in the academic commentary on *Wallace*.[70] Under the *Wallace* doctrine, if employers give reasonable notice of dismissal, they are at liberty to dismiss in a bad-faith manner, with resulting injury to employees. The more important point in the present context, however, is that the dissenting opinion, like the majority opinion, offers no encouragement for the view that Canadian common law is on the brink of recognizing the existence of an independent duty of good faith contractual performance. Advocates of the recognition of such a duty may consider McLachlin J.'s opinion to be somewhat more encouraging than that of the majority. McLachlin J. did not, however, discuss the possible existence of a generalized good faith duty and carefully restricted her analysis to the existence of a good faith duty in the context of manner of dismissal.

D. THE DEFINITION OF GOOD FAITH

In the event that a generalized duty of good faith contractual performance is to be recognized in the Canadian common law of contracts, consideration must be given to the question of whether and, if so, how a definition of good faith should be fashioned. Although no clear consensus appears to have emerged in the American jurisprudence with respect to a definition, a variety of approaches are no doubt possible.

---

68 *Ibid.* at 44.

69 See S.K. O'Byrne, "Bad Faith—Employment Contexts—*Wallace v. United Grain Growers Ltd.*" (1998) 77 Can. Bar Rev. 492; N. Rafferty and P.A. Rowbotham, "Developments in Contract and Tort Law: The 1997–98 Term" (1999) 10 Sup. Ct. L. Rev. (2d) 169 at 171–81; M.C. Crane, "Developments in Employment Law: The 1997-98 Term" (1999) 10 Sup. Ct. L. Rev. (2d) 341 at 349–66.

70 The "obligation" conceived in *Wallace* appears to represent an uneasy compromise between compensatory damages, normally associated with the breach of an enforceable duty, and punitive damages, which are ordered to punish a particularly offensive manner of breaching an enforceable duty.

As a preliminary point, there would appear to be a broad consensus, however, on the proposition that the duty of good faith performance is a lesser obligation than those duties imposed on fiduciaries to act self-lessly in the interests of the person to whom the fiduciary duty is owed. Finn has suggested, for example, that the good faith standard requires individuals to have regard for each other's "legitimate interests" but permits them to otherwise act in their own self interest.[71] A possible definition of good faith, then, might be a requirement to take into account the legitimate interests of the other party. While suggestive, this approach does not appear to offer sufficiently precise guidance for the decision of concrete cases.

Another approach would be to stitch together the existing rules of common law that appear to implement the good faith duty—such as those at issue in the cases examined in this chapter—and consider this a working definition of the concept of good faith. On this basis, the duty might be defined as (1) the duty to exercise discretionary powers conferred by contract reasonably and for the intended purpose; (2) the duty to cooperate in securing performance of the main objects of the contract; and (3) the duty to refrain from strategic behaviour designed to evade contractual obligations.

Some observers, no doubt, would prefer a more abstract and generalized statement of the duty. The Uniform Commercial Code defines "good faith" in Article 1-201 (19) as "honesty in fact in the conduct or transaction concerned." In the sale of goods provisions of the Code, Article 2-103 (1)(b) defines good faith, in the case of a merchant, as "honesty in fact and the observance of reasonable commercial standards of fair dealing in the trade." A leading commentator, however, is of the view that these definitions do not capture the richness of American good faith experience and, accordingly, he suggests that resort must still be made to the common law for definitional purposes.[72] The same writer[73] concedes the difficulty of defining good faith and suggests that more precision can be given to the notion by focusing on bad faith. Bad faith, it is thought, is more easily identified and good faith can be defined as the absence of that conduct. Good faith, on this view, is best understood as an "excluder" concept that is defined in terms of

---

71   P. Finn, "The Fiduciary Principle" in T.G. Youdan, ed., *Equity, Fiduciaries and Trusts* (Agincourt, ON: Carswell, 1989) 1 at 11. And see *Shelanu Inc. v. Print Three Franchising Corp.*, above note 11 at 599, Weiler J.A. (quoting Finn's suggestion with approval).

72   R. Summers, "The General Duty of Good Faith—Its Recognition and Conceptualization" (1982) 67 Cornell L. Rev. 810.

73   Summers, above note 5. See also Belobaba, above note 10.

that which it excludes, that is, performance in bad faith. Shifting attention to the definition of bad faith will, it is argued, give more precision to the definition of good faith.[74]

Other possibilities are suggested by the Canadian jurisprudence. Thus, Kelly J., in *Gateway Realty*, adopted the "bad faith as excluder" analysis and then described bad faith in the following fashion:

> In most cases, bad faith can be said to occur when one party, without reasonable justification, acts in relation to the contract in a manner where the result would be to substantially nullify the bargained objective or benefit contracted for by the other, or to cause significant harm to the other, contrary to the original purpose and expectation of the parties.[75]

Alternatively, one might take as a starting point Iacobucci J.'s requirement, in *Wallace*, that employers "ought to be candid, reasonable, honest and forthright with their employees and should refrain from engaging in conduct that is unfair or is in bad faith by being, for example, untruthful, misleading or unduly insensitive."[76]

E. THE TEST FOR IMPLYING GOOD FAITH DUTIES

If, as some have suggested,[77] the role of the duty of good faith is essentially to serve as an implied term in appropriate circumstances, it must

---

74   Compare with S.J. Burton, "Breach of Contract and the Common Law Duty to Perform in Good Faith" (1980) 94 Harv. L. Rev. 369.

75   Above note 19 at 197. See also *Transamerica Life Canada v. ING Canada* (2003), 234 D.L.R. (4th) 367 at 378 (Ont. C.A.), O'Connor A.C.J.O. ("... courts have implied a duty of good faith with a view to securing the performance and enforcement of the contract made by the parties, or, as it is sometimes put, to ensure that parties do not act in away that eviscerates or defeats the objectives of the parties").

76   Above note 59 at 34. In *1193430 Ontario Inc. v. Boa-Franc (1983) Ltée.* (2003), 68 O.R. (3d) 382 (S.C.J.), in which the parties conceded that their distributorship agreement contained an implied term requiring good faith and good communication, it was held that this term was breached when the distributor failed to disclose a transfer of its ownership to a third party. And see *TSP-Intl Ltd. v. Mills* (2005), 74 O.R. (3d) 461 (S.C.J.). *Venture Capital USA Inc. v. Yorkton Securities Inc.* (2003), 66 O.R. (3d) 760, [2003] O.J. No. 3529, [2003] O.T.C. 819 (S.C.J.), rev'd on appeal (2005), 75 O.R. (3d) 325, [2005] O.J. No. 1885 (C.A.).

77   See, for example, E.A. Farnsworth, "Good Faith Performance and Commercial Reasonableness under the Uniform Commercial Code" (1963) 30 U. Chicago L. Rev. 666.

be asked what the test for such implication is to be. More particularly, one may ask, in the language adopted by the Supreme Court of Canada,[78] whether the implication is based on the "presumed intentions" of the parties or whether the term is implied, regardless of presumed intention, as a "legal incident of a particular class or kind of contract," an incident that is "necessary in a practical sense to the fair functioning of the agreement, given the relationship between the parties."[79] Good faith sceptics, of course, will prefer the former view, that is, the view that a good faith duty should be implied only to give effect to the presumed intentions of the parties. Those who favour a muscular role for good faith, on the other hand, will favour the latter approach, with the attendant risk that the implied duty of good faith will become a vehicle for imposing on the parties duties they would not have willingly assumed. In *Wallace*,[80] it may be noted, McLachlin J., who favoured the implication of a duty to dismiss only in a good faith manner, preferred the latter view on that occasion. The vulnerability of employees, especially at the time of dismissal, provided a basis for imposing such a term on employers as an incident of the contract of employment. Although the line between the two types of implication is difficult to draw, it may be realistic to assume that implied duties of good faith are likely, on occasion at least, to slide into the category of legal incidents rather than mere presumed intentions. Certainly, it would be difficult to defend the implication of terms on each of the cases considered here on the basis of the traditional business efficiency or officious bystander test. In the control of contractual discretion cases,[81] for example, it may be more realistic to suggest that the implied limitation on the exercise of the discretion is intended to give effect to the "reasonable expectations of the parties."[82]

F. CONCLUSION

Although the frequency with which the Canadian common law judiciary has discussed the recognition of a generalized duty of good faith

---

78   *Machtinger v. HOJ Industries Ltd.*, [1992] 1 S.C.R. 986, for discussion of which see Chapter 19, section D(4).
79   *Ibid.* at 1010. For discussion of the rules relating to the implication of contractual terms, see Chapter 19, section D.
80   Above note 59.
81   For discussion of which, see above this Chapter, section B(2).
82   A point made explicitly in *Paragon Finance plc v. Stanton*, above note 40 at 262 (C.A.), Dyson L.J.

performance in contract law suggests that there exists some momentum in the direction of embracing the doctrine, an examination of the *ratio decidendi* in the leading cases indicates that it would be premature to proclaim that this event has occurred. In particular, there is, as yet, little or no evidence of a willingness on the part of the Supreme Court of Canada to recognize the existence of the doctrine in a generalized form. The reasons for this judicial hesitation are a matter of speculation. It may be that it is accepted that Canadian common law can adequately meet problems of bad faith by deploying existing doctrines. Indeed, as the cases analyzed in section C of this chapter indicate, there is a plausible basis for this view. Alternatively, or additionally, it may be that there is judicial concern about the alleged uncertainty of good faith or the dangers of foreign borrowings.

Concerns about the vagueness or uncertainty of the doctrine may recede, however, when one examines the actual cases in which the doctrine has been considered to be applicable by Canadian common law judges. These cases appear to fall into a recognizable pattern resting on three established principles of contractual interpretation. Agreements have, in the past, often been construed to impose implied obligations to cooperate in the accomplishment of the objectives of the agreement,[83] to exercise contractually conferred discretionary powers for the intended purpose[84] and, less frequently perhaps, to refrain from evading contractual duties by doing indirectly what one agreed not to do directly.[85] Unpacking the duty of good faith in this fashion suggests that it is more reckonable than may be feared and that the main effect of a recognition of the doctrine would be simply that of giving expression to an underlying theme in the existing law of contractual interpretation. If and when a recognition of the general duty occurs, it will likely be discovered that not very much has changed in the Canadian common law of contract. Recognition of a good faith duty may facilitate the implication of terms in contracts more aggressively than the traditional doctrines on implied terms would permit. It may also provide a firmer basis than we now have for argument by analogy from the existing categories of good faith cases. Such change as may occur, however, seems likely to fall within the category of gradual adjustment of common law doctrine rather than radical reform.

---

83 See above this Chapter, section B(1).
84 See above this Chapter, section B(2).
85 See above this Chapter, section B(3).

FURTHER READINGS

J. BEATSON & D. FRIEDMANN, eds., *Good Faith and Fault in Contract Law* (Oxford: Clarendon Press, 1995).

E.P. BELOBABA, "Good Faith in Canadian Contract Law" in Law Society of Upper Canada, *Special Lectures 1985, Commercial Law: Recent Developments and Emerging Trends* (Toronto: R. De Boo, 1985).

M. BRIDGE, "Does Anglo-Canadian Contract Law Need a Doctrine of Good Faith?" (1984) 9 Can. Bus. L.J. 385.

R. BROWNSWORD, "'Good Faith in Contracts' Revisited" (1996) 49 Curr. Legal Probs. 112.

R. BROWNSWORD, N.J. Hird & G. Howells, eds., *Good Faith in Contract* (Aldershot, UK: Dartmouth, 1999).

S.J. BURTON, "Breach of Contract and the Common Law Duty to Perform in Good Faith" (1980) 94 Harv. L. Rev. 369.

A.D.M. FORTE, ed., *Good Faith in Contract and Property Law* (Oxford: Hart, 1999).

P. GIRARD, "'Good Faith' in Contract Performance: Principle or Placebo?" (1983) 5 Sup. Ct. L. Rev. 309.

J.D. MCCAMUS, "Abuse of Discretion, Failure to Cooperate and Evasion of Duty: Unpacking the Common Law Duty of Good Faith Contractual Performance" (2004) Advocates' Q. 72.

S.K. O'BYRNE, "Bad Faith—Employment Contexts—*Wallace v. United Grain Growers Ltd.*" (1998) 77 Can. Bar Rev. 492.

S.K. O'BYRNE, "Breach of Good Faith in Performance of the Franchise Contract: Punitive Damages and Damages for Intangibles" (2004) 83 Can. Bar Rev. 431.

S.K. O'BYRNE, "Good Faith in Contractual Performance: Recent Developments" (1995) 74 Can. Bar Rev. 70.

ONTARIO LAW REFORM COMMISSION, *Report on Amendment of the Law of Contract* (Toronto: Ministry of the Attorney General, 1989) c. 9.

E. PEDEN, *Good Faith in the Performance of Contracts* (Sydney: Butterworths, 2003).

R. POWELL, "Good Faith in Contracts" (1956) 9 Curr. Legal Probs. 16.

D. STACK, "The Two Standards of Good Faith in Canadian Contract Law" (1999) 62 Sask. L. Rev. 201.

R.S. SUMMERS, "The General Duty of Good Faith—Its Recognition and Conceptualization" (1982) 67 Cornell L. Rev. 810.

G. TEUBNER, "Legal Irritants: Good Faith in British Law or How Unifying Law Ends Up in New Divergences" (1998) 61 Mod. L. Rev. 11.

R. ZIMMERMAN & S. WHITTAKER, eds., *Good Faith in European Contact Law* (Cambridge: Cambridge University Press, 2000).

PART SIX

REMEDIES

CHAPTER 22

DAMAGES

A. INTRODUCTION

The principal remedy available to a victim of a breach of contract is an award of compensatory damages. Damage awards may be contrasted with court orders that require the party in breach of contract either to perform the contract or to refrain from conduct that amounts to a breach of contract. Such orders, sometimes referred to as "coercive" remedies were granted in exceptional circumstances by courts of equity and will be the subject of treatment in a subsequent chapter.[1] Compensatory damages are, however, the usual remedy for breach of contract. The governing principle for calculating compensatory damages in a claim for damages for breach of contract is the expectancy principle that requires the party in breach to pay, as damages, an amount of money that will provide the victim of the breach with the financial equivalent of performance. In this chapter, we examine the expectancy principle and its operation. Further, an account is offered of the principles that limit or reduce the scope of compensatory damage awards such as the principle that the plaintiff cannot recover for losses that could have been avoided by reasonable steps taken in mitigation by the plaintiff. In the typical case, the subject of compensation is economic loss suffered by the plaintiff. It must be considered, however whether compensation

---

1   See Chapter 23.

may also be awarded for certain intangible losses such as the mental stress and anxiety that the plaintiff may suffer as a result of breach. As we will see, limited recognition has been given by the common law to compensate for injuries of this kind.

Although the expectancy principle is the governing principle, other forms of monetary relief can be imagined. Thus, compensation could be calculated on the basis of a principle that would restore the plaintiff to the position he or she was in prior to entering the contract. On this basis, the plaintiff would be awarded recovery of out-of-pocket expenses incurred in reliance on the contract and other similar losses. This measure of relief, referred to in contract law as the reliance measure, is similar to the general principle for calculating damages in a tort claim. Occasionally, damages calculated on a reliance measure can be awarded in a claim for damages for breach of contract on the basis of the analysis considered further in this chapter. A further alternative measure of relief would be to simply require the party in breach to restore to the plaintiff benefits that the plaintiff has conferred upon the party in breach through performance of the agreement. Such awards are considered to be restitutionary in nature. The availability of restitutionary relief in the context of contract breach will be considered in Chapter 24, which provides a more general examination of the role of restitutionary relief in contract law.[2]

A further possible alternative measure of relief—disgorgement of profits—has emerged in recent years. A party in breach of contract may enjoy a profit as a result of the contract breach. Thus, a seller of goods who refuses to deliver the goods to a first purchaser might profit by selling the very goods in question to a second purchaser at a much higher price, indeed, let us assume a price that is higher than the market price. Under the traditional expectancy analysis, the initial purchaser would be entitled to recover only the difference between the initial sale price and the market price. Thus compensated, the initial purchaser could acquire a substitute in the market and would be in as good a position as he or she would have been in if the contract had been performed. There is recent Canadian and English authority, however, suggesting that in exceptional circumstances, the initial buyer might be entitled to recover all the seller's profits on the second transaction.[3] This type of relief, typically referred to as "disgorgement" relief, is not

---

2   See Chapter 24, section B(1).

3   If in this simple illustration, there are substitute goods readily available to the buyer in the market, the breach is likely to be considered "efficient" and not subject to disgorgement relief. See further Chapter 24, section B(2).

truly compensatory in nature. The seller's profit does not necessarily correspond to any loss suffered by the first buyer. Disgorgement relief is generally considered to be a second type of restitutionary measure of recovery that has as its purpose the stripping of the defendant's ill-gotten gains. It will be examined separately in the context of a more general discussion of restitutionary relief.[4]

As a further alternative to these various forms of compensatory and restitutionary relief, it can be asked whether the victim of a breach of contract may be able to seek punitive or exemplary damages against the party in breach. Such awards would amount, in effect, to civil fines being collected by the plaintiff. Under traditional doctrine, although such awards have been made in a particular range of tort cases, awards of punitive damages have had no place in the law of contract. In recent years, however, the Supreme Court of Canada has recognized the possibility of awarding punitive damages in contract cases.[5] The current Canadian law on this issue will be further considered below.[6]

Finally, the complexity and uncertainties that may complicate the exercise of assessing damages in a breach of contract claim may lead the parties to stipulate in their agreement the monetary consequences of breach of contract. Although provisions of this kind are commonly included in agreements, they are not invariably considered to be enforceable by the courts. The analysis underlying the distinction between those terms that are enforceable and those that are not will be examined in the concluding part of this chapter.

B. THE EXPECTANCY PRINCIPLE

1) The Basic Principle

The basic principle for calculating an award of damages in a contract claim—the expectancy principle—has the objective of providing the plaintiff with a monetary equivalent of performance. The expectancy principle is forward-looking in the sense that it attempts to secure for the plaintiff the benefits of performance rather than merely restoring the plaintiff to the position he or she was in before the contract was created. The latter objective could be served by simply awarding the plaintiff recovery of all the out-of-pocket expenses sustained in reliance on the con-

---

4   See *ibid.*
5   *Whiten v. Pilot Insurance Co.*, [2002] 1 S.C.R. 595.
6   See below this Chapter, section I.

tract. Reimbursement of such losses as have been incurred in reliance on the contract would make the plaintiff whole in the sense of restoring the plaintiff to the financial position the plaintiff was in before entering the contract. Recovery of this kind, often referred to as reliance damages, is, in contrast to the expectancy principle, backward-looking.

The classic exposition of the expectancy principle was set out in *Robinson v. Harman*[7] by Baron Parke as follows: "The rule of the common law is, that where a party sustains a loss by reason of a breach of contract, he is, so far as money can do it, to be placed in the same situation, with respect to damages, as if the contract had been performed."[8] This principle has been recited by the courts in numberless cases. In the decision of the Privy Council in *Sally Wertheim v. Chicoutimi Pulp Company*,[9] it was coupled with the following encomium: "That is a ruling principle. It is a just principle."[10] Although, as we shall see, the question of how to justify the expectancy principle or identify its underlying rationale has attracted some debate among legal theorists,[11] there can be no doubt that the expectancy principle is well established and applied by the courts in calculating damage awards in claims for damages for breach of contract.

The operation of the principle may be portrayed by some illustrations of its application. If an owner of land hires a builder to erect a structure on the land and the builder abandons the project before its completion, the owner would be entitled to claim the difference between the amount remaining to be paid under the contract and the amount required to hire a substitute builder to finish the work.[12] Such an amount would normally place the owner of the land in a position he or she would have been in if the contract had been performed. An employee under a contract of employment at will who is entitled to reasonable notice of termination of the relationship from the employer and who is wrongfully dismissed without such notice would be entitled to recover the wages that would have been earned during that notice period.[13] In a contract for the pur-

---

7   (1848), Exch. 850, 154 E.R. 363.

8   *Ibid.* at 855 (Exch.).

9   [1911] A.C. 301 (P.C.).

10   *Ibid.* at 307.

11   See below this Chapter, section C.

12   In a case where the builder does not commence the work, an interesting question may arise as to whether the expectancy should be calculated on the basis of the measure suggested in the text or, rather, on the basis of the extent to which the completed work would enhance the value of the property. For a discussion of this point, see below this Chapter, section E(3).

13   Subject, however, to the application of the mitigation principle, for discussion of which see below this Chapter, section F(3).

chase and sale of goods, if the seller refuses to deliver the goods, the purchaser is normally entitled to claim the difference between the contract price and the market price of substitute goods.[14] In an appropriate case, the expectancy principle might provide a basis for recovery of what might be considered to be consequential losses. Thus, in a contract to supply a chattel that will be used by the buyer to generate profit, the supplier of a defective chattel may be liable for the loss of profits sustained by the buyer as a result of the breach.[15]

Where it is the purchaser of goods that breaches the contract of sale by refusing to take delivery of goods, however, a more complex picture emerges. In order for the seller to claim expectancy damages in the form of the profit that would have been made by completing the transaction, it must first be determined whether the contract price is higher than the market price. If it is, the seller should be entitled to recover the difference between the two as that amount is required to put the seller in as good a position as the seller would have been in if the contract had been performed. If the contract price and the market price are equivalent, it may appear that no expectancy loss has been sustained. If, however, the seller has, in effect, lost a sale because the seller has access to a supply of such goods that is greater than the potential demand for them, the seller should recover the profit that would have been made on this transaction.[16] Thus, if a car dealer sells the very car that the defaulting purchaser refuses to accept to another purchaser but could, in any event, have obtained a further car from the manufacturer to supply to the second purchaser, the car dealer has suffered a loss in volume of sales and should recover expectancy damages. On the other hand, if the dealer's access to cars is restricted with the result that the dealer can sell every car obtained from the manufacturer, the dealer has suffered no loss in volume and would not be entitled to expectancy damages.[17]

---

14   This common law principle has been enshrined in sale of goods legislation. See, for example, *Sale of Goods Act*, R.S.O. 1990, c. S.1, s. 49(3).

15   Subject, however, to the principle that such losses must have been reasonably foreseeable by the supplier at the time of entering in the contract. For discussion of this principle, see below this Chapter, section F(2).

16   See, for example, *W.L. Thompson Ltd. v. Robinson (Gunmakers) Ltd.*, [1955] Ch. 177; *Victory Motors Ltd. v. Bayda*, [1973] 3 W.W.R. 747 (Sask. Dist. Ct.). See also *Interoffice Telephones v. Robert Freeman Co.*, [1958] 1 Q.B. 190 (C.A.) (equipment rental). See also C. Goetz and R. Scott, "Measuring Sellers' Damages: The Lost Profits Puzzle" (1979) 31 Stan. L. Rev. 323.

17   *Charter v. Sullivan*, [1957] 2 Q.B. 117 (C.A.). See also *Lazenby Garages v. Wright*, [1976] 1 W.L.R. 459 (C.A.) (sale of second-hand car — no lost volume).

In some fact situations, application of the expectancy principle may generate a calculation that appears to replicate reliance damages. For example, if the undertaking that has been breached is one that, if performed, would have led the promisee not to enter the agreement or, at least, not to detrimentally rely on the undertaking in question, application of the expectancy rule may restore the innocent party, in a financial sense, to the position that the party was in before the contract was entered. In an English case,[18] for example, the lessee of a service station entered into the station lease with the lessor oil company on the faith of the lessor's undertaking that a study of the "through-put" or volume of sales likely to be enjoyed at the particular location had been carefully done. In fact, the study carelessly overestimated the volume of the projected sales, and the lessee's business failed. It was held that the lessee was entitled to recover, as damages for breach of contract, his lost investment on the theory that if the study had been carefully done, it would have revealed the sorry prospects for the business and the lessee would never have made that investment. Thus, although the calculation is an expectancy calculation in the sense that it puts the lessee in the position he would have been in if the undertaking concerning the study had been performed, the calculation corresponds with a reliance calculation in the sense that it allows the lessee to recover his out-of-pocket expenses and to be restored to his pre-contractual position. Similarly, it has been held, in the context of a construction contract, that where the employer of the contractor breaches a contractual undertaking to have prepared the site properly before the construction work was to begin, the contractor is entitled to recover as expectancy damages, the expenses incurred in doing the work that should have been done by the employer. The contractor would not, however, be entitled to recover a profit margin on that work. If the employer had performed its undertaking, the work would not have been done by the contractor and no profit would have been enjoyed on that work.[19] In cases of this kind, the expectancy measure of damages thus appears to coincide with the reliance or reimbursement measure of damages that would be applied in a tort claim if the contract had been induced by tortious misconduct.[20] The contractual expectancy measure and the tort measure of indem-

---

18 *Esso Petroleum Co. v. Mardon*, [1976] Q.B. 801.

19 *BG Checo International Ltd. v. British Columbia Hydro & Power Authority*, [1993] 1 S.C.R. 12 at 26, 40–42, La Forest and McLachlin JJ.

20 See *Esso Petroleum Co. v. Mardon*, above note 18 at 820–21, Lord Denning M.R.; *BG Checo International Ltd. v. British Columbia Hydro & Power Authority, ibid.*; *Rainbow Industrial Caterers Ltd. v. Canadian National Railway Co.*, [1991] 3 S.C.R. 3.

nification for injuries sustained will also coincide in a case where the breach of contract, such as careless driving by one's chauffeur, results in personal injury or property damage. Placing the injured employer in the position he or she would have been in if the chauffeur had complied with the contractual obligation to drive carefully requires compensation for the injuries sustained and would not involve a profit element.

2) Exceptions

The expectancy principle admits of few exceptions. Indeed, the pervasiveness of the expectancy principle may be illustrated by the fact that a number of the principal exceptions recognized at common law have been undermined or, indeed, overruled. Thus, an important exception at common law related to the non-payment of money. The traditional position was that where breach consisted of a failure to perform an obligation to pay money, interest on the amount in question would not be awarded at trial in the absence of an explicit agreement to pay interest in such circumstances.[21] This approach may be said to constitute an exception to the expectancy principle as a person who receives the sum that was due on an earlier date only at the time of trial cannot be said to have been placed in as good a position as he or she would have been in if the contract had been performed. In the modern era, however, common law jurisdictions have typically enacted legislation enabling courts to award both pre-judgment interest, running typically from the date of breach until the date of judgment, and post-judgment interest running after that date.[22] The interest awarded is normally simple rather than compound and at the bank rate. It may not, therefore, precisely place the payee in as good a position as he or she would have been in if the contract had been performed. Courts do, however, typically have a discretion to vary the amount of interest. Indeed, and more recently, it has been suggested that the courts are possessed of a discretion to award compound interest, formerly the preserve of courts of equity, in a broader range of cases that may include claims for damages for breach of contract.[23]

An important exception to the expectancy rule at common law arose in the context of contracts for the purchase and sale of land, in

---

21 *London, Chatham and Dover Rwy. Co. v. South Eastern Rwy. Co.*, [1893] A.C. 429 (H.L.). Compare with *Trans Trust S.P.R.L. v. Danubian Trading Co.*, [1952] 2 Q.B. 297 (C.A.).

22 See, for example, *Courts of Justice Act*, R.S.O. 1990, c. C.43, ss. 128–30.

23 *Bank of America Canada v. Mutual Trust Co.*, [2002] 2 S.C.R. 601. See also *Westdeutsche Landesbank Girozentrale v. Islington London Borough Council*, [1996] A.C. 669 (H.L.).

cases where the vendor has been unable to convey title. In the 1776 decision of *Flureau v. Thornhill*,[24] it was established that, in such circumstances, the purchaser is unable to recover damages for loss of the bargain. Virtually the entirety of the four-line judgment of Chief Justice De Grey is taken up by the following sentence: "On a contract for a purchase, if the title proves bad and the vendor is (without fraud) incapable of making a good one, I do not think that the purchaser can be entitled to any damages for the fancied goodness of the bargain which he supposes he has lost."[25] At only slightly greater length, Blackstone J., in a concurring opinion, added that the purchaser would, however, be entitled to "a return of the deposit with interest and costs." That was, he said, "[A]ll that can be expected."[26] The decision thus created an exception to the expectancy principle restricting a disappointed purchaser, absent bad faith on the part of the vendor, to recovery of the deposit and other costs incurred by the purchaser, such as the cost of a survey, in preparing to complete the transaction. Although this recovery is in the reliance measure, later Canadian authority[27] establishes that the purchaser is not entitled to general reliance damages but only to those expenses related to the closing of the transaction.

In 1874, the House of Lords re-examined the doctrine in its famous decision in *Bain v. Fothergill*.[28] This case concerned the sale of a lease of a mining royalty. In the initial lease, the lessees had agreed not to assign the lease without the consent of the lessors. Mistakenly assuming that they would be able to obtain that consent, the lessees entered into a contract to sell the leasehold interest to the plaintiff purchasers. The sale was not conditional on obtaining the lessors' consent. When the lessors refused to consent and the transaction therefore failed to close, the plaintiff purchasers sought the return of their deposit and costs and, as well, damages for their loss of bargain. The plaintiffs thought that such a claim might enjoy success, notwithstanding the decision in *Flureau v. Thornhill*, because there existed some evidence in the case law that the courts had recognized an exception to *Flureau v. Thornhill* in cases where vendors know, at the time of entering the contract of sale, that they do not have the present ability to transfer title.[29] In such

---

24   (1776), 2 Bla. W. 1078, 96 E.R. 635.

25   *Ibid.*

26   *Ibid.*

27   *Ontario Asphalt Block Co. v. Montreuil* (1916), 52 S.C.R. 541 (intending purchaser in possession of land—not entitled to recover the cost of improvements made to the land).

28   (1874), L.R. 7 H.L. 158.

29   *Hopkins v. Grazebrook* (1826), 6 B. & Cress. 31, 108 E.R. 364.

a case, or so the plaintiffs argued, *Flureau v. Thornhill* should not apply
and full damages for loss of bargain should be available. When *Bain v.
Fothergill* surfaced for consideration by the House of Lords, it was held
that no such exception to the rule in *Flureau v. Thornhill* should be
admitted. If, as in the present case, the vendor had acted in good faith,
the fact that the vendor knew that he did not have title at the time of
entering the transaction would not expose him to the full measure of
damages for breach of contract. The rule in *Bain v. Fothergill*, as it came
to be known, was thus firmly established as the governing principle
for the calculation of damages in the context of failure to make title in
contracts for the purchase and sale of interests in land.

The Supreme Court of Canada had occasion to reconsider the rule
in *A.V.G. Management Science Ltd. v. Barwell Developments Ltd.*[30] Barwell
had agreed to sell an apartment building to one Jordan. Mistakenly
believing that the deal with Jordan was not going to proceed, Barwell
then entered into a second agreement to sell the building to the plaintiff. Jordan successfully sought specific performance of its agreement
with Barwell and Barwell was thus unable to convey title to the property to the plaintiff. The plaintiff sought damages for loss of the bargain
and argued that the vendor should not have the benefit of the protection in *Bain v. Fothergill* since the vendor had himself made it impossible to convey title by entering into two separate agreements to convey
the same title to different persons. The plaintiff argued that whether or
not the vendor had acted in bad faith, the special protection of *Bain v.
Fothergill* should not be available to a vendor who engages in "double-
dealing." In other words, the purchaser argued, in effect, that a new exception to the rule in *Bain v. Fothergill* should be recognized, enabling
purchasers to recover full loss of bargain damages in circumstances of
this kind.

The trial judge[31] held that the vendor was not guilty of fraud or bad
faith and, accordingly, that he was entitled to the protection afforded by
Bain v. Fothergill. On appeal, however, a majority of the British Columbia Court of Appeal[32] concluded that the rule should not apply where,
as here, the defect could not be said to be "unexpected." The rule in
Bain v. Fothergill, it was said, was designed to protect a vendor who is
confronted by "unexpected" defects in title. A vendor who caused the
problem himself by entering into two transactions could not claim that
the problem is "unexpected" in the requisite sense. These facts were

30 [1979] 2 S.C.R. 43.
31 [1976] 6 W.W.R. 289 (B.C.S.C.).
32 [1978] 1 W.W.R. 730 (B.C.C.A.).

therefore not captured by the rule in *Bain v. Fothergill* and the plaintiff was entitled to recover damages for loss of bargain. The majority of the Court of Appeal also indicated, however, more general reservations about the very rule in *Bain v. Fothergill* itself and suggested that, if the matter should come before the Supreme Court of Canada, consideration should be given to the possibility of overruling this familiar and well-established rule of contract law.

Upon further appeal to the Supreme Court of Canada,[33] these matters surfaced before a panel of five members of the Court. Writing for a unanimous Court, Laskin C.J.C. agreed with the court below that the present facts fell outside the rule in *Bain v. Fothergill* and that the rule should not protect a vendor who, having title, has "either voluntarily disabled himself from being able to convey or has risked and lost his ability to do so by what were in effect concurrent dealings with two different purchasers." This holding was, of course, sufficient to dispose of the matter, but the Court accepted the invitation of the British Columbia Court of Appeal to consider overturning the rule in *Bain v. Fothergill*. Indeed, Laskin C.J.C. indicated that were it necessary to do so in the present case, the Court would have been prepared to overrule the doctrine. There were a number of reasons for this conclusion. The decision in *Bain v. Fothergill* was a product of the factual context of mid-nineteenth-century England. The original rationale of the rule in *Bain v. Fothergill* rested in the uncertainty, at that time, in the state of English title documents. There was only a voluntary system for registration of land titles in force in England at that time. Proof of title was a notoriously difficult matter. Times had changed. With the adoption of Torrens registration systems in Western Canada and the older registration schemes in the common law East, the problem of uncertainty of titles had ceased to provide a grounding for the rule. The main rationale of the rule had, in effect, "disappeared."[34] The Court also noted in passing that the rule had been the subject of a criticism in a report by the British Columbia Law Reform Commission[35] and that the province of British Columbia, acting on the commission's advice, had enacted legislation abrogating the rule in 1978.[36] The Court further noted that the doctrine had been generally rejected in the common law of the

---

33   Above note 30.

34   Above note 30 at 56.

35   Law Reform Commission of British Columbia, *Report on the Rule in Bain v. Fothergill* (Vancouver: Law Reform Commission of British Columbia, 1976).

36   Legislation that, at the time of this appeal, had not yet been proclaimed. See now *Property Law Act*, R.S.B.C. 1996, c. 377, s. 37.

United States.[37] The Court concluded that the doctrine should be considered to be overruled.

Although Laskin C.J.C.'s observations were technically mere *obiter dicta*, they have had the effect, to say the least, of substantially undermining the authority of *Bain v. Fothergill*. Two provincial appellate courts have suggested that the doctrine has been effectively overruled.[38] Apart from the British Columbia legislation[39] the doctrine has also been overruled by statute in England.[40] At the same time, however, the expectancy rule may be very harsh medicine for an innocent householder or even a commercial vendor who is unable to make title in a rising market. It therefore remains common for real estate transactions to be structured in such a way as to immunize vendors from expectancy damages in the event of title defects.[41]

Another of the traditional exceptions to the awarding of expectancy damages has been more plainly overruled by the Supreme Court of Canada. At common law, if a lessor, confronted by a wrongful repudiation of the lease by the lessee, retook possession of the premises or re-let the premises to a third party, the lease was said to be "surrendered" and the lessor would be unable to claim against the lessee for expectancy damages relating to the unexpired portion of the term.[42] The theory underlying this principle was that a lease is not merely a contract but creates an estate in land. Upon surrender of the lease, the leasehold interest expires and so too, it was thought, does the obligation to pay rent. In *Highway Properties Ltd. v. Kelly Douglas & Co. Ltd.*,[43] the Supreme Court of Canada had an opportunity to reconsider this doctrine in the context of a repudiation of a shopping centre lease

---

37 Referring to A. James Casner, ed., *American Law of Property* (Boston: Little, Brown, 1952–1954) vol. 3 at 169–70.

38 *Brown v. Waterloo Regional Board of Commissioners of Police* (1983), 150 D.L.R. (3d) 729 at 734 (Ont. C.A.), Weatherston J.A., var'g (1982), 37 O.R. (2d) 277 (H.C.J.); *Kopec v. Pyret* (1987), 36 D.L.R. (4th) 1 at 11 (Sask. C.A.), Vancise J.A. On the general issue of the respect to be accorded considered *dicta* of the Supreme Court of Canada, see *R. v. Sellars*, [1980] 1 S.C.R. 527 at 529–30, Chouinard J.

39 Above note 36.

40 *Law of Property Act*, 1989 (U.K.), 1989, c. 34, s. 3.

41 See also *Vendors and Purchasers Act*, R.S.O. 1990, c. V.2, s. 4(c) (statutory default rule providing vendor has 30 days to remove purchaser's objections to title, failing which the vendor must return the deposit but is not otherwise liable).

42 See, for example, *Lyon v. Reed* (1844), 13 M. & W. 285, 153 E.R. 118; *Phene v. Popplewell* (1862), 12 C.B. (N.S.) 334, 142 E.R. 1171, *Attorney-General Saskatchewan v. Whiteshore Salt & Chemical Co.*, [1955] S.C.R. 43; *Goldhar v. Universal Sections and Mouldings Ltd.* (1962), 36 D.L.R. (2d) 450 (Ont. C.A.).

43 [1971] S.C.R. 562.

by a major tenant. The landlord had retaken possession of the premises but served notice that the lessee would be held accountable for full damages with respect to any losses suffered during the unexpired portion of the lease. For a unanimous Court, Laskin J. held that the traditional rule should no longer be followed and that a lessee guilty of a repudiatory breach of the lease would be exposed to a claim for expectancy damages. He observed as follows: "It is no longer sensible to pretend that a commercial lease ... is simply a conveyance and not also a contract. It is equally untenable to persist in denying resort to the full armoury of remedies ordinarily available to redress repudiation of covenants, merely because the covenants may be associated with an estate in land."[44]

The surrender doctrine had also applied to leases of chattels. In the later case of *Keneric Tractor Sales Ltd. v. Langille*,[45] however, the Supreme Court held that, consistently with the *Kelly Douglas* decision, the traditional rule should no longer be considered applicable to chattel leases. Thus, where a lessor of either land or goods, faced with a repudiatory breach by the lessee retakes possession of the property but is unable to re-let the property or is only able to re-let it at a reduced rental, the lessee will be liable to pay expectancy damages, placing the lessor in the position the lessor would have been in if the lessee had not repudiated the lease.

In recent years, however, the Supreme Court of Canada[46] has confirmed the existence of a further exception to the expectancy principle in the form of a presumption that where the party in breach of contract was entitled, under the agreement, to perform in a variety of ways, the damages available will be calculated on the assumption that the defendant would have selected the least burdensome mode of performance.[47] Thus, for example, damages for breach of a contract to deliver 200 tonnes of a particular commodity "5 percent more or less" will be calculated on the basis that the supplier is in breach of an obligation to deliver 190 tonnes.[48] As is sometimes said, "in an action for breach of contract a defendant is not liable for doing that which he

---

44   *Ibid.* at 576.

45   [1987] 2 S.C.R. 440.

46   *Hamilton v. Open Window Bakery Ltd.* (2004), 235 D.L.R. (4th) 193 (S.C.C.).

47   *Cockburn v. Alexander* (1848), 6 C.B. 791; *Abrams v. Reiach (Herbert) Ltd.*, [1922] 1 K.B. 477 (C.A.); *Vecher v. Coplak Enterprises, "The World Navigator"*, [1991] 2 Lloyd's Rep. 23 (C.A.); *Park v. Parsons Brown & Company* (1989), 62 D.L.R. (4th) 108 (B.C.C.A.); *Johnson Matthey Banking v. The State Trading Corp. of India, Ltd.*, [1984] 1 Lloyd's Rep. 427 (Q.B.).

48   *Re Thornett & Fehr*, [1921] 1 K.B. 219.

is not bound to do."[49] In some cases, application of the presumption will correspond with the likely facts and therefore may be considered to apply the expectancy rule. In *Withers v. General Theatre Corp.*,[50] for example, the plaintiff music hall performer had been hired by the defendant, the owner of the London Palladium and various other music halls, to perform a new sketch for a period of weeks. Although both the plaintiff and defendant initially envisaged that the performance would take place at the most prestigious venue, the Palladium, the contract specifically provided that the plaintiff's performance could be transferred to any other of the halls owned or controlled by the defendant. In the course of a one-week preliminary run, at Portsmouth, it became apparent that the sketch was not satisfactory to the defendant and the plaintiff was summarily dismissed. The plaintiff sought damages on the basis that at least a two-week run at the Palladium was envisaged. The court held, however, that since the defendant was not obliged to run the plaintiff's act at the Palladium, damages were to be calculated on the basis that he would only have been permitted to perform in a less prestigious venue. In the circumstances of this case, there was no likelihood that the plaintiff would be permitted to perform at the Palladium and, accordingly, the presumed facts appear to correspond with the likely facts. In *Hamilton v. Open Window Bakery Ltd.*, however, the Supreme Court of Canada clearly indicated that the presumption of least-burdensome performance is not merely an evidentiary presumption but constitutes a strict limitation on the operation of the expectancy principle. In this case, an employee was wrongfully dismissed under an agreement that would have permitted dismissal after twenty-one months of employment. The trial judge held that, but for the employer's breach, the contract would probably have run for a period of time beyond twenty-one months and calculated damages on that basis. The Supreme Court of Canada held, however, that the presumption applies in such circumstances and that the calculation of damages must rest on an assessment of the minimum performance the defendant was required to provide. Accordingly, it should have been presumed that the employer would have terminated the contract after twenty-one months of service. The presumption was stated to be a "long-standing and widely accepted general principle, [which] is sound in policy and is one that leads to predictable and justifiable results."[51] Assuming that the trial judge's finding of fact on the likely length of the employment relation-

---

49   *Lavarack v. Woods of Colchester Ltd.*, [1967] 1 Q.B. 278 at 294 (C.A.), Diplock L.J.
50   [1933] 2 K.B. 536 (C.A.).
51   Above note 46 at 200, Arbour J.

ship was correct, the application of the presumption thus has the effect of precluding the plaintiff from recovering an amount that would place the plaintiff in the position he or she would have been in if the contract had been performed.

C. JUSTIFYING EXPECTANCY

As we have seen, the expectancy principle is well established as the determining principle for the quantification of compensatory damages in a contract damages claim. At a theoretical level, however, justification of the doctrine has proven to be a matter of some contention. The classic defence of the expectancy principle is that set out by Fuller and Perdue in a well-known law review article.[52] The particular problem tackled by Fuller and Perdue was to provide a justification for the granting of expectancy damages in cases where the contract between the parties remains wholly executory and neither party has detrimentally relied on the promise of the other. In such a case, although the promisee may experience a sense of disappointment at losing the advantages of the bargain, it might be argued that the promisee has experienced no actual injury other than that sense of disappointment. The promisee, it might be said, has not lost anything as a result of the breach. As Fuller and Perdue stated, this "seems on the face of things a queer kind of 'compensation.'"[53] We might refer to such cases as involving a "pure" expectancy claim. The expectancy principle holds, however, that in such a case the promisee has experienced an injury in the form of a lost expectation of profit that should be the subject of compensation in a damages claim. Once the agreement has been entered, the benefits due to the promisee are secured by the expectancy principle and damages are awarded for the lost profit or benefit, regardless of whether the promisee has engaged in acts of detrimental reliance.

In defending the application of the expectancy principle, Fuller and Perdue begin by articulating the three principal purposes that might be pursued in awarding contract damages. First, a court could require the promisor to give back any value or benefit received from the promisee, such as a down payment, on the theory that otherwise the promisor would be unjustly enriched at the expense of the promisee. Such awards would protect the promisee's *restitution* interest. A second ob-

---

52 L. Fuller and W. Perdue, "The Reliance Interest in Contract Damages" (1936) 46 Yale L.J. 52.
53 *Ibid.* at 53.

jective could be to compensate the promisee for any detrimental reliance engaged in by the promisee on the assumption that the promisor would perform the agreement. The objective of such an award would be to undo the harm resulting from the promisor's breach and place the promisee in a position he or she was in before the contract was created. Fuller and Perdue identify such awards as achieving protection of the promisee's *reliance* interest. The third alternative, which corresponds to the existing law, is to grant awards that attempt to place the promisee in the position the promisee would have been in if the contract had been performed and this, of course, constitutes protection of the *expectation* interest.

A critical step in the analysis that follows is the observation by Fuller and Perdue that the reliance interest may include lost opportunities to make a profit by dealing with other persons where those opportunities have been forgone in reliance on the promisor's undertaking to perform the agreement. They illustrate the point with the example of a physician who charges a patient for a missed appointment on the theory that an opportunity to provide services to another patient has been forgone in reliance on the first patient's promise to attend. Fuller and Perdue argue that there is nothing in the definition of the reliance interest that would preclude inclusion of this type of lost opportunity to profit as a reliance injury. Thus, protection of the reliance interest could, in principle at least, include compensation both for losses in the sense of out-of-pocket expenses and for forgone opportunities to profit or, in the authors' terminology, "gains prevented."[54] The expectancy interest is broader than the reliance interest because it would include profits secured to the promisee under an agreement even though the promisee had not suffered a forgone opportunity to make a similar profit elsewhere. Returning to the example of the physician, if the physician could demonstrate that the supply of patients exceeded the physician's ability to provide services, a forgone opportunity to profit would be established and the loss of profit on the appointment would be included in a reliance award. If the physician could not offer such proof, however, the profit that would have been secured if the first patient had attended the appointment is only compensable in an expectancy award.

Before turning to their defence of the expectancy principle, Fuller and Perdue dismiss alternative theories that might appear to have some persuasive force. First, they suggest that expectancy might be defended on a psychological basis. Even though, in a pure expectancy case, the promisee may not have suffered an economic injury, there is nonetheless

---

54 *Ibid.* at 55.

a sense of disappointment that is likely to be experienced by a promisee in such circumstances. Rather than attempting to determine the nature of any particular promisee's level of disappointment, however, the law, it might be said, simply assumes the existence of the injury and compensates for it by awarding expectancy losses. The difficulty with this theory, the authors suggest, is that there are many promises that the law does not enforce. Accordingly, an instinct to protect and compensate for disappointed expectations cannot provide an explanation for the law's protection of the expectation interest. Second, they invoke the "will theory" that holds that the law vests in the contracting parties a private legislative power such that the enforcement of the contract merely implements the intentions of the parties. The will theory might be thought to be consistent with the protection of the expectancy interest. Fuller and Perdue reject this suggestion, however, on the basis that even if one accepts that a contract represents a kind of private law, it is a private law that typically is silent on the question of the measure of damages to be awarded in the event of breach of the agreement. Thus, there is nothing in the will theory, as such, that is inconsistent with the awarding of reliance damages as a matter of general principle.

A third approach, described by Fuller and Perdue as an "economic or institutional approach,"[55] locates the rationale for the expectancy principle in the phenomenon of the modern credit economy. The essence of a credit economy, they suggest, is that future values are collapsed into present values. Arguably, it is an inevitable feature of a credit economy that promises of future conduct become, in effect, a species of property that can be traded. Thus, the future breach of a binding promise constitutes a present loss in the sense that the economic modes of thought underlying the credit economy will have attributed value to the promise of future conduct that has now been lost. Such a view, for Fuller and Perdue, "sees law not as the creature but as the creator of social institutions."[56] The principal objection to this justification, in their view, is that it involves a circular argument. A promise has present value because the law enforces it. Enforceability inevitably involves the conferral of present value on future performance and is therefore "not the cause of legal intervention but the consequence of it."[57] Moreover, historically, promises were enforced long before the development of the modern credit economy. Thus, enforceability ought to be seen not as an instrument for creating the credit economy but as a development

---

55   *Ibid.* at 59.
56   *Ibid.* at 60.
57   *Ibid.*

that preceded it and upon which the modern credit economy has been constructed.

Against this background, Fuller and Perdue turned to the justification that they find convincing, which they characterize as the "juristic" explanation. By this term they mean that the explanation is one that is rooted in "some policy consciously pursued by courts and other law makers ... because they have considered it wise to do so, not through a blind acquiescence and habitual ways of thinking and feeling, or through an equally blind deference to the individual will."[58] The juristic explanation for the expectancy principle is twofold. First, the authors argue that even if one were to assume that the purpose to be served in calculating damage awards is to protect the reliance interest of the promisee, one may still defend the expectancy principle on the basis that it offers the most effective protection of that interest. Keeping in mind that the reliance interest, in their view, embraces forgone opportunities to make a profit elsewhere, Fuller and Perdue argue that although such forgone opportunities are involved to some extent in most contracts, it may often be very difficult, if not impossible, to prove their existence. Moreover, once breach has occurred, the promisee will not be allowed to recover compensation for injuries that could be avoided by taking up other opportunities for gain.[59] The existence of the mitigation principle tends to corroborate the view that the purpose underlying the expectancy principle is to compensate the promisee for the loss of other opportunities for gain. In order to ensure that the promisee is adequately compensated for such lost opportunities, the expectancy principle assumes that they have occurred.

Second, not only is the expectancy measure a more effective cure for losses in the form of gains prevented, it is an effective prophylaxis against this kind of injury. The expectancy measure is more easily administered than the reliance measure and thus constitutes a more effective sanction against breach of contract. By enforcing even unrelied-upon promises, the law both encourages performance and facilitates reliance on contractual arrangements. As a more effective prophylaxis, then, the expectancy principle constitutes "a policy in favour of promoting and facilitating reliance on business agreements"[60] with resulting stimulation of business activity. In short, "[t]o encourage reliance we must therefore dispense with its proof."[61] In essence, then,

58   *Ibid.*
59   See below this Chapter, section F(3) for a discussion of the mitigation principle.
60   Above note 52 at 61.
61   *Ibid.* at 62.

the difficulty of proving lost opportunities for gain elsewhere provides an explanation for the conclusion that in order both to achieve more effective compensation of reliance losses and to encourage future reliance on agreements, the expectancy principle is a better instrument for the protection of the reliance losses than a rule merely awarding and therefore requiring proof of reliance losses.

Modern law and economic scholars offer a different justification for the expectancy principle.[62] Pursuant to this school of thought, the rules of contract law are evaluated on the basis of an efficiency criterion in order to assess whether the rule under scrutiny conduces to more efficient behaviour on the part of contracting parties. Measured by this standard, it is argued that the expectancy principle does indeed conduce to efficient behaviour. Thus, for example, a manufacturer confronted with a repudiatory breach by a purchaser should not be encouraged to continue to manufacture the product that the customer no longer wishes to acquire. Assuming that the manufactured product would have negligible value for anyone else, ideally, the common law should encourage the manufacturer to cease production. The expectancy principle, by awarding the manufacturer the profits that it would have made on the entire agreement, successfully accomplishes this objective. Further, if the seller should default, an efficient rule would require the purchaser to seek an alternative supplier. In Posner's view, it would be inefficient to impose an obligation on the seller to find a substitute seller. After all, the buyer will know his or her own needs best.

Thus, requiring the seller to arrange for a substitute would introduce a further and inefficient step in the exercise of acquiring a substitute. By awarding the buyer expectancy damages in preference to insisting that the initial seller arrange the substitute, the common law, again, creates incentives for efficient conduct. More controversially, Posner argues that the expectancy principle is consistent with the criterion of efficiency by encouraging so-called efficient breach. An efficient breach occurs where a party is tempted to breach a contract simply because the opportunities afforded by breach are more profitable than those involved in performance of the contract. In Posner's view, breach of contract in such circumstances ought to be encouraged. It is an efficient breach if, for example, the seller can sell his commodity to another purchaser who is willing to pay more for it. Obviously, the seller will profit from the transaction. The second purchaser, who evidently has a more valuable use for the commodity in question, will

---

62   See, for example, R. Posner, *Economic Analysis of Law*, 6th ed. (New York: Aspen, 2003) at 119–20.

be better off. The initial purchaser, who may suffer the disappointment of breach will, nonetheless, be fully indemnified by expectancy damages. Accordingly, the breach of contract will, in sum, increase the total wealth of the three affected parties and, indeed, society at large as the goods in question are directed to the buyer who has the most profitable use in mind for the goods in question. By not discouraging efficient breaches of this kind, the expectancy principle thus further conduces to efficient outcomes.

Although the theory of efficient breach has proven to be controversial,[63] the less controversial aspects of the economic analysis may be thought to provide a further policy justification for the existing rule. Perhaps the more convincing justification for the rule, however, is that offered by Fuller and Perdue. If the innocent party was to be saddled with the burden of proving reliance in the form of a forgone opportunity to make profits in some other fashion, the innocent party may be unable to prove the existence of losses that actually occurred through lack of evidence. A prudent party who anticipates the possibility of breach and who therefore appreciates the need to be able to prove forgone opportunity to profit would have an incentive to engage in the exercise of documenting such lost opportunities at the time of contracting. As a general matter, such activities may be wasteful of the innocent party's time and others who may become implicated in the innocent party's inquiries.

Although there exists an apparently substantial professional consensus in support of the expectancy rule, there is at least one voice to the contrary. Atiyah has offered a critique of "pure expectancy" damages.[64] In Atiyah's view, the best explanation for the imposition of contractual liability is that the promisee has either conferred a benefit on the promisor or has detrimentally relied on the promisor's undertaking. In the context of a wholly executory agreement where no benefit has been conferred and no detrimental reliance has been suffered, it is arguable, in Atiyah's view, that no claim for expectancy damages should lie. In direct response to the Fuller and Perdue thesis that wholly executory contracts should be enforced in the expectancy measure in order both

63   See I. Macneil, "Efficient Breach of Contract: Circles in the Sky" (1982) 68 Va. L. Rev. 947; D. Friedmann, "The Efficient Breach Fallacy" (1989) 18 J. Legal Stud. 1; R. O'Dair, "Restitutionary Damages for Breach of Contract and the Theory of Efficient Breach: Some Reflections" (1993) 46 Curr. Legal Probs. 113; L. Smith, "Disgorgement of the Profits of Breach of Contract: Property, Contract and 'Efficient Breach'" (1994–95) 24 Can. Bus. L.J. 121.
64   See P.S. Atiyah, "Contracts, Promises and the Law of Obligations" (1978) 94 Law Q. Rev. 193.

to cure reliance in the form of lost opportunities for profit and encourage reliance on agreements, Atiyah has argued[65] that supporters of this view have not explained why a simple shifting of the burden of proof to the defendant to demonstrate the absence of such reliance would not solve the problem. Atiyah's response, however, is unsatisfying. If, as seems likely, the defendant will find the burden of establishing a negative proposition of this kind virtually insurmountable in the typical case, there would be no significant change in the results of the decided cases under Atiyah's proposal. If, on the other hand, serious contests over the question of whether alternative opportunities for profit have been forgone are a realistic possibility, at least in some commercial contexts, unattractive incentives are created for the innocent party to engage in the wasteful exercise of documenting the existence of such opportunities against the chance that it may be necessary to prove their existence. Moreover, the innocent party who lacks legal advice at the time of contracting is not likely to anticipate the need for such preventive measures. On balance, then, the justification for the expectancy principle mounted by Fuller and Perdue appears to emerge relatively unscathed from this critique.

D. RELIANCE AS AN ALTERNATIVE MEASURE

As an alternative to relief in the expectancy measure, a victim of a breach of contract who has incurred expenditures or other losses in reliance on the agreement but who cannot establish that a profit would have been made as a result of full performance of the agreement may wish to seek recovery of those expenses and losses through a claim for reliance damages. Such claims have occasionally enjoyed success, though the circumstances in which they are likely to do so must be examined with some care.

The leading illustration of a successful claim of this type is the decision of the Australian High Court in *McRae v. Commonwealth Disposals Commission*,[66] a case arising in the context of an unsuccessful salvage expedition. During the Second World War, a number of ships, including oil tankers, had been wrecked or stranded in the seas near New Guinea. The defendant commission was empowered to dispose of these vessels. It sold the rights to the vessels to salvers, who, after

---

65   *Ibid.* at 216. See also P.S. Atiyah, *Essays on Contract* (Oxford: Clarendon Press, 1986) c. 2 and 7.

66   (1951), 84 C.L.R. 377 (Aust. H.C.).

the expenditure of significant sums of money, would hope to enjoy a profit from the sale of the salvaged vessel and its contents. The salvers were purchasing, in effect, a chance to make a profit. The plaintiff had purchased from the defendant an oil tanker said by the commission to be located "on Jourmand Reef which is approximately 100 miles north of Samarai."[67] In order to carry out this project, the plaintiff refitted one of its vessels, the *Gippsland*, for salvage work, purchased certain salvage equipment, engaged a crew and a salvage expert and sailed from Sydney toward the Jourmand Reef. In the course of the voyage, the *Gippsland* foundered. Fortunately, no lives were lost. The plaintiff then chartered a second vessel and proceeded to the Jourmand Reef where it was discovered that no sunken vessel was to be found in the location identified by the commission.

The commission's belief that there was such a vessel on Jourmand Reef was erroneous, indeed, recklessly so. The High Court held that the commission was in breach of an implied promise that there was a tanker in the location specified. Obviously, the plaintiff could not establish that if there had been a sunken vessel at that location, the salvage operation would have been successful and enjoyed a profit. Accordingly, the plaintiff framed its claim as one for wasted expenditures and sought to recover the investment it had made in the search for the tanker. The commission defended the claim on the basis that the plaintiff, being unable to disprove the possibility that the expenditures might have been wasted even if a vessel had been found, could not discharge its burden to establish that the damages suffered flowed from the breach. The High Court held, however, that the reliance claim was valid. The Court reasoned that the plaintiff could make out a *prima facie* case for recovery simply by establishing, first, that the expenditures had been incurred because of the commission's promise that such a tanker was in existence and, second, that the fact that there was no such vessel made it certain that the expenditures would be wasted. Once this was established by the plaintiff, the burden would then be thrown upon the defendant to establish that "if there had been a tanker, the expense incurred would equally had been wasted. This, of course, the Commission cannot establish."[68] Thus, in a case where it is the nature of the defendant's breach that has prevented the plaintiff from being able to establish that the agreement would have been profitable, the plaintiff is relieved of the normal burden to establish profitability and the onus shifts to the defendant to establish that the agreement would not have

67   *Ibid.* at 396.
68   *Ibid.* at 414.

been profitable.[69] Where, as in *McRae*, the defendant cannot do so, the plaintiff is then allowed to recover wasted expenditures.

As *McRae* illustrates, however, the plaintiff is not necessarily permitted to recover all out-of-pocket expenses in a reliance claim. In *McRae*, a distinction was drawn between recoverable wasted expenditures that were fairly attributable to this particular project as opposed to unrecoverable investments in capital assets, such as the refitting of the *Gippsland* and the purchase of salvage equipment, which would have been utilized by the plaintiff in a series of salvage projects. In the former category came such items as the wages of the crew and the expert salver, the fee paid to the commission, office expenses, the cost of ship's stores consumed in the voyage and various travel and other related out-of-pocket expenses. The distinction between expenses fairly attributable to this particular project and those that should be spread over the life of the capital assets acquired by the plaintiff is evidently a sound one. On the other hand, there is no reason in principle not to allow the plaintiff in such a case to claim as an expense the depreciation in the value of capital assets that is fairly attributable to the particular venture.[70]

It is an interesting question whether, in addition to the wasted expenditures, the plaintiff in such a case ought to be permitted to recover for the value of the profits that the plaintiff might have enjoyed in another venture that has been passed up or lost in reliance on the contract with the defendant. Such a claim was, in fact, allowed in *McRae*. The plaintiff was allowed to recover the profits that the *Gippsland* would have earned from the non-salvage operations from which it was diverted in order to be employed in salvage work. In favour of this result, it may be argued that such a loss was truly incurred in reliance on the plaintiff's contract with the defendant and, accordingly, ought to be included within a reliance claim. Allowing recovery for the lost opportunity to profit elsewhere arguably enabled the plaintiff to be put more squarely back into the position it would have been in if it had not entered the contract with the defendant. On the other hand, the awarding of lost damages in the form of a lost opportunity to profit

---

69   The plaintiff does not have to affirmatively prove that there would have been no profit. If the plaintiff simply claims reliance losses in such circumstances, the burden to demonstrate loss is imposed on the defendant. See *C.C.C. Films Ltd. v. Impact Quadrant Films Ltd.*, [1985] 1 Q.B. 16.

70   See, for example, *Bowlay Logging Ltd. v. Domtar Ltd.* (1982), 135 D.L.R. (3d) 179 at 182–83 (B.C.C.A.), aff'g (1978), 87 D.L.R. (3d) 325 (B.C.S.C.) (payments on equipment rentals with an option to purchase—included as expenses at trial—held on appeal to contain a capital element that could, however, be offset against a proper depreciation allowance).

elsewhere appears to be inconsistent with the reasoning underlying the shifting burden analysis adopted by the High Court in *McRae*. If the explanation for the granting of the wasted expenditures claim is that the plaintiff, on the one hand, cannot establish profitability, but the defendant, to whom the burden of so demonstrating has shifted, is unable to demonstrate that a loss would have been incurred by the plaintiff, the underlying theory of the award is that the salvage venture is assumed to be a "break-even" operation in which the plaintiff's revenues from the project would at least match its expenses. To allow the additional recovery of lost opportunity to profit elsewhere appears to grant the plaintiff the benefit of a further and, perhaps, generous presumption that the salvage venture would have been at least as profitable an exercise as its normal non-salvage activities.

Some controversy surrounds the question of whether, in a wasted expenditures claim, the plaintiff may claim for expenditures incurred prior to entering into the contract with the defendant. This issue arose in *Anglia Television Ltd. v. Reed*.[71] The plaintiff had undertaken preparations to make a television drama entitled "The Man in the Wood." Arrangements had been made for the location of the filming, the employment of a director and other staff members and various related matters. All of this was done before the plaintiff found the leading man. The filming was to take place between September 9 and October 11 of 1968. Mr. Reed, the defendant, was retained for the lead role on August 30, 1968, shortly before the filming was to commence. Unfortunately, Reed's agents had double-booked him and a few days later, on September 3, he repudiated his agreement with the plaintiff. The plaintiff unsuccessfully sought to find a substitute for Mr. Reed in time to begin filming. Apparently unable to establish that "The Man in the Wood" would have been a profitable item, the plaintiff brought a claim against Reed for its wasted expenditures. The defence raised was that Reed ought to be liable only for such expenditures as occurred after August 30th. The English Court of Appeal rejected that argument and held that the plaintiff was entitled to all of its wasted expenditures. Lord Denning M.R. reasoned that it must have been plain to Mr. Reed when he entered into the contract that many of the expenses would already have been incurred and, further, that if he failed to perform his agreement, all of those expenditures would be wasted.

The decision in *Anglia Television* has been criticized, however, on the basis that the pre-contractual expenditures were incurred not in reliance on the defendant's promise to perform but in the hope that

71 [1972] 1 Q.B. 60 (C.A.).

an agreement with the defendant or some equivalent person would be achieved in timely fashion.[72] Indeed, it is sometimes suggested that, as a general rule, pre-contractual expenditures should be considered irrecoverable. Surely it would be incorrect, however, to hold that pre-contractual expenditures can never be recovered. The chauffeur who negligently destroys his employer's car will be liable for its value whenever the car might have been purchased. The difficulty in the *Anglia Television* case is that the expenditures appear to have been essentially gambled by the television company in the hope that a suitable actor would be found in time. It is therefore at least arguable that Anglia Television was to some extent the author of its own misfortune and should not be able to shift the loss it was about to incur on what was apparently not an obviously profitable venture to the defendant Reed. If Reed had been retained at an earlier point in time, it would be more obvious that Anglia Television's inability to hire a substitute was caused by Reed and it would be more clearly appropriate to impose liability upon him for wasted expenditures, whether they were incurred before or after he agreed to take on the role. As a matter of general principle, then, it appears to be incorrect to suggest that liability for pre-contractual expenses can never be recovered in a wasted expenditures claim. Whether Mr. Reed is appropriately considered liable for them should turn on whether the plaintiff's loss is fairly considered to have resulted from the defendant's breach. In Lord Denning's view, apparently, Reed had caused the loss of the plaintiff's investment.

The plaintiff's ability to bring an alternative claim in the reliance measure is subject to any limitation that might be imposed by application of the expectancy principle. Thus, if the evidence concerning the transaction establishes that the contract was an unprofitable one in the sense that the plaintiff would have lost money through performance, the plaintiff's claim for wasted expenditures is subject to a deduction for the amount of that loss. The governing principle, then, is one of compensation on the basis of the expectancy principle. The plaintiff will not be put in a better position, by the awarding of reliance damages, than the plaintiff would have been in if the contract had been performed. The dominance of the expectancy measure over the reliance measure in this sense is demonstrated in *Bowlay Logging Ltd. v. Domtar Ltd.*[73] The plaintiff had been hired by the defendant to provide logging services. The defendant

---

72   See A.I. Ogus, "Damages for Pre-Contract Expenditure" (1972) 35 Mod. L. Rev. 423. See also D. McLauchlan, "Damages for Pre-Contract Expenditure" (1985) 11 N.Z.U.L. Rev. 346.

73   Above note 70. See also *C. & P. Haulage v. Middleton*, [1983] 1 W.L.R. 1461 (C.A.).

was to haul the logs. In breach of the contract, the defendant failed to provide sufficient trucks to discharge its obligations under the agreement. By the time of the breach, the plaintiff had incurred expenses in the order of $230,000 and had received in return payments of $108,000 on a total contract price of $150,000. The plaintiff claimed the difference between its expenditures and the amount received to date as reliance damages. The evidence at trial revealed, however, that the contract had been drastically underbid by the plaintiff and that if the contract had been fully performed, the plaintiff would likely have incurred losses of an even greater amount than it had incurred to date. Accordingly, the plaintiff was restricted to a claim for nominal damages only. The trial judge, Berger J., upheld on this point by the British Columbia Court of Appeal, explained the result as follows:

> The law of contract compensates a plaintiff for damages resulting from the defendant's breach; it does not compensate a plaintiff for damages resulting from his making a bad bargain. Where it can be seen that the plaintiff would have incurred a loss on the contract as a whole, the expenses he has incurred are losses flowing from entering into the contract, not losses flowing from the defendant's breach. In these circumstances, the true consequence of the defendant's breach is that the plaintiff is released from his obligation to complete the contract or, in other words, he is saved from incurring further losses.[74]

In short, the defendant is not liable for losses sustained by the plaintiff that were not caused by the defendant's breach. The risk that the contract is underbid was assumed by the plaintiff through the negotiation of the agreement and cannot be shifted to the defendant because of the latter's breach of contract. It follows, then, that the claim for reliance losses is not an alternative form of claim that is independent of the expectancy principle. Rather, it is subject to and controlled by the expectancy principle in cases where the plaintiff's expectancy is a negative one.

E. APPLYING THE EXPECTANCY PRINCIPLE

A variety of difficulties may be encountered in applying the general expectancy principle to particular fact situations. Four will be considered here. First, there are a number of different methods that might be

---

74   *Bowlay Logging Ltd. v. Domtar. Ltd., ibid.* at 334–35 (B.C.S.C.).

adopted for calculating expectancy damages and the possibility exists of intermingling or confusing them. Second, disarming complexities may arise when a proposed calculation of the expectancy involves both a capital and an income element. Third, the expectancy principle may be capable of more than one interpretation or application in a particular fact situation and the correct or preferable choice may be unclear. Fourth, it may be considered whether, in a case where the plaintiff can establish only a chance of future profit, some value should be placed on that chance.

1) Two Formulae for Calculating Expectancy Damages

In a simple case, such as a seller's failure to deliver goods to the buyer, it is evident that expectancy damages may be calculated by determining the amount, if any, by which the market value of goods exceeds the contract price. Where the amount is $200, the purchaser will be enabled by its recovery to be put in as good a position as would have been the case by purchasing a substitute. Further, it is obvious that if the purchaser has already paid an amount, say $100, as a deposit or partial payment, this amount must be added to the $200 in order to compensate the purchaser in the full expectancy measure, which, on the revised facts, yields $300. What is less obvious, however, is that there are, broadly speaking, two different approaches or methods of calculation that lead to this result. The method alluded to above involves the calculation of a net profit or surplus value that the purchaser has achieved in this transaction and adds to it a component to reflect any expenditures made to date by the purchaser that are attributable to this transaction. This formula may be expressed as follows:

net profits ($200) + expenditures to date ($100) = expectancy ($300)

If we give precise values to the market value of the goods, say $1,000, and the contract price, say $800, a second method for producing the $300 calculation becomes apparent. One could begin with the gross value to which the purchaser is entitled under the agreement, that is, $1,000, and deduct therefrom an amount reflecting the expenditures that the purchaser would have been required to make under the agreement if performance were completed, that is, $700 (purchase price less moneys already paid to the seller). In a more complicated transactional form, such as the sale of a business or the purchase of equipment to be used in a profit-making venture, calculation of the gross value of the transaction may involve the determination of projected revenues or gross profits, which are the anticipated result of the performance of the transaction. The second approach or formula, may be expressed as follows:

gross value, revenue or "profits" ($1,000) – avoided expense ($700) = expectancy ($300)

Although the choice of one method or formula over another is a matter of mathematical indifference, there may be some practical advantages in the real world, either in matters of calculation or proof, that might lead the plaintiff to prefer one method over the other. While the choice of method may be a matter of indifference, it is of course important that the method chosen is followed consistently. Possibilities for confusion arise, however, because both formulae involve an expense calculation (past expenses in one and future expenses in the other) and both may involve a profit calculation (net profits in the first and gross in the second). In the reported cases, it is not invariably clear which of the two profit calculations has been employed and whether the court has consistently followed the adopted method. In one case, for example, a court appears to have restricted the plaintiff's recovery to past expenses by reason of the fact that net profits did not exceed them.[75] Such an approach would be erroneous. One may recover both profits and expenses, provided that the profits are calculated on a net basis and the expenses in question are those that have already been incurred.

2) Capital vs. Income

It is occasionally suggested that an expectancy calculation cannot include both a capital and an income component. Although this generalization rests upon an unassailable proposition, it is nonetheless likely to mislead and has inspired some confusing discussion in the reported cases.[76] The unassailable proposition is that where the breach involves failure to supply a capital asset, the plaintiff cannot recover both the cost of acquiring a substitute capital asset and the value of the income stream that would be generated by the asset in question. Such a calculation would palpably involve a double recovery. However, it would be incorrect to suggest, as courts occasionally do, that a proper expectancy calculation could never include both a capital and an income element.[77]

---

75   *Sunshine Vacation Villas Ltd. v. Governor and Company of Adventurers of England Trading into Hudson's Bay* (1984), 13 D.L.R. (4th) 93 (B.C.C.A.).

76   *Ibid.* And see *Cullinane v. British "Rema" Manufacturing Co.*, [1954] 1 Q.B. 292 (C.A.).

77   *McRae,* above note 66; *Sunshine Vacation Villas,* above note 75.

Such an approach may be appropriate, for example, where a purchaser of equipment used to generate a profit is in possession of defective equipment for a period of time before returning it to a supplier. Assuming that the purchaser has suffered an income loss during the period of possession as a result of the defects, one possible method for calculating expectancy damages would be to award the plaintiff recovery of the net profits lost during the period of possession, together with sufficient money to replace the defective equipment with used equipment whose value would reflect the depreciation that would normally occur during the period of possession. In short, in an appropriate case, a satisfactory expectancy calculation could include both net profits lost in the past as a result of the breach together with replacement of the capital asset at its depreciated value. Although such an approach was rejected in an English case,[78] it is sound in principle and has been adopted in other cases.[79] Again, then, it would be incorrect to suggest that an expectancy calculation can never include both a capital and an income element. When both elements are included, however, care must be taken to avoid the possibility of double recovery or overcompensation.

3) Conflicting Methods of Application

In some fact situations, the expectancy principle speaks ambiguously in the sense that it offers two different and conflicting methods for calculating the amount of expectancy damages. If a builder refuses to carry out an agreement to build a structure on a parcel of land, for example, one method of calculating the owner's damages would be to calculate the difference, if any, between the contractor's price for the work and the price that would be required to hire a substitute contractor to perform the work. A second method would be to calculate the difference in value between the land unadorned and the land with the completed structure. The former measure is often referred to as "cost of performance" and the latter as the "diminution in value" resulting from the refusal to perform. The two different measures might yield quite different valuations. In the mythical case of a contract to build an ugly fountain for a homeowner, for example, the cost of performance might

---

78   *Cullinane*, above note 76.

79   See, for example, *Sunnyside Greenhouses Ltd. v. Golden West Seeds* (1972), 27 D.L.R. (3d) 434 (Alta. C.A.), aff'd [1973] 3 W.W.R. 288 (S.C.C.). See also N. Biger and A. Rosen, "A Framework for the Assessment of Business Damages for Breach of Contract" (1980–81) 5 Can. Bus. L.J. 302; M. Baer, "Can Contract Damages Based on Wasted Expenses Give the Plaintiff More than the Value of the Promsed Performance?" (1978–79) 3 Can. Bus. L.J. 198.

constitute a substantial number but the diminution in value from not constructing an ugly fountain on one's front lawn might be non-existent. Indeed, the presence of the fountain might reduce the value of the property. This type of contest between the cost of performance measure and the diminution-in-value measure can arise in a variety of factual settings. In broad general terms, the courts attempt to strike a balance in these cases that will avoid unjust enrichment of the plaintiff through overcompensation and, on the other hand, unjust enrichment of the defendant through undercompensation of the plaintiff.

In the case of a partially completed building contract, the cost of performance is the usual measure of recovery. Allowing the plaintiff owner of the property to recover the difference between the contract price and the price required to obtain a substitute performance meets the justice of the case. The owner is likely to complete the structure and, accordingly, such an award will be the preferred measure for placing an owner in the position he or she would have been in if the contract had been performed. This would normally be the result even if the completion of the structure does not result in an enhancement of the value of the property that is equivalent to the cost of performance. Indeed, were the general rule otherwise, the diminution-in-value measure would often apply to building contracts with an unattractive result. In the context of home renovations and repairs, for example, it would often be the case that the cost of doing the work in question would not be matched by an equivalent increase in the value of the property.[80]

When the construction work has been completed defectively or not in compliance with the contract's specifications, however, the diminution-in-value measure may apply if, in the circumstances, it is evident that the owner will not or is very unlikely to cure the defects in question.[81] In such cases, there is a concern that awarding the cost of performance will amount to an overcompensation of the owner. The courts lean in favour of the diminution-in-value measure especially in cases where curing the defect would involve wasteful destruction of all or part of a structure. The well-known decision of Cardozo J. in *Jacobs*

---

80 See *Ruxley Electronics and Construction Ltd. v. Forsyth*, [1995] 3 All E.R. 268 at 276 (H.L.), Lord Mustill (such a result "would be unacceptable to the average householder, and it is unacceptable to me"), rev'g [1994] 3 All E.R. 801 (C.A.).

81 See, for example, *McGarry v. Richards, Ackroyd & Gall Ltd.*, [1954] 2 D.L.R. 367 (B.C.S.C.); *Strata Corp. NW 1714 v. Winkler* (1987), 45 D.L.R. (4th) 741 (B.C.C.A.) In these particular cases, the B.C. courts have suggested that the diminution of value is the general measure of relief to be applied in the context of a contract to bill on another's land. This would appear to be true, however, only in cases where the courts are concerned that work will not be done.

& Youngs, Inc. v. Kent[82] is a case of this kind. The building contract specified that the building incorporate pipes of Reading manufacture. The builder had incorporated Cohoes piping of equivalent quality. Replacing the pipe would have had no impact on the value of the house and would have involved substantial destruction of the walls of the building. In such a case, in Cardozo J.'s view, the "cost of completion is grossly and unfairly out of proportion to the good to be obtained"[83] and the proper measure of relief is the diminution in value. Again, in such cases, there is a concern that the owner is not likely to undertake the work and, accordingly, the cost-of-performance measure would overcompensate the owner. Where the corrective work has actually been undertaken by the time of trial, however, courts will award the cost of performance provided that the conduct of the owner in effecting the work is considered to be reasonable. In a Canadian case, it was suggested that in such a case "one should be careful not to weigh in too fine a set of balances the conduct of the aggrieved party."[84]

A novel approach to the resolution of this particular type of conflict was taken by the House of Lords in *Ruxley Electronics and Construction Ltd. v. Forsyth.*[85] The defendant Forsyth had retained the plaintiff contractor to build an enclosed swimming pool beside his home for a price of approximately £70,000. Although the agreement initially stipulated that the depth of the pool, at the deep end, should be 6 feet 9 inches, Forsyth asked that the depth be increased to 7 feet 6 inches. The contractor agreed to make this change at no extra charge. The relations between the parties were apparently acrimonious and, in due course, the contractor brought a claim against Forsyth for £10,330, the outstanding balance of the contract price. Having discovered that the maximum depth of the pool was merely 6 feet 9 inches, Forsyth counterclaimed for the cost of bringing the pool into compliance with the contract specifications. This would have involved demolishing the existing pool and rebuilding it at a total cost of £21,560. At trial, it was found that the pool, at its present depth, was safe for diving. Accordingly, the lack of stipulated depth did not reduce the value of the pool. Further, the trial judge found that it would be unreasonable to rebuild the pool as the cost of doing so was wholly disproportionate to the advantage to be achieved. The trial judge remained doubtful that the work would be

---

82   129 N.E. 889 (N.Y. 1921).

83   *Ibid.* at 891.

84   *New West Homes Ltd. v. Thunderbird Petroleums Ltd.* (1975), 59 D.L.R. (3d) 292 at 308 (Alta. C.A.), Moir J.A.

85   Above note 80.

undertaken, even though Forsyth professed an intention to do so. Accordingly, the cost of performance was not awarded. The trial judge did, however, award damages for loss of amenities in the amount of £2,500. Although overturned on appeal,[86] the decision at trial was upheld on further appeal to the House of Lords. Lord Jauncey explained that the reasonableness of doing the work could be taken into account in determining the true nature of the loss suffered. As it was unreasonable to do the work in question, Forsyth's loss did not extend to the cost of reinstatement. At the same time, however, Lord Jauncey indicated that if one were to award merely the diminution in value, this would simply enable the contractor, as promisor, to "please himself whether or not to comply with the wishes of the promisee which, as embodied in the contract, form part of the consideration for the price." Their Lordships were unanimous in the view that these two measures of relief were not exhaustive and that the modest award at trial for loss of amenities was a satisfactory device for compensating Forsyth for his actual loss.[87] As Lord Mustill observed, though the amount awarded may be small and difficult to quantify, there was "no reason why the imprecision of the exercise should be a barrier, if that is what fairness demands."[88]

Similar problems may arise in the context of agreements under which one party is to extract minerals or other natural resources from the property of another in return for a price that includes an obligation to restore the land to a useable state once the extraction process is completed. The problem is neatly illustrated by two American cases reaching opposite conclusions on rather similar facts. In *Groves v. John Wonder Co.*[89] the cost of performance of the restoration work was awarded. Groves and Wonder, both of whom were in the business of excavating and screening gravel, were the owners of neighbouring properties. Groves leased his property to Wonder who agreed, in return, to remove the gravel and leave Groves' property at a uniform grade similar to the grade of the existing roadway on the premises. Wonder paid Groves a contract price of $105,000. Wonder then deliberately breached the contract by removing only the best of the gravel and by refusing to restore the property. Groves sued to recover the cost of performing the restorative work, estimated at $60,000. Unrestored, the land was valueless but

---

86   *Ibid.* (C.A.).
87   *Ibid.* at 278 (H.L.), Lord Mustill ("... once this is recognized, the puzzling and paradoxical feature of this case, that it seems to involve a contest of absurdities, simply falls away").
88   *Ibid.* at 278. See also below this Chapter, section H.
89   286 N.W. 235 (Minn. C.A. 1939).

after restoration the value would probably have been only $12,168. For the majority, Stone J. offered a variety of reasons for awarding Groves the cost of doing the work. In his view, the general principle of awarding cost of performance in a building or construction contract ought to apply. Otherwise, an owner of the land would be unable to enter an enforceable agreement to erect structures that do not enhance the value of the land. More generally, inability to recover the cost of performance would defeat the owner's right to plan and build for the future. Moreover, it was significant, for Stone J., that the breach of the defendant was wilful. Stone J. did not emphasize, however, that the awarding of merely the change in value of the land that would be effected by restoration would enable Wonder to enrich himself at Groves' expense by extracting the gravel and then refusing, in effect, to pay the full contract price, a price that included the cost of restoration of the land. Further, Stone J. rejected as inapplicable the economic waste cases such as *Jacob & Youngs Inc. v. Kent* on the ground that they applied only in circumstances where the rectification of defects would involve the destruction of an existing structure. In dissent, Olson J. made the point that the purpose of awarding damages is compensation not punishment, and further that because Groves' apparent intent was to simply hold the property for resale the impact of the breach on its value was the true measure of the expectancy. Less convincingly, he suggested that the parties might have stipulated for the cost of performance as a remedy if they had wished to do so.

Peevyhouse v. Garland Coal & Mining Co.[90] concerned a lease of farm land to a coal mining company under which the lessee was permitted to strip-mine the land. In return, the lessee agreed to undertake certain restorative work at the conclusion of the mining operation. When that work was not done, the farmer sued for the cost of its performance. The filling in of the pits created by the strip-mining operation would have required the moving of many thousands of cubic yards of earth at an estimated cost of twenty-nine thousand dollars. The defendant, relying on *Groves*, argued that the recovery of such a sum amounted to overcompensation. The verdict at trial, awarding five thousand dollars, exceeded the value of the farm land and, indeed, any enhancement of that value that would have been achieved by the remedial work, the latter amount being estimated at three hundred dollars. For the majority, Jackson J. rejected the authority of *Groves* on the basis that the agreement in that case had been mischaracterized as being akin to a

---

90   382 P.2d 109 (Okla. 1962). See J.L. Maute, "*Peevyhouse v. Garland Coal & Mining Co.* Revisited: The Ballad of Willy and Lucille" (1995) 89 Nw. U.L. Rev. 1341.

"building and construction" contract. In his view, the provisions of the lease in *Groves* pertaining to remedial work were merely "incidental."[91] The rule pronounced by the *Peevyhouse* majority, then, as a basis for not interfering with the jury award, was that in the context of a coal mining lease where the remedial work is merely incidental to the purpose of the contract and where the cost of performing the work is grossly disproportionate to the diminution in value resulting from the failure to do the work, the appropriate measure is diminution in value. In dissent, Irwin J. more clearly articulated than did the majority in *Groves* the concern that the mining company had already received the full value of the benefits it was to receive under the contract and that, in the light of that value received, the defendant ought to be required to provide the monetary equivalent of the full consideration it had promised to provide under the agreement, including the cost of doing the remediation work.[92] The dissenting opinion also mentioned the wilful and bad-faith nature of the defendant's breach of contract.

Although there is little basis for suggesting that English and Canadian courts would place significant weight on the question of whether the breach in a case such as this was wilful or not, concerns about the unjust enrichment of the defendant party who has already received full consideration under the agreement are likely to weigh in favour of the cost of performance measure.[93] In an extreme case, however, where the cost of performance is grossly disproportionate to the value to be achieved by performance and where, accordingly, performance of the work appears very unlikely, a discretion to award relief based on diminution of value may be exercised. A more extreme illustration of this phenomenon than the English case of *Tito v. Waddell (No. 2)*[94] is difficult to imagine. This claim arose from a history of phosphate mining on Ocean Island under a series of arrangements that included leases with the local inhabitants, the Balabans, under which the phosphate company was required to replant the worked-out land with trees

---

91   *Peevyhouse v. Garland Coal & Mining Co., ibid.* at 112.
92   See also *Farrell Lines, Inc. v. City of New York*, 281 N.E.2d 162 (N.Y. 1972) (lease of pier imposing duty on lessee to maintain the pier—lessee breaches—lessor subsequently announces intention to demolish the pier—cost of performance awarded because rental likely less when lease includes a covenant to repair).
93   Compare with *Radford v. De Froberville*, [1977] 1 W.L.R. 1262 (Ch.) (vendor sells part of his land to defendant who undertakes, in return to build a stone wall along the boundary—upon purchaser's failure to build the wall, vendor recovers cost of doing so—court was persuaded that vendor intended to build the wall on his own land).
94   [1977] Ch. 106.

and shrubs of various kinds. At the end of the process, five-sixths of the island had been mined, the local inhabitants had been moved to another larger island where they had successfully resettled and Ocean Island itself had become inhabitable. The mining process had the effect of leaving scores of coral pinnacles per acre in the mined-out properties, many standing 60 to 80 feet in height. The Balabans brought this action seeking, as damages, the cost of replanting Ocean Island that, in their view, would require levelling the pinnacles and a massive importation of soil. In the event, it was the trial judge's view that the defendant's obligation to replant was limited by language in the leases and in other pertinent documents to that of conducting the work only where it was practically feasible to do so. The trial judge also held, however, that it was inappropriate to award even the cost of performing this reduced obligation. There was, in his view, simply no prospect that the work would be done.[95]

Contests between cost of performance and diminution of value may also arise in the context of development or joint venture agreements under which an owner of mineral or oil and gas rights enters into an agreement with a potential developer of the property who, in return for the development activity, will obtain partial ownership rights in the property. In cases where the developer breaches an undertaking to perform a certain amount of development work, the owner of the interest may sue for damages for the cost of performance. The developer may resist the claim on the basis that the owner should be restricted to whatever can be established to be the impact of the breach of contract on the value of the owner's interest. In the typical case, the developer who refuses to go forward will not have enjoyed the fruits of the agreement and thus, unlike *Groves v. Wonder*, the situation does not involve a potential unjust enrichment of the developer. Moreover, as a practical matter, if the opportunity is an attractive one, it may well be that the owner will be able to deal the same interest to another developer in return for the same set of obligations and thus reduce or eliminate any loss resulting from breach of the first agreement. Where the owner has not done so, however, and chooses, rather, to bring an action for the cost of the performance of the developmental work against the initial developer, the reported cases indicate that the courts will be concerned to determine whether, in fact, the development work will be undertaken by the owner. Thus, in *Cunningham v. Insinger*,[96] a case involving

---

95   *Ibid.* at 328–38.
96   [1924] 2 D.L.R. 433 (S.C.C.). See also *Sunshine Exploration Ltd. v. Dolly Varden Mines Ltd. (N.P.L.)*, [1970] S.C.R. 2 (emphasis placed on the fact that the parties

the development of a mine, the Supreme Court of Canada held that inasmuch as the work to be done by the defendant formed a necessary part of a development plan for the mine, which the owner plaintiff would complete in the ordinary course, a claim for the cost of performing the work should be allowed. On the other hand, in a case where it seemed unlikely that the owner of oil and gas rights would commence the drilling of an exploratory well, given the evidence of geologists suggesting that the venture would fail, a claim for the cost of undertaking the drilling work failed.[97]

4) Loss of a Chance to Profit

As a general rule, the burden is placed on the plaintiff to establish that the contract that was breached was a profitable one as a prerequisite to obtaining an award of damages on the basis of the expectancy principle. There are, however, exceptional cases in which courts have been prepared to place a valuation on a mere chance to make a profit and to award recovery of that value. The leading case is the decision of the English Court of Appeal in *Chaplin v. Hicks*.[98] The plaintiff in this case was one of fifty finalists in a competition for aspiring actresses run by a theatre manager. There were to be twelve winners of the contest, each of whom would be signed to a three-year acting contract at an average wage of four pounds per week. The final step in the competition was to be interviewed by the defendant manager who would make the ultimate selection of the winners. In what was ultimately held to be a breach of contract, the defendant failed to properly notify the plaintiff of the time and place of the interview and, as a result, she was excluded from the final round of the competition. The theatre manager defended the plaintiff's action for damages on the ground that the question of whether the plaintiff would have enjoyed success in the competition involved so many contingencies that it was impossible to determine whether she had sustained an economic loss. The jury, however, awarded damages of one hundred pounds and this award was upheld by the Court of Appeal. Vaughan Williams L.J. observed that "the fact that damages can-

---

had evidently agreed that the work was worth doing and on the plaintiff's evidence that the work would be done).

97 *Cotter v. General Petroleum Ltd. and Superior Oil Ltd.*, [1950] 4 D.L.R. 609 (S.C.C.) (although Cartwright J. placed emphasis on this factor, he and other members of the Court offered several reasons for denying this form of relief). See M. Sychuk, "Damages for Breach of an Express Drilling Covenant" (1970) 8 Alta. L. Rev. 250.

98 [1911] 2 K.B. 786 (C.A.).

not be assessed with certainty does not relieve the wrong-doer of the necessity of paying damages for his breach of contract."[99] The jury had evidently come to the conclusion that the plaintiff had been deprived of an opportunity that had a monetary value. The Court of Appeal agreed that the jury was correct to do so. Even though the value of the opportunity could not be calculated with precision, the court noted that the plaintiff's chances were about one in four. Further, even though it was true that there was no market for trading in such opportunities, it was clear that if there were such a market, a good price could be obtained for the opportunity. The jury's award, then, which represented a fraction of, if not precisely a quarter of, the average wage to be paid to a winner, was allowed to stand.

The rule that permits the placing of a value on a lost chance to profit, in an appropriate case, is well accepted and has been applied not only in the context of competitions[100] but in more traditional commercial settings.[101] In *Multi-Malls Inc. v. Tex-Mall Properties Ltd.*,[102] for example, the doctrine was applied to a contract for the purchase and sale of land subject to a condition precedent that the property be rezoned by the municipality so as to permit construction of a shopping mall. Before the transaction closed, the vendor began the development of a shopping centre on a nearby site, thereby substantially reducing, if not eliminating, the prospects for a rezoning of the parcel under sale. The vendor's conduct was held to constitute a breach of an implied term imposing an obligation not to do anything likely to prevent the rezoning of the property. Even in the absence of the vendor's misconduct, however, the prospects for rezoning the subject parcel were not buoyant. Indeed, the initial prospects for success in a rezoning application were in the order of a 20-percent chance. Applying *Chaplin v. Hicks*, however, the trial judge awarded the purchaser damages calculated by applying the 20 percent figure to the profit that would have been made by developing the property. The Ontario Court of Appeal confirmed this approach. In another case and on similar facts, however, the same court refused to

---

99   *Ibid.* at 792. See also *Penvidic Contracting Co. Ltd. v. International Nickel Co. of Canada Ltd.*, [1976] 1 S.C.R. 267. And see *Wood v. Grand Valley Ry. Co.* (1915), 51 S.C.R. 283; *Toronto Hockey Club Ltd. v. Arena Gardens of Toronto Ltd.*, [1926] 4 D.L.R. 1 (P.C.); *Carson v. Willitts*, [1930] 4 D.L.R. 977 (Ont. S.C.A.D.); *Capital Trust Corp. Ltd. v. Wilson*, [1937] 3 D.L.R. 178 (Ont. C.A.); *Cloverlawn Investments Ltd. v. MacPherson* (1975), 58 D.L.R. (3d) 212 (B.C.S.C.).

100 *Hawrysh v. St. John's Sportsmen's Club* (1964), 46 D.L.R. (2d) 45 (Man. Q.B.).

101 See, for example, *Mills v. Edmonton (City)* (1987), 46 D.L.R. (4th) 26 (Alta. Q.B.).

102 (1980), 108 D.L.R. (3d) 399 (Ont. H.C.J.), aff'd (1981), 128 D.L.R. (3d) 192 (Ont. C.A.), leave to appeal to S.C.C. refused, [1982] 1 S.C.R. xiii.

apply the *Chaplin v. Hicks* doctrine where the fulfilment of the condition was considered to be "highly unlikely"[103] and "too insubstantial to justify anything more than nominal damages."[104] A 20-percent chance, then, appears to be sufficiently substantial to engage the doctrine.

Little guidance has been offered in the authorities as to the basis for distinguishing cases subject to the *Chaplin v. Hicks* calculation from other cases in which merely nominal damages are awarded because the plaintiff has encountered difficulty in establishing that a profit would be made. One might consider, for example, whether *Chaplin v. Hicks* should apply to the fact situation in *McRae v. Commonwealth Disposals Commission.*[105] The plaintiff in that case was unable to prove that the salvage expedition authorized by the defendant commission would have been a profitable one. As the defendant commission could not prove that it would be unprofitable, however, the Australian High Court allowed the plaintiff's claim for reliance losses. If the plaintiff could have demonstrated that it enjoyed a 25-percent chance of profit, however, the application of *Chaplin v. Hicks* appears, on first impression at least, appealing. A critical difference between the two fact situations, however, is that in *McRae*, but not in *Chaplin*, the plaintiff would, on this assumption, stand a 75-percent chance of enduring substantial losses. Conversely, in *Chaplin*, there is no "downside risk" of this kind. In *McRae*, if it were true that there was merely a 25-percent chance of profit, the defendant would be able to establish a 75-percent likelihood of substantial loss and would prevail. In *Chaplin*, losing the competition would not impose on the plaintiff a substantial loss of investment. The absence of downside risk may also explain the result in the *Multi-Malls* case. If the application for rezoning was unsuccessful, the transaction would not close and the purchaser would not suffer substantial losses. It also appears to be material in these cases that the reason why the plaintiff has merely a chance of profit in cases like *Chaplin* rests on factors that are beyond the control of the plaintiff. Thus, if, in *Chaplin*, the reason why the plaintiff stood only a 25-percent chance of winning the competition was that she was a terribly incompetent actress, the claim would likely be denied.[106]

---

103 *Eastwalsh Homes Ltd. v. Anatal Developments Ltd.* (1993), 100 D.L.R. (4th) 469 at 486 (Ont. C.A.).

104 *Ibid.* at 488.

105 Above note 66 for discussion of which, see above this Chapter, section D. In *McRae* itself, the majority distinguished *Chaplin* on the basis that in *Chaplin* the broken promise was to give the plaintiff a chance whereas in *McRae*, the chance was inherent in the nature of the thing contracted for. See *ibid.* at 412.

106 Compare with *Cohnstaedt v. University of Regina*, [1994] 5 W.W.R. 154 (Sask. C.A.), rev'd [1996] 3 S.C.R. 451. For discussion of this case, see D.H. Clark,

F. LIMITATIONS ON EXPECTANCY DAMAGES

1) Causation

The party in default under an agreement is liable to the plaintiff only for such losses as have been caused by the breach. Issues of causation arise more frequently in the context of tort law than in contract cases. Presumably this is because contract law normally deals with economic loss whereas tort law normally deals with personal injury and property damage. Difficult issues of causation may, however, arise in a contractual setting. Moreover, the causation principle appears to underlie other rules relating to the calculation of contractual damages. Thus, as we have seen,[107] the proposition that a claim in the reliance measure for wasted expenditures is subject to an expectancy limitation is often explained on the basis of a causation principle. The loss resulting from the unprofitability of the agreement is caused by the plaintiff's bad bargaining rather than the defendant's breach. Further, causation issues may arise in cases where intervening forces, such as a decline in market values or the intervention of a careless third party, may have the effect of reducing the value of the defendant's performance to the plaintiff. In such cases, the plaintiff may be unable to establish that all or part of the loss has been caused by the defendant's breach. The plaintiff may argue in such circumstances, however, that *but for* entering into the agreement with the defendant, the loss would not have been sustained. The defendant's response may be that though this is true, it was not the defendant's conduct that was the *effective* cause of the loss. The contest in such a case, then, is between two competing versions of the concept of causation.[108]

Where a claim concerns loss of value in an asset provided to the plaintiff under the agreement by the defendant and where the loss results from the careless intervention of a third party, it is easily seen, on causation principles, that the defendant should not be liable for the loss. The facts of *Canson v. Boughton & Co.*[109] are illustrative. The plaintiff was a purchaser of land under a transaction on which it had been represented by the defendant law firm. The defendant had failed to

---

"Loss of a Chance in (and by) the Supreme Court of Canada" (1996) 75 Can. Bar Rev. 564.

107   See above this Chapter, section D.

108   See generally H.L.A. Hart and A.M. Honoré, *Causation in the Law* (Oxford: Clarendon Press, 1959) c. 5 and 11.

109   [1991] 3 S.C.R. 534.

disclose certain material information to the plaintiff prior to the formation of the agreement. The plaintiff maintained that if all the facts had been disclosed by the defendant, it would not have agreed to purchase the land. Once the parcel had been acquired, the plaintiff built a large warehouse on the property. As a result of negligence on the part of the soils engineers and a pile-driving company, the warehouse sank into the earth and sustained considerable damage. Having failed to obtain complete satisfaction from the engineers and the pile driver, the plaintiff brought an action against the defendant law firm for damages arising from the non-disclosure. Arguably, the conduct of the defendant was either tortious or constituted a breach of contract. On these facts, the plaintiff can argue that *but for* the defendant's misleading conduct, it would not have entered the transaction and, therefore, would not have suffered the loss. The Supreme Court of Canada accepted, however, that in either a tort claim or a claim for damages for breach of contract, the defendants could not be responsible "for the very substantial damages that arose from the actions of the engineering firm and the pile-driving company."[110]

More difficult questions may arise where the asset acquired under the transaction by the plaintiff suffers a loss in value as a result of market forces. In *Waddell v. Blockey*,[111] for example, the plaintiff had instructed the defendant, his agent, to buy a quantity of rupee paper. The defendant sold the plaintiff his own rupee paper, fraudulently representing that it was the rupee paper of third parties. The plaintiff then held on to the rupee paper for a period of months during which the market value of rupee paper declined steeply. The plaintiff sold the rupee paper at a significant loss and sought to recover that amount from the defendant. The claim was rejected on the basis that there was "no natural and proximate connection between the wrong done and the damage suffered."[112] The plaintiff was entitled to recover only such loss, if any, as resulted from the fact that he had sold the plaintiff his own rupee paper rather than that of a third party. The loss in value

---

110 *Ibid.* at 565. The plaintiff argued, however, that the defendant's misconduct also constituted a breach of fiduciary obligation and, accordingly, under the applicable principles of equity, it was not necessary to establish that the defendant's conduct was the effective cause of the injury. The Supreme Court rejected this argument and held that principles of causation also apply in the context of the law of fiduciary obligation. For discussion of this case, see J.D. McCamus, "Prometheus Unbound: Fiduciary Obligation in the Supreme Court of Canada" (1997) 28 Can. Bus. L.J. 107.

111 (1879), 4 Q.B.D. 678 (C.A.).

112 *Ibid.* at 682, Thesiger L.J.

resulted from the plaintiff's decision to hold on to the paper in a declining market. Moreover, one might add, it was the plaintiff's decision, not the defendant's, to invest in rupee paper in the first place. The British Columbia Court of Appeal came to a different result, however, on what might appear to be the similar facts of *Allan v. McLennan*.[113] Allan, the plaintiff, had purchased from the defendant shares in the Bank of Vancouver on the faith of the defendant's false statements that they were shares owned by the bank. The shares were actually owned by the defendant. If they were the bank's own shares, of course, the purchase price would go to the bank. In fact, the price was received by the defendant. The shares were valueless. The trial judge accepted Allan's evidence that he had relied on these representations and been induced by them to purchase the shares. Allan successfully sued the defendant for the loss sustained in purchasing the shares. Although this decision appears, on first impression, to be inconsistent with *Waddell*, the two decisions can be reconciled. The plaintiff in *Waddell* made the decision to invest in rupee paper and to hold it in a declining market. There is nothing in the report in the *Allan* case that suggests that the plaintiff had made a decision to buy shares in the Bank of Vancouver owned by any other party than the bank itself or, indeed, to buy any other shares of any kind. Unlike *Waddell*, then, *Allan* is a case in which there is no decision made by the plaintiff that is independent of the defendant's misrepresentation and that may be said to have occasioned the loss.

The *Waddell* line of authority is, however, difficult to reconcile with the decision of the Supreme Court of Canada in *Hodgkinson v. Simms*.[114] The plaintiff, Hodgkinson, was a stockbroker who had enjoyed a substantial increase in his employment income. As a result, he sought investment advice from the defendant Simms with a view to sheltering as much of his income as possible from taxation. Hodgkinson accepted Simms' advice to invest in four so-called MURBs, a type of tax-sheltered real estate investment, not realizing that Simms had a relationship with the sellers of the MURBs pursuant to which Simms would receive a commission on these sales. With a subsequent downturn in the real estate market, Hodgkinson lost heavily on these investments. At trial, Hodgkinson's evidence was that he would not have entered into these transactions but for Simms' non-disclosure of his conflict of interest. On this basis, he claimed for the losses sustained on the MURB investments. The defendant, relying on the *Waddell* line of authority, argued that given Hodgkinson's interest in tax shelters, he would nonetheless have invested in real estate tax shelters even if he had known of Simms' conflict of interest. Accordingly, Hodgkinson would have sustained similar losses in any event. Hodgkinson's decision to invest in real estate shelters was not induced, or so it was argued, by Simms' non-disclosure. Although the Court divided on this point, a majority held that Hodgkinson was entitled to recover his full losses from Simms. La Forest J. held that the defendant's suggestion that Hodgkinson would in any event have invested in real estate tax shelters simply flew in the face of the findings at trial, which had been upheld in the Court of Appeal. Further, it was his view that in any event, in a case of this kind, "the onus is on the defendant to prove that the innocent victim would have suffered the same loss regardless of the breach."[115] The defendant had not successfully established at trial that Hodgkinson would have invested in real estate in any event. More generally, La Forest J. was of the view that "[f]rom a policy perspective it is simply unjust to place the risk of market fluctuations on a plaintiff who would not have entered into a given transaction but for the defendant's wrongful conduct."[116]

In their dissenting opinion in *Hodgkinson,* however, Sopinka and McLachlin JJ. reasoned as follows:

> In our view, it cannot be concluded that the devaluation of the appellant's investments arose naturally from the respondent's breach of contract. The loss in value was caused by a downturn which did not reflect any inadequacy in the advice provided by the respondent. We would reject application of the *but for* approach to causation in circumstances where the loss resulted from forces beyond the control of the respondent who, the trial judge determined, had provided otherwise sound investment advice.[117]

The minority stopped short, however, of making a clear finding that, in their view, Hodgkinson would have invested in real estate tax shelters even if he had been aware of Simms' conflict of interest.

The *Hodgkinson* court appeared divided over the question of the continuing validity of the *Waddell* line of authority. La Forest J. saw an irreconcilable conflict between *Waddell* and *Allan* and indicated a preference for the latter. Sopinka and McLachlin JJ. placed reliance on

---

115 *Ibid.* at 441, relying on *London Loan & Savings Co. v. Brickenden,* [1934] 2 W.W.R. 545 at 550–51 (P.C.); *Huff v. Price* (1990), 51 B.C.L.R. (2d) 282 at 319–20 (C.A.); *Commercial Capital Trust Co. v. Berk* (1989), 57 D.L.R. (4th) 759 at 763–64 (Ont. C.A.).

116 *Hodgkinson v. Simms, ibid.* at 452.

117 *Ibid.* at 478.

Waddell in departing from a simple "but for" test on the present facts. It is likely, however, that on facts similar to *Waddell*, the claim for investment losses would fail, as it did in that case. If Hodgkinson had made a clear decision to invest in real estate tax shelters before meeting with Simms, his claim would surely have failed. Simms would not have caused the loss. Accordingly, the preferable explanation for the majority view in *Hodgkinson* is that the Court did not accept that Simms had discharged the onus, imposed on him in these particular circumstances, to prove that Hodgkinson would have invested in real estate tax shelters in any event.

2) Remoteness

Damages for breach of contract are recoverable only to the extent that the type of loss that has occurred was reasonably foreseeable by the parties at the time of entering the agreement. The leading nineteenth-century authority articulating this principle, *Hadley v. Baxendale*,[118] has given the rule its name. The plaintiff Hadley was the proprietor of a mill in Gloucester. As a result of the breakage of the mill's crank shaft on May 11th, the mill was stopped. A fracture in the shaft was discovered the next day and it became necessary to send the broken shaft to an engineering firm in Greenwich where it would serve as a model for a new shaft. Accordingly, on the 13th, the plaintiff dispatched one of its clerks to the local office of Pickford & Co., a London carrier, of which the defendant Baxendale was the managing partner. The clerk was assured that if the shaft was delivered to the carrier before noon on any day, it would be delivered the following day in Greenwich. The plaintiff brought the shaft to the carrier on the following day. As a result of the defendant's neglect, however, the delivery to Greenwich was delayed and the plaintiff did not receive the new shaft until several days after what would otherwise have been its date of delivery. As a result, the mill was stopped for a greater period than was necessary. The plaintiff brought an action to recover profits lost as a result of the delay.

On behalf of the Exchequer Court, Baron Alderson articulated the basic principle in the following terms:

> Where two parties have made a contract which one of them has broken, the damages which the other party ought to receive in respect of such breach of contract should be such as may fairly and reasonably be considered either arising naturally, i.e., according to the usual

---

118 (1854), 9 Exch. 341, 156 E.R. 145.

course of things, from such breach of contract itself, or such as may reasonably be supposed to have been in the contemplation of both parties, at the time they made the contract as the probable result of the breach of it.[119]

This classic formulation of the rule, placing emphasis on "the usual course of things" and the "probable result" appears to set a high threshold of foreseeability for a particular consequence to be considered to be within "the contemplation of both parties." Alderson B. went on to state a second principle dealing with situations in which the consequences of breach would be foreseeable only if special circumstances were communicated by one party to the other in the following terms:

Now, if the special circumstances under which the contract was actually made were communicated by the plaintiffs to the defendants, and thus known to both parties, the damages resulting from the breach of such a contract, which they would reasonably contemplate, would be the amount of injury which would ordinarily follow from a breach of contract under these special circumstances so known and communicated. But, on the other hand, if the special circumstances were wholly unknown to the party breaking the contract, he, at the most, could only be supposed to have had in his contemplation the amount of injury which would arise generally, and in the great multiple of cases not affected by any special circumstances, from such a breach of contract.[120]

In Alderson B.'s view, it was this second branch of the rule or, as some would say, this second rule in *Hadley v. Baxendale* that was applicable to the facts at hand. The consequence that the mill was stopped was not foreseeable "in the great multitude of cases of millers sending off broken shafts to third persons by a carrier under ordinary circumstances."[121] Accordingly, the loss was foreseeable, in the requisite sense, only if that fact had been communicated to the carrier. In the court's view "the only circumstances here communicated by the plaintiffs to the defendants at the time the contract was made, were, that the article to be carried was the broken shaft of a mill, and that the plaintiffs were the millers of that mill."[122]

---

119 *Ibid* at 151 (E.R.).
120 *Ibid*.
121 *Ibid*.
122 See *ibid*. The headnote of the report suggests, however, that the clerk had in fact informed the defendant's employee that the mill was stopped. Danzig suggests that this apparent inconsistency may be explained on the basis that under the

The rule in *Hadley v. Baxendale* remains as a governing principle in the calculation of damages for breach of contract. It is often referred to, albeit somewhat elliptically, as a rule requiring that the damages be "reasonably foreseeable" or not too "remote." In *Hadley*, Alderson B. provided an explanation of the underlying rationale of the rule as follows: "For, had the special circumstances been known, the parties might have specially provided for the breach of contract by special terms as to the damages in that case; and of this advantage it would be very unjust to deprive them."[123]

One might add that there are yet further devices available for handling the risk of liability in such circumstances. One might take out insurance or adopt a strategy of self-insurance. Alternatively, a party might agree to shift the risk of loss to the other party in return for an increase in the price to be paid. A risk-adverse party may simply decline to enter into the transaction in the first place. As Alderson B. emphasized, however, the point of the rule is to facilitate private planning with respect to risk allocation and it is thus consistent with the general justification for the expectancy principle that we have considered elsewhere.[124]

Nearly one hundred years later, a similarly influential articulation of the rule in *Hadley v. Baxendale* was set forth by Asquith L.J. in *Victoria Laundry (Windsor) Ltd. v. Newman Industries Ltd.*[125] In this case, Asquith L.J. summarized the then-current learning on the relationship between the expectancy principle and the rule in *Hadley v. Baxendale* in a series of six propositions. Asquith L.J. emphasized that the reasonable foreseeability test rests on the knowledge possessed by the parties at the time of contracting and that such knowledge is either one of two kinds, "actual" or "imputed." Imputed knowledge is knowledge of the "ordinary course of things" that everyone, as a reasonable person, is presumed to have. Actual knowledge is knowledge of special circumstances outside the ordinary course of things that, if communicated to the other party, may attract the second rule in *Hadley v. Baxendale*. Asquith L.J. also emphasized that it is not necessary that the party in breach should have actually contemplated the consequences of breach. "It suffices that, if he had considered the question, he would as a rea-

---

law of agency, as it was then understood, communication to the defendant's employee would not have constituted effective communication to the defendant. See R. Danzig, "*Hadley v. Baxendale*: A Study of the Industrialization of the Law" (1975) 4 J. Legal Stud. 249 at 262–63.

123 *Ibid.*
124 See above this Chapter, section C.
125 [1949] 2 K.B. 528 (C.A.).

sonable man have concluded that the loss in question was liable to result."[126] More controversially, Asquith L.J., in a sixth proposition, articulated the test for the degree of foreseeability that must be present for the rule to apply in the following terms:

> Nor, finally, to make a particular loss recoverable, need it be proved that upon a given state of knowledge the defendant could, as a reasonable man, foresee that a breach must necessarily result in that loss. It is enough if he could foresee it was likely so to result. It is indeed enough ... if the loss (or some factor without which it would not have occurred) is a "serious possibility" or a "real danger." For short, we have used the word "liable" to result. Possibly the colloquialism "on the cards" indicates the shade of meaning with some approach to accuracy.[127]

The controversial aspect of this formulation of the test is that it appears to signal a lowering of the threshold of liability from a requirement that the consequences of breach be so foreseeable as to be, in the words of Alderson B., "either arising naturally, i.e., according to the usual course of things ... or ... the probable result of the breach"[128] to a standard that required merely that the consequence constitutes, in the language of Asquith L.J., "a 'serious possibility' or a 'real danger' ... [or] ... 'liable' to result."[129] As articulated by Asquith L.J., then, it appears that the threshold for establishing foreseeability has been reduced over the century following the decision in *Hadley v. Baxendale*.

In *Koufos v. Czarnikow (C.) (The Heron II)*,[130] the House of Lords gave extensive but inclusive consideration to the question of whether Asquith L.J.'s opinion was intended to lower the threshold for application of the rule in *Hadley* and *Baxendale* and, if so, whether his restatement of the doctrine constituted good law. One member of the panel, Lord Reid, was of the view that the intended effect of Asquith L.J.'s opinion was to reduce the threshold and that it was, in this respect, unacceptable. Lord Reid took particular exception to the phrase "liable to result" that would include cases where an individual foresees "a very improbable result."[131] Lord Reid also found unhelpful the phrases "a serious possibility," "a real danger" and "on the cards."[132] Lord Hodson,

---

126 *Ibid.* at 540.
127 See *ibid.*
128 Above note 118 at 151 (E.R.).
129 Above note 125 at 540.
130 [1969] 1 A.C. 350, [1967] 3 All E.R. 686 (H.L.).
131 *Ibid.* at 389.
132 *Ibid.* at 390.

although he gave pride of place to Alderson B.'s expression "in the great multitude of cases" also found Asquith L.J.'s phrase "liable to result" to be quite satisfactory.[133] Lord Pearce acknowledged that the doctrine had evolved in the period between *Hadley v. Baxendale* and *Victoria Laundry* and indicated that the expressions used by Asquith L.J. in the latter case were correct.[134] At the same time, he did not find the reference to the colloquialism "on the cards" as being a useful test.[135] Lord Upjohn, although he was content to adopt as the test the language of "real danger" or a "serious possibility," was nonetheless of the view that the adoption of such language would not have lead to a different result in *Hadley v. Baxendale* itself.[136] Finally, Lord Morris declined to express a preference for any of the contending phrases. Each of them might help, he suggested, "but so may many others."[137] In sum, then, the formulation of the rule in *Hadley v. Baxendale* set forth by Asquith L.J. in the *Victoria Laundry* case appears to have survived the scrutiny of the House of Lords in *Koufos* relatively unscathed.[138] At the same time, however, no clear consensus emerged from the court as to whether the foreseeability threshold has been reduced over time.

A careful examination of the historical circumstances of *Hadley v. Baxendale* strongly suggests that the apparently higher threshold set forth by Baron Alderson in *Hadley* was a product of its time and that a variety of institutional changes in the legal landscape over the next several decades may well have provided a context in which a lower threshold appeared appropriate. In the middle of the nineteenth century, as Danzig[139] has noted, the undeveloped state of business corporations and insolvency law created an environment in which the proprietors of emerging national businesses were exposed to the possibility of severe personal liability meted out by local juries. The decision in *Hadley v.*

---

133 *Ibid.* at 410–11.

134 *Ibid.* at 415.

135 *Ibid.* ("… I am not sure just what nuance it has either in my own personal vocabulary or in that of others. I suspect that it owes its attraction, like many other colloquialisms, to the fact that one may utter it without having the trouble of really thinking out with precision what one means oneself or what others will understand by it, a spurious attraction which in general makes colloquialism unsuitable for definition …").

136 *Ibid.* at 425.

137 *Ibid.* at 397.

138 For a recent decision in which the *Hadley* and *Victoria Laundry* tests appear to be used interchangeably, see *Jackson v. Royal Bank of Scotland*, [2005] 2 All E.R. 71 (H.L.). See also *Aruna Mills Ltd. v. Dhanrajmal Gobindram*, [1968] 1 Q.B. 655 at 668.

139 See Danzig, above note 122.

Baxendale restricted their vulnerability to such awards. The subsequent development of the limited liability corporation, the improvement of insolvency laws, the growth of insurance and of tort law has arguably created an environment in which the standard imposed by courts applying the rule in *Hadley v. Baxendale* could evolve in the direction of a lower threshold of foreseeability than that set forth by Alderson B. in *Hadley* itself. Certainly, on its facts, the *Koufos* case lends no support to the idea that the threshold requires that the consequences of the breach be foreseeable in the sense of being probable. The claim concerned the late arrival of a cargo of sugar and the resulting loss of its value to the owner. The owner intended to sell the sugar upon arrival. During the delay, the sugar market in Basrah, the port of destination, suffered a decline. It was accepted that there was an even chance of the market either rising or falling during the delay. Thus, neither eventuality could be considered to be "probable." The House of Lords was unanimous, however, in the view that it was not necessary to establish an "odds-on" probability in order to engage the reasonable foreseeability test. Accordingly, the purchaser's claim enjoyed success.

At the other end of the spectrum of likelihood, in attempting to determine how unlikely a consequence might be and still meet the threshold of being "liable to result," one may consider the relationship between the *Hadley v. Baxendale* standard of foreseeability and the reasonable foreseeability test employed in the law of tort. Such a comparison was undertaken by the House of Lords in the *Koufos* case. On this point, a clear consensus emerged to the effect that the standard of foreseeability required in a contract claim is of a higher degree than that required in a tort claim. Lord Reid explained that whereas in contract, the victim of a breach can secure protection from an unusual risk by signifying the existence of the risk to the other party, in tort law, the victim has no opportunity to secure such protection.[140] Hence, liability in tort can be and should be wider.[141] However, another possible explanation for the differences in approach taken to reasonable foreseeability in contract and tort might be that contract normally deals with injuries in the form of economic loss whereas tort typically involves

---

140 Above note 130 at 386.

141 However, compare with *dicta* of the Supreme Court of Canada suggesting that there is no practical difference between the remoteness test in contract and that in tort. See *BG Checo International Ltd. v. British Columbia Hydro & Power Authority*, above note 19 at 42; *Asamera Oil Corp. v. Sea Oil & General Corp.*, [1979] 1 S.C.R. 633 at 673; *B.D.C. Ltd. v. Hofstrand Farms Ltd.*, [1986] 1 S.C.R. 228 at 243–44.

injuries to persons or property.[142] Thus, where the potential result of a negligent act is the death of another person, one would expect that such a risk, even if rather remote, would be considered to be reasonably foreseeable. If, on the other hand, the fall in the sugar market in *Koufos* had been considered to be a rather remote possibility, it is unlikely that the market decline would have been considered to be reasonably foreseeable for purposes of the rule in *Hadley v. Baxendale*.

The law of contracts does not always deal with merely economic loss, however, and accordingly, this insight leads to a further possibility worthy of consideration. It may well be appropriate, in cases where a breach of contract results in physical injury or property damage, that a requirement of reasonable foreseeability more akin to that employed in tort cases should also apply to the contract claim. Indeed, failure to apply a similar standard would lead to anomalous results. If one's chauffeur, for example, engages in a negligent act of driving that would only in very rare circumstances lead to an accident, it would be surprising if a third party injured in the accident would have an easier claim in tort than would the employer who, injured while seated in the back seat of the car, would have a claim for contractual damages. It appears at least conceivable, then, that the standard of reasonable foreseeability will to some extent fluctuate with the nature of the interest injured by the contract breach. Very little direct support for such a concept can be found, however, in the decided authorities. Nonetheless, a suggestion to this effect was made by Lord Denning in *H. Parsons (Livestock) Ltd. v. Uttley Ingham & Co. Ltd.*,[143] a case involving the supply of a defective feed hopper to a pig farmer. As a result of a failure of the ventilator in the hopper, the pig-nuts stored in the hopper became mouldy. When fed to the pigs, the nuts caused illness and ultimately, death, to many of the herd. The farmer sued for the loss of the pigs. At trial, it was held that the loss was not reasonably foreseeable in the sense that it was a consequence that would have been within the contemplation of the parties at the time of contracting. In the Court of Appeal, however, it was held that the loss was sufficiently foreseeable to engage liability in contract. Lord Denning, in particular, suggested that a different approach would be taken in contract cases depending on whether the loss in question was physical injury as opposed to a lost profit. In the latter category, in his view, the test of "reasonable contemplation" and "serious possibility" set out in *Hadley*, *Victoria Laundry* and *Koufos* was

---

142 See generally M. Eisenberg, "The Principle of *Hadley v. Baxendale*" (1992) 80 Cal. L. Rev. 563.

143 [1978] Q.B. 791.

to be applied.[144] In a physical injury case, on the other hand, the party in default would be liable for any loss that he "ought reasonably to have *foreseen* at the time of the breach as a possible consequence, even if it was only a *slight* possibility."[145] Such views remain unorthodox however,[146] even if, as a practical matter, they may assist in predicting the outcome of particular cases.[147]

In applying the rule, a distinction is drawn between the type of injury that occurs and the extent of the loss.[148] The basic principle is that to be recoverable, it is the type of loss that must be foreseen but not necessarily its extent. As the facts of the *Victoria Laundry* case illustrate, however, application of the distinction may, in a particular fact situation, be a subtle matter. The plaintiff laundry had decided to expand its business and had agreed to buy a large boiler from the defendant firm of engineers. The defendant breached the contract by delivering the boiler twenty-odd weeks later than the time for delivery set out in the agreement. The demand for laundry services being apparently insatiable, the plaintiff claimed for the profits lost as a result of the delay and further, claimed for the profits that would have been made on a number of highly profitable dyeing contracts that they would have entered into with the Ministry of Supply. Although the defendant firm was aware that the plaintiffs were in the business of laundering and dyeing, they were unaware of the prospect of the unusually lucrative contracts with the ministry. The Court of Appeal held that the ordinary profits lost during the period of delay could be recovered, whereas the profits on

---

144 *Ibid.* at 803.
145 *Ibid.* (emphasis in original).
146 In the *Parsons* case itself, Scarman L.J., Orr L.J. concurring, rejected Lord Denning's proposed distinction but found, nonetheless, that the loss of the pigs was sufficiently foreseeable to come within the *Hadley v. Baxendale* test. See *ibid.* at 813.
147 Compare with Lord Pearce in *Koufos* who, in formulating an illustration of the proposition that an unlikely consequence may nonetheless be a foreseeable one, offered the example of a negligently repaired ceiling of one of the law courts that collapsed on the heads of those in court. As the room is vacant much of the time, the odds against anyone being injured by the collapse are, he suggested, nearly 10 to 1. Unsurprisingly, the obvious illustration of an unlikely consequence that is nonetheless sufficiently foreseeable was a negligent breach of contract giving rise to personal injuries. See above note 130 at 712 (All E.R.).
148 See, for example, *Vacwell Engineering Co. Ltd. v. BDH Chemicals Ltd.*, [1971] 1 Q.B. 88 (supply of dangerous chemicals without adequate warning—minor explosion foreseeable—supplier liable for consequences of major explosion). See also *H. Parsons (Livestock) Ltd. v. Uttley Ingham & Co. Ltd.*, above note 143 at 813, Scarman L.J.

the particularly lucrative government contracts were not recoverable. It is not entirely obvious, however, that the type of business loss sustained on the government contracts was different in kind rather than in extent. Nonetheless, the court appears to have assumed that the loss on the ministry contracts was different in kind.

In a case such as *Victoria Laundry*, in which the second or special circumstances rule is applied to a claim for lost profits, it is well established that even though the unforeseeable profits are irrecoverable, an award may be made for ordinary profits even though the plaintiff had no intention of conducting ordinary business. Thus, in *Victoria Laundry* itself, the plaintiff was allowed to recover the ordinary profits that might have been made if the capacity of the boiler that would have been devoted to the government contracts had been devoted to ordinary laundering and dyeing work. Asquith L.J. held that the plaintiffs were entitled to recover "some general (and perhaps conjectural) sum for loss of business in respect of dyeing contracts to be reasonably expected."[149] Similarly, in *Cory v. Thames Ironworks Company*,[150] where the parties to the purchase and sale of a hull of a boom derrick had in mind different uses for the chattel, recovery was allowed for the damages that would have been sustained through its ordinary use. The purchasers were coal merchants and the seller reasonably expected that the hull would be used to store coal. In fact, the purchaser had in mind a much more profitable use of the hull in transferring the coal from colliers to barges for shipment. Upon late delivery of the hull, the sellers were held liable only for the loss of profits that would have occurred as a result of using the hull as a storage facility. Thus, where the claim fails under the second rule, it may nonetheless succeed under the first rule on the view, presumably, that since lost profits of some kind were within the contemplation of both parties, the defendant is not prejudiced by being held liable for the amount of lost profit that was reasonably foreseeable.

In determining whether a particular loss is reasonably foreseeable, it may be relevant to consider the occupation of the defendant and the presumed knowledge that a defendant in this particular line of work would be expected to have of the business of the other party. Thus, in *Victoria Laundry*, even though the defendant firm had not manufactured the boiler, it was an engineering firm that, according to Asquith L.J., knew the nature of the plaintiff's business and were aware, to a greater extent than the uninstructed layman, of the commercial uses of boilers. Where, on the other hand, the defendant is a carrier rather

149 Above note 125 at 543.
150 (1868), L.R. 3 Q.B. 181.

than a supplier of goods, it may be that, as in *Hadley v. Baxendale*, the defendant will not be assumed to have sufficiently specific knowledge of the other party's business to render the loss reasonably foreseeable.

Application of the rule may also be affected by circumstances that may be thought to render any expectation that the other party will act, in effect, as an insurer of the first party's business losses to be an unreasonable one. Thus, even where special circumstances leading to such loss have been communicated, it may be held that the nature of the communication was not sufficient to signal the existence of an expectation of this kind. In *Munroe Equipment Sales Ltd. v. Canadian Forest Products Ltd.*,[151] the defendant was urgently seeking a tractor to assist in the removal of cut logs prior to the winter season. Having accidentally encountered a salesman of the plaintiff, the defendant arranged to rent a second-hand tractor from the plaintiff. The plaintiff was made aware of the intended use for the tractor. In the event, however, the tractor proved to be most unsatisfactory and the defendant abandoned the tractor and refused to make a series of monthly payments. The plaintiff lessor sought recovery of the payments and, in response, the defendant counterclaimed for lost profits resulting from its inability to remove all the wood that could have been removed if the tractor had performed in a satisfactory manner. The Manitoba Court of Appeal divided on whether the counterclaim should succeed. For the majority, disallowing the counterclaim, Miller C.J.M. reasoned that insufficient information had been made available to the lessor concerning such matters as the amount of wood ready to be removed and the fact that, as a result of labour difficulties, the removal was an urgent matter. Perhaps the key to understanding the approach of the majority, however, is revealed in the following observations of Miller C.J.M.: "In my opinion it is unreasonable to expect that such a burden of responsibility for damages as now claimed by the defendant should be assumed from the rental of a second-hand unit. Surely no reasonable person could contemplate, under the circumstances of the renting of this machine, that the lessor of one second-hand tractor was underwriting and virtually insuring the removal of all this pulp wood from the bush."

In the minority view, however, sufficient information to engage the second rule in *Hadley v. Baxendale* had been communicated to the plaintiff and accordingly, in their view, the counterclaim should have been allowed. A few years later, in *Scyrup v. Economy Tractor Parts Ltd.*,[152] the same court, again divided, reached the opposite conclusion on rather

151 (1961), 29 D.L.R. (2d) 730 (Man. C.A.).
152 (1963), 40 D.L.R. (2d) 1026 (Man. C.A.).

similar facts. The plaintiff in this case owned a tractor and acquired from the defendant a second-hand hydraulic dozer attachment for the tractor, which it needed to carry out a profitable contract with a third party. The attachment was defective and after a series of performance failures, the third party dismissed the plaintiff from the profitable agreement. The plaintiff successfully sued the defendant for the resulting lost profits. For the majority, the fact that the attachment was required for performance of the contract with the third party had been disclosed to the plaintiff, and the defendant therefore had actual knowledge of the special circumstances giving rise to the loss. In dissent, however, Miller C.J.M. again adopted the view that insufficient information had been provided. In his view, the defendant should not be saddled with a claim for damages for loss of profits "unless it was clearly indicated to the defendant at the time the equipment was purchased exactly what kind of contract was being entered into by the plaintiff, the type of work that was to be done and the magnitude of the operation."[153]

In cases such as these, it is evident that the issue of whether sufficient information concerning the special circumstances has been communicated is a highly manipulable one. Perhaps a better explanation for the denial of relief in the *Munroe* case, then, is that the special circumstances were not communicated in such a way as to signal to a reasonable person that a potential liability was being assumed. Indeed, in earlier cases, it had been suggested that the communication of special circumstances will not confer liability unless the information is brought home to the other party in such fashion as to form part of the agreement between the parties.[154] This requirement of an implicit undertaking to indemnify, however, has disappeared from the law of contract damages.[155] Indeed, strict application of a principle of this kind is simply inconsistent with the basic principle that reasonably foreseeable loss is compensable. Thus, in *Cornwall Gravel Co. Ltd. v. Purolator Courier Ltd.*,[156] a courier company was held liable for the consequen-

---

153 *Ibid.* at 1029.
154 See, for example, *British Columbia and Vancouver's Island Spar, Lumber & Saw-Mill Co., Ltd. v. Nettleship* (1868), L.R. 3 C.P. 499 at 509, Willes J.; *Victoria Laundry (Windsor) Ltd. v. Newman Industries Ltd.*, above note 125. See also *Horne v. Midland Railway Co.* (1873), L.R. 8 C.P. 131 (where a similar view was explained, however, on the basis that the defendant railway, being a common carrier, could not decline to accept the goods for transit after receiving such notice).
155 See *Koufos v. Czarnikow (C.) (The Heron II)*, above note 130 at 422 (A.C.).
156 (1978), 83 D.L.R. (3d) 267 (Ont. H.C.J.). See also *B.G. Linton Construction Ltd. v. C.N.R. Co.*, [1975] 2 S.C.R. 678.

tial loss resulting from late delivery of what it had been informed was a tender when it turned out that, if it had been delivered in time, the tender would have been the winning bid. Though it appears unlikely that the courier understood that it was tacitly assuming the risk of such loss, the court held that since the special circumstances had been communicated and the loss was plainly foreseeable, liability for lost profits on the tendered project followed. Nonetheless, cases such as *Munroe Equipment* suggest that while it is not necessary to establish the existence of an implicit contractual intention to indemnify, there may well be cases where the communication of special circumstances, in a particular factual context, may not sufficiently signal the potential liability to the other party so as to render it appropriate to hold that the loss was within the contemplation of the parties in the requisite sense.

3) Mitigation

The third limitation on the recovery of expectancy damages is that the victim of the breach cannot recover losses that the victim could have avoided by taking reasonable steps subsequent to the breach. Thus, an employee who has been wrongfully dismissed must make reasonable efforts to find alternative employment.[157] Similarly, where a purchaser refuses to close a transaction for the purchase and sale of land, the vendor must make reasonable efforts to sell the property to a third party.[158] A disappointed buyer of goods of inferior quality that were intended to be used in profit-making activities, must take reasonable steps to acquire a substitute, rather than simply continuing to run up losses.[159] A disappointed purchaser of services must proceed diligently to find a substitute service provider.[160] The principle against avoidable loss is applicable in all contractual settings. Thus in *Caines v. Bank of Nova Scotia*,[161] for example, the plaintiff, having discovered that his

---

157 *Cemco Electrical Manufacturing Co. v. Van Snellenberg*, [1964] S.C.R. 121; *Red Deer College v. Michaels* (1975), 57 D.L.R. (3d) 386 (S.C.C.).

158 *100 Main Street Ltd. v. W.B. Sullivan Construction Ltd.* (1978), 88 D.L.R. (3d) 1 (Ont. C.A.), leave to appeal to S.C.C. refused, *ibid.; Woodford Estates Ltd. v. Pollack* (1978), 93 D.L.R. (3d) 350 (Ont. H.C.J.). See also *Hongkong Bank of Canada v. Richardson Greenshields of Canada Ltd.* (1990), 72 D.L.R. (4th) 161 (B.C.C.A.) (sale of bonds).

159 *Wingold Construction Co. Ltd. v. Kramp*, [1960] S.C.R. 556.

160 *Mertens v. Home Freeholds Company*, [1921] 2 K.B. 526 (C.A.); *Armstrong v. Roslyn Park Land Co. Ltd.* (1951), 4 W.W.R. (N.S.) 270 (B.C.S.C.).

161 (1978), 90 D.L.R. (3d) 271 (N.B.C.A.). See also *Hunt v. TD Securities Inc.* (2003), 66 O.R. (3d) 481 (C.A.) (improper sale of client's shares by broker—client obliged to purchase substitute shares).

insurance policy had lapsed as a result of the failure of the defendant bank to discharge its obligation to pay the premiums, did not act reasonably by relying on the bank's assurance that it had indeed made payment and by failing to arrange new insurance immediately. Although it is often said that the principle against avoidable loss imposes a duty to mitigate, a more accurate way of expressing the principle is that a failure to mitigate reduces recoverable loss. The plaintiff is not under a duty to mitigate in the sense that a failure to mitigate gives rise to a cause of action on the part of the party in default.

A variety of explanations have been offered for the mitigation principle.[162] One possible explanation is that the principle is simply an application of the doctrine of causation.[163] The plaintiff cannot recover losses that have, in a sense, been caused by his or her own failure to take reasonable steps to minimize the loss resulting from a breach. Although it is true that none of the losses would have occurred "but for" the defendant's breach, the plaintiff's failure to mitigate may be considered to be an intervening cause exacerbating the loss initially caused by the defendant. Alternatively, it may be suggested that the mitigation doctrine draws its strength from the principle that the plaintiff may recover only such losses as are reasonably foreseeable under the rule in *Hadley v. Baxendale*.[164] On this view, as it is reasonably foreseeable that parties will take reasonable steps to minimize losses resulting from a breach of contract, it is unforeseeable that they will not do so. Hence, losses resulting from a failure to mitigate are not foreseeable in the requisite sense. This rationale is perhaps less convincing than that based on causation. The fact that it is foreseeable that a particular party may not engage in reasonable acts of mitigation would not preclude application of the doctrine. The mitigation principle is thus not simply an application of the doctrine of reasonable foreseeability. A third justification offered for the doctrine is that it serves to encourage economically efficient behaviour.[165] Avoiding the economic waste that might otherwise result from breach of contract serves not only the interests of the party in default but, as well, a more general societal interest in efficient behaviour.

---

162 See generally M. Bridge, "Mitigation of Damages in Contract and the Meaning of Avoidable Loss" (1989) 105 Law Q. Rev. 398.
163 For discussion of causation as a limitation on expectancy, see above this Chapter, section F(1).
164 Above note 118, for discussion of which see above this Chapter, section F(2).
165 C. Goetz and R. Scott, "The Mitigation Principle: Toward a General Theory of Contractual Obligation" (1983) 69 Va. L. Rev. 967.

The taking of reasonable steps may include continued dealings with the party in default. In *Payzu Ltd. v. Saunders*,[166] a buyer of goods, confronted with a wrongful breach by the seller, was obliged to accept an offer by the seller to continue their relationship on altered terms. The goods were to be delivered in instalments. The contract provided for payment for each instalment within one month of delivery. The buyer failed to make the first payment in a punctual fashion and the seller repudiated the agreement but offered to continue to deliver the goods if the purchaser would pay cash on delivery. The buyer rejected that offer and sued for damages when the market price for the goods in question escalated. Although the seller's repudiation was held to be wrongful, the plaintiff could not recover the damages that flowed from the refusal to accept the seller's offer to deal on a cash basis. Not every such offer must be accepted, of course. In the context of a personal services contract, for example, an employee who is dismissed with a false imputation of wrongdoing[167] is not obliged to accept an offer of re-employment nor would a dismissed employee be obliged to accept re-employment that involves a significant demotion in status.[168] In the absence of such considerations, however, it may be reasonable for an employee to accept a suitable offer of re-employment.[169]

Although the plaintiff cannot recover losses that could have been avoided by reasonable steps, it has been suggested that "the measures which [the plaintiff] may be driven to adopt in order to extricate himself ought not be weighed in nice scales at the instance of the party whose breach of contract has occasioned the difficulty."[170] Moreover, the burden of establishing that the plaintiff has failed to take reason-

---

166 [1919] 2 K.B. 581 (C.A.).

167 *Ibid.* at 588, Banks L.J.

168 *Yetton v. Eastwoods Froy Ltd.*, [1967] 1 W.L.R. 104 (Q.B.) (refusal of managing director to accept position of assistant managing director held to be reasonable); *O'Grady v. Insurance Corp. of British Columbia* (1975), 63 D.L.R. (3d) 370 (B.C.S.C.) (corporate secretary and general counsel not obliged to accept position as head of a particular legal department); *Thiessen v. Leduc*, [1975] 4 W.W.R. 387 (Alta. S.C.T.D.) (chief constable not obliged to accept transfer to another unspecified department); *Herrschaft v. Vancouver Community College* (1978), 91 D.L.R. (3d) 328 (B.C.S.C.) (college director of curriculum not obliged to accept position involving acquisition of instructional space).

169 See, for example, *Brace v. Calder*, [1895] 2 Q.B. 253 (C.A.) (employee dismissed as a result of the dissolution of partnership—refusal to accept equivalent position from the partners who acquired the business was held unreasonable).

170 *Banco de Portugal v. Waterlow & Sons Ltd.*, [1932] A.C. 452 at 506 (H.L.), Lord Macmillan.

able steps to mitigate the loss falls upon the defendant.[171] In a close case, then, it appears that the plaintiff who has attempted to mitigate loss may be the beneficiary of some latitude in the interpretation of the standard of reasonableness. Further, should the plaintiff's attempt at mitigation be unsuccessful, it is well established that the plaintiff may recover the costs of mitigation or, indeed, any exacerbation of the original loss resulting from the failed attempt to mitigate.[172] Although the taking of reasonable steps in mitigating of loss—such as acquiring substitute goods[173]—may impose additional expense on the plaintiff,[174] it is nonetheless well established that the "mitigation principle does not impose on the plaintiff an obligation to take any step which a reasonable and prudent man would not ordinarily take in the course of his business."[175] More particularly, the plaintiff is not under an obligation to place assets at significant risk in order to mitigate.[176] The plaintiff is not required, for example, to engage in the expense of litigation, the result of which is speculative, in order to mitigate loss.[177] Further,

---

171 *Red Deer College v. Michaels,* above note 157 at 390, Laskin C.J.C.

172 See *Wilson v. United Counties Bank,* [1920] A.C. 102 at 125 (H.L.), Lord Atkinson; *Lloyds and Scottish Finance Ltd. v. Modern Cars and Caravans (Kingston) Ltd.,* [1966] 1 Q.B. 764 at 782–83, Edmund Davies J.

173 *Startup et al. v. Cortazzi* (1835), 2 C.M. & R. 165, 150 E.R. 71. See also, for example, *Sale of Goods Act,* R.S.O. 1990, c. S.1, s. 49(3). It is occasionally suggested, however, that the duty to mitigate should be imposed only where the breach of contract has made available an "asset" to the plaintiff such as the unpaid purchase price, which can then be devoted to absorbing the cost of mitigation. See, for example, *Peebles v. Pfeifer,* [1918] 2 W.W.R. 877 (Sask. K.B.). However, in *Asamera Oil Corp. v. Sea Oil & General Corp.,* above note 141, the Supreme Court decided that the mitigation principle was not limited by such a requirement. The presence of such an "asset" is but one of many factors that bears on the task of determining in a particular case what is or is not reasonable on the part of the injured party in all the circumstances." See *ibid.* at 658–59, Estey J.

174 See, for example, *Asamera Oil Corp. Ltd.* above note 141 (non-return of loaned shares—obligation either to purchase replacement shares in a rising market or pursue litigation expeditiously). For discussion of the factors relevant to a determination of when mitigation through repurchase of shares wrongfully disposed of by a defendant broker should occur, see *Hunt v. TD Securities Inc.,* above note 161.

175 *British Westinghouse Electric and Manufacturing Co. Ltd. v. Underground Electric Ry. Co. of London Ltd.,* [1912] A.C. 673 at 689, Viscount Haldane L.C. See also *Dunkirk Colliery Co. v. Lever Co.* (1878), 9 Ch. Div. 20.

176 See *Jewelowski v. Propp,* [1944] K.B. 510; *Lesters Leather & Skin Co. Ltd. v. Home & Overseas Brokers Ltd.* (1948), 64 T.L.R. 569 (C.A.). See also *Caine v. Schultz,* [1927] 1 W.W.R. 600 (B.C.C.A.).

177 *Bank of Montreal v. Maddox & MacInnis* (1987), 83 N.B.R. (2d) 342 (C.A.); *Pilkington v. Wood,* [1953] Ch. 770.

the plaintiff is not required to undertake steps that may prejudice its commercial reputation.[178]

It is less clear, however, whether the plaintiff's financial inability to take steps in mitigation provides an excuse for failure to do so. Although the House of Lords in *Liesbosch Dredger v. S.S. Edison*[179] suggested that losses caused by the plaintiff's impecuniosity were not compensable, it is not clear whether the basis for this suggestion was that the loss arising from impecuniosity was not foreseeable or, on the other hand, was not caused by the breach.[180] If the correct explanation is that the loss may not be foreseeable in such a case, the possibility arises that where the injury was foreseeable, the plaintiff's failure to mitigate may not reduce the damage award. A number of Canadian cases appear to have accepted that the *Liesbosch* case set out a general principle against impecuniosity as an excuse for failure to mitigate.[181] More recent English authority has suggested, however, that the correct basis for the *Liesbosch* principle rests on whether the losses exacerbated by impecuniosity were reasonably foreseeable.[182] Further, some Canadian cases appear to have assumed that the proper approach is to consider whether the losses caused by impecuniosity were reasonably foreseeable.[183] In *Freedhoff v. Pomalift Industries Ltd.*,[184] for example, the supplier of a defective ski lift was held liable to the purchaser for the losses involved in attempting to fix the equipment and the lost profits up to the time when the plaintiff would have been reasonably required

---

178 *James Finlay & Co. v. N.V. Kwik Hoo Tong Handel Maatschappij*, [1929] 1 K.B. 400 (C.A.). See also *Kuzych v. Stewart*, [1944] 4 D.L.R. 775 (B.C.S.C.). Similarly, costly steps taken in mitigation in order to preserve commercial reputation may be considered reasonable. See *Banco de Portugal v. Waterlow & Sons Ltd.*, above note 170 (defendant printer unwittingly facilitates unlawful circulation of a second and unauthorized printing of bank notes printed for the plaintiff issuing bank—bank's decision to honour the notes for a period of time, though not required to do so, constituted a reasonable step in mitigation).

179 [1933] A.C. 449 (H.L.).

180 *Ibid.* at 460, Lord Wright.

181 See, for example, *The King v. C.P.R.*, [1947] S.C.R. 185 at 189–90, Kerwin J.; *Stewart v. Industrial Acceptance Corp. Ltd.*, [1949] 3 D.L.R 42 at 51 (B.C.S.C.), Whittaker J.; *Dawson v. Helicopter Exploration Co. Ltd.* (1958), 12 D.L.R. (2d) 1 at 11 (S.C.C.), Rand J.; *Alberta Caterers Ltd. v. R. Volcan (Alta.) Ltd.* (1977), 81 D.L.R. (3d) 672 at 682 (Alta. S.C.T.D.), Cavanagh J.

182 *Trans Trust S.P.R.L. v Danubian Trading Co. Ltd.*, above note 21 at 306 (C.A.), Denning L.J.

183 See, for example, *General Securities Ltd. v. Don Ingram Ltd.*, [1940] S.C.R. 670; *Re 140 Developments Ltd. v. Steveston Meat & Frozen Food Lockers (1973) Ltd.* (1975), 59 D.L.R. (3d) 470 (B.C.S.C.).

184 (1971), 19 D.L.R. (3d) 153 (Ont. C.A.).

to acquire substitute equipment, but not for the further losses resulting from the plaintiff's impecuniosity. As a result of the diminished revenues, the plaintiff was unable to meet mortgage payments with a resulting loss of the property and business. The Ontario Court of Appeal held that such losses did not "meet the test of foreseeability."[185] Similarly, the same court has held that a plaintiff's pre-existing mental condition that incapacitated the plaintiff from taking reasonable steps in mitigation did not excuse the plaintiff's failure to mitigate as the condition was not known to the defendants.[186]

As a matter of general principle, benefits or profits acquired by the plaintiff through steps taken in mitigation of the loss will reduce the defendant's liability in damages. In applying this principle, however, a difficult line must be drawn between profits secured through acts of mitigation and profits that might have been secured by the plaintiff even in the absence of the defendant's breach of contract. The leading case is *British Westinghouse Electric and Manufacturing Co. Ltd. v. Underground Electric Ry. Co. of London Ltd.*,[187] where Viscount Haldane observed: "the subsequent transaction, if to be taken into account, must be one arising out of the consequences of the breach and in the ordinary course of business."[188] In this case, the plaintiff replaced defective machinery supplied by the defendant with more efficient machinery. The resulting increase in the plaintiff's profits was taken into account in reducing the defendant's liability. On the other hand, in a decision of the Supreme Court of Canada, *Karas v. Rowlett*,[189] where the wrongful non-renewal of a lease on which the plaintiff conducted a business provoked the plaintiff to lease another property on which to conduct a

---

185 *Ibid.* at 158. Compare with *R.G. McLean Ltd. v. Canadian Vickers Ltd.* (1970), 15 D.L.R. (3d) 15 at 24 (Ont. C.A.), Arnup J.A. Although the legislation was subsequently repealed, it was held by the House of Lords in a subsequent case that the jurisdiction to award damages in lieu persists nonetheless. See *Leeds Industrial Co-operative Society Ltd. v. Slack*, [1924] A.C. 851 (H.L.). The jurisdiction has typically been retained in legislation in the common law provinces. See, for example, *Courts of Justice Act*, R.S.O. 1990, c. C.43, s. 99.

186 *Turczinski v. Dupont Heating & Air Conditioning Ltd.* (2004), 246 D.L.R. (4th) 95 at 108 (Ont. C.A.), Feldman J.A.

187 Above note 175, quoted with approval in *A.P.E.C.O. of Canada Ltd. v. Windmill Place*, [1978] 2 S.C.R. 385 at 389. See also *Erie County Natural Gas & Fuel Co. v. Carroll*, [1911] A.C. 105 (P.C.). The principle has been extended to tort claims. See *British Columbia v. Canadian Forest Products Ltd.* (2004), 240 D.L.R. (4th) 1 at paras. 106–7 (S.C.C.).

188 *British Westinghouse Electric and Manufacturing Co. Ltd. v. Underground Electric Ry. Co. of London Ltd., ibid.* at 690.

189 [1944] S.C.R. 1.

different business, it was held that since the plaintiff might have, in any event, engaged in the further business, the profits of the new business were not to be taken into account in the reduction of the defendant's liability. Similarly, in *Jewelowski v. Propp*[190] a plaintiff who was fraudulently induced to invest in a business that subsequently went into liquidation, did not have to account for profits subsequently made when the plaintiff later bought assets of the business from the receiver and resold them at a substantial profit.[191]

G. TIME OF MEASUREMENT

As a matter of principle, identification of the time as of which damages should be measured is not normally a matter of difficulty. The victim of a breach of contract is entitled to expectancy damages, subject to the usual limitations, up to the moment in time at which the victim's reasonable steps in mitigation would avoid any further aggravation of the loss resulting from breach. Thus, for example, a wrongfully dismissed employee may recover wages that would have been earned during a reasonable notice period subject to the limitation, however, that if reasonable steps in mitigation would have achieved re-employment during the period, the compensable losses terminate at that point in time. Where the calculation of damages requires the valuation of an asset, however, the question of when the valuation should occur is a more difficult matter. In the context of agreements for the purchase and sale of goods and of realty, a rather crisp rule developed at common law that, in the normal case, the subject matter of the transaction would be valued at the date of breach. Thus, a purchaser of goods faced with non-delivery would be entitled to recover the difference between the contract price and the market value of the goods on the date for delivery. Similarly, a purchaser of land confronted by the vendor's refusal to close the transaction would be entitled to recover the difference between the contract price and the value of the land at the date of closing. Although in some cases, particularly in the context of sale of goods, it may be realistic to assume that the victim of the breach could

---

190 Above note 176.

191 Compare with *Cockburn v. Trusts & Guarantee Co.* (1917), 55 S.C.R. 264 (employee wrongfully dismissed as a result of employer's liquidation—plaintiff attended liquidation sale and purchased company assets subsequently resold by him at a profit—profits taken into account in reduction of the defendant's liability).

in fact mitigate on the date of the breach, there must be many cases in which an expectation that a purchaser would immediately mitigate by acquiring substitute property is quite unrealistic. Accordingly, the normal rule can only be defended as a rule of convenience that provides some stability or predictably in the calculation of damages in these contexts. The normal rules are capable of working a hardship, however, especially in cases involving the sale of land, where, for a variety of reasons, it may be quite unrealistic to expect the disappointed purchaser of land to mitigate by acquiring a substitute property. In order to address this difficulty, English and Canadian courts have recognized, in recent decades, the existence of greater flexibility in the normal rule than was traditionally thought to be the case. For a time, it was thought that principles of equity might be called upon to intervene, at least in the context of land sales, in cases of this kind. More recently, however, it has become clear that the normal rule, the common law rule, is sufficiently flexible to permit a court to measure the value of the subject matter of the transaction at a later point of time than breach and, more particularly, at the time of trial.

The difficulties occasioned by the normal rule and the potential for an equitable solution is illustrated in the decision of Megarry J. in *Wroth v. Tyler*,[192] a case involving a transaction for the purchase and sale of a residential property. Tyler had agreed to sell his home, occupied by himself and his wife, to the Wroths for six thousand pounds. As the property was the matrimonial home of the Tylers, however, Tyler's wife's consent was required to close the transaction. Mrs. Tyler, in due course, withheld her consent. Accordingly, the transaction did not close. The Wroths brought an action seeking specific performance of the agreement of sale or, in the alternative, a claim for damages. As time wore on, the value of the property escalated. The property was worth seventy-five hundred pounds at the time of closing and eleven thousand five hundred pounds at the date of trial. For the Wroths, a young couple of modest means, specific performance was obviously the preferred remedy. In return for the payment of the purchase price, they would receive a home worth eleven thousand five hundred pounds. Megarry J., however, denied this form of relief.[193] Under the governing matrimonial property legislation, the wife could not to be evicted from the home, even when title passed to the purchaser. Although the husband was entitled to bring an application to terminate his wife's right, it would not be appropriate, in the view of Megarry J., to grant a decree of specific performance with

---

192 [1974] Ch. 30.
193 For consideration of the availability of specific relief, see Chapter 23.

vacant possession that would require a husband to commence litigation against his wife. Moreover, it appeared that if specific performance were granted and the transaction closed, the Wroths would be unable to evict Mrs. Tyler but they probably would be able to evict the husband and daughter. For Megarry J. this provided an additional reason for refusing a decree of specific performance. Accordingly, Megarry J. turned to consider the damages claim.

Megarry J. began his damages analysis by reciting the expectancy principle and observing that for the Wroths to be put in a position they would have been in if the contract had been performed, they would now require an additional fifty-five hundred pounds in order to acquire a substitute home. He accepted that the Wroths were without any additional financial means beyond the initial six thousand pounds purchase price with which to mitigate their loss by acquiring a substitute forthwith after the defendant's breach. Further, although the claim for specific performance failed, it was a proper claim that it was reasonable for the Wroths to pursue. If damages were to be calculated under the normal rule, however, and therefore calculated as of the date of breach, the Wroths would not be placed in as good a position as they would have been in if the contract had been performed. While fifteen hundred pounds would have enabled mitigation at the date of breach, that amount would be quite inadequate by the time of trial. Although Megarry J. suggested that the common law rule might not be so inflexible as to preclude valuation at the time of trial, he held that it was unnecessary to rely on the common law doctrine since this was a case in which damages were being awarded in lieu of specific performance and were therefore equitable in nature. Prior to the enactment of the *Chancery Amendment Act 1858*,[194] traditionally referred to as *Lord Cairns' Act*, a party who unsuccessfully sought specific performance in a court of equity could only pursue a damages claim by commencing a further action in a court of common law. *Lord Cairns' Act* provided, however, that a court competent to grant decrees of specific performance for an injunction is able "if it shall think fit, to award damages to the party injured, either in addition to or in substitution for such injunction or specific performance, and such damages may be assessed in such man-

---

194 (U.K.), 21 & 22 Vict. c. 27. Although the legislation was subsequently repealed, it was held by the House of Lords in a subsequent case that the jurisdiction to award damages in lieu persists nonetheless. See *Leeds Industrial Co-operative Society Ltd. v. Slack*, [1924] A.C. 851 (H.L.). The jurisdiction has typically been retained in legislation in the common law provinces. See, for example, *Courts of Justice Act*, R.S.O. 1990, c. C.43, s. 99.

ner as the court shall direct."[195] If damages were to be awarded that would truly be "in substitution for" a decree of specific performance, the damages calculation must be made, in Megarry J.'s view, as of the time of trial. Accordingly, the Wroths were awarded damages of fifty-five hundred pounds.

The consequence of Megarry J.'s holding that damages calculated at the time of trial could be awarded under *Lord Cairns' Act* left open the possibility that at common law a more rigid rule requiring measurement of damages at the time of breach would apply. Thus, the more flexible approach would be available only in a case in which the case was one in which it could be said that a court of equity would have had jurisdiction to grant a decree of specific performance or an injunction.[196] In *Johnson v. Agnew*,[197] however, the House of Lords held that the common law principles upon which damages are to be calculated are sufficiently flexible to accommodate the result in *Wroth v. Tyler*. Lord Wilberforce, having observed that the expectancy principle normally leads to an assessment of damages in a sale of goods case as of the date of breach went on to state that "this is not an absolute rule: if to follow it would give rise to injustice, the court has the power to fix such other date as may be appropriate in the circumstances."[198] Although the decision in *Wroth v. Tyler* was thus not overruled, the House of Lords did further indicate that *Lord Cairns' Act* did not facilitate an assessment of damages on principles other than those of the common law. Thus, both at common law and in equity, damages would normally be calculated as of the date of breach but where a purchaser of land reasonably attempts to seek specific performance of the contract, damages should be calculated as of the date when that attempt fails.[199] Canadian courts accepted and applied the decision in *Wroth v. Tyler*,[200] and the subsequent clarification of both the common law rule and the assessment of damages under *Lord Cairns' Act* set forth by the House of Lords in *Johnson v. Agnew*.[201]

---

195 *Ibid.*, s. 2.
196 For discussion of the jurisprudence examining the nature of this limitation on jurisdiction, see P.M. McDermott, *Equitable Damages* (Sydney: Butterworths, 1994) c. 4.
197 [1980] A.C. 367.
198 *Ibid.* at 401.
199 *Ibid.*
200 See, for example, *306793 Ontario Ltd. in Trust v. Rimes* (1979), 25 O.R. (2d) 79 (C.A.).
201 *Semelhago v. Paramadevan*, [1996] 2 S.C.R. 415. See also *Kinbauri Gold v. IAM-GOLD International African Mining Gold Corp.* (2004), 246 D.L.R. (4th) 595 (Ont. C.A.) (relevance of absence of market for shares at date of breach for date

H. INTANGIBLE INJURIES

Thus far, we have considered compensation for injuries to the economic interests of the victims of contract breach. A breach of contract may also cause intangible injuries of various kinds. The victim of a breach may, for example, suffer resulting annoyance, humiliation, distress or, indeed, serious psychological trauma. We here consider whether these sorts of intangible injuries may attract compensation. The position under traditional Canadian and English common law doctrine was that such damages were not available. In the latter part of the twentieth century, however, English and then Canadian courts recognized claims of this kind. The leading English case, *Jarvis v. Swans Tours Ltd.*,[202] is a classroom favourite in which a solicitor's high hopes for a pleasurable two-week Swiss vacation—fuelled by claims made in the defendant's brochure—were dashed when virtually all of the advertised virtues of the experience proved to be either non-existent or below par. The Court of Appeal awarded damages for the resulting mental aggravation. The nature of this case and subsequent authorities provided a basis for a conclusion that in English law, at least, such claims were restricted to contractual contexts in which the object of the agreement was to provide a pleasurable experience or, at least, to ensure one's peace of mind.[203] The House of Lords recently clarified the English doctrine on this point in *Farley v. Skinner.*[204] The plaintiff, a prospective purchaser of a country property, retained the defendant surveyor to inspect the property and, *inter alia,* asked him to investigate whether the property would be seriously affected by aircraft noise given its proximity to Gatwick International Airport. Reassured on the latter point by the defendant, the plaintiff acquired the property and, upon moving in,

---

of determining the market capitalization value of defendant—court divided—majority favours calculation of value as of date of breach).

202 [1973] Q.B. 233 (C.A.).

203 Thus, claims have been allowed against solicitors whose failure to provide service at a reasonable level of skill and care foreseeably caused mental distress to the client. See, for example, *Heywood v. Wellers*, [1976] Q.B. 446 (C.A.) (mishandled attempt on behalf of female client to restrain a man from molesting her); *Hamilton Jones v. David & Snape (a firm)*, [2004] 1 All E.R. 657 (Ch.) (negligent failure to prevent removal of client's children from jurisdiction). See also *P.A. Wournell Contracting Ltd. v. Allen* (1979), 100 D.L.R. (3d) 62 (N.S.S.C.T.D.), rev'd on other grounds (1980), 108 D.L.R. (3d) 723 (N.S.S.C.A.D.) (solicitor's failure to incorporate company); *Boudreau v. Benaiah* (2000), 182 D.L.R. (4th) 569 (Ont. C.A.) (negligent conduct of defence to criminal charges).

204 [2001] 4 All E.R. 801 (H.L.).

discovered that the defendant's advice on this point was seriously in error. The purchaser brought a claim for non-pecuniary damages for the loss of tranquility resulting from the substantial presence of aircraft noise on the property. The defendant argued in response that such damages could only be claimed where the very object of the contract is to provide pleasure, relaxation or peace of mind and that a contract with a surveyor to inspect a property does not come within that category of agreements. The House of Lords allowed the claim, however, on the basis that it was sufficient if "a major or important object of the contract is to give pleasure, relaxation or peace of mind."[205] Thus, in this case, where the contract to inspect included a particular undertaking concerning airplane noise that had such an object, damages for consequential mental distress were available.

In Canada, however, it is unlikely that even this limitation exists on the availability of damages for mental distress. Canadian courts have applied the *Jarvis* doctrine in cases in which the agreements breached cannot be characterized as providing for pleasure or peace of mind.[206] They have also accepted that the *Jarvis* doctrine may apply in the context of wrongful dismissal cases.[207] Recovery in the latter context, however, has been rendered problematic by the 1989 decision of the Supreme Court of Canada in *Vorvis v. Insurance Corp. of British Columbia*,[208] or, rather, by subsequent interpretations of the majority reasoning in *Vorvis*. In this case, the plaintiff lawyer had been abruptly terminated by his employer, a government automobile insurance plan, without cause and without reasonable notice. Prior to the dismissal, his supervisor, who considered the plaintiff to be conscientious to a fault, engaged in detailed and, perhaps, heavy-handed supervision of

---

205 *Ibid.* at 812.

206 See, for example, *Zuker v. Paul* (1982), 135 D.L.R. (3d) 481 (Ont. Div. Ct.) (breach of warranty of title to automobile); *Taylor v. Gill*, [1991] 3 W.W.R. 727 (Alta. Q.B.) (non-completion of sale of residential premises); *Gourlay v. Osmond* (1991), 19 R.P.R. (2d) 59 (N.S.S.C.T.D.) (non-completion of purchase of residential premises); *Kempling v. Hearthstone Manor Corp.* (1996), 137 D.L.R. (4th) 12 (Alta. C.A.) (non-completion of sale of condominium unit).

207 See, for example, *Brown v. Waterloo Regional Board of Commissioners of Police*, above note 38 (Ont. C.A.). And see *Kopij v. Metropolitan Toronto (Municipality)* (1996), 29 O.R. (3d) 752 (Gen. Div.). Further, in *Wallace v. United Grain Growers Ltd.*, [1997] 3 S.C.R. 701, a majority of the Supreme Court accepted that even though contracts of employment are not peace of mind contracts, foreseeable mental distress is compensable, provided that it results from "an independent actionable wrong." See *ibid.* at 734, Iacobucci J. With respect to the latter requirement, see further, the discussion below in this Chapter, this section.

208 [1989] 1 S.C.R. 1085.

the plaintiff's work. In addition to the claim for wages that would have been earned during a reasonable notice period, the plaintiff sought aggravated and punitive damages. The term, "aggravated" damages, the Court opined, should be reserved for compensation for intangible injuries. In the Court's view, although aggravated damages can be awarded for a breach of contract, it would have been inappropriate to do so on the fact of *Vorvis*. The plaintiff's claim for aggravated damages was for the mental distress suffered by the plaintiff as a result of the defendant's conduct. With respect to this claim, McIntyre J., on behalf of a majority of the Court, emphasized that it was necessary to find that the mental injury resulted from an independently actionable wrong. The purport of the opinion in this respect is simply to suggest that where the mental injury results from employer behaviour preceding the wrongful dismissal, it is necessary to show that the employer's behaviour is itself actionable. In dissent, Wilson J. stated more directly that the governing Canadian principle is to the effect that "aggravated damages for mental suffering may be awarded in breach of contract cases .... [where] the parties should reasonably have foreseen mental suffering as a consequence of a breach of the contract at the time the contract was entered into." On this view, presumably, the English requirement that the contract contain at least an aspect of which is designed to provide pleasure or peace of mind is considered to be simply a proxy for the reasonable foreseeability test. Accordingly, there is no compelling reason not to simply apply the foreseeability test itself. Although a peace of mind contract thus might be the typical case where mental distress is a foreseeable outcome of breach, it is not the only situation in which mental distress is foreseeable. Thus, for example, where the defendant knew or ought to have known that the plaintiff suffered from a mental condition making mental distress a foreseeable outcome of breach, damages for such distress are recoverable.[209] In *Vorvis*, Wilson J. appears to have accepted that the manner of wrongfully dismissing an employee might give rise to a claim of this kind.[210] The majority did not clearly consider this question, having determined that the employer conduct that *preceded* the wrongful dismissal itself did not breach a duty owed to the plaintiff.

As far as a claim for damages for mental distress resulting from the manner of a wrongful dismissal is concerned, the *Vorvis* doctrine appears to provide a basis for reconsidering the traditional position of English common law that no compensation is available for injured

---

209 *Turczinski v. Dupont Heating & Air Conditioning Ltd.,* above note 186 at 105.
210 Above note 208 at 1118.

feelings resulting from wrongful termination of a contract of employ-ment.[211] Under *Vorvis*, such injuries should be compensable, provided that they are reasonably foreseeable at the time of contracting. Subse-quent interpretations of the *Vorvis* decision, however, have created a point of difficulty. It now appears to be generally accepted by Canadian courts that damages for mental distress cannot be awarded in this con-text unless there exists an independent and actionable wrong in addi-tion to the wrongful dismissal.[212] The reason why a separate actionable wrong was thought to be required by MacIntyre J. in *Vorvis*, as he at-tempted to explain, was that the failure to give reasonable notice that constituted the breach in that case was not in fact the conduct that caused the plaintiff's intangible injuries. The allegedly wrongful act in *Vorvis* was not the manner of giving insufficient notice but, rather, the careful supervision or, from the employee's perspective, the harass-ment that preceded his dismissal. McIntyre J.'s point, then, was that the conduct complained of must itself constitute a breach of a contractual or tortious duty. He did not plainly hold either that compensable ag-gravated damages could never arise from a wrongful dismissal or that the existence of a second wrong in addition to the wrongful dismissal was an indispensable prerequisite to success. To be sure, it may well have been his view that the manner of communicating a wrongful dis-missal is unlikely to cause intangible injuries, but McIntyre J. did not absolutely preclude this possibility. By misinterpretation, it seems, of McIntyre J.'s remarks in *Vorvis*, the law of wrongful dismissal has thus arrived at an unsatisfactory state in Canadian law.[213] If the apparent inability of Canadian courts to award damages for mental distress re-

---

211 *Addis v. Gramophone Co. Ltd.*, [1909] A.C. 488 (H.L.). This remains the position in English law. The enactment of legislation providing statutory remedies for dismissal that does not include compensatory damages for injured feelings has been held to constitute a barrier to reform of the law on this point as a matter of common law. See *Johnson v. Unisys Ltd.*, [2003] 1 A.C. 518 (H.L.); *Dunnachie v. Kingston-upon-Hull City Council*, [2004] 3 All E.R. 1011 (H.L.), rev'g [2004] 2 All E.R. 501 (C.A.). See also *Eastwood v. Magnox Electric plc*, [2004] 3 All E.R. 991 (H.L.) (financial loss resulting from psychiatric or other illness caused by unfair treatment prior to the wrongful dismissal held compensable).

212 See *Wurster v. Universal Environmental Services Inc.* (1998), 167 D.L.R. (4th) 166 (Ont. C.A.); *Noseworthy v. Riverside Pontiac-Buick Ltd.* (1998), 168 D.L.R. (4th) 629 (Ont. C.A.).

213 See further *Whiten v. Pilot Insurance Co.*, above note 5 (discussing the exist-ence of the requirement in a claim for punitive damages). Nothing in the *Pilot Insurance* decision, however, appears to resolve the difficulty. It unhelpfully preserves the independent actionable wrong requirement required for punitive damages and offers no guidance with respect to damages for mental distress.

lating to the manner in which the decision to dismiss is communicated is considered problematic, the most coherent solution to the problem would be, as McLachlin J. suggested in her dissenting opinion in *Wallace v. United Grain Growers Ltd.*,[214] to imply a term not to engage in bad-faith conduct in the course of dismissing an employee. The breach of such a term could give rise to a claim for damages for mental distress. As we have seen,[215] however, the majority in *Wallace* rejected this approach and favoured the surprising view that where a dismissal is conducted in a bad-faith manner, the period of reasonable notice may be extended. The extension of the notice period, for the *Wallace* majority, is intended to achieve compensation for "humiliation, embarrassment, and damage to one's self-worth and self-esteem,"[216] but where the bad-faith conduct "affects employment prospects [it] may be worthy of considerably more compensation than that which does not."[217] By this rather complex and indirect route, then, the Supreme Court has, in effect, achieved a form of compensation for intangible injuries resulting from the manner of a wrongful dismissal.

I. PUNITIVE DAMAGES

As a matter of general principle, damages for breach of contract or tort are compensatory in nature. Common law courts, however, have also assumed a jurisdiction to award "exemplary" or "punitive" damages in some kinds of civil cases. The imposition of such damages is a rare phenomenon and is typically imposed only in the context of certain types of tort claims. The anomalous nature of punitive or exemplary damage awards in civil cases has often been the subject of comment in the decisions of courts within the British Commonwealth. Thus, in the leading opinion of the decision of the House of Lords in *Rookes v. Barnard*,[218] Lord Devlin observed that their recognition, which he favoured to a limited degree, involved "admitting into the civil law a principle which ought logically to belong to the criminal."[219] The lack of procedural safeguards normally associated with punishment, the enrichment

---

214 Above note 207.
215 For discussion of this aspect of the *Wallace* decision, see Chapter 21, section C.
216 Above note 207 at 745.
217 *Ibid.* at 746.
218 [1964] A.C. 1129 (H.L.). See also *Kuddus v. Chief Constable of Leicestershire Constabulary*, [2002] 2 A.C. 122 (H.L.).
219 *Rookes v. Barnard, ibid.* at 1226.

of the plaintiff rather than the state by the imposition of a civil fine and the inherent difficulty of quantifying such awards with resulting doctrinal uncertainty have conspired, in the English tradition at least, to justify caution and restraint in the making of such awards. Indeed, in *Rookes v. Barnard* itself, the English law of punitive damages approached the brink of extinction. Such awards were preserved in that case for application only in tort law and essentially in only two types of cases; first, claims arising from oppressive, arbitrary or unconstitutional acts of public servants or as Lord Devlin described it, "the arbitrary and outrageous use of executive power"[220] and second, those in which the defendant's conduct was calculated to make a profit that exceeds the compensation available to the plaintiff. Until quite recently, the rules set forth in *Rookes v. Barnard* settled the boundaries for punitive damage awards in English law.

At the same time, however, some support for the making of such awards can be found. Lord Devlin himself expressed the view that punitive damage awards played a very useful role in the two categories of cases identified in *Rookes v. Barnard*. Further, the restriction of English awards to these two categories of cases has attracted criticism over the years. More particularly, the English Law Commission, in its report, *Aggravated, Exemplary and Restitutionary Damages*,[221] recommended a much broader potential availability of such awards in the context of tort law and in claims arising from equitable wrongdoing. Even for such enthusiasts, however, the extension of damage awards into the context of claims for damages for breach of contract, where no tort has been committed, have typically been considered to be beyond the pale. Thus, the Law Commission itself recommended against extending awards of punitive damages into the contractual context. A number of reasons were offered in support of this recommendation. Thus, "a contract is a private arrangement in which parties negotiate rights and duties, whereas the duties which obtain under the law of tort, are imposed by law; it can accordingly be argued that the notion of state punishment is more readily applicable to the latter than

---

220 *Ibid.* at 1223. And see *Cassell & Co. Ltd. v. Broome*, [1972] A.C. 1027 at 1077–78 (H.L.) (doctrine also applies to police and other local authorities applying rights of search or arrest without warrant).

221 U.K., Law Commission, *Aggravated, Exemplary and Restitutionary Damages* (Law Com.; no. 247) (London: HMSO, 1997). For a critical assessment, see P. Jaffey, "The Law Commission Report on Aggravated, Exemplary and Restitutionary Damages" (1998) 61 Mod. L. Rev. 860. See also Ontario Law Reform Commission, *Report on Exemplary Damages* (Toronto: The Commission, 1991).

to the former."[222] It was further argued that "the need for certainty" is perceived to be greater in relation to contract than tort, thus rendering the discretionary features of exemplary damage awards unattractive. The commission noted that exemplary damages have never been awarded for breach of contract in the past, that the awarding of exemplary damages would tend to discourage efficient breach of contract[223] and that contract, unlike tort law, typically involves pecuniary rather than non-pecuniary losses with respect to which exemplary awards are less appropriate. Other considerations may be thought to weigh against punitive damages in contract. It can be argued that, to the extent that punitive damage awards punish defendants who have inflicted anxiety and other mental suffering on plaintiffs, such injuries can be more directly and appropriately addressed by awards of compensatory damages relating to such injuries.[224]

It is well-established Canadian law that punitive damages are not narrowly restricted to the two categories of tort claims identified by the House of Lords in *Rookes v. Barnard.*[225] Punitive damages are considered to be generally available in the context of tort claims where the conduct is "deserving of punishment because of its harsh, vindictive, reprehensible and malicious nature."[226] More particularly, punitive damages may be awarded for negligence, provided that the negligence exhibits a degree of callousness that warrants such an award. In the leading case, *Robitaille v. Vancouver Hockey Club,*[227] the plaintiff was a professional hockey player who suffered a serious spinal injury that was misdiagnosed by the defendant team's physician. After an initial injury, Robitaille's request for medical treatment was ignored, his continuing complaints concerning symptoms were considered to be unfounded and he was pressured by the team's management to continue playing by threats of suspension. In a subsequent game, Robitaille was further injured and suffered a permanent and disabling spinal cord in-

---

222 *Ibid.*, s. 5.72.

223 For description of the efficient breach concept, see above this Chapter, section C.

224 Farnsworth reports that American courts also exhibit a reluctance to grant awards of punitive damages in the context of pure contractual breach and explains this phenomenon on the basis that damages for breach of contract are essentially compensatory in nature. See E.A. Farnsworth, *Contracts*, 2d ed., vol. III (New York: Aspen Law & Business, 1998) at 192–96.

225 Above note 218.

226 *Vorvis v. Insurance Corp. of British Columbia*, above note 208 at 1108, McIntyre J.

227 (1981), 124 D.L.R. (3d) 228 (B.C.C.A.). See also *A v. Bottrill*, [2003] 1 A.C. 449 (P.C.) (negligent medical advice).

jury. The British Columbia Court of Appeal upheld an award of punitive damages at trial on the basis that the negligence of the defendants
was "such as to merit condemnation."[228] Although the test for the availability of punitive damages in a tort context has been variously stated,
the Supreme Court emphasized in *Norberg v. Wynrib*[229] that it is not
necessary to meet the threshold of "harsh, vindictive or malicious"
conduct suggested in *Vorvis*[230] but it was sufficient to establish that the
conduct was "reprehensible and it was of a type to offend the ordinary
standards of decent conduct in the community."[231] As *Robitaille* itself
illustrates, punitive damages have been awarded for breach of contract
where the breach of contract also constitutes a tort. In recent years,
however, the awarding of punitive damages for non-tortious or pure
breaches of contract received the blessing of the Supreme Court of Canada. This development was reaffirmed in the decision of the Supreme
Court in *Whiten v. Pilot Insurance Co.*[232]

The Canadian embrace of punitive damages for pure breach of contract arose in the context of wrongful dismissal cases and, more particularly, in the context of dismissal coupled with with an imputation of
wrongdoing. In a contract of employment of indefinite duration, there
is an implied term requiring the employer to give reasonable notice to
the employee of an impending dismissal. Thus, in the typical wrongful
dismissal case, the employee who has not received reasonable notice
sues for damages for breach of that implied term. Where the wrongful
dismissal is accompanied with false allegations of employee misconduct or other forms of harassment, it may be considered whether additional damages may be awarded to an employee who claims to have
been injured by conduct of this kind. The traditional response of English law, followed until recent years in common law Canada, was that
no such damages claim was available on a breach of contract theory.
In the 1909 decision in *Addis v. Gramophone Co. Ltd.*,[233] the House of
Lords held that, in a wrongful dismissal claim, no compensation can be
awarded for the manner of dismissal. To the extent that the employee

---

228 *Robitaille v. Vancouver Hockey Club, ibid.* at 251.
229 [1992] 2 S.C.R. 226.
230 Above note 208.
231 Above note 229 at 268.
232 Above note 5. For discussion, see J.D. McCamus, "Prometheus Bound or Loose
Cannon? Punitive Damages for Pure Breach of Contract" (2004) 41 San Diego
L. Rev. 1491; J. Swan, "Punitive Damages for Breach of Contract: A Remedy in
Search of a Justification" (2004) 29 Queen's L.J. 596.
233 [1909] A.C. 488 (H.L.). And see *Johnson v. Unisys Ltd.*, above note 211; *Eastwood
v. Magnox Electric plc*, above note 211.

had suffered injuries as a result of, for example, defamation, the employee should be left to whatever tort remedies might be available.

The novel idea that punitive damages might be awarded in the wrongful dismissal context was taken up by the Supreme Court of Canada in *Vorvis v. Insurance Corp. of British Columbia*[234] in 1989. On this occasion, the Court offered the view that although such an award would be inappropriate on the facts of that case, punitive damages could indeed be awarded in the context of a claim for damages for breach of contract. The Supreme Court majority acknowledged the anomalous or "peculiar" nature of punitive damages awarded "in the absence of the procedural protections for the defendant [which are] always present in criminal trials where punishment is ordinarily awarded."[235] Nonetheless, the Court held that "while it may be very unusual to do so, punitive damages may be awarded in cases of breach of contract."[236] For such an award to be appropriate, the conduct of the defaulting party must be "of such a nature as to be deserving of punishment because of its harsh, vindictive, reprehensible and malicious nature."[237] Again, "the conduct must be extreme in its nature and such that by any reasonable standard it is deserving of full condemnation and punishment."[238] On the facts of the case, the wrongful dismissal had been preceded by a period of aggressive supervision perpetrated by the plaintiff's supervisor. Although it was true that the supervisor had treated the plaintiff "in a most offensive manner"[239] the conduct was not of such a nature as to justify an award of punitive damages.

For the majority, McIntyre J. indicated an awareness of the problematic aspects of extending awards of punitive damages from their then-existing home of tort actions to cases of breach of contract. In a tort case, the defendant is "under a legal duty to use care not to injure his neighbour, and the neighbour has in law a right not to be so injured and an additional right to compensation where injury occurs."[240] On the other hand, "[i]n an action based on a breach of contract, the only link between the parties for the purpose of defining their rights and

---

234 Above note 208, the facts of which are briefly described above in the text at note 206. For an earlier suggestion to this effect, see *Brown v. Waterloo Regional Board of Commissioners of Police*, above note 38 (Ont. H.C.J.), Linden J., var'd 150 D.L.R. (3d) 729 (Ont. C.A.).

235 *Vorvis v. Insurance Corp. of British Columbia, ibid.* at 1104.

236 *Ibid.* at 1107.

237 *Ibid.* at 1108.

238 *Ibid.*

239 *Ibid.* at 1107.

240 *Ibid.*

884 THE LAW OF CONTRACTS

obligations is the contract. Where the defendant has breached the contract, the remedies open to the plaintiff must arise from the contractual relationship, that 'private law,' which the parties agreed to accept."[241] In the view of McIntyre J., however, the distinction between the nature of tortious liability and liability for breach of contract did not provide a reason to refuse to extend punitive damages into the latter context. Rather, it served as a basis for surmising that an award of punitive damages will be "very rare in contract cases."[242] Beyond this suggestion that the difference between the two forms of liability does not preclude the awarding of punitive damages in the contractual context, the Court offered no reasoned explanation for the proposition that punitive damages should be extended into the purely contractual arena. Presumably, the Court felt that it was necessary or desirable to do so in order to provide a disincentive for conduct that, although "harsh, vindictive, reprehensible and malicious," is not tortious in nature.

The reason offered by McIntyre J. for declining to award punitive damages on the facts of *Vorvis*, though clearly expressed and quite defensible, has created a trail of confusion in subsequent cases. McIntyre J. was of the view that the heavy-handed supervision exercised by the plaintiff's supervisor was not "sufficiently offensive, standing alone, to constitute actionable wrong."[243] McIntyre J. indicated that the only basis for the imposition of punishment "must be a finding of the commission of an actionable wrong which caused the injury complained of by the plaintiff."[244] Such an approach, he noted,[245] was consistent with the American rule that awarded punitive damages in a contract case only when the breach of contract also constituted a tort for which punitive damages would be recoverable. The heavy-handed supervision engaged in by the supervisor appeared to be neither tortious nor a breach of any term of the contract of employment. More particularly, it appears to have been McIntyre J.'s view that this conduct did not constitute a breach of the term requiring the employer to give reasonable notice of termination. This reasoning appears unexceptionable. McIntyre J. was

---

241 *Ibid.*

242 *Ibid.*

243 *Ibid.* at 1110. The result could be otherwise if a campaign of harassment of an employee itself amounted to constructive dismissal. For a decision allowing recovery for intangible losses of this kind under the applicable provision (s. 123) of the *Employment Rights Act 1996*, see *Dunnachie v. Kingston-upon-Hull City Council*, above note 211 (C.A.).

244 *Vorvis v. Insurance Corp. of British Columbia, ibid.* at 1106.

245 *Ibid.*, referring to American Law Institute, *Restatement of Contracts 2d* (St. Paul: American Law Institute, 1981) s. 355.

simply reiterating the proposition that in the absence of a breach of a duty of some kind, punitive damages cannot be awarded. In subsequent cases, however, it has been assumed by courts, including the Supreme Court of Canada, that McIntyre J. simply precluded the possibility that punitive damages could ever be awarded for the offensive manner in which a notice of dismissal is effected. Further, later courts have struggled with the notion of whether an award of punitive damages is permissible, then, only where there exists an independent "actionable wrong" other than the principal breach of contract with respect to which damages are claimed. The answer to this question, surely, should be that if the principal breach of contract in issue is sufficiently offensive in nature, the holding in *Vorvis* suggests that punitive damages would be available, notwithstanding the absence of any additional breach of duty, whether tortious or contractual. The problem, as McIntyre J. saw it in *Vorvis*, was that the allegations of offensive conduct related to the manner of supervision prior to dismissal rather than to the manner in which the requirement of reasonable notice was breached by the employer. While it may be difficult to imagine circumstances where the manner of giving unreasonable notice is so offensive as to warrant an award of punitive damages, nothing in the reasoning of McIntyre J. in *Vorvis* precludes this possibility.

Wilson J., dissenting on this point, would have awarded punitive damages. Wilson J. disagreed with what she characterized as McIntyre J.'s view that "punitive damages" can only be awarded when the misconduct is in itself an "actionable wrong."[246] Rather, in her view, "the correct approach is to assess the conduct in the context of all the circumstances and determine whether it is deserving of punishment because of its shockingly harsh, vindictive, reprehensible or malicious nature."[247] On the present facts, the employer had engaged in "reprehensible conduct … towards a sensitive, dedicated and conscientious employee. The appellant was harassed and humiliated and, …. ultimately dismissed for no cause after a sustained period of such treatment."[248] Thus, Wilson J. appears to have suggested that even in the absence of a breach of duty, whether tortious or contractual, punitive damages may be awarded. Another plausible interpretation of her view, however, is that the humiliating nature of the notice of dismissal renders the breach of the requirement to give reasonable notice a sufficiently offensive character to attract an award of punitive damages. To this in-

---

246 Above note 208 at 1130.
247 *Ibid.*
248 *Ibid.* at 1130–31.

886   THE LAW OF CONTRACTS

terpretation of Wilson J.'s views, however, one might object that a clear distinction was not drawn by Wilson J. between the conduct leading up to the decision to dismiss and the manner of the dismissal itself, a distinction that is implicit in the reasoning of McIntyre J. and that does appear to ground his decision.

Subsequently, Canadian courts have taken the view that the decision in *Vorvis* does require that in addition to finding that a principal breach of contract sounding in damages has occurred, one must find, in order to grant an award of punitive damages, that the offensive conduct constitutes a separate actionable wrong in the form of either tortious misconduct or an additional breach of contract.[249] Indeed, in the particular context of wrongful dismissal, the Supreme Court of Canada has taken the view that punitive damages cannot be awarded with respect to an offensive manner of giving notice of termination on the theory that punitive damages can only be awarded where there is, in addition to the failure to give reasonable notice, a separate actionable wrong. In *Wallace v. United Grain Growers Ltd.*,[250] this view was affirmed. The Court went on to hold, however, that an employer who engages in "callous and insensitive treatment"[251] in dismissing an employee, though not liable for punitive damages, may attract liability in the form of an extension of the period of required reasonable notice. This is so, in the Court's view, even though the misconduct cannot be held to be a breach of an implied term to dismiss only in good faith. Such a term, in the majority's view, should not be implied into the contract of employment as it would constitute an undesirable fetter on the employer's capacity to dismiss without cause and upon reasonable notice. Thus, in the wrongful dismissal context at least, the Court has adopted the rather surprising position that even in the absence of a breach of duty, be it tortious or contractual, compensation can be awarded. In a vigorous dissent, McLachlin J. suggested that a clearer

---

249 See, for example, *Marshall v. Watson Wyatt & Co.* (2002), 209 D.L.R. (4th) 411 (Ont. C.A.); *Schimp v. RCR Catering Ltd.* (2004), 236 D.L.R. (4th) 461 (N.S.C.A.). In New Brunswick, however, this confusion has been cleared up by legislation providing that "in a claim for aggravated, exemplary or punitive damages, it is not necessary that the matter in respect of which those damages are claimed be an actionable wrong independent of the alleged wrong for which the proceedings are brought. See *Law Reform Act*, S.N.B. 1993, c. L-1.2, s. 3.

250 Above note 207.

251 *Ibid.* at 740. Iacobucci J. further characterized such conduct as "bad faith conduct in the manner of dismissal" and offered as illustrations thereof, "conduct that is unfair or is in bad faith by being, for example, untruthful, misleading or unduly insensitive." See *ibid.* at 740 and 743.

and sounder approach would be to hold that a term is to be implied in the contract of employment that the employer must not engage in such conduct, breach of which could thus clearly and directly lead to an award of damages, including potentially, punitive damages.

To some extent, these difficulties arise from a failure to draw a clear distinction between the manner in which the decision to dismiss is reached as opposed to the manner of the dismissal itself. The approach advocated by McLachlin J. in dissent avoids the confusion that results from this deficiency by implying a term imposing obligations of good faith conduct relating to the dismissal of an employee.[252] Calculation of the notice period, for McLachlin J., then, can be and should be restricted to an assessment of those factors, including the manner of dismissal, that may have an impact on the "difficulty of finding replacement employment."[253] In the majority view, however, the Canadian law of wrongful dismissal appears now to have reached the position where punitive damages relating to the manner of dismissal are not available but, curiously, an employer who behaves in a "callous and insensitive" manner relating to the dismissal of an employee is vulnerable to an extension of the period of reasonable notice even though the conduct in question may not, in itself, constitute a breach of either tortious or contractual duties.[254]

Putting to one side the unsatisfactory complexities of current Canadian law on wrongful dismissal, it was clearly established, as a result of the decision in *Vorvis*, that punitive damages had become potentially available in Canadian law for breach of contract. It was only in the later decision in *Whiten v. Pilot Insurance Co.*,[255] however, that the Supreme Court of Canada actually approved an award of this kind. In this case, the Court upheld an award of one million dollars in punitive damages against a defendant insurer who had breached its implied contractual

---

252 See *ibid.* at 762, placing reliance on academic commentary supporting the recognition of an implied term of this kind. See, for example, R.B. Schai, "Aggravated Damages and the Employment Contract" (1991) 55 Sask. L. Rev. 345; G. England, "Recent Developments in the Law of the Employment Contract, Continuing Tension between the Rights Paradigm and the Efficiency Paradigm" (1995) 20 Queen's L.J. 557.

253 *Ibid.* at 751.

254 In the wake of *Wallace*, several Canadian courts have awarded damages calculated on the basis of an extended notice period in order to reflect harsh treatment in the manner of dismissal. See, for example, *Cassady v. Wyeth-Ayerst Canada Inc.* (1998), 163 D.L.R. (4th) 1 (B.C.C.A.); *Montague v. Bank of Nova Scotia* (2004), 69 O.R. (3d) 87 (C.A.).

255 Above note 5.

duty to handle claims by an insured in such fashion as to meet a standard of good faith and fair dealing. The defendant had conceded that it had breached this duty on the facts of this case. The facts were propitious for a punitive damages claim. The claimant's home had been destroyed by an accidental fire. The claim under her insurance policy with the defendant was met with scepticism and, ultimately, indefensibly harsh treatment. Indeed, over advice to the contrary of an independent insurance adjuster, the insurance industry's "Crime Prevention Bureau," the fire department and an engineering expert and a firefighter, the last two of whom it had retained, the defendant insurer persisted in the theory that the fire resulted from an act of arson committed by the plaintiff and her husband. Acting on this theory, the insurer terminated interim payments to the claimant, knowing full well that she and her husband were in precarious financial circumstances, in an apparent attempt to coerce an unfairly low settlement amount. Further, the defendant forced the claimant to litigate her claim at an estimated cost of three hundred and twenty thousand dollars. At trial, the jury awarded approximately three hundred and twenty-five thousand dollars in compensatory damages and an additional amount of one million dollars as punitive damages. In the Ontario Court of Appeal, the punitive damage award was reduced to one hundred thousand dollars, though one dissenting member of the panel would have dismissed the appeal.

On further appeal to the Supreme Court of Canada, however, the jury award was restored. Characterizing the conduct of the defendant insurer as that of having "behaved abominably"[256] the Court had no difficulty in finding that the defendant had behaved in a "malicious, oppressive and high-handed manner that 'offends the court's sense of decency.'"[257] On this occasion, however, the Court engaged in an extended analysis of the history and purposes of the awarding of punitive damages. This led the Court to offer a series of conclusions concerning the general nature and role of the punitive damages award. On behalf of the majority, Binnie J. stated: "[p]unishment is a legitimate objective not only of the criminal law but of the civil law"[258] and that punitive damages "serve a need that is not met by either the pure civil law or the pure criminal law."[259] Thus, in the present case, no one other than the claimant could be rationally expected to invest three hun-

---

256   *Ibid.* at para 37.
257   *Ibid.* at para. 36, quoting from the Court's previous decision in *Hill v. Church of Scientology of Toronto*, [1995] 2 S.C.R. 1130 at para. 196.
258   *Ibid.* at para. 37.
259   *Ibid.*

dred and twenty thousand dollars of costs in the attempt to prove that the defendant had acted in bad faith. An award that undoubtedly over-compensates the plaintiff is given "in exchange for this socially useful service."[260] After a lengthy survey of developments in England, Australia, New Zealand, Ireland and the United States, Binnie J. concluded that the English attempt to limit punitive damages by "categories" did not work and had been rightly rejected by Canadian courts.[261] Further, he indicated that there exists a "substantial consensus"[262] that the general objectives served by punitive damages are retribution, deterrence of the wrongdoer and others and denunciation. Third, while conceding that the primary vehicle of punishment is the criminal law and that successful prosecution has in some jurisdictions been held to preclude punitive damages, it was Binnie J.'s view that prior punishment of the defendant for the misconduct in issue should be considered to be merely another factor to be considered in making an award of punitive damages, "albeit a factor of potentially great importance."[263] Further, Binnie J. expressed the view that the incantation of "time-honoured pejoratives, ('high-handed,' 'oppressive,' 'vindictive,' etc.) provides insufficient guidance."[264] In formulating more satisfactory guidance, emphasis was to be placed, in his view, on the need to promote rationality, proportionality and sensitivity to the particular circumstances of the case in making such awards. Finally, he suggested that it may be rational to employ a punitive damages award to relieve a wrongdoer of its profit. Binnie J. returned to a number of these themes in attempting to fashion a set of control mechanisms that are intended to preclude the making of excessive punitive damages awards.

While the majority's analysis admirably set the stage for the attempt to craft limitations on the granting of punitive damages, less analytical rigour was applied to the question of whether punitive damage awards ought to be extended beyond tort to the context of pure contractual breach. On this point, the majority essentially adopted the view that this matter had been settled by the Court previously in the *Vorvis* case. Unfortunately, however, the Court perpetuated the notion that had plagued reasoning in the lower courts after *Vorvis* that such awards could be made only if the offensive conduct constituted a separate "actionable wrong." The Court backed into this difficulty by asking

---

260 *Ibid.*
261 *Ibid.* at para. 67.
262 *Ibid.* at para. 68.
263 *Ibid.* at para. 69.
264 *Ibid.* at para. 70.

whether breach of contract, rather than tort, could constitute such a separate actionable wrong. In answering this question, the majority placed emphasis on the fact that McIntyre J. chose to use the expression "actionable wrong"[265] rather than the term "tort" that is employed in the American *Restatement of Contracts 2d.*[266] Further, it was noted that the possibility of punitive damages for breach of contract appeared to have been conceded by the Court in a subsequent case.[267] Third, it was suggested that "the requirement of an independent tort would unnecessarily complicate the pleadings, without in most cases adding anything of substance."[268] The majority's survey of comparative experience did not observe that in the jurisdictions in question, punitive damages, even in the United States, is not typically awarded in pure breach of contract claims. The recent recommendation of the English Law Commission[269] to the effect that exemplary or punitive damages ought not to be awarded in the context of contractual breach was not referred to nor was any response offered to the arguments made by the commission in support of that recommendation.

In order to grant an award for punitive damages on the facts of *Pilot Insurance*, then, it would be necessary to find that, in addition to the breach of contract constituted by the failure to pay the claim, a further independent actionable wrong, whether a tort or a breach of contract, also occurred. This requirement was met on the facts of *Pilot Insurance*, in the Court's view, by virtue of the fact that the defendant's abominable behaviour constituted a breach of the insurer's implied duty of good faith and fair dealing that requires the insurer to process claims in a prompt and fair manner.[270] No explanation was given for the proposition that although one single breach of duty suffices for punitive damages in a tort context, punitive damages in contract require two breaches of duty. Indeed, it appears that no coherent justification can be offered for the latter requirement. It thus appears likely that, in

---

265 *Ibid.* at para. 80.

266 Above note 245, s. 355.

267 Above note 5 at para. 81, referring to *Royal Bank of Canada v. W. Got & Associates Electric Ltd.*, [1999] 3 S.C.R. 408 at para. 26.

268 *Ibid.* at para. 82.

269 Above note 221.

270 See *Fidler v. Sun Life Assurance Co. of Canada* (2004), 239 D.L.R. (4th) 547 (B.C.C.A.), applying *Whiten* on this point. See also *Princeton Light & Power Co. v. MacDonald* (2005), 254 D.L.R. (4th) 431 (B.C.C.A.) (imposing a similar duty on an electrical utility because of its practical monopoly on the supply of a commodity of fundamental importance to the public—punitive damages awarded for utility's unreasonable treatment of customer).

due course, Canadian appellate courts, including the Supreme Court of Canada, will come to the conclusion, in an appropriate case, that the circumstances of a single breach of contract could be such as to give rise to an appropriate award of punitive damages.

An important feature of the decision in *Pilot Insurance* is an extensive set of guidelines set out by the Court for both trial judges and appellate courts designed to rein in and control the potential for excessive punitive damage awards. Essentially, three different types of guidelines were identified. First, the Court sought to structure the trial judge's charge to the jury in a fashion that would caution, if not ensure, restraint in the making of such awards.[271] Second, the Court indicated that the level of scrutiny exercised by appellate courts in reviewing such awards was to be at a higher level than that normally exercised in supervising damage awards. Third, the Court crafted an extensive set of guidelines setting a standard of "rationality" that must be met by punitive damage awards.

In general terms, Binnie J. suggested that the jury charge should not leave the jurors "to guess what their role and function is."[272] To that end, in his view, it would be helpful if the jury charge placed emphasis on a number of points. First, the exceptional nature of punitive damages should be stressed, placing emphasis on the usual string of pejoratives identifying conduct that "departs to a marked degree from ordinary standards of decent behaviour."[273] The jury should be advised that damages are to be assessed in an amount "reasonably proportionate to such factors as the harm caused, the degree of the misconduct, the relative vulnerability of the plaintiff and any advantage or profit gained by the defendant."[274] As well, it should be explained to the jury that the purpose of punitive damages is not compensation but rather to give the defendant his or her just dessert, to deter the defendant and others from similar misconduct in the future and to mark the community's collective condemnation of what has happened. Punitive damages

---

271 For an account of experimental studies offering discouraging evidence of the ability and/or willingness of juries to follow even rather precise instructions on how to calculate punitive damages, see W.K. Viscusi, "Punitive Damages: How Jurors Fail to Promote Efficiency" (2002) 39 Harv. J. on Legis. 139. See also R. Sunstein, D. Kahneman and D. Schkade, "Assessing Punitive Damages" (with Notes on Cognition and Valuation in Law) (1998) 107 Yale L.J. 2071; D. Schkade, "Erratic by Design: A Task Analysis of Punitive Damages Assessment" (2002) 39 Harv. J. on Legis. 121.

272 Above note 5 at para. 93.

273 *Ibid.* at para. 94.

274 *Ibid.*

are to be awarded only where compensatory damages are inadequate to accomplish these purposes and only in an amount that is no greater than necessary to accomplish their purpose rationally. The jury also should be plainly told that the plaintiff will keep the punitive damages as a "windfall"[275] in addition to compensatory damages and that judges and juries in our system of law have usually found that "moderate awards ... are generally sufficient."[276] The jury should be advised to have regard to other fines or penalties suffered by the defendant and to award punitive damages only where the misconduct would be otherwise unpunished or inadequately punished. Although Binnie J. concluded by indicating that the use of any particular expression was not obligatory, it was nonetheless incumbent on the trial judge to "emphasize the nature, scope and exceptional nature of the remedy, and fairness to both sides."[277]

In exercising supervision over awards of punitive damages, the role of appellate courts was envisaged by the *Pilot Insurance* majority to be a more muscular one than is exercised with respect to general damage awards. With respect to the latter, courts may only intervene if the award is "so exorbitant or so grossly out of proportion [to the injury] as to shock the court's conscience and sense of justice."[278] In the context of punitive damages, however, Binnie J. indicated that the emphasis must be on the appellate court's obligation to ensure that the award is the product of reason and rationality. In his view, "[t]he focus is on whether the Court's sense of reason is offended rather than on whether its conscience is shocked."[279] The applicable standard of review—"rationality"—was spelled out in great detail by Binnie J. in an attempt to set a standard that will effectively confine the discretion exercised by judge or jury at trial. What is envisaged, however, is a discretion to award punitive damages within a range bounded by rationality at either end of the range. The Supreme Court did not opt, then, for the type of *de novo* appellate review adopted in the modern U.S. authorities.[280]

---

275 *Ibid.*

276 *Ibid.*

277 *Ibid.* at para. 95.

278 *Ibid.* at para. 108, quoting from *Hill v. Church of Scientology of Toronto*, above note 257 at para. 159.

279 *Ibid.*

280 *Cooper Industries Inc. v. Leatherman Tool Group Inc.* 121 S. Ct. 1678 (2001). And see L. Litwiller, "Has the Supreme Court Sounded the Death Knell for Jury Assessed Punitive Damages? A Critical Re-Examination of the American Jury" (2002) 36 U.S.F. L. Rev. 411.

The standard of rationality to be applied in appellate scrutiny of punitive damage awards is obviously a device designed to structure and confine the discretion of judge and jury to award punitive damages at trial. This test of rationality applies both to the threshold question of whether to award punitive damages at all and to the issue of quantum. With respect to the threshold question, it must be considered whether the award of punitive damages constituted a "rational response" to the misconduct of the defendant. One must assess whether the award of punitive damages was rationally required to meet the objectives served by punitive damages. On the facts of *Pilot Insurance*, the Court concluded that the award had apparently answered the jury's perceived need for "retribution, denunciation and deterrence." The Court agreed that this was "an exceptional case that justified an exceptional remedy."[281]

Turning to the question of quantum, however, the Court developed a much more elaborate set of guidelines for attempting to determine "whether a reasonable jury, properly instructed, could have concluded that an award in that amount, *and no less*, was rationally required to punish the defendant's misconduct."[282] In determining the critical issue of "rationality," the key to applying that standard rests on a concept of "proportionality." "A disproportionate award overshoots its purpose and becomes irrational."[283] In the Court's view, there are six aspects to the proportionality criterion. The award must be proportionate to the "blameworthiness" of the defendant's conduct, to the degree of vulnerability of the plaintiff,[284] to the actual or potential harm directed specifically at the plaintiff, to the need for deterrence[285] in the light of other penalties, both civil and criminal, to which the defendant has been or will likely be subject and, finally, to the advantage gained or profits made through the misconduct. In applying this test to the actual

---

281 Above note 5 at para 105.
282 *Ibid.* at para. 107 (emphasis added).
283 *Ibid.* at para. 111.
284 This factor militates against the award of punitive damages in most commercial situations. Indeed, in the Court's contemporaneously released decision in *Performance Industries Ltd. v. Sylvan Lake Golf & Tennis Club Ltd.*, [2002] 1 S.C.R. 678, the Court struck down an award of punitive damages of $200,000 in the context of a dispute concerning a proposed real estate development. Although the defendant's conduct had been fraudulent and reprehensible, the Court emphasized that this was a commercial relationship between two businessmen and, further, that the facts did not reveal an "abuse of a dominant position." See *ibid.* at para. 88. In the particular circumstances, then, neither the award of punitive damages itself nor the particular quantum met the test of rationality.
285 Above note 5 at paras. 119 and 121 (perhaps in light of the "financial power" of the defendant—the punishment "should 'sting'").

award in *Pilot Insurance*, Binnie J. indicated that although he would not himself have awarded one million dollars in punitive damages on these facts, the award was, nonetheless, "within the rational limits within which a jury must be allowed to operate."[286] The jury had been adequately instructed that it should make an award of punitive damages "if, but only if"[287] the award of compensatory damages was insufficient. "The award was not so disproportionate as to exceed the bounds of rationality."[288] In response to the defendant's objection that prior to this judgment, the highest previous punitive damages award in a bad-faith insurance case was fifty thousand dollars, the Court observed that "one of the strengths of the jury system is that it keeps the law in touch with evolving realities, including financial realities."[289]

In the aftermath of *Pilot Insurance*, there is some evidence in recent appellate decisions that Canadian courts will exercise the supervisory jurisdiction committed to them to control the awarding of punitive damages at trial. In *Ferme Gérald Laplante & Fils Ltée v. Grenville Patron Mutual Fire Insurance Company*,[290] for example, a jury award of punitive damages in another bad-faith insurer case was reversed. Following upon a fire at the plaintiff's farm, a hard-fought dispute took place between the plaintiff farmer and the defendant insurer. By the time of trial, although the insurer had already paid out to the plaintiff $1.17 million, a number of disputed items remained. The jury awarded a further $488,389 in compensatory damages and $750,000 in punitive damages. The Ontario Court of Appeal held that although it was open to the jury on the facts to find that a breach of the good-faith duty had occurred, the jury could not rationally conclude that an award of punitive damages was required to punish the defendant's misconduct. Similarly, in a wrongful dismissal case, *Prinzo v. Baycrest Centre for Geriatric Care*,[291] the same court set aside a five-thousand-dollar award for punitive damages. Even though the employer, in its treatment of the plaintiff at the time of dismissal, had committed the tort of intentional infliction of mental suffering, that conduct had been effectively compensated by an award of damages for mental distress. Accordingly, in the court's view, an award of punitive damages was not necessary for deterrence purposes and served no rational purpose. Even though the

---

286 *Ibid.* at para. 128.
287 *Ibid.* at para. 129.
288 *Ibid.* at para. 128.
289 *Ibid.* at para. 136.
290 (2002), 217 D.L.R. (4th) 34 (Ont. C.A.).
291 (2002), 60 O.R. (3d) 474, 215 D.L.R. (4th) 31 (C.A.).

same court upheld a substantial award of punitive damages in another case,[292] such decisions indicate a willingness to carefully scrutinize punitive damage awards.

Nonetheless, doubts will linger as to the soundness of the Supreme Court's innovation in *Pilot Insurance*. It is not obvious that the doctrine pronounced in *Pilot Insurance* was necessary to the result of that case. Under prior Canadian law, the defendant insurer would be vulnerable to a claim for punitive damages if its conduct had been tortious. Although no finding on this point was made by the Court, there can be little doubt that Pilot Insurance had committed a tort. Even if one accepts the position taken by its representatives that they genuinely believed that Mrs. Whiten had committed arson, their conduct appears negligent and, further, would appear to meet the threshold set out in the *Robitaille*[293] case of manifesting a callous disregard for the interests of the plaintiff. If this is correct, it then follows that the entire discussion of the awarding of punitive damages for pure breach of contract is simply unnecessary to the decision in the *Pilot Insurance* case. More generally, there is very little basis for thinking that punitive damages should have a role to play in circumstances where an insurer is guilty of lesser forms of wrongdoing. If the insurer had merely engaged in negligent conduct that did not manifest a callous disregard for the interests of the insured, even the *Pilot Insurance* court would not likely have awarded punitive damages. Further, it is all the more unlikely that such an award would be made in a case where the conduct of the insurer fell short of negligence but nonetheless exposed the insured's liability for a non-tortious breach of the implied covenant to process the insurer's claim in good faith. Apart from cases already covered by the *Robitaille* principle, then, the role for punitive damages for pure breach of contract may, as a practical matter, be very limited.

When one considers the application of the aggravated or mental distress damages line of authority to the *Pilot Insurance* fact situation, it seems doubtful that the *Pilot Insurance* principle itself was properly applied to the facts of that case. Under Canadian law, prior to *Pilot Insurance*, it is clearly established that damages for mental distress may be awarded in a case where the mental distress results from bad-faith

292 *Khazzaka v. Commercial Union Assurance Co. of Canada* (2002), 66 O.R. (3d) 390 (C.A.) (facts similar to *Whiten*—jury award of $200,000.00 in punitive damages upheld). See also *Fidler v. Sun Life Assurance Co. of Canada,* above note 270.
293 Above note 227.

conduct of an insurer in the course of processing a plaintiff's claim.[294] Curiously, in *Pilot Insurance*, no claim for aggravated damages to compensate Mrs. Whiten for her undoubted mental distress was advanced. It is unclear why this was the case. Even an unusually resilient personality would have suffered a great deal of distress as a result of the abysmal treatment afforded to the Whitens by the defendant insurer. Their distress was surely many times more severe than the level of anxiety suffered by solicitor Jarvis as a result of his disappointing Swiss vacation[295] and a substantial award on this basis would appear to have been warranted. Thus, it is not actually correct to suggest, as the Supreme Court suggested in *Pilot Insurance*,[296] that the *Pilot Insurance* jury applied its collective mind to the question of whether punitive damages should be awarded "if but only if," compensatory damages were insufficient to meet the needs of the situation. The whole range of compensatory damages was simply not considered by the jury. Arguably, then, the *Pilot Insurance* principle itself was misapplied. It is possible, of course, that the *Pilot Insurance* jury might have awarded punitive damages on top of a substantial award for mental distress. It is of interest, however, that in *Prinzo*,[297] the Ontario Court of Appeal overturned an award for punitive damages at trial on the basis that the misconduct in question had resulted in an award of damages for the plaintiff's resulting mental distress and, accordingly, a further award of punitive damages "is not necessary for deterrence purposes ... [and therefore] serves no rational purpose."[298] It might well be, then, that the *Pilot Insurance* jury, if properly instructed, might have made a substantial award for damages for mental distress and come to a similar conclusion. On this ground as well, then, the practical application of the *Pilot Insurance* doctrine of punitive damages for pure as opposed to tortious breach of contract may be severely limited.

---

294 See, for example, *Warrington v. Great-West Life Assurance Co.* (1996), 139 D.L.R. (4th) 18 (B.C.C.A.); *McIsaac v. Sun Life Assurance Co. of Canada* (1999), 173 D.L.R. (4th) 649 (B.C.C.A.); *Eddie v. Unum Life Insurance Co. of America* (1999), 177 D.L.R. (4th) 738 (B.C.C.A.); *Clarfield v. Crown Life Insurance Co.* (2000), 50 O.R. (3d) 696 (S.C.J.).
295 *Jarvis v. Swans Tours Ltd.*, above note 202.
296 Above note 5 at para. 129.
297 Above note 291.
298 *Ibid.* at 56 (D.L.R.). Compare with *Asselstine v. Manufacturers Life Insurance Co.* (2005), 254 D.L.R. (4th) 464 (B.C.C.A.) (bad faith conduct by insurer—both aggravated and punitive damages awarded).

J. PENALTIES AND LIQUIDATED DAMAGES

The parties to an agreement may wish to stipulate the remedy or remedies available in the event of breach for a variety of reasons. They may wish to avoid the uncertainties and expense of litigation by clear agreement with respect to the consequences of breach. Alternatively, one of the parties may wish to stipulate for a severe penalty in the event of the other party's breach in order to increase the pressure on the other party to perform. Such provisions are often said to be intended to have an *in terrorem* effect. We here consider the enforceability of contractual terms aligned to either one of these purposes. In the further alternative, however, a party might wish to stipulate a remedy that minimizes or, indeed, eliminates that party's exposure to liability in the event of breach. Clauses of this type, normally referred to as exclusion clauses or limitation of liability clauses, are considered elsewhere in this volume.[299] We will consider here, however, the effect of clauses that, though inserted by the innocent party for an *in terrorem* purpose, accidentally underestimate the amount of loss that actually occurs and ask whether, in such circumstances, the clause should constitute a cap on the *quantum* of relief available to the innocent party. Parties may also attempt to control the consequences of breach by stipulating that moneys or other values already transferred by the party in breach will be forfeited upon breach. The enforceability of these arrangements would normally be tested in the context of an attempt by the party in breach to seek restitution of the value being forfeited. This issue is considered elsewhere in a more general treatment of the restitutionary remedies of parties in the context of a breach of contract.[300]

Where the parties to an agreement engage in the exercise of attempting to predict the financial consequences of breach and stipulate for the payment of an equivalent sum in the event of breach in order to avoid the risks of litigation, their purpose is considered benign and such arrangements are generally held to be enforceable. An enforceable term of this kind is characterized as a "liquidated damages" clause. On the other hand, a term that is designed to operate *in terrorem* by stipulating payment of an amount that exceeds the likely damages caused by breach is characterized as a "penalty" and held to be unenforceable. The rule striking down penalty clauses represents an extension of a traditional equitable doctrine relating to penal bonds to apply to contractual provisions in a more general way. Penal bonds were typically sealed instruments

299 See Chapter 20.
300 See Chapter 24, section C.

providing that a certain sum of money would be paid unless the promisor performed a particular contractual undertaking. Upon breach of that undertaking, then, the promise to pay the penalty became enforceable at common law. As early as the late-seventeenth century, however, courts of equity intervened and prevented collection of the penal sum leaving the victim of the breach to pursue a claim for damages for breach at common law.[301] Similarly, under contemporary practice, if a penalty clause is struck down, the innocent party is entitled to pursue a claim for damages for breach of contract in the normal fashion.

In order to determine the effect of a particular stipulated remedies provision, then, it is necessary to consider whether the clause is correctly characterized as either a liquidated damages clause or a penalty clause. The basic test for distinguishing between the two was described in the following terms by Fitzpatrick C.J.C. in a decision of the Supreme Court of Canada: "A penalty is the payment of a stipulated sum on breach of the contract, irrespective of the damage sustained. The essence of liquidated damages is a genuine covenanted pre-estimate of damage."[302]

The underlying rationale of the rule striking down penalty clauses was described by Laskin C.J.C. in *H.F. Clarke Ltd. v. Thermidaire Corp.*[303] as follows: "The primary concern in breach of contract cases … is compensation, and judicial interference with the enforcement of what the Courts regard as penalty clauses is simply a manifestation of a concern for fairness and reasonableness rising above contractual stipulation, whenever the parties seek to remove from the Courts their ordinary authority to determine not only whether there has been a breach but what damages may be recovered as a result thereof."[304] The question in each case, then, is whether the stipulated sum is "considered to be a *bona fide* pre-estimate of the damage."[305] The rule thus effects a substantial limitation on the ability of the parties to fix damages in advance. Indeed, in another decision of the Supreme Court,[306] Dickson J. observed that "the power to strike down a penalty clause is a blatant inference with freedom of contract."[307]

---

301 The power of the courts to grant relief from penalties has been given statutory expression in many jurisdictions. See, for example, *Courts of Justice Act*, R.S.O. 1990, c. C.43, s. 98.

302 *Canadian General Electric Co. v. Canadian Rubber Co. of Montreal* (1915), 52 S.C.R. 349 at 351.

303 [1976] 1 S.C.R. 319.

304 *Ibid.* at 331.

305 *Shatilla v. Feinstein*, [1923] 3 D.L.R. 1035 at 1038 (Sask. C.A.), Martin J.A.

306 *J.G. Collins Insurance Agencies Ltd. v. Elsley Estate*, [1978] 2 S.C.R. 916.

307 *Ibid.* at 937.

Application of the test is easiest in a stark case where the "sum stipulated for is extravagant and unconscionable in amount in comparison with the greatest loss that could conceivably be proved to have followed from the breach."[308] Where the *in terrorem* nature of the clause is less evident, however, application of the test may prove to be a subtle matter. The fact that the parties may describe the stipulated sum as "liquidated damages" or, as is often stipulated, "as liquidated damages and not as a penalty" is not dispositive.[309] Conversely, although a prudent drafter would not describe such a term explicitly as a penalty, the use of that term would not preclude a court from determining that the stipulation is a liquidated damages clause.[310] In each case, the court must look behind the language of the provision and attempt a proper classification of the term.

A number of guidelines have emerged in the jurisprudence applying the distinction.[311] Thus, a stipulation requiring payment of a larger sum for breach of a covenant to pay a lesser sum is penal in nature. Where the consequences of the breach may vary in severity, the fact that the stipulated sum also varies in a manner proportionate to the severity of loss points in the direction of liquidated damages.[312] On the other hand, where the provision stipulates for the payment of a single sum with respect to the occurrence of any one of a number of possible breaches, some of which may be important but others of which may be trivial, the stipulation is more likely to be characterized as penal. Thus, in *Shatilla v. Feinstein*,[313] a stipulation in a contract for the sale of a wholesale dry goods business provided that the sum of ten thousand dollars would be payable for each and every breach of a non-competition covenant given by the vendor. The non-competition clause was drafted very broadly and, as Martin J.A. pointed out, the provision could be breached in a serious way by, for example, opening up a competing business or, on

---

308   *Dunlop Pneumatic Tyre Co. Ltd. v. New Garage and Motor Co. Ltd.*, [1915] A.C. 79 at 87 (H.L.), Lord Dunedin.

309   See, for example, *Shatilla v. Feinstein*, above note 305.

310   *Elphinstone v. Monkland Iron & Coal Co.* (1886), 11 App. Cas. 332 (H.L.); *Clydebank Engineering & Shipbuilding Co. v. Yzquierdo-y-Castaneda, Don Jose Ramos*, [1905] A.C. 6 (H.L.).

311   A leading statement of them by Lord Dunedin in *Dunlop Pneumatic Tyre Co. Ltd.*, above note 308, has been adopted in a number of Canadian cases. See *Shatilla v. Feinstein*, above note 305; *Waugh v. Pioneer Logging Co. Ltd.*, [1949] S.C.R. 299.

312   *Public Work Commissioner v. Hills*, [1906] A.C. 368 at 376 (P.C.), Lord Dunedin. See also *Clydebank Engineering & Shipbuilding Co. v. Yzquierdo-y-Castaneda, Don Jose Ramos*, above note 310.

313   Above note 305.

the other hand, in a trivial fashion by, for example, taking employment as a clerk in a similar business or, indeed, purchasing a few shares in a company operating a similar business. Martin J.A. relied on Lord Dunedin for the proposition that in circumstances of this kind, "the strength of the chain must be taken to be its weakest link."[314] Accordingly, the stipulation was held to be penal in nature. If, on the other hand, the various breaches that might occur are essentially of the same kind, the fact that individual breaches may differ in their degree of severity will not preclude a finding that the stipulation is a liquidated damages clause.[315] The fact that pre-estimation or quantification of the loss may be difficult does not preclude a finding of liquidated damages. Indeed, it is in just such a case that the parties may have attempted to eliminate such uncertainty by agreeing to a liquidation of damages clause.[316] Especially difficult will be cases where the party inserting the stipulation may have mixed motives. Thus, a court may lean in the direction of a liquidated damages finding for a party who stipulates a remedy in order to encourage performance but, at the same time, does not stipulate an amount that is unreasonable.[317]

Under the logic of the traditional test, the question of whether there has been a genuine pre-estimate of loss would focus on the intentions of the parties at the time of contracting and require consideration of whether such an estimate was intended by them. In *H.F. Clarke Ltd. v. Thermidaire Corp.*,[318] however, the Supreme Court of Canada appears to have suggested that the stipulated damages provision can also be assessed in the light of the circumstances as they ultimately transpire after breach. In this case, a distributor breached a non-competition clause that was to apply for three years following the termination of its relationship with the manufacturer. Upon termination, the distributor established and conducted a competitive business. The breach continued throughout the three-year period. The plaintiff manufacturer sought to enforce a stipulated damages clause that provided for recovery of the "*gross* trading profit" secured by the distributor through breach of the non-competition clause. On this formula, the plaintiff's recovery was

---

314 *Dunlop Pneumatic Tyre Co.,* above note 308 at 89, quoted by Martin J.A. in *Shatilla v. Feinstein,* above note 305 at 1043.

315 *Shatilla v. Feinstein,* above note 305 at 1038, Martin J.A.

316 *Dunlop Pneumatic Tyre Co. Ltd.,* above note 308 at 88, Lord Dunedin.

317 *Dunlop Pneumatic Tyre Co. Ltd., ibid.,* appears to be a case of this kind. Dunlop had stipulated that the wholesale purchaser of its tires should pay £5 for each and every time it ignored the requirement to sell the tires at the manufacturer's list price. The House of Lords held that the clause was enforceable.

318 Above note 303.

estimated at $239,449.05. The defendant's *net* trading profit, however, was estimated at $92,017.00, a figure that might be thought to approximate the plaintiff's actual loss. Although there was thus a wide disparity between the figure produced by the stipulated formula and actual trading losses, evidence of the parties was accepted at trial to the effect that the more inclusive gross trading profits formula was adopted in order to take account of the difficulty of quantifying injuries such as loss of product identification and goodwill and depreciation of the plaintiff's customer and trade relations that would result from the defendant's unlawful activities. The Ontario Court of Appeal concluded that the provision was the product of a genuine attempt to pre-estimate loss and held it enforceable. This reasoning appears unexceptionable under the traditional analysis. The formula, being time-based, was sensitive to the severity of the losses. The gap between gross trading profits and net trading profits was agreed to by the parties as a means of quantifying categories of loss that would be difficult to prove with certainty.

On further appeal, however, the Supreme Court reversed and held that the clause, at least as applied to the entire three-year period, constituted a penalty. The precise ground for this conclusion is not entirely clear. The Court observed that the gross trading profit formula "departs markedly from any reasonable approach to recoverable loss or actual loss since all the elements of costs and expenses which would be taken into account to arrive at net profit are excluded from consideration."[319] The inappropriateness of the formula, presumably, is a matter that could have been determined by the parties at the time of entering the agreement. On this basis, then, it appears that the Supreme Court in this case is simply imposing a reasonableness requirement on the formula selected by the parties, notwithstanding whatever good intentions they may have had at the time of formation of the contract. On the other hand, the Court stated at various points in the judgment that the plaintiff had not attempted at an earlier stage to seek an interlocutory injunction and bring the loss of profits to an end. The Court stated that "the proper course is to look at the situation (as in fact it was at the time of trial) as one where each party was content to have the issue of liquidated damages or penalty determined according to the consequences of a breach over the entire period of the covenant."[320] Thus, the Court appears to suggest that the validity of the provision can be assessed in the light of the actual consequences of breach rather than on the basis of a simple determination of whether the parties had engaged in a

319 *Ibid.* at 332, Laskin C.J.C.
320 *Ibid.* at 336.

genuine or *bona fide* attempt to estimate loss. The majority of the Court concluded by characterizing "the exaction of gross trading profits for *a three-year period* as a penalty and not as giving rise to a sum claimable as compensation by way of liquidated damages."[321] The Court thus left open the possibility that a clause that might be enforceable in the context of a breach lasting for a short period of time might be considered to be penal in the event that the breach persisted for a lengthy period of time.[322] The suggestion, albeit tacit, that courts may engage in a second look at the enforceability of a provision in light of the actual circumstances of breach is inconsistent with the traditional doctrine and may be thought to unduly complicate the exercise of negotiating and drafting provisions of this kind. Moreover, with respect to such matters as goodwill, the Court directed that the plaintiff should be provided an opportunity to demonstrate the existence of such losses in a further reference on the matter. This approach certainly defeats the apparent intention of the parties to avoid the difficulties inherent in proving losses of this kind. On the other hand, it may be argued that the very difficulty of predicting and quantifying such losses makes it attractive to enable the courts to engage in a second look at the time of actual breach, in order to determine whether the clause has an unreasonable effect and, if so, withhold its enforcement.[323]

The typical penalty clause stipulates a sum to be paid that will likely handsomely exceed the actual loss sustained as a result of breach, thus providing a powerful incentive for performance. Where, however, the actual loss itself exceeds the penal sum, an interesting question arises as to whether the penalty ought to constitute an upper limit on recovery. This issue was addressed by the Supreme Court of Canada in *J.G. Collins Insurance Agencies Ltd. v. Elsley Limited.*[324] The Collins agency had purchased the general insurance business of its competitor, D.C. Elsley Limited. The agreement of purchase and sale contained a non-competition provision under which the vendor, the defendant Elsley, agreed not to carry on the business of a general insurance agent within the neighbouring area for ten years. The provision stipulated a penalty to be paid to the purchaser of one thousand dollars for each and every breach of this covenant. In due course, Collins employed Elsley, himself, to man-

---

321   *Ibid.* at 339 (emphasis added).

322   A similar idea relating to the enforceability of limitation of liability or exclusion clauses was articulated by Wilson J. in *Hunter Engineering Co. Inc. v. Syncrude Canada Ltd.*, [1989] 1 S.C.R. 426, for discussion of which, see Chapter 21.

323   See, for support of an approach of this kind, M. Eisenberg, "The Limits of Cognition and the Limits of Contract" (1995) 47 Stan. L. Rev. 211.

324   Above note 306.

age the newly combined businesses on an employment contract that contained a similar non-competition clause. Upon the eventual termination of their relationship, Elsley recommenced his own general insurance business in breach of the non-competition clause and, in so doing, inflicted severe economic harm on the business of the Collins agency. In response to the claim by the Collins agency for these substantial losses, Elsley defended on the basis that the stipulated remedy provision limited the plaintiff's recovery to one thousand dollars.

In a unanimous judgment, the Supreme Court held that the penalty clause did create an upper limit on the plaintiff's recovery. Dickson J. explained that the sole purpose of the rule permitting courts to strike down penalty clauses is to provide relief against oppression of the party required to pay the stipulated sum. Where the actual loss exceeds the sum, however, the penalty obviously has no oppressive effect on the party in breach. Dickson J. reasoned as follows: "The party imposing the penalty should not be able to obtain the benefit of whatever intimidating force the penalty clause may have in inducing performance, and then ignore the clause when it turns out to be to his advantage to do so. A penalty clause should function as a limitation on the damages recoverable, while still being ineffective to increase damages above the actual loss sustained when such loss is less than the stipulated amount."[325]

Dickson J. thus appears to assume that the clause was inserted by Collins in the expectation that it would have an *in terrorem* effect upon Elsley. The fact that the clause actually substantially underestimated the losses that might occur was simply Collins' bad judgment or poor luck and Collins ought, therefore, to be restricted in its recovery to the stipulated sum. Dickson J. did not consider, however, whether the clause might have been intended by Elsley to have an oppressive effect on the Collins agency, substantially reducing the effect of the non-competition clause. If that was the intention, and if, as seems likely, the clause could not be defended as resting upon a genuine attempt to pre-estimate loss, there would be much to be said for the proposition that the clause should be held to be unenforceable. Indeed, such a clause appears to act as a limitation of liability and, presumably, should be analyzed on that basis.[326] It may be, then, that the *Elsley* doctrine should be considered applicable only to cases where what was intended as an *in terrorem* penalty clause accidentally or unforeseeably has the effect of

---

325 *Ibid* at 937.
326 For a discussion of the law applicable to limitation of liability clauses, see Chapter 20.

underestimating the actual loss sustained by the innocent party. Even in such cases, however, it is difficult to articulate a convincing basis for enforcement of the clause as a limit on the innocent party's ability to recover full compensation for losses resulting from the breach.[327]

FURTHER READINGS

P.S. ATIYAH, *Essays on Contract* (Oxford: Clarendon Press, 1986) c. 2 and 7.

M. BRIDGE, "Mitigation of Damages in Contract and the Meaning of Avoidable Loss" (1989) 105 Law Q. Rev. 398.

M.G. BRIDGE, "Expectation Damages and Uncertain Future Losses" in J. Beatson and D. Friedmann, eds., *Good Faith and Fault in Contract Law* (Oxford: Clarendon Press, 1995).

J. CASSELS, *Remedies: The Law of Damages* (Toronto: Irwin Law, 2000).

D.H. CLARK, "Loss of a Chance in (and by) the Supreme Court of Canada" (1996) 75 Can. Bar Rev. 464.

R. DANZIG, "*Hadley v. Baxendale*: A Study of the Industrialization of the Law" (1975) 4 J. Legal Stud. 249.

M.A. EISENBERG, "The Limits of Cognition and the Limits of Contract" (1995) 47 Stan. L. Rev. 211.

M.A. EISENBERG, "The Principle of *Hadley v. Baxendale*" (1992) 80 Cal. L. Rev. 563.

E.A. FARNSWORTH, "Legal Remedies for Breach of Contract" (1970) 70 Colum. L. Rev. 1145.

D. FRIEDMANN, "The Efficient Breach Fallacy" (1989) 18 J. Legal Stud. 1.

L. FULLER & W. PERDUE, "The Reliance Interest in Contract Damages" (1936) 46 Yale L.J. 52.

---

327 Canadian courts, however, appear to have assumed that penalty clauses underestimating loss are enforceable. See, for example, *Fern Investment Ltd. v. Golden Nugget (1987) Ltd.* (1994), 19 Alta. L.R. (3d) 442 (C.A.); *Lee v. Occo Developments Ltd.* (1996), 181 N.B.R. (2d) 241 (C.A.); *Re iTV Games Inc.* (2002), 21 B.L.R. (3d) 258 (B.C.C.A.); *McNamara Construction Co. v. Newfoundland Transshipment Ltd.* (2002), 213 Nfld. & P.E.I.R. 1 (Nfld. S.C.T.D.).

C. GOETZ & R. SCOTT, "The Mitigation Principle: Toward a General Theory of Contractual Obligation" (1983) 69 Va. L. Rev. 967.

H.L.A. HART & A.M. HONORÉ, *Causation in the Law* (Oxford: Clarendon Press, 1959) c. 5 and 11.

M.B. KELLY, "The Phantom Reliance Interest in Contract Damages" (1992) Wis. L. Rev. 1755.

D.W. MACLAUCHLAN, "Damages for Pre-Contract Expenditure" (1985) 11 N.Z.U.L. Rev. 346.

I. MACNEIL, "Efficient Breach of Contract: Circles in the Sky" (1982) 68 Va. L. Rev. 947.

J.L. MAUTE, "*Peevyhouse v. Garland Coal & Mining Co.* Revisited: The Ballad of Willy and Lucille" (1995) 89 Nw. U.L. Rev. 1341.

J.D. MCCAMUS, "Prometheus Bound or Loose Cannon? Punitive Damages for Pure Breach of Contract" (2004) 41 San Diego L. Rev. 1941.

H. MCGREGOR, *McGregor on Damages*, 17th ed. (London: Sweet & Maxwell, 2003).

R. O'DAIR, "Restitutionary Damages for Breach of Contract and the Theory of Efficient Breach: Some Reflections" (1993) 46 Curr. Legal Probs. 113.

ONTARIO LAW REFORM COMMISSION, *Report on Exemplary Damages* (Toronto: Ministry of the Attorney General, 1991).

C.R. SUNSTEIN, D. Kahneman & D. Schkade, "Assessing Punitive Damages" (with Notes on Cognition and Valuation in Law) (1998) 107 Yale L.J. 2071.

J. SWAN, "Punitive Damages for Breach of Contract: A Remedy in Search of a Justification" (2004) 29 Queen's L.J. 596.

G.H. TREITEL, *Remedies for Breach of Contract* (Oxford: Clarendon Press, 1988).

W.K. VISCUSI, "Punitive Damages: How Jurors Fail to Promote Efficiency" (2002) 39 Harv. J. on Legis. 139.

S.M. WADDAMS, *The Law of Damages*, 4th ed. (Aurora: Canada Law Book, 2004).

SPECIFIC PERFORMANCE AND INJUNCTIONS

A. INTRODUCTION

As an alternative to the claim for damages for breach of contract, the victim of a breach may be able to pursue specific relief in the form of an order of specific performance or an injunction.[1] An order of specific performance is a court order that directs the party in breach to perform the very acts that the party in breach promised to perform in the agreement. An order granted against a defaulting seller of goods under a contract for the purchase and sale of goods would require the seller to deliver the goods to the buyer. An injunction is a court order directing that the party in breach refrain from doing something that the party in breach promised in the agreement not to do. An employee who breached a postemployment non-competition clause, for example, might be enjoined from competing with his or her former employer. For the victim of a breach of contract, the availability of specific relief might appear to be the perfect expression of the expectancy principle.[2]

---

1   See generally R. Sharpe, *Injunctions and Specific Performance*, 3d ed. (Aurora: Canada Law Book, 2000); G. Jones and W. Goodhart, *Specific Performance*, 2d ed. (London: Butterworths, 1996); E. Yorio, *Contract Enforcement: Specific Performance and Injunctions* (Boston: Little Brown & Co., 1989). For a more general account of equitable remedies, see J. Berryman, *The Law of Equitable Remedies* (Toronto: Irwin Law, 2000).

2   See generally Chapter 22, section B.

By obtaining an order that the plaintiff will either do or not do the very thing promised in the agreement, the innocent party will be placed, it might seem, in precisely the position he or she would have been in had the contract been performed.

The remedies of specific performance and injunction are equitable in nature in the sense that they were developed by the Courts of Equity rather than the Courts of Common Law.[3] The equitable origins of these remedies are significant for a number of reasons. First, the enforcement mechanisms of Courts of Equity and Courts of Common Law were starkly different. The typical order of a court of common law is an order that the defendant pay a certain amount of money to the plaintiff. Should the defendant fail to comply with the order, the plaintiff may invoke the enforcement machinery of the common law that essentially enables the state to seize and realize the value of some of the defendant's assets in order to obtain the resources to satisfy the plaintiff's judgment. At common law, a writ of execution would be issued enabling the sheriff to seize as much of the assets of the defendant as was necessary to carry out this objective. The enforcement mechanism of the Courts of Equity was very different. The form of the order of an equity court was to direct the defendant personally to do or not do that which had been promised to be done or not to be done. Failure to carry out the order constituted a contempt of the court, thereby exposing the defendant to proceedings for criminal contempt or, indeed, to civil proceedings for civil contempt at the instigation of the plaintiff. Such proceedings, in either case, could result in the imposition of the sanction of imprisonment. In explaining the difference between these two modes of enforcement, it is often said that the common law acted *in rem* or against the property of the defendant, whereas equitable decrees operated *in personam* or against the defendant personally. Thus, in considering whether or not to grant equitable rather than common law relief, courts have taken into consideration the potentially more oppressive effect of equitable forms of relief.

A second implication of the equitable origins of specific relief arises from the essentially curative role performed by courts of equity. The animating principle of equity jurisprudence is that equity has a jurisdiction to cure defects in the common law. To the extent that courts of equity remain true to this mandate, they would intervene with the development of new rights and remedies only in circumstances where the rights and remedies available at common law were in some sense

---

3   For a brief discussion of the historical division between Common Law and Equity, see Chapter 1, section B.

inadequate. Accordingly, it is well established that equitable relief and, in particular, specific relief for breach of contract, is available only in circumstances where the common law remedy of damages does not provide adequate relief to the plaintiff. A third implication is that equitable relief is generally considered to be discretionary in nature. Accordingly, courts of equity, in granting such relief, assert the existence of a discretion to withhold or grant relief depending on the circumstances of the particular case, including the morality of the conduct of either one or both of the parties. Although the most common grounds for exercising that discretion have crystallized in the form of well-recognized limitations on or defences to the granting of relief, further considered later in this chapter, it is doubtful that the discretionary nature of the remedies can be completely defined or confined by such doctrines.

In subsequent sections of this chapter, we will discuss the grounds upon which specific relief in the form of decrees of specific performance or injunctions are made available to the innocent party for breach of contract. Consideration will then be given to the potential impact on that availability of contractual stipulations that purport to constrain or facilitate such relief.

B. SPECIFIC PERFORMANCE

1) Introduction

The basic principle concerning the awarding of decrees of specific performance requiring the party in breach personally to perform the obligation that has been breached is that such relief is available only on an exceptional basis. In the normal case, then, the innocent party must be content with a claim for damages for breach of contract. The central limitation on the availability of such relief is a general rule that specific relief is available only where the remedy of damages at common law is, in some sense, inadequate. We will examine later the general nature of that test as it is applied in the context of certain standard types of transactions. There are, however, other limiting principles. Thus, it is commonly said that equity will not grant such a decree where it potentially involves the court in the supervision of complex tasks or obligations to be performed over a long period of time. Further, and less defensibly, specific relief will not be available, or so it is said, when the remedy is not one that is potentially available to both parties. This so-called doctrine of mutuality has been a source of considerable confusion in the law relating to specific performance. Specific relief is denied where the order operates unfairly by privileging an unworthy plaintiff or imposing undue hardship on a party. In some contexts, relief is denied on grounds of public policy that is relevant to the particular transaction type. Further, other equitable principles of more general application may have the effect of confining the availability of the decree. Each of these limitations on the availability of specific relief will be further considered later. Finally, the manner in which awards of specific performance can be coupled with or replaced by monetary awards will be considered.

Although the exceptional nature of specific relief may seem to follow logically or naturally from the curative role historically performed by the courts of equity, it is less than obvious that the restricted availability of this form of relief can be otherwise defended on policy grounds. Specific relief is generally more widely available in civilian systems. Before turning to consider the doctrines constraining the availability of such relief in the common law system, it may be useful to speculate on the basis on which the more restrictive approach can be defended if, indeed, such a defence is possible. Identification of the possible rationale for severely limiting specific relief has been of particular interest to law and economics scholars. Two of the leading contributors to the literature reach opposite conclusions.

Kronman,[4] on the one hand, defends the existing rule on the basis that most contracting parties, if they had considered the matter at the time of contracting, probably would have agreed that specific relief should be available only where the subject matter of the contract is unique in such a way as to render damages at common law an inadequate form of relief. Kronman begins with the proposition that where goods are unique, damages at common law run the risk of undercompensation. Where, for example, goods are readily available in the marketplace, courts are more likely to have an information base upon which to calculate more or less accurately the value of the goods to the purchaser. As the subject matter of the contract becomes increasingly unique, however, the court's ability to calculate the value of the particular goods to the plaintiff becomes more difficult with consequent risk of undercompensation. Further, although damages generally do not compensate for the purchaser's search costs, the search costs related to goods that are readily available in the market is likely to have produced information of continuing use to the purchaser. Where the goods

---

4   A.T. Kronman, "Specific Performance" (1978) 45 U. Chicago L. Rev. 351. For a survey of the history of the remedy, emphasizing liberalizing tendencies, see J. Berryman, "The Specific Performance Damages Continuum: An Historical Perspective" (1985) 17 Ottawa L. Rev. 295.

are unique, this is less likely to be the case. Accordingly, a rational promisee would be willing to pay more for a right to compel specific performance in cases where the risks of undercompensation are at their highest, that is, in the context of an agreement to purchase a unique commodity. While promisors would, of course, be generally reluctant to agree to specific relief, a promisor is likely to be most concerned about yielding such a right in cases where better offers for the purchase of the subject matter of the contract are a distinct possibility. In general, the likelihood of such offers should diminish as the goods become more and more unique. Accordingly, a promisor who fully intends to perform is less likely to resist a contractual stipulation of specific relief in circumstances where the goods are unique. In the context of unique chattels, then, the promisee may be especially willing to pay a premium for a right to specific relief and the promisor may be especially willing to sweeten the price in return for granting the promisee an entitlement of this kind. On this view, then, the existing rule replicates the bargain that rational parties would construct and, by doing so, promotes efficient conduct by reducing the cost of negotiating agreements.

Schwartz,[5] on the other hand, favours the civilian approach of making specific performance routinely available. Schwartz offers three reasons for this. First, contract damages are likely to be undercompensatory or inadequate as they fail to compensate for certain incidental losses — such as the costs of finding a substitute performance — upon which it is difficult to place and prove a financial value. Second, promisees are likely to prefer money damages at law in cases where substitute performance is obtained with relative ease and money damages are therefore an adequate remedy. A rational promisee would prefer a substitute supplier rather than to continue dealings with a reluctant promisor or, indeed, to endure the delays inherent in the pursuit of equitable relief. Where damages are adequate, the rational promisee will prefer to arrange a substitute supplier promptly and, if necessary, sue for damages in due course rather than await the outcome of a claim for specific relief. Third, promisees are likely to be better than courts in making a judgment as to whether damages constitute an adequate remedy for the promisee and, further, the nature of the difficulties involved in coercing the promisor to perform. Promisees are thus more likely than the courts to be able to accurately predict whether a decree of specific performance would induce satisfactory performance from the promisor. As promisees are more likely than courts to be able to determine whether specific performance is an appropriate remedy, courts

---

5   A. Schwartz, "The Case for Specific Performance" (1979) 89 Yale L.J. 271.

ought to defer to their judgment on this point. This is essentially the civilian approach.

There are additional considerations that may be thought to support the existing common law rule. The current rule may be defended on the basis of the policies that underlie the doctrine of mitigation.[6] To the extent that an innocent party may reasonably pursue specific relief, the need to engage in mitigation is, temporarily at least, suspended. If the duty of mitigation is defensible on the basis of efficiency concerns, such arguments thus run in favour of a restrictive approach to specific performance. An additional concern with a more expansive approach to specific performance rests on the capacity of such decrees to result in an overcompensation of the innocent party. One who seeks specific performance of a contract for the purchase of land, for example, can avoid the duty to mitigate at the time of breach and, if the subject matter of the contract inflates in value by the time of the trial, enjoy what may be considered to be an unearned windfall. The purchaser may be in a better position than if the contract had been performed in a timely fashion. Where, in the typical case of the purchase of a residential property, the purchaser owns an existing home that he or she will sell upon completion of the transaction in question, the purchaser may have enjoyed a substantial increase in the value of the existing property by the time of trial and will add to this profit the increase in the value of the subject matter of the sale. Moreover, the purchaser may have avoided the carrying costs associated with the subject property during the period from the date of breach until the time of trial. If specific performance of the transaction enjoys success, the purchaser will enjoy the increased value of the subject matter of the sale without being required to offset saved expenses of this kind and may enjoy, as well, the increase in value of the property retained by the purchaser during this period. The ultimate test of this proposition arises in the context of the calculation of damages in lieu of specific performance. In that context, the Supreme Court of Canada has recently held that neither the saved expenses nor the profit from the increase in value of the purchaser's existing property can be deducted from the claim.[7] On that occasion, the Court conceded that damages unaffected by these calculations constituted a windfall for the plaintiff purchaser[8] but felt that such a windfall was necessary in order to replicate the inherent characteristics of a specific performance decree. Interestingly, the Court further asserted,

---

6   See generally Chapter 22, section F(3).
7   *Semelhago v. Paramadevan*, [1996] 2 S.C.R. 415.
8   *Ibid.* at para. 19.

in light of this analysis, that a restrictive view should be taken of the availability of specific performance in cases of this kind. In short, the capacity of specific performance to overcompensate the plaintiff suggests that the current approach of restricted availability can draw support from the policies underlying the common law's general approach to calculating contract damages of allowing the innocent party to recover compensation but no more than compensation for losses sustained as a result of the breach.[9]

2) Inadequacy of Damages Test

The general principle that specific performance will be available only in a case where damages at common law prove to be inadequate is the central fulcrum of the balance determining whether or not a decree will be made available in a particular case. The principle is of general application. Thus, if in a particular fact situation, it is established that damages are inadequate, this constitutes a powerful argument for granting the decree. In *Beswick v. Beswick*, for example, where a nephew had promised his uncle that after the uncle's death, the nephew would look after his widowed aunt as part of the purchase price for a business being sold to the nephew by the uncle, consideration was given to the possibility that the damages claim by the uncle's estate against the nephew might prove to be inadequate. After the uncle's death, the nephew refused to comply with his undertaking. The ultimate beneficiary of the nephew's promise, the aunt, was held unable to sue as a mere third-party beneficiary of the promise on the basis of the doctrine of privity.[10] The potential difficulty with the claim brought by the uncle's estate is that the correct view might be that the uncle's estate has suffered no loss as a result of the nephew's breach of promise. Faced with the potential inadequacy of damages, the House of Lords concluded that the estate should be entitled to a decree of specific performance that would force the nephew to make the requisite payments to his aunt. Where damages are inadequate, the decree may be available in the context of a current breach and, as well, in the context of a pro-

---

9   For an analysis of the recent suggestion that, in appropriate cases, a plaintiff should be entitled to seek disgorgement of the profits of a breach of contract from the party in default, see Chapter 24, section B(2). As is further suggested below, the windfall benefit achieved by specific performance in some cases might be defended, in part at least, on the basis that such decrees effect a disgorgement of the profits that would otherwise be secured by the party in breach. See below this Chapter, section B(4).

10   See generally Chapter 9.

spective or threatened future breach of contract.[11] In the event that damages are not inadequate, of course, the general principle stands as a major obstacle to a decree of specific performance. Application of the principle can be usefully illustrated by examining three different contractual settings in which the principle has played a central role in either granting or denying relief: sale of land, sale of goods and sale of shares in corporations.

a) Sale of Land

Traditionally, Canadian courts accepted the position adopted in English law that specific performance is granted as a matter of course in the context of agreements for the purchase and sale of land.[12] This view is typically grounded on the basis of a presumption that land is unique.[13] On this approach, land is simply deemed to be unique on the theory that each parcel of land has its own special characteristics. Accordingly, an award of damages at common law would be an inadequate form of relief. There could be no guarantee that, armed with a damages award, the disappointed purchaser could acquire an equivalent parcel elsewhere. This presumption will often and perhaps usually correspond to the reality that, from the typical purchaser's perspective at least, no two parcels of land, especially residential properties, are precisely the same. On the other hand, there may well be situations, especially where, for example, land is being purchased for investment or resale, in which the purchaser might be to some extent indifferent to the precise characteristics of a particular parcel of land. Canadian courts, especially in more recent years, have taken the view that where, from a factual point of view, the argument for uniqueness is less than convincing, an exception should be made to the general rule and specific performance ought to be denied.[14]

These developments were confirmed by the Supreme Court of Canada in *obiter dicta* discussing the application of the inadequacy of dam-

---

11 See, for example, *Kloepfer Wholesale Hardware & Automotive Co. Ltd. v. Roy*, [1952] 2 S.C.R. 465. With respect to anticipatory repudiation, see generally Chapter 16.

12 See, for example, *Hall v. Warren* (1804), 9 Ves. 605; *Kloepfer Wholesale Hardware & Automotive Co. Ltd. v. Roy, ibid.* at 472, Kerwin J.; *Nepean Carleton Developments Ltd. v. Hope*, [1987] 1 S.C.R. 427.

13 See, for example, *Adderley v. Dixon* (1824), 1 Sim. & St. 607, 57 E.R. 239; *Flint v. Corby* (1853), 4 Gr. 45.

14 See, for example, *Chaulk v. Fairview Construction Ltd.* (1977), 14 Nfld. & P.E.I.R. 13 (Nfld. C.A.); *Domowicz v. Orsa Investment Ltd.* (1993), 15 O.R. (3d) 661 (Gen. Div.); *1110049 Ontario Ltd. v. Exclusive Diamonds Inc.* (1995), 25 O.R. (3d) 417 (C.A.).

ages doctrine to real estate transactions in *Semelhago v. Paramadevan*.[15] For the Court, Sopinka J. described the traditional common law position in the following terms: "Under the common law every piece of real estate was generally considered to be unique. Blackacre had no readily available equivalent. Accordingly, damages were an inadequate remedy and the innocent purchaser was generally entitled to specific performance."[16]

Having noted that the rigid presumption in favour of uniqueness applicable to the sale of land did not apply to contracts for the sale of goods, Sopinka J. observed, however, that Canadian courts had to some extent moved away from this absolutist position. He provided the following justification for this development:

> While at one time the common law regarded every piece of real estate to be unique, with the progress of modern real estate development this is no longer the case. Residential, business and industrial properties are all mass produced much in the same way as other consumer products. If a deal falls through for one property, another is frequently, though not always, readily available.
>
> It is no longer appropriate, therefore, to maintain a distinction in the approach to specific performance as between realty and personalty. It cannot be assumed that the damages for the breach of contract for the purchase and sale of real estate would be an inadequate remedy in all cases.[17]

Under Canadian law, then, the presumption of uniqueness is merely a presumption and is subject to being overturned in cases where the lack of uniqueness of the subject matter of the sale suggests that the remedy of damages at common law would constitute an adequate response to the breach of contract.

It is not entirely clear why the Supreme Court felt it necessary to discuss this issue in the *Semelhago* case. Indeed, in a concurring opin-

---

15   Above note 7. There is a vast literature on this case. See, for example, N. Siebrasse, "Damages in Lieu of Specific Performance: *Semelhago v. Paramadevan* (1998) 76 Can. Bar Rev. 551; O. Da Silva, "Case Comment: The Supreme Court of Canada's Lost Opportunity: *Semelhago v. Paramadevan*" (1998) 23 Queen's L.J. 475; D.H. Clark, "Will That Be Performance ... or Cash?: *Semelhago v. Paramadevan* and the Notion of Equivalence" (1999) 37 Alta. L. Rev. 589; J. Lem, "Blackacre Had No Readily Available Equivalent: Specific Performance and Equitable Damages After *Semelhago v. Paramadevan*" in Law Society of Upper Canada, *Special Lectures 2002, Real Property Law: Conquering the Complexities* (Toronto: Irwin Law, 2003).

16   *Semelhago v. Paramadevan, ibid.* at para. 14.

17   *Ibid.* at paras. 20–21.

ion, Mr. Justice La Forest noted that the issue was not truly before the Court and indicated his preference for postponing consideration of the matter to another and more appropriate occasion.[18] The issue before the Court in *Semelhago* was the correct manner of calculating the damages in lieu of specific performance, a topic to which we will return.[19] Semelhago was the intending purchaser of a new subdivision home from Paramadevan for a price of $205,000. Semelhago had planned to pay $75,000 cash and raise the remaining $130,000 of the price by a mortgage on the new home. At the time of trial the subject matter of the sale was worth $325,000 and Semelhago, as plaintiff, elected to pursue damages for breach of contract rather than a decree of specific performance. It was his position that as damages were being calculated as a substitute for specific performance, the full difference between the contract price and the market price at the date of trial should be awarded to him. The vendor's position was that Semelhago should be required to take into account the increase in the capital value of Semelhago's existing home, which had significantly increased in value, and the notional interest earned on the $75,000 payment, which Semelhago was not required to make from the date of breach to the time of trial. Taking into account these offsetting amounts would have very substantially reduced Semelhago's damages claim. In this case, the Court confirmed the approach taken in earlier cases that offsetting deductions of this kind would not be made when calculating damages in lieu of specific performance. It would appear, however, that the Court held some misgivings with respect to the potential for overcompensation inherent in this approach. Immediately prior to the passage quoted above, suggesting that specific performance should be reserved for cases of truly unique real estate, Sopinka J. observed the following with respect to a court's decision to refrain from making deductions of the kind requested by Paramadevan: "This approach may appear to be overly generous to the respondent in this case and other like cases and may be seen as a windfall. In my opinion, this criticism is valid if the property agreed to be purchased is not unique."[20]

It was against this background, then, that the Court strongly questioned the strength of the presumption in favour of the inadequacy of damages in the context of agreements for the purchase and sale of land. Another solution to the windfall problem, of course, might have been to exercise a discretion in favour of allowing such offsets in appropriate

---

18   *Ibid.* at para. 1.
19   See below this Chapter, section B(4).
20   Above note 7 at para. 20.

cases. Be that as it may, *Semelhago* offers strong support for the position that in Canadian common law, the courts have moved some distance away from a rigid presumption in favour of the uniqueness of every single parcel of real estate.

There is, of course, some force in the point made by Sopinka J. that under modern conditions, residential and commercial properties are to some extent mass produced. Nonetheless, it may be questioned whether the approach adopted in *Semelhago* will achieve a substantial difference in the outcome of decided cases. If one considers the residential housing market in a large city, for example, the vast majority of transactions will involve the purchase and sale of existing housing stock in which the existing owner and resident sells to a purchaser who will reside in the premises. In the context of such transactions, the argument in favour of uniqueness of particular residential properties is likely to enjoy success. In the context of commercial properties being acquired for a commercial use by the purchaser, it also appears likely that the attributes that made the parcel attractive to the purchaser will also ground a claim that the parcel is unique. In *John E. Dodge Holdings v. 805062 Ontario Ltd.*,[21] for example, a defaulting vendor of a parcel of serviced but undeveloped land to a purchaser who wished to build a hotel on the property resisted the buyer's claim on the basis that there were other similar properties in the neighbourhood. The Court of Appeal affirmed the trial judge's finding that the location of the parcel closer than the other parcels to a large amusement park and a projected mall, with slightly better zoning and traffic patterns than the others, established the requisite degree of uniqueness. Nonetheless, in cases involving the purchase of building lots that are indistinguishable from their neighbours or new mass-produced properties or properties acquired for investment, it may be expected that Canadian courts will accept the argument that common law damages constitute an adequate remedy and specific performance will be denied.[22]

The presumed or actual uniqueness of individual parcels of real estate may provide a basis for a conclusion that damages are an inadequate remedy for the purchaser of a particular parcel. The uniqueness of the property does not begin to provide an explanation, however, for the fact that, under traditional doctrine, the vendor is also presumed

---

21   (2003), 63 O.R. (3d) 304 (C.A.).
22   See, for example, *McMurray Imperial Enterprises Ltd. v. Brimstone Acquisitions and Asset Management Inc.* (1997), 210 A.R. 97; *Corse v. Ravenwood Homes Ltd.* (1998), 226 A.R. 214; *1174538 Ontario Ltd. v. Barzel Windsor (1984) Inc.* (1999), 28 R.P.R. (3d) 256.

to be entitled to a decree of specific performance against a defaulting purchaser. In the typical case, the purchaser will be providing a money price, perhaps coupled with a debt secured on the property in question, as the consideration given to the vendor in return for the vendor's transfer of title. Although some courts have attempted to justify the vendor's general entitlement to specific performance on the basis that parcels of real estate are unique,[23] it is evident that uniqueness of the property is normally irrelevant from the seller's point of view unless perhaps, the property is so unusually unique that it is virtually unsaleable. In the typical case, however, the vendor's only real interest is in receiving a money consideration for the property. Accordingly, the vendor's interest would appear to be adequately protected by a common law damages claim for the difference between the contract price with the initial purchaser and the price at which the vendor is able to sell the property to a third party. Nonetheless, the general entitlement of vendors to specific performance is well established.[24] The availability of specific performance for the vendor has often been justified on the basis of the doctrine of mutuality, that is, the proposition that since the purchaser is normally entitled to a decree of specific performance so, in fairness, should the vendor.[25] Although, as we shall see, the doctrine of mutuality does not appear to offer a very convincing explanation for the availability of specific performance decrees, the idea may appeal to a basic sense of fairness in the context of the typical sale of residential premises. In such transactions, the likely financial importance of the transaction for both parties, the vexation involved in negotiating such agreements and the potentially negative consequences of breach in circumstances where the parties may have committed themselves to the purchase and sale of other properties[26] might suggest that the remedies available to the parties should be seen by the laypersons involved in such transactions as being even-handed. Nonetheless, the presumption in favour of specific redress for the vendor, whose interest in the transaction is essentially monetary, remains difficult to defend. The undermining of the presumption in claims brought by the purchaser,

23 See, for example, *Taylor v. Sturgeon* (1996), 12 R.P.R. (3d) 107 (N.S.S.C.); *Landmark of Thornhill Ltd. v. Jacobson* (1995), 25 O.R. (3d) 628 (C.A.).

24 *Lewis v. Lord Lechmere* (1722), 10 Mod. 503, 88 E.R. 828; *Walker v. Eastern Counties Rwy Co.* (1848), 6 Hare 594, 67 E.R. 1300; *Eastern Counties Rwy. Co. v. Hawkes* (1855), 5 H.L.C. 331, 10 E.R. 928; *Dick v. Dennis* (1991), 20 R.P.R. (2d) 264 (Ont. Ct. Gen. Div.).

25 See, for example, *Eastern Counties Rwy. Co. v. Hawkes, ibid.*; *Walker v. Eastern Counties Rwy. Co., ibid.*

26 See Sharpe, above note 1 at 8–9.

effected in *Semelhago*, may thus lead to a reconsideration of its role in the context of vendor claims.

b) Sale of Goods

The inadequacy of damages test leads to a different approach to the availability of specific performance contracts for the purchase and sale of goods. In the context of the sale of ordinary articles of commerce, at least, the buyer will normally be able to obtain a substitute for the goods the seller has refused to deliver in the marketplace. Accordingly, expectancy damages that would enable the buyer to acquire such a substitute would normally constitute an adequate remedy. Unlike sale of land cases, then, the presumptive remedy in a sale of goods case is common law damages.[27] In the case of breach by the seller, those damages would normally be calculated as the difference between contract price and the market price at the date of breach.[28] In the case of buyer's default, damages would be the difference between the contract price and the market price at the date of breach, assuming that the market value of the goods is less than the contract price at that point in time.[29] A disappointed buyer seeking the remedy of specific performance must demonstrate, then, that the subject matter of the contract is sufficiently rare or unique that a substitute is not readily available in the marketplace and, accordingly, damages are not an adequate remedy. Thus, in *Falcke v. Gray*,[30] which involved a contract to purchase two large oriental jars that had apparently been of some interest to King George IV, it was held that the jars were of such "unusual distinction and curiosity that a substitute would not readily be available."[31] Kindersley V.C. also noted that the unique qualities of the goods made it "altogether

---

27   Where a sale of residential premises is coupled with a sale of the contents, however, specific performance of the sale of the contents may be ordered. See *Record v. Bell*, [1991] 1 W.L.R. 853. A different result may obtain, however, where a sale is coupled with an obligation to provide the purchaser with a one-fifth share of crops grown on the land by the vendor. See *Mennonite Land Sales v. Friesen* (1921), 62 D.L.R. 344 (Sask. K.B.) (value of crops easily determined — damages an adequate remedy).

28   See, for example, *Sale of Goods Act*, R.S.O. 1990, c. S.1, s. 49(3).

29   *Ibid.*, s. 48(3).

30   (1859), 29 L.J. Ch. 28. See also *Pusey v. Pusey* (1684), 1 Vern. 273, 23 E.R. 465 (ancient horn with alleged connection to King Canute); *Duke of Somerset v. Cookson* (1735), 3 P. Wms. 390 (antique silver altar piece inscribed in Greek); *Fells v. Read* (1796), 3 Ves. Jr. 70, 30 E.R. 899 (ornamented silver tobacco box owned by private club of former overseers of the poor); *Thorn v. Public Works Commissioners* (1863), 32 Beav. 490, 55 E.R. 192 (stones from historic bridge).

31   *Falcke v. Gray, ibid.* at 30.

doubtful what price they will fetch."[32] By way of contrast, in *Cohen v. Roche*[33] an agreement under which a buyer agreed to purchase a lot of "Hepplewhite chairs" was denied specific performance on the basis that the chairs in question were simply "ordinary Hepplewhite furniture."[34] McCardie J. also noted that the plaintiff, a dealer in furniture, had purchased the chairs "in the ordinary way of his trade for the purchase of ordinary resale at a profit,"[35] thus suggesting that the fact that the plaintiff appeared to have no special or personal interest in acquiring the particular chairs undermined the claim for specific performance.

The requisite quality of uniqueness is not limited, however, to objects possessing rare or sentimental personal value. In a few cases, courts have determined that the commercial uniqueness of a particular chattel rendered a contract for its purchase specifically enforceable. The classic illustration of this proposition is *Behnke v. Bede Shipping Co.*,[36] a case involving the purchase of a British steamship by a German purchaser. Further, the purchaser had an immediate need for the vessel. The steamship, though an old vessel, had been refitted with boilers that were of sufficient quality to satisfy the German regulations of the time. The fact that the vessel was therefore immediately registrable in Germany made it especially attractive to the purchaser. The evidence at trial suggested that a substitute was not likely to be readily available in the marketplace. Accordingly, the commercial uniqueness of the vessel met the inadequacy of damages threshold and the seller was directed to perform the agreement. Similarly, ordinary chattels, such as taxicabs, that are licensed to be utilized in a particular form of business in circumstances where such licences are of restricted availability may be considered to be sufficiently unique in the requisite sense.[37] In other cases, the mere difficulty of obtaining substitutes for what are otherwise quite ordinary chattels may provide a basis for specific relief. In a series of pre-Confederation Ontario cases, owners of sawmills were able to specifically enforce agreements to supply logs on the basis that the logs could be transported by river to the mills only for limited per-

---

32   *Ibid.*
33   [1927] 1 K.B. 169. See also *Simmons & McBride Ltd. v. Kirkpatrick*, [1945] 3 W.W.R. 557 (B.C.S.C.) (second-hand Cadillac uniquely suited to buyer's undertaking business — no available market for substitute — specific performance ordered).
34   *Cohen v. Roche, ibid.* at 179.
35   *Ibid.*
36   [1927] 1 K.B. 649.
37   *Dougan v. Ley* (1946), 71 C.L.R. 142 (Aust. H.C.).

iods of time and were not available in abundant quantities, thus making it quite difficult to obtain an alternative source of supply.[38]

Application of the rules related to specific performance to sale of goods contracts is complicated, to some degree, by the fact that the *Sale of Goods Act* specifically provides for the availability of the remedy in the following terms: "In an action for breach of contract to deliver specific or ascertained goods, the court may, if it thinks fit, direct that the contract be performed specifically, without giving the defendant the option of retaining the goods on payment of damages, and may impose such terms and conditions as to damages, payment of the price, and otherwise, as to the court seems just."[39] Provincial sale of goods legislation typically defines specific goods as those "identified and agreed upon at the time the contract of sale is made."[40] The concept of ascertained goods was left by the statute for elaboration at common law and, broadly speaking, refers to the identification of goods that are to be the specific subject matter of the sale at a time later than formation of the contract.[41] Unascertained goods, on the other hand, would include goods described in the agreement but not yet segregated from a larger bulk of similar goods or not yet acquired by the seller from a third party or, indeed, not yet manufactured.

On the foregoing basis, then, the statutory provision may be taken to suggest that until the goods have been specifically identified as being the goods subject to sale, no decree of specific performance may be made available. On the other hand, it is not entirely clear from the wording of the provision that it is designed to exclude the availability of specific performance in other circumstances. In *Re Wait*,[42] however, an English court denied specific performance of a contract to sell a quantity of wheat on the ground that the wheat had not yet been segregated from a larger bulk of the commodity. Accordingly, as the goods were neither specific nor ascertained, the statute was inapplicable and, it was assumed, specific performance must therefore be denied. The result in the case is perhaps explicable on the basis that, as the seller had

---

38   *Farwell v. Wallbridge* (1851), 2 Gr. 332; *Stephenson v. Clarke* (1854), 4 Gr. 540; *Flint v. Corby,* above note 13. See also *Fuller v. Richmond* (1850), 2 Gr. 24.

39   See, for example, *Sale of Goods Act*, R.S.O. 1990, c. S.1, s. 50. The same provision, with some minor variations, appears in the sale of goods legislation of all of the common law provinces.

40   See, for example, *Sale of Goods Act*, R.S.O. 1990, c. S.1, s. 1.

41   See, for example, *Re Wait*, [1927] 1 Ch. 606 (C.A.); *Re Western Canada Pulpwood Co. Ltd.*, [1930] 1 D.L.R. 652 (Man. C.A.); *Karlshamns Oljefabriker v. East Port Navigation Corp.*, [1982] 1 All E.R. 208 (Q.B.).

42   *Re Wait, ibid.*

become insolvent, the granting of specific relief would in effect grant priority in the insolvency to the buyer who, on the merits, should probably rank simply as an unsecured creditor of the seller. Nonetheless, the decision in *Re Wait* has been interpreted by subsequent courts as support for the proposition that specific performance is available only in cases where goods are either specific or ascertained.[43] So restrictive a reading of the provision, however, seems neither necessary or desirable. The statute does not explicitly say that specific performance will not be available in other circumstances.[44] Further, it would be undesirable to restrict the availability of specific performance to sales agreements involving specific or ascertained goods as that would absolutely preclude the availability of the remedy in the context of long-term agreements for the supply or purchase of fungible goods. Such agreements might be critical to the commercial welfare of either the seller or the buyer. Further, the calculation of damages in such cases may prove to be extremely difficult if not impossible. For both of these reasons, there may well be agreements of this kind in which the inadequacy of damages threshold should be considered to be met and specific performance should be decreed.

In more recent cases, there is some indication of a willingness to grant specific relief in the context of long-term supply agreements of this kind. A leading illustration is *Sky Petroleum v. V.I.P. Petroleum*,[45] a case in which an interlocutory injunction was granted in circumstances where the court acknowledged that such relief was inconsistent with the traditional position that specific performance should not be granted in the context of goods that are neither specific nor ascertained. In this case, the plaintiff was obliged under requirements of the contract to acquire, subject to certain minimum annual quantities, all its motor gasoline and diesel fuel from the defendant for a ten-year per-

---

43   See, for example, *Re Western Canada Pulpwood Co. Ltd.*, above note 41; *Humboldt Flour Mills Co. Ltd. v. Boscher* (1974), 50 D.L.R. (3d) 477 (Sask. Q.B.).

44   Indeed, it is assumed that specific performance may occasionally be available to sellers, a point not touched upon by the provision. See, for example, *Elliott v. Pierson*, [1948] 1 All E.R. 939 at 942 (Ch.). Further, the provision does not touch injunctive relief that, when awarded in favour of a buyer of goods that are neither specific nor ascertained, may have a similar effect to a decree of specific performance. See, for example, *Sky Petroleum v. V.I.P. Petroleum*, [1974] 1 W.L.R. 576 (Ch.).

45   *Sky Petroleum v. V.I.P. Petroleum, ibid.* See also *Marquest Industries Ltd. v. Willows Poultry Farms Ltd.* (1967), 63 D.L.R. (2d) 753 (B.C.S.C.), rev'd on other grounds (1968), 1 D.L.R. (3d) 513 (B.C.C.A.) (five-year contract for the supply of chicken offal — specific performance decreed).

iod, subject to renewal at certain fixed prices. As the economic circumstances of the gasoline and petroleum markets changed, the defendant
purported to terminate the agreement. This placed the plaintiff, in the
court's view, in a very difficult situation with no great prospect of finding an alternative supplier and a serious prospect of being forced out
of business. Goulding J. held that the traditional rule precluding specific performance of the contract for the supply of unascertained goods
was that damages are normally a sufficient remedy in such cases. That
rationale did not apply, in his view, to the present circumstances. Accordingly, interim injunctive relief was decreed. While it may be appropriate that such relief be awarded only sparingly in the context of
long-term contracts for the supply of goods of this kind, a rule that
altogether precluded such relief is unattractive on policy grounds. As
Goulding J. suggests, there may well be cases where damages do not
constitute an adequate remedy and specific relief would meet the needs
of justice in the particular situation.

A second issue of interpretation concerning the legislative provision raises for consideration the very relevancy of the inadequacy of
damages test. The statutory provision makes no reference to the test
and it may be considered, therefore, whether a more expansive role
for specific relief was envisaged by the statute. It is at least a plausible
view that the failure to refer to the inadequacy of damages test in the
statutory provision is some evidence of a legislative intention merely to
broaden the basis for specific relief in the context of agreements for the
sale of specific or ascertained goods rather than to create a complete
code, as it were, confining the remedy to such cases.[46] A further potential source of complication is that in a claim for detinue at common law,
courts also retained the possibility of awarding specific relief. Thus, in
the context of a contract for the purchase and sale of goods, if title has
passed the buyer, such a claim could result in a common law order that
the seller deliver the goods to the buyer. In *Cohen v. Roche*,[47] McCardie

---

46   Indeed, the intent of the original legislation upon which this provision is
     based appears to have been one of broadening the availability of the remedy,
     thus more closely aligning English law with the Scottish civilian model. See
     G.H. Treitel, "Specific Performance in the Sale of Goods" [1966] J. Bus. L. 211;
     Ontario Law Reform Commission, *Report on Sale of Goods*, vol. III (Toronto:
     Ministry of the Attorney General, 1979). The Commission recommended that
     the provision be reformed by deleting the reference to "specific or ascertained
     goods" and suggested that the remedy ought not be restricted to cases of
     "unique" goods. See *ibid.* at 443–44.
47   Above note 33. See also *Société Des Industries Metallurgiques S.A. v. Bronx Engin-
     eering Co. Ltd.*, [1975] 1 Lloyd's Rep. 465.

J. was required to consider whether these three sources of specific relief — specific performance in equity, under the statute and in detinue — applied different tests with respect to the availability of such relief. It was McCardie J.'s view that, in each instance, an inadequacy of damages test was to be applied. The same principle was applicable in any claim for specific relief in the context of an agreement for the purchase and sale of goods regardless of the precise formulation of the plaintiff's claim. As indicated above, it was McCardie J.'s view that the lot of Hepplewhite chairs at issue in that case were not sufficient to engage the inadequacy of damages test. This rejection of the idea that specific relief would be more broadly available in cases covered by the statutory provision has been broadly accepted.

c) Sale of Shares

Although specific performance is often available in the context of agreements for the purchase and sale of securities, such relief is not normally available where the securities in question, securities in publicly traded companies being the obvious illustration, are readily available in the market.[48] Allowing a plaintiff buyer to pursue specific performance relief in the context of publicly traded shares essentially allows the plaintiff to speculate at the defendant seller's expense and pick an opportune moment in which to seek relief. Rather than encourage such conduct, courts generally prefer to restrict the buyer to a damages claim at common law, thereby providing an incentive for the buyer to mitigate loss by securing substitute shares in the market.[49] Where the shares in question are privately traded, however, specific performance of the purchase agreement is more likely to be specifically enforced.[50] Such shares may be difficult to evaluate and, moreover, substitute shares would not typically be available from another source.

Common law damages will not constitute an adequate remedy in circumstances where the shares have a particular value to the plaintiff that is not reflected in their market value. The most obvious illustra-

---

48 See, for example, *Cud v. Rutter* (1719), 1 P. Wms. 570 at 571, 24 E.R. 521, Parker L.C.; *Re Schwabacher* (1908), 98 L.T. 127 at 128 (Ch.), Parker J.; *Asamera Oil Corp. Ltd. v. Sea Oil & General Corp.*, [1979] 1 S.C.R. 633 at 644–45, Estey J. Occasionally, however, specific performance of agreements to sell shares traded publicly has been awarded. See, for example, *W.C. Pitfield & Co. Ltd. v. Jomac Gold Syndicate Ltd.*, [1938] 3 D.L.R. 158 (Ont. C.A.).

49 See, for example, *Asamera Oil Corp. Ltd. v. Sea Oil & General Corp.*, *ibid.* at 660, Estey J.

50 *Eansor v. Eansor*, [1946] S.C.R. 54; *Gilbert v. Barron* (1958), 13 D.L.R. (2d) 262 (Ont. H.C.J.); *Fleisher v. Rosenbloom* (1988), 53 Man. R. (2d) 247 (Q.B.).

tion of this point is the purchase and sale of a control block of shares. Such agreements are typically subject to specific performance decrees. *Gilbert v. Barron*,[51] for example, concerned an agreement among three principal shareholders of a company who wished to preserve their control of the company. The agreement provided that should any of the three purchase further shares in the company, he would offer one-third to each of the other two at the cost price to him. The defendant acquired an additional group of shares from another source and, with a view to securing his own control of the corporation, refused to transfer shares to the other two principal shareholders. The other two brought a claim for breach of the agreement and successfully sought the remedy of specific performance. More generally, however, specific performance is in principle available in any case where valuation difficulties or other circumstances render damages an inadequate form of relief.[52]

3) Other Limitations

a) Mutuality

The doctrine of mutuality of remedies suggests that specific relief ought to be available to both parties, in a particular case, or neither. The doctrine may be stated in both a positive and negative version. Thus, the positive version of the rule is that if one party is entitled to specific performance, then the other party to the agreement should also be so entitled. In this affirmative version, then, the doctrine of mutuality provides a reason to extend specific relief to a party. The negative version of the doctrine states that if one party is not entitled to specific relief, then neither should the other party. In this version, the rule may be seen to provide a defence to a claim for specific relief. As is often pointed out, the two versions of the rule simply cannot stand together. If we assume on the basis of the principle of inadequacy of damages, for example, that one party should be entitled to specific performance but the other should not, the two versions of the rule point incoherently to equal and opposite results. The affirmative version of the rule sug-

---

51   *Ibid.* See also *Dobell v. Cowichan Copper Co. Ltd.* (1967), 65 D.L.R. (2d) 440 (B.C.S.C.). See generally Note, "Specific Performance of Contracts for a Controlling Interest in a Corporation" (1935) 49 Harv. L. Rev. 122.

52   See, for example, *Odessa Tramways Co. v. Mendel* (1878), 8 Ch. D. 235 (C.A.) (sale of treasury shares to acquire needed capital — previous attempt to sell in the market unsuccessful); *MacDonald v. Soulis*, [1925] 2 D.L.R. 926 (N.S.S.C.) (employer agreement to repurchase shares sold to employee); *McDougall Segur Exploration Co. of Canada Ltd. v. Solloway Mills & Co. Ltd.*, [1931] 2 W.W.R. 516 (Alta. S.C.).

gests that both parties should be entitled to specific relief. The negative version will suggest that neither of them should be so entitled. This fundamental incoherence of the rule — itself a rather damning indictment — is not the only difficulty with this now essentially discredited doctrine. The doctrine simply lacks a convincing rationale. Neither in its affirmative nor its negative form does the mere fact of lack of equal access to specific relief by the parties to an agreement provide a reasoned justification for the conclusion that such relief should be either granted or denied to both of them.

The principal work done by the affirmative version of the rule is to provide a justification, where it might be otherwise lacking, for the proposition that since a purchaser of real estate is entitled to specific performance, so too is the vendor. As suggested earlier in this chapter,[53] however, the mere fact that the purchaser may be entitled to specific performance where damages would prove to be an inadequate remedy does not, in itself, appear to provide a convincing reason for providing the vendor with a similar remedy in the event of a default by the purchaser. There would be nothing incoherent with a rule that stipulated that a purchaser may be entitled to specific relief but that a vendor, whose only interest in the transaction being performed is monetary, would normally be limited to the remedy of damages and subject, as a result, to a duty to engage in acts of mitigation following the default by the purchaser. The mere fact that the property may, in the requisite sense, be unique and thus justify specific relief to the purchaser does not mean that the monetary consideration to be received in return by the vendor is in some sense unique, thus legitimating or requiring the special characteristics of specific redress. As has been suggested by others,[54] the most plausible explanation for the development of the affirmative mutuality principle rests in the pre-*Judicature Act* division between proceedings in common law and those in equity. The concern may have been if one party was afforded the advantage of equitable relief, it would be unattractive to bifurcate the proceedings concerning the transaction and leave the other party to the tender mercies of juries in the courts of common law. In other words, the concern may have been with mutuality of jurisdiction rather than mutuality of remedy as such. This justification for the doctrine obviously does not survive the late-nineteenth-century merger of the proceedings of the courts of

---

53   See above this Chapter, section B(2).

54   See, for example, Sharpe, above note 1 at 7–43; referring, *inter alia*, to *Lewis v. Lord Lechmere*, above note 24; *Clifford v. Turrell* (1841), 1 Y. & C.C.C. 138, 62 E.R. 826.

common law and equity under the *Judicature Act* regime.[55] If specific performance for the vendor of real estate is to be supported, then, it must be on some basis other than a doctrine of mutuality.[56]

The negative version of the mutuality principle has been stated in various forms over the years. It appears now to be accepted, however, that the correct version of the principle is that stated in the following terms by Professor Ames: "Equity will not compel specific performance by a defendant if, *after performance*, the common law remedy of damages would be his *sole security* for the performance of the plaintiff's side of the contract."[57]

Earlier statements of the doctrine had suggested that mutuality of remedies must be established at the time of contracting. In *Price v. Strange*,[58] however, it was clearly established that the principle does not apply if the defendant, against whom specific performance may be ordered, will not be left, after performing, with a mere remedy in damages. In other words, the Ames definition plainly indicates that the underlying concern of mutuality doctrine, in this context, is not a concern to establish an absolute equality of access to specific relief from the point of contract formation but, rather, a concern about the insecurity of the defendant's position in circumstances where the defendant is required to specifically perform but cannot be guaranteed of a return performance from the plaintiff. In such circumstances, the plaintiff's claim for specific performance may fail on the basis that granting the decree would place the defendant in an untenable or insecure position. Once this underlying purpose of the negative version of the principle is accepted, a number of implications with respect to the operation of the rule are clarified.

First, the rule only applies in circumstances where the contract does not require performance of the plaintiff's obligation before that of the defendant. If the plaintiff has already performed its obligations by the time the decree would be issued, there is no insecurity with respect to that performance. Accordingly, specific performance can be awarded without unfairly exposing the defendant to the risk of the plaintiff's non-performance. Indeed, in *Price v. Strange*, this principle is applied to circumstances where part of the plaintiff's responsibilities were discharged by the defendant. In this case, an overholding subtenant had

---

55   For brief discussion of which, see Chapter 1, section B.
56   See further above this Chapter, section B(2), the discussion of "Sale of Land."
57   J.B. Ames, "Mutuality in Specific Performance" in J.B. Ames, *Lectures on Legal History* (Cambridge: Harvard University Press, 1913) at 371 (emphasis added).
58   [1978] Ch. 337.

entered into an oral agreement with the head tenant whereby the sub-tenant agreed to do certain repair work on the premises in return for a renewal of the sublease. The plaintiff commenced the work in question but was ordered by the defendant to desist before completion of the work. The defendant then completed the work herself and, though she continued to accept for some months rental payments from the plaintiff at the renewal rate, she refused to execute the sublease. The subtenant sought specific performance of the obligation to execute the sublease and enjoyed success. Goff L.J. observed that in the circumstances the "defendant is not at risk of being ordered to grant the underlease and having no remedy except in damages for subsequent non-perform-ance of the plaintiff's agreement to put the premises in repair."[59] The plaintiff's decree of specific performance was conditioned, however, on reimbursement of the defendant for the portion of the repair work that she had performed.

Further, once it is appreciated that the object of the negative mu-tuality principle is to prevent hardship to the defendant who is ordered to specifically perform without satisfactory assurance that the plaintiff will perform in due course, it becomes apparent that the principle is in the nature of a discretionary defence rather than an absolute bar to a decree of specific performance. This point has also been confirmed in *Price v. Strange*.[60] In turn, once the discretionary nature of the defence is appreciated, it may be that a broader range of factors relating to the exercise of the discretion may come into view. Thus, if, by definition, the issue arises in circumstances where the defendant has voluntarily entered into an agreement in which the plaintiff's performance does not precede the defendant's performance and where the defendant has not, by contract, ensured security of some kind for the plaintiff's performance, it may be questioned whether the discretionary defence should defeat the plaintiff's claim for specific performance as a mat-ter of course. The plaintiff, having successfully made out the case that damages are an inadequate remedy, has a strong claim, it seems, to a de-cree of specific performance. Conditioning that relief on a requirement that the plaintiff has already performed or has provided security in some form for that performance appears to improve the position of the defendant over that secured by the terms of the contract. On the other hand, by granting the decree of specific performance, the defendant is deprived of the self-help remedy of breach of contract in circumstances where the defendant may be reasonably concerned that the plaintiff

---

59   *Ibid.* at 357–58.
60   *Ibid.* at 359.

will not ultimately perform. Moreover, the fact that the parties are engaged in litigation with respect to performance of the contract suggests that the defendant may have reasons to be insecure about the plaintiff's willingness to perform that were not present at the time of formation of the agreement. On balance, then, it may be that the traditional position that courts will withhold specific performance unless the defendant's position with respect to the plaintiff's performance is in some sense secure may often have merit. The important point, however, for present purposes is that the courts possess a discretion in these cases to determine whether the legitimate interest of the defendant in not being exposed to lack of security with respect to the plaintiff's performance should trump the plaintiff's legitimate interest in securing a decree of specific performance.

The discretionary nature of the doctrine also suggests that there may be some scope for judicial creativity in determining the manner in which security of the plaintiff's performance might be obtained as a condition of granting the plaintiff a decree of specific performance. There is significant evidence of a willingness to exercise a discretion of this kind in the existing cases. Thus, in a Canadian case[61] involving an agreement to exchange land in Saskatchewan for a property in Iowa, the Supreme Court of Canada rejected a mutuality defence and held that it would be possible to order the defendant to transfer the Saskatchewan property into the hands of an officer of the court pending plaintiff's transfer of the Iowa property to the defendant. Similarly, in a recent English case[62] involving a transfer of shares by the defendant in return for a consideration calculated in accord with a formula that could only be applied in the two years following the transfer, the English court held that the shares should be initially transferred to the plaintiff's solicitors who would hold the shares as stakeholders until such time as the plaintiff's payment was made.

Finally, it may be noted that the underlying rationale of ensuring security of performance does appear to be evident in earlier cases applying the negative mutuality principle. Thus, specific relief was traditionally denied on mutuality grounds to plaintiffs who are minors.[63] In such cases, courts were evidently concerned that the legal status of minors rendered it impossible to secure the return performance of the

---

61   *Jones v. Tucker* (1916), 53 S.C.R. 431.
62   *Langen & Wind Ltd. v. Bell*, [1972] Ch. 685.
63   See, for example, *Flight v. Bolland* (1828), 4 Russ. 298, 38 E.R. 817; *Lumley v. Ravenscroft*, [1895] 1 Q.B. 683 (C.A.).

plaintiff. In *Gretzky v. Ontario Minor Hockey Association*,[64] for example, an attempt by a promising fourteen-year-old hockey player, described presciently by the trial judge as "exceptionally gifted,"[65] to force a Toronto hockey league to permit him to move away from his home in Brantford to play in Toronto failed on the ground of lack of mutuality of remedy. The defendant league would obviously be quite incapable of requiring the plaintiff to live up to his side of the bargain.

b) Difficulty in Supervision

Courts are reluctant to grant decrees of specific performance that might require difficult or long-term exercises in supervision of the performance of a party. There are a number of reasons for this reluctance. The ordering of specific performance of a complex task may require difficult judgments as to whether the promisor has successfully complied with the decree. Not only is the resulting adjudicative task a burdensome one, the promisor may be placed in a difficult situation when determining the level of performance required on pain of being exposed, in the event of error, to a citation for contempt. There is a risk, in other words, that the effect of the order on the defendant may be harsh or oppressive. These problems will be exacerbated if the task is not defined with sufficient precision and such vagueness will, in itself, provide a basis for refusing to grant specific performance.[66] Courts will also be reluctant to decree specific performance of tasks that require an extended period of time on the ground that such decrees create the potential for a series of judicial interventions with resulting strain on judicial resources.[67] For reasons such as these, it is well established, for example, that a decree is not available to require specific performance of a promise to carry on a business. In *Co-operative Insurance Society Ltd. v. Argyll Stores (Holdings) Ltd.*,[68] for example, the House of Lords held that an obligation of a major tenant in a shopping mall to operate the business of a supermarket on the leased premises during usual business hours could not be specifically enforced. In explaining this result, Lord Hoffmann referred to the risk of an indefinite series of rul-

64   (1975), 64 D.L.R. (3d) 467 (Ont. H.C.J.).

65   *Ibid.* at 467.

66   See, for example, *Brace v. Wehnert* (1858), 25 Beav. 348, 53 E.R. 670.

67   *Ryan v. Mutual Tontine Westminster Chambers Assoc.*, [1893] 1 Ch. 116 at 123 (C.A.), Lord Esher M.R.; *City of Kingston v. Kingston Portsmouth & Cataraqui Electric Rwy.* (1898), 25 O.A.R. 462 at 466, Moss J.A.

68   [1997] 3 All E.R. 297 (H.L.). See also *S.B.I. Management Ltd. v. Wabush (Carol) Co-op Society Ltd.* (1985), 51 Nfld. & P.E.I.R. 257 (Nfld. S.C.T.D.); *Toulon Development Corporation v. Loblaws* (1995), 161 N.B.R. (2d) 313 (Q.B.).

ings on compliance, the oppressive nature of the contempt sanction, imprecision in the terms of the obligation and the potential enrichment of the plaintiff at the defendant's expense if the defendant was required to carry on the business at a loss.[69]

For similar reasons, it is often said that decrees of specific performance will not normally be awarded in the context of building or construction agreements.[70] Nonetheless, an exception to this general principle has developed in circumstances where the interest of the plaintiff in specific performance is particularly compelling. Thus, a series of nineteenth-century cases involving railways held that where a railway had acquired ownership of land on the vendor's faith, in part, of its undertaking to build an accommodation work, such as a road, bridge, wharf or siding for the benefit of the vendor, who retained adjacent land, the obligation to build the accommodating work will be specifically enforced.[71] Where the accommodation work was not described with sufficient precision in the agreement, however, such relief was denied.[72] In *Wolverhampton Corp. v. Emmons*,[73] it was accepted that the principle was of general application and therefore applied to circumstances in which a municipal corporation transferred land to the defendant who, in turn, covenanted that he would build houses on the land within a specific period of time. Although the particulars of the houses to be constructed were agreed upon, the defendant, having acquired the land, refused to proceed with the project and was held subject to a decree of specific performance.

In a similar Ontario case, *Tanenbaum v. W.J. Bell Paper Co. Ltd.*,[74] the vendor of a parcel of land retained a parcel that, after the sale, was separated from the nearest public roadway by the transferred parcel. The purchaser, as part of the agreement of purchase and sale, had agreed to construct a road across the purchased parcel equivalent in quality to the public roadway to accommodate the vendor by providing access to the public roadway. The purchaser also agreed to install an accommodat-

---

69   A different result is possible in civilian jurisdictions. See *Propriétés Cité Concordia Ltée v. Royal Bank*, [1983] R.D.J. 524 (Que. C.A.).

70   See, for example, *Powell Duffryn Steam Coal Co. v. Taftvale Rwy. Co.* (1874), 9 Ch. App. 331.

71   *Storer v. Great Western Rwy. Co.* (1842), 2 Y. & C.C.C. 48, 63 E.R. 21; *Sanderson v. Cockermouth and Worthington Rwy. Co.* (1849), 11 Beav. 497, 50 E.R. 909; *Wilson v. Furness Rwy. Co.* (1869) L.R. 9 Eq. 28.

72   See, for example, *Wilson v. Northampton and Banbury Junction Rwy. Co.* (1874), 9 Ch. App. 279 (undertaking to construct "a station").

73   [1901] 1 K.B. 515.

74   (1956), 4 D.L.R. (2d) 177 (Ont. H.C.J.).

ing water main that would provide water to the parcel retained by the vendor. The Ontario Court relied on English authority for the general proposition that, in such circumstances, a decree of specific performance can be awarded. Gale J. also accepted English authority[75] for the proposition that it was not necessary that the defendant have acquired the property on which the accommodating work is to be constructed under the agreement in question. The doctrine is engaged merely by virtue of the fact that the defendant is in possession of the land on which the work is to be done. Thus, in the English decision, where the vendor had retained land on which the accommodation work was to be constructed for the benefit of the purchaser, a decree of specific performance was awarded. Gale J. further relied on an American treatise[76] for the following suggestion that the modern trend of the cases leans in the direction of granting specific performance: "The basis of equity's disinclination to enforce building contracts specifically is the difficulty of enforcing a decree without an expenditure of effort disproportionate to the value of the results. But where the inadequacy of damages is great, and the difficulties not extreme, specific performance will be granted and the tendency in modern times has been increasingly towards granting relief, where under the particular circumstances of the case, damages are not an adequate remedy."[77] In principle, then, courts must balance the degree of difficulty of supervision with the intensity of the plaintiff's interest in specific performance, granting specific performance in cases where the suppression of concerns about supervision is necessary in order to achieve a just result.

The practical problems of supervising contract performance is often said to be one of the principal reasons for refusing to specifically enforce contracts of personal services or employment.[78] Although the traditional principle of denying specific relief for breach of contracts for personal services is well established,[79] the courts have also indicated

---

75 *Carpenters Estates Ltd. v. Davies,* [1940] Ch. 160.
76 S. Williston, *A Treatise on the Law of Contracts,* rev. ed., vol. 5 (New York: Baker, 1936–45).
77 *Ibid.* s. 1423 at 3976–77, quoted in *Tanenbaum v. W.J. Bell Paper Co. Ltd.,* above note 74 at 204.
78 *Ryan v. Mutual Tontine Westminster Chambers Association,* above note 67.
79 See, for example, *Clarke v. Price* (1819), 2 Wils. Ch. 157, 37 E.R. 270; *Baldwin v. Society for the Diffusion of Useful Knowledge* (1838), 9 Sim. 393, 59 E.R. 409; *Pickering v. Bishop of Ely* (1843), 2 Y. & C.C.C. 249, 63 E.R. 109; *Ogden v. Fossick* (1862), 4 De G. F. & J. 426, 45 E.R. 1249; *Southern Foundries (1926) Ltd. v. Shirlaw,* [1940] A.C. 701 (H.L.). And see *Dupré Quarries Ltd. v. Dupré,* [1934] S.C.R. 528; *Field v. C.N.R.,* [1934] 3 D.L.R. 383 (N.S.S.C.); *Kapp v. B.C. Lions Football*

932   THE LAW OF CONTRACTS

a greater flexibility with respect to the availability of specific relief. In particular, the force of the argument that difficulties in supervision lead inescapably to a denial of specific relief has been significantly undermined. In a well-known passage from his opinion in *C.H. Giles & Co. Ltd. v. Morris*,[80] Megarry J. reasoned as follows:

> One day, perhaps, the courts will look again at the so-called rule that contracts for personal services or involving the continuous performance of services will not be specifically enforced. Such a rule is plainly not absolute and without exception, nor do I think that it can be based on any narrow consideration such as difficulties of constant superintendence by the court. ... The reasons why the court is reluctant to decree specific performance of a contract for personal services (and I would regard it as a strong reluctance rather than a rule) are, I think, more complex and more firmly bottomed on human nature. If a singer sang flat, or sharp, or too fast, or too slowly, or too loudly, or too quietly, or resorted to a dozen of the manifestations of temperament traditionally associated with some singers, the threat of committal would reveal itself as a most unsatisfactory weapon: for who could say whether the imperfections of performance were natural or self-induced? To make an order with such possibilities of evasion would be vain; and so the order will not be made. However, not all contracts of personal service or for the continuous performance of services are as dependent as this on matters of opinion and judgment, nor do all such contracts involve the same degree of the daily impact of person upon person. In general, no doubt, the inconvenience and mischief of decreeing specific performance of most of such contracts will greatly outweigh the advantages, and specific performance will be refused. But I do not think that it should be assumed that as soon as any element of personal service or continuous services can be discerned in a contract the court will, without more, refuse specific performance.[81]

As Megarry J. observes, there are many employment contexts in which the difficulty of supervision rationale would be less than convincing. Where employment tasks are well defined, lack any significant element of opinion or judgment and are easily monitored, a decree of specific performance is not likely to impose a substantial burden of supervision

---

Club (1967), 64 D.L.R. (2d) 426 (B.C.S.C.); *Red Deer College v. Michaels*, [1976] 2 S.C.R. 324.

80   [1972] 1 W.L.R. 307.

81   *Ibid.* at 318.

upon a court. Moreover, modern experience with labour arbitration, where reinstatement of a grieving employee is a commonplace order, provides abundant evidence that, at least in the context of claims brought by the employee, specific performance is often a perfectly viable remedy.[82]

Nonetheless, instances of courts actually awarding specific performance or, in the more likely case, issuing an injunction[83] that will have the effect of requiring specific performance on an employment contract are rare indeed. A leading illustration of the phenomenon is *Hill v. C.A. Parsons & Co. Ltd.*[84] in which an injunction was issued ordering an employer not to dismiss a long-term employee who was close to retirement age. The employee had been dismissed by the employer under pressure from a closed-shop union that the plaintiff had refused to join. Damages were inadequate as they would not fully compensate the employee for the loss of pension and other retirement benefits. Moreover, prolonging the plaintiff's employment would also likely bring him within the protection of a new statutory scheme that prohibited dismissal for refusal to join a trade union. Although the facts of this case are both unusual and ideally suited to test the availability of specific relief in an employment context,[85] there have been similar awards in subsequent English[86] and Canadian[87] cases. Notwithstanding the existence of such authorities, the general rule against specific relief in the employment context remains securely established. As we will see in "Public Policy"

---

82 See R. Brown, "Contract Remedies in a Planned Economy: Labour Arbitration Leads the Way" in B. Reiter and J. Swan, eds., *Studies in Contract Law* (Toronto: Butterworths, 1980) c. 4.

83 For discussion of injunctions see below this Chapter, section C.

84 [1972] Ch. 305.

85 A point noted by Lord Denning M.R. in *Chappell v. Times Newspapers Ltd.*, [1975] 1 W.L.R. 482 at 501.

86 See, for example, *Jones v. Lee*, [1980] I.C.R. 310 (C.A.) (dismissal of teacher without due process enjoined); *Irani v. Southampton and South-West Hampshire Health Authority*, [1985] I.R.L.R. 203 (Ch.) (termination of employment without due process enjoined); *Powell v. London Borough of Brent*, [1987] I.R.L.R. 466 (C.A.) (injunction to protect a promised promotion).

87 See, for example, *Shephard v. Colchester Regional Hospital Commission* (1991), 103 N.S.R. (2d) 361 (S.C.T.D.), leave to appeal to C.A. refused 106 N.S.R. (2d) 239 (S.C.A.D.) (temporary restoration of hospital privileges to a physician); *McCaw v. United Church of Canada* (1991), 82 D.L.R. (4th) 289 (Ont. C.A.) (restoration of status of cleric). See also *International Brotherhood of Electrical Workers v. Winnipeg Builders Exchange*, [1967] S.C.R. 628 (injunction prohibiting a strike).

later in this section,[88] the general rule is more stoutly defended on various public policy grounds.

c) Unfairness

More generally, courts retain a general discretion to refuse to grant awards of specific performance where to do so would produce an unfair or unjust result. The various circumstances taken into account in exercising this discretion, referred to here as circumstances of "unfairness," can be divided, broadly speaking, into two categories. First, there are a variety of contexts within which the conduct of the plaintiff is such that it appears unfair to grant the plaintiff the advantages of specific relief. Second, there are situations in which the circumstances of the defendant are such that specific relief would impose an unfair burden on either the defendant or the plaintiff. No clear distinction is drawn between these two types of considerations in the case law and, in the circumstances of a particular case, elements of both kinds of unfairness may be present. Specific performance may be denied, for example, on the basis that the defendant has been induced into the agreement on the basis of a misrepresentation.[89] As we have seen,[90] misrepresentation may also provide a ground for rescission of the agreement. It has been suggested, however, that the nature of the representation required to establish a defence to a claim for specific performance may be less severe than that required to ground a claim for rescission.[91] Thus, where a misrepresentation relates to a collateral matter that could not ground rescission, it may nonetheless provide a defence to a claim for specific performance.[92] A failure to disclose information that might not constitute misrepresentation might nonetheless provide a defence.[93] Further, the fact that the right to rescind for misrepresentation may have been lost by, for example, affirmation of the contract does not preclude a defendant's reliance on the misrepresentation as a defence to a claim for specific performance.[94] The fact that a

---

88   See below this Chapter, section B(3)(d).

89   See, for example, *Henderson v. Thompson* (1909), 41 S.C.R. 445; *Whitney v. MacLean*, [1932] 1 W.W.R. 417 (Alta. C.A.); *Davis v. Moranis and Smith*, [1949] 4 D.L.R. 433 (Ont. C.A.).

90   See Chapter 10.

91   *Re Terry & White's Contract* (1886), 32 Ch. D. 14 at 29 (C.A.), Lindley L.J.; *Whitney v. MacLean*, above note 89 at 450, McGillivray J.A.

92   *Holliday v. Lockwood*, [1917] 2 Ch. 47.

93   See, for example, *Walters v. Morgan* (1861), 3 De G. F. & J. 718 at 724, 45 E.R. 1056, Westbury L.J.; *Falcke v. Gray*, above note 30.

94   See, for example, *Shaw v. Masson*, [1923] S.C.R. 187; *Panzer v. Zeifman* (1978), 88 D.L.R. (3d) 131 (Ont. C.A.)

defendant was labouring under a mistake when entering the agreement may also constitute a defence to a claim for specific performance. In a leading case,[95] however, it was suggested that mere mistake on the defendant's part was insufficient. The plaintiff must be implicated to some extent in the error. Subject to this limitation, mistake is a recognized defence to a plea for specific performance[96] and is all the more likely to be available in a case where specific relief would impose hardship on the defendant.[97] An agreement entered into in circumstances of unfairness in the sense that an unfair advantage has been taken by the plaintiff of the defendant's inequality of bargaining power will not enjoy success.[98] Although unfairness in this context is related to, if not co-extensive with, the modern doctrine of unconscionability[99] giving rise to a right of rescission, there is some possibility that the defence may be available in circumstances that would not provide a basis for rescission.[100] Mere inadequacy of consideration is not, in itself, a sufficient basis for refusing specific performance.[101] Further, notwithstanding statements to the contrary in the traditional authorities,[102] it appears to be accepted that written undertakings given without consideration, but under seal, may be specifically enforced.[103]

Courts retain a discretion to refuse a decree of specific performance in circumstances where specific relief would impose great hardship on either one of the parties. It has been suggested that the circumstances

95 *Tamplin v. James* (1880), 15 Ch. D. 215 (C.A.). See also *Hobbs v. Esquimalt & Nanaimo Railway Co.* (1899), 29 S.C.R. 450; *Freeman v. Kaltio* (1963), 39 D.L.R. (2d) 496 (B.C.S.C.).

96 See, for example, *Omnium Securities Co. v. Richardson* (1884), 7 O.R. 182 (H.C.J.); *Drummond Mines Co. v. Fernholm* (1906), 8 O.W.R. 864 (Div. Ct.).

97 See, for example, *Hope v. Walter*, [1900] 1 Ch. 257 (C.A.) (sale of investment property — unbeknownst to vendor and purchaser, property was being used as a brothel — vendor's claim for specific performance denied).

98 See, for example, *McColl-Frontenac Oil Co. v. Saulnier & Saulnier*, [1949] 3 D.L.R. 208 (N.B.S.C.A.D.), leave to appeal to S.C.C. refused, [1949] 3 D.L.R. 777 (N.B.S.C.A.D.); *McCorkell v. McFarlane*, [1952] O.W.N. 653 (H.C.J.); *Hnatuck v. Chretian* (1960), 31 W.W.R. 130 (B.C.S.C.); *Knupp v. Bell* (1960), 67 D.L.R. (2d) 256 (Sask. C.A.); *Huttges v. Verner* (1975), 64 D.L.R. (3d) 374 (N.B.S.C.A.D.).

99 See Chapter 11, section D.

100 See, for example, *McCorkell v. McFarlane*, above note 98; *Huttges v. Verner*, above note 98.

101 See, for example, *Coles v. Trecothick* (1804), 9 Ves. 234, 32 E.R. 592; *Western v. Russell* (1814), 3 Ves. & B. 187, 35 E.R. 450; *Haywood v. Cope* (1858), 25 Beav. 140, 53 E.R. 589.

102 See, for example, *Jefferys v. Jefferys* (1841), Cr. & Ph. 138, 41 E.R. 443; *Savereux v. Tourangeau* (1908), 16 O.L.R. 600 (Div. Ct.).

103 *Mountford v. Scott*, [1974] 1 All E.R. 248 (Ch.).

amounting to hardship must be present as, a general rule, at the time the contract is entered into.[104] Indeed, in some cases it has been suggested, more strictly, that hardship resulting from subsequent events is immaterial.[105] Nonetheless, there are both traditional and modern authorities taking into account hardship resulting from subsequent events as a basis for denying specific performance.[106] Modern illustrations include *Patel v. Ali*[107] in which the subsequent events creating a hardship were not in any way attributable to the conduct of the plaintiff. The defendant vendors were a married couple who had agreed to sell their home to the plaintiffs. Shortly thereafter, the wife gave birth to a second child and the husband was imprisoned for a period of time. After his release, a third child was born. As a result of illness associated with the latter pregnancy, the wife became physically dependent on the support of friends and relatives, one of whom lived nearby. The court held that forced removal of the defendant wife from the premises would be a great hardship and the plaintiff's claim for specific performance was dismissed.

Similarly, in an Ontario decision, *1110049 Ontario Ltd. v. Exclusive Diamonds Inc.*,[108] a claim for specific performance of a contract to sell a jewellery business was successfully resisted on hardship grounds. The defendant had carried on a jewellery business in a mall with his wife. Depressed, as a result of the brutal murder of his wife, he agreed to sell the business to another jeweller. The defendant subsequently decided that he wished to continue the business. The Court of Appeal held that there would be substantial hardship resulting from the forced sale of the business. Further, hardship to a third party may provide a basis for declining a decree of specific performance. In another Ontario case, *Mitz v. Wiseman*,[109] specific performance of a contract to transfer a cottage property was denied on the basis that a second purchaser from the same vendor, who had taken possession of the property and made substantial improvements, would suffer considerable hardship if a decree were issued in favour of the first purchaser.

104 *Matthews v. McVeigh*, [1954] 2 D.L.R. 338 (Ont. C.A.); *Stewart v. Ambrosina* (1975), 63 D.L.R. (3d) 595 (Ont. H.C.J.), aff'd (1977), 78 D.L.R. (3d) 125 (Ont. C.A.).
105 *Stewart v. Ambrosina, ibid.* at 602 (Ont. H.C.J.), Cory J.
106 See, for example, *City of London v. Nash* (1747), 1 Ves. Sen. 12, 27 E.R. 859; *Webb v. Direct London & Portsmouth Railway Co.* (1852), 1 De G.M. & G. 521, 42 E.R. 654; *Blackwood v. Paul* (1854), 4 Gr. 550; *Hill v. Buffalo & Lake Huron Rwy. Co.* (1864), 10 Gr. 506.
107 [1984] Ch. 283.
108 Above note 14.
109 (1971), 22 D.L.R. (3d) 513 (Ont. H.C.J.).

d) Public Policy

As indicated earlier in this section,[110] the more persuasive justification for the traditional reluctance of the courts to enforce contracts for personal services or employment is that there are significant reasons of public policy for refusing to specifically enforce such agreements. With respect to claims brought by employers, specific relief requiring an unwilling employee to serve a plaintiff employer is traditionally considered to constitute an inappropriate intrusion upon the defendant employee's freedom of action. Indeed, one judge colourfully noted that a decree of specific performance in such circumstances would "turn contracts of service into contracts of slavery."[111] As far as claims brought by the employee are concerned, the rationale for denying specific relief is often explained in terms of a policy against forcing upon the employer an employment relationship where the employer's trust and confidence in the employee has been significantly undermined.[112] The existence of such a relationship of trust and confidence may vary in degree, however, from one type of employment to another. Thus, where successful performance rests on the integrity and loyalty of the employee, and the employer lacks confidence in the employee's capacity for faithful service, such considerations are likely to provide a basis for refusing specific relief.[113] On the other hand, where such concerns are not present, either because of the nature of the employment or the nature of the relationship between the particular employer and employee, one might anticipate a greater judicial willingness to grant specific relief in the perhaps unusual circumstances where damages would not constitute an adequate remedy for the employee. It should be noted that the policy against imposing relationships of trust and confidence upon unwilling parties may apply in other than employment settings. Thus, it is well established, for example, that an agreement to enter into and carry on a partnership is not specifically enforceable.[114]

Public policy considerations may arise in other contexts. Thus, for example, the possibility of awarding specific relief in the context of the defendant's insolvency raises policy issues of some subtlety. Where the plaintiff would be entitled to specific relief in any event, as in the

---

110 See above this Chapter, section B(3)(b).

111 *De Francesco v. Barnum* (1890), 45 Ch. D. 430 at 438, Fry L.J.

112 See, for example, *Pickering v. Bishop of Ely*, above note 79 at 267 (Y. & C.C.C.); *Page One Records Ltd. v. Britton*, [1968] 1 W.L.R. 157 (Ch.); *Red Deer College v. Michaels*, above note 79.

113 See, for example, *Chappell v. Times Newspapers*, above note 85.

114 See, for example, *New Brunswick and Canada Rwy. and Land Co. v. Muggeridge* (1859), 4 Drew. 686, 62 E.R. 263; *Scott v. Rayment* (1868), L.R. 7 Eq. 112.

context of a sale of rare or unique goods, a strong argument can be made for allowing specific relief, notwithstanding the defendant's insolvency. Moreover, where title to the goods has been transferred by the defendant to the plaintiff purchaser, the granting of specific relief offers an attractive result even though the point appears not to have been clearly settled. The more difficult question, however, is whether the fact of the defendant's insolvency renders damages an inadequate remedy thus providing, in itself, a basis for specific relief that might not otherwise be present. The better view, arguably, is that the decree of specific performance ought not to be a device whereby plaintiffs are entitled to get an undeserved priority over other unsecured creditors.[115] A policy favouring even-handed distribution of the insolvent's estate is an obstacle to the granting of specific relief. In cases where the very agreement itself is unenforceable[116] on grounds of public policy, of course, a decree of specific performance is unavailable[117] as are all other remedies for breach of contract.

e) Delay

As we have seen previously,[118] in the context of a discussion of the effect of misrepresentations in equity, the equitable defence of laches is available in proceedings in circumstances where the plaintiff had engaged in unreasonable delay before seeking rescission of the transaction. This general equitable defence is also applicable in the context of claims for specific performance. As in other contexts, the defence is engaged not merely by delay but in circumstances where delay has been coupled with prejudice of some kind. In *Bark-Fong v. Cooper*,[119] Duff J. made this point in the following terms: "The doctrine of laches, it has been frequently said, is not a technical doctrine and in order to constitute a defence there must be such a change of position as would make it inequitable to require the defendant to carry out the contract. The delay must be of such a character to justify the inference that the

---

115 See *Anders Utkilens Rederi A/S v. O/Y Lovisa Stevedoring Co. A/B, The Golfstraum*, [1985] 2 All E.R. 669 at 674 (Ch.), Goulding J. And see H. Horack, "Insolvency and Specific Performance" (1917–18) 31 Harv. L. Rev. 702; H. McClintock, "Adequacy of Ineffective Remedy at Law" (1932) 16 Minn. L. Rev. 233. See also *Re Wait*, above note 41.

116 See Chapter 12 for discussion of the doctrines that have the effect of rendering agreements unenforceable on grounds of public policy.

117 See, for example, *Finney v. Township of McKellar* (1982), 133 D.L.R. (3d) 351 (Ont. C.A.).

118 See Chapter 10, section E.

119 (1913), 49 S.C.R. 14.

plaintiffs intended to abandon their rights under the contract or otherwise make it unjust to grant specific performance."[120]

4) Monetary Awards

Orders of specific performance and injunctions are equitable remedial alternatives to a claim for monetary damages at common law. It is important to note, however, that specific relief can, in certain circumstances, be coupled with a monetary award. The most common form of such awards is made in the context of real estate transactions and in circumstances where the vendor is not able to provide the type of ownership rights or quality of land promised in the agreement of purchase and sale. Such awards typically take the form of a reduction in the purchase price and are referred to as "specific performance with an abatement." Further, in the nineteenth century, a statutory power was conferred upon courts of equity to award damages as an alternative to or in substitution for the granting of an injunction or a decree of specific performance.[121] The statute, the *Chancery Amendment Act*,[122] commonly known as *Lord Cairns' Act*, was enacted in 1858 with a view to solving a procedural problem inherent in the pre-*Judicature Act* system in which the Courts of Equity and Courts of Common Law were completely separate institutions. A plaintiff who failed in equity to secure a decree of specific performance and who wished to obtain relief in the form of a damages award would be required to launch a second action in the Courts of Common Law. The legislation cured this procedural defect by enabling a court of equity, in such circumstances, to substitute a damages award for the equitable relief unsuccessfully sought by the plaintiff. Although this jurisdiction has been preserved to the present day in the Canadian common law provinces,[123] the procedural merger of the courts of common law and equity effected by the *Judicature Acts*[124] and equivalent Canadian developments,[125] made this procedural problem disappear. Since that time, an action for common law

---

120 *Ibid.* at 23. See also *Lindsay Petroleum Co. v. Hurd* (1874), L.R. 5 P.C. 221; *Lazard Brothers & Co. Ltd. v. Fairfield Properties Co. (Mayfair) Ltd.* (1977), 121 Sol. Jo. 793 (Ch.).

121 See generally P. McDermott, *Equitable Damages* (Sydney: Butterworths, 1994).

122 1858, (U.K.), 21 & 22 Vict., c. 27.

123 See, for example, *Courts of Justice Act*, R.S.O. 1990, c. C.43, s. 99. In some provinces, the jurisdiction is preserved as part of the general equity jurisdiction preserved by statute; see, for example, *Judicature Act*, R.S.N.S. 1989, c. 240, s. 41.

124 1873 (U.K.), 36 & 37 Vict. c. 66; 1875 (U.K.), 38 & 39 Vict., c. 77.

125 See, for example, *Courts of Justice Act*, R.S.O. 1990, c. C.43, s. 96.

damages can be combined with a claim for equitable relief in the now procedurally unified court system. The question that remains, however, is whether contemporary courts, in the exercise of their equitable jurisdiction to grant damages in lieu of specific relief, simply apply common law principles for the calculation of damages or, on the other hand, retain a jurisdiction to apply equitable principles that may function differently from those at common law. Both types of monetary awards — specific performance with abatement and damages in lieu of specific relief — will be briefly considered here.

Awards of specific performance with an abatement in the context of real estate transactions may be granted either to the vendor or the purchaser. The common sense underlying the remedy is perhaps more obvious in the context of claims by a purchaser. Where a vendor is unable to transfer either the promised title[126] or quality[127] of land, allowing the purchaser to accept whatever it is the vendor can convey, subject to an appropriate deduction, may accord with the reasonable expectations of the purchaser and, perhaps, the vendor as well. Although the cases illustrate a variety of techniques for calculating the abatement,[128] the exercise is essentially similar to calculating damages for breach of contract. Where the remedy is available to the purchaser, it is essentially an option that the purchaser may prefer to the right to treat the contract as discharged or terminated by the vendor's repudiatory breach[129] and pursue the vendor for return of the deposit[130] or for damages for breach of contract.[131] The availability of the remedy is subject to a number of limitations. It is available only for a breach of a term rather than a misrepresentation inducing the agreement. The

---

126 See, for example, *Kennedy v. Spence* (1911), 24 O.L.R. 535 (H.C.J.); *Burrow v. Scammell* (1881), 19 Ch. D. 175; *Hurley v. Roy* (1921), 64 D.L.R. 375 (Ont. S.C.A.D.).

127 See, for example, *Butler v. Purcell* (1956), 2 D.L.R. (2d) 317 (N.S.S.C.); *Lavine v. Independent Builders Ltd.*, [1932] 4 D.L.R. 569 (Ont. C.A.); *Levy and Levy v. Rodewalt* (1959), 18 D.L.R. (2d) 77 (Alta. S.C.A.D.).

128 Various methods are reviewed in *Sokoloff v. 5 Rosehill Avenue Developments Inc.* (1998), 21 R.P.R. (3d) 176 (Ont. Ct. Gen. Div.). Those methods include a rateable reduction in the price, reimbursing the purchaser for the cost of remedying the defect and awarding the purchaser the difference between the value of the land with and without the defect. See also *Topfell Ltd. v. Galley Properties Ltd.*, [1979] 1 W.L.R. 446 (Ch.). See generally C. Harpum, "Specific Performance with Compensation as a Purchaser's Remedy — A Study in Contract and Equity" (1981) 40 Cambridge L.J. 47.

129 See Chapter 15.

130 See Chapter 24, section B(1).

131 See Chapter 22.

misrepresentee is left to the remedy of rescission[132] and any potential damages claim in tort.[133] If the purchaser was aware of the particular defect at the time of contracting, the agreement may be interpreted as one in which the purchaser agreed to take the property with defects at the contract price.[134] Relief may be denied where the defect was not relevant to the manner in which the price was calculated.[135] Such relief has also been denied where it would work undue hardship on the vendor.[136] Where the defect results from a common and fundamental error of the parties, the more appropriate remedy may be to rescind the agreement.[137] The remedy will not be available to the purchaser after the transaction has closed.[138] Finally, it is not uncommon for vendors to insist on including provisions in the agreement that have the effect of precluding the remedy. Agreements will often stipulate, for example, that in the event the vendor is unable to remove an objection to title made by the purchaser, the vendor shall have the right to terminate the agreement. Such provisions essentially confer a discretion on the vendor to terminate in the event of a difficulty of this kind. Although such provisions are enforceable, the discretion must not, however, be exercised in an arbitrary or capricious fashion.[139]

The rationale for allowing a defaulting vendor to force specific performance with an abatement on an unwilling purchaser may be less obvious. The rationale for granting such relief is one of denying to a purchaser the ability to terminate an agreement on the basis of what might appear to be a minor or technical defect for what may be, essentially, ulterior reasons. The test for making the relief available to the vendor is whether a purchaser, acting reasonably, would be willing to accept the property with defects, subject to a reasonable reduction

---

132 See Chapter 10, section E.

133 See Chapter 10, section F.

134 *Bullen v. Wilkinson* (1912), 2 D.L.R. 190 (Ont. C.A.).

135 *Rudd v. Lascelles*, [1900] 1 Ch. 815.

136 *Osborne v. Farmers' & Mechanics' Building Society* (1855), 5 Gr. 326; *Martens v. Burden* (1974), 45 D.L.R. (3d) 123 (Alta. S.C.T.D.); *Patel v. Ali*, above note 107.

137 *Earl of Durham v. Legard* (1865), 34 Beav. 611, 55 E.R. 771; *Hyrski v. Smith* (1969), 5 D.L.R. (3d) 385 (Ont. H.C.J.). See Chapter 13, section C.

138 *Allen v. Richardson* (1879), 13 Ch. D. 524; *Di Cenzo Construction Co. Ltd. v. Glassco* (1978), 90 D.L.R. (3d) 127 (Ont. C.A.).

139 See *Hurley v. Roy*, above note 126; *Mason v. Freedman*, [1958] S.C.R. 483; *Le Mesurier v. Andrus* (1986), 25 D.L.R. (4th) 424 (Ont. C.A.), leave to appeal to S.C.C. refused (1986), 63 O.R. (2d) x. For discussion of the general principle that contractual discretions must be exercised in good faith, see Chapter 21, section B(2).

in the price.[140] Relief will not be available to the vendor in cases where the defect has a significant impact on the intended use of the property by the purchaser[141] or would leave the purchaser with an unmarketable title.[142] Relief to the vendor will most obviously be available where the defect is a trivial one[143] but, provided that the defect does not have a significant impact on the purchaser's use and enjoyment of the property, the defect may be such as to have a substantial impact on the value of the property.[144]

Turning to the question of calculating damages in lieu of specific performance under *Lord Cairns' Act*[145] and its Canadian equivalents, the critical question is whether the damages are to be calculated simply on the basis of common law principles or whether there are special features to the calculation that derive from the equitable origins of the jurisdiction to grant such awards. As we have noted,[146] it was considered for a time that the timing of the calculation of damages might have an equitable approach differing from the common law. In *Wroth v. Tyler*[147] Megarry J. held that in the particular circumstances of that case, damages in lieu would be calculated as of the date of trial whereas, at common law, they would normally be calculated as of the date of breach. The case involved a sale of a matrimonial home by a husband to a young married couple. Upon default of the vendor, the purchasers' claim for specific performance was defeated on the basis that granting such relief would work an undue hardship on the vendor's wife who had refused to yield her legal interest in the matrimonial home. In a rising market, the purchasing couple was unable to purchase an equivalent substitute and sought damages in lieu calculated as of the date of trial. Megarry J. was of the view that in order to render the damages truly in substitution for a decree of specific performance, they should be calculated on an equitable basis as of the date of trial. Accordingly, the plaintiffs were awarded the difference between the contract price and the value of the subject property at the time of trial. The view that equitable damages in lieu

140 *Le Mesurier v. Andrus, ibid.*
141 *Flight v. Booth* (1834), 1 Bing. (N.C.) 370, 131 E.R. 1160.
142 *Pyrke v. Waddingham* (1852), 10 Hare 1, 68 E.R. 813; *Danby v. Stewart* (1979), 97 D.L.R. (3d) 734 (Ont. H.C.J.).
143 See, for example, *Stefanovska v. Kok* (1990), 73 O.R. (2d) 368 (H.C.J.); *Green v. Kaufman* (1996), 95 O.A.C. 183 (C.A.).
144 See, for example, *Powell v. Elliot* (1875), L.R. 10 Ch. App. 424; *Shepherd v. Croft,* [1911] 1 Ch. 521.
145 Above note 122.
146 See Chapter 22, section G.
147 [1974] Ch. 30.

were different from common law damages was, however, short-lived. In *Johnson v. Agnew*[148] the House of Lords held that damages in lieu of specific performance under *Lord Cairns' Act* were to be calculated on the basis of common law principles. Further, however, the court held that the general principle that damages at common law in a sale of land case were to be calculated at the date of breach is sufficiently flexible that courts could fix another date where it is appropriate to do so in order to avoid an injustice. Although the result in *Wroth v. Tyler* was thus not overruled, Megarry J.'s account of the special nature of equitable damage calculations was flatly rejected. Canadian courts have also accepted that damages in lieu of specific performance are to be calculated on the basis of common law principles.[149]

The decision in *Johnson v. Agnew* provided a further indication of the approach to be taken in fixing a date for calculating damages in a sale of land case. The claim in this case had been brought by vendors who had agreed to sell to the defendant a parcel of land that they had previously mortgaged to a third party. The price to be paid by the defendant would more than meet the vendors' outstanding obligations under the mortgage. In reliance on this transaction, the vendors entered into a further agreement to purchase a new property, expecting to use the proceeds from the sale to the defendant, together with borrowed moneys, to meet their obligations as purchaser under the second agreement. Upon default of the defendant, the vendors sought specific performance of the agreement. The vendors obtained summary judgment for specific performance on June 27, 1974. In due course, the vendors having defaulted under the mortgage, the mortgagee took possession of the parcel and sold it for a price that did not fully meet the vendors' obligations under the mortgage. This action occurred on April 3, 1975 and, from this point on, specific performance of the agreement was obviously impossible. On November 5, 1976, the vendors pursued a claim for damages in lieu of specific performance on the theory that the contract had been repudiated by the purchaser. The House of Lords held that such a claim was viable. The fact that specific performance had been awarded did not preclude an alternative claim in damages where the decree had not been fulfilled. As for the date for calculating damages, Lord Wilberforce suggested that, provided the vendor had reasonably pursued specific relief, the date for calculation should be that at which "(otherwise than by his default) the contract is lost."[150] On the present

---

148 [1980] A.C. 367.
149 *Semelhago v. Paramadevan*, above note 7.
150 Above note 148 at 401.

facts, the possibility of obtaining specific performance was lost upon the sale of the property by the mortgagee. Accordingly, damages were to be calculated as of April 3, 1975. Implicit in this approach, however, is the possibility that where specific performance remains potentially available up to the date of trial, but is denied, calculation of damages as of the date of trial may be appropriate. Certainly, the Supreme Court of Canada confirmed in *Semelhago v. Paramadevan*[151] that calculation of damages as of the time of trial may be appropriate when calculating damages in lieu of specific performance in the context of a contract for the sale of land.[152]

Notwithstanding the convergence of equitable damages in lieu of specific performance and common law damages, there is one aspect of damages in lieu that appears inconsistent with the basic common law principle that damages are to be awarded on the basis of the expectancy principle, placing the plaintiff in as good a position, so far as an award of money can do so, as the plaintiff would have been if the contract had been performed.[153] It appears now to be well established that when granting damages in lieu, a court will not take into account offsetting gains enjoyed by the plaintiff, thus potentially placing the plaintiff in a better position than he or she would have been in if the contract had been performed. The issue arose in the decision of the Ontario Court of Appeal in *306793 Ontario Ltd. v. Rimes*,[154] in which a purchaser claimed for specific performance of an agreement to sell a parcel of land for development purposes. The trial judge awarded damages in lieu calculated as of the date of trial but deducted savings effected during the delay by the purchaser who had not been required to pay the carrying charges for the land up to that point in time. An appeal enjoyed success, however, on the basis that no such deduction should be made. It was the Court of Appeal's view that since the vendor would, after judgment, remain in possession of the land, the vendor was in a position to recoup the carrying charges upon resale of the property. Although the implicit suggestion is that if the purchaser is forced to deduct the carrying costs this will create a windfall for the vendor, this appears to ignore the fact that the vendor is being ordered to pay damages measured by the full difference between the contract price and the market price at the date of trial. Thus, even if it is true that the vendor could be fully reimbursed for carrying costs upon resale of the property

---

151 Above note 7.

152 See also *306793 Ontario Ltd. v. Rimes* (1979), 100 D.L.R. (3d) 350 (Ont. C.A.).

153 See generally Chapter 22, section B.

154 Above note 152.

at the increased market price, the vendor is being forced, under the *Rimes* decision, to turn over all of that surplus value to the purchaser. Thus, under *Rimes*, the vendor remains out-of-pocket for the carrying costs and the purchaser receives a windfall benefit in the sense that the purchaser has avoided an expense that otherwise would have been endured if the contract had been performed in a timely fashion.

The approach taken in *Rimes* has been confirmed, however, by the Supreme Court of Canada in *Semelhago v. Paramadevan*.[155] In this case, Semelhago had agreed to purchase from the defendant Paramadevan a house in a new subdivision at a contract price of $205,000 which Semelhago intended to meet with $75,000 in cash and a mortgage of $130,000. Upon the vendor's breach, Semelhago launched a claim for specific performance or damages in lieu thereof. Five years later, at the time of trial, the market value of the property was $325,000, an increase in value of $120,000. In light of the *Rimes* principle, Semelhago took the position that he was entitled to the full $120,000 as damages in lieu of specific performance. The defendant urged that there should be deductions for various offsetting benefits enjoyed by Semelhago, such as the carrying costs under the mortgage that Semelhago did not have to pay prior to trial. More strikingly, the defendant urged that the property retained by Semelhago, which he unquestionably would have sold if their deal had closed, had similarly escalated in value from $190,000 to $300,000, an increase of $110,000, and that as this was a profit enjoyed by Semelhago as a result of the breach, this amount also ought to be deducted from the plaintiff's damages claim. The Supreme Court held, however, that the making of any of these deductions was inconsistent with the principle of *Rimes*. The general principle was defended by Sopinka J. on the following basis: "Damages are to be substituted for the decree of specific performance. I see no basis for deductions that are not related to the value of the property which was the subject of the contract. To make such deductions would depart from the principle that damages are to be a true equivalent of specific performance."[156]

The suggestion that Semelhago's profit of $110,000 is in some sense "unrelated" may not be found convincing once it is accepted that Semelhago's retention of the property is directly attributable to the defendant's breach of contract. Perhaps a more convincing reason for refusing the deduction is that if the defendant Paramadevan is not required to pay Semelhago the full measure of the increase in value of the subject property without making that deduction, Paramadevan

155 Above note 7.
156 *Ibid.* at para. 19.

946 THE LAW OF CONTRACTS

will, in effect, profit handsomely from his breach of contract. Even if it is true, then, that Semelhago is properly seen as suffering an actual loss of only $10,000 because of the increase in value of his own property, the refusal to deduct Semelhago's profit is, in effect, a required disgorgement of the profit made by Paramadevan through his breach of contract. Accordingly, it is arguable that the refusal to deduct the purchaser's gain in a case like this is yet another precursor of the more recently recognized principle to the effect that, in certain limited circumstances at least, the innocent victim of a breach of contract may be entitled to seek disgorgement of a profit secured by the defaulting party through breach.[157]

Disgorgement of profit cannot, however, explain the refusal to deduct the carrying charges in *Rimes*. The carrying charges absorbed by the vendor in *Rimes* that would have been paid by the purchaser if the transaction had closed in a timely fashion represented a straight out-of-pocket loss for the vendor rather than a profit secured through breach. In *Semelhago*, Sopinka J. did not refer to disgorgement as a possible rationale for refusing to deduct Semelhago's gain but did acknowledge that such a result "may appear to be overly generous to the respondent in this case and other like cases and may be seen as a windfall."[158] Acknowledgment of the windfall nature of the award led directly to Sopinka J.'s suggestion that a more restrictive view should be taken of the availability of specific performance in real estate cases.[159] In *Semelhago*, Sopinka J. suggested that the traditional principle that land is presumed to be unique, and therefore that agreements for its sale should be specifically enforceable should no longer be considered good law. In the view of the Supreme Court of Canada, then, the fact that damages in lieu of specific performance may, in effect, overcompensate the plaintiff, offers a justification for applying vigorously the principle that such relief should only be made available where damages at common law are inadequate. In this respect, then, the capacity of damages in lieu to achieve an overcompensation of a purchaser in cases like *Rimes* and *Semelhago* does appear to constitute a feature of damages in lieu that is different from and inconsistent with basic common law principles for calculating contract damages.

---

157 See Chapter 24, section B(2).
158 Above note 7 at para. 20.
159 For discussion see above this Chapter, section B(2), "Sale of Land."

C. INJUNCTIONS

Where a party has given a contractual undertaking not to do something, an order of specific relief would take the form of an injunction. Injunctions are of essentially two kinds, "prohibitory" and "mandatory."[160] A prohibitory injunction is a court order requiring the defendant to refrain from doing that which the defendant promised not to do. A mandatory injunction requires the defendant to undertake a positive act of some kind, normally a positive act that will have the effect of undoing something the defendant has done in breach of a contractual obligation. By way of illustration, in *Gross v. Wright*,[161] the Supreme Court of Canada confirmed a mandatory injunction ordering the defendant to demolish a party wall that had been constructed in breach of an agreement with his neighbour. The contract stipulated that the wall was to be two feet or more in thickness, half on each side of the property line. The wall complied with the contractual requirements on the plaintiff's side but had been narrowed by the defendant on his own side of the line. By requiring demolition of the wall, the mandatory injunction had the effect of restoring the *status quo* that existed prior to the breach. A prohibitory injunction, on the other hand, simply requires the defendant to refrain from acting inconsistently with a negative undertaking.

As we have seen earlier in this chapter,[162] a plaintiff seeking an order of specific performance must demonstrate that damages at common law do not constitute an adequate remedy and, as well, must avoid offending the limiting principle that an order of specific performance will not be granted that requires the court to engage in extensive supervision of complex or long-term obligations. It is generally assumed that these limitations will not be as strictly applied to the specific enforcement of negative obligations. The classic statement is found in *Doherty v. Allman*,[163] where Lord Cairns L.C. explained as follows:

> If parties, for valuable consideration, with their eyes open, contract that a particular thing shall not be done, all that a Court of Equity has to do is to say, by way of injunction, that which the parties have already said by way of covenant, that the thing shall not be done; and in such a case the injunction does nothing more than give the sanction of the process of the Court to that which already is the con-

---

160 See Sharpe, above note 1, c. 9.
161 [1923] S.C.R. 214.
162 See this Chapter, sections B(2) and (3).
163 (1878), 3 App. Cas. 709 (H.L.).

tract between the parties. It is not then a question of the balance of convenience or inconvenience, or of the amount of damage or of injury — it is the specific performance, by the Court of that negative bargain which the parties have made, with their eyes open, between themselves.[164]

Although Lord Cairns suggested that the court has essentially "no discretion to exercise"[165] in such circumstances, it is accepted that the courts retain a discretion to decline a request for an injunction and that the presumption in favour of injunctive relief is not an absolute one.[166] This greater willingness to order defendants to refrain from breaching express or, indeed, implied[167] negative covenants rather than to specifically perform positive obligations appears to rest on an assumption that the enforcement of negative obligations is a more straightforward matter than ordering the specific performance of a positive obligation. Ordering the defendant to refrain from conduct is, indeed, less likely to involve the court in difficulties of supervision than an order to carry out a positive act. It is also less invasive of the defendant's freedom of action. When one turns to consider mandatory injunctions, however, the courts evidence a much greater willingness to assess the appropriateness of the decree. Thus, for example, mandatory injunctions will not be issued in circumstances where the burden imposed thereby on the defendant is severely disproportionate to the benefit to be enjoyed by the plaintiff.[168]

The distinction between positive and negative undertakings is not easily drawn. Many positive covenants could be interpreted as containing implicit negative covenants and *vice versa*. A positive promise to provide exclusive services to an employer is implicitly a negative covenant not to provide such services to a third party. A promise not to terminate a particular employment relationship is implicitly a positive covenant to continue the employment. A positive covenant to purchase all requirements of a particular item from a particular supplier is implicitly a negative covenant not to purchase such items from third parties. Such illustrations can be easily multiplied. Moreover, the distinction is man-

---

164 *Ibid.* at 720.

165 *Ibid.*

166 See, for example, *Servicemaster Industries Inc. v. Servicemaster of Victoria Ltd.* (1979), 101 D.L.R. (3d) 376 (B.C.S.C.).

167 *Metropolitan Electric Supply Co. v. Ginder*, [1901] 2 Ch. 799; *Lord Strathcona Steamship Co. Ltd. v. Dominion Coal Co. Ltd.*, [1926] A.C. 108 (P.C.).

168 See, for example, *Haggerty v. Latreille* (1913), 14 D.L.R. 532 (Ont. S.C.A.D.); *Redland Bricks Ltd. v. Morris*, [1970] A.C. 652 (H.L.).

ipulable. A drafter who wished to take advantage of the rule in *Doherty v. Allman* could craft what might appear to be in substance a positive obligation in terms of a negative covenant not to do all else. Accordingly, in determining whether a covenant is positive or negative, courts are obliged to determine whether the covenant in question is positive or negative as a matter of substance rather than form.[169]

Further, courts will not enforce a negative covenant by injunction where the effect of doing so is to specifically enforce a positive contractual obligation.[170] Application of this principle in the context of employment contracts is a matter of some subtlety. As we have seen,[171] courts are generally unwilling to specifically enforce either the employer's or the employee's obligations under such agreements. At the same time, however, courts are willing to enforce to some extent negative covenants obliging the employee to refrain from providing services to a third party. In theory, at least, courts will withhold injunctive relief of such provisions if the effect of the injunction would be to effectively coerce the defendant employee to provide services to the plaintiff employer. The classic authority on point is *Lumley v. Wagner*.[172] Benjamin Lumley was the manager of Her Majesty's Theatre Haymarket. He had retained the services of a famous opera singer, Johanna Wagner, to perform at his theatre for a period of three months. Wagner also agreed not to perform for anyone else during this period. In due course, however, she signed an agreement to provide similar services during the same period with Frederick Gye. Gye was the proprietor of the opera theatre at Covent Garden and was Lumley's chief competitor.[173] Lumley sought to enjoin Wagner from working for Gye. The court noted that under existing principles it would not order specific performance of Wagner's undertaking to perform for Lumley. The court did, however, order Wagner to refrain from working for Gye, even though, as the court conceded, the granting of the injunction might well encourage Wagner

169 *Wolverhampton and Walsall Rwy. Co. v. London & North-Western Rwy. Co.* (1873), L.R. 16 Eq. 433; *Manchester Ship Canal Co. v. Manchester Racecourse Co.*, [1901] 2 Ch. 37 (C.A.); *Metropolitan Electric Supply Co. Limited v. Ginder*, above note 167.

170 *Fothergill v. Rowland* (1873), L.R. 17 Eq. 132; *Whitwood Chemical Co. v. Hardman*, [1891] 2 Ch. 416 (C.A.).

171 See above this Chapter, sections B(3)(b) and (c).

172 (1852) 1 De G. M. & G. 604, 42 E.R. 687 (Ch.). For an examination, *inter alia*, of the historical context of this decision, see S. Waddams, "Johanna Wagner and the Rival Opera Houses" (2001) 117 Law Q. Rev. 431.

173 Lumley brought a successful and precedent-setting action against Gye for inducing breach of contract. See *Lumley v. Gye* (1853), 2 El. & Bl. 216, 118 E.R. 749.

to perform her agreement with Lumley. In the particular circumstances of this case, it may be noted, the short-term nature of the engagement and Wagner's star status no doubt had the consequence that Wagner, as a practical matter, was not necessarily compelled by the injunction to work for Lumley. Indeed, in the event, Wagner sang for neither Lumley nor Gye.

In the later case of *Warner Bros. Picture Inc. v. Nelson*,[174] the defendant Nelson, the famous film actress known as Bette Davis, had entered into a potentially much longer commitment to provide services exclusively to Warner Brothers. Under an agreement that could be renewed annually by Warner Brothers for several years at increasing rates of salary, Davis also agreed that she would not provide her services to any other photographic, stage or motion picture producer "or engage in any other occupation"[175] without the express written consent of Warner Brothers. In due course, however, "for no discoverable reason except that she wanted more money"[176] Davis left the United States and entered into an agreement to provide her services to a third party in England. Warner Brothers, relying on *Lumley v. Wagner*, sought to enjoin Davis from pursuing this opportunity on the basis of the negative covenant in her employment contract. Branson J., after reviewing relevant authorities concluded as follows: "where a contract of personal service contains negative covenants, the enforcement of which will not amount to a decree of specific performance of the positive covenants of the contract or to the giving of a decree under which the defendant must either remain idle or perform those positive covenants, the Court will enforce those negative covenants."[177] As Branson J. noted, a simple injunction ordering the defendant not to "engage in any other occupation" could not be awarded as it would "force the defendant to perform her contract or remain idle."[178]

A more limited injunction restraining Davis from providing her services as an actress to others, however, would not offend the general principle. It was Branson J.'s view that Bette Davis could simply take up another line of work. As he observed:

> The defendant is stated to be a person of intelligence, capacity and means, and no evidence was produced to show that, if enjoined from doing the specific acts otherwise than for the plaintiffs, she will not

174 [1937] 1 K.B. 209.
175 *Ibid.* at 213.
176 *Ibid.*
177 *Ibid.* at 217.
178 *Ibid.* at 219.

be able to employ herself both usefully and remuneratively in other spheres of activity, though not as remuneratively as in her special line. She will not be driven, although she may be tempted to perform the contract, and the fact that she may be so tempted is no objection to the granting of an injunction.[179]

Branson J. further limited the injunction, however, to a three-year period and to a restraint that operated only within the geographic scope of the United Kingdom. Unsurprisingly, history records that Bette Davis went back to work for Warner Brothers and it may be questioned, of course, whether the suggestion that Ms. Davis might simply have taken up another line of work is a practical or realistic one.[180] For a particular employee, changing one's career path could involve a substantial and perhaps irreparable loss of intellectual or reputational capital. Certainly, subsequent courts appear to have been somewhat more sympathetic to the notion that depriving an individual of an ability to carry on his or her normal trade through injunctive relief constitutes a practical compulsion to carry out the positive aspects of the employment contract and is thus unacceptably close to an order of specific performance of those obligations.[181]

A more practical approach to the question of the degree of compulsion to perform positive covenants that will preclude injunctive relief is to be found in more recent cases dealing with applications for injunctions brought by service providers. In *Page One Records Ltd. v. Britton*,[182] the defendants were a group of musicians known as "The Troggs" who had a falling out with the plaintiff, their manager and agent. The Troggs purported to dismiss the plaintiff and retained the services of a new agent. The plaintiff sought an injunction ordering the defendants to refrain from doing so on the basis of a negative provision to this effect in their agreement. In response to the defendant's argument that the granting of such an injunction would effectively force them to work with the plaintiff, in whom they had lost confidence, the plaintiff urged that The Troggs could either act as their own managers or seek employment of another nature. Stamp J. dismissed these suggestions, noting that such groups require managers and that self-management was a capacity that fell outside the skillset of The Troggs. Stamp J. distinguished *Lumley*

179 *Ibid.*
180 B. Davis, *The Lonely Life* (New York: GP Putnam's Sons, 1962) c. 11 and 12.
181 See, for example, *Capitol Records — EMI of Canada Ltd. v. Gosewich* (1977), 17 O.R. (2d) 501 (H.C.J.); *Warren v. Mendy*, [1989] 1 W.L.R. 853 at 867 (C.A.), Nourse L.J.
182 Above note 112.

v. *Wagner* on the basis that, in the present circumstances, the defendants would be obliged, as a practical matter, to continue to employ the plaintiff as their agent and manager. Accordingly, he denied injunctive relief. Similarly, in *Warren v. Mendy*,[183] the defendant boxer had wrongfully dismissed the plaintiff, his manager. The plaintiff sought to enjoin the defendant from retaining the services of another manager. The court denied relief on the basis that the practical effect of such an order would be to force the defendant to continue to employ the plaintiff.

The typical defendant in this line of cases is a celebrity of some sort whose refusal to abide by a negative covenant will visit significant economic injury on the plaintiff. In *Lumley v. Wagner*, for example, Lumley was no doubt legitimately concerned that Gye's gain would be Lumley's loss. Loss of The Troggs as a client would no doubt visit economic injury on Page One Records. Warner Brothers had similar concerns about the attempted defection of Bette Davis. It may be considered, then, whether injunctive relief of this kind should be limited to this type of fact situation. Certainly, a Canadian decision is consistent with the view that the prospect of economic injury to the plaintiff is a necessary element in a claim for injunctive relief of this kind. In *Detroit Football Club v. Dublinski*,[184] the Detroit Football Club sought to enjoin Tom "Dubber" Dublinski from playing football with the Toronto Argonauts in contravention of a negative stipulation in his employment contract with the Detroit team. By the time the matter came on for trial, the Detroit contract had expired. Nonetheless, McRuer C.J.H.C. considered whether injunctive relief might have been available during the term of the agreement. He observed that a court of equity would not enforce a negative covenant by injunction where the injunction would protect no interest of the plaintiff other than "the interest flowing from the positive covenant."[185]

Noting that the Detroit and Toronto teams played in different leagues and in different countries, McRuer C.J.H.C. suggested that the fact that Dublinski would play quarterback for the Argonauts would do no more harm to the Detroit club than if Dublinski had simply remained idle. Accordingly, in McRuer C.J.H.C.'s view, injunctive relief would not have been available, in any event, to the plaintiff. This suggestion of a need to establish a legitimate economic interest on the part of the plaintiff in order to obtain an injunction in the employment con-

---

183 Above note 181.
184 (1956), 4 D.L.R. (2d) 688 (Ont. H.C.J.), rev'd (1957), 7 D.L.R. (2d) 9 (Ont. C.A.) (the Court of Appeal did not consider the availability of injunction).
185 *Ibid.* at 706–7 (Ont. H.C.J.).

text would significantly restrict the availability of injunctions on *Lumley v. Wagner* grounds.[186] To enjoy success, the plaintiff employer would have to establish that the stature of the employee is such that loss of the services in question would visit economic harm on the plaintiff. An argument in support of this approach would be that given the tendency of such injunctions to indirectly enforce positive obligations to provide services, the *Lumley v. Wagner* injunction ought to be reserved to cases where the employer has a strong economic interest in enforcing the negative covenant. Numerous English cases, however, have refrained from applying an analysis of this kind. Injunctions have been granted in cases where neither the particular skillset nor the reputation of the defendant was such as to warrant this type of analysis.[187] The *Dublinski* decision, however, provides Canadian courts with an opportunity to make the *Lumley v. Wagner* injunction available only on a more restricted basis.

Quite apart from the distinction between prohibitory and mandatory injunctions, injunctions may be subdivided between those that are "permanent" or "perpetual" in nature and those that are "interim" or "interlocutory." Interlocutory injunctions are awarded by a court pending trial. Permanent or perpetual injunctions are issued after a trial as the final and binding order of the court. The use of the adjectives "perpetual" or "permanent" are not intended to suggest that the effect of such injunctions will last forever. It is commonplace for permanent injunctions to have a limited period of duration. Rather, the connotation is one of indicating that such injunctions represent the final judicial determination of the rights of the parties in dispute and are to be distinguished from interim or interlocutory injunctions that are of a temporary nature and operative during the period prior

---

186 Such a requirement is reminiscent of restraint of trade doctrine. It is generally accepted, however, that negative restraints on employment with third parties that operate during the term of employment are not subject to scrutiny on restraint of trade grounds. For discussion see Chapter 12, section B(4). In the *Dublinski* case, however, McRuer C.J.H.C. was of the view that since Dublinski had refused to provide his services to the Detroit club, the contract had *de facto* come to an end and restraint of trade analysis therefore became relevant to the question of whether an injunction would lie. See above note 184 at 697–709 (Ont. H.C.J.). At the same time, however, McRuer C.J.H.C. did not question the enforceability of the positive covenant to play for the Detroit club in the contract and the potential existence of a claim for damages against Dublinski for its breach. See *ibid.* at 697 (Ont. H.C.J.).

187 See, for example, *Lanner v. Palace Theatre (Ltd.)* (1893), 9 T.L.R. 162 (Ch.); *William Robinson & Co. Ltd. v. Heuer*, [1898] 2 Ch. 451 (C.A.); *Marco Productions Ltd. v. Pagola*, [1945] K.B. 111.

to the final determination of the rights of the parties. In the present context, an interlocutory injunction would typically order a party to refrain from breaching the contract in issue pending final determination of the rights of the parties. An interim injunction might be said to be a subspecies of interlocutory injunctions. An interim injunction is typically of even shorter duration and is intended to maintain the *status quo* between the parties until a full and proper determination of the appropriateness of a full interlocutory injunction may be made. Applications for interim injunctions are normally made on notice to the other party. In particularly urgent cases, however, such applications may be made without notice and are referred to as *ex parte*. In a particular case, an *ex parte* injunction could be followed by an interim injunction, then by a full interlocutory injunction pending trial and, ultimately, by a permanent injunction issued at the conclusion of the trial.

The power to issue interlocutory injunctions of various kinds is typically conferred by statute.[188] The issuance of an interlocutory injunction is often a contentious matter. The decision to issue such an order will typically be made on a very limited evidentiary basis. The issuance of a decree may, on the one hand, be necessary to preserve the *status quo* in order to facilitate effective relief for one of the parties or, on the other hand, may, by causing irreparable harm to the enjoined party, prejudge the outcome of the trial in a manner that proves to be mistaken. Accordingly, a rather complex body of jurisprudence has developed with respect to the granting of interim injunctions, including those issued to restrain a breach of contract.[189] In the present context, however, it must be noted that the principle of *Doherty v. Allman* does not apply in the usual fashion in the context of interlocutory injunctions issued to restrain a breach of contract.[190] Broadly speaking, in considering whether to grant interlocutory injunctions, courts have considered a shopping list of relevant factors. Although the jurisprudence concerning each of the factors is itself rather complex, it is sufficient to note for present purposes that courts will generally consider the relative strength of the plaintiff's case and the defendant's defence, the question of whether the injunction is necessary to avoid irreparable

---

188 See, for example, *Courts of Justice Act,* R.S.O. 1990, c. C.43, s. 101 (interlocutory injunctions may be ordered "where it appears to a judge of the court to be just or convenient to do so").

189 See generally Sharpe, above note 1, c. 2.

190 See *Texaco Ltd. v Mulberry Filling Station Ltd.,* [1972] 1 W.L.R. 814 (Ch.); *Crampton v. Robertson,* [1977] 6 W.W.R. 99 (B.C.S.C.).

harm of the party seeking its protection and finally, the balance of convenience or, one might say, inconvenience between the parties.

With respect to the first factor, the traditional treatment of this issue was to consider whether the plaintiff had established a strong *prima facie* case.[191] Typically, in the absence of a strong *prima facie* case, courts would refuse to issue an injunction prior to trial.[192] In the leading decision of the House of Lords in *American Cyanimid Co. v. Ethicon Ltd.*,[193] however, it was held that it would be sufficient if the plaintiff established that the claim "is not frivolous or vexatious; in other words, that there is a serious question to be tried."[194] Canadian courts have adopted this apparent watering down of the *prima facie* case test.[195] Nonetheless, it appears likely that, at least in contracts cases, the strength of the plaintiff's case will remain an important consideration.[196] A showing of irreparable harm requires the applicant to establish that failure to issue the injunction would result in harm that either cannot be quantified in monetary terms or cannot be subsequently cured.[197] The third factor, "balance of convenience," requires the court to consider "which of the two parties will suffer the greater harm from the granting or refusal of an interlocutory injunction, pending a decision on the merits."[198] It

---

191 See, for example, *J.T. Stratford & Son Ltd. v. Lindley*, [1965] A.C. 269 (H.L.).

192 See, for example, *Bain v. Bank of Canada*, [1935] 4 D.L.R. 112 (B.C.C.A.); *Cradle Pictures (Canada) Ltd. v. Penner* (1975), 63 D.L.R. (3d) 440 (Ont. H.C.J.).

193 [1975] A.C. 396 (H.L.).

194 *Ibid.* at 407.

195 *Metropolitan Store (MTS) Ltd. v. Manitoba Food & Commercial Workers, Local 832*, [1987] 1 S.C.R. 110; *RJR-MacDonald Inc. v. Canada (Attorney General)*, [1994] 1 S.C.R. 311. Compare with *Z.I. Pompey Industrie v. ECU-Line N.V.* (2003), 224 D.L.R. (4th) 577 (S.C.C.).

196 See, for example, *Toronto Marlborough Major Junior "A" Hockey Club v. Tonelli* (1975), 67 D.L.R. (3d) 214 (Ont. H.C.J.); *Dialadex Communications Inc. v. Crammond* (1987), 34 D.L.R. (4th) 392 (Ont. H.C.J.); *Series 5 Software Ltd. v. Clarke*, [1996] 1 All E.R. 853 (Ch. D.); *Z.I. Pompey Industrie v. ECU-Line N.V.*, *ibid.* For an analysis of the now extensive body of jurisprudence considering these issues, see Sharpe, above note 1 at 2-10 to 2-24.

197 *RJR-MacDonald Inc. v. Canada (Attorney General)*, above note 195 at 341, Sopinka and Cory JJ. There are a number of cases suggesting, however, that, in the context of negative covenants, it is either unnecessary to establish irreparable harm or that less emphasis will be placed on it in this context. See, for example, *Montreal Trust Co. v. Montreal Trust Co. of Canada* (1988), 48 D.L.R. (4th) 385 at 393 (B.C.C.A.), McLachlin J.A.; *Miller v. Toews*, [1991] 2 W.W.R. 604 (Man. C.A.). Sharpe, above note 1 at 2-26 to 2-27 suggests that this proposition is applicable only where a clear case on the merits has been established by the plaintiff.

198 *RJR-MacDonald Inc. v. Canada (Attorney General)*, above note 195 at 342.

also appears to be accepted that this list of factors operates as a series of guidelines to channel judicial discretion in issuing interlocutory injunctions, rather than a rigid three-step test.[199]

Application of the test in a contractual setting may be illustrated by the decision of the Manitoba Court of Appeal in *Zipper Transportation Services Ltd. v. Korstrom*.[200] In this case, the defendant had supplied courier, messenger, cartage and delivery services as an independent contractor for various customers of the plaintiff. Their agreement included a post-termination non-competition clause under which the defendant had agreed to refrain from competing with the plaintiff for a specified period of time. The defendant gave notice to the plaintiff that he was terminating their relationship. Shortly thereafter, Piston Ring, one of the plaintiff's customers, terminated its agreement with the plaintiff. When the plaintiff learned that the defendant was now providing similar services to Piston Ring, an action was commenced together with an application for an interlocutory injunction to enforce the non-competition clause. The trial judge[201] issued the injunction on the basis that the non-competition covenant was a reasonable one and that the defendant's conduct constituted a plain and uncontested breach. Accordingly, in his view, the injunction should issue. The Court of Appeal, however, was of the view that the trial judge had failed to give adequate attention to the irreparable harm and balance of convenience factors. As far as irreparable harm was concerned, the court was of the view that the damages that would be suffered by the plaintiff were ascertainable and monetarily compensable. With respect to balance of convenience, the court's view was that since there was no reason to think that if the injunction was issued, Piston Ring would return as a customer to the plaintiff, the injunction would confer no economic benefit on the plaintiff. Further, as the injunction would plainly harm the defendant, the balance of convenience weighed in favour of refusing to issue the injunction. Accordingly, the injunction issued at trial was set aside.

D. CONTRACTUAL STIPULATION OF SPECIFIC RELIEF

Contracting parties who are concerned about their inability to predict the remedies that might be available in the event of the other party's

199 *Apotex Fermentation Inc. v. Novopharm Ltd.* (1994), 95 Man. R. (2d) 241 (C.A.).
200 (1998), 126 Man. R. (2d) 126 (C.A.), rev'g (1997), 122 Man. R. (2d) 139 (Q.B.).
201 *Ibid.*

breach of contract often attempt to stipulate the nature of those remedies within their contractual arrangements. Indeed, parties enjoying a strong hand in the negotiations may wish to strengthen the other party's incentives for performance by stipulating the remedies for breach in a rather aggressive manner. As we have seen,[202] it is commonplace for parties to specifically provide in their agreement that, in the event of the other party's breach of contract, that party will be obliged to pay damages in a specific amount or in accord with a particular formula. As we have also seen, courts have jealously guarded their ability to scrutinize such arrangements and will not enforce such clauses where they appear to have been inserted in the bargain by the stronger party with a view to imposing a severe penalty in the event of breach, thus increasing the pressure on the other party to perform. Such stipulated remedies clauses will be enforced only if they are considered to constitute a legitimate pre-estimate of damage. A distinction is thus drawn between "liquidated damages" clauses, that are enforceable, and "penalties," that are not. Here we consider the effect of an enforceable liquidated damages clause on the possibility of specific relief. If parties have negotiated and agreed to a clause stipulating that damages calculated in a particular fashion should be paid in the event of breach, it may be considered whether there is any room left by such an arrangement for the innocent party to seek redress in the form of an order of specific performance or an injunction. Here we also consider the treatment accorded contractual stipulations that provide for specific relief in some form. Typically, such clauses will acknowledge the unique value of the performance to be rendered by the promisor, concede that irreparable harm would be caused to the promisee by the promisor's breach of contract and provide the promisor's agreement that, in the event of breach, specific relief either in the form of a decree of specific performance or an injunction should be issued by a court.

The courts do not generally consider that the presence of an enforceable liquidated damages clause in an agreement constitutes an admission by the innocent party that damages are an adequate remedy. Accordingly, the presence of such a clause does not preclude the innocent party from seeking a decree of specific performance.[203] Exceptionally, however, courts may find that the substance of the agreement between the parties is that the party in breach has been granted what is

---

202 See Chapter 22, section J.
203 *Howard v. Hopkyns* (1742), 2 Atk. 371, 26 E.R. 624; *Crutchley v. Jerningham* (1817), 2 Mer. 502, 35 E.R. 1032; *Long v. Bowring* (1864), 33 Beav. 585, 55 E.R. 496; *Fleischer v. Rosenbloom* (1988), 53 Man. R. (2d) 247 (Q.B.).

essentially an option either to perform the undertaking or pay the stipulated sum.[204] Similarly, the presence of a liquidated damages clause will typically not preclude successful application for an injunction. In *Elsley v. J.G. Collins Insurance Agencies Ltd.*,[205] the Supreme Court of Canada granted an injunction to enforce a non-competition clause against an insurance agent, notwithstanding the presence of a liquidated damages clause in the agent's contract of employment. In short, then, the presence of a binding liquidated damages clause in an agreement does not normally preclude a claim for specific relief.

There has been much less judicial discussion of the effect to be given to contractual stipulations that provide that the promisor will agree to specific relief in the event of breach either in the form of a decree of specific performance or an injunction. Such authority as exists suggests that the courts will give some weight to such provisions in exercising the discretion to grant specific relief but will not simply defer to the wishes of the parties. A leading authority concerns an agreement to the issuance of an injunction in the event of breach of a non-competition clause. In *Warner Brothers Pictures Inc. v. Nelson*,[206] it will be recalled, Bette Davis had agreed to provide services exclusively to Warner Brothers for a particular period of time and not to render services during that period to any other theatre, film or photographic business without the consent of Warner Brothers. In the agreement, Davis conceded the unique and extraordinary value of her services and the irreparable nature of the injury that would result from her breach of contract; she explicitly agreed that Warner Brothers should be entitled to an injunction in the event of breach. With respect to this provision, Branson J. observed: "Of course, parties cannot contract themselves out of the law; but it assists, at all events, on the question of evidence as to the applicability of an injunction in the present case, to find the parties formally recognizing that in cases of this kind injunction is a more appropriate remedy than damages."[207] In sum, such provisions are of assistance but not controlling. Indeed, it would be surprising if the courts would yield to contractual stipulation their ability to consider the various limitations on and discretionary defences to specific relief, especially those relating to the potentially oppressive effect of

---

204 See, for example, *Legh v. Lillie* (1860), 6 H. & N. 165, 158 E.R. 69.

205 [1978] 2 S.C.R. 916. See also *National Provincial Bank of England v. Marshall* (1888), 40 Ch. D. 112 (C.A.); *Mills v. Gill*, [1952] 3 D.L.R. 27 (Ont. H.C.J.).

206 Above note 174.

207 *Ibid.* at 221. See also *Toronto Blue Jays Baseball Club v. Tri-Tickets Inc.* (1991), 85 D.L.R. (4th) 422 (Ont. Ct. Gen. Div.).

such orders on defendants and their impact on the deployment of judicial resources.[208]

FURTHER READINGS

J.B. AMES, "Mutuality in Specific Performance" (1903) 3 Colum. L.R. 1.

W. BAKER, "Interlocutory Injunctions — A Discussion of the 'New Rules'" (1977) 42 Sask. L. Rev. 53.

J. BERRYMAN, *The Law of Equitable Remedies* (Toronto: Irwin Law, 2000).

J. BERRYMAN, "The Specific Performance Damages Continuum: An Historical Perspective" (1985) 17 Ottawa L. Rev. 295.

W.J. BISHOP, "Choice of Remedy for Breach of Contract" (1985) 14 J. Legal Stud. 299.

R.G. HAMMOND, "Interlocutory Injunctions: Time for a New Model" (1980) 30 U.T.L.J. 241.

C. HARPUM, "Specific Performance with Compensation as a Purchaser's Remedy — A Study in Contract and Equity" (1981) 40 Cambridge L.J. 47.

D.R. HARRIS, "Specific Performance — A Regular Remedy for Consumers?" (2003) 119 Law Q. Rev. 541.

A.T. KRONMAN, "Specific Performance" (1978) 45 U. Chicago L. Rev. 351.

J. LEM, "Blackacre Had No Readily Available Equivalent: Specific Performance and Equitable Damages after *Semelhago v. Paramadevan*" in Law Society of Upper Canada, *Special Lectures 2002, Real Property Law: Conquering the Complexities* (Toronto: Irwin Law, 2003) 837.

P. LINZER, "On the Amorality of Contract Remedies — Efficiency, Equity and the Second Restatement" (1981) 81 Colum. L. Rev. 111.

P.M. MCDERMOTT, *Equitable Damages* (Sydney: Buttersworths, 1994).

P.M. PERELL, "The Interlocutory Injunction and Irreparable Harm" (1989) 68 Can. Bar Rev. 538.

---

208 See generally Sharpe, above note 1 at 7-39 to 7-41.

A. SCHWARTZ, "The Case for Specific Performance" (1979) 89 Yale L.J. 271.

R.J. SHARPE, *Injunctions and Specific Performance*, 3d. ed. (Aurora: Canada Law Book, 2000).

N. SIEBRASSE, "Damages in Lieu of Specific Performance: *Semelhago v. Paramadevan*" (1997) 76 Can. Bar Rev. 551.

S.M. WADDAMS, "The Choice of Remedy for Breach of Contract" in J. Beatson & D. Friedmann, eds., *Good Faith and Fault in Contract Law* (Oxford: Clarendon Press, 1995).

E. YORIO, "In Defence of Money Damages for Breach of Contract" (1982) 82 Colum. L. Rev. 1365.

CHAPTER 24

RESTITUTION AND DISGORGEMENT

A. INTRODUCTION

The law of contracts and torts adopted its modern shape in the nineteenth century as the law was gradually transformed from its origins in medieval common law and equity into a set of modern categories or subjects of the law recognizable to the contemporary lawyer.[1] It was not until the twentieth century, however, that a similar process gathered together various doctrines of common law and equity and reshaped them as the modern law of restitution. The invention or recognition of the subject occurred in the United States in the first half of the century. In 1937, the American Law Institute published its ground-breaking *Restatement of Restitution*.[2] The subtitle of the volume, *Quasi-Contracts and Constructive Trust*, signalled to the reader that the *Restatement* incorporated doctrines of the common law often referred to as the law of quasi-contracts and certain doctrines of equity related to the law of trusts. The organizing premise or thesis of the *Restatement* was that

---

1   See generally J.H. Baker, *An Introduction to English Legal History*, 4th ed. (London: Butterworths LexisNexis, 2002), c. 11, 16 and 17.

2   American Law Institute, *Restatement of Restitution, Quasi-Contracts and Constructive Trusts* (St. Paul: American Law Institute, 1937). For the early history and development of the analytical framework underlying the *Restatement*, see A. Kull, "James Barr Ames and the Early Modern History of Unjust Enrichment" (2005) 25 Oxford J. Legal Stud. 297.

these seemingly disparate materials could be organized and restated on the basis of a common underlying principle, termed the principle against unjust enrichment. The underlying principle was stated boldly in the first section of the *Restatement* in the following terms: "A person who has been unjustly enriched at the expense of another is required to make restitution to the other."[3] The work then proceeds to restate, in the manner of the American restatements, the various rules and doctrines of common law and equity that the institute considered to be unified by or explained by that principle. Subsequent chapters of the volume restated the rules relating to the recovery of benefits conferred in an emergency, by mistake, under coercion or under ineffective transactions and of benefits acquired through wrongful conduct of various kinds, including breach of fiduciary obligation.

Recovery of money paid under a mistake provides a simple illustration. Under traditional law, moneys paid under mistake of fact—as where the payor mistakenly believes he is indebted to the payee or mistakenly believes that the payee is some other person—has been considered recoverable. Obviously, such recovery is not grounded on either contract or tort. There is no contract under which the payee is committed to repay the money nor is the receipt of mistaken payment itself tortious. Though the idea had developed that relief could be explained on the basis of an implied undertaking to repay, the institute adopted the view that the implied contract was a mere fiction and that the preferable, indeed coherent, explanation for recovery was that, otherwise, the mistakenly paid party would be unjustly enriched.

In response to the institute's initiative, recognition of restitution as a separate discipline or subject of the law developed rather quickly in American law.[4] Recognition came only more slowly, however, in other common law jurisdictions. Thus, as recently as 1978, an English judge stated: "[T]here is no general doctrine of unjust enrichment recognized in English law."[5] In recent decades, however, the basic approach adopted in the *Restatement* appears to have been accepted in the older

---

3   *Ibid.*, s. 1.
4   Some evidence of this is to be found in the subsequently published and updated volumes 2 and 3 of the *Restatement*, above note 2, which consist of brief summaries of thousands of American cases referring to and applying sections of the *Restatement*. See also G. Palmer, *The Law of Restitution*, (Boston: Little, Brown, 1978). Although it is true that the Institute's attempt to develop a second restatement faltered after publishing a series of tentative drafts, substantial progress has now been made on a third restatement, now titled, *Restatement of Restitution and Unjust Enrichment 3d.*
5   *Orakpo v. Manson Investment Ltd.*, [1978] A.C. 95 at 104 (H.L.), Lord Diplock.

commonwealth jurisdictions and lengthy treatises on the subject have appeared in England,[6] Australia,[7] New Zealand[8] and Canada.[9] Indeed, in Canada, recognition came more quickly than in the other commonwealth jurisdictions. The American approach was essentially adopted by the Supreme Court of Canada in a remarkable series of decisions beginning in 1956 with *Deglman v. Guaranty Trust Co. of Canada.*[10]

In this chapter, we consider various restitutionary claims that may arise in a transactional or contractual setting. Of principal concern are the restitutionary remedies available upon discharge of an agreement by breach.[11] As we shall see, for the innocent party, the victim of the breach of contract, a claim in restitution for the value of benefits conferred on the other party may provide an attractive alternative to the claim for damages for breach of contract. In recent years, it has been suggested that a further alternative claim available to the innocent party may be a claim to recover the profits secured by the party in breach as a result of the breach of contract. This type of claim, here referred to as a claim for disgorgement of profits, is well recognized in the context of other kinds of wrongful conduct and, although the point is not free from contention, the *Restatement* and modern treatises on the law of restitution include an account of disgorgement claims as an aspect of the law of restitution. Thus, for example, claims for the disgorgement of profits may arise where a defendant has profited through crime,[12] tort,[13] breach of fiduciary obligation[14] and breach of confidence.[15] Until recently, however, it has been assumed that such a claim did not lie where the defendant has merely committed a breach of contract. In

---

6 Lord Goff and G. Jones, *The Law of Restitution*, 6th ed. (London: Sweet & Maxwell, 2002); A. Burrows, *The Law of Restitution*, 2d ed. (London: Butterworths, 2002); G. Virgo, *The Principles of the Law of Restitution* (Oxford: Oxford University Press, 1999); S. Hedley and M. Halliwell, eds., *The Law of Restitution* (London: Butterworths LexisNexis, 2002).

7 K. Mason and J.W. Carter, *Restitution Law in Australia* (Sydney: Butterworths, 1995).

8 R.B. Grantham and C.E.S. Rickett, *Enrichment and Restitution in New Zealand* (Oxford: Hart, 2000).

9 P.D. Maddaugh and J.D. McCamus, *The Law of Restitution,* 2d ed. (Aurora: Canada Law Book, 2004); G.H.L. Fridman, *Restitution*, 2d ed. (Toronto: Carswell, 1992).

10 [1954] S.C.R. 725.

11 See Chapter 15.

12 See, for example, Maddaugh and McCamus, above note 9, c. 23.

13 *Ibid.*, c. 24.

14 *Ibid.*, c. 27.

15 *Ibid.*, c. 28.

recent years, however, such claims have become a plainly recognized feature of English[16] and, perhaps, Canadian law.

Upon discharge of a contract for breach, the party who has breached the contract may also be entitled to bring a claim for the value of benefits conferred on the other party. Thus, for example, a party who has paid a rather large down payment under a contract for the purchase of goods and is then unable to perform may be able to claim for recovery of the payment on the theory that otherwise, the seller, albeit an innocent party in this context, would be unjustly enriched by retention of so large an amount. As we shall see, however, claims for the value of goods and services supplied by the defaulting party are less securely recognized and accordingly, in the context of services rendered, a doctrine of substantial performance has emerged that may, in an appropriate case, allow the defaulting party to enforce the very contract itself. The restitutionary claims of the guilty party and the doctrine of substantial performance will both be considered later in this chapter.

Finally, as the *Deglman*[17] case itself illustrates, restitutionary claims may arise in the context of transactions that are ineffective for one reason or another. In *Deglman*, the transaction was ineffective because it failed to comply with the *Statute of Frauds*.[18] The plaintiff, who had provided services under the unenforceable agreement, was held entitled to recover their value in a restitutionary claim. The general principles under which such claims lie, both at common law and in equity, will be briefly considered in section D of this chapter, "Restitution under Ineffective Transactions."

Before turning to specifics, however, it will be useful to draw out two consequences of the late recognition of the unity and underlying principle of restitutionary doctrine, one terminological and the other substantive. As far as terminology is concerned, even contemporary judicial decisions in this area frequently employ the traditional language of the medieval writs in describing particular claims. Thus, a claim for restitution of money paid to the defendant is often still described as a claim for "money had and received," a claim for the value of money paid to a third party that benefited the defendant as a claim in "money paid" and claims for the value of goods and services provided as claims in *quantum valebat* and *quantum meruit*. Although a modern approach would simply describe each of these claims as being a claim for restitution, a termino-

---

16   *Attorney General v. Blake*, [2001] 1 A.C. 268 (H.L.), aff'g [1998] 1 All E.R. 833 (C.A.).

17   Above note 10.

18   For discussion of which see Chapter 6, section B.

logical shift of this kind is inhibited, to some extent, by the substantive implications of late recognition. The study of the underlying coherence and similarity of a body of case law is likely to lead to its reformulation as courts and others develop a clearer view of the similarities between cases and appreciate the need for their similar resolution. This gradual process of refinement and improvement of doctrine and the elimination of anomalous results has occurred to a lesser degree in the context of restitutionary doctrine than in the older disciplines of contract and tort. Accordingly, anomalous results persist in particular areas of restitutionary doctrine and they are linked, to some extent, to the differences between money claims and claims for the value of non-monetary benefits conferred. Although the shift to a more modern terminology based on the elements of the unjust enrichment principle is well underway,[19] its completion is likely to be accompanied by some further adjustment or refinement of restitutionary doctrine.

B. REMEDIES UPON BREACH: THE INNOCENT PARTY

1) Restitution of Benefits Conferred

When confronted by a repudiatory breach of contract,[20] the innocent party may elect either to affirm or disaffirm the contract. In either case, the innocent party is entitled to pursue a claim for damages for losses resulting from the breach.[21] If the innocent party affirms the contract, the executory obligations of the parties remain enforceable and the innocent party's remedies are restricted to a claim for the damages sustained as a result of the breach. On the other hand, if the innocent party disaffirms the contract, the executory obligations of the parties are discharged by the breach and, as an alternative to the claim for damages, the innocent party may pursue restitutionary relief. Historically, the claim would be for money had and received if the innocent party had paid money to the party in breach or in *quantum meruit* or *quantum valebat* for the value of services rendered or goods supplied. The innocent party may prefer the claim in restitution to a damages claim in cases where the actual quantum of damages is difficult or inconvenient to prove or where, the contract being an unprofitable one,

---

19   See, for example, Maddaugh and McCamus, above note 9, c. 3.
20   See Chapter 15.
21   See Chapter 22.

the claim for restitution of benefits conferred may yield a higher meas-ure of relief than a claim for damages.

Under traditional English doctrine, the claim in money had and received could be met by a defence that the plaintiff had received some value under the agreement and, accordingly, there did not exist the requisite "total failure of consideration." The requirement of a total fail-ure of consideration is typically illustrated by the two contrasting cases of *Hunt v. Silk*[22] and *Giles v. Edwards*.[23] In *Hunt v. Silk*, a landlord had agreed to execute a lease for nineteen years within ten days and per-form some repairs on the subject property, the tenant having paid a de-posit of ten pounds. The tenant took immediate possession and, when the ten days elapsed without the repairs being made, the tenant tried to require the landlord to undertake them. When his overtures failed to enjoy success, the tenant quit the premises and sought return of the ten pounds. The claim was rejected on the basis that the tenant had enjoyed an interim occupation of the premises. In *Giles v. Edwards*, by way of contrast, a claim to recovery of a deposit paid by a purchaser of lumber enjoyed success on the basis that the purchaser had apparently not taken delivery of any lumber. The supplier had refused to cord all the required lumber and the purchaser, it was said, was not obliged to take part of the wood only. A strict requirement of this kind that resti-tution is contingent upon a showing of a total failure of consideration is very difficult to justify. In a case like *Hunt v. Silk*, it appears obvious that the justice of the defendant's position could be met by simply de-ducting the value of the interim enjoyment of the premises from the plaintiff's restitutionary claim. Traditionally, however, the requirement was considered to be a strict one and it was understood that the com-mon law would refuse to apportion value in such circumstances.

Although there are some modern English and Australian author-ities applying the total failure requirement, none of the recent cases offer a modern justification for the doctrine. Moreover, they tend to underscore the unsatisfactory nature of the doctrine. In *Baltic Shipping Company v. Dillon*,[24] for example, the Australian High Court would have denied restitutionary recovery of a fee paid for a fourteen-day pleasure cruise on the basis of the doctrine. Eight days into the cruise, the ship sank. The plaintiff sued to recover both damages and the fee. The lat-ter claim was denied on the unexceptionable ground that one could not recover both damages and the fee. This would amount to double

---

22   (1804), 5 East 449, 102 E.R. 1142.
23   (1797), 17 T.R. 181, 101 E.R. 920.
24   (1993), 176 C.L.R. 344 (Aust. H.C.).

recovery. The court went on to suggest, however, that, in any event, the restitutionary claim for the fee would fail because of the partial performance of the contract and the resulting lack of a total failure of consideration. The manipulability of the requirement is evident in the decisions at various levels in this case. Both the trial judge and the court of appeal would have held that the fee could be recovered on the basis that in such circumstances the entire value of the cruise had been destroyed by its catastrophic end. The consideration had totally failed. In the High Court's view, however, part of the consideration had been received during the first eight days. Although the concept of "consideration" is manipulable, the doctrine is rigid in its "all or nothing" approach. Either there has or there has not been a total failure of consideration. In cases like *Hunt v. Silk*, however, recovery subject to a deduction for value received seems an appropriate but, under traditional doctrine, unattainable result.

For a variety of reasons, it appears unlikely that Canadian courts would apply the total failure requirement strictly in the context of money claims. First, the requirement has simply been ignored by Canadian courts in a number of cases. Thus, in the context of sale of defective goods, interim use of the goods does not prevent restitutionary recovery.[25] Similarly, restitutionary recovery of moneys paid for defective services has been allowed.[26] Further, under traditional English doctrine, the total failure requirement is simply inapplicable to claims in *quantum meruit* and *quantum valebat*.[27] One can recover the value of goods or services supplied subject to a deduction for moneys received to date. There appears to be no sound reason for treating money claims so differently from claims for the value of goods and services. Further, Canadian courts have simply ignored the requirement in the context of monetary restitutionary claims brought by the party in default.[28] It would appear anomalous to allow greater restitutionary relief to the party in default than to the innocent party. Finally, it appears that the total failure requirement is of diminishing significance in English law.

---

25 See, for example, *Lightburn v. Belmont Sales Ltd.* (1969), 6 D.L.R. (3d) 692 (B.C.S.C.); *Gibbons v. Trap Motors Ltd.* (1970), 9 D.L.R. (3d) 742 (B.C.S.C.); *Wojakowski v. Pembena Dodge Chrysler Ltd.*, [1976] 5 W.W.R. 97 (Man. Q.B.).

26 *Patson v. Abalon Construction Ltd.* (1996), 110 Man. R. (2d) 2 (C.A.) (recovery subject to a deduction for the value of the services rendered).

27 See, for example, *Alkok v. Grymek*, [1968] S.C.R. 452; *Gettle Bros. Construction Co. Ltd. v. Alwinsal Potash of Canada Ltd.* (1969), 5 D.L.R. (3d) 719 (Sask. C.A.), aff'd [1971] S.C.R. 320.

28 See, for example, *Stephenson v. Bromley*, [1928] 4 D.L.R. 737 (Man. C.A.) and see below this Chapter, section C.

In the recent decision in *Goss v. Chilcott*,[29] the Privy Council allowed monetary restitutionary recovery, notwithstanding the receipt of some consideration by the plaintiff "at least in cases in which apportionment can be carried out without difficulty."[30] The facts of the case concern recovery of moneys advanced on a mortgage loan from which, of course, it would be a simple matter to deduct the value of payments already received by the lender. Presumably, however, this authority could be applied in any situation in which the apportionment is not considered to be beyond the fact-finding capacities of a court. Under *Goss*, then, a more sensible result could be achieved in *Hunt v. Silk*. A simpler solution, however, would be simply to dispense with the total failure requirement and this, indeed, appears to be the Canadian position.

In cases where the contract in question is an unprofitable one for the innocent party, the question arises as to whether a restitutionary claim ought to be available to the innocent party, even though it might have the effect of granting a greater quantum of relief than that available in a contractual damages claim. As we have seen,[31] the measure of relief in a claim for contract damages is in the expectancy measure, that is, a monetary award that will, to the extent that money can do so, place the innocent party in the position he or she would have been in if the contract had been performed. Thus, in the simple case of a contract for the purchase of goods having a market value of one hundred dollars and a price of ninety dollars, breached by the seller who refuses to deliver the goods, the disappointed purchaser will be fully compensated in the expectancy measure by an award of ten dollars. The purchaser can combine the ninety dollars he would have spent, together with the ten-dollar award and acquire a satisfactory substitute in the marketplace. If the numbers are reversed, however, and the buyer had agreed to purchase goods having a market value of ninety dollars at a price of one hundred dollars, the expectancy principle yields no recovery. The purchaser will be as well off, indeed better off, by purchasing substitute goods at the market rate. If, in the latter case, the purchaser had, however, paid a down payment of twenty dollars, the logic of the expectancy principle would yield recovery only of ten dollars on the basis that the award of ten dollars coupled with the unspent eighty

---

29   [1996] A.C. 788 (P.C.). See also *Westdeutsche Landesbank Girozentrale v. Islington L.B.C.*, [1996] A.C. 669 (H.L.). For criticism of the doctrine, see P.B.H. Birks, "Failure of Consideration" in F.D. Rose, ed., *Consensus ad Idem* (London: Sweet & Maxwell, 1996) c. 9.

30   *Goss v. Chilcott*, *ibid.* at 798, Lord Goff of Chieveley.

31   See Chapter 22.

dollars could yield a satisfactory substitute at the market rate. In such a case, then, the seller would profit to the extent of ten dollars from the breach of contract as a result of having astutely taken a down payment. In such a case, the buyer would prefer to bring a restitutionary claim for the entire down payment, thus preventing what would otherwise appear to be the unjust enrichment of the defendant. In such a case, it is trite law[32] that the full down payment is recoverable. The expectancy principle imposes no limit on the extent of restitutionary recovery in this situation.

A more difficult case arises, however, in the context of partial performance of a contract to supply goods or services. When confronted by a repudiatory breach, the supplier who is committed under the contract to an unprofitable price will no doubt prefer to bring a restitutionary claim for the full value of the goods and services supplied in a *quantum valebat* or *quantum meruit* claim, rather than pursue what would be, at best, a claim for nominal damages for breach of contract. Interestingly, such commonwealth,[33] including Canadian,[34] authority as exists on the point uniformly holds that the alternative restitutionary claim, untrammelled by either the contract price or the expectancy principle, will enjoy success. Such results may be defended on the basis that, as in the case of the down payment made on an unprofitable contract, the defendant, who has repudiated the contract, ought not to be able to rely on an advantageous price term in order to secure a profit from the arrangement that has not been earned by full performance. Alternatively, the result in the case of partial performance might be defended on the basis that the damages claim is not likely to be fully compensatory, either because it will not fairly reflect the economies of scale that would have been achieved by full performance, or that it will fail to reflect other benefits to be achieved through full performance or the true cost of losses caused by the disruption of performance. Nonetheless, the

---

32   See, for example, *Wilkinson v. Lloyd* (1845), 7 Q.B. 27, 115 E.R. 398; *Jay Trading Corp. v. Ifax Export & Import Ltd.*, [1954] 2 D.L.R. 110 (N.S.S.C.); *Dawood Ltd. v. Heath Ltd.*, [1961] 2 Lloyd's Rep. 512 (Q.B.).

33   See, for example, *Lodder v. Slowey*, [1904] A.C. 442 (P.C.); *Renard Constructions (ME) Pty. Ltd. v. Minster for Public Works* (1992), 26 N.S.W.L.R. 234 (C.A.); *Iezzi Constructions Pty. Ltd. v. Currumbin Crest Development Pty. Ltd.* (1994), 10 Bldg. & Constr. Law 403 (Qld. C.A.).

34   See, for example, *Lindsay v. Sutton*, [1947] O.W.N. 951 (H.C.J.), rev'd on other grounds [1948] O.W.N. 252; *Van Wetzel v. Risdon*, [1953] 2 D.L.R. 382 (Alta. S.C.); *Leo Gushue Construction v. Thistle* (1990), 8. Nfld. & P.E.I.R. 220 (Nfld. S.C.); *Potter Station Power Co. v. Inco Ltd.* (1998), 78 O.T.C. 161, 43 C.L.R. (2d) 53, supp. reasons [1998] O.J. No. 5349 (Gen. Div.).

rule has attracted its critics[35] and arguably generates unjust results in cases where substantial performance has been rendered in a drastically underbid contract. The well-known American case of *Boomer v. Muir*[36] colourfully illustrates the problem. The plaintiff contractor had agreed to build a large dam in return for a contract price involving monthly progress payments. At the time of the employer's wrongful repudiation of the agreement, a mere twenty thousand dollars in progress payments remained to be paid but the contractor's alternative claim in restitution for the value of the work done netted an award of two hundred and fifty-eight thousand dollars.

Critics of the rule suggest that such results are unsupportable and typically propose either that the expectancy rule should be applied with the result that the plaintiff in *Boomer v. Muir* would recover nothing or, at the least, that the contract price, here an additional twenty thousand dollars, would constitute an upper limit on the award. A number of points are typically taken in support of such proposals. First, as we have seen,[37] it is clearly established that the expectancy principle sets an upper limit on claims for reliance losses as an alternative to the expectancy claim. The rationale for that rule, arguably, is that the party who has underbid the contract should not be able to shift the loss, occasioned by poor bargaining, to the party guilty of breach, simply because the breach has occurred. If this reasoning is persuasive in the context of claims for reliance losses, it seems obvious, or so the argument goes, that it should also apply to a restitutionary claim. A partial reply to this point, at least, might be that in the reliance context there is no necessary equivalence between the plaintiff's reliance losses and the defendant's gain. In the restitution claim, however, the defendant is merely being required to pay for the value of what has been received under a contract that the defendant has now repudiated. Critics of the rule also point out that if the contract had been fully performed by the contractor in *Boomer v. Muir*, there is no question but that the contractor would be restricted to a claim of twenty thousand dollars, that is, to a claim enforcing the price term in the contract.[38] A similar limit ought to be placed, it is argued, on a claim for the value of partial rather than complete performance. In response, however, it may be observed that

---

35   See, for example, N.R. Rafferty, "Contracts Discharged through Breach: Restitution for Services Rendered by the Innocent Party" (1999) 37 Alta. L. Rev. 51.

36   24 P.2d 570 (Cal. App. 1933).

37   See Chapter 22, section D.

38   See, for example, *Morrison-Knudsen Co. Inc. v. British Columbia Hydro & Power Authority* (1978), 85 D.L.R. (3d) 186 (B.C.C.A.).

the limitation imposed by the contract price in cases of full performance can be explained on the basis that, in such circumstances, plaintiff contractors acquire precisely what they expected to receive under
the agreement. That is not the case where performance is only partial.

The arguments for and against the existing rule—allowing an uncapped restitutionary claim for partial performance—are thus rather
delicately balanced. It does not appear, however, to be clearly the case
that the existing rule is indefensible as a matter of general principle. It
is perhaps, therefore, unlikely to change. Although American law also
supports the existing rule, a few cases have applied the contract price as
a numerical cap on recovery.[39] On this view, the plaintiff contractor in
Boomer v. Muir should be limited to a claim for a further twenty thousand dollars. This rule, however, seems the most difficult to defend. The
limit set on recovery appears arbitrary. It responds neither to the extent
of the alleged unjust enrichment of the defendant nor, on the other hand,
to the arguments in favour of applying the expectancy measure on the
theory that an independent and uncapped restitutionary claim should
not be allowed to unwind the risks allocated by the contract price.

In the typical case, services provided at the request of a defendant will be beneficial in the sense that they create value in some form.
The defendant in *Boomer v. Muir* received a partially constructed dam.
In other cases, however, the services might be of such a nature that
they do not produce wealth in the hands of the defendant. Examples
would include the provision of legal services in a failing cause or geo-
logical services that reveal no exploitable mineral deposits. In other
cases, the decision of the defendant to breach the contract may deprive
the services of any value in the sense of enhanced wealth. In *Planche
v. Colburn*,[40] for example, the plaintiff had been hired to write a book
to be published in the defendant's "Juvenile Library" series. Before the
work was completed, the defendant abandoned the projected series and
wrongfully terminated the contract with the plaintiff. Notwithstanding
the fact that the incomplete manuscript was of no value to the defendant, the plaintiff successfully recovered in *quantum meruit* for the value
of the services rendered. This result can be defended on the basis that
the performance of a requested service *per se* should be considered to
be beneficial and of value to the defendant.[41] Thus, the client of the

---

39   See, for example, *Johnson v. Bovee*, 574 P.2d 513 (Col. App. 1978); *Wuchter v.
     Fitzgerald*, 163 P. 819 (Or. 1917).
40   (1831), 8 Bing. 14, 131 E.R. 305.
41   See American Law Institute, *Restatement of Restitution,* above note 2 at 12. And
     see *Pacific National Investments Ltd. v. Victoria (City)* (2004), 245 D.L.R. (4th)

professional who provides advice that does not generate wealth can, without artificiality, be said to have had the "benefit" of those services and, when the professional is wrongfully dismissed, a *quantum meruit* claim for their market value should lie. When a person expends effort providing requested services on the understanding that they are compensable, it is arguably immaterial to the restitution claim that the services either inherently or, as a result of a decision by the employer, do not create wealth in the form of a marketable asset.

2) Disgorgement of Profits Secured

One possible motive for a deliberate breach of contract could be a decision to attempt to secure a greater profit from performance than was provided under the existing agreement. Thus, a seller, for example, might refuse to perform an existing contract for the sale of goods in order to supply the goods at a higher price to a third party. Under traditional doctrine, the nature and extent of any profits secured through breach is irrelevant to the calculation of the buyer's claim for damages for breach of contract. Under the governing expectancy principle, buyers in such circumstances are entitled only to recovery of sufficient money to put them in the position they would have been in if the contract had been performed.[42] The purchaser, for example, could recover only the difference, if any, between the contract price and the market price the buyer would be required to pay in order to acquire substitute goods. In a particular set of facts, of course, the buyer's expectancy damages may be equivalent to the seller's profit as, for example, where the seller breaches the contract in order to sell the goods at the market price to a third party. Where the seller's price to the third party is higher than the market price, however, the excess over the market price is not recoverable by the buyer. In its recent decision in *Attorney General v. Blake*,[43] however, the House of Lords held that in exceptional circumstances the victim of a breach of contract may sue for an accounting of profits as an alternative to the claim for damages for breach of contract. As noted above,[44] this may be viewed as an extension to the context of

---

211 at para. 17 (S.C.C.), Binnie J.

42　See Chapter 22.

43　Above note 16. See J.D. McCamus, "Disgorgement for Breach of Contract: A Comparative Perspective" (2003) 36 Loy. L.A. L. Rev. 943; M. McInnes, "Gain-Based Relief for Breach of Contract: *Attorney General v. Blake*" (2001) 35 Can. Bus. L.J. 72. And see generally J. Edelman, *Gain-Based Damages* (Oxford: Hart, 2002).

44　See this Chapter, section A.

contractual breach of a general principle, considered by many to be an aspect of the law of restitution, that enables the victims of wrongdoers to recover profits secured by the wrongful acts.

The traditional reluctance of the common law to award an account of profits for breach of contract is often defended on the basis that it is generally accepted, even by its proponents, that the remedy should be available only in unusual circumstances and, accordingly, creates a need to distinguish between normal as opposed to outrageous or cynical or bad-faith breaches of contract that would attract the special remedy. Such a distinction, it is argued, introduces an unattractive element of uncertainty if not morality in the law of contract.[45] Law and economics scholars offer a further defence of the traditional rule on the basis of the theory of "efficient breach."[46] Under this theory, the seller who can breach the contract and sell the goods to a third party wishing to pay more than the contract price, ought to be encouraged to do so. Such breaches are efficient in the sense that the seller has improved his or her position, the third party who places a higher premium on acquiring the goods improves his or her position and the purchaser who has suffered a loss will be fully compensated for it by the expectancy rule. Accordingly, the net effect of the breach is to increase wealth. On this view, then, a rule permitting an accounting of profits would discourage efficient behaviour. Many find this a persuasive view and, indeed, in the *Blake* decision, the House of Lords was careful to distinguish cases of efficient breach from those in which an accounting of profits might be made available. The theory of efficient breach has attracted criticism, however.[47] The principal criticism is that the alleged efficiency gains are illusory in the sense that they require one to ignore the potential costs resulting from the likely dispute between the seller and the first purchaser. Further, it is suggested that the theory fails to recognize the general desirability of encouraging contract performance.[48]

---

45   A view that may draw support from the famous statement of O.W. Holmes that a contractual obligation is nothing more than "a prediction that you must pay damages if you do not keep it—and nothing else," a view, he suggested, that "stinks in the nostrils of those who think it advantageous to get as much ethics into the law as they can." See O.W. Holmes, "The Path of the Law" (1897) 10 Harv. L. Rev. 457 at 462.

46   See, for example, R. Posner, *Economic Analysis of Law*, 6th ed. (New York: Aspen, 2003) at 119–20.

47   See, for example, I.R. Macneil, "Efficient Breach of Contract: Circles in the Sky" (1982) 68 Va. L. Rev. 947; D. Friedmann, "The Efficient Breach Fallacy" (1989) 18 J. Legal Stud. 1.

48   The efficient breach analysis does not necessarily exclude entirely the possibility of an accounting of profits. Thus, where the breach is merely "opportunistic" in the sense that though the seller, for example, profits through breach (by, for

A third argument made in support of the traditional approach is that the availability of an accounting of profits remedy might undermine the general principle requiring the victim of a breach to undertake reasonable efforts to mitigate resulting loss.[49] In theory at least, the victim of a breach might be encouraged by the availability of such relief to decline to mitigate and eventually sue the seller either for the profit made on a resale or for the value of the goods at the date of trial.[50] In particular fact situations, however, it may be that even purchasers who are aware of the rule might nonetheless adopt the prudent course of mitigating their losses.

The principal argument in favour of granting this form of relief in a contractual context is that some breaches of contract are as offensive or wrongful as many breaches of fiduciary obligation or breaches of confidence. Accordingly, just as the accounting of profits remedy is available in these other contexts, so too it should be available in the context of a heinous or unusually wrongful breach of contract. A further and perhaps more persuasive argument in support is that courts will, in any event, order disgorgement of profits in a case of contract breach where any other result would be unjust, even in the absence of an explicit doctrine permitting the granting of such relief. Accordingly, explicit recognition of the doctrine would subject such cases to a more open and principled analysis.

The latter argument draws support from the fact that a number of authorities, decided prior to the decision in *Blake*, have awarded what appears to be disgorgement relief, typically in circumstances where the expectancy damages calculation seems to offer an inadequate response to the defendant's misconduct. The decision in *British Motor Trade Association v. Gilbert*[51] is a leading illustration of this phenomenon. This case arose in the context of a regulatory scheme designed to control the resale prices of cars for a period of time in the context of a market shortage. Purchasers of cars agreed to resell them only to the plaintiff association at a controlled price. The defendant, however, breached this

---

example, reinvesting the price paid by the purchaser) but the goods are not transferred to a third party willing to pay more for the goods, the breach is not efficient in the requisite sense and the accounting of profits ought to lie. Lionel Smith argues that this move "contradicts completely" the efficient breach theory by attacking the profit motive. See L. Smith, "Disgorgement of the Profits of Breach of Contract: Property Contract and 'Efficient Breach'" (1994) 24 Can. Bus. L.J. 121 at 135.

49   See Chapter 22, section F(3).

50   See S.M. Waddams, "Breach of Contract and the Concept of Wrongdoing" (2000) 12 Sup. Ct. L. Rev. 1 at 9.

51   [1951] 2 All E.R. 641 (Ch.).

undertaking and sold his car on the black market, thereby profiting from his breach of contract. The expectancy rule could not reach those profits. If the defendant had performed his agreement, no profit would have been enjoyed. Under the expectancy calculation, then, the plaintiff association required no compensation in order to be put in the position it would have been in if the contract had been performed. Nonetheless, the court awarded the plaintiff the profits secured by the defendant through his breach of contract. The unconvincing reason offered by the court for this unusual result was that the plaintiff ought to be able to take into account, in calculating damages, the cost of substitution in the black market. A better explanation for the result would be that the accounting of profits was awarded because of the inadequacy of the damages remedy in this context. If the accounting remedy is not available, an agreement of this kind, evidently in the public interest, would simply not be enforceable.

Similarly, in *Wrotham Park Estate Co. Ltd. v. Parkside Homes Ltd.*,[52] the relief awarded appears to effect a disgorgement of profits achieved through a breach of contract. In this case, a developer had purchased land that was subject to a restrictive covenant imposing limitations on use of the land for a residential development. Nonetheless, the developer proceeded with a project that ignored the restrictions. In response, the covenantees, who were, in fact, the successors in title to the vendors, sought to enjoin the project. Although that relief was refused, the plaintiffs were allowed a damages claim. Although the loss sustained by the plaintiffs as a result of the breach was insubstantial in expectancy terms, they were allowed to recover a sum of money that would represent the amount the developer would likely have been required to pay for a relaxation of the covenant. If such an award was not made, the court held, the developer would be left "in undisturbed possession of the fruits of [its] wrongdoing."[53] To be sure, this decision does not offer unambiguous evidence of a disgorgement calculation. Such an award might be rationalized with the traditional principle on the basis that it offers compensation for the plaintiffs' lost opportunity to bargain for such a sum.[54] Moreover, the decision remained controversial for some time.[55] In *Blake*,[56] however, the House of Lords confirmed the correct-

52 [1974] 1 W.L.R. 798 (Ch.).
53 *Ibid.* at 812.
54 R. Sharpe and S. Waddams, "Lost Opportunity to Bargain" (1982) 2 Oxford J. Legal Stud. 290.
55 Compare with *Surrey C.C. v. Bredero Homes Ltd.*, [1993] 3 All E.R. 705 (C.A.) (similar facts—*Wrotham Park* not applied) with *Jaggard v. Sawyer*, [1995] 2 All E.R. 189 (C.A.) (similar facts—*Wrotham Park* applied).
56 Above note 16.

ness of the decision in *Wrotham Park* and placed the result squarely on the basis of a disgorgement principle. Indeed, Lord Nicholls[57] identified *Gilbert* and *Wrotham Park* and other similar cases,[58] as important precursors of a more explicit recognition of the principle that disgorgement relief can be made available in a breach of contract setting.

The facts of the *Blake* decision made it an appealing context within which to consider recognition of disgorgement relief. The defendant Blake was a traitor who had betrayed his country by divulging valuable secret information to the Soviet Union acquired during his service in the Security Intelligence Service in the period following the Second World War. Uncovered as a spy in 1961, he was convicted of spying and given a lengthy sentence. In 1966, however, he escaped from Wormwood Scrubs, eventually making his way to Moscow where he proceeded to write a memoir entitled *No Other Choice*. The book was eventually published in England in September of 1990. Some of the information in the book pertained to his activities as an intelligence officer. By the time of publication, however, the information, in part no doubt because of the revelations of other former spies, was no longer confidential nor was its disclosure damaging to the public interest. Nonetheless, the writing and publication of the memoir constituted a clear breach of an undertaking Blake had given when taking up employment in the security service not to divulge any official information acquired during the course of his employment as an intelligence officer. By the time the attorney general became aware of the publication, the publisher had already paid Blake sixty thousand pounds under the publishing contract. The attorney general commenced an action, however, to recover the ninety thousand pounds that was still to be paid and was therefore, as a practical matter, potentially recoverable. Obviously, if Blake had performed his agreement, no book would have been written. Thus, under the expectancy principle, the damages suffered by the Crown were non-existent. An attractive opportunity was thereby afforded for consideration of the appropriateness of granting an accounting of profits remedy for breach of contract.[59]

In the leading opinion, Lord Nicholls canvassed the various non-contractual contexts in which disgorgement relief is traditionally

---

57   *Ibid.* at 282–85 (H.L.).

58   *Reid-Newfoundland Company v. Anglo-American Telegraph Company*, [1912] A.C. 555 (P.C.); *Lake v. Bayliss*, [1974] 1 W.L.R. 1073 (H.C.).

59   On similar facts, it had previously been suggested that an accounting of profits might be available on the basis of breach of confidence. See *Attorney-General v. Guardian Newspapers Ltd. (No. 2)*, [1990] 1 A.C. 109 (H.L.). See also *Snepp v. United States*, 444 U.S. 507 (1980).

awarded and, as well, the contract cases such as *Gilbert* and *Wrotham Park* in which disgorgement relief was awarded without explicit consideration of a principled basis for disgorgement. Lord Nicholls concluded that there was no reason in principle why an account of profits could not be awarded in a contract case. He emphasized, however, that "[n]ormally the remedies of damages, specific performance and injunction, coupled with the characterization of some contractual obligations as fiduciary, will provide an adequate response to a breach of contract"[60] and, indeed, that it is only in cases where such "remedies are inadequate"[61] that an accounting of profits should be awarded. Lord Nicholls declined, however, to offer more specific guidance as to when the remedy might be appropriate. He explained as follows:

> No fixed rules can be prescribed. The court will have regard to all the circumstances, including the subject matter of the contract, the purpose of the contractual provision which has been breached, the circumstances in which the breach occurred, the consequences of the breach and the circumstances in which relief is sought. A useful general guide, although not exhaustive, is whether the plaintiff had a legitimate interest in preventing the defendant's profit-making activity and, hence, in depriving him of his profit.
>
> It would be difficult, and unwise, to attempt to be more specific.[62]

The facts of *Blake* itself offer an illustration of the application of this principle. Obviously, the Crown had a legitimate interest in preventing the type of activity at issue in this case. Further, Lord Nicholls placed considerable emphasis on the importance of confidentiality in the work of the security service and on the fact that Blake's activities threatened to jeopardize the very effectiveness of an important public institution. Although Blake's writing career did not constitute a breach of fiduciary obligation to the Crown, the situation was "closely akin"[63] to a fiduciary relationship, a context in which an accounting of profits is the standard remedy. The conduct also involves the commission of a criminal offence. Thus, this particular breach of contract is very similar to the kinds of activities that traditionally engage the accounting remedy.[64]

Beyond this, however, Lord Nicholls merely suggested some factors that would not give rise to the accounting of profits remedy. Following

---

60 Above note 16 at 285 (H.L.).
61 *Ibid.*
62 *Ibid.*
63 *Ibid.* at 287.
64 See generally Maddaugh and McCamus, above notes 12–15.

the lead of the Court of Appeal,[65] Lord Nicholls agreed that the mere fact that a particular breach was cynical and deliberate would not constitute a basis for disgorgement relief. Further, Lord Nicholls indicated that the mere fact that the breach was undertaken in order to enjoy a more profitable contract with a third party would not, in itself, provide a basis for disgorgement. Thus, the *Blake* decision preserves the traditional position that the remedy for a so-called efficient breach remains compensatory damages. Lord Nicholls rejected, however, a suggestion made in the Court of Appeal that the disgorgement remedy would be particularly appropriate in cases of "skimped performance." Cases of skimped performance are those in which the defendant has promised to provide a particular service and even though the defendant skimped on the level of service provided, no harm resulted.[66] In such cases, in Lord Nicholls' view, a simple claim in damages would be sufficient. Lord Nicholls also rejected the Court of Appeal's suggestion that disgorgement should be allowed in any case where the defendant breached an undertaking not to do something. In his view, to allow disgorgement in any case of a negative undertaking would make the remedy too broadly available.[67]

In sum, then, the *Blake* decision adopts a rather open-textured or open-ended principle as a basis for awarding disgorgement relief for contract breach. The doctrine has been applied on a few occasions in England[68] and it appears likely that the doctrine will be accepted into Canadian common law as well. A number of pre-*Blake* Canadian decisions have awarded relief in the disgorgement measure. In *Jostens Canada Limited Ltd. v. Gibsons Studio Ltd.*,[69] for example, the defendant, a school photographer who had served for years as the local representa-

---

65   *Attorney General v. Blake*, above note 16 at 845 (C.A.).
66   See, for example, *City of New Orleans v. Firemen's Charitable Association,* 9 So. 486 (La. 1891) (defendant provider of fire-fighting services skimped on the contractually required number of fire fighters, horses and length of hose—no fire occurred—nominal damages awarded).
67   *Attorney General v. Blake*, above note 16 at 286 (H.L.).
68   *Esso Petroleum Co. Ltd. v. Niad Ltd.*, [2001] 1 All E.R. (D) 824 (defendant service station participates in "Pricewatch" program, receiving discounts on oil purchases from plaintiff Esso in return for a promise to lower prices to consumers on order from the plaintiff—the defendant profits by not lowering prices—excess profits recoverable); *Experience Hendrix v. PPX Enterprises Ltd.*, [2003] EWCA Civ. 323 (C.A.) (unauthorized licensing of master recordings—damages calculated with reference to defendant's gain).
69   (1999), 174 D.L.R. (4th) 351 (B.C.C.A.). See also *Arbutus Park Estates Ltd. v. Fuller* (1976), 74 D.L.R. (3d) 257 (B.C.S.C.) (applying *Wrotham Park*, above note 52).

tive of the plaintiff national firm, was required to disgorge profits made by wrongfully negotiating on its own account contracts to supply services to various schools. The *Blake* doctrine itself has been applied in a recent authority[70] and, indeed, the Supreme Court of Canada itself appears to have accepted the existence of such a doctrine.[71]

C. REMEDIES UPON BREACH: THE GUILTY PARTY

1) Introduction

For the party in breach, the possibility of restitutionary recovery holds out the only prospect for relief. A party that has conferred value, through performance of the agreement, on the other party but that has become incapable or unwilling to perform the remainder of the contract may have committed a repudiatory breach of contract.[72] In such circumstances, the innocent party is entitled to treat the contract as discharged by the breach and terminate or sever the relationship between the parties. If the innocent party has suffered loss, a claim can be brought for damages for breach of contract.[73] The guilty party has no such claim, of course—the innocent party is not in breach of contract—but may wish to pursue a claim for the value of benefits conferred on the innocent party. Such benefits were conferred at the defendant's request. Compensation for them from the innocent party would have been received if the contract had been fully performed. It is not obvious that the innocent party ought to be able to acquire the benefits for free, simply because the contract has been breached. Thus, for example, if the guilty party has paid a large down payment under a contract for the purchase and sale of goods only to subsequently cancel the order, the defaulting purchaser will wish to seek recovery of that down payment on the theory that the seller, who has accepted the repudiatory breach as the termination of the contract, has provided no consideration in return for the amount and that the retention by

---

70   *Amertek Inc. v. Canadian Commercial Corporation* (2003), 229 D.L.R. (4th) 419 (Ont. S.C.J.), rev'd on other grounds [2005] O.J. No. 2879 (C.A.).

71   *Bank of America Canada v. Mutual Trust Co.,* [2002] 2 S.C.R. 601. And see M. McInnes, "Restitutionary Damages for Breach of Contract: *Bank of America (Canada) v. Mutual Trust Co.*" (2002) 37 Can. Bus. L.J. 125.

72   See Chapter 15.

73   See Chapter 22.

the seller, therefore, constitutes an unjust enrichment. To the extent that the seller has actually suffered a loss as a result of the breach, the purchaser will argue, the seller is fully protected by the claim for damages for breach of contract. Restitutionary relief for the guilty party is indeed allowed, on this basis, in certain circumstances. The precise rules permitting recovery in such cases, however, differ between cases in which the defaulting party seeks recovery of monies paid to the innocent party and cases where the defaulting party seeks to recover the value of goods and services provided to the innocent party.

2) Money Paid

As a matter of general principle, monies paid by the guilty party to the innocent party are recoverable in a restitutionary claim unless the agreement between the parties has stipulated that the monies paid are to be forfeited in the event of breach. An arrangement of this kind is normally inferred when the payment is described by the parties as a "deposit." In the leading case, *Howe v. Smith*,[74] an initial payment of five hundred pounds on a contract for the purchase and sale of land was described as "a deposit and in part payment of the purchase-money."[75] The payment was described as a part payment, presumably, in order to make it clear that the monies paid would be credited toward the purchase price. Use of the term "deposit," however, clearly indicated, in the court's view, that the payment was not merely a part payment. It is "also an earnest to bind the bargain so entered into, and creates by the fear of its forfeiture a motive in the payer to perform the rest of the contract."[76] Use of the term "deposit" is not necessarily dispositive, however, and in a recent case, it has been held that where the so-called deposit is an unreasonably large amount, the payment may not constitute a true deposit and may be recoverable, subject to the innocent party's counterclaim for losses suffered as a result of the breach.[77]

As a general rule, then, monies paid as a part payment rather than a deposit are recoverable. In the leading case, *Dies v. British International Mining & Finance Corp. Ltd.*,[78] a purchaser had paid a down payment of two hundred and seventy thousand pounds on a contract for the sup-

---

74   (1884), 27 Ch. D. 89 (C.A.).

75   *Ibid.*

76   *Ibid.* at 101, Fry L.J.

77   *Workers Trust & Merchant Bank Ltd. v. Dojap Investments Ltd.*, [1993] A.C. 573 (P.C.).

78   [1939] 1 K.B. 724. See also *Mason v. Clouet*, [1924] A.C. 980 (P.C.).

ply of a large quantity of rifles and ammunition. The purchaser failed to take delivery and the seller disaffirmed the contract. The defaulting purchaser was allowed to recover the monies paid subject to the seller's counterclaim for losses suffered as a result of the breach. Similar recovery has been granted in Canadian cases.[79] It has been suggested[80] that because the plaintiff's claim is for money had and received, it is necessary to establish that the plaintiff has suffered a total failure of consideration. This view has the unattractive consequence that if the purchaser had taken delivery of a first few rifles in the *Dies* case, restitutionary recovery would be denied. It is clearly established Canadian law, however, that the receipt of partial consideration by the party in default does not preclude a restitutionary claim for monies paid to the innocent party.[81]

If the innocent party has suffered loss in the form of expenses wasted in preparation for performance, such losses are compensable in the innocent party's claim for damages for breach of contract. Thus, in *Stevenson v. Colonial Homes*,[82] where a purchaser of a prefabricated cottage defaulted, the supplier was allowed to recover expenses of this kind that it could not otherwise recoup, including the cost of converting the prefabricated materials to another use. Recent English authority[83] suggests that in the context of a contract to provide work and materials that requires payment of the purchase price by instalments, it is arguable that the payments were intended to fund the work in progress and are therefore not recoverable. The cases in question involved the construction of large ships and, although the claims were made against the guarantors of the buyer's obligations under the shipbuilding contracts,

---

79   *Stephenson v. Bromley*, above note 28; *Hirst v. Moore*, [1955] 1 D.L.R. 514 (B.C.S.C.); *Stevenson v. Colonial Homes Ltd.* (1961), 27 D.L.R. (2d) 698 (Ont. C.A.); *Radley Bros. (Oshawa) Ltd. v. A to Z Rental Canada Ltd.* (1973), 32 D.L.R. (3d) 521 (Ont. H.C.J.), var'd 46 D.L.R. (3d) 686 (Ont. C.A.); *Case v. Floral Studio Ltd.* (1998), 56 O.T.C. 210 (Gen. Div.).

80   See, for example, *Hyundai Heavy Industries Co. Ltd. v. Papadopoulos*, [1980] 1 W.L.R. 1129 at 1135–36 (H.L.), Viscount Dilhorne.

81   See, for example, *Stephenson v. Bromley*, above note 28 (purchaser of hotel business takes possession for one year before defaulting—down payment recoverable subject to a deduction for the value of the interim use of the property and the depreciation in the value of the assets of the business). See also *Westcott v. Day*, [1945] 1 W.W.R. 281 (Man. K.B.); *Hirst v. Moore*, above note 79. See also Maddaugh and McCamus, above note 9, c. 4.200.10.

82   Above note 79.

83   *Hyundai Heavy Industries Co. Ltd. v. Papadopoulos*, above note 80; *Hyundai Shipbuilding & Heavy Industries Co. Ltd. v. Pournaras*, [1978] 2 Lloyd's Rep. 502 (C.A.).

the guarantors argued that they ought to be able to defend the claim on the basis of the *Dies* principle. If the monies had been paid by the buyer, the guarantors argued, they would be recoverable on the basis of *Dies* and, accordingly, this should also constitute a defence to the claim against them. The English courts held, however, that in an instalment contract of this kind, *Dies* would not apply and, accordingly, the guarantors were liable. As the shipbuilders would be fully protected by their claim for damages for breach of contract, this seems to be a generous interpretation of the agreement in their favour and it may be that Canadian courts would insist on a clearer signal in the agreement that the instalment payments were to be forfeited in the event of breach.[84]

As we have seen, contractual stipulations that provide for forfeiture of payments made by the party in default will normally preclude restitutionary relief by the payor. In exceptional circumstances, however, such stipulations may themselves be held unenforceable, in which case, a restitution claim for the monies paid would lie. In *Stockloser v. Johnson*,[85] Denning L.J. articulated the following two-step test for identifying circumstances in which the forfeiture provision will become ineffective: "First, the forfeiture clause must be of a penal nature, in this sense, that the sum forfeited must be out of all proportion to the damage, and secondly, it must be unconscionable for the seller to retain the money."[86]

The first branch of the test draws on the traditional distinction between penalties and liquidated damages clauses[87] and extends to the phenomenon of pre-payments the thrust of the general principle that penalty clauses are unenforceable. Denning L.J.'s approach is defensible, then, on the basis that if penalty clauses are unenforceable, monies paid under such clauses should, in principle, be recoverable. The second branch of the test suggests, however, that there may be circumstances where penal forfeitures can be justified. On the very facts of *Stockloser* itself—forfeiture of instalment payments on a contract to purchase quarrying machinery and plant—Denning L.J. was of the view that the purchaser had taken the risk that the venture would prove to be

---

84   An alternative explanation for the denial of recovery, under English law, may be that the buyers had received partial consideration in the form of the work in progress and, accordingly, that the buyers' claim would fail on the basis of inability to meet the total failure of consideration requirement. If this is the correct explanation for the result, under English law, it is clear that the results would be incorrect under Canadian law, which has abandoned the total failure of consideration requirement. See above note 81.

85   [1954] 1 Q.B. 476 (C.A.).

86   *Ibid.* at 490.

87   See Chapter 22, section J.

unprofitable. Accordingly, it was not unconscionable for the vendor to retain the instalment payments. Denning L.J. went on, however, to provide illustrations of cases where recovery would be appropriate. Thus, where a valuable piece of jewellery is purchased on the instalment plan under a contract that provides for forfeiture of payments to date in the event of purchaser default, it would be unjust to allow the jeweller to retain 80 percent of the payments made and recover the piece of jewellery, an appreciating asset, as well. Similarly, a defaulting purchaser under a contract for the purchase and sale of land who has paid a 50-percent deposit ought to enjoy recovery subject to the vendor's counterclaim for damages resulting from the breach. The *Stockloser* principle appears to have been accepted by Canadian courts.[88]

3) Goods and Services Supplied

In principle, there is no reason why value transferred by the defaulting party in the form of goods and services should be treated differently for purposes of a restitutionary claim than money paid. There are, indeed, a number of cases in which defaulting parties have recovered for a partial supply of professional[89] and other services.[90] As with the recovery of monies paid, the restitutionary claim would be defeated by a contractual stipulation that, in the event of breach, the value transferred would be forfeited. In the context of building contracts, for example, the courts have inferred forfeiture stipulations on the basis of the doctrine of so-called entire contracts. An entire contract is one in which payment is to be made to the builder in a lump sum at the conclusion of the work. From such an arrangement it is traditionally inferred that the builder has agreed that in the event of default, the value of the work done prior to the breach would be forfeited and no restitutionary

---

88   See, for example, *Wilkinson v. Rena-Ware Distributors Ltd.* (1955), 16 W.W.R. 376 (Alta. Dist. Ct.); *Buck v. Cooper* (1955), 1 D.L.R. (2d) 282 (B.C.S.C.); *Popyk v. Western Savings & Loan Association* (1969), 3 D.L.R. (3d) 511 (Alta. S.C.A.D.); *Re Provinces & Central Properties Limited and City of Halifax* (1969), 5 D.L.R. (3d) 28 (N.S.S.C.A.D.); *Hughes v. Lukuvka* (1970), 14 D.L.R. (3d) 110 (B.C.C.A.); *Craig v. Mohawk Metal Ltd.* (1975), 61 D.L.R. (3d) 588 (Ont. H.C.J.); *Deber Investments Ltd. v. Roblea Estates Ltd.* (1976), 21 N.S.R. (2d) 158 (S.C.T.D.); *Canadian Union College v. Camsteel Industries Ltd.* (1979), 17 A.R. 98 (Dist. Ct.); *Tymo v. Wild Rose Properties Ltd.* (1983), 43 A.R. 54 (Q.B.); *Athabasca Realty Co. Ltd. v. Graves* (1979), 106 D.L.R. (3d) 473 (Alta. Q.B.). See also *Bayda v. Canada North Dakota Land Co., Ltd.* (1913), 13 D.L.R. 1 (Sask. S.C.).

89   *Campbell, Albo, Low Ltd. v. Black* (1995), 26 O.R. (3d) 111 (Gen. Div.).

90   *Tanenbaum v. Wright-Winston Ltd.* (1965), 49 D.L.R. (2d) 386 (Ont. C.A.). Compare with *Bolliver v. Hirtle Estate* (1990), 71 D.L.R. (4th) 381 (N.S.S.C.A.D.).

claim in *quantum meruit* would lie for the value of the work done. In the leading case of *Sumpter v. Hedges*,[91] the plaintiff builder had agreed to erect two houses and a stable on the defendant's land for a lump sum, but abandoned the work after partial completion as a result of financial difficulties. The plaintiff was held unable to recover the value of the work done in a *quantum meruit* claim. Collins L.J. explained as follows: "Where, as in the case of work done on land, the circumstances are such as to give the defendant no option of whether he will take the benefit of the work or not, then one must look to other facts than the mere taking the benefit of the work in order to ground the inference of a new contract ... the mere fact that a defendant is in possession of what he cannot help keeping, or even has done work upon it, affords no ground for such an inference."[92]

This reasoning is inconsistent with the modern American and Canadian view that restitutionary liability is grounded on the unjust enrichment principle rather than on an implied contractual obligation to pay for value received.[93] On the facts of *Sumpter v. Hedges*, the employer of the builder has received a valuable benefit that the employer wanted and for which he was prepared to pay. Thus, there can be no objection that the employer has received something for which it is unjust to require payment. In principle, then, just as moneys paid in part performance are recoverable, so too the value of services rendered in these circumstances should be compensable in a restitutionary claim.

The unsatisfactory nature of the rule in *Sumpter v. Hedges* is ameliorated by two rules that restrict its potentially harsh application by permitting enforcement of all or part of the building contract. First, if the defaulting builder can establish that the contract is a divisible one, enforcement of the divisible portion of the contract that has been performed is allowed.[94] Second, the doctrine of substantial performance holds that where the builder's work is defective but the contract can be said to have been substantially performed, the builder is entitled to bring a claim to enforce the price term of the agreement subject, of course, to the employer's counterclaim for losses resulting from the de-

---

91   [1898] 1 Q.B. 673 (C.A.). See also *Lacroix Bros. & Co. Ltd. v. Cook*, [1926] 4 D.L.R. 747 (Sask. C.A.).

92   *Sumpter v. Hedges, ibid.* at 676.

93   See above this Chapter, section A.

94   See, for example, *Manitoba Fisheries Ltd. v. Drake Construction Co. Ltd.* (1963), 42 D.L.R. (2d) 351 (Man. Q.B.) (arrangement to pay ship captain bonus calculated on number of trips—severable rather than payable at the end of the season). The divisibility of employment contracts is typically provided for by statute. See, for example, *Apportionment Act*, R.S.O. 1990, c. A.23, s. 13.

fective work.[95] Application of the doctrine rests on a distinction between incomplete work in the sense of a refusal by the builder to perform part of the contract and completed work that is, however, defectively done. Under the traditional doctrine, it is only in the latter context that the doctrine applies and enables the builder to sue for the contract price. The doctrine is likely to be strictly applied against a contractor who withholds performance for strategic reasons. Thus, in *Fairbanks Soap Co. v. Sheppard*,[96] the supplier of a machine for manufacturing soap chips withheld installation of critical pieces of the machinery in order to coerce payment from the purchaser of monies to which the supplier was not then entitled under the agreement. The Supreme Court of Canada held that the doctrine was inapplicable. In more sympathetic circumstances, however, where the supplier or builder has essentially completed the work, albeit defectively, the doctrine is likely to apply. Thus, in another Canadian case in which a builder had, according to the trial judge, not fully performed the contract and had done some of the work badly, the doctrine was nonetheless applied by the court "based more on the fact of work badly done than on work not entirely done."[97] The doctrine of substantial performance thus appears to be a somewhat manipulable device for restricting the scope of the *Sumpter v. Hedges* rule.[98] Whether Canadian courts will reconsider the status of the rule in *Sumpter v. Hedges* in the light of recent developments in Canadian restitutionary doctrine remains to be seen. There is, however, some support in the Canadian authorities for the view that even in the context of incomplete performance, a claim in *quantum meruit* ought to lie for the value of services rendered by a defaulting party.[99]

---

95   H. Dakin Co. Ltd. v. Lee, [1916] 1 K.B. 566 (C.A.); Hoenig v. Isaacs, [1952] 2 All E.R. 176 (C.A.); Taylor Hardware Co. v. Hunt, [1917] 35 D.L.R. 504 (Ont. S.C.A.D.); Fairbanks Soap Co. v. Sheppard, [1953] 1 S.C.R. 314; Markland Associates Ltd. v. Lohnes (1973), 33 D.L.R. (3d) 493 (N.S.S.C.T.D.).
96   Ibid.
97   Markland Associates Ltd. v. Lohnes, above note 95.
98   Indeed, in Hoenig v. Isaacs, above note 95, Denning L.J. suggested that the doctrine of substantial performance would apply in any case where the supplier's default did not constitute a repudiatory breach. This view has the attraction of apparently extending the scope of the doctrine of substantial performance, thus further restricting the scope of Sumpter v. Hedges and applying it, essentially, only to cases where the builder or supplier has refused to complete performance of the agreement, conduct that would normally constitute a repudiatory breach. On the other hand, this view is not easily reconciled with the traditional distinction between incomplete and complete but defective performance.
99   See, for example, Kemp v. McWilliams (1978), 87 D.L.R. (3d) 544 (Sask. C.A.). In Kemp, the Saskatchewan court awarded quantum meruit in a case of plainly

D. RESTITUTION UNDER INEFFECTIVE TRANSACTIONS

1) Introduction

As we have seen, restitutionary remedies may be available in the context of a contractual breach either to the innocent party or, indeed, to the party in default. Restitutionary remedies may also be available to parties in the context of transactions that are ineffective in the sense of being unenforceable for one of the various reasons canvassed in this volume.[100] The nature of the remedial device employed to achieve restitutionary relief depends, as a general matter, on whether the reason for the ineffectiveness of the agreement was developed by the courts of common law or the courts of equity. Where, for example, a contract is unenforceable because of failure to comply with the *Statute of Frauds*,[101] courts of common law considered such agreements to be void. If benefits had been conferred by one party upon the other, the conferring party would be entitled to bring a common law restitutionary claim. Under traditional doctrine, the characterization of the claim would depend on the type of benefit conferred and would be referred to by the shorthand reference to the medieval writ employed historically to achieve restitution of the particular type of benefit conferred. Thus, claims for money paid to a defendant would lie in a claim for money had and received. Claims for money paid to a third party that had the effect of conferring a benefit on the defendant would lie in a claim for money paid. Claims for goods and services would lie in claims for *quantum valebat* and *quantum meruit,* respectively.

In cases where the reason for the ineffectiveness of the transaction was developed by the courts of equity, however, the agreement would be enforceable at common law and merely voidable, as opposed to void, in equity. An agreement that is voidable in equity can be set aside or

---

incomplete performance. Although the court purported to rely on the doctrine of substantial performance, it did not enforce the contract price term and is thus properly seen as a case of restitutionary relief for incomplete performance. See also *McMahon v. Coffee* (1844), 1 U.C.R. 110; *Hamilton v. Raymond* (1852), 2 U.C.C.P. 392; *Barton v. Fisher* (1846), 3 U.C.R. 75; *Brazeau v. Wilson* (1916), 30 D.L.R. 378 (Ont. S.C.A.D.).

100 See Chapters 10–14.

101 1677 (U.K.), 29 Car. II, c. 3, adopted in Canadian common law provinces either by incorporation of English law or by explicit enactment. See, for example, *Statute of Frauds*, R.S.O. 1990, c. S.19. And see J.E. Côté, "The Introduction of English Law into Alberta" (1964) 3 Alta. L. Rev. 262.

rescinded on equitable grounds. One of the prerequisites of the availability of rescissionary relief, however, is that there can be a giving back and taking back of the value of benefits conferred on either party. As part of the rescissionary decree, then, orders are typically made to achieve that objective. In equity, then, restitution will be accomplished as part and parcel of the exercise of setting aside the agreement. In the typical case of a transaction void at common law, by way of contrast, the obtaining of restitutionary relief is independent from the determination that the contract is unenforceable at common law. The transaction is unenforceable regardless of whether a giving back and taking back of assets transferred is either possible or desired by the parties.

Although the distinction between void at common law and voidable in equity holds for many different kinds of ineffective transactions, the distinction between common law and equitable relief has been blurred in two particular contexts, those of misrepresentation and duress. In these contexts, though doctrines of common law recognized agreements induced by fraudulent misrepresentation or duress to be unenforceable, such agreements were considered by common law courts to be voidable in the equitable manner rather than void.[102]

2) At Common Law

Broadly speaking, benefits conferred under agreements that are void for some reason at common law are recoverable in claims for money had and received, money paid, *quantum meruit* and *quantum valebat*. Taking as illustrative, claims for restitutionary recovery of money conferred under agreements void for failure to comply with the *Statute of Frauds*,[103] services rendered under such an agreement may be the subject of restitutionary recovery in a *quantum meruit* claim. The leading decision of the Supreme Court of Canada in *Deglman v. Guaranty Trust Co. of Canada*[104] is a case of this kind. A nephew who had provided services to his aunt on the faith of the latter's unenforceable oral undertaking to leave real property to him in her will in return for the services rendered was allowed to recover their value in a restitutionary claim. Similarly, a purchaser of land under an unenforceable oral agreement to purchase land is entitled to recover money paid as a deposit or part payment in a claim for money had and received. Although it is sometimes suggested that such claims will fail where the plaintiff has

---

102 See generally Chapters 10 and 11, section A.
103 Above note 101.
104 Above note 10.

already received a partial consideration and therefore cannot establish the requisite total failure of consideration,[105] it is unlikely that a contemporary Canadian court would apply such a requirement. Certainly, in cases where the claim is for the value of services rendered under an informal agreement, the partial receipt of consideration does not preclude recovery.[106] There is simply no convincing reason for denying recovery in a money claim rather than simply deducting the value of the benefit received from the award in cases of this kind. Indeed, Canadian courts have simply ignored the requirement in the informality context[107] and in the context of other kinds of agreements considered to be unenforceable at common law.[108] Although, as a matter of general principle, similar relief is available in the context of benefits conferred under agreements rendered void at common law for other reasons, the application of the principle does vary to some extent from one context to another. Thus, the rather detailed rules that have developed in the context of agreements unenforceable on grounds of illegality or frustration have been separately examined elsewhere in this volume.[109]

3) In Equity

Agreements that are voidable in equity on grounds of misrepresentation,[110] undue influence,[111] unconscionability[112] or on the basis of fundamental mistake[113] are vulnerable to an equitable decree of rescission that has the effect of setting aside the agreement and rendering it unenforceable. There are several prerequisites to the granting of a decree of rescission. The most important for present purposes is the requirement that in order to obtain rescission, the parties must be able to effect a *restitutio in integrum* or a restoration of the *status quo ante* by effecting a giving back and a taking back of benefits conferred by the parties one on the other. Thus, in order to set aside an agreement in equity, restitution of benefits conferred by both parties must be possible. The decree of rescission, then, may contain specific orders designed to achieve that

---

105 See, for example, *Thomas v. Brown* (1876), 1 Q.B.D. 714.
106 See, for example, *Giles v. McEwan* (1896), 11 Man. R. 150 (C.A.).
107 See, for example, *Hill v. Stanton* (1845), 2 U.C.R. 149.
108 See, for example, *Stephenson v. Bromley*, above note 28.
109 See Chapters 12 and 14.
110 See Chapter 10.
111 See Chapter 11, section B.
112 See Chapter 11, section C.
113 See Chapter 13, section C.

objective.[114] If an order requires the restitution of benefits conferred *in specie*, the order obviously has a proprietary effect.[115] Although the specific application of the doctrine of rescission in the context of different kinds of voidable contracts is considered elsewhere in this volume,[116] the points of general application will be briefly reviewed here.

The requirement of *restitutio in integrum* is not always strictly applied in the sense that where assets have been transferred under a voidable agreement and have subsequently deteriorated in value, an order requiring return of the asset may be coupled with an award of monetary compensation for that loss in value.[117] More generally, courts of equity may make whatever allowances or require whatever accounting of profits may be necessary in order to achieve what is "practically just."[118] Indeed, courts of equity have often asserted a broader jurisdiction to impose terms requiring one of the parties, for example, to be willing to enter into a substitute agreement with the other party on fairer terms.[119]

The other principal limitations on the availability of rescissionary relief are the requirements that the parties seeking relief have not affirmed the agreement, that there have not been laches or undue delay in seeking relief and that the subject matter of the contract has not become subject to the rights of third parties. The application of these limitations or bars to relief may vary from one type of voidable agreement to another. As a general matter, however, affirmation may be constituted either by words or conduct.[120] Laches or undue delay is likely to support a denial of relief only in circumstances where the delay has resulted in prejudice of some kind to the other party.[121] The third require-

---

114 See, for example, *Whittington v. Seale-Hayne* (1900), 82 L.T. 49, for discussion of which see Chapter 10, section E.

115 See generally S. Worthington, "The Proprietary Consequences of Rescission" [2002] R.L.R. 28.

116 See Chapters 10, 11, sections B and C, and 13, section C.

117 See, for example, *Addison v. Ottawa Auto & Taxi Co.* (1913), 16 D.L.R. 318 (Ont. S.C.A.D.); *Wiebe v. Butchart's Motors Ltd.*, [1949] 4 D.L.R. 838 (B.C.C.A.).

118 See, for example, *Erlanger v. New Sombrero Phosphate Co.* (1878), 3 App. Cas. 1218 at 1278–79 (H.L.), Lord Blackburn.

119 See, for example, *Solle v. Butcher*, [1950] 1 K.B. 671 (C.A.), for discussion of which see Chapter 13, section C; *Bank of Montreal v. Murphy*, [1986] 6 W.W.R. 610 (B.C.C.A.), for discussion of which see Chapter 10, section E. See also *Instone v. A. Schroeder Music Publishing Co. Ltd.*, [1974] 1 All E.R. 171 (C.A.), aff'd [1974] 3 All E.R. 616 (H.L.).

120 *Grant Campbell & Co. v. Devon Lumber Co. Ltd.* (1914), 7 O.W.N. 209 (S.C.A.D.); *Panzer v. Zeifman* (1978), 88 D.L.R. (3d) 131 (Ont. C.A.).

121 See, for example, *Lindsay Petroleum Company v. Hurd* (1874), L.R. 5 P.C. 221 at 239–40, Sir Barnes Peacock.

ment is applicable where a third party who is *bona fide*[122] in the sense of being unaware of the circumstances giving rise to the voidability of the agreement, purchases the subject matter of the agreement for value. Under traditional doctrine, a claim for rescission should be dismissed in such circumstances in order to protect the rights of the third party. A *restitutio in integrum* has therefore become impossible.[123]

Under the traditional view, if one of the bars to rescission was applicable and the decree of rescission was therefore denied, the plaintiff would simply be left without any relief whatsoever. In the result, then, if property was acquired, for example, under an agreement induced by undue influence, the intervention of third-party rights would preclude rescissionary relief and, accordingly, the party exercising the improper influence would be left in possession of the profit secured through the wrongful conduct. Although the case for allowing a monetary restitution claim in such circumstances to restore to the victim the value of benefit secured through misconduct appears quite compelling, traditional equitable doctrine refrained from granting such relief on the basis that the awarding of compensation was essentially a jurisdiction exercised by the courts of common law rather than the courts of equity.[124] In recent years, however, English and Canadian courts have begun to recognize that this no longer constitutes a sound reason for denying relief in this form and orders of compensation have been granted in such circumstances. In *Mahoney v. Purnell*,[125] for example, where an asset was acquired through undue influence and then resold to a third party, the plaintiff was awarded the difference between the value initially received for the interest transferred under undue influence and the sale price to the third party. Such an award is arguably restitutionary in nature, restoring to the victim the true value of the asset transferred under undue influence. A series of Canadian decisions have granted

---

122 *Lancashire Loans Ltd. v. Black*, [1934] 1 K.B. 380 (C.A.); *Avon Finance Co. Ltd. v. Bridger*, [1985] 2 All E.R. 281 (C.A.).

123 See, for example, *Clough v. London & North Western Ry.* (1871), L.R. 7 Exch. 26; *Laverty v. Eastern Sales Ltd.* (1955), 37 M.P.R. 254 (N.B.S.C.A.D.); *Wilson v. Harrison* (1979), 35 N.S.R. (2d) 499 (S.C.T.D.); *Coldunell Ltd. v. Gallon*, [1986] Q.B. 1184 (C.A.); *Baranick v. Counsel Trust Co.* (1994), 12 B.L.R. (2d) 39, 37 R.P.R. (2d) 202 (Ont. Ct. Gen. Div.), aff'd 17 B.L.R. (2d) 140 (Ont. C.A.); *Foy v. Royal Bank of Canada* (1995), 37 C.P.C. (3d) 262 (Ont. Ct. Gen. Div.).

124 Although courts of equity, from an early stage, possessed a jurisdiction to award compensation, such awards were not commonly made. See P.M. McDermott, "Jurisdiction of the Court of Chancery to Award Damages" (1992) 108 Law Q. Rev. 652.

125 [1996] 3 All E.R. 61 (Q.B.).

compensation of this kind in lieu of rescission in cases of misrepresentation,[126] undue influence[127] and unconscionability.[128] Support for the awarding of restitutionary compensation in these cases may be drawn from the modern Canadian recognition of the unjust enrichment analysis underlying restitutionary relief. There appears to be no sound reason for holding that restitutionary claims of this kind would lie in the context of contracts rendered ineffective for reasons recognized by the common law but not in the context of those recognized historically in equity. Further, the Supreme Court of Canada in recent decades has more openly recognized that courts of equity have an inherent jurisdiction to grant awards of compensation.[129] It appears likely, therefore, that compensation in this restitutionary form will continue to be potentially available in the cases where rescission cannot be awarded.

FURTHER READINGS

P.B.H. BIRKS, "Failure of Consideration" in F.D. Rose, ed., *Consensus ad Idem* (London: Sweet & Maxwell, 1996).

D. CAMPBELL & D. HARRIS, "In Defence of Breach: A Critique of Restitution and the Performance Interest" (2002) 22 Legal Stud. 208.

S.W. DELONG, "The Efficiency of Disgorgement as a Remedy for Breach of Contract" (1989) 22 Ind. L. Rev. 737.

J. EDELMAN, *Gain-Based Damages* (Oxford: Hart, 2002).

E.A. FARNSWORTH, "Your Loss or My Gain? The Dilemma of the Disgorgement Principle in Breach of Contract" (1982) 94 Yale L.J. 1339.

D. FRIEDMANN, "Restitution of Benefits Obtained through the Appropriation of Property or the Commission of a Wrong" (1980) 80 Colum. L. Rev. 504.

---

126 See, for example, *Dusik v. Newton* (1985), 62 B.C.L.R. 1 (C.A.); *Bank of Montreal v. Murphy*, [1986] 6 W.W.R. 610 (B.C.C.A.). See also *Fleischhaker v. Fort Garry Agencies Ltd.* (1957), 11 D.L.R. (2d) 599 (Man. C.A.).

127 See, for example, *Treadwell v. Martin* (1976), 67 D.L.R. (3d) 493 (N.B.S.C.A.D.).

128 See, for example, *Paris v. Machnick* (1972), 32 D.L.R. (3d) 723 (N.S.S.C.T.D.); *Junkin v. Junkin* (1978), 86 D.L.R. (3d) 751 (Ont. H.C.J.). See also *McCarthy v. Kenny*, [1939] 3 D.L.R. 556 (Ont. Sup. Ct.).

129 See generally J.D. McCamus, "Equitable Compensation and Restitutionary Developments" in *Special Lectures of the Law Society of Upper Canada, 1995 — Law of Remedies* (Toronto: Carswell, 1995) at 295.

D. FRIEDMANN, "The Efficient Breach Fallacy" (1989) 18 J. Legal Stud. 1.

P. JAFFEY, "Efficiency, Disgorgement and Reliance in Contract" (2002) 22 J. Legal Stud. 570.

A. KULL, "Disgorgement for Breach, the 'Restitution Interest' and the Restatement of Contracts" (2001) 79 Tex. L. Rev. 2021.

I.R. MACNEIL, "Efficient Breach of Contract: Circles in the Sky" (1982) 68 Va. L. Rev. 947.

P.D. MADDAUGH & J.D. McCAMUS, *The Law of Restitution*, 2d ed. (Aurora: Canada Law Book, 2004) c. 19 and 25.

J.D. McCAMUS, "Disgorgement for Breach of Contract: A Comparative Perspective" (2003) 36 Loy. L.A. L. Rev. 943.

M. McINNES, "Gain-Based Relief for Breach of Contract: *Attorney General v. Blake*" (2001) 35 Can. Bus. L.J. 72.

M. McINNES, "Restitutionary Damages for Breach of Contract: *Bank of America (Canada) v. Mutual Trust Co.*" (2002) 37 Can. Bus. L.J. 125.

G.E. PALMER, "The Contract Price as a Limit on Restitution for Defendant's Breach" (1959) 20 Ohio St. L.J. 264.

N.R. RAFFERTY, "Contracts Discharged through Breach: Restitution for Services Rendered by the Innocent Party" (1999) 37 Alta. L. Rev. 51.

R. SHARPE & S. WADDAMS, "Lost Opportunity to Bargain" (1982) 2 Oxford J. Legal Stud. 290.

L. SMITH, "Disgorgement of the Profits of Breach of Contract: Property, Contract and 'Efficient Breach'" (1994) 24 Can. Bus. L.J. 121.

S.M. WADDAMS, "Breach of Contract and the Concept of Wrongdoing" (2000) 12 Sup. Ct. L. Rev. 1.

E.J. WEINRIB, "Restitutionary Damages as Corrective Justice" (2000) 1 Theor. Inq. L. 1.

S. WORTHINGTON, "The Proprietary Consequences of Rescission" (2002) R.L.R. 28.

TABLE OF CASES

100 Main Street Ltd. v. W.B. Sullivan Construction Ltd. (1978), 20 O.R. (2d)
    401, 88 D.L.R. (3d) 1 (C.A.), leave to appeal to S.C.C. refused (1978),
    20 O.R. (2d) 401n, 88 D.L.R. (3d) 1n, 24 N.R. 359n (S.C.C.) 680, 865
1043545 Ontario Inc. v. 2748355 Canada Inc., [1998] O.J. No. 2781,
    70 O.T.C. 267, 19 R.P.R. (3d) 190 (Gen. Div.) 714
1110049 Ontario Ltd. v. Exclusive Diamonds Inc. (1995), 25 O.R.
    (3d) 417, [1995] O.J. No. 2690, 83 O.A.C. 391 (C.A.) 913, 936
1174538 Ontario Ltd. v. Barzel Windsor (1984) Inc., [1999] O.J. No. 5091,
    28 R.P.R. (3d) 256 (S.C.J.) 916
1193430 Ontario Inc. v. Boa-Franc (1983) Ltée. (2003), 68 O.R.
    (3d) 382, [2003] O.J. No. 5138, [2003] O.T.C. 1103 (S.C.J.) 805
306793 Ontario Ltd. v. Rimes (1979), 25 O.R. (2d) 79, 100 D.L.R.
    (3d) 350, 10 R.P.R. 257 (C.A.) 874, 944
872899 Ontario v. Iacovoni (1998), 40 O.R. (3d) 715, 163 D.L.R. (4th) 263,
    [1998] O.J. No. 2797 (C.A.), aff'g (1997), 33 O.R. (3d) 561, 147 D.L.R.
    (4th) 333, [1997] O.J. No. 1917 (Gen. Div.), leave to appeal to the S.C.C.
    refused (1999), 236 N.R. 199, [1998] S.C.C.A. No. 476 ...... 259, 262, 264, 265
947101 Ontario Ltd. v. Barrhaven Town Centre Inc., [1995] O.J. No. 15,
    121 D.L.R. (4th) 748, 17 B.L.R. (2d) 186 (Gen. Div.) 793
968703 Ontario Ltd. v. Vernon (2002), 58 O.R. (3d) 215,
    [2002] O.J. No. 580, 155 O.A.C. 386 (C.A.) 636
978011 Ontario Ltd. v. Cornell Engineering Co. (2001), 53 O.R. (3d) 783,
    198 D.L.R. (4th) 615, [2001] O.J. No. 1446 (C.A.) 140, 192, 335–36

A & K Lick-a-Chick Franchises Ltd. v. Cordiv Enterprises Ltd. (1981),
    44 N.S.R. (2d) 159, 119 D.L.R. (3d) 440, [1981] N.S.J. No. 335
    (T.D.) 414, 425, 740

A v. Bottrill (2002), [2002] UKPC 44, [2003] 1 A.C. 449 (P.C.) 881

A.L. Gullison & Sons Ltd. v. Corey (1979), 24 N.B.R. (2d) 638, [1979] N.B.J.
   No. 49 (Q.B.), rev'd (1980), 29 N.B.R. (2d) 86, [1980] N.B.J. No. 41 (C.A.)... 563

A.P.E.C.O. of Canada Ltd. v. Windmill Place, [1978] 2 S.C.R. 385,
   82 D.L.R. (3d) 1, 19 N.R. 124 870

A.V.G. Management Science Ltd. v. Barwell Developments Ltd. (1976),
   69 D.L.R. (3d) 741, [1976] 6 W.W.R. 289 (B.C.S.C.), aff'd (1977),
   83 D.L.R. (3d) 702, [1978] 1 W.W.R. 730, 3 R.P.R. 90 (B.C.C.A.),
   rev'd (1978), [1979] 2 S.C.R. 43, 92 D.L.R. (3d) 289, 24 N.R. 554 ...20, 821–22

Abba Ventures Inc. v. Royal Trust Corp. of Canada (1996), 176 N.B.R.
   (2d) 33, [1996] N.B.J. No. 131, 25 B.L.R. (2d) 211 (Q.B.) 129

Abbot of Westminster v. Clerke (1536-37) 1 Dyer 27a, 73 E.R. 59
   (K.B.) 568, 573

Abel v. McDonald, [1964] 2 O.R. 256, 45 D.L.R. (2d) 198 (C.A.) 332

Aberfoyle Plantations Ltd. v. Cheng, [1960] A.C. 115 (P.C.) 675–76

Abraham v. Wingate Properties Ltd. (1985), [1986] 1 W.W.R. 568,
   [1985] M.J. No. 156, 36 Man.R. (2d) 264 (C.A.) 661

Abram Steamship Co. v. Westville Shipping Co., [1923] A.C. 773 (H.L.) 339

Abrams v. Reiach (Herbert) Ltd., [1922] 1 K.B. 477 (C.A.) 824

Ackerman v. Thomson & McKinnon, Auchincloss, Kohlmeyer, Inc. (1974),
   4 O.R. (2d) 240, 47 D.L.R. (3d) 524 (C.A.)... 172

Active Customs Brokers Limited Ltd. v. Sack, [1987] O.J. No. 1082,
   25 O.A.C. 305, 37 B.L.R. 229 (Div. Ct.)... 166

Adam v. General Paper Co. Ltd. (1978), 19 O.R. (2d) 574, 85 D.L.R.
   (3d) 736 (H.C.J.) 170

Adams v. Union Cinemas Ltd., [1939] 3 All E.R. 136 (C.A.) 168

Adanac Realty Ltd. v. Homes Development Ltd., [1986] O.J. No. 1248,
   43 R.P.R. 88 (H.C.J.) 375

Adderley v. Dixon (1824), 1 Sim. & St. 607, 57 E.R. 239 (V.C.)....................... 913

Addis v. Gramophone Co. Ltd., [1909] A.C. 488 (H.L.)..................... 799, 878, 882

Addison v. Ottawa Auto & Taxi Co. (1913), 16 D.L.R. 318 (Ont. S.C.A.D.) 989

Adolph Lumber Co. v. Meadowcreek Lumber Co. (1919), 58 S.C.R. 306,
   45 D.L.R. 579, [1919] 1 W.W.R. 823 655

Advance Rumely Thresher Co. v. Yorga, [1926] S.C.R. 397, [1926]
   3 D.L.R. 517 461

Afovos Shipping Co. S.A. v. Pagnan, [1983] 1 W.L.R. 195 (H.L.) 656

Agrifoods International Corp. v. Beatrice Goods Inc., [1997] B.C.J. No. 393,
   34 B.L.R. (2d) 294 (S.C.) 634

Ahone v. Holloway (1988), 30 B.C.L.R. (2d) 368, [1988] B.C.J. No. 1603
   (C.A.) 205–6

Ailsa Craig Fishing Co. Ltd. v. Malvern Fishing Co. Ltd., [1983]
   1 W.L.R. 964, [1983] 1 All E.R. 101 (H.L.)............................358, 724, 764

Aita v. Silverstone Towers Ltd. (1978), 19 O.R. (2d) 681, 86 D.L.R. (3d) 439,
   4 B.L.R. 92 (C.A.)... 728

Alampi v. Swartz, [1964] 1 O.R. 488, 43 D.L.R. (2d) 11 (C.A.)........................ 711

Alati v. Kruger (1955), 94 C.L.R. 216 (A.H.C.).. 403

Albert E. Daniels Ltd. v. Sangster (1976), 12 O.R. (2d) 512 (Co. Ct.) 464
Albert v. Albert (1981), 33 N.B.R. (2d) 689, [1981] N.B.J. No. 60 (Q.B.) 387
Alberta Caterers Ltd. v. R. Volcan (Alta.) Ltd. (1977), 10 A.R. 501,
    81 D.L.R. (3d) 672, [1977] A.J. No. 777 (S.C.T.D.) 869
Alberta Turkey Producers v. Leth Farms Inc. (1998), 1998 ABQB 887,
    [1999] 7 W.W.R. 12, [1998] A.J. No. 1187 464
Alderslade v. Hendon Laundry, Ltd., [1945] K.B. 189 (C.A.) 358
Alec Lobb v. Total Oil GB, [1985] 1 All E.R. 303 (C.A.) 484
Alessio v. Jovicka (1973), 42 D.L.R. (3d) 242, [1974] 2 W.W.R. 126
    (Alta. S.C.A.D.) 360
Alevizos v. Nirula, 2003 MBCA 148, 234 D.L.R. (4th) 352, [2003]
    M.J. No. 433 352
Alexander Hamilton Institute v. McNally (1919), 53 N.S.R. 303 (App. Div.) 655
Alexander v. Railway Executive, [1951] 2 K.B. 882 755
Alexander v. Rayson, [1936] 1 K.B. 169 (C.A.) 431
Alkok v. Grymek, [1968] S.C.R. 452, 67 D.L.R. (2d) 718 967
Allan v. Bushnell T.V. Co. Ltd. (1968), [1969] 1 O.R. 107, 1 D.L.R.
    (3d) 534 (H.C.J.) 738
Allan v. McLennan, (1916), 31 D.L.R. 617 (B.C.C.A.) 852
Allcard v. Skinner (1887), 36 Ch. D. 145 386
Allegheny College v. National Chautauqua County Bank of Jamestown,
    159 N.E. 173 (N.Y.C.A. 1927) 231, 273
Allen v. Rescous (1676), 2 Lev. 174, 83 E.R. 505 (K.B.) 429, 430
Allen v. Richardson (1879), 13 Ch. D. 524 941
Allen v. Robles, [1969] 3 All E.R. 154 (C.A.) 659, 665
Alliance Bank v. Broom (1864), 2 Drew. & Sm. 289, 62 E.R. 631 (Ch.) 226
Alpenstow Ltd. v. Regalian Properties Plc., [1985] 1 W.L.R. 721 (Ch.) 127
Altantic Paper Stock Ltd. v. St. Anne-Nackawic Pulp & Paper Co. (1975),
    [1976] 1 S.C.R. 580, 56 D.L.R. (3d) 409, 4 N.R. 539 725
Aluminium Co. of America v. Essex Group Inc., 499 F. Supp. 53
    (W.D. Pa. 1980) 589
Amalgamated Investment Property Co. v. John Walker and Sons Ltd.,
    [1976] 3 All E.R. 509 (C.A.) 593–94
Amalgamated Society of Railway Servants v. Osborne, [1910] A.C. 87 (H.L.) 444
Amber Size & Chemical Co. v. Menzel, [1913] 2 Ch. 239 744
American Cyanimid Co. v. Ethicon Ltd., [1975] A.C. 396 (H.L.) 955
American Home Assurance Co. v. Brett Pontiac Buick GMC Ltd. (No. 2)
    (1992), 116 N.S.R. (2d) 319, 96 D.L.R. (4th) 485, [1992] N.S.J. No. 378
    (C.A.) 442
American Ins. Co. v. El Paso Pipe & Supply Co., 978 F.2d 1185
    (10th Cir. 1992) 65
American National Red Cross v. Geddes Bros. (1920), 61 S.C.R. 143,
    55 D.L.R. 194, [1921] 1 W.W.R. 185 660
Amertek Inc. v. Canadian Commercial Corp. (2003), 229 D.L.R. (4th) 419,
    [2003] O.J. No. 3177, [2003] O.T.C. 742 (S.C.J.), rev'd on other grounds
    [2005] O.J. No. 2789 (C.A.) 349, 979

Amoco Australia Pty. v. Rocca Bros. Motor Engineering Co., [1975]
    A.C. 561 (P.C.) 484
Anders Utkilens Rederi A/S v. O/Y Lovisa Stevedoring Co. A/B,
    The Golfstraum, [1985] 2 All E.R. 669 (Ch.) 938
Anderson v. Anderson, [1895] 1 Q.B. 749 725
Andrews Bros. (Bournemouth), Ltd. v. Singer & Co. Ltd., [1934]
    1 K.B. 17 (C.A.) 755
Andrews v. Calori (1907), 38 S.C.R. 588 .... 54, 61
Andrews v. Hopkinson, [1957] 1 Q.B. 229 327
Andronyk v. Williams (1985), 21 D.L.R. (4th) 557, [1985] M.J. No. 148,
    36 Man.R. (2d) 161 (C.A.), leave to appeal to S.C.C. refused (1986),
    69 N.R. 77n, [1986] 4 W.W.R. lxviii, 42 Man. R. (2d) 242n (S.C.C.) 327
Angers v. Gauthier, [1924] S.C.R. 479, [1924] 4 D.L.R. 1035 445
Anglia Television Ltd. v. Reed, [1972] 1 Q.B. 60 (C.A.) 835
Angus v. Scully, 57 N.E. 674 (Mass. S.J.C. 1900) 607
Anns v. Merton London Borough Council, [1978] A.C. 728 (H.L.) 154
Apotex Fermentation Inc. v. Novopharm Ltd., [1994] 7 W.W.R. 420,
    [1994] M.J. No. 357, 95 Man. R. (2d) 241 (C.A.) 956
Appleby v. Myers (1867), L.R. 2 C.P. 651 (Ex. Ch.) 580, 605
Appleton v. Ritchie Taxi, [1942] O.R. 446, [1942] 3 D.L.R. 546 (C.A.) 185
Apthorp v. Neville & Co. (1907), 23 T.L.R. 575 (K.B.) 430
Arbutus Park Estates Ltd. v. Fuller (1976), 74 D.L.R. (3d) 257, [1977]
    1 W.W.R. 729, 2 R.P.R. 126 (B.C.S.C.) 978
Archbolds (Freightage) Ltd. v. S. Spanglett Ltd., [1961] 1 Q.B. 374 (C.A.) 478
Archer v. Brown, [1985] Q.B. 401 349
Archibald v. McNerhanie (1899), 29 S.C.R. 564 170
Armhouse Lee Ltd. v. Chappel, [1996] E.W.J. No. 211 (C.A.) 436
Armstrong v. Gage (1877), 25 Gr. 1, [1877] O.J. No. 199 (Ch.) 369
Armstrong v. Roslyn Park Land Co. Ltd., (1951) 4.W.W.R. (N.S.) 270
    (B.C.S.C.) 865
Arnold Nemetz Engineering Ltd. v Tobien, [1971] 4 W.W.R. 373 (B.C.C.A.).... 102
Arrowhon Exploration Ltd. v. Northstar Energy Corp. (1993), 108 D.L.R.
    (4th) 709 (Alta. Q.B.) 714
Arthur Andersen Inc. v. Toronto-Dominion Bank (1994), 17 O.R. (3d) 363,
    [1994] O.J. No. 427, 71 O.A.C. 1 (C.A.) 711, 715, 722
Aruna Mills Ltd. v. Dhanrajmal Gobindram, [1968] 1 Q.B. 655 858
Asamera Oil Corp. Ltd. v. Sea Oil & General Corp. (1978), [1979]
    1 S.C.R. 633, 98 D.L.R. (3d) 1, 23 N.R. 181 669
Asamera Oil Corp. v. Sea Oil & General Corp. (1978), [1979]
    1 S.C.R. 633, 89 D.L.R. (3d) 1, 23 N.R. 181 .... 859, 868, 923
Asselstine v. Manufacturers Life Insurance Co., 2005 BCCA 292,
    254 D.L.R. (4th) 464, [2005] B.C.J. No. 1152 896
Assicurazioni Generali & Schenker & Co. v. S.S. Bessie Morris & Co. Ltd.,
    [1892] 2 Q.B. 652 (C.A.) 590
Associated Japanese Bank (International) Ltd. v. Credit du Nord SA,
    [1989] 1 W.L.R. 255, [1988] 3 All E.R. 902 (Q.B.) 538, 540–41, 545, 550

Astley Industrial Trust Ltd. v. Grimley, [1963] 1 W.L.R. 584, [1963]
    2 All E.R. 33 (C.A.) 756
Astley v. Reynolds (1731), 2 Str. 915, 93 E.R. 939 (K.B.) 370
Athabasca Realty Co. Ltd. v. Graves (1979), 23 A.R. 65, 106 D.L.R.
    (3d) 473, [1979] A.J. No. 595 (Q.B.) 983
Atkinson v. Ritchie (1809), 10 East 530, 103 E.R. 877 (K.B.) 568, 574
Atlantic Paperstock Ltd. v. St. Anne-Nackawic Pulp & Paper Co., [1976]
    1 S.C.R. 580, 56 D.L.R. (3d) 409, 4 N.R. 539 .... 599, 601–2
Atlantic Shipping and Trading Co. v. Louis Dreyfus and Co.,
    [1922] 2 A.C. 250 (H.L.) 764
Atlas Express Ltd. v. Kafco (Importers and Distributors) Ltd.,
    [1989] Q.B. 833 374
Atlas Supply Co. of Canada Ltd. v. Yarmouth Equipment Ltd. (1991),
    103 N.S.R. (2d) 1, [1991] N.S.J. No. 178, 37 C.P.R. (3d) 38 (S.C.A.D.),
    leave to appeal to S.C.C. granted but discontinued, [1991] 3 S.C.R. ix,
    108 N.S.R. (2d) 270n, [1991] S.C.C.A. No. 256 .... 421, 775
Atlific (Nfld.) Ltd. v. Hotel Buildings Ltd. (1994), 120 Nfld. & P.E.I.R. 91,
    [1994] N.J. No. 224 (C.A.), leave to appeal to S.C.C. refused (1995),
    185 N.R. 400n, [1994] S.C.C.A. No. 383 709
Atmospheric Diving Systems Inc. v. International Hard Suits Inc., [1994]
    5 W.W.R. 719, [1994] B.C.J. No. 493, 89 B.C.L.R. (2d) 356 (S.C.) 106, 787
Attica C. Carriers Corp. v. Ferrostaal Poseidon Bulk Reederei G.m.b.H.,
    [1976] 1 Lloyd's Rep. 250 (C.A.) 670
Attorney General of Australia v. Adelaide Steamship Co., [1913] A.C. 781
    (P.C.) 456
Attorney General of British Columbia v. Deeks Sand & Gravel Co. Ltd.,
    [1956] S.C.R. 336, 2 D.L.R. (2d) 305 226
Attorney General v. Blake (2000), [2000] UKHL 45, [2001] 1 A.C. 268,
    [2000] H.L.J. No. 47 (H.L.) aff'g (1997), [1998] 1 All E.R. 833,
    [1997] E.W.J. No. 1320 (C.A.) 964, 975–76, 977, 978
Attorney-General Saskatchewan v. Whiteshore Salt & Chemical Co. (1954),
    [1955] S.C.R. 43, [1955] 1 D.L.R. 241 823
Attorney-General v. Guardian Newspapers Ltd. (No. 2), [1990] 1 A.C. 109
    (H.L.) 976
Attwood v. Lamont, [1920] 3 K.B. 571 (C.A.) 453, 455, 488
Attwood v. Small (1838), 6 Cl. & F. 232, 7 E.R. 684 (H.L.) 331
Augdome Corp. v. Gray (1974), [1975] 2 S.C.R. 354, 49 D.L.R. (3d) 372,
    3 N.R. 235 .... 558, 559, 563
Austera Tanks Pty. Ltd. v. Running, [1982] 2 N.S.W.L.R. 840 (S.C.) 451
Austin v. Gordon (1872), 32 U.C.R. 621, [1872] O.J. No. 51 (Q.B.) 238
Avco Financial Services Realty Ltd. v. Norman (2003), 64 O.R. (3d) 239,
    226 D.L.R. (4th) 175, [2003] O.J. No. 1255 (C.A.) 352
Avery v. Bowden (1855), 5 El. & Bl. 714, 119 E.R. 647 (K.B.) 667
Avon Finance Co. Ltd. v. Bridger, [1985] 2 All E.R. 281 (C.A.) 990
Awwad v. Geraghty & Co., [2000] 1 All E.R. 608 (C.A.) 443

B. (D.C.) v. Zellers (1996), 138 D.L.R. (4th) 309, [1996] 8 W.W.R. 100,
 [1996] M.J. No. 362 (Q.B.), aff'd [1996] 10 W.W.R. 689, 113 Man. R.
 (2d) 198, [1996] M.J. No. 499 (C.A.), leave to appeal to S.C.C. refused,
 [1996] 10 W.W.R. 689 .... 226, 227
B. (J.F.) v. B (M.A.) (1999), 178 D.L.R. (4th) 340, [1999] O.J. No. 3214,
 1 R.F.L. (5th) 339 (S.C.J.), aff'd (2001), 203 D.L.R. (4th) 738, [2001]
 O.J. No. 1361, 14 R.F.L. (5th) 1 (C.A.) 410, 419
B.C.C.I. v. Ali (2001), [2001] UKHL 8, [2002] 1 A.C. 251, [2001]
 2 W.L.R. 735 (H.L.).. 710
B.D.C. Ltd. v. Hofstrand Farms Ltd., [1986] 1 S.C.R. 228, 26 D.L.R.
 (4th) 1, [1986] S.C.J. No. 13 .... 154, 859
BG Checo International Limited v. British Columbia Hydro and Power
 Authority, [1993] 1 S.C.R. 12, 99 D.L.R. (4th) 577, [1993]
 S.C.J. No. 1 ....696, 700, 701, 717, 818, 859
B.G. Linton Construction Ltd. v. C.N.R. Co. (1974), [1975] 2 S.C.R. 678,
 49 D.L.R. (3d) 548, 3 N.R. 151 .... 183, 765–66, 767, 768, 864
B.I.H. Investments v. Kim, [1996] B.C.J. No. 49 (S.C.)............................... 146
B.P. Exploration Co. (Libya) Ltd. v. Hunt (No. 2), [1979] 1 W.L.R. 783
 (Q.B.), aff'd [1981] 1 W.L.R. 232 (C.A.), aff'd [1983] 2 A.C. 352 (H.L.) 608
B.P. Refinery (Westernport) Pty. Ltd. v. Shire of Hastings (1977),
 52 A.J.L.R. 20 (P.C.).. 736
Baggots Brass Beds Ltd. v. Neal Leasing Inc., [1989] O.J. No. 1049,
 4 R.P.R. (2d) 316 (H.C.J.)...797, 798
Bagnell's Cleaners & Launderers Ltd. v. Eastern Automobile Co. (1991),
 111 N.S.R. (2d) 51, [1991] N.S.J. No. 527 (S.C.T.D.)................................ 775
Baily v. De Crespigny (1869), L.R. 4 Q.B. 180..574
Bain v. Bank of Canada, [1935] 4 D.L.R. 112 (B.C.C.A.) 955
Bain v. Fothergill (1874), L.R. 7 H.L. 158... 820
Bainbridge v. Firmstone (1838), 8 Ad. & El. 743, 112 E.R. 1019 (Q.B.)............. 223
Baker v. Guaranty Savings & Loan Association (1930), [1931] S.C.R. 199,
 [1931] 1 D.L.R. 968...331
Baker v. Jones, [1954] 2 All E.R. 553 (Q.B.)..440
Baker v. Lintott (1980), 25 A.R. 512, [1980] A.J. No. 885, 54 C.P.R. (2d) 200
 (Q.B.).. 457
Baldwin & Francis Ltd. v. Patents Appeal Tribunal, [1959] A.C. 663 (H.L.).... 716
Baldwin v. Canada Foundry (1914), 6 O.W.N. 152, [1914] O.J. No. 322 (S.C.),
 aff'd (1914), 17 D.L.R. 834, 6 O.W.N. 364 (S.C.A.D.) 727
Baldwin v. Society for the Diffusion of Useful Knowledge (1838),
 9 Sim. 393, 59 E.R. 409 (V.C.).. 931
Balfour v. Balfour, [1919] 2 K.B. 571 (C.A.)...............................111, 129–30
Ball v. Hesketh (1697), Comb. 381, 90 E.R. 541 (K.B.) 238
Baltic Shipping Company v. Dillon (1993), 176 C.L.R. 344 (A.H.C.) 966
Banbury v. Bank of Montreal, [1918] A.C. 626 (H.L.)................................. 163
Banco de Portugal v. Waterlow & Sons Ltd., [1932] A.C. 452 (H.L.) 867, 869
Bank Line Ltd. v. Arthur Capel & Co., [1919] A.C. 435 (H.L.)........................ 582

Bank of America Canada v. Mutual Trust Co., 2002 SCC 43, [2002]
 2 S.C.R. 601, [2002] S.C.J. No. 44 ....819, 979
Bank of British Columbia v. Wren (1973), 38 D.L.R. (3d) 759 (B.C.S.C.) 333
Bank of Commerce v. Jenkins (1888), 16 O.R. 215, [1888] O.J. No. 117 (H.C.J.) ... 256
Bank of Credit and Commerce International SA v. Aboody, [1992]
 4 All E.R. 955 (C.A.) 383, 384
Bank of Montreal v. Crosby Group Ltd. (1977), 26 N.S.R. (2d) 331,
 [1977] N.S.J. No. 643 (S.C.T.D.) 263
Bank of Montreal v. Duguid (2000), 47 O.R. (3d) 737, 185 D.L.R. (4th) 458,
 [2000] O.J. No. 1356 (C.A.) 387, 402
Bank of Montreal v. Korico Enterprises Ltd. (2000), 50 O.R. (3d) 520,
 190 D.L.R. (4th) 706, [2000] O.J. No. 3290 (C.A.) 723
Bank of Montreal v. Maddox & MacInnis (1987), 83 N.B.R. (2d) 342,
 [1987] N.B.J. No. 1018, 47 R.P.R. 188 (C.A.) 868
Bank of Montreal v. Murphy (1985), [1986] 6 W.W.R. 610, [1985]
 B.C.J. No. 1767, 6 B.C.L.R. (2d) 169 (C.A.) ....203 , 347–48, 989, 991
Bank of Montreal v. Sperling Hotel Ltd. (1973), 36 D.L.R. (3d) 130,
 [1973] 4 W.W.R. 417, [1973] M.J. No. 88 (Q.B.) 262
Bank of Montreal v. Stuart (1910), [1911] A.C. 120, 103 L.T. 641,
 27 T.L.R. 117 (P.C.) 387, 388
Bank of Montreal v. University of Saskatchewan (1953), 9 W.W.R.
 (N.S.) 193 (Sask. Q.B.) 714
Bank of New Zealand v. Simpson, [1900] A.C. 182 (P.C.) 711
Bank of Nova Scotia v. Forest F. Ross & Son (1982), 40 N.B.R. (2d) 563,
 [1982] N.B.J. No. 228 (Q.B.) 263
Bank of Nova Scotia v. MacLellan (1977), 25 N.S.R. (2d) 181, 78 D.L.R.
 (3d) 1, [1977] N.S.J. No. 622 (S.C.) 223
Bank of Nova Scotia v. Zackheim (1983), 44 O.R. (2d) 244, 3 D.L.R. (4th) 760,
 1 O.A.C. 372 (C.A.) 203
Bank of Toronto v. Perkins (1882), 8 S.C.R. 603 .... 460, 461
Banks v. Biensch (1977), 5 A.R. 83, 3 Alta. L.R. (2d) 41, [1977] A.J. No. 544
 (S.C.T.D.) 735
Banque Brussels Lambert SA v. Australian National Industries Ltd. (1989),
 21 N.S.W.L.R. 502 (S.C.) 92, 122–23
Banque Canadienne Nationale v. Soucisse, [1981] 2 S.C.R. 339, 43 N.R. 283 ... 783
Baranick v. Counsel Trust Co., [1994] O.J. No. 4, 12 B.L.R. (2d) 39,
 37 R.P.R. (2d) 202 (Gen. Div.), aff'd [1994] O.J. No. 3476, 17 B.L.R.
 (2d) 140 (C.A.) 990
Barclay v. Prospect Mortgages Ltd., [1974] 1 W.L.R. 837 (Ch.) 474
Barclays Bank plc v. O'Brien (1993), [1994] 1 AC 180, [1993] 4 All E.R. 417
 (H.L.) 388, 399, 400
Barclays Bank plc v. Thomson, [1997] 4 All E.R. 816 (C.A.) 401
Bark-Fong v. Cooper (1913), 49 S.C.R. 14, 16 D.L.R. 299, 5 W.W.R. 633..... 938–39
Barnett and Wise v. Wise, [1961] O.R. 97, 26 D.L.R. (2d) 321 (C.A.) 131
Barnett v. Harrison, [1976] 2 S.C.R. 531, 57 D.L.R. (3d) 225, 5 N.R. 131,
 aff'g [1973] 2 O.R. 176, 33 D.L.R. (3d) 272 (C.A.) 619, 684, 685–86, 687

Barrick Estate v. Clark (1950), [1951] S.C.R. 177, [1950] 4 D.L.R. 529 58
Barron Estate v. Kelly (1918), 56 S.C.R. 455, 41 D.L.R. 590, [1918]
    2 W.W.R. 131 342
Barry v. Davies, [2000] 1 W.L.R. 1962 (C.A.) 48
Barton v. Armstrong, [1976] A.C. 104 (P.C.) 368, 369
Barton v. Fisher (1846), 3 U.C.R. 75, [1846] O.J. No. 47 (Q.B.) 986
Battle v. Fidelity & Casualty Co. of New York (1923), 54 O.L.R. 24,
    [1923] O.J. No. 89 (H.C.), aff'd (1924), 55 O.L.R. 330, [1924]
    O.J. No. 30 (S.C.A.D.) 662
Bauer v. Bank of Montreal, [1980] 2 S.C.R. 102, 110 D.L.R. (3d) 424,
    32 N.R. 191 .... 197, 198
Baughman v. Rampart Resources Ltd. (1995), 124 D.L.R. (4th) 252,
    [1995] 6 W.W.R. 99, [1995] B.C.J. No. 752 (C.A.) 55
Bawitko Investments Ltd. v. Kernels Popcorn Ltd. (1991), 79 D.L.R.
    (4th) 97, [1991] O.J. No. 495, 53 O.A.C. 314 (C.A.) 101
Bayda v. Canada North Dakota Land Co., Ltd., (1913), 13 D.L.R. 1
    (Sask. S.C.) 983
Bayoil S.A. v. Seawind Tankers Corp., [2001] 1 Lloyd's Rep. 533
    (Q.B. Div. Commercial Ct.) 727
Beattie v. Dinnick (1896), 27 O.R. 285, [1896] O.J. No. 131 (Q.B.) 166
Beauchamp v. Beauchamp (1972), [1973] 2 O.R. 43, 32 D.L.R. (3d) 693,
    2 N.R. 76 (C.A.), aff'd [1974] S.C.R. v, 40 D.L.R. (3d) 160, 2 N.R. 76...684–85
Beaufort Developments (N.I.) Ltd. v. Gilbert-Ash N.I. Ltd. (1998), [1999]
    1 A.C. 266, [1998] 2 W.L.R. 860, [1998] H.L.J. No. 19 719
Beaufort Realties (1964) Inc. v. Belcourt Construction (Ottawa) Ltd.,
    (sub nom. Chomedy Aluminum Co. Ltd. v. Belcourt Construction
    (Ottawa) Ltd.) (1979), 24 O.R. (2d) 1, 97 D.L.R. (3d) 170 (C.A.),
    aff'd [1980] 2 S.C.R. 718, 116 D.L.R. (3d) 193, 33 N.R. 460 .... 767, 776
Beer v. Bowden, [1981] 1 W.L.R. 522 (C.A.) 146
Beer v. Lea (1912), 7 D.L.R. 434 (Ont. H.C.), aff'd (1913), 14 D.L.R. 236
    (Ont. S.C.A.D.) 56, 88
Beer v. Townsgate I Ltd. (1997), 36 O.R. (3d) 136, 152 D.L.R. (4th) 671,
    [1997] O.J. No. 4276 (C.A.) 355, 358. 465
Behnke v. Bede Shipping Co., [1927] 1 K.B. 649 919
Bell v. Lever Brothers Ltd. (sub. nom. Lever Brothers Ltd. v. Bell),
    [1931] 1 K.B. 557 (C.A.), rev'd [1932] A.C. 161 (H.L.) 495, 528, 530, 531,
    532–35, 549, 553
Bellamy v. Debenham (1890), 45 Ch. D. 481, aff'd on other grounds
    [1891] 1 Ch. 412 (C.A.) 54, 55, 61
Belle River Community Arena Inc. v. W.J.C. Kaufmann Co. (1978),
    20 O.R. (2d) 447, 87 D.L.R. (3d) 761, 4 B.L.R. 231 (C.A.) 506–7
Belvoir Finance Co. Ltd. v. Stapleton, [1971] 1 Q.B. 210 (C.A.) 482
Bennett v. Bennett, [1952] 1 K.B. 249 (C.A.) 484
Bentsen v. Taylor, Sons & Co., [1893] 2 Q.B. 274 667

Bercovici v. Palmer (1966), 59 D.L.R. (2d) 513 (Sask. Q.B.), aff'd (1966),
   59 D.L.R. (2d) 516 (Sask. C.A.) 558, 559, 787

Berg v. Sadler and Moore, [1937] 2 K.B. 158 430

Berkeley Street Church v. Stevens (1875), 37 U.C.Q.B. 9 229

Berliner Gramophone Co. Ltd. v. Scythes (1916), 31 D.L.R. 789 (Sask. S.C.).... 222

Bernard-Norman Specialties Co. v. S.C. Time Inc. (1989), 71 O.R.
   (2d) 278, [1989] O.J. No. 2311, 31 C.P.R. (3d) 158 (H.C.J.) 740

Berne Developments Ltd. v. Haviland (1983), 40 O.R. (2d) 238,
   27 R.P.R. 56 (H.C.J.)... 475

Berryere v. Berryere (1972), 26 D.L.R. (3d) 764, 7 R.F.L. 82 (B.C.S.C.) 131

Bertolo v. Bank of Montreal (1986), 57 O.R. (2d) 577, 33 D.L.R. (4th) 610,
   [1986] O.J. No. 1377 (C.A.) 401, 409

Beswick v. Beswick, [1968] A.C. 58 (H.L.), aff'g [1966] Ch. 538
   (C.A.) 294–95, 299, 300, 315, 316

Bettini v. Gye (1876), 1 Q.B.D. 183 622

Beury v. Canada National Fire Ins. Co. (1917), 35 D.L.R. 790 (Ont. S.C.),
   aff'd (1917), 37 D.L.R. 105 (Ont. S.C.A.D.)... 662

Bigg v. Boyd Gibbons Ltd., [1971] 1 W.L.R. 913 (C.A.)...................................... 35

Bigos v. Bousted, [1951] 1 All E.R. 92 (K.B.) 430, 473

Birrell v. Dryer (1884), 9 App. Cas. 345 (H.L.) 723

Bisset v. Wilkinson, [1927] A.C. 177 (P.C.) 327

Black Gavin & Co. v. Cheung (1980), 20 B.C.L.R. 21, [1980] B.C.J. No. 39
   (S.C.) 677

Black Swan Mines v. Goldbelt Resources Ltd. (1996), [1997] 1 W.W.R. 605,
   [1996] B.C.J. No. 1458, 78 B.C.A.C. 193 (C.A.).. 712

Black v. Wilcox (1976), 12 O.R. (2d) 759, 70 D.L.R. (3d) 192 (C.A.)......... 405, 409

Black, Gavin & Co. v. Cheung (1980), 20 B.C.L.R. 21, [1980] B.C.J. No. 39
   (S.C.) 220

Blackburn v. Flavelle (1881), 6 App. Cas. 628 (P.C.)... 726

Blackler v. New Zealand Rugby Football League, [1968] N.Z.L.R. 547 (C.A.)..... 458

Blackwood v. Paul (1854), 4 Gr. 550 (U.C. Ch. in Appeal) 936

Blair v. Western Mutual Benefit Association, [1972] 4 W.W.R. 284
   (B.C.C.A.)... 49, 233

Blanchard v. Jacobi (1918), 43 O.L.R. 442, [1918] O.J. No. 149 (H.C.) 369

Blanchette v. Shabatowski (1981), 29 A.R. 158, [1981] A.J. No. 740 (Q.B.) 340

Blanco v. Nugent, [1949] 3 D.L.R. 19 (Man. K.B.)... 727

Bleakley v. Smith (1840), 59 E.R. 831, 11 Sim. 150 (Ch.) 173

Bliss & Laughlin Industries Incorporated v. Doerner (1978), 5 B.L.R. 132,
   42 C.P.R. (2d) 74 (Ont. C.A.), aff'd [1980] 2 S.C.R. 865, 117 D.L.R.
   (3d) 547, 34 N.R. 168... 450, 456

Bodmin Bros. v. Langestone & Lavery (1911), 31 N.Z.L.R. 200 (S.C.) 450

Bolliver v. Hirtle Estate (1990), 97 N.S.R. (2d) 247, 71 D.L.R. (4th) 381,
   [1990] N.S.J. No. 179 (S.C.A.D.) 983

Bolton v. Madden (1873), L.R. 9 Q.B. 55... 222

Bomek v. Bomek (1983), 146 D.L.R. (3d) 139, [1983] 3 W.W.R. 634, [1983]
  M.J. No. 96 (C.A.) 409
Bonisteel v. Saylor (1890), 17 O.A.R. 505, [1890] O.J. No. 37 (C.A.) 431
Boomer v. Muir, 24 P.2d 570 (Cal. App. 1933) 970
Boon v. Bell and Bell, [1932] 2 W.W.R. 304 (Sask. C.A.)..................................... 655
Boon v. Fair (1916), 11 O.W.N. 177, 27 O.W.R. 623, [1916] O.J. No. 429 (H.C.).....439
Boone v. Eyre (1779), 1 H. Bl. 273n, 126 E.R. 160 (C.P.)............................... 621–22
Boothby v. Sowden (1812), 3 Camp. 175, 170 E.R. 1346 (Nisi Prius) 252, 254
Botjar v. Parker (1979), 24 O.R. (2d) 694, 99 D.L.R. (3d) 147 (H.C.J.), aff'd
  on other grounds (1979), 26 O.R. (2d) 705, 103 D.L.R. (3d) 577 (C.A.) 223
Boudreau v. Benaiah (2000), 46 O.R. (3d) 737, 182 D.L.R. (4th) 569,
  [2000] O.J. No. 278 (C.A.) 875
Boulevard Heights v. Veilleux (1915), 52 S.C.R. 185, 26 D.L.R. 333,
  9 W.W.R. 742.. 482
Boult Enterprises Ltd. v. Brissett (1985), 21 D.L.R. (4th) 730, [1985]
  B.C.J. No. 1872, 67 B.C.L.R. 273 (C.A.) 97, 103
Bowater Newfoundland Ltd. v. Newfoundland & Labrador Hydro (1978),
  15 Nfld. & P.E.I.R. 301, [1978] N.J. No. 14 (C.A.)..717
Bowlay Logging Ltd. v. Domtar Ltd. (1982), 135 D.L.R. (3d) 179, [1982]
  6 W.W.R. 528, [1982] B.C.J. No. 1916 (C.A.), aff'g (1978), 87 D.L.R.
  (3d) 325, [1978] 4 W.W.R. 105 (B.C.S.C.) 834, 836, 837
Bowmakers Ltd. v. Barnet Instruments Ltd., [1945] 1 K.B. 65 (C.A.) 478
Boyd v. International Utility Structures Inc., 2002 BCCA 438, 216 D.L.R.
  (4th) 139, [2002] B.C.J. No. 1770 (C.A.).. 487, 488
Boydell v. Drummond (1809), 11 East. 142, 103 E.R. 958 (K.B.).......................171
Boyers and Co. v. D. & R. Duke, [1905] 2 I.R. 617 (K.B.D.)................................ 36
Brace v. Calder, [1895] 2 Q.B. 253 (C.A.) 867
Brace v. Wehnert (1858), 25 Beav. 348, 53 E.R. 670 (M.R.) 929
Bradlaugh v. Newdegate (1883), 11 Q.B.D. 1 442
Braithwaite v. Foreign Hardwood Co., [1905] 2 K.B. 543 (C.A.) 663
Brandon Gas & Power v. Brandon Creamery Co. (1912), 8 D.L.R. 191
  (Man. C.A.)... 220
Brantford General Hospital Foundation v. Marquis Estate (2003),
  67 O.R. (3d) 432 (Ont. S.C.J.) 231
Brauer & Co. (Great Britain) Ltd. v. James Clark (Brush Materials) Ltd.,
  [1952] 2 All E.R. 497 (C.A.) 589, 600, 739
Brazeau v. Wilson (1916), 36 O.L.R. 396, 30 D.L.R. 378 (Ont. S.C.A.D.) 986
Bremer Handelsgesellschaft mbH v. C. Mackprang Jr., [1979] 1 Lloyd's
  Rep. 221 (C.A.) 602
Bremer Handelsgesellschaft mbH v. Vanden Avenne-Izegem PVBA, [1978]
  2 Lloyd's Rep. 109 (H.L.) 643
Brewster v. Kitchell (1697-98), 1 Salk. 198, 91 E.R. 177 (K.B.)...........................574
Bridge v. Cage (1605), Cro. Jac. 103, 79 E.R. 89 (K.B.) 239
Brikom Investments Ltd. v. Carr, [1979] Q.B. 467 (C.A.) 695

Brinkibon Ltd. v. Stahag Stahl Und Stahlwarenhandelsgesellschaft mbH,
[1983] 2 A.C. 34 (H.L.) 78–79
Brisbois v. Chamberland (1990), 1 O.R. (3d) 417, 77 D.L.R. (4th) 583,
[1990] O.J. No. 1790 (C.A.) 557
Bristol, Cardiff and Swansea Aërated Bread Co. v. Maggs (1890),
44 Ch. D. 616 .... 54, 219
Britain v. Rossiter (1879), 11 Q.B.D. 123 (C.A.) 169
British & American Telegraph Co. v. Colson (1871), L.R. 6 Ex. Ch. 108 76
British & Beningtons Ltd. v. North Western Cachar Tea Co. Ltd., [1923]
A.C. 48 (H.L.) 642, 662, 663
British Columbia (Ministry of Crown Lands) v. Cressy Development Corp.
[1992] 4 W.W.R. 357, 66 B.C.L.R. (2d) 146, [1992] B.C.J. No. 646 (S.C.) ... 595
British Columbia and Vancouver's Island Spar, Lumber & Saw-Mill Co., Ltd.
v. Nettleship (1868), L.R. 3 C.P. 499 864
British Columbia v. Canadian Forest Products Ltd., 2004 SCC 38,
240 D.L.R. (4th) 1, [2004] 2 S.C.R. 74 870
British Crane Hire Corp. v. Ipswich Plant Hire Ltd., [1975] Q.B. 303 (C.A.) 188
British Motor Trade Association v. Gilbert, [1951] 2 All E.R. 641 (Ch.) 974
British Movietonews Ltd. v. London and District Cinemas, [1951]
1 K.B. 190 (C.A.), rev'd on appeal [1952] A.C. 166 (H.L.) 571, 577
British Reinforced Concrete Engineering Co. v. Schelff, [1921] 2 Ch. 563 449
British Road Services Ltd. v. Arthur B. Crutchley and Co. Ltd., [1967] 2 All
E.R. 785 (Liverpool Winter Assizes), aff'd [1968] 1 All E.R. 811 (C.A.) 60
British Russian Gazette and Trade Outlook Ltd. v. Associated Newspapers
Ltd., [1933] 2 K.B. 616 (C.A.) 251–52
British Steel Corp. v. Cleveland Bridge and Engineering Co., [1984]
1 All E.R. 504 (Q.B.) 98
British Westinghouse Electric and Manufacturing Co. Ltd. v. Underground
Electric Ry. Co. of London Ltd., [1912] A.C. 673 (H.L.) 868
British Whig Publishing Co. v. E.B. Eddy Co. (1921), 62 S.C.R. 576,
59 D.L.R. 77 727
Brodie v. Brodie, [1917] P. 271 433
Brody v. Brody (1976), 1 A.R. 470, [1976] A.J. No. 524 (S.C.T.D.) 131
Brown v. Brown, [1980] 1 N.Z.L.R. 484 (C.A.) 450
Brown v. Moore (1902), 32 S.C.R. 93 .... 461, 481
Brown v. Waterloo Regional Board of Commissioners of Police (1982),
37 O.R. (2d) 277, 136 D.L.R. (3d) 49, 17 B.L.R. 299 (H.C.J.), var'd
(1983), 43 O.R. (2d) 113, 150 D.L.R. (3d) 729, 4 Admin. L.R. 113
(C.A.) 823, 876, 883
Brownscombe v. Public Trustee of Alberta, [1969] S.C.R. 658, 5 D.L.R.
(3d) 673, 68 W.W.R. 483 177
Bruce v. Tolton (1879), 4 O.A.R. 144, [1879] O.J. No. 10 (C.A.) 54, 61
Bruner v. Moore, [1904] 1 Ch. 305 284
Buchanan v. Canadian Imperial Bank of Commerce (1979), 100 D.L.R.
(3d) 624, 15 B.C.L.R. 373, [1979] B.C.J. No. 322 (S.C.), var'd (1980),
125 D.L.R. (3d) 394, 23 B.C.L.R. 324, [1980] B.C.J. No. 696 (C.A.) 408

Buck v. Cooper (1955), 1 D.L.R. (2d) 282 (B.C.S.C.) 983
Buckley v. Tutty (1971), 125 C.L.R. 353 (A.H.C.)... 458
Buday v. Locator of Missing Heirs Inc. (1993), 16 O.R. (3d) 257,
     108 D.L.R. (4th) 424, [1993] O.J. No. 2999 (C.A.) 442, 443
Bullen v. Wilkinson (1912), 2 D.L.R. 190 (Ont. C.A.)..................................... 941
Bundy v. Johnson (1856), 6 U.C.C.P. 221, [1856] O.J. No. 229 35
Bunge Corp., New York v. Tradax Export S.A., Panama, [1981]
     1 W.L.R. 711, [1981] 2 All E.R. 513 (H.L.) 630–31
Burgess v. Zimmerli (1914), 17 D.L.R. 708 (B.C.C.A.)...................................... 470
Burgoyne v. Murphy, [1951] 2 D.L.R. 556, 27 M.P.R. 195 (N.B.S.C.) 222
Burns v. Brouse (1923), 24 O.W.N. 585, [1923] O.J. No. 600 (S.C.A.D.) 328
Burrow v. Scammell (1881), 19 Ch. D. 175... 940
Butcher v. Stapely (1685), 1 Vern. 363 (Ch.) 174
Butler Machine Tool Co. Ltd. v. Ex-Cell-O Corp. (England) Ltd., [1979]
     1 All E.R. 965 (C.A.)...60, 61, 62
Butler v. Purcell (1956), 2 D.L.R. (2d) 317 (N.S.S.C.) 940
Buttcon Ltd. v. Toronto Electric Commissioners (2003), 65 O.R.
     (3d) 601, [2003] O.J. No. 2796, [2003] O.T.C. 638 (S.C.J.) 47, 117–18, 156
Buyers v. Begg (1951), [1952] 1 D.L.R. 313, 3 W.W.R. (N.S.) 673 (B.C.C.A.) 105
Byers v. McMillan (1887), 15 S.C.R. 194 201
Byle v. Byle (1990), 65 D.L.R. (4th) 641, [1990] B.C.J. No. 258,
     46 B.L.R. 292 (C.A.)... 368, 369
Byrne v. Van Tienhoven (1880), 5 C.P.D. 344 .... 82, 83, 84
Byron v. Tremaine (1898), 31 N.S.R. 425 (S.C.), aff'd (1898), 29 S.C.R. 445 430

C. & P. Haulage v. Middleton, [1983] 1 W.L.R. 1461 (C.A.) 836
C. Battison & Sons Inc. v. Mauti (1986), 58 O.R. (2d) 82, 34 D.L.R.
     (4th) 700, [1986] O.J. No. 1373 (Div. Ct.) 464
C.C.C. Films Ltd. v. Impact Quadrant Films Ltd., [1985] 1 Q.B. 16 834
C.H. Giles & Co. Ltd. v. Morris, [1972] 1 W.L.R. 307 (Ch.)............................. 932
Cahan v. Fraser, [1951] 4 D.L.R. 112, 3 W.W.R. (N.S.) 665 (B.C.C.A.).............. 572
Caine v. Schultz (1926), 38 B.C.R. 332, [1927] 1 W.W.R. 600, [1926]
     B.C.J. No. 90 (C.A.)... 868
Caines v. Bank of Nova Scotia (1978), 22 N.B.R. (2d) 631, 90 D.L.R.
     (3d) 271, [1978] N.B.J. No. 172 (C.A.).. 865
Caisse Populaire de La Salle Credit Union Ltd. v. River Ridge Properties Ltd.
     (1997), 115 Man. R. (2d) 115, [1997] M.J. No. 88 (C.A.) 524
Calgary Hardwood & Veneer Ltd. v. Canadian National Railway Co. (1977),
     5 A.R. 582, 74 D.L.R. (3d) 284, [1977] A.J. No. 454 (S.C.T.D.), aff'd (1979),
     16 A.R. 52, 100 D.L.R. (3d) 302, [1979] A.J. No. 831 (S.C.A.D.)............35, 101
Calgary v. Northern Construction Co.(1985), 67 A.R. 95, [1986]
     2 W.W.R. 426, [1985] A.J. No. 741 (C.A.) 495, 508, 554
California Standard Co. v. Chiswell, [1955] 5 D.L.R. 119, 14 W.W.R. 456
     (Alta. S.C.T.D.) 200
Callisher v. Bischoffsheim (1870), L.R. 5 Q.B. 449 226
Calmusky v. Karaloff, [1947] S.C.R. 110 222

Calvan Consolidated Oil & Gas v. Manning, [1959] S.C.R. 253, 17 D.L.R.
(2d) 1 .... 103, 128
Campbell, Albo, Low Ltd. v. Black (1995), 26 O.R. (3d) 111, [1995]
O.J. No. 3295 (Gen. Div.) 983
Canada (Attorney General) v. Becker (1998), 1998 ABCA 283,
223 A.R. 59, [1999] 4 W.W.R. 347 465
Canada Cycle and Motor Co. Ltd. v. Mehr (1919), 48 D.L.R. 579
(Ont. S.C.A.D.) 222
Canada Egg Products Ltd. v. Canadian Doughnut Co. Ltd., [1955]
S.C.R. 398, [1955] 3 D.L.R. 1 .... 659, 660
Canada Law Book Co. v. Boston Book Co. (1922), 64 S.C.R. 182,
66 D.L.R. 209 709
Canada Life Assurance Co. v. Stewart (1994), 132 N.S.R. (2d) 324,
118 D.L.R. (4th) 67, [1994] N.S.J. No. 345 (S.C.A.D.) 368
Canada Square Corp. Ltd. v. Versafood Services Ltd. (1981), 34 O.R.
(2d) 250, 130 D.L.R. (3d) 205, 15 B.L.R. 89 (C.A.) 97, 103, 104, 128, 709
Canada Steamship Lines Ltd. v. The King, [1952] A.C. 192, [1952]
2 D.L.R. 786, 5 W.W.R. (N.S.) 609 (P.C.) 358, 724
Canada West Loan Co. Ltd. v. Virtue (1920), 29 B.C.R. 76, [1921]
1 W.W.R. 730 (S.C.) 328
Canada West Tree Fruits Ltd. v. T.G. Bright & Company, [1990]
6 W.W.R. 89, [1990] B.C.J. No. 1712, 48 B.C.L.R. (2d) 91 (C.A.),
leave to appeal to S.C.C. refused, [1991] 1 S.C.R. xiv, [1991]
2 W.W.R. lxvii, 52 B.C.L.R. (2d) xxxviiin 219, 246
Canadian Bank of Commerce v. Foreman, [1927] 2 D.L.R. 530
(Alta. S.C.A.D.) 192
Canadian Doughnut Co. Ltd. v. Canada Egg Products Ltd., [1954]
2 D.L.R. 77, 11 W.W.R. (N.S.) 193 (Sask. C.A.), aff'd [1955] S.C.R. 398,
[1955] 3 D.L.R. 1 635
Canadian Dyers Association Ltd. v. Burton (1920), 47 O.L.R. 259, [1920]
O.J. No. 138 (H.C.J.) 34, 35
Canadian General Electric Co. Ltd. v. Pickford & Black Ltd. (1970), [1971]
S.C.R. 41, 2 N.S.R. (2d) 497, 14 D.L.R. (3d) 372 296
Canadian General Electric Co. v. Canadian Rubber Co. of Montreal
(1915), 52 S.C.R. 349, 27 D.L.R. 294 898
Canadian General Securities Co. v. George (1918), 42 Ont. L.R. 560,
43 D.L.R. 20 (Ont. S.C.A.D.), rev'd on other grounds (1919),
59 S.C.R. 641, 52 D.L.R. 679 170
Canadian Government Merchant Marine Ltd. v. Canadian Trading Co.
(1922), 64 S.C.R. 106, 68 D.L.R. 544, [1922] 3 W.W.R. 197 582
Canadian Hockey Club Inc. v. Arena Amusements Ltd., [1930]
1 D.L.R. 127 (S.C.C.) 222
Canadian Imperial Bank of Commerce v. Boudreau (1982), 41 N.B.R.
(2d) 365, [1982] N.B.J. No. 262 (Q.B.) 369
Canadian Imperial Bank of Commerce v. Dene Mat Construction Ltd., [1988]
4 W.W.R. 344, [1988] N.W.T.J. No. 25, [1988] N.W.T.R. 174 (S.C.) 263

Canadian Imperial Bank of Commerce v. Kean (1985), 55 Nfld. & P.E.I.R. 88,
[1985] N.J. No. 210 (S.C.T.D.) 263

Canadian Imperial Bank of Commerce v. Ohlson (1997), 209 A.R. 140,
154 D.L.R. (4th) 33, [1997] A.J. No. 1185 (C.A.) 422

Canadian Imperial Bank of Commerce v. P.E.I. Mussel King Inc. and
Vandenbrent (1984), 49 Nfld. & P.E.I.R. 173, [1984] P.E.I.J. No. 64 (S.C.) 524

Canadian Imperial Bank of Commerce v. Titus (1980), 28 O.R. (2d) 52,
110 D.L.R. (3d) 219 (H.C.J.) 171

Canadian Indemnity Co. v. Okanagan Mainline Real Estate Board
(1970), [1971] S.C.R. 493, 16 D.L.R. (3d) 715, [1971]
1 W.W.R. 289 ....193, 202, 752

Canadian Market Place Ltd. v. Fallowfield (1976), 13 O.R. (2d) 456,
71 D.L.R. (3d) 341 (H.C.J.) 54, 61

Canadian Pacific Airlines Ltd. v. British Columbia, [1989] 1 S.C.R. 1133,
59 D.L.R. (4th) 218, [1989] S.C.J. No. 43 329

Canadian Pacific Forest Products Ltd. v. Belships (Far East) Shipping
(Pte.) Ltd., [1999] 4 F.C. 320, 175 D.L.R. (4th) 449, [1999]
F.C.J. No. 938 (C.A.) 724, 776

Canadian Pacific Hotels Ltd. v. Bank of Montreal, [1987] 1 S.C.R. 711,
40 D.L.R. (4th) 385, [1987] S.C.J. No. 29 .... 730, 733, 734, 735–36, 743

Canadian Taxpayers Federation v. Ontario (Minister of Finance) (2004),
73 O.R. (3d) 621, [2004] O.J. No. 5239, [2004] O.T.C. 1115 (S.C.J.) 445

Canadian Union College v. Camsteel Industries Ltd. (1979), 17 A.R. 98,
[1979] A.J. No. 572, 9 Alta. L.R. (2d) 167 (Dist. Ct.) 983

Canadian Williston Minerals Ltd. v. Forseth and Imperial Oil Ltd. (1962),
33 D.L.R. (2d) 72 (Sask. C.A.) 224

Canadian-Dominion Leasing Corporation Ltd. v. Suburban Super Drug Ltd.
(1966) 56 D.L.R. (2d) 43, 55 W.W.R. 396 (Alta. S.C.A.D.) 765

Canson v. Boughton & Co., [1991] 3 S.C.R. 534, 85 D.L.R. (4th) 129,
[1991] S.C.J. No. 91 850

Cantor Art Services Ltd. v. Kenneth Bieber Photography Ltd., [1969]
1 W.L.R. 1226 (C.A.) 729

Can-Truck Transportation Ltd. v. Fenton's Auto Paint Shop Ltd. (1993),
101 D.L.R. (4th) 562, [1993] O.J. No. 944, 62 O.A.C. 376 (C.A.) 607

Capital Quality Homes Ltd. v. Colwyn Construction Ltd. (1975),
9 O.R. (2d) 617, 61 D.L.R. (3d) 385 (C.A.) 573, 577, 593, 594–95

Capital Trust Corp. Ltd. v. Wilson, [1937] 3 D.L.R. 178 (Ont. C.A.) 848

Capitol Records—EMI of Canada Ltd. v. Gosewich (1977), 17 O.R.
(2d) 501, 80 D.L.R. (3d) 737, 36 C.P.R. (2d) 36 (H.C.J.) 951

Car and Universal Finance Co. Ltd. v. Caldwell, [1965] 1 Q.B. 525
(C.A.) 339, 343

Carleton Condominium Corp. No. 32 v. Camdev Corp., [1999]
O.J. No. 3448, 124 O.A.C. 352, 47 C.L.R. (2d) 224 (C.A.) 773

Carlill v.Carbolic Smoke Ball Co., [1893] 1 Q.B. 256 (C.A.) 40–41, 69-70, 86

Carlisle & Cumberland Banking Co. v. Bragg, [1911] 1 K.B. 489 (C.A.).......... 521

Carman Construction Ltd. v. Canadian Pacific Railway Co., [1982]
1 S.C.R. 958, 136 D.L.R. (3d) 193, 42 N.R. 147.............. 198, 201, 356–57, 359
Carmichael v. Bank of Montreal (1972), 25 D.L.R. (3d) 570, [1972]
3 W.W.R. 175, [1972] M.J. No. 71 (Q.B.).. 56, 57
Carney v. Herbert, [1985] 1 All E.R. 438 (P.C.).. 484
Carow Towing Co. v. The "Ed McWilliams" (1919), 46 D.L.R. 506 (Ex. Ct.) 73
Carpenters Estates Ltd. v. Davies, [1940] Ch. 160 931
Carr v. Fama Holdings Ltd. (1989), 63 D.L.R. (4th) 25, [1989]
B.C.J. No. 1888, 45 B.L.R. 42 (C.A.) 643
Carr v. Lynch, [1900] 1 Ch. 613... 173
Carr-Harris v. Canadian General Electric Co. (1921), 61 D.L.R. 434
(Ont. S.C.A.D.)... 446
Carson v. Willitts, [1930] 4 D.L.R. 977 (Ont. S.C.A.D.)................................ 848
Case v. Floral Studio Ltd. (1998), 56 O.T.C. 210, [1998] O.J. No. 761
(Gen. Div.) 981
Cassady v. Wyeth-Ayerst Canada Inc. (1998), 163 D.L.R. (4th) 1, [1999]
3 W.W.R. 74, [1998] B.C.J. No. 1876 (C.A.)................................ 887
Cassell & Co. Ltd. v. Broome, [1972] A.C. 1027, [1972] 1 All ER 801 (H.L.) 880
Cassidy v. Canada Publishing Corp., [1989] B.C.J. No. 135, 41 B.L.R. 223
(S.C.)... 608
Casson v. Roberts (1862), 31 Beav. 613 (M.R.)................................. 174, 179
Caton v. Caton (1867), L.R. 2 H.L. 127 172
Causeway Shopping Centre Ltd. v. Muise, [1969] S.C.R. 274......................... 109
Ceccol v. Ontario Gymnastic Federation (2001), 55 O.R. (3d) 614,
204 D.L.R. (4th) 688, [2001] O.J. No. 3488 (C.A.) 745
Cehave NV v. Bremer Handelsgesellschaft mbH (1975), [1976] Q.B. 44,
[1975] 3 All E.R. 739 (C.A.)... 632, 633
Cemco Electrical Manufacturing Co. v. Van Snellenberg (1946), [1947]
S.C.R. 121, [1946] 4 D.L.R. 305... 865
Central & Eastern Trust Co. v. Rafuse, [1986] 2 S.C.R. 147, 31 D.L.R.
(4th) 481, [1986] S.C.J. No. 52... 351
Central London Property Trust Ltd. v. High Trees House Ltd., [1947]
1 K.B. 130 .... 277, 279–80, 282, 289, 290
Chandler v. Webster, [1904] 1 K.B. 493 (C.A.) 604
Chandris v. Isbrandtsen-Moller Co. Inc., [1951] 1 K.B. 240........................ 725
Chant v. Infinitum Growth Fund Inc. (1986), 55 O.R. (2d) 366, 28 D.L.R.
(4th) 577, [1986] O.J. No. 584 (C.A.) 199
Chapelton v. Barry Urban District Council, [1940] 1 K.B. 532 (C.A.) 185
Chaplin v. Hicks, [1911] 2 K.B. 786 (C.A.)................................. 847–48
Chapman v. Kopitoski (1972), 31 D.L.R. (3d) 479, [1972] 6 W.W.R. 525,
[1972] S.J. No. 195 (Q.B.)... 172
Chappell v. Times Newspapers Ltd., [1975] 1 W.L.R. 482 (C.A.)...............933, 937
Charles Rickards Ltd. v. Oppenheim, [1950] 1 K.B. 616 (C.A.) 277, 281, 289
Charrington & Co. v. Wooder, [1914] A.C. 71 (H.L.)................................. 709
Charter v. Sullivan, [1957] 2 Q.B. 117 (C.A.) 817

Charterhouse Credit Co. Ltd. v. Tolley, [1963] 2 Q.B. 683 (C.A.) 756

Chaulk v. Fairview Construction Ltd. (1977), 14 Nfld. & P.E.I.R. 13,
[1977] N.J. No. 35, 3 R.P.R. 116 (C.A.) 913

Chichester v. Cobb (1866), 14 L.T. (N.S.) 433 (Q.B.) 171

Chilliback v. Pawliuk (1956), 1 D.L.R. (2d) 611, 17 W.W.R. 534
(Alta. S.C.T.D.) 257

Chillingworth v. Esche, [1924] 1 Ch. 97 127

Chilton v. Co-operators General Insurance Co. (1997), 32 O.R. (3d) 161,
143 D.L.R. (4th) 647, [1997] O.J. No. 579 (C.A.) 723

Chinook Aggregates Ltd. v. Abbotsford (Municipal District) (1989), [1990]
1 W.W.R. 624, 40 B.C.L.R. (2d) 345, 35 C.L.R. 241 (C.A.)........... 149, 741, 742

Chrispen v. Topham (1986), 28 D.L.R. (4th) 754, 48 Sask. R. 106, [1986]
S.J. No. 455 (Q.B.), aff'd on other grounds (1987), 39 D.L.R. (4th) 637,
59 Sask. R. 145, [1987] S.J. No. 392 (C.A.) 134, 435

Christie v. York Corporation, [1940] S.C.R. 139, [1940] 1 D.L.R. 81 40

Churchward v. The Queen (1865), L.R. 1 Q.B. 173 222

CIBC Mortgage Corporation v. Rowatt (2002), 61 O.R. (3d) 737, 220 D.L.R.
(4th) 139, [2002] O.J. No. 4109 (C.A.) 383

CIBC Mortgages plc v. Pitt, [1993] 4 All E.R. 433 (H.L.) 385, 394, 400

City and Westminster Properties (1934) Ltd. v. Mudd, [1959] Ch. 129 201

City of Kingston v. Kingston Portsmouth & Cataraqui Electric Rwy. (1898),
25 O.A.R. 462, [1898] O.J. No. 51 (C.A.)... 929

City of London v. Nash (1747), 1 Ves. Sen. 12, 27 E.R. 859 (Ch.).................... 936

City of Los Angeles v. Superior Court, 333 P.2d 745 (Cal. 1951) 104

City of New Orleans v. Firemen's Charitable Association, 9 So. 486
(La. 1891).. 978

Clarfield v. Crown Life Insurance Co. (2000), 50 O.R. (3d) 696, [2000]
O.J. No. 4074, [2000] O.T.C. 757 (S.C.J.)... 896

Clarion Ltd. v. National Provident Institution, [2000] 2 All E.R. 265 (Ch.)..... 541

Clarke v. Price (1819), 2 Wils. Ch. 157, 37 E.R. 270 (Ch.) 931

Clarke v. The Earl of Dunraven (sub nom. The Satanita), [1897] A.C. 59
(H.L.), aff'g [1895] P. 248 (C.A.) 302

Claude Neon General Advertising Ltd. v. Singh, [1942] 1 D.L.R. 26
(N.S.S.C.) 583

Clausen v. Canada Timber and Lands Ltd., [1923] 4 D.L.R. 751, [1923]
3 W.W.R. 1072 (P.C.)..655, 657

Clayton v. Clayton (1998), 40 O.R. (3d) 24, [1998] O.J. No. 2028,
38 R.F.L. (4th) 320 (Gen. Div.)... 410

Clea Shipping Corp. v. Bulk Oil International Ltd. (No. 2), [1984]
1 All E.R. 129 (Q.B.) 671

Cleveland Petroleum Co. v. Dartstone Ltd., [1969] 1 All E.R. 201 (C.A.) 458

Cleveland v. Boak (1906), 39 N.S.R. 39 (C.A.) 200

Clifford Davis Management Ltd. v. W.E.A. Records Ltd., [1975]
1 W.L.R. 61 (C.A.) 413, 458

Clifford v. Turrell (1841), 1 Y. & C.C.C. 138, 62 E.R. 826 (V.C.) 925

Clifford v. Watts (1870), L.R. 5 C.P. 577 583

Clifton v. Palumbo, [1944] 2 All E.R. 497 (C.A.) 35–36

Clive v. Beaumont (1848), 1 De G. & Sm. 397, 63 E.R. 1121 (V.C.) 54, 61

Clough v. London & North Western Ry. (1871), L.R. 7 Exch. 26...................... 990

Cloverlawn Investments Ltd. v. MacPherson (1975), 58 D.L.R. (3d) 212,
    21 C.P.R. (2d) 174 (B.C.S.C.) 848

Clydebank Engineering & Shipbuilding Co. v. Yzquierdo-y-Castaneda,
    Don Jose Ramos, [1905] A.C. 6 (H.L.) 899

Coastal States Pty. Ltd. v. Melevende, [1965] V.R. 433 (S.C.) 342

Cockburn v. Alexander (1848), 6 C.B. 791, 136 E.R. 1459 (C.P.) 824

Cockburn v. Trusts & Guarantee Co. (1917), 55 S.C.R. 264, 37 D.L.R. 701...... 871

Codelfa Construction Pty. Ltd. v. State Rail Authority of NSW (1982),
    149 C.L.R. 337 (A.H.C.) 590

Coderre (Wright) v. Coderre, [1975] 2 W.W.R. 193 (Alta. S.C.T.D.).......... 558, 559

Cohen v. Roche, [1927] 1 K.B. 169 919

Cohnstaedt v. University of Regina (1994), 113 D.L.R. (4th) 178, [1994]
    5 W.W.R. 154, [1994] S.J. No. 124 (C.A.), rev'd [1996] 3 S.C.R. 451,
    131 D.L.R. (4th) 605, [1995] S.C.J. No. 76... 849

Coldunell Ltd. v. Gallon, [1986] Q.B. 1184 (C.A.) 990

Cole v. Booker (1913), 29 T.L.R. 295 (K.B.).. 443

Coles v. Trecothick (1804), 9 Ves. 234, 32 E.R. 592 (Ch.) 172, 935

Collins v. Blantern (1767), 2 Wils. K.B. 341, 95 E.R. 847 (K.B.)....................... 439

Collins v. Godefroy (1831), 1 B. & Ad. 950, 109 E.R. 1040 (K.B.)..............241, 438

Colonial Investment of Winnipeg, Manitoba v. Borland (1911),
    1 W.W.R. 171, 19 W.L.R. 588, [1911] A.J. No. 5 (S.C.T.D.),
    aff'd (1912), 6 D.L.R. 211, 2 W.W.R. 960, 22 W.L.R. 145,
    5 Alta. L.R. 71 (S.C.), aff'd (1912), 2 W.W.R. 960 (Alta. C.A.) 192, 503

Colquhoun v. Brooks (1887), 19 Q.B.D. 400, aff'd (1889),
    14 App. Cas. 493 (H.L.)... 726

Combe v. Combe, [1951] 2 K.B. 215 (C.A.) 280

Commercial Bank of Australia Ltd. v. Amadio (1983), 151 C.L.R. 447
    (A.H.C.)... 412

Commercial Capital Trust Co. v. Berk (1989), 68 O.R. (2d) 257,
    57 D.L.R. (4th) 759, [1989] O.J. No. 614 (C.A.).. 853

Commercial Plastics Ltd. v. Vincent, [1965] 1 Q.B. 623 (C.A.) 453

Commissioner for the New Towns v. Cooper, [1995] 2 All E.R. 929 (C.A.)...... 560

Commonwealth Bank of Australia v. TLI Management Pty. Ltd., [1990]
    V.R. 510 (S.C.).. 122

Commonwealth Construction Co. v. Imperial Oil Ltd. (1976), [1978]
    1 S.C.R. 317, 1 A.R. 161, 69 D.L.R. (3d) 558...310

Commonwealth of Australia v. Verwayen (1990), 170 C.L.R. 394 (A.H.C.)...... 290

Compagnie Française de Chemins de Fer Paris-Orleans v. Leeston
    Shipping Co. Ltd. (1919), 1 Ll. L.R. 235.. 346

Computer Centre Personnel Ltd. v. Lagopoulous (1975), 8 O.R. (2d) 480,
    58 D.L.R. (3d) 352, 19 C.P.R. (2d) 16 (H.C.J.) 455–56

Computer Workshops Ltd. v. Banner Capital Market Brokers Limited
    (1988), 64 O.R. (2d) 266, 50 D.L.R. (4th) 118, [1988] O.J. No. 223
    (H.C.J.), aff'd (1990), 1 O.R. (3d) 398, 74 D.L.R. (4th) 767, [1990]
    O.J. No. 2449 (C.A.) 636
Con-force Products Ltd. v. Luscar Limited (1982), 27 Sask. R. 299, [1982]
    S.J. No. 976 (Q.B.) 735
Connaught Laboratories Ltd. v. Canada, [1983] F.C.J. No. 1002,
    49 N.R. 332 (C.A.) 642
Connors Bros. Ltd. v. Connors, [1940] 4 All E.R. 179 (P.C.) 449, 450, 456
Consolidated Investments Ltd. v. Acres (1917), 32 D.L.R. 579 (Alta. S.C.) 346
Consolidated-Bathurst Export Ltd. v. Mutual Boiler & Machinery
    Insurance Co. (1979), [1980] 1 S.C.R. 888, 112 D.L.R. (3d) 49,
    32 N.R. 488 .... 705, 717, 719, 723
Continental Insurance Co. v. Law Society of Alberta (1984), 56 A.R. 98,
    14 D.L.R. (4th) 256, [1985] 1 W.W.R. 481 (C.A.) 727
Cook v. Cook (1968), 66 D.L.R. (2d) 285, 5 N.S.R. (1965-69) 202 (S.C.T.D.) 717
Cook v. Lister (1863), 13 C.B. (N.S.) 543, 143 E.R. 215 (C.P.) 252, 254, 255
Cook v. Wright (1861), 1 B. & S. 559, 121 E.R. 822 (K.B.) 227
Cooke v. Anderson and Anderson, [1945] 2 D.L.R. 698, [1945]
    1 W.W.R. 657 (Alta. S.C.A.D.) 715
Cooke v. CKOY Ltd., [1963] 2 O.R. 257, 39 D.L.R. (2d) 209 (H.C.J.) 737, 740
Cooper Industries Inc. v. Leatherman Tool Group Inc., 532 U.S. 424,
    121 S. Ct. 1678 (2001) 892
Cooper v. Critchley, [1955] 1 Ch. 431, [1955] 1 All E.R. 520............................170
Cooper v. Martin (1803), 102 E.R. 759 (K.B.) 238
Cooper v. Phibbs (1867), L.R. 2 H.L. 149 .... 527, 537, 547
Co-operative Insurance Society Ltd. v. Argyll Stores (Holdings) Ltd.
    (1997), [1998] A.C. 1, [1997] 3 All E.R. 297, [1997] H.L.J. No. 18 (H.L.)... 929
Cope v. Harasino (1964), 48 D.L.R. (2d) 744, 50 W.W.R. 639,
    47 C.P.R. 36 (B.C.C.A.) 450
Cope v. Rowlands (1836), 2 M. & W. 149, 150 E.R. 707 (Ex.)............................ 461
Copycats v. Rosney, [1989] M.J. No. 680, 62 Man. R. (2d) 308 (Q.B.) 219
Corey Developments Inc. v. Eastbridge Developments (Waterloo) Ltd.
    (1997), 34 O.R. (3d) 73, [1997] O.J. No. 2836, 34 B.L.R. (2d) 259
    (Gen. Div.), aff'd on other grounds (1999), 44 O.R. (3d) 95, [1999]
    O.J. No. 1788, 120 O.A.C. 278 (C.A.) 205
Cornwall Gravel Co. Ltd. v. Purolator Courier Ltd. (1978), 18 O.R.
    (2d) 551, 83 D.L.R. (3d) 267, 32 N.R. 597 (H.C.J.)....................................... 864
Corse v. Ravenwood Homes Ltd., 1998 ABQB 380, 226 A.R. 214, [1998]
    A.J. No. 509..916
Cory v. Thames Ironworks Company (1868), L.R. 3 Q.B. 181............................ 862
Coss (Trustee of) v. Shuckett (1990), 65 Man.R. (2d) 161, [1990]
    M.J. No. 196, 79 C.B.R. (N.S.) 149 (C.A.)... 524
Cotter v. General Petroleums Ltd. (1950), [1951] S.C.R. 154, [1950]
    4 D.L.R. 609..727, 728, 847

Couchman v. Hill, [1947] K.B. 554.. 201

Cougle v. Maricevic (1983), [1992] 3 W.W.R. 475, 64 B.C.L.R. (2d) 105,
[1983] B.C.J. No. 1563 (C.A.) 411

Couldery v. Bartrum (1881), 19 Ch. D. 394 (C.A.)..................................... 252, 255

Coulls v. Bagot's Executor & Trustee Co. Ltd. (1967), 119 C.L.R. 460
(A.H.C.)...294–95

Council of London Bureau Council v. Twickenham Garden Developments
Ltd., [1971] Ch. 233... 669

Courtney and Fairbairn Ltd. v. Tolaini Brothers (Hotels) Ltd., [1975]
1 All E.R. 716 (C.A.) 97–98, 101–2, 142

Courtwright v. C.P. Ltd. (1983), 45 O.R. (2d) 52, 5 D.L.R. (4th) 488,
26 B.L.R. 17 (H.C.J.), aff'd (1985), 50 O.R. (2d) 560, 18 D.L.R.
(4th) 639 (C.A.) 335

Couturier v. Hastie (1852), 8 Exch. 40, 155 E.R. 1250, rev'd on other
grounds (1856), 5 H.L.C. 673, 10 E.R. 1065, [1843–60]
All E.R. Rep. 280 ....166, 527

Cowan v. Boyd (1921), 61 D.L.R. 497 (Ont. S.C.A.D.) 53

Cox v. Adams (1904), 35 S.C.R. 393... 386

Crabb v. Arun District Council, [1976] Ch. 179 (C.A.)..................... 288, 290, 291

Cradle Pictures (Canada) Ltd. v. Penner (1975), 10 O.R. (2d) 444,
63 D.L.R. (3d) 440, 24 C.P.R. (2d) 79 (H.C.J.) 792, 955

Craig v. Mohawk Metal Ltd. (1975), 9 O.R. (2d) 716, 61 D.L.R. (3d) 588
(H.C.J.)... 983

Craighampton Investments Ltd. v. Ayerswood Developments Ltd., [1984]
O.J. No. 107, 4 O.A.C. 124 (C.A.)... 712

Crampton v. Robertson, [1977] 6 W.W.R. 99 (B.C.S.C.) 954

Crane v. Hegeman-Harris Co. Inc., [1939] 1 All E.R. 662 (Ch.) 557

Credit Lyonnais Bank Nederland NV v. Burch, [1997] 1 All E.R. 144
(C.A.) 387, 388, 397, 398, 400

Creditel of Canada Ltd. v. Faultless (1977), 18 O.R. (2d) 95, 81 D.L.R.
(3d) 567, 2 B.L.R. 239 (Ont. H.C.J.) 455

Crediton Gas Co. v. Crediton Urban District Council, [1928] 1 Ch. 174.......... 740

Cricklewood Property and Investment Trust Ltd. v. Leighton's Trust
Investment Ltd., [1945] A.C. 221 (H.L.) 591–92

Croll v. Kelly (1983), 48 B.C.L.R. 306, [1983] B.C.J. No. 1875 (S.C.)................. 486

Cromwell v. Morris, (1917), 34 D.L.R. 305, [1917] 2 W.W.R. 377
(Alta. C.A.) 656, 657, 666–67

Crosse v. Gardner (1689), Carth. 90, 90 E.R. 656 (K.B.) 692

Crutchley v. Jerningham (1817), 2 Mer. 502, 35 E.R. 1032 (Ch.) 957

Crystalline Investments v. Domgroup Ltd., 2004 SCC 3, [2004]
1 S.C.R. 60, [2004] S.C.J. No. 3 165–66

CTN Cash and Carry Ltd. v. Gallaher Ltd., [1994] 4 All E.R. 714 (C.A.)......374, 380

Cud v. Rutter (1719), 1 P. Wms. 570, 24 E.R. 521 (Ch.) 923

Cullinane v. British "Rema" Manufacturing Co., [1954] 1 Q.B. 292
(C.A.) 839, 840

Cummer-Yonge Investments Ltd. v. Fagot, [1965] 2 O.R. 157n, 50 D.L.R.
(2d) 30n, 8 C.B.R. (N.S.) 62n (C.A.), aff'g [1965] 2 O.R. 152, 50 D.L.R.
(2d) 25, 8 C.B.R. (N.S.) 62 (H.C.J.) 165–66
Cundy v. Lindsay (1878), 3 App. Cas. 459 (H.L.)...510, 538
Cunningham v. Insinger, [1924] S.C.R. 8, [1924] 2 D.L.R. 433....................... 846
Currie v. Misa (1875), L.R. 10 Ex. 153, aff'd (1876), 1 App. Cas. 554
(H.L.) 216, 217
Currie v. Thomas (1985), 19 D.L.R. (4th) 594, [1985] B.C.J. No. 1922,
3 C.P.C. (2d) 42 (C.A.)...178
Curtis v. Chemical Cleaning & Dyeing Co., [1951] 1 K.B. 805, [1951]
1 All ER 631 (C.A.) 193, 202,751
Czarnikow v. Roth, Schmidt & Co., [1922] 2 K.B. 478 (C.A.)...........................440

D. & C. Builders Ltd. v. Rees, [1966] 2 Q.B. 617 (C.A.) 254, 282, 283, 290
D.P.P. for Northern Ireland v. Lynch, [1975] A.C. 653 (H.L.) 368, 394
Dagle v. Dagle Estate (1990), 81 Nfld. & P.E.I.R. 245, 70 D.L.R. (4th) 201,
[1990] P.E.I.J. No. 54 (C.A.), leave to appeal to S.C.C. refused, [1991]
1 S.C.R. viii, 88 Nfld. & P.E.I.R. 180n, 74 D.L.R. (4th) viii...................... 480
Dagley v. Dagley (1905), 38 N.S.R. 313 (S.C.) 178–79
Dahl v. Nelson (1881), 6 App. Cas. 38 (H.L.)... 572
D'Amore v. McDonald, [1973] 1 O.R. 845, 32 D.L.R. (3d) 543 (H.C.J.),
aff'd (1973), 1 O.R. (2d) 370, 40 D.L.R. (3d) 354 (C.A.) 470–71
Danby v. Stewart (1979), 23 O.R. (2d) 449, 97 D.L.R. (3d) 734 (H.C.J.) 942
Darcy v. Allen (The Case of Monoplies) (1602), Moore (K.B.) 671,
11 Co. Rep. 84 b, 77 E.R. 1260.. 447
Darlington Borough Council v. Wiltshier Northern Ltd., [1995]
1 W.L.R. 68 (H.L.) 299
Darlye's Case (1631), Het. 175.. 239
Daulia Ltd. v. Four Millbank Nominees Ltd., [1978] Ch. 231, [1978]
2 All E.R. 557 (C.A.) 56, 87
David v. Arnott-Smith Timber Co. (1952), 7 W.W.R. (N.S.) 306 (B.C.S.C.)....... 734
Davidson v. Norstrant (1921), 61 S.C.R. 493, 57 D.L.R. 377, [1921]
1 W.W.R. 993 224
Davidson v. Three Spruces Realty Ltd. (1977), 79 D.L.R. (3d) 481, [1977]
6 W.W.R. 460 (B.C.S.C.) 766, 770, 771, 772
Davis Contractors Ltd. v. Fareham Urban District Council, [1956]
A.C. 696 (H.L.) 548, 570, 571–72, 579, 581, 583, 588, 589
Davis v. Moranis and Smith, [1949] 4 D.L.R. 433 (Ont. C.A.)........................... 934
Davis v. Shaw (1910), 21 O.L.R. 474, [1910] O.J. No. 151 (Div. Ct.).................. 219
Dawood Ltd. v. Heath Ltd., [1961] 2 Lloyd's Rep. 512 (Q.B.)........................... 969
Dawson v. Helicopter Exploration Co. Ltd. (1958), 12 D.L.R. (2d) 1 (S.C.C.) 869
Dawson v. Helicopter Exploration Co., [1955] S.C.R. 868, [1955]
5 D.L.R. 404.. 86–87, 221
De Francesco v. Barnum (1890), 45 Ch. D. 430 937
De la Bere v. Pearson, [1908] 1 K.B. 280 (C.A.) 223
Deacons (A Firm) v. Bridge, [1984] A.C. 705 (P.C.)... 457

Deber Investments Ltd. v. Roblea Estates Ltd. (1976), 21 N.S.R. (2d) 158,
[1976] N.S.J. No. 516 (S.C.T.D.) 983

Decro-Wall v. Practitioners in Marketing Ltd., [1971] 1 W.L.R. 361,
[1971] 2 All E.R. 216 (C.A.) 656–57

Deglman v. Guaranty Trust Co., [1954] S.C.R. 725, [1954]
3 D.L.R. 785 .... 176–77, 179, 609, 963, 964

Delaney v. Cascade River Holidays Ltd. (1983), 44 B.C.L.R. 24, [1983]
B.C.J. No. 476, 24 C.C.L.T. 6 (C.A.) 193

DeLaval v. Bloomfield, [1938] 3 D.L.R. 405 (Ont. C.A.) 102

Delisle v. Bulman Group Ltd., [1991] 4 W.W.R. 637, [1991] B.C.J. No. 585,
54 B.C.L.R. (2d) 343 (S.C.) 714

Dell'Aquila Estate v. Mellof, [1996] 6 W.W.R. 445, 143 Sask. R. 8, [1996]
S.J. No. 188 (Q.B.) 390

Dellelce Construction and Equipment v. Portec Inc. (1990), 73 O.R.
(2d) 396, [1990] O.J. No. 844, 44 C.P.C. (2d) 165 (H.C.J.) 694

Deluxe French Fries v. McArdle (1976), 10 Nfld. & P.E.I.R. 414, [1976]
P.E.I.J. No. 52 (S.C.) 247

Denmark Productions Ltd. v. Boscobel Productions Ltd., [1969]
1 Q.B. 699 (C.A.) 657

Denny, Mott & Dickson v. James B. Fraser & Co. Ltd., [1944]
A.C. 265 (H.L.) 571, 579

Denton v. Great Northern Rwy. Co. (1856), 5 El. & Bl. 860, 119 E.R. 701
(K.B.) 36

Derry v. Peek (1889), 14 A.C. 337 (H.L.) 326, 347

Detomac Mines Ltd. v. Reliance Flourspar Mining Syndicate Ltd., [1952]
O.R. 423, [1952] 3 D.L.R. 464 (H.C.J.), aff'd [1952] O.R. 783, [1952]
4 D.L.R. 385 (C.A.) 728

Detroit Football Co. v. Dublinski, [1956] O.R. 744, 4 D.L.R. (2d) 688 (H.C.J.),
rev'd on other grounds [1957] O.R. 58, 7 D.L.R. (2d) 9 (C.A.) 458, 952–53

Devald v. Zigeuner (1958), 16 D.L.R. (2d) 285, [1958] O.W.N. 381
(H.C.J.) 557, 562

DeWolfe v. Mansour (1986), 73 N.S.R. (2d) 110, [1986] N.S.J. No. 62,
33 B.L.R. 135 (S.C.) 376

Di Cenzo Construction Co. Ltd. v. Glassco (1978), 21 O.R. (2d) 186,
90 D.L.R. (3d) 127 (C.A.) 941

Dialadex Communications Inc. v. Crammond (1987), 57 O.R. (2d) 746,
34 D.L.R. (4th) 392, [1987] O.J. No. 88 (H.C.J.) 955

Diamond Developments Ltd. v. Crown Assets Disposal Corp. (1972),
28 D.L.R. (3d) 207, [1972] 4 W.W.R. 731 (B.C.S.C.) 102

Dick Bentley Productions Ltd. v. Harold Smith (Motors) Ltd., [1965]
1 W.L.R. 623 (C.A.) 692–93

Dick v. Dennis, [1991] O.J. No. 2347, 20 R.P.R. (2d) 264 (Gen. Div.) 917

Dickinson v. Dodds (1876), 2 Ch. D. 463 (C.A.) 82, 85, 219

Dies v. British International Mining & Finance Corp. Ltd., [1939]
1 K.B. 724 980

Dillwyn v. Llewelyn (1862), 4 De G.F. & J. 517 (C.A.) 287

Dimmock v. Hallett (1866), L.R. 2 Ch. App. 21 327

Dimskal Shipping Company S.A. v. International Transport Workers
     Federation (sub nom. The Evia Luck), [1992] 2 A.C. 152 (H.L.) 371, 374

Dinicola v. Huang & Danczkay Properties (1996), 29 O.R. (3d) 161,
     135 D.L.R. (4th) 525, [1996] O.J. No. 1733 (Gen. Div.), aff'd on
     other grounds (1998), 40 O.R. (3d) 252, 163 D.L.R. (4th) 286,
     [1998] O.J. No. 2570 (C.A.) 597

Dmyterko Estate v. Kulikowsky, [1992] O.J. No. 1912, 47 E.T.R. 66
     (Gen. Div.) 390

Dobell v. Cowichan Copper Co. Ltd. (1967), 65 D.L.R. (2d) 440,
     61 W.W.R. 594 (B.C.S.C.) 924

Doherty v. Allman (1878), 3 App. Cas. 709 (H.L.) 947–48

Dominion Building Corp. Ltd. v. The King, [1933] A.C. 533, [1933]
     3 D.L.R. 577, [1933] 2 W.W.R. 417 (P.C.) 70–71

Dominion Coal Co. v. Lord Strathcona Shipping Co. Ltd., [1926]
     A.C. 108 (P.C.) 584

Dominion Fire Insurance Co. v. Nakata (1915), 52 S.C.R. 294,
     26 D.L.R. 722, 9 W.W.R. 1084 436

Domowicz v. Orsa Investment Ltd. (1993), 15 O.R. (3d) 661, [1993]
     O.J. No. 2214 (Gen. Div.) 913

Donaldsonv. Tracy, [1951] N.Z.L.R. 684 (S.C.) 682

Donoghue v. Stevenson [1932] A.C. 562 (H.L.) 305

Doon v. Wilks, [1996] B.C.J. No. 3091, 5 R.P.R. (3d) 282 (S.C.) 332

Doran v. McKinnon (1916), 53 S.C.R. 609, 31 D.L.R. 307 171

Dot Developments Ltd. v. Fowler (1980), 118 D.L.R. (3d) 371, [1980]
     B.C.J. No. 137, 18 R.P.R. 10 (S.C.) 659

Dougan v. Ley (1946), 71 C.L.R. 142 (A.H.C.) 919

Douglas Lake Capital Co. v. Smith (1991), 78 D.L.R. (4th) 319, [1991]
     B.C.J. No. 484, 54 B.C.L.R. (2d) 52 (C.A.) 205

Drake International Ltd. v. Miller (1976), 9 O.R. (2d) 652, 61 D.L.R.
     (3d) 420, 21 C.P.R. (2d) 129 (H.C.J.) 452

Dreger (Litigation Guardian of) v. Dreger (1994), 91 Man. R. (2d) 171,
     [1994] M.J. No. 75 (Q.B.), aff'd [1994] 10 W.W.R. 293, 97 Man. R.
     (2d) 39, [1994] M.J. No. 520 (C.A.) 480

Dresser Industries Inc. v. Raven Muds Ltd. (1976), 1 A.R. 616, [1976]
     A.J. No. 527 (S.C.A.D.) 659

Drewry v. Percival (1909), 19 O.L.R. 463, [1909] O.J. No. 145 (Div. Ct.) 226–27

Drummond Mines Co. v. Fernholm (1906), 8 O.W.R. 864, [1906]
     O.J. No. 788 (Div. Ct.) 935

Dugas v. Dugas' Estate (1978), 23 N.B.R. (2d) 199, [1978] N.B.J. No. 217
     (App. Div.) 131

Duke of Somerset v. Cookson (1735), 3 P. Wms. 390, 24 E.R. 1114 (Ch.) 918

Dunkirk Colliery Co. v. Lever Co. (1878), 9 Ch. Div. 20 (C.A.) 868

Dunlop Pneumatic Tyre Co. Ltd. v. New Garage and Motor Co. Ltd.,
     [1915] A.C. 79 (H.L.) 899, 900

Dunlop Pneumatic Tyre Co. Ltd. v. Selfridge & Co. Ltd., [1915]
A.C. 847 (H.L.) 214, 294, 296, 297–98, 299, 303
Dunnachie v. Kingston-upon-Hull City Council, [2004] UKHL 36,
[2004] 3 All E.R. 1011 (H.L.), rev'g [2004] EWCA Civ 84, [2004]
2 All E.R. 501 (C.A.) 878, 884
Dunton v. Dunton (1892), 18 V.L.R. 114 (S.C.) 219
Dupré Quarries Ltd. v. Dupré, [1934] S.C.R. 528, [1934] 4 D.L.R. 618 931–32
Durrell v. Evans (1862), 1 H. & C. 174, 158 E.R. 848 (Ex. Ch.) 172
Dusik v. Newton, [1985] B.C.J. No. 18, 62 B.C.L.R. 1 (C.A.) 991
Dutton and Wife v. Poole (1678), 2 Lev. 210, 83 E. R. 523 (K.B.) 297
Dwight v. Ellsworth (1852), 9 U.C.R. 539, [1852] O.J. No. 118 (Q.B.) 439
Dyck v. Manitoba Snowmobile Association Inc., [1985] 1 S.C.R. 589,
18 D.L.R. (4th) 635, [1985] S.C.J. No. 34 302–3
Dynamex Canada Inc. v. Miller (1998), 161 Nfld. & P.E.I.R. 97, [1998]
N.J. No. 56, 37 C.C.E.L. (2d) 41 (C.A.) 557
Dynamic Transport Ltd. v. O.K. Detailing Ltd., [1978] 2 S.C.R. 1072,
85 D.L.R. (3d) 19, 20 N.R. 500 .... 173, 680, 682, 739, 787, 788

E & R Distributors v. Atlas Drywall Ltd. (1980), 118 D.L.R. (3d) 339,
25 B.C.L.R. 394, [1980] B.C.J. No. 1213 (C.A.) 399
E.P. Chester Ltd. v. Mastorkis (1968), 4 N.S.R. (1965–69) 256, 70 D.L.R.
(2d) 133, 56 C.P.R. 139 (S.C.A.D.) 450, 488
Eadie v. Township of Brantford, [1967] S.C.R. 573, 63 D.L.R. (2d) 561 376
Eansor v. Eansor, [1946] S.C.R. 54, [1946] 2 D.L.R. 781 923
Earl of Aylesford v. Morris (1873), 8 Ch. App. 484 382
Earl of Durham v. Legard (1865), 34 Beav. 611, 55 E.R. 771 (M.R.) 941
Earl of Northumberland's Case (1583), 4 Leon. 91, 74 E.R. 750 (K.B.) 369
Earl of Oxford's Case (1615), 1 Rep. Ch. 1 10
Eastern Counties Rwy. Co. v. Hawkes (1855), 5 H.L.C. 331, 10 E.R. 928 917
Eastern Power Ltd. v. Azienda Comunale Energia & Ambiente (1999),
178 D.L.R. (4th) 409, [1999] O.J. No. 3275, 125 O.A.C. 54 (C.A.) 80
Eastham v. Newcastle United Football Club Ltd., [1964] Ch. 413 458
Easton v. Sinclair (1912), 3 D.L.R. 652 (Ont. H.C.J.) 408
Eastwalsh Homes Ltd. v. Anatal Developments Ltd. (1993), 12 O.R.
(3d) 675, 100 D.L.R. (4th) 469, [1993] O.J. No. 676 (C.A.) 849
Eastwood v. Kenyon (1840), 11 Ad. & El. 438, 113 E.R. 482 (Q.B.) .. 232, 237, 238
Eastwood v. Magnox Electric plc, [2004] UKHL 35, [2004] 3 All E.R. 991
(H.L.) 878, 882
Eccles v. Bryant and Pollock, [1948] Ch. 93 127
Eddie v. Unum Life Insurance Co. of America, 1999 BCCA 507, 177 D.L.R.
(4th) 738, [1999] B.C.J. No. 2013 896
Edgington v. Fitzmaurice (1885), 29 Ch. Div. 459 (C.A.) 152, 328
Edper Brascan Corp. v. 117373 Canada Ltd. (2000), 50 O.R. (3d) 425,
[2000] O.J. No. 4012, [2000] O.T.C. 722 (S.C.J.) 146
Edwards v. Skyways Ltd., [1964] 1 All E.R. 494 (Q.B.) 113, 120, 233
Egerton v. Brownlow (1853), 4 H.L. Cas. 1, 10 E.R. 359 445

Elderslie Steamship Co. Ltd. v. Borthwick, [1905] A.C. 93 (H.L.) 717

Electric Power Equipment v. R.C.A. Victor Co. (1964), 41 D.L.R. (2d) 727,
    var'd (1965), 46 D.L.R. (2d) 722, 49 W.W.R. 193 (B.C.C.A.) 572–73

Eli Lilly and Co. v. Novopharm Ltd., [1998] 2 S.C.R. 129, 161 D.L.R.
    (4th) 1, [1998] 2 S.C.R. 129 .... 710, 723

Eliason v. Henshaw, 4 Wheaton 225 (U.S.S.C. 1819) 56

Elite Bailiff Services Ltd. v. British Columbia, 2003 BCCA 102, 223 D.L.R.
    (4th) 39, [2003] B.C.J. No. 376 149

Elliott v. Pierson, [1948] 1 All E.R. 939 (Ch.) 921

Ellis v. Barker (1871), L.R. 7 Ch. App. 104 385

Elphinstone v. Monkland Iron & Coal Co. (1886), 11 App. Cas. 332 (H.L.) 899

Elsley v. J.G. Collins Insurance Agencies Ltd., [1978] 2 S.C.R. 916,
    83 D.L.R. (3d) 1, 20 N.R. 1 958

Emerald Resources Ltd. v. Sterling Oil Properties Management Ltd. (1969),
    3 D.L.R. (3d) 630 (Alta. S.C.A.D.), aff'd (1971), 15 D.L.R. (3d) 256 (S.C.C.) 170

Empire Gas Corp. v. American Bakeries Co., 840 F.2d 1333 (7th Cir. 1988) ... 220

Empress Towers Ltd. v. Bank of Nova Scotia (1990), 73 D.L.R. (4th) 400,
    50 B.C.L.R. (2d) 126, [1990] B.C.J. No. 2054 (C.A.) 144–45

Enderby Town Football Club v. Football Association Ltd., [1971] Ch. 591 440

Eng v. Evans (1991), 83 Alta. L.R. (2d) 107, [1991] A.J. No. 900 (Q.B.) 134

England v. Davidson (1840), 11 Ad. & El. 856, 113 E.R. 640 (K.B.) 240

Ennis v. Klassen (1990), 70 D.L.R. (4th) 321, [1990] 4 W.W.R. 609, [1990]
    M.J. No. 219 (C.A.) 345

Entores Ltd. v. Miles Far East Corp., [1955] 2 All E.R. 493 (C.A.) 79

Erie County Natural Gas & Fuel Co. v. Carroll, [1911] A.C. 105 (P.C.) 870

Erlanger v. New Sombrero Phosphate Co. (1878), 3 App. Cas. 1218
    (H.L.) 338, 340, 989

Errington v. Errington and Woods [1952] 1 K.B. 290 (C.A.) 85, 88, 133

Ertel Bieber & Co. v. Rio Tinto Co., [1918] A.C. 260 (H.L.) 446

Erwin v. Snelgrove, [1927] 4 D.L.R. 1028 (Ont. S.C.A.D.) 471

Esso Petroleum Co. Ltd. v. Harper's Garage (Stourport) Ltd., [1968]
    A.C. 269 (H.L.) 447, 457

Esso Petroleum Co. Ltd. v. Niad Ltd., [2001] EWHC Ch 458, [2001]
    1 All E.R. (D) 824 (Ch.) 978

Esso Petroleum Co. v. Mardon, [1976] Q.B. 801 (C.A.) 326, 328, 350, 354, 694,
    696, 818

Estate-Gard Services of Canada Ltd. v. Loewen Management Corp. (1989),
    38 B.C.L.R. (2d) 362, [1989] B.C.J. No. 1298 (C.A.) 657

Evans v. Hoare, [1892] 1 Q.B. 593 172

Ev's Truck & Equipment Inc. v. Mack Canada Inc., [1993] B.C.J. No. 1272,
    50 C.P.R. (3d) 94 (S.C.) 740

Experience Hendrix v. PPX Enterprises Ltd., [2003] EWCA Civ. 323,
    [2003] E.W.J. No. 1384 (C.A.) 978

F. & B. Transport Ltd. v. White Truck Motor Sales Manitoba Ltd. (1965),
    49 D.L.R. (2d) 670, 51 W.W.R. 124 (Man. C.A.) 330, 765

F. Crocker v. Sundance Northwest Resorts Ltd., [1988] 1 S.C.R. 1186,
    51 D.L.R. (4th) 321, [1988] S.C.J. No. 60 193
F.T. Developments Ltd. v. Sherman, [1969] S.C.R. 203, 70 D.L.R. (2d) 426 685
Fairbanks Soap Co. v. Sheppard, [1953] 1 S.C.R. 314, [1953] 2 D.L.R. 193 985
Fairweather v. McCullough (1918), 43 D.L.R. 525 (Ont. S.C.A.D.) 471
Falcke v. Gray (1859), 29 L.J. Ch. 28 .... 918, 919, 934
Famous Foods Ltd. v. Liddle (1941), 56 B.C.R. 372, [1941] 3 D.L.R. 525,
    [1941] 3 W.W.R. 708 (C.A.) 226–27
Farley v. Skinner, [2001] UKHL 49, [2001] 4 All E.R. 801 875–76
Farrar v. MacPhee (1971), 1 Nfld. & P.E.I.R. 341, 19 D.L.R. (3d) 720,
    [1971] P.E.I.J. No. 39 (S.C.) 134, 435
Farrell Lines, Inc. v. City of New York, 281 N.E.2d 162 (N.Y. 1972) 845
Farwell v. Wallbridge (1851), 2 Gr. 332, [1851] O.J. No. 257 (U.C. Ch.) 920
Fausset v. Carpenter (1831), 2 Dow & Cl. 232, 6 E.R. 715 (H.L.) 729
Federal Deposit Insurance Corporation v. W.R. Grace & Co., 877 F.2d 614
    (7th Cir. 1989) 334
Fell v. Whittaker (1871), L.R. 7 Q.B. 120 370
Fells v. Read (1796), 3 Ves. Jr. 70, 30 E.R. 899 (Ch.) 918
Felthouse v. Bindley (1862), 11 C.B. (N.S.) 869, 142 E.R. 1037 (Ex. Ch.) 70
Fender v. St. John-Mildmay, [1938] A.C. 1 (H.L.) 433
Fercometal S.A.R.L. v. Mediterranean Shipping Co. S.A., [1989] A.C. 788
    (H.L.) 666
Ferland v. Keith (1958), 15 D.L.R. (2d) 472, [1958] O.W.N. 445 (C.A.) 201
Ferme Gérald Laplante & Fils Ltée v. Grenville Patron Mutual Fire
    Insurance Company (2002), 61 O.R. (3d) 481, 217 D.L.R. (4th) 34,
    [2002] O.J. No. 3588 (C.A.) 894
Fern Investment Ltd. v. Golden Nugget (1987) Ltd. (1994), 149 A.R. 303,
    19 Alta. L.R. (3d) 442, [1994] A.J. No. 400 (C.A.) 904
Fibrosa Spolka Akcyjna v. Fairbairn Lawson Combe Barbour Ltd., [1943]
    A.C. 32 (H.L.) 605
Fidler v. Sun Life Assurance Co. of Canada, 2004 BCCA 273, 239 D.L.R.
    (4th) 547, [2004] B.C.J. No. 982 .... 890, 895
Field v. C.N.R., [1934] 3 D.L.R. 383 (N.S.S.C.) 932
Financings Ltd. v. Stimson, [1962] 1 W.L.R. 1184 (C.A.) 56
Findlay v. Findlay, [1951] 1 D.L.R. 185 (Ont. C.A.), aff'd (1951), [1952]
    1 S.C.R. 96, [1951] 4 D.L.R. 769 368
Findon v. Parker (1843), 11 M. & W. 675, 152 E.R. 976 (Ex. Ct.) 442
Finelli v. Dee, [1968] 1 O.R. 676, 67 D.L.R. (2d) 393 (C.A.) 668
Finlay Investments Ltd. v. Abraham, [1982] B.C.J. No. 1505, 26 R.P.R. 188
    (S.C.) 109
Finney v. Township of McKellar (1982), 36 O.R. (2d) 47, 133 D.L.R.
    (3d) 351, 18 M.P.L.R. 11 (C.A.) 445, 938
First City Capital Ltd. v. Petrosar Ltd. (1987), 61 O.R. (2d) 193, 42 D.L.R.
    (4th) 738, [1987] O.J. No. 849 (H.C.J.) 625
First City Investments Ltd. v. Fraser Arms Hotel Ltd. (1979), 104 D.L.R.
    (3d) 617, [1979] 6 W.W.R. 125, 13 B.C.L.R. 107 (C.A.) 100, 129

First City Trust Co. v. Triple Five Trust Corp. Ltd. (1989), 57 D.L.R.
(4th) 554 (Alta. C.A.) 625

First National Securities Ltd. v. Jones, [1978] Ch. 109, [1978] 2 All E.R. 221
(C.A.) 263

Fisher v. Appollinaris (1875), 10 Ch. App. 297 .... 439, 440

Fisher v. Bell, [1961] 1 Q.B. 394 37

Fitch v. Dewes, [1921] 2 A.C. 158 (H.L.) 454

Fitch v. Snedaker, 38 N.Y. 248 (1868) 51

Fitzgerald v. Dressler (1859), 7 C.B. (N.S.) 374, 141 E.R. 861 (C.P.) 166

Fleischer v. Rosenbloom, [1988] M.J. No. 5, 53 Man. R. (2d) 247 (Q.B.) 957

Fleischhaker v. Fort Garry Agencies Ltd. (1957), 11 D.L.R. (2d) 599,
23 W.W.R. 390. 65 Man.R. 339 (C.A.) 991

Fleisher v. Rosenbloom (1988), 53 Man. R. (2d) 247, [1988] M.J. No. 5
(Q.B.) 923

Fleming v. Bank of New Zealand, [1990] A.C. 577 (P.C.) 216

Fleming v. Boultbee (1929), 37 O.W.N. 293, [1929] O.J. No. 345 (H.C.) 331

Fleming v. Mair, [1921] 2 W.W.R. 421 (Sask. C.A.) 222

Fletton Ltd. v. Peate Marwick (1988), 50 D.L.R. (4th) 729, [1988]
B.C.J. No. 479, 27 B.C.L.R. (2d) 209 (C.A.), leave to appeal to
S.C.C. refused (1988), 50 D.L.R. (4th) vii, 91 N.R. 254n (S.C.C.) 666

Flexi-Coil Ltd. v. Smith-Roles Ltd. (1980), [1981] 1 F.C. 632, 50 C.P.R.
(2d) 29 (T.D.), aff'd [1982] 1 F.C. 553 (C.A.) 438

Flight v. Bolland (1828), 4 Russ. 298, 38 E.R. 817 (C.A.) 928

Flight v. Booth (1834), 1 Bing. (N.C.) 370, 131 E.R. 1160 (C.P.) 942

Flint v. Corby, 4 Gr. 45, [1853] O.J. No. 236 (U.C. Ch.) 913, 920

Florida Power & Light Co. v. Westinghouse Electric Co., 826 F.2d 239
(4th Cir. 1987) 589

Flureau v. Thornhill (1776), 2 Bla. W. 1078, 96 E.R. 635 (C.P.) 820

Foakes v. Beer (1884), 9 App. Cas. 605 (H.L.) 25, 251, 272, 275, 281, 290

Focal Properties Ltd. v. George Wimpey Canada Ltd. (1975), 14 O.R.
(2d) 295, 73 D.L.R. (3d) 387 (C.A.), aff'd on other grounds (1977),
[1978] 1 S.C.R. 2, 78 D.L.R. (3d) 129, 16 N.R. 71 .... 573, 595–96

Foley v. Classique Coaches Ltd., [1934] 2 K.B. 1 (C.A.) 96

Foot v. Rawlings, [1963] S.C.R. 197, 37 D.L.R. (2d) 695, 41 W.W.R. 650 253

Forbes v. Git (1921), [1922] 1 A.C. 256, 61 D.L.R. 353, [1922]
1 W.W.R. 250 (P.C.) 727

Fores v. Johnes (1802), 4 Esp. 97, 170 E.R. 654 (Nisi Prius) 430

Foster v. Driscoll, [1929] 1 K.B. 470 446

Foster v. Mackinnon (1869), L.R. 4 C.P. 704 520–21

Fothergill v. Rowland (1873), L.R. 17 Eq. 132 949

Foundling Hospital (Governors and Guardians) v. Crane, [1911] 2 K.B. 367 ... 266

Fournier Van & Storage Ltd. v. Fournier, [1973] 3 O.R. 741, 38 D.L.R.
(3d) 161 (H.C.J.) 304

Fowler Estate v. Barnes (1996), 142 Nfld. & P.E.I.R. 223, [1996] N.J. No. 206,
13 E.T.R. (2d) 150 (S.C.T.D.) 394

Foy v. Royal Bank of Canada, [1995] O.J. No. 1422, 37 C.P.C. (3d) 262
(Gen. Div.) 990
Francis v. Canadian Imperial Bank of Commerce (1994), 21 O.R. (3d) 75,
120 D.L.R. (4th) 393, [1994] O.J. No. 2657 (C.A.) 246, 292
Francis v. Trans Canada Trailer Sales Ltd. (1969), 6 D.L.R. (3d) 705,
69 W.W.R. 748 (Sask. C.A.) 201
Frank H. Davis of Georgia Inc. v. Rayonier Canada (B.C.) Ltd. (1968),
65 W.W.R. 251 (B.C.S.C.)..127
Fraser Jewellers (1982) Ltd. v. Dominion Electric Protection Co. (1997),
34 O.R. (3d) 1, 148 D.L.R. (4th) 496, [1997] O.J. No. 2359 (C.A.) 421, 773–74
Fraser River Pile & Dredge Ltd. v. Can-Dive Services Ltd., [1999]
3 S.C.R. 108, 176 D.L.R. (4th) 257, [1999] S.C.J. No. 48................311–12, 313
Fraser v. Morrison (1958), 12 D.L.R. (2d) 612, 25 W.W.R. 326 (Man. C.A.).....219
Fredrickson v. Insurance Corp. of British Columbia (1986), 28 D.L.R.
(4th) 414, [1986] 4 W.W.R. 504, [1986] B.C.J. No. 366 (C.A.), aff'd
[1988] 1 S.C.R. 1089, 49 D.L.R. (4th) 160, [1988] S.C.J. No. 54.................442
Freedhoff v. Pomalift Industries Ltd., [1971] 2 O.R. 773, 19 D.L.R.
(3d) 153 (C.A.)...869
Freeman v. Kaltio (1963), 39 D.L.R. (2d) 496 (B.C.S.C.) 935
Freeth v. Burr (1874), L.R. 9 C.P. 208...635, 655
Friedmann Equity Developments Inc. v. Final Note Ltd., 2000 SCC 34,
[2000] 1 S.C.R. 842, 188 D.L.R. (4th) 269 ....257, 259, 260, 264, 265, 268
Frind v. Sheppard, [1940] O.R. 448, [1940] 4 D.L.R. 455, 74 C.C.C. 386
(C.A.), rev'd [1941] S.C.R. 531, [1941] 4 D.L.R. 497 441
Frost v. Knight (1872), L.R. 7 Ex. 111 654
Fry v. Lane (1888), 40 Ch. D. 312...405
Fuller v. DePaul University, 12 N.E.2d 213 (Ill. App. 1938)............................335
Fuller v. Richmond (1850), 2 Gr. 24, [1850] O.J. No. 301 (U.C. Ch.) 920
Fuller v. Stoltze, [1938] 1 D.L.R. 635 (Sask. C.A.), aff'd [1939] 1 D.L.R. 1
(S.C.C.)...439
Fullerton v. Provincial Bank of Ireland, [1903] A.C. 309 (H.L.) 226
Funke v. Paist, 52 A.2d 655 (Pa. 1947)...682
Furtado v. Rogers (1802), 3 Bos. & P. 191, 127 E.R. 105 (C.P.)......................446

G. Ford Homes Ltd. v. Draft Masonry (York) Co. Ltd. (1983), 43 O.R.
(2d) 401, 1 D.L.R. (4th) 262, 2 O.A.C. 231 (C.A.)............................730, 738
Gaar Scott Co. v. Ottoson (1911), 19 W.L.R. 472 (Man. C.A.) 257
Gaertner v. Fiesta Dance Studios Ltd. (1973), 32 D.L.R. (3d) 639 (B.C.S.C.).....411
Galati v. Edwards Estate, [1998] O.J. No. 4128, 77 O.T.C. 215, 27 C.P.C.
(4th) 123 (Gen. Div.) 443
Gallen v. Butterley (1984), 9 D.L.R. (4th) 496, [1984] B.C.J. No. 1621,
53 B.C.L.R. 38 (C.A.) 204
Gamerco S.A. v. ICM/Fair Warning (Agency) Ltd., [1995] 1 W.L.R. 1226
(Q.B.)...608
Gange v. Sullivan (1966), 116 C.L.R. 418 (A.H.C.)..682

Garbutt Business College Ltd. v. Henderson, [1939] 4 D.L.R. 151,
[1939] 3 W.W.R. 257 (Alta. C.A.) 488

Gardner v. Coutts & Co., [1968] 1 W.L.R. 173 (Ch.) 793

Garland v. Consumers Gas Co., [1998] 3 S.C.R. 112, 40 O.R. (3d) 479,
[1998] S.C.J. No. 76 485

Gateway Hotel (1985) Ltd. v. Schur (1990), 66 Man. R. (2d) 305, [1990]
M.J. No. 400 (Q.B.) 471

Gateway Realty Ltd. v. Arton Holdings Ltd. and LaHave (No. 3) (1991),
106 N.S.R. (2d) 180, [1991] N.S.J. No. 362 (S.C.T.D.), aff'd (1992),
112 N.S.R. (2d) 180, [1992] N.S.J. No. 175 (S.C.A.D.) 785–86, 787, 805

GATX Corp. v. Hawker Siddeley Canada Inc., [1996] O.J. No. 1462,
1 O.T.C. 322, 27 B.L.R. (2d) 251 (Gen. Div.) 794–95

Geffen v. Goodman Estate, [1991] 2 S.C.R. 353, 81 D.L.R. (4th) 211,
[1991] S.C.J. No. 53 .... 386, 387, 388, 389–90, 391–93, 394, 395, 396–97

Geipel v. Smith (1872), L.R. 7 Q.B. 404 578

General Refractories Co. of Canada v. Venturedyne, Ltd., [2002]
O.J. No. 54, [2002] O.T.C. 10 (S.C.J.) 62

General Securities Ltd. v. Don Ingram Ltd., [1940] S.C.R. 670, [1940]
3 D.L.R. 641 869

Genesee County v. Pailthorpe, 224 N.W. 418 (Mich. S.C. 1929) 57

Gennis v. Madore (1988), 72 Nfld. & P.E.I.R. 104, [1988] P.E.I.J. No. 22
(S.C.T.D.) 108, 678

George Mitchell Ltd. v. Finney Lock Seeds Ltd., [1983] Q.B. 284 (C.A.),
aff'd [1983] 2 A.C. 803 (H.L.) 763, 764, 765

Georgia Construction Co. v. Pacific Great Railway Co., [1929] S.C.R. 630,
[1929] 4 D.L.R. 161 733

Gettle Bros. Construction Co. Ltd. v. Alwinsal Potash of Canada Ltd.
(1969), 5 D.L.R. (3d) 719 (Sask. C.A.) aff'd (1970), [1971] S.C.R. 320,
15 D.L.R. (3d) 128 967

Giannone & Stampeder Motor Hotel Ltd. (1963), 41 D.L.R. (2d) 242
(Alta. S.C.T.D.) 449

Gibbons v. Proctor (1891), 64 L.T. 594 (Q.B.) 51

Gibbons v. Trapp Motors (1970), 9 D.L.R. (3d) 742 (B.C.S.C.) 766, 967

Gibson v. Manchester City Council, [1978] 2 All E.R. 583 (C.A.), rev'd
[1979] 1 W.L.R. 294, [1979] 1 All E.R. 972 (H.L.) 37

Gibson v. McVeigh, [1922] 1 W.W.R. 151 (Alta. S.C.) 219

Gilbert Steel Ltd. v. University Construction Ltd. (1976), 12 O.R. (2d) 19,
67 D.L.R. (3d) 606 (C.A.) 219, 246, 275, 281, 289

Gilbert v. Barron (1958), 13 D.L.R. (2d) 262, [1958] O.W.N. 98 (H.C.J.) 923

Gilbert v. Campbell (1869), 12 N.B.R. 474 (S.C.) 655

Gilchrist Vending Ltd. v. Sedley Hotel Ltd. (1967) (1967), 66 D.L.R. (2d) 24,
[1967] S.J. No. 150 (Sask. Q.B.) 225

Giles v. Edwards (1797), 17 T.R. 181, 101 E.R. 920 (K.B.) 966

Giles v. McEwan (1896), 11 Man. R. 150 (C.A.) 988

Gillespie Bros. v. Cheney, Eggar & Co., [1896] 2 Q.B. 59 204

Gillespie Brothers & Co. Ltd. v. Roy Bowles Transport Ltd., [1973]
Q.B. 400 (C.A.) 766
Gillett v. Gillett (1979), 18 A.R. 1, 100 D.L.R. (3d) 247, [1979] A.J. No. 64
(S.C.T.D.) 409
Gindis v. Brisbourne, 2000 BCCA 73, 183 D.L.R. (4th) 431, [2000]
B.C.J. No. 162 410
Ginter v. Chapman & Keen (1967), 60 W.W.R. 385, [1967] B.C.J. No. 27
(C.A.) 660
Gissing v. T. Eaton Co. (1911), 25 O.L.R. 50, [1911] O.J. No. 8 (C.A.) 410
Gladu v. Edmonton Land Co. (1914), 19 D.L.R. 688 (Alta. S.C.) 409
Glasbrook Bros. v. Glamorgan County Council, [1925] A.C. 270 (H.L.) 240
Glasner v. Royal LePage Real Estate Services Ltd., [1992] B.C.J. No. 2454,
28 R.P.R. (2d) 72 (S.C.) 193, 502
Glencore Grain Rotterdam BV v. Lebanese Organisation for International
Commerce, [1997] EWCA Civ 1958, [1997] 4 All E.R. 514 (C.A.) 642–43
Gloge Heating & Plumbing Ltd. v. Northern Construction Co. (1986),
67 A.R. 150, 27 D.L.R. (4th) 264, [1986] A.J. No. 10 (C.A.) 46
Glynn v. Margetson & Co., [1893] A.C. 351 (H.L.) 727
Godson v. P. Burns & Co. (1919), 58 S.C.R. 404, 46 D.L.R. 97, [1919]
1 W.W.R. 848 102
Gold v. Rosenberg, [1997] 3 S.C.R. 767, 35 O.R. (3d) 736, 152 D.L.R.
(4th) 385 399
Gold v. Stover (1920), 60 S.C.R. 623, 57 D.L.R. 64, [1920] 3 W.W.R. 429 654
Golden Properties Ltd. v. Imbrook Properties Ltd., [1991] B.C.J. No. 2011,
17 R.P.R. (2d) 245 (C.A.) 127
Goldhar v. Universal Sections and Mouldings Ltd. (1962), [1963] 1 O.R. 189,
36 D.L.R. (2d) 450 (C.A.) 823
Goldsoll v. Goldman, [1915] 1 Ch. 292 .... 449, 450
Goldsworthy v. Brickell, [1987] 1 All E.R. 853 (C.A.) 387, 389
Goldthorpe v. Logan, [1943] 2 D.L.R. 519, [1943] O.W.N. 215 (C.A.) 42
Good v. Cheesman (1831), 2 B & Ad. 328, 109 E.R. 1165 (K.B.) 252, 254
Goodfriend v. Goodfriend (1971), [1972] S.C.R. 640, 22 D.L.R. (3d) 699,
6 R.F.L. 60 471
Gordon v. Ferguson (1961), 30 D.L.R. (2d) 420, 46 M.P.R. 177,
38 C.P.R. 1 (N.S.S.C.) 488
Gordon v. Gordon (1819), 3 Swans. 400, 36 E.R. 910 (Ch.) 333
Gordon v. Roebuck (1992), 9 O.R. (3d) 1, 92 D.L.R. (4th) 670, [1992]
O.J. No. 1499 (C.A.) 377–78, 380
Gorog v. Kiss (1977), 16 O.R. (2d) 569, 78 D.L.R. (3d) 690 (C.A.),
leave to appeal to S.C.C. refused (1977), 18 N.R. 484 479
Goss v. Chilcott, [1996] A.C. 788 (P.C.) 968
Gourlay v. Osmond (1991), 104 N.S.R. (2d) 155, 19 R.P.R. (2d) 59, [1991]
N.S.J. No. 318 (S.C.T.D.) 876
Graham v. Mosson (1839), 5 Bing (N.C.) 603, 132 E.R. 1232 (C.P.) 172
Graham v. Pitkin, [1992] 1 W.L.R. 403, [1992] 2 All E.R. 235 (P.C.) 107, 682

Graham v. Voth Bros. Construction (1974) Ltd., [1982] 6 W.W.R. 365,
[1982] B.C.J. No. 850, 39 B.C.L.R. 305 (Co. Ct.) 256

Graham v. Wagman (1976), 14 O.R. (2d) 349, 73 D.L.R. (3d) 667 (H.C.J.),
var'd on another point (1978), 21 O.R. (2d) 1, 89 D.L.R. (3d) 282 (C.A.) 597

Grainger & Son v. Gough, [1896] A.C. 325 (H.L.) 36

Grand Restaurants of Canada Ltd. v. Toronto (City) (1981), 32 O.R.
(2d) 757, 123 D.L.R. (3d) 349 (H.C.J.) 352

Grant Campbell & Co. v. Devon Lumber Co. Ltd. (1914), 7 O.W.N. 209,
[1914] O.J. No. 684 (S.C.A.D.) 342, 989

Grant v. Von Alvensleben (1913), 4 W.W.R. 1303 (B.C.C.A.) 232

Granville Savings and Mortgage Corp. v. Campbell (1992), 93 D.L.R.
(4th) 268, [1992] 5 W.W.R. 1, [1992] M.J. No. 309 (C.A.) 406

Great Eastern Oil & Import Co. Ltd. v. Chafe, [1956] 4 D.L.R. (2d) 310
(Nfld. S.C.) 222

Great Northern Rwy. Co. v. Witham (1873), L.R. 9 C.P. 16 220

Great Peace Shipping Ltd. v. Tsavliris Salvage (International) Ltd., [2002]
EWCA Civ No. 1407, [2002] 4 All E.R. 689, [2002] E.W.J. No. 4397
(C.A.) 538, 540, 542, 545, 546, 547–49, 550, 551, 552–53, 585

Green v. Kaufman, [1996] O.J. No. 4007, 95 O.A.C. 183, 31 C.L.R.
(2d) 87 (C.A.) 942

Green v. Perley (1989), 103 N.B.R. (2d) 181, [1989] N.B.J. No. 1149 (Q.B.) 397

Greenberg v. Lake Simcoe Ice Supply Co. (1917), 39 O.L.R. 32, [1917]
O.J. No. 203 (H.C.J.) 220

Greenberg v. Meffert (1985), 50 O.R. (2d) 755, 18 D.L.R. (4th) 548,
9 O.A.C. 69 (C.A.), leave to appeal to S.C.C. refused (1985),
30 D.L.R. (4th) 268n (S.C.C.) 739, 790–91

Greening Industries Ltd. v. Penny (1966), 53 D.L.R. (2d) 643 (N.S.S.C.) 449

Greenwood Shopping Plaza Ltd. v. Beattie, [1980] 2 S.C.R. 228,
39 N.S.R. (2d) 119, 111 D.L.R. (3d) 257 .... 296, 308, 314

Greenwood v. Greenwood (1863), 2 De G. J. & S. 28, 46 E.R. 285 (Ch.) 333

Gretzky v. Ontario Minor Hockey Association (1975), 10 O.R. (2d) 759,
64 D.L.R. (3d) 467, 24 C.P.R. (2d) 275 (H.C.J.) 929

Griesshammer v. Ungerer and Miami Studios of Dancing (1958),
14 D.L.R. (2d) 599, 25 W.W.R. 689 (Man. C.A.) 411

Griffin v. Martens (1988), 27 B.C.L.R. (2d) 152, [1988] B.C.J. No. 828
(C.A.) 92, 108–9, 144, 678

Griffith v. Brymer (1903), 19 T.L.R. 434 (K.B.) 567

Griffith v. Tower Publishing Co. Ltd. and Moncrieff, [1897] 1 Ch. 21 307

Grist v. Bailey (1966), [1967] Ch. 532, [1966] 2 All E.R. 875 540

Gronau v. Schlamp Investments Ltd. (1974), 52 D.L.R. (3d) 631, [1974]
M.J. No. 223 (Q.B.) 332

Gross v. Wright (1922), [1923] S.C.R. 214, [1923] 2 D.L.R. 171, [1923]
1 W.W.R. 882 947

Groves v. John Wonder Co., 286 N.W. 235 (Minn. C.A. 1939) 843

Guarantee Co. of North America v. Gordon Capital Corp., [1999]
3 S.C.R. 423, 178 D.L.R. (4th) 1, [1999] S.C.J. No. 60, rev'g
(1998), 38 O.R. (3d) 563, 157 D.L.R. (4th) 643, [1998]
O.J. No. 1197 (C.A.) 339, 617, 643–44, 662, 697-99, 720, 721

Guerin v. Canada, [1984] 2 S.C.R. 335, 13 D.L.R. (4th) 321, 55 N.R. 161 403

Gutka v. Cargill Ltd. (1994), 127 Sask R. 126, [1994] S.J. No. 624 (Q.B.) 740

H. Dakin Co. Ltd. v. Lee, [1916] 1 K.B. 566 (C.A.) 985

H. Parsons (Livestock) Ltd. v. Uttley Ingham & Co. Ltd., [1978]
Q.B. 791 860–61

H.F. Clarke v. Thermidaire Corp. Ltd., [1973] 2 O.R. 57, 33 D.L.R. (3d) 13,
9 C.P.R. (2d) 203 (C.A.), rev'd on other grounds (1974), [1976]
1 S.C.R. 319, 54 D.L.R. (3d) 385, 17 C.P.R. (2d) 1 .... 556, 898, 900–02

H.I.H. Casualty & General Insurance Ltd. v. New Hampshire Insurance
Co., [2001] 2 Lloyd's Rep. 161 (C.A.) 713

Hadfield v. Hadfield (1996), 30 B.C.L.R. (3d) 131, [1996] B.C.J. No. 2583
(S.C.) 440

Hadley v. Baxendale, (1854), 9 Exch. 341, 156 E.R. 145 854–56

Hadley v. Clark (1799), 8 T.R. 259, 101 E.R. 1377 (K.B.) 568

Haggar v. de Placido, [1972] 1 W.L.R. 716 (Crown Ct.) 131

Haggerty v. Latreille (1913), 14 D.L.R. 532 (Ont. S.C.A.D.) 948

Hain S.S. Co. Ltd. v. Tate & Lyle Ltd., [1936] 2 All E.R. 597,
41 Com. Cas. 350 (H.L.) 667, 755

Hall v. More, [1928] 1 D.L.R. 1028 (B.C.C.A.) 488

Hall v. Warren (1804), 9 Ves. 605 (H.L.) 913

Hamelin v. Seven Mile High Group Inc., [1994] 6 W.W.R. 251, [1994]
B.C.J. No. 694, 42 B.C.A.C. 241 (C.A.) 200

Hamer v. Sidway (1891), 27 N.E. 256 (N.Y. 1891) 217, 218

Hamilton Gear & Machine Co. Ltd. v. Lewis Brothers Ltd., [1924]
3 D.L.R. 367 (Ont. C.A.) 69

Hamilton Jones v. David & Snape (a firm) (2003), [2003] EWHC 3147,
[2004] 1 All E.R. 657 (Ch.) 875

Hamilton v. Open Window Bakery Ltd. (2003), 2004 SCC 9, [2004]
1 S.C.R. 303, 235 D.L.R. (4th) 193 .... 824, 825

Hamilton v. Raymond (1852), 2 U.C.C.P. 392, [1852] O.J. No. 155 986

Hamilton v. Watson (1845), 12 Cl. & F. 109 (H.L.) 334

Hammond v. Small (1859), 16 U.C.Q.B. 371 229

Hanau v. Ehrlich, [1912] A.C. 39 (H.L.) 168

Harbutt's "Plasticine" Ltd. v. Wayne Tank & Pump Co. Ltd., [1970]
1 Q.B. 447 (C.A.) 758–59

Harding v. Harding (1972), 28 D.L.R (3d) 358, 8 R.F.L. 1 (B.C.S.C.) 224

Hardwick Game Farm v. Sussex Agricultural Poultry Producers
Association, [1969] 2 A.C. 31 (H.L.) 188

Hardwick v. Johnson, [1978] 2 All E.R. 935 (C.A.) 131

Hardy v. Elphick, [1974] Ch. 65 (C.A.) 171

Hare v. Horton (1833), 5 B. & Ad. 715, 110 E.R. 954 (K.B.) 726

Hargreaves Transport Ltd. v. Lynch, [1969] 1 W.L.R. 215 (C.A.).....................680
Hargreaves v. Fleming (1995), 129 Sask. R. 136, [1995] S.J. No. 149
   (Q.B.)..147, 156
Harling v. Eddy, [1951] 2 K.B. 739...201
Harnam Singh v. Jamal Pirbhai, [1951] A.C. 688 (P.C.)............................278
Harrington v. Victoria Graving Dock Co. (1878), 3 Q.B.D. 549 430
Harris v. Great Western Railway Co. (1876), 1 Q.B.D. 515.......................184
Harris v. Lindeborg, [1931] S.C.R. 235, [1931] 1 D.L.R. 945....................170
Harris v. Nickerson (1873), L.R. 8 Q.B. 286...48
Harris v. Sheffield United Football Club Ltd., [1988] Q.B. 77 240
Harris v. Watson (1791), Peake 101, 170 E.R. 94 (Nisi Prius).............244–45
Harrison v. Harrison, [1910] 1 K.B. 35...433
Harry v. Kreutziger (1978), 95 D.L.R. (3d) 231, 9 B.C.L.R. 166
   (C.A.) 408, 409, 410–11, 425
Hart v. Boutilier (1916), 56 D.L.R. 620 (S.C.C.)..............................558, 563
Hart v. O'Connor, [1985] A.C. 1000 (P.C.) 412
Hartley v. Ponsonby (1857), 7 El. & Bl. 872, 119 E.R. 1471 (K.B.)...........245
Hartog v. Colin & Shields, [1939] 3 All E.R. 566 (K.B.)............................502
Harty v. Gooderham (1871), 31 U.C.R. 18, [1871] O.J. No. 29 (Q.B.)..........35, 36
Harvey v. Facey, [1893] A.C. 552 (P.C.)...34
Harvey v. Perry, [1953] 1 S.C.R. 233, [1953] 2 D.L.R. 465 55
Harvey v. Young (1603), Yel. 21, 80 E.R. 15 (K.B.).....................................692
Harvie v. Gibbons (1980), 109 D.L.R. (3d) 559, 12 Alta. L.R. (2d) 72,
   16 R.P.R. 174 (Alta. C.A.)...171
Hasham v. Zenab, [1960] A.C. 316 (P.C.) 667
Hassard v. Peace River Co-operative Seed Growers Association, [1954]
   2 D.L.R. 50 (S.C.C.) 727
Haug & Nellermoe v. Murdoch (1916), 26 D.L.R. 200 (Sask. S.C.) 470
Hawkes v. Saunders (1782), 1 Cowp. 289 (K.B.)......................................236
Hawrish v. Bank of Montreal, [1969] S.C.R. 515, 2 D.L.R. (3d) 600,
   66 W.W.R. 673 ....197, 198, 200, 201
Hawrysh v. St. John's Sportsmen's Club (1964), 46 D.L.R. (2d) 45,
   49 W.W.R. 243 (Man. Q.B.)...848
Hayne v. Cummings (1864), 16 C.B. (N.S.) 421, 143 E.R. 1191 (C.P.) 728
Haynes v. Doman, [1899] 2 Ch. 13 (C.A.)...455
Hayward v. Mellick (1984), 45 O.R. (2d) 110, 5 D.L.R. (4th) 740,
   2 O.A.C. 161 (C.A.)..358–59
Haywood v. Cope (1858), 25 Beav. 140, 53 E.R. 589 (M.R.) 935
Healthcare Developers Inc. v. Newfoundland (1996), 141 Nfld. &
   P.E.I.R. 34, 136 D.L.R. (4th) 609, [1996] N.J. No. 149 (C.A.) 140, 148
Hedley Byrne & Co. v. Heller & Partners Ltd. (1963), [1964] A.C. 465,
   [1963] 2 All E.R. 575 (H.L.)..............................163, 326, 349, 355
Heglibiston Establishments v. Heyman (1978), 36 P. & C.R. 351 (C.A.)...........435
Heilbut, Symons & Co. v. Buckleton, [1913] A.C. 30 (H.L.)................691–92
Heisler v. Anglo-Dal Ltd., [1954] 2 All E.R. 770 (C.A.)..............................643

Helm v. Simcoe & Erie General Insurance Co. (1979), 19 A.R. 326,
    108 D.L.R. (3d) 8, [1979] A.J. No. 506 (C.A.) 267
Henderson v. Thompson (1909), 41 S.C.R. 445 934
Hendry v. Zimmerman, [1947] 4 D.L.R. 550 (Man. K.B.) 438
Henthorn v. Fraser, [1892] 2 Ch. 27 73
Herbert Morris Ltd. v. Saxelby, [1916] 1 A.C. 688 (H.L.) 452
Hercules Managements Ltd. v. Ernst & Young, [1997] 2 S.C.R. 165,
    146 D.L.R. (4th) 577, [1997] S.C.J. No. 51 .... 154, 351
Hermann v. Charlesworth, [1905] 2 K.B. 123 (C.A.) 434, 472
Herne Bay Steam Boat Company v. Hutton, [1903] 2 K.B. 683 (C.A.) 577, 582
Heron Garage Properties Ltd. v. Moss, [1974] 1 All E.R. 421 (Ch.) 682
Herring v. Dorell (1840), 8 Dowl. 604 239
Herrschaft v. Vancouver Community College (1978), 91 D.L.R. (3d) 328
    (B.C.S.C.) 867
Heyman v. Darwins Ltd., [1942] A.C. 356 (H.L.) 654, 655, 661
Heywood v. Wellers, [1976] Q.B. 446 (C.A.) 875
Highway Properties Ltd. v. Kelly, Douglas & Co. Ltd. (1971), [1971]
    S.C.R. 562, 17 D.L.R. (3d) 710, [1972] 2 W.W.R. 28 .... 664–65, 823–24
Hill v. Archbold, [1968] 1 Q.B. 686 (C.A.) 442
Hill v. Buffalo & Lake Huron Rwy. Co. (1864), 10 Gr. 506 (U.C. Ch.) 936
Hill v. C.A. Parsons & Co. Ltd., [1972] Ch. 305 933
Hill v. Church of Scientology of Toronto (1995), 24 O.R. (3d) 865, [1995]
    2 S.C.R. 1130, [1995] S.C.J. No. 64 .... 888–90, 892
Hill v. Nova Scotia (Attorney General), [1997] 1 S.C.R. 69, 142 D.L.R.
    (4th) 230, [1997] S.C.J. No. 7 178
Hill v. Stanton (1845), 2 U.C.R. 149, [1845] O.J. No. 58 (Q.B.) 988
Hillas and Co. Ltd. v. Arcos Ltd., [1932] All E.R. Rep. 494, 147 L.T. 503
    (H.L.), rev'g. (1932), 40 Lloyd's Rep. 307 (C.A.) 94, 95, 101, 103, 141,
    728-29
Hillis Oil & Sales Ltd. v. Wynn's Canada Ltd., [1986] 1 S.C.R 57,
    25 D.L.R. (4th) 649, [1986] S.C.J. No. 9 .... 718, 723
Hinchey v. Gonda, [1955] O.W.N. 125 (H.C.J.) 330
Hirachand Punamchand v. Temple, [1911] 2 K.B. 330 .... 252, 255
Hirji Mulji v. Cheong Yue S.S. Co. Ltd., [1926] A.C. 497 (P.C.) 571, 603
Hirst v. Moore (1954), [1955] 1 D.L.R. 514, 12 W.W.R. (N.S.) 609 (B.C.S.C.) 981
Hi-Tech Group Inc. v. Sears Canada Inc. (2001), 52 O.R. (3d) 97, [2001]
    O.J. No. 33, 141 O.A.C. 56 (C.A.) 709
Hnatuk v. Chretian (1960), 31 W.W.R. 130 (B.C.S.C.) 408, 935
Hobart Investment Corp. Ltd. v. Walker (1977), 76 D.L.R. (3d) 156,
    [1977] 4 W.W.R. 113, 1 R.P.R. 187 (B.C.C.A.) 661
Hobbs v. Esquimalt & Nanaimo Railway Company (1899),
    29 S.C.R. 450 .... 499, 935
Hobbs v. TDI Canada Ltd. (2004), 246 D.L.R. (4th) 43, [2004] O.J. No. 4876,
    192 O.A.C. 141 (C.A.) 246
Hochster v. De La Tour (1853), 2 El. & Bl. 678, 118 E.R. 922 (Q.B.) 652–53

Hodgkinson v. Simms, [1994] 3 S.C.R. 377, 117 D.L.R. (4th) 16, [1994]
S.C.J. No. 84 852–53

Hoenig v. Isaacs, [1952] 2 All E.R. 176 (C.A.) 985

Hoffman v. Red Owl Stores, 133 N.W.2d 267 (Wis. 1965) 138

Hogan v. Newfoundland (Attorney General), 2000 NFCA 12, 189 Nfld. &
P.E.I.R. 183, 183 D.L.R. (4th) 225 445

Hogar Estates in Trust v. Shebron Holdings Ltd. (1979), 25 O.R. (2d) 543,
101 D.L.R. (3d) 509 (H.C.J.) 332

Holliday v. Lockwood, [1917] 2 Ch. 47 934

Hollier v. Rambler Motors (A.M.C.) Ltd., [1972] 2 Q.B. 71 (C.A.) 186

Hollinger Consolidated Gold Mines Ltd. v. Northern Canadian Power,
[1923] 4 D.L.R. 1205 (Ont. S.C.A.D.) 598

Holman v. Johnson (1775), 1 Cowp. 341, 98 E.R. 1120 (K.B.) 468, 470, 477

Holwell Securities v. Hughes, [1974] 1 W.L.R. 155 (C.A.) 75

Homburg Houtimport B.V. v. Agrosin Private Ltd. (2003), [2003] UKHL 12,
[2004] 1 AC 715, [2003] 2 W.L.R. 711 727

Home Counties Dairies Ltd. v. Skilton, [1970] 1 All E.R. 1227 (C.A.) 455

Homestar Industrial Properties Ltd. v. Philps (1992), [1993] 1 W.W.R. 163,
[1992] B.C.J. No. 2237, 72 B.C.L.R. (2d) 69 (C.A.) 666–67

Hong Kong Fir Shipping Co. Ltd. v. Kawasaki Kisen Kaisha Ltd., [1962]
2 Q.B. 26 (C.A.) 625, 627–28, 633, 656

Hongkong Bank of Canada v. Richardson Greenshields of Canada Ltd.
[1990], 72 D.L.R. (4th) 161, [1990] 6 W.W.R. 1, [1990] B.C.J. No. 1721
(C.A.) 865

Hoolahan v. Hivon, [1944] 4 D.L.R. 405, [1944] 3 W.W.R. 120 (Alta S.C.A.D.)... 256

Hope v. Walter, [1900] 1 Ch. 257 (C.A.) 935

Hopkins v. Grazebrook (1826), 6 B. & Cress. 31, 108 E.R. 364 (K.B.) 820

Horlock v. Beal, [1916] 1 A.C. 486 (H.L.) 577, 578

Horne v. Midland Railway Co. (1873), L.R. 8 C.P. 131 864

Houle v. Banque Canadienne Nationale, [1990] 3 S.C.R. 122, 74 D.L.R.
(4th) 577, [1990] S.C.J. No. 120 783

Household Fire & Carriage Accident Insurance Co. v. Grant (1879),
4 Ex. D. 216 (C.A.) 73, 74, 75, 76

Household Movers & Shippers Ltd. v. Fitzhugh (1989), 79 Nfld. &
P.E.I.R. 171, [1989] N.J. No. 180 (S.C.T.D.) 191–92

Howard Marine & Dredging Co. Ltd. v. A. Ogden & Sons (Excavations)
Ltd., [1978] Q.B. 574 (C.A.) 60, 69

Howard v. Hopkyns (1742), 2 Atk. 371, 26 E.R. 624 (Ch.) 957

Howard v. Pickford Tool Co. Ltd., [1951] 1 K.B. 417 (C.A.) 641

Howard v. Shirlstar Container Transport Ltd., [1990] 3 All E.R. 366 (C.A.) 464

Howatson v. Webb, [1907] 1 Ch. 537, aff'd [1908] 1 Ch. 1 (C.A.) 524, 525

Howe v. Smith (1884), 27 Ch. D. 89 (C.A.) 980

Howell v. Coupland (1876), 1 Q.B.D. 258 587

Hubbard v. Walker (1856), 13 U.C.R. 205, [1856] O.J. No. 28 (Q.B.) 607

Hubbs v. Black (1918), 44 O.L.R. 545, [1918] O.J. No. 48 (S.C.A.D.) 223

Hudson Bay Oil & Gas Co. v. Dynamic Petroleums Ltd. (1958),
26 W.W.R. 504 (Alta. S.C.T.D.) 102
Huff v. Price (1990), 76 D.L.R. (4th) 138, 51 B.C.L.R. (2d) 282, [1990]
B.C.J. No. 2692 (C.A.) 853
Huggard v. Ontario & Saskatchewan Land Co. (1908), 8 W.L.R. 866
(Sask. C.A.) 267
Hughes v. Lukuvka (1970), 14 D.L.R. (3d) 110, 75 W.W.R. 464 (B.C.C.A.) 983
Hughes v. Metropolitan Rwy. Co. (1877), 2 App. Cas. 439 (H.L.) 277, 284, 285,
286
Hull v. Pearson (1899), 56 N.Y. Supp. 518 (C.A.) 230
Humboldt Flour Mills Co. Ltd. v. Boscher (1974), 50 D.L.R. (3d) 477, [1974]
S.J. No. 237 (Q.B.) 921
Hunt v. Silk (1804), 5 East 449, 102 E.R. 1142 (K.B.) 966
Hunt v. TD Securities Inc. (2003), 66 O.R. (3d) 481, 229 D.L.R. (4th) 609,
[2003] O.J. No. 3245 (C.A.) 865, 868
Hunter Engineering Co. Inc. v. Syncrude Canada Ltd., [1989] 1 S.C.R. 426,
57 D.L.R. (4th) 321, [1989] S.C.J. No. 23 .... 421, 633, 640, 753, 754, 763,
764, 768–69, 770–73, 776–77, 902
Hurley v. Roy (1921), 64 D.L.R. 375 (Ont. S.C.A.D.) 940, 941
Huron v. Armstrong (1868), 27 U.C.R. 533, [1868] O.J. No. 78 (Q.B.) 266
Huttges v. Verner (1975), 12 N.B.R. (2d) 473, 64 D.L.R. (3d) 374, [1975]
N.B.J. No. 196 (S.C.A.D.) 935
Hutton v. Warren (1836), 1 M. & W. 466, 150 E.R. 517 (Ex.) 732–33
Hyde v. Dean of Windsor, (1597), Cro. Eliz. 552, 78 E.R. 798 .... 568, 573
Hyde v. Wrench (1840), 3 Beav. 334, 49 E.R. 132 (M.R.) 53
Hydro Electric Power Commission of Ontario v. Coniagas Reduction
Co. Ltd., [1933] 3 D.L.R. 337 (P.C.) 737
Hylton v. Hylton (1754), 2 Ves. Sr. 547, 28 E.R. 349 (H.L.) 386
Hyrsky v. Smith, [1969] 2 O.R. 360, 5 D.L.R. (3d) 385 (H.C.J.) 542, 941
Hyundai Heavy Industries Co. Ltd. v. Papadopoulos, [1980] 1 W.L.R. 1129
(H.L.) 981
Hyundai Shipbuilding & Heavy Industries Co. Ltd. v. Pournaras, [1978]
2 Lloyd's Rep. 502 (C.A.) 981

Iezzi Constructions Pty. Ltd. v. Currumbin Crest Development Pty. Ltd.
(1994), 10 Bldg. & Constr. Law 403 (Qld. C.A.) 969
Imperial Bank of Commerce v. Ohlson (1997), 209 A.R. 140, 154 D.L.R.
(4th) 33, [1997] A.J. No. 1185 (C.A.) 416
Imperial Brass Ltd. v. Jacob Electric Systems Ltd. (1989), 72 O.R. (2d) 17
(Ont. H.C.J.) 635
Imperial Glass Ltd. v. Consolidated Supplies Ltd. (1960), 22 D.L.R.
(2d) 759 (B.C.C.A.) 35, 505–6
Imperial Grain & Milling Co. v. Slobinski Bros. & Sons, [1922]
3 W.W.R. 221 (Man. K.B.) 734
Imperial Life Assurance Co. of Canada v. Colmenares, [1967] S.C.R. 443,
62 D.L.R. (2d) 138 74

In re Cory (1912), 29 T.L.R. 18 (Ch. D.) 230
In re Davstone Estates Ltd.'s Leases, [1969] 2 Ch. 378 440
In Re Gloucester Municipal Election Petition, [1901] 1 K.B. 683 220
In re Greene (1930), 45 F.2d 428 (S.D.N.Y.) 225
In re Hudson (1885), 33 W.R. 819 (Ch. D.) 230
In re Trepca Mines Ltd. (No. 2), [1963] Ch. 199 (C.A.) 442, 443
In re: Estate of Wheeler, 1 N.E.2d 425 (Ill. 1936) 228
Inche Noriah v. Shaik Allie Bin Omar, [1929] A.C. 127 (P.C.) 387, 397
Independent Lumber Co. v. David (1911), 1 W.W.R. 134 (Sask. C.A.) 727
Industrial & Technical Press v. Jack Canuck Publishing Co. Ltd. (1920),
    17 O.W.N. 409, [1920] O.J. No. 610 (S.C.) 716
Ingram v. Little, [1961] 1 Q.B. 31 (C.A.) 512–13
Inntrepreneur Pub. Co. v. East Crown, [2000] 2 Lloyd's Rep. 611 (Ch.) 695
Instone v. A. Schroeder Music Publishing Co. Ltd., [1974] 1 All E.R. 171
    (C.A.), aff'd [1974] 3 All E.R. 616 (H.L.) 989
Interfoto Picture Library Ltd. v. Stiletto Visual Programmes Ltd. (1988),
    [1989] Q.B. 433, [1988] 2 W.L.R. 615, [1988] 1 All E.R. 348
    (C.A.) 189–90, 780
International Brotherhood of Electrical Workers v. Winnipeg Builders
    Exchange, [1967] S.C.R. 628, 65 D.L.R. (2d) 242, 61 W.W.R. 682 933
Interoffice Telephones v. Robert Freeman Co., [1958] 1 Q.B. 190 (C.A.) 817
Investors Compensation Scheme Ltd. v. West Bromwich Building Society,
    [1998] 1 W.L.R. 896 (H.L.) 710
Inwards v. Baker, [1965] 2 Q.B. 29 (C.A.) 287
Ipswich Tailors' Case (1614), 77 E.R. 1218 (K.B.) 447
Irani v. Southampton and South-West Hampshire Health Authority, [1985]
    I.R.L.R. 203 (Ch.) 933
Irving v. Irving, [1988] B.C.J. No. 2373, 17 R.F.L. (3d) 318 (S.C.) 237
Island Properties Ltd. v. Entertainment Enterprises Ltd. (1983), 41 Nfld. &
    P.E.I.R. 80, 146 D.L.R. (3d) 505, [1983] N.J. No. 269 (S.C.T.D.), var'd (1986),
    58 Nfld. & P.E.I.R. 151, 26 D.L.R. (4th) 347, [1986] N.J. No. 12 (C.A.) 76
ITO — International Terminal Operators Ltd. v. Miida Electronics Inc.,
    [1986] 1 S.C.R. 752, 28 D.L.R. (4th) 641, [1986] S.C.J. No. 38 ...... 302, 358, 724
Ivanochko v. Sych (1967), 60 D.L.R. (2d) 474, 58 W.W.R. 633 (Sask. C.A.) 542

J. Clark & Son Ltd. v. Finnamore (1972), 5 N.B.R. (2d) 467, 32 D.L.R.
    (3d) 236, [1972] N.B.J. No. 109 (S.C.A.D.) 310, 312
J. Evans & Son (Portsmouth) Ltd. v. Merzario (Andrea) Ltd., [1976]
    1 W.L.R. 1078 (C.A.) 201, 204, 206, 207, 693, 727, 752
J. Lauritzen A.S. v. Wijsmuller B.V. (The Super Servant Two), [1989] 1 Lloyd's
    Rep. 148 (Q.B.), aff'd [1990] 1 Lloyd's Rep. 1 (C.A.) 597, 598, 599, 602
J. Nunes Diamonds Ltd. v. Dominion Electric Protection Co., [1972]
    S.C.R. 769, 26 D.L.R. (3d) 699 349
J. Spurling Ltd. v. Bradshaw, [1956] 2 All E.R. 121 (C.A.) 186, 187
J.G. Collins Insurance Agencies Ltd. v. Elsley Estate, [1978] 2 S.C.R. 916,
    83 D.L.R. (3d) 1, 20 N.R. 1 ...... 449, 451, 452, 453, 454, 456, 488, 898, 902–3

J.T. Stratford & Son Ltd. v. Lindley, [1965] A.C. 269 (H.L.). 955

Jackson v. Jackson (1960), 26 D.L.R. (2d) 686, 34 W.W.R. 431 (B.C.S.C.) 131

Jackson v. Macauley Nicholls Maitland & Co. Ltd. (1942), 57 B.C.R. 492,
   [1942] 2 D.L.R. 609, [1942] 2 W.W.R. 33 (C.A.) 102

Jackson v. Royal Bank of Scotland, [2005] UKHL 3, [2005] 2 All E.R. 71
   (H.L.) 858

Jackson v. Union Marine Insurance Co. (1874), L.R. 10 C.P. 125 578

Jacobs & Youngs, Inc. v. Kent, 129 N.E. 889 (N.Y. 1921) 842

Jacques v. Lloyd D. George & Partners Ltd., [1968] 1 W.L.R. 625 (C.A.) 192, 202

Jaggard v. Sawyer, [1995] 2 All E.R. 189 (C.A.) 975

Jakeman v. Cook (1878), 4 Ex. D. 26 238

James Finlay & Co. v. N.V. Kwik Hoo Tong Handel Maatschappij, [1929]
   1 K.B. 400 (C.A.) 869

James Miller & Partners Ltd. v. Whitworth Street Estates (Manchester) Ltd.,
   [1970] A.C. 583 (H.L.) 714

James Thorley Ltd. v. Orchis Steamship Co. Ltd., [1907] 1 K.B. 660 (C.A.) 755

Janson v. Driefontein Consolidated Mines Ltd., [1902] A.C. 484 (H.L.) 446

Jarvis v. Swans Tours Ltd., [1973] Q.B. 233 (C.A.) 799, 875, 896

Jay Trading Corp. v. Ifax Export & Import Ltd., [1954] 2 D.L.R. 110
   (N.S.S.C.) 969

Jefferys v. Jefferys (1841), Cr. & Ph. 138, 41 E.R. 443 (Ch.) 935

Jenyns v. Public Curator (1953), 90 C.L.R. 113 (H.C.A.) 385

Jewelowski v. Propp, [1944] K.B. 510 .... 868, 871

Joel v. Law Union and Insurance Co., [1908] 2 K.B. 863 (C.A.) 333

John Burrows Ltd. v. Subsurface Surveys Ltd., [1968] S.C.R. 607,
   68 D.L.R. (2d) 354 284–85

John E. Dodge Holdings v. 805062 Ontario Ltd. (2003), 63 O.R. (3d) 304,
   223 D.L.R. (4th) 541, [2003] O.J. No. 350 (C.A.) 916

Johnson Matthey Banking v. The State Trading Corp. of India, Ltd., [1984]
   1 Lloyd's Rep. 427 (Q.B.) 824

Johnson v. Agnew, [1980] A.C. 367 (H.L.) 661, 874, 943

Johnson v. Bovee, 574 P.2d 513 (Col. App. 1978) 971

Johnson v. Calvert, 19 Cal. Rep. 2d 494 (1993) 437

Johnson v. Forbes, [1932] 1 D.L.R. 219 (Alta. S.C.A.D.) 232, 233, 237

Johnson v. Lazzarino (1998), 39 O.R. (3d) 724, [1998] O.J. No. 1941,
   63 O.T.C. 151 (Gen. Div.), aff'd (1999), 43 O.R. (3d) 253n, [1999]
   O.J. No. 1431, 122 O.A.C. 311 (C.A.) 444, 465

Johnson v. Musselman, [1917] 2 W.W.R. 444 (Alta. C.A.) 439

Johnson v. Unisys Ltd., [2003] 1 A.C. 518 (H.L.) 878, 882

Johnston Bros. v. Rogers Bros. (1899), 30 O.R. 150, [1899] O.J. No. 130
   (Div. Ct.) 35

Johnston v. St. Andrews Church (Montreal), (1877), 1 S.C.R. 235 792

Johnstone v. Boyes, [1899] 2 Ch. 73 48

Johnstone v. Milling (1886), 16 Q.B.D. 460 (C.A.) 659, 661, 667

Jones v. DeWolfe (1883), 23 N.B.R. 356 (C.A.) 658

Jones v. Jones (1840), 6 M. & W. 84 (Exch.) 173, 179
Jones v. Lee, [1980] I.C.R. 310 (C.A.) 933
Jones v. Merionethshire Permanent Benefit Building Society, [1892]
    1 Ch. 173 439
Jones v. Padavatton, [1969] 2 All E.R. 616 (C.A.) 130, 132
Jones v. Tucker (1916), 53 S.C.R. 431, 30 D.L.R. 228, 10 W.W.R. 1117 928
Jones v. Wate (1839), 5 Bing. N.C. 341 (C.P.) 242
Jorden v. Money (1854), 5 H.L. Cas. 185 278
Joscelyne v. Nissen, [1970] 1 All E.R. 1213 (C.A.) 557, 558
Joseph Constantine S.S. Line Ltd. V. Imperial Smelting Corp. Ltd., [1942]
    A.C. 154 (H.L.) 571
Jostens Canada Limited Ltd. v. Gibsons Studio Ltd., 1999 BCCA 273,
    174 D.L.R. (4th) 351, [1999] B.C.J. No. 972 978
Junior Books Ltd. v. Veitchi Co. Ltd., [1983] 1 A.C. 520 (H.L.) 306
Junkin v. Junkin (1978), 20 O.R. (2d) 118, 86 D.L.R. (3d) 751 (H.C.J.) 419, 991

K.(E.) v. K.(D.), 2003 BCSC 1296, 233 D.L.R. (4th) 101, [2003] B.C.J.
    No. 1961 440
Kamlee Construction Ltd. v. Town of Oakville (1960), 26 D.L.R. (2d) 166,
    [1960] S.C.J. No. 1 660
Kanitz v. Rogers Cable Inc. (2002), 58 O.R. (3d) 299, [2002] O.J. No. 665,
    [2002] O.T.C. 143 (S.C.J.) 81
Kapp v. B.C. Lions Football Club (1967), 64 D.L.R. (2d) 426, 61 W.W.R. 31
    (B.C.S.C.) 932
Karas v. Rowlett (1943), [1944] S.C.R. 1, [1944] 1 D.L.R. 241 870
Karlshamns Oljefabriker v. East Port Navigation Corp., [1982] 1 All E.R.
    208 (Q.B.) 920
Karsales (Harrow) Ltd. v. Wallis, [1956] 1 W.L.R. 936, [1956]
    2 All E.R. 866 (C.A.) 754–55, 765, 766
Kasprzycki v. Abel (1986), 55 O.R. (2d) 536 (Dist. Ct.) 470–71
KBK No. 138 Ventures Ltd. v. Canada Safeway Ltd., 2000 BCCA 295,
    185 D.L.R. (4th) 650, [2000] B.C.J. No. 938 595
Kearley v. Thomson (1890), 24 Q.B.D. 742 (C.A.) 438, 472
Keefe v. Fort (1978), 27 N.S.R. (2d) 353, 89 D.L.R. (3d) 275, [1978]
    N.S.J. No. 554 (C.A.) 766
Keelan v. Norray Distributing Ltd. (1967) 62 D.L.R. (2d) 466,
    60 W.W.R. 129 (Man. Q.B.) 765
Keir v. Leeman (1844), 6 Q.B. 308, 115 E.R. 118, aff'd (1845), 9 Q.B. 371,
    115 E.R. 1315 (Ex. Ch.) 439, 440
Kellogg Brown & Root Inc. v. Aerotech Herman Nelson Inc.,
    2004 MBCA 63, 238 D.L.R. (4th) 594, [2004] M.J. No. 181 342
Kelly v. Mack Canada Inc. (1988), 66 O.R. (2d) 68, 53 D.L.R. (4th) 476,
    [1988] O.J. No. 1436 (C.A.) 232
Kelly v. Watson (1921), 61 S.C.R. 482, 57 D.L.R. 363, [1921] 1 W.W.R. 958 102
Kemp v. McWilliams (1978), 87 D.L.R. (3d) 544, [1978] S.J. No. 195
    (C.A.) 985–86

Kempling v. Hearthstone Manor Corp. (1996), 184 A.R. 321, 137 D.L.R.
(4th) 12, [1996] A.J. No. 654 (C.A.) 876
Kencor Holdings Ltd. v. Saskatchewan, [1991] 6 W.W.R. 717, [1991]
S.J. No. 439, 96 Sask. R. 171 (Q.B.)... 149, 741
Kendrick v. Barkey (1907), 9 O.W.R. 356, [1907] O.J. No. 288 (H.C.J.)............. 304
Keneric Tractor Sales Ltd. v. Langille, [1987] 2 S.C.R. 440, 43 D.L.R.
(4th) 171, [1987] S.C.J. No. 61 824
Kennedy v. Spence (1911), 24 O.L.R. 535, [1911] O.J. No. 99 (H.C.J.) 940
Kentucky Fried Chicken v. Scott's Food Service Inc., [1998] O.J. No. 4368,
114 O.A.C. 357, 41 B.L.R. (2d) 42 (C.A.) 712
Kerridge v. Simmonds (1906), 4 C.L.R. 253 (A.H.C.) 439, 440
Kesarmal S/O Letchman Das v. N.K.V. Valliappa Chettiar S/O Nagappa
Chettiar, [1954] 1 W.L.R. 380 (P.C.) 369
Kesmat Investments Inc. v. Industrial Canadian Indemnity Co. (1985),
70 N.S.R. (2d) 341, [1985] N.S.J. No. 109, 21 C.L.R. 171 (S.C.A.D.)... 582, 590
Khazzaka v. Commercial Union Assurance Co. of Canada (2002),
66 O.R. (3d) 390, [2002] O.J. No. 3110, 162 O.A.C. 293 (C.A.)................ 895
Kinbauri Gold v. IAMGOLD International African Mining Gold Corp.
(2004), 246 D.L.R. (4th) 595, [2004] O.J. No. 4568, 192 O.A.C. 24
(C.A.) 874
Kinetic Construction Ltd. v. Comox-Strathcona (Regional District),
2004 BCCA 485, 245 D.L.R. (4th) 262, [2004] B.C.J. No. 2247................ 150
King v. Walmar Ventures Ltd. (1986), 10 B.C.L.R. (2d) 15, [1986]
B.C.J. No. 597, 38 C.C.L.T. 51 (C.A.) 340
King's Norton Metal Co. Ltd. v. Edridge, Merrett & Co. Limited (1897),
14 T.L.R. 98 (C.A.)..511
Kingshott v. Brunskill (1952), [1953] O.W.N. 133, [1952] O.J. No. 312
(C.A.) 432, 462, 466, 469
Kingswood Estate Co. v. Anderson (1962), [1963] 2 Q.B. 169, [1962]
3 All E.R. 593 (C.A.)..175
Kingu v. Walmar Ventures Ltd. (1986), 10 B.C.L.R. (2d) 15, [1986]
B.C.J. No. 597, 38 C.C.L.T. 51 (C.A.).. 351
Kinzie v. Harper (1908), 15 O.L.R. 582, [1908] O.J. No. 165 (Div. Ct.)...... 173, 179
Kiriri Cotton Co. Ltd. v. Dewani, [1960] A.C. 192 (P.C.) 470
Kitimat (District) v. Alcan, Inc., 2005 BCSC 44, 250 D.L.R. (4th) 144,
[2005] B.C.J. No. 58..316
Kleinwort Benson Limited v. Lincoln City Council (1998), [1999]
2 A.C. 349, [1998] 4 All E.R. 513 (H.L.) 19, 20
Kleinwort Benson Ltd. v. Malaysia Mining Corp. Bhd., [1989]
1 All E.R. 785 (C.A.), rev'g [1988] 1 All E.R. 714 (Q.B.), leave
to appeal to H.L. refused [1989] 1 All E.R. 785 (C.A.) 118–20
Kloepfer Wholesale Hardward & Automotive Co. v. Roy, [1952]
2 S.C.R. 465, [1952] 3 D.L.R. 705.. 654
Kloepfer Wholesale Hardware & Automotive Co. v. Roy, [1952]
2 S.C.R. 465, [1952] 3 D.L.R. 705..667, 913

Knight Sugar Co. v. Webster, [1930] S.C.R. 518, [1930] 4 D.L.R. 343 727
Knight v. Cushing (1912), 1 D.L.R. 331 (Alta. S.C.) 170
Knowles v. Anchorage Holdings Co. Ltd. (1964), 43 D.L.R. (2d) 300,
    46 W.W.R. 173 (B.C.S.C.)... 765
Knowlton Realty Ltd. v. Wyder (1971), 23 D.L.R. (3d) 69, [1972]
    1 W.W.R. 713 (B.C.S.C.) 127
Knox v. Bunch (1913), 11 D.L.R. 377 (Alta. S.C.T.D.) 328
Knupp v. Bell (1968), 67 D.L.R. (2d) 256 (Sask C.A.), aff'g (1966),
    58 D.L.R. (2d) 466 (Sask. Q.B.)..................................406, 408, 409, 419, 935
Knutson v. Bourkes Syndicate, [1941] S.C.R. 419, [1941]
    3 D.L.R. 593 .... 371, 374–75, 381
Kocotis v. D'Angelo (1957), [1958] O.R. 104, 13 D.L.R. (2d) 69 (C.A.) 461
Koe v. Earl (1993), 82 Man. R. (2d) 297, [1993] M.J. No. 52 (Q.B.) 471
Koffman v. Fischtein (1984), 49 O.R. (2d) 124, 14 D.L.R. (4th) 380,
    35 R.P.R. 257 (H.C.J.), var'd (1986), 53 O.R. (2d) 671 (C.A.)...................... 262
Kopec v. Pyret (1987), 36 D.L.R. (4th) 1, [1987] 3 W.W.R. 449, [1987]
    S.J. No. 204 (C.A.) 823
Kopij v. Metropolitan Toronto (Municipality) (1996), 29 O.R. (3d) 752,
    [1996] O.J. No. 2408, 8 O.T.C. 86 (Gen. Div.)................................ 876
Korogonas v. Andrew (1993), [1994] 2 W.W.R. 173, [1993] A.J. No. 811,
    14 Alta. L.R. (3d) 153 (C.A.) 54, 61
Koufos v. Czarmikow (C.) (The Heron II) (1967), [1969] 1 A.C. 350,
    [1967] 3 All E.R. 686 (H.L.) 857–58, 864
Krawchuk v. Ulrychova (1996), 188 A.R. 372, 40 Alta. L.R. (3d) 196,
    [1996] A.J. No. 579 (Prov. Ct.)....................................625, 633, 635
Krell v. Henry, [1903] 2 K.B. 740 (C.A.) 566, 575, 579, 580, 585
Kuddus v. Chief Constable of Leicestershire Constabulary (2001),
    [2001] UKHL 29, [2002] 2 A.C. 122 (H.L.)................................ 879
Kupchak v. Dayson Holdings Co. Ltd. (1965), 53 D.L.R. (2d) 482,
    53 W.W.R. 65 (B.C.C.A.)..................................341, 342, 344, 346, 347, 403
Kutsenko v. Wasilenko (1959), 19 D.L.R. (2d) 665 (Sask. C.A.) 435
Kuzych v. Stewart, [1944] 4 D.L.R. 775 (B.C.S.C.)................................ 869

L. Schuler A.G. v. Wickman Machine Tool Sales Ltd., [1972]
    2 All E.R. 1173 (C.A.), aff'd (1973), [1974] A.C. 235, [1973]
    2 All E.R. 39 (H.L.)..................................637–38, 648, 721-22
L.C.D.H. Audio Visual Ltd. v. I.S.T.S. Verbatim Ltd., [1988] O.J. No. 633,
    40 B.L.R. 128 (H.C.), aff'd. (Sept. 11, 1991, Doc. No. C.A. 425/88).............. 98
L.K. Oil & Gas Ltd. v. Canalands Energy Corp. (1989), 98 A.R. 161,
    60 D.L.R. (4th) 490, [1989] A.J. No. 577 (C.A.), leave to appeal
    to S.C.C. refused (1990), 103 A.R. 240n, 65 D.L.R. (4th) viii,
    [1990] 1 W.W.R. lxxi (S.C.C.)..331
Lac Minerals Ltd. v. International Corona Resources Ltd., [1989]
    2 S.C.R. 574, 61 D.L.R. (4th) 14, [1989] S.C.J. No. 83 137
Lacroix Bros. & Co. Ltd. v. Cook, [1926] 4 D.L.R. 747 (Sask. C.A.)..............984
Lake v. Bayliss, [1974] 1 W.L.R. 1073 (H.C.).. 976

Lamont v. Canadian Transfer Co. Ltd. (1909), 19 O.L.R. 291, [1909]
O.J. No. 127 (C.A.) 185
Lampel v. Berger (1917), 38 D.L.R. 47 (Ont. S.C.) 447
Lampleigh v. Braithwait (1615), Hobart 105, 80 E.R. 255 (K.B.) 233
Lancashire Loans Ltd. v. Black, [1934] 1 K.B. 380 .... 386, 990
Landmark of Thornhill Ltd. v. Jacobson (1995), 25 O.R. (3d) 628, [1995]
O.J. No. 2819, 85 O.A.C. 179 (C.A.) 917
Landymore v. Hardy and White Rose Properties Ltd. (1991), 110 N.S.R.
(2d) 2, [1991] N.S.J. No. 533, 21 R.P.R. (2d) 174 (S.C.T.D.) 795
Langen & Wind Ltd. v. Bell, [1972] Ch. 685 928
Langley Lo-Cost Builders Ltd. v. 474835 B.C. Ltd., 2000 BCCA 365,
[2000] 7 W.W.R. 46, [2000] B.C.J. No. 1187 712
Langston v. Langston (1834), 2 Cl. & F. 194, 5 E.R. 908 (H.L.) 728
Lanka Contracting Ltd. v. Brant County Board of Education (1986),
54 O.R. (2d) 414, 26 D.L.R. (4th) 708, [1986] O.J. No. 234 (C.A.) 69
Lanner v. Palace Theatre (Ltd.) (1893), 9 T.L.R. 162 (Ch.) 953
Lapointe v. Messier (1913), 49 S.C.R. 271, 17 D.L.R. 347 482
Larkin v. Gardiner (1895), 27 O.R. 125, [1895] O.J. No. 83 (Div. Ct.) 67
Larrinaga v. Société Franco-Américaine des Phosphates de Medulla,
Paris (1922), 29 Com. Cas. 1, [1923] All E.R. Rep. 1 (H.L.) 577, 584
Lasenby v. Lamp Holdings & Developments Ltd., (1980), 29 O.R.
(2d) 794, 117 D.L.R. (3d) 181(Div. Ct.) 464
Latimer v. Fontaine (1905), 2 W.L.R. 191 (N.W.T.S.C.).............................. 450
Laurence v. Lexcourt Holdings Ltd., [1978] 2 All E.R. 810, [1978]
1 W.L.R. 1128 (Ch.) 540
Lavarack v. Woods of Colchester Ltd., [1967] 1 Q.B. 278 (C.A.) 825
Laverty v. Eastern Sales Ltd. (1955), 37 M.P.R. 254 (N.B.S.C.A.D.).................... 990
Lavine v. Independent Builders Ltd., [1932] 4 D.L.R. 569 (Ont. C.A.).............. 940
Lazard Brothers & Co. Ltd. v. Fairfield Properties Co. (Mayfair) Ltd.
(1977), 121 Sol. Jo. 793 (Ch.) 939
Lazarenko v. Barowsky Estate, [1966] S.C.R. 556, 57 D.L.R. (2d) 577............. 134
Lazenby Garages v. Wright, [1976] 1 W.L.R. 459 (C.A.)..................................817
Le Mesurier v. Andrus (1986), 54 O.R. (2d) 1, 25 D.L.R. (4th) 424,
[1986] O.J. No. 2371 (C.A.), leave to appeal to S.C.C. refused,
[1986] 2 S.C.R. v, 63 O.R. (2d) x, 74 N.R. 239n.............................789, 941–42
Leaf v. International Galleries, [1950] 2 K.B. 86 (C.A.)......................345, 347, 695
Lebeaupin v. Richard Crispin & Co., [1920] 2 K.B. 714............................ 600, 602
Lee v. Occo Developments Ltd. (1996), 181 N.B.R. (2d) 241, [1996]
N.B.J. No. 438, 5 R.P.R. (3d) 203 (C.A.) 903
Lee v. Showmen's Guild of Great Britain, [1952] 2 Q.B. 329 (C.A.).................. 440
Leeds Industrial Co-operative Society Ltd. v. Slack, [1924] A.C. 851
(H.L.) 870, 873
Lee-Parker v. Izzet (No. 2), [1972] 1 W.L.R. 775 (Ch.).................................. 107
Lefkowitz v. Great Minneapolis Surplus Store, 86 N.W.2d 689
(Minn. S.C. 1957) 36

Leggatt v. Brown (1899), 30 O.R. 225 (H.C.J.) 439

Legh v. Lillie (1860), 6 H. & N. 165, 158 E.R. 69 (Ex.) 958

Lehndorff Canadian Pension Properties Ltd. v. Davis Management Ltd. (1989),
59 D.L.R. (4th) 1, [1989] 5 W.W.R. 481, [1989] B.C.J. No. 990 (C.A.) 625

Leitch Gold Mines Ltd. v. Texas Gulf Sulphur Co. (1968), [1969] 1 O.R. 469,
3 D.L.R. (3d) 161 (Ont. H.C.J.) 711, 714

Leitz v. Saskatoon Drug & Stationery Co. Ltd.; T.C. Distributers (1970) Ltd.,
Third Party (1980), 112 D.L.R. (3d) 106, 4 Sask. R. 35, [1980]
S.J. No. 197 (Q.B.) 305

Lemenda Trading Co. v. African Middle East Petroleum Co., [1988] Q.B. 448 ... 446

Leo Gushue Construction v. Thistle (1990), 8 Nfld. & P.E.I.R. 220, [1990]
N.J. No. 62, 38 C.L.R. 214 (S.C.) 969

Leopold v. Leopold (2000), 51 O.R. (3d) 275, [2000] O.J. No. 4604,
12 R.F.L. (5th) 118 (S.C.J.) 410

Les Affréteurs Réunis Société Anonyme v. Leopold Walford (London) Ltd.,
[1919] A.C. 801 (H.L.) 304

Lesters Leather & Skin Co. Ltd. v. Home & Overseas Brokers Ltd. (1948),
64 T.L.R. 569 (C.A.) 868

L'Estrange v. F. Graucob Ltd., [1934] 2 K.B. 394 (C.A.) 190

Letkeman v. Zimmermann (1977), [1978] 1 S.C.R. 1097, 79 D.L.R. (3d) 508,
17 N.R. 564 .... 431, 472

Levison v. Patent Steam Carpet Cleaning Co. Ltd., [1978] Q.B. 69 (C.A.) 766

Levy and Levy v. Rodewalt (1959), 18 D.L.R. (2d) 77 (Alta. S.C.A.D.).............. 940

Lewis v. Averay, [1972] 1 Q.B. 198 (C.A.).. 514, 539, 552

Lewis v. Lord Lechmere (1722), 10 Mod. 503, 88 E.R. 828 (K.B.).............. 917, 925

Lieberman v. Roseland Theatre Ltd., [1946] 1 D.L.R. 342 (N.S.S.C.)................ 590

Liesbosch Dredger v. S.S. Edison [1933] A.C. 449 (H.L.) 869

Lightburn v. Belmont Sales Ltd. (1969), 6 D.L.R. (3d) 692, 69 W.W.R. 734
(B.C.S.C.) 766, 967

Lindsay Petroleum Co. v. Hurd (1874), L.R. 5 P.C. 221 .... 345–46, 939, 989

Lindsay v. Sutton, [1947] O.W.N. 951 (H.C.J.) rev'd on other grounds
[1948] O.W.N. 252 (C.A.) 969

Lindsey v. Heron & Co. (1921), 50 O.L.R. 1, 64 D.L.R. 92, [1921]
O.J. No. 75 (S.C.A.D.) 499, 500

Linton v. Royal Bank of Canada, [1967] 1 O.R. 315, 60 D.L.R. (2d) 398
(H.C.J.) 263

Lister v. Romford Ice & Cold Storage Co. Ltd., [1957] A.C. 555 (H.L.)......743, 744

Littlewoods Organisation Ltd. v. Harris, [1978] 1 All E.R. 1026 (C.A.).... 452, 455

Liverpool City Council v. Irwin, [1976] Q.B. 319 (C.A.), var'd [1977]
A.C. 239 (H.L.) 733, 736, 743

Livingston v. Evans, [1925] 4 D.L.R. 769 (Alta. S.C.) 53

Llanelly Railway & Dock Co. v. London & North Western Railway Co.
(1875), L.R. 7 H.L. 550 739

Lloyd v. Lloyd (1837), 2 My. & Cr. 192, 40 E.R. 613 (Ch.) 716

Lloyds and Scottish Finance Ltd. v. Modern Cars and Caravans (Kingston)
Ltd., [1966] 1 Q.B. 764 868

Lloyds Bank v. Bundy, [1975] Q.B. 326 (C.A.)...............................365–67, 387, 424

Lloyd's v. Harper (1880), 16 Ch. D. 290 (C.A.) 294, 304

Lockett v. Norman-Wright, [1925] Ch. 56... 127

Lodder v. Slowey, [1904] A.C. 442 (P.C.)... 969

Lodge v. National Union Investment Co. Ltd., [1907] 1 Ch. 300 474

London & Lancashire Fire Insurance Co. Ltd. v. Bolands Ltd., [1924]
   A.C. 836 (H.L.) 716

London Assurance v. Mansel (1879), 11 Ch. D. 303 333

London Drugs Ltd. v. Kuehne & Nagel International Ltd., [1992]
   3 S.C.R. 299, 97 D.L.R. (4th) 261, [1992] S.C.J. No. 84.......... 299, 300, 308–9,
   311, 315, 317, 743

London Loan & Savings Co. v. Brickenden, [1934] 3 D.L.R. 465, [1934]
   2 W.W.R. 545 (P.C.) 853

London, Chatham and Dover Rwy. Co. v. South Eastern Rwy. Co., [1893]
   A.C. 429 (H.L.) 819

Long v. Bowring (1864), 33 Beav. 585, 55 E.R. 496 (M.R.) 957

Long v. Lloyd, [1958] 1 W.L.R. 753 (C.A.) 342

Long v. Smith (1911), 23 O.L.R. 121, [1911] O.J. No. 111 (H.C.J.) 201

Lord Kennedy v. Panama, New Zealand and Australian Royal Mail Co.
   (Ltd.) (1867), L.R. 2 Q.B. 580 (Q.B.) 29, 531

Lord Strathcona Steamship Co. Ltd. v. Dominion Coal Co. Ltd., [1926]
   A.C. 108 (P.C.) 948

Lovell & Christmas Ltd. v. Wall (1911), 104 L.T. 85 (C.A.)............................... 716

Love's Realty & Financial Services Ltd. v. Coronet Trust (1989),
   94 A.R. 341, 57 D.L.R. (4th) 606, [1989] A.J. No. 214 (C.A.)......................465

Low v. Fry (1935), 152 L.T.R. 585 (K.B.) 173, 179

Lowe v. Suburban Developers Ltd., [1962] O.R. 1029, 35 D.L.R. (2d) 178
   (C.A.) 340

Lucas v. Dixon (1889), 22 Q.B.D. 357 (C.A.) 171

Lumley v. Gye (1853), 2 El. & Bl. 216, 118 E.R. 749 (Q.B.)...............................949

Lumley v. Ravenscroft, [1895] 1 Q.B. 683 (C.A.) 928

Lumley v. Wagner (1852) 1 De G. M. & G. 604, 42 E.R. 687 (Ch.) 949

Luxor (Eastbourne) Ltd. v. Cooper, [1941] A.C. 108 (H.L.) 730

Lyon v. Reed (1844), 13 M. & W. 285, 153 E.R. 118 (Ex.)............................... 823

Lyons v. Multari (2000), 50 O.R. (3d) 526, [2000] O.J. No. 3462,
   136 O.A.C. 281 (C.A.)... 454

Lysaght v. Edwards (1876), 2 Ch. D. 499 593

M v. H., [1999] 2 S.C.R. 3, 171 D.L.R. (4th) 577, [1999] S.C.J. No. 23............. 134

M.(N.) v. A.(A.T.), 2003 BCCA 297, 13 B.C.L.R. (4th) 73, [2003]
   B.C.J. No. 1139.. 292

M. F. Whalen (The) v. Pointe Anne Quarries Ltd. (1921), 63 S.C.R. 109,
   63 D.L.R. 545 ....557, 559

M.J.B. Enterprises Ltd. v. Defence Construction (1951) Ltd., [1999]
   1 S.C.R. 619, 170 D.L.R. (4th) 577, [1999] S.C.J. No. 17...............45, 116, 140,
   149, 737, 741–42

Mabley & Carew Co. v. Borden, 195 N.E. 697 (Ohio 1935).............................. 233
MacDonald v. ADGA Systems International Ltd., [1999] O.J. No. 146,
    117 O.A.C. 95, 41 C.C.E.L. (2d) 5 (C.A.), leave to appeal to S.C.C.
    refused (1999), 127 O.A.C. 396n, [1999] S.C.C.A. No. 147 746
MacDonald v. Soulis, [1925] 2 D.L.R. 926 (N.S.S.C.)..................................... 924
Machtinger v. HOJ Industries Ltd., [1992] 1 S.C.R. 986, 91 D.L.R.
    (4th) 491, [1992] S.C.J. No. 41..730, 743, 744, 806
MacKenzie v. Royal Bank of Canada, [1934] A.C. 468 (P.C.) 329
MacLauchlan v. Soper (1965), 50 M.P.R. 339 (P.E.I.S.C.) 224
MacLeod v. Ruck (1985), 3 B.C.L.R. (2d) 35, [1985] B.C.J. No. 2266 (C.A.) 332
MacNaughton v. Stone (1949), [1949] O.R. 853, [1950] 1 D.L.R. 330 (H.C.J.) 661
Maddison v. Alderson (1883), 8 App. Cas. 467 (H.L.) 175
Madison Developments Ltd. v. Plan Electric Co. (1997), 36 O.R. (3d) 80,
    152 D.L.R. (4th) 653, [1997] O.J. No. 4249 (C.A.), leave to appeal to
    S.C.C. refused (1997), 157 D.L.R. (4th) vii, [1997] S.C.C.A. No. 659 311
Magee v. Pennine Ins., [1969] 2 Q.B. 507, [1969] 2 All E.R. 891 (C.A.)............. 540
Magrath v. Sydenham Mutual Fire Ins. Co., [1923] 3 D.L.R. 44 (Ont. S.C.) 662
Mahoney v. Purnell, [1996] 3 All E.R. 61 (Q.B.) 403, 990
Maier v. E&B Exploration Ltd. (1986), 69 A.R. 239, [1986] 4 W.W.R. 275,
    [1986] A.J. No. 302 (C.A.) 233
Main v. Main, [1955] 2 D.L.R. 588 (B.C.S.C.), aff'd (1956), 2 D.L.R. (2d) 341
    (B.C.C.A.).. 219
Majdpour v. M&B Acquisition Corp. (2001), 56 O.R. (3d) 481, 206 D.L.R.
    (4th) 627, [2001] O.J. No. 4932 (C.A.).. 635, 640
Manchester Diocesan Council for Education v. Commercial & General
    Investments Ltd., [1969] All 3 E.R. 1593 (Ch. D.) 55, 56, 57, 58, 70
Manchester Ship Canal Co. v. Manchester Racecourse Co., [1901] 2 Ch. 37
    (C.A.) 797, 949
Manitoba Development Corporation v. Columbia Forest Products Ltd. (1973),
    43 D.L.R. (3d) 107, [1974] 2 W.W.R. 237, [1973] M.J. No. 64 (Man. C.A.) 714
Manitoba Fisheries Ltd. v. Drake Construction Co. Ltd. (1963), 42 D.L.R.
    (2d) 351 (Man. Q.B.).. 984
Mann v. St. Croix Paper Co. (1912), 5 D.L.R. 596 (N.B.C.A.) 727
Mannpar Enterprises Ltd. v. Canada, 1999 BCCA 239, 173 D.L.R. (4th) 243,
    [1999] B.C.J. No. 850 .... 146, 147, 156
Manulife Bank of Canada v. Conlin, [1996] 3 S.C.R. 415, 139 D.L.R.
    (4th) 426, [1996] S.C.J. No. 101.. 723
Maple Flock Co. Ltd. v. Universal Furniture Products (Wembley) Ltd.,
    [1934] 1 K.B. 148 (C.A.) 635
Marathon Realty Co. v. Toulon Construction Corp. (1987), 80 N.S.R.
    (2d) 390, [1987] N.S.J. No. 310, 45 R.P.R. 233 (S.C.T.D.)........................... 127
Marco Productions Ltd. v. Pagola, [1945] K.B. 111....................................... 953
Maredelanto Compania Naviera SA v. Bergbau-Handel G.m.b.H.
    "The Mihalis Angelos," [1971] 1 Q.B. 164 (C.A.)....................................... 662

Marentette Bros. Ltd. v. City of Sudbury (1974), 3 O.R. (2d) 305,
45 D.L.R. (3d) 321 (C.A.) 738

Mariani v. Lemstra, [2003] O.J. No. 750, 26 C.L.R. (3d) 137 (S.C.J.) 327

Marinangeli v. Marinangeli (2003), 66 O.R. (3d) 40, 228 D.L.R. (4th) 376,
[2003] O.J. No. 2819 (C.A.) 737, 738

Marion White Ltd. v. Frances, [1972] 3 All E.R. 857 (C.A.) 455

Maritime National Fish Ltd. v. Ocean Trawlers, [1935] A.C. 524, [1935]
3 D.L.R. 12, [1935] 2 W.W.R. 606 (P.C.)...577, 597

Mark 7 Development Ltd. v. Peace Holdings Ltd. (1991), 53 B.C.L.R.
(2d) 217, [1991] B.C.J. No. 239, 15 R.P.R. (2d) 101 (C.A.) 677–78

Markland Associates Ltd. v. Lohnes (1973), 11 N.S.R. (2d) 181, 33 D.L.R.
(3d) 493, [1973] N.S.J. No. 160 (S.C.T.D.) 985

Marquest Industries Ltd. v. Willows Poultry Farms Ltd. (1967), 63 D.L.R.
(2d) 753, 61 W.W.R. 227 (B.C.S.C.), rev'd on other grounds (1968),
1 D.L.R. (3d) 513, 66 W.W.R. 477 (B.C.C.A.)... 921

Marquis Camden v. Inland Revenue Commissioners, [1914] 1 K.B. 641 (C.A.) ...716

Marshall v. Bernard Place Corp. (2002), 58 O.R. (3d) 97, [2002] O.J. No. 463,
156 O.A.C. 377 (C.A.).. 791

Marshall v. Canada Permanent Trust Co. (1968), 69 D.L.R. (2d) 260
(Alta. S.C.T.D.) 408, 409, 411–12, 419

Marshall v. Watson Wyatt & Co. (2002), 57 O.R. (3d) 813, 209 D.L.R.
(4th) 411, [2002] O.J. No. 84 (C.A.) 886

Martel Building Ltd. v. Canada, 2000 SCC 60, [2000] 2 S.C.R. 860,
193 D.L.R. (4th) 1 .... 46, 116, 148, 149, 150, 153–55, 157, 742, 743

Martell v. Consett Iron Co. Ltd., [1955] Ch. 363 (C.A.) 442

Martens v. Burden (1974), 45 D.L.R. (3d) 123, [1974] 3 W.W.R. 522
(Alta. S.C.T.D.) 941

Martin v. Haubner (1896), 26 S.C.R. 142...170

Martin v. Meles, 60 N.E. 397 (Mass. 1901) 229

Martin-Baker Aircraft Co. Ltd. v. Canadian Flight Equipment Ltd., [1955]
2 Q.B. 556 740

Martselos Services Ltd. v. Arctic College (1994), 111 D.L.R. (4th) 65, [1994]
3 W.W.R. 73, [1994] N.W.T.J. No. 4 (C.A.), leave to appeal to S.C.C.
refused, [1994] 3 S.C.R. viii, [1994] S.C.C.A. No. 130 148

Marvco Color Research Ltd. v. Harris, [1982] 2 S.C.R. 774, 141 D.L.R.
(3d) 577, 45 N.R. 302... 520, 523

Marwood v. Charter Credit Corp. (1971), 2 N.S.R. (2d) 743, 20 D.L.R.
(3d) 563, [1971] N.S.J. No. 117 (S.C.A.D.)... 542

Maschinenfabrik Seydelmann K-G. v. Presswood Bros. Ltd. (1965),
53 D.L.R. (2d) 224 (Ont. C.A.), rev'g on other grounds (1964),
47 D.L.R. (2d) 214 (Ont. H.C.J.) 464, 481, 482

Maskell v. Horner, [1915] 3 K.B. 106... 370

Mason v. Clouet, [1924] A.C. 980 (P.C.)... 980

Mason v. Freedman, [1958] S.C.R. 483, 14 D.L.R. (2d) 529 ....789, 941

Mason v. Provident Clothing & Supply Co., [1913] A.C. 724
(H.L.) 452, 455, 488, 491

Massey v. Midland Bank plc, [1995] 1 All E.R. 929 (C.A.) 400, 401

Mastercraft Construction Corp. v. Baker (1978), 19 O.R. (2d) 652,
    86 D.L.R. (3d) 121, 3 R.P.R. 65 (H.C.J.), aff'd (1979), 26 O.R.
    (2d) 389n 104 D.L.R. (3d) 767n (C.A.) 662

Matheson v. Smiley, [1932] 2 D.L.R. 787 (Man. C.A.) 236

Mathias v. Yetts, (1882), 46 L.T. (N.S.) 497 (C.A.) 331

Matson v. Emory, 676 P.2d 1029 (Wash. App. 1984) 797

Matsoukis v. Priestman & Co., [1915] 1 K.B. 681 600

Matthews v. McVeigh, [1954] O.R. 278, [1954] 2 D.L.R. 338 (C.A.) 936

Maughan v. International Harvester Co. of Canada Ltd. (1980), 38 N.S.R.
    (2d) 101, 112 D.L.R. (3d) 243, [1980] N.S.J. No. 380 (S.C.A.D.) 232

May and Butcher Ltd. v. The King, [1934] 2 K.B. 17 (H.L.) 93, 94, 103

McAllister v. Cardinal (1964), [1965] 1 O.R. 221, 47 D.L.R. (2d) 313,
    47 C.P.R. 28 (H.C.J.) 449, 450

McCallum v. Proctor (1914), 26 O.W.R. 481, 6 O.W.N. 556, [1914]
    O.J. No. 424 (S.C.A.D.)..331

McCallum v. Zivojinovic (1977), 16 O.R. (2d) 721, 79 D.L.R. (3d) 133,
    2 R.P.R. 164 (C.A.), leave to appeal to S.C.C. refused (1977),
    19 N.R. 539 (S.C.C.).. 661

McCannell v. Mabee McLaren Motors Ltd. (1926), 36 B.C.R. 369, [1926]
    1 D.L.R. 282, [1926] B.C.J. No. 102 (C.A.) 301–2

McCarthy v. Kenny, [1939] 3 D.L.R. 556 (Ont. Sup. Ct.) 991

McCauley v. McVey (1979), [1980] 1 S.C.R. 165, 98 D.L.R. (3d) 577,
    27 N.R. 604 687

McCaw v. United Church of Canada (1991), 4 O.R. (3d) 481, 82 D.L.R.
    (4th) 289, [1991] O.J. No. 1225 (C.A.)... 933

McClelland & Stewart Ltd. v. Mutual Life, [1981] 2 S.C.R. 6, 125 D.L.R.
    (3d) 257, 37 N.R. 190...717, 722, 723

McColl-Frontenac Oil Co. v. Saulnier & Saulnier, [1949] 3 D.L.R. 208
    (N.B.S.C.A.D.), leave to appeal to S.C.C. refused, [1949] 3 D.L.R. 777
    (N.B.S.C.A.D.) 935

McCorkell v. McFarlane, [1952] O.W.N. 653, [1952] O.J. No. 186 (H.C.J.)........ 935

McCowan v. McKay (1901), 13 Man. R. 590 (C.A.) 659, 666

McCutcheon v. David MacBrayne Ltd., [1964] 1 All E.R. 430 (H.L.) 186–87

McDonald v. Fellows (1979), 17 A.R. 330, 105 D.L.R. (3d) 434, [1979]
    A.J. No. 841 (C.A.) 473

McDonald v. Murray (1883), 2 O.R. 573, [1883] O.J. No. 249 (H.C.J. C.P.)....... 102

McDougall Segur Exploration Co. of Canada Ltd. v. Solloway Mills & Co.
    Ltd., [1931] 2 W.W.R. 516 (Alta. S.C.) 924

McFarlane v. Daniell (1938), 38 S.R. (N.S.W.) 337 (Dist. Ct. App.) 484

McGarry v. Richards, Ackroyd & Gall Ltd., [1954] 2 D.L.R. 367 (B.C.S.C.)..... 841

McGrath v. MacLean (1979), 22 O.R. (2d) 784, 95 D.L.R. (3d) 144 (C.A.),
    leave to appeal to S.C.C. refused April 7, 1979 333

McGrath v. Shah (1987), 57 P. & C.R. 452 (H.C.)................................... 695

McGregor v. McGregor (1888), 21 Q.B.D. 424 (C.A.) 168, 241

McIntyre Estate v. Ontario (Attorney General) (2002), 61 O.R. (3d) 257, 218 D.L.R. (4th) 193, [2002] O.J. No. 3417 (C.A.), rev'g (2001), 53 O.R. (3d) 137, 198 D.L.R. (4th) 165, [2001] O.J. No. 713 (S.C.J.)........ 442, 443, 444

McIntyre v. Spiernburg (1979), 41 N.S.R. (2d) 584, [1979] N.S.J. No. 771 (S.C.T.D.)................171

McIsaac v. Sun Life Assurance Co. of Canada, 1999 BCCA 299, 173 D.L.R. (4th) 649, [1999] B.C.J. No. 1120 896

McKay v. Clow, [1941] S.C.R. 643, [1941] 4 D.L.R. 273 390

McKenzie v. Bank of Montreal (1975), 7 O.R. (2d) 521, 55 D.L.R. (3d) 641 (H.C.J.), aff'd (1976), 12 O.R. (2d) 719, 70 D.L.R. (3d) 113 (C.A.)........416, 425

McKenzie v. Dwight (1885), 11 O.A.R. 381, [1885] O.J. No. 112 (C.A.) 329

McKenzie v. Walsh (1920), 61 S.C.R. 312, 57 D.L.R. 24, [1921] 1 W.W.R. 1017 172

McKinlay Motors Ltd. v. Honda Canada Inc. (1989), 80 Nfld. & P.E.I.R. 200, [1989] N.J. No. 332, 46 B.L.R. 62 (S.C.T.D.) 791

McKinney v. McKinney, [1980] B.C.J. No. 56, 17 R.F.L. (2d) 308 (S.C.)..............130

McKinnon v. McPherson (1910), 44 N.S.R. 402 (C.A.) 386

McKnight v. Robertson (1910), 17 O.W.R. 454, [1910] O.J. No. 435 (C.A.)........ 715

McLellan v. Winston (1886), 12 O.R. 431, [1886] O.J. No. 70 (H.C.J. (C.P.)) 666

McMahon v. Coffee (1844), 1 U.C.R. 110, [1844] O.J. No. 48 (Q.B.)..............986

McMaster University v. Wilchar Construction Ltd., [1971] 3 O.R. 801, 22 D.L.R. (3d) 9 (H.C.J.), aff'd (1973), 12 O.R. (2d) 512n, 69 D.L.R. (3d) 400n (C.A.) 502, 506, 541

McMillen v. Chapman and S.S. Kresge Co. Ltd., [1953] O.R. 399, [1953] 2 D.L.R. 671 (C.A.) 561

McMurray Imperial Enterprises Ltd. v. Brimstone Acquisitions and Asset Management Inc. (1997), 210 A.R. 97, [1997] A.J. No. 985 (Q.B.)..............916

McMurray v. Spicer (1868), L.R. 5 Eq. 527..............173

McNamara Construction Co. v. Newfoundland Transshipment Ltd. (2002), 213 Nfld. & P.E.I.R. 1, [2002] N.J. No. 127, 20 C.L.R. (3d) 1 (S.C.T.D.).....904

McRae v. Commonwealth Disposals Commission (1951), 84 C.L.R. 377 (A.H.C.)..............527, 832, 839, 849

MDS Health Group Ltd. v. King Street Medical Arts Centre Ltd., [1994] O.J. No. 630, 12 B.L.R. (2d) 209, 55 C.P.R. (3d) 360 (Gen. Div.).......... 792–93

Mechanical Pin Resetter Co. Ltd. v. Canadian Acme Screw & Gear Ltd. (1970), [1971] S.C.R. 628, 15 D.L.R. (3d) 475, 65 C.P.R. 150..............715

Medina v. Stoughton (1700), 1 Salk. 210, 91 E.R. 1297 (K.B.) 692

Meditek Laboratory Services Ltd. v. Purolator Courier Ltd. (1995), 125 D.L.R. (4th) 738, [1995] 6 W.W.R. 738, [1995] M.J. No. 233 (C.A.) 724, 776

Melady v. Jenkins Steamship Co. (1909), 18 O.L.R. 251, [1909] O.J. No. 194 (Div. Ct.)..............73

Melanson v. Dominion of Canada General Insurance Co., [1934] 2 D.L.R. 459 (N.B.S.C.A.D.)..............658

Mellco Developments Ltd. v. Portage La Prairie (City), 2002 MBCA 125, 222 D.L.R. (4th) 67, [2002] M.J. No. 381 ....47, 116–17, 118, 156

Menard v. Genereux (1982), 39 O.R. (2d) 55, 138 D.L.R. (3d) 273 (H.C.J)........431

Mendelssohn v. Normand Ltd. (1969), [1970] 1 Q.B. 177, [1969]
3 W.L.R. 139, [1969] 2 All E.R. 1215 (C.A.)........................185, 202 752, 776
Mennonite Land Sales v. Friesen (1921), 62 D.L.R. 344 (Sask. K.B.)..................918
Merritt v. Merritt, [1970] 2 All E.R. 760 (C.A.) 130–31, 434
Mertens v. Home Freeholds Company, [1921] 2 K.B. 526 (C.A.) 865
Mesa Operating Ltd. Partnership v. Amoco Canada Resources Ltd. (1992),
129 A.R. 177, [1992] A.J. No. 287 (Q.B.), aff'd (1994), 149 A.R. 187,
19 Alta. L.R. (3d) 38, [1994] A.J. No. 201 (C.A.) 788–89
Metropolitan Electric Supply Co. Limited v. Ginder, [1902] 2 Ch. 799 ....948, 949
Metropolitan Store (MTS) Ltd. v. Manitoba Food & Commercial Workers,
Local 832, [1987] 1 S.C.R. 110, 38 D.L.R. (4th) 321, [1987] S.C.J. No. 6.... 955
Metropolitan Trust Co. of Canada v. Pressure Concrete Services Ltd.,
[1973] 3 O.R. 629, 37 D.L.R. (3d) 649 (H.C.J.), aff'd (1975), 9 O.R.
(2d) 375, 60 D.L.R. (3d) 431 (C.A.).. 739
Metropolitan Water Board v. Dick, Kerr & Co. Ltd., [1918] A.C. 119
(H.L.) 566, 574
Meyer v. Davies, [1989] B.C.J. No. 913, 45 B.L.R. 92 (S.C.) 127
Midland Railway Co. v. Ontario Rolling Mills (1882), 2 O.R. 1,
[1882] O.J. No. 63 (H.C.J. (Q.B.D.)), aff'd (1884), 10 O.A.R. 677,
[1884] O.J. No. 93 (C.A.) 655
Milani v. Banks (1997), 32 O.R. (3d) 557, 145 D.L.R. (4th) 55, [1997]
O.J. No. 1171 (C.A.) 487, 488
Miles v. New Zealand Alford Estate Co. (1886), 32 Ch. D. 266................. 226, 227
Miller v. Emcer Products Ltd., [1956] Ch. 304 726
Miller v. Karlinski (1945), 62 T.L.R. 85 (C.A.) 484
Miller v. Toews (1990), [1991] 2 W.W.R. 604, [1990] M.J. No. 643,
70 Man.R. (2d) 4 (C.A.) 955
Milliken v. Young, [1929] 3 D.L.R. 64 (Sask. C.A.)................................716, 717
Mills v. Continental Bag & Paper Co. (1918), 45 D.L.R. 389 (Ont. S.C.A.D.) ... 716
Mills v. Edmonton (City) (1987), 83 A.R. 1, 46 D.L.R. (4th) 26, [1987]
A.J. No. 950 (Q.B.) 848
Mills v. Gill, [1952] O.R. 257, [1952] 3 D.L.R. 27, 16 C.P.R. 46 (H.C.J.) 454, 958
Mira Design Co. Ltd. v. Seascape Holdings Ltd., [1982] 4 W.W.R. 97,
36 B.C.L.R. 355, [1982] B.C.J. No. 51 (S.C.) 486
Mitchell v. Homfray (1881), 8 Q.B.D. 587 (C.A.).. 385
Mitchell v. Mortgage Company of Canada (1919), 59 S.C.R. 90,
48 D.L.R. 420, [1919] 3 W.W.R. 324 172
Mitsui & Co. (Canada) Ltd. v. Royal Bank of Canada, [1995] 2 S.C.R. 187,
123 D.L.R. (4th) 449, [1995] S.C.J. No. 37 .... 99, 100
Mitz v. Wiseman (1971), [1972] 1 O.R. 189, 22 D.L.R. (3d) 513 (H.C.J.) 936
Mizon v. Pohoretzky (1917), 40 O.L.R. 239, [1917] O.J. No. 77 (S.C.A.D.)........ 450
Modular Windows of Canada v. Command Construction (1984),
11 C.L.R. 131 (Ont. H.C.J.)... 246
Mohamed v. Alaga & Co. (1998), [1998] EWCA Civ 1654, [1999]
3 All E.R. 699 (C.A.)... 471
Molsons Bank v. Cranston (1918), 45 D.L.R. 316 (Ont. S.C.A.D.) 266

Monnickendam v. Leanse (1923), 39 T.L.R. 445 (K.B.) 174, 179

Montague v. Bank of Nova Scotia (2004), 69 O.R. (3d) 87, [2004]
    O.J. No. 13, 180 O.A.C. 381 (C.A.) 887

Montefiore v. Menday Motor Components Co., [1918] 2 K.B. 241 445

Monteith v. Calladine (1964), 47 D.L.R. (2d) 332, 49 W.W.R. 641
    (B.C.C.A.) 442, 443

Monticchio v. Torcema Construction Ltd. (1979), 26 O.R. (2d) 305,
    102 D.L.R. (3d) 462, 8 B.L.R. 225 (H.C.J.) 474

Montreal Trust Co. of Canada v. Birmingham Lodge Ltd. (1995),
    24 O.R. (3d) 97, 125 D.L.R. (4th) 193, [1995] O.J. No. 1609 (C.A.)............ 715

Montreal Trust Co. v. Montreal Trust Co. of Canada (1988), 48 D.L.R.
    (4th) 385, [1988] B.C.J. No. 410, 24 B.C.L.R. (2d) 238 (C.A.) 955

Moojelsky v. Rexnord Canada (1989), 96 A.R. 91, [1989] A.J. No. 313
    (Q.B.) 170, 171

Morgan v. Griffith (1871), L.R. 6 Ex. 70 200

Morgan v. Hudson Bay Mining & Smelting Co., [1930] 2 D.L.R. 587
    (Man. K.B.) 717

Morgan v. McFee (1908), 18 O.L.R. 30 (C.A.) 440

Morin v. Anger (1930), 66 O.L.R. 327, [1930] O.J. No. 50 (S.C.A.D.) 340

Morrell v. Cserzy, [2002] O.J. No. 698, [2002] O.T.C. 147, 14 C.L.R.
    (3d) 94 (Ont. S.C.J.) 465

Morris v. Baron & Co., [1918] A.C. 1 (H.L.) 247

Morrison Lamothe Inc. v. Bedok (1986), 55 O.R. (2d) 129, 29 D.L.R.
    (4th) 255, [1986] O.J. No. 518 (H.C.J.) 285

Morrison v. Coast Finance Ltd., (1965), 55 D.L.R. (2d) 710,
    54 W.W.R. 257 (B.C.C.A.) 406, 407–8, 409, 415–16, 417–18, 420

Morrison-Knudsen Co. Inc. v. British Columbia Hydro & Power Authority
    (1978), 85 D.L.R. (3d) 186, [1978] 4 W.W.R. 193 (B.C.C.A.) 970

Morton Construction Co. Ltd. v. City of Hamilton (1961), [1962] O.R. 154,
    31 D.L.R. (2d) 323 (C.A.) 375

Morton v. Morton, [1942] 1 All E.R. 273 (P.D.) 101

Moschi v. Lep Air Services Ltd., [1973] A.C. 331 (H.L.) 643–44, 654

Moscovitch Estate v. South End Development Co. Ltd. (1968), 4 N.S.R.
    (1965–69) 182 (S.C.A.D.), aff'd [1968] S.C.R. vi 74

Mountford v. Scott, [1974] 1 All E.R. 248 (Ch.), aff'd [1975] Ch. D. 258,
    [1975] 1 All E.R. 198 (C.A.) 235, 935

Mule v. Royal Bank of Canada (1997), 156 N.S.R. (2d) 347, 147 D.L.R.
    (4th) 268, [1997] N.S.J. No. 13 (C.A.) 471

Multi-Malls Inc. v. Tex-Mall Properties Ltd. (1980), 28 O.R. (2d) 6,
    108 D.L.R. (3d) 399, 9 B.L.R. 240 (H.C.J.), aff'd (1981), 37 O.R.
    (2d) 133, 128 D.L.R. (3d) 192n (C.A.), leave to appeal to S.C.C.
    refused (1982), 41 N.R. 360n (S.C.C.) 680, 739, 788, 848

Mundinger v. Mundinger (1968), [1969] 1 O.R. 606, 3 D.L.R.
    (3d) 338 (C.A.), aff'd [1970] S.C.R. vi, 14 D.L.R. (3d) 256..................409, 410

Munro v. French (1979), 103 D.L.R. (3d) 91, [1979] S.J. No. 276,
    10 R.P.R. 179 (Q.B.) 478

Munroe Equipment Sales Ltd. v. Canadian Forest Products Ltd. (1961),
  29 D.L.R. (2d) 730 (Man. C.A.).. 863
Murphy v. McSorley, [1929] S.C.R. 542, [1929] 4 D.L.R. 247........................... 102
Murray McDermid Holdings Ltd. v. Thater (1982), 42 B.C.L.R. 119,
  [1982] B.C.J. No. 1842 (S.C.) 221, 677
Murray v. Sperry Rand Corp. (1979), 23 O.R. (2d) 456, 96 D.L.R. (3d) 113,
  5 B.L.R. 284 (H.C.J.)...231, 304–5, 691, 694
Mutual Life Assurance v. Evatt, [1971] 1 All E.R. 150 (P.C.) 351

Napier v. National Business Agency Ltd., [1951] 2 All E.R. 264 (C.A.)......431, 484
Nash v. Inman, [1908] 2 K.B. 1 (C.A.)..238
National Bank of Canada v. Digest Reporting Service Limited, [1985]
  6 W.W.R. 481, 35 Man.R. (2d) 284, [1985] M.J. No. 142 (C.A.) 524
National Bank of Canada v. Taylor (1986), 71 A.R. 343, 45 Alta. L.R.
  (2d) 301, [1986] A.J. No. 526 (Q.B.) 524
National Carriers Ltd. v. Panalpina (Northern) Ltd., [1981] A.C. 675
  (H.L.) 580–81, 584, 592–93
National Provincial Bank of England v. Marshall (1888), 40 Ch. D. 112
  (C.A.) 958
National Trust Co. v. Palace Theatre Ltd., [1928] 2 D.L.R. 739
  (Alta. S.C.A.D.) 718
National Westminster Bank plc v. Morgan, [1985] A.C. 686, [1985]
  1 All E.R. 821 (H.L.) 385, 388–89, 390–91, 425
Natuk v. Kawula (1979), 104 D.L.R. (3d) 288, 1 Man.R. (2d) 25,
  [1979] M.J. No. 152 (C.A.) 409
Naylor Group Inc. v. Ellis-Don Construction Ltd. (1999), 43 O.R. (3d) 325,
  171 D.L.R. (4th) 243, [1999] O.J. No. 913 (C.A.), var'd 2001 SCC 58,
  [2001] 2 S.C.R. 943, [2001] S.C.J. No. 56 ....46, 116, 148, 572
Neider v. Carda of Peace River District Ltd., [1972] S.C.R. 678, 25 D.L.R.
  (3d) 363, [1972] 4 W.W.R. 513 462
Nelson Coke & Gas Co. v. Pellatt (1902), 4 O.L.R. 481, [1902] O.J. No. 179
  (C.A.) 257
Nelson Lumber Co. Ltd. v. Koch (1980), 111 D.L.R. (3d) 140, [1980]
  4 W.W.R. 715, [1980] S.J. No. 138 (C.A.) 351
Nelson v. Nelson (1995), 184 C.L.R. 53 (A.H.C.)........................476–77, 480
Nepean Carleton Developments Ltd. v. Hope, [1978] 1 S.C.R. 427,
  71 D.L.R. (3d) 609, 13 N.R. 7 913
Neville v. Dominion of Canada News Co. Ltd., [1915] 3 K.B. 556 (C.A.)..........446
Neville v. London Express Newspaper Ltd., [1919] A.C. 368 (H.L.) 443
New Brunswick and Canada Rwy. and Land Co. v. Muggeridge (1859),
  4 Drew. 686, 62 E.R. 263 (V.C.) 937
New Brunswick v. Olsen (1984), 57 N.B.R. (2d) 321, [1984] N.B.J. No. 290
  (Q.B.).. 262
New West Homes Ltd. v. Thunderbird Petroleums Ltd. (1975), 59 D.L.R.
  (3d) 292, [1975] A.J. No. 345 (C.A.)... 842

New Zealand Shipping Co. Ltd. v. A.M Satterthwaite & Co. Ltd. (sub nom.
  The Eurymedon) (1974), [1975] A.C. 154, [1974] 2 WLR 865,
  [1974] 1 All ER 1015 (P.C.) 242, 302, 303
Newbigging v. Adam (1886), 34 Ch. D. 582 (C.A.)...340
Newcourt Credit Group Inc. v. Hummel Pharmacy Ltd. (1998), 38 O.R.
  (3d) 82, [1998] O.J. No. 314, 113 O.A.C. 389 (Div. Ct.)...........................773
Newell v. Royal Bank of Canada (1997), 156 N.S.R. (2d) 347, 147 D.L.R.
  (4th) 268, [1997] N.S.J. No. 13 (C.A.) 439
Newfoundland & Labrador Housing Corp. v. Suburban Construction Ltd.
  (1987), 66 Nfld. & P.E.I.R. 347, 38 D.L.R. (4th) 150, [1987] N.J. No. 173
  (C.A.) 259, 265
Newfoundland and Labrador Drilling Ltd. v. Miller (1992), 97 Nfld. &
  P.E.I.R. 140, [1992] N.J. No. 27 (S.C.T.D.) 376
Newswander v. Giegerich (1907), 39 S.C.R. 354.. 443
Nichols v. Jessup, [1986] 1 N.Z.L.R. 237 (N.Z.C.A.)... 412
Nickoll & Knight v. Ashton Edridge & Co., [1901] 2 K.B. 126 (C.A.) 574
Nicolene Ltd. v. Simmonds, [1953] 1 Q.B. 543 (C.A.)...........................54, 61, 105
Nieckar v. Sliwa (1976), 67 D.L.R. (3d) 378, [1976] S.J. No. 118 (Q.B.) 56
Norberg v. Wynrib, [1992] 2 S.C.R. 226, 92 D.L.R. (4th) 449, [1992]
  S.C.J. No. 60...882
Nordenfelt v. Maxim Nordenfelt Guns & Ammunition Co., [1894]
  A.C. 535 (H.L.) 448, 450
Norfolk v. Aikens (1989), 64 D.L.R. (4th) 1, [1989] B.C.J. No. 2256,
  41 B.C.L.R. (2d) 145 (C.A.)...666–67
Norman v. Cole (1800), 3 Esp. 253, 170 E.R. 606 (Nisi Prius) 445
North Eastern Rwy. Co. v. Hastings, [1900] A.C. 260 (H.L.) 716
North Ocean Shipping Co. Ltd. v. Hyundai Construction Co. Ltd.
  (sub nom. The Atlantic Baron) (1978), [1979] Q.B. 705, [1978]
  3 All E.R. 1170 ....368, 371, 377
North Saskatchewan Seeds Ltd. v. Couch, [1960] S.J. No. 60,
  32 W.W.R. 253 (Dist. Ct.) 470
Northeast Marine Services Ltd. v. Atlantic Pilotage Authority, [1995]
  2 F.C. 132, 179 N.R. 17, [1995] F.C.J. No. 99 (C.A.)................................... 148
Northern & Central Gas Co. Ltd. v. Hillcrest Collieries Ltd. (1976),
  59 D.L.R. (3d) 533, [1976] 1 W.W.R. 481 (Alta. S.C.A.D.) 328
Northern Messenger & Transfer Ltd. v. Fabbro (1964), 45 D.L.R. (2d) 73,
  49 W.W.R. 115 (Man. Q.B.)..453
Northwestern Mechanical Installations Ltd. v. Yukon Construction Co.
  (1982), 37 A.R. 132, 136 D.L.R. (3d) 685, [1982] A.J. No. 727 (C.A.) 714
Norton v. Margesson, [2001] O.J. No. 3985, [2001] O.T.C. 744, 47 R.P.R.
  (3d) 237 (S.C.J.) 714
Norwich Union Fire Insurance Society Ltd. v. Wm. H. Price Ltd., [1934]
  A.C. 455 (H.L.) 547
Noseworthy v. Riverside Pontiac-Buick Ltd. (1998), 168 D.L.R. (4th) 629,
  [1998] O.J. No. 5346, 116 O.A.C. 265 (C.A.)...878
Nottingham Patent Brick and Tile Co. v. Butler (1886), 16 Q.B.D. 778 (C.A.) .. 332

Nowlan v. Midland Transport (1996), 174 N.B.R. (2d) 81, [1996]
  N.B.J. No. 88 (C.A.), leave to appeal to S.C.C. refused (1996),
  179 N.B.R. (2d) 319, [1996] S.C.C.A. No. 191 648
Nutt v. Read (1999), 32 H.L.R. 761 (C.A.) 541

O'Calaghan v. Coady (1912), 8 D.L.R. 316 (P.E.I.S.C.) 266
Obde v. Schlemeyer, 353 P.2d 672 (Wash. 1960) 334
Occidental Worldwide Investment Corp. v. Skibs A/S Avanti (sub nom.
  The Siboen and The Sibotre), [1976] 1 Lloyd's Rep. 293 (Q.B.) 371
Ocean Tramp Tankers Corp. v. V/O Sovfracht (The Eugenia), [1964]
  2 Q.B. 226 (C.A.) 582, 586
O'Connor v. Beatty (1876), 27 U.C.C.P. 203, [1876] O.J. No. 78 (C.P.)............... 266
Odeco Drilling of Canada Ltd. v. Hickey Estate (1985), 54 Nfld. &
  P.E.I.R. 116, [1985] N.J. No. 245 (S.C.T.D.), aff'd (1986), 59 Nfld. &
  P.E.I.R. 150, [1986] N.J. No. 13, 9 C.P.C. (2d) 238 (C.A.)............................ 656
Odessa Tramways Co. v. Mendel (1878), 8 Ch. D. 235 (C.A.) 924
O'Flaherty v. British Acceptance Corp. Ltd. (1964), 48 D.L.R. (2d) 562,
  50 W.W.R. 485 (B.C.S.C.) 278
Ogden v. Fossick (1862), 4 De G. F. & J. 426, 45 E.R. 1249 (Ch.) 931
O'Grady v. Insurance Corp. of British Columbia (1975), 63 D.L.R.
  (3d) 370 (B.C.S.C.).. 867
Oldershaw v. King (1857), 2 H. & N. 517, 157 E.R. 213 (Ex. Ch.) 226
Olley v. Marlborough Court Ltd., [1949] 1 All E.R. 127 (C.A.) 185
Olympia Enterprises v. Dover Financial Corp. (1995), 147 N.S.R. (2d) 121,
  [1995] N.S.J. No. 528 (S.C.) 487
Omnium Securities Co. v. Richardson (1884), 7 O.R. 182, [1884]
  O.J. No. 35 (H.C.J.) 935
Ontario Asphalt Block Co. v. Montreuil (1916), 52 S.C.R. 541, 27 D.L.R. 514 820
Oom v. Bruce (1810), 12 East 225, 104 E.R. 87 (K.B.)..470
Orakpo v. Manson Investment Ltd., [1978] A.C. 95 (H.L.) 962
O'Reilly v. Marketers Diversified Inc. (1968), 1 D.L.R. (3d) 387 (B.C.C.A.),
  rev'd [1969] S.C.R. 741, 6 D.L.R. (3d) 631, 69 W.W.R. 251 .... 685, 686
Osborne v. Farmers' & Mechanics' Building Society (1855), 5 Gr. 326
  (U.C. Ch.) 941
Oscar Chess Ltd. v. Williams, [1957] 1 W.L.R. 370 (C.A.) 693
Osmack v. Stan Reynolds Auto Sales Ltd. (1973), 14 N.R. 48, [1974]
  1 W.W.R. 408 (Alta S.C.A.D.), aff'd (1975), 14 N.R. 46, [1976]
  2 W.W.R. 576, [1975] S.C.J. No. 1 661
Osorio v. Cardona (1984), 15 D.L.R. (4th) 619, [1984] B.C.J. No. 3068,
  59 B.C.L.R. 29 (S.C.).. 135, 409
Ostopowich v. Crown Trust Co. (1959), 20 D.L.R. (2d) 514, 29 W.W.R. 89
  (Man. C.A.).. 131
O'Sullivan v. Management Agency and Music Ltd., [1985] Q.B. 428,
  [1985] 3 All E.R. 351 (C.A.).. 403
Oswald Hickson Collier & Co. v. Carter-Ruck, [1984] 2 All E.R. 15 (C.A.) 457
OTM Ltd. v. Hydranautics, [1981] 2 Lloyd's Rep. 211 (Q.B.D.)....................... 52, 60

Ottawa (City) Non-Profit Housing Corp. v. Canvar Construction
(1991) Inc., [1999] O.J. No. 1972, 96 O.T.C. 391, 46 C.L.R.
(2d) 116 (Gen. Div.), rev'd [2000] O.J. No. 1078, 13 O.A.C. 11,
3 C.L.R. (3d) 55 (C.A.) 508, 554–55
Outson v. Zurowski (1985), 18 D.L.R. (4th) 563, 63 B.C.L.R. 89,
[1985] B.C.J. No. 2181 (C.A.) 470–71
Owen Sound Public Library Board v. Mial Developments Ltd. (1979),
26 O.R. (2d) 459, 102 D.L.R. (3d) 685, 8 R.P.R. 113 (C.A.) 284

P.A. Wournell Contracting Ltd. v. Allen (1979), 35 N.S.R. (2d) 250,
100 D.L.R. (3d) 62, [1979] N.S.J. No. 804 (S.C.T.D.), rev'd on other
grounds (1980), 37 N.S.R. (2d) 125, 108 D.L.R. (3d) 723, [1980]
N.S.J. No. 367 (S.C.A.D.) 875
P.J. Van der Zijden v. Tucker & Cross, [1975] 2 Lloyd's Rep. 240 (Q.B.) 602
Pachal v. Schiller (1914), 20 D.L.R. 851 (Sask. S.C.) 439
Pacific National Investments Ltd. v. Victoria (City), 2000 SCC 64, [2000]
2 S.C.R. 919, [2000] S.C.J. No. 64 .... 445, 737
Pacific National Investments Ltd. v. Victoria (City), 2004 SCC 75, [2004]
3 S.C.R. 575, 245 D.L.R. (4th) 211 ....738, 971–72
Paddon-Hughes Development Co. v. Chiles Estate (1991), [1992]
3 W.W.R. 519, [1991] A.J. No. 980, 1 Alta. L.R. (3d) 76 (Q.B.) 714
Page One Records Ltd. v. Britton, [1968] 1 W.L.R. 157 (Ch.) 937, 951
Paine v. Meller (1801), 6 Ves. 349, 31 ER 1088 (Ch.) 593, 596
Palachik v. Kiss, [1983] 1 S.C.R. 623, 146 D.L.R. (3d) 385, 47 N.R. 148 180
Palasky v. Palasky (1993), 89 Man. R. (2d) 1, [1993] M.J. No. 368 (Q.B.) 714
Pamarta Holdings Ltd. v. Routledge (1974), 6 O.R. (2d) 70, 52 D.L.R.
(3d) 19 (H.C.J.) 667
Panchaud Frères SA v. Etablissements General Grain Company, [1970]
1 Lloyd's Rep. 53 (C.A.) 643
Panzer v. Zeifman (1978), 20 O.R. (2d) 502, 88 D.L.R. (3d) 131
(C.A.) 342, 934, 989
Pao On v. Lau Yiu Long, [1980] A.C. 614 (P.C.) 234, 243, 368, 371, 372, 380
Paradine v. Jane (1647) Aleyn 26, 82 E.R. 897 (K.B.) 568, 573
Paragon Farms Ltd. v. H.D. Linn Dev. Services Inc., [1988] 6 W.W.R. 417,
[1988] S.J. No. 504, 69 Sask. R. 214 (Q.B.) 657
Paragon Finance Plc. v. Staunton (2001), [2001] EWCA CIV 1466, [2002]
1 W.L.R. 685, [2002] 2 All E.R. 248 (C.A.) 791, 806
Paris v. Machnick (1972), 7 N.S.R. (2d) 634, 32 D.L.R. (3d) 723, [1972]
N.S.J. No. 190 (S.C.T.D.) 409, 419, 991
Park v. Parsons Brown & Company (1989), 62 D.L.R. (4th) 108, [1989]
B.C.J. No. 1528, 39 B.C.L.R. (2d) 107 (C.A.) 824
Parker v. South Eastern Railway Co. (1877), 2 C.P.D. 416
(C.A.) 183, 184, 185, 190
Parkinson v. College of Ambulance, [1925] 2 K.B. 1 445
Parrish & Heimbecker Ltd. v. Gooding Lumber Ltd., [1968] 1 O.R. 716,
67 D.L.R. (2d) 495 (C.A.) 577, 587–88

Parsons Bros. Ltd. v. Shea (1965), 53 D.L.R. (2d) 86 (Nfld. S.C.) 580, 607

Partridge v. Crittenden, [1968] 1 W.L.R 1204 (Q.B.D.)................................ 36

Pasley v. Freeman (1789), 3 T.R. 51, 100 E.R. 450 (K.B.) 348, 692

Patel v. Ali, [1984] Ch. 283.. 936, 941

Paterson v. Houghton (1909), 19 Man. R. 168 (C.A.)................................ 84

Patson v. Abalon Construction Ltd. (1996), 110 Man. R. (2d) 2, [1996]
  M.J. No. 43, 26 C.L.R. (2d) 155 (C.A.) 967

Pavey and Matthews Pty Ltd. v. Paul, [1987] HCA 5, 162 CLR 221,
  69 A.L.R. 577 476

Payne v. Cave (1789), 3 Term Rep. 148, 100 E.R. 502 (K.B.) 47

Payzu Ltd. v. Saunders, [1919] 2 K.B. 581 (C.A.) 867

Pearce v. Brooks (1866), L.R. 1 Ex. 213 (Ex. Ch.)............................... 435–36

Pearce v. Transportation Fire & Casualty Co. (1977), 18 O.R. (2d) 569,
  83 D.L.R. (3d) 259 (Dist. Ct.)... 74

Pearson v. Adams (1912), 27 O.L.R. 87, [1912] O.J. No. 9 (Div. Ct.), rev'd (1913),
  28 O.L.R. 154, [1913] O.J. No. 43 (C.A.), rev'd (1914), 50 S.C.R. 204 726

Pearson v. Simmonds Precision Products, 624 A.2d 1134 (Vt. 1993) 335

Peebles v. Pfeifer, [1918] 2 W.W.R. 877 (Sask. K.B.) 868

Peek v. Gurney (1873), L.R. 6 H.L. 377 352

Peel Condominium Corp. No. 505 v. Cam-Valley Homes Ltd. (2001),
  53 O.R. (3d) 1, 196 D.L.R. (4th) 621, [2001] O.J. No. 714 (C.A.)........ 158, 335

Peevyhouse v. Garland Coal & Mining Co., 382 P.2d 109 (Okla. 1962) 844–45

Pellow v. Ivey (1933), 49 T.L.R. 422 (Ch.) 450

Pennsylvania Shipping Company Co. v. Compagnie Nationale de Navigation,
  [1936] 2 All E.R. 1167 (K.B.) 346

Penvidic Contracting Co. Ltd. v. International Nickel Co. of Canada Ltd.
  (1975), [1976] 1 S.C.R. 267, 53 D.L.R. (3d) 748, 4 N.R. 1 .... 738, 848

Peoples' Bank of Halifax v. Johnson (1892), 20 S.C.R. 541 439

Performance Industries Ltd. v. Sylvan Lake Golf & Tennis Club Ltd.,
  2002 SCC 19, [2002] 1 S.C.R. 678, [2002] S.C.J. No. 20.................... 893

Perkins Oil Co. v. Fitzgerald, 121 S.W. 2d 877 (Ark. 1938)....................380

Permaform Plastics Ltd. v. London & Midland General Insurance Co., [1996]
  7 W.W.R. 457, 110 Man.R. (2d) 260, [1996] M.J. No. 322 (C.A.) 379

Perry v. Brandon (1914), 32 O.L.R. 94, [1914] O.J. No. 114 (S.C.A.D.)............... 729

Peter Kiewit Sons' Co. of Canada Ltd. v. Eakins Construction Ltd., [1960]
  S.C.R. 361, 22 D.L.R. (2d) 465 ....370, 375, 572

Peters v. Parkway Mercury Sales Ltd. (1975), 10 N.B.R. (2d) 703,
  58 D.L.R. (3d) 128, [1975] N.B.J. No. 74 (S.C.A.D.) 351, 766

Petridis v. Shabinsky (1982), 35 O.R. (2d) 215, 132 D.L.R. (3d) 430,
  22 R.P.R. 297 (H.C.J.)..284, 289

Petrofina (Great Britain) Ltd. v. Martin, [1966] Ch. 146 447

Petterson v. Pattberg, 161 N.E. 428 (N.Y.C.A. 1928) 56, 88

Peyman v. Lanjani (1984), [1985] Ch. 457, [1984] 3 All E.R. 703 .... 342, 343

Pharmaceutical Society of Great Britain v. Boots Cash Chemists
  (Southern) Ltd., [1953] 1 Q.B. 401 (C.A.) 38

Phelps v. Herro, 137 A.2d 159 (Md. 1957) 658

Phene v. Popplewell (1862), 12 C.B. (N.S.) 334, 142 E.R. 1171 (C.P.) 823
Phillips v. Brooks, [1919] 2 K.B. 243 512
Phillips-Renwick v. Renwick Estate (2003), 229 D.L.R. (4th) 158,
    [2003] O.J. No. 3156, 41 R.F.L. (5th) 337 (S.C.J.)..................................410
Philpott v. Wallet (1682), 3 Lev. 65, 83 E.R. 579 (K.B.)............................. 167
Phoenix General Ins. Co. of Greece S.A. v. Halvanon Ins. Co. Ltd.,
    [1988] Q.B. 216 (C.A.) 464
Photo Production Ltd. v. Securicor Transport Ltd., [1980] A.C. 827
    (H.L.) 617, 633, 643–44, 753, 759, 760–62, 765, 768, 769
Pickering v. Bishop of Ely (1843), 2 Y. & C.C.C. 249, 63 E.R. 109 (V.C.).............931
Pielak v. Crown Forest Industries Ltd., [1992] 3 W.W.R. 592,
    64 B.C.L.R. (2d) 207, [1992] B.C.J. No. 437 (S.C.) 442
Pierce v. Empey, [1939] S.C.R. 247, [1939] 4 D.L.R. 672................................. 796
Pietrobon v. McIntyre (1987), 15 B.C.L.R. (2d) 350, [1987] B.C.J. No. 1571
    (S.C.) 107, 678
Pilgrim v. Milner (1997), 155 Nfld. & P.E.I.R. 221, [1997] N.J. No. 224 (C.A.)...... 84
Pilkington v. Wood, [1953] Ch. 770...868
Pillans and Rose v. Van Mierop & Hopkins (1765), 3 Burr. 1663,
    97 E.R. 1035 (K.B.) 213
Pimvicska v. Pimvicska (1974), 50 D.L.R. (3d) 569, [1974] 6 W.W.R. 512
    (Alta. S.C.T.D.) 482
Pinnel's Case (1602), 5 Co. Rep. 117, 77 E.R. 237 (C.P.) 251
Pitt v. PHH Asset Management Ltd., [1993] 4 All E.R. 961 (C.A.).................... 126
Planche v. Colburn (1831), 8 Bing. 14, 131 E.R. 305 (C.P.) 971
Plant v. Bourne, [1879] 2 Ch. 281 (C.A.)... 173
Plas-Tex Canada Ltd. v. Dow Chemical of Canada Ltd., 2004 ABCA 309,
    357 A.R. 139, 245 D.L.R. (4th) 650...................................... 774–75
Plimmer v. Wellington Corp. (1884), 9 App. Cas. 699 (P.C.) 287
Pobasco Ltd. v. Cogan (1990), 72 O.R. (2d) 254, [1990] O.J. No. 303,
    38 E.T.R. 193 (H.C.J.) 134
Pople v. Dauphin (1921), 60 D.L.R. 30 (Man. C.A.) 370
Poplett v. Stockdale (1825), Ry. & Mood. 337, 171 E.R. 1041 (Nisi Prius) 430
Popyk v. Western Savings & Loan Association (1969), 3 D.L.R. (3d) 511,
    67 W.W.R. 684 (Alta. S.C.A.D.) 983
Pordage v. Cole (1669), 1 Wms. Saund. 319, 85 E.R. 449 (K.B.)....................... 620
Porter v. Freudenberg, [1915] 1 K.B. 857 .... 446, 447
Porter v. Pelton (1903), 33 S.C.R. 449, 23 C.L.T. 213........................ 258, 265, 268
Potter Station Power Co. v. Inco Ltd. (1998), 78 O.T.C. 161, [1998]
    O.J. No. 4522 43 C.L.R. (2d) 53 (Gen. Div.), supp. reasons
    [1998] O.J. No. 5349 (Gen. Div.) 969
Potter v. Duffield (1874), L.R. 18 Eq. 4... 173
Potucek v. Cordeleria Lourdes, 310 F.2d 527 (10th Cir. 1962)..................515, 543
Powder Mountain Resorts Ltd. v. British Columbia, [1999] 11 W.W.R. 168,
    [1999] B.C.J. No. 1954, 47 C.L.R. (2d) 32 (S.C.), aff'd 2001 BCCA 619,
    [2001] 11 W.W.R. 488, [2001] B.C.J. No. 2172 .... 47, 117
Powell Duffryn Steam Coal Co. v. Taftvale Rwy. Co. (1874), 9 Ch. App. 331 ... 930

Powell v. Elliot (1875), L.R. 10 Ch. App. 424 942

Powell v. London Borough of Brent, [1987] I.R.L.R. 466 (C.A.) 933

Powell v. Powell, [1900] 1 Ch. 243 397

Powers & Son v. Hatfield & Scott, (1916), 10 O.W.N. 198, [1916] O.J. No. 558
   (H.C.J.), aff'd (1916), 27 O.W.R. 666, [1916] O.J. No. 453 (S.C.A.D.) 54, 61

Practice Statement (Judicial Precedent), [1966] 1 W.L.R. 1234 20

Prather v. King Resources Co. (1972), 33 D.L.R. (3d) 112, [1973]
   1 W.W.R. 700 (Alta. S.C.A.D.) 328

Prenn v. Simmonds [1971] 1 W.L.R. 1381 (H.L.) 709, 710, 711–12, 713

Presbyterian Church of Albany v. Cooper (1889), 112 N.Y. Rep. 517,
   20 N.E. 352 229

Price v. Strange, [1978] Ch. 337 (C.A.) 926–27

Pridmore v. Calvert (1975), 54 D.L.R. (3d) 133 (B.C.S.C.) 408, 410

Prince v. Elm Investment Co. Inc., 649 P.2d 820 (Utah 1982) 797

Princeton Light & Power Co. v. MacDonald, 2005 BCCA 296, 254 D.L.R. (4th)
   431, [2005] B.C.J. No. 1189 890

Printing & Numerical Registering Company v. Sampson (1875),
   L.R. 19 Eq. 462 24

Prinzo v. Baycrest Centre for Geriatric Care (2002), 60 O.R. (3d) 474,
   215 D.L.R. (4th) 31, [2002] O.J. No. 2712 (C.A.) 894

Privest Properties Ltd. v. Foundation Co. of Canada Ltd. (1977), 145 D.L.R.
   (4th) 729, [1997] B.C.J. No. 935, 34 B.L.R. (2d) 281 (C.A.) 709

Procopia v. D'Abbondanzo, [1973] 3 O.R. 8, 35 D.L.R. (3d) 641 (H.C.J.),
   var'd (1975), 8 O.R. (2d) 496, 58 D.L.R. (3d) 368 (C.A.) 263

Prokop v. Kohut (1965), 54 D.L.R. (2d) 717 (B.C.S.C.) 435

Promech Sorting Systems B.V. v. Bronco Rentals and Leasing Ltd. (1995),
   123 D.L.R. (4th) 111, [1995] 4 W.W.R. 484, [1995] M.J. No. 100 (C.A.) 184

Property & Bloodstock Ltd. v. Emerton; Bush v. Property & Bloodstock
   Ltd. (1967), [1968] Ch. 94 (C.A.) 676–77

Propriétés Cité Concordia Ltée v. Royal Bank, [1983] R.D.J. 524 (Que. C.A.) .. 930

Provincial Bank of Canada v. Whiteoak Construction Ltd. (1976),
   15 N.B.R. (2d) 408, [1976] N.B.J. No. 209 (S.C.Q.B.) 263

Provincial Court Judges Association (Saskatchewan) v. Saskatchewan
   (Minister of Justice), [1995] 6 W.W.R. 626, 133 Sask. R. 115, [1995]
   S.J. No. 309 (Q.B.), rev'd on other grounds [1996] 2 W.W.R. 129,
   137 Sask. R. 204, [1995] S.J. No. 692 (C.A.) 445

Provincial Insurance Co. v. Connolly (1879), 5 S.C.R. 258 716

Provincial Sanatorium v. McArthur, [1935] 4 D.L.R. 255 (P.E.I.S.C.),
   leave to appeal to S.C.C. refused, [1935] 4 D.L.R. 458 (P.E.I.S.C.) 230

Prudential Trust Co. Ltd. v. Cugnet, [1956] S.C.R. 914, 5 D.L.R.
   (2d) 1 ....521, 524, 526

Public Work Commissioner v. Hills, [1906] A.C. 368 (P.C.) 899

Pugsley v. Fowler (1909), 4 N.B. Eq. 122 (N.B.S.C.) 655

Punjab National Bank v. de Boinville, [1992] 1 W.L.R. 1138 (C.A.) 713

Pusey v. Pusey (1684), 1 Vern. 273, 23 E.R. 465 (Ch.) 918

Putsman v. Taylor, [1927] 1 K.B. 637, aff'd [1927] 1 K.B. 741 (C.A.) 488
Pym v. Campbell (1856), 6 E. & B. 370, 119 E.R. 903 (Q.B.)..................... 199, 204
Pyrke v. Waddingham (1852), 10 Hare 1, 68 E.R. 813 (V.C.)............................ 942

Qualico Developments Ltd. v. Calgary (City) (1987), 81 A.R. 161, [1987]
   5 W.W.R. 361, [1987] A.J. No. 530 (Q.B.) 709
Quance v. Brown (1926), 58 O.L.R. 578, [1926] 2 D.L.R. 824, [1926]
   O.J. No. 131 (App. Div.) 168
Québec (Sous-ministre du Revenu) v. Simpsons-Sears Ltd., [1986]
   R.L. 37 (Que. C.A.)... 36
Quebec Pharmaceutical Ass'n. v. T. Eaton Co. (1931), 56 C.C.C. 172
   (Que. C.A.).. 36
Queen v. Cognos Inc., [1993] 1 S.C.R. 87, 99 D.L.R. (4th) 626, [1993]
   S.C.J. No. 3 351

R. v. Marshall, [1999] 3 S.C.R. 456, 177 D.L.R. (4th) 513, [1999]
   S.C.J. No. 55.. 736
R. v. Bell, [1979] 2 S.C.R. 212, 98 D.L.R. (3d) 255, 26 N.R. 457 20
R. v. Bermuda Holdings Ltd. (1969), 9 D.L.R. (3d) 595, 70 W.W.R. 754,
   [1970] 3 C.C.C. 374 (B.C.S.C.) 37
R. v. Big M Drug Mart Ltd. et al., [1985] 1 S.C.R. 295, 18 D.L.R. (4th) 321,
   [1985] S.C.J. No. 17... 462
R. v. CAE Industries Ltd. (1985), [1986] 1 F.C. 129, 20 D.L.R. (4th) 347,
   61 N.R. 19 (C.A.), leave to appeal to S.C.C. refused (1985),
   20 D.L.R. (4th) 347n, 63 N.R. 158n, [1986] 2 W.W.R. lxi...................... 106
R. v. Clarke (1927), 40 C.L.R. 227 (A.H.C.) 50–51, 56
R. v. Commercial Credit Corp. (1983), 61 N.S.R. (2d) 410, 4 D.L.R.
   (4th) 314, [1983] N.S.J. No. 316 (S.C.A.D.)....................................... 73
R. v. Dawood)(1975), [1976] 1 W.W.R. 262, 27 C.C.C. (2d) 300,
   31 C.R.N.S. 382 (Alta. C.A.)... 38
R. v. Goodman, [1939] S.C.R. 446, [1939] 4 D.L.R. 361, 72 C.C.C. 305.... 442, 443
R. v. Sellars, [1980] 1 S.C.R. 527, 110 D.L.R. (3d) 629, 32 N.R. 70 823
R.G. McLean Ltd. v. Canadian Vickers Ltd. (1970), [1971] 1 O.R. 207,
   15 D.L.R. (3d) 15 (C.A.) 766, 870
R.H. Peden Construction Ltd. v. Resolute Construction (1977) Ltd. (1980),
   31 A.R. 453, [1980] A.J. No. 826 (Q.B.) 351
Radford v. De Froberville, [1977] 1 W.L.R. 1262 (Ch.)............................845
Radley Bros. (Oshawa) Ltd. v. A to Z Rental Canada Ltd., [1973] 1 O.R. 823,
   32 D.L.R. (3d) 521 (H.C.J.), var'd (1974), 3 O.R. (2d) 766, 46 D.L.R.
   (3d) 686 (C.A.) 981
Raffles v. Wichelhaus (1864), 2 H. & C. 906, 159 E.R. 375 (Ex.)..................... 496
Raggow v. Scougall & Co. (1915), 31 T.L.R. 564 (K.B. Div'l Ct.)...................... 247
Rainbow Industrial Caterers Ltd. v. C.N.R., [1991] 3 S.C.R. 3, 84 D.L.R.
   (4th) 291, [1991] S.C.J. No. 67 ....351, 354, 818
Rainbow Industrial Caterers Ltd. v. Canadian National Railway Co. (1988),
   54 D.L.R. (4th) 43, [1988] B.C.J. No. 1710, 30 B.C.L.R. (2d) 273 (C.A.) 328

Ralli Bias v. Compania Naviera Sota & Aznar, [1920] 2 K.B. 287 (C.A.) 574
Ralston v. Tanner (1918), 43 O.L.R. 77, [1918] O.J. No. 109 (S.C.) 385
Ramrod Investments Ltd. v. Matsumoto Shipyards Ltd. (1990),
    47 B.C.L.R. (2d) 86, [1990] B.C.J. No. 1340, 11 R.P.R. (2d) 36 (C.A.)........ 625
Ramsden v. Dyson (1866), L.R. 1 H.L. 129 291
Rann v. Hughes (1778), 4 Brown P.C. 27, 2 E.R. 18 (H.L.)................................ 213
Rapatax (1987) Inc. v. Cantax Corp. (1997), 196 A.R. 200, 145 D.L.R.
    (4th) 419, [1997] A.J. No. 313 (C.A.), leave to appeal to S.C.C. refused
    (1997), 149 D.L.R. (4th) vii, [1997] S.C.C.A. No. 307.............................. 740
Rasch v. Horne, [1930] 3 D.L.R. 647 (Man. C.A.) 327, 328
RDA Film Distribution Inc. v. British Columbia Trade Development Corp.
    (2000), 2000 BCCA 674, [2001] 2 W.W.R. 88, [2000] B.C.J. No. 2550....... 643
Re 140 Developments Ltd. v. Steveston Meat & Frozen Food Lockers
    (1973) Ltd. (1975), 59 D.L.R. (3d) 470 (B.C.S.C.) 869
Re Baby M, 537 A.2d 1227 (N.J. 1988) 436
Re Berker Sportcraft Limited's Agreements (1947), 177 L.T. 420 (Ch. D.) 740
Re Birks, [1900] 1 Ch. 417... 718
Re Brocklehurst [1978] Ch. 14 (C.A.)... 397
Re Broughton Collieries Ltd., [1944] 1 D.L.R. 530, 17 M.P.R. 258 (N.S.C.A.)...... 712
Re Calford Properties Ltd. and Kelly's Billiards Ltd. (1973), 37 D.L.R.
    (3d) 300, [1973] 4 W.W.R. 532 (Alta. S.C.T.D.).. 102
Re Canadian National Railway and Canadian Pacific Ltd. (1978),
    95 D.L.R. (3d) 242, [1979] 1 W.W.R. 358 (B.C.C.A.)................................ 714
Re Casey's Patents, [1892] 1 Ch. 104 234
Re Craig (1970), [1971] Ch. 95, [1970] 2 All E.R. 390.............................. 384, 388
Re Dennis Commercial Properties Ltd. v. Westmount Life Insurance Co.,
    [1969] 2 O.R. 850, 7 D.L.R. (3d) 214 (H.C.J.), aff'd (1969), [1970]
    1 O.R. 698n, 8 D.L.R. (3d) 688n (C.A.)... 593
Re George & The Goldsmiths & General Burglary Insurance Assoc. Ltd.,
    [1899] 1 Q.B. 595... 716
Re Gonin, [1979] Ch. 16... 131
Re Grosch, [1945] 3 D.L.R. 63 (Alta. S.C.A.D.) 232
Re Hammond, [1938] 3 All E.R. 308 (Ch.)... 727
Re Hogg Estate (1987), 83 A.R. 165, [1987] A.J. No. 1009 (Q.B.) 224
Re Hoyle, [1893] 1 Ch. 84...170
Re Imperial Land Co. v. Marseilles (1872), L.R. 7 Ch. App. 587 .... 54, 61
Re iTV Games Inc., 2002 BCCA 38, [2002] B.C.J. No. 93, 21 B.L.R. (3d) 258..... 904
Re Lang Estate, [1919] 1 W.W.R. 651 (Sask. Q.B.)... 200
Re Loblaw, [1933] 4 D.L.R. 264 (Ont. S.C.)... 229
Re MacNeil Estate (2002), 2003 NSSC 50, 212 N.S.R. (2d) 133, [2002]
    N.S.J. No. 575.. 266
Re Metropolitan Theatres Ltd. (1917), 40 O.L.R. 345, [1917] O.J. No. 94
    (H.C.) 266
Re Mirams, [1891] 1 Q.B. 594... 445
Re Nishi Industries (1978), 28 C.B.R. (N.S.) 261 (B.C.C.A.)............................. 99

Re Penn Central Transportation Co. v. Canada Southern Railway Co.,
[1971] 3 O.R. 247, 20 D.L.R. (3d) 135 (H.C.J.) 792

Re Provinces & Central Properties Limited and City of Halifax (1969),
2 N.S.R. (1965–69) 221, 5 D.L.R. (3d) 28 (S.C.A.D.) 983

Re Schwabacher (1908), 98 L.T. 127 (Ch.) 923

Re Selectmove Ltd., [1995] 2 All E.R. 531 (C.A.) 253

Re Solicitor (1907), 14 O.L.R. 464, [1907] O.J. No. 159 (H.C.J.) 443

Re Spenborough Urban District Council's Agreement, [1968] Ch. 139 740

Re Strand Music Hall Co. Ltd. (1865), 35 Beav. 153, 55 E.R. 853 (M.R.) 719

Re Terry & White's Contract (1886), 32 Ch. D. 14 (C.A.) 934

Re Thornett & Fehr, [1921] 1 K.B. 219 824

Re Wait, [1927] 1 Ch. 606 (C.A.) 920

Re Western Canada Pulpwood Co. Ltd., [1930] 1 D.L.R. 652
(Man. C.A.) 920–21

Re Whissel Enterprises Ltd. and Eastcal Developments Ltd. (1980),
25 A.R. 92, 116 D.L.R. (3d) 174, [1980] A.J. No. 882 (C.A.) 173

Re Zamikoff v. Lundy, [1970] 2 O.R. 8, 9 D.L.R. (3d) 637 (C.A.) 259, 265, 268

Reardon Smith Line Ltd. v. Yngvar Hansen-Tangen, [1976] 1 W.L.R. 989
(H.L.) 633, 709

Record v. Bell, [1991] 1 W.L.R. 853 (Ch.) 918

Red Deer College v. Michaels (1975), [1976] 2 S.C.R. 324, 57 D.L.R.
(3d) 386, 5 N.R. 99 .... 865, 868, 932, 937

Redgrave v. Hurd (1881), 20 Ch. D. 1 (C.A.) 325, 330, 331, 352

Redican v. Nesbitt (1923), [1924] S.C.R. 135, [1924] 1 D.L.R. 536,
[1924] 1 W.W.R. 305 344

Redland Bricks Ltd. v. Morris, [1970] A.C. 652 (H.L.) 948

Reference re Farm Products Marketing Act, [1957] S.C.R. 198,
7 D.L.R. (2d) 257 20

Regazzoni v. K.C. Sethia (1944) Ltd., [1958] A.C. 301 (H.L.) 446

Regina v. Whitaker, [1914] 3 K.B. 1283 445

Reid-Newfoundland Company v. Anglo-American Telegraph Company,
[1912] A.C. 555 (P.C.) 976

Reif v. Page (1882), 55 Wisc. 496 240

Reigate v. Union Manufacturing Co., [1918] 1 K.B. 592 (C.A.) 735, 740

Rei-Mar Investment Ltd. v. Christie (1974), 48 D.L.R. (3d) 315 (B.C.S.C.) 219

Renard Constructions (ME) Pty. Ltd. v. Minister for Public Works (1992),
26 N.S.W.L.R. 234 (C.A.) 791, 969

Richardson v. Snipes, 330 S.W.2d 381 (Tenn. 1959) 682

River Wear Commissioners v. Adamson (1877), 2 App. Cas. 743 (H.L.) 709

Riverlate Properties v. Paul, [1975] Ch. 133 (C.A.) 560

RJR-MacDonald Inc. v. Canada (Attorney General), [1994] 1 S.C.R. 311,
111 D.L.R. (4th) 385, [1994] S.C.J. No. 17 955

Robb v. Green, [1895] 2 Q.B. 315 (C.A.) 744

Robert Bell Engine & Thresher Co. v. Farquharson (1918), 39 D.L.R. 625,
1 W.W.R. 924 (Sask. S.C.A.D.) 656

Robert Simpson Regina Ltd. v. Dominion Electric Protection Co. (1971),
19 D.L.R. (3d) 218, [1971] 3 W.W.R. 721, [1971] S.J. No. 59 (Q.B.) 358

Roberts & Co. Ltd. v. Leicestershire County Council, [1961] Ch. 555 ..... 560, 562

Roberts v. Montex Development Corporation (1979), 100 D.L.R. (3d) 660,
[1979] 4 W.W.R. 306, [1979] B.C.J. No. 1067 (S.C.) 55

Robertson v. French (1803), 4 East 130, 102 E.R. 779 (K.B.)......................716, 727

Robichaud v. Caisse Populair de Pokemouche Ltée. (1990), 69 D.L.R.
(4th) 589, [1990] N.B.J. No. 213, 105 N.B.R. (2d) 227 (C.A.) 252

Robinson v. Davison (1871), L.R. 6 Ex. 269..574

Robinson v. Harman (1848), Exch. 850, 154 E.R. 363...................................816

Robitaille v. Vancouver Hockey Club (1981), 124 D.L.R. (3d) 228, [1981]
3 W.W.R. 481, [1981] B.C.J. No. 555 (C.A.) 881, 882, 895

Rochdale Credit Union Ltd. v. Barney (1984), 48 O.R. (2d) 676, 14 D.L.R.
(4th) 116, 7 O.A.C. 9 (C.A.)... 385

Rochefoucauld v. Boustead, [1897] 1 Ch. 196 (C.A.) 178

Roenish v. Bangs (1993), 138 A.R. 15, 8 Alta. L.R. (3d) 148, [1993]
A.J. No. 166 (Q.B.) 376, 394

Rogalsky Estate v. Rogalsky (1984), [1985] 2 W.W.R. 699, 32 Man. R.
(2d) 223, [1984] M.J. No. 515 (Q.B.) 131

Rogers v. Hewer (1912), 5 Alta. L.R. 227, 8 D.L.R. 288, 3 W.W.R. 477
(Alta. C.A.) 172

Rogers v. Leonard (1973), 1 O.R. (2d) 57, 39 D.L.R. (3d) 349 (H.C.J.) 462

Rommerill v. Gardner (1962), 35 D.L.R. (2d) 717, 40 W.W.R. 265 (B.C.C.A.)... 256

Ron Engineering & Construction Eastern Ltd. v. Ontario, [1981]
1 S.C.R. 111, 119 D.L.R. (3d) 267, 35 N.R. 40 ....44, 115, 147, 504, 507,
508, 554, 741

Ronald Elwyn Lister Ltd. v. Dunlop Canada Ltd. (1978), 19 O.R. (2d) 380, 8
5 D.L.R. (3d) 321, 4 B.L.R. 1 (H.C.J.), rev'd on other grounds (1979),
27 O.R. (2d) 168, 105 D.L.R. (3d) 684, 9 B.L.R. 290 (C.A.), but restored
on further appeal [1982] 1 S.C.R. 726, 135 D.L.R. (3d) 1,
42 N.R. 181 .... 226–27, 356, 376

Rooke v. Dawson, [1895] 1 Ch. 480 36

Rookes v. Barnard, [1964] A.C. 1129, [1964] 1 All ER 367(H.L.) 879, 880

Rose and Frank Company v. J.R. Crompton and Brothers Ltd., [1923]
2 K.B. 261 (C.A.), aff'd [1925] A.C. 445 (H.L.).............. 113–14, 116, 120, 728

Rosen v. Rosen (1994), 18 O.R. (3d) 641, 3 R.F.L. (4th) 267, [1994]
O.J. No. 1160 (C.A.) 410

Rosher v. Williams (1875), L.R. 20 Eq. 210, 44 L.J. Ch. 419............................ 219

Ross v. Caunters, [1980] Ch. 297 306

Ross v. Hern, [2003] O.J. No. 1659, [2003] O.T.C. 375 (S.C.J.) 135

Ross v. Ross (1977), 28 N.S.R. (2d) 260, 80 D.L.R. (3d) 377,
[1977] N.S.J. No. 696 (S.C.T.D.)... 266

Rossiter v. Miller (1878), 3 App. Cas. 1124 (H.L.)... 173

Routh v. Jones, [1947] 1 All E.R. 758 (C.A.).. 454, 457

Royal Bank of Canada v. Bermuda Holdings Ltd. (1975), 67 D.L.R.
(3d) 316 (B.C.S.C.)... 263

Royal Bank of Canada v. Gill (1986), 31 D.L.R. (4th) 61, 6 B.C.L.R.
(2d) 359, [1986] B.C.J. No. 795 (S.C.), aff'd [1988] 3 W.W.R. 441,
23 B.C.L.R. (2d) 176, [1988] B.C.J. No. 147 (C.A.) 524
Royal Bank of Canada v. Grobman et al. (1977), 18 O.R. (2d) 636 (H.C.J.) 460
Royal Bank of Canada v. Hinds (1978), 20 O.R. (2d) 613, 88 D.L.R.
(3d) 428, 4 B.L.R. 241 (H.C.J.) 425
Royal Bank of Canada v. Hislop (1989), 62 D.L.R. (4th) 228, [1989]
B.C.J. No. 1779, 39 B.C.L.R. (2d) 392 (C.A.) 334
Royal Bank of Canada v. Hussain (1997), 37 O.R. (3d) 85, [1997]
O.J. No. 5233, 67 O.T.C. 170 (Gen. Div.) 409
Royal Bank of Canada v. W. Got & Associates Electric Ltd., [1999]
3 S.C.R. 408, 178 D.L.R. (4th) 385, [1999] S.C.J. No. 59 890
Royal Bank of Scotland v. Etridge (No. 2), [2001] UKHL 44, [2001]
3 W.L.R. 1021, [2001] 4 All E.R. 449 .... 334, 383, 392, 393, 394–96,
397, 398, 400, 401–2
Royal Bank v. Kiska, [1967] 2 O.R. 379, 63 D.L.R. (2d) 582
(C.A.) 216, 222, 226, 260, 261–62
Royal Boskalis Westminster NV v. Mountain, [1999] Q.B. 674 446
Rudd v. Lascelles, [1900] 1 Ch. 815 941
Rudder v. Microsoft Corp., [1999] O.J. No. 3778, 40 C.P.C. (4th) 394,
2 C.P.R. (4th) 474 (S.C.J.) 81
Rule v. Pals, [1928] 3 D.L.R. 295 (Sask C.A.) 329
Rupar v. Rupar (1964), 46 D.L.R. (2d) 553, 49 W.W.R. 226 (B.C.S.C.) 480
Rutkowski Estate v. Brandhorst (1997), 206 A.R. 313, [1997] A.J. No. 879,
19 E.T.R. (2d) 209 (C.A.) 390
Ruxley Electronics and Construction Ltd. v. Forsyth, [1995] 3 All E.R. 268
(H.L.), rev'g [1994] 3 All E.R. 801 (C.A.) 841, 842, 843
Ryan v. Mutual Tontine Westminster Chambers Assoc., [1893] 1 Ch. 116
(C.A.) 929, 931

S.(F.) v. H.(C.) (1994), 120 D.L.R. (4th), 432, [1994] O.J. No. 2630,
22 C.C.L.T. (2d) 292 (Gen. Div.), aff'd on other grounds (1996),
133 D.L.R. (4th) 767, [1996] O.J. No. 1303, 22 R.F.L. (4th) 226 (C.A.) 333
S. v. K. (1986), 55 O.R. (2d) 111, 10 C.P.C. (2d) 252 (Dist. Ct.) 443
S.B.I. Management Ltd. v. Wabush (Carol) Co-op Society Ltd., (1985),
51 Nfld. & P.E.I.R. 257, [1985] N.J. No. 316 (S.C.T.D.) 929
S.F. Silver Falcon Holding Co. v. Agricultural Development Co. of
Saskatchewan (1990), 81 Sask. R. 195, [1990] S.J. No. 20 (Q.B.) 597
S.S. Magnhild v. McIntyre Bros. & Co., [1920] 3 K.B. 321 725
S.W. Strange Ltd. v. Mann, [1965] 1 All E.R. 1069 (Ch.) 454
S-244 Holdings Ltd. v. Seamore Building Systems Ltd., [1994]
8 W.W.R. 185, [1994] B.C.J. No. 598, 41 B.C.A.C. 272 (C.A.) 344, 348
Sail Labrador Ltd. v. Challenge One (1998), [1999] 1 S.C.R. 265,
169 D.L.R. (4th) 1, [1998] S.C.J. No. 69 .... 292, 633, 647
Saint John Tug Boat Co. v. Irving Refinery Ltd., [1964] S.C.R. 614,
46 D.L.R. (2d) 1, 49 M.P.R. 284 68–69

Sally Wertheim v. Chicoutimi Pulp Company, [1911] A.C. 301 (P.C.) 816

Salmon River Logging Co. Ltd. v. Burt (1953), [1953] 2 S.C.R. 117,
[1954] 1 D.L.R. 1.. 358, 724

Samson v. Lockwood (1998), 40 O.R. (3d) 161, [1998] O.J. No. 2471, 110 O.A.C.
301 (C.A.).. 643

Samuel Smith & Sons v. Silverman, [1961] O.R. 648, 29 D.L.R. (2d) 98 (C.A.)....185

Samuel v. Black Lake Asbestos and Chrome Co. (1920), 58 D.L.R. 270 (Ont.
S.C.A.D.), rev'd on other grounds (1921), 62 S.C.R. 472, 63 D.L.R. 617 598

Samuel v. Jarrah Timber and Wood Paving Corp. Ltd., [1904] A.C. 323
(H.L.) 715

Sanderson v. Cockermouth and Worthington Rwy. Co. (1849), 11 Beav. 497,
50 E.R. 909 (M.R.)... 930

Saner v. Bilton (1878), 7 Ch. D. 815... 725

Sanitary Refuse Collectors v. Ottawa (City) (1971), [1972] 1 O.R. 296,
23 D.L.R. (3d) 27 (H.C.J.)...257, 330

Sanko Steamship Co. v. Eacon Timber Sales Co. (1986), 32 D.L.R. (4th) 269,
[1986] B.C.J. No. 1088, 8 B.C.L.R. (2d) 69 (S.C.)... 635

Santellii v. Bifano Enterprises Ltd. (1981), 33 B.C.L.R. 266, [1981]
B.C.J. No. 1472 (S.C.)... 109

Saperstein v. Drury (1943), 59 B.C.R. 281, [1943] 4 D.L.R. 191, [1943]
3 W.W.R. 193 (C.A.), aff'd. [1944] S.C.R. 148, [1944] 2 D.L.R. 511 172

Sarbit v. Hanson & Booth Fisheries (Canada) Co., [1950] 4 D.L.R. 34,
[1950] 2 W.W.R. 545 (Man. K.B.) rev'd on other grounds (1950),
58 Man. R. 377, [1951] 2 D.L.R. 108, 1 W.W.R. (N.S.) 115 (C.A.).............. 166

Sargent v. Nicholson (1915), 25 D.L.R. 638 (Man. C.A.) 228, 229

Saskatchewan River Bungalows Ltd. v. Maritime Life Assurance Co. (1992),
127 A.R. 43, 92 D.L.R. (4th) 372, [1992] A.J. No. 512 (C.A.), rev'd
[1994] 2 S.C.R. 490, 115 D.L.R. (4th) 478, [1994] S.C.J. No. 59 87

Saunders v. Anglia Building Society, [1971] A.C. 1004
(H.L.) 519–20, 521, 522-23, 524, 526, 539

Saunders v. Edwards, [1987] 1 W.L.R. 1116 (C.A.) 349, 477

Savereux v. Tourangeau (1908), 16 O.L.R. 600, [1908] O.J. No. 154 (Div. Ct.).....935

Sawyer v. Pringle (1891), 18 O.A.R. 218, [1891] O.J. No. 9 (C.A.) 655

Saxon v. Saxon, [1976] 4 W.W.R. 300, 24 R.F.L. 47 (B.C.S.C.), aff'd [1978]
4 W.W.R. 327, [1978] B.C.J. No. 810, 5 R.F.L. (2d) 25 (C.A.) 368, 369

Scally v. Southern Health & Social Services Board, [1992] 1 A.C. 294 (H.L.)...743

Scammell and Nephew Ltd. v. Ouston, [1941] A.C. 251 (H.L.)................91, 104–5

Scandinavian Trading Co. A/B v. Zodiac Petroleum S.A. and William
Hudson Ltd. (The "Al Hofuf"), [1981] 1 Lloyd's Rep. 81 (Q.B.) 642

Scanlon v. Standish (2002), 57 O.R. (3d) 767, 155 O.A.C. 96, 24 R.F.L.
(5th) 179 (C.A.)... 53

Scarborough Tire & Spring Service Ltd. v. Campbell Graphics Inc., [1994]
O.J. No. 2092, 17 B.L.R. (2d) 118, 7 M.V.R. (3d) 125 (Gen. Div.) 775

Scarf v. Jardine (1882), 7 App. Cas. 345 (H.L.) 659

Schara Tzedeck v. Royal Trust Co., [1951] 2 D.L.R. 228, 1 W.W.R. (N.S.) 760
(B.C.S.C.), aff'd [1952] 2 D.L.R. 298, 5 W.W.R. (N.S.) 279 (B.C.C.A.),
aff'd on other grounds (1952), [1953] 1 S.C.R. 31, [1952] 4 D.L.R. 529 734
Schebsman, In re, [1944] Ch. 83 (C.A.) 304
Scheel v. Henkelman (2001), 52 O.R. (3d) 1, 195 D.L.R. (4th) 531, [2001]
O.J. No. 55 (C.A.) 410
Scheuerman v. Scheuerman, [1916] 52 S.C.R. 625, 28 D.L.R. 223,
10 W.W.R. 379.. 479
Schiller v. Fisher, [1981] 1 S.C.R. 593, 124 D.L.R. (3d) 577, 37 N.R. 350........... 67
Schimp v. RCR Catering Ltd., 2004 NSCA 29, 221 N.S.R. (2d) 379,
236 D.L.R. (4th) 461..886
Schmidt v. International Harvester Co. of Canada Ltd. (1962),
38 W.W.R. 180 (Man. Q.B.) 765
Schneider v. Norris (1814), 2 M. & S. 287 (K.B.) 172
Schnell v. Nell (1861), 17 Ind. 29... 225
Schroeder Music Publishing Co. Ltd. v. MacAulay, [1974] 1 W.L.R. 1308,
[1974] 3 All E.R. 616 (H.L.) 413, 418, 451, 458
Scivoletto v. De Dona (1961), 35 W.W.R. 44 (Alta. D.C.) 223
Scotson v. Pegg (1861), 6 H. & N. 295, 158 E.R. 121 (Ex. Ch.) 242
Scott v. Avery (1856), 5 H.L. Cas. 881 440
Scott v. Brown, Doering, McNab & Co., [1892] 2 Q.B. 724 (C.A.) 431
Scott v. Coulson, [1903] 2 Ch. 249 (C.A.)............................... 528, 529, 544, 549
Scott v. Hanson (1829), 1 Russ. & M. 128, 39 E.R. 49 (Ch.) 327
Scott v. Rayment (1868), L.R.7 Eq. 112 937
Scott v. Wawanesa Mutual Insurance Co., [1989] 1 S.C.R. 1445, 59 D.L.R.
(4th) 660, [1989] S.C.J. No. 55 .... 312, 726
Scragg v. United Kingdom Temperance & General Provident Institution,
[1976] 2 Lloyd's Rep. 227 (Q.B. (Com. Ct.)) 716
Scriven Brothers & Co. v. Hindley & Co., [1913] 3 K.B. 564 503
Scruttons Ltd. v. Midland Silicones Ltd., [1962] A.C. 446 (H.L.)...................... 296
Scyrup v. Economy Tractor Parts Ltd. (1963), 40 D.L.R. (2d) 1026,
43 W.W.R. 49 (Man. C.A.) 863
Sealand of the Pacific Ltd. v. Ocean Cement Ltd. (1973), 33 D.L.R. (3d) 625,
[1973] 3 W.W.R. 60 (B.C.S.C.), var'd (1974), 51 D.L.R. (3d) 703, [1974]
6 W.W.R. 724 (B.C.C.A.).. 351
Seddon v. North Eastern Salt Co. Ltd., [1905] 1 Ch. 326 344
Semelhago v. Paramadevan, [1996] 2 S.C.R. 415, 136 D.L.R. (4th) 1, [1996]
S.C.J. No. 71 .... 874, 911, 914–15, 943–44, 945, 946
Series 5 Software Ltd. v. Clarke, [1996] 1 All E.R. 853 (Ch. D.)........................ 955
Servicemaster Industries Inc. v. Servicemaster of Victoria Ltd. (1979),
101 D.L.R. (3d) 376, [1979] B.C.J. No. 392, 13 B.C.L.R. 15 (S.C.)..............948
Shadwell v. Shadwell (1860), 9 Cl. & F. 99, 9 C.B. (N.S.) 159 (C.P.) 242
Shanklin Pier Ltd. v. Detel Products Ltd., [1951] 2 K.B. 854..................... 231, 304
Shatford v. B.C. Wine Growers Ltd., [1927] 2 D.L.R. 759 (B.C.S.C.) 57
Shatilla v. Feinstein, [1923] 3 D.L.R. 1035 (Sask. C.A.) 898, 899, 900

Shaw Cablesystems Manitoba Ltd. v. Canadian Legion Memorial Housing
    Foundation (Manitoba) (1996), 135 D.L.R. (4th) 501, [1996]
    6 W.W.R. 640, [1996] M.J. No. 267 (Q.B.) 740
Shaw v. Groom, [1970] 2 Q.B. 504 (C.A.) 464
Shaw v. Masson (1922), [1923] S.C.R. 187 934
Shelanu Inc. v. Print Three Franchising Corp. (2003), 64 O.R. (3d) 533,
    226 D.L.R. (4th) 577, [2003] O.J. No. 1919 (C.A.) 158, 625, 635, 782, 804
Shelley v. Paddock, [1980] 1 Q.B. 348 (C.A.) 477
Shepard & Co. v. Rhodes (1863), 7 R.I. 470 225
Shephard v. Colchester Regional Hospital Commission (1991), 103 N.S.R.
    (2d) 361, [1991] N.S.J. No. 204 (S.C.T.D.), leave to appeal to C.A.
    refused (1991), 106 N.S.R. (2d) 239, [1991] N.S.J. No. 378 (S.C.A.D.) 933
Shepherd v. Croft, [1911] 1 Ch. 521 942
Sherk v. Horwitz, [1972] 2 O.R. 451, 25 D.L.R. (3d) 675, 5 C.P.R.
    (2d) 135 (H.C.J.), aff'd on other grounds (1972), [1973] 1 O.R. 360,
    31 D.L.R. (3d) 152, 9 C.P.R. (2d) 119 (C.A.), leave to appeal to
    S.C.C. refused (1972), 9 C.P.R. (2d) 119n (S.C.C.) 456, 457
Sherman v. Monarch Chrome Furniture Co. Ltd. (1958), 15 D.L.R.
    (2d) 6 (Ont. C.A.) 168
Sherwood v. Walker, 33 N.W. 919 (Mich. S.C. 1887) 528
Shiesel v. Kirsch, [1931] O.R. 41 (Ont. C.A.) 446
Shirlaw v. Southern Foundries (1926) Ltd., [1939] 2 K.B. 206 (C.A.) 735
Shogun Finance Ltd. v. Hudson (2001), [2001] EWCA Civ 1000, [2002]
    4 All E.R. 572 (C.A.), aff'd (2003), [2003] UKHL 62, [2004]
    1 A.C. 919, [2004] 1 All E.R. 215 .... 516-18, 539, 552
Shoppers Trust Co. v. Dynamic Homes Ltd. (1992), 10 O.R. (3d) 361,
    96 D.L.R. (4th) 267, [1992] O.J. No. 2000 (Gen. Div.) 409
Shopsky and Shopsky v. Danyliuk (1959), 23 D.L.R. (2d) 501,
    30 W.W.R. 647 (Alta. S.C.) 483
Shorb v. Public Trustee (1953), 8 W.W.R. (N.S.) 657 (Alta. S.C.),
    aff'd (1954), 11 W.W.R. (N.S.) 132 (Alta. C.A.) 563
Shore v. Wilson (1842) 9 Cl. & F. 355, 8 E.R. 450 (H.L.) 716
Shun Cheong Holdings B.C. Ltd. v. Gold Ocean City Supermarket Ltd.,
    2002 BCCA 451, 216 D.L.R. (4th) 392, [2002] B.C.J. No. 1853 (C.A.) 634
Sibree v. Tripp (1846), 15 M. & W. 23, 153 E.R. 745 (Ex. Ch.) 253
Sibtac Corp. Ltd. v. Soo; Lienster Investments Ltd., Third Party (1978),
    18 O.R. (2d) 395. 83 D.L.R. (3d) 116 (H.C.J.) 74
Sidmay Ltd. v. Wehttam Investments Ltd., [1967] 1 O.R. 508, 61 D.L.R.
    (2d) 358 (C.A.), aff'd [1968] S.C.R. 828, 61 D.L.R. (2d) 358 ....464, 465, 474
Sigvaldason v. Hitsman (1922), 65 D.L.R. 317 (Sask. C.A.) 174, 179
Silver Dollar City v. Kitzmiller Construction Co., 931 S.W. 2d 909
    (Mo. App. 1996) 515, 543
Simmons & McBride Ltd. v. Kirkpatrick (1945), 61 B.C.R. 467, [1945]
    4 D.L.R. 134, [1945] 3 W.W.R. 557 (S.C.) 919
Simmons v. U.S., 308 F.2d 160 (4th Cir. 1962) 52
Simpkins v. Pays, [1955] 3 All E.R. 10 (H.C.) 135

Simpson v. Hughes (1897), 66 L.J. Ch. 334 (C.A.) 54, 61

Singh v. Ali, [1960] A.C. 167, [1960] 2 W.L.R. 180, [1960] 1 All E.R. 269
    (P.C.) 482

Singh v. Kulubya, [1964] A.C. 142 (P.C.) 482

Sirius International Insurance Co. (Publ) v. FAI General Insurance Ltd.
    (2004), [2004] UKHL 54, [2005] 1 All E.R. 191 .... 710, 719–20

Skeate v. Beale (1841), 11 Ad. & El. 983, 113 E.R. 688 (Ex.) 370–71

Skipp v. Kelly, (1926), 42 T.L.R. 258 (J.C.P.C.) 433

Sky Petroleum v. V.I.P. Petroleum, [1974] 1 W.L.R. 576 (Ch.) 921

Sky Ranches Ltd. v. Nelson (1980), 30 B.C.L.R. 162, [1980] B.C.J. No. 887
    (C.A.) 675

Slator v. Nolan (1876), 11 I.R. Eq. 367 405

Smallman v. Smallman, [1971] 3 All E.R. 717 (C.A.) 680

Smirnis v. Toronto Sun Publishing Co. (1997), 37 O.R. (3d) 440, [1997]
    O.J. No. 4717, 44 O.T.C. 304 (Gen. Div.) 52, 56–57

Smith & Osberg Ltd. v. Hollenback (1938), 53 B.C.R. 296, [1938]
    3 W.W.R. 704 (S.C.) 73

Smith & Snipes Hall Farm v. River Douglas Catchment Board, [1949]
    2 K.B. 500 (C.A.) 299

Smith Newcourt Securities Ltd. v. Scrimgeour Vickers (Asset Management)
    Ltd. (1996), [1997] A.C. 254, [1996] 4 All ER 769, [1996] H.L.J. No. 38.... 352

Smith v. Chadwick (1882), 20 Ch. D. 27 715

Smith v. Chadwick (1884), 9 App. Cas. 187 (H.L.) 331

Smith v. Cuff (1817), 6 M. & S. 160, 105 E.R. 1203 (K.B.) 471

Smith v. Dawson (1923), 53 O.L.R. 615, [1923] O.J. No. 173 (S.C.A.D.) 245

Smith v. Gold Coast and Ashanti Explorers Ltd., [1903] 1 K.B. 285, aff'd
    [1903] 1 K.B. 538 (C.A.) 168

Smith v. Hughes (1871), L.R. 6 Q.B. 597 (Div'l Ct.) 331, 337, 496, 499, 501, 506

Smith v. Land and House Property Corp. (1884), 28 Ch. Div. 7 (C.A.) 328

Smith v. Spencer (1918), 42 D.L.R. 269 (Sask. C.A.) 172

Smith v. Westhall (1697), 1 Ld. Raym. 316, 91 E.R. 658 (K.B.) 168

Smythers v. Armstrong (1989), 67 O.R. (2d) 753, 57 D.L.R. (4th) 174,
    [1989] O.J. No. 92 (H.C.J.) 442

Snepp v. United States, 444 U.S. 507 (1980) 976

Snipes Mountain Co. v. Benz Bros. & Co., 298 P. 714 (Wash. 1931) 588

Societa Italiana Assicurazioni Transporti v. Canadian Marine Underwriters
    Ltd., [1994] O.J. No. 3131, 26 C.C.L.I. (2d) 283 (Gen. Div.) 442

Société Des Industries Metallurgiques S.A. v. Bronx Engineering Co.
    Ltd., [1975] 1 Lloyd's Rep. 465 (C.A.) 922

Société Franco Tunisienne D'Armement v. Sidermar, [1961] 2 Q.B. 278... 585, 587

Société Italo-Belge pour le Commerce et L'Industrie S.A. v. Palm and
    Vegetable Oils (Malaysia) Sdn. Bhd., [1982] 1 All E.R. 19
    (Q.B.) 282–83, 289, 290

Sodd Corporation Inc. v. Tessis (1977), 17 O.R. (2d) 158, 79 D.L.R.
    (3d) 632, 25 C.B.R. (N.S.) 16 (C.A.) 326, 356, 694

Sokoloff v. 5 Rosehill Avenue Developments Inc., [1998] O.J. No. 4911,
    83 O.T.C. 56, 21 R.P.R. (3d) 176 (Gen. Div.) 940
Solle v. Butcher, [1950] 1 K.B. 671 (C.A.) 504, 535–37, 538, 539, 989
Solway v. Davis Moving & Storage Inc. (2002), 62 O.R. (3d) 522,
    222 D.L.R. (4th) 251, [2002] O.J. No. 4760 (C.A.) 421, 752, 773
Souder v. Wereschuk, 2004 ABCA 339, 357 A.R. 173, 245 D.L.R.
    (4th) 385 .... 332, 333
Southern Foundries (1926) Ltd. v. Shirlaw, [1940] A.C. 701 (H.L.) 931
South-West Oxford Township v. Bailack (1990), 75 O.R. (2d) 360,
    73 D.L.R. (4th) 411 (Gen. Div.) 262
Southwood Mall Ltd. v. Scardina, [1981] 6 W.W.R. 569, [1981] M.J. No. 19,
    13 Man.R. (2d) 26 (Co. Ct.) 330
Spear v. Bank of Nova Scotia (1973), 6 N.B.R. (2d) 377, 37 D.L.R. (3d) 130,
    [1973] N.B.J. No. 63 (S.C.A.D.) 263
Spencer v. C.P.R. (1913), 13 D.L.R. 836 (Ont. S.C.A.D.) 185
Spencer v. Hemmerde, [1922] 2 A.C. 507 (H.L.) 238
Spiers v. Hunt, [1908] 1 K.B. 720 433
Spiro v. Lintern, [1973] 1 W.L.R. 1002 (C.A.) 278
Spooner v. Starkman, [1937] 2 D.L.R. 582 (Ont. C.A.) 185
Sprucegrove (Town) v. Yellowhead Regional Library Board (1982),
    44 A.R. 48, 143 D.L.R. (3d) 188, [1982] A.J. No. 669 (C.A.) 216
Squillante v. California Lands, 42 P.2d 81 (Cal. Dist. Ct. App. 1935) 588
St. John Shipping Corp. v. Joseph Rank Ltd., [1957] 1 Q.B. 267 .... 431, 463–64,
    467, 475
Staffordshire Area Health Authority v. South Staffordshire Waterworks
    Co., [1978] 1 W.L.R. 1387 (C.A.) 740
Staiman Steel Ltd. v. Commercial & Home Builders Ltd. (1976),
    13 O.R. (2d) 315, 71 D.L.R. (3d) 17 (H.C.) 500, 503
Stanco Projects Ltd. v. British Columbia (Ministry of Water, Land and
    Air Protection), 2004 BCSC 1038, 242 D.L.R. (4th) 720, [2004]
    B.C.J. No. 1644 742
Standard Realty Co. v. Nicholson (1911), 24 O.L.R. 46, [1911] O.J. No. 49
    (H.C.) 172
Startup et al. v. Cortazzi (1835), 2 C.M. & R. 165, 150 E.R. 71 (Ex.) 868
Steadman v. Steadman, [1976] A.C. 536 (H.L.) 175
Stefanovska v. Kok, 73 O.R. (2d) 368, [1990] O.J. No. 865, 12 R.P.R.
    (2d) 80 (H.C.J.) 942
Steinberg Inc. v. Tilak Corp. (1991), 2 O.R. (3d) 165, [1991] O.J. No. 97,
    15 R.P.R. (2d) 146 (Gen. Div.) 719
Steinberg v. Cohen (1929), [1930] 2 D.L.R. 916 (Ont. S.C.A.D.) 474, 482
Steinberg v. Steinberg (1963), 45 D.L.R. (2d) 162, 45 W.W.R. 562, [1963]
    S.J. No. 133 (Q.B.) 131
Stellar Properties Ltd. v. Botham Holdings Ltd., [1994] 8 W.W.R. 639,
    [1994] B.C.J. No. 639, 94 B.C.L.R. (2d) 42 (C.A.) 541
Stenhouse Australia Ltd. v. Phillips, [1974] A.C. 391 (P.C.) 455

Stephens v. Gulf Oil (1975), 11 O.R. (2d) 129, 65 D.L.R. (3d) 193, 25 C.P.R.
    (2d) 64 (C.A.), leave to appeal to S.C.C. refused, [1976] 1 S.C.R. xi,
    11 O.R. (2d) 129n, 65 D.L.R. (3d) 193n 451, 458
Stephenson v. Bromley, [1928] 4 D.L.R. 737 (Man. C.A.) 967, 981, 988
Stephenson v. Clarke (1854), 4 Gr. 540, [1854] O.J. No. 212 (U.C. Ch.) 920
Stephenson v. Hilti (Canada) Ltd. (1989), 93 N.S.R. (2d) 366, 63 D.L.R.
    (4th) 573, [1989] N.S.J. No. 346 (S.C.T.D.) 408
Stevenson v. Colonial Homes Ltd., [1961] O.R. 407, 27 D.L.R. (2d) 698 (C.A.) ... 981
Stevenson, Jacques & Co. v. McLean (1880), 5 Q.B.D. 346 .... 54, 61, 73, 219
Stewart v. Ambrosina (1975), 10 O.R. (2d) 483, 63 D.L.R. (3d) 595 (H.C.J.),
    aff'd (1977) 16 O.R. (2d) 221, 78 D.L.R. (3d) 125 (C.A.) 936
Stewart v. Industrial Acceptance Corp. Ltd., [1949] 3 D.L.R 42 (B.C.S.C.) 869
Stilk v. Myrick (1809), 2 Camp. 317, 170 E.R. 1168 (Nisi Prius) 245
Still v. Minister of National Revenue (1997), [1998] 1 F.C. 549,
    154 D.L.R. (4th) 229, [1997] F.C.J. No. 1622 (C.A.) 460, 466, 476, 481
Stockloser v. Johnson, [1954] 1 Q.B. 476 (C.A.) 982
Stocznia Gdanska S.A. v. Latvian Shipping Co. (No. 2), [2002] EWCA
    Civ 889, [2002] 2 Lloyd's Rep. 436, [2002] E.W.J. No. 2917 (C.A.) 659
Stocznia Gdanska SA v. Latvian Shipping Co. (1996), [1997] 2 Lloyd's
    Rep. 228, [1996] E.W.J. No. 5146 (C.A.), rev'd on other grounds,
    [1998] 1 W.L.R. 574, [1998] 1 All E.R. 883, [1998] H.L.J. No. 9 66
Stolze v. Fuller (1938), [1939] S.C.R. 235, [1939] 1 D.L.R. 1,
    71 C.C.C. 36 .... 384, 471
Storer v. Great Western Rwy. Co. (1842), 2 Y. & C.C.C. 48, 63 E.R. 21 (V.C.) 930
Storer v. Manchester City Council, [1974] 3 All E.R. 824 (C.A.) 37, 62
Stott v. Merit Investment Corp. (1988), 63 O.R. (2d) 545, 48 D.L.R.
    (4th) 288, [1988] O.J. No. 134 (C.A.) 227, 368, 376–77, 380, 381
Strata Corp. NW 1714 v. Winkler (1987), 45 D.L.R. (4th) 741, [1987]
    B.C.J. No. 2340, 20 B.C.L.R. (2d) 16 (C.A.) 841
Stribbell v. Bhalla (1990), 73 O.R. (2d) 748, [1990] O.J. No. 999,
    42 C.P.C. (2d) 161 (H.C.J.) 443
Strickland v.Turner (1852), 7 Ex. 208, 155 E.R. 919 .... 528, 549
Stromdale & Ball Ltd. v. Burden, [1952] Ch. 223 260
Strongman (1945) Ltd. v. Sincock, [1955] 2 Q.B. 525 (C.A.) 478
Stuart v. Kingman (1978), 21 O.R. (2d) 650, 91 D.L.R. (3d) 142 (H.C.J.) 431
Stuart v. Mott (1894), 23 S.C.R. 384 170
Stubbs v. Erickson (1981), 34 B.C.L.R. 45, [1981] B.C.J. No. 1896 (S.C.) 409
Sturgeons Ltd. v. Municipality of Metropolitan Toronto, [1968] 2 O.R. 526,
    70 D.L.R. (2d) 20 (S.C.) 127
Sudbrook Trading Estate Ltd. v. Eggleton, [1983] 1 A.C. 444 (H.L.) 99, 100
Suisse Atlantique Société d'Armement Maritime S.A. v. N.V. Rotterdamsche
    Kolen Centrale, [1967] 1 A.C. 361 (H.L.) 754, 756–58, 762, 765, 768, 769
Sullivan v. Gray, [1942] 3 D.L.R. 269, [1942] O.W.N. 329 (H.C.J.) 307
Sumpter v. Hedges, [1898] 1 Q.B. 673 (C.A.) 984, 985
Sun Fire Office v. Hart (1889), 14 App. Cas. 98 (H.L.) 725

Sunnyside Greenhouses Ltd. v. Golden West Seeds (1972), 27 D.L.R.
(3d) 434, [1972] 4 W.W.R. 420 (Alta. C.A.), aff'd (1973), 33 D.L.R.
(3d) 384, [1973] 3 W.W.R. 288, [1973] S.C.J. No. 21 840

Sunshine Exploration Ltd. v. Dolly Varden Mines Ltd. (N.P.L.) (1969),
[1970] S.C.R. 2, 8 D.L.R. (3d) 441, 70 W.W.R. 418................................... 846

Sunshine Vacation Villas Ltd. v. Governor and Company of Adventurers
of England trading into Hudson's Bay (1984), 13 D.L.R. (4th) 93,
[1984] B.C.J. No. 1794, 58 B.C.L.R. 33 (C.A.) 839

Surrendra Overseas Ltd. v. Government of Sri Lanka, [1977] 1 W.L.R. 565
(Q.B.).. 238

Surrey C.C. v. Bredero Homes Ltd., [1993] 3 All E.R. 705 (C.A.)..................... 975

Swanson Construction Co. v. Government of Manitoba (1963), 40 D.L.R.
(2d) 162, 43 W.W.R. 385 (Man. C.A.) 572–73

Swim v. Amos (1895), 33 N.B.R. 49 (C.A.)... 172

Switzer's Investments Ltd. v. Burn (1964), 47 D.L.R. (2d) 280,
49 W.W.R. 627 (Alta. S.C.).. 174, 179

Sydall v. Castings Ltd., [1967] 1 Q.B. 302 (C.A.) 716

Sylan Industries Ltd. v. Fairview Sheet Metal Works Ltd. (1994), 113 D.L.R.
(4th) 493, 89 B.C.L.R. (2d) 18, [1994] B.C.J. No. 468 (C.A.)......................311

Sylvan Lake Golf & Tennis Club v. Performance Industries Ltd.,
2002 SCC 19, [2002] 1 S.C.R. 678, 209 D.L.R. (4th) 318............ 557, 558, 559,
560, 562-64

Sylvio Construction Co. v. 678192 Ontario Ltd., [1993] O.J. No. 1423,
11 B.L.R. (2d) 148, 11 C.L.R. (2d) 136 (Gen. Div.)..................................... 127

Symington v. Vancouver Breweries Ltd., [1931] 1 D.L.R. 935 (B.C.C.A.) 438

Syros Shipping Co. SA v. Elaghill Trading Co. (The Proodos C), [1980]
2 Lloyd's Rep. 390 (Q.B.) 227

Sze Hai Tong Bank Ltd. v. Rambler Cycle Co. Ltd., [1959] A.C. 576 (P.C.) 755

Tai Hing Cotton Mill Ltd. v. Kamsing Knitting Factory, [1979] A.C. 91 (P.C.).... 667

Tamplin Steamship Co. v. Anglo Mexican S.S. Co., [1916] 2 A.C. 397
(H.L.) 570, 576, 578, 584

Tamplin v. James (1880), 15 Ch. D. 215 (C.A.) 935

Tanenbaum v. W.J. Bell Paper Co. Ltd., [1956] O.R. 278, 4 D.L.R.
(2d) 177 (H.C.J.) 930, 931

Tanenbaum v. Wright-Winston Ltd., [1965] 2 O.R. 1, 49 D.L.R. (2d) 386
(C.A.) 983

Tank Lining Corp. v. Dunlop Industrial Ltd. (1982), 40 O.R. (2d) 219,
140 D.L.R. (3d) 659, 68 C.P.R. (2d) 162 (C.A.) 450, 456, 458

Tarmac Canada Inc. v. Hamilton-Wentworth (Regional Municipality),
[1999] O.J. No. 3273, 125 O.A.C. 72, 48 C.L.R. (2d) 236 (C.A.) 148, 149

Taylor Hardware Co. v. Hunt, [1917] 35 D.L.R. 504 (Ont. S.C.A.D.)................. 985

Taylor v. Armstrong (1979), 24 O.R. (2d) 614, 99 D.L.R. (3d) 547 (H.C.J.) 409

Taylor v. Bhail, [1996] C.L.C. 377 (C.A.) 484

Taylor v. Bowers (1876), 1 Q.B.D. 291 (C.A.)... 472

Taylor v. Caldwell (1863) 3 B. & S. 826, 122 E.R. 309 (K.B.) 566, 569, 573, 579, 597, 603

Taylor v. Gill (1991), 113 A.R. 38, [1991] 3 W.W.R. 727, [1991] A.J. No. 133 (Q.B.) 876

Taylor v. Johnson (1983), 151 C.L.R. 422 (A.H.C.) 503, 504, 551

Taylor v. Oakes Roncoroni & Co. (1922), 127 L.T. 267 (C.A.) 643, 663

Taylor v. Smith (1995), 26 O.R. (3d) 50, 128 D.L.R. (4th) 548, [1995] O.J. No. 2841 (Gen. Div.) 135

Taylor v. Sturgeon (1996), 156 N.S.R. (2d) 147, [1996] N.S.J. No. 559, 12 R.P.R. (3d) 107 (S.C.) 917

TCB Ltd. v. Gray, [1986] Ch. 621 262

Techform Products Ltd. v. Wolda (2001), 56 O.R. (3d) 1, 206 D.L.R. (4th) 171, [2001] O.J. No. 3822 (C.A.), rev'g (2000), 5 C.P.R. (4th) 25 (Ont. S.C.J.) 292, 379, 380

Templin v. Alles, [1944] 1 D.L.R. 733, [1944] O.W.N. 96, [1944] O.J. No. 22 (C.A.) 727

ter Neuzen v. Korn, [1995] 3 S.C.R. 674, 127 D.L.R. (4th) 577, [1995] S.C.J. No. 79 730

TerraCan Corp. v. Pine Projects Ltd.(1993), 100 D.L.R. (4th) 431, [1993] 3 W.W.R. 724, [1993] B.C.J. No. 203 (C.A.) 487, 488

Texaco Ltd. v Mulberry Filling Station Ltd., [1972] 1 W.L.R. 814 (Ch.) 954

Thackwell v. Barclays Bank Plc, [1986] 1 All E.R. 676 (Q.B.) 477

Thai Trading Co. v. Taylor, [1998] Q.B. 781 444

The Athinoula, [1980] 2 Lloyd's Rep. 481 (Q.B. (Com. Ct.)) 727

The Concadoro, [1960] 2 A.C. 199 (P.C.) 600

The Curfew, [1891] P. 131 711

The Governors of Dalhousie College at Halifax v. The Estate of Arthur Boutilier, [1934] S.C.R. 642, [1934] 3 D.L.R. 593 .... 229, 230

The King v. C.P.R., [1947] S.C.R. 185, [1947] 2 D.L.R. 1 869

The Mihalis Angelos, [1971] 1 Q.B. 164 632

The Moorcock (1889), L.R. 14 P.D. 64 735

The Pas v. Porky Packers Ltd. (1976), [1977] 1 S.C.R. 51, 65 D.L.R. (3d) 1, 7 N.R. 569 349

The Queen v. McLean (1884), 8 S.C.R. 210 220

Thermo-Flow Corp. Ltd. v. Kuryluk (1978), 28 N.S.R. (2d) 699, 84 D.L.R. (3d) 529, [1978] N.S.J. No. 598 (S.C.T.D.) 262

Thiessen v. Leduc, [1975] 4 W.W.R. 387 (Alta. S.C.T.D.) 867

Thirkell v. Cambi, [1919] 2 K.B. 590 170

Thomas & Co. v. Brown (1899), 4 Com. Cas. 186 .... 310, 312

Thomas Brown & Sons Ltd. v. Fazal Deen (1962), 108 C.L.R. 391 (A.H.C.) 482

Thomas v. Brown (1876), 1 Q.B.D. 714 .... 174, 179, 988

Thomas v. Grace (1865), 15 U.C.C.P. 462, [1865] O.J. No. 193 228

Thomas v. Thomas (1842), 2 Q.B. 851, 114 E.R. 330 ....224, 225, 237

Thompson v. Guaranty Trust Co. (1973), [1974] S.C.R. 1023, 39 D.L.R. (3d) 408, [1973] 6 W.W.R. 746 177

Thompson v. Skill (1909), 13 O.W.R. 887, [1909] O.J. No. 706 (C.A.) 262

Thomson Groceries Ltd. v. Scott, [1943] O.R. 290, [1943] 3 D.L.R. 25
(C.A.) 102, 105–6

Thorn v. Public Works Commissioners (1863), 32 Beav. 490,
55 E.R. 192 (M.R.) 918

Thornton v. Shoe Lane Parking Ltd., [1971] 2 Q.B. 163 (C.A.) 185, 186

Thoroughgood's Case (1582), 2 Co. Rep. 9a, 76 E.R. 408 (C.P.) 519

Thorp v. Thorp (1702), 12 Mod. 455, 88 E.R. 1448 (K.B.) 215

Thrupp v. Fielder (1798), 2 Esp. 628, 170 E.R. 477 (Nisi Prius) 238

Tilden Rent-A-Car Company v. Clendenning (1978), 18 O.R. (2d) 601,
83 D.L.R. (3d) 400, 4 B.L.R. 50 (C.A.) 191, 192

Tillmanns & Co. v. S.S. Knutsford Ltd., [1908] 2 K.B. 385 720

Tinn v. Hoffman (1873), 29 L.T. 271 (Ex. Ch.).. 32, 56

Tinsley v. Milligan, [1993] 3 All E.R. 65 (H.L.).. 479

Tito v. Waddell (No. 2), [1977] Ch. 106 845

Tiverton Estates Ltd. v. Wearwell Ltd., [1975] Ch. 146 (C.A.) 171

Tobias v. Dick and T. Eaton Co., [1937] 4 D.L.R. 546 (Man. K.B.) 220, 222

Tobin v. McComb, 156 S.W. 237 (Tex. C.A. 1913) 57

Tony and Jim's Holdings Limited v. Silva (1999), 43 O.R. (3d) 633,
170 D.L.R. (4th) 193, [1999] O.J. No. 705 (C.A.)....................................316–17

Tool Metal Manufacturing Co. Ltd. v. Tungsten Electric Co. Ltd., [1955]
1 W.L.R. 761 (H.L.)... 286

Topfell Ltd. v. Galley Properties Ltd., [1979] 1 W.L.R. 446 (Ch.)..................... 940

Torchia v. Royal Insurance Co. of Canada (2003), 64 O.R. (3d) 775,
[2003] O.J. No. 2199, [2003] O.T.C. 493 (S.C.J.) 726

Toronto Blue Jays Baseball Club v. Tri-Tickets Inc. (1991), 6 O.R. (3d) 15,
85 D.L.R. (4th) 422, [1991] O.J. No. 2002 (Gen. Div.) 958

Toronto Dominion Bank v. Fortin (No. 2) (1978), 88 D.L.R. (3d) 232, [1978]
5 W.W.R. 302, 27 C.B.R. (N.S.) 232 (B.C.S.C.)..................................... 541

Toronto Gravel Road & Concrete Co. v. County of York (1885),
12 S.C.R. 517.. 737

Toronto Hockey Club Ltd. v. Arena Gardens of Toronto Ltd., [1926]
4 D.L.R. 1, [1926] 3 W.W.R. 26 (P.C.)... 848

Toronto Marlborough Major Junior "A" Hockey Club v. Tonelli (1975),
11 O.R. (2d) 664, 67 D.L.R. (3d) 214, 25 C.P.R. (2d) 175 (H.C.J.) 955

Toronto Transit Commission v. Gottardo Construction Ltd. (2003),
68 O.R. (3d) 356 (S.C.J.)...117

Toronto Type Foundry Ltd. v. Miehle-Goss-Dexter (1968), [1969]
2 O.R. 431, 5 D.L.R. (3d) 578, [1968] O.J. No. 597 (Ont. H.C.J.) 740

Toronto-Dominion Bank v. Leigh Instruments Ltd. (Trustee of), [1998]
O.J. No. 2637, 63 O.T.C. 1, 40 B.L.R. (2d) 1 (Gen. Div.), aff'd (1999),
45 O.R. (3d) 417, 178 D.L.R. (4th) 634, [1999] O.J. No. 3290 (C.A.),
leave to appeal to S.C.C. refused (1999), 188 D.L.R. (4th) vi,
[1999] S.C.C.A. No. 521 ....121–22, 709, 712

Total Oil (Great Britain) Ltd. v. Thompson Garages (Biggin Hill) Ltd.,
[1972] 1 Q.B. 318 (C.A.).. 665

Toulon Development Corporation v. Loblaws (1995), 161 N.B.R. (2d) 313,
[1995] N.B.J. No. 219 (Q.B.)... 929

Towers v. Affleck (1973), [1974] 1 W.W.R. 714, [1974] I.L.R. 1-599 (B.C.S.C.)...410

Town of Fort Frances v. Boise Cascade Canada Ltd., [1983] 1 S.C.R. 171,
143 D.L.R. (3d) 193, 46 N.R. 108 41

Trans Canada Credit Corporation Ltd. v. Royal Insurance Co. of Canada
(1983), 58 N.S.R. (2d) 280, 149 D.L.R. (3d) 280, [1983] N.S.J. No. 440
(S.C.A.D.) 312

Trans Trust S.P.R.L. v. Danubian Trading Co., [1952] 2 Q.B. 297 (C.A.).......... 819

Transamerica Life Canada v. ING Canada (2003), 68 O.R. (3d) 457,
234 D.L.R. (4th) 367, [2003] O.J. No. 4656 (C.A.) 805

TransCanada Pipelines Ltd. v. Northern & Central Gas Corp. (1983),
41 O.R. (2d) 447, 146 D.L.R. (3d) 293 (C.A.) 711

TransCanada Pipelines Ltd. v. Potter Station Power Limited Partnership
(2003), 226 D.L.R. (4th) 262, [2003] O.J. No. 2440, 172 O.A.C. 379
(C.A.) 723

Transport North American Express Inc. v. New Solutions Financial Corp.,
2004 SCC 7, [2004] 1 S.C.R. 249, 235 D.L.R. (4th) 385, rev'g (2002),
60 O.R. (3d) 97, 214 D.L.R. (4th) 44, [2002] O.J. No. 2335 (C.A.),
rev'g (2001), 54 O.R. (3d) 144, 200 D.L.R. (4th) 560, [2001]
O.J. No. 1948 (S.C.J.) 483, 484, 488–92

Treadwell v. Martin (1976), 13 N.B.R. (2d) 137, 67 D.L.R. (3d) 493,
[1976] N.B.J. No. 49 (S.C.A.D.).. 404, 991

Treen Gloves & Safety Products Ltd. v. Degil Safety Products (1989) Inc.,
[1990] B.C.J. No. 1672, 33 C.P.R. (3d) 74 (S.C.).................................... 740

Trendtex Trading Corporation v. Credit Suisse, [1980] Q.B. 629
(C.A.) 441, 442, 443

Trethewey v. Girard (1983), 149 D.L.R. (3d) 359, [1983] B.C.J. No. 1918
(S.C.) 327

Tribe v. Tribe, [1995] 4 All E.R. 236 (C.A.)..................................... 473, 480

Trident General Insurance Co. Ltd. v. McNiece Bros. Pty. Ltd. (1988),
165 C.L.R. 107 (A.H.C.).................................20, 299, 313, 314, 316

Trigg v. M.I. Movers International Transport Services Ltd. (1991),
4 O.R. (3d) 562, 84 D.L.R. (4th) 504, [1991] O.J. No. 1548 (C.A.),
leave to appeal to S.C.C. refused, [1992] 1 S.C.R. ix, 7 O.R.
(3d) xiin, 88 D.L.R. (4th) vii...193, 202, 751

Trollope & Colls Ltd. v. Atomic Power Constructions Ltd., [1962]
3 All E.R. 1035 (Q.B.)... 53

Trueman Maritime Auto & Trailer Sales Ltd. (1977), 19 N.B.R. (2d) 8,
[1977] N.B.J. No. 199 (S.C.A.D.).. 232

Trueman v. Fenton (1777), 2 Cowp. 544, 98 E.R. 1232 (C.A.) 238

Trust & Loan Company of Upper Canada v. Ruttan (1877), 1 S.C.R. 564........ 266

Trustees of Baker University v. Clelland, 86 F.2d 14 (8th Cir. 1936)................ 229

Tsakiroglou & Co. v. Noblee Thorl G.m.b.H. (1961), [1962] A.C. 93, [1961]
2 All E.R. 179 (H.L.) 566, 586, 588

Tsiribis v. Panopoulos, [1981] O.J. No. 713, 21 R.P.R. 58 (H.C.J.) 715

TSP-Intl Ltd. v. Mills (2005), 74 O.R. (3d) 461, [2005] O.J. No. 616, [2005] O.T.C. 132 (S.C.J.) 805

Tucker Estate v. Gillis (1988), 90 N.B.R. (2d) 391, 53 D.L.R. (4th) 688, [1988] N.B.J. No. 805 (C.A.) 431

Turczinski v. Dupont Heating & Air Conditioning Ltd. (2004), 246 D.L.R. (4th) 95, [2004] O.J. No. 4510, 191 O.A.C. 350 (C.A.) 870, 877

Turner v. Clark (1983), 49 N.B.R. (2d) 340, [1983] N.B.J. No. 29, 30 R.P.R. 164 (C.A.) 593

Turner v. Royal Bank of Scotland, [1999] 2 All E.R. (Comm) 664 (C.A.) 733, 734

Turney v. Zhilka, [1959] S.C.R. 578, 18 D.L.R. (2d) 447 ......173, 619, 682–83, 686

Tweddle v. Atkinson (1861), 1 B. & S. 393, 121 E.R. 762 (Q.B.) 296, 297, 298

Tymo v. Wild Rose Properties Ltd. (1983), 43 A.R. 54, 24 Alta. L.R. (2d) 351, [1983] A.J. No. 558 (Q.B.) 983

Tywood Industries Ltd. v. St. Anne-Nackawic Pulp & Paper Co. Ltd. (1979), 25 O.R. (2d) 89, 100 D.L.R. (3d) 374 (H.C.J.) 62

United Dominion Promotion Sales Inc. v. Shaw (1957), 9 D.L.R. (2d) 759, 119 C.C.C. 380 (N.B. Co. Ct.) 430

United Dominions Trust Ltd. v. Western (1975), [1976] Q.B. 513, [1975] 3 All E.R. 1017 (C.A.) 524

United Shoe Machinery of Canada v. Brunet, [1909] A.C. 330, [1909] C.R.A.C. 148, 18 B.R. 511 (P.C.) 342

United States v. Motor Trucks Ltd., [1924] A.C. 196 (P.C.) 556

United Systems Ltd. v. Clearwater Lobsters Ltd. (1986), 58 Nfld. & P.E.I.R. 138, [1986] N.J. No. 100 (Nfld. S.C.T.D.)...................................... 635

Universal Cargo Carriers Corp. v. Citati, [1957] 2 Q.B. 401, [1957] 2 All E.R. 70, [1957] 1 Lloyd's Rep. 174, aff'd on other grounds [1957] 1 W.L.R. 979, [1957] 3 All E.R. 234, [1957] 2 Lloyd's Rep. 191 (C.A.) ...655, 657

Universe Tankships of Monrovia v. International Transport Workers' Federation, [1983] 1 A.C. 366 (H.L.) 373–74, 380

Upfill v. Wright, [1911] 1 K.B. 506 436

Utica City National Bank v. Gunn, 118 N.E. 607 (N.Y. 1918) 709

Vachon Construction Ltd. v. Cariboo (Regional District) (1996), 136 D.L.R. (4th) 307, [1996] B.C.J. No. 1409, 78 B.C.A.C. 43 (C.A.) 148, 149, 742

Vacwell Engineering Co. Ltd. v. BDH Chemicals Ltd., [1971] 1 Q.B. 88........... 861

Valley Equipment Ltd. v. John Deere Ltd. (2000), 223 N.B.R. (2d) 264, [2000] N.B.J. No. 28, 4 B.L.R. (3d) 282 (Q.B.) 791

Van Kruistum v. Dool (1997), 35 O.R. (3d) 430, [1997] O.J. No. 6336 (Gen. Div.) 377

Van Wetzel v. Risdon (1952), [1953] 2 D.L.R. 382, 7 W.W.R. (N.S.) 646 (Alta. S.C.) 969

Vancouver Malt and Sake Brewing Co. Ltd. v. Vancouver Breweries Limited, [1934] A.C. 181 (P.C.) 448

Vancouver Milling & Grain Co. v. C.C. Ranch Co. (1924), [1924] S.C.R. 671, [1925] 1 D.L.R. 185 588

Vancouver v. Registrar of Vancouver Land Registration District, [1955]
2 D.L.R. 709, 15 W.W.R. 351 (B.C.C.A.) 445

Vandekerkhove v. Litchfield (1993), 103 D.L.R. (4th) 739, [1993]
B.C.J. No. 1355, 84 B.C.L.R. (2d) 252 (S.C.), rev'd on other grounds
(1995), 121 D.L.R. (4th) 571, 1 B.C.L.R. (3d) 70, [1995] B.C.J. No. 146
(C.A.), leave to appeal to S.C.C. refused (1995), 126 D.L.R.
(4th) vii, [1995] S.C.C.A. No. 131 ....487, 488, 541

Vandepitte v. Preferred Accident Insurance Co. (1932), [1933]
A.C. 70, [1933] 1 D.L.R. 289, [1932] 3 W.W.R. 573 (P.C.) 304, 312, 316

Vandewal v. Vandewal, [2003] O.J. No. 3269 (C.A.) 316

Vantage Navigation Corporation v. Suhail and Saud Bahwan Building
Materials LLC (sub nom. The Alev), [1989] 1 Lloyd's Rep. 138 (Q.B.)........374

Veba Oil Supply & Trading GmbH v. Petro Trade Inc. (2001), [2001]
EWCA Civ. 1832, [2002] 1 All E.R. 703 (C.A.) 648

Vecher v. Coplak Enterprises, "The World Navigator", [1991]
2 Lloyd's Rep. 23 (C.A.) 824

Venture Capital USA Inc. v. Yorkton Securities Inc. (2003), 66 O.R.
(3d) 760, [2003] O.J. No. 3529, [2003] O.T.C. 819 (S.C.J.), rev'd
(2005), 75 O.R. (3d) 325, [2005] O.J. No. 1885, 197 O.A.C. 264........ 738, 805

Victoria Electrical Co. v. Monarch Electrical Co. Ltd. (1917),
13 O.W.N. 141, [1917] O.J. No. 324 (Ex.)... 35

Victoria Laundry (Windsor) Ltd. v. Newman Industries Ltd., [1949]
2 K.B. 528 (C.A.)... 856–57, 862, 864

Victoria Queen Investments Ltd. v. The Savarin Ltd. (1980),
25 O.R. (2d) 489, 101 D.L.R. (3d) 353, 10 R.P.R. 32 (H.C.J.) 681

Victoria Wood Development Corp. v. Ondrey (1977), 14 O.R.
(2d) 723, 74 D.L.R. (3d) 528, 1 R.P.R. 141 (H.C.J.).................................... 596

Victory Motors Ltd. v. Bayda, [1973] 3 W.W.R. 747 (Sask. Dist. Ct.)..................817

Vincent v. Premo Enterprises (Voucher Sales) Ltd., [1969] 2 Q.B. 609 (C.A.)..... 267

Vita Food Products Inc. v. Unus Shipping Co., [1939] A.C. 277 (P.C.) 463

Vitol S.A. v. Norelf Ltd., [1996] A.C. 800 (H.L.) 642

Von Hatzfeldt-Wildenburg v. Alexander, [1912] 1 Ch. 284 ....126–27, 128

Vorvis v. Insurance Corporation. of British Columbia, [1989]
1 S.C.R. 1085, 58 D.L.R. (4th) 193, [1989] S.C.J. No. 46............800, 876, 877,
881, 882, 883, 885

W.C. Pitfield & Co. Ltd. v. Jomac Gold Syndicate Ltd., [1938] 3 D.L.R. 158
(Ont. C.A.) 923

W.J. Alan & Co. Ltd. v. El Nasr Export & Import Co., [1972] 2 Q.B. 189
(C.A.) 282, 284, 289, 290

W.J. Tatem v. Gamboa, [1939] 1 K.B. 132.. 582, 584

W.L. Thompson Ltd. v. Robinson (Gunmakers) Ltd., [1955] Ch. 177................817

W.R. Grace & Co. of Canada Ltd. v. Sare (1980), 28 O.R. (2d) 612, 111 D.L.R.
(3d) 204, 51 C.P.R. (2d) 83 (H.C.J.) 455

Waddell v. Blockey (1879), 4 Q.B.D. 678 (C.A.) 851

Wakeham v. MacKenzie, [1968] 2 All E.R. 783 (Ch.) 175

Walford v. Miles, [1992] 1 All E.R. 453 (H.L.) 142–43, 152

Walker v. Eastern Counties Rwy Co., (1848), 6 Hare 594, 67 E.R. 1300 (V.C.)....917

Wallace v. United Grain Growers Ltd., [1997] 3 S.C.R. 701, 152 D.L.R. (4th) 1, [1997] S.C.J. No. 94 ....7, 799, 800, 801–03, 805, 806, 876, 879, 886–87

Wallersteiner v. Moir (No. 2), [1975] Q.B. 373 (C.A.) 443

Walters v. Morgan (1861), 3 De G. F. & J. 718, 45 E.R. 1056 (Ch.) 934

Walters v. Walters, [1946] 3 W.W.R. 497 (Sask. C.A.) 226-27

Walton v. Waterhouse (1673), 2 Wms. Saund. 420, 85 E.R. 1233 (K.B.) 568

Waltons Stores (Interstate) Pty. Ltd. v. Maher (1988), 164 C.L.R. 387 (A.H.C.).. 290, 291-92

Wanderers' Hockey Club v. Johnson (1913), 18 B.C.R. 367, 5 W.W.R. 117, [1913] B.C.J. No. 70 (S.C.) 431

Wandinger v. Lake (1977), 16 O.R. (2d) 362, 78 D.L.R. (3d) 305, 2 B.L.R. 39 (H.C.J.) 340

Ward v. Byham, [1956] 1 W.L.R. 496, [1956] 2 All E.R. 318 (C.A.)............219, 241

Wardle v. Manitoba Farms Loans Association, [1954] 4 D.L.R. 572, 13 W.W.R. (N.S.) 49 (Man. C.A.), rev'd on other grounds (1955), [1956] S.C.R. 3, [1955] 5 D.L.R. 673... 719

Warlow v. Harrison (1858), 1 El. & El. 309, 120 E.R. 925 (Ex.) 48

Warner Bros. Picture Inc. v. Nelson, [1937] 1 K.B. 209 ....451, 950–51

Warren & Co. v. Agdeshman (1922), 38 T.L.R. 588 (K.B.) 222

Warren v. Mendy, [1989] 1 W.L.R. 853 (C.A.) 951, 952

Warrington v. Great-West Life Assurance Co. (1996), 139 D.L.R. (4th) 18, [1996] 10 W.W.R. 691, [1996] B.C.J. No. 1944 (C.A.) 896

Waters v. Donnelly (1884), 9 O.R. 391 (Ch.) 404–5, 408

Watkins v. Olafson, [1989] 2 S.C.R. 750, 61 D.L.R. (4th) 577, [1989] S.C.J. No. 94 19

Watson v. Haggitt, [1928] A.C. 127 (P.C.) 718

Waugh v. Pioneer Logging Co. Ltd., [1949] S.C.R. 299, [1949] 2 D.L.R. 577....899

Wauton v. Coppard, [1889] 1 Ch. 92.. 329

Webb v. Direct London & Portsmouth Railway Co. (1852), 1 De G.M. & G. 521, 42 E.R. 654 (Ch.)... 936

Webb v. McGowin, 168 So. 196 (Ala. App. 1935) 237

Webster v. Higgin, [1948] 2 All E.R. 127 (C.A.)... 201

Welby v. Drake (1825), 1 Car. & P. 557, 171 E.R. 1315 (Nisi Prius).......... 252, 255

Wells (Merstham) Ltd. v. Buckland Sand and Silica Ltd., [1965] 2 Q.B. 170 304

Welton Tool Rental Ltd. v. Douglas Aircraft Co. (1978), 28 N.S.R. (2d) 636, [1978] N.S.J. No. 597 (S.C.T.D.).. 69

Wenzoski v. Klos, [1940] 2 D.L.R. 195, [1940] 1 W.W.R. 523 (Man. C.A.) 709

West Coast Securities Ltd. v. Continental Ins. Co. (1975), 66 D.L.R. (3d) 278, [1976] 2 W.W.R. 444 (B.C.S.C.) 662

West Sussex Properties Ltd. v. Chichester DC, [2000] All E.R. (D) 887 (C.A.) 541

West Texas Transmission L.P. v. Enron Corporation, 907 F.2d 1554 (5th Cir. 1990), cert. denied, 499 U.S. 906, 915 F.2d 695 (1991) 797

West v. Houghton (1879), 4 C.P.D. 197 (P.C.).. 294, 300

Westcom TV Group Ltd. v. CanWest Global Broadcasting Inc. (1996),
    [1997] 1 W.W.R. 761, [1996] B.C.J. No. 1638, 29 B.L.R. (2d) 123
    (S.C.) 151, 152

Westcott v. Day, [1945] 1 W.W.R. 281 (Man. K.B.) 981

Westdeutsche Landesbank Girozentrale v. Islington L.B.C., [1996]
    A.C. 669 (H.L.) 819, 968

Western Log Exchange Ltd. v. Soucie Construction Ltd., [1979]
    B.C.J. No. 502, 14 B.C.L.R. 293, 8 B.L.R. 1 (S.C.), aff'd on other
    grounds [1980] B.C.J. No. 702, 21 B.C.L.R. 57 (C.A.)......................... 200

Western Processing and Cold Storage Ltd. v. Hamilton Construction
    Co. Ltd. (1965), 51 D.L.R. (2d) 245, 51 W.W.R. 354 (Man. C.A.).............. 765

Western v. Russell (1814), 3 Ves. & B. 187, 35 E.R. 450 (Ch.) 935

Westlake v. Adams (1858), 5 C.B. (N.S.) 248, 141 E.R. 99 (C.P.)...................... 222

Westward Farms Ltd. v. Cadieux (1982), 138 D.L.R. (3d) 137, [1982]
    5 W.W.R. 1, [1982] M.J. No. 96 (C.A.) 109

Weyerhauser Can. v. IWA Can., Local 1-207, 2003 ABQB 372, 338 A.R. 89,
    16 Alta. L.R. (4th) 321 714

Wheeler v. Klaholt, 59 N.E. 756 (Mass. S.C.J. 1901)...................................... 72

White & Carter (Councils) Ltd. v McGregor, [1962] A.C. 413 (H.L.) 667–68

White v. Bluett (1853), 23 L.J. Ex. 36 ....218, 219

White v. Central Trust Co. (1984), 54 N.B.R. (2d) 293, 7 D.L.R. (4th) 236,
    [1984] N.B.J. No. 147 (C.A.) 710

White v. John Warwick & Co. Ltd., [1953] 1 W.L.R. 1285 (C.A.)...................... 299

White v. Jones, [1995] 2 A.C. 207 (H.L.).. 299, 306

Whiten v. Pilot Insurance Co., 2002 SCC 18, [2002] 1 S.C.R. 595,
    [2002] S.C.J. No. 19 .... 7, 815, 878, 882, 887, 890, 891–92, 893–94, 896

Whitney v. MacLean, [1932] 1 W.W.R. 417 (Alta. C.A.).................................... 934

Whittington v. Seale-Hayne (1900), 82 L.T. 49 (Ch.).................................340, 989

Whitwood Chemical Co. v. Hardman, [1891] 2 Ch. 416 (C.A) 949

Wiebe v. Bobsien (1984), 14 D.L.R. (4th) 754, [1985] 1 W.W.R. 644,
    59 B.C.L.R. 183 (S.C.), aff'd (1985), 20 D.L.R. (4th) 475, [1986]
    4 W.W.R. 270, [1985] B.C.J. No. 1742 (C.A.) 107, 618, 678–79, 681

Wiebe v. Butchart's Motors Ltd., [1949] 4 D.L.R. 838 (B.C.C.A.) 989

Wiebe v. Gunderson, 2004 BCCA 456, 243 D.L.R. (4th) 1, [2004]
    B.C.J. No. 1844 354

Wild v. Tucker, [1914] 3 K.B. 36.. 238

Wilgross Investments Ltd. v. Goldshlager (1974), 5 O.R. (2d) 687,
    51 D.L.R. (3d) 343, 19 R.F.L. 360 (Div. Ct.).. 369

Wilkinson v. Lloyd (1845), 7 Q.B. 27, 115 E.R. 398 (K.B.) 969

Wilkinson v. Rena-Ware Distributors Ltd. (1955), 16 W.W.R. 376
    (Alta. Dist. Ct.) 983

William Cory & Son Ltd. v London Corporation, [1951] 1 K.B. 8, aff'd
    [1951] 2 K.B. 476 (C.A.) 590

William E. Thomson Associates Inc. v. Carpenter (1989), 69 O.R. (2d) 545, 61 D.L.R. (4th) 1, [1989] O.J. No. 1459 (C.A.), leave to appeal to S.C.C. refused (1990), 71 O.R. (2d) x, 65 D.L.R. (4th) viii, 105 N.R. 397n 485, 487

William Robinson & Co. Ltd. v. Heuer, [1898] 2 Ch. 451 (C.A.) 953

William Sindall plc v. Cambridgeshire County Council, [1994] 3 All E.R. 932, [1994] 1 W.L.R. 1016 (C.A.) 541, 545, 550

Williams & Clyde Coal Co. v. English, [1938] A.C. 57 (H.L.) 744

Williams v. Bayley (1866), L.R. 1 H.L. 200 .... 384, 471

Williams v. Carwardine (1833), 4 B. & Ad. 621, 110 E.R. 590, 172 E.R. 1101 (K.B.) 50, 438

Williams v. Downey-Waterbury (1994), 120 D.L.R. (4th) 737, [1995] 2 W.W.R. 609, [1994] M.J. No. 687 (C.A.) 390

Williams v. Fleetwood Holdings Ltd. (1973), 41 D.L.R. (3d) 636 (Sask. C.A.) 431

Williams v. Lloyd, (1629) Jones, W. 179, 82 E.R. 95 (K.B.) 569

Williams v. Roffey Bros. & Nicholls (Contractors) Ltd., [1990] 1 All E.R. 512 (C.A.) 248–49, 252

Williams v. Williams, [1957] 1 All E.R. 305 (C.A.) 241

Wilson v. Belfast Corp. (1921), 55 I.L.T. 205 (C.A.) 49

Wilson v. Carnley, [1908] 1 K.B. 729 (C.A.) 433

Wilson v. Clarke Simpkins Ltd. (1961), 30 D.L.R. (2d) 745 (B.C.C.A.) 200

Wilson v. Furness Rwy. Co. (1869) L.R. 9 Eq. 28 930

Wilson v. Harrison (1979), 35 N.S.R. (2d) 499, [1979] N.S.J. No. 825 (S.C.T.D.) 990

Wilson v. Northampton and Banbury Junction Rwy. Co. (1874), 9 Ch. App. 279 930

Wilson v. United Counties Bank, [1920] A.C. 102 (H.L.) 868

Windhill Local Board of Health v. Vint (1890), 45 Ch. D. 351 439

WindPower Inc. v. Saskatchewan Power Corp., 2002 SKCA 61, 217 Sask. R. 193, [2002] S.J. No. 287 47

Wingold Construction Co. Ltd. v. Kramp, [1960] S.C.R. 556, 23 D.L.R. (2d) 350 865

Winn v. Bull, (1877), 7 Ch. D. 29 127

Winnipeg Condominium Corp. No. 36 v. Bird Construction Co., [1995] 1 S.C.R. 85, 121 D.L.R. (4th) 193, [1995] S.C.J. No. 2 306

Winnipeg Livestock Sales Ltd. v. Plewman, 2000 MBCA 60, 192 D.L.R. (4th) 525, [2000] M.J. No. 429 454

Winter Garden Theatre (London) Ltd. v. Millennium Productions Ltd., [1948] A.C. 173 (H.L.) 740

Wirth v. Kutarma, [1955] 5 D.L.R. 785, 17 W.W.R. 223 (Sask. C.A.) 461

Wise v. Axford (1954), [1955] 1 D.L.R. 508, [1954] O.J. No. 273, [1954] O.W.N. 822 (C.A.) 563

With v. O'Flanagan, [1936] Ch. 575 (C.A.) 332

Withers v. General Theatre Corp., [1933] 2 K.B. 536 (C.A.) 825

Wojakowski v. Pembena Dodge Chrysler Ltd., [1976] 5 W.W.R. 97, [1976] M.J. No. 277 (Q.B.) 967

Wolverhampton and Walsall Rwy. Co. v. London & North-Western Rwy.
Co. (1873), L.R. 16 Eq. 433..949
Wolverhampton Corp. v. Emmons, [1901] 1 K.B. 515 (C.A.) 930
Wong v. DiGrazia, 386 P.2d 817 (Cal. 1963) 104
Wood Preservation, Ltd. v. Prior (Inspector of Taxes), [1968]
2 All E.R. 849 (Ch.), aff'd [1969] 1 All E.R. 364 (C.A.) 682
Wood v. Grand Valley Ry. Co. (1915), 51 S.C.R. 283, 22 D.L.R. 614,
25 C.R.C. 117..848
Wood v. Lucy, Lady Duff-Gordon, 118 N.E. 214 (N.Y. 1917)...........................221
Wood v. Roberts (1818), 2 Stark. 417, 171 E.R. 691 (Nisi Prius)...............252, 254
Woodar Investment Development Ltd. v. Wimpey Construction U.K. Ltd.,
[1980] 1 W.L.R. 277 (H.L.)..299
Woodford Estates Ltd. v. Pollack (1978), 22 O.R. (2d) 340, 93 D.L.R.
(3d) 350 (H.C.J.) 865
Woods v. Borstel (1962), 34 D.L.R. (2d) 68 (Alta. S.C.A.D.)...............346, 697–98
Woods v. Hubley (1995), 146 N.S.R. (2d) 97, 130 D.L.R. (4th) 119,
[1995] N.S.J. No. 459 (C.A.), leave to appeal to S.C.C. refused
(1996), 136 D.L.R. (4th) vii, [1996] S.C.C.A. No. 11 410
Woolf v. Collis Removal Service, [1948] 1 K.B. 11 (C.A.).................................755
Workers Trust & Merchant Bank Ltd. v. Dojap Investments Ltd.,
[1993] A.C. 573 (P.C.)...980
Wright v. Carter, [1903] 1 Ch. 27 (C.A.) 385
Wroth v. Tyler, [1974] Ch. 30 ....872, 942
Wrotham Park Estate Co. Ltd. v. Parkside Homes Ltd., [1974] 1 W.L.R. 798
(Ch.)..975, 978
Wuchter v. Fitzgerald, 163 P. 819 (Or. 1917)..971
Wurster v. Universal Environmental Services Inc. (1998), 167 D.L.R.
(4th) 166, [1998] O.J. No. 3920, 113 O.A.C. 360 (C.A.).............................878

Xenos v. Wickham (1866), L.R. 2 H.L. 296..266, 267

Y.M.C.A. v. Rankin (1916), 27 D.L.R. 417 (B.C.C.A.)   229
Y.M.C.A. v. Wood (1916), 27 D.L.R. 420 (B.C.C.A.) 229
Yanke v. Fenske (1959), 21 D.L.R. (2d) 419 (Sask. C.A.) 266
Yeoman Credit Ltd. v. Apps (1961), [1962] 2 Q.B. 508, [1961] 2 All E.R. 281...756
Yerkey v. Jones (1939), 63 C.L.R. 649 (A.H.C.)..386
Yetton v. Eastwoods Froy Ltd., [1967] 1 W.L.R. 104 (Q.B.) 867
Yorkshire Bank plc v. Tinsley, [2004] EWCA Civ 816, [2004] 3 All E.R. 463,
[2004] 1 W.L.R. 2380 (C.A.) 400
Yorkwood Homes (Georgetown) Inc. v. Law Development Group
Georgetown (No. 2) Ltd. (1999), 45 O.R. (3d) 257, [1999]
O.J. No. 3276, 27 R.P.R. (3d) 17 (C.A.) 722
Yoshimoto v. Canterbury Golf International Ltd., [2001] 1 N.Z.L.R. 523
(C.A.) 713
Young v. Young, [1993] 4 S.C.R. 3, 108 D.L.R. (4th) 193, [1993]
S.C.J. No. 112 442

Yukong Line Ltd. of Korea v. Rendsburg Investments Corp. of Liberia,
[1996] 2 Lloyd's Rep. 604, [1996] E.W.J. No. 464 (C.A.) 659

Z.I. Pompey Industrie v. ECU-Line N.V., 2003 SCC 27, [2003]
1 S.C.R. 450, 224 D.L.R. (4th) 577 955
Zell v. American Seating Co., 138 F.2d 641 (2d Cir. 1943)..................... 196
Zipper Transportation Services Ltd. v. Korstrom, [1998] M.J. No. 82,
126 Man. R. (2d) 126 (C.A.), rev'g [1997] M.J. No. 476,
122 Man. R. (2d) 139 (Q.B.) 956
Zippy Print Enterprises Ltd. v. Pawliuk (1994), [1995] 3 W.W.R. 324,
[1994] B.C.J. No. 2778, 100 B.C.L.R. (2d) 55 (C.A.) 355
Zuker v. Paul (1982), 37 O.R. (2d) 161, 135 D.L.R. (3d) 481,
2 P.P.S.A.C. 53 (Div. Ct.).. 876
Zurich Life Insurance Co. of Canada v. Davies, [1981] 2 S.C.R. 670,
130 D.L.R. (3d) 748, 39 N.R. 457 723
Zwicker v. Zwicker Estate (1899), 29 S.C.R. 527................................... 266

INDEX

Acceptance of offers, 52–67
  battle of the forms, 59–67, 69
  communication of offers, 67–82
  counteroffers, rejections and failed acceptance, 52–59
  instantaneous communications, 76–82
  postal acceptance rule, 73–76
  revocation of offers, 74, 82–89
  silence as acceptance, 68–73
  timeliness and, 57–59
Act for the Prevention of Frauds and Perjuries, An see Statute of Frauds
Act Respecting Champerty, An, 441, 444
Actual undue influence, 384–385
Addis v. Gramaphone Co. case, 799
Affirmation of transaction in misrepresentation, 342–343
Agreement execution in misrepresentation, 343–345
Agreements
  conditional, 4, 672–688
  oral, 160, 168, 174, 175, 187, 194, 195, 197, 198, 199, 200, 201, 202, 204
  partly oral and written, 160
  standard form, 182–183, 192
  written, 1, 3, 160–208

Agreements contrary to public policy at common law, 430–459
  agreements facilitating immoral conduct or undermining marriage, 432–437
  agreements to commit an unlawful act: crime, tort, defrauding third parties, 430–432
  agreements undermining other state interests, 444–447
  agreements undermining the administration of justice, 438–444
  covenants in restraint of trade, 447–459
  Kingshott v. Brunskill case, 432
Agreements to agree, 101–104, 117, 141, 156
Agreements to transfer interests in land and frustration, 591–596
  leases and, 591–593
  sale of land and, 593–596
Ambiguous agreements, 498–504
  consensus ad idem and, 498, 499, 500
American Cyanimid Co. v. Ethicon Ltd. case, 955
Anns test, 154
Anticipatory repudiation, 4, 651–671
  doctrine of, 653, 654, 656

elements of, 655–658
Highway Properties Ltd. v. Kelly Douglas & Co. Ltd. case, 664–665
Hochster v. De La Tour case, 652
loss mitigation in, 668
remedy of specific performance and,
669, 670
rescission and, 661
right to affirm, 654, 665–670
right to affirm vs. waiver of proposed
breach, 666
right to disaffirm, 654, 658–665, 666,
667, 670
White & Carter (Councils) Ltd. v. Mc-
Gregor case, 667, 668, 669, 670
Anticompetitive practices, see Covenants
in restraint of trade
Assignment of contractual rights
third-party beneficiaries and, 306–
307
Assumpsit, 160, 163
Attorney General v. Blake case, 972, 973,
974, 975, 976, 977, 978, 979
Auctions
negotiations and offers and, 47–48
without reserve, 48

Baggots Brass Beds Ltd. v. Neal Leasing
Inc. case, 797, 798
Baily v. De Crespigny case, 574
Bain v. Fothergill case, 820–821, 822,
823
Balfour v. Balfour case, 129–130, 133
Bank of British Columbia v. Wren case,
333, 334, 335
Banque Brussels Lambert SA v. Australian National Industries Ltd. case,
122–123, 124
Barclays Bank plc v. O'Brien case, 399,
400
Bargain theory, 27, 212, 214–232
certainty, 218–219
charitable subscriptions, 228–231
definition of consideration, 214–219
firm offers, 219–220
forbearance, 226–228
Hamer v. Sidway case, 217
illusory consideration, 220–221
implied consideration, 221–222
manufacturers' warranties, 231–232

nominal consideration, 223–226
peppercorn theory, 222–223
Wood v. Lucy, Lady Duff-Gordon case,
221
Bargaining in good faith, 2, 137–159
Anns test, 154
certainty of terms, 141–143
conduct of tendering process, 147–
151, 156, 157
fair and equal treatment, 148–151
Martel Building Ltd. v. Canada case,
153, 155, 157
non-disclosure as misrepresentation,
140
options to renew leases, 144–147,
153, 157
when there is no contract yet, 151–
156, 157
Barnett v. Harrison case, 619
Battle of the forms
acceptance of offers and, 59–67, 69
Uniform Commercial Code (U.C.C.)
Section 2-207 and, 63–67
Beaufort Realties 1964 Inc. v. Belcourt
Construction Ottawa Ltd. case, 767,
769
Behnke v. Bede Shipping Co. case, 919–
920
Bell v. Lever Brothers Ltd. case, 530–531,
534, 535, 536, 541, 542, 544, 545,
547, 549, 551, 552n, 553
Bettini v. Gye case, 622–623
BG Checo International Ltd. v. British
Columbia Hydro & Power Authority
case, 700
B.G. Linton Construction Ltd. v. C.N.R.
Co. case, 765
Bigos v. Bousted case, 473
Bilateral contract, 68, 70, 86, 88, 215,
733
definition of, 32
Blue pencil test, 450, 483, 488, 489, 490
Boomer v. Muir case, 970–971
Boone v. Eyre case, 621–622
Bowmakers Ltd. v. Barnet Instruments
Ltd. case, 478, 479
Brinkibon Ltd. v. Stahag Stahl Und
Stahlwarenhandelsgesellschaft mbH
case, 78, 79, 80, 81

British Motor Trade Association v. Gilbert case, 974–975, 976, 977
British Westinghouse Electric and Manufacturing Co. Ltd. v. Underground Electric Ry. Co. London Ltd. case, 870
Brownscombe v. Public Trustee of Alberta case, 177
Business efficacy test, 87, 735, 736, 738, 741, 743

Canada Square Corp. Ltd. v. Versafood Services Ltd. case, 97, 103
Canons of construction, 716–729
Carbolic Smoke Ball case, 40–42, 69, 70
Carlisle & Cumberland Banking Co. v. Bragg case, 521
Central London Property Trust Ltd. v. High Trees House Ltd. case, 277, 279, 280, 281, 282n, 285, 286
Certainty of agreement terms, 91–110
   agreements to agree and, 101–104, 117, 141, 156
   bargaining in good faith and, 141–143
   consideration and, 218–219
   Courtney and Fairbairn Ltd. v. Tolaini Brothers (Hotels) Ltd. case, 142
   doctrine of certainty and, 92
   Hillas and Co. Ltd. v. Arcos Ltd. case, *see* Incompleteness of agreement terms
   incompleteness and, 93–100
   vagueness and, 104–110
   Walford v. Miles case, 142–143, 152
C.H. Giles & Co.Ltd. v. Morris case, 932
Champerty, 441, 443
   Act Respecting Champerty, An, 441, 444
   McIntyre Estate v. Ontario (Attorney General) case, 444
Chaplin v. Hicks case, 848, 849
Charitable subscriptions, consideration and, 228–231
Cohabitation agreements, *see* Domestic and social arrangements
Collateral agreements, 88, 89, 200, 201, 360
Collateral claims, 477–481
   Bowmakers Ltd. v. Barnet Instruments Ltd. case, 478, 479

claims on collateral agreements, 477–478
   enforcement of property rights, 477, 478–479
   Saunders v. Edwards case, 477
   Tinsley v. Milligan case, 479, 480, 481
   tort claims, 477
Collateral contract analysis, 690, 691n
Collateral contracts
   third-party beneficiaries and, 304–305
Comfort letters in commercial agreements, 118–125
   Banque Brussels Lambert SA v. Australian National Industries Ltd. case, 122–123, 124
   Kleinwort Benson Ltd. v. Malaysia Mining Corp. case, 118–121, 123, 124
   Toronto-Dominion Bank v. Leigh Instruments Ltd. (Trustee of) case, 121–122, 123, 124, 125
Commercial arrangements
   comfort letters and, 118–125
   explicit agreements not to be bound, 113–115
   honour pledge clause, 113, 114, 115
   intentions to create, 113–129
   preliminary agreements, letters of intent and agreements "subject to contract", 125–129
   tendering processes and, 115–118
Commitment letters, 128–129
Common law
   Court of Chancery and, 9, 10
   definition of, 7–9
   equity and, 9–13, 19, 907–908
   Royal courts of, 9
Common mistakes, 496
Communication of offer, 48–52
Communication of offer acceptance, 67–82
   consensus ad idem theory, 67, 71
   Felthouse v. Bindley case, 70–71, 73
   instantaneous communications, 76–82
   mistaken communications, 82
   negative option billing, 72
   postal acceptance rule, 67, 73–76, 77, 83–84

Saint John Tug Boat Co. v. Irving Refinery Ltd. case, 68
silence as acceptance, 68–73
waiver principle, 69, 70
Concurrent conditions, 674
Concurrent liability in contract and tort, 18, 700–701
   BG Checo International Ltd. v. British Columbia Hydro & Power Authority case, 700
   doctrine of concurrent liability, 701
Condition-warranty dichotomy: criticisms and cure, 624–629, 630
   applying the *Hong Kong Fir* test, 633–636, 639, 640
   conditions vs. promises, 624–625, 673
   conditions vs. warranties, 625–629, 632
   Hong Kong Fir Shipping Co. Ltd. v. Kawasaki Kisen Ltd. case, 625–628, 629, 630, 633, 634
   innominate vs. intermediate terms, 627
   refinement of the *Hong Kong Fir* analysis, 629–633
Conditional agreements, 4, 672–688
   concurrent conditions, 674
   conditions defined, 672
   conditions precedent to an agreement, 673, 675–681, 686
   conditions subsequent, 673, 675
   implied subsidiary obligations, 679–681
   non-promissory condition precedent, 673, 674, 675, 683
   non-promissory condition subsequent, 673, 675
   non-promissory conditions, 673, 674
   promissory conditions, 672
   promissory condition precedent, 674, 683
   "true" condition precedent, 675, 683
   unilateral waiver, 682, 684, 686
   waiver and "true" conditions precedent, 682–688
Conditions precedent, 673, 675–681, 686
Conditions subsequent, 673, 675

Conditions, warranties and repudiatory breach, 615–650
   Bettini v. Gye case, 622–623
   Boone v. Eyre case, 621–622
   concurrent conditions, 621
   condition-warranty dichotomy: criticisms and cure, 624–629, 630
   conditions, 616, 618, 619, 620, 623, 624, 625, 627, 629, 630, 631, 632, 633, 636–639, 640, 672, 673, 675
   contractual conditions, 636
   definition of repudiatory breach, 639–641
   doctrine of independency, 621
   doctrine of the dependent and independent terms, 620, 621
   doctrine of "true" condition precedent, 619
   refinement of *Hong Kong Fir* test analysis, 629–633, 640
   Hong Kong Fir test application, 633–636
   innocent party and, 615–616, 617
   is there a doctrine of "material" breach?, 646–649
   non-promissory condition precedent, 619
   obligations concerning the whole, 621, 622
   perfect tender rule, 646
   promises and conditions, 617–624, 625
   promissory condition precedent, 619
   remedies for repudiatory breach, 641–646
   repudiation, 616
   rescission, 616, 617, 645
   Sale of Goods Act of 1893, 623, 624, 628, 632, 640
   warranties, 616, 617, 623, 629
   when is a contractual condition not a "true" condition, 636–639
Consensus ad idem, 2, 31, 48, 52, 55, 67, 71, 83, 85, 91, 112, 182, 364, 495, 497, 498, 499, 500, 501, 502, 503, 504, 506, 507, 509, 510
Consideration, 214–256
   bargain theory, the, 214–232
   certainty, 218–219

charitable subscriptions and, 228–231

definition of, 214–218

firm offers, 219–220

forbearance and, 226–228

illusory consideration, 220–221

implied consideration, 221–222

manufacturers' warranties, 5, 231–232

moral consideration, 233n, 236–237

nominal consideration, 223–226

Pao On v. Lau Yiu Long case, 234–235, 243, 244, 248, 371–372, 373, 374, 375, 376, 377, 378, 379

partial payment of a debt, 250–256, 275–276

past consideration, 232–238

peppercorn theory and, 222–223, 224, 232

pre-existing duty rule, 239–250

Consideration and form, 211–274

consideration, 214–256

formality: promises under seal, 256–269

reform of, 269–273

Construction of agreements

avoiding commercially unreasonable or absurd outcomes, 719–722

construction *contra proferentum* principle, 722–724

construction of the agreement as a whole, 717–718

earlier vs. later inconsistent terms, 727–728

ejusdem generis principle, 724–725

explicit references: *expressio unius est exclusio alterius* principle, 726

giving effect to all parts of the agreement, 719

handwritten vs. printed terms, 726–727

Hillas and Co. Ltd. v. Arcos Ltd. case, 728

preference for one that preserves validity of agreement, 728–729

verba ita sunt intelligenda ut res magis valeat quam pereat principle, 728

Constructive trust

restitution, as a, 179–180

Contingency fee agreements, 443, 444

Contract law

continuity and change in, 18–23

general principles of interpretation, 6

modern trends in, 23–27

Contract, tort and restitution, 13–18

Contracts of adhesion, 182

Contractual obligations, primary and secondary, 656n

Contractual representations

disaffirming the offer, 698

rescission, 698, 699

rescission *ab initio*, 698, 699

Court of Chancery, 9, 10

Courtney and Fairbairn Ltd. v. Tolaini Brothers Hotels Ltd. case, 142

Couturier v. Hastie case, 527

Covenants, 259

Covenants in restraint of trade, 447–459

blue pencil test, 450, 483, 488

J.G. Collins Insurance Agencies Ltd. v. Elsley case, 453, 454, 456

Nordenfelt test, 449, 451, 456, 457

Nordenfelt v. Maxim Nordenfelt Guns & Ammunition Co. case, 448–449, 450

solus agreements, 457

test for reasonableness of restraint, 448–449

Vancouver Malt and Sake Brewing Co. Ltd. v. Vancouver Breweries Limited case, 448

Coverage of third parties in insurance contracts, 312–313

Cundy v. Lindsay case, 510, 511, 512, 515, 516, 518, 538–539

Damages, 5, 813–905

asset valuation in calculation of, 871–872

calculating the expectancy principle, 837–849

coercive remedies, 813

disgorgement relief, 814

expectancy principle, 813, 814, 815–826

intangible injuries, 875–879

justifying expectancy, 826–832

limitations on expectancy damages, 850–871

Lord Cairns' Act, 873, 874, 939

penalties and liquidated damages, 897–904

punitive (exemplary), 815, 879–896

reliance as an alternative measure, 832–837

reliance measure, 814

repudiatory breach, for, 644

restitutionary, 814

scope of, 813

specific performance, in lieu of, 174–175

time of measurement of, 871–875

Davis Contractors test, 572, 579, 580, 581, 583, 589

Deed of conveyance, 36

Deglman v. Guaranty Trust Co. case, 176, 177, 179, 987

Del credere agent, 166

Derry v. Peek case, 348

Dies v. British International Mining & Finance Corp. Ltd. case, 980–981, 982

Disgorgement of profits secured, 912n, 972–979

    Attorney General v. Blake case, 972, 973, 974, 975, 976, 977, 978, 979

    British Motor Trade Association v. Gilbert case, 974–975, 976, 977

    cases of skimped performance, 978

    theory of efficient breach, 973, 978

Doctrine of accord and satisfaction, 251–252

Doctrine of actual undue influence, 384, 385

Doctrine of anticipatory breach, 652, 664

Doctrine of anticipatory repudiation, 653, 654, 656, 658, 664, 665

Doctrine of causation, 866

Doctrine of *caveat emptor*, 502

Doctrine of certainty, 92

Doctrine of champerty, 441

Doctrine of commercial impracticability, 589

Doctrine of concurrent liability, 701

Doctrine of consideration, 3, 112, 211–212, 213, 214, 215n, 217, 223, 269, 275, 276, 381

    Pilans and Rose v. Van Mierop & Hopkins case, 213

    Rann v. Hughes case, 213

Doctrine of constructive notice, 400, 401, 402, 403, 415, 416

Doctrine of contractual performance, 795, 796, 803

Doctrine of duress, 364, 367, 384, 424

Doctrine of economic duress, 365, 381, 382

Doctrine of entire contracts, 983

Doctrine of equitable mistake, 537, 538, 540, 541, 542

    rejection of by English Court of Appeal, 545–553

    Solle v. Butcher case, 535, 536–537, 538n, 539, 540, 542, 545, 547, 548, 551, 552

Doctrine of *error in substantialibus*, 360

Doctrine of frustration, 4, 532, 548, 549, 566, 567, 580, 581, 583, 590, 591, 603

    commercial purpose, of, 576, 577

    construction theory, 572, 573

    Davis Contractors test, 572, 579, 580, 581, 583, 589

    development of, 568–573

    implied-term theory, 569, 570, 572

    leases and, 591–593

    Paradie v. Jane case, 568, 573

    reasonableness standard, 570, 571

    sale of land and, 593–596

    self-induced frustration and, 597, 599

    Tamplin v. Anglo Mexican S.S. Co. case, 570

    Taylor v. Caldwell case, 569, 573, 574, 575, 579, 603n

Doctrine of fundamental breach, 421, 640, 707, 724, 750, 752, 753, 754

    anticipatory secondary obligation, 761–762

    Beaufort Realties (1964) Inc. v. Belcourt Construction (Ottawa) Ltd. case, 767, 769

    B.G. Linton Construction Ltd. v. C.N.R. Co. case, 765

    Canadian reception of, 765–776

    construction approach, 765, 776

    contra proferentum approach, 762, 763, 764, 776

doctrine of unconscionability and, 770–771, 772, 773, 774, 775, 776, 777, 778

Fraser Jewellers (1982) Ltd. v. Dominion Electric Protection Co. case, 773–774

Harbutt's "Plasticine" Ltd. v. Wayne Tank & Pump Co. Ltd. case, 758, 759

Hunter Engineering Co. Inc. v. Syncrude Canada Ltd. case, 768–769, 771, 776, 777, 778

Karsales (Harrow) Ltd. v. Wallis case, 755–756, 758, 765

Photo Production Ltd. v. Securicor Transport Ltd., 759, 760, 763, 768, 769, 772

repudiatory breach and, 752–754

rise and fall in English law, 754–764

Suisse Atlantique Societe d'Armement Maritime S.A. v. N.V. Rotterdamsche Kolen Centrale case, 756, 759, 760, 762, 765, 766, 767, 768, 769

Unfair Contracts Terms Act 1977, 759–760, 762, 763, 764, 767, 769, 773, 776, 777

Doctrine of good faith performance, 781, 782, 784, 786, 787, 807

Doctrine of impossibility by destruction of specific subject matter, 573, 574, 575, 576, 589

Baily v. De Crespigny case, 574

implied-contract theory, 574, 579

Doctrine of independency, 621

Doctrine of intention, 112

Doctrine of *locus poenitentiae*, 471–472, 473, 474

Doctrine of maintenance, 441

Doctrine of "material" breach, 646–649

Doctrine of mistaken assumptions, 509, 530, 531, 532, 536, 538, 541, 542, 548, 551, 552, 585

Doctrine of mitigation, 911

Doctrine of mutuality, 908, 917, 924, 926

Doctrine of *non est factum*, 518, 519, 520, 521, 522, 524

Carlisle & Cumberland Banking Co. v. Bragg case, 521

Foster v. Mackinnon case, 520

Prudential Trust Co. Ltd. v. Cugnet case, 521, 523, 524n, 525, 526

Saunders v. Anglia Building Society case, 519–520, 521, 522, 523, 524, 525, 526

Thoroughgood's Case, 519

Doctrine of notional severance, 491

Doctrine of part performance, 174–178

Doctrine of "practical compulsion", 374–375

Doctrine of privity of contract, 3, 8n, 27, 217, 229n, 254n, 294, 343

Doctrine of promissory estoppel, 214, 252n, 279–287, 382, 503, 643, 659n

intended to be acted upon, 281–283

nature of the undertaking, 283–285

reassertion of rights upon notice, 285–287

sword vs. shield?, 280–281, 286

Doctrine of reasonable foreseeability, 866

Doctrine of repudiatory breach, 656, 752, 753, 754, 757

Doctrine of restraint of trade, 458, 459

Doctrine of resulting trust, 479, 480, 481

Doctrine of severability, 450, 455, 483, 485, 487, 488, 489, 490

Doctrine of substantial performance, 964, 984–985

Doctrine of the dependent and independent terms, 620, 621

Doctrine of the unilateral mistake, 505, 509

Doctrine of "true" condition precedent, 619, 682, 684

Barnett v. Harrison case, 619

Turney v. Zhilka case, 619, 682–683, 684, 685, 686, 687, 688

Doctrine of unconscionability, 26, 365, 405, 406, 407, 411, 412, 413, 417–419, 420, 421, 422, 424, 770–771, 935

Doctrine of undue influence, 365, 382, 392, 394, 404, 406, 424

presumptive undue influence, 365, 383

Doctrine of waiver, 277–279, 643

Hughes v. Metropolitan Rwy Co. case, 277, 280, 282, 285

Dohery v. Allman case, 947–948, 949, 954

Domestic and social arrangements, 129–135
  Balfour v. Balfour case, 129–130, 133
  intentions to create, 129–135, 167

Dominating influence test, 388–391

Duress, 367–382
  duress of goods, 370–371
  duress to the person, 369–370
  economic, 367, 369, 371–382, 409n, 415
  illegitimate pressure test, 373–374, 376
  overborne will threshold, 373, 376
  Skeate v. Beale case, 370–371
  Stott v. Merrit Investment Corp. case, 376–377, 380n, 381

Duress, undue influence and unconscionability, 4, 26n, 284, 364–427
  duress, 367–382
  Lloyds Bank v. Bundy case, 365–366, 424, 425
  traditional categories of, 369–371
  unconscionability, 404–424
  undue influence, 382–404
  Universe Tankships of Monrovia v. International Transport Workers' Federation case, 373, 375, 376, 377, 378, 379, 380

Duty owed to a third party, enforceability, 242–244

Duty owed to the promisor, enforceability, 244–250

Dynamic Transport Ltd. v. O.K. Detailing Ltd. case, 679–680, 682, 787–788

E-commerce acceptances of offers, *see* Instantaneous communications of offers

Ejusdem generis principle, 724–725

Enforceability of agreements, 3, 160, 162, 164, 209–321
  consideration and form, 211–274
  privity of contract, 294–321
  waiver and promissory estoppel, 275–293

English Law Reform Frustrated Contracts Act of 1943, 603

Entire agreement and exemption clauses, 207, 354–361, 694, 695

Equitable compensation, 403, 404

Equity, common law and, 9–13, 19

Estoppel, *see* Waiver and promissory estoppel

Exculpatory clauses, 5, 749–779
  Canadian reception of the doctrine of fundamental breach, 765–776
  doctrine of fundamental breach, 750
  doctrine of fundamental breach vs. repudiatory breach, 752
  implied duty to perform in good faith, 780–809
  parol evidence rule, 751, 752
  related doctrines, 750
  rise and fall of fundamental breach in English law, 754–764
  rule of law, 750, 756, 757, 758, 759, 761
  rules of incorporation, 751

Expectancy damages limitations, 850–871
  British Westinghouse Electric and Manufacturing Co. Ltd. v. Underground Electric Ry. Co. London Ltd. case, 870
  causation issues, 850–854
  doctrine of causation and, 866
  Hadley v. Baxendale case, 854, 855, 856, 858, 859, 860, 863, 865
  impecuniosity, 869, 870
  implicit undertaking to indemnify, 864, 865
  Koufos v. Czarnikow (C.) (The Heron II) case, 857–858, 859, 860, 861n
  mitigation, 865–871, 872
  principle against avoidable loss, 865, 866
  remoteness, 854–865
  standard of reasonable foreseeability (*Hadley* rule), 856, 857, 859, 860, 861, 862, 863, 864, 865, 866, 867, 868, 869, 870, 873, 877
  Victoria Laundry (Windsor) Ltd. v. Newman Industries Ltd. case, 856–857, 858, 860, 861, 862

Expectancy principle, 813, 814, 815–826, 820, 873, 906, 972, 976

Bain v. Fothergill case, 820–821, 822, 823
basic principle of, 815–819
calculation of, 837–849
capital vs. income component in calculation of, 839–840
Chaplin v. Hicks case, 847–848, 849
cost of performance vs. diminution in value measures of calculation of, 840–847
economic approach to, 828–829, 831
efficient behaviour and, 830–831
exceptions to, 819–826
expectation interest and, 827
Groves v. John Wonder Co. case, 843–844, 845, 846
Highway Properties Ltd. v. Kelly Douglas & Co. Ltd. case, 823–824
Jacobs & Youngs, Inc. v. Kent case, 841–842, 844
juristic explanation for, 829
justifying expectancy, 826–832
land purchase and sale contracts and, 819–820
limitations on expectancy damages, 850–871
mitigation principle and, 829
non-payment of money and, 819
Peevyhouse v. Garland Coal & Mining Co. case, 844--845
presumption of least-burdensome performance and, 824, 825–826
reliance damages and, 818, 829, 830, 832–837
reliance interest and, 827
restitution interest and, 826
Robinson v. Harman case, 816
Ruxley Electronics and Construction Ltd. v. Forsyth case, 842–843
Sally Wertheim v. Chicoutimi Pulp Company case, 816
surrender doctrine and, 824
Tito v. Waddell (No. 2) case, 845–846
two formulae to calculate expectancy damages, 838–839
value for lost profits from breach, 847–849
will theory and, 828
Explicit commercial agreements not to be bound, 113–115

Rose and Frank Company v. J.R. Crompton and Brothers Ltd. case, 113–115, 116
Expressio unius est exclusio alterius principle, 726

Face-to-face principle, 510, 511, 513, 515, 516, 517
Factual matrix, 709, 710, 712
Fair and equal treatment, *see* Bargaining in good faith
Faxed acceptance of offers, *see* Instantaneous communications of offers
Felthouse v. Bindley case, 70–71, 73
Fertility contracts, 437
Fiduciary law, 17
Fiduciary obligation, *see* Bargaining in good faith
Firm offers, 82, 85, 219–220, 257, 269, 271
Flagpole problem and its solutions, 85–89
Foakes v. Beer case, 8n, 251, 252, 253, 254, 255, 272, 273, 275, 276, 277, 278, 281, 282, 290, 823
Foley v. Classique Coaches Ltd. case, 96, 97
Forbearance, 226–228
Force majeure, 567, 599, 600
Force majeure clauses, 599–602, 725
principle of *contra proferentum*, 602, 722–724
Formality: promises under seal, 3, 164, 256–269
cautionary function of, 267, 268
chanelling function of, 267, 268
delivery as an escrow, 266–267
evidentiary function of, 267, 268
sealed contract rule, 258–259
Formation of agreements, 29–208
agreements in writing, 160–208
bargaining in good faith and, 137–159
certainty of terms, 91–110
insufficient terms preventing, 34
intention to create legal relations, 111–136
offer and acceptance, 31–90
Foster v. Mackinnon case, 520

Fraser Jewellers 1982 Ltd. v. Dominion Electric Protection Co. case, 773–774

Fraud and misrepresentation, 192

Frustrated Contracts Act, 604

Frustration, 4, 566–611, 604
  adventure, of the, 578
  agreements to transfer interests in land, 591–596
  commercial impracticability, 588–590
  consequences of, 603–609
  development of doctrine of, 568–573
  English Law Reform (Frustrated Contracts) Act, 603
  force majeure, 567, 599, 600
  force majeure clauses, 599–602, 725
  Frustrated Contracts Act, 604
  Geipel v. Smith case, 578
  impossibility, 573–574, 585, 586
  Jackson v. Union Marine Insurance Co. case, 578
  Krell v. Henry case, 575, 576, 577, 579, 580
  Maritime National Fish Ltd. v. Ocean Trawlers Ltd. case, 597–598
  mistaken assumptions and, 576, 577, 584–585
  modern restatement of: risk-allocation analysis, 579–588
  purpose, of, 575–577
  self-induced, 597–599
  standard categories of, 573–579
  Taylor rule, 575
  temporary impossibility, 578–588
  Uniform Act, 604, 608, 609
  Uniform Frustrated Contracts Act, 603, 606, 607, 608

Fundamental breach: the rise and fall in English law, 754–764

Gallen v. Butterley case, 204, 205

Gardner v. Coutts & Co. case, 793, 795, 796

Gateway Realty Ltd. v. Arton Holdings Ltd. case, 785–787, 788, 792, 805

GATX Corp. v. Hawker Siddeley Canada Inc. case, 794–795, 796, 798

Geffen v. Goodman Estate case, 386–387, 388n, 389, 390, 391, 393, 395n, 396, 397

Geipel v. Smith case, 578

General principles of interpretation, 705–748
  commercial setting or background, 708–711
  construction canons, 716–729
  doctrine of fundamental breach, 707
  ejusdem generis principle, 725
  expressio unius est exclusio alterius principle, 726
  extrinsic aids for, 707
  factual matrix, 709, 710, 712
  identification of the target of interpretation, 707, 708
  implied terms in agreements, 729–747
  latent ambiguity, 711
  law of interpretation of agreements, 705, 706, 707
  meaning of words, 716
  parol evidence rule, 708, 727
  Prenn v. Simmonds case, 709, 711
  principle of inadmissibility, 708
  prior negotiations, drafts and antecedent agreements, 711–713
  process of implication, 707
  Reardon Smith Line Ltd. v. Yngvar Hansen-Tangen case, 709
  related agreements, 715
  sources for, 706, 707–716
  subsequent conduct of parties, 713–715
  true intentions of parties and, 705, 706, 707
  verba ita sunt intelligenda ut res magis valeat quam pereat principle, 728

Gilbert Steel Ltd. v. University Construction Ltd. case, 246, 247, 248, 275, 281

Giles v. Edwards case, 966

Good faith in performance of agreements, *see* Implied duty to perform in good faith

Goods sales and specific performance, 914, 918–923
  Behnke v. Bede Shipping Co. case, 919–920

inadequacy of damages test and, 922–923
long-term supply agreements and, 921–922
Sale of Goods Act, 920
Sky Petroleum v. V.I.P. Petroleum case, 921–922
uniqueness of goods, 918–919
Gratuitous promises, 275, 291
Greenberg v. Meffert case, 790
Groves v. John Wonder Co. case, 843–844, 845, 846
Guarantees under the *Statute of Frauds* of 1677, 165–167
del credere agent and, 166

Hadley v. Baxendale case, 854, 855, 856, 858, 859, 860, 863, 865
Hamer v. Sidway case, 217
Harbutt's "Plasticine" Ltd. v. Wayne Tank & Pump Co. Ltd. case, 758, 759
Hedley Bryne & Co. v. Heller & Partners case, 349, 350, 355, 357
Heilbut, Symons & Co. v. Buckleton case, 691, 693, 694
Hermann v. Charlesworth case, 434, 472
H.F. Clarke Ltd. v. Thermidaire Corp. case, 898, 900
Highway Properties Ltd. v. Kelly Douglas & Co. Ltd. case, 664–665, 823–824
Hill v. C.A. Parsons & Co. Ltd. case, 933
Hillas and Co. Ltd. v. Arcos Ltd. case, 94, 95, 96, 97, 101, 141, 728
Hire Purchase Act, 1964, 516
Hochster v. De La Tour case, 652
Holman v. Johnson case, 468, 470, 477
Hong Kong Fir Shipping Co. Ltd. v. Kawasaki Kisen Ltd. case, 625–628, 629, 633, 634
applying the test of, 633–636
innominate term of analysis of, 632, 633, 640
recognition of "true" conditions, 630
refining the analysis of, 629–633, 640
Honour pledge clause, *see* Commercial arrangements
Howe v. Smith case, 980
Hughes v. Metropolitan Rwy Co. case, 277, 280, 282, 285

Hunt v. Silk case, 966, 967, 968
Hunter Engineering Co. Inc. v. Syncrude Canada Ltd. case, 768–769, 771, 776, 777, 778
Hutton v. Warren case, 732

Illegality, 4, 428–493
agreements contrary to public policy of common law, 428, 429, 430–459
agreements to commit an unlawful act: crime, tort, defrauding third parties, 430–432
consequences of, 467–483
severance, 483–492
statutory, 428, 429, 430, 432, 459–467
Illegality consequences
Bigos v. Bousted case, 473
collateral claims, 477–481
doctrine of *locus poenitentiae*, 471–472, 473, 474
Holman v. Johnson case, 468, 470, 477
in pari delicto, 470, 471, 474, 476
Kiriri Cotton Co. Ltd. v. Dewani case, 470
passage of property, 481–483
potior est conditio defendentis, 468, 470
repentance and, 471, 473
restitution claims and, 470–477
Illusory consideration, 220–221
Implication of terms
anticipatory repudiation and, 653
business efficacy test, 87
Implied consideration, 221–222
Implied duty to perform in good faith, 5, 780–809, 784
Addis v. Gramaphone Co. case, 799
Baggots Brass Beds Ltd. v. Neal Leasing Inc. case, 797, 798
contra proferentum principle, 790
Dynamic Transport Ltd. v. O.K. Detailing Ltd. case, 787–788
Gardner v. Coutts & Co. case, 793, 795, 796
Gateway Realty Ltd. v. Arton Holdings Ltd. case, 785–787, 788, 792, 805
GATX Corp. v. Hawker Siddeley Canada Inc. case, 794–795, 796, 798

good faith and control of discretionary powers conferred by contract,
788–791
good faith and duty to not evade contractual obligations, 792–798
good faith, best efforts and duty to
cooperate, 785–788
good faith, definition of, 803–805
good faith duties, test for implying,
805–806
good faith, Supreme Court of Canada
and: *Wallace v. United Grain Growers Ltd.* case, 798–803, 805, 806
Greenberg v. Meffert case, 790
*Landymore v. Hardy and White Rose
Properties Ltd.* case, 795, 796
law of contractual interpretation and,
792, 807
leading cases in, 784–798
LeMesurier v. Andrus case, 789–790
*Manchester Ship Canal Co. v. Manches-
ter Racecourse Co.* case, 797, 798
*MDS Health Group Ltd. v. King Street
Medical Arts Centre Ltd.* case, 792
*Mesa Operating Ltd. Partnership v.
Amoco Canada Resources Ltd.* case,
788–789
presumed intentions of party and,
806
recognition of duty of good faith performance, 782, 783, 784
Restatement of Contracts (American),
781, 785
Uniform Commercial Code (American)
and, 781, 804
*Vorvis v. Insurance Corporation of
British Columbia* case, 800
Implied subsidiary obligations, 679–681
*Dynamic Transport Ltd. v. O.K. Detail-
ing Ltd.* case, 679–680, 682
Implied terms in agreements, 729–747
business efficacy test, 735, 736, 738,
741, 743
Hutton v. Warren case, 732
implied statutory terms, 732, 746–
747
necessity standard, 736, 743
officious bystander test, 735, 736,
738, 741

presumed intention of party, 730,
731, 732, 736, 737, 743
term implied from custom or usage,
730, 731, 732–735
term implied in fact, 730, 731, 732,
735–743
terms implied by law, 730, 732,
743–746
Impossibility to perform contract, *see*
Frustration, impossibility
Impracticability to perform contract, *see*
Frustration, commercial imprac-
ticability
Incompleteness of agreement terms,
93–100
*Canada Square Corp. Ltd. v. Versafood
Services Ltd.* case, 97, 103
Foley v. Classique Coaches Ltd. case,
96, 97
Hillas and Co. Ltd. v. Arcos Ltd. case,
94, 95, 96, 97, 101, 141
*L.C.D.H. Audio Visual Ltd. v. I.S.T.S.
Verbatim Ltd.* case, 98–99
May and Butcher Ltd. v. The King case,
93–94, 95, 96, 103n
Incurable uncertainty, 107, 109
Inducement and misrepresentation, 331
Inequality of bargaining power, *see* Dur-
ess, undue influence and uncon-
scionability
Influence peddling, 445, 446
Informal trust arrangements
Statute of Frauds of 1677 and, 178
Ingram v. Little case, 512–513, 514, 515,
517
Injunctions, 947–956
American Cyanimid Co. v. Ethicon Ltd.
case, 955
Dohery v. Allman case, 947–948, 949,
954
ex parte, 954
interim or interlocutory, 953, 954
Lumley v. Wagner case, 949–950,
951–952, 953
mandatory, 947, 953
permanent or perpetual, 953
positive vs. negative undertakings,
947, 948, 949, 950
prima facie test, 955–956
prohibitory, 947, 953

Instantaneous communications of offers, 76–82
  Brinkibon Ltd. v. Stahag Stahl Und Stahlwarenhandelsgesellchaft mbH case, 78, 79
Insurance contracts
  coverage of third parties in insurance contracts, 312–313
  doctrine of privity of contact and, 309–313
  waiver of rights against third parties in insurance contracts, 310–312
Intangible injuries and damages, 875–879, 895–896
  aggravated damages, 877
  Jarvis v. Swans Tours Ltd. case, 875, 876
  Vorvis v. Insurance Corporation of British Columbia case, 876, 877, 878
  Wallace v. United Grain Growers Ltd. case, 879
Intention to create legal relations, 111–136
  commercial arrangements and, 113–129
  domestic and social arrangements, 129–135
Intention to misrepresent, 328
Inter praesentes, 76, 77, 78
Interpretation of agreements, 5, 703–810
  exculpatory clauses, 749–779
  general principles of interpretation, 705–748
  implied duty to perform in good faith, 780–809
Invitation to treat, 33, 34, 36

Jackson v. Union Marine Insurance Co. case, 578
Jacobs & Youngs, Inc. v. Kent case, 841–842, 844
Jarvis v. Swans Tours Ltd. case, 875, 876
J.G. Collins Insurance Agencies Ltd. v. Elsley case, 453, 454, 456, 902–904
Judicature Acts of 1873 and 1875, 10

Karsales Harrow Ltd. v. Wallis case, 755–756, 758, 765
King's Norton Metal Co.Ltd. v. Edridge, Merrett & Co. Limited case, 511

Kingshott v. Brunskill case, 432, 462, 466, 469
Kingswood Estate Co. v. Anderson case, 175
Kiriri Cotton Co. Ltd. v. Dewani case, 470
Kleinwort Benson Ltd. v. Malaysia Mining Corp. case, 118–121, 123, 124
Koufos v. Czarnikow C. The Heron II case, 857–858, 859, 860, 861n
Krawchuk v. Ulrychova case, 635
Krell v. Henry case, 575, 576, 577, 579, 580

Laches in misrepresentation, 345–346, 402, 938
Land sales and specific performance, 913–918
  doctrine of mutuality and, 917
  Semelhago v. Paramadevan case, 914–915, 916, 918
  uniqueness of land, 912, 913, 916–917
Landymore v. Hardy and White Rose Properties Ltd. case, 795, 796
Last shot rule, acceptance of offers and, 60, 61
Law of interpretation of agreements, 705, 706, 707
Law of agency, see Doctrine of privity of contract
  New Zealand Shipping Co. Ltd. v. A.M. Satterthwaite & Co. Ltd. case, 302, 303
  third-party beneficiaries and, 301–303, 304
Law of contracts
  continuity and change in, 18–23
  tracing modern developments in, 23–27
Law of contractual interpretation, 792, 807
Law of offer and acceptance, 505
Law of performance, conditions and warranties in, 26
Law of restitution, 963
Law of restraint of trade, 413
Law of trusts, third-party beneficiaries and, 303–304
L.C.D.H. Audio Visual Ltd. v. I.S.T.S. Verbatim Ltd. case, 98–99

Lease renewal options
  bargaining in good faith and, 144–147, 153, 157
LeMesurier v. Andrus case, 789–790
L'Estrange v. Graucob rule, 190, 192, 193
Letters of intent, 127–128
Lewis v. Averay case, 514, 515, 517, 552n
Liability in tort, 348–354, 357
  Derry v. Peek case, 348
  Hedley Bryne & Co. v. Heller & Partners case, 349, 350, 355
  tort of deceit, 348, 352
  tort of negligence, 349, 350, 351, 352, 353, 357, 358, 359
Limited liability of employees, doctrine of privity of contact and, 308–309
Lindsay Petroleum oil Co. v. Hurd case, 345
Liquidated damages, *see* Damages
Lloyds Bank v. Bundy case, 365–366, 424, 425
London Drugs Ltd. v. Kuchne & Nagel International Ltd. case, 299n, 308, 311, 313, 314, 315, 317, 319
Lord Kennedy v. Panama, New Zealand and Australian Royal Mail Co. Ltd. case, 529, 530, 531, 535
Lumley v. Wagner case, 949–950, 951–952, 953

Maddison v. Alderson case, 175, 176, 177
Mahoney v. Purnell case, 403, 404
Mailbox rule, *see* Postal acceptance rule
Maintenance, 441, 442n
Manchester Ship Canal Co. v. Manchester Racecourse Co. case, 797, 798
Manifest disadvantage, 391–395, 396, 397
  Royal Bank of Scotland (No. 2) v. Etridge case, 393, 395, 396, 398, 400, 401n
Manufacturer's warranties, 231–232
Marine National Fish doctrine, 598
Maritime National Fish Ltd. v. Ocean Trawlers Ltd. case, 597–598
Marriage brokage contracts, 434, 472
  Hermann v. Charlesworth case, 434, 472
Martel Building Ltd. v. Canada case, 153, 155, 157

Material breach, *see* Repudiatory breach
Materiality and misrepresentation, 329–330, 331, 648, 697
May and Butcher Ltd. v. The King case, 93–94, 95, 96, 103n
McGrath v. MacLean case, 333, 334, 335
McIntyre Estate v. Ontario Attorney General case, 444
McRae v. Commonwealth Disposals Commission case, 832–835
MDS Health Group Ltd. v. King Street Medical Arts Centre Ltd. case, 792
Mellco Developments Ltd. v. Portage La Prairie City case, 116–117, 118
Mesa Operating Ltd. Partnership v. Amoco Canada Resources Ltd. case, 788–789
Mirror image rule, 31, 52, 64, 65
Misrepresentation, 4, 12, 18, 152, 158, 162, 163, 325–363, 502n, 509n, 512, 514, 689, 690, 693, 698, 699, 701, 934, 938
  Bank of British Columbia v. Wren case, 333, 334, 335
  elements of, 326–331
  entire agreement and exemption clauses, 354–361, 694, 695
  inducement, 331
  intention, 328
  liability in tort, 348–354
  materiality, 329–330, 331, 648, 697
  McGrath v. MacLean case, 333, 334, 335
  non-disclosure and good faith, 334–337
  non-disclosure as, 331–334
  overview of, 360–361
  rescission and restitution, 337–348, 699n
  remedies for, 360–361
  sales talk, 326, 327
  statement of opinion, 327–328
  statements of law, 329–330
  statutory reform in, 361–362
  uberrima fides, 332, 334
Misrepresentation Act, 362
Mistaken assumptions, 495, 496, 526–555, 567, 576, 584, 585
  assumed foundation test, 531

Bell v. Lever Brothers Ltd. case, 530–531, 534, 535, 536, 541, 542, 544, 545, 547, 549, 551, 552n, 553
  common law, at, 526, 527–535
  Couturier v. Hastie case, 527
  difference in kind test, 534, 535
  equity, in, 535–545
  fundamental basis test, 531n
  Lord Kennedy v. Panama, New Zealand and Australian Royal Mail Co. (Ltd.) case, 529, 530, 531, 535
  material affect of, 543
  mistaken assumptions principle, 543, 576
  rejection of doctrine of equitable mistake by English Court of Appeal, 545–553
  res extincta, 527, 531, 540, 542
  res sua, 527, 528, 531, 537, 542, 547
  subject-matter test, 530, 531, 532, 533, 535, 536, 537, 542, 549
  Toronto Dominion Bank v. Fortin (No. 2) case, 541–542
  unilateral mistake in, 527, 553–555
  void for mistake, 539, 540, 541, 542, 551
Mistaken bids, 504–509
  consensus ad idem, 509
  mistake as to terms, 505, 506, 509
  Ron Engineering & Construction Eastern Ltd. v. Ontario case, 504, 505, 506, 508, 509, 554
  snapping up an offer, 505, 506, 508
Mistakes, 4, 494–565
  common law, 496
  integration, in, 495–496, 555–564
  mistaken assumptions, 495, 496, 509, 526–555, 567
  misunderstandings, 495, 496–526
  "motive", as to, 495
  negative consent and, 495n
  nullified consent and, 495n
  "terms", as to, 495
Mistakes as to identity of other party, 497, 504, 509–518, 511, 551n
  consensus ad idem, 509, 510
  correspondence dealings, 510, 511, 517
  Cundy v. Lindsay case, 510, 511, 512, 515, 516, 518, 538–539

  face-to-face dealings, 510, 511, 513, 515, 516, 517
  Hire Purchase Act, 1964, 516
  Ingram v. Little case, 512–513, 514, 515, 517
  King's Norton Metal Co.Ltd. v. Edridge, Merrett & Co. Limited case, 511
  Lewis v. Averay case, 514, 515, 517, 552n
  Phillips v. Brooks case, 512, 513
Mistakes in integration, 555–564
  defences and bars to relief, 563–564
  proving the antecedent agreement, 556–559
  unilateral mistake and rectification, 559–562, 564
Misunderstandings, 495, 496–526
  ambiguity, 498–504
  consensus ad idem and, 497, 498, 499, 500, 501, 502, 503, 504, 506, 507, 509
  consensus and, 497, 502
  context of mistaken bids, in the, 504–509
  doctrine of *caveat emptor*, 502
  mistake as to identity of other contracting party, 497, 504, 509–518
  non est factum: mistakenly signed documents, 192, 498, 504, 518–526, 539
  objective theory of contract formation, 500, 501, 503
  rogue, 498, 510, 511, 512, 514, 515, 516
  unilateral mistakes as to terms, 496, 501–504, 505, 506
Monetary awards and specific performance, 939–946
  damages in lieu of specific relief, 940, 943, 944, 945
  specific performance with an abatement, 939, 940, 941
Moral consideration, 233n, 236–237
Morrison v. Coast Finance Ltd. case, 407–408, 409, 420
Mutuality in specific performance, 924–929
  affirmative version of doctrine of, 924, 925

C.H. Giles & Co.Ltd. v. Morris case, 932

Hill v. C.A. Parsons & Co. Ltd. case, 933

negative version of doctrine of, 924, 925, 926, 927, 928

National Westminister Bank plc v. Morgan case, 388–389, 391

Negative option billing, 72

New Zealand Shipping Co. Ltd. v. A.M. Satterthwaite & Co. Ltd. case, 302, 303

Nominal consideration, 223–226

Non-disclosure and good faith, 334–337

Non-disclosure as misrepresentation, 331–334, 553n

Non est factum: mistakenly signed documents, 192, 498, 504, 518–526, 539

  carelessness, 523, 524

  problems with the doctrine, 519

Non-presumptive relational undue influence, 395–397

Non-promissory condition precedent, 619, 673, 674, 675, 679, 682, 683

Non-promissory condition subsequent, 673, 675

Non-promissory conditions, 673, 674, 686

  implied subsidiary obligations, 679

  subsidiary promissory obligations, 674, 675

  waiver and "true" conditions precedent, 682–688

Nordenfelt test, 449, 451, 456, 457

Nordenfelt v. Maxim Nordenfelt Guns & Ammunition Co. case, 448–449, 450

Notional severance, 491, 492

Nudum pactum, 215

Objective theory of contract formation, 500, 501, 503

Offer and acceptance, 2, 31–90

  bilateral vs. unilateral contracts and, 32–33

  consensus ad idem, 2, 31

  mirror image rule, 31

  offer, the, 33–52

  rules of, 112

Offers, 33–52

  acceptance of, 52–67

  auctions, 47–48

  Carlill v. Carbolic Smoke Ball Co. case, 40–42

  communication of, 48–52

  communication of acceptance of, 67–82

  definition of, 33

  firm, 82, 85

  offers to general public: rewards and other unilateral contracts, 40–42

  preliminary negotiations and, 34–48

  R. v. Ron Engineering & Construction (Eastern) Ltd. case, 44, 45, 46, 47, 115, 117, 147

  retail sales, 37–40

  revocation of, 82–89

  tenders, 43–47

Officious bystander test, 735, 736

  Moorcock, The, case, 735

  Shirlaw v. Southern Foundries (1926) Ltd. case, 735

Open-textured "principled exception", 313–317

Opinion statements as misrepresentation, 327–328

Overborne will threshold, 373, 376

Pacta sunt servanda, 14

Pao On v. Lau Yiu Long case, 234–235, 243, 244, 248, 371–372, 373, 374, 375, 376, 377, 378, 379

Paradie v. Jane case, 568, 573

Parker v. South Eastern Railway Co. case, 183–184, 185, 190

Parol evidence rule, 3, 161, 193–207, 708, 727, 751, 752

  Canadian reception of modern version of, 203–206

  exceptions to, 199–203

  Gallen v. Butterley case, 204, 205

  merger and entire agreement clauses in, 206–207

  Pym v. Campbell case, 199–200

  scope and operation of, 197–199

  traditional vs. modern version of, 195–196, 197, 198, 199, 201, 203, 207

Parrish & Heimbecker Ltd. v. Gooding Lumber Ltd. case, 587

Partial payment to discharge a debt enforceability, 250–256, 275–276

Foakes v. Beer case, 8n, 251, 252, 253, 254, 255, 272, 273, 275, 276, 277, 279, 281, 282, 283

Passage of property in illegality, 481–483

no passage of property rule, 481, 482, 483

Past consideration, 232–238, 273

threefold test for exception to, 234–236

Pearce v. Brooks case, 435–436

Peevyhouse v. Garland Coal & Mining Co. case, 844–-845

Penalties and liquidated damages, 897–904

H.F. Clarke Ltd. v. Thermidaire Corp. case, 898, 900

J.G. Collins Insurance Agencies Ltd. v. Elsley case, 902–904

terrorem, in, 897, 899, 903

Penalties, *see* Damages

Peppercorn theory, 222–223, 224, 232

Perfect tender rule, 646

Performance and breach of contracts, 613–702

anticipatory repudiation, 651–671

conditional agreements, 672–688

conditions, warranties and repudiatory breach, 615–650

representation and warranty, 689–702

Performance doctrine, acceptance of offers and, 60

Phillips v. Brooks case, 512, 513

Photo Production Ltd. v. Securicor Transport Ltd. case, 759, 760, 763, 768, 769, 772

Pilans and Rose v. Van Mierop & Hopkins case, 213

Postal acceptance rule, 73–76, 77, 78, 80, 83–84

Pre-contractual representation as warranty, 690–695, 696

animus contrahendi, 692, 693

collateral contract analysis, 690, 691n

entire agreement clause, 694, 695

Heilbut, Symons & Co. v. Buckleton case, 691, 693, 694

"intention" test, 693, 694

non-careless misrepresentation and, 690

unilateral contracts, 690, 691

Pre-existing duty rule, 239–250, 382

duty owed to promisor, 244–250

duty owed to third party, 242–244

Gilbert Steel Ltd. v. University Construction Ltd. case, 246, 247, 248

public duty, 239–242

Stilk v. Myrick case, 248, 249, 250

Williams v. Roffey Bros. & Nicholls (Contractors) Ltd. case, 248, 250, 252, 253

Precedent, 18, 20, 22

Preliminary agreements in commercial arrangements, 125–129

Preliminary negotiations and offers, 34–48

auctions, 47–48

deed of conveyance, 36

invitation to treat, 33, 34, 36

quotations, 35, 36

retail sales, 37–40

tenders, 43–47

Prenn v. Simmonds case, 709, 711

Presumptive undue influence, 385–395, 402, 425

dominating influence and, 388–391

establishing the presumption, 385–388

Geffen v. Goodman Estate case, 386–387, 388n, 389, 390, 391, 393, 395n, 396, 397

manifest disadvantage, 391–395

National Westminister Bank plc v. Morgan case, 388–389, 391

Privity of contract, 294–321

additional exceptions to at common law, 308–319

assignment of contractual rights, 306–307

collateral contracts, 304–305

coverage of third parties in insurance contracts, 312–313

crystallization of third party's rights, 318

development and rationale of rule, 296–301

insurance contracts, 309–313

law of agency, 301–303, 304

law of trusts, 303–304

limitations on and exceptions to rule, 301–319

limited liability of employees, 308–309

London Drugs Ltd. v. Kuchne & Nagel International Ltd. case, 299n, 308, 311, 313, 314, 315, 317, 319

open-textured "principled exception" to, 313–317, 313–317

resale price maintenance scheme, 297

statutory exceptions to, 307–308

subsequent variation or annulment of promise, 317–319

third-party beneficiary rule, 295, 296, 297, 298

tort law, 305–306, 309

Tweddle v. Atkinson case, 296, 297, 298

waiver of rights against third parties in insurance contracts, 310–312

Promises, 1, 2

Promises and conditions of contracts, *see* Conditions, warranties and repudiatory breach

Promissory condition precedent, 674, 683

Promissory conditions, 672, 674, 686

Proprietary estoppel, 287–289

Prostitution contracts, 435–436

Pearce v. Brooks case, 435–436

Prudential Trust Co. Ltd. v. Cugnet case, 521, 523, 524n, 525, 526

Public duty enforceability, 239–242

Public vs. private law, 14

Punitive (exemplary) damages in civil cases, 815, 879–896

Robitaille v. Vancouver Hockey Club case, 881–882

Rookes v. Barnard case, 879–881

test of rationality for, 893, 894

Vorvis v. Insurance Corporation of British Columbia case, 883, 884, 886, 887, 889

Wallace v. United Grain Growers Ltd. case, 886

Whiten v. Pilot Insurance Co. case, 887–888, 890, 891, 892, 893, 894, 895, 896

Pym v. Campbell case, 199–200

Quantum meruit, 179

Quotations, 35, 36

Rann v. Hughes case, 213

Reardon Smith Line Ltd. v. Yngvar Hansen-Tangen case, 709

Rescission, 12, 616, 617, 645

Rescission and restitution and misrepresentation, 337–348, 934

ab initio effect, 338, 368, 643, 698, 699

affirmation of transaction, 342–343, 641–643, 644

doctrine of *error in substantialibus*, 360

equitable rescission, 338–339

execution of the agreement, 343–345

intervention of third-party rights, 343

laches, 345–346

limitations to rescissionary relief, 338

Lindsay Petroleum Oil Co. v. Hurd case, 345

merger in subsequent warranty, 346–347

Redican v. Nesbitt case, 344

restitution without rescission, 347–348

restoration of the *status quo ante*, 339–342, 402, 403

Redican v. Nesbitt case, 344

Reliance as an alternative to expectancy measure, 832–837

McRae v. Commonwealth Disposals Commission case, 832–835

Remedies for breach of contract, 5, 14, 174, 811–992

damages, 813–905

in personam, 12

restitution and disgorgement, 961–992

specific performance and injunctions, 906–960

Remedies upon breach for guilty party, 979–985
  Dies v. British International Mining & Finance Corp. Ltd. case, 980–981, 982
  doctrine of entire contracts, 983
  doctrine of substantial performance, 984–985
  forfeiture provision test, 982–983
  goods and services supplied, 983–985
  Howe v. Smith case, 980
  money paid, 980–983
  Stockloser v. Johnson case, 982, 983
  Sumpter v. Hedges case, 984, 985
Remedies upon breach for innocent party, 965–979
  Boomer v. Muir case, 970–971
  disgorgement of profits secured, 972–979
  Giles v. Edwards case, 966
  Hunt v. Silk case, 966, 967, 968
  partial performance of a contract, 969–971
  restitution of benefits conferred, 965–972
  total failure of consideration, 966, 967, 968
Report on Amendment on the Law of Contract, 22
Representation and warranty, 5, 689–702
  concurrent liability in contract and tort, 700–701
  contractual representations, 696–699
  materiality and, 648, 697
  measure of relief, 695–696
  pre-contractual representation as warranty, 690–695, 696
Repudiatory breach, 4, 616, 617, 636, 637, 638, 645, 651, 654, 655, 657, 698, 699, 720, 752, 753, 758, 761, 830, 969, 979
  applying the Hong Kong Fir test, 633–636, 639, 640
  damages, 644
  definition of, 639–641
  doctrine of fundamental breach, 640
  doctrine of "material" breach?, is there a, 646–649

Krawchuk v. Ulrychova case, 635
perfect tender rule, 646
refinement of the Hong Kong Fir analysis, 629–633
remedies for, 641–646
rescission and, 645, 661
restitution, 644–646
right to disaffirm, 641–643, 654, 661
Shun Cheong Holdings B.C. Ltd. v. Gold Ocean City Supermarket Ltd. case, 634–635
Resale price maintenance scheme, 297
Restatement of Contracts (American), 276, 289, 290, 291, 292, 320, 334, 543, 544, 555, 646, 781, 785, 890
Restatement of Restitution, 15, 16, 961, 962, 963
Restitutio in integrum, 338, 340
Restitution
  disgorgement and, 6, 961–992
  law of, 15, 16, 17, 961
  repudiatory breach, for, 644–646
  restatement of, 15, 16
  Statute of Frauds of 1677 and, 179–180
  total failure of consideration and, 644–645
Restitution and disgorgement, 961–992
  disgorgement of profits, 963
  doctrine of restitution, 964
  late recognition of the unity, 964
  principle of restitutionary doctrine, 964
  remedies upon breach: the guilty party, 979–985
  remedies upon breach: the innocent party, 965–979
  restitution under ineffective transactions, 986–991
Restitution in illegal contracts, 470–477
Restitution under ineffective transactions, 986–991
  common law, at, 987–988
  Deglman v. Guaranty Trust Co. case, 987
  equity, in, 988–991
  laches and, 989
  restitutio in integrum and, 988, 989, 990
  status quo ante and, 988

atute of Frauds of 1677 and, 986, 987
restitution without rescission in misrepresentation, 347–348
Retail sales, negotiations and offers in, 37–40
Revocation of offers, 74, 82–89
  communication of revocation, 83–85
  flagpole problem and its solutions, 85–89
Risk-allocation analysis, 579–588
  mistaken assumptions and, 584–585
  Parrish & Heimbecker Ltd. v. Gooding Lumber Ltd. case, 587
  Societe Franco Tunisienne D'Armemennt v. Sidermar case, 585, 586
  Tsakiroglou & Co. v. Noblee Thorl G.m.b.H. case, 586, 587
Robinson v. Harman case, 816
Robitaille v. Vancouver Hockey Club case, 881–882
Rogue, 498, 510, 511, 512, 514, 515, 516
Ron Engineering & Construction Eastern Ltd. v. Ontario case, 44, 45, 46, 47, 115, 117, 147, 505, 506, 508, 509, 554
Ron Engineering doctrine, 509, 554
Rose and Frank Company v. J.R. Crompton and Brothers Ltd. case, 113–115, 116
Royal Bank of Scotland No. 2 v. Etridge case, 393, 395, 396, 398, 400, 401n
Royal courts of common law, 9
Rule of law, 18, 750, 756, 757, 758, 759, 761
Rule of recognition, 3, 213
Rules of incorporation, 751
Ruxley Electronics and Construction Ltd. v. Forsyth case, 842–843

Saint John Tug Boat Co. v. Irving Refinery Ltd. case, 68
Sale of Goods Act of 1893, 623, 624, 628, 632, 640
Sales talk as misrepresentation, 326, 327
Sally Wertheim v. Chicoutimi Pulp Company case, 816

Saunders v. Anglia Building Society case, 519–520, 521, 522, 523, 524, 525, 526
Saunders v. Edwards case, 477
Schroeder Music Publishing Co. Ltd. v. Macaulay case, 413–414, 418
Sealed contract rule, 258–259, 265n
Seals used in promises, 3, 212–213, 256–269
Semelhago v. Paramadevan case, 914–915, 916, 918, 944, 945, 946
Severance in illegality, 483–492
  blue pencil test, 483, 488, 489, 490
  notional severance, 484, 491, 492
  Section 347 of the Criminal Code and, 485, 486, 487, 491
  test for, 483, 484, 487
  William E. Thomson Associates Inc. v. Carpenter case, 485–486, 487, 489, 491, 492
Shares sales and specific performance, 923–924
Shirlaw v. Southern Foundries 1926 Ltd. case, 735
Shun Cheong Holdings B.C. Ltd. v. Gold Ocean City Supermarket Ltd. case, 634–635
Signed documents
  Tilden Rent-A-Car Company v. Clendenning case, 191–192
  written agreements and, 190–193
Silence as offer acceptance, 68–73
Skeate v. Beale case, 370–371
Sky Petroleum v. V.I.P. Petroleum case, 921–922
Societe Franco Tunisienne D'Armemennt v. Sidermar case, 585, 586
Solle v. Butcher case, 535, 536–537, 538n, 539, 542, 545, 547, 548, 551, 552
Solus agreements, 457
Specialties, 259
Specific performance, 908–946
  civilian approach to, 910–911
  common law approach to, 909–910, 911, 912
  delay, 938–939
  difficulty in supervision of performance, 929–934
  doctrine of mitigation, 911

doctrine of mutuality, 908, 917, 924, 926, 928
general principle of, 912, 913
inadequacy of damages test, 912–924
limiting principles of, 908–909
monetary awards, 939–946
mutuality, 924–929
other limitations of, 924–939
overcompensation of plaintiff, 911–912
public policy considerations, 937–938
sale of goods, 914, 918–923
sale of land and, 913–918
sale of shares, 923–924
unfairness circumstances, 934–936
Specific performance and injunctions, 5–6, 906–960
contractual stipulation of specific relief, 956–959
decrees of specific performance, 908–946
equitable remedies of, 907–908
injunctions, 947–956
Specific performance with an abatement, 939, 940, 941
St. John Shipping Corp. v. Joseph Rank Ltd. case, 463, 464, 467, 481
Standard form agreements, 182–183, 192, 260–261
Stare decisis, 18, 20
Statements of law and misrepresentation, 329–330
Status quo ante, 338, 339–342, 402, 403, 661
Statute of Frauds of 1677
agreements not to be performed within one year and, 168–169
Brownscombe v. Public Trustee of Alberta case, 177
contracts for sale of any interest in land and, 169–170
criticism of, 163–165
Deglman v. Guaranty Trust Co. case, 176, 177, 179
doctrine of part performance and, 174–178
formality of making agreements in writing and, 180–181

guaranteeing the obligations for debt, default or miscarriages to a third party, 165–167
informal trust arrangements and, 178
Kingswood Estate Co. v. Anderson case, 175
Maddison v. Alderson case, 175, 176, 177
other statutory writing requirements, 180–181
promise by executor or administrator to answer damages out of their own estate and, 167–168
promises made on consideration of marriage and, 167
purpose of, 161–162
relief from effects of non-compliance to, 174–180
restitution claims and, 179–180
Section 4 formalities and the effect of non-compliance to, 170–174
Steadman v. Steadman case, 175, 176, 177
Thompson v. Guaranty Trust case, 177
undertakings subject to Section 4, 165–170
use of to perpetrate a fraud, 178–179
Statutory illegality, 459–467
Kingshott v. Brunskill case, 462, 466, 469
St. John Shipping Corp. v. Joseph Rank Ltd. case, 463, 464, 467, 476, 481
Still v. Minister of National Revenue case, 466, 476, 481
traditional vs. modern approach to, 460–462, 466
Statutory unconscionability, 422–424
trade or business practices, 422–424
Unconscionable Transactions Relief Act, 422
Steadman v. Steadman case, 175, 176, 177
Stilk v. Myrick case, 248, 249, 250
Still v. Minister of National Revenue case, 466, 476, 481
Stipulation of specific relief for breach, 956–959
liquidated damages and, 957–958
Stockloser v. Johnson case, 982, 983
Stott v. Merrit Investment Corp. case, 376–377, 380n, 381

ct to contract", 37n, 127, 142, 171
sidiary promissory obligations, 674, 675
Suisse Atlantique Societe d'Armement Maritime S.A. v. N.V. Rotterdamsche Kolen Centrale case, 756, 759, 760, 762, 765, 766, 767, 768, 769
Sumpter v. Hedges case, 984, 985

Tamplin v. Anglo Mexican S.S. Co. case, 570
Taylor v. Caldwell case, 569, 573, 574, 575, 579, 603n
Taylor v. Johnson case, 503, 504
Telexed acceptance of offers, *see* Instantaneous communications of offers
Tendering processes to create legal relations, 115–118
   bargaining in good faith and, 140, 147–151, 156, 157
   Mellco Developments Ltd. v. Portage La Prairie (City) case, 116–117, 118
Tenders, negotiations and offers and, 43–47
Third-party beneficiary, *see* Privity of contract
Thompson v. Guaranty Trust case, 177
Thoroughgood's Case, 519
Ticket cases, 3, 183–190
Tilden Rent-A-Car Company v. Clendenning case, 191–192
Tinsley v. Milligan case, 479, 480, 481
Tito v. Waddell No. 2 case, 845–846
Toronto Dominion Bank v. Fortin No. 2 case, 541–542
Toronto-Dominion Bank v. Leigh Instruments Ltd. (Trustee of) case, 121–122, 123, 124, 125
Tort, 17
   claims in collateral agreements, 477
   claims in representation and warranty cases, 700, 701
   deceit, 348, 352
   inducement of breach of contract, 430
   law, third-party beneficiaries and, 305–306, 309
   negligence, 348, 349, 350, 351, 352, 353, 357, 358, 359
   Saunders v. Edwards case, 477

Total failure of consideration principle, 644–645
"True" condition precedent, 27, 675, 683
Trusts, *see* Doctrine of privity contract
Tsakiroglou & Co. v. Noblee Thorl G.m.b.H. case, 586, 587
Turney v. Zhilka case, 619, 682–683, 684, 685, 686, 687, 688
Tweddle v. Atkinson case, 296, 297, 298

Uberrima fides, 332, 334
Unconscionability, 404–424, 554n, 555, 560, 770–771, 772, 773, 774, 775, 776, 777, 778
   effects on third parties, 415–416
   elements of, 407–415
   justification for the doctrine of, 417–419
   Morrison v. Coast Finance Ltd. case, 407–408, 409, 420
   procedural, 406, 418, 421
   remedies for, 419–421
   Schroeder Music Publishing Co. Ltd. v. Macaulay case, 413–414, 418
   statutory, 422–424
   substantive, 406, 413, 414, 416, 417, 418, 421
   two-fold test of, 410, 411
Unconscionable Transactions Relief Act, 422
Undue influence, 382–404, 425
   Barclays Bank plc v. O'Brien case, 399, 400
   constructive notice and, 400, 401, 402, 403
   effects on third parties, 398–402
   equitable compensation, 403, 404
   independence of the plaintiff, 397–398
   Mahoney v. Purnell case, 403, 404
   remedies for, 402–404
   type 1: actual undue influence, 384–385
   types 2A and B: presumptive undue influence, 385–395, 425
   type 3: non-presumptive relational undue influence, 395–397
Uniform Act, 604, 608, 609
Uniform Frustrated Contracts Act, 603, 606, 607, 608

Unilateral contract, 33n, 36, 48, 52, 56, 68, 85, 86, 88, 89, 215, 269, 271, 305, 690, 691, 696
  definition of, 32–33
  offers to general public, 40–42
  rewards and other unilateral contracts to general public, 40–42, 70
Unilateral mistakes as to contract terms, 496, 501–504, 505, 509
  consensus ad idem and, 501, 502, 503, 504, 506
  consensus approach, 502, 503, 506
  estoppel and, 503
  snapping up an offer, 502, 505, 506, 508
  Taylor v. Johnson case, 503, 504
Universe Tankships of Monrovia v. International Transport Workers' Federation case, 373, 375, 376, 377, 378, 379, 380
Unsigned documents
  Parker v. South Eastern Railway Co. case, 183–184, 185, 190
  written agreements and, 183–190

Vagueness in agreement terms, 104–110
Vancouver Malt and Sake Brewing Co. Ltd. v. Vancouver Breweries Limited case, 448
Verba ita sunt intelligenda ut res magis valeat quam pereat principle, 728
Victoria Laundry (Windsor) Ltd. v. Newman Industries Ltd. case, 856–857, 858, 860, 861, 862
Vitiating factors, 3, 323–611
  duress, undue influence and unconscionability, 364–427
  frustration, 566–611
  illegality, 428–493
  misrepresentation, 325–363
  mistakes, 494–565
Vorvis v. Insurance Corporation of British Columbia case, 800, 876, 877, 878, 883, 884, 886, 887, 889

Waiver and promissory estoppel, 3, 275–293, 343
  Central London Property Trust Ltd. v. High Trees House Ltd. case, 277, 279, 280, 281, 282n, 285, 286
  doctrine of promissory estoppel, 279–287
  Foakes v. Beer case, 276, 277, 278, 279, 281, 282, 283, 290
  proprietary estoppel, 287–289
  waiver, estoppel by representation and *Foakes v. Beer*, 277–279
  Walton Stores (Interstate) Pty. v. Maher: inching towards Section 90 of the *Restatement of Contracts*, 289–292
Waiver and "true" conditions precedent, 682–688
  Turney v. Zhilka case, 682–683, 684, 685, 686, 687, 688
Waiver of proposed breach, 666
Waiver of rights against third parties in insurance contracts, 310–312
Waiver principle, 70
Walford v. Miles case, 142–143, 152
Wallace v. United Grain Growers Ltd. case, 799, 800, 802, 803, 805, 806, 879, 886
Walton Stores (Interstate) Pty. v. Maher case, 290, 291, 292
Warranties, 5, 231–232, 617
White & Carter (Councils) Ltd. v. McGregor case, 667, 668, 669
  anticipatory repudiation, 670
Whiten v. Pilot Insurance Co. case, 887–888, 890, 891, 892, 893, 894, 895, 896
William E. Thomson Associates Inc. v. Carpenter case, 485–486, 487, 489, 491, 492
Williams v. Roffey Bros. & Nicholls Contractors Ltd. case, 248, 250, 252, 253
Wood v. Lucy, Lady Duff-Gordon case, 221
Written agreements, 1, 3, 160–208
  agreements not to be performed within one year and, 168–169
  contracts for sale of any interest in land, 169–170
  entire agreement clauses in, 207
  incorporation of written terms in, 181–193
  other statutory writing requirements, 180–181

ol evidence rule, 193–207
romise by executor or administrator
to answer damages out of his or
her own estate, 167–168
promises made upon consideration of
marriage, 167
promises to answer for debt, default
or miscarriages of another person,
165–167
relief from non-compliance, 174–180
Section 4 of statute formalities and
effect of non-compliance, 170–174
signed documents and, 190–193
Statute of Frauds of 1677, 161–181
undertakings subject to Section 4 of
statute, 165–170
unsigned documents and, 183–190
Wrongful dismissal, *see* Damages

ABOUT THE AUTHOR

John D. McCamus, B.A., M.A., LL.B., LL.M., L.S.M., is a Professor of Law and University Professor at Osgoode Hall Law School of York University, a faculty which he served as Dean from 1982-1987. He is a member of the Ontario Bar. Prior to joining the faculty at Osgoode, he spent a year as a law clerk at the Supreme Court of Canada for Chief Justice Laskin. At Osgoode, his principal areas of research and teaching have included private law, especially restitution and contract, commercial law and information practices law. His published work includes numerous books, articles and government reports on these and other topics, a text, co-authored with P.D. Maddaugh, *The Law of Restitution*, 2d ed. (2004) and a casebook, *Cases and Materials on Contracts*, 3d ed. (2005), co-edited with Professors Waddams, Trebilcock, Neyers and Waldron. From 1990 to 1993, he was a member and then, from 1993 to 1996, Chair of the Ontario Law Reform Commission. In 1998, he was appointed by the American Law Institute to the Advisory Committee for the *Restatement of Restitution and Unjust Enrichment 3d*. Since 2000, he has also been an Associated Scholar in the Toronto office of Davies Ward Phillips & Vineberg LLP.